BIBLIOGRAPHY OF
BRITISH HISTORY

STUART PERIOD, 1603–1714

BIBLIOGRAPHY OF
BRITISH HISTORY

STUART PERIOD, 1603–1714

ISSUED UNDER THE DIRECTION OF
THE AMERICAN HISTORICAL ASSOCIATION
AND THE ROYAL HISTORICAL SOCIETY
OF GREAT BRITAIN

EDITED BY

GODFREY DAVIES
FIRST EDITION

MARY FREAR KEELER
SECOND EDITION

OXFORD
AT THE CLARENDON PRESS
1970

Oxford University Press, Ely House, London W. 1

GLASGOW NEW YORK TORONTO MELBOURNE WELLINGTON
CAPE TOWN SALISBURY IBADAN NAIROBI DAR ES SALAAM LUSAKA ADDIS ABABA
BOMBAY CALCUTTA MADRAS KARACHI LAHORE DACCA
KUALA LUMPUR SINGAPORE HONG KONG TOKYO

FIRST EDITION 1928
SECOND EDITION 1970

PRINTED IN GREAT BRITAIN

PREFACE TO THE SECOND EDITION

ECAUSE the Introduction by the distinguished editor of the volume on the Stuart Period in the *Bibliography of British History*, published in 1928, explains the planning of the project under the joint sponsorship of the American Historical Association and the Royal Historical Society, it has been reprinted below. For the work of Godfrey Davies and those who collaborated with him in preparing the first edition all who follow must be grateful. In accepting in 1957 responsibility for the revision of that volume, as authorized by the Councils of both organizations, with the financial sponsorship of the Ford Foundation, the present editor has been able to build upon strong foundations.

Several developments since the time when the Davies edition was compiled have dictated changes in the selection and the arrangement of materials. The lively interest of scholars in the seventeenth century has led to a greatly increased volume of publication, and also to a widened range of emphasis. Reflections of such changes may be noted, for example, in the enlarged sections in this edition on economic and social history, on local history, on cultural history and various aspects of the intellectual trends of the period, and on the non-English areas. Some attention has had to be given to the remarkable developments in the organizing of archival and library materials, particularly since the Second World War, and to the availability for the research worker of resources such as those on microfilm. Not available to Davies were the *Short-title catalogue of books . . . 1478–1640*, published in 1926, and the companion volume by Donald Wing for 1641–1700. Those works have made it possible to insert titles useful to the student on particular subjects and to point out the abundance of other seventeenth-century imprints. In the interest of students of the period to whom the repositories of such riches may not be readily accessible, the present edition includes a considerable number of additional references to such titles.

The work of other bibliographers since Davies has been drawn upon extensively. Clyde L. Grose's *Select bibliography of British history* for the period of 1660–1760 supplements the Davies volume in many respects, particularly with its references to manuscript materials, and has been especially useful. For the period of Queen Anne there is the excellent bibliography by William T. Morgan. The shorter bibliographies prepared by P. H. Hardacre, P. Zagorin, and R. Walcott under the direction of Elizabeth Furber for the Conference on British Studies, and now collected in a single volume, have helped guide the selecting of modern works. The plans for other bibliographies to be prepared under the auspices of the

Conference offer hope to the student who may be disappointed by the absence of titles from the most recent years in the present volume.

As in the other volumes of this series, by Read for the Tudors and Pargellis for the eighteenth century, the lists of titles have been determined on a selective basis, with a stress on materials from the century itself and on those later works whose interpretations have been significant. Titles relating to a particular subject have frequently been grouped in a single paragraph, with the order of titles indicating more often differences in approach than relative importance. The most useful edition of a work, as well as its first edition, is usually given. More of the older titles from the Davies lists might have been eliminated; many have been retained because their interpretations still have value. Numerous articles drawn from scholarly journals have been added, the result of an intensive search of a wide list of periodicals up to and through the volume for 1958 and of a smaller list for the subsequent five years. For books, the emphasis has been on those published before 1961 or 1962, although a few later titles have been inserted.

The arrangement of subjects of the present volume differs in many respects from that followed by Davies. Decisions have been made partly to accommodate the changing views among scholars as to what is important, and partly to adjust to editorial plans. The elimination of a separate chapter on voyages is a case in point, although through its disappearance some flavour of the age may have been lost. New subdivisions in the chapters on economic and social history suggest some of the trends of scholarly interest. The choice of where to place a particular title has had to be the editor's, however. The fuller table of contents and index will, it is hoped, make up for inconveniences to the reader arising from such decisions.

Changed also is the arrangement of titles within sections. In general the order is first the bibliographies, in some cases with reference to manuscript resources, next the source materials, and then the selected later works. The Davies plan of adhering to a chronological order according to the date of the first edition has been replaced by alphabetical order in most of the sections that are not sources. For works published during the Stuart period the order is generally chronological, chiefly according to the date of the first edition, but in some instances according to the date of writing or of the events with which the contents are concerned. In several sections in which geographical areas are significant an alphabetical arrangement according to the names of the areas has been followed.

Omitted from this edition are most of the descriptions relating to size and format. Also omitted are most of the references to London as the place of publication; if no place of publication is given, London is to be understood. The Davies titles taken from periodical literature have been checked so that in most cases numbers for volume and page could be given, as well as the year of publication. Although the index must be depended upon for many cross-references, a number that seem particularly useful are cited in the text, with the number of the title referred to enclosed within parentheses. Square brackets have been reserved chiefly for supplying information useful for dating or otherwise establishing the identity of a work.

In the preparation of this revised edition many scholars have assisted with suggestions, some have prepared the preliminary draft of a chapter or a section, and others have given time to review certain portions critically. Decisions on the final form have in most cases been the responsibility of the editor, however. The responsibility for any shortcomings of the new volume must be mine.

For their encouragement and suggestions offered in the early stages of the work—without whose persuasions, in fact, the task would not have been undertaken—my special acknowledgements are due to the late Wallace Notestein and the late Conyers Read. Their enthusiasm for the bibliographical effort was impelling. To Sir John Neale for helpful advice at the beginning of the project, and to H. Hale Bellot, the late Helen Cam, Edgar B. Graves, and T. F. T. Plucknett, members of the Joint Anglo-American Committee, for their confidence and their continuing support even though the work moved more slowly than had been planned, and to the officials of the Ford Foundation, appreciation is expressed. The advice of E. B. Graves, from his own experience in connection with the volume on the medieval period, was especially valuable. The encouragement and the friendly prodding of Boyd C. Shafer, who had hoped to see the volume completed before the end of his service as Executive Secretary of the American Historical Association, and the continued encouragement and patience of his successor, Paul Ward, have been helpful. Special appreciation must be expressed to the late Stanley Pargellis, chairman of the committee for the Association, who served as my mentor and counsellor. He was always ready with advice, and considerate and encouraging through periods of delay and frustration. His death while the volume was going through the press has made this recognition of his contributions to the Stuart bibliography come too late. It is no exaggeration, however, to say that without his steady support the work could not have been finished.

Aid on several sections of the bibliography has been given by former associates of mine at Yale University. Hartley Simpson reviewed and made valuable suggestions for the chapter on Political History, as did Basil D. Henning. Alexander M. Witherspoon did likewise for the section on Literature, and Franklin L. Baumer for other parts of the chapter on Cultural History. Mildred Campbell of Vassar organized the section on Land and wrote the introductions. From Caroline Robbins of Bryn Mawr came many helpful suggestions relating to Political History, especially pamphlets, and to Parliament; and others from Margaret Judson of Rutgers relating to Political Theory. Walter L. Woodfill wrote the section on Music, and Robert Westfall that on Science.

Assistance on various parts came also from scholars in the British Isles. I am indebted for suggestions on Economic History to Christopher Hill and several of his colleagues, including G. D. Ramsay. For the initial work on the Foreign Relations section, and especially the references to collections of manuscripts, my thanks are due to D. H. Pennington, J. P. Cooper, and others. Ellis Waterhouse of Birmingham gave advice for Fine Arts and supplied the lists of catalogues. The chapter on Scotland was compiled by Donald Gordon of Edinburgh, and that on Wales by A. H. Dodd, both at a fairly early stage of the work. R. Dudley Edwards of Dublin made invaluable contributions to the chapter on bibliographical resources, which he kindly read and criticized in an early draft; he also prepared the plan for the chapter on Ireland, and supplied most of the materials for its first section, and portions of later parts.

Others have assisted me in special ways. Mrs. Margaret Gay Davies generously made available her husband's interleaved copy of the first edition, with his notes on supplementary titles. For the privilege of using study space in the Library of Congress and access to its shelves for several years I am indebted to the courtesy of Colonel Willard Webb, Chief, Stock and Reader Division. For extended hospitality provided for me and my assistants by the Folger Shakespeare Library, and the interest and encouragement always offered by its distinguished director, Louis B. Wright, and his staff, I warmly express my gratitude.

Assisting me in the early years of the revision process were, in turn, Joan Kennedy, Alicia Faxon, and Mary Caperton Rosenberger. Without their help the project would have foundered at the start. For their aid in the tedious task of typing the manuscript my thanks go to Nancy Baker Freeman and Doris Gilbert, and for assistance with the index, to Juanita Smith. To the staff of the Clarendon Press I am indebted for firm but kindly criticism in preparing the volume for its final stages of production.

MARY FREAR KEELER

Hood College
Frederick, Maryland
15 November 1969

INTRODUCTION TO THE FIRST EDITION

THE late H. R. Tedder read a paper on 19 March 1914 before the Royal Historical Society on 'The forthcoming bibliography of modern British History', and his authoritative account is the basis of the following summary of the progress of the undertaking until the appointment of the present editor.

In 1909 the American Historical Association and the Royal Historical Society both named committees to discuss the question of co-operating in order to continue Gross's *Sources and literature of English history from the earliest times to about 1485*. They planned a series of three volumes, each in two parts. The first was to be general, comprising an introduction on the scope and arrangement of the work, accounts of publications of learned societies and historical periodicals, etc., and lists of authorities covering the whole period 1485–1910. The second was to contain the special authorities for 1485–1714, and the third those for 1714–1910. In 1912 the late Sir George Prothero became general editor and committees were appointed for both the Tudor and Stuart periods. Much work had been performed by 1914, when the outbreak of war completely suspended it. Sir George Prothero was never again able to give much attention to it, and his death in July 1922 left it unfinished. A special committee of the Royal Historical Society sat in that year to discuss the continuance of the bibliography, and a change of plan was adopted. In view of the length of time which had elapsed since the project was first mooted, it was imperative to complete at least a part of it as speedily as possible. As the preparations for the original volume two were the most advanced, it was decided to proceed with it. Now the Tudor and Stuart periods were each to be allotted a separate volume. A committee of American scholars, with E. P. Cheyney as chairman, has charge of the Tudor volume, which is nearing completion.

I was nominated editor of the volume covering 1603–1714 in February 1923, but other literary commitments prevented my assuming my duties for more than a year. Owing to the urgency, as well as the extent of the work still to be accomplished, the original idea of including manuscripts was abandoned, although considerable information about them is incorporated in the notes. The indefinite postponement of the general introductory volume, and the impossibility of referring to it or to the Tudor volume, have necessitated the insertion in this book of a number of works not confined to the period. It is now designed to be complete in itself. Otherwise the contents correspond to the scheme prepared by Sir George Prothero and the committee of 1912, except that whereas they contemplated about 2,500 titles, there are now over 3,800 numbered, besides 1,500 to 2,000 in the footnotes.

It is my pleasant task to express the profound gratitude of the Royal Historical Society to the late Sir George Prothero and to those who have assisted in the production of this volume. It is most unfortunate that owing to the change of editorship there is neither a complete list of the original contributors nor a precise record of their services. So far as is known the following compiled the whole or parts of the sections which are inserted in brackets after their names, and in a number of cases have recently revised them: C. H. Collins Baker (Art); E. A. Benians (Voyages and Travels); Arthur Berry (Science); Sir Reginald Blomfield (Architecture); the late P. Hume Brown (Scotland); R. Dunlop (Ireland); the late H. E. Egerton (Colonies); Lord Ernle (Agriculture); the Bishop of Truro [W. H. Frere] (Anglican Church to 1660); Sir Henry Hadow (Music); B. L. K. Henderson (Economic and Social History); H. D. Hazeltine (Legal Sources); the late A. M. Hyamson (Judaism); the late Colonel E. M. Lloyd (Military); J. E. Lloyd (Wales); H. E. Malden (Local History); J. G. Muddiman (Newspapers); the late Sir A. E. Shipley (Science); W. T. Whitley (Nonconformity).

It is possible to specify more particularly the debt of gratitude due to those whose assistance dates from 1923. E. R. Adair took charge of Administration, read the typescripts of the political and constitutional and the economic sections, and made many improvements; W. H. Burgess dealt with Unitarianism; the late E. H. Burton with Roman Catholicism; Miss E. Jeffries Davis virtually compiled all the entries on London; A. H. Dodd and J. G. Edwards added many titles to the Welsh bibliography; D. Hay Fleming doubled the size of the section on Scotland and subjected what had already been done to a very fruitful revision; C. S. S. Higham assumed control of Voyages and Travels and the East and West Indies, and wrote their introductions; M. W. Jernegan lent me his notes on the American colonies and made many valuable suggestions; Norman Penney revised and considerably augmented Quakerism; W. G. Perrin made himself responsible not only for the contents but also for the arrangement of the Naval section; H. G. Richardson revised Agriculture so systematically as to transform it, and penned its introduction; and W. R. Scott dealt with foreign trade and wrote part of the introduction to economic history.

One name deserves especial mention. Sir Charles Firth compiled the section on ballads, but this was the least of his services. He has assisted at every stage of the growth of this bibliography: his library and unrivalled stores of knowledge were always open to me. He has read the typescripts and the proofs, and encouraged me in every way. Nevertheless the final responsibility rests on my shoulders, not on his.

In spite of all this assistance, however, it is certain that much remains still to be accomplished. I have only been able to devote my leisure hours to this volume, and these perforce were mainly employed in compiling not less than a third of the entries. Consequently I am only too conscious that I have neglected many of my editorial duties. Yet those whose opinion is far weightier than mine believe that the interests of historical scholarship will be better served by the appearance of this volume now with all its imperfections than by delaying it for further revision. After all, the absence of such improvements as I could effect will matter little, if scholars will note such errors as they find and communicate them to the Honorary Secretary of the Royal Historical Society, 22 Russell Square, London, W.C. 1, by whom they will be acknowledged. Subjected to the revision of all who study the Stuart period, this book in a second edition will become more worthy of the two great historical bodies under whose direction it is issued.

In a bibliography of this kind the two main difficulties are those of selection and arrangement. In deciding what works to include or omit, the necessity of covering the whole field has been the ruling principle. In each section the aim has been to ensure that every aspect of its subject-matter shall be presented however inadequate the means may be. In dealing with controversial questions an attempt has been made to give fair representation to opposing schools of opinion whether contemporary or modern. Care has been taken to provide a selection of the historical literature of succeeding generations, so that the reader may trace the progress of knowledge and the different interpretations of events in each age. It has been impossible to include many pamphlets, but usually at least one tract of a prolific writer has been listed, so that his name can be turned up in the catalogue of a library such as the British Museum in order to discover what else he wrote. Most space has been devoted to the normal activities of the inhabitants of Stuart Britain. In the more specialized topics, such as art or science, the first consideration has been the needs of the general historian, in the hope that when he has occasion to tread these unfrequented paths he may find the guidance he requires.

The arrangement has been dictated by the avoidance of repetition and convenience of reference. Thus the desire not to do the same thing twice is responsible for putting peers in the alphabetical order of their titles in biographical sub-sections, since they are listed under their family names in the index. The usual arrangement of each section is to enumerate first the bibliographies, then the sources, and finally the later works. These all follow the chronological order of the date of the first edition unless there is an obvious reason for a deviation from this rule. Instances of such deviations are biographies arranged alphabetically, regimental histories which conform to the order of the Army List, or local histories which are arranged geographically. In a few small sub-sections, as in foreign relations or naval history, sources and later works are grouped together to save space, but such instances are rare. To keep the size of the bibliography within moderate limits certain devices have been adopted. Cross references, which are enclosed in round brackets, are only given when their absence cannot be supplied by the index. Many works have been inserted in footnotes—occasionally some strange bedfellows appear—but the more important are all indexed. Descriptions of books are necessarily brief. No distinction is made between small, medium, and large quartos. All others are octavos, or, if shorter, duodecimos, if taller, folios. Whenever possible the number of volumes, the size, the place and the date of publication of the first edition of each work is given, but no attempt is made to enumerate all later editions. The ideal has been, however, to note later editions whenever the rarity of the first, or the superior utility of the later, editions makes this desirable. When the format of the later edition is similar to the first, the description has not been repeated but the date alone is supplied. Thus an entry of the type 1 vol. 8vo. Lond. 1672 and 1701, would imply that the edition of 1701 was identical with that of 1672 in its format. On the other hand, if any detail of the description of the later volume is different, then all are repeated.

As regards the index, all authors and all editors, when there are no authors, are included, and the relatively few subject-matter entries are intended merely to supplement the table of contents. Titles are only inserted for anonymous works for which no subject-matter entry easy of reference could be found. When a book has both author and editor, the editor is only indexed if he has contributed materially to its value, or if there seems to be a reasonable chance that the reader will seek for it under the editor's name rather than under the author's. In short, practical utility has in all things been the chief guide of the editor.

CONTENTS

Contents

ABBREVIATIONS

Acad.	Academy
add.	additions, additional
Add. MSS.	Additional Manuscripts, British Museum
A.H.A.	American Historical Association
A.H.R.	*American Historical Review*
Anon.	Anonymous
Antiq.	Antiquarian, Antiquities
app.	appendix
Arch.	Architecture, Archaeological
Arch. Hib.	*Archivium Hibernicum*
Bibl.	Bibliography, Bibliographical
Biog.	Biography, Biographical
Bodl.	Bodleian
B.M., Br. Mus.	British Museum
Bull.	Bulletin
B.B.C.S.	*Bulletin of the Board of Celtic Studies*
C.S.P.	*Calendar of State Papers*
Camb.	Cambridge
C.B.E.L.	*Cambridge Bibliography of English Literature*
ch., chap.	chapter
c.	*circa*
Coll.	Collection
comp.	compiler, compiled
Conn.	Connecticut
cor.	corrected
D.N.B.	*Dictionary of National Biography*
Doc.	Document
Eccles.	Ecclesiastical
Econ.	Economic
Econ. Hist. Rev.	*Economic History Review*
Edin.	Edinburgh
ed.	editor, edited
edn.	edition
Eng.	England, English
E.H.R.	*English Historical Review*
enl.	enlarged
Harl.	Harleian
Hist.	History, Historical, Historische
H.M.C.	Historical Manuscripts Commission

H.C.	House of Commons
illus.	illustration
Inst.	Institute
intro.	introduction
I., Ir., Ire.	Ireland, Irish
I.M.C.	*Irish Historical Manuscripts Commission*
I.H.Stud.	*Irish Historical Studies*
J.H.S.E.	Jewish Historical Society of England
Jour., Journ.	Journal
J.M.H.	*Journal of Modern History*
Lancs.	Lancashire
Lang.	Language
Lib.	Library
Lit.	Literary, Literature
Lond.	London
Mag.	Magazine
MS., MSS.	Manuscript, Manuscripts
Mass.	Massachusetts
Med.	Medieval, Medical
Misc.	Miscellany
Mod.	Modern
Nat.	Natural
N.S.	New Series
N.Y.	New York
n.d.	no date
no.	number
Oxf.	Oxford
Parl. papers	Parliamentary papers
pt.	part
Penn.	Pennsylvania
Phila.	Philadelphia
Phil.	Philosophy, Philosophical
pl.	plate
ports.	portraits
pr.	printed
Proc.	Proceedings
pseud.	pseudonym
P.R.O.	Public Record Office
P.M.L.A.	*Publications of the Modern Language Association*
pub., publ.	published, publication
Quart.	Quarterly
Rec.	Record
repr.	reprint, reprinted

rev.	review, revised
Roy.	Royal
R.H.S. Trans.	*Royal Historical Society Transactions*
R.S.A.I.	Royal Society of Antiquaries of Ireland
s.a.	no date of publication given
Scot.	Scotch, Scottish
S.H.R.	*Scottish Historical Review*
Ser.	Series
Sess.	Session
S.T.C.	*Short-Title Catalogue*
s.l.	no place of publication given
Soc.	Society
suppl.	supplement
Trans.	Transactions, Translated
Univ.	University
V.C.H.	*Victoria County History*
vol.	volume
Wash.	Washington
Yorks.	Yorkshire

I

I. GENERAL REFERENCE WORKS

A. BIBLIOGRAPHIES AND CATALOGUES

1. BIBLIOGRAPHY OF BIBLIOGRAPHY

1 BESTERMAN, T. A world bibliography of bibliographies and of bibliographical catalogues ... 2 vols. 1939–40. 3rd edn. rev. 4 vols. Geneva. 1955–6.

Useful particularly for continental countries. Compare also *Bibliographic index, a cumulative bibliography of bibliographies 1937–42* (1945), *1943–6* (1948), *1947–50* (1951), *1951–5* (1956), *1956–9* (1961), *1960* (1961), N.Y. Important also is *The British national bibliography*, 1950+, based upon Br. Mus. books; *Index 1950–4*, 1955. For bibliographies of the main western European states see Read (11 n., *infra*, 1959 edn.), p. 3. For current titles to mid 1954 see H. F. Conover, ed., *Current national bibliographies*, Wash., 1955 (a continuation of the work under the same title ed. by L. Heyl, Wash., 1933, 1942, and continued in serial form in the Library of Congress *Quarterly Journal of Current Acquisitions*, 1949–53). See also the annual *International bibliography of historical sciences*, Paris, 1926+ (publ. 1930+), published by the International Committee of Historical Sciences; and C. M. Winchell, *Guide to reference books* (American Library Assoc.), 7th edn., Chicago, 1951; supplements, 1950–2 (1954), 1953–5 (1956), 1956–8 (1960).

The American Historical Association's guide to historical literature, ed. by G. F. Howe et al., N.Y., 1961, is of somewhat uneven value for British history, and does not completely supersede the 1931 edn. by G. M. Dutcher.

2 COURTNEY, W. P. A register of national bibliography, with a selection of the chief bibliographical books and articles printed in other countries. 3 vols. 1905–12.

Not well organized, but still of some value.

2. CATALOGUES AND BIBLIOGRAPHIES RELATING TO BRITISH HISTORY

See also *British national bibliography* (1 n.).

3 A SHORT-TITLE CATALOGUE of books printed in England, Scotland, and Ireland, and of English books printed abroad, 1475–1640. By A. W. Pollard, G. R. Redgrave, et al. 1926. Repr. 1946.

Most valuable. A revision is in progress at Harvard by W. Jackson. With Wing (4), the 'S.T.C.' supersedes all previous bibliographies for the period, such as the list by William London, 1658, and suppl. 1660 [–61]. Several check lists and supplements have been printed, such as that for titles in the Huntington Library (by C. K. Edmonds, *Hunt. Lib. Bull.* 4 (1933), 1–152); in the Newberry Library (by G. L. Woodward, Chicago, 1939); *American copies . . .*, by W. W. Bishop, Ann Arbor, 2nd edn., 1950; and a list of books printed abroad, compiled by A. F. Johnson, *Library*, 5th Ser. 4

(1950), 273–6. The Folger Library has a MS. copy of additions also. See also D. Ramage, *Finding list of English books to 1640 in libraries in the British Isles, excluding the national libraries . . .*, Durham, 1958. P. G. Morrison compiled an index of printers, publishers, and booksellers listed in the *Short-title catalogue* (Bibliographical Society of the University of Virginia), 1950. Still of value on publishers is E. Arber, ed., *A transcript of the registers of the company of stationers 1554–1640*, 5 vols., 1875–94 (later edn., 5 vols., N.Y., 1950); and the continuation, 1640–1708, ed. by H. R. Plomer, 3 vols., 1913–14.

4 SHORT-TITLE CATALOGUE of books printed in England, Scotland, Ireland, Wales, and British America, and of English books printed in other countries, 1641–1700. By D. G. Wing. N.Y. 1945–51.

Continuation of the above. See supplements, titles at the Huntington Library, by M. I. Fry and G. Davies (*Hunt. Lib. Quart.*, 1953); Christ Church (Oxf.), by W. G. Hiscock, Oxf. 1956; Ireland, by J. Alden, 1955; and French translations, by J. E. Tucker, 1955. There is an index of printers, etc. by P. G. Morrison, 1955.

For the period after 1700 no such complete catalogue exists. Useful, however, are Edward Arber, ed., *The term catalogues 1668–1709 with a number for Easter term 1711*, 3 vols., 1903–6, which is based on booksellers' catalogues and has a good index; and W. Bent, *A general catalogue of books . . . printed in Great Britain . . .* [1700–86], 1786.

5 ANNUAL BULLETIN OF HISTORICAL LITERATURE, 1911+. 1912+.

Published by the Historical Association, this is a useful selective bibliography of the books and articles, with annotations. Index for vols. 1–12, 1923. For an annual list of articles see the July issue of *E.H.R.* (35).

6 CAMBRIDGE BIBLIOGRAPHY OF ENGLISH LITERATURE. Ed. by F. W. Bateson. 4 vols. Camb. 1941. Suppl. by G. Watson. Camb. 1957.

Includes books on historical and social background as well as titles relating to literature; valuable, though mostly without critical comment. Still useful are the more detailed bibliographies in the *Cambridge history of English literature* (2579). In vols. vii–ix are valuable sections on 'Historical and political writings' that are of special interest for the period.

For additional titles on general background (1660–1800), see the current bibliographical lists in the *Philological Quarterly* (2572).

7 CAMBRIDGE MODERN HISTORY. Ed. by A. W. Ward, G. W. Prothero, and S. Leathes. 13 vols. and atlas. Camb. 1902–12. Rev. edn. vol. i+. Camb. 1957+.

Extensive though not always selective bibliographies in the first edn.; not included in the new edn. Useful for continental as well as English affairs. See vol. iii for 1603–25; vol. iv, 1625–60; vol. v, 1660–1714.

8 FREWER, L. B. Bibliography of historical writings published in Great Britain and the Empire, 1940–5. Oxf. 1947.

Published in co-operation with the International Committee of the Historical Sciences (see no. 1). A partial continuation for the next decade is provided by J. C. Lancaster, *Bibliography of historical works issued in the United Kingdom 1946–1956*, published by the Institute of Historical Research, 1957.

9 GEROULD, J. T., ed. Sources of English history of the seventeenth century 1603–1689 in the University of Minnesota library, with a selection of secondary material. Minneapolis. 1921.

An excellent guide. Enumerates the separate items in collections of pamphlets, etc. Very useful also are the selected bibliographies in A. Browning, ed., *English Historical Documents*, vol. viii (1660–1714), 1953.

10 GROSE, C. L. A select bibliography of British history, 1660–1760. Chicago. 1939. Repr. N.Y. 1966.

Valuable, especially for inclusion of many references to periodicals. Cf. his bibliographical articles on British history, 1660–1760 in *J.M.H.* 2 (1930), 448–71, and 12 (1940), 515–34. See also the articles by C. H. Firth, 'The development of the study of seventeenth century history', *R.H.S. Trans.* 3rd Ser. 7 (1913), 25–48, and 8 (1914), 1–16; and W. A. Shaw, ed., *A bibliography of the historical works of Dr. Creighton . . . Dr. Stubbs . . . Dr. S. R. Gardiner and Lord Acton*, 1903, and *A bibliography of the writings of Sir Charles Firth*, Oxf. 1928.

11 GROSS, C. The sources and literature of English history from the earliest times to about 1485. 1900. 2nd rev. edn. 1915. Repr. N.Y. 1951.

Many general items are useful for later periods. A third edn., to become a part of the *Bibliography of British history* series, is in progress. Volumes for other periods in this series which contain titles useful also for the 17th century are: C. Read, ed., *Bibliography of British history, Tudor period, 1485–1603*, Oxf. 1933, 2nd edn., Oxf. 1959; G. Davies, ed., *Bibliography of British history, Stuart period, 1603–1714*, Oxf. 1928; and S. Pargellis and D. J. Medley, eds., *Bibliography of British history, the eighteenth century, 1714–1789*, Oxf. 1951. See also Morgan (15).

12 HALKETT, S. and LAING, J. Dictionary of anonymous and pseudonymous English literature. New and enl. edn. by J. Kennedy, W. A. Smith, and A. F. Johnson. 7 vols. 1926–34.

The standard work, first published in 4 vols., Edin. 1882–8. An eighth volume for 1900–50 appeared in 1956. See also A. Taylor and F. J. Mosher, *Bibliographical history of anonyma and pseudonyma*, Chicago, 1950.

13 McKERROW, R. B., ed. A dictionary of printers and booksellers in England, Scotland, and Ireland, and of foreign printers of English books 1557–1640. Bibliographical Soc. London. 1910.

A volume continuing the list from 1640 to 1667, and ed. by H. R. Plomer, was published in 1907; A. Esdaile edited *A dictionary of the printers . . ., 1668–1725*, Oxf. 1922.

14 MILNE, A. T., ed. Writings on British history, 1934+. 1937+.

Valuable annual series, covering to date the publications for 1935–45, and published under the auspices of the Royal Historical Society of Great Britain.

15 MORGAN, W. T. A bibliography of British history (1700–1715) with special reference to the reign of Queen Anne. 5 vols. Bloomington, Ind. 1934–42.

Full, with useful lists (chronological) of 'pamphlets and memoirs', and helpful comments on MS. collections for the early 18th century.
    A useful series of bibliographical articles, published under the auspices of the Conference on British Studies (publ. in book form under the editorship of E. Furber, Camb. (Mass.) 1966), includes the following relating to the 17th century: P. Zagorin, 'English history, 1558–1640', *A.H.R.* 68 (1963), 364–84; P. H. Hardacre, 'Writings on Oliver Cromwell since 1929', *J.M.H.* 33 (1961), 1–14; and R. Walcott, 'The later Stuarts (1660–1714)', *A.H.R.* 67 (1962), 352–70. See also S. B. Baxter, on William III, *J.M.H.* 38 (1966), 256–66.

16 PEDDIE, R. A. Subject index of books published before 1880. 4 vols. 1933–48.

Useful for searching the period not included in the Br. Mus. *Subject index* (17 n.). An older index which, though still helpful, must be used with caution is Robert Watt, *Bibliotheca Britannica; or a general index to British and foreign literature*, 4 vols., Edin. 1824. Lists of the writings of many 17th-century authors are included in the first two volumes which are arranged alphabetically by author; the subject index occurs in the other volumes.

B. LIBRARY RESOURCES

GUIDES AND CATALOGUES

The leadership of the British Museum and the Library of Congress in providing union catalogues has greatly simplified the search for printed materials in numerous libraries. For a general guide, indicating the types of information on special subjects to be found in libraries in Great Britain and Ireland up to 1928, see G. B. Barwick, ed., *The ASLIB directory, a guide to sources of special information in Great Britain and Ireland* (Assoc. of Special Libraries and Information Bureaux), 1928. For American libraries see R. B. Downs, *American library resources, a bibliographical guide*, Chicago, 1951, suppl. 1962· L. Ash, *Subject collections*, N.Y., 1958; and P. M. Hamer, ed., *Guide to archives and manuscripts* (19 n.). Although the printed catalogues of special libraries are no longer of great value, each library has its unpublished card catalogue. For guides to materials relating to America see Crick and Alman (p. 10 *infra*). For several other special guides, see Pargellis (11 n.) no. 19.

17 BRITISH MUSEUM. DEPARTMENT OF PRINTED BOOKS. Catalogue of printed books. 95 vols. 1881–1900 (repr. in 58 vols., ed. by J. W. Edwards. Ann Arbor. 1946). Suppl. 15 vols. 1900–5 (repr. in 10 vols., ed. by J. W. Edwards, 1950). Rev. edn. General catalogue of printed books. 263 vols. 1931–66.

Cf. *Subject index of the modern works added to the British Museum library 1881–1900*, ed. by G. K. Fortescue, 3 vols., 1902–3, which has been continued by further subject indexes at five-year intervals. See also the British Museum's union catalogue, published as *British national bibliography*, 1950+ (publ. 1951+).

18 CLARK, G. KITSON, and ELTON, G. R. Guide to research facilities in history in the universities of Great Britain and Ireland. Camb. 1963.

Does not list library resources in detail, but provides comments on the types of resources, both in printed collections and manuscript materials, at the principal libraries. Included are Aberdeen University Library, with its important MacBean Collection on the period; the University of Edinburgh Library and the National Library of Scotland; the Welsh libraries at Aberystwyth and Bangor; the Irish institutions at Belfast and Dublin; and the libraries of the various English universities.

19 U.S. LIBRARY OF CONGRESS. A catalogue of books represented by Library of Congress printed cards issued [1898] to July 31, 1952. Assoc. of Research Libraries. Ann Arbor, Mich. 1942+.

Valuable, though not a complete catalogue of the library's collections. For books in other American libraries, see the Library of Congress, *National Union Catalogue*, 1953+ (publ. 1958+). See also Union Theological Seminary (N.Y.) *Catalogue of the McAlpin collection of British history and theology*, 5 vols., N.Y. 1927–30; and C. M. Winchell, *Locating books for inter-library loan, with a bibliography of printed aids* . . ., N.Y. 1930. For the extensive collections of materials on the period in the Folger Shakespeare Library, the Huntington Library, and the Newberry Library there are no complete printed catalogues, but their various *Bulletins* should be consulted. See also P. M. Hamer, *Guide to archives and manuscripts in the United States*, New Haven, 1961; and *The national union catalog of manuscript collections 1959–1961*, Ann Arbor, 1962.

20 HALE, R. J., Jr. Guide to photocopied historical materials in the United States and Canada. Ithaca. 1961.

Cf. *Union list of microfilms*, U.S. and Canada, 1942; rev. edn. by J. W. Edwards, Ann Arbor, 1951; *Cumulation 1949–59*, 1961.

C. PERIODICALS AND SOCIETY PUBLICATIONS

1. BIBLIOGRAPHIES AND GUIDES

21 YEAR-BOOK OF THE SCIENTIFIC AND LEARNED SOCIETIES of Great Britain and Ireland. 1884+.

An annual compilation, with lists of publications of most of the societies. The principal societies, libraries, and research institutions are listed in *The world of learning*, 8th edn., 1957.

22 BRITISH UNION—CATALOGUE OF PERIODICALS. A record of periodicals of the world from the seventeenth century to the present day in British libraries. By J. D. Stewart, M. E. Hammond, and E. Saenger. 4 vols. 1955–8.

For the standard work on American libraries, *Union list of serials in libraries of the United States and Canada* . . ., 2nd edn., N.Y. 1943; suppl. 1944–9; *New serial titles*, N.Y. 1949+. Cf. *Ulrich's periodical directory, or a classified guide to a select list of current periodicals, foreign and domestic*, 9th edn. by E. C. Graves, N.Y. 1959.

23 INSTITUTE OF HISTORICAL RESEARCH. The historical publications of the societies of England and Wales. Suppls. nos. 1–13. 1929–46.

Publication of these supplements to the *Bull. Inst. Hist. Research* was suspended in 1946. For publication of record materials see R. Somerville, *Handlist of record publications*, Brit. Rec. Assoc. Pub. Pamphlet, no. 3, 1951; P. Gouldesbrough *et al.*, *Handlist of Scottish and Welsh record publications*, pamphlet no. 4 in the series; and E. L. C. Mullins, *Texts and calendars*, Royal Historical Society Guides and Handbooks, no. 7, 1958.

24 READERS' GUIDE TO PERIODICAL LITERATURE [Poole's Index]. N.Y. 1882+.

Lists chiefly American periodicals. Some British journals are covered in the *Supplement, 1907–19*, and the continuation, *International index to periodicals*, 1920+. The best guide to English periodicals is *The subject index to periodicals* . . ., 1915–16+, publ. by the Library Assoc., 1919+.

2. Serial Publications

See also Ch. X *infra*, §§ I and J on Newspapers and Printing. Journals devoted primarily to special subjects or localities are listed in later sections, rather than in the following general list. For others, such as library publications, see Ulrich (22 n.).

25 AMERICAN HISTORICAL REVIEW. American Historical Assoc. N.Y. 1895+.

A quarterly; lists of articles dealing with English history appear regularly.

26 ARCHAEOLOGIA; or miscellaneous tracts relating to antiquity. Society of Antiquities of London. 1770+.

An index for the first fifty volumes was compiled by M. Stephenson, 1889; notices concerning separate items appear also in Gerould *supra* (9), and Gomme *infra* (3101).

27 BULLETIN OF THE INSTITUTE OF HISTORICAL RESEARCH. (London University.) 1923+.

Prints news of migration of MSS., and summaries of theses, as well as documents and articles. Contains addenda and corrigenda to *D.N.B.*

28 CANADIAN HISTORICAL REVIEW. Toronto. 1920+.

Includes bibliographical articles and reviews.

29 CHURCH QUARTERLY REVIEW. 1876+.

30 DUBLIN REVIEW. 1836+.

Title changed, 1960, to *Wiseman's review.*

31 ECONOMIC HISTORY REVIEW. 1927+.

Prints lists of publications dealing with English economic history.

32 ECONOMIC JOURNAL: the journal of the British Economic Assoc. 1891+.

33 ECONOMICA. London School of Economics and Political Science. 1921+.

34 EDINBURGH REVIEW. Edin., Lond., N.Y. 1803–1929.

35 ENGLISH HISTORICAL REVIEW. Lond., N.Y. 1886+.

Published quarterly, with bibliographical issue each July.

36 HISTORICAL JOURNAL. Camb. 1957+ [*Cambridge historical journal*, 1925–56].

An annual.

37 HISTORISCHE ZEITSCHRIFT. Munich. 1859+.

Valuable reviews.

38 HISTORY: the quarterly journal of the Historical Association. 1916+.

Publishes lists of new books. See also the pamphlet series, *Annual bulletin of historical literature.*

39 IRISH HISTORICAL STUDIES. Dublin. 1938+.

Prints annually lists of writings in Irish history and research theses completed and in progress.

40 JOURNAL OF BRITISH STUDIES. Hartford (Conn.). 1961+.

41 JOURNAL OF MODERN HISTORY. Chicago. 1929+.

42 LAW QUARTERLY REVIEW. 1885+.

43 NOTES AND QUERIES. 1849+.

44 POLITICAL SCIENCE QUARTERLY. Boston. 1886+.

45 QUARTERLY JOURNAL OF ECONOMICS. Boston. 1887+.

46 REVUE D'HISTOIRE ECCLÉSIASTIQUE. Louvain. 1900+.

Contains useful bibliographical materials.

47 REVUE DES QUESTIONS HISTORIQUES. Paris. 1866+.

48 REVUE HISTORIQUE. Paris. 1876+.

49 ROYAL HISTORICAL SOCIETY, LONDON. TRANSACTIONS. 1869+. 1872+.

For index see H. Hall, *List and index of the publications of the Royal Historical Society 1871–1924, and of the Camden Society, 1840–1897,* 1925.

50 SCOTTISH HISTORICAL REVIEW. Glasgow. 1903–28, 1947+.

Not published, 1928–47.

51 VIERTEL JAHRSCHRIFT für sozial- und wirtschaftsgeschichte. Leipzig. 1903+.

Articles in English and French, as well as German.

D. WORKS OF REFERENCE ON SPECIAL SUBJECTS

A useful series of handbooks relating to many special subjects is *Helps for students of history,* ed. by C. Johnson and J. P. Whitney, 51 vols., S.P.C.K., 1918–24. Examples are guides to various MS. collections, such as P.R.O. (no. 4, 1918), Br. Mus. (no. 31, 1920); Bodleian Library (no. 47, 1922).

52 BEATSON, R. Political index to the histories of Great Britain and Ireland. Edin. 1786. 3rd edn. 3 vols. 1806.

Includes lists of officials, peers, etc. Cf. lists for 1660–1714 in App. ii of *English Hist. Docs.* viii (261), Powicke (56), and Haydn (2408).

53   CHUBB, T. The printed maps in the atlases of Great Britain and Ireland. A bibliography, 1579–1870. 1927.

> See also *A map of XVII century England* . . . (Ordnance Survey Publ.), Southampton, 1930; and the London Topographical Society's publications in facsimile of various 17th-century maps, especially vols. 14 (1928) and 20 (1952).

54   DICTIONARY OF NATIONAL BIOGRAPHY. Ed. by L. Stephen and S. Lee. 63 vols. 1885–1900.

> Supplements; repr. 22 vols. 1908–9. Corrections and additions in *Bull. Inst. Hist. Research*. A standard reference work.

55   HARRIS, JOHN. Lexicon technicum: or, an universal English dictionary of arts and sciences. 1704. 2nd edn. 2 vols. 1708–10.

> The first general encyclopedia of the modern type, E. Chambers, *Cyclopaedia*, did not appear until 1728; but useful for information on many subjects are E. Chamberlayne's *Angliae notitiae* . . . (2353) and the similar work of Miège (2353 n.).

56   POWICKE, F. M., ed. Handbook of British Chronology. (Royal Historical Soc. guides and handbooks, no. 2.) 1939. 2nd edn. 1961.

> Cf. C. R. Cheney, *Handbook of dates* (no. 4 in the series), 1945, rev. edn., 1955. See also Samuel Clarke, *The historian's guide* (1600–75), 1676, later editions with continuations, for a contemporary date book. See also N. Luttrell (344) and A. Boyer (374).

E. PAMPHLET COLLECTIONS

For this type of historical material, in which the century is so rich, there is no complete guide. Valuable collections on special subjects exist; there are also famous general collections gathered by individuals, many of which are now housed in libraries in England, Scotland, Ireland, Canada, and the United States. The description of the *types* of library collections in Pargellis (11 n.), pp. 11–12, is applicable in general also to the 17th century. Noteworthy for special subjects and special collections in London, in addition to the British Museum, are Friends' House (Quakers), Guildhall Library, University of London Library (economics), Westminster Abbey (sermons), and Dr. Williams's Library (theology); in Durham, the University (Jacobites); in Scotland, the National Library at Edinburgh (Jacobites, and Scottish history since 1585); and Public Library, Charleville Hall, Dublin (Ireland), as well as others listed in Clark and Elton's *Guide* (18).

There are rich collections in America at W. L. Clements Library, Ann Arbor, Mich. (America), Harvard College, Yale University (the Wagner collection on economic tracts and the Civil War); other libraries referred to on p. 5 *supra*. For the collection at the Folger Shakespeare Library there is a useful card catalogue arranged by date of publication. Subject references to many of these materials can be traced through *The ASLIB directory*, Downs, *American library resources*, and Ash, *Subject collections* (see p. 4 *supra*).

For the titles of pamphlets written by or attributed to particular authors, and locations of copies of the tracts, see *S.T.C.* and Wing (4). Examples of famous pamphlets have been listed under the appropriate topics in many of the later sections of this volume; others may be traced in the index by the names of their authors, such as Defoe, Halifax, Swift, and Temple.

Cited below are several useful catalogues and printed collections. Of the latter the most important are nos. 58 and 61.

57   CATALOGUE OF ENGLISH broadsides, 1505–1897. (Bibliotheca Lindesiana.) [Aberdeen.] 1898.

A special list, stopping at 1684, is W. H. Hart, *Index expurgatorius anglicanus, or a descriptive catalogue of the principal books printed or published in England which have been suppressed or burned by the common hangman*, 5 pts., 1872–84. Useful catalogues of collections are: J. O. Halliwell, *Catalogue of proclamations, broadsides . . . [at] the Chetham Library*, Manchester, 1851; R. Lemon, ed., *Catalogue of a collection of printed broadsides in the possession of the Society of Antiquaries*, 1866; *Catalogue of a collection of historical tracts, 1561–1800* (Redpath Library, McGill Univ., Montreal), 1901; and *A catalogue of pamphlets . . . 1506 to 1700 . . . Lincoln's Inn*, 1908.

58   CATALOGUE of the pamphlets . . . collected by George Thomason, 1640–1661 [in the British Museum]. Ed. by G. K. Fortescue. 2 vols. 1908.

A famous collection, usually referred to as the 'Thomason tracts', which is invaluable for the history of the civil war, the interregnum, and the early restoration. See also Maseres (1578).
    A Compleat catalogue of all the stitch'd books relating to the popish plot, 1678–1680, was published in 1680.

59   HARLEIAN MISCELLANY: or a collection of scarce, curious, and entertaining tracts . . . found in the late Earl of Oxford's library. Ed. by W. Oldys. 8 vols. 1744–6. Ed. by T. Park. 10 vols. 1808–13.

See *Contents of the Harleian miscellany* with an index, Sidney, 1885. The contents are listed also in the *Catalogue of the London Library*, 2 vols., 1913–14.

60   THE PHENIX, or a revival of scarce and valuable pieces. 2 vols. 1707–8.

Repr. in 1721 as *A collection*. . . . See also J[ohn] Morgan's collection, *Phoenix Britannicus*, 1732; and one somewhat antiquarian in nature by Francis Peck, *Desiderata curiosa*, 2 vols., 1732–5, later edn., 2 vols., 1779. Because it includes miscellaneous papers from the Nalson MSS., Peck is useful especially for *c.* 1645–60.

61   [SOMERS TRACTS.] Collection of scarce and valuable tracts . . . selected from . . . public as well as private libraries, particularly that of the late Lord Somers. 16 vols. 1748–51. Later ed. by Sir W. Scott. 13 vols. 1809–15.

A table of contents of this valuable collection is included in the *Catalogue of the London Library* (59 n.).

62   STUART TRACTS. 1603–1693. Ed. by C. H. Firth. Westminster. 1903.

Cf. G. A. Aitken, ed., *Later Stuart tracts*, Westminster, 1903. Both of these collections were parts of the 1903–4 edition of E. Arber's *English Garner* (1st edn., 8 vols., 1877–96). See also A. Lang's *Social England* (2173 n.). Other useful collections on selected topics are W. H. Dunham and S. M. Pargellis, *Complaint and reform in England, 1436–1714*, N.Y. 1937; and W. Haller, *Tracts on liberty* (960). For tracts relating chiefly to Newcastle upon Tyne in the 17th century see M. A. Richardson's *Reprints of rare tracts . . .*, 7 vols., Newcastle, *c.* 1847–9.

F. MANUSCRIPTS

Listed in this section are general collections of manuscripts that are useful for the study of the 17th century. Special collections, including most of those for Scotland and Ireland, are referred to in a number of the later subdivisions of this volume. The major repositories in England are the Public Record Office and the British Museum, but there are valuable collections in smaller institutions in London, Oxford, Cambridge, and Manchester as well. For accessions and migrations of MSS., the student should consult, before 1957, the *Bull. Inst. Hist. Research* (27), and since 1957, the National Register of Archives, annual *List of accessions* (p. 13, *infra*). Excellent for general use as well as for locating materials pertaining to America is B. R. Crick and M. Alman, *A guide to manuscripts relating to America in Great Britain and Ireland*, 1961. For manuscripts in American repositories, see *National union catalog of manuscript collections,* 1962+ (19 n.); and P. M. Hamer, ed., *Guide to archives and manuscripts* (19 n.). For references to foreign archives, see Ch. II *infra*, § G on Foreign Relations. See also p. 12 *infra* on the Historical Manuscripts Commission, and Ch. XI.

1. GENERAL

63   ARCHIVES. 1949+.

The journal of the British Records Association, which contains articles on many repositories of manuscripts, both in the British Isles and abroad. This publication, with the *Bulletin* of the National Register of Archives (p. 13 *infra*), has largely superseded the *Repository of British archives,* ed. by H. Hall. 1920.

2. GOVERNMENT OFFICIAL ARCHIVES

In addition to the types of government records described in *Reports* (64) and in various guides to the Public Record Office, there are the valuable collections constituting virtually the archives of Parliament which are housed in the House of Lords Record Office. For descriptions of the latter see Bond (783) and the *Guide* by Crick and Alman.

For the P.R.O. collection there is no complete printed guide. Many MS. catalogues at the P.R.O. supplement the printed indexes and guides that are mentioned here.

64   REPORTS OF THE ROYAL commission on public records . . . England and Wales. Parl. papers. 3 vols. 1912–19.

Vol. i, *P.R.O. and central administration;* vol. ii, *Government departments;* vol. iii, *Local records* (3106).

65   GUIDE TO THE CONTENTS OF THE PUBLIC RECORD OFFICE 2 vols. 1963.

Vol. i, *Legal records;* vol. ii, *State papers and departmental records.* This important publication from the Stationery Office was preceded by the introductory volume, *Guide to the public records,* 1949 (repr. 1950). Though more condensed, it supersedes the

former standard *Guide* by M. S. Guiseppi, 2 vols., 1923–4, and all previous ones. Still
useful are several briefer guides, such as C. Johnson, *The Public Record Office* (Helps
for students of history, no. 4), 1918; V. H. Galbraith, *An introduction to the use of the
public records*, rev. edn., 1952. See also Mullins (23 n.).

66 REPORT[S] of the Deputy keeper of the public records. Parl. papers.
1840+.

Although the annual *Reports* are brief, many of those published before 1890 contain
valuable appendices of lists of officials and calendars of documents (e.g. the *30th, 43rd,*
and *48th reports*). These are continued in the *P.R.O. Lists and indexes*, 1892+. Indexes
to the early *Reports* were printed in 1865 and 1880. For contents of the *Lists and indexes*,
and for the printing of papers from the P.R.O. collection, consult *List of record publications* (rev. 1960), published by H.M. Stationery Office, or, to 1914, Gross (11), no. 473.
A project for reprinting the *Lists and indexes* series, using the amended copies at the
P.R.O., is in progress.

3. British Museum

67 BRITISH MUSEUM. The catalogues of the manuscript collections. 1951.

A handbook compiled by the deputy keeper of manuscripts as a guide to the catalogues
of the various collections. It should be supplemented by the notes in the *Bull. Inst.
Hist. Research* and by Nat. Register Archives, *List of acquisitions by repositories*, 1957+.
Among the collections most useful for the Stuart period, besides those in 'Add. MSS.',
are the Egerton, Harley, Lansdowne, and Stowe. There is no satisfactory index by
subjects, although the class catalogue in the MS. reading room is of value for some
purposes. For descriptions see Crick and Alman (p. 10 *supra*), and the older J. P.
Gilson, *Student's guide to the manuscripts in the British Museum* (Helps for students of
history, no. 31), 1920. A record of B.M. MSS. which have been microfilmed and are
available in American libraries is in Hale (20).

4. Other Libraries and Repositories

The most useful recent guide to the various repositories is Crick and Alman
(p. 10 *supra*), but short descriptions of the types of manuscripts with the names
of some collections, are given in Clark and Elton, *Guide to research facilities* (18).
Mostly out of date now is L. Newcombe, *The university and college libraries of
Great Britain and Ireland*, 1927. For manuscript collections of Scotland, Ireland,
and Wales, see the separate chapters on those regions.

(a) *Cambridge*

68 A CATALOGUE of the manuscripts preserved in the library of the University of Cambridge. Ed. by C. Hardwick and H. R. Luard. 5 vols. Camb.
1856–67.

More up to date are the valuable catalogues of the manuscripts of many of the
colleges, many of which are by M. R. James.

(b) *London*

69 GUILDHALL. A guide to the records in the Corporation of London
records office and the Guildhall library muniments room. By P. E. Jones and
R. Smith. 1951.

Detailed descriptions of two collections, which include official records of the City government, of London parishes, and of some of the livery companies.

Other important MSS. in London are at the College of Arms, the Inns of Court (a Lincoln's Inn catalogue was printed in 1838), and the Society of Antiquaries; for ecclesiastical history, those at Lambeth Palace Library (out-of-date catalogue by H. J. Todd, 1812), the Dr. Williams's Library, Gordon Square, and the Friends Reference Library, Euston Road. Chiefly of antiquarian interest is R. A. Rye, *Students' guide to the libraries of London*, 1927.

(c) *Manchester*

70 JOHN RYLANDS LIBRARY. 'Hand-list of the collection of English manuscripts in the John Rylands library, 1928.' By M. Tyson. *John Rylands Lib. Bull.* 13 (1929), 152–219.

See ibid. 19 (1935), 230–54, 458–85, for additions to 1935. Of special interest to students of the history of Parliament are the 19th-century papers of W. D. Pink.

(d) *Oxford*

71 BODLEIAN LIBRARY. A summary catalogue of western manuscripts. Ed. by F. Madan and H. H. E. Craster. Oxf. 1895+.

A useful *Student's guide to the manuscripts relating to English history in the seventeenth century in the Bodleian Library* was compiled by G. Davies (Helps for students of history, no. 47), 1922. Among the important ones for the century are the Ashmolean MSS., Clarendon MSS. (see no. 257 for published portions), Tanner MSS., and Rawlinson MSS., as well as the Gough topographical collections. Notable accessions are frequently listed in the *Bodleian Quarterly Record*.

For other collections at Oxford see H.M.C. (236). A *Catalogue of the manuscripts of Balliol College* was compiled by R. A. B. Mynors, N.Y. 1963.

G. HISTORICAL MANUSCRIPTS COMMISSION REPORTS

The *Reports*, which began in 1870 and have continued to date, list the materials available in many private collections, and in borough and cathedral archives. Excerpts and partial calendars were included in appendices of the earlier volumes; since 1899 the calendaring has been more full, and separate volumes and series have been issued for many collections, including some which were briefly surveyed before.

There is no complete guide to the series. A brief account is provided in R. A. Roberts, *The reports of the Historical MSS. Commission* (Helps for students of history, no. 22), 1920. The Commission has published the following indexes: Part I, *Topographical* (to 1911), 1914; Part II, *Persons* (to 1911), by F. Bickley, 2 vols., 1935–8, a 'selective' index only; and *Guide to the reports of the Historical Manuscripts Commission 1911–57*, ed. by A. C. S. Hall, 3 vols., 1966, an index of persons in the vols. publ. from 1911 to 1957. For subject indexes see that by F. G. Davenport on diplomatic history, *18th report*, 1917; and that by

E. S. Upton and G. P. Winship, entitled *Guide to sources of English history* [1603–1660], Wash. 1952. The latter, which provides a subject index for the collections listed in the *Reports* 1–9, has been revised, N.Y. 1964. The index in Mullins (23 n.) also may be consulted. The *18th report* prints an alphabetical list of the collections examined, with some indication of the periods with which they are related; in the *19th report* (1926) and the *22nd report* (1946) appear lists of the owners, collections, and place of deposit for 1925 and 1946 respectively. The most recent information is in United Kingdom Government publications, *Publications of the royal commission on historical manuscripts*, Sectional list no. 17 revised to 30 June 1960, H.M.S.O., 1960. Notes on the migration of MSS. appear in the *Bull. Inst. Hist. Research* (27); E. Upton's notes on the location of 17th-century documents appear in vol. 15 (1937), pp. 73–8. See also Crick and Alman (p. 10 *supra*), Hale (20), Hamer (19 n.), and Mullins.

Since 1948 information about manuscript collections has appeared in *The Bulletins of the National Register of Archives*, published by the Commission. Its *List of accessions to repositories*, beginning with the accessions of 1957, has become a publication of the Stationery Office, 1958+.

I. General History, in Private or Family Collections

The following list is not intended as an exhaustive guide to the 17th-century materials in the *Reports*. It cites the collections of major importance for the century: Bath (80), Buccleuch (89), Cowper (see Coke, 101), Danby (113), Dartmouth (114), De La Warr (117), De L'Isle (118), Downshire (see Trumbull, 225), Finch (136), Fitzherbert (137), Harley (153), Hastings (155), Hodgkin (159), House of Lords (162), Morrison (188), Ormonde (195), Portland (204), Rutland (211), Sackville (see Cranfield, 108), Salisbury (212), Stuart (221), and *Various collections*, as well as some that are of particular value for Scotland, Ireland, and Wales. The list indicates also where the papers of many 17th-century individuals or families are to be found. The names of modern owners have been used only for large collections. The number of the report is indicated by an arabic numeral; parts of reports are indicated by roman numerals.

72 AILESBURY, MARQUESS OF. Correspondence of Bruce family *c.* 1650–1714; and letters of Edward Cooke. 15 VII Ailesbury MSS.

73 ANGLESEY, EARL OF. Letters, 1661–77. 6 I Leconsfield MSS.: 316*b*–318. Diary, 1671–4. 13 VI Lyttelton–Annesley MSS.

74 ANNANDALE, WILLIAM, EARL AND MARQUESS OF. Correspondence, 1690–1715. 15 IX J. J. Hope-Johnstone MSS.

75 ASHBURNHAM, EARL OF. 8 III. Many official papers in an artificial collection, which are now in the Stowe MSS. in Br. Mus.

76 BANKES, SIR JOHN, Chief Justice. Papers *temp.* Charles I and II. 8 I R. Bankes MSS.

77 BARKER, SIR ABEL. Letterbook, 1642–65; Barker family corresp. 1604–1760; various papers relating to taxation and public affairs. 5 E. Field MSS.: 387–404.

78 BARRINGTON, SIR THOMAS. Family papers, 1573–1675, including those of Sir Thomas Barrington, bart. 7 I G. A. Lowndes MSS.: 537–78.

79 BASKERVILLE, THOMAS. Journeys in England, *temp.* Charles II. 13 II Portland MSS. ii.

80 BATH, MARQUESS OF. 3, 4, and vols. i–iii, 1904–8.

A rich collection described in *3rd* and *4th reports*, with more elaborate selections printed in the later volumes. i: Harley papers, 1643–1714; ii: papers of Harley, Holles, and H. Savile; iii: Prior papers, valuable for the treaty of Ryswick. *3rd report* includes extracts from papers of the Thynne family and some of Bulstrode Whitelocke; *4th report* gives a catalogue of foreign correspondence of Henry Coventry.

81 BAXTER, RICHARD. Letters. 3 Dr. Williams's Library MSS.: 365–8.

82 BEAUFORT, DUKE OF. 12 IX. Contains letters of Charles I to the Marquess of Worcester 1639–45; journal of the siege of Colchester, family letters *temp.* Charles I; parliamentary diary 18 Dec. 1680–8. Jan. 1681.

83 BEDFORD, FRANCIS, Fourth EARL OF. 2 Duke of Bedford MSS. Letters and papers of the Russell family at Woburn Abbey; include commonplace books of the fourth earl, and materials on William, the fifth earl. Other Russell correspondence is in the Frankland–Russell–Astley MSS., 1900.

84 BELASYSE, JOHN, LORD. Correspondence of the Belasyse family, *c.* 1655–97, Frankland–Russell–Astley MSS., 1900; papers of Lord Fauconberg after 1660, and on the Yorkshire families of Belasyse and Fairfax, *Various collections*, ii, 1903, G. Wombell MSS. John Moone, 'A brief relation of the life . . . of John Lord Belasyse', is in Ormonde MSS., N.S. ii, 1903, pp. 376–99.

85 BERKELEY, GEORGE, Bishop. Letters. 7 I Egmont MSS.

86 BRADSHAW, RICHARD. Letters from abroad, 1650–9. 6 Miss ffarington MSS.: 426–44. Some letters from this collection have been printed by the Chetham Soc., 1853, 1856.

87 BRAMHALL, JOHN, Bishop. Correspondence, 1634–63. R. R. Hastings MSS. iv.

88 BRAYE, LORD. 10 VI. The Braye MSS. relate chiefly to the 17th century, being chiefly from the collections of John Browne, Clerk of the Parliaments, *c.* 1621–80, Sir Thomas Cave, and others. Some correspondence of John Mordaunt, 1658–9.

89 BUCCLEUCH AND QUEENSBERRY, DUKE OF. Papers relating largely to Scottish affairs after 1670, 158 MSS. at Drumlanrig Castle, i–ii, 1897–1903. In the Montagu House MSS., i–iii, 1899–1926, are i: papers of Sir Ralph Winwood, 1564–1628; the Montagu family, Thomas Osborne, and the Holles family; ii: Shrewsbury papers; iii: Montagu papers, including parliamentary diaries, *temp.* James I and Charles I. See also Montagu of Beaulieu (184).

90 BUCKINGHAM, DUKE OF. Letters, early 17th century. 2 G. M. Fortescue MSS. Others are in 10 Drummond Moray MSS.

91 BUFTON, JOSEPH. Late 17th-century diaries. *Various collections*, viii, S. P. Unwin MSS.

92 BULSTRODE, SIR RICHARD, envoy. Letters, 1677. 9 II Alfred Morrison MSS. See also the 'Bulstrode Papers', 1897, in the 'catalogue' of the Morrison collection by A. W. Thibaudeau.

93 CAPELL, ARTHUR. Papers of the Capell family, including letters of Arthur Capell, *Various collections*, vii, Earl of Essex MSS.

94 CHARLES I. Naseby letters, 1644–7, 6 I House of Lords MSS. (described also in *1st report*, App., 1–9); 12 IX Beaufort MSS.; 9 Alfred Morrison MSS.

95 CHESTERFIELD, PHILIP, Second EARL OF. Correspondence, *temp.* Anne. 5 E. P. Shirley MSS.

96 CHEVALIER, JEAN. Journal, on events in Jersey during the civil war. 2 Hoskins MSS.: 158–165.

97 CLARKE, WILLIAM. Papers, 1650–61, with autobiography of Dr. George Clarke, useful for Williamite wars in Ireland, and account of the restoration by J. Collins. Leyborne Popham MSS., 1899.

98 CLIFFORD FAMILY. Papers, 1578–1660, of the Cliffords, earls of Cumberland, 11 VII Hothfield MSS.

99 CLIFTON, SIR GERVASE. Letters, 17th century. *Various collections*, vii, 1914, Sir Hervey Bruce MSS.

100 COFFIN, RICHARD. News-letters and family correspondence of a Devonshire H.S., *c.* 1685–1700. Extracts, 5 Pine Coffin MSS., 1876; MSS. described in *4th report*, 1874.

101 COKE, SIR JOHN, Secretary. Calendared papers of Sir John and his sons, 1603–44, especially relating to his secretaryship 1625–39; third vol. has letters of Thomas Coke, *temp.* Anne. 12 I–III Cowper MSS.

102 CONINGSBY FAMILY. Papers, including those of Fitzwilliam Coningsby, 1618–35, and affairs of Monmouthshire in the 17th century. 7 I Webb MSS.

103 COOKE, EDWARD. Letters from Ireland, *temp.* Charles II. 15 VII Ailesbury MSS.

104 CORNWALLIS FAMILY. Letters, 17th century. 8 I Lord Braybrooke MSS.

105 COTTRELL FAMILY. Letters of the royalist Cottrells and the Dormer family. 2 Cottrell–Dormer MSS.

106 COVENTRY, SIR THOMAS, Lord Keeper. Official papers of Sir Thomas, 1626–39. 1 Earl of Coventry MSS.

107 COWPER, COUNTESS, MSS. Transactions in Parliament, 17 March–26 June 1627; valuable for naval history. 2 Cowper–Lucas MSS.: p. 5.

108   CRANFIELD, LIONEL. Mercantile correspondence of L. Cranfield, with editorial annotations by A. P. Newton. *Sackville MSS.*, i, 1940; other correspondence, 4 De La Warr MSS.: 276–317. See an earlier report on the Sackville MSS. 7 I, 1879.

109   CRAWFORD, WILLIAM, EARL OF. Correspondence, 1689–98. 15 IX J. J. Hope-Johnstone MSS.

110   CRESWICKE FAMILY. Papers of a Bristol family. 5 Ellacombe MSS.: 323–9.

111   CROKE, SIR JOHN, Speaker. Calendar and extracts from papers of the Croke family of Chequers Court, including papers of Sir John, recorder of London, and Speaker of the House. Mrs. Frankland–Russell–Astley MSS., 1900.

112   CROMWELL, OLIVER. Letters, calendared. 2 Mrs. Prescott MSS.: 97–8; 8 I G. H. Finch MSS.: 640.

113   DANBY, THOMAS OSBORNE, EARL OF (later Duke of Leeds). Papers of Osborne, earl of Danby and duke of Leeds, chiefly 1660–1700. 11 VII Leeds MSS.

Other papers of Osborne are in 15 II Hodgkin MSS. and Buccleuch MSS. at Montagu House, i, 1899; important papers of 1667–88 are in Earl of Lindsey MSS., 1942, which were described in 14 IX Lindsey MSS., 1895, 367–457. Many papers of the earl of Danby are in Br. Mus. Add. MSS. 28040–54, 28071–94, 38849B. See also Crick and Alman (p. 10 *supra*).

114   DARTMOUTH, EARL OF. Valuable collection in three volumes, of which vols. i and iii relate especially to naval affairs, chiefly after 1660; include correspondence of the royalist Col. William Legge, letters on Tangiers, and on the 1688 revolution. 11 V, 14 X, and 15 I Dartmouth MSS., 1887–96.

115   DAVIES, SIR JOHN. Correspondence, 1603–19. IV R. R. Hastings MSS., 1947.

116   DELAVAL FAMILY. Papers relating to naval affairs, 1611–1797. 13 VI Delaval MSS.

117   DE LA WARR, EARL OF. Correspondence of Richard Sackville, earl of Dorset, Lionel Cranfield, earl of Middlesex, and others. 4 De La Warr MSS.: 276–317. Cf. 7 I Sackville MSS., 1879; and *Sackville MSS.*, i, 1940.

118   DE L'ISLE AND DUDLEY MANUSCRIPTS. Papers chiefly of the Sidney family at Penshurst Place, including those of Sir Robert Sidney, Viscount Lisle, 1603–7, and others for the years 1608–11. Described in 3 Lord De L'Isle and Dudley MSS.: 227–33; calendared, vols. i–vi, 1925–66, with vols. iii–vi covering 1603–98. See also 3 Duke of Northumberland MSS.

119   DENBIGH, EARL OF. Family letters, including those of the first and second earls, 17th century. 4 I Denbigh MSS.; 6 I; 7 I; 8 I; and *Earl of Denbigh*, 1911. The latter volume includes letters of Basil, Lord Feilding, during his Venetian embassy.

120   DEVONSHIRE, DUKE OF. Letters and household accounts, chiefly pertaining to the northern shires, 1551–1685. 3 Devonshire MSS.: 36–45.

121   DIGBY, SIR JOHN. Correspondence of Lord Digby, afterwards earl of Bristol, who was ambassador at Madrid, 1611–12. 8 I G. Wingfield–Digby MSS.; and 10 I. The Digby correspondence was used by S. R. Gardiner.

122   DILLON, VISCOUNT. Letters of social interest, including some from Charles II and James II. 2 Dillon MSS.

123   DRYDEN FAMILY. Letters, 17th and 18th century, of Sir John Dryden, bart., John Dryden, the poet, and others. 2 Dryden MSS.

124   DYCKVELT, BARON DE. Letters, 1672–1702. *Earl of Denbigh*, pt. 5, 1911.

125   EARLE, ERASMUS, serjeant-at-law. Papers, *c.* 1630–63. 10 IV Misses Boycott MSS.

126   EDGCUMBE FAMILY. Letters, *c.* 1622–85, of Colonel Piers Edgcumbe and Sir Richard Edgcumbe. 2 Earl of Mount Edgcumbe MSS.: 21–3.

127   EDMONDES, SIR THOMAS. Letterbook. Salisbury MSS., pt. 18, 1940.

128   EGERTON, SIR THOMAS. Legal papers of Sir Thomas Egerton, Lord Ellesmere. 11 VII Bridgwater Trust MSS. Many published by the Camden Society, 1840.

129   EGLINTON FAMILY. Letters, 1569–1658. 10 I Earl of Eglinton MSS.

130   ELIOT, SIR JOHN. Papers of the family, including much that is valuable for parliamentary history. 1 Eliot MSS.: 41–4.

131   ELLACOMBE MSS. Papers concerning the Monmouth rebellion, and the Creswicke family of Bristol. 5 H. T. Ellacombe MSS.: 323–9.

132   ERSKINE, SIR CHARLES. Letters, especially as a commissioner to the Westminster Assembly. 4 Mrs. Erskine-Murray MSS.: 521–8.

133   ESSEX, Second EARL OF. Letters. 12 IX W. W. B. Hulton MSS.

134   FAIRFAX FAMILY. Papers at Leeds Castle, which formed the basis for the four volumes of *Fairfax Correspondence*. 6 I P. Wykeham Martin MSS.

135   FANSHAWE, SIR RICHARD, BARONET. Correspondence, while in Portugal and Spain, 1661–6, calendared. Heathcote MSS., 1899.

136   FINCH, HENEAGE (later Earl of Winchelsea). Letters and papers of the Finch family, earls of Winchelsea and Nottingham, valuable especially for Winchelsea's Turkish embassy, 1660–8 (vol. i), and for the correspondence of the first and second earls of Nottingham, 1670–91 (vols. ii–iii). 7 I G. H. Finch MSS., 1879, and calendared, Finch MSS., 1913–61.

137   FITZHERBERT, SIR WILLIAM, BARONET. Papers, 1626–1745, including letters of General Monck, Sir George Treby (1671–1700); and papers relating to the Popish plot. 13 VI Sir William Fitzherbert MSS.

138   FLEMING, SIR DANIEL. Accounts, 1656–88, and letters, including valuable series of news-letters, *c.* 1660–1700. 12 VII S. H. Le Fleming MSS.

139 FRANKLAND–RUSSELL–ASTLEY, Mrs. Papers of Sir John Croke; Belasyse–Russell–Falkland correspondence, 1655–97; papers of the Cutts and Revett families, 1687–1708. Mrs. Frankland–Russell–Astley MSS., 1900.

140 GARNET, HENRY. Papers concerning Garnet, the Jesuit, in 1606. Salisbury MSS., pt. 18, 1940.

141 GASCOIGNE, SIR BERNARD. Draft letters, *temp.* Charles II and James II. 15 II J. Eliot Hodgkin MSS.

142 GAWDY FAMILY. Important letters and papers relating to numerous East Anglian families, *c.* 1572–*c.* 1675. 7 I Frere MSS.: 518–30; 10 II Gawdy MSS. The Frere collection is now in Br. Mus. Add. MSS. 36988–9.

143 GELL, SIR JOHN. Letters and accounts of civil war activities. 9 II H. Chandos–Pole–Gell MSS.: 384–8.

144 GORDON, SIR ROBERT. Accounts of estate management, 1616–22. 2 Duke of Sutherland MSS.: 179.

145 GRAHAM, COLONEL JAMES. Letters. 10 IV J. F. Bagot MSS.

146 GRAHAM, SIR RICHARD. Papers of a courtier and royalist, *temp.* James I and Charles I. 6 I Sir Reginald Graham MSS.

147 GRAHAM, SIR RICHARD, VISCOUNT PRESTON. Official papers, especially concerning his embassy in Paris, 1682–8. 6 I Sir F. U. Graham MSS.; 7 I Graham MSS.: 261–428.

148 GRIFFITH, JOHN. Papers of John Griffith, lawyer and courtier, *temp.* James I, and other North Wales families. 5 Conway Griffith MSS.: 405–23.

149 GRIMSTON, SIR HARBOTTLE. Papers, personal accounts, travel records, valuable for social history. Verulam MSS., 1906. See also papers of the Yorkshire Grimstons in Lady Du Cane MSS., 1905.

150 HALIFAX, GEORGE SAVILE, MARQUESS OF. Letters of the Savile and other north country families prior to 1660; correspondence and notes of the first George Savile, Lord Halifax, 1664–1700. 2 Earl of Spencer MSS.

151 HAMILTON, DUKES OF. Miscellaneous letters and papers of the marquesses (later dukes) of Hamilton, 1570–1707, 11 VI Duke of Hamilton MSS.; calendared in Supplement, 1932; letters of William Douglas, third duke, 15 VIII Buccleuch and Queensberry MSS. at Drumlanrig I: 215–64. Some letters (1635–50) were edited by S. R. Gardiner, Camden Soc., 1880; cf. *Camden Soc. Misc.* ix.

152 HARE, FRANCIS. Letters of a chaplain to Marlborough, 1704–70. 14 IX T. J. Hare MSS.

153 HARLEY FAMILY. Correspondence, period of the civil war and *temp.* Anne, Bath MSS. i–iii, 1904–8; family correspondence, 1603–1700, and official papers of Robert Harley, *temp.* Anne, 14 II and 15 IV Portland MSS. iii–iv; and Portland MSS. v–x (6 vol. series, 1899–1931).

154 HARVEY, JOHN. Partial diary, 1710. 2 J. T. Harvey MSS.

155 HASTINGS FAMILY. Family papers and 17th-century letters; parliamentary notes, 1614, 1621; news-letters. MSS. of R. R. Hastings, 4 vols.,
1928–47. Cf. nos. 87, 115, 208. Now in Huntington Library, California. Cf.
Hunt. Lib. Bull. 5 (1934), 1–67.

156 HERBERT, SIR EDWARD, LORD HERBERT OF CHERBURY.
Papers of Lord Herbert and others of the family. 10 IV Powiss MSS.

157 HEVENINGHAM, ARTHUR. Miscellaneous papers of Sir John,
Arthur, and others of the family. 9 II Earl of Leicester MSS.

158 HOBART FAMILY. Papers, 1601 to mid 18th century, of an influential
Norfolk family. Marquess of Lothian MSS., 1905.

159 HODGKIN MANUSCRIPTS. An artificial collection from all parts of
the century, but especially rich in letters of the period of 1665–7, and 1702–19.
15 II J. E. Hodgkin MSS., 1897.

See *E.H.R.* 18 (1903), 390–2, for a notice on some items. Parts were publ. in full in
3 vols. of *Rariora: being notes of some of the printed books, manuscripts . . . collected
1858–1900 by John Eliot Hodgkin*, 1902.

160 HOLLES, SIR JOHN. Papers of Sir John and others of the Holles family.
13 II Portland MSS. ii; letter-book, *temp.* James I, Portland MSS. ix, 1923;
Duke of Buccleuch MSS. (Montagu House), i, 1899; Bath MSS. ii.

161 HOPKINSON, REV. FRANCIS, MSS. Letters relating to the Exchequer, early Stuart period. 3 Hopkinson MSS.: 264–7.

162 HOUSE OF LORDS MSS. 1450–1678. *Reports 1–9*, House of Lords
MSS., which include, besides a calendar of acts and petitions, calendars of
important undertakings, such as the Laudian visitation of 1634 (*2nd report*),
John Dury's mission to the continent, 1631–40 (*4th report*); lists of extant
protestation returns, 1642 (*5th report*); Naseby letters of Charles I (*Reports 1
and 5*). The calendar for 1678–93 is continued in 4 vols., *Reports 11–14*.

A new series, of which 11 volumes have appeared (1900–62), gives the calendar, 1693–
1714, including with the 4th volume, 1699–1702, the journal of the House of Lords of
the protectorate, 1657–9. Draft journals of 1610 and 1625 and other early materials are
in N.S. vol. 11. For Nalson's papers, 1641–60, see 13 I Duke of Portland MSS. i. See
also p. 113 *infra.*

163 HUTTON, SIR RICHARD, Judge. Diary, 1614–39. 12 IX J. H.
Gurney MSS.

164 INGRAM, SIR ARTHUR. Papers, 17th century, relating to the Ingrams
of Temple Newsam, Yorkshire. *Various collections*, viii, 1913, F. Lindley
Wood MSS.

165 JAMES II. Letters and miscellaneous papers, a number from the period
of Charles II. 8 I, pt. 2, Lord Braybrooke MSS.; 10 VI B. R. T. Balfour
MSS.; 15 V Foljambe MSS.; 15 VIII Buccleuch MSS. at Drumlanrig I.

166 JERVOISE, SIR THOMAS. Papers, including Hampshire affairs and
parliamentary items. *Various collections* iv, F. H. T. Jervoise MSS.

167 JESSOP, WILLIAM, Clerk of the House of Commons. 17th-century
papers of Jessop. 12 IX W. W. B. Hulton MSS.

168　LANGDALE, SIR MARMADUKE. Miscellaneous letters, especially from exiled royalists to Sir Marmaduke Langdale, 1650-60. *Various collections* ii, Mrs. Harford MSS.

169　LECHMERE, SIR NICHOLAS, Baron of the Exchequer. Papers, 1651-1701. 5 Lechmere MSS.: 299-300.

170　LEE MSS. Notebook of an unknown barrister, 1616-18, described briefly. 3 J. H. Lee MSS.: 267-9.

171　LEGH FAMILY. Papers, 1609-1743, of the Leghs of Lyme Hall, Cheshire. 3 W. J. Legh MSS.: 268-70.

172　LE STRANGE FAMILY. Account books, estate and family letters of the Le Strange family of Norfolk, with much on the 17th century. 11 VII Le Strange MSS., calendared; some excerpts, with earlier description, 3 Le Strange MSS.: 271-3.

173　LEVESON, SIR RICHARD. Letters, *temp*. Charles I and the civil war especially. 5 Duke of Sutherland MSS.: 136-214.

174　LINDSEY MSS. Important collection, including Osborne papers, 1672-1713; treasury accounts, 1671-88; papers relating to the treasury; the coal trade, etc.; and Charles Bertie's diary of a trip to France, 1660-2. MSS. of the Earl of Lindsey (ed. C. G. O. Bridgeman and J. C. Walker, 1942), supplementing the earlier report, 14 X, 1895.

175　LODER FAMILY. Papers, largely 17th century, including Loder farm and household account book, 1610-20. 13 IV Loder-Symonds MSS.

176　LONSDALE MSS. Papers of the Lowther family, 1626-1815, with parliamentary diaries of 24 Apr.-12 June 1626, and 4 June 1628-25 Feb. 1629. 13 VII Earl of Lonsdale MSS.

177　LYTTLETON, SIR THOMAS. Letters, civil war period, in Worcestershire. 2 Lord Lyttleton MSS.: 36.

178　MACCLESFIELD MSS. Correspondence of George Stepney, 1694-1707, and James Cressett, 1693-1703. 1 Earl of Macclesfield MSS.

179　MALET MSS. Miscellaneous correspondence, 17th century, of various political figures, including Arthur Hopton, Edward Hyde, Bulstrode Whitelocke, and Windebank. 5 Malet MSS.: 308-21; and 7 I Malet MSS.: 429-33.

180　MANCHESTER, EARLS OF. Papers and correspondence of the earls of Manchester, Lord Mandeville, and others at Kimbolton. 8 II Duke of Manchester MSS., 1881; reissued, 1910.

181　MARLBOROUGH, JOHN, First DUKE OF. Papers relating to the first duke and related families, including documents on St. Albans. 8 I, pt. 1, Duke of Marlborough MSS.; 2 Lord Lyttleton MSS.: 36.

182　MILDMAY MSS. Papers, especially some relating to the Jewel House, 1588-1660. 7 H. G. St. J. Mildmay MSS.: 590-6.

183　MONCK, GEORGE (later Duke of Albemarle). Correspondence, mid 17th century. 5 Stanhope Grove MSS.: 360-1. Other papers in 13 VI Fitzherbert MSS.; and R. R. Hastings MSS. ii.

184 MONTAGU FAMILY. Correspondence, mainly first half of the 17th century. Lord Montagu of Beaulieu MSS., 1900. See also Buccleuch MSS. (89).

185 MOORE, JOHN, member of Parliament. Correspondence, civil war period. 10 IV Captain Stewart's MSS.: 83–99.

186 MORAY, EARL OF. Miscellaneous papers, including royal household accounts, *temp.* James I, and letters to the earl of Somerset. 6 Earl of Moray MSS.: 634–73.

187 MORE, SIR GEORGE. The 17th-century papers relate chiefly to Sir George More of Losely, Surrey, his son Robert, and other Surrey families. 7 W. More–Molyneux MSS.: 596–681.

Some of the papers are printed in Kempe, *Losely MSS.* (284). Many of the papers are now in the Folger Library, Washington.

188 MORRISON MSS. Miscellaneous collection of Alfred Morrison, containing many 17th-century items. 9 II Alfred Morrison MSS.

See A. W. Thibaudeau, ed., *Catalogue of collections of . . . Alfred Morrison,* 6 vols., 1883–92; and a second series, 7 vols., 1893–7, including the important 'Bulstrode papers', which relate to 1667–75.

189 MOSTYN PAPERS. News-letters, 1673–92, especially. 1 and 4 Lord Mostyn MSS.

190 NALSON, JOHN. Papers, 1628–*c.* 1660, collected by Nalson, chiefly from the office of the Clerk of the Parliaments. 13 I Duke of Portland MSS. i, 1891.

191 NEVILLE FAMILY. Letters, the Nevilles of Holt, 3 Peake MSS.: 277–8. Some papers of the Berkshire Nevilles are in 8 I, pt. 2, Lord Braybrooke MSS.

192 NEWPORT, FRANCIS LORD. Letters, *temp.* civil war, excerpts. 5 Duke of Sutherland MSS.

193 NEWTON, SIR ISAAC. Papers concerning the Mint. 8 I Earl of Portsmouth MSS.: 60–92; several letters in 10 VI Balfour MSS.

194 NORTHUMBERLAND, DUKE OF, MSS. Miscellaneous papers of the Percy family, including letters of Algernon, earl of Northumberland, and of Prince Rupert, calendared. 3 Duke of Northumberland MSS., Alnwick, pp. 45–118; 6 Duke of Northumberland MSS., Syon, pp. 221–33.

195 ORMONDE, DUKE OF. Collection formerly at Kilkenny Castle, now in the National Library, Dublin, which includes valuable correspondence of Robert Southwell with the first duke of Ormonde, 1677–85, a calendar of petitions, 1666–9, and many other documents important for Irish history, 1572–1713.

Abstracts in the first two volumes, and fuller calendars in the new series (8 vols.). Descriptions and abstracts, *2nd report,* app., pp. 209–10; *3rd report,* app., pp. 425–30; *4th report,* app., pp. 539–73; *6th report,* app., pp. 719–80; *7th report,* app., pp. 737–834; *8th report,* i, pp. 499–552; *9th report,* pt. 2, pp. 126–81; calendars, 2 vols. and index, Ormonde MSS., 1895–1909; new series, 8 vols., 1902–20. Other correspondence of Ormonde is 15 II J. Eliot Hodgkin MSS.

196 ORRERY, EARL OF. Letters to the earl from the earl of Anglesey, 1661–77. 6 I Leconfield MSS.

197 PASTON FAMILY. Letters to Sir Robert Paston, 1661–79. 6 I Inglesby
MSS.: 363–91. Copies of Paston family letters. 12 IX R. W. Ketton MSS.

198 PENNINGTON, ADMIRAL. Logs, 1631–6. 10 IV Lord Muncaster
MSS.: 275–96.

199 PEPYS, SAMUEL. Papers, 1661–1702. 15 II J. Eliot Hodgkin MSS.
See also Magdalene College (Camb.) MSS., 1911.

200 PERCEVAL [PERCIVAL] FAMILY. Letters, 1640–5, 1701–30. Extracts, 7 Earl of Egmont MSS.; and i–ii, Egmont MSS., 1905–9. Later papers,
including a journal of Sir John Percival, 1686. 3 vols. Egmont MSS., 1920–3.

201 PHELIPS FAMILY. Chiefly papers of Sir Edward Phelips, Speaker, his
son, Sir Robert Phelips, and others, 1607–85. I W. Phelips MSS.: 57–8;
calendar, 3 Phelips MSS.: 281–6.

202 PITT, THOMAS, Governor. Papers, 1698–1709, with other family
papers. 13 III and 14 V J. B. Fortescue MSS. i–ii.

203 POPHAM, EDWARD. Naval papers, *temp.* Commonwealth, with papers
also of William Clarke, 1650–61, and Dr. George Clarke. Calendared.
Leyborne–Popham MSS., 1899.

204 PORTLAND MSS. See nos. 153, 190.

205 PROGER, EDWARD. Letters and papers, 1637–1715. 10 IV N. Story
Maskelyne MSS.

206 PYM, JOHN. 17th-century papers of John Pym, Charles Pym, and others.
10 VI P. P. Bouverie MSS.

207 PYNE, JOHN. Letters, mid 17th century, of Colonel John Pyne. 9
W. Pyne MSS.

208 RAWDON FAMILY. Correspondence, 1641–94. R. R. Hastings MSS. ii.

209 RIGBY, ALEXANDER, clerk of the peace. Papers relating chiefly to
Lancashire in the 17th century preserved by Rigby and his family. 14 IV
Lord Kenyon MSS.

210 RINUCCINI MSS. 'Memoirs' of the nuncio to Ireland. 9 Earl of
Leicester MSS. ii, 340–57. See also no. 4114.

211 RUTLAND MSS. Papers of the Manners family, including a diary of
the earl of Rutland of 1639; calendared, with extracts. 12 IV–V, Duke of
Rutland MSS., 1888–91.

212 SALISBURY, MARQUESS OF. Papers, including those of the Cecils,
1603–24 and later, described in *Reports 3* and *7*; calendar in progress, 19 vols.,
1883–1965, with vols. xv–xix covering 1603–7. See Read (11 n.), no. 185.
Microfilm of these important papers is in the Br. Mus. and in the Folger
Library, Washington.

213 SALVETTI, AMERIGO. Dispatches, 1625–8. 11 I H. D. Skrine MSS.

214 SALWEY, RICHARD, MAJOR. Letters and papers, 1653–85. 10 IV
A. Salwey MSS.

215 SLINGSBY, HENRY. Papers, *temp.* Charles II. 6 I Sir Reginald Graham MSS.

216 SMYTH, JOHN, of Nibley. Papers concerning Gloucestershire and other border counties, collected by Smyth, steward of Lord Berkeley. 5 R. Cholmondeley MSS.: 333–60.

217 SOMERSET MSS. Correspondence of the Seymour family, relating especially to the civil war and to Anne's reign. 15 VII Duke of Somerset MSS.

218 SPELMAN, HENRY. Papers. 12 IX J. H. Gurney MSS.

219 STOPFORD-SACKVILLE MSS. Papers relating to Monmouth's rebellion. Described in *9th report*, pt. 3; calendared in 2 vols., 1904–10.

220 STRICKLAND, ROBERT. Correspondence, 1638–85, of Robert Strickland of Sizergh. 5 W. C. Strickland MSS.: 329–32.

221 STUART PAPERS. Calendar of the Stuart papers at Windsor Castle, chiefly of interest for period after 1714, but with vols. i, ii, iv, and vi including earlier materials. 7 vols. 1902–23.

222 SUTHERLAND MSS. Valuable collections of news-letters for the civil war and restoration periods. Described in *2nd report*; excerpts in 5 Duke of Sutherland MSS.: 135–214.

223 THROCKMORTON FAMILY. Papers of the Throckmorton family, including some regarding Titus Oates. 10 IV Sir N. W. Throckmorton MSS.

224 TILLARD, WILLIAM. Diary during voyage to India, 1699–1705. Described, 15 X Sir Walter Corbet MSS.

225 TRUMBULL PAPERS. Correspondence of Sir William Trumbull, 1645–1728, i, pts. 1–2; papers of William Trumbull the elder, 1605–14, largely diplomatic, and some of the Spanish embassy of Fanshawe, 1661–6, ii–iii. Marquess of Downshire MSS., 4 vols., 1924–40.

226 TUFTON FAMILY. 11 VII Lord Hothfield MSS.

227 VANE FAMILY. Letters, Sir Harry Vane, Sir Walter Vane, and others, 1632–74. *Various collections*, iii, 1904, P. R. Papillon MSS.: 256–8.

228 VERE FAMILY. 17th-century papers of the Veres, earls of Oxford. 14 IX J. Round MSS.; and Portland MSS. ii.

229 VERNEY MSS. Letters of Sir Edmund, Sir Ralph, and Sir John Verney especially. 7 Sir H. Verney MSS.: 433–509.

230 VERNON, JAMES. Correspondence during embassy to Copenhagen 1704–7. Portland MSS. ix, 1923.

231 WARREN, SIR WILLIAM. Naval accounts. 1668–75. Earl of Lindsey MSS., 1942.

232 WENTWORTH FAMILY. Papers, 17th and 18th centuries. *Various collections*, ii, 1903, Mrs. Wentworth of Woolley Park MSS.; and iii, 1904, Sir T. Barrett Lennard MSS. (calendared): 155–255.

233 WOODFORDE, ROBERT, steward. Diary, 1637–41 (extracts). 9, pt. 2, A. J. Woodforde MSS.

234 WORTLEY, SIR FRANCIS. Family papers, relating to Yorkshire. Described, 3 Lord Wharncliffe MSS.

235 WROTTESLEY FAMILY. 17th-century letters, Hugh and Walter Wrottesley especially. 2 Lord Wrottesley MSS.

2. Local Collections

(a) *Colleges*

(1) *Oxford*

236 Balliol, 4. Corpus Christi, 2: 126. Exeter, register, 2: 127–30. Jesus, 2: 130. Lincoln, 2: 130–2. Magdalen, 4. New, 2: 132–6. Oriel, 2: 136–7. Queen's, 2: 137–42; 4. St. John's, 4. Trinity, 2: 142–3. Wadham, 5: 479–80. Worcester, 2: 143.

(2) *Cambridge*

237 The University, miscellaneous, 1: 73–4. Clare, accounts, 2: 110–16. Downing, accounts, 3: 320–7. Emmanuel, accounts, 4: 417–21. Gonville and Caius, registers and accounts, 2: 116–17. Magdalene, 5: 481–4, and Pepys MSS., calendared, 1911. Pembroke, 5: 484. Sidney Sussex, registers, 3: 327–9. St. Catherine's, order book, etc., 4: 423–4. Trinity Hall, registers and accounts, 2: 121–3.

(3) *Dublin*

238 Trinity College, 4: 598–9.

(b) *Counties of England*

239 Essex, sessions records, 10 IV: 502–7. Somerset, sessions and other records, 7, pt. 1: 694–5. Suffolk, sessions and military records, 13 IV Woodhouse MSS. Wiltshire, sessions and other records, *Various collections*, i, 1901. Worcestershire, sessions records, ibid. Yorkshire (West and North Ridings), 9 I.

(c) *Municipal Corporations (England)*

The records are chiefly accounts and registers, with court records in some cases. Few are fully calendared.

240 Abingdon, 1. Aldeburghe, *Various collections*, iv, 1907. Axbridge, 3: 300–3. Barnstaple, 9 I. Berwick-upon-Tweed, 3: 308–10; *Various collections*, i, 1901. Beverley, *Corporation of Beverley*, 1900. Bishops Castle, 10 IV. Bridgnorth, 10 IV. Burford, *Various collections*, i, 1901. Bury St. Edmunds, 14 VIII. Cambridge, 1. Canterbury, 9 I. Carlisle, 9 I. Chester, 8 I: 355–403. Coventry 1; 15 X. Dunwich, *V arious collections*, vii, 1914. Eye, 10 IV. Exeter, full records, *City of Exeter*, 1916. Glastonbury, 1. Gloucester, 12 IX. Great Grimsby, 14 VIII. Hastings, 13 IV. Hereford, 13 IV. High Wycombe, 5: 554–65. Higham Ferrars, 12 IX. Hythe, 2: 91–2; 4. Ipswich, 9 I. Kendal,

10 IV. King's Lynn, 11 III. Kingston-on-Thames, 3. Leicester, 8 I: 403–41. Lincoln, 14 VIII. Lostwithiel, *Various collections*, i, 1901. Minehead, 10 VI Luttrell MSS. New Romney, 4. Newark, 12 IX. Norwich, 1. Nottingham, 1. Orford, *Various collections*, iv, 1907. Plymouth, 9 I; 10 IV. Pontefract, 8 I: 269–76. Reading, 11 VII. Rochester, 9 I. Rye, 13 IV. St. Albans, 5: 565–8. Salisbury, *Various collections*, iv, 1907. Sandwich, 5: 568–71. Shrewsbury, 15 X. Southampton, 11 III. Stratford-upon-Avon, 9 I. Thetford, *Various collections*, vii, 1914. Totnes, 3: 341–50. Wells, 1; 3: 350–1. Wenlock, 10 IV. Weymouth and Melcombe Regis, 5: 575–90. Wisbech, 9 I. Yarmouth (Norfolk), 9 I. York, 1.

(d) *Manuscripts of Ecclesiastical Institutions*

241   Church of England registers and documents (Bishoprics, deans and chapters): Bristol, 1. Canterbury, 6 I; 9 I; *Various collections*, i, 1901. Carlisle, 9 I. Chichester, *Various collections*, i, 1901. Ely, 12 IX. Exeter, *Various collections*, iv, 1907. Gloucester, 12 IX; *Various collections*, vii, 1914. Lichfield, 14 VIII. Lincoln, 12 IX. London, *Various collections*, vii, 1914. Norwich, 1. Peterborough, 12 IX. Salisbury, *Various collections*, i, 1901, and iv, 1907. Southwell, 12 IX. Wells, 1; 10 III; *MSS. of the Dean and chapter of Wells*, i–ii, 1907–14. Westminster, 1. Windsor, *Various collections*, vii, 1914. Worcester, 14 VIII. York, 1.

242   Parishes (see also Pargellis (11 n.), no. 4443): Carisbrooke, 6 I. Cheddar (Somerset), churchwardens and other 17th-century accounts, 3 : 329–31. Hartland (Devon), 5: 571–5. Hunstanton vicarage, 9 I. Parkham (Devon), overseers' books, 4: 468–9. Mendlesham (Suffolk), 5: 592–7.

243   Non-Anglican Protestantism: Dr. Williams's Library. See Baxter (81).

244   Roman Catholic institutions: Dominican Friars at Woodchester near Stroud, 2: 146–9. Roman Catholic chapter of London, 5: 463–70. Roman Catholic archbishop of Westminster, 5: 470–6. Stonyhurst College, 3: 334–41 and 10 IV: 176–99. College of Irish Franciscans, Louvain, 4: 599–614. *Franciscan MSS.* at Killiney, Dublin, 1906. See also 10 V Earl of Fingall MSS.

(e) *Other Institutions or Repositories in England*

245   Chetham Library, Manchester. Miscellaneous documents, 16th–17th centuries, many relating to Ireland. 2 Chetham Library MSS. Christ's Hospital, Abingdon, 1. Royal College of Physicians, 8 I, pt. 1. Corporation of Trinity House, 8 I, pt. 1. Inner Temple, 11 VII. Post Office records (1673–7), 10, pt. 4, Mainwaring MSS. Merchant Adventurers (York) and Yorkshire Philosophical Society, 1.

(f) *Ireland*

Collections in the preceding pages which include significant Irish documentation are the following: Cowper i–ii (see Coke, 101); De La Warr, *3rd, 4th*, and *7th Reports* (117); Downshire (see Trumbull, 225); House of Lords (162); Laing (253); Portland (see 153 and 190); Salisbury (212); and Stuart (221).

In addition, materials in the following relate specifically to Ireland. See also Ch. XV *infra*.

246 Municipal Corporations. Cork, 1, 1874. Dublin, 1. Galway, 10 V: 45–6. Kilkenny, 1. Limerick, 1. Waterford, 1; 10 V.

247 Collections with materials specifically described as Irish:

Ailesbury (72). Cooke on restoration and Charles II.
Ashburnham (75). Essex viceroyalty; T. Taylor's books of survey.
Chetham Library (245). Loftus; Church of Ireland.
Clements (*Various collections*, viii). Irish Lords Journal, 1639–41.
De Ros (4: 317–25). Ginkell, Irish campaign.
Drogheda (9 II Drogheda MSS.: 293–330). Loftus. See also *Various collections*, iii, Barrett Lennard MSS., 1904.
Egmont (200). Perceval, Castle Chamber.
Franciscan (244). Irish college of Louvain.
Hastings vol. iv (155). Bramhall; Sir John Davies.
Leconfield (73). Anglesey.
Leicester (210). Rinuccini.
Leyborne Popham (97, 203). George Clarke, William III's campaign.
Lyons (2: 235–48). Archbishop King.
Ormonde (195).
Rosse (1; 2: 217–23). Sir W. Parsons.
Talbot of Malahide (8 I, pt. 1, pp. 493 ff.). Richard Talbot, duke of Tyrconnel, 1689.

(g) *Scotland*

For Scottish history, collections in the *Reports* listed above that are of especial importance are: Annandale [Hope-Johnstone MSS.] (74); Buccleuch (89); Fleming [Le Fleming MSS.] (138); Crawford [Hope-Johnstone MSS.] (109); Eglinton (129); Hamilton (151); Harley [Portland MSS.] (153); Moray (186). See also C. S. Terry, *Index to papers relating to Scotland . . . H.M.C. reports* (3695).

In addition to the collections listed below, selected because of their considerable quantity of material relating specifically to Scotland, others relating to Scottish history are listed in Mullins (23 n.).

248 CORPORATION (MUNICIPAL) MSS. Official documents of Aberdeen, Edinburgh, and Glasgow. Described, *1st report*, 1874.

249 ATHOLE MSS. Royal letters; papers relating affairs of Murray, the first duke, *temp.* William and Anne. 12 VIII Duke of Athole MSS.

250 LAING MSS. An artificial collection, assembled by David Laing, now at the Univ. of Edinburgh; contains many papers of value for general Scottish history; calendared. Vol. i goes to 1699. Laing MSS. i–ii, 1914–25.

251 MAR AND KELLIE MSS. Papers of the Erskine family, especially of the earl of Mar at the time of the union. Earl of Mar and Kellie MSS., 1904; suppl., ed. by H. Paton, 1930.

252 MARCHMONT MSS. Papers of the earls of Marchmont especially of Patrick Hume, the first earl, who was Lord Chancellor of Scotland (1696–1702). 14 III Earl of Marchmont MSS.: 56–173. Other correspondence was pub-

lished, *Selection from the papers of the earls of Marchmont . . .*, ed. by G. H. Rose, 3 vols., 1831.

253 MONTROSE MSS. Description and abstracts of papers at Buchanan Castle, relating especially to James, first marquis of Montrose (1626–50); some Lennox and Monteith papers in the *2nd report*. 2 Duke of Montrose MSS.: 165–77; 3 Duke of Montrose MSS.: 377–80, 395–6, 399–402.

254 SEAFIELD MSS. Correspondence of Seafield, Lord Chancellor *temp.* Anne. Seafield MSS., 1894. See also the volumes of correspondence edited by J. Grant and P. Hume Brown for the Scot. Hist. Soc., Edin., 1912, 1915. (See no. 3757.)

(h) *Wales*

255 WELSH LANGUAGE, Manuscripts in. Includes papers of Lord Mostyn, W. R. M. Wynne, and others. 2 vols. in 7, 1898–1910.

Although these volumes are mainly relevant to earlier periods, some 17th-century verse is calendared.

Among the *Reports* of the Historical Manuscripts Commission the following contain material on 17th-century Wales:

Beaufort (82).
Brogyntyn (*2nd report*).
Carreglwyd and Berw (*5th report*).
Cecil (212), vols. xv–xviii.
Chirk Castle (*2nd report*).
Cholmondeley (*5th report*).
De L'Isle and Dudley (118), vol. iii.
Earl of Denbigh (119).
Gwysaney (*6th report*).
House of Lords (162).
Kenyon (*14th report*, ix).
Portland (204).
Puleston of Emral (*2nd report*) and of Worthenbury (*15th report*, vii).

II
POLITICAL HISTORY

A. GENERAL, 1603–1714

The reader will wish to check the various chronological subdivisions of this section for works which, because they relate primarily to a particular phase of political history, have been classified in the list for that period. For collections of manuscripts and tracts, consult pp. 36–8 *infra* and nos. 257, 258. Somewhat similar to modern yearbooks or almanacs are Chamberlayne, *Angliae notitia* and Miège, *The new state of England* (2353). See also *infra*, Chs. V, VI, VII, and IX. For sections on Parliament and Proclamations see Ch. III. Particular persons may be traced by the index.

1. Sources

(a) *State Papers*

256 CALENDAR OF STATE PAPERS, Domestic series. 1603–1704. 81 vols.+. 1857–1947+.

Invaluable, with much material on foreign affairs as well as domestic matters. The first two vols. of the series for James II (Feb. 1685–May 1687), 1960–4, reduce the earlier gap of 1685–9. Cf. S. C. Lomas, 'The State papers of the early Stuarts and the interregnum', *R.H.S. Trans.*, 2nd Ser. 16 (1902), 97–132. Comments on domestic affairs appear frequently in the Venetian state papers, for which there are *Calendars*, 1864–1947, with vols. 10–38 relating to 1603–75. The foreign state papers have not been completely calendared for the period.

257 CLARENDON, EDWARD, EARL OF. State papers collected by Edward, earl of Clarendon, commencing 1621. Ed. by R. Scrope and T. Monkhouse. 3 vols. Oxf. 1767–86.

A valuable collection from the Clarendon MSS. in the Bodleian Library, extending to 1660. See the *Calendar of the Clarendon state papers*, ed. by O. Ogle, W. H. Bliss, and W. D. Macray, 3 vols., Oxf. 1869–76; vol. iv (1657–60) ed. by F. J. Routledge, 1932.

258 HARDWICKE, P. YORKE, EARL OF, ed. Miscellaneous state papers, 1501–1726. 2 vols. 1778.

Selected chiefly from the Hardwicke papers in the Br. Mus. (Add. MSS. 35349–36278). Includes papers pertaining to the Spanish match and the marriage of Charles I, correspondence of Buckingham, documents on the Bishops' Wars and on Monmouth's rebellion, correspondence of various statesmen (to 1709), and of William III. In a *Supplement to state papers* (s.l., s.a.) are letters of James I and of Argyle (1641–2), and documents pertaining to Portland in 1697.

(b) *Letters, Memoirs, and Miscellaneous Collections*

259 COLLINS, A., ed. Letters and memorials of state in the reigns of Queen Mary, Queen Elizabeth, King James, King Charles I, part of the reign of King Charles II, and Oliver's usurpation . . . from the originals at Penshurst . . . and from his majesty's Office of Papers. 2 vols. 1746.

Commonly called 'Sydney Papers'. Valuable collection of letters of members of this family. Cf. *Sydney papers, consisting of a journal of the earl of Leicester,* 1646-61, and *Original letters of Algernon Sydney* (1659-61), ed. by R. W. Blencowe, 1825; and no. 118.

260   ELLIS, SIR H., ed. Original letters illustrative of English history. 11 vols. 1824-46.

A good selection, in three series. See also E. Harington's edn. of Sir John Harington's *Nugae antiquae, being a collection of original papers in prose and verse,* 2 vols., 1769-75; later edn. by T. Clark (2 vols., 1804) includes a repr. of Harington's *Brief view of the state of the Church* [to 1608], originally publ. 1653. Sir G. Bromley edited a *Collection of original royal letters* (Charles I, Charles II, and James II), 1787. For other collections of letters see nos. 337, 338, 371, 375, and § F in this chapter on Correspondence, Journals, and Biographies. Not to be trusted is James Howell's *Epistolae Ho-Elianae* (2432).

261   BROWNING, ANDREW, ed. English historical documents, 1660-1714. 1953.

Vol. viii of the series under the general editorship of D. C. Douglas. Contains a valuable introduction as well as carefully selected documents and bibliography.

(c) *Early Histories*

For useful comments on the earliest historians see C. H. Firth, 'The undeserved neglect of earlier English historians by their successors', *Bull. Inst. Hist. Research,* 5 (1927-8), 65-9. His earlier article, 'The development of the study of seventeenth-century history', *R.H.S. Trans.,* 3rd Ser. 7 (1913), 25-48, is also valuable. See also Ch. X *infra,* nos. 3005-8.

262   KENNET [KENNETT], WHITE, Bishop of Peterborough. A complete history of England [to William III]. 3 vols. 1706. 2nd edn. 1719.

Vols. i-ii comprise histories collected by J. Hughes, including Camden's *Annals of James I* and Wilson's *History of King James* (282). Kennet's Whiggish narrative (1625-1702) in vol. iii evoked responses such as Echard (263) and North (342 n.). See also no. 342.

263   ECHARD, LAURENCE. The history of England [to 1688]. 3 vols. 1707-18. 3rd edn. 1720.

Tory reply to Kennet, but a less careful work. Cf. Echard, *An appendix . . . of several explanations and amendments,* 1720; and his *History of the revolution and the establishment of England in 1688,* 1725. See also comments in preface to Aiken, *Nottingham* (483).

264   RAPIN-THOYRAS, PAUL DE. The history of England. Translated [from French] . . . with additional notes [and a continuation to the accession of George II] by Nicholas Tindal. 28 vols. 1726-47. 3rd edn. 5 vols. 1743-5.

First publ. in French in 10 vols., 1723-7, this is a valuable work by a Huguenot exile, and constitutes a source for the period of the 1688 revolution. Bibliographical notes are included in the biography written by Raoul de Cazenove, Paris, 1866; in Lowndes, p. 2047; and in *D.N.B.*

2. LATER HISTORIES

See also *Cambridge Modern History* (7), vols. iii-v.

265   ASHLEY, M. P. England in the seventeenth century. 1952. Bibl.

An excellent brief account in the 'Pelican' series. By Ashley also an essay in *Life under the Stuarts* edited by J. E. Morpurgo and others, 1954. Another single-volume account is I. D. Jones, *The English revolution . . . 1603–1714*, 1931. See also D. Ogg, *Europe in the seventeenth century*, 8th edn., 1960; and F. L. Nussbaum, *The triumph of science and reason* (1660–85), N.Y. 1953. Useful chapters on various subjects relating to the period are in *Historical essays, 1600–1750, presented to David Ogg*, ed. by H. E. Bell and R. L. Ollard, N.Y. 1963.

266 CARTE, T. A general history of England . . . from the earliest times [to 1654]. 4 vols. 1747–55.

Though largely outdated, still of some value.

267 CLARK, G. N. The later Stuarts, 1660–1714. (Oxford history of England.) Oxf. 1934. 2nd edn. Oxf. 1955. Bibl.

One of the best for the period, including sections on cultural as well as political matters. Also by Clark, *The seventeenth century*, Oxf. 1929; rev. edn., Oxf. 1947. See also the volume by Sir R. Lodge in the 'Political History of England' series (vol. viii), 1910 (271).

268 DAVIES, G. The early Stuarts, 1603–1660. Oxf. 1937. Repr. with corrections. 1945. 1952. 2nd edn. 1959.

A detailed account, following the traditional Whig interpretation; a companion volume to no. 267. A useful bibliography of Davies's works, compiled by P. Hardacre, was printed in the volume by Davies entitled *Essays on the later Stuarts*, San Marino, 1958. For other useful volumes dealing with the early part of the century, see J. D. Mackie, *Cavalier and Puritan*, 1930 (N.Y., 1936); Sir J. A. R. Marriott, *The crisis of English liberty*, Oxf. 1930; and J. Mackinnon, *A history of modern liberty*, vols. iii and iv, 1908–41. The latter is virtually a general history of England and Scotland. The second and third vols. of Sir Winston Churchill's *History of the English-speaking peoples*, N.Y. 1956–7, contain some excellent sketches of political and military leaders.

269 FIRTH, SIR C. Essays, historical and literary. N.Y. 1938.

Includes comments on Raleigh, Milton, and Clarendon, among others. Other valuable essays on varied subjects, such as Monmouth's rebellion, witchcraft, and Lady Arabella Stuart, are contained in F. A. Inderwick, *Side-lights on the Stuarts*, 1888; later edn., 1891. See also W. Notestein, *The Stuart period: unsolved problems*, Wash. 1919; and W. A. Aiken and B. D. Henning, eds., *Conflict in Stuart England: essays in honor of Wallace Notestein*, Lond. and N.Y. 1960.

270 HUME, D. The history of Great Britain. 2 vols. Edin. and Lond. 1754–7. Later edn. 8 vols. 1770.

The first edn. (1603–88) was extended back to 1485 in the later edn.; various continuations were made by T. Smollett and others. Tory in viewpoint and long a classic, Hume's work was unscholarly and is considered now as of little historical value. Largely written in criticism of Hume is G. Brodie, *History of the British empire from the accession of Charles I to the restoration*, 4 vols., Edin. 1820; later edn., 3 vols., 1866.

271 HUNT, W. and POOLE, R. L., eds. The political history of England. 12 vols. 1905–10. Bibl.

A standard work. Vol. vii (1603–1660) is by F. C. Montague, 1907; vol. viii (1660–1702) is by Sir R. Lodge, 1910; and vol. ix (1702–60) is by I. S. Leadham, 1909. That by Lodge especially presents an objective and clear account of political developments.

272 KENYON, J. P. The Stuarts: a study in English kingship. 1958. Bibl.

Essentially political history, with modern interpretations, but not without flaw. A somewhat loosely organized study of the period is Sir C. Petrie, *The Stuarts*, 1937, later edn., 1958.

273   LINGARD, J. A history of England to 1688. 8 vols. 1819–30. Later edn. 10 vols. 1854–5 and several reprints, with an abridgement and continuation by H. N. Birt, 1903, 1912.

A careful survey from a moderate Roman Catholic point of view.

274   OLDMIXON, J. The critical history of England. 2 vols. 1724–6.

Criticizes Clarendon and Echard, but defends Burnet. Strongly Whig in viewpoint also is his *History of England, during the reigns of the royal house of Stuart,* 1730. The *Critical history* led to considerable controversy, provoking replies from Zachary Grey (*Defence of our ancient and modern historians,* 1725), and Francis Atterbury (*Vindication,* 1731). Oldmixon continued his *History of England* through the reign of George I in 1 vol., 1735; and wrote also *The secret history of Europe . . . for 50 years past, with original papers,* 4 pts., 1712–15.

275   RANKE, L. VON. A history of England principally in the 17th century. 6 vols. Oxf. 1875.

Translated from the German, *Englische geschichte,* 7 vols., Berlin, 1859–69. Especially useful for foreign relations in the latter part of the period; has valuable appendices of documents, including dispatches in French of the Brandenburg agent, 1690–5, and William's letters in Dutch to Heinsius, 1692–1702.

276   TREVELYAN, G. M. England under the Stuarts. 1904. Maps. Bibl. 25th edn. 1949.

Excellent, including much of social and cultural interest. Cf. A. B. Allen, *Stuart England: the complete background book,* 1954, as a brief guide to materials on many aspects of the period.

277   TURBERVILLE, A. S. Commonwealth and restoration. 1928. Rev. edn. 1936.

Useful as an outline of political history; views somewhat outdated.

B. 1603–1640

1. SOURCES

For collections of constitutional documents and for the developing conflict between king and Parliament see *Constitutional History.* For the Gunpowder Plot see *Ecclesiastical History* (1484–8). The order in the list below is roughly chronological according to content. See also pp. 50–73 in this chapter.

278   STOW, JOHN and HOWES, EDMUND. Annales or a general chronicle of England. 1631.

Stow's *Chronicle* was augmented and continued by Howes, 1600–31. See comment on Stow's work in Read (11 n., 1959), p. 28.

279   BAKER, SIR RICHARD. A chronicle of the kings of England, from the time of the Romans . . . unto the death of King James the First. 1641. Later edns. 1665 and 1733.

Edns. after 1660 have a continuation by E. Phillips which is a valuable authority for 1658–60, and based on the papers of Sir Thomas Clarges, Monck's brother-in-law, but this section was much abridged in edns. after 1674. Cf. T. Blount's *Animadversions upon Sir Richard Baker's chronicle* . . ., Oxf. 1672. Other early accounts are Thomas Frankland, *The annals of King James and King Charles the First* (1612–42), 1681; and Robert Johnston, *Historia rerum Britannicarum* . . . (1572–1628), Amsterdam, 1655.

280   TRUTH BROUGHT TO LIGHT; or, the history of the first 14 years of King James I. 1692.

Includes an account of the royal revenue, with the receipts, issues, etc. A less complete edn. of 1651 has the title: *The narrative history of King James . . . for the first fourteen years.* Repr. in *Somers tracts,* 2nd edn. (61), vol. ii. For proclamations, law cases, etc., see *The connexion, being choice collections of some principal matters in King James his reign,* 1681; see also *infra,* nos. 716, 1060.

281   THOU, JAQUES AUGUSTE DE. Jacobi Augusti Thuani historiarum sui temporis [Monsieur de Thou's History of his own time]. 2 vols. 1729.

Translated into English from the 1620 Geneva edn., which carried Thou's narrative to 1618 (originally publ. in 5 vols., Paris, 1604–8). Contains an account of the early years of James I, with comments on the Gunpowder Plot and on toleration. Thou was influential on early history writing of the period.

282   WILSON, ARTHUR. The history of Great Britain, being the life and reign of King James the First. 1653.

Repr. in Kennet (262). Cf. Wilson's autobiography in Peck (60 n.), ii. 460; and the intro. to Wilson's play, *The Swisser,* ed. by A. Feuillerat, Paris, 1904. Useful but prejudiced; to be used with caution.

283   SCOTT, SIR WALTER, ed. Secret history of the court of James the First. 2 vols. Edin. 1811.

Comprises: Francis Osborne's *Some traditionall memoyres on the raigne of King James the First,* 1658; Sir Anthony Weldon's *The court and character of King James,* 1650, from the 1651 edn. in which was added *The court of King Charles; Aulicus Coquinariae,* 1650, an answer to Weldon attributed to Sir William Sanderson; *A perfect description of the people and country of Scotland,* 1659; Sir Edward Peyton's *Divine catastrophe of the kingly family of the house of Stuarts,* 1652; and *The court and kitchin of Elizabeth, commonly called Joan Cromwell, wife of the late usurper,* 1664. All of these should be used with caution. On Weldon see a valuable article in *Retrospective Review,* 3, pt. 2 (1821), and 7 (1823), under the title of 'Sir Anthony Weldon's court of King James'. Weldon also wrote a satirical account of James I, *A cat may look at a king,* 1652. Facsimile repr. of Weldon's *Court* and other tracts of the period are in *Smeeton's historical & biographical tracts,* 2 vols., Westminster, 1820.

284   THE LOSELEY MANUSCRIPTS . . . from the reign of Henry VIII to that of James I. Preserved . . . at Loseley House, in Surrey. Ed. by A. J. Kempe. 1836.

Has some letters of James I, and some documents illustrating Sir George Chaworth's embassy to the Infanta Isabella Clara Eugenia (1621). Cf. H.M.C. (187) regarding these papers. Another valuable collection illustrative of the reigns of Elizabeth and James I is *The Egerton papers,* ed. by J. P. Collier, Camden Soc., 1840; see H.M.C. (128).

285   GOODMAN, GODFREY. The court of King James the First . . . to which are added letters . . . of the most distinguished characters of the court. Ed. by J. S. Brewer. 2 vols. 1839.

The MS. of Bishop Goodman's work is in the Bodl. Libr. Cf. J. E. B. Mayor, ed.,

'Original letters of Godfrey Goodman together with materials for his life', *Camb. Antiq. Soc.* 2 (1864). See no. 1247.

286 HALLIWELL, J. O., ed. Letters of the kings of England. 2 vols. 1846.

Vol. ii contains many letters of James I and Charles I. Cf. E. Lodge, ed., *Illustrations of British history . . . in the reigns of Henry VIII . . . and James I exhibited in a series of original papers selected from the manuscripts of the noble families of Howard, Talbot and Cecil* [in the College of Arms], 3 vols., 1791, 2nd edn., 3 vols., 1838; for the reign of James I see vol. iii. See also *Cabala sive scrinia sacra: mysteries of state and government in letters of . . . great ministers of state . . . in the reigns of King Henry the Eighth . . . King Charles*, 2 pts., 1654, later edns., 1663, 1691 (the best), which contains many papers addressed to Buckingham.

287 COURT AND TIMES of James the First; illustrated by authentic and confidential letters. Ed. by R. F. Williams. 2 vols. 1849.

Mainly news-letters of John Chamberlain and J. Mead, transcribed by Thomas Birch, the originals of which are now mostly in the Domestic State Papers (P.R.O.) and the Winwood papers in the Br. Mus. A modern edn., greatly superior for completeness and accuracy is by N. E. McClure, *The letters of John Chamberlain*, 2 vols., Phila., 1939. On Chamberlain see E. P. Statham, *A Jacobean letter-writer, c.* 1920; and W. Notestein, *Four Worthies* (2444).

Williams edited also from Birch's transcripts, *The court and times of Charles the First . . . including memoirs of the mission in England of the Capuchin friars by Father Cyprien de Gamache*, 2 vols., 1848, mainly from originals in P.R.O. Cf. no. 1450 n.

288 GARDINER, S. R., ed. The Fortescue papers; consisting chiefly of letters relating to state affairs, collected by J. Packer, secretary to George Villiers, [first] duke of Buckingham. Camd. Soc. 1871.

From MS. in the possession of the Hon. J. M. Fortescue. See also Gardiner's edn. of letters of Diego Sarmiento de Acuna, Count of Gondomar, concerning the earl of Somerset, *Archaeologia*, 41 (1867), 151–86; and of letters (1619–21) from Lord Bacon to Christian IV, King of Denmark, ibid. 219–69.

289 L'ESTRANGE, HAMON. The reign of King Charles (to 1641). 1655. 2nd edn. 1656.

The 'enlarged' 1656 edn. contains an appendix 'The observator observed', in reply to Peter Heylyn's criticisms, *Observations*, 1656. Heylyn continued his attack in *Extraneus vapulans*, 1656, and *Examen historicum*, 1659. See also Sir E. Walker, *Historical discourses* (1583); and no. 418.

290 RUSHWORTH, JOHN. Historical collections of private passages of state, weighty matters of law, remarkable proceedings in five parliaments (1618–29). 7 vols. 1659–1701. Later edns. 8 vols. 1680–1701. 1721.

Title is from first volume; subsequent volumes extend the collection to 1649. Valuable storehouse of material. See *D.N.B.*, Rushworth.

See also a compilation of *Reprints* of contemporary tracts, mainly relating to political matters, 1644–1715, published by the Clarendon Historical Society, 2 vols., Edin. 1882–6.

291 NALSON, JOHN, ed. An impartial collection of the great affairs of state from the beginning of the Scotch rebellion in the year 1639 to the murther of King Charles I. 2 vols. 1682–3.

Intended as an antidote to Rushworth. Prints many documents from public records (see intro. to no. 190), but extends only to 1642. Partial in narrative, but useful for its documents.

292 FAIRFAX. Memoirs of the reign of Charles the First [Fairfax correspondence, 1 and 2, to 1642]. Ed. by G. W. Johnson. 2 vols. 1848.

Volumes 3 and 4 of the Fairfax correspondence were edited by R. Bell, as *Memorials of the Civil War*, 1849 (1579 n.).

293 WALLINGTON, NEHEMIAH. Historical notices of the reign of Charles I, 1630–46. Ed. by R. Webb. 2 vols. 1869.

Notices of events arranged under subjects and compiled from news-letters and newspapers.

2. LATER WORKS

294 D'ISRAELI, I. Commentaries on the life and reign of Charles I. 5 vols. 1828–31. Later edn. 2 vols. 1851. Ed. by B. Disraeli aft. earl of Beaconsfield.

Another of the older histories, containing a few original documents, is F. P. G. Guizot's *History of Charles the First and the English revolution* (1625–49), trans. by A. R. Scoble, 2 vols., 1854; a later one-vol. trans. by W. Hazlitt, 1856.

295 EUSDEN, J. D. Puritans, lawyers and politics in early seventeenth-century England. New Haven. 1958. Bibl.

Scholarly. Concerned with the relationships between Puritanism and the common law. Cf. J. F. MacLear, 'Puritan relations with Buckingham', *Hunt. Lib. Quart.* 21 (1957–8), 111–32; and G. Davies, 'English political sermons, 1603–1640', ibid. 3 (1939), 1–22.

296 GARDINER, S. R. History of England from the accession of James I to the outbreak of the civil war, 1603–42. 10 vols. 1883–4. Maps. Plans.

This is the second and revised edition of this standard *History*, originally published in five series of two vols. each, 1863–82. The introductions in the first edn. contain accounts of the authorities used which are omitted in the second edn. Cf. Usher (320 n.).
By Gardiner also, *The first two Stuarts and the Puritan revolution, 1603–1660* [Epochs of Modern History], 1876; many later reprints. See also no. 320.

297 HINTON, R. W. K. 'Government and liberty under James I.' *Camb. Hist. Jour.* 11 (1953), 48–64.

Analyses Sir John Eliot's political views and parliament's plea for liberty in 1610.

298 McELWEE, W. The murder of Sir Thomas Overbury. Lond. and N.Y 1952.

A compilation of the evidence in the form of a chronological narrative, but not improving upon Gardiner's account in the second volume of his *History*. E. A. Parry's *The Overbury mystery*, 1925, is a semi-popular account.

299 USHER, R. G. 'James I and Sir Edward Coke.' *E.H.R.* 18 (1903), 664–75.

Sets other accounts against Coke's own and concludes that Coke did not 'successfully beard the king'.

300 WEDGWOOD, C. V. The great rebellion. Vol. i. The king's peace. Vol. ii. The king's war. 1955–8.

The first two volumes of a projected series, in which the author, utilizing the products of the latest research, provides a fresh synthesis of the history of the period. Vol. i draws upon Strafford materials recently opened to study. Brilliant in style.

By the same author, 'Anglo-Scottish relations, 1603–40', *R.H.S. Trans.*, 4th Ser. 32 (1950), 31–48; and no. 310 n. A useful comment on literature as a source is her *Poetry and politics under the Stuarts*, Camb. 1960.

C. 1640–1660

See also Ch. VI *infra* for narratives of the civil war. See also Ch. XI for such matters as Protestation returns. Important materials are to be found in pamphlet collections (nos. 58, 62 n.), in Ch. III, and in Ch. IV. For ballads such as *Rump Songs* (2659 n.), see Ch. X.

1. SOURCES (roughly chronological order by content)

301 BATE, GEORGE. Elenchi motuum nuperorum in Anglia. Pars prima; simulac juris regii & parlamentarii brevis enarratio. Paris. 1649.

A second part to 1660 was added in 1661, Lond. and a third [to 1669], *Motus compositi*, by Thomas Skinner, 1676. A trans. in three parts appeared in 1685, *Elenchus motuum . . .*, or *A short historical account of the rise and progress of the late troubles in England*. A trans. of part i was ed. by E. Almack under the English title, 1902. Cf. Robert Pugh's *Elenchus elenchi . . .*, Paris, 1664, replying to Bate; and *Clarke papers* (308).

302 BRUCE, J., ed. Notes of the treaty carried on at Ripon between King Charles I and the covenanters of Scotland, A.D. 1640, taken by Sir J. Borough, Garter King of Arms. Camd. Soc. 1869.

Cf. B. M. Gardiner, ed., 'The secret negociation with Charles the First 1643–4', *Camd. Soc. Misc.* viii., 1883 (from Tanner MSS. in Bodl. Lib.). For a critical study of the text of the Solemn League and Covenant see an article by S. W. Carruthers, *Scottish Church Hist. Soc. Records*, 6 (1936), 232–51.

303 STACE, M., ed. Cromwelliana. A chronological detail of events in which Oliver Cromwell was engaged (1642–58). Westminster. 1810. Plates.

Extracts from newspapers becoming more detailed after 1649. Useful for dates is Sir William Dugdale, *A short view of the late troubles . . . [with a] narrative of the treaty of Uxbridge . . .*, Oxf. 1681.

304 HOBBES, THOMAS. Behemoth, or an epitome of the civil wars (1640–1660). 1679. Later edn., including suppressed passages, ed. by F. Tönnies. 1889.

Repr. in Maseres (1578). Cf. J. Heath, *A brief chronicle of the late intestine warr* (1637–53), 1663, a later edn. of which, 1676, continues the account, 1662–75, by J. Phillips. On Hobbes, see also nos. 968, 2697.

305 CLARENDON, EDWARD HYDE, EARL OF. The history of the rebellion and civil wars in England. 3 vols. Oxf. 1702–4. Later edn. by B. Bandinel. 7 vols. Oxf. 1849. Ed. by W. D. Macray. 6 vols. Oxf. 1888. Repr. 1958.

The most important single authority for the two decades it covers, Anglican and royalist in point of view; for evaluations see Ranke (275), vi, C. H. Firth in *E.H.R.* 19 (1904), and C. Hill, in *History Today* (Oct. 1953), 695–703. The 1849 edn. includes *History of the rebellion in Ireland* and Warburton's notes. On the MS. see Macray, *Annals of the Bodleian* (Oxf. 1890), p. 225. See also nos. 257, 422.

306 WHITELOCKE, BULSTRODE. Memorials of the English affairs (1625–60). 1682. Later edn. 4 vols. Oxf. 1853.

Has some personal memoirs, but mainly a compilation from newspapers; useful for commonwealth and protectorate. Cf. J. Oldmixon, *Clarendon and Whitlock compar'd*, 1727, which elicited answers by J. Davys, F. Curll, and J. Burton. There are valuable Whitelocke MSS. in Br. Mus., Add. MSS. 37341–7.

307 NICHOLAS, EDWARD. The Nicholas papers: correspondence of Sir Edward Nicholas Secretary of State. Ed. by Sir G. F. Warner. Camd. Soc. 4 vols. 1886–1920.

1641–60. Selected from Br. Mus. Egerton MSS. See also Peck's *Desiderata curiosa* (60 n.) for 1645–60. For Strafford's trial see Rushworth (865).

308 CLARKE PAPERS. Selections from the papers of William Clarke, secretary to the council of the army 1647–9 and to General Monck and the commanders of the army in Scotland 1651–60. Ed. by C. H. Firth. 4 vols. Camd. Soc. 1891–1901.

MSS. at Worcester College, Oxf. Especially valuable for the debates of the Army Council. The latest edition of the army debates is by A. S. P. Woodhouse, *Puritanism and liberty*, 1938, 2nd edn., 1950.

Important tracts relating to the debates are in the collection entitled *A declaration of the engagements, remonstrances, representations . . . from His Excellency Sir Tho. Fairfax and the generall councel of the army*, 1647; the Leveller pamphlet by John Wildman, *Putney projects, or the old serpent in new forme*, 1647; and *Jonah's cry out of the whale's belly or certaine epistles writ by Lieu. Col. J.[ohn] Lilburne unto Lieu. Gen. Cromwell*, 1647. See a bibl. of Lilburne by E. Peacock in *Notes & Queries*, 7th Ser., vol. 5. See also 962.

309 STEVENSON, G. S., ed. Charles I in captivity, from contemporary sources. 1927.

Includes, among others, the whole of Sir Thomas Herbert's *Memoirs of the last two years of the reign of King Charles I* (originally publ. 1678, later edns. 1702, 1813), with the narratives of Col. Edward Cooke, Major Huntingdon, and Henry Firebrace. Cf. *Narrative of John Ashburnham of his attendance on King Charles the First . . . to which is prefixed A Vindication of his character and conduct*, 2 vols., 1830, the vindication being in reply to criticisms by Clarendon; an appendix includes 'Memoirs of Sir John Berkley'.

On the king's captivity see also *Letters between Col. Robert Hammond . . . and the committee . . . at Derby House . . . relating to King Charles I while he was confined in Carisbrook Castle*, ed. by T. Birch, 1764.

310 NALSON, JOHN. A true copy of the journal of the high court of justice for the tryal of King Charles I. 1684.

Cf. *England's black tribunal*, 1660, 6th edn., 1737. The 1660 edn. has the trial of Charles I; the edn. of 1737 adds 'The loyal martyrology', a register of persons slain in the royal cause, and of those imprisoned or banished. Cf. *The trial of Charles I . . . from the memoirs of Sir Thomas Herbert and John Rushworth*, ed. by R. Lockyer, 1959. See H. W. Randall, 'The rise and fall of a martyrology: sermons on Charles I', *Hunt. Lib. Quart.* 10 (1947), 135–67. C. V. Wedgwood, *A coffin for King Charles*, N.Y. 1964 (English edn. title, *The trial of Charles I*), gives an account of the trial based upon recent scholarship.

311 THURLOE, JOHN. A collection of state papers of John Thurloe, esq., secretary first to the council of state and afterwards to the two protectorates. Ed. by T. Birch. 7 vols. 1742.

The main authority for the protectorate, drawn from the Rawlinson MSS. A, vols. 1–73, in the Bodl. Lib., and Br. Mus. Add. MSS. 415–19, and other sources. Cf. *Original letters and papers of state addressed to Oliver Cromwell . . . (1649–1658), found among the political collection of . . . John Milton*, edited by J. Nickolls, 1743, from MSS. in the possession of the Society of Antiquaries.

A list of tracts important for the years 1649–51 is given by J. M. Wallace in his article on the date of John Tatham's drama, 'The distracted state', in *Bull. of N.Y. Public Library*, 64 (1960), 29–40.

312 DEEDES, C., ed. Royal & loyal sufferers. 1903.

Repr. C. Wase, *Electra of Sophocles presented to . . . the Lady Elizabeth*, The Hague, 1649; *An exact narrative . . . of his . . . majesties escape from Worcester*, 1660; *ΕΙΚΩΝ ΒΑΣΙΛΙΚΗ or the true pourtraiture of . . . Charles II*, 1660; *The loyal sacrifice . . . Sir Charles Lucas and Sir George Lisle*, 1648.

For lists of royalists see the *Compounding Papers* (761 n.); Underdown, *Royalist Conspiracy* (323 n.); and indexes compiled by M. G. W. Peacock for the Index Society, 1879, and W. P. W. Phillimore, Index Library, 1889.

313 A COLLECTION of several letters and declarations . . . sent by General Monk unto the Lord Lambert . . . 2 pts. in 1 vol. 1660. Later edn. 1714.

Edn. of 1714 was issued, together with *The Art of restoring*, as a warning against a second restoration. Cf. G. Keynes's edn. (Los Angeles, 1951) of John Evelyn's *Apologie for the royal party*, 1659, and *A panegyric to Charles II*, 1661.

2. LATER WORKS

For chiefly military narratives, see *infra*, Ch. VI or Ch. XI. See also Ch. III, § F on Political Theory; on Political Parties see Ch. III.

On the important matter of causation, particularly the interpretations of the Marxists, see nos. 314, 328, 990, 994. A useful commentary on these interpretations is by R. B. Schlatter in *Jour. Hist. Ideas*, 4 (1943), 349–67. See also no. 325.

314 BERNSTEIN, E. Cromwell and communism, socialism, and democracy in the great English revolution. Trans. by H. J. Stenning. 1930.

The German original, 'Kommunistische and demokratish-sozialistische Strömungen...', was printed in *Die Geschichte des Sozialismus* by E. Bernstein and C. Kautsky, Stuttgart, 1895. Deals especially with the Levellers and other radical groups. See also Pease (990).

315 CARLSON, L. H. 'A history of the Presbyterian party from Pride's purge to the dissolution of the Long Parliament.' *Church History* 11 (1942), 83–122.

Narrative of their public and secret political activity until their submission to Cromwell.

316 CATTERALL, R. C. H. 'The failure of the humble petition and advice.' *A.H.R.* 9 (1903–4), 36–65.

Cf. two articles on Cromwell and the Crown by C. H. Firth, *E.H.R.* 17 (1902), 429 ff., and 18 (1903), 54 ff.

317 COATE, M. Cornwall in the great civil war and interregnum, 1642–1660: a social and political study. Oxf. and N.Y. 1933.

Broader than its title indicates, this study of a region is an important contribution to the history of the period. See studies on the county committees, such as Everitt's on Kent (1607).

318 FIRTH, SIR C. H. The last years of the protectorate. 2 vols. 1909. Bibl.

A continuation, on the same scale, of Gardiner (320). G. Davies, *The restoration* . . . (358) is designed to finish Firth's narrative. Cf. the articles by Firth and R. F. D. Palgrave on the insurrection of 1655 in *E.H.R.* 3 (1888) and 4 (1889); also by Firth, ed. by G. Davies, 'The royalists under the protectorate', ibid. 52 (1937), 634–48. See also the biog. by Firth, *Oliver Cromwell and the rule of the Puritans in England* (430). A *Bibliography of the writings of Sir Charles Firth* was publ., Oxf. 1928.

Firth's work largely supersedes A. Bisset, *Omitted chapters of the history of England from the death of Charles I to the battle of Dunbar*, 2 vols., 1864–7, and its second edn., *History of the commonwealth* . . ., 2 vols. 1867.

319 FREUND, M. Die große Revolution in England. Anatomie eines Umsturzes. Hamburg. 1951. Bibl.

Attributes the revolution to the ambitions of a small group; anti-Puritan view. Cf. A. Gross, *Der Streit um das Widerstandsrecht*, Berlin, 1929.

320 GARDINER, S. R. History of the great civil war, 1642–9. 3 vols. 1886–91. Maps. Rev. edn. 4 vols. 1893. Maps.

Continued in his *History of the commonwealth and protectorate* (1649–56), 3 vols., 1894–1901, maps; later edn., 4 vols., 1903. The latter edn. has a number of corrections and references to new authorities by C. H. Firth. See continuations by Firth and Davies (318, 358); and Gardiner's work on the earlier period (296).

For comments on Gardiner's methods see F. York Powell in *E.H.R.* 17 (1902), 278; C. H. Firth in *Quart. Rev.* 391 (1902) and *Athenaeum*, 1902, based on conversations with Gardiner; R. G. Usher, *A critical study of the historical method of Samuel Rawson Gardiner with an excursus on the historical conception of the Puritan revolution from Clarendon to Gardiner*, St. Louis, 1915; and *Times Lit. Suppl.*, 25 Sept. to 18 Dec. 1919.

321 GODWIN, W. History of the commonwealth of England. From its commencement to the restoration of Charles the Second. 4 vols. 1824–8.

Stops in 1658; useful for pamphlet literature.

322 GUIZOT, F. P. G. History of Oliver Cromwell and the English commonwealth (1649–58). Trans. by A. R. Scoble. 2 vols. 1854.

Still useful for documents from French and Spanish archives. Tr. from *Histoire de la république d'Angleterre et de Cromwell*, 2 vols., Paris, 1854. The 1862 edition of Guizot's *Histoire* contains also *Histoire du protectorat de Richard Cromwell et du rétablissement des Stuarts*.

323 HARDACRE, P. H. The royalists during the Puritan revolution. The Hague. 1956.

An introductory study, moving away from the traditional focus on the parliamentary leaders. The same author uses the biographical approach in 'The royalists in exile during the Puritan revolution, 1642–1660', *Hunt. Lib. Quart.* 16 (1953), 353–70. Cf. Firth (318). D. Underdown, in *Royalist conspiracy in England, 1649–1660*, New Haven, 1960, uses thorough scholarship to trace the continuity of activity by royalists in England, without which, he concludes, a non-violent restoration could not have been accomplished. Cf. M. Hollings, 'Thomas Barret: a study in the secret history of the interregnum', *E.H.R.* 43 (1928), 33–65; and D. Underdown's article on Sir Richard Willys, ibid. 69 (1954), 373–87. On the Penruddock uprising of 1655 a good brief account is by A. H. Woolrych, 1955.

324 HEXTER, J. H. The reign of King Pym. Camb. (Mass.). 1941. Repr. 1960.

Valuable, using a detailed study of Pym's parliamentary tactics to show his leadership of a moderate group in opposition to Charles I. A valuable supplement to Hexter is L. Glow, 'Pym and Parliament; the methods of moderation', *J.M.H.* 36 (1964), 373–97. Written with a Tory, Anglo-Catholic bias is J. Lane, *The reign of King Covenant*, Fair Lawn, N.J., 1957.

325 HILL, C., ed. English revolution, 1640. 3rd edn. 1955.

Three essays, illustrative of the Marxist interpretation: C. Hill, 'The English revolution'; M. James, 'Contemporary materialist interpretations of society in the English revolution'; E. Rickword, 'Milton: the revolutionary intellectual'. C. Hill and E. Dell edited from the sources a volume entitled *The good old cause, the English revolution of 1640–1660: its causes, course, and consequences*, 1949. See also Hill, *Puritanism and revolution: studies in interpretation of the English revolution of the 17th century*, 1958, and his article on the same theme in *History*, 41 (1956), 67–87; *Intellectual origins of the English revolution*, Oxf. 1965; and no. 1195.

326 INDERWICK, F. A. The interregnum, 1648–1660: studies of the commonwealth, legislative, social and legal. 1891. Facsimiles of coins.

Cf. E. Jenks, *The constitutional experiments of the commonwealth*, Camb. 1890, and C. H. Firth's review in *E.H.R.* 6 (1891).

327 JAMES, M. 'The political importance of the tithes controversy in the English revolution.' *History*, 26 (1941), 1–18.

See also her important study on social problems (2518); her essay in no. 325; and her edition, with M. Weinstock, of a source book for this period, *England during the interregnum*, 1935.

328 KOSMINSKII, E. A., ed. Angliiskaya burzhuaznaya revolyutziya xvii veka [The English bourgeois revolution, 17th century]. Moscow. 1954.

Essays of ten Soviet scholars presenting 'the first synthesized statement of the interpretation of the English revolution in Marxist terms'. See the review by C. Hill in *E.H.R.* 71 (1956).

Other works by Soviet scholars, in addition to Petegorskii (966 n.), include (titles Anglicized here): N. G. Dmitrievskii, editor [*Legal aspect of the English revolution*], Moscow, 1946; V. M. Lavrovskii and M. A. Barg [*The English bourgeois revolution*], Moscow, 1958; and A. Kudryavtsev ['The English revolution in the light of the newest bourgeois historiography'], *Istoricheskii Sbornik*, 2 (1934), 214–34.

Useful comments on the Marxist interpretation are: C. Hill, 'Soviet interpretations of the English interregnum', *Econ. Hist. Rev.* 8 (1938), 159–67; and his 'The English civil war interpreted by Marx and Engels', *Science and Society*, 12 (1948), 130–56. But see also Hill (325).

329 MUDDIMAN, J. G., ed. Trial of King Charles the First. Edin. and Lond. 1928.

Includes repr. of Bradshaw's journal and some new material on the regicides. Cf. H. R. Williamson, *The day they killed the king*, 1957; and Sir H. Halford, *Essays and orations*, 1831, which contains 'An account of the opening of the tomb of King Charles I at Windsor' in 1813. Cf. Wedgwood (310 n.).

330 RANNIE D. W. 'Cromwells major-generals.' *E.H.R.* 10 (1895), 471–506.

For Colchester under army control see the article by J. H. Round, ibid. 15 (1900), 641–64. On the 1659 rebellions see R. Petty, 'The rebellion of Sir George Booth, August, 1659', *Jour. Chester and North Wales Arch. Arch. Hist. Soc.*, N.S. 33 (1939), 119–37; and A. H. Woolrych, 'The good old cause and the fall of the Protectorate', *Camb. Hist. Jour.* 13 (1957), 133–61.

331 SANFORD, J. L. Studies and illustrations of the great rebellion. 1858.

Somewhat out of date but still useful. Some of the essays are: Constitutional returns to the Long Parliament; Parliamentary Royalism; The Earl of Essex; Cavalier and roundhead letters 1645 (mainly from Tanner MS. 60 Bodl. Lib.). Cf. M. C. Wren, 'The disputed elections in London in 1641', *E.H.R.* 64 (1949), 34–52.

332 SOLT, L. F. Saints in arms: Puritanism and democracy in Cromwell's army. Stanford. 1959.

Solt disagrees with some interpretations on the relationship between Puritan and liberty as presented by Woodhouse (308 n.) and others. See also his article, 'Revolutionary Calvinist parties in England under Elizabeth I and Charles I', *Church History*, 27 (1958), 234–9, and on the army chaplain, William Dell, in *Church Quart. Rev.* 153 (1952), 43–55.

333 STERN, A. Geschichte der Revolution in England. Berlin. 1881.

A volume in the standard series under the general editorship of W. Oncken, Berlin, 1878+. Stern's volume deals chiefly with the years 1640–59.

Examples of recent brief studies by German historians are G. Lenz, *Demokratie und Diktatur in der englischen Revolution, 1640–1660*, Munich, 1933; and R. Stadelman, *Geschichte der englischen Revolution*, Wiesbaden, 1954.

334 TURBERVILLE, A. S. Commonwealth and restoration. 1928. Later edn. 1936.

335 ZAGORIN, P. 'The English revolution 1640–1660.' *Jour. of World History*, 2, no. 3 (1955).

D. 1660–1689

Important for this period especially, as well as for earlier ones are: Rapin-Thoyras (264) and the tracts in the Harleian and Somers collections (59, 61). For the Popish Plot see Ch. V *infra* (1489–97). See also § G in this chapter on Foreign Relations; Ch. III, § D on Parliament; and *H.M.C.* (80, 114, 179).

1. SOURCES

(a) *General*

An important MS. source for this period, listed at the Dr. Williams's Library as the Roger Morrice Collection MSS. P, Q, and R, is a three-volume set of 'Entring Books', or historical registers kept by a Presbyterian clergyman and friend of Baxter (1677–91). It contains material valuable for political, parliamentary, and religious history. Plans for editing this collection are in the hands of D. R. Lacey, Annapolis (U.S. Naval Academy).

The arrangement of printed sources is in roughly a chronological order according to content, first general and then the specific occurrences.

336 STATE TRACTS: in two parts. The first being a collection of several treatises relating to the government, privately printed in the reign of King Charles II; the second part consisting of a further collection . . . 1660 to 1689. 2 pts. 1692–3.

Printed by Richard Baldwin and sometimes referred to as 'Baldwin Tracts'. Pt. 1 was publ. separately in 1689. See also 370.

337 BROWN, THOMAS, ed. Miscellanea aulica: or a collection of state treatises. 1702.

Contains letters of Charles II and James, Duke of York, and documents, 1660–75, illustrating foreign relations and Scottish history.
A useful collection of news-letters written from the secretary of state's office is *Letters addressed from London to Sir Joseph Williamson . . . 1673 and 1674*, ed. by W. D. Christie, 2 vols., Camden Soc., 1874.

338 COOPER, W. D., ed. Savile correspondence. Camden Soc. 1858.

Letters of Henry Savile, envoy at Paris, 1679–82, and vice-chamberlain to Charles II and James II, with some letters from George Marquess of Halifax, 1679–86. Other letters of value for the period are: J. H. Wilson, ed., *The Rochester–Savile letters, 1671–1680*, Columbus, 1941; E. M. Thompson, ed., *Correspondence of the family of Hatton being chiefly letters addressed to Christopher, first Viscount Hatton, 1601–1704*, 2 vols., Camden Soc., 1878, which are drawn from Br. Mus. Add. MSS. 29548–96.

339 DALRYMPLE, SIR JOHN. Memoirs of Great Britain and Ireland [1681–92]. 2 vols. Lond. and Edin. 1771–3. Cont. to 1702 in vol. 3. Edin. 1788. Later edn. 3 vols. 1790.

Valuable as a collection of correspondence, partly from state papers in P.R.O., but especially important are the documents in vol. ii, selected from the correspondence of French ambassadors in the Archives des Affaires Étrangères in Paris. The first edn. is the best. For a guide and index by M. Jolliffe, see *Bull. Inst. Hist. Research*, 20 (1946), 119–30. For other correspondence see Kemble (548).

340 GUIZOT, F. P. G., ed. Collection des mémoires relatifs à la révolution d'Angleterre. 25 vols. Paris. 1827.

The prefaces were publ. separately as *Portraits politiques des hommes des différents partis*, 1851 and 1874, and trans. by A. R. Scoble as *Monk's contemporaries*, 1851.
Includes memoires of Buckingham, Burnet, Clarendon, Charles II, and Reresby, as well as of persons active in the 1640–60 era. Many have been separately edited since Guizot's time. See § F of this chapter.

341 BURNET, GILBERT. Bishop Burnet's history of his own time. 2 vols. 1724–34. Later edn. by M. J. Routh. 6 vols. Oxf. 1823 and 1833. Ed. by O. Airy [to 1685]. 2 vols. Oxf. 1897–1900; suppl. by H. C. Foxcroft. Oxf. 1902.

Important, though prejudiced and not infallible. The best edn. is Routh's (1833). The Foxcroft supplement is valuable, including portions from the original draft. For a bibliography see Clarke and Foxcroft (1229), pp. 551–2. For critical estimates see Ranke (275), vi. 45–87; and C. H. Firth's intro. to Clarke and Foxcroft. Some of Burnet's letters [1680] were ed. by Foxcroft in *Camden Soc. Misc.* xi, 1907.

Some replies provoked by the Whiggish viewpoint of Burnet are: Thomas Salmon, *Impartial examination*, 2 vols., 1724; and Bevil Higgons, *Historical and critical remarks*, 1725; 1727.

Much less valuable than Burnet, but also provocative of controversy, was Bishop Samuel Parker's *History of his own time* (1660–80), translated from the Latin original, 1726, by T. Newlin, 1727.

342 KENNET, WHITE. A register and chronicle ecclesiastical and civil . . . 1728.

Useful for 1660–2. Materials for this register and for a continuation to 1679 are in Br. Mus. Lansdowne MSS. 1002–10, and form the basis for Bishop Kennet's *Complete history* (262). Original material is included in some of the Tory replies to Kennet's *History*, such as Roger North's *Examen: or an enquiry into the credit and veracity of a pretended complete history*, 1740, the materials for which are in Br. Mus. Add. MSS. 32518–20, 32525. See also Echard (263).

343 JONES, DAVID. The secret history of White-Hall from the restoration of Charles II down to the abdication of K. James. 6 pts. 1697. 2nd edn. 2 vols. 1717.

A continuation . . . to 1696 was publ. in 1697, and included, with material to 1714, in the 1717 edn. Not reliable. Also to be used with caution is *Secret history of the reigns of King Charles II and King James II*, [? Lond.], 1690, a reply to which is entitled *The blatant beast muzzled, or reflections on a late libel . . .*, 1691.

344 LUTTRELL, NARCISSUS. A brief relation of state affairs from September 1678 to April 1714. 6 vols. Oxf. 1857.

A daily record of public events, extracted chiefly from news-letters and newspapers. Not always accurate but valuable as a guide to what the public of the day knew.

Collected also by Luttrell, *Narcissus Luttrell's Popish Plot catalogues*, ed. by F. C. Francis, Oxf. 1956. See also 1489.

345 RALPH, JAMES. The history of England during the reigns of King William, Queen Anne and King George I, with an introductory review of the reigns of the royal brothers, Charles and James. 2 vols. 1744–6.

Vol. i, 1660–88; vol. ii, 1689–1702. A careful compilation of much contemporary material, especially pamphlets from the collection by Somers. Cf. Rapin-Thoyras (264). For a Whig interpretation by the physician to William and Mary see James Welwood, *Memoirs of the most material transactions in England for the last hundred years* [to 1688], 1700, later edn. by F. Maseres, 1820. A Roman Catholic history is P. J. D'Orléans, *The history of the revolutions in England under the family of the Stuarts* (1603–90), trans. by J. Stevens, 1711 and 1722, from the French edn., Paris, 1793–4.

(b) *Special Events*

(1) *Restoration*

346 PRICE, JOHN. The mystery and method of his majesty's happy restauration. 1680.

Repr. in Maseres, *Select tracts* (1578). Valuable because Price accompanied Monck. See also no. 1666 .

347 MEMOIRS relating to the impeachment of Thomas earl of Danby . . . in . . . 1678 . . . with an appendix containing the proceedings in Parliament. 1710.

Cf. Browning's *Danby* (433), and the two volumes of documents printed with the life.

348 [WRIGHT, JAMES]. Compendious view of the late tumults and troubles in this kingdom, by way of annals [1678–85]. 1685.

For titles relating to the 1678 'Popish Plot' see Shaftesbury (503) and nos. 1489–97.

349 NEVILLE, HENRY. Plato redivivus or a dialogue concerning government. 1681 [1680?]. Later edns. 1681, 1698, 1763.

As in other writings, Neville here advocated limits on the royal prerogative; there were numerous replies, such as *The apostate Protestant, a letter to a friend*, 1681; *Oceana and Britannia*, 1681 (repr. as Marvell's in Grosart's *Marvell*); *Antidotum Britannicum . . .* by W. W., 1681, which was answered in turn by *Reflections on Antidotum* by William Atwood; *A seasonable address* (possibly G. Saville or Halifax), repr. in *Somers Tracts* (61); T. Otway, *Venice preserved or A plot discovered*, 1682.

Numerous other tracts of the period relate particularly to the succession question, of which the following are examples: William Dugdale, *A short view of the late troubles*, Oxf. and Lond. 1681; [Elkanah Settle], *Character of a popish successor*, 1681, which passed through several editions in the same year, and was supplemented by a second part and a defence by [John Phillips], 1681; Sir Roger L'Estrange's replies, entitled *The papist in masquerade*, 1681, and *A reply to the second part . . .*, 1681.

In defence of the king are: John Dryden, *His majesty's declaration defended*, 1681 (repr. Augustan Repr. Soc. 23, Los Angeles, 1950), and *The medall*, 1682; [Halifax?], *Observations upon a late libel . . . concerning the king's declaration*, 1681 (ed. by H. MacDonald, Camb. and N.Y. 1940); and several tracts by John Nalson: *The common interest of king and people*, 1677, 1678; *The king's prerogative*, 1680, *Foxes and firebrands*, 1680, 1681, Dublin, 1682, and *The complaint of liberty and property*, 1681.

For others, see Ch. III *infra*, § B on the Crown, § D on Parliament, and § F on Political Theory, especially the work of R. Brady (976), R. Filmer (975), and Lord Somers (977 n.). See also biographies of Sidney (509) and Russell (499).

(3) *Rye House Plot and Monmouth Rebellion*

350 SPRAT, THOMAS. A true account and declaration of the horrid conspiracy against the late King . . . together with copies of the informations as they were ordered to be printed by his late majesty. 1685. Later edn. (vol. xiv of *Collectanea Adamantaea*). Edin. 1886.

Official account of the Rye House plot. Most of the informations are calendared in *C.S.P. Domestic, 1683*.

For a private account see *The secret history of The Rye House plot and of Monmouth's rebellion written by Ford Lord Grey in 1685. Now first published from a manuscript sign'd by himself before the Earl of Sunderland*, 1754. See also William Lord Russell (499).

351 DOBLE, C. E., ed. 'Correspondence of Henry earl of Clarendon and James earl of Abingdon, chiefly relating to the Monmouth insurrection (1683–5).' *Oxf. Hist. Soc.* 32 (1896), 245–78.

Cf. A. L. Humphreys, ed., 'Some sources of history for the Monmouth rebellion . . .', *Somersetshire Arch. and Nat. Hist. Soc. Proc.* 38 (1892), 312–26. Narratives by Monmouth supporters are: John Coad, *A memorandum of the wonderful providences of God,*

1849, and H. Pitman (*Stuart Tracts* (62)); by an opponent is Adam Wheeler's *Iter bellicosum*, edited by H. E. Malden, *Camd. Misc.* xii (1910), 151–68.

J. G. Muddiman, *The Bloody Assizes*, Edin. and Lond. 1929, reprints the text of *The Western martyrology* and gives a critical analysis of the records of the celebrated trial of the rebels.

(4) *1685–1688*

352 GUTCH, J., ed. Collectanea curiosa. 2 vols. Oxf. 1781.

Useful for the reign of James II, especially for the trial of the seven bishops. Most of the papers are in the Tanner MSS., Bodl. Lib. Useful also for this period is *The Ellis correspondence* (1686–8), ed. by G. J. W. Agar-Ellis, Lord Dover, 2 vols., 1829, later edn., 2 vols., 1831, from Br. Mus. Add. MSS. 4194. Other Ellis papers are ibid. 28875–956.

See also Ch. V *infra*, § F on Roman Catholicism.

(5) *The Revolution of 1688*

353 MULLER, P. L., ed. Willem III von Oranien und Georg Friedrich von Waldeck. 2 vols. The Hague. 1873–80.

Contains correspondence in French, of William and Waldeck, 1675–92, and is valuable for English history, 1688–90. For correspondence of William with Charles II, at the time of the exclusion controversy, see letters ed. by J. P. Kenyon in *Bull. Inst. Hist. Research*, 30 (1957), 95–101.

354 SPEKE, HUGH. Some memoirs of the most remarkable passages and transactions on the late happy revolution in 1688. Dublin. 1709. Later edn. Dublin [1710–13?].

A useful daily record of events by one of William's army chaplains is John Whittle, *An exact diary of the late expedition . . .*, 1689.

Cf. The documents in Edmund Bohun's *History of the desertion or an account of all publick affairs in England* (Sept. 1688–12 Feb. 1689), 1689. Almost pure propaganda is *Revolution politicks: being a complete collection of all reports, lyes and stories which were forerunners of the great revolution in 1688*, 1733.

355 A COLLECTION of papers relating to the present juncture of affairs in England. 12 pts. 1688–9.

Valuable contemporary series.

2. LATER WORKS

356 BELOFF, M. Public order and popular disturbances, 1660–1714. Oxf. and N.Y. 1938.

Relates economic and political causes for various uprisings. On particular uprisings see: W. C. Abbott, 'English conspiracy and dissent', *A.H.R.* 14 (1909), 503–28, 699–722; C. Burrage, 'The fifth monarchy insurrections', *E.H.R.* 25 (1910), 722–47; Sir W. Foster, 'Venner's rebellion [1661]', *London Topographical Rec.* 18 (1952), 27–33; H. Gee, 'The Derwentdale plot, 1663', *R.H.S. Trans.*, 3rd Ser. 11 (1917), 125–42, and a similar article in *Arch. Aeliana*, 3rd Ser. 14 (1917), 145–56; and J. Walker, 'The Yorkshire plot, 1663', *Yorks. Arch. Jour.* 31 (1934), 348–59, and his 'Dissent and republicanism after the restoration', *Baptist Quart.* 8 (1937), 263–80.

357   CRAWFORD, C. C. 'The suspension of the Habeas Corpus Act and the revolution of 1689.' *E.H.R.* 30 (1915), 613–30.

See also new material on Habeas Corpus in H. Nutting, 'The most wholesome law', *A.H.R.* 65 (1960), 527–43.

358   DAVIES, G. The restoration of Charles II, 1658–1660. San Marino and Lond. 1955.

Valuable for the limited period on which it concentrates. A good many French dispatches are included in F. P. G. Guizot, *History of Richard Cromwell and the restoration,* tr. by A. R. Scoble, 2 vols., 1856; see also M. Coate, 'William Morice and the restoration of Charles II', *E.H.R.* 33 (1918), 367–77; and P. Morrah, *The year of the restoration,* 1960. See also 268 n.

359   EMERSON, W. R. Monmouth's rebellion. 1951.

A useful essay based on printed sources. See also B. Little, *The Monmouth episode,* 1956.

360   FOX, C. J. A history of the early part of the reign of James the Second. Ed. by V. Fox, Lord Holland. 1808.

Appendix includes corresp. of Barillon, French ambassador at London, Dec. 1684–Dec. 1685. See commentaries by G. Rose, *Observations on the historical work of . . . Charles James Fox, with a narrative of . . . The enterprise of the Earl of Argyle in 1685,* by Sir P. Hume, 1809; and S. Heywood, *Vindication of Mr. Fox's history,* 1811.

361   MACAULAY, T. B. The history of England, from the accession of James II. 5 vols. 1849–65. Illus. edn. by Sir C. H. Firth. 6 vols. 1913–15.

Brilliant and detailed; a classic which, though strongly Whig in bias, is based upon wide research. The edn. by T. F. Henderson (1 vol., 1907; 5 vols., Oxf. 1931) adds useful notes. Of the numerous criticisms of Macaulay's writing the following are examples: J. M. Kemble in *Frazer's Magazine,* Feb. 1856; J. Paget, 'The new "Examen"', published in *Blackwood's Magazine* and repr. in his *Paradoxes and puzzles,* Edin. 1874; Firth, *A commentary on Maclaulay's history,* 1938.

See also Macaulay's *Critical and historical essays contributed to the 'Edinburgh Review',* 3 vols., 1843, later edn. by F. C. Montague, 1903.

362   MACKINTOSH, SIR J. History of the revolution in England in 1688. 1834. Later edns.

Chapters 1–11 are by Mackintosh. Important appendix of documents, now in Br. Mus. Add. MSS. 34487–526, that were used by Macaulay for his *History* (361). The latter's review, repr. in his *Essays,* is useful.

Useful for its extracts from the French ambassador's dispatches is F. A. J. Mazure, *Histoire de la révolution de 1688 en Angleterre,* 3 vols., Paris, 1825. An excellent modern critique is G. M. Trevelyan, *The English revolution, 1688–1689,* 1938. On the role of William III see L. Pinkham, *William III and the respectable revolution,* Camb. 1954, K. H. D Haley, *William of Orange and the English opposition, 1672–4,* Oxf. 1953, and Haley's article in *E.H.R.* 69 (1954), 302–6. I. Morley in *A thousand lives: an account of the English revolutionary movement, 1660–1685,* 1954, provides only an inadequate treatment of the subject.

363   MILNE, D. J. 'The results of the Rye House plot and their influence upon the revolution of 1688.' *R.H.S. Trans.,* 5th Ser. 11 (1951), 91–108.

Argues that government handling of the plot tended in the end to weaken its position. Important for the plot and Jacobite intrigues is J. Ferguson, *Robert Ferguson the plotter,* Edin. 1887.

364   OGG, D. England in the reign of Charles II. 2 vols. Oxf. 1934. Bibl.
Rev. edn. 2 vols. Oxf. 1955.

Important work, more complete than Macaulay for this period. By Ogg also, *England in the reigns of James II and William III*, Oxf. 1955, which is somewhat overcritical in its treatment of James II. See also no. 265 n. Useful for the relations of business and politics in the period is D. C. Coleman, *Sir John Bankes, baronet and businessman*, N.Y. 1963.

365   RONALDS, F. S. The attempted Whig revolution of 1678–1681. Urbana, Ill. 1937. Bibl.

Biographical articles on persons concerned with the Popish Plot and the Exclusion Bill. Compare with J. R. Jones, *The first Whigs* (922). See also *Eccles. Hist.* nos. 1489–97.

366   SACRET, J. H. 'The Restoration government and municipal corporations.' *E.H.R.* 45 (1930), 232–59.

Valuable. Cf. R. Austin, 'The city of Gloucester and the regulation of corporations, 1662–63', *Bristol and Glouc. Arch. Soc.* 58 (1936), 257–74; and T. Pape, *The Restoration government and . . . Newcastle-under-Lyme*, Manchester, 1940.

367   SOMERVILLE, T. The history of political transactions and of parties from the restoration of King Charles the Second to the death of King William. 1792.

Still useful, as is the same author's *History of Great Britain during the reign of Queen Anne*, 1798.

E. 1689–1714

Several titles listed in the general political section or for the period of 1660–89 are important for this period also. Good general accounts are contained in Clark (267) and Leadham (271 n.). Macaulay (361) and Ranke (275) are classics for this as well as for the preceding period. Important works will be found also in Chs. III, VI, and XIV *infra*. On the Stuarts in exile see nos. 386–7, 2337–8, 3695 a. Useful bibliographies occur in Clark and Leadham. Manuscripts of special value are Bath, Downshire, and Portland (H.M.C., nos. 80, 225, 204).

I. SOURCES

Arranged roughly in chronological order according to content.

368   CUNNINGHAM, ALEXANDER. The history of Great Britain (1688–1714). Ed. by W. Thomson. 2 vols. Lond. and Edin. 1787.

Trans. from Latin. Interesting, but to be used with caution.

369   MACPHERSON, JAMES, ed. Original papers containing the secret history of Great Britain (1660–1714). 2 vols. 1775.

Principally after 1688. Contains extracts from the *Life of James II* (ed. by J. S. Clarke), and Jacobite correspondence from the Nairne papers. For corrections and criticisms see articles by A. Parnell, *E.H.R.* 12 (1897), 254–84; by J. F. Chance, ibid. 13 (1898), 533–49; and by G. Davies, ibid. 35 (1920), 367–76. Macpherson is the author of a *History of Great Britain* (1660–1714), 2 vols., 1775.

370 A COLLECTION OF STATE TRACTS, published on occasion of the late revolution in 1688 and during the reign of King William III. 3 vols. 1705–7.

Important. Cf. *A choice collection of papers relating to state affairs during the late revolution*, 1703. Repr. as *A collection of scarce and valuable papers*, 1712. Not to be confused with no. 336. See also G. M. Trevelyan, ed., *Select documents for Queen Anne's reign* (1702–7), 1929.

371 VERNON, JAMES. Letters illustrative of the reign of William III from 1696 to 1708 addressed to the Duke of Shrewsbury ... by J. Vernon, Secretary of State. Ed. by G. P. R. James. 3 vols. 1841.

Valuable, especially for 1696–1702. See corrections by D. H. Somerville, *E.H.R.* 48 (1933), 624–30.

372 [ABBADIE, JACQUES.] The history of the late conspiracy against the king ... with a particular account of the Lancashire plot. 1696.

An 'official' account of the Assassination plot. Another *History*, with documents, by R[ichard] K[ingston] was published in 1698. Other sources on early Jacobitism are: L. Tate, editor, 'Letter-book of Richard Talbot', *Analecta Hibernica*, 4 (1932), 99–138, concerning the Jacobite army, 1689–90; W. Gandy, *The Association oath rolls of 1696* (Lancashire), 1921; Matthew Smith, *Memoirs of secret service*, 1699, by one who was employed to hunt for conspirators (cf. a pamphlet by Smith [1700], Wing, S 4132); and John Macky, *Memoirs of the secret services of John Macky* (William III, Anne, and George I), 1733, repr. for Roxburghe Club, 1895. See also no. 378; Pargellis (11 n.), pp. 406–7; and *Scottish History*.

373 FULLER, WILLIAM. The whole life of Mr. William Fuller ... together with a true discovery of the intrigues for which he lies now confin'd. 1703.

Autobiography of a perjuror, including his *Brief discovery of the true mother of the pretended Prince of Wales*, 1696. His *Life* had appeared in 2 parts, 1701. In 1704 was printed his *Sincere and hearty confession* of the design to put forth Mrs. Mary Grey as the mother of the prince.

374 BOYER, ABEL. History of the reign of Queen Anne digested into Annals (1703–13). 11 vols. 1703–13.

Essentially the base for his useful *History of the life and reign of Queen Anne*, 1722. A monthly publication under the title of *The political state of Great Britain* (1711–40), 60 vols., 1711–40, continued the history. The volumes for 1711–14 were published in a 5-vol. edn., 1718–20. The tone of Boyer is Whiggish, but his work is valuable, especially for developments in Parliament. A microfilm copy of the original edition is in Lib. of Congress.

375 WENTWORTH PAPERS 1705–1739 selected from the ... correspondence of Thomas Wentworth Lord Raby, created in 1711 Earl of Strafford. Ed. by J. J. Cartwright. 1883.

Especially useful for the period of Utrecht; selected from private and official correspondence, 1685–1755, in Br. Mus. Add. MSS. 22192–267, 31128–52. Cf. letters of Strafford's secretary, Ayerst, in *E.H.R.* 3 (1888), 751–60; 4 (1889), 131–43, 338–50, 539–47.
  For other important collections of correspondence see Coke (101), Oxford (486), Shrewsbury (504). See also news-letters in *Le Fleming papers* (138).

376 KENNET, WHITE. The wisdom of looking backward to judge the better of one side and t'other by the speeches, writings, actions . . . for the four years last past. 1715.

Valuable analysis of pamphlets, etc. Cf. John Asgill, *A collection of tracts* (1700–15), 1715. Other examples of tracts of importance are: Thomas Burnet, *The necessity of impeaching the late ministry*, 1715; [Daniel Defoe?], *Minutes of the negotiations of Monsr. Mesnager at the court of England toward the close of the last reign*, 1717, 1736, which should be compared with T. Bateson, 'Relations of Defoe and Harley', *E.H.R.* 15 (1900), 238–50; and [George Smyth, possibly Gilbert Burnet?], *A memorial offered . . . to the Princess Sophia . . . containing a delineation of the constitution and policy of England . . .*, 1703, ed. by J. G. H. Feder, 1815. See also Swift (377).

377 SWIFT, JONATHAN. History of the last four years of the Queen. 1758.

The latest edition, with an intro. by Harold Williams, is in the Herbert Davis edn. of Swift's *Prose Works*, vol. vii (Oxf. 1951). Other invaluable political writings of Swift, besides his *Journal to Stella*, which relates to the years 1710–13, are printed in two volumes of *Political tracts* (1711–13 and 1713–19), vols. vi and viii of the Davis edn. Oxf. 1951 and 1953, and in the earlier Temple Scott edn. (2598). Cf. a separate edn. of *An enquiry into the behavior of the queen's last ministry*, by I. Ehrenpreis, Bloomington, 1956.

378 ALLARDYCE, J., ed. Historical papers relating to the Jacobite period, 1699–1750. (New Spalding Club.) 2 vols. Aberdeen. 1895–6.

Important collection. Useful also are Cavelli, *Les Derniers Stuarts* (2337); and L. G. W. Legg, 'Extracts from Jacobite correspondence 1712–14', *E.H.R.* 30 (1915), 501–18. An account of papers concerning the Lancashire plot is presented by T. C. Porteus in *Lanc. & Cheshire Antiq. Soc. Trans. for 1934–5*, 50 (1937), 1–64. See also no. 372, Beamont (1070), and Terry (3695a).

2. Later Works

379 DAVIES, G. 'The fall of Harley in 1708.' *E.H.R.* 66 (1951), 246–54.

Reviews the historical arguments regarding the cause of Harley's fall.

380 KENYON, J. P. 'The earl of Sutherland and the king's administration, 1693–1695.' *E.H.R.* 71 (1956), 576–602.

Argues that the Junto was only one of several political elements before 1696. For biographical sketches of individuals see T. Merz, *The junto*, Newcastle, 1907.

381 KLOPP, O. Der Fall des Hauses Stuart und die Succession des Hauses Hannover (1660–1714). 14 vols. in 7. Vienna. 1875–88.

The best account of English foreign relations, especially from about 1678; based largely on Austrian dispatches. Also drawing heavily upon foreign archives, but with Tory bias, is F. Salomon, *Geschichte des letzten Ministeriums Königin Annas von England, 1710–14, und der englischen Thronfolgefrage*, Gotha, 1894. Useful for the European background to 1710 is C. F. J. von Noorden, *Europäische Geschichte im achtzehnten Jahrhundert*, 3 vols., Düsseldorf, 1870–82. Cf. M. A. Thomson, 'The safeguarding of the Protestant succession, 1702–18', *History*, 39 (1954), 39–53.

382 LAPRADE, W. T. Public opinion and politics in eighteenth-century England to the fall of Walpole. N.Y. 1936.

First seven chapters deal with 1700–14; draws upon published correspondence, pamphlets, and periodicals; has bibliographical footnotes. Cf. M. Foot, *The pen and the sword*, 1957, relating to the political crisis on the issue of terminating the war, 1710–12.

383   NOBBS, D. England and Scotland, 1560–1707. N.Y. 1952.

An interpretive essay on the background of the union. Cf. T. Keith, 'The economic causes of the Scottish union', *E.H.R.* 24 (1909), 44–60; W. L. Burn, 'The Scottish policy of John, sixth earl of Mar, 1707–1715', *Hunt. Lib. Quart.* 2 (1939), 439–48; and nos. 3727, 3767, 3774.

384   STANHOPE, PHILIP HENRY, EARL. History of England comprising the reign of Queen Anne until the Peace of Utrecht, 1701–1713. 1870. 4th edn. 2 vols. 1872.

Still useful; written to fill the gap between Macaulay (361) and the opening of Stanhope's own history of eighteenth-century England. A scholarly study of one religious-political episode of the period, which confirms earlier interpretations, is A. T. Scudi, *The Sacheverell affair*, N.Y. 1939, bibl.

385   TREVELYAN, G. M. England under Queen Anne. 3 vols. 1930–4.

The best modern account, notable for literary style as well as for scholarship, by Macaulay's grandnephew. The older history by F. W. Wyon, 2 vols., 1876, has still some value; several useful chapters on Anne's period are to be found in M. Wolfgang, *England under George I*, 1936; a good deal of interesting as well as trivial material appears in J. R. Sutherland, *Background for Queen Anne*, 1939.

3. LATER WORKS: JACOBITISM

386   JONES, G. H. The main stream of Jacobitism. Camb. (Mass.). 1954.

An able modern study, showing especially relationships to foreign policies of Britain and continental countries. On earlier aspects, see G. L. Cherry, 'The legal and philosophical position of the Jacobites, 1688–1689', *J.M.H.* 22 (1950), 309–21. See also H. N. Fieldhouse, 'Oxford, Bolingbroke, and the pretender's place of residence', *E.H.R.* 52 (1937), 289–96. For a Jacobite bibliography, 1897–1939, see D. Guthrie and C. L. Grose, *J.M.H.* 11 (1939), 49–60. See also nos. 2337 and 3695a.

387   PETRIE, SIR C. A. The Jacobite movement. 1932. Rev. edn. 2 vols. 1948–50. Rev. 1-vol. edn. 1959.

Vol. i of the 1948–50 edn. covers the years 1688–1716. An American edn., Boston, 1933, was entitled *The Stuart pretenders: the Jacobite movement, 1688–1807*. A valuable work, with useful bibliography; some inaccuracies. The 1959 edn. supersedes the earlier ones.

F. CORRESPONDENCE, JOURNALS, AND BIOGRAPHIES

The biographical materials in this section relate chiefly to English political figures. A more general list will be found in Ch. IX *infra*; and persons whose roles were chiefly in connection with the church, the law, the army or navy, or who are most famous as writers, are listed in the corresponding sections of this volume. See also H.M.C., nos. 72–235. A number of names, such as Bacon, Milton, Swift, appear in several places, and should be traced through the index. There are biographical sections also for Ireland, Scotland, and Wales. The titles that follow are selections only, since there is an increasing volume of biographical writing. Definitive biographies on numerous major figures, especially those of the later decades, are still lacking. An alphabetical rather than a chronological arrangement of individuals has been followed.

1. COLLECTED BIOGRAPHIES

See Ch. IX, § F *infra* for more general guides to biographical study, family history, and genealogical research. The famous general collections by Aubrey (2439), Fuller (2442), Walton (2448), and others are there.

388 CARLYLE, T. Historical sketches of notable persons and events in the reigns of James I and Charles I. Ed. by A. Carlyle. 1898.

> Pym and Cromwell are the subjects of lectures by Goldwin Swift in *Three English statesmen . . .*, 1867, later edn., 1868. Biographies of Hampden, Strafford, and others, in popular style, are in P. Lindsay, *For king and parliament*, 1949.

389 LLOYD, DAVID. State worthies, or the statesmen and favourites of England since the reformation. 1665. Later edn. 2 vols. 1766.

> By Lloyd also, *Memoires of the lives . . . of those . . . personages that suffered . . . for the Protestant religion and . . . allegiance to their soveraigne . . . from 1637 to 1660, and from thence continued to 1666*, 1668. Cf. James Heath, *A new book of loyal English martyrs and confessors*, 1663 [1665?]. Both authors are royalist in view.

390 NOBLE, M. The lives of the English regicides. 2 vols. 1798.

> The best-known collection on the subject. See also the two 1661 collections of brief lives by 'W. S.', *A compleat collection of the lives . . . of those persons lately executed*, and *Rebels no saints: or a collection of the speeches . . . of those persons lately executed*; and the anonymous *History of king-killers . . .*, 1719. On three regicides who fled to America, Dixwell, Goffe, and Whalley, see Ezra Stiles, *History of three of the judges of Charles I*, Hartford (Conn.), 1794.

391 SANFORD, F. A genealogical history of the kings of England (1066– 1677). 1677. Ports. Later edn., to 1707, by S. Stebbing. 1707.

> In her *Six Stuart sovereigns, 1521–1701*, 1935, Eva Scott gives revisionist interpretations of the various reigns, but contributes little that is new.

392 STEBBING, W. Some verdicts of history reviewed. 1887.

> Includes studies of Shaftesbury, Cowley, Prior, and Bolingbooke. Cf. T. Lewis, *Lives of the friends and contemporaries of Lord Chancellor Clarendon*, 3 vols., 1852. See also Merz (380 n.).

393 STRICKLAND, A. Lives of the queens of England. 12 vols. 1840–8. Many edns. Ed. by J. F. Kirk. 16 vols. Phila. 1902–3.

> Useful, but uncritical. See also the useful but uneven *Lives of the princesses of England* (to Charles I), by M. A. E. Green, 6 vols., 1849–55. See also R. S. Rait, ed., *Five Stuart princesses*, 1902, 1908; and no. 2337.

394 WALKER, E., *et al.* Historical portraits. 4 vols. Oxf. 1909–19. Ports.

> Essentially a history of portraiture, but with brief biographical sketches. Vol. ii covers 1600–1700; vol. iii, 1700–1800. Useful. See also E. Lodge, *Portraits of illustrious personages of Great Britain*, 12 vols., 1823–40, ports.; later edn., 12 vols., 1835.

395 WINSTANLEY, W. England's worthies. Select lives of the most eminent persons of the English nation from Constantine the Great to the death of Oliver Cromwell. 1660. Later edn. 1684.

The 1684 edn. contains new lives ending with Rupert, but omits Cromwell.

2. INDIVIDUALS: PAPERS AND BIOGRAPHIES

AILESBURY, THOMAS BRUCE, EARL OF. 1656–1741

396 Memoires. Ed. by W. E. Buckley. 2 vols. Roxburghe Club. 1890.

Important, especially for 1678–1714, but must be used with caution because the author was writing in his very old age. See criticisms by W. Burghclere in *Quart. Rev.* 103 (1905), 548–71. *The life and loyalties of Thomas Bruce . . . earl of Ailesbury and Elgin, gentleman of the bedchamber to Charles II and James II,* by the Earl of Cardigan, 1951, though based on the *Memoires* and other sources, is written in popular style for the general reader.

ALBEMARLE, CHRISTOPHER MONCK, DUKE OF. 1653–88

397 Ward, E. F. Christopher Monck, duke of Albemarle. 1915.

For George Monck, the first duke, see no. 1666.

ANGLESEY, ARTHUR ANNESLEY, EARL OF. 1614–86

398 Memoirs of . . . Arthur Earl of Anglesey late privy seal intermixt with moral political and historical observations. Ed. by Sir P. Pett. 1693.

Anglesey's diary 1671–5 is in H.M.C. (73), pp. 261–78; a continuation to 1684 is in Br. Mus. Add. MS. 18730.

ANNE, QUEEN. 1665–1714

399 The letters and domestic instructions of Queen Anne. Ed. by B. C. Brown. 1935. Bibl.

The first collection, from numerous sources, of Anne's correspondence. Several letters were ed. by G. Davies in *S.H.R.* 19 (1922), 190–5. A satisfactory biography is yet to be written. H. W. Paul, *Queen Anne,* 1906, is too brief; M. R. Hopkinson, *Anne of England,* 1934 and rev. 1938, is lively but faulty in its scholarship; scholarly but popular is Neville Connell's biography, 1937. A popular interpretation of Anne was attempted by B. C. Brown, the editor of her letters, 1929.

A biography of Anne's only son, the Duke of Gloucester (d. 1700), was written by H. W. Chapman, 1954, bibl.

See also the contemporary histories of her reign by Boyer (374) and Swift (377).

ARLINGTON, HENRY BENNET, EARL OF. 1618–85

400 The right honourable the earl of Arlington's letters. . . . Ed. by Thomas Bebington. 2 vols. 1701.

Official letters to Sir William Temple (vol. i) and to the several ambassadors to Spain (vol. ii), which are useful for foreign relations rather than personal history. The excellent biography by Violet Barbour, *Henry Bennet, earl of Arlington,* Washington, 1914, bibl., is brief and based upon materials now somewhat dated.

ARUNDEL, THOMAS HOWARD, EARL OF. *c.* 1585-1646

401 Hervey, M. F. S. The life, correspondence, and collections of Thomas Howard, earl of Arundel. Camb. 1921.

ASHBURNHAM, JOHN. 1603-71

402 A narrative by John Ashburnham of his attendance on King Charles the First . . . to which is prefixed a vindication of his character and conduct. 2 vols. 1830.

Ashburnham, who attended Charles 1646-8, replied to Clarendon's criticisms. The appendices include 'Memoirs' of Sir John Berkley.

BACON, FRANCIS. 1561-1626

403 The works of Francis Bacon. Ed. by James Spedding *et al.* 14 vols. 1857-74.

Vols. viii-xiv, subtitled 'Life and letters', include all of the occasional papers of Bacon, letters, speeches, and non-philosophical writings, and are arranged in chronological order with a biographical and historical commentary by Spedding. By Spedding, also, *An account of the life and times of Francis Bacon*, 2 vols., Boston, 1880, and *Evenings with a reviewer* (defence of Bacon against the charges of Macaulay in his 'Essay on Bacon'), 2 vols., 1881. Brief lives are by R. W. Church [English Men of Letters], 1884, E. Abbott, 1884, C. Williams, 1933, A. Dodd, 1949. Dodd in *The martyrdom of Francis Bacon*, 1945, argues Bacon's innocence on the charges of bribery. A *Life of Alice Barnham*, Bacon's wife, was publ. by A. C. Bunten, 1928. In *Francis Bacon: the first statesman of science*, 1960, J. G. Crowther attempts in part ii to show some of the problems of the scientist in the political world. See also the interpretive biography by C. D. Bowen, Boston (Mass.), 1963.

See H. Wheeler, 'The constitutional ideas of Francis Bacon', *Western Political Quart.* 9 (1956), 927-36. See also nos. 2695, 2904.

BANKES, SIR JOHN. 1627-99

404 Coleman, D. C. Sir John Bankes, baronet and businessman: a study of business, politics and society in later Stuart England. Oxf. and N.Y. 1963.

Valuable.

BOLINGBROKE, HENRY ST. JOHN, VISCOUNT. 1678-1751

405 Letters and correspondence, public and private, of . . . Henry St. John, Lord Viscount Bolingbroke during the time he was Secretary of State [1710-14]. Ed. by G. Parke. 4 vols. 1798; also 2 vols. 1798.

Other correspondence with James Brydges, ed. by G. Davies and M. Tinling, is printed in *Hunt. Lib. Bull.* 8 (1935), 153-70, and 9 (1936), 119-66. *Memoirs of the life and ministerial conduct . . . of the late Lord Viscount Bolingbroke*, publ. in 1752, may have been compiled by D. Mallet, who edited Bolingbroke's philosophical *Works*, 5 vols., 1754, 8 vols., 1809. The best biography is still W. Sichel, *Bolingbroke and his times*, 2 vols., 1901-2, the first volume of which extends to 1714. Older lives by T. Macknight, 1863, and A. Hassell, 1889 (Oxf. 1915) are still of some value. Two useful articles by H. W. Fieldhouse are printed in *E.H.R.* 52 (1937), 443-59 and 673-82; and another by Fieldhouse is in *History*, 23 (1938), 41-56. Popular but of little value are lives by M. R. Hopkinson, 1936, C. Petrie, 1937, and D. Harkness, 1957; but see Sir C. G. Robertson, *Bolingbroke* [Historical Assoc., G. 6], 1947.

BOTELER, WILLIAM

406   Hardacre, P. H. 'William Boteler: a Cromwellian oligarch.' *Hunt. Lib. Quart.* 11 (1947), 1–11.

Brief account of one of the most hated major-generals.

BRAMSTON, SIR JOHN

407   Braybrooke, Lord, ed. The autobiography of Sir John Bramston of Skreens. Camd. Soc. 1845.

Notices of public affairs as well as of domestic life; valuable especially for the reign of James II, but continues to 1699.

BRISTOL, GEORGE DIGBY, EARL OF. 1612–77

408   Townshend, D. George Digby, second earl of Bristol. 1924.

Useful. Cf. H. M. Digby's *Sir Kenelm Digby and George Digby, earl of Bristol*, 1912.

BROOKE, ROBERT GREVILLE, LORD. 1608?–43

409   Strider, R. E. L. Robert Greville, Lord Brooke. Camb., Mass. 1958. Bibl.

Little new material on life, which constitutes the first part; useful on literary role.

BUCKINGHAM, GEORGE VILLIERS, DUKE OF. 1592–1628

410   Letters of the duke and duchess of Buckingham chiefly addressed to King James I of England. Ed. by T. G. Stevenson[?]. Edin. 1834.

Still useful, though dated, is K. Thomson, *Life and times of George Villiers, duke of Buckingham*, 3 vols., 1860. Of modern biographies, the best is by H. R. Williamson, 1940; popularly written, reasonably accurate is that by M. A. Gibb, 1936. Famous contemporary evaluations are the 'character' by Clarendon (*History*, no. 305), and the essays by Henry Wotton (*Reliquiae Wottoniae*, no. 2648). Over-apologetic and romanticized are the interpretations by P. Gibbs, 1908, new edn. 1930; and C. R. Cammell, 1939. A more moderate revisionist evaluation by P. Erlanger, *L'énigme du monde: George Villiers, duc de Buckingham*, Paris, 1951, was trans. by L. Smith-Gordon, Lond., 1953. See also no. 792.

BUCKINGHAM, GEORGE VILLIERS, DUKE OF. 1628–87

411   Burghclere, W., Lady. George Villiers, second duke of Buckingham, 1628–1687. 1903.

Still the best life, though not definitive. A popular portrait, based chiefly on printed materials, is H. W. Chapman, *Great Villiers*, 1949, bibl.; popular in style but based on scholarly research is J. H. Wilson, *The rake and his times: George Villiers, 2nd duke of Buckingham*, N.Y. 1954.

BUCKINGHAM, JOHN SHEFFIELD, DUKE OF. 1648–1721

412   [Memoirs of the duke of Buckingham.] By John Sheffield, earl of Mulgrave, marquis of Normandy, and duke of Buckingham.

Two sets of memoirs relating to the period of Charles II and another, 'Some account of the revolution of 1688', exist. They are printed in the second edn. of his *Works*, 2 vols., The Hague, 1726; the latter part is said to have been suppressed from the first edn., 2 vols., 1723, and was separately printed at The Hague in 1727. The memoirs appear in later edns. and two parts are included in vol. xxi of Guizot's *Collections* (340). A short life appears in *Miscellanea from the works* ..., Halifax, 1933. See also no. 2612.

BULSTRODE, SIR RICHARD. 1610–1711

413 Bulstrode, Sir Richard. Memoirs and reflections upon the reign and government of King Charles the Ist and K. Charles the IId. 1721.

Cf. Sir C. Firth's article on Bulstrode's Memoirs in *E.H.R.* 10 (1895), 266–75, which shows that added to Bulstrode's own memoirs in his old age are materials from Clarendon and Warwick. His *Original letters . . . to the earl of Arlington* [1674] were ed. by Edward Bysshe in 1712. The *Bulstrode papers* (Morrison collection, H.M.C., no. 92), news-letters sent to him at Brussels, 1667–75, are valuable.

CAESAR, SIR JULIUS. 1558–1636

414 Lodge, E. Life of Sir Julius Caesar, a privy councillor to King James and Charles the First, with memoirs of his family and descendants. 1827.

Useful.

CAREW, GEORGE, LORD. 1557–1629

415 Letters from George Lord Carew to Sir Thomas Roe. Ed. by J. Maclean. Camden Soc. 1860.

Originals in P.R.O. Dom. S.P. Covers the period Jan. 1615–Jan. 1618.

CATHERINE OF BRAGANZA. 1638–1705

416 Davidson, L. C. Catherine of Braganza, infanta of Portugal and queen-consort of England. 1908.

The more recent life by J. Mackay, 1937, bibl., has no great depth and is based chiefly on printed sources. Entirely in popular style is M. B. Jones, *Restoration carnival: Catherine of Braganza at the court of Charles II*, 1937. Cf. C. L. Grose, 'Anglo-Portuguese marriage of 1662', *Hispanic Amer. Hist. Rev.* 10 (1930), 313–52. Letters of Catherine are in Br. Mus. Add. MS. 22548 and Eg. 1534.

CHANDOS, JAMES BRYDGES, DUKE OF. 1673–1744

417 Robinson, J. R. The princely Chandos: a memoir of James Brydges, paymaster-general to the forces abroad ... 1705–11, afterwards the first duke of Chandos. 1893.

Portions of the Brydges papers, accounts, etc., now at the Huntington Lib., have been printed in its *Bull.* 2 (1931), 123–47. See his correspondence with Bolingbroke, no. 405. C. H. C. and M. I. Baker, in *The life and circumstances of James Brydges, first duke of Chandos*, Oxf. 1949, do not go much beyond social and literary history.

CHARLES I

418 The letters, speeches and proclamations of King Charles I. Ed. by Sir C. Petrie. 1935. Bibl.

The fullest collection. Other collections of letters are those ed. by J. Bruce for the Camden Soc., vol. 63 (1856), under the title, *Charles I in 1646*; the early collections: *Reliquiae sacrae Carolinae*, 2 pts., The Hague, 1649, *Bibliotheca regia, or the royall library*, 1659, and G. Bromley's *Collection* (260 n.). The authorship of *Eikon basilike*, 'The king's book', 1648–9, by recent scholarship is considered to be shared by the king and John Gauden. Milton's reply, *Eikonoklastes*, was printed in 1649. On the literature of the Eikon, see F. F. Madan, *A new bibliography of the Eikon basilike*, Oxf. Bibl. Soc. Pub., N.S. 3, 1950 (which supersedes the 1896 bibl. by E. Almack). See also Trevor-Roper's article in *History Today*, 1 (1951), 7–12.

Early lives tended to be strongly partisan. Among the hostile ones are: *The non-such Charles and his character*, 1651, which is attributed to Balthazar Gerbier; and *The life and reign of King Charles or the pseudo-martyr discovered*, 1651; for contrast see John Arnway, *The tablet, or moderation of Charles the I, martyr*, The Hague, 1649, later edn. by W. Rider, Lond., 1661; Sir William Sanderson, *A compleat history of the life and raigne of King Charles . . .*, 1658, which was a reply to the works of L'Estrange and Heylyn (289), and which produced a series of replies by Heylyn, 1658 (Wing, H 1732), and 1659 (Wing, H 1706), with rejoinders by Sanderson, 1650 (Wing, S 650) and 1659 (Wing, S 649). For the civil-war period see Thomas Manley, *Iter Carolium . . .* (Jan. 1641/2–9), 1660, which has been repr. in Gutch's *Collectanea curiosa*, ii, 1781; *Somers tracts*, vol. v; and by H. S. Wheatley-Crowe, from the original MS., in *Royalist revelations*, 1922. Of little value is William Lilly's *True history of King James the First and King Charles the First*, 1715.

419   Charles I, a study. By F. M. G. Higham. [1932.]

A biography which is moderate in its interpretation and is based on sources but without notes. Examples of the reaction to the Whig interpretations of the 19th century are A. Fea, *Memoirs of the martyr king* (1646–9), 1905; H. Belloc, *Charles the first*, Phila., 1933, 2nd edn., 1936; those by C. W. Coit, 1924, and J. Brookes, 1934, which are extreme in their revisionism while presenting no new evidence; and the ambitious series, in popular style, by E. Wingfield-Stratford, *Charles, king of England*, 3 vols., 1948–50. (The account for 1600–43 in vols. i–ii was first publ. as *King Charles and the conspirators*, 1937.) E. John (*pseud.* for E. J. Simpson), *King Charles I*, 1933 (2nd edn., 1952), is more objective and follows the Tawney thesis in accounting for the attack of the gentry upon the prerogative. Revisionist studies with emphasis on Charles's later years are G. M. Young, *Charles I and Cromwell*, 1935, rev. edn., 1950; and H. Ross Williamson, *Charles and Cromwell*, 1946. See also the brief life by M. P. F. Pakenham [Great Lives series], 1936, bibl.; and no. 310 n. and four essays by C. V. Wedgwood *et al.*, *King Charles I, 1649–1949* [Historical Assoc., G. 11], 1949.

CHARLES II

420   The letters, speeches and declarations of King Charles II. Ed. by A. Bryant. 1935.

A selection only. Two speeches, 1663, 1672, were ed. by K. Feiling for *E.H.R.* 45 (1930), 291–3. Many contemporary accounts relating to Charles's escape after Worcester and his period of exile are listed in W. A. Horrox, ed., *A bibliography of the literature relating to the escape . . .*, Aberdeen, 1924; see also various reprints, including the account dictated by Charles himself to Pepys, and Thomas Blount's *Boscobel*, 1660, in *The Boscobel tracts relating to the escape . . .*, ed. by J. Hughes, Edin. and Lond., 1830, later edn. 1857; a collection ed. by A. Fea, *The flight of the king*, 1897, 1908; and another group of tracts, ballads, etc., ed. by A. M. Broadley, under the title of *The royal miracle*, 1912. H. P. Kingston's *Wanderings of Charles II in Staffordshire and Shropshire*, Birmingham, 1933, combines contemporary accounts with narrative; S. E. Hoskins, *Charles the Second in the Channel Islands*, 2 vols., 1954, is based on Chevalier's *Journal* (96); and the *Nicholas papers* (307) are important for the period to 1660. Relating to this period in Charles's life also are two works by E. Scott, *The king in exile* (1646–54), 1905, and *The travels of King Charles II in Germany and Flanders, 1654–1660*, 1907.

421   Bryant, A. King Charles II. 1931. Rev. edn. 1955.

The best life, defensive against the Whig interpretation; also still valuable is O. Airy's *Charles II*, 1901, 1904. Cf. C. L. Grose, 'Charles the Second of England', *A.H.R.* 43

(1938), 533-41; G. Davies, 'Charles II in 1660', *Hunt. Lib. Quart.* 19 (1956) 245-75. On special aspects of his character and reign see also A. C. A. Brett, *Charles II and his court*, 1910; C. H. Hartmann, *Charles II and madame* [Henrietta, Duchess of Orleans], 1934, reissued 1954 as *The king my brother*; and popular lives by J. Drinkwater, 1926, and D. Wheatley, 1933, 1938. J. E. E. D. Lord Acton, 'Secret history of Charles II', in *Home and Foreign Review* (1882), 146-74 (repr. in Acton's *Historical essays and studies*, ed. by J. N. Figgis and R. V. Laurence, 1907), is concerned mainly with James de la Cloche.

CLARENDON, EDWARD HYDE, EARL OF. 1609-74

422   Clarendon, Edward Hyde, earl of. The life of Edward, earl of Clarendon. Being a continuation of the History of the Great Rebellion from the restoration to his banishment in 1667. Oxf. 1759. Later edn. 2 vols. Oxf. 1857.

Original in Bodl. Lib. Clarendon MS. 123. Earlier portions of an earlier life, written before 1671, were incorporated by Clarendon in his *History* (305); the *Continuation*, though less accurate, is of great importance for the early years of the restoration and for Clarendon's second exile. For Clarendon's state papers see no. 257.

   Still the best biography of Clarendon is T. H. Lister, *Life and administration of Edward, first earl of Clarendon*, 3 vols., 1837-8, the third vol. of which comprises correspondence from MSS. at the Bodl. Lib. (see Lister's reply to a critical review, *Quart. Rev.* 62 (1838), 505-66). Also useful, with new materials but less impartial, is H. Craik's *Life*, 2 vols., 1911. C. H. Firth's incisive evaluation, *Edward Hyde, earl of Clarendon*, as historian and statesman, delivered as a lecture, Oxf. 1909, was repr. in his *Essays, historical and literary* (269). B. H. G. Wormald challenges the view that Clarendon was a mediocre statesman in *Clarendon: politics, history, and religion, 1640-1660*, Camb. 1951 (repr. 1965), an expansion of his article, 'How Hyde became a royalist', *Camb. Hist. Jour.* 8 (1945), 65-92. Notes by G. Davies and K. Feiling are in *E.H.R.* 32 (1917), 405-7, and 44 (1929), 289-91.

CLARENDON, HENRY HYDE, EARL OF. 1638-1709

423   Singer, S. W., ed. The correspondence of Henry Hyde, earl of Clarendon, and of his brother, Laurence Hyde, earl of Rochester, with the diary of Lord Clarendon from 1687 to 1690. 2 vols. 1828.

Important especially for the period of James II. Some additional papers were ed. by C. E. Doble (351).

CLIFFORD, THOMAS CLIFFORD, LORD. 1630-73

424   Hartmann, C. H. Clifford of the Cabal, 1630-1673. 1937.

Useful; based on papers of Clifford, Lord High Treasurer.

COKE, SIR EDWARD. 1552-1634

425   Bowen, C. D. The lion and the throne: the life and times of Sir Edward Coke, 1552-1634. 1957. Bibl.

Excellent on career of the distinguished lawyer, though somewhat weak on legal procedure of the period; should be checked with the brilliant 1952 Selden Society lecture, *Sir Edward Coke*, by S. E. Thorne, 1957. Less valuable are the biographies by H. Lyon and H. Block, Boston (Mass.), 1929, and C. W. James, 1929. Some biographical material is in L. L. Norsworthy, *The lady of Bleeding Heart Yard: Lady Elizabeth Hatton, 1578-1646*, 1935. See also no. 1079.

COKE, SIR JOHN. 1563–1644

426   Coke, D. The last Elizabethan: Sir John Coke, 1563–1644. 1937.

Useful biography of a secretary of state for Charles I, drawing heavily upon the family correspondence. See H.M.C. (101).

COVENTRY, SIR WILLIAM. 1628?–86

427   Shelley, R. J. A. Sir William Coventry: a patron of Pepys. 1932.

Active in naval affairs *temp.* Charles II.

CROMWELL, HENRY. 1628–74

428   Ramsey, R. W. Henry Cromwell. 1933.

Based largely on Henry Cromwell's correspondence.

CROMWELL, OLIVER. 1599–1658

429   Abbott, W. C., ed. The writings and speeches of Oliver Cromwell. 4 vols. Camb. (Mass.). 1937–47.

The definitive edition, with valuable appendices of documents relating to foreign affairs, and bibliography (see below), as well as a biographical sketch. Still useful is T. Carlyle's classic edition of *Oliver Cromwell's letters and speeches, with elucidations*, 2 vols., 1845; the best edition is by S. C. Lomas, 3 vols., 1904, bibl., with an intro. by C. H. Firth, dealing with Carlyle as an editor and with the 'Squire papers'; on the latter see also notes by W. A. Wright, S. R. Gardiner, and W. Rye in *E.H.R.* 1 (1896), 311–48, 517–22, 744–56, and Firth's *The early history of the Ironsides* (1586 n.). C. L. Stainer also ed. *Speeches of Oliver Cromwell, 1644–58*, 1901. W. C. Abbott published an excellent *Bibliography of Oliver Cromwell: a list of printed materials*, Camb. (Mass.) 1929, and a supplement (to 1944) in vol. iv of the *Writings*. These are supplemented by P. H. Hardacre's important bibliographical essay (1929–60) in *J.M.H.* 33 (1961), 1–14.

430   [Fletcher, Henry.] The perfect politician, or a full view of the life and actions, military and civil, of O. Cromwell. 1660.

Regarded as the 'only early life of any value' (*D.N.B.*). The extreme royalist view set forth in James Heath, *Flagellum or the life . . . of O. Cromwell*, 1663, later edn., 1679, and echoed in Clarendon's *History* (305) set the key for the most partisan attacks. Representative of the revisionist history of the 19th century are the life by S. R. Gardiner, 1899, later edn., 1901; and the classic biography by C. H. Firth, *Oliver Cromwell and the rule of the Puritans in England* [Heroes of the Nations], N.Y. 1900, which has gone through many edns. (latest 1953); cf. Firth, 'Cromwell and the crown', *E.H.R.* 17 (1902), 429–42, and 18 (1903), 52–80. For others, see Abbott's *Bibliography* (above). Biographies of the period of 1930–40 tended to focus on Cromwell as a dictator, ranging from M. P. Ashley, *Oliver Cromwell, the conservative dictator*, 1937, H. Oncken, *Cromwell: vier essays uber die führung einer nation*, Berlin, 1935, to M. T. Blauvelt, *Oliver Cromwell, a dictator's tragedy*, N.Y. 1937. E. Barker's essay, *Oliver Cromwell and the English people*, Camb. 1937, draws the parallel with modern dictators less sharply; and moderate in tone are the lives by J. Buchan, 1934, 1944, C. V. Wedgwood, 1939, 1947, and P. Young, 1962. In a re-evaluation by M. P. Ashley, *The greatness of Oliver Cromwell*, 1957, the author attempts to deal with the paradoxes of his career and stresses Cromwell's struggle for liberty of conscience. Concerned especially with the religious issue are M. Brosch, *Oliver Cromwell und die puritanische revolution*, Frankfort on Main, 1886; H. Kittel, *Oliver Cromwell, seine religion und sendung*, Berlin, 1928, and R. S. Paul, *The Lord-Protector: religion and politics in the life of Oliver Cromwell*, 1955. On Cromwell's family, see R. Tangye, *The two protectors,*

Oliver and Richard Cromwell, 1899; J. Waylen, *The house of Cromwell*, 1880 (ed. by J. G. Cromwell, 1897); and R. W. Ramsey, *Studies in Cromwell's family circle*, N.Y. 1930.

431 Hill, C. Oliver Cromwell, 1658–1958. [Historical Assoc., G. 38.] 1958.

A pamphlet that presents the paradoxes of Cromwell's career, and the problems of biographers in interpreting them. For other essays on the changing interpretations see Abbott's 'The fame of Oliver Cromwell', in vol. iv of the *Writings*; D. H. Pennington, 'Cromwell and the historians', *History Today*, 8 (1958), 598–605; and the first ch. of Ashley, *The greatness of Oliver Cromwell*.

CROMWELL, RICHARD. 1626–1712

432 Burn, A. S., ed. 'Correspondence of Richard Cromwell.' (c. 1675–1708.) *E.H.R.* 13 (1898), 93–124.

The fullest modern biography is R. W. Ramsey, *Richard Cromwell, protector of England*, 1935. See also no. 430.

DANBY, THOMAS OSBORNE, EARL OF [*later* DUKE OF LEEDS]. 1632–1712

433 Browning, A. Thomas Osborne, earl of Danby and duke of Leeds, 1632–1712. 3 vols. Glasgow. 1944–51.

Outstanding work, based upon extensive use of sources, and revealing much of fiscal policy and party development. Vol. i, Life; vol. ii, Letters; vol. iii, Appendices. Compare the author's prize essay of same title, 1 vol., Oxf. 1913. See also A. M. Evans, 'The imprisonment of Lord Danby in the Tower, 1679–1684', *R.H.S. Trans.*, 4th Ser. 12 (1929), 105–35. See also H.M.C. (113). Other MSS. are in the Leeds–Godolphin MSS. in Br. Mus. Add. MSS. 28040–95, and in Add. MS. 39757.

DENBIGH, WILLIAM FEILDING, EARL OF. ?–1643 and BASIL FEILDING, 2nd EARL OF. c. 1608–75

434 Denbigh, Cecelia Mary Feilding, Countess of. Royalist father and Round-head son; being the memoirs of the first and second earls of Denbigh, 1600–1675. 1915. Illus.

Cf. no. 119.

DERBY, JAMES STANLEY, EARL OF. 1607–51

435 Private devotions and miscellanies of James, seventh earl of Derby, K.G., with a prefatory memoir and an appendix of documents. Ed. by F. R. Raines. 3 vols. Chetham Soc. Manchester. 1867.

The intro. is a full biography.

DIGBY, SIR JOHN. 1605–45

436 Bernard, G., ed. 'Life of Sir John Digby 1605–1645'. *Camd. Soc. Misc. xii*, 3rd Ser., vol. 18. 1910.

DIGBY, SIR KENELM. 1603–65

437 Private memoirs of Sir Kenelm Digby, gentleman of the bed chamber to King Charles the First . . . Ed. by Sir N. H. Nicholas. 1827.

The expurgated passages are included in E. W. Bligh, *Sir Kenelm Digby and his Venetia*, 1932. See *Journal of a voyage* (1628), ed. by J. Bruce, Camden Soc., 1868. Biographies are by T. Longueville, 1896; J. F. Fulton, 1937; R. T. Petersson, *Sir Kenelm Digby, the ornament of England, 1603–1665*, 1956, bibl.; and V. Gabrieli, *Sir Kenelm Digby, un Inglese italianato*, Rome, 1957.

DOWNING, SIR GEORGE. *c.* 1624–84

438 Beresford, J. The godfather of Downing Street: Sir George Downing, 1623–1684. 1925.

Cf. R. C. H. Catterall, 'Sir George Downing and the regicides', *A.H.R.* 17 (1912), 268–89. One ch. on Downing and Pepys is included in H. Bolitho, *No. 10 Downing Street, 1660–1900*, 1957.

DYVE, SIR LEWIS. 1599–1669

439 Tibbutt, H. G. The life and letters of Sir Lewis Dyve, 1599–1669. [Bedfordshire Hist. Rec. Soc. 27.] Streatley. 1948.

The only biography of the royalist governor of Abingdon (1642–4), who eventually followed the king into exile.

ELIOT, SIR JOHN. 1592–1632

440 Hulme, H. The life of Sir John Eliot, 1592–1632: a struggle for parliamentary freedom. N.Y. 1957.

Valuable; based upon careful use of MSS. at Port Eliot. Less laudatory of Eliot's abilities and leadership than was J. Forster in *Sir John Eliot: a biography*, 2 vols., 1864. See also H. R. Williamson, *Four Stuart portraits*, 1949. Hulme ed. Eliot's probate inventory, 1633, for *Camd. Misc.* xvi (1936), pp. 1–14. A. B. Grosart ed. Eliot's *An apology for Socrates* (i.e. a vindication of himself) and *Negotium posterorum* (an account of parliamentary opposition), 2 vols., 1881. On Eliot's role in parliament see also no. 823.

ELIZABETH, PRINCESS PALATINE. 1596–1662

441 Letters of Elizabeth, Queen of Bohemia. Ed. by L. M. Baker. 1953.

Correspondence covering the years 1603–62. Standard older biographies are by M. A. E. Green (393 n.), revised by S. C. Lomas under the title of *Elizabeth Electress Palatine and Queen of Bohemia*, 1909; and Sir A. W. Ward, ed. by T. F. Tout and J. Tait, 1902. There are later biographies by A. Buchan, *A Stuart portrait*, 1934; and C. M. A. Oman, *Elizabeth of Bohemia*, 1938.

FALKLAND, LUCIUS CARY, VISCOUNT. *c.* 1610–43

442 Marriott, Sir J. A. R. The life and times of Lucius Viscount Falkland. Lond. and N.Y. 1907. 2nd edn. Lond. 1908.

K. Weber presents a study of Falkland and his circle in *Lucius Cary, second Viscount Falkland*, N.Y. 1940. See also K. B. Murdock, *The sun at noon: three biographical sketches*, 1939.

FALMOUTH, CHARLES BERKELEY, VISCOUNT FITZHARDINGE and EARL OF. 1630–65

443 Hartmann, C. H. The King's friend: the life of Charles Berkeley, Viscount Fitzhardinge, Earl of Falmouth, 1630–1665. 1951.

Biography of the courtier credited in his day with great influence over Charles II; based on state papers and personal papers.

FANSHAWE, ANN, LADY. 1625–80

444 Memoirs of Lady Fanshawe, wife of . . . Sir Richard Fanshawe, ambassador . . . to the Court of Madrid in 1665. To which are added extracts from the correspondence of Sir Richard Fanshawe. Ed. by C. R. Fanshawe. 1829. Later edn. by H. C. Fanshawe. 1907.

There are other edns., but that of 1907 has new notes and a better text. Valuable for the civil-war period and for diplomatic history later. See also nos. 135 and 657.

FINCH, JOHN, LORD. 1584–1660

445 Terry, W. H. The life and times of John, Lord Finch: Speaker of the House of Commons, Speaker of the House of Lords, Lord Chief Justice and Lord Keeper of England. 1936.

FIREBRACE, SIR HENRY. 1619–91

446 Firebrace, C. W. Honest Harry, being the biography of Sir Henry Firebrace, Knight, 1619–1691. 1932.

Useful biography of a one-time parliamentarian who turned to the king, and became a court official after 1660.

FOX, SIR STEPHEN. 1627–1716

447 Memoirs of the life of Sir Stephen Fox. 1717.

Throws some light on Charles II's court in exile.

GODOLPHIN, SIDNEY, EARL. *c.* 1645–1712

448 Elliot, H. F. H. The life of Sidney, Earl Godolphin, lord high treasurer of England, 1702–1710. 1888.

Still the most satisfactory life (see review in *Edin. Rev.* 169 (1889), 301–27), although Sir T. Lever published a sketchy biography in 1952. Useful on Godolphin's administration are I. S. Leadham, 'Finance of Lord Treasurer Godolphin', *R.H.S. Trans.*, 3rd Ser. 4 (1910), 21–32; and C. Buck and G. Davies, eds., 'Letters on Godolphin's dismissal in 1710', *Hunt. Lib. Quart.* 3 (1940), 225–42. Some Godolphin MSS. correspondence is in H.M.C., *14th Rep.*, pt. 3 (1894), pp. 191–238, and Br. Mus. Add. MSS. 28052, 29055–7, and 28071.

GORING, GEORGE, LORD. 1608–57

449 Wedgwood, C. V. 'George Goring: soldier and rake.' *Sussex County Mag.* 9 (1935), 164–9.

GRAFTON, HENRY, DUKE OF. 1663–90

450 Fitzroy, Sir A. Henry Duke of Grafton 1663–1690. 1921.

Brief life of the son of the Duchess of Cleveland.

HALIFAX, CHARLES MONTAGU, EARL OF. 1661–1715

451 The works and life of . . . Charles late Earl of Halifax. 1715.

In the Natl. Lib. of Scotland are Halifax Papers, containing banking schemes studied by Halifax in planning for the Bank of England.

HALIFAX, SIR GEORGE SAVILE, MARQUIS OF. 1663–95

452 Foxcroft, H. C. The life and letters of Sir George Savile, Bart., first Marquis of Halifax. With a new edn. of his works. 2 vols. 1898.

An excellent biography, with a bibliography and appendices containing reprints of his works. The latter include: *Character of a trimmer* (1688, attributed by some contemporaries to William Coventry); and *Character of Charles II*. The *Complete Works* were separately ed. by Sir W. Raleigh (979). Some additional letters are in *E.H.R.* 26 (1911), 535–42. See also *Savile corresp.* (338). Additional notes on Halifax's early life were supplied by Foxcroft in *History*, 26 (1941), 176–87; and the author published a condensed version of her original work, without the documentation, under the title, *The character of a trimmer*, Camb. 1946. A brief life by K. Klose was published in Breslau, 1936.

HAMPDEN, JOHN. 1594–1643

453 Nugent, George Grenville, Lord. Some memorials of John Hampden, his party and his times. 2 vols. 1831. 2nd edn. 2 vols. 1832. 3rd edn. 1 vol. 1854.

Still the standard full-length life, though it contains many inaccuracies. Macaulay's review (*Edin. Rev.* 54 (1831), 505–50; repr. in his *Essays* (361 n.)) brought various replies (see C. H. Firth's article on Hampden in *D.N.B.*). A good modern biography, drawing upon the Eliot MSS., but somewhat biased against the Stuarts, has been written by H. R. Williamson, 1933, bibl. notes. A sketch of Hampden appears in C. E. Lucas-Phillips, *Cromwell's captains*, Lond. and Toronto, 1938.

HENRIETTA MARIA. 1609–69

454 Letters of Queen Henrietta Maria. Ed. by M. A. E. Green. 1857.

Other letters, including many from French archives, were ed. by Charles, Comte de Baillon, Paris, 1877; and others (1628–66), by H. Ferrero, Turin, 1881. Early lives were by John Davincey, 1660; one repr. in Smeeton's tracts (283 n.); a *Memoir by Madame de Mottville, on the life of Henrietta Maria*, ed. by M. G. Hanotaux, *Camd. Soc. Misc.* viii, 1883; and C. Cotolendi, *Vie de . . . Henriette-Marie de France*, Paris, 1690. Useful modern biographies are by I. A. Taylor, 2 vols., 1905, H. Haynes, 1912, and C. Oman, 1936, 1951, bibl. On her daughter, Henrietta, see no. 2348.

HENRY, PRINCE OF WALES. 1594–1612

455 Birch, T. The life of Henry Prince of Wales, eldest son of King James I. 1760.

The earliest *Life*, written by his tutor, Sir Charles Cornwallis, was published in 1641. Cf. E. C. Wilson, *Prince Henry and English literature*, Ithaca, 1946. Bibl. footnotes.

HERBERT, SIR THOMAS. 1606–82

456 Herbert, Sir Thomas. Memoirs of the last two years of the reign of . . . King Charles I. 1702. Later edn. pr. by W. Nicoll. 1813.

Includes also narratives by Col. Edward Cooke, Major Huntingdon, and Henry Firebrace. Herbert's narrative was first published in 1678 with the title *Threnodia Carolina*. Cf. N. Mackenzie, 'Sir Thomas Herbert of Tintern: a parliamentary "royalist"', *Bull. Inst. Hist. Research*, 28 (1955–6), 32–86, which portrays Herbert as a political opportunist.

HOLLES, DENZIL, LORD. 1599–1680

457 Memoirs of Denzil, Lord Holles (1641–8). 1699.

Repr. in Maseres's *Select tracts* (1578). Cf. W. L. Grant, 'A Puritan at the court of

Louis XIV', in *Queen's Univ. Bull.*, no. 8 (Kingston, Ontario, 1913), which is an account of his embassy to Paris, 1663–6.

On Holles's father, John Holles, see biographical article by A. Thomson, *J.M.H.* 8 (1936), 145–72. See also Gervase Holles, *Memorials of the Holles family* (2480).

HOPKINS, EDWARD. d. 1736

458   'Memoirs of . . . Edward Hopkins, M.P. for Coventry.' Ed. by M. D. Harris. *E.H.R.* 34 (1919), 491–504.

Mainly William III to Anne.

HOSKYNS, JOHN. 1566–1638

459   Osborn, L. B. The life, letters and writings of John Hoskyns, 1566–1638. New Haven and Lond. 1937.

Includes personal letters and literary work of a lawyer, writer, and critic, who was also an M.P. Bibl. notes.

IRETON, HENRY. 1611–51

460   Ramsey, R. W. Henry Ireton. 1949. Bibl.

Based upon sound scholarship, drawing heavily upon the Clarke Papers.

JAMES I. 1566–1625

461   The workes of the most high and mighty prince James. Ed. by James Montagu. 1616.

For other edns. of the political works see no. 959. J. Craigie ed. *The poems of James VI of Scotland*, Edin. 1955. For correspondence see Ellis, *Letters* (260); Halliwell (286); and two volumes of correspondence before 1603, with Queen Elizabeth and with Sir Robert Cecil, ed. by J. Bruce for the Camden Society, 1849 and 1861. Letters concerning Scottish affairs are in Laing (3853). On correspondence with Cecil (Hatfield MSS.), 1604–11, see F. G. Marcham, 'James I of England and the "little beagle" letters', in *Persecution and liberty: essays in honor of George Lincoln Burr*, N.Y. 1931. Contemporary (1603–4) complaints against King James, with texts and bibliographical comments, were published by J. D. Mackie, *S.H.R.* 23 (1925), 1–17. His observations as the French ambassador in 1603 were recorded by Maximilian de Béthune, Duc de Sully, in his *Mémoires*, 2 vols. [Amsterdam], 1638, later vols. (Various later edns.; English trans. of 5th edn. by C. Lennox, 6 vols., Dublin, 1781.)

462   Sanderson, Sir William. A compleat history of the lives and reigns of Mary Queen of Scotland, and of her son . . . James the Sixth . . . in vindication of him against two scandalous authors [Sir Anthony Weldon and A. Wilson]. 2 pts. 1656.

On Weldon and Wilson see nos. 282, 283. A reply to Sanderson was made by Sir Carew Raleigh, *Observations on a book entitled A complete history . . . by a lover of truth*, 1656, to which Sanderson answered in *An answer to a scurrilous pamphlet . . .*, 1656 (Wing, S 644). W. Harris's *Historical and critical account of the life and writings of James the First . . .*, 1753, was combined with similar lives of Charles I, 1758, Cromwell, 1762, and Charles II, 2 vols., 1766, in a 5-volume edn., 1814; it is of value only for its copious footnotes. The best book on James is D. H. Willson, *King James VI and I*, 1956, bibl. footnotes. H. G. Stratford's study, *James VI of Scotland and the throne of England*, N.Y. 1940, is excellent for the years 1587 to 1603. Biographies in more popular style are by C. W. S. Williams, 1934 and 1951; H. R. Williamson, 1935; and C. and H. Steeholm, 1938. Useful interpretations of this complex monarch are: I. Disraeli, *An inquiry into the literary and political character of James I*, 1816; C. J.

Sisson, 'King James the First of England as a poet and political writer', in *Seventeenth century studies presented to Sir Herbert Grierson*, Oxf. 1938; G. Davies, 'The character of James VI and I', *Hunt. Lib. Quart.* 5 (1941), 33–63; D. H. Willson, 'James I and his literary assistants', ibid. 8 (1949), 35–58; 'James I and Anglo-Scottish unity', in *Conflict in Stuart England*, 1960; and W. McElwee, *The wisest fool in Christendom*, N.Y. 1958.

JAMES II. 1633–1701

463 Clarke, J. S., ed. Life of James II . . . collected out of memoirs writ of his own hand . . . 2 vols. 1816.

Useful, but to be used with caution. The *Life* was published from Stuart MSS., at the time in Carlton House, and now at Windsor; for an account of the MSS. on which Clarke's *Life* is based see intro. to no. 221. Portions from the memoirs, the originals of which were in large part lost, and which were apparently notes by James with additions filled in by persons close to him after 1688, especially by William Dicconson, have appeared in several places, notably J. Macpherson's *Original Papers* (369); and T. Carte's *Life of Ormonde* (1735–6; 2nd edn., 6 vols., Oxf. 1851); for an account of various publications see A. Ward on 'James II' in *D.N.B.*; for a critical evaluation of the *Life* see Ranke (275), vi. 29–45. One portion of the original memoirs (1652–60), was presented by James in 1696 to the family of the Marshal of Turenne, and a version was included in A. M. Ramsay's *History of . . . Viscount de Turenne* (no. 1688); subsequent to the rediscovery of the MS. memoirs in France in 1954, an edition collating this portion with that included in the Clarke edition, has been published as *The Memoirs of James II, his campaigns as Duke of York: 1652–1660*, trans. by A. L. Sells, with an intro. by Sir A. Bryant, Bloomington, 1961. G. Davies ed. James's *Papers of devotion* for the Roxburghe Club, Oxf. 1925.

464 Turner, F. C. James II. N.Y. and Lond. 1948.

The best and least partisan biography. Less dependable is F. M. G. Higham, *James the second*, 1934. A few documents of value are in [D. Jones?], *The life of James the second* [*c.* 1702]. See also T. Longueville, *The adventures of King James II of England*, 1904; A. Fea, *James II and his wives*, 1908. Popular in form and strongly partisan are the biographies by H. Belloc, 1928, and M. V. Hay, 1938. On the years in exile, see Cavelli, *Les derniers Stuarts* (2337).

LAMBERT, JOHN. 1619–84

465 Dawson, W. H. Cromwell's understudy; the life and times of General John Lambert and the rise and fall of the protectorate. 1938. 1942.

Scholarly and definitive. Has an appendix listing tracts in the Thomason collection that relate to Lambert. See also M. Ashley, *Cromwell's generals* (1665 n.).

LANGDALE, MARMALUKE, LORD. 1598–1661

466 Sunderland, F. H. Marmaluke Lord Langdale and some events of his time. 1926.

Includes some original letters of this Yorkshire royalist from the Harford collection, but is otherwise based on the usual printed sources; provides few references for documents quoted.

LAUD, WILLIAM, ARCHBISHOP. 1573–1645

467 Trevor-Roper, H. R. Archbishop Laud, 1573–1645. 1940. 2nd rev. edn. 1962.

A biography based on the most recent scholarship. Other modern lives are by A. S. Duncan-Jones, 1927, and R. P. T. Coffin, N.Y. 1930. Cf. J. H. R. Moorman, 'In commemoration of Archbishop Laud . . .', *Bull. John Rylands Lib.* 29 (1945), 106–20. For Laud's *Works* and references mainly relating to his career as a churchman, see Ch. V, no. 1266.

LILBURNE, JOHN. *c.* 1614–57

468 Gibb, M. A. John Lilburne the Leveller, a Christian democrat. 1947. Bibl.

Sympathetic, scholarly. Cf. P. Gregg, *Free-born John: a biography of John Lilburne,* 1961. A valuable early bibliography was compiled by E. Peacock, *N. & Q.,* 7th Ser. 5 (1888), Jan.–June. A list of his pamphlets appears in D. M. Wolfe, *Milton in the Puritan revolution* (967 n.), pp. 469–79; and many have been repr. in recent works on the Levellers (see nos. 960, 962).

LOCKE, JOHN. 1632–1704

469 See nos. 978, 2701.

LONSDALE, JOHN LOWTHER, VISCOUNT. 1655–1700

470 Lonsdale, John Lowther, Viscount. Memoir of the reign of James II. York. 1808.

A continuation, ed. by Sir C. H. Firth from Br. Mus. Add. MS. 34516, is in *E.H.R.* 30 (1915), 90–7.

LUDLOW, EDMUND. 1617?–92

471 Memoirs of Edmund Ludlow. 3 vols. Vivay in Bern. 1698–9. Later edn. by Sir C. H. Firth. 2 vols. Oxf. 1894.

Autobiography of a republican. Many documents and elaborate notes are in the 1894 edition.

MARLBOROUGH, SARAH CHURCHILL, DUCHESS OF. 1660–1744
For the Duke of Marlborough see no. 1703.

472 Private correspondence of Sarah Duchess of Marlborough . . . with her sketches and opinions of her contemporaries, and the select correspondence of her husband. 2 vols. 1838.

Mainly letters to the duchess, and from Coxe's *Transcripts of papers at Blenheim. Letters of Sarah, duchess of Marlborough,* 1875, are chiefly from her exile (1712–14), and written to a relative, Sarah Jennings. Many letters between the duchess and Queen Anne are included in the important *Account of the conduct of the . . . duchess of Marlborough from her first coming to the court to . . . 1710,* 1742 (ed. by W. King, as *Memoirs,* 1930), which was written in her defence, and is generally attributed to Nathaniel Hooke. It produced various replies, such as James Ralph, *The other side of the question,* 1742 and 1744, and [Henry Fielding,] *Full vindication of the dutchess,* 1742. Useful for the duchess as well as the duke is A. L. Rowse, *The early Churchills,* 1956. *John and Sarah, duke and duchess of Marlborough,* by S. J. Reid, 1914, is based on unpublished MSS. at Blenheim, but is too defensive. A lively modern interpretation, based on materials in print, is L. Kronenberger, *Marlborough's duchess,* N.Y. 1958. Cf. K. Thomson, *Memoirs of Sarah, duchess of Marlborough,* 2 vols., 1839, and a biography by K. Campbell, 1932. Popular biographies are by F. Molloy, 2 vols., 1901; O. Colville, 1904; and F. B. Chancellor, 1932.

MARTEN, HENRY. 1602–80

473 Coll. Henry Marten's familiar letters to his lady of delight. 1662. 1663.

A few of his papers are referred to in H.M.C., *13th report* pt. 4, p. 47. Early lives are in *Ath. Oxon.* (2427) and Noble's *Regicides* (390). J. Forster contributed a biography to vol. iv. of *Lardner's Cabinet Cyclopaedia*, 1838. Some additional notes by J. C. Cole are in *Berks. Arch. Jour.* 49 (1946), 23–40.

MARY II. 1662–94

474   Bathurst, A. B., ed. Letters of two queens. 1924.

Mainly letters of Queen Mary (*c.* 1673–88); those of Anne are repr. in Brown (399). *Lettres et mémoires de Marie Reine d'Angleterre . . .*, ed. by Mechtild, Comtesse Bentinck, The Hague, 1880, contains corresp. of James II and Mary (1687–8); of Anne and Mary (1688, an Engl. version in Dalrymple (339)); and Mary to Electress Sophia *et al.* (1689–93). Other letters are included in R. Doebner, ed., *Memoirs of Mary Queen of England (1689–93)*, Lond. and Leipzig, 1886. Cf. Gilbert Burnet, *Essay on the memory of the late queen*, 1695, later edn., Edin. 1842; and E. Fowler, *Memoirs . . . of . . . Queen Mary*, 2nd edn. 1712. The best biography is N. M. Waterson, *Mary II, Queen of England*, Durham (N.C.), 1928, but useful also are M. Bowen, *The third Mary Stuart*, 1929, which includes many letters; and H. W. Chapman, *Mary II*, 1953, which draws upon Dutch as well as English materials. The life by M. F. Sandars, 1913, is uncritical.

MARY OF MODENA. 1658–1718

475   Haile, M. Queen Mary of Modena. Her life and letters. 1905.

Based on unpublished materials in foreign archives, with many notes from correspondence. In *Queen over the water: Mary Beatrice of Modena, queen of James II*, 1953, M. Hopkirk presents a sympathetic account of the queen in exile. See also F. Madan, ed., *Stuart papers* (2337 n.).

MATHEW, SIR TOBIE. 1577–1655

476   Mathew, D. Sir Tobie Mathew. 1950.

Short biography of a courtier and Catholic convert, *temp.* Charles I. Cf. Alban Butler, *Life of Sir Tobie Matthew*, 1795, which drew upon a MS. account of his conversion (ed. by A. H. Mathew, *The true historical relation . . . of Sir Tobie Matthew*, 1904); and A. H. Matthew and A. Calthrop, *The life of Sir Tobie Matthew*, 1907.

MIDDLESEX, LIONEL CRANFIELD, EARL OF. 1575–1645

477   Tawney, R. H. Business and politics under James I: Lionel Cranfield as merchant and minister. 1958. Bibl.

Based upon extensive use of MS. materials, particularly those in the Sackville collection (108); deals effectively with practices in finance, *temp.* James I, as well as with the career of Cranfield in his years of greatest power.

MILTON, JOHN. 1608–74

478   Raymond, D. N. Oliver's secretary: John Milton and the era of revolt. N.Y. 1932.

Scholarly study of Milton's political career and his pamphlets, with bibl. footnotes. The standard full-scale life is Masson (2634). On the legal background for Milton's political writings see J. M. French, *Milton in Chancery*, N.Y. 1939. For studies of his political thought see no. 967.

MONMOUTH, JAMES SCOTT, DUKE OF. 1649–85

479   Roberts, G. The life, progresses and rebellion of James, duke of Monmouth. 2 vols. 1844.

Still useful, though out of date. Cf. A. Fea, *King Monmouth: being a history of the career of James Scott 'the Protestant duke'*, 1902. Letters of Monmouth after his capture in 1685 were edited by G. Duckett, *Camd. Misc.* viii (1883); an early life, *Historical account of the heroick life*, 1683, is repr. in Smeeton (283 n.), and in an appendix of the popular biography by L. Melville, *Mr. Crofts, the king's bastard*, 1929. Popular, but with some new material, is the life by E. D'Oyley, 1938. D. J. Porritt's short life, Ilfracombe, 1953, is drawn from materials in print. See also nos. 350, 351.

MORDAUNT, JOHN, VISCOUNT. 1626–75

480 The letter book of John, Viscount Mordaunt, 1658–1660. Ed. by M. Coate. Camden Soc. 1945.

Edited from MS. letter-book in the John Rylands Lib.; abstracts only of those letters of Mordaunt, a leading royalist, that have already been printed or calendared elsewhere (e.g. *C.S.P. Dom. 1659–60*; H.M.C., 10 VI, Braye MSS.).

NICHOLAS, EDWARD. 1593–1669

481 Nicholas, D. Mr. Secretary Nicholas, 1593–1669; his life and letters. 1955.

A chronological report, rather than an interpretive biography, using chiefly letters already in print (see G. F. Warner's volumes, ed. for the Camden Soc. (307), *C.S.P. Dom.*, etc.), but a few from Eg. MSS. in Br. Mus.

NORTH, SIR DUDLEY. 1602–77
and FRANCIS NORTH, BARON GUILFORD. 1637–85

482 North, Roger. The lives of . . . Francis North, Baron Guilford, . . . Sir Dudley North; and . . . Rev. Dr. John North . . . with the autobiography of [Roger North]. Ed. by A. Jessopp. 3 vols. 1890.

The valuable biographies were originally publ. 1742–4, and again in 1820; and the autobiography in 1887. The latter and the life of Guilford are valuable for the history of law and politics; the life of Sir Dudley North is important for the history of trade. All present the Tory view characteristic of the later years of Charles II. For MSS. of the Lives see Br. Mus. Add. MSS. 32506–17.

NOTTINGHAM, DANIEL FINCH, EARL OF. 1647–1730

483 Aiken, W. H., ed. The conduct of the earl of Nottingham, 1688–93. New Haven. 1941.

A compilation from contemporary MSS. by Nottingham and others, especially Finch MSS.; arranged in chronological order so as to provide a narrative extension of Echard's *History* (263). For Nottingham's correspondence, see H.M.C. (136).

OATES, TITUS. 1649–1705

484 Dakers, E. (J. Lane, pseud.). Titus Oates, the first biography. 1949.

Overdrawn and not fully reliable, but the only full-scale account of Oates's life. See nos. 1489–97.

OVERBURY, SIR THOMAS. 1581–1613

485 Gough, C. E. The life and characters of Sir Thomas Overbury. Norwich. 1909.

Cf. E. A. Parry, *The Overbury mystery . . .*, 1925; and M. A. De Ford, *The Overbury affair . . .*, Phila. 1960.

OXFORD, ROBERT HARLEY, EARL OF. 1661–1724

486   Roscoe, E. S. Robert Harley, Earl of Oxford. 1902. Bibl.

No full-scale biography has been written. Very brief accounts are by O. B. Miller, Oxf. 1925, and J. H. Davis, *Robert Harley as secretary of state, 1704–8*, Chicago, 1934, which is an abstract from a doctoral thesis. Some correspondence (1710–13) with James Brydges, ed. by G. Davies and M. Tinling, is in *Hunt. Lib. Quart.* 1 (1938), 457–72. See also Merz, *Junto* (380 n.).

PETER, HUGH. 1598–1660

487   Stearns, R. P. The strenuous Puritan: Hugh Peter, 1598–1660. Urbana. 1954.

Virtually definitive biography of the radical Puritan divine and popular propagandist of the civil war. Also by Stearns, 'Hugh Peter and his biographers', *Bostonian Soc. Proc. for 1935* (1935), 27–50; and 'Letters and documents by or relating to Hugh Peter', *Essex Inst. Hist. Coll.* 71 (1935), 303–18. Earlier lives are by J. Felt, Boston, 1851, and J. M. Patrick, Buffalo, 1946.

PORTER, ENDYMION. 1587–1649

488   Huxley, G. Endymion Porter: the life of a courtier, 1587–1649. 1959.

Well documented biography of a courtier and patron of the arts. Still useful is D. Townshend, *Life and letters of Mr. Endymion Porter*, 1897.

PORTLAND, WILLIAM BENTINCK, EARL OF. *c.* 1645–1709

489   Grew, M. E. William Bentinck and William III (Prince of Orange). The life of Bentinck, Earl of Portland from the Welbeck correspondence. 1924.

Based upon the Portland MSS. (204). Some additional letters, though chiefly 18th century, are in Br. Mus. Eg. MSS. 1704–56. See also no. 524.

PRIOR, MATTHEW. 1664–1721

490   Legg, L. G. W. Matthew Prior: a study of his public career and correspondence. Camb. 1921. Bibl.

Careful study of a court official and diplomat, who was also a poet. Cf. F. Bickley, *The life of Matthew Prior*, 1914; C. K. Eves, *Matthew Prior, poet and diplomatist*, N.Y. 1939; and R. W. Ketton-Cramer, *Matthew Prior*, 1957. See also nos. 80, 153, 552 n., 2638.

On George Stepney [1663–1707], an associate of Prior, see an essay by H. T. Swedenburg, Jr., *Hunt. Lib. Quart.* 10 (1946), 1–34.

PRYNNE, WILLIAM. 1600–69

491   Kirby, E. W. William Prynne: A study in Puritanism. Camb. (Mass.). 1931.

Scholarly and able biography based largely on Prynne's pamphlets. See Wing for a list of Prynne's publications, P 3886–4130, and a list in *Hunt. Lib. Quart.* 20 (1956), 53–93. A modern work is W. M. Lamont, *Marginal Prynne, 1660–1669*, Toronto, 1963. See also no. 747 n.

PYM, JOHN. 1584?–1643

492   Brett, S. R. John Pym: the statesman of the Puritan revolution. 1940. 1943.

Not completely satisfactory because it fails to deal with the techniques of parliamentary control. For the latter, see J. H. Hexter, *The reign of King Pym*, 1941 (324). Still useful is C. E. Wade, *John Pym*, 1912.

RADCLIFFE, SIR GEORGE. 1593–1657

493 Whitaker, T. D. The life and original correspondence of Sir George Radcliffe . . . the friend of the Earl of Strafford. 1810.

Includes letters of Radcliffe's family as well as letters from Strafford to him.

RALEIGH [RALEGH], SIR WALTER. *c.* 1552–1618

494 The works of Sir Walter Raleigh . . . [with an] account of his life by T. Birch. 2 vols. 1751. Later edn. 8 vols. Oxf. 1829.

See T. N. Brushfield's *Bibliography of Sir Walter Ralegh*, 2nd edn., Exeter, 1908, and *Camb. hist. English lit.* iv, 515–18. Raleigh's letters are printed in E. Edwards, *The life of Sir Walter Raleigh, together with his letters*, 2 vols., 1868. Of the older lives, still useful is that by W. Stebbing, Oxf. 1891, 1899, bibl. Probably the best modern life is by W. M. Wallace, Princeton, 1959. Other modern lives are by E. Thompson, 1935, and H. R. Williamson, 1951. For comments on Raleigh's writing see C. H. Firth, 'Sir Walter Raleigh's *History of the world*', *Proc. British Academy*, 8 (1918), 427–46 (the *History* was publ. 1614); and E. C. Strathmann, *Sir Walter Raleigh: a study in Elizabethan skepticism*, 1951. See also Read (11 n.), pp. 274–5 and index.

ROCHESTER, JOHN WILMOT, EARL OF. 1647–80

495 Burnet, Gilbert. Some passages of the life and death of John Earl of Rochester, written by his own direction on his death-bed. 1680. Later edns. by R. Gower. 1875.

A well documented modern biography, with a bibliography of his works and of writings on him is J. Prinz, *John Wilmot, Earl of Rochester: his life and writings*, Leipzig, 1927, 1930. Cf. C. W. S. Williams, *Rochester*, 1935. See also no. 2641.

ROMNEY, HENRY SIDNEY, EARL OF. 1641–1704

496 Blencowe, R. W., ed. Diary of the times of Charles the Second by Henry Sidney, including his correspondence with the countess of Sunderland and other distinguished persons. 2 vols. 1843.

Valuable diary, 1679–82, with correspondence 1679–81 and 1684–9. The diary is in Br. Mus. Add. MS. 32682, and the correspondence in Br. Mus. Add. MSS. 32680–1. On Dorothy Sidney, countess of Sunderland, see J. Cartwright (Mrs. H. Ady), *Sacharissa . . . 1617–1684*, 1893, 3rd edn. 1901, 4th edn. 1926.

RUDYARD, SIR BENJAMIN. 1572–1658

497 Manning, J. A. Memoirs of Sir Benjamin Rudyard. 1841.

Contains speeches, poems, and a few personal papers.

RUPERT, PRINCE PALATINE. 1619–82

498 Scott, E. Rupert, Prince Palatine. Westminster. 1899.

Still the best life. Among later lives are J. Cleugh, 1934; C. Wilkinson, 1934; G. A. Edinger, 1936; B. Fergusson, 1952. Some official papers of Rupert are in H.M.C. (114, 159).

RUSSELL, WILLIAM, LORD. 1639–83

499   Russell, Lord John. Life of William Lord Russell. 1819. 4th edn. 1853.

A careful study of the times, as well as a biography. Of the numerous tracts relating
to the trial and execution of Lord Russell in connection with the Rye House plot,
examples are: *A true narrative of the whole proceedings*, 1683; *The trials of Walcott,
Hone, Lord William Russell* . . ., 1683 (also in *State trials*, ix); *Last speech*, 1683 (repr.
as *Dying speech*, 1689); [Roger L'Estrange,] *Considerations upon a printed sheet entitled
The Speech*, 1683 (repr. in *Clarendon Hist. Soc. Reprints*, Ser. 1 (1882–4), pp. 253–92);
F. N. W., *Historical review of the late horrid plot*, 1684. A modern brief account in
popular style is H. Armitage, *Russell and the Rye House*, Letchworth, 1948. See also
no. 350.

SACHEVERELL, WILLIAM. 1638–91

500   Sitwell, Sir G. The first Whig: an account of the parliamentary career of
William Sacheverell. Scarborough. 1894.

Use with reservations. Much of the material reappears in the same author's *Letters of
the Sitwells and Sacheverells* . . ., 2 vols., Scarborough, 1900–1, which are illustrative
of social history. For corrections on Sitwell, see J. R. Jones, 'The Green Ribbon Club',
Durham Univ. Jour., N.S. 18, pp. 17–20.

SALISBURY, ROBERT CECIL, EARL OF. 1565–1612

501   Cecil, A. A life of Robert Cecil, first earl of Salisbury.

Still the only full-length life. See also no. 212, and a short article by J. Hurstfield,
History Today, 7 (1957), 279–84, and Read (11 n.), no. 783.

SELDEN, JOHN. 1584–1654

502   See Ch. IV, no. 1075.

SHAFTESBURY, ANTHONY, EARL OF. 1621–83

503   Brown, L. F. The first earl of Shaftesbury. N.Y. 1933.

The best life. Still valuable also is W. D. Christie's *Life*, 2 vols., 1871, which is based
on papers of Shaftesbury in the P.R.O., and other MSS., and which incorporates most
of the *Memoirs, letters and speeches* . . ., ed. by Christie, 1859 (see calendar of Shaftesbury
MSS. included in *Reports of the Deputy Keeper of the Public Record Office*, 33, 34, 39
(1871–7)). Early biographies, both possibly by P. Misopappas [pseud.?], *The compleat
statesman* . . . *Anthony, earl of Shaftesbury*, 1683, and *Rawleigh redivivus*, 1683, are
commented on by J. R. Tanner in *E.H.R.* 5 (1890), 118–20. G. W. Cooke ed. a
Life by B. Martyn and A. Kippis (1st edn. ? 1790), 2 vols., 1836, which includes
materials now missing, but is inaccurate.

SHREWSBURY, CHARLES TALBOT, DUKE OF. 1660–1718

504   Private and original correspondence of Charles Talbot, duke of Shrewsbury, with King William, the leaders of the Whig party . . . from the family
papers . . . of . . . the duchess of Buccleuch. Ed. by W. Coxe. 1821.

Important. For the Buccleuch MSS. see no. 89. Other MSS. are in the Bath MSS.,
vol. i (80). Cf. Vernon correspondence (371). For a biography see T. C. Nicholson
and A. S. Turberville, *Charles Talbot, duke of Shrewsbury*, Camb. 1930.

STAFFORD, SIR WILLIAM HOWARD, VISCOUNT. 1612–80

505   D., S. N. Sir William Howard, Viscount Stafford, 1612–1680. 1929.

Cf. A bibliographical note by R. E. Grun, 'A note on William Howard, author of "A
patterne of Christian loyaltie" ', *Cath. Hist. Rev.* 42 (Oct. 1956).

STRAFFORD, THOMAS WENTWORTH, EARL OF. 1593–1641

506   The Earl of Strafford's letters and despatches with an essay towards his life by Sir George Radcliffe . . . Ed. by W. Knowler. 2 vols. in one. 1739.

Correspondence to 1639, from Earl Fitzwilliam's MSS. Other Strafford papers are in *Camd. Misc.*, vols. viii and ix, 1883, 1885. 'Private letters . . . to his third wife' were ed. by R. M. Milnes, Lord Houghton, *Philobiblon Soc. Misc.* 1 (1854). The most satisfactory biography, making use especially of the Fitzwilliam MSS., is C. V. Wedgwood, *Strafford*, 1935, rev. edn., 1962. See also her interpretative essay in *History Today*, Jan. 1951, 18–24. Of the earlier lives, that by E. Cooper, 2 vols., 1874, has no value except for a few letters. Robert Browning's *Prose life of Strafford* (first publ. under the name of J. Forster in 1836), ed. by C. H. Firth and F. J. Furnivall, 1892, is chiefly of literary interest. Other recent lives are by W. A. H. Gardner, Lady Burghclere, 2 vols., 1931, which is marred by some inaccuracies; and F. W. F. Smith, Earl of Birkenhead, 1938. On Strafford's wealth see J. P. Cooper's essay in *Econ. Hist. Rev.*, 2nd Ser. 11 (1958), 227–48; on his Irish career see H. Kearney, *Strafford in Ireland*, Manchester, 1957; on his trial see no. 865.
  Various tracts on Strafford are in the *Somers Collection* (61), vol. iv.

STUART, JAMES FRANCIS EDWARD. 1688–1766

507   Haile, M. James Francis Edward, the Old Chevalier. 1907.

Includes material from foreign archives, but not a definitive life of the 'Old Pretender'. Cf. A. N. and H. Tayler, *The Old Chevalier*, 1934. See also nos. 386, 387.

SUNDERLAND, ROBERT SPENCER, EARL OF. 1641–1702

508   Kenyon, J. P. Robert Spencer, earl of Sunderland, 1641–1702. 1958.

Important, the only biography, based upon wide research; bibl. footnotes.

[SYDNEY.] SIDNEY, ALGERNON. 1622–83

509   Ewald, A. C. The life and times of the Hon. Algernon Sydney 1622–1683. 2 vols. 1873.

To be used with caution, though the only full-length biography. Other lives are by: G. W. Meadley, 1813, and G. M. I. Blackburne, 1885. The *Works of Algernon Sidney*, 1772, contain letters as well as his philosophical works. His *Letters . . . to the honourable H. Savile*, 1679, were publ. 1742. On his *Discourse concerning government*, 1698, and its influence on 18th-century thought, particularly in America, see C. Robbins, *William and Mary Quart.*, 3rd Ser. 4 (1947), 267–96. See also no. 977. See also Blencowe, ed., *Sydney papers* (259 n.). Many tracts on Sidney were printed at the time of his trial and execution, e.g. *Sidney redivivus, his dying speech, and others*, 1684.

TANKERVILLE, FORD GREY, EARL OF. 1655–1701

510   Price, C. Cold Caleb: the scandalous life of Ford Grey, 1st earl of Tankerville. 1956. Bibl.

The only biography of the Whig politician, dealing especially with his role in Monmouth's rebellion. For Grey's confession, 1685, published as *The secret history of the Rye House plot: and of Monmouth's rebellion*, 1754, see no. 350 n.

TEMPLE, SIR RICHARD. 1634–97

511   Davies, G. 'The political career of Sir Richard Temple (1634–1697) and Buckingham politics.' *Hunt. Lib. Quart.* 4 (1940), 47–83.

Shows the relations of an M.P. with his borough constituents. On the family's wealth see E. F. Gay's articles, ibid. 1 (1937), 367–90; 2 (1938), 404–37; and 6 (1942), 255–91.

TEMPLE, SIR WILLIAM. 1628–99

512   The works of Sir William Temple, Bart., to which is prefix'd some account of the life and writings of the author. Ed. by Jonathan Swift. 2 vols. 1720. Later edns. 4 vols. Edin. 1754. 4 vols. 1814.

Included are *Observations upon the United Provinces* (1673; repr. Camb. 1933); *Memoirs*, 1672–79 (1692; ed. by Swift, with a continuation to 1680, 2 vols., 1709); *Letters* (3 vols., publ. by Swift, 1700–3). Other volumes of letters are: David Jones's edn. of his *Letters* (from the Hague Embassy), 1699; and *Select letters to the Prince of Orange . . .*, 1701. See also no. 2497.

The *Memoirs* are useful for the period of Charles II. On Temple's life and writing see T. P. Courtenay, *Memoirs of the life, works and correspondence of Sir William Temple, Bart.*, 2 vols., 1836, and Macaulay's essay reviewing Courtenay's book, in *Edin. Rev.* 68 (1838), 113–87, repr. in his *Essays* (2599 n.).

Although a definitive life has not yet appeared, a good brief biography is M. L. R. Beaven, *Sir William Temple*, Oxf. 1908. On the literary importance of Temple see no. 2599.

THURLOE, JOHN. 1616–68

513   Bischoffshausen, S. F. von. Die politik des Protectors Oliver Cromwell in der auffassung and thätigkeit seines Ministers des Staats-Secretärs John Thurloe. Innsbruck. 1899.

Has an appendix of documents. A recent short biography, based chiefly upon his state papers, is D. L. Hobman, *Cromwell's master spy: a study of John Thurloe*, 1961.

TWYSDEN, SIR ROGER. 1597–1672

514   Larking, L. B., ed. 'Sir Roger Twysden's journal.' *Archaeologia Cantiana.* 1–4 (1858).

From the Roydon Hall MSS. Twysden wrote to expose his persecution as a royalist in Kent, 1641–8.

VANE, SIR HENRY. 1613–62

515   Hosmer, J. K. The life of young Sir Harry Vane. Boston and Lond. 1888.

The best life. Other lives by: J. Forster (vol. iv of *Lardner's Cabinet Cyclopaedia*, 1838); W. W. Ireland, 1905; and J. Willcock, 1913. For contemporary comment see *Tryal of Sir Henry Vane*, 1662; and [George Sikes,] *Life and death of Sir Henry Vane*, 1662.

WALLER, SIR WILLIAM. c. 1597–1668

516   Waller, Sir W. Vindication of the character and conduct of Sir William Waller. 1793.

Vague defence of his conduct in 1647. Waller's recollections, which are scattered anecdotes, are printed at the end of *The Poetry of Anna Matilda*, 1788. MS. in Wadham College Libr., Oxf.

WALPOLE, SIR ROBERT. 1676–1745

517   Coxe, W. Memoirs of the life and administration of Sir Robert Walpole. 3 vols. 1798. 3rd edn. 4 vols. 1816.

A standard work, with many documents; the correspondence before 1714 deals chiefly with 1710. See also G. R. S. Taylor, *Robert Walpole and his age*, 1931, bibl., and J. H. Plumb, *Robert Walpole: the making of a statesman*, 1956, the first volume of a projected two-volume work.

WALWYN, WILLIAM. *fl.* 1649+

518 Schenk, W. 'A seventeenth-century radical.' *Econ. Hist. Rev.* 14 (1944), 74–83.

Brief account of his career. See also nos. 990, 994.

WARWICK, SIR PHILIP. 1609–83

519 Memoires of the reigne of King Charles I . . . with a continuation to the happy restauration of King Charles II. 1701. 1702. Later edn. by Sir W. Scott. Edin. 1813.

A royalist memoir, MS. in Br. Mus. Add. MS. 34714.

WHEELWRIGHT, JOHN. 1592–1679

520 Heard, J. John Wheelwright. N.Y. 1930.

Brief life of one of the New England settlers, a friend of Winthrop and Cromwell, who returned to England for a time during the protectorate.

WHITELOCKE, BULSTRODE. 1605–76?

521 Whitelocke, R. H. Memoirs, biographical and historical, of Bulstrode Whitelocke. 1860.

His MS. 'Annals' are in Br. Mus. Add. MS. 37343. See his published *Memorials* (306) and also no. 634. See also *Liber famelicus of James Whitelocke* (1035).

WILBRAHAM, SIR ROGER. 1553–1616

522 The journal of Sir Roger Wilbraham, solicitor general in Ireland and master of requests, 1593–1616, together with notes in another hand . . . 1642–1649. Ed. by H. S. Scott. *Camd. Soc. Misc.* x. 1902.

Pr. from MS. in the possession of the earl of Lathom.

WILDMAN, JOHN. *c.* 1621–93

523 Ashley, M. John Wildman, plotter and postmaster: a study of the English republican movement in the seventeenth century. New Haven and Lond. 1947.

A readable life, based on extensive research. See also no. 963.

WILLIAM III

524 Correspondentie van Willem III en van Hans Willem Bentinck, eersten graf van Portland. Ed. by N. Japikse. 6 vols. The Hague. 1927–37.

From William III's voluminous correspondence, partly from collections at Welbeck Abbey (see no. 204) and the P.R.O., partly from the Netherlands archives. Important publications from the latter are *Archives de la Maison d'Orange-Nassau* (673). See also his correspondence with Waldeck (353), and correspondence with Charles II and others (673 n.).
    No completely satisfactory biography has been written. Early lives are: an anonymous *History of the most illustrious William, Prince of Orange*, 1688; Abel Boyer, *History of King William the Third*, 3 vols., 1702–3; and Nicholas Chevalier, *Histoire de Guillaume III*, Amsterdam, 1692. The standard biography is N. Japikse, *Prins Willem III, de stadhouder-koning*, 2 vols., Amsterdam, 1930–3. Of those in English A. H. Trevor's *Life*, 2 vols., 1835–6, includes some documents; H. D. Traill's *William the Third*, 1888,

is useful but much out of date; and good but too brief are the accounts by G. J. Renier, 1932, and D. Ogg, 1956.

On special aspects of William's life see M. Bowen, *William Prince of Orange . . . his early life*, 1928; Haley (362 n.); Pinkham (362 n.); M. C. Trevelyan, *William the Third and the defence of Holland, 1672–1674*, 1930. See also G. van Alphen, *De Stemming van de Engelsche tegen de Hollenders in Engeland tisjens de regeering van den koning-stadhouder Willem III*, Assen, 1938. For bibl. see Baxter (15 n.).

YONGE, WALTER. 1579–1649

525 Diary of Walter Yonge esq., Justice of the Peace and M.P. for Honiton . . . from 1604 to 1628. Ed. by G. Roberts. Camden Soc. 41 (1848).

Notes on public events as well as on personal affairs.

YORK, ANNE HYDE, DUCHESS OF. 1637–71

526 Henslowe, J. R. Anne Hyde, Duchess of York. *c.* 1915.

Popular.

G. FOREIGN RELATIONS

1. GENERAL

(a) *Bibliography*

527 DAVENPORT, F. G. Materials for English diplomatic history 1509–1783 calendared in the reports of the Historical Manuscripts Commission, with references to similar materials in the British Museum. Historical Manuscripts Comm. *18th report* (1917), pp. 357–402.

See the section on Historical Manuscripts Commission Reports in Ch. I *supra*, especially: De La Warr (117); Fanshawe (135); Heneage Finch, earl of Winchelsea, and John Finch (136); Sir Richard Graham (147); Marlborough (181); Montagu in Buccleuch and Queensberry (89); Nottingham (136); Matthew Prior in Bath MSS. (80) and Portland, v (153); Shrewsbury (89); Sir Robert Sidney, later viscount Lisle, and papers on the United Provinces (118); William Trumbull the elder and Sir William Trumbull (225); Winwood in Buccleuch and Queensberry (89) and the important Portland MSS. (153).

528 LIST of volumes of state papers, foreign, preserved in the Public Record Office. 1547–1782. Lists and indexes no. 19. 1904.

Classified mainly by countries.

529 THOMAS, D. H. and CASE, L. M., eds. Guide to the diplomatic archives of Western Europe. Phila. 1959.

By countries, with bibliography of published documents; descriptions of main reposi-tories.

See also V. E. Hrabar, *De legatis et legationibus tractatus varii* and *De legatorum jure tractatuum catalogus completus*, Dorpat, 1905 and 1918 (guides to early treatises on ambassadors, the first down to 1625, the second 1625–1700).

Foreign bibliographies useful for the period include: E. Bourgeois and L. André, *Les sources de l'histoire de France dix-septième siècle 1610–1715*, 8 vols., Paris, 1913–35, especially vol. v, 'Histoire politique et militaire'; F. C. Dahlmann and G. Waitz, *Quellenkunde der deutschen Geschichte*, 9th edn., H. Haering, Leipzig, 1931; J. H. Gosse and N. Japikse, *Handboek tot de staatkundige geschiednis van Nederland*, The Hague,

1927; and B. Sanchez Alonso, *Fuentes de la historia espanola*, 3rd edn., Madrid, 1952. For other regions, see the bibliographies in *Cambridge Modern History* (7). See also Ch. XV, § A 4 (b).

(b) *Sources*

(1) *Manuscripts*

530 PUBLIC RECORD OFFICE: State Papers Foreign.

Arranged for this period by countries. Listed in Giuseppi (65 n.), vol. ii, pp. 19–22.

531 BRITISH MUSEUM: Many letter-books and collections of correspondence of British ambassadors and envoys abroad include:

Add. 18639–42, Add. 34310–11. Letter-books of Sir Isaac Wake, May 1615–October 1623 (on embassies to Savoy and Venice).

Egerton 2592–7: Correspondence of James Hay, earl of Carlisle. On embassies in Germany, France, and Spain, 1616–36. Includes material on the negotiations for the marriage of Prince Charles to Henrietta Maria.

Add. 22919–20: Diplomatic papers of Sir George Downing, ambassador at The Hague, 1644–82.

Add. 9796–9804: Letters, papers, and memoirs of Sir William Temple, 1665–80.

Add. 34329–38, 35099M: Letter-books of Sir Robert Southwell. On negotiations in Portugal, 1665–9. (Also letter-books of Francis Parry, resident in Portugal, Add. 35100–1.)

Add. 34329–36, 35099–101: Southall papers.

Add. 37979–92: Correspondence of envoys abroad with William Blathwayt and Edward earl of Conway, 1669–1701.

Add. 15892, 15898, 15901–2, 15943, 17012–9: Correspondence and papers of Lawrence Hyde, earl of Rochester, 1676–81.

Add. 29548–96: Correspondence of Daniel Finch, earl of Nottingham, 1702–4.

Add. 37348–62: Whitworth Papers. Charles Whitworth, later Baron Whitworth, represented England at the Diet of Ratisbon 1702, and was afterwards envoy to various courts and congresses, 1702–25.

Add. 22193–267: Papers of Thomas Wentworth, earl of Strafford (ambassador to Prussia, 1703, to Holland and at Utrecht, 1711–14).

Other manuscripts in the Br. Mus. and in private collections down to 1917 are listed in Davenport (527). Among the many collections in other libraries the Clarendon (257), Tanner (71), and Rawlinson MSS. in the Bodl. Lib., Oxf., have materials on foreign affairs. Transcripts in the Br. Mus. include: Transcripts of State Papers, 1603–25, made by S. R. Gardiner from originals at Simancas and Venice (Add. 31111–2) and State Correspondence between England and the Netherlands, 1576–1764, 102 vols. (Add. 17677A–KKK2b). Bodl. Lib.

Several other groups of Br. Mus. MSS. are added in the later sections on separate regions in this chapter, pp. 84–94.

(2) *Collections of Treaties*

(a) General

532 MYERS, D. P. Manual of collections of treaties and of collections relating to treaties. Camb., Mass. 1922.

A valuable bibliography. See also *Catalogue of an exhibition of treaties at the Public Record Office*, Historical MSS. Comm. Office, 1948.

533 RYMER, T. and SANDERSON, R., eds. Foedera, conventiones, literae, et cujuscunque generis acta publica, inter reges Angliae et alios quosvis imperatores, reges, pontifices, principes, vel communitates ab . . . anno 1101, ad nostra usque tempora, habita aut tractata; ex autographis . . . fideliter exscripta. 20 vols. 1704–32.

The collection goes to 1654, the period from 1603 being covered in vols. 16–20, ed. by Sanderson. See Sir T. D. Hardy's *Syllabus*, 3 vols., 1869–85, for later edns., contents, index, etc., and life of Rymer. A better version of the Dutch correspondence is in Thurloe.

534 DUMONT, J., ed. Corps universel diplomatique du droit des gens; contenant un recueil des traitez d'alliance, de paix . . . faits en Europe depuis la règne de l'Empereur Charlemagne jusques à présent. 8 vols. Amsterdam. 1726–31.

A *Supplément* was ed. by J. Rousset de Missy, 5 vols., Amsterdam, 1739. Cf. J. Y. de Saint-Prest, *Histoire des traités de paix, et autres négotiations du dix-septième siècle*, 2 vols., Amsterdam, 1725; and vol. i of G. F. von Martens, *Supplément au recueil des principaux traités . . . depuis 1761 . . . précédé de traités du 18ᵉ siècle antérieurs à cet époque . . .*, 4 vols., Göttingen, 1802–8.

535 [HARRIS, W.], ed. Complete collection of all marine treaties subsisting between Great Britain and France, Spain . . . etc. (1546–1763). 1779.

See also Tétot, *Répertoire des traités de paix, de commerce, . . . [1648] jusqu'à nos jours*, 2 vols., Paris, 1866–73.

536 DAVENPORT, F. G., ed. European treaties bearing on the history of the United States and its dependencies. 4 vols. Wash. 1917–37. Bibl.

Vol. i to 1648; vol. ii, 1650–97; vol. iii, 1697–1715.

(b) Chiefly after 1648

(Treaties were not regularly published by royal authority until after 1667.)

537 SEVERAL TREATIES of peace and commerce concluded between the late king . . . and other princes and states. 1686.

The first English collection, published by royal permission. Another early collection, incomplete and containing inaccuracies, is *A general collection of treaties . . . (1648–1731)*, 4 vols., 1710–32.

538 JENKINSON, C., 1st Earl of Liverpool, ed. A collection of all treaties of peace, alliance and commerce between Great Britain and other powers (1648–1783). 3 vols. 1785.

Jenkinson ed. an early volume with the same title extending from 1619 to 1734, in 1781. He gives translations only, but his collection is fuller than the *Collection of treaties . . .* by G. Chalmers, 2 vols., 1790.

539 VAST, H., *comp.* Les grands traités du règne de Louis XIV. 3 pts. Paris. 1893–9.

Valuable bibl. notes for each treaty. Other useful European collections are C. G. de Koch, *Abrégé de l'histoire des traités de paix entre les puissances depuis la paix de Westphalie*, 4 vols., Basel, 1796–7 (enl. by M. S. Friedrich Schoell, 15 vols., Paris,

1817–18; later edn., 4 vols., Brussels, 1837–8); and A. Faber (i.e. C. L. Leucht), *Europäische Staats-Cantzley*, 120 vols., Nuremberg, etc., 1697–1760, a periodical containing treaties and diplomatic documents. For Portuguese treaties see J. Ferreira, Visconde de Borges de Castro, ed., *Collecção dos tratados . . . entre a coroa de Portugal e as mais potencias . . .* (1640–), 8 vols., Lisbon, 1856–8. Supplementary vols., 1872–80, with vols. 9–10 relating to this period.

(3) *Printed Correspondence and Instructions*

The printed correspondence of various envoys, secretaries of state, and others is listed in § F of this chapter: e.g. Queen Anne (399), Arlington (400), Bolingbroke (405), Elizabeth of Bohemia (401), Fanshawe (444), Shrewsbury (504), Temple (512), William III (524). See also Dalrymple (339), Vernon (371), Wotton (574), and individuals listed *sub* Davenport (527) and in the section on materials published by the Hist. MSS. Com. (pp. 12–27). See also Campana de Cavelli, *Les derniers Stuarts* (2337). Other collections are in the sections on regions *infra*.

540 CALENDARS OF STATE PAPERS.

The volumes in the English 'Domestic' series (256) contain many papers on foreign affairs. Numerous comments on foreign affairs generally occur in the *Calendar of state papers . . . Venice*, ed. by H. F. Brown and A. B. Hinds, vols. 10–38 (1603–75), 1900–40+; those on Milan (1385–1618), ed. by A. B. Hinds, 1912, have little major material.

For collections published by foreign states see the separate regions below. Many are described in Thomas and Case (529). For lists of ambassadors, see L. Bittner and L. Gross, eds., *Reportorium der diplomatischen vertreter aller länder* (since 1648), vol. i (1648–1715), Berlin, 1936. A short *List of diplomatic visitors to England in 1670* was publ. by C. S. S. Higham, Manchester, 1926.

541 RECUEIL DES INSTRUCTIONS données aux ambassadeurs de France. Vols. xxiv–xxv. Angleterre, 1648–90. Ed. by J. J. Jusserand. Paris. 1929.

The rest of the series, with full introductions, is valuable also.

542 BRITISH DIPLOMATIC INSTRUCTIONS, 1689–1789. 7 vols. 1922–34.

Edited for the Royal Historical Society. The series includes 2 vols. on Sweden ed. by J. F. Chance, 1922; 1 vol. on Denmark ed. by Chance, 1926; and 4 vols. on France ed. by L. C. W. Legg, 1925. Also ed. for the society is D. B. Horn, *British diplomatic representatives, 1689–1789* (Camden Soc.), 1932. See also C. H. Firth and S. C. Lomas (578); B. Spuler, 'Europäische diplomaten in Konstantinopel . . .' (to 1739), *Jahrb. Gescht. Osteuropas*, 1 (1936), 229–62, 383–440; and the note in Pargellis (11 n.), p. 35.

543 BIRCH, T., ed. An historical view of the negociations between the courts of England, France, and Brussels [1592–1617], extracted chiefly from the MS. state papers of Sir Thomas Edmondes. 1749.

Other important sources for foreign relations *temp*. James I are Winwood's *Memorials* during his service as British agent in Holland, 1603–14 (671); Halliwell's *Letters* (286); the works of Bacon (Spedding, no. 403), and Raleigh (Birch, no. 494); and Sir Henry Wotton's *Letters* (574).

544 PHILIPS, E., ed. Letters of state written by Mr. John Milton to most of the sovereign princes and republicks of Europe (1649–1659). 1694.

Cf. Masson (2634), vi. 791 seq. for earlier edns. The chief source for foreign policy in the interregnum, however, is Birch, *Collection of state papers of John Thurloe* (311); for which a supplement is Von Bischoffshausen, *Politik des Protectors Oliver Cromwell* (513). For Cromwell's correspondence see no. 429; for earlier parliamentary policy see Rushworth (290) and Cary (1577); for Royalist foreign relations, *Clarendon state papers* (257).

545 WYNNE, W. The life of Sir Leoline Jenkins . . . ambassador and pleni-potentiary for the general peace at Cologn and Nimeguen, and secretary of state to K. Charles II and a compleat series of letters from the beginning to the end of those two important treaties. 2 vols. 1724.

The letters are chiefly for 1673–9; additional letters of Jenkins are in Br. Mus. Add. MSS. 34341–6. On an incident related to the Cologne negotiations, see K. Spiegel, *Wilhelm Egon von Furstenbergs Gefangenschaft und ihre Bedeutung für die Friedensfrage, 1674–79*, Bonn, 1936.

546 COLLECTIONS of all the acts, memorials, and letters that pass'd in the negotiation of the peace, with the treatise concluded at Nimeguen. 1679.

Cf. *Actes et mémoires de negociations de la paix de Nimègue*, 4 vols., Amsterdam, 1679–80.

547 WICQUEFORT, A. VAN. Mémoires touchant les ambassadeurs et les ministres publics. 2 vols. Cologne. 1676–9.

By the same author, *Ambassadeur et ses functions*, 2 vols., The Hague, 1681, 1680; trans. by John Digby, 1716. Cf. François de Collières, *De la manière de négocier avec les souverains*, Paris, 1716 (Engl. trans. by A. F. Whyte, 1919). Sir E. M. Sotow's *Guide to diplomatic practice*, 2 vols., 1917, rev. edn. 1922, is a standard modern manual. On ministerial etiquette see *Finetti philoxenis: some choice observations of Sir John Finett . . . touching the reception . . . of forren ambassadors*, ed. by J. Howell, 1656.

548 KEMBLE, J. M., ed. State papers and correspondence, illustrative of the social and political state of Europe (1686–1707). 1857.

Mainly about Germany, from German sources; important. See also *Lettres historiques* (3080 n.).

549 'The diary of Élie Bouhéreau', ed. by E. Johnston. *Huguenot Soc. London Proc.* 15 (1934), 46–68.

Excerpts from the notes of an émigré who was secretary for two diplomatic missions, *temp.* William III.

550 [BERNARD, JACQUES, ed.] Actes et mémoires des négociations de la paix de Ryswick. 4 vols. The Hague. 1699. 2nd edn. 5 vols. The Hague. 1707. 3rd edn. 5 vols. The Hague. 1725.

One vol. appeared in England, 1698, as *Acts and negotiations*. See also: Jean Dumont, *Mémoires politiques pour servir à la parfait intelligence de l'histoire de la paix de Ryswick*, 4 vols., The Hague, 1699; M. Bowen [pseud.], '*Luctor et emergo*', being an historical essay on the state of England at the peace of Ryswick, 1697, The Hague, 1924, Newcastle, 1925; and Legrelle (594). An article on 'Economic aspects of the negotiations at Ryswick' by W. T. Morgan is in *R.H.S. Trans.*, 4th Ser. 14 (1931), 225–49. Some papers pertaining to Viscount Townshend's embassy to The Hague, 1709–11, are in the Townshend MSS., H.M.C., *11th rep.*, pt. 4, 1887.

551 COLE, C., ed. Memoirs of affairs of state containing letters written by ministers employed in foreign negotiations. 1733. Repr. as Historical and political memoirs. 1735.

Mainly letters of the duke of Manchester, 1697–1708, which are calendared briefly in H.M.C., *8th rep.*, pt. 2 (180). Of use for this period and later is G. de Lamberty, *Mémoires pour servir* *a l'histoire du xviii siècle* . . ., 14 vols., The Hague and Amsterdam, 1724–40, 2nd edn., 1730–40, which is a collection of state papers extracted from Gazettes, etc., covering *c.* 1700–18.

552 TORCY, J. B. COLBERT, MARQUIS DE. Mémoires . . . pour servir à l'histoire des négociations depuis le traité de Riswick jusqu'à la paix d'Utrecht. 3 vols. The Hague. 1756. Later edn. 3 vols. Lond. 1757.

Repr. in most French collections. For Torcy's other memoirs and correspondence see Bourgeois and André (529 n.), vol. ii. Useful in connection with Torcy is Wickham Legg's *Matthew Prior* (490), and his article on Prior in *E.H.R.* 29 (1914), 525–32. Prior's *History of his own time* . . ., 1740, though it should be used with caution, relates to his negotiations (see also H.M.C., Portland MSS. and Bath MSS.).

553 HOFF, B. VAN, ed. The correspondence, 1701–1711, of John Churchill, first duke of Marlborough, and Anthony Heinsius, Grand Pensionary of Holland. Utrecht. 1951.

Valuable. See also Marlborough MSS. (181).

554 SWIFT, JONATHAN. The conduct of the allies, and of the late ministry, in beginning and carrying on the present war. 2nd edn. 1711.

See also Swift's *Some remarks on the barrier treaty*, 1712. For a list of pamphlets replying to Swift's defence of Harley's policy, see C. L. Grose (10), p. 314.

555 [FRESCHOT, CASIMIR.] Histoire de congrès et de la paix d'Utrecht, comme aussi de celle de Rastadt et de Bade. Utrecht. 1716.

Tr. of *Actes, mémoires* . . . *concernant la paix d'Utrecht*, 3 vols., Utrecht, 1713; 6 vols., Utrecht, 1714–15. Important also are the *Wentworth Papers* (375), selected from Br. Mus. Add. MSS. 22192–267, 31128–52; other letters of Strafford in Bodl. Lib. Rawl. A. 285–6, C. 391–2; and papers of Ch. Boyle, earl of Orrery, envoy to Flanders and Utrecht, 1713–14, in Br. Mus. Add. MS. 37209.

A bibliography relating to the treaty is in *Camb. Mod. Hist.*, vol. v, 854–6. See also *Bolingbroke's defence of the Treaty of Utrecht, being letters vi–viii of 'The study and use of history'*, with intro. by G. M. Trevelyan, Camb. 1932.

556 WALPOLE, ROBERT. Report from the committee of secrecy appointed by order of the house of commons to examine . . . papers . . . relating to the late negociations of peace and commerce (9 June 1715). 1715.

Prints many valuable state papers. Repr. in Cobbett, vii, in Appendix. Cf. D. A. E. Harkness, 'Opposition to the 8th and 9th articles of the commercial treaty of Utrecht', *S.H.R.* 21 (1924), 219–26.

(c) *Later Works*

Several titles in Ch. III, § C relate to the conduct of foreign affairs, e.g. Barbour (726). See also *Travel*, *Economic History*, *Military History*, and *Naval History*. Good short accounts are in Ranke's *History of England* (275) and in Davies (268) and Clark (267).

557 ADAIR, E. R. The extraterritoriality of ambassadors in the sixteenth and seventeenth centuries. 1929.

See also by Adair, 'Law of nations and the common law of England: a study of 7 Anne cap. 12', *Camb. Hist. Jour.* 2 (1926–8), 290–7.

558   CLARK, G. N. 'The character of the Nine Years' War 1688–97.' *Camb. Hist. Jour.* 11 (1954), 168–82.

559   EHRMAN, J. 'William III and the emergence of a Mediterranean naval policy, 1692–4.' *Camb. Hist. Jour.* 9 (1949), 269–92.

560   FEILING, K. British Foreign Policy, 1660–72. 1930. Bibl.

The most important study of foreign relations under Charles II. See also Ogg (364) and Hartmann, *Charles II and Madame* (421 n.). On one detail, see D. K. Clark, 'Edward Backwell as a royal agent', *Econ. Hist. Rev.* 9 (1938), 45–55.

561   GERARD, J. W. The peace of Utrecht. N.Y. and Lond. 1885.

Includes much general diplomatic history of the period of Louis XIV. The best survey of the peace is O. Weber, *Der Friede von Utrecht . . . 1710–1713*, Gotha, 1891. See also Sir A. W. Ward's chapter in *Camb. Mod. Hist.*, vol. v, and no. 555. Articles relating to the peace are L. C. M. Delavand, 'Scènes de la vie diplomatique . . . 1712–14', *Rev. du dix-huitième siècle*, 2 (1914), 141–60, 258–74; E. E. Rich, 'The Hudson's Bay Company and the treaty of Utrecht', *Camb. Hist. Jour.* 11 (1954), 183–203; G. M. Trevelyan, 'The "Jersey" period of the negotiations . . .', *E.H.R.* 49 (1934), 100–5; and H. N. Fieldhouse, 'A note . . .', *A.H.R.* 40 (1935), 274–8.

562   HEAD, F. W. The fallen Stuarts. Camb. 1901.

On the use of the exiled Stuarts in diplomacy and war. See also O. Klopp, *Der fall des Hauses Stuart* (381).

563   HEEREN, A. H. L. 'Historical development of the rise and growth of the continental interests of Great Britain.' In his Historical treatises. Oxf. 1836. Pp. 199–422.

564   HORN, D. B. 'Rank and emolument in the British diplomatic service, 1689–1789.' *R.H.S. Trans.*, 5th Ser. 9 (1959), 19–49.

Valuable. This and other aspects are treated in Horn's *British diplomatic service 1689–1789*, Oxf. 1961. For lists of ambassadors see no. 542. See also M. Lane, 'The diplomatic service under William III', *R.H.S. Trans.*, 4th Ser. 10 (1927), 87–109, and her lighter article in *Nineteenth Century*, 102 (1927), 558–64; and S. T. Bindoff, 'A bogus envoy from James I', *History*, 27 (1942), 15–37. On the special royal messengers, see the general account by A. B. Wheeler-Holohan, *The history of the King's messengers*, 1935.

565   IMMICH, M. Geschichte des europäischen Staatensystems. 1905.

Useful manual on relations of the European states. See also E. Kaeber, *Die Idee des Europäischen Gleichgewichts in der publicistischen Literatur vom 16. bis zur Mitte des 18. Jahrhunderts*, Berlin, 1907; E. M. G. Routh, 'The attempts to establish a balance of power in Europe during the second half of the seventeenth century', *R.H.S. Trans.*, N.S. 18 (1904), 33–76, and A. F. Pollard's brief comment in *History*, N.S. 5 (1920), 103–4. See also R. Lodge, 'English foreign policy 1660–1715', ibid. 15 (1930), 296–307. Some important documents are printed in A. H. Gaedecke, *Politik Österreichs in der spanischen Erbfolgefrage*, 2 vols., Leipzig, 1877.

566 JESSUP, P. C. and DEAK, F. Neutrality. Its history, economics, and law. Vol. I: the origins. N.Y. 1935. Bibl.

Scholarly; covers 15th to mid 18th century. See also C. J. Kulsrud, 'Armed neutralities to 1780', *Am. Jour. Internat. Law,* 29 (1935), 423–47.

567 JUSSERAND, J. A. A. J. 'School for ambassadors.' *A.H.R.* 27 (1922), 426–64.

Surveys writings on diplomacy, mainly in the 16th and 17th centuries. Cf. D. P. Heatley, *Diplomacy and the study of international relations,* Oxf. 1919.

568 KOCH, G. Die Friedensbestrebungen Wilhelms III von England in den Jahren 1694–1697. Ein Beitrag zur Geschichte des Rijswijker Friedens. Ed. by W. Michael. Tübingen and Leipzig. 1903.

Cf. C. Ringhoffer, *Die Flugschriften-Literatur zu Beginn des spanischen Erbfolgekriegs,* Berlin, 1881.

569 MACKIE, J. D. Negotiations between James I and Ferdinand I. Oxf. 1926.

570 PRESTWICH, M. 'Diplomacy and trade in the Protectorate.' *J.M.H.* 22 (1950), 103–121.

On the conflict between commercial advantage and the Protestant interest. See also J. N. Bowman, *The Protestant interest in Cromwell's foreign relations,* Heidelberg, 1900.

571 ROUTLEDGE, F. J. England and the Treaty of the Pyrenees. Liverpool. 1953.

See also by Routledge, 'The negotiations between Charles II and the Cardinal de Retz, 1658–59', *R.H.S. Trans.,* 5th Ser. 6 (1956), 49–68. Cf. C. E. Quainton, 'Colonel Lockhart and the Peace of the Pyrenees', *Pacific Hist. Rev.* 4 (1935), 267–80.

572 ROWEN, H. H. The ambassador prepares for war: the Dutch embassy of Arnauld de Pomponne, 1669–71. The Hague. 1957.

Useful.

573 SEELEY, SIR J. R. The growth of British policy. 2 vols. Camb. 1895. 2nd edn. 1897.

Still valuable. Other general works with chapters on the 17th century include: H. E. Egerton, *British foreign policy in Europe to the end of the nineteenth century,* 1917; C. Scarfoglio, *England and the continent,* 1939 (trans. from Italian edn., Rome, 1937).

574 SMITH, L. P. The life and letters of Sir Henry Wotton. 2 vols. Oxf. 1907. Illus.

Valuable. App. I contains a complete list of Wotton's letters and dispatches. Cf. *Letters and dispatches from Sir Henry Wotton . . . 1617–1620,* Roxburghe Club, 1815, and A. W. Ward's biog., Westminster, 1898.

575 TURNER, E. R. 'Parliament and foreign affairs.' *E.H.R.* 34 (1919), 172–97.

See also Thomson (820).

576 WEDGWOOD, C. V. 'King Charles I and the Protestant cause.' *Proc. Huguenot Soc. London,* 19 (1954), 19–27.

2. FRANCE

(a) *Sources*

For the background of French policy, containing much that is related to British history, the following general works are useful, Lavisse being the best: G. Hanotaux, ed., *Histoire de la nation française*, 15 vols., Paris, 1920–7 (vol. ix, diplomatic history); E. Lavisse, *Histoire de France*, 9 vols., Paris, 1900–11; and V. L. Tapié, *La politique étrangère de la France et le début de la guerre de trente ans* (1608–21), Paris, 1934, bibl.

The arrangement of the titles below is roughly in chronological order by content.

577 BASCHET, A. Lists of French ambassadors &c. in England . . . 1509–1714 with remarks on their correspondence. Rep. of the Deputy Keeper, xxxvii, 1876.

Baschet edited a *List of despatches* of the French ambassadors of the same period, ibid. xxxix, 1878. See also ibid., vols. xl–xlvii for his account of his transcripts of documents in French archives. See also *Recueil des instructions* (541).

578 FIRTH, C. H. and LOMAS, S. C., eds. Notes on the diplomatic relations of England and France 1603–1688. Oxf. 1906.

A similar list for 1689–1763 was compiled by L. G. W. Legg, Oxf. 1909. Both have full references to published dispatches. Cf. *British diplomatic instructions* (542), Birch (543), and Winwood's *Memorials* (671).

579 LA BRODERIE, A. L. Ambassades de M. de la Broderie en Angleterre sous le règne d'Henri IV et la minorité de Louis XIII (1606–11). 5 vols. [Paris.] 1750.

Other collections of the papers of individual French envoys in the first half of the century are: François de Bassompierre, *Ambassades du Maréchal de Bassompierre en Espagne, en Suisse et en Angleterre* (1626), 4 vols., Cologne, 1668; Bassompierre's *Journal de mon vie*, ed. by de Chanterac, 4 vols., Paris, 1870–7; and J. W. Crocker's translation of the *Memoirs of the embassy . . . to the court of England in 1626*, 1819; C. Hippeau, ed., *Mémoirs inédits du Comte Leveneur de Tillières . . . Charles I*, Paris, 1863; M. Houssaye, 'L'ambassade de M. de Blainville à la cour de Charles I', *Rev. des Questions Hist.* 33 (1878), 176–204.

580 D'ESTRADES, GODEFROY L., COMTE. Lettres, mémoires, et négociations (1663–8). 5 vols. Brussels. 1709. Later edn. 9 vols. Lond. 1743.

The later editions include earlier materials, from 1637, as well as later [to 1677]. Incomplete, and to be used with caution. See critical comments in Bourgeois and André (519 n.), ii. 262–4, and C. L. Grose (10), p. 272. A modern edition of parts of D'Estrades was begun by A. R. de Saint Leger and L. Lemaire (2 vols., Paris, 1924–35). E. Combe translated the letters of 1662 in his *Sale of Dunkirk . . .*, 1728. An article on D'Estrades in London in 1661 was publ. by L. Lemaire, *Soc. Hist. de France Annuaire Bull.* 71 (1934), 181–226.

581 CURRAN, M. B. Despatches of William Perwich, English agent in Paris, 1669–77. Camden Soc. 3rd Ser. 5. 1903.

Published correspondence of other English envoys to France are: Henry Savile (1679–82) in *Saville correspondence* (338); Lord Preston (1682–8) in H.M.C., Graham MSS. (145).

582 LEEDS, THOMAS OSBORNE, DUKE OF, ed. Copies and extracts of some letters written to and from the earl of Danby (1676–8). 1710.

Danby's defence: illustrate foreign policy, particularly towards France. See Browning (433) and H.M.C. (159).

583 D'AVAUX, JEAN ANTOINE DE MESMES, COMTE DE. Négociations du comte d'Avaux en Hollande. 6 vols. Paris. 1752–3.

English tr. Lond. 1754. Valuable for preparations of William of Orange, 1687–8.

584 GRIMBLOT, P., ed. Letters of William III and Louis XIV and their ministers (1697–1709). 2 vols. 1848.

Important, especially for the Spanish Succession question. See also C. Hippeau, *Avénement des Bourbons au trône d'Espagne: correspondance inédite du Marquis d'Harcourt*, 2 vols., Paris, 1875; and the documents published in H. Reynald, *Succession d'Espagne* . . ., 2 vols., Paris, 1883. Documents and excerpts are included also in Legrelle (594). Other titles are in C. L. Grose (10), pp. 329–31, and in the general section above (Cole, etc.).

(b) *Later Works*

585 BIGBY, D. A. Anglo-French relations, 1641–1649. 1933.

Useful, well documented. Also by Bigby, 'An unknown treaty between England and France', *E.H.R.* 28 (1913), 337–41.

586 CLARK, R. E. Sir William Trumbull in Paris, 1685–1686. Camb. 1938.

Scholarly monograph; shows especially Trumbull's efforts to assist the Huguenots. See also H.M.C. (225).

587 GALTIER DE LAROQUE, A. de. Marquis de Ruvigny, député général des églises réformées auprès du roi, et les protestants à cour de Louis XIV, 1643–85. Paris. 1892.

There were several missions to England, 1660–76. Cf. D. R. Serpell, *The condition of Protestantism in France and its influence on the relations of France and England, 1650–1654*, Paris, 1934.

588 GARDINER, S. R. 'Cromwell and Mazarin in 1652.' *E.H.R.* 11 (1896), 479–509.

See also C. H. Firth, ed., *The journal of Joachin Hane . . . during his employment by Oliver Cromwell in France* (1653–4), Oxf. 1896, and Firth's article, 'Cromwell's instructions to Colonel Lockhart in 1656', *E.H.R.* 21 (1906), 742–6.

589 GEORGE, R. H. 'Financial relations of Louis XIV and James II.' *J.M.H.* 3 (1931), 392–414.

590 GROSE, C. L. 'England and Dunkirk.' *A.H.R.* 39 (1934), 1–27.

Also by Grose, 'The Dunkirk money, 1662', *J.M.H.* 5 (1933), 1–18. Cf. A. R. de Saint-Léger, 'Acquisition de Dunkerque . . .', *Rev. d'Hist. Mod. et Contemporaine*, 2 (1901), 233–45; and S. A. Swaine, 'English acquisition and loss of Dunkirk', *R.H.S. Trans.*, N.S. 1 (1883), 93–118.

591 GROSE, C. L. 'Louis XIV's financial relations with Charles II and the English parliament.' *J.M.H.* 1 (1929), 177–204.

See also documents edited by Grose in *E.H.R.* 44 (1929), 625–8, and articles on the treaty of Dover by F. A. Middlebush and E. S. de Beer, ibid. 38 (1923), 258–60 and 39 (1924), 86–9; and articles on Henrietta Stuart, duchess of Orleans, by K. Feiling, ibid. 43 (1928), 394–8, and 47 (1932), 642–5. For a revisionist article on the role of Arlington in relation to the treaty, see M. D. Lee in *Jour. of Brit. Studies*, 1 (1961), 58–70. On 'Anglo-French trade relations under Charles II', see D. G. E. Hall in *History*, 7 (1922), 17–30. See also [Abbe Primi] in *State tracts* (336), i. 1–30.

592 JUSSERAND, J. J. A French ambassador at the court of Charles the second. Le Comte de Cominges from his unpublished correspondence. 1892.

Extracts from French dispatches are in app. See also C. M. de Ligne, 'Une ambassade à Londres au xviiᵉ siècle', (1660), *Rev. Paris*, 43 (1936), 578–92; and W. L. Grant's short account of Denzil Holles's embassy to France, 1663–6, in *Queen's Univ. Bull.*, no. 8 (Kingston, 1913).

593 LAFFLEUR DE KERMAINGANT, P. P. Mission de Christophe de Harlay Comte de Beaumont (1602–5). 2 vols. Paris. 1895.

Valuable narrative and documents. Part of the series, *L'ambassade de France en Angleterre sous Henri IV*, 4 vols., Paris, 1886–95. Cf. Mme Saint-René Taillandier, 'Une ambassade de Sully à Londres (1603)', *Rev. Paris*, 44 (1937), 622–53; and A. Desclozeaux, 'L'ambassade de Sully en Angleterre en 1610 et les économies royales', *Revue Historique*, 44 (1890), 68–71. See also J. Nouaillac, 'Le règne de Henri IV (1589–1610): sources, travaux et questions à traiter', *Rev. d'Hist. Moderne et Contemporaine*, 9 (1907–8), 104–23, 348–63.

594 LEGRELLE, A. La diplomatie Française et la succession d'Espagne. 4 vols. Ghent. 1888–92. Later edn. 6 vols. Braine-le-Comte. 1895–1900.

Later edn. has a continuation. Valuable sequel to Mignet, containing many details, the comments favouring Louis XIV. Also by Legrelle, *Notes et documents sur la paix de Ryswick*, Lille, 1894; and *Une négociation inconnue entre Berwick et Marlborough 1708–9*, Ghent, 1893. Cf. M. Thomson, 'Louis XIV and William III', *E.H.R.* 76 (1961), 37–58; and 'Louis XIV and the grand alliance, 1703–10', *Bull. Inst. Hist. Research*, 34 (1961), 16–35.

595 MIGNET, F. A. M., ed. Négociations relatives à la succession d'Espagne sous Louis XIV. 4 vols. Paris. 1835–42.

Narrative to 1679, with excerpts from principal documents; the most valuable account for the period. Continued by Legrelle. Based chiefly on Mignet is H. Lonchay, *Rivalité de la France et de l'Espagne aux Pay-Bas, 1635–1700*, Brussels, 1896. See also C. F. S. de Grovestins, *Histoire des luttes et rivalités politiques entre les puissances maritimes et la France dans la dernière moitié du XVIIᵉ siècle*, 8 vols., Paris, 1851–4, later edn., 1868; includes many documents, especially in vol. iv (1677–84), and a list of MS. materials in vol. viii.

596 PICAVET, C. G. La diplomatie française au temps de Louis XIV . . . institutions, mœurs, et coutumes. Paris. 1930. Bibl.

597 SÉGUR-DUPEYRON, P. de. Histoire des négociations commerciales et maritime de la France au XVIIᵉ et XVIIIᵉ siècles. 3 vols. Paris. 1872–3.

See also C. Bastide (2175); and H. Schorer, 'Englisch-französische Handelsvertrag vom Jahre 1713', *Hist. Jahrbuch*, 21 (1900), 353–87, 715–42.

3. GERMANY AND CENTRAL EUROPE

(a) *Sources*

The best bibliographical guide is Dahlman–Waitz (529 n.). Several collections of MSS. in the British Museum are cited in C. L. Grose (10), p. 332. These include correspondence of William D. Colt, envoy to Hanover and Zell, 1690–3 (Add. MSS. 34095–6, 36662); letters of Robert Wolseley, envoy to the elector of Bavaria at Brussels, 1691–4 (Add. MSS. 34352); transcripts from Berlin of L. Friedrich Bonnet, London resident for Brandenberg 1696–1701 (Add. MSS. 30000A–E); papers of George Stepney, envoy to Berlin and Vienna 1698–1706 (Add. MSS. 7058–79, 21551, 34354, 37155–6); and letters of William Aldersey, agent at Hamburg 1701 (Add. MSS. 34357). See also the Hanover papers 1695–1714 (Stowe MSS. 222–32), described by P. M. Thornton, *E.H.R.* 1 (1886), 756–77. For the P.R.O. collections, see no. 530. Many dispatches are printed in Ranke's *History of England* (275).

598 PRIBRAM, A. F. Österreichische staatsverträge. England, Bd. I. 1526–1748. Innsbruck. 1907.

599 GARDINER, S. R., ed. Letters and other documents illustrating the relations between England and Germany at the commencement of the Thirty Years' War (1618–20). 2 vols. Camd. Soc. (nos. 90, 98). 1865–8.

See also *Letters of Elizabeth, Queen of Bohemia* (441); and *Fortescue papers* (288).

600 ORLICH, L. VON, ed. Briefe aus England [1674–78] in Gesandtschafts-berichten des Ministers Otto von Schwerin des Jüngern an den Grossen Kürfursten Friedrich Wilhelm. Berlin. 1837.

Cf. *E.H.R.* 14 (1899), 609. See M. Hein, *Otto von Schwerin*, Königsberg, 1929. On English affairs, see also *Letters . . . to Sir Joseph Williamson*, ed. by Christie (337 n.).

601 ROSENFELD, S., ed. The letter book of Sir George Etherege (1685–8). 1928.

Relates to Etherege's mission to Ratisbon; more interesting for social than for diplomatic history. Cf. Rosenfeld's article in *Rev. English Studies*, 10 (1934), 177–89.

602 CHANCE, J. F. Notes on the diplomatic relations of England and Germany. List of diplomatic representatives and agents, England and North Germany 1689–1727. Ed. by C. H. Firth. Oxf. 1907.

603 MANNERS-SUTTON, H., ed. The Lexington papers . . . from the official and private correspondence of Robert Sutton, Lord Lexington, British minister at Vienna, 1694–8. 1851.

Letters from almost every court in Europe.

604 TOLAND, JOHN. An account of the courts of Prussia and Hanover sent to a minister of state in Holland. 1705.

605 HÖFLER, K. A. C., ed. 'Diplomatische Correspondenz des Grafen Johann Wenzel Gallas, kaiserlichen Gesandten in London und Haag, während

des spanischen Successions-krieges.' *Archiv fur Österreichische Gesch.* 41 (1869), 291–311.

606 ERDMANNSDORFFER, B. *et al.*, eds. Urkunden und Actenstücke zur Geschichte des Kurfürsten Friedrich Wilhelm von Brandenburg. 21 vols. Berlin. 1864–1915.

See also C. E. Doble, ed., 'Letters of Rev. Wm. Ayerst, 1706–21', *E.H.R.* 3 (1888), 751–60; 4 (1889), 131–43, 338–50, 539–47. Ayerst was a chaplain to the Earl of Strafford (see *Wentworth Papers*, no. 375).

607 BRIEF HISTORY of the poor Palatine refugees lately arriv'd in England. 1709.

(b) Later Works

608 BELLER, E. A. 'The negotiations of Sir Stephen Le Sieur.' *E.H.R.* 40 (1925), 22–33.

609 BRINKMANN, C. 'The relations between England and Germany, 1660–88.' *E.H.R.* 24 (1909), 247–77, 448–69.

Valuable. Brinkmann has also given an excellent account of trade relations with the Hanseatic towns, ibid. 23 (1908), 683–708. Cf. Sir William Swan's 'Narrative', *Archaeologia* 37 (1857), 147–57, and R. Fester, *Augsburger allianz von 1686*, Munich, 1893.

610 FIRTH, C. H., ed. 'England and Austria in 1657.' *E.H.R.* 32 (1917), 407–11.

Deals with Cromwell's attempt to prevent the election of a Hapsburg as emperor. See also important correspondence of the Oldenburg envoy to Cromwell in Oncken's *Cromwell* (430 n.).

611 KING, H. L. Brandenburg and the English revolution of 1688. Oberlin. 1914.

See also R. Wiebe, *Untersuchungen über die Hilfeleistung der deutschen Staaten für Wilhelm III von Oranien im Jahre 1688*, Göttingen, 1939; and articles on military support for William in 1688 by C. Jany, *Forschungen zur Brandenburgischen und Preussischen Gesch.* 2 (1889), 99–124; E. E. K. E. Danckelman, *Preussische Jahrbücher*, 187 (1922), 337–45; and *Archiv für Urbundenforschung*, 8 (1923), 194–200.

612 MOWAT, R. B. 'The mission of Sir Thomas Roe to Vienna 1641–2.' *E.H.R.* 25 (1910), 264–75.

Cf. E. A. Beller, 'The mission of Sir Thomas Roe to the conference at Hamburg, 1638–40', ibid. 41 (1926), 61–77.

613 PRIBRAM, A. F. Franz Paul Freiherr von Lisola, 1613–1674. Leipzig. 1894.

Also by Pribram, 'Franz von Lisola und der ausbau der Tripleliga . . . (1670–1)', *Mitteilungen des Instituts für Österreichische Gesch.* 30 (1909), 444–500. Cf. H. Reynald, 'Le Baron de Lisola, sa jeunesse et sa première ambassade en Angleterre', *Revue Historique*, 27 (1885), 300–51.

614 REESE, W. Ringen um Frieden und Sicherheit in den Entscheidungs-jahren des spanischen Erbfolgekrieges, 1708 bis 1709. Munich. 1933.

615 WARD, A. W. The Electress Sophia and the Hanoverian succession. 1903. 2nd edn. 1909.

Important, with survey of authorities in 1909 edn. Cf. Ward's article on the subject in *E.H.R.* 1 (1886), 470–506, and his earlier work, *Great Britain and Hanover*, Oxf. 1899. Useful also are: W. Michael, *Englische Geschichte in achtzehnten Jahrhundert*, vol. i, 1895 (trans. under title of *England under George I*, 1936); and G. Schnath, *Geschichte Hannovers im Zeitalter der neunten Kur und der englischen Sukzession 1674–1714*, i (1674–92) (Veröff. der Hist. Kommission für Hannover, 18), 1938.

616 WHITELOCK, W. W. Verhältnis Max Emanuels von Bayern zu Wilhelm III von England. Munich. 1893.

Cf. G. F. Preuss, 'Konig Wilhelm III, Bayern und die Grosse Allianz, 1701', *Hist. Zeitschrift*, 93 (1904), 193–229.

4. ITALY

(a) *Sources*

Since British relations were with separate Italian states, and there is no satisfactory bibliography for them separately or as a group, the student must usually search for references under the names of the individual states. Savoy had the most important diplomatic relations, especially in the later part of the Stuart period, and the Venetian archival material is extensive; but there is material, especially in manuscript form, for relations with Genoa, Rome, Sicily and Naples, and Tuscany (Leghorn).

The repositories of manuscripts in the various states are listed in Thomas and Case (529). A particularly rich collection at Turin, containing many letters of the Stuart period, and only briefly noted in the 1876 *Guide* by N. Bianchi, was described in the *Times Lit. Supp.*, 16 Sept. 1939, p. 544. On the Venetian materials see no. 540. See also Ch. XV, *infra*, pp. 569–71.

Of manuscript collections in England, those at the P.R.O. may be located chiefly under 'State Papers Foreign' and 'Foreign Entry Book' (*Lists and Indexes*, no. 19), either under the heading of 'Italian states and Rome', or by separate state names. At the P.R.O. also are the important transcripts of Venetian MSS. by Rawdon L. Brown (see *Rep. Dep. Keeper Pub. Rec.* 46 (1886), App. 2, pp. 337–81), calendared to date up to 1675. Most of those in private collections have been described in the H.M.C. *Reports*, and can be traced by Davenport's list in *18th report* (527). Valuable for Italy are papers of Salvetti (Skrine MSS., no. 213), and of the earl of Denbigh (Denbigh MSS., no. 119). Some materials are at the Bodleian Library, such as Rawl. A. 185 and Western MSS. 15004–26. Davenport lists also various MSS. in the Br. Mus.

617 BRITISH MUSEUM ADD. MSS. 27962A–W. Transcripts from archives at Florence of correspondence of Florentine ambassadors in England (1616–79).

Also at the Br. Mus. are documents of 1610–52 in Stowe MSS. 135; transcripts of dispatches of Piedmont envoys (1611–13), in Add. MSS. 32023A and B; and letters of English envoys Thomas Higgons (Venice, 1674–7), Add. MSS. 32094–5; Lambert

Blackwell (Florence and Genoa, 1700–3), Add. MSS. 34356; and Richard Hill (Savoy), Add. MSS. 37529–30.

618   TRAITÉS PUBLICS de la royale maison de Savoie avec les puissances étrangères depuis la paix de Château-Cambresis jusqu'à nos jours publiés par ordre du Roi. 8 vols. Turin. 1836–61.

Cf. *Manuale di storia diplomatica. Cronologia dei principali trattati internazionali di pace* (1496 B.C. to A.D. 1885), Turin, 1886.

619   BAROZZI, N. and BERCHET, G., eds. Relazioni degli Stati Europei lette al Senato degli ambasciatori Veneti nel Secolo decimo settimo. III Ser. Italia. IV Ser. Inghilterra. Venice. 1861–3.

See also the *Calendars of state papers . . . Venice* (540), and the article on them by E. R. Adair in *History*, 20 (1935), 124–37.

620   MACKIE, J. D. Negotiations between King James VI. and I. and Ferdinand I., Grand Duke of Tuscany: a selection of documents transcribed from the Denmilne manuscripts in the national library of Scotland and from a manuscript in the Staats-Bibliothek at Munich. 1927.

621   PRAYER, C., ed. Olivero Cromwell dalla battaglia di Worcester alla sua morte. Genoa. 1882.

Repr. of the Genoese ambassador's dispatches. The material was used by E. Momigliano in his *Cromwell* (English tr. by L. E. Marshall, 1930). Cf. O. Pàstine, 'Genova e Inghilterra da Cromwell a Carlo II', in *Rivista storica Italiana*, 66 (1954), 309–47.

622   MORLAND, SIR SAMUEL. History of the evangelical churches of the valleys of Piedmont. 1658.

Cf. Vaughan's *Dell and Morland correspondence* (694).

623   ELLIS, H., ed. 'Relation of the Lord Fauconberg's embassy to the states of Italy in . . . 1669.' *Archaeologia*, 37 (1857), 158–88.

From Br. Mus. Sloane MSS. 2752. Cf. H.M.C. *Var. Coll.* ii (1903), 130–63. See also R. W. Ramsey, *Studies in Cromwell's family circle and other papers*, 1930, pp. 35–118.

624   POGGI, F. Lettere di Carlo Ottone, proconsole genovese in Londra, al governo della Republica di Genova (1670–1). Genoa. 1915.

625   BLACKLEY, W., ed. The diplomatic correspondence of . . . Richard Hill envoy extraordinary . . . to the duke of Savoy . . . from July 1703 to May 1706. 2 vols. 1845.

Valuable. For relations with Savoy see also J. Savage's trans. of *Memoires of the transactions of Savoy during this war, wherein the duke of Savoy's foul play . . . and his secret correspondence with the French king are . . . demonstrated*, 1697; and H. M. Fieldhouse, 'St. John and Savoy in the war of Spanish Succession', *E.H.R.* 50 (1935), 278–91.

(b) *Later Works*

626   ALBION, G. Charles I and the court of Rome. 1935.

Scholarly study.

627 BERCHET, G. Cromwell e la republicca di Venezia. Venice. 1864.

Cf. N. Conigliani, *Giovanni Sagredo*, Venice, 1934, on the Venetian envoy to Cromwell.

628 CARUTTI, D. Storia del regno di Vittorio Amadeo II. Firenze. 1863.

Needs to be supplemented by later works. For a general Italian background, though not fully reliable, see E. Callegari's *Preponderanzo straniere* (Milan, 1900) in E. Vallardi *et al.*, *Storia politica d'Italia*, 10 vols., Milan, 1897+.

629 MORANDI, C., ed. Relazioni di ambasciatori sabaudi, genovesi e veneti durante il periodo della Grande Alleanza e della Successione di Spagna (1693–1713). Vol. i. Bologna. 1935.

Of more value for comments on English affairs than on foreign policy. Cf. G. Gigli, 'Il nunzio pontificio d'Adda e la seconda rivoluzione inglese', *Nuova Riv. Stor.* 23 (1939), 285–342. See also Campagna de Cavelli, *Les derniers Stuarts* (2337).

630 PASSAMONTI, E. Relazione anglo-sabaude dal 1603 al 1625. Turin. 1934.

Extracted from *Boll. Storico-Bibliog. Subalpino*, 36 (1934), 264–317, 488–543.

5. NORTHERN POWERS

(a) *Scandinavian Kingdoms*

(1) *Sources*

631 BLISS, W. H. and MACRAY, W. D. 'Reports on materials relating to England in Swedish archives and libraries.' *Rep. Dep. Keeper Pub. Rec.* 43 (1882), App. 2, pp. 1–52; 45, App. 2, pp. 57–62.

Macray's similar report on Danish archives is printed, ibid. 45–7 (1885–6), particularly 46. See also references to the Scandinavian archives in *C.M.H.*, vol. v, pp. 876–82.
  Among MSS. in England that pertain to Scandinavia, see H.M.C., Hamilton, Supplementary, 1932 (151); Bonde, Whitelocke, Robinson. For diplomatic instructions, see Chance (542).

632 GARDINER, S. R., ed. Letters relating to the mission of Sir Thomas Roe to Gustavus Adolphus 1629–30. *Camden Soc. Misc.* vii (N.S. 14), 1875.

Valuable modern histories of the period are M. Roberts, *Gustavus Adolphus: a history of Sweden, 1611–1632*, 2 vols., 1953–8, bibl.; A. Rydfors, *De diplomatiska förbindelserna mellan sverige och England 1624–maj 1630*, Uppsala, 1890; and A. Heimer, *De diplomatiska förbindelserna* (Sweden and England, 1633–54), Lund, 1893. On Roe's attempts at mediation, a useful work is M. Cichocki, *Medjacja Francji w rozejmie altmarskim* (French mediation in the truce of Altmark), Krakow, 1928.

633 BONDE, CHRISTER. 'Diarium' in *Rep. Dep. Keeper Pub. Rec.* 43 (1882), App. 2.

Abbreviated, but little of importance is omitted. Transcripts of dispatches of Bonde and also of Peter Coyet and I. Barkman (Swedish envoys to Cromwell), prepared for S. R. Gardiner, are in Br. Mus. Add. MSS. 31800. Cf. P. Riks-rådet Frih. Kalling, *Christer Bondes ambassad till England 1655*, Uppsala, 1851. See also Johan Ekeblad, *Letters*, ed. by N. Sjöberg, Stockholm, 1911 (Letters from England, 1655–6 in vol. i, 405–43).

634 WHITELOCKE, BULSTRODE. Journal of the Swedish embassy in the years 1653 and 1654. Ed. by C. Morton. 2 vols. 1772. Later edn. by H. Reeve. 2 vols. 1855.

MS. in Br. Mus. 4902.

635 JENKS, E., ed. 'Some correspondence of Thurloe and Meadowe.' *E.H.R.* 7 (1892), 720–42.

On Meadowe's peace mission to Denmark, 1657–8, see also Thurloe Papers (544 n.). See also Sir Philip Meadowe's later account, *Narrative of the principal actions occurring in the war betwixt Sweden and Denmark before and after the Roschild treaty*, publ. 1677. Important Swedish works on this period, based on diplomatic correspondence, are J. L. Carlbom, *Karl X Gustav från Weichseln . . . 1657 . . . 1658*, Stockholm, 1910; C. G. Weibull, *Freden i Roskilde*, Malmo, 1958; and T. Gibl, *Sveriga och Vastmakterna . . .* (Sweden and the Western powers . . .), Uppsala, 1913.

636 MIÈGE, GUY. A relation of three embassies from . . . Charles II to the Grand Duke of Muscovy, the King of Sweden and the King of Denmark performed by the Earl of Carlisle (1663 and 1664). 1669.

For later contacts with Denmark, see 'Copies of several letters . . . by . . . Charles Bertie . . . envoy . . . to . . . Denmark (1670–2)', *Retrospective Rev.*, 2nd Ser. 2 (1828), 177–205.

637 WESTERGAARD, W., ed. The first triple alliance: the letters of Christopher Lindenov, 1668–1672. New Haven. 1947.

Pertain chiefly to Denmark. For a scholarly account of Sweden's foreign policy, 1660–8, with much on British policy, see B. Fahlborg, *Sverige yttre politik 1660–1664*, Stockholm, 1932; and *Sverige yttre politik 1664–1668*, 2 vols., Stockholm, 1949.

638 MOLESWORTH, ROBERT, VISCOUNT. An account of Denmark as it was in the year 1692. 1694.

Repr. in Harris (2144), vol. ii. Attacked the Danish government as tyrannical (see no. 980). Molesworth's correspondence, 1689–1744, is in H.M.C. *Various Coll.* viii. 214–417. A report of the parallel mission of William Duncombe to Sweden, 1689–92, ed. by J. F. Chance, is in *E.H.R.* 39 (1924), 571–87.

639 ROBINSON, JOHN. An account of Sweden. 1694. 3rd edn. 1717.

Most valuable of the contemporary sources. Robinson was in Sweden, 1680–1709. Important correspondence with Blathwayt (1692–1702) and Harley (1704–7) are in Br. Mus. Add. MSS. 35105–6 and 34677, respectively. Articles relating to Robinson are: J. Milne, *R.H.S. Trans.*, 4th Ser. 30 (1948), 75–93; and R. M. Hatton, *Bull. Inst. Hist. Research*, 28 (1955), 128–59.

(2) *Later Works*

640 CHANCE, J. F. Notes on the diplomatic relations of England with the north of Europe. Lists of English diplomatic representatives . . . in Denmark, Sweden, and Russia, and of those countries in England, 1689–1762. Ed. by C. H. Firth. Oxf. 1913.

Useful articles on post-1688 relations are: J. F. Chance, 'England and Sweden in the time of William III and Anne', *E.H.R.* 16 (1901), 676–711, which emphasizes the importance of the Baltic trade; M. Lane, 'The relations between England and the northern powers, 1689–1697, Part I. Denmark', *R.H.S. Trans.*, 3rd Ser. 5 (1911),

157–91; A. E. Stamp, 'The meeting of the duke of Marlborough and Charles XII at Altranstadt (1707)', ibid., N.S. 12 (1898), 103–16; and J. J. Murray, 'Robert Jackson's mission to Sweden (1709–1717)', *J.M.H.* 21 (1949), 1–16.

641 GRAUERS, S. Sverige och den forsta engelska navigationsakten (Historiska studier tillagnade Ludvig Stavenow). Stockholm. 1924.

Also on trade in the Cromwellian period: O. A. Johnson, *Navigasjonsakten av 1651* . . . (The navigation act of 1651), Oslo, 1934; and M. Prestwich, 'Diplomacy and trade under the protectorate', *J.M.H.* 22 (1950), 103–21.

642 JONES, G. The diplomatic relations between Cromwell and Charles X Gustavus of Sweden. Lincoln, Nebraska. 1897.

See also J. L. Carlbom, *Sverige och England* (1655–7), Göteborg, 1900; J. N. Bowman, *The Protestant interest in Cromwell's foreign relations*, Heidelberg, 1900; and B. Grabe, 'Den nordiska alliastanken under holländsk–engelska kriget', *Historisk Tidskrift* (Stockholm), 2nd Ser. 1 (1938), 272–82 (the idea of a Nordic alliance during the Dutch–English war, 1652–5). Important recent studies are N. F. Noordam, *De republik en de Noordse Oorlog*, Assen, 1940, and M. Roberts, 'Cromwell and the Baltic', *E.H.R.* 76 (1961), 402–46.

643 LOSSKY, A. Louis XIV, William III, and the Baltic crisis of 1683. Berkeley (Cal.). 1954.

Valuable. On Sweden's foreign policy 1681–4, see K.-E. Rudelius, *Sveriges utrikespolitik 1681–1684* . . ., Uppsala, 1942.

644 MITCHELL, T. History of the Scottish expedition to Norway in 1612. 1886.

645 SCHOOLCRAFT, H. L. 'England and Denmark, 1660–1667.' *E.H.R.* 25 (1910), 457–79.

Cf. H. Bohrn, *Sverige, Danmark och Frankreich, 1672–1674*, Stockholm, 1933.

646 THYRESSON, B. Sverige och det protestantiska Europa från Knaredfreden till Rigas erövring [Sweden and Protestant Europe from the peace of Knäred to the capture of Riga, 1613–1621]. Uppsala. 1928.

Important.

(b) *Russia and Poland*

(1) *Sources*

647 SBORNIK IMPERATORSKAGO RUSSKAGO ISTORICHESKAGO OBSHCHESTVA. (Publs. Imperial Russian Hist. Soc.) 148 vols. St. Petersburg. 1867–1916.

Publishes a variety of diplomatic correspondence, much transcribed from foreign archives, including English dispatches from P.R.O. and Br. Mus. Vols. xxxix, l, and lxi contain dispatches relating to the later Stuarts, esp. corresp. of the English ministers, Charles Whitworth (1704–12) and George Mackenzie (1714–15). For a review of this series see *Rev. d'Hist. Dipl.* 2 (1888), 410–24. See also nos. 530, 640, and bibl. in *Camb. Mod. Hist.* (7), vol. v, pp. 861–75.

648 LUBIMENKO, I. 'Letters illustrating the relations of England and Russia in the seventeenth century.' *E.H.R.* 32 (1917), 92–103.

By the same author, 'The correspondence of the first Stuarts with the first Romanovs', *R.H.S. Trans.*, 4th Ser. 1 (1918), 77–91; and 'The struggle of the Dutch with the English for the Russian market in the seventeenth century', ibid. 7 (1924), 27–51.

649 WHITWORTH, CHARLES. An account of Russia as it was in the year 1701. Strawberry Hill Press. 1758.

For Whitworth's correspondence, see no. 647.

(2) *Later Works*

650 ANDERSON, M. S. Britain's rediscovery of Russia, 1553–1815. N.Y. 1958.

Good modern account, documented. By Anderson also, 'English views of Russia in the seventeenth century', *Slavonic and East Eur. Rev.*, Dec. 1954, 140–60. Cf. L. Loewenson, 'The first interviews between Peter I and William III in 1697', ibid., June 1958.

651 COLLYER, A. D. 'Notes on the diplomatic correspondence between England and Russia in the first half of the 18th century.' *R.H.S. Trans.*, N.S. 14 (1900), 143–74.

Cf. V. N. Aleksandrenko, 'Beiträge zur Geschichte der diplomatischen Verhandlungen zwischen Russland und England im xviii. Jahrhundert (to 1760)', *Jahrbuch der internationalen Vereinigung*, 1898, pp. 227–44; 1905, pp. 409–25; and E. Borshak, 'Early relations between England and Ukraine', *Slavonic Rev.* 10 (1932), 138–60.

652 KONOVALOV, S. 'Anglo-Russian relations 1617–18.' 'Anglo-Russian relations 1620–24.' *Oxford Slavonic Papers*, 1 (1950), 64–103; and 4 (1953), 71–131.

Cf. by Konovalov, 'Two documents concerning Anglo-Russian relations in the early 17th century', ibid. 2 (1951), 129–44. See also S. Yakobson, 'Early Anglo-Russian relations (1553–1613)', *Slavonic Rev.* 13 (1935), 597–610; and O. Odložílik, 'Karel of Zerotín and the English court, 1564–1636', ibid. 15 (1937), 413–25.

653 LUBIMENKO, I. Les relations commerciales et politiques de l'Angleterre avec la Russie avant Pierre le Grand. Paris. 1934. Bibl.

By Lubimenko also, 'A project for the acquisition of Russia by James I', *E.H.R.* 29 (1914), 246–56; and 'The Anglo-Russian relations during the first English revolution', *R.H.S. Trans.*, 4th Ser. 11 (1928), 39–59. See also L. Loewenson, 'Did Russia intervene after the execution of Charles I?', *Bull. Inst. Hist. Research*, 18 (1940), 13–20.

654 PRZEZDZIECKI, R. Diplomatic ventures and adventures: Some experiences of British envoys at the court of Poland. 1953.

References to an incident in Cromwell's period are in chap. 5. See also J. Jasnowski, 'England and Poland in the sixteenth and seventeenth centuries', *Polish Science and Learning*, 7 (1948).

6. SPAIN, PORTUGAL, AND THE LOW COUNTRIES

(a) *Bibliographies and Sources*

The best bibliography for Spanish history is Sánchez Alonzo (529 n.), but there are good critical bibliographies also in A. Ballesteros y Beretta, *Historia de*

España, Barcelona, 1922–6 (vol. iv to 1700). A bibliography of English works on Portugal is included in the commemorative volume of the Instituto de Coimbra, Comemorações das seculares relações entre a Inglaterra e Portugal, *Instituto*, Ser. 4, 20 (1937), 111–96. On the Low Countries, see H. Pirenne, *Bibliographie de l'histoire de Belgique* . . . (1598–1630), Ghent, 1893, later edns., Brussels, 1902, 1931; and Pirenne's *Histoire de Belgique*, 7 vols. Brussels, 1920–32 (3rd rev. edn., 4 vols., Brussels, 1948–52). See also no. 673. Numerous State Papers relating to Spain, Portugal, Flanders, and Holland, at the P.R.O., are listed in *Lists and Indexes*, vol. 19, but have not been calendared for the Stuart period. See also Davenport (527). The Portuguese and Spanish archives, described in Thomas and Case (529), chapters 10 and 11, should be searched for additional material. See also Ch. XV *infra*, pp. 569–71.

655 LONCHAY, H. and CUVELIER, J., eds. Correspondance de la cour d'Espagne sur les affaires des Pays-Bas au XVIIᵉ siècle. 6 vols. Brussels. 1923–7.

Published under the auspices of the Belgian Commission Royale d'Histoire. See also the Trumbull papers in H.M.C. (225); and E. Bysshe, ed., *Original letters written [in 1674] to the earl of Arlington by Sir R[ichard] Bulstrode envoy at the court of Brussels*, 1712.

656 JESUS, FRAY FRANCISCO de. Narrative of the Spanish marriage treaty. Ed. by S. R. Gardiner. Camd. Soc. 1869.

Translated from the Spanish narrative, a copy of which is in Br. Mus. Add. MS. 14043. Gardiner edited *The earl of Bristol's defence of his negotiations in Spain*, Camd. Soc., 1871 (*Camd. Misc.* vi). See also a note by P. Revill and F. W. Steer in *Bull. Inst. Hist. Research*, 31 (1958), 141–58.

657 ORIGINAL LETTERS and negotiations of . . . Sir Richard Fanshaw, the earl of Sandwich, the earl of Sunderland and Sir William Godolphin, wherein divers matters between the three crowns of England, Spain and Portugal are set in a clearer light than is any where else extant. 2 vols. 1724.

An important collection. Cf. H.M.C. Heathcote MSS. (135), from Fanshawe's correspondence, 1661–6; and the *Memoirs* (444).

658 CARTE, T. The history of the revolutions of Portugal . . . to 1667 with letters of Sir Robert Southwell, during his embassy there, to the duke of Ormond. 1740.

Southwell's letters cover June to Dec. 1667. Other Southwell corresp., 1654–1700, is in Br. Mus. Add. MSS. 35099–101; and additional Portuguese materials are in Add. MSS. 20844–45.

659 WALFORD, A. R., ed. 'Private letter from the Rev. J. Colbatch to the bishop of Salisbury, 1696 [and] the bishop of Salisbury's reply (1697).' *Hist. Assoc. Lisbon Branch Ann. Repts.* 2 (1938), 99–149.

Concerns the Lisbon factory and the consul Methuen.

660 MAHON, PHILIP H. STANHOPE, VISCOUNT, ed. Spain under Charles II, or extracts from the correspondence of . . . Alexander Stanhope, British minister to Madrid, 1690–99. 1840. 2nd edn. 1844.

Important for the Partition Treaties. See also 'Cartas del duque de Montalto a don Pedro Ronquillo, embajador de S.M.C. en Inglaterra (1685–8)', *Colección de documentos inéditos para la historia de España*, 79 (1882), 299–475. Pamphlets relating to the partition treaties are [Andrew Fletcher], *Discorso delle cose di Spagna*, Naples [Edin.], 1698 and 1755, in Fletcher's *Political works*; and Defoe's *Two great questions consider'd* . . ., 1700, and his *Two great questions further considered*, 1700.

(b) *Later Works*

661   GIRARD, A. 'Notes sur les consuls étrangers en Espagne avant le traité des Pyrénées.' *Rev. Hist. Moderne*, N.S. 9 (1934), 120–38.

Includes English consuls, 1532–1659. Cf. M. S. Jayne, 'British consuls in Lisbon, from 1583', *Hist. Assoc. Lisbon Branch Ann. Repts.* 2 (1938), 78–84; and J. Meos, 'Het consulaatswezen in België tijdens vroegere eerwen', *Bijd. Gesch.* 26 (1935), 107–36 (includes English consuls in Belgium and Belgian consuls in England).

662   GROSE, C. L. 'Anglo-Portuguese marriage of 1662.' *Hispanic Amer. Hist. Rev.* 10 (1930), 313–52.

Valuable calendar of documents on the negotiations are in vols. xvii–xviii of M. F. de Barros (visconde de Santarem), *Quadro elementar das relações politicas e diplomaticas*, 18 vols., Paris and Lisbon, 1842–72. A pamphlet by the Portuguese envoy in England is Francisco de Mello e Torres (marques de Sande), *Relaçam da forma*, Lisbon, 1661. Cf. John Colbach, *Examination of . . . Echard's account of the marriage treaty*, Camb. 1733.

663   HUME, M. A. S. Un gran diplomático español: el conde de Gondomar en Inglaterra. Revista Nuestro Tiempo. Madrid. 1902.

Cf. B. C. Pérez, *El conde de Gondomar y su intervención al proceso, prisión y muerte de Sir Walter Raleigh*, Santiago, 1928.

664   MACKIE, J. D. 'James VI and I and the peace with Spain, 1604.' *S.H.R.* 23 (1926), 241–9.

Cf. L. B. Wright, 'Propaganda against James I's "appeasement" of Spain', *Hunt. Lib. Quart.* 6 (1943), 149–72. A diary relating to the peace is included in the later editions of R. Watson's *History of the reign of Philip the Third*, ed. by W. Thomson, 1783; 2nd edn., 2 vols. 1786; 7th edn., 1 vol., 1839. See also, in *Ocios diplomáticos*, by W. R. de Villa-Urrutia, marqués de Villa-Urrutia (Madrid, 1927), 'Jornada del condestable de Castilla a Inglaterra para las paces de 1604' and 'La embajada de Lord Nottingham a Espaňa en 1605'. See also A. J. Loomie, *Toleration and diplomacy: the religious issue in Anglo-Spanish diplomacy, 1603–1605* (Amer. Phil. Soc.), Phila., 1963.

665   McLACHLAN, J. O. Trade and peace with old Spain, 1667–1750; a study of the influence of commerce on Anglo-Spanish diplomacy in the first half of the eighteenth century. Camb. 1940.

Cf. P. A. Means, *The Spanish Main, focus of envy, 1492–1700*, N.Y. 1935; and I. A. Wright, 'The Spanish resistance to the English occupation of Jamaica', *R.H.S. Trans.*, 4th Ser. 13 (1930), 117–47. For the Spanish background of the whole period, 1621–1700, see R. Trevor-Davies, *Spain in decline*, 1957, bibl. See also no. 2121. On Tangier see Abbey (3420 n.).

666   PRESTAGE, E. The diplomatic relations of Portugal with France, England and Holland from 1640 to 1668. Watford. 1925.

A good survey, based on Portuguese records. By Prestage also: *Dr. Antonio de Sousa de Macedo, residente de Portugal em Londres* (1642–6), Lisbon, 1916 (repr., with another article by Prestage in *Bull. of the Acad. das Sciencias of Lisbon*, 10 (1916); 'The Anglo-Portuguese alliance', *R.H.S. Trans.*, 4th Ser. 17 (1934), 69–100; and *Chapters in Anglo-Portuguese relations*, Watford, 1935 (including articles by several authors). See also R. Lodge, 'Methuen treaties of 1703', *History*, 18 (1934), 33–5; and Chapman (2121).

667 ABBOTT, W. C. An introduction to the documents relating to the international status of Gibraltar, 1704–1934. N.Y. 1934. Bibl.

Useful introduction, though emphasis is on the period after 1713. This is true also of S. Conn's *Gibraltar in British diplomacy in the eighteenth century*, New Haven, 1942. No thorough history of Gibraltar exists, though there is a brief one by E. R. Kenyon (1911, rev. edn. 1938); and Sir C. Petrie ed. J. Plá's *Gibraltar* (trans. by D. Round), 1955.

7. UNITED PROVINCES

There are abundant materials on Anglo-Dutch relations, both in print and in MS. Works on the Netherlands background by Dutch historians include P. J. Blok, *Geschiedenis van het Nederlandsche volk*, 8 vols., Groningen, 1892–1908, English trans., by R. Putman *et al.*, 5 vols., N.Y. and Lond., 1898–1912 (vols. iii and iv on the period), bibliographies in both edns.; P. Geyl, *The Netherlands in the seventeenth century*, pt. 1, 1609–48, N.Y. 1961, bibl. (tr. by S. T. Bindoff from the 2nd rev. edn. of the work, first publ. in 1936; pt. 2, 1648–1702, to follow); and the *Algemene geschiedenis der Nederlanden*, by various authors, 12 vols., Utrecht, 1948–58.

The major archives of the Netherlands, both the Dutch Republic and the provinces, are described in ch. 8 of Thomas and Case (529). For state papers at the P.R.O. see *Lists and Indexes*, xix. At the Br. Mus. are 'Transcripts from the Hague', state correspondence (1576–1764), Add. MSS. 17677A–KKK2b; related documents are in 34339–40, 35852, and 34507–12. The correspondence of James D. Dayrolles, 1706–12, is in Add. MSS. 15866–75. Pertaining to the peace negotiations of Utrecht are Add. MS. 37209 and Bodl. Lib. Rawl. A. 285–6, C. 391–2.

MSS. in the H.M.C. *Reports* of importance are vol. iii of De L'Isle and Dudley (118); Portland, vols. iv, v, and ix (153); and Townshend, *11th report*, App. IV, 1887. See also the general list at the beginning of this section (p. 74 *supra*) and the titles under 'France' (pp. 81–2 *supra*).

(a) *Bibliographies*

668 NIJHOFF, N. Bibliotheca historico-Neerlandica. Catalogue des livres et manuscrits concernant l'histoire et la topographie des Pays-Bas. The Hague. 1871. Later edns. 1899. 1932.

A bookseller's catalogue. See also his *Bibliotheca juridica; catalogus van alle boeken sedert 1837 in het Koningrijk der Nederlanden verschenen*, 1874. The standard modern guide is Gosses and Japikse (529 n.). *A guide to Dutch bibliographies* was publ. by B. H. Wabeke, Wash. 1951.

669 KNUTTEL, W. P. C. Catalogus van de pamfletten-verzameeling . . . in Koninklijke Bibliothek. 9 vols. The Hague. 1889–1920.

The best index to pamphlet literature in the Royal Library. Other guides to pamphlet collections are by L. D. Petit (for the Bibliotheca Thysiana at Leyden), 2 vols., The Hague, 1882–4; and J. C. van der Wulp (Univ. Library, Ghent), 3 vols., Amsterdam, 1866–8. Knuttel published also *Lijst van Engelsche vlugschriften, betrekking hebbende op de Nederlandsche geschiedenis tot 1640*, 1886.

670 CLARK, G. N. List of authorities on British relations with the Dutch 1603–1713. s.l. 1920.

Cf. *Bijdragen voor vaderlandsche geschiedenis*, 5th Ser., vols. iii–iv (1916–17), which includes a list by S. J. van den Bergh on Anglo-Dutch relations.

(b) *Sources*

671 WINWOOD, SIR RALPH. Memorials of affairs of state in the reigns of Queen Elizabeth and King James I, collected chiefly from the original papers of Sir Ralph Winwood. Ed. by E. Sawyer. 3 vols. 1725.

Important for 1603–14. Other Winwood papers are in H.M.C. (89).

672 CARLETON, SIR DUDLEY. Letters from and to Sir Dudley Carleton during his embassy in Holland (1616–1620). Ed. by Philip Yorke, 2nd earl of Hardwicke. 1757. Later edn. 1780.

Cf. *Sir Dudley Carleton's state letters during his embassy at the Hague* (1627), ed. by Sir Thomas Phillipps, s.l., 1841.

673 ARCHIVES . . . de la maison d'Orange-Nassau. 2nd Ser. 1584–1688. Ed. by G. G. van Prinsterer. 5 vols. Leyden and Utrecht. 1857–61. 3rd Ser. 1689–1702. Ed. by F. J. L. Krämer. 3 vols. Leyden. 1907–9.

Both valuable, the second series especially for the correspondence of William III and Heinsius. See also *Correspondentie van Willem III en van Portland* (524). For the correspondence at the Dutch Pensionaries, see R. Fruin and N. Japikse, eds., *Brieven aan de Witt*, 2 vols., Amsterdam, 1919–22; and E. W. Kernkamp and N. Japikse, eds., *Brieven aan de Witt*, 4 vols., Amsterdam, 1906–13. See also R. Sanderson, ed., *Original letters from William III then Prince of Orange to King Charles II, etc.* [translated], 1704; and the Marlborough corresp. (181).

674 VERBAAL van de ambassade van Aerssen, Joachimi en Burmania naar Engeland 1625. Utrecht. 1867.

675 AITZEMA, LIEUWE VAN. Saken van staet en oorlogh. 6 vols. The Hague. 1669–72. Cont. by Lambertus Sylvius [i.e. Lambert van den Bos], as Historien onses tyds. 2 vols. Amsterdam. 1685–99.

There are various editions of Aitzema's work, which continued its account to 1669.

676 COLENBRANDER, H. T. Bescheiden uit vreemde archiven omtrent de groote Nederlandsche zeeoorlogen, 1652–76. 2 vols. The Hague. 1919.

For the first Dutch war, see Gardiner (1808 n.); for the second, see letters printed in vol. iii of Lister's *Clarendon* (422 n.). See also C. H. Firth, ed., 'Secretary Thurloe on the relations of England and Holland', *E.H.R.* 21 (1906), 319–27.

677 THE RIGHT HONOURABLE EARL OF ARLINGTON's letters to Sir William Temple . . . [1665–1670] giving a perfect and exact account of the

treaties of Munster, Breda, Aix-la-Chapelle, and the Triple Alliance. Ed. by
T. Bebington. 1701.

See also Sir William Temple's, *Observations upon the United Provinces of the Netherlands,*
1673 (repr. Camb. 1933; also in *Works* (512)); Temple's *Memoirs* (512 n.); and [Henry
Stubbs], *Justification of the present war against the United Netherlands,* 1672 (also in
Harl. Misc., vol. viii). For further bibl. on this period, see *Camb. Mod. Hist.,* vol. v,
1908. On the Treaty of Dover see Grose (591).

678   LANE, M. 'A relation of the present state of affairs in the United Provinces
1675.' *E.H.R.* 30 (1915), 304–17.

From state papers in P.R.O.

679   MIDDLEBUSH, F. A., ed. Dispatches of Thomas Plott (1681–2) and
Thomas Chudleigh (1682–5), English envoys at the Hague. The Hague. 1926.

680   [WITHERS, JOHN.] Dutch better friends than the French to the
monarchy, church, and trade of England. 1713.

(c) *Later Works*

681   ALPHEN, G. van. De stemming van de Engelschen tegen de Hollanders
in Engeland . . . 1688–1702. Assen. 1938.

682   BASNAGE de BEAUVAL, J. Annales des Provinces-Unies depuis les
négociations pour la paix de Munster. 2 vols. The Hague. 1719–26.

Cf. G. A. Lefèvre-Pontalis, *John de Witt,* 2 vols., 1885 (1st edn., French, 2 vols., Paris,
1884); and N. Japikse, *Johan de Witt,* Amsterdam, 1915.

683   CLARK, G. N. The Dutch alliance and the war against French trade
1688–97. Manchester. 1923.

Also by Clark, 'Dutch influence in British history', *Niewe Gids,* 38 (1923), 505–15;
'Dutch missions in England in 1689', *E.H.R.* 35 (1920), 529–57; 'Neutral commerce in
the War of the Spanish Succession and the Treaty of Utrecht', *British Year-Book of
International Law,* 1928, pp. 69–83; an article in *Econ. Hist. Rev.* (1927–8), 262–80;
and Clark and W. J. M. Eysinga (2117). See also J. F. Bense, *Anglo-Dutch relations . . .
to the death of William III,* 1925; and C. H. Firth in *R.H.S. Trans.,* 3rd Ser. 9 (1915),
1–20.

684   COOMBS, D. The conduct of the Dutch: British opinion and the Dutch
alliance during the War of the Spanish Succession. The Hague. 1958.

Important; includes useful bibl. of pamphlet literature. See also his articles in *Econ.
Hist. Rev.* 10 (1957), 94–103; and in *E.H.R.* 72 (1957), 642–61. Cf. A. J. Veenendaal,
Het Engels-Nederlands condominium in Zuidelijke Nederlander, vol. i, Utrecht, 1945; and
P. Geyl, 'Nederlands staatkunde in de Spaanser Successie-Oorlog', in *Kernproblemen
van onze geschiedenis,* Utrecht, 1937.

685   EDMUNDSON, G. Anglo-Dutch rivalry during the first half of the
seventeenth century. Oxf. 1911. Bibl.

The Ford lectures at Oxf. in 1910. Still valuable for the period to 1609 are J. L.
Motley's *History of the United Netherlands . . .,* 4 vols., 1860–7 (many later edns.), and
The life . . . of John of Barneveld, 2 vols., 1874.

686 ELIAS, J. E. Het Voorspel van den Eersten Engelschen Oorlog. [The Hague, 1920].

Cf. his *De Tweede Engelsche Oorlog als Keerpunt in onze Betrekkingen met England*, The Hague, 1930; R. J. Fruin, 'Prins Willem III in sijn verhouding tot Engeland', in *Verspreide geschriften* (10 vols., The Hague, 1900–5), v. 1–193; cf. also ibid. iv. 338–76; G. D. J. Schotel, 'Briefwisseling tusschen Karel II . . . en Willem III . . . in 1672', *Bijdragen voor vaderlandsche geschiedenis*, N.S. 4 (1866), 1–19; Elizabeth H. Korvezce, 'Zendingen van Frederik van Reede naar Engeland . . . 1672–4', ibid., 6th Ser. 7 (1928), 243–58; E. H. W. Pahlow, 'Anglo-Dutch relations, 1671–2', *Ann. Rep. Amer. Hist. Assoc. 1911*, i. 121–7.

687 GEIKIE, R. and MONTGOMERY, I. A. The Dutch barrier, 1705–19. Camb. 1930.

Study of an issue of special interest to England. Cf. R. Dollot, *Origines de la neutralité de la Belgique et le système de la barrière (1609–1830)*, Paris, 1902, bibl.

688 GEYL, P. Oranje en Stuart, 1641–1672. Utrecht. 1939. Antwerp. 1963.

Work of important Dutch scholar, whose revisionist studies should be consulted in relation to older histories. See also G. Mitsukuri, *Englisch-niederländische Unionsbestrebungen im Zeitalter Cromwells*, Tübingen, 1891; R. R. Goodison, 'England and the Orangist party, 1665–72', *Bull. Inst. Hist. Research*, 13 (1936), 173–6; and articles by Geyl and by Goodison relating to the Buat intrigue in *Bijd. en Mededeel. Hist. Genoots. Utrecht*, 60 (1939), 209–12, and 57 (1936), 1–61.

689 GROSE, C. L. 'The Anglo-Dutch alliance of 1678.' *E.H.R.* 39 (1924), 349–72, 526–51.

Useful study of a complicated situation. Cf. K. H. D. Haley, 'The Anglo-Dutch rapprochement of 1677', ibid. 78 (1958), 614–48; Haley's *William of Orange and the English opposition* (362 n.); and M. C. Trevelyan, *William III and the defence of Holland, 1672–1674*, 1930. Relating to the years 1678–85 see J. J. Doesburg's articles in *Tijdschrift voor geschiedenis*, 1891, and *Tijdschrift en aardrijkskunde*, 1892.

690 JAPIKSE, N. De verwikkelingen tusschen de republiek en Engeland (1660–5). Leiden. 1900.

By Japikse also, 'Louis XIV et la guerre anglo-hollandaise de 1665–7', *Revue Historique*, 98 (1908), 22–60. Cf. C. Ballhausen, *Die drei englisch-holländischen Seekriege (1652–74)*, vol. i, The Hague, 1923; H. A. Hansen, 'Opening phase of the third Dutch war', *J.M.H.* 21 (1949), 97–108; and C. Brinkmann, 'Charles II and the bishop of Munster in the Anglo-Dutch war of 1665–66', *E.H.R.* 21 (1906), 686–98. See also C. Wilson's studies of the wars, *Profit and power* (2118). W. del Court wrote on 'Sir William Davidson in Nederland (1661–71)', *Bijdragen voor vaderlandsche geschiedenis*, 4th Ser. 5 (1906), 375–425; see also H. H. Rowen (572) and Anderson (1812).

691 SCHOOLCRAFT, H. L. 'The capture of New Amsterdam.' *E.H.R.* 22 (1907), 676–93.

Cf. C. H. Wilson, 'Who captured New Amsterdam?', ibid. 72 (1957), 469–74.

692 VAN DEN HAUTE, G. Les relations anglo-hollandaises au début du XVIIIe siècle, d'après la correspondance d'Alexandre Stanhope, 1700–1706. Louvain. 1932.

8. OTHER EUROPEAN AREAS

(a) *Hungary*

693 MAKKAI, C. 'The Hungarian puritans and the English revolution.' *Acta Historica* (Budapest). 5 (1958), 13–45.

The influence of English ideas, 1600–60.

(b) *Switzerland*

694 VAUGHAN, R., ed. The protectorate of Oliver Cromwell and the state of Europe . . . illustrated in a series of letters between Dr. John Pell, resident ambassador with the Swiss cantons, Sir Samuel Morland, Sir William Lockhart, Mr. Secretary Thurloe. 2 vols. 1839.

See also articles showing Cromwell's interest in the relief of the Vaudois, by B. Gagnebin, in *Boll. Soc. Stud. Valdesi*, 58 (1939), 237–54, and *Proc. Huguenot Soc. London*, 18 (1948), 158–80. Cf. A. Stern, 'Oliver Cromwell und die evangelischen Kantone der Schweiz', *Hist. Zeit.* 40 (1878).

695 KILCHENMANN, F. Mission des englischen Gesandten, Thomas Coxe, in der Schweiz, 1689–92. Zürich. 1914.

Cf. L. A. Robertson's article, based on MSS. at P.R.O. and Br. Mus., 'The relations of William III with the Swiss Protestants, 1689–1697', *R.H.S. Trans.*, 4th Ser. 12 (1929), 137–62.

696 MEIER, M. Die diplomatische Vertretung Englands in Schweiz in 18. Jahrhundert (1689–1789). Basle. 1952.

See also B. Bucher, *Abraham Stanyon, 1704–14: die englische Diplomatie in der Schweiz zur Zeit des Spanischen Erbfolgekrieges*, Zürich, 1951.

(c) *Turkey*

In addition to the titles below, see also the Trumbull papers (225), and *Economic History*, nos. 2132, 2385. The standard history of Turkey is J. W. Zinkeisen, *Geschichte des Osmanischen Reiches*, 7 vols., Hamburg, 1840–63, vols. iii, iv, and v.

697 ROSS, Sir E. D. 'A letter from James I to the Sultan Ahmad.' *School of Oriental Studies Bull.* 7 (1934), 299–306.

Related to imprisonment of Sir Thomas Sherley (see no. 2385).

698 ABBOTT, G. F. Under the Turk in Constantinople: a record of Sir John Finch's embassy, 1674–81. 1920.

Important. See also Finch MSS. (136); A. Malloch, *Finch and Baines, a 17th century friendship*, Camb. 1917; and Paul Rycaut, *Present state of the Ottoman empire*, 1668 (by Winchelsea's secretary, 1661, and afterwards consul at Smyrna). See also *Lives of the Norths* (482).

699 SUTTON, SIR ROBERT. The despatches of Sir Robert Sutton, ambassador in Constantinople 1710–14. Ed. by A. N. Kurat. Camd. Soc. 3rd Ser. 78. 1953.

Valuable reports on internal politics and external pressures.

700   WOOD, A. C. 'The English embassy at Constantinople, 1660–1762.'
E.H.R. 40 (1925), 533–61.

On the brief period spent by Etherege as embassy secretary, see T. H. Fujimura,
P.M.L.A. 71 (1956), 465–81. See also B. Spuler, 'Europäische Diplomaten in Konstantinopel bis zum Frieden von Belgrad (1739)', *Jahrb. Gesch. Osteuropas*, 1 (1936),
229–62, 383–440, which includes a list of English ambassadors; and D. M. Vaughan,
Europe and the Turk: a pattern of alliances, 1350–1700, Liverpool, 1954.

9. NON-EUROPEAN REGIONS

See also *Colonial History*.

701   STODART, ROBERT. The journal of Robert Stodart, being an account
of his experience as a member of Sir Dodmore Cotton's mission in Persia in
1628–29. Luzac. 1935.

From MS. in Bodl. Lib., with notes by E. D. Ross. See also J. R. Childs, 'The evolution
of British diplomatic representation in the Middle East', *Roy. Central Asian Soc. Jour.*
26 (1939), 634–47.

702   ANDERSON, J. English intercourse with Siam in the 17th century. 1890.

703   MUTŌ, C. A short history of Anglo-Japanese relations. Tokyo. 1936.

Deals chiefly with 1600–23.

704   PRITCHARD, E. H. Anglo-Chinese relations during the 17th and 18th
centuries. Urbana. 1931.

III

CONSTITUTIONAL HISTORY

Interest of scholars in the Stuart period, which tended to focus in the earlier works on the major conflict between king and Parliament, has expanded more recently to include studies of administration, both central and local. An increasing amount of published source materials relating to the Privy Council, the Treasury, and less well known branches of the royal administration provides the basis for future studies of the functioning of central authority. Parliamentary history, profiting likewise from valuable publication of debates and diaries, especially for the first half of the period, has also attracted wide attention; its full history remains to be written. On the studies of political ideas of the period, a separate introductory paragraph appears in the appropriate section.

A. GENERAL

1. BIBLIOGRAPHY AND SOURCES

705 CAM, H. M. and TURBERVILLE, A. S. Bibliography of English constitutional history. 1929.

Historical Association Leaflet no. 75. See the 1958 bibliography compiled for the Association by S. B. Chrimes and I. A. Roots (Helps for students of history, no. 58). See also Ch. IV.

706 DYKES, D. O., ed. Source book of constitutional history from 1660. 1930.

See also D. L. Keir and F. H. Lawson, *Cases in constitutional law*, Oxf. 1928 (rev. edn., 1933), which has helpful introductions; and C. G. Robertson, ed., *Select statutes cases and documents to illustrate English constitutional history 1660–1832, with a Supplement from 1832 to 1894*, 1904, 2nd edn., 1913, 6th edn., 1935, useful notes.

707 STEPHENSON, C. and MARCHAM, F. G., eds. Sources of English constitutional history: a selection of documents from A.D. 600 to the present. N.Y. and Lond. 1937.

Other valuable collections are: J. R. Tanner, *Constitutional documents of the reign of James I*, Camb. 1930; S. R. Gardiner, ed., *The constitutional documents of the Puritan revolution, 1628–1660*, Oxf. 1889, later edns., 1899 and 1906; and Sir G. W. Prothero, ed., *Select statutes and other constitutional documents . . . Elizabeth and James*, Oxf. 1894; later edns., 1898, 1906, 1913, and 1949 repr. of the 1913 edn. Useful also is P. L. Hughes and R. F. Fries, *Crown and Parliament in Tudor–Stuart England . . .*, N.Y. 1959.

2. LATER WORKS

708 AMOS, A. The English constitution in the reign of King Charles the second. 1857.

Deals with special problems such as dispensing power, king and Parliament, habeas corpus, liberty of the press, and others. Cf. B. Behrens, 'The Whig theory of the constitution in the reign of Charles II', *Camb. Hist. Jour.* 7 (1941), 42–71; and C. C. Crawford's articles on habeas corpus in *Amer. Law Rev.* 42 (1908), 481–99, and *E.H.R.* 30 (1915), 613–30.

709   ANSON, SIR W. R. The law and custom of the constitution. Vol. i, Parliament. Vol. ii, The Crown. 2 vols. 1886–92. 2nd edn. 1892–6. 3rd edn. (vol. ii in 2 pts.) 1897–1908. Vol. i, 4th edn. 1909. 5th edn. ed. by Maurice L. Gwyer. 1922. Vol. ii, 4th edn. ed. by A. B. Keith. 1935.

Standard authority on the modern constitution. Cf. E. Jenks, 'Anson on the constitution', *Soc. Comparative Legislation Jour.*, 3rd Ser. 18 (1936) 71–7.

710   DICEY, A. V. Lectures introductory to the study of the law of the constitution. 1885. 4th edn. 1893. 9th edn. with intro. and app. by E. C. S. Wade. 1939.

Cf. D. M. Griffith, *Questions and answers in constitutional law and legal history*, 1935.

711   HALLAM, H. The constitutional history of England from the accession of Henry VII to the death of George II. 2 vols. 1827. 8th edn. 3 vols. 1855. Later edn. 3 vols. 1930.

Still of use, though out of date and strongly Whig in bias.

712   JENNINGS, W. I. The law and the constitution. 1933. 4th edn. 1952.

713   KEIR, D. L. The constitutional history of modern Britain, 1485–1937. 1938. 3rd edn. 1946. 5th edn. 1953.

Excellent survey. Another useful summary is D. J. Medley's *Student's manual of English constitutional history*, Oxf. 1894, 6th edn., 1925. T. P. Taswell-Langmead, *English constitutional history*, in the 10th edn. by T. F. T. Plucknett, 1946, is also useful.

714   MAITLAND, F. W. The constitutional history of England. Ed. by H. A. L. Fisher. Camb. 1908. Repr. 1920.

A standard work, though brief. Cf. Lord John Russell, *An essay on the history of the English government and constitution, from the reign of Henry VII to the present time*, 1821, 2nd edn. enl., 1823, new edn., 1865; J. Hatschek, *Englische Verfassungsgeschichte*, Munich and Berlin, 1913, which is useful though it contains some imperfections; and M. A. Thomson, *A constitutional history of England, 1642–1801*, 1938, which is vol. iv of a 5-vol. work by the same title under the editorship of R. F. Treharne.

715   TANNER, J. R. English constitutional conflicts of the seventeenth century. 1603–1689. Camb. 1928.

Excellent study of major events. B. Kemp's *King and commons, 1660–1832*, N.Y. 1957, is less substantial. For the different documents entitled 'Agreement of the people', see J. W. Gough in *History*, 15 (1931), 334–41. See also *Political theory*, pp. 137–44.

B. THE CROWN AND HOUSEHOLD

1. BIBLIOGRAPHY AND SOURCES

See also *Political Theory* (nos. 959, 971, 975), and the various rulers listed in *Political Biography*.

716 BIBLIOTHECA LINDESIANA. A bibliography of royal proclamations of the Tudor and Stuart sovereigns and others published under authority 1485–1714. Ed. by R. R. Steele. 2 vols. Oxf. 1910.

I. England and Wales. II. Scotland and Ireland. Has excellent indexes and a valuable introduction.
   A later publication of *Some proclamations of Charles I* was issued in the *Bodleian Quart. Rec.*, vol. 8, no. 90. Suppl., Oxf. 1936. See also listings in Wing under each sovereign (e.g. William, W 2309–2497; William and Mary, W 2498–2637).

717 A COLLECTION OF ORDINANCES and regulations for the government of the royal household, from Edward III to King William and Queen Mary. 1790.

Published for the Society of Antiquaries.

718 'A TRUE COLLECTION as well of all the Kinges Majesties offices and fees in any of the courtes at Westminster, as of all the offices and fees of His Majesties honorable household.' *Archaeologia*, 15 (1806), 72–91.

A list for 1606. See ibid. 14 (1803), 249–61, for 1610 orders for the household of Prince Henry.

719 DOCUMENTS on the State Paper Office. Ed. by W. N. Sainsbury. 30th Report of Dep. Keeper of Public Records (App., pp. 212–93). 1869.

See also *An index to bills of Privy Signet, commonly called Signet bills 1584 to 1596 and 1603 to 1624 with a calendar of writs of privy seal 1601 to 1603*, ed. by W. P. W. Phillimore, Brit. Record Soc., Index Lib., 1890. There is also a calendar of Privy Seals 1–7 Charles I in the *43rd Rep. Dep. Keeper Pub. Rec.* (App., pp. 1–205), and 8–11 Charles I in the *48th Report* (App., pp. 451–560).

720 VAN THAL, H. The royal letter book. Being a collection of royal letters from the reign of William I to George V. 1937.

See also nos. 374, 399, 418.

721 'A LIST of the department of the Lord Chamberlain of the household, autumn, 1663.' *Bull. Inst. Hist. Research*, 19 (1941), 13–24.

2. LATER WORKS

For Crown lands, surveys, and sales of, see no. 1951.

722 KEARSLEY, R. H. His majesty's bodyguard of the honourable corps of gentlemen-at-arms. 1937.

Cf. C. de W. Crookshank's article on the corps in *Archaeol. Jour. for 1936*, 93 (1937); see also 'The court', Ch. IX, p. 336.

723 WORMUTH, F. D. The royal prerogative, 1603–1649. A study in English political and constitutional ideas. Ithaca and Lond. 1939.

By Wormuth also is *The origins of modern constitutionalism*, N.Y. 1949. On special powers of the monarch see valuable studies by E. F. Churchill, 'The dispensing power and the defense of the realm', *Law Quart. Rev.* 37 (1921), 412–41; 'The dispensing power of the crown in ecclesiastical affairs', ibid. 38 (1922), 297–316, 420–34; and 'Dispensations under the Tudors and Stuarts', *E.H.R.* 34 (1919), 409–15; and Sir W. Holdsworth, 'The treaty-making power of the Crown', *Law Quart. Rev.* 58 (1942), 175–83.

C. CENTRAL ADMINISTRATION

Since the Privy Council was the main-spring of the whole central administration, Adair (733) supplies a guide to the materials, both printed and manuscript, for administrative history. Other guides are Gerould (9) and the bibliographies on special offices or councils by Evans (751), Reid (750), and Skeel (3497). For the various departments useful short descriptions are given by Andrews, *Guide* (3330). Reference may also be made to the 'Whitehall Series' of department histories, ed. by Sir James Marchant, although they are mainly modern in emphasis, e.g. Sir H. L. Smith, *The board of trade*, [1928]; Sir E. Murray, *The Post Office*, [1927]; and Sir T. L. Heath, *The treasury*, [1927]. Lists of office-holders, *post* 1669, based upon Chamberlayne and Miège (2353 n.) and compiled by M. M. S. Arnett and M. Joliffe, are printed in *Bull. Inst. Hist. Research*, 15 (1937), 24–30, and 17 (1940), 130–8.

Much may be learned of administrative history also from works dealing with local government, with the law courts, with taxation, and with other aspects of government regulation in matters of religion, trade, or publication.

I. General: Sources and Later Works

724 DEFOE, DANIEL. 'Maxims and instructions for ministers of state.' Ed. by G. F. Warner. *E.H.R.* 22 (1907), 130–43.

From Br. Mus. Lansdowne MS. 98, pp. 223–46. Describes the functions of government about 1704.

725 AYLMER, G. E. The king's servants: The civil service of Charles I, 1625–1642. Lond. and N.Y. 1961.

An important study of the growing bureaucracy, with valuable lists and tables. See articles by Aylmer: 'Attempts at administrative reform, 1625–40', *E.H.R.* 72 (1957), 229–59; 'The last years of purveyance 1610–1660', *Econ. Hist. Rev.*, 2nd Ser. 10 (1957), 81–93; 'Charles I's commission on fees, 1627–40', *Bull. Inst. Hist. Research*, 31 (1958), 58–67; and 'Office holding as a factor . . . 1625–42', *History*, 44 (1959), 228–40.

726 BARBOUR, V. 'Consular service in the reign of Charles II.' *A.H.R.* 33 (1928), 553–78.

727 CLARK, D. K. 'Edward Backwell as a royal agent.' *Econ. Hist. Rev.* 9 (1938–9), 45–55.

728 NOBLE, M. A history of the College of Arms and the lives of all the kings, heralds and pursuivants from the reign of Richard III . . . until the present time. 1804.

729 NOTESTEIN, W. 'The establishment of the committee of both kingdoms.' *A.H.R.* 17 (1912), 477–95.

Cf. Glow (888).

730 THOMAS, F. S. Notes of materials for a history of the public departments. 1846.

Valuable for the secretary of state and the Signet Office.

731 RICHINGS, M. G. Le service secret de la couronne d'Angleterre depuis le moyen âge jusqu'à nos jours. Paris. 1935.

Published in English, 1934, under the title *Espionage*. See also J. Walker, 'The secret service under Charles II and James II', *R.H.S. Trans.*, 4th Ser. 15 (1932), 211–42; and J. Y. Akerman, ed., *Moneys received and paid for secret services (1679–1688)*, Camden Soc., 1851.

732 WALLIS, J. P. 'Cromwell's constitutional experiments.' *19th Century*, 47 (1900).

On the experiences of an 'intelligencer' under Cromwell see Thomas Scot's account ed. by C. H. Firth, *E.H.R.* 12 (1897), 116–26.

2. PRIVY COUNCIL AND CABINET

(a) *Bibliography and Sources*

733 ADAIR, E. R. The sources for the history of the council in the sixteenth and seventeenth centuries. 1924.

Has many references to MSS. as well as to pr. sources. Adair wrote also, 'The privy council registers', *E.H.R.* 30 (1915), 698–704; and 'The rough copies of the privy council register', *E.H.R.* 38 (1923), 410–22.

734 THE PRIVATE DIARY of William first Earl Cowper. Ed. by E. C. Hawtrey. Roxburghe Club. 1833.

Valuable for history of the cabinet, 1703–10.
Cf. *Notes which passed at meetings of the privy council between Charles II and the Earl of Clarendon 1660–7*, ed. by W. D. Macray, Roxburghe Club, 1896 (from Bodl. Lib. Clarendon MSS. 100–1). See also no. 481.

735 ACTS OF THE PRIVY COUNCIL of England 1613–1631+. 1921–64+.

Those portions of the 17th- and 18th-century registers of the privy council that refer to the colonies were published by W. Grant and J. Munro (3317). The introductions to these volumes (especially vols. i and ii) are most valuable for the working of the privy council. (There is a list of privy councillors for the period in the Addendum to vol. v.) Extracts from the privy council registers concerning the drama have been printed by E. K. Chambers and W. W. Greg, *Dramatic records from the privy council register 1603–42* (The Malone Society's Collections, pts. iv and v, pp. 370–95, 1911).

(b) *Later Works*

736 ANSON, SIR W. R. 'The cabinet in the seventeenth and eighteenth centuries.' *E.H.R.* 29 (1914), 56–78.

Other important articles on the development of the cabinet are by E. I. Carlyle, 'Committees of council under the earlier Stuarts [1603–40]', ibid. 21 (1906), 673–85, and 'Clarendon and the privy council 1660–7', ibid. 27 (1912), 251–73; by G. Davies, 'Council and cabinet 1679–88', ibid. 37 (1922), 47–66; J. H. Plumb, 'The organization of the cabinet in the reign of Queen Anne', *R.H.S. Trans.*, 5th Ser. 7 (1957), 137–57; and H. W. V. Temperley, 'Inner and outer cabinet privy council 1697–1783', *E.H.R.* 27 (1912), 682–99, with its appendix of 'Documents illustrative of the powers of the privy council in the 17th century', ibid. 28 (1913), 127–31. These articles, though differing in some of their conclusions, should be read to correct some of the conclusions in Turner (740).

737   CORBETT, SIR J. S. 'Queen Anne's defence committee.' *Monthly Rev.*, May 1904, pp. 55–65.

> Examines Nottingham's notes, May 1702–Jan. 1703 in Br. Mus. Hatton–Finch MSS. (Add. MS. 29591).

738   FITZROY, SIR A. The history of the privy council. 1928.

> Popular treatment.

739   ROBERTS, C. 'Privy Council schemes and ministerial responsibility in later Stuart England.' *A.H.R.* 64 (1959), 564–82.

> By the same author, 'The growth of ministerial responsibility to Parliament in later Stuart England', *J.M.H.* 28 (1956), 215–33. Cf. C. B. Anderson's article, ibid. 34 (1962), 381–9.

740   TURNER, E. R. (*a*) The privy council of England in the seventeenth and eighteenth centuries, 1603–1784. 2 vols. Baltimore. 1927–8. (*b*) The cabinet council of England in the seventeenth and eighteenth centuries, 1662–1784. 2 vols. Baltimore. 1930–2.

> Vol. ii of the latter work was edited by G. Megaro. These works, though weak on the earlier period and in some of the conclusions, are important for collecting materials from extensive research which provide a basis for all subsequent research on the nature of the cabinet. For a criticism of Turner see *E.H.R.* 46 (1931), 130–3. See also the following important articles by Turner: 'The origin of the cabinet council [to 1640]', *E.H.R.* 38 (1923), 171–205; 'Committees of the council and the cabinet 1660–88', *A.H.R.* 19 (1914), 772–93; 'The privy council of 1679', *E.H.R.* 30 (1915), 251–70; 'The development of the cabinet 1688–1760', *A.H.R.* 18 (1913), 751–68, and 19 (1913), 27–43; 'Privy council committees 1688–1760', *E.H.R.* 31 (1916), 545–72; 'The lords of the committee of the council', *A.H.R.* 22 (1916), 90–4; and 'The lords justices of England', *E.H.R.* 29 (1914), 453–76. See also Anson (736). These studies supersede the earlier works by Blauvelt, 1902, and Torrens, 2 vols., 1894.

741   WILLSON, D. H. The privy councillors in the house of commons, 1604–1629. Minneapolis. 1940.

> See also *Parliament*.

3. PRIVY COUNCIL AND COLONIAL ADMINISTRATION

See *Board of Trade* (777–82) and *Colonial History* (3316–19).

742   KAYE, P. L. English colonial administration under Lord Clarendon 1660–1667. Johns Hopkins Univ. Studies in Historical and Political Science No. 23. Baltimore. 1905.

> An earlier work by the same author, 'The colonial executive prior to the Restoration' (Johns Hopkins Univ. Studies in Historical and Political Science, No. 18, 1900), is also of some value for the colonial control exercised by the home government.

743   RUSSELL, E. B. The review of American colonial legislation by the king in council. Columbia Univ. Studies in History, Economics, and Public Law. 64, no. 2. N.Y. 1915.

> Chap. 1 deals with the period to 1696.

744 SMITH, J. H. Appeals to the privy council from the American plantations. N.Y. and Lond. 1950. Bibl.

Intro. essay by J. Goebel. Valuable account of development of appelate jurisdiction and
procedure. See J. F. Macqueen, *A practical treatise on the appelate jurisdiction of the
House of Lords and privy council*, 1842; H. D. Hazeltine, *Appeals from colonial courts . . .
with a special reference to Rhode Island* (Papers from the Historical Seminary of Brown
Univ., No. 7), Providence, R.I., 1896; and A. M. Schlesinger, 'Colonial appeals to the
privy council', *Pol. Sci. Quart.* 28 (1913), 279–97, 433–50.

4. STAR CHAMBER AND SPECIAL COUNCILS

(a) *Sources*

745 HAWARDE, J. Les reportes del cases in camera stellata 1593–1609. Ed.
by W. P. Baildon. 1894.

746 HUDSON, WILLIAM. A treatise on the court of star chamber. Ed. by
F. Hargrave. In Hargrave's Collectanea Juridica, vol. ii, pp. 1–240. 2 vols.
1792.

Written *c.* 1620. The treatise exists in many versions; probably the best is Add. MS.
11681. See also p. vi of the bibl. in Scofield (749); and 'An outline of the history of the
star chamber', *Archaeologia*, 25 (1834), 342–93, by John Bruce, which is derived from
Hudson. A similar treatise by Isaac Cotton written in 1622 is in Br. Mus. Stowe MS.
418.

747 REPORTS of cases in the courts of star chamber and high commission.
Ed. by S. R. Gardiner. Camden Soc. 1886.

From Harl. MS. 4130, and Rawlinson A. 128; star chamber cases Easter Term 1631 to
Trinity Term 1632; high commission cases Oct. 1631 to June 1632; shows ordinary
course of business in these courts. There are reports of other star chamber cases 1625–8
in Rushworth, vol. ii, pt. 2. See also Gardiner's edition of *Speech of Sir Robert Heath . . .
in the case of Alexander Leighton in the star chamber, 4 June 1630 (Camden Soc. Misc.*
vii, 1875); *Documents relating to the proceedings against William Prynne in 1634 and 1637,*
ed. by J. Bruce and S. R. Gardiner, Camden Soc., N.S. 18, 1877, with an app. containing
a list of Prynne's works; and William Laud's *Speech delivered in the star chamber* [14 June
1637] . . . *at the censure of John Bastwick, Henry Burton, and William Prinn,* 1637, repr.
in *Harl. Misc.*

(b) *Later Works*

748 BURN, J. S. The star chamber: notices of the court and its proceedings.
1870.

749 SCOFIELD, C. L. A study of the court of star chamber largely based on
manuscripts in the British Museum and the Public Record Office. Chicago.
1900. Bibl.

A careful treatise, in parts outdated, with a valuable bibliography. See also E. P. Cheyney, 'The court of star chamber', *A.H.R.* 18 (1913), 727–50; A. P. Keep, 'Star chamber
proceedings against the Earl of Suffolk and others', *E.H.R.* 12 (1898), 716–29, which is
based on contemp. MSS. in possession of Pye family, proceedings in 1619; and H. E. I.
Phillips, 'The last years of the court of star chamber, 1630–41', *R.H.S. Trans.*, 4th Ser.
21 (1939), 103–31.

750 REID, R. R. The King's Council of the North. Lond. and N.Y. 1921.

Excellent guide to sources on this branch of government to 1640. For Council of the Marches of Wales, see *Wales*. For the Court of Wards, see *Legal History*.

5. SECRETARY OF STATE

751 EVANS, F. M. G. [Mrs. C. S. S. Higham.] The principal secretary of state. A survey of the office from 1558 to 1680. Manchester, N.Y., and Lond. 1932. Bibl.

A valuable study; it contains an excellent account of the original records of the secretary's office. See the author's article on emoluments of the secretaries of state, *E.H.R.* 35 (1920), 513–28. Cf. D. G. C. Allan, 'Charles II's secretaries of state', *History Today*, Dec. 1958, and M. A. Thomson, *Secretaries of state, 1681–1782* Oxf. 1932, bibl.

752 FRASER, P. The intelligence of the secretaries of state and their monopoly of licensed news, 1660–1688. Camb. 1956.

753 JACOBSEN, G. A. William Blathwayt, a late seventeenth-century administrator. New Haven. 1932.

Good account of an official, 1668–1717. See also M. Lane's article on Blathwayte in *Contemp. Rev.* 125 (1934), 639–44; and R. A. Preston, 'William Blathwayt and the evolution of a royal personal secretariat', *History*, 34 (1949), 28–43.

6. ADMIRALTY

(a) *Sources*

See also Chs. IV, VII, and XII.

754 SHILTON, D. O. and HOLWORTHY, R. eds. High court of admiralty examinations, 1637–1638. Lond. and Wash. 1932.

See also R. G. Marsden, *A digest of cases relating to shipping, admiralty, and insurance law (temp.* Elizabeth to 1897), 1899.

755 THE SERGISON PAPERS. Selected and ed. by Comdr. R. D. Merriman. 1949 (1950). Navy Rec. Soc. Pub. Vol. 89.

Relate to 48 years of a clerk in the Admiralty, but especially to 1691–9.

(b) *Later Works*

756 DOTY, J. D. The British admiralty board as a factor in colonial administration, 1689–1763. Phila. 1930.

See also R. G. Marsden, 'The high court of admiralty in relation to national history, commerce, and the colonisation of America, A.D. 1550–1650', *R.H.S. Trans.*, N.S. 16 (1902), 69–96; and A. R. G. McMillan, 'Admiralty patronage in Scotland in 1702–1705', *Juridical Rev.* 50 (1938), 81–6.

757 JAMES, G. F. and SHAW, J. F. S. 'Admiralty administration and personnel, 1619–1714.' *Bull. Inst. Hist. Research*, 14 (1936), 10–24, 166–83.

Also by G. F. James, 'Some further aspects of admiralty administration, 1689–1714', ibid. 17 (1939), 13–27, and 'Josiah Burchett, secretary to the Lords Commissioners of the Admiralty, 1695–1742', *Mariner's Mirror*, 23 (1937), 477–98.

758 MURRAY, SIR O. A. R. 'The admiralty.' *Mariner's Mirror*, 23 (1937), 13–35, 129–47, 316–31.

Historical account by a modern official. Cf. G. Robinson, 'Admiralty and naval affairs, May 1660 to March 1674', *Mariner's Mirror*, 36 (1950), 12–40.

7. TREASURY AND EXCHEQUER

(a) *Bibliography and Sources*

See also Ch. VIII, pp. 295–7. In Appendix (vol. iii) of A. Browning's *Thomas Osborne Earl of Danby* (433) are printed various papers on the revenue, 1673–9. Descriptions of MS. materials in P.R.O. occur in *Rep. Dep. Keeper Pub. Rec.* 38 (1877), 41 (1880), and 42 (1881); and in *Lists and Indexes*, nos. 2 (1893), 37 (1912), and 46 (1921). See also Grose (10), p. 90, on Br. Mus. MSS.

759 DEVON, F., ed. Issues of the Exchequer; being payments made out of His Majesty's revenue during the reign of King James I. 1836.

Extracts from the records in the Pell office.

760 RETURN of the whole amount of the national debt of Great Britain and Ireland . . . from 1691 to Jan. 5, 1857. Parl. Papers, 1857–8, vol. 33, pp. 2–105.

See also *Accounts of the net public income and expenditure* (1688–1801), pt. i, s.l., 1869 (Parl. papers, 1868–9, vol. 35).

761 CALENDAR OF THE PROCEEDINGS of the Committee for Advance of Money, 1642–1656. Ed. by M. A. E. Green. 3 vols. 1888.

Also ed. by M. A. E. Green, *Calendar of the proceedings of the Committee for Compounding, 1643–60*, 5 vols., 1889–92.
Both series are valuable for the period of the civil war and interregnum. Various records of compounding proceedings are in print, such as Lancashire (Rec. Soc. Lanc. and Cheshire, 1891–1942) or Yorkshire (Yorks. Arch. Soc. Rec. Ser., 1893–5); see Mullins (23 n.).

762 CALENDAR OF TREASURY BOOKS, 1660–1718. Ed. by W. A. Shaw *et al.* 32 vols. 1904–62.

Volumes i–xxviii cover the years 1660–1714. Shaw's introductions, of which the last appeared in 1952, are especially valuable. See also his 'Beginnings of the national debt' in *Historical Essays . . .*, ed. by T. F. Tout and J. Tait, 1902 (repr. Manch., 1907). Miscellaneous papers addressed to the Treasury, chiefly after 1688, were edited by J. Redington as *Calendar of treasury papers, 1556–(1728)*, 6 vols., 1868–89.

763 SUMMARY LIST of the customs and excise records preserved in various official repositories. Second Rept. of the Royal Comm. on Public Records, part 2 (pp. 239–48), 1914.

Cf. G. G. Dixon, 'Notes on the records of the Custom House, London', *E.H.R.* 34 (1919), 71–84.

(b) *Later Works*

764 ASHTON, R. 'The disbursing official under the early Stuarts: the cases of Sir William Russell and Philip Burlamachi.' *Bull. Inst. Hist. Research*, 30 (1957), 162–74.

Cf. A. V. Judges, 'Philip Burlamachi', *Economica* 6 (1926), 286 ff. See also no. 2062.

765 BAXTER, S. B. The development of the Treasury, 1660–1702. London and Camb., Mass. 1957.

Emphasizes the administrative work of this department as it emerged from the Exchequer. A general history of the department is Sir T. L. Heath, *The Treasury*, 1927. See also no. 477.

766 CRAIG, SIR J. H. McC. The Mint. A history of the London mint (287–1948). Camb. 1953.

By the same author: *Newton at the Mint*, Camb. 1946.

767 DIETZ, F. C. English public finance, 1558–1641. Lond. and N.Y. 1932.

Also by Dietz, *Receipts and issues of the exchequer during the reigns of James I and Charles I*, Northampton, Mass., 1928.

768 GILL, D. M. 'The Treasury, 1660–1714.' *E.H.R.* 46 (1931), 600–22.

Also by Gill, 'The relationship between the treasury and the excise and customs commissioners (1660–1714)', *Camb. Hist. Jour.* 4 (1932), 94–9. Both are valuable studies.

769 HAMILTON, R. An inquiry concerning the rise and progress, the redemption and present state and the management of the national debt of Great Britain and Ireland. Edin. 1813. 3rd edn. enl. 1818.

770 HUGHES, E. Studies in administration and finance 1553–1825 with special reference to the history of salt taxation in England. Manchester. 1934.

Excellent for the special subjects to which it relates.

771 LEADAM, I. S. 'The finance of Lord Treasurer Godolphin.' *R.H.S. Trans.*, 3rd Ser. 4 (1910), 21–32.

772 NEWTON, A. P. 'The establishment of the great farm of the English customs.' *R.H.S. Trans.*, 4th Ser. 1 (1918), 129–56.

Describes the system in use in 1600 and the great reform of 1604–5. Cf. 'A list of Records of the Greencloth extant in 1610', also by Newton, *E.H.R.* 34 (1919), 237–41. See also nos. 2069–70.

773 RICHARDS, R. D. 'The exchequer in Cromwellian times.' *Econ. Hist.* 2 (1931), 213–33.

Cf. W. O. Scroggs, 'English finance under the Long Parliament', *Quart. Jour. of Economics*, 21 (1907).

8. POST OFFICE

The library at the General Post Office (North London) contains many books and MSS. relating to the Post Office from 1672. Important MSS. are Mainwaring

MSS., 10 vols., Post Office records, chiefly 1673–7. See H.M.C. *Rep. 10*, pt. 4 (1885), 209.

774 CLEAR, C. R. Thomas Witherings and the birth of the postal service. Together with a copy and a transcription of the proclamation of King Charles I establishing the first postal system . . . (Post Office Green Papers, no. 15). 1935.

775 HEMMEON, J. C. The history of the British Post Office. Camb., Mass. 1912.

A standard work. Also valuable are H. Joyce, *The history of the Post Office*, 1893; and J. W. Hyde, *The early history of the post in grant and farm* (to 1685), 1894.

776 MARSHALL, C. F. D. The British Post Office from its beginnings to 1925. 1926. Bibl.

Appendices and bibl. are useful. For some special aspects see C. H. Firth, 'Thurloe and the Post Office', *E.H.R.* 13 (1898), 527–33; and E. R. Turner, 'The secrecy of the post', ibid. 33 (1918), 320–7.

9. BOARD OF TRADE

See also *Privy Council* and *Colonial History*.

777 JOURNALS OF THE COMMISSIONERS FOR TRADE AND PLANTATIONS from . . . 1704 . . . to 1782. 14+ vols. 1920–38+.

The first two vols. include the period 1704–15.

778 ANDREWS, C. M. British committees, commissions and councils of trade and plantations, 1622–1675. Baltimore. 1908.

See also the bibliography in Andrews, *Colonial self-government 1652–89* (American Nations Series, vol. v), 1904, and no. 3335.

779 BIEBER, R. P. The lords of trade and plantations 1675–1696. Allentown, Pa. 1919.

This subject is also dealt with by W. T. Root in 'The lords of trade and plantations 1675–96', *A.H.R.* 23 (1917), 20–41. Bieber has also published 'The British plantation councils of 1670–4', *E.H.R.* 40 (1925), 93–106.

780 DICKERSON, O. M. American colonial government 1696–1765. Cleveland. 1912.

See also M. P. Clarke, 'The board of trade at work', *A.H.R.* 17 (1911), 17–43.

781 LEES, R. M. 'Parliament and the proposal for a council of trade, 1695–6.' *E.H.R.* 54 (1939), 38–66.

See also his article on the Commissioners for Wool, 1689, in *Economica*, 40 (1933) 147–68, 264–74.

782 SMITH, SIR H. L. The Board of Trade. 1928.

A department history in the Whitehall series.

D. PARLIAMENT

1. BOTH HOUSES

There is still no authoritative history of Parliament either *in extenso* or for the Stuart period. The student must depend upon Cobbett (789), the old *Parliamentary history* (790), and the sources from which they are drawn. More recent scholarship, notably that of S. R. Gardiner and of Wallace Notestein and his students, has produced an increasing volume of carefully edited materials relating to particular parliaments of this century. These are in less abundance for the years after 1660, but valuable articles and monographs and several shorter diaries have helped to fill the gaps.

783　BOND, M. F. 'The records of Parliament', i, ii. *The Amateur Historian,* 4, nos. 6 and 7 (1959–60; 1960).

Excellent bibliographical articles, dealing with the Lords. Mr. Bond is an authority on the MSS. in the House of Lords library, and is the editor of the *Record Office Memorandum,* irregularly published, which includes useful information on the parliamentary records housed there. See also Woods (p. 112).

(a) *Statutes: General and Individual Collections*

784　STATUTES OF THE REALM [to 1713]. Ed. by T. E. Tomlins *et al.* 11 vols. 1810–28.

An official publication with chronological and alphabetical indexes in vols. x and xi. There are inaccuracies, but this is the most complete collection. Valuable also, but selected and somewhat abridged is the collection that was privately printed by Tomlinson and J. Raithby as *Statutes at large* [1225–1800], 20 vols., 1811. In the extended edition by D. Pickering, *The statutes at large from Magna Carta to 1806,* 46 vols., Camb. 1762–1807, vols. vii–xiii cover the 17th century; for other editions see Lowndes, *Bibliographer's manual,* 2499–2500. Examples of the numerous digests of the statutes are: R. P. Tyrhwhitt and T. W. Tyndale, *A digest of the public general statutes from . . . 1224–5 to . . . 1821,* 2 vols., 1822, and G. Grabb, *Digest and index . . . of all statutes* (1215 to *temp.* Victoria), 3 vols., 1841–4.

785　ANNO REGNI Jacobi regis Angliae . . . 21 at the Parliament begun . . . 19 . . . February in the 21 yeere of the reigne . . . and . . . continued untill the 29 day of May following. 1624.

Cf. *A collection in English, of the statutes now in force, continued from the beginning of Magna Carta . . . untill the end of the parliament holden in the 7. yere of . . . King James . . .* Pr. for the Society of Stationers, 1615. Texts of statutes. These are examples of many similar publications.

786　THE LAWES RESOLUTIONS OF WOMENS RIGHTS; or the lawes provision for women. 1632.

For collections of statutes dealing with particular subjects, such as the above, see *S.T.C.* and Wing. Some useful ones are: *A collection of so much of the statutes in force, as contain and enjoyn the taking of the several oaths of supremacy and allegiance . . .,* 1661; *An abridgement; or a summary account of all the statute[s] . . . made against Jesuits,* 1666 (later collections, 1675, 1679, are Wing, E 863 and E 862); *An abstract of all such acts of parliament now in force as relate to the admiralty and navy of England,* 1697; *A collection of acts . . . relative to those protestant dissenters . . . usually called . . . Quakers, from the year 1688,* 1757; and William Nelson, *The laws of England concerning game; of hunting, hawking, fishing, and fowling,* etc. . . . 3rd edn., 1736.

787   FIRTH, C. H. and RAIT, R. S., eds. Acts and ordinances of the interregnum 1642–1660. 3 vols. 1911.

Vol. iii contains an Introduction by Prof. Firth giving account of sources, chronological
table, and index. This edn. fills an important gap in *Statutes of the realm*. Various collections, printed for Edward Husband, printer to the House of Commons, and listed
by Firth, were published in 1643 (Dec. 1641–March 1643); 1646 (9 March 1642–Dec.
1646) and 1649–1653 (16 Jan. 1649–8 April 1653), 2 vols. Henry Scobell, clerk of the
House of Commons, edited a *Collection of several acts, . . . whereunto are added some
ordnances of Parliament* (1648–51), 1651, and a later edn. for 1640–1656, in 2 vols. in
1656. For this period also see *A collection of all the proclamations, declarations . . . passed
by his Highness the Lord Protector and his Council . . .* (16 Dec. 1653–2 Sept. 1654), 1654.

788   HUGHES, WILLIAM, ed. Exact abridgment of all the statutes in force
(1642–63). 1663. Later edns. cont. to 1708.

Continues a work by Edmund Wingate, 1642, and an earlier abridgment (1640–56)
publ. by Hughes, 1657. See Thomas Manby's 1667 edn. of the *Statutes made in the
reigns of King Charles I and King Charles II* [to 1667], and its continuation, with earlier
statutes also, as *Collection of all the statutes now in use*, 1670.

(b) *Journals and Debates (General)*

The debates and records pertaining to particular Parliaments or periods are listed
separately below. See also the records of the separate houses, filed respectively
under 'House of Lords' and 'House of Commons'. An excellent, though not
exhaustive, guide to parliamentary materials is [John A. Woods], *A bibliography
of parliamentary debates of Great Britain* (House of Commons Library, Doc.
no. 2), H.M. Stationery Office, 1956.

789   COBBETT, WILLIAM, ed. The parliamentary history of England
[1066–1803]. 36 vols. 1806–20.

Vols. i–vi cover the period to 1714, with some interesting pamphlets of the later 17th
cent. repr. in vols. iv and vi. Cobbett is out of date, and must be supplemented with
the published diaries. Cobbett's work was continued afterwards by Hansard. Cobbett
drew upon earlier printed books, such as Richard Chandler, *History and proceedings of
the House of Commons* [1660–1743], 14 vols., 1742–4, and Boyer's *Political State* (374 n.).
See also [John Torbuck], *A collection of Parliamentary debates in England* (1688–1741),
21 vols., 1739–42; 2nd edn., 24 vols., 1741–9; 3rd edn., bearing Torbuck's name, 21
vols., 1741–2. For the sources used by Cobbett, and other materials, see H. H. Bellott
et al., 'General collections of reports of Parliamentary debates for the period since 1660',
Bull. Inst. Hist. Research 10 (1932–3), 171–7.

790   THE PARLIAMENTARY or constitutional history of England from the
earliest times to the restoration of Charles II. 24 vols. 1751–62.

Commonly known as the *Old Parliamentary history*. Valuable, especially for copious
extracts from contemporary pamphlets, 1640–60, and for the inclusion in the part dealing
with 1660 of an otherwise unavailable MS. diary. Must be used with caution, however,
because of uncritical methods of compilation. The sources are analysed in Woods
(*supra*).

(c) *Journals and Debates (Individual Parliaments or Periods)*

Materials from debates are included in many modern writings on particular
Parliaments, such as Relf (824), Firth (825 n.), and others. Stock's *Proceedings*

and debates of the British Parliaments respecting North America (3320), is useful for a study of Parliament as well as of colonial matters. Important for 1610 is E. R. Foster (857 n.).

791 RICKARD, R. L., ed. Account of the courts of record, beginning with the two houses of Parliament, by R. Robinson. *Camd. Soc. Misc.* ii. 1953.

Pertains to *c.* 1592, but revised *temp.* James I. In the same volume are 'The Hastings journal', edited by Lady de Villiers, which gives new information on proceedings in the House of Lords in 1621; and O. C. Williams, ed., 'Minute book of James Courthope', for parliamentary sessions of Dec. 1697–May 1699.

792 GARDINER, S. R., ed. Documents illustrating the impeachment of Buckingham in 1626. Camd. Soc. 1889.

Copies of documents relating to five of the charges, from papers in P.R.O. and Harleian MSS. Cf. *The earl of Bristol's defence of his negotiations in Spain* (*Camd. Soc. Misc.* vi), 1871.

793 FULLER, THOMAS, ed. Ephemeris Parliamentaria; or A faithfull register of the transactions in Parliament, in the third and fourth years of the reign of King Charles. 1654. Later edns. 1657 [1658?] and 1660.

A collection of legal arguments and speeches probably first issued as separates, includes also a version of the *True relation* for 1629. Title of later edition is: *The sovereigns prerogative and the subjects priviledge.*

794 HISTORICAL COLLECTIONS or a brief account of the most remarkable transactions of the two last Parliaments. 1681.

795 MANTOUX, P. 'French reports of British parliamentary debates in the 18th century.' *A.H.R.* 12 (1907), 244–69.

Valuable as indicating the existence of detailed reports of proceedings among the Correspondance politique: Angleterre, of the French Foreign Office. He quotes a report of some proceedings of the 1679 session. Transcripts of most of the French ambassador's dispatches of the 17th century are deposited in P.R.O.

(d) *Parliamentary Papers*

Of special importance are the widely varied papers in the MSS. of the House of Lords, some of which came into the Lords' custody because they were addressed to the speaker of that house, or because they were secured for the purpose of a parliamentary inquiry. Since the Lords always demanded the original documents, refusing copies, they are most valuable. Included are minute books, drafts of bills with amendments marked, copies of bills that never became law, and much other material that illustrates the *Journals*. See comments by Maurice Bond (783); and the description of the calendaring of the House of Lords MSS. (162). They have been microfilmed for the Library of Congress. For the House of Commons see no. 796.

For guides to printed papers, see the catalogues and indexes by H. H. Bellot in *Bull. Inst. Hist. Research*, 11 (1933–4), 24–30, and 85–96; and H. B. Lees-Smith, *A guide to parliamentary and official papers*, 1924.

796 CATALOGUE OF PARLIAMENTARY REPORTS, and a breviate of their contents, arranged . . . according to the subjects, 1696–1834. Parl. Papers. 1834.

Cf. P. and G. Ford, editors, *Hansard's Catalogue and breviate of parliamentary papers, 1696–1834,* Oxf. 1953; and the same editors' *Guide to parliamentary papers,* Oxf. 1955, 2nd edn., Oxf. 1956.

(e) *Treatises*

(1) *Contemporary*

See also several titles under *Political Theory* (*infra,* pp. 137 ff.), and Ch. X, *Scholarship.* The following titles are arranged in rough chronological order by date of publication or the life of the author.

797 RALEIGH, SIR WALTER. The prerogative of Parliaments in England: proved in a dialogue . . . between a councillor of state and a justice of peace . . . Midelburghe. 1628.

798 [ANON.] Privileges and practice of Parliaments in England. 1640.

Repub. in slightly altered form, 1680.

799 MAY, THOMAS. The history of the Parliament of England which began November 3, 1640, with a short and necessary view of some precedent years. 1647.

Based on newspaper and official manifestos. For estimate see *D.N.B.,* sub May. Repr. with an appendix of documents, by F. Maseres, 1812, later edn. Oxf. 1854. This last edn. restored the original text which Maseres amended. See also no. 1578 n.

800 TWYSDEN, SIR ROGER. The commoners liberty: or the English-Mans birthright. 1648.

801 COTTONI POSTHUMA: divers choice pieces of that renowned antiquary, Sir Robert Cotton. Ed. by J. Howell. 1651. Later edns. 1672. 1679. 1884.

A collection of tracts. See also William Prynne's *Plea for the House of Lords, or a short . . . vindication of the judiciary and legislative power* . . . 1648, later edn., 1658.

802 HOBART, JOHN. 'Letters concerning the dissolution of Cromwell's last Parliament, 1658.' Ed. by C. H. Firth. *E.H.R.* 7 (1892), 102–10.

From correspondence of Hobart among Tanner MSS. in Bodleian Library.

803 ELSYNGE, HENRY. The ancient method and manner of holding Parliaments in England. 1660. 3rd edn. 1675.

An account of established parliamentary procedure: drawn largely from the *Modus tenendi Parliamenti,* 1659, but (especially in the edn. of 1675) with much new matter.
    See Elsynge's notes on debates, and the commentary, probably by him, on procedures in the Lords in his own day (nos. 838, 839). His *Methods of passing bills in Parliament,* 1685, is repr. in *Harleian* (59), vol. v. For procedures on special subjects see below (pp. 117–18), and see sections on the separate houses.

804 SELDEN, JOHN. Of the judicature in Parliaments, a posthumous
treatise: wherein, the controversies and precedents belonging to that title, are
methodically handled [? 1681].

805 HALE, MATTHEW. The jurisdiction of the Lords House, or Parliament
considered according to ancient records. Ed. by F. Hargrave. 1796.

Hale died in 1676. *The original institution, power and jurisdiction of Parliaments*, 1707,
bears Hale's name also, but his authorship is doubtful. Sir John Pettus's *Constitution
of Parliaments in England deduced from the time of King Edward the Second, illustrated
by King Charles the Second* (1661–79), 1680, is incomplete and deals only with the
Lords.

806 SOME CONSIDERATIONS upon the question whether the Parliament
is dissolved by prorogation for fifteen months. 1676.

Probably by Denzil Holles, possibly by H. Cary (H.M.C., 9 II, p. 69). Among the
numerous pamphlets relating to the dissolution question, in addition to those reporting
debates (see nos. 843, 872), are the following: *Reasons to prove the last prorogation of the
Parliament illegal*, 1676 (pr. in Grey, iv. 57–8) and Cobbett, iv. 816; [Marvell?], *A
seasonable question . . .*, 1676 (pr. in the Thompson edn. of Marvell's *Works*, ii. 523–54);
Vox populi [*sic*], [1677?], pr. in H.M.C , 9 II, 70; Marchamont Nedham's reply for the
court in answer to the above, *A second packet of advices*, 1677; *The grand question
concerning the prorogation of this Parliament for a year and three months*, 1676, possibly
by Holles (abstr. in H.M.C., 9 II, 70–3); and *The question is, whether a prorogation . . .
be not . . . dissolution*, 1676 (pr. in Grey, iv. 55–7, and Cobbett, iv. 813–15).

807 [SHERIDAN, THOMAS.] A discourse of the rise and power of Parliament. 1677.

Cf. T[heobald], F[rancis](?), *A discourse concerning the basis of government*, 1667.

808 PETYT, WILLIAM. The antient right of the commons of England
asserted. 1680.

Also by Petyt are: *Miscellanea Parliamentaria: containing presidents* (1) *of freedom from
arrests*, (2) *of censures . . .*, 1680; and *Jus Parliamentarium: or the ancient power, jurisdiction, rights and liberties . . . of Parliament*, 1739. Petyt kept records in the Tower and
collected many tracts. A list of the Petyt MSS., which are valuable for parliamentary
history, is in *Catalogue of the printed books and manuscripts in the library of the Inner
Temple*, 1833; they were reported on also by H.M.C., *Rep.* 2 (1871), pp. 151–6, and 11
(see no. 245).

809 [CARE, HENRY.] English liberties or the freeborn subject's inheritance.
Containing I. Magna Carta, the Petition of Right; the Habeas Corpus Act . . .
II. The proceedings in appeal of murther; the work and power of Parliament . . .
III. All laws against . . . dissenters. 1680. Later edns. 1691. 1719.

The 1719 edn. is considerably enlarged; another, brought out in 1766 by John Almon,
was entitled *British liberties*.

810 RYMER, THOMAS. Of the antiquity, power and decay of parliaments.
Being a general view of government, and civil policy in Europe. 1684. Later
edns. 1704. 1714.

Has been wrongly attributed to Sidney by Ralph (*Hist. of England*, 1744–6).

811 DUGDALE, SIR WILLIAM. A perfect copy of all summons of the nobility to the Great Councils and Parliaments of the realm (from 49 Henry III). 1685.

812 ATKYNS, SIR ROBERT. The power, jurisdiction and priviledge of Parliament; and the antiquity of the House of Commons asserted. 1689.

Atkyns, a judge, was the author of numerous pamphlets.

813 [SOMERS, JOHN LORD.] A vindication of the proceedings of the late Parliament of England, A.D. 1689 . . . 1690.

Attributed in some library catalogues to A. Sidney or William Jones.

814 A SHORT HISTORY of the Parliament. 1713.

This was attributed to Sir Robert Walpole. There were several edns. in 1713.

(2) *Later Works*

(a) General

815 HINTON, R. W. K. 'The decline of parliamentary government under Elizabeth I and the early Stuarts.' *Camb. Hist. Jour.* 13 (1957), 116–32.

Argues the greater activity of royal officials in this period. Cf. Weston (996), Willson (741), and C. Roberts (739).

816 KUEHNER, E. Ideen zur Parlamentsreform im England im 17. Jahrhundert. Freiburg. 1931.

817 KEMP, B. King and Commons 1660–1832. N.Y. 1957.

Lacks adequate documentation.

818 McILWAIN, C. H. The high court of Parliament. New Haven (Conn.) and Lond. 1910. Repr. 1934.

A classic stressing the judicial functions in earlier periods, but useful for background.

819 POLLARD, A. F. The evolution of Parliament. 1920. Amended 1926. Repr. 1934.

Useful especially for the historical development before 1603. Cf. W. Wilding and P. Laundy, *An encyclopaedia of Parliament*, N.Y. 1958, which, though modern, contains a good many articles of a historical nature.

820 THOMSON, M. A. 'Parliament and foreign policy, 1689–1714.' *History*, 38 (1953), 234–43.

Points out the growth of parliamentary responsibility in this area.

(b) Particular Periods

821 WALLACE, W. M. Sir Edwin Sandys and the first Parliament of James I. Phila. 1940.

Portion of a doctoral dissertation.

822   MOIR, T. L. The Addled Parliament of 1614. N.Y. 1958.

Scholarly; revised interpretation.

823   FULLER, M. B. In the time of Sir John Eliot: (1) Eliot and the case of John Nutt, a pirate. (2) The Parliament of 1621. (3) Negotium Posterorum and the Parliament of 1625. Northampton (Mass.). 1919.

Cf. H. Hulme, *The leadership of Sir John Eliot in the Parliament of 1626*, Chicago, 1932.

824   RELF, F. H. The Petition of Right. (University of Minnesota, Studies in the Social Sciences, no. 8.) Minneapolis. 1917.

Useful also as a guide to sources relating to the session of 1628. Cf. H. Hulme's summary of the debate of 3 May 1628 in *E.H.R.* 50 (1935), 302–6.

825   BRETT, S. R. 'The Long Parliament.' *Quart. Rev.* 275 (1940), 107–17.

Cf. E. A. McArthur, 'Women petitioners and the Long Parliament', *E.H.R.* 24 (1909), 698–709. A full examination of the sources regarding the expulsion of this Parliament is in the series of articles by C. H. Firth, *History*, 2, nos. 7 and 8 (1917–18), 129–43, 193–206. Some original documents relating to this event were published by Firth in *E.H.R.* 8 (1893), 526–7. See also W. Michael, 'Oliver Cromwell und die Auflösung des Langen Parlaments', *Historische Zeitschrift*, 63 (1889), 56–78; Glow (888); and Keeler (915).

826   GLASS, H. A. The Barebone Parliament and the religious movements of the 17th century culminating in the protectorate system of church government. 1899.

Cf. A. Woolrych, 'The calling of Barebone's Parliament', *E.H.R.* 80 (1965), 492–513.

827   ABBOTT, W. C. 'The Long Parliament of Charles II.' *E.H.R.* 21 (1906), 21–56 and 254–85.

Other articles relating to the period of Charles II are: L. F. Brown, 'The religious factors in the Convention Parliament', ibid. 22 (1907), 51–63; G. F. Trevallyn Jones, 'The composition . . . of the Presbyterian party in the Convention', ibid. 79 (1964), 307–54; A. Zimmermann, 'Karl II. und sein Konflikt mit seinem unduldsamen anglikanischen Parlament', *Historisches Jahrbuch*, 26 (1905), 549–66; C. E. Fryer, 'The royal veto under Charles II', *E.H.R.* 32 (1917), 103–11; D. T. Whitcombe, 'The Cavalier House of Commons: the session of 1663', *Bull. Inst. Hist. Research*, 32 (1959), 181–91; C. Robbins, 'The Oxford session of the Long Parliament of Charles II', ibid. 21 (1948), 214–24. See also C. Roberts, 'Sir Richard Temple's discourse on the Parliament of 1667–1668', *Hunt. Lib. Quart.* 20 (1957), 137–44; and C. Robbins, 'The repeal of the Triennial Act', ibid. 12 (1949), 121–40.

828   BATE, F. The declaration of indulgence 1672: a study in the rise of organised dissent, 1908. Bibl.

829   CHERRY, G. L. 'The role of the Convention Parliament (1688–89) in parliamentary supremacy.' *Jour. Hist. Ideas*, 17 (1956), 390–406.

Useful articles showing relationships between Parliament and the central administration on economic matters in the later years are by R. M. Lees (781 and 2158 n.).

(f) *Procedure: Sources and Later Works on Special Subjects*

830   ADAIR, E. R. and EVANS, F. M. G. 'Writs of assistance.' *E.H.R.* 36 (1921), 356–72.

Deals with the position of persons summoned to attend the House of Lords as assistants.

831 CLIFFORD, F. A history of private-bill legislation. 2 vols. 1885–7.

Useful also for local government. An excellent modern work is O. C. Williams, *Historical development of private bill procedure*, 2 vols., 1948–9.

832 HATSELL, J. Precedents of proceedings in the House of Commons. 4 vols. 1781. Later edns. 1785. 1796. 1818.

An early *Collection of the rights and priviledges of Parliament* was printed in 1642 (Wing). Sir T. E. May's *Treatise on the law . . . and usage of Parliament*, 1844, and later edns., 1893, 1924, has historical portions that are of some use.

833 WILLSON, D. H. 'Summoning and dissolving Parliament, 1603–25.' *A.H.R.* 45 (1940), 279–300.

See also *Elections, infra.*

834 WITTKE, C. History of English parliamentary privilege. Columbus. 1921.

Must be used with caution. Cf. A. S. Turberville, 'The "protection" of servants of members of Parliament', *E.H.R.* 42 (1927), 590–600; and G. W. Prothero, 'The parliamentary privilege of freedom from arrest, and Sir Thomas Shirley's case, 1604', with important documents, ibid. 8 (1893), 733–40.

2. HOUSE OF LORDS

(a) *Journals, Debates, Procedure*

(1) *General*

See also *Parliamentary Papers*, and H.M.C. (89, 162). The earliest private journals in print 1610 (ed. by E. R. Foster (857 n.)) and 1614 (in H.M.C., Hastings MSS., 1947 (155)).

835 JOURNALS of the House of Lords 1578–1714 [vols. 2–19]. 1767+.

Based on MS. Minutes, with records of bills, letters, and other business but not the debates after 1628; lists of peers present. Of particular value for the civil war period. There is also a single volume, extracted from the journals, *Compleat collection of all the standing orders of the House of Lords*, 1748.

836 ROGERS, J. E. T., ed. A complete collection of the protests of the Lords . . . with historical introductions. 3 vols. Oxf. 1875.

Also edited from the *Journals*; scholarly. Vol. i, 1624–1741. Cf. *A complete collection of protests made in the House of Lords . . . 1641–1737*, 1737, and a similar publication for 1641–1745, printed in 1745.

837 [TIMBERLAND, E., publ.] The history and proceedings of the House of Lords from . . . 1660 to the present time. 8 vols. 1741–2.

Vol. i covers 1660–97. Often referred to by the publisher's name.

(2) *Debates and Diaries of Particular Parliaments*

The order is roughly chronological. For 1610 see no. 857 n.

838 GARDINER, S. R., ed. Notes of the debates in the House of Lords, officially taken by Henry Elsing, clerk of the parliaments, A.D. 1621. Camden Soc. 1870.

Ed. from MSS. at Crowcombe Court once in the possession of Lieutenant-Col. Carew. Many gaps in this edition are filled by *Notes of the debates in the House of Lords officially taken by Robert Bowyer and Henry Elsing, 1621, 1625, 1628*, ed. by F. H. Relf, Camden Soc., 1929. Additional notes on 1621, taken by the earl of Huntingdon, were ed. by Lady de Villiers, *Camd. Soc. Misc.* xx (1953). For 1628 see also Relf's 'Debates in the House of Lords, 1628', *R.H.S. Trans.*, 4th Ser. 8 (1925), 38–55; and [H. Elsyng?], 'The moderne forme of the parliaments of England, with a foreword by C. S. Sims', *A.H.R.* 53 (1948), 288–305. See also no. 803.

839 GARDINER, S. R., ed. Notes of the debates in the House of Lords officially taken by Henry Elsing . . . 1624 and 1626. Camden Soc. 1879.

Also from Crowcombe Court MSS.

840 SCOBELL, HENRY. Remembrances of some methods, orders, and proceedings heretofore used and observed in the House of Lords, extracted out of the Journals of that House. 1657.

841 HOLLES, DENZIL. The grand question concerning the judicature of the House of Peers stated and argued, and the case of Thomas Skinner . . . 1669.

Vindicates jurisdiction of peers. Also by Holles, *The case stated of jurisdiction of the . . . Lords in the point of impositions*, 1676, which supports the Lords' claim to moderate, though not to institute or increase, rates on merchandise voted by the Commons.

842 A NARRATIVE of some passages in, or relating to, the Long Parliament. By a person of honour. 1670.

Attributed to Francis North, Lord Guilford. For the next year see *Lord Lucas's speech*, 1671 (repr. in *State tracts* (336), p. 454), which was widely circulated and ordered by the House to be burned.

843 TWO SPEECHES. I. The earl of Shaftesbury's speech . . . [20 Oct. 1675]. II. The D. of Buckingham's speech . . . [16 Nov. 1675]. Together with the protestation . . . the day the Parliament was prorogued, Nov. 22nd, 1675. Amsterdam [probably Lond.]. 1675.

Repr. in *State tracts* (336), pp. 57–64. Illustrates country party's manœuvres. Cf. *A letter from a person of quality, to his friend in the country*, 1675 (repr. in *State tracts*, pp. 41–56, and in Cobbett's *Parliamentary history*), which was probably written under Shaftesbury's supervision. In 1676 appeared an answer by Marchamont Nedham: *A pacquet of advices and animadversions, sent from London to the men of Shaftesbury*. For other pamphlets relating especially to the dissolution question see nos. 806, 872.

844 E., J. A narrative of the cause and manner of the imprisonment of the lords: now close prisoners in the Tower of London. Amsterdam [probably Lond.]. 1677.

Important on proceedings of February 1676/7.

845 SIMPSON, A. 'Notes of a noble lord, 29 January to 12 February, 1688/9.' *E.H.R.* 52 (1937), 87–97.

Bibliographical article, relating to notes (original lost) apparently by Henry Hyde, second earl of Clarendon.

846 AN ACCOUNT of the proceedings of the House of Peers upon the observations of the commissioners for taking, examining, and stating the publick accounts . . . together with the papers referred to in these proceedings. 1702.

847 THE PROCEEDINGS of the House of Lords concerning the Scottish conspiracy and the papers laid before that house by her majesties command relating thereunto. 1704.

848 THE REPORT of the Lords committees appointed to take into consideration the report of the commissioners . . . for . . . examining . . . the publick accompts . . . so far as relates to the accompts of . . . Edward earl of Orford, late treasurer of the navy. 1704.

(b) *Later Works*

849 COLLINS, A. Proceedings, precedents, and arguments, on claims and controversies, concerning baronies by writ and other honours. With the arguments of Sir F. Bacon . . . and others . . . Published from the manuscript collections of R. Glover . . . Sir W. Dugdale . . . and others. 1734.

Compare Dugdale (811).

850 DE BEER, E. S. 'The House of Lords in the Parliament of 1680.' *Bull. Inst. Hist. Research*, 20 (1943), 22–37.

851 FIRTH, C. H. The House of Lords during the civil war (1603–60). 1910.

Cf. Weston (996 n.).

852 MACQUEEN, J. F. A practical treatise on the appellate jurisdiction of the House of Lords and privy council. 1842.

Cf. T. Beven, 'The appellate jurisdiction of the House of Lords', *Law Quart. Rev.* 17 (1901), 155–70, 357–71.

853 PIKE, L. O. A constitutional history of the House of Lords. Lond. and N.Y. 1894.

Standard; valuable especially for the legal side.

854 TURBERVILLE, A. S. The House of Lords in the reign of William III. Oxf. 1913.

By same author: 'The House of Lords under Charles II', *E.H.R.* 44 (1929), 400–17; 45 (1930), 58–77; and *The House of Lords in the XVIIIth Century*, Oxf. 1927. See also W. S. Holdsworth, 'The House of Lords, 1689–1783', *Law Quart. Rev.* 45 (1929), 307–42, 432–58.

3. HOUSE OF COMMONS

(a) *Journals and Debates*

Various additional Commons debates in MS. are in the process of being edited by American scholars under the Yale University Diaries Project: those for 1610 by Elizabeth Read Foster (857 n.); those for 1624, 1626, and 1628, at the University of California, Los Angeles. Mark H. Curtis has worked on those for 1624. Many proceedings for the period of 1670–89 are in a Roger Morrice MS. (Dr. Williams's Lib.), which is to be edited by D. R. Lacey (Annapolis).

855   JOURNALS of the House of Commons 1547–1714 [vols. 1–17]. 17 vols. 1742+.

On the printing of the *Journals* see H. H. Bellot, *Bull. Inst. Hist. Research*, 11 (1933), 85–91. For each session after 1680 there are also less full *Votes of the House of Commons*. There are several general indexes, but none that are complete.

856   BOWYER, R. The parliamentary diary of Robert Bowyer, 1606–1607. Ed. by D. H. Willson. Minneapolis. 1931.

857   GARDINER, S. R., ed. Parliamentary debates in 1610 ... from the notes of the House of Commons. Camden Soc. 1862.

From Br. Mus. Add. MS. 4210, with illustrative papers from Harleian and Lansdowne MSS. Included in H.M.C., *MSS. of House of Lords*, xi (N.S.), Addenda 1514–1714, ed. by M. F. Bond (1962), pp. 117–25, is 'Ewens's draft journal of 1610'. The latter was mentioned but incorrectly described in *3rd Rep.*, App., p. 12. Cf. E. R. Foster, ed., *Proceedings in Parliament 1610*, 2 vols., New Haven (Conn.), 1966, a work of major importance; vol. i, The Lords; vol. ii, The Commons.

858   NOTESTEIN, W., RELF, F. H., and SIMPSON, H., eds. Commons debates, 1621. 7 vols. New Haven. 1935.

A scholarly edition of several texts of diaries and accounts dealing with this Parliament. See also the earlier *Proceedings and debates* . . . by [Edward Nicholas], edited by T. Tyrwhitt, 2 vols., 1766. Some of Nicholas's notes among the State Papers are mentioned in *C.S.P. Dom., 1619–23*, and some of his notes on the 1624 Parliament are referred to, ibid. *1623–4*.

For useful review articles on the edition by Notestein *et al.*, see Sir W. Holdsworth in *Law Quart. Rev.* 52 (1936), 481–93; and C. H. McIlwain in *J.M.H.* 9 (1937), 206–14.

859   GARDINER, S. R., ed. Debates in the House of Commons in 1625, edited from a MS. in the library of Sir Rainald Knightley, bart. Camden Soc. 1873.

From MSS. at Fawsley, Northants. Notes by Richard Knightley, M.P., an active opponent of the Court. See also 'Draft journal and committee book, 1625', ed. by M. F. Bond, in H.M.C., *MSS. of House of Lords*, xi (N.S.), Addenda 1514–1714 (1962), pp. 177–207.

860   ARCHBOLD, W. A. J. 'A diary of the Parliament of 1626.' *E.H.R.* 17 (1902), 730–7.

Gives extracts from diary in Camb. Univ. Library (MSS. DD. 12, 20–2). Writer possibly Bulstrode Whitelocke. Cf. Lonsdale MSS. (176) for parliamentary diaries 24 April–12 June 1626, 4–26 June 1628, 20 Jan.–25 Feb. 1629.

861   NOTESTEIN, W. and RELF, F., eds. The Commons' debates for 1629. Minneapolis. 1921.

Prints the *True relation*, the notes of Sir Edward Nicholas (from S.P. Dom. Chas. I, see *C.S.P. Dom., 1628–9*, pp. 31, 466), and the diary of Sir Richard Grosvenor. The excellent introduction deals with sources of the debates of the House of Commons in the first half of the century. Versions of the *True relation* for the 1629 session were printed as *The diurnall occurrences ... in parliament ... which ended 10 March ... 1628*,

1641; and Sir T. Crew, *The proceedings and debates . . . 20 Jan.–10 March 1628 . . .*, ed. by J. Parkhurst, 1707. See also E. Hughes, 'A Durham manuscript of the Commons debates of 1629', *E.H.R.* 74 (1959), 672–9.

862 NOTESTEIN, W., ed. The journal of Sir Simonds D'Ewes. New Haven (Conn.). 1923.

An important journal (3 Nov. 1640–20 March 1641) derived from Br. Mus. Harl. MSS. 162, 164, and 165, and collated with several other diaries of the Long Parliament. A second, though not consecutive volume of D'Ewes's *Journal*, ed. by W. H. Coates, New Haven, 1942, covers the period of 12 Oct. 1641–10 Jan. 1642; an appendix describes the various issues of *Diurnal occurrences* relating to the period covered. A microfilm copy of the D'Ewes MSS. is in the Folger Shakespeare Library. See also important notes kept by Dering, Northcote, Palmer, and Verney (nos. 863, 864). Printed speeches were collected as *Speeches and passages of this great and happy Parliament* [3 Nov. 1640–June 1641], 1641.

863 LARKING, L. B., ed. Proceedings, principally in the county of Kent in connection with the parliaments called in 1640 and especially with the committee of religion. Camd. Soc. 1862.

From Sir Edward Dering's papers. Informative on elections and on discussions of the Laudian regime. Useful for the early days, 3 Nov.–18 Dec. 1640, and 4 Jan. 1641, are the notes of Geoffrey Palmer, ed. from a Camb. Univ. Lib. MS. (Nk. 6. 38) by W. A. J. Archbold, in *E.H.R.* 16 (1901), 730–73. The *Notebook of Sir John Northcote* (M.P. for Ashburton, Devon), ed. by A. H. A. Hamilton, 1877, relates to the period of 24 Nov. to 28 Dec. 1640; included from the Northcote family MSS. also are memoranda pertaining to the session 18 May–21 June 1661.

864 BRUCE, J., ed. Verney papers: Notes of proceedings in the Long Parliament temp. Charles I . . . from memoranda . . . by Sir Ralph Verney. Camd. Soc. 1845.

An important diary, the notes extending from Dec. 1640 to 27 June 1642, with a document of uncertain date in an app. See H.M.C. (229).

865 RUSHWORTH, J. The tryal of Thomas, Earl of Strafford (1641) . . . 1680.

Based mainly on notes taken by Rushworth, as he daily attended the trial. Cf. Abraham Wright, *Novissima Straffordii*, ed. by P. Bliss and B. Bandinel, Roxburghe Club: Historical Papers, 1846; and S. R., *A briefe and perfect relation of the answers and replies of Thomas Earle of Strafford*, 1647, which is of greater value than Wright.

866 FORSTER, J., ed. The debates on the Grand Remonstrance (Nov.–Dec. 1641) . . . with an introductory essay. 1860.

Strong parliamentary bias, although based upon MSS. in P.R.O., D'Ewes's *Journal* (Harl. MSS.), and various printed materials; should be compared with H. L. Schoolcraft, *The genesis of the Grand Remonstrance*, Urbana, 1902, although this is almost entirely from the printed sources then available; and W. H. Coates, 'Some observations on "The Grand Remonstance"', *J.M.H.* 4 (1932), 1–17. J. Forster wrote also *Arrest of the five members by Charles the First*, 1860.

867 RUTT, J. T., ed. Diary of Thomas Burton Esquire, member in the Parliaments of Oliver and Richard Cromwell [1656–1659] . . . with an introduction containing an account of the Parliament of 1654. 4 vols. 1828.

From Burton's notebooks now in Br. Mus. (Add. MSS. 15859–64) and Goddard's Journal (Add. MSS. 5138).

868   MARGOLIOUTH, H. M., ed. The poems and letters of Andrew Marvell. 2 vols. Oxf. 1927. 2nd enl. edn. 2 vols. Oxf. 1952.

Important letters (vol. ii) written to Hull on parliamentary proceedings, 1660–78. In the earlier edition by A. B. Grosart of Marvell's *Complete works*, 4 vols., s.l., 1872–5, the letters are in vol. ii. Two additional Marvel letters were publ. by C. Robbins in the *Times Literary Supplement*, 15 Dec. 1958 and 20 Mar. 1959. On a source used for the *Parliamentary history* (790) for this period see C. Robbins, 'Seymour Bowman, M.P., diarist of the Convention of 1660', *N. & Q.* 196, no. 3, 3 Feb. 1951; also see her edition of five speeches by Sir John Holland, 1661–3, in *Bull. Inst. Hist. Research*, 28 (1955), 189–202. See also ibid. 29 (1956), 244–52, and the memoranda of 18 May 1661–21 June 1661 in Northcote (863 n.).

869   DEBATES of the House of Commons from the year 1667 to the year 1694, collected by Hon. Anchitel Grey [M.P. for Derby]. 10 vols. 1763.

A very valuable collection. Two smaller but important diaries of the period of Charles II are: *The diary of John Milward . . . September, 1666 to May, 1668*, edited by C. Robbins, Camb. 1938; and *The parliamentary diary of Sir Edward Dering, 1670–1673*, edited by B. D. Henning, New Haven, 1940.

870   PROCEEDINGS in the House of Commons touching the impeachment of Edward, late earl of Clarendon . . . 1667. With many debates and speeches . . . 1700.

An important collection, apparently made at the period, and widely circulated in MS.; used in Cobbett's *Parliamentary history*, vol. iv. See the article by C. Roberts on the impeachment in *Camb. Hist. Jour.* 13 (1957), 1–18.

871   A RELATION of the most material matters handled in Parliament: relating to religion, popery, and the liberty of the subject. [London? possibly Holland.] 1673.

Proceedings on various days in Feb., March, Oct., and Nov. 1673, together with various lists; written by a country-party extremist; repr. in *State tracts* (336), pp. 26–36. Other notes on proceedings, 29 March and 20 Oct.–4 Nov. 1673, are in *Votes and addresses of the honourable House of Commons . . . 1673, concerning popery and other grievances*, 1673; for the 1673/4 session, reports of political proceedings, with texts of various bills, are in *A journal of the proceedings of the House of Commons the last session* [7 Jan. 1673/4–24 Feb. 1673/4] *. . . printed at Rome . . . at the request of . . . the duke of York.* [Probably Holland.] 1674.

872   TWO SEASONABLE DISCOURSES concerning this present Parliament. Oxf. 1675.

Reports, probably by Shaftesbury, of the debate of 20 Nov. 1675, giving the arguments for dissolution. This may have been published with T. E., *A letter from a Parliament man . . . concerning the proceedings . . . begun the 13th of October 1675*, s.l., 1675, which gives the composition of the House. The first is in Cobbett, iv, app. vi and vii; both are repr. in *State tracts* (336), pp. 65–9. For satirical lists of members, both possibly by Marvell, see *Seasonable argument* (Amsterdam, 1677/8; pr. in Cobbett and in Thompson edn. of *Works*); and *Flagellum parliamentarium* [1672?], ed. by H. Nicholas from Br. Mus. Lansdowne MS. 805, fols. 83–9, in 1827; repr. in Aungervyle Soc. Reprints, 1st Ser., Edin. 1881–2.

For other comments on the dissolution question see Marvell and nos. 806, 843.

873   MARVELL, A. The growth of popery. 1677.

A more or less accurate report of the debates of the spring of 1676–7. Repr. in *State tracts* (336). On the following year, see *A collection of some memorable and weighty transactions in Parliament in the year 1678, and afterwards, in relation to the impeachment of Thomas, earl of Danby, 1695.*

874 AN EXACT COLLECTION of the debates of the House of Commons held at Westminster October 21, 1680 . . . with the debates . . . at Oxford. 1689.

Included with other matter on 1685 in *A Faithful register . . .*, 1689. See also *Historical collections, or a brief account of the most remarkable transactions of the Parliament* [1681], 1689. There is an interesting diary for December, 1680, in the Beaufort MSS., H.M.C., *12th Report*, app. ix, 98–115 (82).

875 DEBATES AT LARGE, between the House of Lords and House of Commons . . . 1688 [1689]. 1695. 2nd edn. corr. 1710.

A third edn. (1714), was entitled *The parliamentary right of the crown of England asserted.* See also the notes by Lord Somers on debates of 1689 in vol. ii of Hardwicke, *Miscellaneous state papers* (258). The Bill of Rights and other materials relating to 1689 are repr. in *The judgment of whole kingdoms* (982 n.).

876 A COLLECTION of the debates and proceedings in Parliament in 1694 and 1695 upon the inquiry into the late briberies and corrupt practices. s.a.

For note on committees, 1697–8, 1698–9, see no. 884.

877 [DRAKE, JAMES.] The history of the last Parliament began at Westminster the tenth day of February . . . 1700[–1]. 1702.

Cf. *A state[ment] of the proceedings . . . with relation to the impeached lords . . .*, 1701, which is a report from the journals, printed by order of the House.

878 MACKWORTH, HUMPHREY. Free Parliaments: or a vindication of the fundamental right of the Commons to be sole judges of all those privileges of the electors and the elected. 1704.

Relates to a disputed election at Aylesbury. An abstract, first pr. in 1705, is repr. in the 1751 and 1809 edns. of *Somers Tracts*. On Mackworth (M.P. 1701–13) see an article by M. Ransome, *Univ. Birmingham Hist. Jour.* I (1948), 232–54. Also pertaining to the first Parliament of Anne, and printed by House order is *The bill entitled an act for preventing occasional conformity . . . and the reports of several conferences . . . and the proceedings thereupon*, 1702.

879 REPORT of the commissioners for taking examinations and stating the public accounts of the kingdom with examinations and depositions relating thereunto. 1711.

(b) *Procedure*

(1) *General*

880 CAMPION, G. F. M. Introduction to the procedure of the House of Commons. 1929. 2nd edn. 1947. Repr. with corr. 1950. Bibl.

This is a handbook on modern practice, but the first chapter is on historical development. Also modern, but with useful background material, is J. Redlich, *The procedure of the House of Commons . . .* tr. from the German by A. S. Steinthal, 3 vols., 1908. See also Chand er (789 n.) and Hatsell (832).

881   SCOBELL, H. Rules and customs which by long practice have obtained the name of orders of the House . . . Dublin. 1692.

Cf. Scobell's 'Memorials of the manner of passing bills' in *Miscellania parliamentaria,* 1685; and G[eorge] P[etyt], *Lex Parliamentaria, a treatise on the laws and customs of Parliament,* 1690, 1707. See also pp. 114–16 *supra.*

(2) *The Speaker and Other Officials*

882   [HAKEWILL, WILLIAM.] ' "The Speaker of the House of Commons", with a foreword by C. S. Sims.' *A.H.R.* 45 (1939), 90–5.

883   DASENT, A. I. The Speakers of the House of Commons from the earliest times . . . Lond. and N.Y. 1911.

Useful, though popular in style. Cf. M. MacDonagh, *The Speaker of the House,* 1914; and A. Manning, *The lives of the Speakers of the House of Commons,* 1850. On the privy councillors in the House see Willson (741).

884   WILLIAMS, O. C. The clerical organization of the House of Commons. N.Y. 1954.

See also the brief monograph by Williams, *The officials of the House of Commons,* 1909; and his edn. of the minute book of James Courthope, a clerk (1697–8 and 1698–9) in *Camd. Soc. Misc.* xx (1953).

(3) *Division Lists*

885   BROWNING, A. and MILNE, D. J., eds. 'An Exclusion Bill division list.' *Bull. Inst. Hist. Research,* 23 (1950), 205–25.

See also R. R. Walcott, ed., 'Division lists of the House of Commons, 1689–1715', ibid. 14 (1936), 25–36.

(c) *Later Works*

There is no complete study of the Commons for this period. Porritt (890) provides much general information, and Notestein (889) draws conclusions that are significant on the work within the House. On matters of patronage, and control, in addition to the titles here, see also *Elections, Lists of Members,* and *Privy Council.*

886   BROWN, L. F. 'Ideas of representation from Elizabeth to Charles II.' *J.M.H.* 11 (1939), 23–40.

Cf. R. L. Bushman, 'English franchise reform in the seventeenth century', *Jour. Brit. Studies,* 3 (1963), 36–56.

887   CRISSEY, M. H. and DAVIES, G. 'Corruption in Parliament, 1660–1677.' *Hunt. Lib. Quart.* 6 (1942), 106–14.

Many of the patterns of court patronage in the period of Elizabeth described in Sir John Neale's Raleigh lecture, *The English political scene,* 1948 (repr. from *Proc. Brit. Academy,* 34 (1948), 97–117) appear in the seventeenth century.

888   GLOW, L. 'The committee of safety.' *E.H.R.* 80 (1965), 289–313.

Valuable article dealing with a committee that assumed executive responsibility. Cf. Notestein (729). Also by Glow, 'Pym and Parliament' (324 n.); and 'The manipulation of committees in the Long Parliament, 1641–1642', *Jour. Brit. Studies,* 5 (1965), 31–52.

889 NOTESTEIN, W. 'The winning of the initiative by the House of Commons.' *Proc. Brit. Acad.* 11 (1924–5), 125–75. Repr. 1926 and 1949.

Supersedes earlier interpretations, as in R. G. Usher, *The institutional history of the House of Commons 1547–1641*, Washington Univ. Studies 11, 1924.

890 PORRITT, E. and PORRITT, A. G. The unreformed House of Commons: parliamentary representation before 1832. 2 vols. Camb. 1903. 1909.

Vol. i, England and Wales; vol. ii, Scotland and Ireland. A standard work, still of great value, though it should be supplemented by the use of recent studies on numerous details.

891 VILLIERS, E. DE. 'Parliamentary boroughs restored by the House of Commons, 1621–41.' *E.H.R.* 68 (1952), 175–202.

A careful study, supporting the view of pressure for seats being exercised by politically active classes. Cf. V. F. Snow, 'Parliamentary reapportionment proposals in the Puritan revolution', ibid. 74 (1959), 409–42.

892 WITMER, H. E. The property qualifications of the House of Commons: a history of the Qualifications Act of 1710. N.Y. 1943. Bibl.

Mostly modern, but with two chapters on 1710 background. On the related subject of salaries for members earlier in the Stuart period see R. C. Latham, 'Payment of parliamentary wages—the last phase', *E.H.R.* 66 (1951), 27–50.

(d) *Elections*
(1) *General*
(a) Sources

893 PRYNNE, WILLIAM. A brief register, kalendar, and survey . . . of parliamentary writs. 4 vols. in 3. 1659–64.

894 BOHUN, W., ed. A collection of debates, reports, orders, and resolutions of the House of Commons, touching the right of electing members to serve in Parliament for the several counties, cities, boroughs, and towns corporate in England and Wales. 1702.

'Most of the cases reported fall within the years 1674–1700': Gross, *A bibliography of British municipal history* (3102), p. 61, where there is a list of the boroughs concerned.

895 [CAREW (THOMAS).] An historical account of the rights of elections of the several counties, cities, and boroughs of Great Britain; collected from public records and the journals of Parliament to . . . [1754]. 1755.

'For the period covered [c. 1600–1754] this is the most exhaustive parliamentary history of boroughs': Gross, p. 62, where there is a list of the boroughs concerned. Very useful for 1624 is John Glanville, *Reports of certain cases, determined and adjudged by the Commons in Parliament, in the twenty-first and twenty-second years of the reign of King James the First*, ed. by J. Topham, 1775.

896 ALL THE PROCEEDINGS in relation to the Aylesbury men committed by the House of Commons and the report of the Lords journal and reports of the conferences. 1704 (1705?).

Cf. *Ashby and White: or the great question whether an action lies at common law for an elector, who is deny'd his vote for members of Parliament?* s.l., 1705.

(b) Later Works

897 CHERRY, G. L. 'Influence of irregularities in contested elections upon election policy during the reign of William III.' *J.M.H.* 27 (1955), 109–24.

898 OLDFIELD, T. H. B. The representative history of Great Britain and Ireland. 6 vols. 1816.

This supersedes the same author's *An entire and complete history of the boroughs of Great Britain*, 3 vols., 1792.
    Cf. Robert Brady, *An historical treatise of cities and burghs*, 1690, 2nd edn. 1704; and B. Willis, *Notitia Parliamentaria* (914).

899 ROWE, V. A. 'The influence of the earls of Pembroke on parliamentary elections, 1625–41.' *E.H.R.* 50 (1935), 242–56.

Cf. L. Stone, 'The electoral influence of the second earl of Salisbury, 1614–68', ibid. 71 (1956), 384–400.

900 SACRET, J. H. 'The restoration government and municipal corporations.' *E.H.R.* 45 (1930), 232–59.

Deals with interference by the government with the freedom of borough elections. See the articles by R. H. George on the 1688 charters and the Bill of Rights as they relate to borough elections, ibid. 55 (1940), 47–56, and *A.H.R.* 42 (1937), 670–9.

(2) *Particular Elections*

901 WRIGHT, T. The case between Sir Francis Goodwin and Sir John Fortescue, 1604, as it shows upon the journals of the House of Commons. 1778.
Hargrave's *State trials*, vol. vii. See also M. E. Bohannon, 'The Essex election of 1604', *E.H.R.* 48 (1933), 395–413.

902 FARNHAM, E. 'The Somerset election of 1614.' *E.H.R.* 46 (1931), 579–99.
Cf. T. L. Moir, 'The parliamentary elections of 1614', *The Historian*, Spring 1954.

903 ATKINSON, W. A. 'A parliamentary election in Knaresborough in 1628.' *Yorks. Arch. Jour.* 34 (1939), 213–21.

904 KERSHAW, R. N. 'The elections for the Long Parliament, 1640.' *E.H.R.* 38 (1923), 496–508.

A continuation is this author's 'The recruiting of the Long Parliament 1645–7' in *History*, 8 (1923), 169–79. See also M. R. Frear, 'The election at Great Marlow in 1640', *J.M.H.* 14 (1942), 433–48; and A. H. Dodd, 'The Caernarvonshire election dispute of 1640–41 and its sequel', *Bull. Board Celtic Studies*, 14 (1950), 42–5, as well as a previous article by Dodd, ibid. 12, 44–8.

905 DAVIES, G. 'The election of Richard Cromwell's Parliament, 1658–9.' *E.H.R.* 53 (1948), 488–501.

906 MUKERJEE, H. W. 'Elections for the Convention and Cavalier Parliaments.' *N. & Q.* 166 (1934), 398–403, 417–21.

Useful, though not always reliable on identifications. Also relating to this period are: K. G. Feiling, 'A letter of Clarendon during the elections of 1661', *E.H.R.* 42 (1927),

407–8; C. Robbins, ed., 'Election correspondence of Sir John Holland . . . [1667]', in *Original Papers* publ. by Norfolk and Norwich Arch. Soc. 21, ii (1950); G. Davies, 'The by-election at Grantham, 1678', *Hunt. Lib. Quart.* 7 (1944), 179–82; and documents on Aldborough elections, 1660–90, edited by J. W. Walker in *Yorks. Arch. Jour.* 34 (1938), 25–34.

907 LIPSON, E. 'The elections to the Exclusion Parliaments 1679–1681.' *E.H.R.* 28 (1913), 59–85.

Compare a supplementary article by M. D. George, ibid. 45 (1930), 552–78; 'The Essex petition of 1679–80', edited by W. G. Benham in *Essex Rev.* 43 (1934), 193–203; and O. W. Furley, 'The Whig exclusionists: pamphlet literature . . . 1679–81', *Camb. Hist. Jour.* 13 (1957), 19–36. Useful documents and comments on the 1681 elections appear in C. S. Emden, *The people and the constitution*, 1933.

908 GEORGE, R. H. 'Parliamentary elections and electioneering in 1685.' *R.H.S. Trans.*, 4th Ser. 19 (1936), 167–95.

Cf. C. H. Josten, 'Elias Ashmole and the 1685 Lichfield election . . .', *Hist. Coll. Staffs.* (1950–1), pp. 215–27.

909 PLUMB, J. H. 'The elections to the Convention Parliament of 1689.' *Camb. Hist. Jour.* 5 (1937), 235–54.

See also his dissertation, 'Elections to the House of Commons in the reign of William III' (*Camb. Univ. Abstr. of Diss., 1935–36* (1937), 70–1).
On the Cirencester election of 1695 three letters edited by A. L. Browne are in *Bristol and Glouc. Arch. Soc. Trans. for 1935*, 57 (1936), 269–74.

910 BROWNE, A. L., ed. 'Lord Halifax and the Malmesbury election in 1701.' *Wilts. Arch. and Nat. Hist. Mag.* 47 (1936), 500–3.

See also G. Davies, 'The election at Hereford in 1702', *Hunt. Lib. Quart.* 12 (1949), 322–7; and 'A Norfolk poll list, 1702', in *Norfolk Rec. Soc.* 8 (1936), 41–70.

911 SYKES, N. 'The cathedral chapter of Exeter and the general election of 1705.' *E.H.R.* 45 (1930), 260–72.

912 MORGAN, W. T. 'An 18th century election in England, 1710.' *Political Science Quart.* 37 (1922), 585–604.

See also M. E. Ransome, 'The general election of 1710', *Bull. Inst. Hist. Research*, 17 (1939), 95–7, and 'The press in the general election of 1710', *Camb. Hist. Jour.* 6 (1939), 209–11, and another article by her in *E.H.R.* 56 (1941), 76–89; also, C. R. Hudleston and R. Austin, 'Gloucestershire voters in 1710', *Bristol and Glouc. Arch. Soc. Trans. for 1936*, 58 (1937), 195–205.
On the parliamentary career of an individual see M. Ransome's article on Sir Humphrey Mackworth in *Univ. of Birmingham Hist. Jour.* 1 (1948), 232–54.

(e) *Lists of Members*
(1) *Lists of Members by Parliaments*

913 RETURN OF THE NAMES of every member returned to serve in each Parliament. 2 vols. 1878.

Pr. from writs and returns in the P.R.O. The indexes, publ. *c.* 1891, contain valuable addenda et corrigenda. Commonly called *Official returns of members of Parliament.* Cf. W. W. Bean, *The parliamentary returns of members of the House of Commons, c.* 1883. See also *Interim report of the committee on the House of Commons personnel and politics, 1264–1832*, H.C. 1931–2 (Cmd. 4130), x. 545, with bibl.

914 WILLIS, BROWNE. Notitia Parliamentaria. 3 vols. 1715–50.

Vols. i and ii deal with parliamentary representation in a very detailed way, taking the
counties alphabetically, but reaching only as far as Durham. Vol. iii gives brief notes
for cities sending members to Parliament, and lists of speakers and M.P.s from 1542
to 1660. Useful, but often unreliable. Useful also is *The Parliamentary register containing lists of the 24 Parliaments from 1660 to 1714*, 1741, with a valuable preface added
in the second edition. Among the Thomason Tracts (58) are various lists of M.P.s for
particular Parliaments or years in the 17th century.

    Cf. J. Foster, 'Members of Parliament . . . 1529–1881', in *Collectanea Genealogica*,
2 (1883), which gives biog. sketches for those whose names begin with A; and the
frequent notes and answers by W. D. Pink in the historical magazines of various
counties. For a description of Pink MS. notes, now in the John Rylands Library,
Manchester, see page 11 of the *Interim report* (913).

915 KEELER, M. F. The Long Parliament, 1640–1641 : a biographical study
of its members. Phila. 1954.

Includes biographical sketches of the original members, with evidence on their social
background. An important work, supplementing and extending the study for the
whole period of the Parliament, is D. Brunton and D. H. Pennington, *Members of the
Long Parliament*, Camb. 1954. See also V. F. Snow, 'Attendance trends . . . in the
Long Parliament', *Hunt. Lib. Quart.* 18 (1955), 301–6, and G. Davies and E. L. Klotz,
'List of members expelled from the Long Parliament', ibid. 2 (1939), 479–88. By Davies
and Klotz also, 'Membership in Richard Cromwell's Parliament', ibid. 6 (1943), 219–20.

916 REX, M. B. University representation in England, 1604–1690. With a
preface by R. L. Schuyler. Lond. and N.Y. 1954.

Definitive treatment of the unusual constituency.

(2) *Lists by County and Borough*

917 BEAN, W. W. The parliamentary representation of the six northern
counties of England . . . and their cities and boroughs (1603–1886). With lists
of members and biographical notices. Hull. 1890.

To be used with caution.

    Biographical notes on the members of several counties have been published in county
magazines, such as J. J. Alexander's notes on Devon M.P.s, C. H. Hunter Blair's notes
for Northumberland, and H. T. Weyman's for Shropshire. See *Interim report* (913).

    For lists of members, arranged according to constituencies and usually with some
biographical data, see the following:

Lists for Counties

Cambridge. D. Cook. A dissertation summarized in *Bull. Inst. Hist. Research*, 15
    (1937), 42–4.
Cornwall. W. P. Courtney, 1889. Contains data regarding borough influences, but not
    full biographical data. Cf. W. T. Lawrance, Truro [1925]; A. de C. Glubb, Truro,
    1934.
Cumberland. R. S. Ferguson, *Cumberland and Westmorland M.P.s*. Lond. and
    Carlisle. 1871.
Gloucester. W. R. Williams. Hereford. 1898. Biog. data.
Hereford. W. R. Williams. Brecknock. 1896.
Kent. J. Cave-Brown, in *Archaeologia Cantiana*, 21 (1895), 198–243.
Lancashire. W. D. Pink and A. B. Beaven. 1889. Cf. W. R. Williams, *Official lists*,
    Brecon, 1901.
Northamptonshire. E. G. Forrester. 1941. Deals with elections, 1695–1882.
Oxfordshire. W. R. Williams. Brecknock. 1899.

Somerset. S. W. Bates Harbin. Taunton. 1939. See parts previously publ. in *Somerset Arch. Soc. Proc.* 80 (1935).
Staffordshire. J. C. Wedgwood. 2 vols. William Salt Soc. 1919–20. A later vol. deals with 1714–.
Surrey. J. E. Smith. 1927.
Sussex. W. D. Cooper. Lewes. 1834. Not infallible.
Wales. W. R. Williams. Brecknock. 1895. Cf. A. H. Dodd, in *Trans. Soc. Cymmr.* 1942 (1944), 8–72.
Wiltshire. F. H. Manley, in *Wilts. Arch. and Nat. Hist. Soc. Mag.* 47 (1935), 177–264; and R. G. Stuckey, ibid. 54 (1951–2), 289–304. See also W. B. Crouch, on Cricklade borough members, published by the Cricklade Historical Soc., Minety, 1949.
Worcestershire. W. R. Williams. Hereford. 1897.
Yorkshire. A. Gooder. *York. Arch. Soc. Rec. Ser.*, 2 vols., Wakefield, 1935–8; and the earlier and less reliable work by G. R. Park, Hull, 1886.

Lists for Boroughs

Bewdley (P. Styles, in *Univ. of Birmingham Hist. Jour.* 1 (1947), 92–133); Coventry (T. W. Whitley, Coventry, 1894); Helston (H. S. Toy in *E.H.R.* 46 (1931), 452–7); Honiton (W. H. Wilkin in *Devon. Asso. Rep. and Trans.* 66 (1934), 253–78); Horsham (W. Albery, Lond., N.Y., and Toronto, 1927); Preston (W. Dobson, 1856; 1868); Reading (A. Aspinall *et al.*, 1962); Rochester (F. F. Smith, 1933).

4. POLITICAL PARTIES

(a) *Sources*

918 HONESTY'S BEST POLICY; or penitence the sum of prudence: Being a brief discourse in honour of the Right Honourable Anthony Earl of Shaftsbury's humble acknowledgment and submission for his offences . . . (25 Feb. 1677/8). [1678].

Satirical advice to Shaftesbury. Important account of the rise of the country party. See also a court–party satire on the country party and the Scottish Covenanters entitled, *A letter from Amsterdam to a friend in England*, 1678.

(b) *Later Works*

919 ABBOTT, W. C. 'The origin of English political parties.' *A.H.R.* 24 (1919), 578–602.

See also G. M. Trevelyan's 1926 lecture, 'The two-party system in English political history', printed in his *Autobiography and other essays*, 1949.

920 BROWNING, A. 'Parties and party organization in the reign of Charles II.' *R.H.S. Trans.*, 4th Ser. 30 (1948), 21–36.

The best analysis for the period. Cf. E. S. de Beer, 'Members of the court party, 1670–8', *Bull. Inst. Hist. Research*, 11 (1933), 1–23; J. R. Jones, 'Court dependents in 1664', ibid. 34 (1961), 81–91; and various lists of members compiled for Danby's purposes in the third volume of Browning's biography (433). Other lists have been printed, for 1679, in *Bull. Inst. Hist. Research*, 30 (1957), 232–41, and for 1688–1715, ibid. 14 (1936), 25–36 and 19 (1942), 65–6. See also ibid. 23 (1950) 205–25 for a division on the Exclusion Bill. See also *Flagellum parliamentarium* (872 n.).

921 FEILING, K. A history of the Tory party 1649–1714. Oxf. 1924.

Outstanding. Supersedes similar works by C. B. R. Kent, 1908, and M. Woods, 1924; and the older G. W. Cooke, *The history of party*, vol. i, 1666–1714, 1836. An attempt to give 'the people's idea of politics' is G. B. Hertz [Hurst], *English public opinion after the restoration*, 1902.

922   JONES, J. R.   The first Whigs: The politics of the exclusion crisis, 1678–1683. Oxf. 1961.

Good analysis. See the same author's article on Norfolk Whigs in *Durham Univ. Jour.*, N.S. 15, pp. 13–21. Cf. Ronalds (365).

923   MITCHELL, W. M.   The rise of the revolutionary party in the English House of Commons. [1603–1629.] N.Y. 1957.

Draws chiefly upon *Journals*, and is somewhat inconclusive. See also articles by T. K. Rabb on Sir Edwin Sandys in 1604, *A.H.R.* 69 (1964), 646–70; by J. N. Ball on Eliot in 1625 in *Bull. Inst. Hist. Research*, 28 (1955), 113–27; and by I. H. C. Fraser on 1629 events, ibid. 30 (1957), 86–95. See also Hexter (324) and Keeler (915).

924   MORGAN, W. T.   English political parties and leaders in the reign of Queen Anne 1702–1710. New Haven. 1920. Bibl.

Based on much research. Cf. Morgan's 'The ministerial revolution of 1710 in England', *Pol. Sci. Quart.* 36 (1921), 184–210, and 'Eighteenth-century election in England' (1710), ibid. 37 (1922), 585–604. See also W. F. Lord, 'The development of political parties during the reign of Queen Anne', *R.H.S. Trans.*, N.S. 14 (1900), 69–121, and Salomon (381 n.).

925   WALCOTT, R.   English politics in the early eighteenth century. Oxf. and Camb. (Mass.). 1956.

Centres about the period 1701–2. See the useful earlier study of the lower house by Walcott, 'English party politics (1688–1714)' in *Essays in . . . honour of W. C. Abbott*, 1941. See also C. Robbins, 'Discordant parties', *Pol. Sci. Quart.*, Dec. 1958. Useful for the era of Bolingbroke is K. Kluzen, *Das Problem der politischen Opposition*, Munich, 1956.

926   WILLSON, D. H.   'The earl of Salisbury and the "court" party in Parliament, 1604–1610.' *A.H.R.* 36 (1931), 274–94.

Emphasizes the declining influence of privy councillors. Cf. L. Stone, 'The electoral influence of the 2nd earl of Salisbury, 1614–68', *E.H.R.* 71 (1956), 384–400.

927   YULE, G.   The Independents of the English civil war. Camb. 1958.

Concerned with political activity as well as religious views. Cf. H. R. Trevor-Roper, 'Oliver Cromwell and his Parliaments', in *Essays presented to Sir Lewis Namier* (ed. by R. Pares and A. J. P. Taylor), 1956, which deals with the problem of managing Parliaments. See also Hexter (324), and Hexter's article in *A.H.R.* 44 (1938–9), 29–49.

E. LOCAL GOVERNMENT

The study of local government, as well as of other aspects of local history, has attracted increased attention in recent years. Of great importance has been the publishing of official records, which are invaluable for their revelations of many aspects of community life as well as of local government. The standard work on local government is by the Webbs (930).

The guides to local history, especially nos. 3102–4, are useful for local government. See also the guide, *County Records*, compiled by F. G. Emmison and

I. Gray (Historical Assoc., Ser. 3), 1948; and the valuable guides to materials on the justices of the peace by B. H. Putman, *Bull. Inst. Hist. Research*, 4 (1926), 144–56, and T. G. Barnes and A. H. Smith, ibid. 32 (1959), 221–42. For lists of printed texts and calendars, especially those by local societies, see the subject index in Mullins (23 n.) *sub* 'Sessions records', 'Borough records', etc. For the lord lieutenant and county military organization see Read (11 n.), pp. 108–9.

See also *Local History*, *Military History* (especially for committees of the civil war period), H.M.C., and Ch. IX, *Social Problems*.

1. Manuscripts

Manuscript materials for the study of local government are abundant, and are to be found not only in localities but in the P.R.O., the Br. Mus., and other libraries. The State Papers contain much correspondence relating to military as well as civil matters. A few examples of local collections are: Manuscript records of quarter sessions of Cheshire from 1559 (the Castle, Chester); Devon minute books from 1592 (Castle at Exeter); Essex session rolls (calendared) and sessions papers (Shire Hall, Chelmsford); Norfolk (Shire Hall, Norwich); Nottinghamshire minute books from 1603 (Shire Hall, Nottingham); Lindsey (Lincolnshire) sessions records (Shire Hall, Lincoln); Wiltshire sessions records (Devizes); Huntingdonshire (Br. Mus. Add. MSS. 34300–400).

The manuscript records of most of the cities and towns are described in H.M.C. *Reports*, pp. 24–5. Examples of the records of parish officials at the P.R.O. are State Papers 16, CXVIII, CCCXCV, and CCCLXXXVIII; at the Br. Mus., Add. MSS. 10457, 34400, 36981. Of accounts of bridgewardens a good collection is in the Essex MSS. in the Chelmsford Shire Hall. For churchwardens' accounts see Ch. XI, *Diocese and Parish*.

2. General Works

928　BARNES, T. G. Somerset 1625–1640: a county's government during the 'personal rule'. Camb. (Mass.). 1961.

Valuable local study. Cf. R. G. H. Whitty, *The court of Taunton in the 16th and 17th centuries*, Taunton, 1934.

929　HURSTFIELD, J. 'County government c. 1530–c. 1660.' *V.C.H. Wilts.* v (1957), 80–110.

930　WEBB, S. and B. English local government from the revolution to the municipal corporations act, 1689–1885. 9 vols. 1906–29.

The standard work. Includes separate descriptions of 'The parish and county'; 'The manor and borough'; 'The King's highway'; 'Statutory authorities for special purposes', as well as volumes on community problems. A good report on local institutions in the earlier part of the century is in vol. ii of E. P. Cheyney, *History of England from the defeat of the Armada to the death of Elizabeth*, 2 vols., N.Y., 1914–26; 1948.

931　WILLCOX, W. B. Gloucestershire: a study in local government, 1590–1640. New Haven. 1940.

Excellent monograph based on a wide variety of records of a single county. Cf. J. J. G. Taylor, 'The civil government of Gloucester, 1640–6', *Trans. Bristol and Glouc. Arch. Soc.* 67 (1949), 59–118; and Dowdell (938).

3. The Shires

(a) *Military Affairs*

932 HARLAN, J., ed. The Lancashire lieutenancy under the Tudors and Stuarts. 2 vols. Chetham Soc. 49–50. 1859.

Documents, chiefly from the Shuttleworth MSS. at Gawthorpe Hall, illustrative of civil and military government. Less on the seventeenth than on the sixteenth century.

933 MILITIA ROLL from Pirehill hundred (*c.* 1685). *Hist. Coll. Stafford-shire*, 1941, pp. 116–24.

See ibid. 1931, pp. 284–5, for a list of deputy lieutenants, 1689.

934 THOMSON, G. S., ed. The Twysden lieutenancy papers, 1583–1668. (Kent Arch. Soc., *Records* 10.) Ashford. 1926.

A good comment on the sources appears in the same author's *Lords lieutenant in the sixteenth century*, 1923. Cf. Thomson's article in *E.H.R.* 40 (1925), 351–74; and A. Clark, 'A lieutenancy book of Essex (1608–1639)', *Essex Rev.* 17 (1908), 157–69.

935 WAKE, J., ed. A copy of papers relating to musters, beacons, subsidies, &c. in . . . Northampton, A.D. 1586–1623. Northampton Rec. Soc. 3. Peterborough. 1926.

Papers of the deputy lieutenant. Useful intro. by J. E. Morris. See also Wake's edn. of *The Montagu musters books*, 1602–23, Northampton Rec. Soc. 7, Peterborough, 1935.

(b) *Quarter Sessions*

Some titles relating to quarter sessions are included in the chapter on *Local History*, under the individual counties. Useful introductions are provided with many editions of the printed records.

(1) *Printed Sources*

936 COUNTY OF BUCKINGHAM: calendar to the sessions records (1678–1718). Ed. by W. Le Hardy and G. Reckitt. 4 vols. Aylesbury. 1934–51.

One of the increasing number of printed records (see Mullins, 23 n., and Ch. XI). Among them the best are:

Cheshire. *Quarter sessions and other records* (1559–1760), ed. by J. H. E. Bennett and J. C. Dewhurst, Rec. Soc. Lancs. and Ches., 94 (1940); *Charges to the grand jury (1660–1677)*, ed. by E. M. Halcrow, Chetham Soc., 3rd Ser. 5, 1953. The records are described in *Jour. Chester and N. Wales Arch., Arch. and Hist. Soc.*, N.S. 32 (1937), 53–63.

Hertfordshire. *Hertfordshire county records*, ed. by W. Le Hardy, 9 vols., Hertford, 1905–39, including Notes and extracts from the sessions rolls (1581–1894), vols. i–iii, 1905–10; and Calendar of the sessions books, vols. iv–ix (1619–1833), 1905–39. Vols. v–vi include 1619–1700.

Lancashire. *Lancashire quarter sessions records*, vol. i, Quarter sessions rolls, 1590–1606, ed. by J. Tait, Chetham Soc. 77 (1917); *Lancashire quarter sessions* [Manchester], vol. i, 1616–1622/3, ed. by E. Axon, Rec. Soc. Lancs. and Ches. 42 (1901).

Lincoln. *Minutes of proceedings in quarter sessions held for the parts of Kesteven in the county of Lincoln, 1674–1695,* ed. by S. A. Peyton, 2 vols. Lincoln Rec. Soc. Publ. 25–6 (1931).

Middlesex. *Middlesex county records,* ed. by J. C. Jeaffreson and W. Le Hardy, 7 vols., Middlesex County Rec. Soc., 1886–92, 1935–7. Excerpts from the sessions records of the 17th century are in vols. ii–iv of the first series; vols. i–iii of the later series are calendars for 1612–16. See also W. J. Hardy, ed., *Calendar of sessions books, 1689–1709,* 1905.

Norfolk. *Norfolk quarter sessions order book, 1656–57,* ed. by D. E. H. James, Norfolk Rec. Soc. Publ. 26 (1955).

Northamptonshire. *Quarter session records of the county of Northampton,* 2 vols. (1586–1623; 1630, 1657–8), ed. by J. Wake, Northamp. Rec. Soc. 1924–6.

Nottinghamshire. *Nottingham county records. Notes and extracts . . . of the 17th century,* ed. by H. H. Copnall, Nottingham, 1915.

Shropshire. *Shropshire county records. Orders of the Shropshire quarter sessions* (1638–1782), ed. by R. L. Kenyon and O. Wakeman, 2 vols. (vols. 14 and 17), s.l., s.a.

Somerset. *Quarter sessions records for the county of Somerset* (1607–77), ed. by E. H. Bates-Harbin and M. C. B. Dawes, 4 vols., Somerset Rec. Soc. 23–4, 28, 34 (1907–19); also T. G. Barnes, ed., *Somerset assize orders, 1629–1640,* ibid. 65 (1959).

Staffordshire. *Staffordshire quarter sessions rolls* (1603–1609), by S. A. H. Burne and D. H. G. Salt, 2 vols., Staff. Rec. Soc. 1940–9 (1950). For earlier vols., 1581–1602, see Read (11 n.), no. 1303.

Surrey. *Surrey quarter sessions records: order book and sessions rolls* (1659–88), ed. by H. Jenkinson and D. L. Powell, 4+ vols., Surrey Rec. Soc. Publ., 1934–51+.

Sussex. *Quarter sessions order book, 1642–1649,* ed. by B. C. Redwood, Sussex Rec. Soc. Publ. 54 (1954).

Warwickshire. *Warwick county records: quarter sessions order books* (1625–90), ed. by S. C. Ratcliff and H. C. Johnson, 8 vols., Warwick County Council, 1935–53.

Worcestershire. *Worcester county records: quarter sessions rolls, 1591–1643,* ed. by J. W. Willis-Bund, Worc. Hist. Soc. 1899–1900.

Yorkshire. *West Riding sessions records* (1597/8–1642), ed. by J. Lister, 2 vols., Yorks. Arch. Soc., Rec. Ser. 3, 54 (1888–1915); [*North Riding*] *quarter sessions records,* ed. by J. C. Atkinson, 9 vols., North Riding Rec. Soc. 1–9 (1884–92).

937 SHEPPARD, WILLIAM. Survey of the county judicatures commonly called the county court, hundred court, and court baron. 1656.

(2) *Later Works*

938 DOWDELL, E. G. A hundred years of quarter sessions: the government of Middlesex from 1660 to 1760. Camb. 1932.

A useful monograph. Still useful also is A. H. A. Hamilton, *Quarter sessions from Queen Elizabeth to Queen Anne,* 1878, which deals chiefly with Devon. See also Holdsworth (1024).

939 FURLEY, J. S. Quarter sessions government in Hampshire in the seventeenth century. Winchester. 1937.

Articles relating to the county courts are T. H. Lewis, 'Attendance of justices and grand jurors at the courts of quarter sessions, 16th to 18th century', *Trans. Soc. Cymmr.* 44 (1942), 108–22; and W. B. Willcox, 'Lawyers and litigants in Stuart England: a county sample', *Cornell Law Quart.* 24 (1939), 533–56.

(c) *Justices of the Peace*

In addition to the titles below, there are useful titles on the office in the sixteenth century, as well as general studies of the development of the office, in Read (11 n.), pp. 109–10. Some are listed in Webb (930), vol. i, p. 295 n. See also *The Stiffkey papers* (3217).

940 DALTON, MICHAEL. The countrey justice, containing the practice of the justices of peace out of their sessions. Enl. edn. 1622. Later edns. 1630. 1661. 1705.

Earlier edns. were in 1618 and 1619.

941 WINGATE, EDMUND. Justice revived being the whole office of a country justice of the peace. 1661.

942 SHEPPARD, WILLIAM. Whole office of the country justice of the peace. 1650. 1652.

Describes the duties and some of the problems likely to be encountered. In his *New survey of the justice of the peace his office*, 1659, Sheppard urged improvements. He wrote also *A sure guide for his majesties justices of peace*, 1663. See also Joseph Keble, *An assistance to justices of peace*, 1683.

943 GRETTON, M. S. Oxfordshire justices of the peace in the seventeenth century. Oxf. 1934 [1935].

Oxfordshire Rec. Soc. Publ. 16. Contains a calendar of quarter sessions records, 1687–9.

(d) *Sheriffs, Constables, and Other Officers*

Titles in addition to those below are given in Holdsworth (1024), vi. 692–3.

(1) *Sources*

944 LAMBARD, WILLIAM. The duties of constables, borsholders, tything-men and such other lowe ministers of the peace. 1602.

First publ. in 1582, this manual went through ten editions in the seventeenth century. See also William Sheppard, *Offices and duties of constables*, 1641. R. S. France ed. a useful 'High constable's register, 1681', *Trans. Lancs. Ches. Hist. Soc.* 107 (1956), 55–87.

945 WILKINSON, JOHN. A treatise ... concerning the office and authoritie of coroners and sherifes ... court leet, court baron, hundred court, etc. 1618. 1628. 1638.

Useful.

946 DALTON, MICHAEL. The office and authoritie of the sherifs. Gathered out of the statutes, and bookes of the common lawes of this kingdome. 1623. 1682. 1700.

The classical description.

947 LIST OF SHERIFFS, for England and Wales, from the earliest time to 1831. *P.R.O. Lists and indexes*, no. 9 (1898).

Invaluable. There are various local lists in Gross (3102). One for Lincolnshire was printed in a supplement to *Lincs. N. & Q.* 24 (1936).

948　KARRAKER, C. H. The seventeenth-century sheriff: a comparative study of the sheriff in England and the Chesapeake colonies, 1607–1689. Chapel Hill. 1930.

Well documented. For a comment on appointment of sheriffs see J. S. Wilson, 'Sheriffs' rolls of the sixteenth and seventeenth centuries', *E.H.R.* 47 (1932), 31–45.

949　WELLINGTON, R. H. The king's coroner, being a complete collection of statutes relating to the office, together with a short history of the same. 2 vols. 1905–6.

4. Courts Leet, Baron, Manorial Courts

On manorial courts see also Ch. VIII, nos. 1911, 1917, 1919. See also Ch. IV, nos. 1090–3.

950　THE ORDER of keeping a court leet and a court baron . . . Pr. by Thomas Wight. 1603. Later edn. 1625.

A standard work, which originated about 1506 as *Modus tenend' cuȓ baroñ.*

951　A BRIEFE DECLARATION for what manner of speciall nusance concerning private dwelling houses, a man may have his remedy by assise, or other action. . . . 1636. 1639.

Includes also comments on customs of towns, on application of statute law in parishes, and on the powers of churchwardens and constables.

952　SHEPPARD, WILLIAM. The court-keeper's guide. 1641. 1656 and other later edns. to 1791.

A popular manual for stewards of manors. Of a similar type are Jonas Adams, *The order of keeping a court leet and a court baron*, 1641, 1650 (earlier edns., 1593, 1615); Sir William Scroggs, *The practice of courts leet and courts baron*, 1702, 1728; and Giles Jacob, *The compleat court keeper, or land steward's assistant*, 1713, 1715, later edns.

953　GREENWOOD, WILLIAM. The authority, jurisdiction and method of keeping county courts, courts leet, courts baron . . . 1668. 1730.

See also David Jenkins, *Pacis consultum; a directory to the publick peace*, 1657, in which various types of local courts are described.

5. Cities, Boroughs, and Parishes

Ch. XI, *Local History*, should be examined for references to particular towns, especially for published records of corporations and parishes. See also Webb (930).

954　MELLOWS, W. T., ed. Peterborough local administration, 1541–1689: Parochial government from the Reformation to the Restoration. Northamp. Rec. Soc. 10. 1937.

Documents illustrating land management and other aspects of administration. See also a study of the accounts of the officials of Ayleston, in *Linc. Arch. and Arch. Soc.* 38 (1926), 106–65.

955   PAPE, T. The Restoration government and the corporation of Newcastle-under-Lyme. Manchester. 1940.

Cf. R. Austin, 'The city of Gloucester and the regulation of corporations, 1662–63', *Bristol and Glouc. Arch. Soc. Trans.* 58 (1937), 257–74; and R. H. George, 'The charters granted to English parliamentary corporations in 1688', *E.H.R.* 55 (1940), 47–56.

956   PARSLOE, C. G. 'The corporation of Bedford, 1647–64.' *R.H.S. Trans.*, 4th Ser. 29 (1947), 151–65.

Deals with the pre-restoration trend toward democratic local government. See also no. 3125 n. For other articles on developments in towns see: P. Styles on Bewdley (*Univ. of Birmingham Hist. Jour.* 1 (1947–8), 92–133); M. C. Wren on London (*Econ. Hist. Rev.*, 2nd Ser. 1 (1948), 46–53); A. B. Clarke on Nottingham mayors (*Thoroton Soc. Trans.* for 1937, 35–75); H. Beaumont on Shrewsbury (*Shrops. Arch. and Nat. Hist. Soc. Trans.* 52 (1947), 79–113).

957   WEINBAUM, M., ed. British borough charters, 1307–1660. 1943.

F. POLITICAL THEORY

The Stuart succession and the later events of the century provided occasion for much speculation about the nature of government. There was first the elaboration and later the decline of the theory of the divine right of kings. During the civil war and the interregnum emerged the wave of democratic or radical movements, toward which recent scholarship has increasingly turned its attention. The theory of sovereignty as enunciated by Hobbes, and afterwards the theories by which the power of the monarch might be limited, particularly as expressed by Locke, represent further important contributions of the seventeenth century to political thought. The idea of political liberty, related to greater freedom in religion and in the social sphere, claimed attention especially in the revolutionary periods. The partisan views of royal power, aided by an eager search into the history of institutions, and taking form eventually in a Whig or a Tory interpretation, make manifest likewise an awakened political consciousness.

Of the works relating to divine right, the chief ones are James I (959), Filmer (975), and Figgis (983). On sovereignty, the treatises of Hobbes (968) overshadow all others. The democratic ideas as set forth in the hundreds of pamphlets of the fourth and fifth decades and the army debates (see *Clarke Papers* [308]), are illustrated in Haller (960), Lilburne (962), Winstanley (966), or Vane (972), and have received able comment in Gooch (984), Laski (984 n.), Pease (990), and Zagorin (997). On theories concerning the limits on kingly power, in addition to the works of Locke (978), valuable modern comments will be found in Judson (988), Robbins (992), and Sabine (993).

In addition to the works listed in this section, others related to political theory will be found in *Political History*; *Political Biography* (e.g. Warwick, no. 519); *Ecclesiastical History*; *Legal History*; and *Military History* (the standing-army issue, no. 1526).

1. SOURCES

The arrangement is generally chronological by date of publication, rather than alphabetical, in order that relationships with political developments may more easily be traced.

958 FORSETT, EDWARD. A comparative discourse of the bodies natural and politique wherein . . . is set forth the true forme of a commonweale. 1606.

The author's later work, *A defence of the right of kings*, 1624, was dedicated to James I.

959 JAMES I. Workes. 1616. The Political Works. Ed. by C. H. McIlwain. Camb. (Mass.). 1918.

See no. 461. His *Basilicon Doron*, written in 1598 for the instruction of Prince Henry, was ed. by J. Craigie, 2 vols., Edin. 1944–50, bibl.; cf. Craigie's bibliographical article in *The Library*, 5th Ser. 3 (1948), 22–32; and his article on political poems by James, *S.H.R.* 29 (1950), 134–42.

960 HALLER, W., ed. Tracts on liberty in the Puritan revolution, 1638–1647. 3 vols. N.Y. 1934.

See also W. Haller and G. Davies, eds., *The Leveller tracts, 1647–1653*, N.Y. 1944; and D. M. Wolfe, ed., *Leveller manifestoes of the Puritan revolution*, N.Y. 1944; repr. N.Y. 1967. Haller's interpretative volume, *Liberty and reformation in the Puritan revolution*, N.Y. 1955, should be compared with Solt, *Saints in arms* (332).

961 DIGGES, DUDLEY. The unlawfulnesse of subjects taking up arms against their soveraigne in what case soever. 1643.

Other pamphlets by this royalist advocate of passive obedience, are listed in Wing, D 1454–1467A. See also the royalist arguments of Bishop Henry Ferne in pamphlets such as *The resolving of conscience*, Camb. 1642; *A reply unto several treatises pleading for the armes*, Oxf. 1643 (see Wing, F 786–806); Philip Hunton, *A treatise of monarchie* . . ., 1643, defending mixed monarchy (cf. C. H. McIlwain's article in *Politica*, 1 (1935), 243–73); and Michael Hudson, *The divine right of government natural and politique*, 1647. For later defenders of monarchy see Gee (971).

962 LILBURNE, JOHN. The legall fundamental liberties of the people of England revived, asserted, and vindicated. 1649.

For the numerous other tracts by this celebrated Leveller see Gibb (468); numerous excerpts are printed in H. W. Wolfram's article on Lilburne in *Syracuse Law Review*, 3 (1952), 213–58. See also Haller (960) and Frank (990 n.). Richard Overton, who assisted with the publication of some of Lilburne's tracts, was the author of other Leveller pamphlets, such as *Articles of high treason*, 1642, *A remonstrance of many thousand citizens*, 1646 (repr. in vol. iii of Haller's *Tracts on liberty*), and others which are listed by Firth in his article on Overton in *D.N.B.*, and in Wing, O 618–636. Overton, and a third important Leveller, William Walwyn, are dealt with also by Frank.

963 WILDMAN, JOHN. The case of the army truly stated. 1647.

Other works by this spokesman for the Levellers are listed in Wing (W 2167–2173), including especially his *Putney projects*, 1647. For recent editions see Woodhouse, *Puritanism and liberty* (308 n.). Cf. Frank, *The Levellers* (990 n.), and Solt (332).

964 BACON, NATHANIEL. An historical discourse of the uniformity of the government of England. 2 vols. in one. 1647–51.

In the nature of a constitutional history, anti-royalist in tone. An edition of 1665 was repressed, but was reissued in 1689.

965 ASCHAM, ANTONY. A discourse: showing what is particularly lawful . . . 1648.

The first of several tracts by Ascham dealing with the transfer of allegiance from a sovereign. See Wing, A 3919–3924. His *Seasonable discourse* . . . was reprinted in 1689. In 1650 he replied to criticisms from Dr. Hamond and Dr. Sanderson.

966 WINSTANLEY, GERRARD. Works. Ed. by G. H. Sabine. Ithaca. 1941.

Excellent edition with valuable intro. Cf. L. Hamilton's edn. of *Selections from the works of Gerrard Winstanley*, 1944. An example of the Digger movement, Winstanley has received much attention from Marxist historians. Cf. D. W. Petegorsky's study, *Left-wing democracy in the English civil war*, 1940; his article in *Science and Society*, 6 (1942), 111–32; and article by W. S. Hudson in *J.M.H.* 17 (1946), 1–21.

967 MILTON, JOHN. The readie and easie way to establish a free commonwealth, and the excellence thereof compared with the inconveniences and dangers of readmitting kingship in this nation. 1660.

See also *Defense, Eikonoklastes,* and nos. 478, 2634. A reply to Milton is G.S. (971 n.). On Milton's political thought, A. Barker deals with *Milton and the Puritan dilemma, 1641–1660*, Toronto, 1942; cf. D. M. Wolfe, *Milton in the Puritan revolution*, N.Y. 1941. Comparisons are made by A. K. Hesselberg, *A comparative study of the political theories of Ludovicus Molina, S.J., and John Milton*, Washington, 1952; and R. Mohl, *Studies in Spencer, Milton, and the theory of monarchy*, N.Y. 1949. Useful articles are: D. M. Wolfe, 'Milton, Lilburne, and the people', *Mod. Philology*, 31 (1934), 253–72; G. F. Sensabaugh, 'Milton in the revolution settlement', *Hunt. Lib. Quart.* 9 (1946), 175–208, and 'Milton and the doctrine of passive obedience', ibid. 13 (1949), 19–54; also by Sensabaugh, *That grand Whig, Milton*, Stanford, 1952. His views on Christian liberty are discussed by A. Sewell in *Mod. Lang. Rev.* 30 (1935), 13–18, and by H. J. C. Grierson, ibid. 39 (1944), 97–107.

968 HOBBES, THOMAS. Leviathan, or the matter, forme, and power of a commonwealth ecclesiastical and civil. 1651. Many later edns. Ed. by A. R. Waller. Camb. 1904. Ed. by W. G. Pogson Smith. Oxf. 1909.

Cf. *The English works of Thomas Hobbes, now first collected*, edited by W. Molesworth, 11 vols., 1839–45 (see also his *Behemoth*, no. 304). Hobbes's famous treatise in defence of absolutism based on natural law provoked numerous criticisms in his own period. Examples are George Lawson, *An examination of the political part of Mr. Hobbes his Leviathan*, 1657 (see Wing, L 705–12); William Lucy, *Observations . . .*, 1663; Clarendon, *A brief view and survey*, Oxf. 1676, repr. in his *Miscellaneous works*, 1727, 1751. A useful recent study is J. Bowle, *Hobbes and his critics*, 1951. Lives of Hobbes have been written by G. C. Robertson, Edin. 1886, L. Stephen, 1904, and J. Laird, 1934. On his life and thought see F. Tönnies, *Thomas Hobbes Leben und Lehre*, Stuttgart, 1896, 3rd edn., 1925; his *Thomas Hobbes der Mann und der Denker*, Osterweick, 1912; L. Strauss, *The political philosophy of Hobbes*, Oxf. 1936; and H. Warrender, *The political philosophy of Hobbes*, Oxf. 1957. The article by W. R. Sorley in *Camb. Hist. Eng. Lit.* vii (1911), 312–44, contains a bibl. See also *C.B.E.L.*

969 NEDHAM, MARCHAMONT. The excellencie of a free state. 1656. Repr. 1767.

Nedham published in 1650 *The case of the commonwealth stated*, and was a frequent contributor to *Mercurius Politicus*. On Nedham's influence see Robbins (992).

970 HARRINGTON, JAMES. Commonwealth of Oceana. 1656. Later edn. by John Toland [with life and other works]. 1700. Ed. by H. Morley. 1883. Ed. by S. B. Lilijegren. Heidelberg. 1924.

A valuable recent interpretation is C. Blitzer, *An immortal commonwealth: the political thought of James Harrington*, New Haven, 1960, bibl. Blitzer also edited selections from Harrington's *Political Writings*, N.Y. 1956. Cf. H. F. Russell Smith, *Harrington and his Oceana*, Camb. 1914; J. W. Gough, 'Harrington and contemporary thought', *Pol.*

Sci. Quart. 45 (1930), 395–404; and R. H. Tawney, *Harrington's interpretation of his age*, 1942 (Raleigh Lecture, 1941, also pr. in *Proc. Brit. Acad.* 27 (1941), 199–224).

971 GEE, EDWARD. The divine right and originall of the civill magistrate from God. 1658.

Written by a Presbyterian divine to express his dissatisfaction with the Commonwealth. Another important criticism of the Commonwealth was William Sancroft, *Modern policies taken from Machiavel . . .*, [? Lond.,] 1653 (repr. from the 7th edn., 1657, in D'Oyley (1278) and in Somers Tracts, vol. vii, 1809 edn.). See also such well-known tracts in defence of kingship in the period 1649–79 as G. S., *The dignity of kingship asserted*, 1660, which has been attributed to Gilbert Sheldon, but in its latest edn. (W. R. Parker, N.Y. 1942), to George Starkey, author of *Royal and other innocents bloud*, 1660; and *The common interest of king and people*, 1677, 1678, by John Nalson, the historian and royalist pamphleteer (see no. 291). See also Filmer (975).

972 VANE, HENRY. The trial of Sir Henry Vane. 1662.

Vane's republican views are clearly stated in 'The people's case stated', which is included in the papers relating to his trial and execution, and is repr. in J. Forster's *Sir Henry Vane the younger* (Lives of . . . British statesmen, vol. iv). See also Vane's speech, *Healing question propounded*, 1656 (repr. in Somers Tracts, vol. vi, and Forster); his printed speeches, his reply to *Oceana* in a letter to Harrington, and other works are listed in C. H. Firth's article on Vane in *D.N.B.* and in the biography by J. Willcock, 1913, appendix. For other lives see no. 515.

973 WHITELOCKE, BULSTRODE. Notes upon the king's writ for choosing members of Parlement, 13 Charles II, being disquisitions on the government of England by King, lords, and commons. Ed. by C. Morton. 2 vols. 1766.

974 MARVELL, ANDREW. The complete works in prose and verse of Andrew Marvell, M.P. . . . Ed. by A. B. Grosart. 4 vols. 1872–5.

Among Marvell's most influential political tracts are *The rehearsal transposed*, 1672, a plea for liberty of conscience; *Account of the growth of popery and arbitrary government*, Amsterdam, 1677 (repr. in State Tracts), 1689, 1693; and *A seasonable argument . . . for a new Parliament*, Amsterdam, 1677 (with a list of 'labourers' for arbitrary power). On Marvell's political thought see P. Legouis, *André Marvell, poète, Puritaine, patriote*, Oxf. 1928, and Fink and Robbins (992). Cf. A study by D. M. Schmitter (microfilm), Ann Arbor, 1955. See also nos. 868, 2632.

975 FILMER, SIR ROBERT. Patriarcha and other political works of Sir Robert Filmer. Ed. by P. Laslett. Oxf. 1949.

The first collection of Filmer's political writings. The most influential, *Patriarcha*, though first publ. in 1680, and frequently reprinted, had been written long before, possibly in the late 1630s. His *Freeholders grand inquest . . .*, first publ. 1648, was reissued in 1679. The publication of Filmer's Tory pamphlets at the time of the exclusion controversy, was followed by Brady (*infra*), and provoked several notable Whig replies. Cf. P. Laslett, 'Sir Robert Filmer: the man versus the Whig myth', *William and Mary Quart.* 5 (1948), 523–46.

976 BRADY, ROBERT. The great point of succession discussed and particular answer to the late pamphlet entitled a brief history of the succession . . . 1681.

The historian's contribution to Tory defence of the hereditary right of succession, replying to John, Lord Somers (977 n.). Cf. J. G. A. Pocock's article on Brady in

Camb. Hist. Jour. 10 (1951), 186–204. See also John Nalson, *The king's prerogative,* 1680; and Sir George Mackenzie, *Jus regium or . . . monarchy . . . maintain'd . . .* Edin. 1684.

977   SIDNEY, ALGERNON. Discourses concerning government published from the author's original manuscript. 1698.

Posthumous publication of the work written shortly after the publ. of Filmer, in reply to his argument (see also no. 509). Also arguing against the Tory views on the exclusion question were John, Lord Somers, *A brief history of the succession to the crown of England,* 1680 (repr. 1689); and Henry Neville, *Plato redivivus* (349). Sir James Tyrell, who published *Patriarcha non monarcha* in 1681, extended his views after 1688 into a valuable statement of the Whig case, *Bibliotheca politica: or an enquiry . . . wherein all the chief arguments as well against as for the late revolution are . . . considered,* 1694, later edn., 1727.

978   LOCKE, JOHN. The works of John Locke. 3 vols. 1714. 8th edn. (with life) by E. Law. 4 vols. 1777. 12th edn. 9 vols. 1824.

Locke's important *Two treatises of government,* 1689, which because of the publication date have generally been treated as written to justify the revolution, have been shown by recent scholarship to belong to Locke's thought of 1679–80, and therefore replying to the arguments of Filmer and others of that period; see P. Laslett's critical edition of the *Two treatises,* Camb. 1960, and his article in *Camb. Hist. Jour.* 12 (1956), 40–55. On Locke's political thought see Sir F. Pollock and A. C. Fraser in *Proc. Brit. Acad.,* 1903–4, pp. 221–49; S. P. Lamprecht, *The moral and political philosophy of John Locke,* N.Y. 1918; W. Kendall, *John Locke and the doctrine of majority rule,* Urbana, 1941; J. W. Gough, *John Locke's political philosophy,* 1950; and R. H. Cox, *Locke on war and peace,* N.Y. 1960. The lives by Peter, Lord King, 1829 (3rd edn., 1858), and H. R. Fox Bourne, 2 vols., 1876, are largely superseded by Cranston (2701 n.); these should be supplemented with T. Forster's edn. of *Original letters of Locke, Algernon Sidney, and Anthony, Lord Shaftesbury,* 1830 (2nd edn., 1847), and B. Rand, ed., *Correspondence of John Locke and Edward Clark* (1682–1704), 1927. For bibl. see W. R. Sorley in *Camb. Hist. Eng. Lit.* viii (1912), pp. 328–48; and H. O. Christopherson, *Bibliographical introduction to the study of John Locke,* Oslo, 1930. See also Ch. X (nos. 2701, 2946); and titles in Walcott's bibl. article in *A.H.R.* 67 (1962), 364–5.

979   HALIFAX, GEORGE SAVILE, MARQUIS OF. Complete works. Ed. by Sir W. Raleigh. Oxf. 1912.

See also no. 452. Chief works are *Character of a trimmer,* 1688, many edns.; *Anatomy of an equivalent,* 1688; *Letter to a dissenter,* 1687; and *Character of King Charles II, and reflections,* 1750. Cf. L. Stapleton, 'Halifax and Raleigh', *Jour. Hist. Ideas,* 2 (1941), 211–24.

980   MOLESWORTH, ROBERT (later Viscount). An account of Denmark as it was in the year 1692. 1694. Later edns.

Probably in print by December, 1693. Based upon the author's observations while serving as envoy to the Danish government, which is portrayed as arbitrary and tyrannical, the *Account* was virtually a political tract reflecting Molesworth's strong Whig views on liberties, both political and religious. It provoked many replies. Its author's views on education exerted considerable influence also. A portion of the tract is repr. in Somers Tracts, xi (1814), pp. 577–84. On Molesworth see C. Robbins, *Commonwealth men* (992); C. H. Brasch, *Om Robert Molesworth's skrift . . .,* Copenhagen, 1879; and J. Toland, ed., *The Letters of Lord Shaftesbury to Molesworth,* 1721.

981   TOLAND, JOHN. Anglia libera: or the limitation and succession of the crown of England explain'd and asserted. 1701.

Toland defends the Acts of 1689 and 1701. Earlier Whiggish works on the succession were William Atwood's not too accurate *Jus Anglorum*, 1681, and *The fundamental constitution . . .*, 1690; and Samuel Johnson, *An argument proving that the abrogation of King James by the people . . . was according to the constitution . . .*, 1692.

982 DEFOE, DANIEL. The original power of the collective body of the people of England. 3rd edn. 1702.

Probably also by Defoe, but possibly by Lord Somers, is *The judgment of whole kingdoms and nations concerning the rights, power, and prerogative of kings, and the rights, priviledges and properties of the people*, 1710, later edn. 1771.

2. Later Works

983 FIGGIS, J. N. The theory of the divine right of kings. Camb. 1896. 2nd edn. 1914.

The standard work. Cf. F. D. Wormuth, *The royal prerogative, 1603–1649* (723). See also P. Birdsall, '"Non obstante", a study of the dispensing power of English kings', in *Essays in honor of C. H. McIlwain*, Camb. (Mass.), 1936. See also C. A. Edie, 'Succession and monarchy . . .', *A.H.R.* 70 (1965), 350–70; and no. 723 n.

984 GOOCH, G. P. The history of English democratic ideas in the seventeenth century. Camb. 1898. 2nd edn. by H. J. Laski. Camb. 1927.

Cf. his *Political thought in England from Bacon to Halifax* (Home University Libr.), 1914–15; and, in the same series, H. J. Laski, *Political thought from Locke to Bentham*, 1920. See also C. Borgéaud, *The rise of modern democracy in old and New England*, trans. by B. Hill, 1894. A 'somewhat summary' treatment is J. W. Allen, *English political thought, 1603–1660*, of which vol. i (1603–44) was publ. in 1938.

985 GOUGH, J. W. Fundamental law in English constitutional history. Oxf. 1955. Bibl.

Deals largely with the seventeenth century, 'the heyday' of fundamental law. See also his *The social contract: a critical study of its development*, Oxf. 1936, and an article, 'Political trusteeship', *Politica*, 4 (1939), 220–47.

986 HEARNSHAW, F. J. C., ed. Social and political ideas of some great thinkers of the sixteenth and seventeenth centuries. 1926.

Lectures by several authors. See also, by the same ed., *The social and political ideas of some English thinkers of the Augustan Age, 1650–1750*, 1928, repr. N.Y. 1950.

987 JORDAN, W. K. Men of substance, a study in the thought of two English revolutionaries, Henry Parker and Henry Robinson. Chicago. 1942. Bibl.

Important study of political and religious ideas of two Cromwellian officials. Cf. M. A. Judson, 'Henry Parker and the theory of parliamentary sovereignty', in *Essays in honor of C. H. McIlwain*, Camb. (Mass.), 1936.

988 JUDSON, M. A. The crisis of the constitution: an essay in constitutional and political thought, 1603–1645. New Brunswick. 1949.

Valuable and well documented; should be compared with no. 996.

989 MOSSE, G. L. The struggle for sovereignty in England from the reign of Queen Elizabeth to the Petition of Right. East Lansing. 1950. Repr. N.Y. 1968.

Useful. See also his *Holy pretense* (1328).

990 PEASE, T. C. The Leveller movement, a study in the historical and political theory of the English great civil war. Wash. and Oxf. 1916. Bibl.

Valuable. J. Frank, in *The Levellers*, Camb. (Mass.), 1955, deals with Lilburne, Overton, and Walwyn, and provides an excellent bibliography. A shorter work on the Levellers is by H. Holorenshaw, 1939. Cf. E. Bernstein, *Cromwell and Communism* (314), Inderwick (326), Schenk (994); and R. C. Latham's review article, 'English revolutionary thought, 1640–1660', *History*, 30 (1945), 38–59. H. N. Brailsford's *Levellers and the English revolution*, ed. by C. Hill, Stanford, 1961, is scholarly but tends to undervalue religious convictions.

991 POCOCK, J. G. A. The ancient constitution and the feudal law. Camb. 1957.

Important. Deals with the effects of scholarship relating to the feudal past on political thought of the seventeenth century. Some aspects of the historical background of political theory are dealt with also by S. Kliger in *The Goths in England: a study in seventeenth- and eighteenth-century thought*, Camb. (Mass.), 1952. See also Fox (3007) and Fussner (3008).

992 ROBBINS, C. The eighteenth-century commonwealthman: studies in the transmission, development and circumstance of English liberal thought from the restoration . . . until the war with the thirteen colonies. Camb. (Mass.). 1959. Bibl.

Valuable. Traces relationships between the Real Whigs of the Augustan age and their seventeenth-century forebears. Cf. Z. S. Fink, *The classical republicans*, Evanston, 1945; and B. Behrens, 'The Whig theory of the constitution in the reign of Charles II', *Camb. Hist. Jour.* 7 (1941), 42–71.

993 SABINE, G. H. A history of political theory. 1937.

Includes the best account of the period in a general history of political theory. Still of some value are W. Graham, *English political philosophy from Hobbes to Maine*, 1899; and L. Stephen, *History of English thought in the eighteenth century*, 2 vols., 1876, 3rd edn., 1949. A provocative recent survey is C. B. McPherson, *The political theory of possessive individualism: Hobbes to Locke*, N.Y. 1962.

994 SCHENK, W. The concern for social justice in the Puritan revolution. 1948. Bibl.

Cf. D. B. Robertson, *The religious foundations of Leveller democracy*, N.Y. 1951. An earlier work emphasizing the religious foundations for the radical movements is Ernst Troeltsch, *The social teaching of the Christian churches*, tr. by O. Wyon, N.Y. 1931 (from the German edn., 1912). See also J. Downie, *Peter Cornelius Plockboy, Pioneer of the first cooperative commonwealth, 1659*, Manchester, 1934.

995 SMITH, A. L. English political philosophy in the seventeenth and eighteenth centuries. Camb. Mod. Hist. vi. 1909. Bibl.

See also W. R. Sorley, *History of English philosophy*, Camb. 1920, bibl., which is based on his chapter in *Camb. Hist. Eng. Lit.*

996 WESTON, C. C. 'The theory of mixed monarchy under Charles I and after.' *E.H.R.* (1960), 426–43.

A companion article is R. W. K. Hinton, 'Constitutional theories from Sir John Fortescue to Sir John Eliot', ibid. 410–25. Both argue a wider acceptance of the theory of mixed monarchy than do Judson (988) or Wormuth (723). Cf. C. C. Weston, *English constitutional theory and the House of Lords, 1556–1832*, 1965.

997 ZAGORIN, P. A history of political thought in the English revolution. 1954. Repr. N.Y. 1966.

Useful re-examination of the major figures, including Harrington, Hobbes, and Filmer.

IV

LEGAL HISTORY

No attempt is made in this volume to list the manuscript sources for the legal history of the period. Many of the groups of manuscripts at the P.R.O. that are listed by Pargellis, pp. 82–5, i.e. Chancery, Exchequer, King's Bench, Common Pleas, etc., contain seventeenth-century material; listings for the period in the records of these courts and in others should be checked in the *Guide* (65), 1963, and in the appropriate volumes of the P.R.O. *Lists and Indexes.*

The nature of legal sources is clearly explained by Holdsworth (1000) and Winfield (1003). The sections on *Political History* and *Constitutional History*, especially *Statutes*, should be referred to for additional titles. Many of the works listed under 'History of Law' in Read (11 n.), pp. 129–50, relate to the seventeenth century. The catalogues of the libraries of the Inns of Court also should be consulted (see Gross (11), nos. 501, 521, 523–4). For the activities of numerous lawyers, the general histories and the biographies of individuals should be consulted, in addition to the titles listed below.

A. REFERENCES AND SOURCES

I. BIBLIOGRAPHIES

998 BASSETT, THOMAS. A catalogue of the common and statute law-books of this realm . . . with an account of the best editions. 1670. 1682.

A bookseller's catalogue.

999 COWLEY, J. D. Bibliography of abridgments, digests, dictionaries, and indexes of English law to . . . 1800. Selden Society. 1932.

Publications by the Selden Society that relate to the period are described in the *General guide to the Society's publications*, by A. K. R. Kiralfy and G. H. Jones, publ. by the society in 1960.

1000 HOLDSWORTH, W. S. Sources and literature of English law. 1925. Repr. 1928. 1952.

Describes various types of legal material; less detail than Winfield. See also the bibliographies in Holdsworth (1024).

1001 INDEX TO LEGAL PERIODICALS and law library journals. N.Y. 1908+.

A quarterly, covering 71 English and American law journals. For journals before 1908 see L. A. Jones, *Index to legal periodical literature*, 3 vols., 1888–1918.

1002 MAXWELL, W. H. and MAXWELL, L. F. A legal bibliography of the British commonwealth of nations. 5 vols. 2nd edn. 1955–7.

Vol. i, English law to 1800; vol. iv, Irish law; vol. v, Scottish law. See also W. H. Maxwell's *Bibliography of English law . . .*, 1925, with supplements (1939–49), parts of

Sweet and Maxwell's *Complete law book catalogue*. Still of some use is the older *Lega bibliography* by J. G. Marvin, Phila. 1847.

1003 WINFIELD, P. H. The chief sources of English legal history. Camb. (Mass.). 1925.

Valuable. A reprint by microfilm process was publ. at Ann Arbor, 1959. Cf. Winfield's article in *Law Quart. Rev.* 30 (1914), 190–200.

1004 WORRALL, J. Bibliotheca legum Angliae . . . or a catalogue of the common and statute law books of this realm . . . New edn. 2 vols. 1788.

First edn. 1732 by Worrall; later edns. by various compilers, including E. Brooke, 1788, 1800; John Clarke, 1806, 1808; and T. H. Horne, 1819. Chiefly a bookseller's catalogue, and often referred to as *Clarke's catalogue*. See also R. W. Bridgman, *A short view of legal bibliography*, 1807; and J. and H. Butterworth, *A general catalogue of law books*, 1815, later edns.

2. DICTIONARIES

1005 COWELL, JOHN. The interpreter: or book containing the signification of words, wherein is set forth the true meaning of all . . . such words and termes as are mentioned in the law writers or statutes . . . requiring any exposition . . . Camb. 1607. Later edns. 1637. 1701.

The most useful law dictionary of its day; first edn. attracted attention because certain definitions enhanced the royal prerogative. Later edns. were revised somewhat by Thomas Manley and by Kennet. For its history see McIlwain's edn. of *Works of James I* (959), pp. xxxvii–ix, and S. B. Chrimes, 'The constitutional ideas of Dr. John Cowell', *E.H.R.* 64 (1949), 461–83. Cowell's work resembled somewhat John Rastell's *Les termes de la ley*, which was compiled in France *c.* 1527, and published in English in various edns., Lond., 1629, 1636, 1641, and later.

1006 BLOUNT, THOMAS. A law dictionary and glossary. 1670.

For other dictionaries, see Cowley (999).

3. JUDICIAL DECISIONS

(a) *Law Reports*

A general discussion of law reports of the century is in Winfield (1003), pp. 183–7, and valuable tables of the reporters to 1700 are in Holdsworth (1024), v. 355–78 and vi. 551–74. See also the tables in C. L. Grose (10), pp. 40–1. For assessment of the value of particular sets of reports, see J. W. Wallace, *The reporters arranged and characterized* . . ., 4th edn. by F. F. Heard, Boston (Mass.), 1882; and V. V. Veeder, 'The English reports, 1292–1865', *Harvard Law Rev.* 15 (1901), 1–21, 109–57. In addition to the reports compiled by lawyers of the Stuart period, later edns. of Edmund Plowden's *Commentaries* (publ. 1571–8) appeared, 1613, 1684.

1007 THE ENGLISH REPORTS. 166 vols. 1865–1900; repr. 176 vols. 1900–30.

Reprints reports on English cases, with original footnotes, from 14th to 19th century. See comments on the series by W. T. S. Daniels, *The history and origin of the law reports*, 1884 (abbr. by N. Lindley in *Law Quart. Rev.* 1 (1885), 137–49).

1008   COKE, SIR EDWARD. Les reports de Edward Coke. 13 vols. 1600–
15, 1656, 1659.

The first five volumes deal mainly with Elizabethan cases; vols. xii and xiii were
published posthumously and in English. For later edns. see Lowndes, pp. 489–90.
See also T. F. T. Plucknett, 'The genesis of Coke's reports', *Cornell Law Quart.* 27
(1942), 190–213. The later *Lord Chancellor Egerton's observations on the Lord Coke's
reports*, edited by George Paul [1710], is of doubtful authorship (see Holdsworth, *History
of English law*, v. 478).

1009   CROKE, SIR GEORGE. Reports. 3 vols. 1657–61.

Less valuable than Coke, and extending from Elizabeth to 1641. Of various later
editions, the best is that in 4 vols., 1790–2. *An abridgment . . .* was publ. by William
Hughes, 1665.

1010   ROLLE, HENRY. Les reports de Henry Rolle, de divers cases en le
court del' banke le roy, en le temps del' reigne de roy Jaques . . . 1675.

(b) Abridgements

1011   HUGHES, WILLIAM. The grand abridgment of the law . . . a collection of the principal cases and points of common law of England, from the
first of Elizabeth to this present time. 3 vols. 1660–3.

The first of the period, but less valuable than Rolle.

1012   ROLLE, HENRY. Un abridgment des plusieurs cases et resolutions del
common ley. 1668.

Edited by Matthew Hale. Rolle's *Abridgment* is even more valuable than his *Reports*,
and is the best for the century. Rolle's law French was translated in part by Knightley
D'Anvers, *A general abridgment of the common law* (3 vols., 1705); and his work was the
base also for Charles Viner's *General abridgment*, 23 vols., Aldershot, 1742–[51]. William
Sheppard's *Grand abridgment* (3 vols., 1675) is less valuable than Rolles, but is in
English.

B. HISTORY AND THE LEGAL PROFESSION

1. HISTORY OF THE LAW

(a) Early Histories

For legal treatises and commentaries, see section D *infra*.

1013   SPELMAN, SIR HENRY. Archaeologus. In modum glossarii . . .
2 vols. 1626–64.

Cf. *Reliquiae Spelmannianae, the posthumous works of Sir H. Spelman relating to the laws
and antiquities of England . . .*, Oxf. 1698. See also John Clayton, *Topicks in the laws
of England . . . also an exposition of severall words not touched by former glossaries*, 1646.

1014   ZOUCHE, RICHARD. Descriptio juris et judicii feudalis, . . . pro
introductione ad studium jurisprudentiae Anglicanae. Oxf. 1634.

By Zouche also, *Elementa jurisprudentiae definitionibus, regulis et sententiis selectioribus
juris civilis illustrata . . .*, Oxf. 1636; and *Juris et judicii fecialis, sive juris inter gentes . . .*,

Oxf. 1650. There were various later edns. of the latter work (e.g. Leyden, 1651, Mainz, 1661), and it was republ. with translation by J. L. Brierly and ed. by T. E. Holland, Wash. 1911. See also nos. 1084, 1772.

1015 POWELL, RICHARD. A treatise of the antiquity etc. of the ancient courts of leet . . . 1641. 1642. Later edns.

1016 DUCK, ARTHUR. De usu et authoritate juris civilis Romanorum . . . 1653. Later edns. 1679. 1689.

1017 PHILIPPS, FABIAN. The antiquity, legality, reason, duty and necessity of prae-emption and pourveyance for the king. 1663.

The author wrote numerous other legal treatises. See *D.N.B.*

1018 DUGDALE, WILLIAM. Origines juridiciales, or historical memorials of the English laws, courts of justice, forms of tryall. . . . Also a chronology of the lord chancellors, justices [etc.]. 1666. 1680. Later edns.

The 1680 edn. is the best.

1019 [HALE, SIR MATTHEW.] The history and analysis of the common law. Written by a learned hand. 1713. 3rd edn. 1733. 6th edn. 2 vols. 1820.

The history and the analysis were also published separately. On Hale and his other writings see an article by W. S. Holdsworth, *Law Quart. Rev.* 39 (1923), 402–26, and no. 1083 n. There is a contemporary life by Gilbert Burnet, 1682.

(b) *Later Works*

1020 AMES, J. B. Lectures on legal history. Camb. (Mass.). 1913. Bibl. Repr. 1930.

Valuable. Traces the history of actions and of doctrines of common law and equity. Cf. P. B. Waite, 'The struggle of prerogative and common law in the reign of James I', *Canadian Jour. Econ. and Pol. Sci.*, 1959.

1021 CHURCHILL, E. F. 'Monopolies.' *Law Quart. Rev.* 41 (1925), 275–96.

Continues to 1685 the earlier account (to 1658) by W. Price, *English patents of monopoly* (2160). See also D. S. Davies, 'Further light on the case of monopolies', *Law Quart. Rev.* 48 (1932), 394–414; and 2160 n.

1022 DUNCAN, J. L. 'The end and aim of law: legal theories in England in the sixteenth and seventeenth centuries.' *Juridical Rev.* 47 (1935), 157–77; 50 (1938), 257–81, 404–38.

1023 HAVIGHURST, A. F. 'The judiciary and politics in the reign of Charles II.' *Law Quart. Rev.* 66 (1950), 62–78, 229–52.

By the same author, 'James II and the twelve men in scarlet', ibid. 69 (1953), 522–46.

1024 HOLDSWORTH, W. S. A history of English law. 3 vols. 1903–9. 13 vols. 1922–52. 7th edn. Vol. i. 1956.

The most comprehensive account, containing much on constitutional development; valuable bibliographical notes. Vols. v and vi deal especially with the Stuart period. By Holdsworth also, 'Defamation in the 16th and 17th centuries', *Law Quart. Rev.* 40 (1924), 302–15, 397–412; 41 (1925), 13–31. See also his *The influence of the legal profession on the growth of the English constitution*, Oxf., 1924.

1025   JENKS, E. A short history of English law. 1912. Bibl. 6th edn. 1949.

Useful brief survey. Also by Jenks, *The history of the doctrine of consideration,* 1892, which includes a chapter on the abridgements. A useful *Concise history of the common law,* by T. F. T. Plucknett, was published in a 5th edn., 1956.

1026   JENKS, E. 'The story of habeas corpus.' *Law Quart. Rev.* 18 (1902), 64–77.

Good account of the origin of habeas corpus. Cf. C. C. Crawford, 'Writ of habeas corpus', *Amer. Law Rev.* 42 (1908), 481–99.

1027   MAITLAND, F. W. Collected papers. Ed. by H. A. L. Fisher. 3 vols. Camb. 1911.

English legal history of the Stuart period is dealt with, *inter alia,* in the following: vol. i, 'The mystery of seisin' and 'The beatitude of seisin'; vol. ii, 'The survival of archaic communities'; vol. iii, 'Records of . . . Lincoln's Inn', 'The corporation sole', and 'The crown as corporation'.

1028   OGILVIE, SIR C. The king's government and the common law, 1471–1641. Oxf. 1958.

1029   POTTER, H. An historical introduction to English law and its institutions. 2nd rev. edn. 1943. 3rd edn. 1948.

1030   SELECT ESSAYS in Anglo-American legal history. Ed. by a Committee of the Association of American Law Schools. 3 vols. Boston (Mass.). 1907–9.

More than seventy essays, many relating to the Stuart period, e.g. in vol. i, T. E. Scrutton, 'Roman law in chancery, church courts, admiralty and law merchant'; W. S. Holdsworth, 'The development of the law merchant'; P. S. Reinsch, 'The English common law in the early American colonies'. In the second and third volumes are essays on special topics such as sources, the courts, procedure, contracts, wills, etc.

1031   SMITH, G. 'The reform of the laws of England, 1640–1660.' *Univ. of Toronto Quart.* 10 (1941), 469–81.

1032   WINFIELD, P. H. The history of conspiracy and the abuse of legal procedure. Camb. 1921.

2. THE LEGAL PROFESSION

(a) *Lawyers and Judges*

See also Ch. II, *Biography*; other lawyers may be traced by the index. On political activities of lawyers see Eusden, *Puritans, lawyers and politics* (295).

1033   FOSS, E. The judges of England [1066–1864]. 9 vols. 1848–64.

The standard reference work, of which there is an abridgement in one vol., *Biographia juridica,* 1870. Valuable also is his *Tabulae curiales: or Tables of the superior courts of Westminster Hall* . . ., 1865, which lists judges, attorney- and solicitor-generals, 1066–1864. Less reliable are the two works by John, Lord Campbell, *The lives of the lord chancellors and keepers of the great seal of England,* 8 vols., 1845–69, 10 vols., 1868; and *The lives of the chief justices of England . . . till the death of Lord Mansfield,* 3 vols., 1849–57, 4 vols., 1874. Selected biographies were published by the earl of Birkenhead, *Fourteen English judges,* 1926; and Sir W. S. Holdsworth, *Some makers of English law,* Camb. 1938. See also Turner, 'The lord justices' (740 n.).

1034 PULLING, A. The order of the coif. 1884. 1887.

The only complete account of the serjeants-at-law. See also H. W. Woolrych, *Lives of eminent serjeants-at-law on the English bar*, 2 vols., 1869.

1035 WHITELOCKE, JAMES. Liber famelicus of Sir James Whitelocke, a judge of the court of king's bench in the reigns of James I and Charles I. Ed. by J. Bruce. Camd. Soc. 1858.

Contains notes on judges and legal matters *temp.* James I.

1036 HOSKYNS, JOHN. The life, letters and writings of John Hoskyns, 1566–1638. Ed. by L. B. Osborn. New Haven. 1937.

1037 ROKEBY, THOMAS. A brief memoir of Mr. Justice Rokeby comprising his religious journal and correspondence. Ed. by J. Raine. Surtees Miscellanea. 1861.

The letters begin in 1665, the journal in 1688.

1038 HYDE, H. M. Judge Jeffreys. 1940. 2nd edn. 1948.

The best life, but not completely definitive. Earlier ones by H. W. Woolrych, 1827; H. B. Irving, 1898; and S. Schofield, 1937. For letters see no. 3510.

(b) *Inns of Court*

For a bibliography of the printed registers of the inns of court see Raven-hart and Johnson (2925). Cf. D. S. Bland, 'The records of the inns of court, a bibliographical aid', *Amateur Historian*, 1962 (Spring). A list of numerous later works relating to the history of the inns and the course of study there is in Read (11 n.), pp. 143–4. For contemporary comment, see Dugdale, *Origines juridiciales* (1018); for the best modern account, Holdsworth (1024), ii. 484–512.

1039 THE PENSION BOOKS OF GRAY'S INN 1569–1800. Ed. by R. J. Fletcher. 2 vols. 1901–10.

'The earliest extant minute book of the ruling body.'

1040 THE RECORDS OF THE HONOURABLE SOCIETY of Lincoln's Inn. Ed. by W. P. Baildon. 4 vols. 1897–1902.

Vols. ii and iii, 1568–1775. These are the minute books. See also *The Records of . . . Lincoln's Inn: admissions, 1420–1893 . . .*, 2 vols., 1896. Modern works are William Ball, *Lincoln's Inn, its history and tradition*, 1947; and G. Hurst, *Short history of Lincoln's Inn*, 1946.

1041 CALENDAR OF INNER TEMPLE RECORDS 1505–1714. Ed. by F. A. Inderwick. 3 vols. 1896–1901.

The series was cont. by R. A. Roberts, vols. iv–v, 1933–6.

1042 MIDDLE TEMPLE RECORD: minutes of parliament, 1501–1703. Ed. by C. T. Martin. 4 vols. 1904–5.

See also C. H. Hopwood, ed., *Calendar of Middle Temple records*, 1902; H. A. C. Sturgess, ed., *Register of admissions to . . . the Middle Temple, from the fifteenth century to . . . 1944*, 3 vols., 1949; and *Master Worsley's book on the history and constitution of the . . . Middle Temple* (written in 1733), ed. by A. R. Ingpen, 1910. Useful also are Ingpen's *Middle Temple bench books . . .*, 1912, containing a historical introduction; and J. B. Williamson, *History of the Temple*, 1924.

C. COURTS, PROCEDURE, AND TRIALS

1. COURTS AND PROCEDURE

(a) *General*

The best descriptions of the various courts and their work are given in Holdsworth (1024), vols. i and v. See Read (11 n.), pp. 144–50, for a brief listing of the courts, those of common law, chancery, and prerogative jurisdiction, with references to their records. There are references to some of these (e.g. Admiralty, Exchequer, Star Chamber) in the section on *Central Administration*, Ch. III, and in *Naval History*, nos. 1767–80. For local courts and their officers see *Local Government* (nos. 928–57).

1043 LIST OF PLEA ROLLS of various courts, preserved in the Public Record Office. *P.R.O. Lists and Indexes*, no. 4. 1894. Rev. edn. 1910.

Among those relating to the Stuart period are rolls of king's bench, common pleas, exchequer, the palatinate of Lancaster, Chester, Wales, and others. For reports on the surviving records of the courts, see vol. i of Guiseppi and of the 1963 *Guide* (65).

1044 RULES AND ORDERS of the several courts of king's bench, common pleas, chancery, and exchequer, 3rd edn. cont. to 1724. 1724.

Based upon earlier collections, several of which pertained to individual courts, such as *Rules and orders for the court of common pleas*, 1654, 1682 (Wing, R 2249, 2251); Sir Thomas Fanshaw's *Practice of exchequer court*, 1658, and William Brown's *Compendium of several branches of practice in the court of exchequer*, 1688. The rules of king's bench, sanctioned by Parliament in 1604, are included in the 1747 (2nd) edn. of George Cooke, *Rules . . . in the court of common pleas*.

(b) *Particular Courts*

(i) *Chancery*

See also nos. 746–9, 1033, 1094–5.

1045 INDEX OF CHANCERY PROCEEDINGS, preserved at the P.R.O. Ser. ii, 1558–1660. 3 vols. 1896–1909.

P.R.O. Lists and indexes, 7, 24, 30. Vols. 24 and 30 list cases of 1579–1621 and 1621–60 respectively. Other important indexes of proceedings are those for Bridges's division, 1613–1714, *P.R.O. Lists and indexes*, nos. 39, 42, 44, 45 (1913–17); and Reynardson's division, 1649–1714, Brit. Rec. Soc., *Index Lib.*, vols. 29, 32 (1903–4).

1046 ACTA CANCELLARIA, or selections from the records of the court of chancery (1558–1624). By C. Monro. 1847.

Includes some extracts from the period of James I. J. Ritchie edited *Reports of cases decided by Francis Bacon, 1617–1621*, 1932.

1047 SANDERS, G. W., ed. Orders of the high court of chancery and statutes of the realm relating to chancery. 2 pts. 1845.

The most complete edition, showing the growth of the court throughout its history.

1048 YALE, D. E. C., ed. Lord Nottingham's chancery cases. 2 vols. (Selden Society, 73, 79.) 1957–61.

Important evidences on the court of equity, 1673–82.

1049 CERTAINE OBSERVATIONS concerning the office of lord chancellor. [By Thomas Egerton, Lord Ellesmere?] 1651.

Usually attributed to Lord Ellesmere (e.g. Wing, Ell. 539), but erroneously (see Holdsworth, *Sources* [1000], p. 181, noting it as inferior work). Dubious also is Ellesmere's authorship of the 1641 tract usually attributed to him, *Privileges and prerogatives of the high court of chancery*. The 'best tract' of this period on the work of the court is the anonymous 'Treatise of the maister of chauncery', which is repr. in Hargrave, *Collection of tracts* (1071).

1050 SELDEN, JOHN. A brief discourse touching the office of lord chancellor of England. Ed. by William Dugdale. 1672. Later edn. 1677. 1811.

1051 BROWN, WILLIAM. Praxis almae curiae cancellariae: A collection of precedents by bill and answer . . . in causes . . . in the high court of chancery for more than thirty years past . . . 1694.

The volume, perhaps edited from MSS. of Robert Heath, contains a preliminary discourse upon the practice of chancery in equity cases. Brown, who was a clerk of the court of common pleas, wrote also *The clerks tutor in chancery* (1687, 2nd edn., 1694), with instructions on procedure. An earlier work is William Tothill, *Transactions of the high court of chancery, both by practice and precedent*, 1649, 1671; it relates to the court from 1559 to 1646.

(2) Other Courts

1052 HALE, W. H. A series of precedents and proceedings in criminal causes . . . 1475–1640 extracted from act books of ecclesiastical courts in the diocese of London. 1847.

With introductory essay on English ecclesiastical law, and jurisdiction of ecclesiastical courts.

1053 ROSCOE, E. S. The Admiralty jurisdiction and practice of the high court of justice. 1931.

By Roscoe also, *Studies in the history of the admiralty and prize courts*, 1932, and no. 1779.

1054 SQUIBB, G. D. The high court of chivalry: a study of the civil law in England. N.Y. 1959.

Cases for 1634–40 are useful for history of the 'Earl Marshal's Court' in a period of criticism of royal policy.

1055 THORNE, S. E. 'The constitution and the courts: a re-examination of the famous case of Dr. Bonham.' *In* The constitution reconsidered. Ed. by C. Read. N.Y. 1938.

On a famous case in common pleas. Also printed in *Law Quart. Rev.* 54 (1938), 543–52.

(c) Procedure

1056 POWELL, THOMAS. The attornies almanacke. Provided . . . for the use of all such as shall have occasion to remove any . . . cause . . . from an inferior court to any higher courts at Westminster. 1627.

Also by Powell, *The attorney's academy*, 1630 (first pr. 1623).

1057 BROWN, WILLIAM. The entring clerk's vade mecum. Being an exact collection of precedents for declarations and pleadings in most actions. 1678.

See also *Regula placitandi*, 1691. The earlier *Maxims and rules of pleading*, by Robert Heath (d. 1649), was publ. in 1964, probably edited by Brown.

1058 BROWN, WILLIAM. A compendious and accurate treatise of recoveries upon writs of entry in the post, and fines upon writs of covenant. 1678. Later edns.

See also Sir Anthony Fitzherbert, *New natura brevium*, 1534, a standard work used by lawyers, which went through various 17th-century and later editions (1598, 1604, 1616, 1635, 1652).

1059 GLISSON, WILLIAM and GULSTON, ANTHONY. The common law epitomiz'd: with directions how to prosecute and defend personal actions. 2nd edn. enl. 1679.

2. TRIALS

Trials regarding particular causes can be found in several other sections; e.g. *Popish Plot, Jacobitism, Witchcraft*, or under the name of an individual.

(a) *Collections*

1060 COBBETT'S complete collection of state trials and proceedings for high treason and other crimes . . . from the earliest period to the present time. 34 vols. 1809–28.

Ed. by W. Cobbett, T. B. Howell, and others, and based on earlier compilations; mainly reprints of pamphlets, uncritically selected. Vol. ii starts with 1603. J. G. Muddiman in *State trials . . .*, Edin. 1930, pleads for a new and revised edn. Other collections of trials are by J. W. Willis-Bund, *Selection of cases from the state trials*, 2 vols., Camb. 1879–82; and H. L. Stephen, *State trials*, 4 vols., 1899–1902.

1061 A DISPLAY OF TYRANNY or remarks upon the illegal and arbitrary proceedings in the courts of Westminster and Guild-hall London [1678–88]. 2 vols. 1689–90.

Possibly by Titus Oates.

1062 LANG, A. The valet's tragedy and other studies. 1903.

Includes essays on the mystery of James de la Cloche and that of Sir Edmund Berry Godfrey. Cf. Lang's *Historical mysteries*, 1904. Essays on various trials will be found also in *Famous trials of history* by F. E. Smith, earl of Birkenhead, 1926; and the second earl's *More famous trials*, 1938. Another collection is by H. Hodge, 1941. See also 'Notable British Trials Series', which includes J. Bent, *The Bloody Assizes*, Edin. 1929; and D. Carswell, ed., *Trial of Guy Fawkes and others: The gunpowder plot*, 1934.

(b) *Separate Trials*

1063 STEPHEN, H. L. 'The trial of Sir Walter Raleigh.' *R.H.S. Trans.*, 4th Ser. 2 (1919), 172–87.

1064 AMOS, A. The great oyer of poisoning. 1846.

The trial of Somerset for poisoning Overbury.

1065 THE ARGUMENTS OF SIR RICHARD HUTTON . . . and Sir George Croke . . . upon a scire facias brought . . . in the court of exchequer against John Hampden esquire. 1641.

The ship-money case. Cf. S. R. Gardiner, ed., 'Notes of the judgment delivered by Sir George Croke in the case of ship-money', *Camd. Soc. Misc.* vii, 1875. See also D. L. Keir, 'The case of ship-money', *Law Quart. Rev.* 52 (1936), 546–74.

1066 HALE, SIR MATTHEW. A tryal of witches, at the assizes held at Bury St. Edmonds 10 March 1664 before Sir M. Hale. 1682.

Also printed in 1683, as an addition to Hale's *Short treatise touching sheriffs' accompts*.

1067 THE DUKE OF NORFOLK'S case: or the doctrine of perpetuities fully set forth and explained. 1688.

1068 HAWLES, JOHN. Remarks upon the tryals of Edw. Fitzharris, Stephen Colledge, Count Coningsmark. The Lord Russell [etc.] as also on the earl of Shaftesburys grand jury . . . 1689.

1069 A TRUE NARRATIVE of the proceedings against the lord bishop of London, in the council chamber of Whitehall, by the lords commissioners . . . 1689.

Simple report, without comment, on the proceedings against Compton.

1070 BEAMONT, W., ed. The Jacobite trials at Manchester in 1694. Chetham Soc. 1853.

Narrative by an anonymous spectator. Illustrative of the so-called 'Lancashire Plot' are the accounts ed. by A. Goss, *The narrative of Richard Abbott, servant of Caryll Lord Molyneux (1689–91);* [and] *An account of the tryalls at Manchester October 1694*, 1864.

D. LEGAL TREATISES AND COMMENTARIES

1. GENERAL

1071 HARGRAVE, F., ed. Collection of tracts relative to the law of England. 1787.

A miscellany by various authors. Also compiled by Hargrave, *Collectanea juridica*, 2 vols., 1791–2.

1072 BACON, FRANCIS. Law tracts. 1737.

Contains: A proposition for compiling and amendment of our laws. The elements of the common laws of England. Reading on the statute of uses. Most of these are included in vol. vii of the *Works*, ed. by Spedding (403). See also C. H. L. Ewen, 'Bacon and the moneylenders', *Baconiana*, 3rd Ser. 21 (1934), 235–53; and P. H. Kocher, 'Bacon and the science of jurisprudence', *Jour. Hist. Ideas*, 18 (1957), 1–26.

1073 FULBECKE, WILLIAM. A parallele or conference of the civil law, the canon law, and the common law of this realm . . . 2 pts. 1601–2. Later edn. 1618.

Differences pointed out in a series of dialogues. Sir T. Ridley publ. his *View of the civile and ecclesiastical law* in 1607, later edn., Oxf. 1634.

1074   COWELL, JOHN. Institutiones juris Anglicani ad methodum et seriem institutionum imperialium compositae et digestae. Camb. 1605. (Trans. into English by W. G., 1651.)

1075   SELDEN, JOHN. Opera omnia. Ed. by D. Wilkins. 3 vols. 1726.

Important early publications are: *Jani Anglorum facies altera*, 1610, 1681; and his notes on Fortescue and Hengham that were published with his *De laudibus legum Angliae written by Sir John Fortescue* . . . [and] *two sums of Sir R. de Hengham*, 1616, 1672. For his treatises on titles and *Mare clausum* see nos. 1096 and 1771. Sir F. Pollock ed. *Table talk of John Selden*, for the Selden Society, 1927. On his library see D. M. Barrett in *Bodleian Libr. Record*, 3 (1951), 128–42, 208–13. See also E. G. M. Fletcher, 'John Selden . . . and his contribution to international law', *Grotius Soc. Trans. for 1933*, 19 (1934), 1–12.

1076   FINCH, SIR HENRY. Nometechnia, c'est a scavoir un description del common leys d'Angleterre solonque les rules del art. 1613.

A similar but larger work, translated into English from a French version, is Finch's *Law, or discourse thereof*, 1627, 2nd edn., 1636.

1077   YELVERTON, SIR HENRY. A treatise conteining divers benefits, and priviledges, and the power of authoritie granted to the patentee, who hath his Maiesties license . . . under the Great Seale of England. s.l. 1617.

1078   CALLIS, ROBERT. The reading of . . . Robert Callis, esq., upon the statute of sewers . . . at Gray's Inn in August, 1622. 1647.

Ed. by W. J. Broderip, 1824. Another important reading is Sir Robert Holborne's *Reading in Lincolnes-Inn, Feb. 28, 1641, upon the statute . . . of treasons*, Oxf. 1642. A collection of readings, including one on jury trial, was published by Thomas Williams under the title of *The excellency and preheminance of the law of England* . . ., 1680.

1079   COKE, EDWARD. Institutes of the lawes of England. 4 vols. 1628–44. Later edn. of part i, ed. by F. Hargrave and C. Butler. 1788.

The first part is the famous 'Commentarie upon Littleton', including a reprint of Littleton's *Tenures*, with Coke's commentaries; the second part deals with various statutes from 1215 to *temp*. James I; the third relates to criminal law; and the fourth is valuable in describing the jurisdiction of the various courts of law. There are various later editions of all four parts. It was to the fourth part that W. Prynne replied in *Brief animadversions on . . . the fourth part of the institutes*, 1669. Other publications by Coke are his *Reports* (1008), and *A booke of entries*, 1616. T. Asche ed. portions from Coke in *Fasciculum florum* . . ., 1618; and W. Hawkins published *Three law tracts*, 1764, including 'The compleat copyholder'. Other works are listed in *D.N.B.* on Coke. For evaluations of Coke see Holdsworth (1024), v. 456–93, his article in *Cambridge Law Jour.* 5 (1935), 332–46, and his essay in P. Vinagradoff, ed., *Essays in legal history*, Oxf. 1914; F. D. MacKinnon in *Law Quart. Rev.* 61 (1935), 289–98; and S. E. Thorne's Selden Society lecture, *Sir Edward Coke, 1552–1952*, 1957. See also C. Hill's evaluation in *Intellectual origins of the English revolution* (325 n.); and D. O. Wagner, 'Coke and the rise of economic liberalism', *Econ. Hist. Rev.* 6 (1935), 30–144. On his library see W. O. Hassall's *Catalogue of the library of Sir Edward Coke*, New Haven, 1950, and *Br. Mus. Quart.* 17 (1952), 23–39. For biography see no. 425.

1080   N[OY], W[ILLIAM]. A treatise of the principall grounds and maxims of the lawes of this kingdome. 1641.

1081 MANTELL, WALTER. A short treatise of the lawes of England: with the jurisdiction of the high court of Parliament with the liberties and freedoms of the subjects. 1644.

Repr. in *Harl. Misc.* iv, 1810 edn. Other works of this period include: John Warr, *The corruption and deficiency of the laws of England*, 1649, repr. in *Harl. Misc.* iii, 1809 edn.; and Henry Robinson, *Certaine proposals in order to a new modelling of the lawes*, 1652, 1653. See also Francis Thorpe, *Sergeant Thorpe . . . his charge to the grand-jury at York Assizes . . .* [1648/9, on] *the severall estates and conditions of men*, 1649.

1082 JENKINS, DAVID. Lex terrae. [1647.]

Deals largely with constitutional law. See also his *Pacis consultum* (953 n.). On Jenkins's treatment by Parliament see W. H. Terry, ed., *Judge Jenkins* (3484).

1083 HOBBES, THOMAS. The elements of law natural and politic. Later edn. by F. Tonnies. 1889. Repr. Camb. 1928.

This originally appeared in two parts: *Humane nature, or the fundamental elements of policie*, 1650 (2nd edn. 1651); and *De corpore politico, or the elements of law, moral, and politick*, 1650. Tonnies collates the printed with the MS. versions. Hobbes's criticism of Coke's position as obsolete in his *Dialogue of the common laws* (pr. in his *Works* (968), vol. vi), provoked a reply by Sir Matthew Hale, which is printed from Harl. MS. 711 in Holdsworth (1024), v, app.

1084 ZOUCHE, RICHARD. Cases and questions resolved in civil law. Oxf. 1652.

Also by Zouche, *Quaestionum juris civilis centuria in decem classes distributa*, Oxf. 1660, 3rd edn. Lond. 1682; and *Solutio quaestionis veteris et novae*, Oxf. 1657 (printed afterwards in Cologne, 1662, Berlin, 1669, Jena and Lond., 1717), in which the question of liability of criminal sovereigns and ambassadors to local jurisdiction is treated. See also no. 1014.

1085 WINGATE, EDMUND. The body of the common law of England as it stood in force before it was altered by statute, or acts of parliament, or state. 2nd edn. 1655.

Includes a collection of statutes, and tables. He printed in 1658 his *Maximes of reason, or the reason of the common law of England*. At the same period Michael Hawke published *The grounds of the lawes of England*, 1657; and Robert Wiseman defended civil law under the title of *The law of laws: or the excellency of the civil law, above all other humane laws whatsoever*, 1657.

1086 SHEPPARD, WILLIAM. The faithful councellor: or the marrow of the law in English. 2 pts. 1651–3.

Pt. 1 deals with common-law actions, and pt. 2 with Chancery. Also by Sheppard, *Of corporations, fraternities, and guilds*, 1659. See also nos. 937, 942, 952.

2. SPECIAL FIELDS OF LAW

See also *Economic History*, *Political Theory*, and *Foreign Relations*. *Maritime Law* is in the chapter on *Naval History*.

(a) *Criminal Law*

1087 PULTON, FERDINANDO. De pace regis et regni. 1609. Later edns. 1610. 1615. 1623.

A treatise on criminal law.

1088　HALE, SIR MATTHEW. Historia placitorum coronae. The history of the pleas of the crown. Ed. by S. Emlyn. 2 vols. 1736. Later ed. by T. Dogherty. 2 vols. 1800.

Valuable. Compiled by the distinguished judge as a history of criminal law, near the end of Charles I's reign, the brief *Pleas of the crown* was printed first, 1678; the full *Historia* (1736) was ed. from transcripts of Hale's manuscripts (Br. Mus. Hargrave MSS. 758–64). See also no. 1019, and others listed in the index.

1089　STEPHEN, J. F. A history of the criminal law of England. 3 vols. 1883.

The standard work, useful for legal procedure. See also L. O. Pike's *History of crime* (2550); and J. Goebel, Jr., *Felony and misdemeanor, a study of the history of English criminal procedure*, 1937. One aspect of criminal law reform is dealt with by S. Rezneck in 'The statute of 1696', *J.M.H.* 2 (1930), 5–26.

(b) *Land Law*

1090　COKE, SIR EDWARD. The complete copy-holder. 1641. Later edns. 1650. 1668. 1673.

A supplement by Charles Calthrop was added for the 1650 edition, and other supplements appeared in the later ones. Cf. Samuel Carter, *Lex custumaria, or a treatise of copy-hold estates*, 1696, later edn. 1701. See also no. 1911.

1091　SHEPPARD, WILLIAM. The touchstone of common assurances: or a plain . . . treatise, opening the learning of the common assurances or conveyances of the kingdom. 1641. Later edn. 1784. Ed. by R. Preston. 2 vols. 1820.

Two other works by Sheppard on common assurances were *Precedent of precedents . . .,* 1655; and *The law of common assurances, touching deeds in general*, 1669. He compiled also *Actions upon the case for deeds*, 2nd edn., 1675.

1092　BRIDGMAN, SIR ORLANDO. Conveyances: being select precedents of deeds and instruments concerning the most considerable estates in England. 2nd edn. 1689. 5th edn. 1725.

1093　SIMPSON, A. W. B. An introduction to the history of the land law. 1961. Bibl.

Largely supersedes the former standard work by Holdsworth, *An historical introduction to the land law* (1949). There are several chapters on the Stuart period in T. E. Scrutton, *Land in fetters* (1952 n.).

(c) *Equity*

See also *Chancery* (nos. 1045–51).

1094　MAITLAND, F. W. Equity: a course of lectures. Ed. by A. H. Chaytor and W. R. Whittaker. Rev. by J. Bremyate. Camb. 1936.

First publ. 1909. Valuable.

1095　SPENCE, G. The equitable jurisdiction of the court of chancery; comprising its rise, progress, and final establishment. 2 vols. 1846–9.

The standard work; contains numerous references to the Stuart period.

(d) *Ecclesiastical Law*

1096 SELDEN, JOHN. The historie of tithes. 1618.

An answer to Selden was publ. in 1619 by Richard Tillesley, entitled *Animadversions upon Mr. Selden's History of Tithes*. Other books on the controversy are listed by R. G. Usher in *Reconstruction of the English Church* (1202).

1097 SPELMAN, SIR HENRY. Concilia, decreta, leges, constitutiones, in re ecclesiarum orbis Britannici. 2 vols. 1639–64.

Vol. ii was ed. by Dugdale 1664. See also no. 3019.

1098 SPELMAN, SIR HENRY. The larger treatise concerning tithes . . . together with some other tracts of the same authour, and a fragment of Sir Francis Bigot. . . . Ed. by J. Stephens. 1647.

Later works on tithes are W[illiam] S[heppard], *The parsons guide: or the law of tithes*, 1654; and Sir Simson Degge, *The parson's counsellor, with the law of tithes and tithing*, 1676, later edns. to 1820.

1099 ENGLAND'S INDEPENDENCY upon the papal power historically and judicially stated, by Sir John Davis and by Sir Edw. Coke, in two reports selected from their greater volumes. With a preface by Sir John Pettus. 1674.

Cf. M. H. Maguire, 'Attack of the common lawyers on the oath *ex officio* as administered in the ecclesiastical courts in England', in *Essays in honor of C. H. McIlwain*, Camb. (Mass.), 1936.

1100 GODOLPHIN, JOHN. Reportorium canonicum: or an abridgment of the ecclesiastical laws of this realm. 1678.

A good summary of the existing practice of ecclesiastical law. Special subjects are treated in: William Hughes, *Parsons law: or a view of advowsons*, 3rd edn., 1673; and William Lawrence, *Marriage by the morall law of God vindicated against all ceremoniall laws of popes and bishops destructive to filiation aliment and succession . . .*, 1680.

1101 ATKYNS, SIR ROBERT. A discourse concerning the ecclesiastical jurisdiction in the realm of England: occasioned by the late commission in ecclesiastical causes. 1689.

(e) *Wills*

1102 GODOLPHIN, JOHN. The orphans legacy: or a testamentary abridgement. In three parts. I. Of last wills and testaments. II. Of executors and administrators. III. Of legacies and devises. 1674. Later edns. 1677. 1685. 1701.

1103 WENTWORTH, THOMAS. The office and duty of executors; or a treatise of wills and executors. To which is added an appendix by J. [T?] M[anley]. 1676. Later edns. 1763. 1774. 1829.

V

ECCLESIASTICAL HISTORY

A. GENERAL AND MISCELLANEOUS

Because ecclesiastical historians have dealt too exclusively with particular bodies, Stoughton (1140), though out of date, is still the principal general history of religious developments. Certain developments in religious thought have received somewhat more attention. Rationalism has been treated by Lecky (1132) and Tulloch (1141); toleration most recently by Jordan (1146); and the interrelationship between religious ideas and the pressure for political and social change by Haller (1325), Hill (325), Woodhouse (308 n.), and others. Many useful articles will be found in *The Church Quarterly Review* and *Church History*.

The elaborate study by Shaw is still the best for the years 1640–60; and the volumes by Frere and Hutton provide the best summary for the whole period from the Anglo-Catholic viewpoint. The post-1660 period, although it has attracted more attention recently, has no complete account, and there is still no adequate bibliography. The influence of the Anglican church upon political and social developments has not been definitively evaluated, although studies in other areas have pointed to reasons for the decline of clerical influence.

Titles relating to matters of religion will be found also in Ch. II and §§ D and F of Ch. III *supra*; and in Chs. IX, X, and XIII–XV *infra*.

1. BIBLIOGRAPHY AND SOURCES

(a) *Bibliographies and Lists*

1104 CASE, S. J., McNEILL, J. T., *et al.*, eds. A bibliographical guide to the history of Christianity. Chicago. 1931. Repr. N.Y. 1951.

A selective handbook. Ch. *b* deals with the British Isles. Elementary but useful also is J. P. Whitney, *A bibliography of church history* (The Historical Association), 1923. Useful on nonconformity is W. R. Powell, 'The sources for the history of Protestant nonconformist churches in England', *Bull. Inst. Hist. Research*, 25 (1952), 213–27. For recent publications (1940–55) relating to the Reformation, and arranged by countries of publication, see the *Bibliographie de la Réforme*, 1450–1648, published under the auspices of the Commission internationale d'histoire ecclésiastique comparée . . ., vols. i, ii, Leyden, 1958–60+.

1105 DARLING, J. Cyclopaedia bibliographica: a library manual of theological and general literature. 2 vols. 1854–9.

Valuable reference work, providing a guide to many collections.

1106 OLLARD, S. L., *et al.* Dictionary of English church history. [1912.] 2nd edn. 1919. 3rd edn. 1948. Bibl. notes.

See also J. S. Purvis, *An introduction to ecclesiastical records*, 1953, which includes some 17th-century materials.

1107 KENNEDY, W. P. M. 'List of visitation articles and injunctions, 1604–1715.' *E.H.R.* 40 (1925), 586–92.

Continuation of the visitation articles edited by W. H. Frere and W. Kennedy for 1535–75, and for 1576–1603 by W. Kennedy. These provide an index to both printed works and MS. collections relating to episcopal government. See also Wake (1181).

(b) *Official Records*

The sources listed here and below are indicative of the types of materials which abound.

1108 ANON. 'Statistics of the Church of England, 1603, regarding recusants, revenues, and number of churches.' (From Harleian and Stowe MSS.) *Trans. Congregational Hist. Soc.* 6 (1913–15).

Cf. T. Richards, The religious census of 1676 (suppl. *Trans. Hon. Soc. Cymmrodorion*, 1925–6); and S. A. Peyton's article thereon in *E.H.R.* 48 (1933), 99–104.

1109 SHAW, W. A., ed. Minutes of the Committee for Plundered Ministers ... relating to Lancashire and Cheshire, 2 vols. (Record Soc. ... Lancashire and Cheshire, 28, 34.) 1893–6.

See appendices in vol. ii of Shaw (1139), with excerpts and descriptions of MS. collections relating to this and other committees at the time of the Long Parliament.

(c) *Sermons*

1110 MacCLURE, M. The Paul's Cross sermons, 1534–1642. 1958.

There are collections of the sermons of individuals such as Richard Allestree, 1684; and John Donne (ed. by G. R. Potter and E. Simpson, vol. i, 1952; the Easter sermons, ed. by H. H. Umbach, Ithaca, 1934); see also Donne's *Works* (1240); and Thomas Reeve, *God's plea to Nineveh ...*, 1657. See also biography sections in this chapter.

1111 PHILLIPS, J. Speculum crape-gownorum or a looking-glass for the young academicks ... with reflections on some late high flown sermons. 2 pts. 1682.

1112 MITCHELL, W. F. English pulpit oratory from Andrewes to Tillotson: a study of its literary aspects. Lond. and N.Y. 1932. Bibl.

Well-documented survey of 17th-century preaching. Cf. C. F. Richardson, *English preachers and preaching, 1640–70*, 1928. See also articles dealing with sermons as they influenced public opinion and political issues by G. Davies, *Hunt. Lib. Quart.* 3 (1939), 1–22, and E. W. Kirby, *A.H.R.* 44 (1939), 528–48. See also White (2585).

(d) *General Sources* (chronologically arranged)

For particular authors, see the biographical sections in this chapter.

1113 THE AUTHORIZED VERSION OF THE ENGLISH BIBLE, 1611. 1611. Later edn. by W. A. Wright. 5 vols. Camb. 1909.

Cf. A. W. Pollard, *Records of the English Bible: the documents relating to the translation and publication of the Bible in English, 1525–1611*, Lond. and N.Y. 1911. Of the numerous histories of the English Bible (see Read, 1959, pp. 168–70), that by B. F. Wescott, 1905, is among the best.

1114 HINDLE, C. J., ed. 'A bibliography of the printed pamphlets and broadsides of Lady Eleanor Douglas, the 17th century prophetess.' *Edin. Bibliog. Soc. Pubns.* 15 (1934), 35–54.

Pamphlets range from 1625 to 1652. Also publ. in *Edin. Bibliog. Soc. Trans.* 1 (1936), 69–98.

1115 [ROBINSON, HENRY?] Liberty of conscience or the sole means to obtain peace and truth. 1943. Repr. 1945.

On authorship see C. H. Firth, *E.H.R.* 9 (1894), 715–17. For similar pamphlets see *Thomson Tracts* under 'Liberty of conscience'. See also E. B. Underhill, ed., *Tracts on liberty of conscience, 1614–1661* (Hanserd Knollys Soc., no. 1), 1846; Jordan (1146); and Haller (960).

1116 WILLIAMS, ROGER. The bloudy tenent of persecution for cause of conscience discussed in a conference betweene truth and peace . . . 1644. 2nd edn. 1644.

This well-known work by Williams was reprinted under the editorship of E. B. Underhill (Hanserd Knollys Soc., no. 4), 1848. For excerpts and comment see also P. Miller, *Roger Williams*, Indianapolis [1953], bibl.

1117 TAYLOR, JEREMY. A discourse of the liberty of prophesying, showing the unreasonableness of prescribing to other men's faith, and the iniquity of persecuting different opinions. 1647.

Wing, T 400.

1118 DUNCON, JOHN. The returnes of spiritual comfort and grief in a devout soul, represented (by intercourse of letters) to the Right Honourable the Lady Lettice, Viscountess Falkland, &c. [1648]. 2nd edn. 1649.

By the same author: *The holy life and death of . . . Letice, Vi-Countess Falkland*, 3rd edn., 1653.

1119 EVELYN, JOHN. A devotionarie book of John Evelyn of Wotton, 1620–1706. Now first published, with an introduction by W. Frere. 1936.

See other books of devotions mentioned in chap. xviii of Hutton (1197).

1120 BLOXAM, J. R., ed. Magdalen College and King James II, 1686–88. (Oxf. Hist. Soc. Publ. Vol. 6.) 1886.

Documents relating to the controversy growing out of the king's attempt to appoint Catholics to office.

1121 LOCKE, JOHN. Epistola de tolerantia . . . Tergou. 1689.

Translated into English by W. Popple, and publ. in Lond. in the same year, 1689. A second, and a third, letter concerning toleration, were publ. in Lond. 1690, 1692. His *The reasonableness of Christianity as delivered in the scriptures* was publ. 1695.

1122 TOLAND, JOHN. Christianity not mysterious: or, a treatise shewing that there is nothing in the Gospel contrary to reason nor above it. 1696. 2nd edn. enl. 1696.

Started the deist controversy. Toland is author of various works, including *Memorial of the state of England in vindication of the Queen, the church, and the administration*, 1705. Cf. F. H. Heinemann, *John Toland and the Age of Enlightenment*, 1944.

1123 PATERSON, JAMES. Pietas Londinensis: or the present ecclesiastical state of London, containing an account of all the churches and chapels of ease ... the names of the present dignitaries ministers and lecturers. 1714.

Cf. Richard Newcourt, *Repertorium ecclesiasticum parochiale Londinense. An ecclesiastical parochial history of the diocese of London*, 2 vols., 1708–10; and George Hennessy, *Novum Repertorium parochiale Londinense*, 1898.

2. LATER WORKS

(a) *General*

1124 BOSHER, R. S. The making of the restoration settlement; the influence of the Laudians, 1649–1662. N.Y. 1951. Repr. 1957.

Important scholarly monograph on the nature of the religious restoration.

1125 BRAUER, K. Die Unionstätigkeit John Duries unter dem Protektorat Cromwells. Ein Beitrag zur Kirchengeschichte des siebzehnten Jahrhunderts. Marburg. 1907.

See also no. 1241.

1126 COX, R. The literature of the Sabbath question. 2 vols. Edin. 1865.

1127 DAVIES, G. 'Arminian versus Puritan in England, ca. 1620–1640.' *Hunt. Lib. Bull.* 5 (1934), 157–79.

Reviews familiar story but makes use of fresh illustrations.

1128 HEATH, C. Social and religious heretics in five centuries. 1936.

Includes essays on 'The Anabaptist movement', 'Winstanley and the diggers', 'The early Quakers'.

1129 HIGHAM, F. M. G. Faith of our fathers: the men and movements of the seventeenth century. 1939.

Brief survey. Cf. H. H. Henson, ed., *Studies in English religion in the seventeenth century*, 1903. See also W. S. Hudson, ed., 'The Scottish effort to presbyterianize the Church of England . . .,' *Church history*, 8 (1939), 255–82, and his 'Denominationalism as a basis for ecumenicity: a seventeenth century conception', ibid. 24 (1955), 32–50; and S. E. Mead, 'From coercion to persuasion', ibid. 25 (1956), 317–37.

1130 HUNT, J. Religious thought in England from the reformation to the end of the last century. 3 vols. 1870–3.

'A broadly conceived and still useful study.' Cf. M. Kaufmann, 'Latitudinarianism and pietism', *Camb. Mod. Hist.* v (1908), ch. 24, and bibl.; and J. B. Mullinger, 'Platonists and latitudinarians', *Camb. Hist. Engl. Lit.* viii (1912), ch. 11.

1131 KIRBY, E. W. 'The Cromwellian establishment.' *Church Hist.* 10 (1941), 144–58.

1132 LECKY, W. E. H. The history of the rise and influence of the spirit of rationalism in Europe. 2 vols. 1865.

Many editions, the most recent being in one vol., N.Y. 1955. See also H. McLachlan, *The religious opinions of Milton, Locke and Newton*, Manchester, 1941.

1133 LUCKOCK, H. M. The bishops in the tower: a record of stirring events affecting the church and nonconformists from the restoration to the revolution. 1887. 2nd edn. 1887.

See *Proceedings and tryall* . . ., 1688, later edn. 1689; and A. Strickland, *Lives* . . ., 1866.

1134 MacLEAR, J. F. 'Popular anticlericalism in the Puritan Revolution.' *Jour. Hist. Ideas*, 17 (1956), 443–70.

Examines non-doctrinal causes.

1135 REIMERS, H. Jonathan Swift, Gedanken und Schriften über Religion und kirche. Hamburg. 1935.

1136 RUPP, E. G. Six makers of English religion, 1500–1799. [1957.]

A study of six works of Engl. Protestantism and their authors: Tyndale, Cranmer, Fox, Milton, Bunyan, and Watts.

1137 SCHNEIDER, H. W. The Puritan mind. 1931.

Cf. S. W. Sachs, *Der typisch puritanische Ideengehalt in Bunyan's 'Life and Death of Mr. Badman'*, Zwönitz, 1936. See also Haller (1325), Woodhouse (308 n.), Whiting (1315).

1138 SERPELL, D. R. The condition of Protestantism in France and its influence on the relations of France and England, 1650–1654. Toulouse and Paris. 1934.

See also English interest in Jansenism in Clark (1465), and W. A. Shaw, 'The English government and the relief of Protestant refugees', *E.H.R.* 9 (1894), 662–83.

1139 SHAW, W. A. A history of the English church during the civil wars and under the commonwealth 1640–1660. 2 vols. 1900.

A standard work, based upon sound use of sources. Contains valuable appendices of documents, with descriptions of MS. collections.

1140 STOUGHTON, J. History of religion in England. 6 vols. 1881. 4th edn. 8 vols. 1901.

Originally publ. in parts, vols. i–iv, 1867–70, and v–vi, in 1878.
  Somewhat out of date, but still useful. Vols. i–v deal with the period. On political aspects see W. A. Barker, *Religion and politics, 1559–1642* (Historical Assoc. Aids for Teachers series, no. 2), 1957.

1141 TULLOCH, J. Rational theology and Christian philosophy in England in the 17th century. 2 vols. Edin. 1872. Later edn. 2 vols.

Should be checked by the more recent work of Cassirer and Powicke (2691).

1142 WOOD, T. English casuistical divinity during the seventeenth century. 1952.

Introduction to the work of leading Anglican and Puritan moralists. Cf. H. R. McAdoo, *The structure of Caroline moral theology*, 1949, bibl.

1143 WORDSWORTH, C., ed. Ecclesiastical biography . . . from the . . . reformation to the revolution. 6 vols. 1810. Later edns. 1818. 4 vols. 1853.

Many of the lives are extracts or reprints from earlier works. Includes lives of Baxter, Ferrar, H. Hammond, M. Hale, Bp. Sanderson, etc.

1144 WRIGHT, L. B. Religion and empire. The alliance between piety and commerce in English expansion. Chapel Hill. 1943. Repr. 1965.

First full and adequate treatment of the subject, drawing upon contemporary propagandist literature.

(b) *Ideas of Toleration*

See also Ch. III *supra*, § F, on Political Theory, and no. 1416.

1145 GWATKIN, H. M. 'Religious toleration in England.' *Camb. Mod. Hist.* v (1908), 324–37. Bibl.

A good introduction to the subject. Also by Gwatkin, *Church and state in England to the death of Queen Anne*, 1917. Cf. R. W. Battenhouse, 'The grounds of religious toleration in the thought of John Donne', *Church Hist.* 11 (1942), 217–48; M. Freund, *Die Idee der Tolerantz im England der Grossen Revolution*, Halle, 1927; T. Lyon, *The theory of religious liberty in England, 1603–39*, Camb. 1937. See also D. Nobbs, 'Phillip Nye on Church and State', *Camb. Hist. Jour.* 5 (1935), 41–59.

1146 JORDAN, W. K. The development of religious toleration in England. 4 vols. Camb. (Mass.) 1932–40.

The definitive work for the period from the Reformation to 1660. The second volume covers 1603–40; vols. iii and iv cover 1640–60. Cf. Jordan's related articles in *Hunt. Lib. Quart.* 3 (1940), 197–223, 289–314, 403–18.

1147 RUSSELL-SMITH, H. F. The theory of religious liberty in the reigns of Charles II and James II. Camb. 1911. Bibl.

Cf. A. A. Seaton, *The theory of toleration under the Stuarts*, Camb. 1911, bibl.; and C. F. Mullett, 'Toleration and persecution in England', *Church Hist.* 18 (1949), 18–43.

1148 SCHLATTER, R. B. The social ideas of religious leaders, 1660–1688. Oxf. 1940.

Shows how the churches had much in common on ideas of toleration, etc.

1149 SYKES, N. 'Ecumenical movements in Great Britain in the seventeenth and eighteenth centuries.' In R. Rouse and S. C. Neil, eds., *History of the ecumenical movements, 1517–1948*. Phila. 1954. Bibl.

(c) *Hymnology*

See also Ch. X *infra*, pp. 400–6 on Music.

1150 JULIAN, J., ed. Dictionary of hymnology. 1892. Later edns. 2 vols. N.Y. 1957.

Cf. *Hymns ancient and modern . . . historical edition with notes on the origin of both hymns and tunes . . . illustrated with facsimiles and portraits*, 1909; and L. F. Benson, *The English hymn, its development and use in worship*, N.Y. 1915.

1151 DAVIS, A. P. Isaac Watts: his life and works. N.Y. 1943.

B. ANGLICAN CHURCH

1. GENERAL

The literature on doctrinal and liturgical history is enormous, and much is to be found in collected works of eminent divines. A useful guide is Darling (1105). For documents on constitutional development see Cardwell (1153); for an outline of the history of the Church of England see Makower (1198). See also Ch. XI *infra*, nos. 3301–14; and also nos. 2415–16. Modern scholars have contributed some important biographies.

(a) *Bibliography and Sources*

1152   JENKINS, C. Ecclesiastical records. 1920.

Helps for Students of History series. See also Whitney (p. 159), and *Church Quarterly Review.*

1153   CARDWELL, E., ed. Documentary annals of the reformed Church of England; being a collection of injunctions, declarations, orders, articles of inquiry . . . from the year 1546 to the year 1716, with notes, historical and explanatory. 2 vols. Oxf. 1839. Later edn. 2 vols. 1844.

Cf. by Cardwell, *Synodalia: A collection of articles of religion, canons and proceedings of convocations in the province of Canterbury from . . . 1547 to . . . 1717*, 2 vols., Oxf. 1842. A useful small collection is H. Gee and W. J. Hardy, eds., *Documents illustrative of English church history* [314–1701], 1896.

1154   WILKINS, D., ed. Concilia Magnae Britanniae et Hiberniae [446–1717]. 4 vols. 1737.

The latter part of vol. iv deals with the 17th century. This work is an amplification of Henry Spelman's *Concilia . . . leges . . . Britannici*, 2 vols., 1639–64.

1155   LEGG, J. W. English orders for consecrating churches in the 17th century, together with forms for the consecration of churchyards. Henry Bradshaw Soc. 1911.

Cf. the same writer's 'On the form and consecration of the church and churchyard of Fulmer in 1610, as used by William Barlow, Bishop of Lincoln', in *Trans. St. Paul's Eccles. Soc.* 6 (1907).

1156   LEGG, L. G. W., ed. English coronation records. Westminster. 1901.

From the earliest times to the coronation of Queen Victoria. See by J. W. Legg, *The coronation order of King James I*, 1902; and *Three coronation orders* (Henry Bradshaw Soc.), 1900. Cf. *The manner of the coronation of King Charles the First of England*, ed. by C. Wordsworth (Henry Bradshaw Soc.), 1892.

1157   KITCHIN, G. W., Dean of Durham, ed. The records of the northern convocation [1279–1710]. Durham. 1907. Surtees Soc. Vol. 113.

1158   WAKE, WILLIAM. Primary visitation charge. 1707.

See also W. P. M. Kennedy (1107); S. L. Ollard and P. C. Walker, *Archbishop Herring's visitation returns, 1743* (5 vols., Yorks. Arch. Soc., 1928–31), the most complete published collections, with a good introduction. The Winchester College articles (1635) are printed in full in *H.M.C.*, iv. 149, from the Lambeth MSS. Cf. no. 3302.

1159 MORE, P. E. and CROSS, F. L. Anglicanism: the thought and practice of the Church of England, illustrated from the religious literature of the seventeenth century, 1935.

Cf. *Anglican liturgies*, ed. by J. H. Arnold, foreword by the Dean of Chichester, 1939. For a devotional manual see [Richard Allestree,] *The whole duty of man . . . necessary for all families. With private devotions for several occasions*, 1658, later edns. (see 2200), on the authorship of which see P. Elmen, 'Richard Allestree and the whole duty of man', *Library*, 5th Ser. 6 (1951), 19–27. See also *A devotionarie book of John Evelyn of Wotton* (1119).

1160 BARLOW, [BISHOP] WILLIAM. The summe and substance of the conference, which it pleased his excellent maiestie to have . . . at Hampton Court, January 14, 1603. 1604.

Repr. in Cardwell, *History of Conferences*. See M. H. Curtis, 'The Hampton Court conference and its aftermath', *History*, 44 (1961), 1–16.

1161 CONSTITUTIONS AND CANONS ecclesiastical treated upon by the Bishop of London president of the Convocation for the province of Canterbury and the rest of the bishops and clergie . . . and agreed upon with the kings . . . licence. 1604. Later ed. by C. H. Davis. 1869. Ed. by M. E. C. Walcott. Oxf. and Lond. 1874. Ed. by J. V. Bullard. 1934.

See also Sparrow (1173).

1162 HUTTON, TIMOTHY [THOS.?]. Reasons for refusal of subscription to the booke of Common Praier under the handes of certaine ministers of Devon and Cornwall. 2 pts. Oxf. 1605. Later edn. part 2. 1606.

For the controversy provoked by this see tracts by T. Sparke and S. ['Hieron'], *S.T.C.* nos. 23020 and 13395.

1163 MASON, F. Of the consecration of the bishops in the Church of England . . . as also of the ordination of priests and deacons. Five bookes wherein they are cleared from the slanders . . . of Bellarmine Sanders . . . and other Romanists. 1613.

Also in Latin, 1625. For defence of other aspects of Anglicanism see Richard Mocket, *Doctrina et politia Ecclesiae Anglicanae . . . quibus ejusdem Ecclesiae apologia praefigitur*, 1617, which contains esp. Jewel's 'Apology', The Prayer Book Catechism, A more advanced Catechism, The 39 Articles—with summary of two books of homilies, The ordinal and *Ecclesiae Anglicanae disciplina et politia*, an account of the organization of the Church of England, authority of king, jurisdiction of bishops, etc. See also Thomas Morton, *A defence of the Innocencie of the three ceremonies of the Church of England*, 1619, replies to which by Wm. Ames and John Burges are *S.T.C.* nos. 559 and 4113. See also Richard Crakanthorp, *Defensio Ecclesiae Anglicanae contra M. Antonii de Dominis . . . iniurias*, ed. by J. Barkham, 1625, repr. in Anglo-Catholic Library, 1847.

1164 MONTAGU, RICHARD. Appello Caesarem: A iust appeale from two uniust informers. 1625.

The central work of the controversy which raged round Montagu. For details see *D.N.B.*

1165 WILLIAMS, JOHN. The holy table, name and thing, more anciently, properly and literally used under the New Testament, than that of an altar.

Written long ago by a minister in Lincolnshire, in answer to D. Coal, a judicious divine of Q. Maries dayes. Printed for the dioc. of Lincoln. 1637.

Cf. Peter Heylyn's *Antidotum Lincolniense or an answer to a book entituled The Holy Table*, 1637.

1166 HALL, JOSEPH. An humble remonstrance to the high court of parliament by a dutifull sonne of the Church. 1640.

This provoked 'An answer' by Smectymnuus, 1641, Bishop Hall replied with *A defence of the humble remonstrance*, 1641, Smectymnuus issued *A vindication of the answer*. . . . To this, and to a further reply to the 'Defence' called *Animadversions upon the remonstrants defence*, by Milton, Hall replied further (see Wing H 417, 393; Hall's *Works*; and Masson's *Life of Milton*, ii. 213).

1167 ASTON, SIR THOMAS. A remonstrance against Presbitery. Exhibited by divers of the nobilitie, gentrie, ministers and inhabitants of the county palatine of Chester . . . Together with a short survey of the Presbyterian discipline . . . 1641.

Includes (1) the Chester remonstrance to the House of Lords against Presbyterian government, with (2) A letter in support of it, and (3) A petition against it.

1168 HEWES [HUGHES], L [LEWIS]. Certaine grievances, or the errours of the service-booke plainely layd open . . . s.l. 1641.

A summary of Puritan objections with interesting illustrative matter.

1169 WHITE, JOHN. The first century of scandalous, malignant priests made and admitted into benefices by the prelates . . . to . . . 1643.

An account of sequestrated clergy, mainly in Essex, by the chairman of committee of inquiry.

1170 FULLER, THOMAS. The church history of Britain [to 1648]. 6 pts. 1655. Ed. by J. S. Brewer. 6 vols. Oxf. 1845. Ed. by J. Nichols. 3 vols. 1868.

In the edn. of 1845 vols. v and vi contain the reigns of James I and Charles I. Appendices include: (A) Sir Thomas Herbert's memoirs; (B) Bishop Cosin and his accusers; (C) Bishop Montague and his accusers. On Fuller's *Holy and profane state*, 1642, see no. 2169.

1171 SPARROW, ANTHONY. A rationale upon the book of common prayer.

The date of the earliest edn. is doubtful. There are copies of that of 1657 at the Bodleian Library and at Queens' College, Camb. After the revision of the Prayer Book in 1662 the *Rationale* was altered accordingly and appeared in many edns. See also P. Heylyn, '*Ecclesia vindicata, or the Church of England justified*', 1657, which includes 'The historie of episcopacie', publ. by the author in 1642 under the pseudonym of Theophilus Churchman.

1172 PEARSON, JOHN. An exposition of the creed. 1659. Later edn. by W. Bowyer. 1710. Ed. by E. Burton. Oxf. 1890.

The standard work on the creed. Cf. *The minor theological works of . . . John Pearson, 1659-82*, ed. by E. Churton, 2 vols., Oxf. 1844.

1173 [SPARROW, ANTHONY], ed., A collection of articles, injunctions, canons, orders, ordinances, and constitutions ecclesiastical, with other publick records of the Church of England chiefly in the times of K. Edward VI, Q. Elizabeth, K. James, and K. Charles I. 1661. Later edn. 1699.

Pref. by Sparrow. Most of the material is now more easily found in the publications of Cardwell. Cf. Edmund Gibson, *Codex juris ecclesiastici anglicani: or, The statutes, constitutions, canons, rubricks and articles of the Church of England*, 2 vols., 1713, 2nd edn., 2 vols., Oxf. 1761; and E. Cardwell's edn. of Gibson's *Synodus anglicana, or the constitution and proceedings of an English convocation shown from the acts and registers thereof to be agreeable to the principles of an episcopal church* (1702, later edns., 1730), Oxf. 1854. See also no. 1161.

1174 EACHARD, JOHN. The grounds and occasions of the contempt of the clergy and religion enquired into. 1670. Many later edns.

Repr. in *Critical essays and literary fragments*, intro. by J. C. Collins, Westminster, 1903. For a series of tracts evoked by this famous criticism, see Wing S 188; E 60, 65, 66; B 4213, and T 4.

1175 [LLOYD, WILLIAM.] Seasonable discourse shewing the necessity of maintaining the established religion, in opposition to popery. 1673. 5th edn. 1673.

See *Enchiridion theologicum anti-Romanum*, 3 vols., Oxf. 1836–7, for reprints of tracts against Roman Catholicism by Jeremy Taylor, Isaac Barrow, Wake, and others.

1176 OVERALL, JOHN. Bishop Overall's convocation-Book MDCVI concerning the government of God's catholic church and the kingdoms of the whole world. 1690. Later edn. Oxf. 1844.

1177 [LONG, THOMAS.] Vox cleri, or the sense of the clergy concerning the making of alterations in the established liturgy. 1690.

1178 SHERLOCK, WILLIAM. The case of the allegiance due to sovereign powers stated and resolved according to scripture and reason and the principles of the Church of England. 1691.

Cf. Macaulay (361) for a summary of this controversy, pp. 457–9, 543 (edn. 1907). Cf. Sherlock's *Discourses preached . . . on several occasions*, 4 vols., Oxf. 1812.

1179 VALOR BENEFICIORUM, or a valuation of all ecclesiastical preferments in England and Wales. 1695.

Cf. John Ecton, *Liber valorum et decimarum . . .* 1711; later edns. 1723, 1728.

1180 GARDINER, JAMES. Advice to the clergy of the diocese of Lincoln. 1697.

Reveals much on condition of the clergy. See also *Brief memoir of Mr. Justice Rokeby* (1037); D. Robertson, ed., *Diary of Francis Evans: secretary to Bishop Lloyd, 1699–1706*, Oxf. 1903; R. Gibbon, 'John Lambe, dean of Ely, 1693–1708', *Church Quart. Rev.* 119 (1935), 226–56; G. C. Moore Smith, ed., *Extracts from the papers of Thomas Woodcock, Camden Soc. Misc.* xi (1907); and *The rector's book, Clayworth, Notts. 1672–1701*, ed. by H. Gill and E. L. Guilford, Nottingham, 1910.

1181 WAKE, WILLIAM. The authority of Christian princes over their ecclesiastical synods asserted with particular respect to the convocations of the clergy of the realm and Church of England. 1697.

This provoked a lively controversy. Cf. Francis Atterbury, *The rights, powers, and privileges of an English convocation stated and vindicated*, 1700. Wake replied in *The state of the Church and clergy of England in their councils, synods, convocations . . . historically deduced from the conversion of the Saxons to the present times*, 1703. There is a useful bibliography on this controversy in Hutton (1197), pp. 280–1; and in Sykes, *Church and State . . . 18th cent.* (1200 n.). Cf. N. Sykes's excellent bibliography in his *William Wake, Archbishop of Canterbury 1657–1737*, 2 vols., N.Y. and Camb. 1957; and J. H. Lupton, *Archbishop Wake and the project of union* [1717–20] *between the Gallican and Anglican churches*, 1896.

1182 DRAKE, J. The memorial of the Church of England, humbly offered to the consideration of all true lovers of our church and constitution. 1705. Later edn. [with life]. 1711.

1183 HICKES, GEORGE. Two treatises, one of the Christian priesthood, the other of the dignity of the episcopal order. 1707. Later edns. 2 vols. 1711. 3 vols. Oxf. 1847–8.

1184 COLLIER, JEREMY. An ecclesiastical history of Great Britain from the first planting of Christianity to the end of the reign of King Charles II. 2 vols. 1708–14. Later edn. by T. Lathbury. 9 vols. 1852.

1185 WALKER, JOHN. An attempt towards recovering an account of the numbers and sufferings of the clergy of the Church of England who were sequester'd, harass'd &c. in the grand rebellion. 1714.

Walker's MS. collections which formed the basis of the above work are in the Bodleian, and contain a mass of biographical material which appears only in part in the above work. G. B. Tatham's *Dr. John Walker and the sufferings of the clergy* (Camb. 1911) supplies a study of Walker's work and a catalogue of his MSS. See A. G. Matthews, *Walker revised*, Oxf. and Lond. 1948.
　　See also [John Johnson], *The clergy-man's vade-mecum: or, An account of the ancient and present church of England; the duties and rights of the clergy; and of their privileges and hardships . . .*, 2 vols. 3rd edn. 1709, 4th edn., rev. and corr., 1715.

1186 HESSELS, J. H., ed. Ecclesiae Londino-Batavae Archivum. Vol. iii. Epistulae et tractatus cum Reformationis tum ecclesiae Londino-Batavae historiam illustrantes [1523–1874]. 2 parts. Camb. 1897.

Cf. *E.H.R.* 15 (1900), 788–800.

(b) *Later Works*

1187 ABBEY, C. J. and OVERTON, J. H. The English church in the eighteenth century. 2 vols. 1878.

Useful also for the previous period. Cf. Overton's *Life in the English church* [1660–1714], 1885, bibl. See also C. L. Grose, 'Religion of restoration England', *Church Hist.* 6 (1937), 3–12, and Abbott and Burrage (356 n.).

1188 ADDLESHAW, G. W. O. The High Church tradition: a study in the liturgical thought of the 17th century. 1941.

1189 BABINGTON, C. Mr. Macaulay's character of the clergy in the latter part of the seventeenth century considered. Camb. 1849.

Cf. P. H. Ditchfield, 'The errors of Lord Macaulay in his estimation of the squires and parsons of the seventeenth century', *R.H.S. Trans.*, 3rd ser. 9 (1915), 77–93; and C. H. Mayo, 'The social status of the clergy in the seventeenth and eighteenth centuries', *E.H.R.* 37 (1922), 258–66. See also A. T. Hart, *The country clergy in Elizabethan and Stuart times, 1558–1660,* 1958, bibl.; and also by Hart, *The eighteenth century country parson, 1689–1830,* Shrewsbury, 1955; and E. H. Day, 'The country clergy to the restoration period', *Theology,* 25 (1937), 354–60.

1190 [BOYER, A.] An impartial history of the occasional conformity and schism bills, containing the rise and progress of those two acts, with all the debates . . . 1717.

Advocates repeal.

1191 CARDWELL, E. A history of conferences and other proceedings connected with the revision of the Book of Common Prayer from the year 1558 to the year 1690. Oxf. 1840. 3rd edn. Oxf. 1849.

1192 CRAGG, G. R. From puritanism to the age of reason: a study of changes in religious thought within the Church of England, 1660 to 1700. Lond. and Camb. 1950.

An excellent study of the factors responsible for the eclipse of Calvinism after the restoration and of the new solution of religious problems offered by the Christian Platonists and the Latitudinarians, as well as the impact of the new science. See also A. Whiteman, 'The re-establishment of the Church of England, 1660–1663', *R.H.S. Trans.*, 5th ser. 6 (1955), 111–31; N. Pocock, 'The restoration settlement of the English church', *E.H.R.* 1 (1886), 677–98; and *History of non-conformity as it was argued and stated by commissioners on both sides in 1661,* 1704, 2nd edn., 1708.

1193 EVERY, G. The High Church party, 1688–1718. 1956.

Broader in content than the title suggests, dealing with the components of the High Church group, but also with the opposition elements. See also G. M. Straka, *Anglican reaction to the revolution of 1688,* Madison (Wisc.), 1962.

1194 FRERE, W. H. The English church in the reigns of Elizabeth and James I. 1904. Bibl. notes.

Scholarly; a companion volume to Hutton (1196). For a modern interpretation of the ideology of the church see C. H. and K. George, *The protestant mind of the English reformation, 1570–1640,* Princeton, 1961.

1195 HILL, C. Economic problems of the Church from Archbishop Whitgift to the Long Parliament. Oxf. 1956.

Careful survey of the economic problems of the established Church, 1580–1640. Cf. M. James, 'The political importance of the tithes controversy in the English revolution, 1640–60', *History,* 26 (1941), 1–18.

1196 HUTTON, W. H. The English church from the accession of Charles I to the death of Anne. (Part vi of A history of the English Church, ed. by W. R. W. Stephens and W. Hunt.) 1903. Bibl. notes.

A standard work. Cf. H. O. Wakeman, *History of the Church of England,* 1912, for a useful short account. For Anglicanism in the colonies see Cross (3338 n.).

1197 HUTTON, W. H. Caroline divines. *Camb. Hist. of Eng. Lit.* Vol. vii. 1911. Bibl.

Chap. 6; continued in his 'Divines of the Church of England 1660–1700', ibid. viii (1912), chap. 12, bibl.

1198 MAKOWER, F. The constitutional history and constitution of the Church of England. Trans. from the German. 1895.

See also T. Lathbury, *A history of the convocation of the Church of England* [to 1742], 1842, 2nd edn., 1853.

1199 PROCTER, F. and FRERE, W. H. A new history of the Book of Common Prayer. 1901.

Cf. J. H. Blunt, ed., *The annotated Book of Common Prayer*, 1866, bibl., later edns. 1884 and 1903, bibl.; and E. C. Ratcliff, *The Booke of Common Prayer of the Church of England: its making and revisions, 1549–1661*, 1949, with numerous illustrations.

1200 SYKES, N. Old priest and new presbyter. Camb. 1956.

Lectures on the *via media* by a modern authority. By Sykes also: *The Church of England and non-episcopal churches in the 16th and 17th centuries*, 1948; 'Queen Anne and the episcopate', *E.H.R.* 1 (1935), 433–64; *Church and state in England in the eighteenth century*, Camb. 1934, bibl.; and *From Sheldon to Secker; aspects of English church history, 1660–1768*, Camb. 1959. Cf. H. H. Henson, *The relationship of the Church of England to the other reformed churches*, Edin. 1911.

1201 TATHAM, G. B. The Puritans in power (1640–60). Camb. 1913. Bibl. footnotes.

Deals with the ejected clergy, the visitation of the universities, and the disposal of church property. Also by Tatham: 'The sale of episcopal lands, during the Civil Wars and commonwealth', *E.H.R.* 23 (1908), 91–108, including valuable tables from the P.R.O. Close Rolls, 1647–59.

1202 USHER, R. G. The reconstruction of the English church. 2 vols. Lond. and N.Y. 1910. Bibl.

Deals chiefly with the work and times of Bancroft. Appendices of documents and studies. Also by Usher: *The rise and fall of the high commission*, Oxf. 1913, bibl.

1203 WILSON, F. W. The importance of the reign of Queen Anne in English church history. Oxf. 1911. Bibl.

Cf. A. Savidge, *The foundation and early years of Queen Anne's bounty*, 1955, bibl.

2. SPECIAL SUBJECTS

(a) *Non-Jurors*

1204 [SELLER, ABEDNIGO.] History of passive obedience . . . Amsterdam. 1689. Enl. edn. 1690.

By a non-juror. Several replies are listed in B.M. *Catalogue*—e.g. [Thomas Bainbridge,] *Seasonable reflections on a late pamphlet*, 1689–90 (Wing, B 474).

1205 LATHBURY, T. A history of the nonjurors, their controversies and writings. 1845.

See also J. H. Overton, *The nonjurors, their lives, principles and writings*, 1902, with an alphabetical list on pp. 467–96. See also Ken (1262) and Kettlewell (1264).

1206 HAWKINS, L. M. Allegiance in Church and State, the problem of the nonjurors in the English revolution. 1928.

(b) *Religious Societies*

See also *Social History*, and Ch. X, *Education.*

1207 WOODWARD, JOSIAH. Account of the rise of the religious societies in . . . London. 1697. 2nd edn. 1698. 4th edn. 1712.

> Similar works erroneously attributed to Woodward and to Defoe: *Account of the societies for reformation of manners,* 1699, 5th edn., 1701; and *Account of the progress of the reformation of manners,* 3rd edn., 1701, 14th edn., 1706. Cf. White Kennett, *Account of the Society for Propagating the Gospel in Foreign Parts,* 1706.

1208 ALLEN, W. O. B. and McCLURE, E. Two hundred years: the history of the Society for Promoting Christian Knowledge, 1698–1898. 1898.

> Cf. McClure, *Chapter in church history, being the minutes of the Society for Promoting Christian Knowledge . . . 1698–1704,* 1888; and W. K. L. Clarke, *Short History of S.P.C.K.,* 1919.

1209 PORTUS, G. V. Caritas Anglicana, or, an historical inquiry into those religious and philanthropical societies that flourished in England between the years 1678 and 1740. 1912.

1210 THOMPSON, H. P. Thomas Bray. 1954.

> Probably the definitive biography of the zealous promoter of the societies for the reformation of manners, the S.P.C.K. and the S.P.G., the charity school movement, and the movement for setting up parochial libraries. See B. C. Steiner, *Rev. Thomas Bray: his life and selected works relating to Maryland,* Baltimore, 1901; and two articles on Bray by S. C. McCullough in *William and Mary Quart.,* 3rd ser. 2 (1945), 15–32, 333–48.

3. COLLECTED BIOGRAPHY

1211 CASSAN, S. H. Lives of the bishops of Bath and Wells from the earliest to the present period. 2 vols. in one. 1829–30.

> Cassan wrote similar works for Sherborne and Salisbury, Salisbury, 1824; and for Winchester, 2 vols., 1827.

1212 COLLINS, W. E., ed. Typical English churchmen from Parker to Maurice. A series of lectures. 1902.

> Includes Chillingworth, Usher, Bramhall, Jeremy Taylor, Burnet.

1213 DUNTON, JOHN. The life and errors of John Dunton . . . written by himself in solitude . . . with the lives and characters of more than a thousand contemporary divines, and other persons of literary eminence. 1705. Later edn. by J. B. Nichols. 2 vols. 1818.

1214 HOOK, W. F. Lives of the archbishops of Canterbury (to Juxon). 12 vols. with index. 1860–84.

> See R. A. Christopher's bibliography relating to Archbishop George Abbott (d. 1633), publ. by the Univ. of Va. Press, 1966.

1215 LE NEVE, JOHN. Fasti Ecclesiae Anglicanae: or, an essay towards deducing a regular succession of all the principal dignitaries in each cathedral, collegiate church or chapel . . . in . . . England and Wales . . . to this present year 1715. 1716. Later edn. by T. D. Hardy. 3 vols. Oxf. 1854.

Edn. of 1854 corrected and continued to 1854.

1216 POPE, W. Life of Seth [Ward] Lord Bishop of Salisbury . . . with a brief account of Bishop Wilkins, Dr. Isaac Barrow, Mr. Lawrence Rooke, Dr. Turberville and others. 1697.

1217 SALMON, N. The lives of the English bishops from the restauration to the revolution. 1733.

A useful compilation containing seventy-four lives. Originally publ. in three parts, 1731–3. It was anonymous. Cf. John Le Neve, *The lives and characters . . . of all the protestant bishops of the Church of England since . . . 1559*, 1720, of which only one volume, dealing with archbishops, appeared. A biography of Matthew Wren, Bishop of Ely, is in C. Wren, *Parentalia* (2760 n.).

4. INDIVIDUALS: BIOGRAPHIES, PERSONAL NARRATIVES, AND COLLECTED WORKS

ANDREWES, LANCELOT

1218 [Works] by Lancelot Andrewes. Ed. by J. P. Wilson and J. Bliss. 9 vols. Oxf. 1841–54.

Includes *Tortura Torti sive ad Matthai Torti librum responsio*, 1609, and *Responsio ad Apologiam Cardinalis Bellarmini . . .*, 1610, being two important parts of the controversy about the oath of allegiance; and, among the 'Minor Works', *An exact narration of the life & death of . . . Lancelot Andrewes . . . faithfully collected by Henry Isaacson*, 1650; and *Two answers to Cardinal Perron, and Two speeches in the Starr-Chamber by . . . Lancelot late Bishop of Winchester*, 1629. Standard biographies are A. T. Russell, *Memoirs of the life and works of . . . Lancelot Andrewes, Lord Bishop of Winchester*, Camb. 1860; and R. L. Ottley, *Lancelot Andrewes*, 1894. Recent lives are by F. Higham, 1952, and P. A. Welsby, 1958. For an analysis of his thought, particularly as revealed in his sermons, see M. F. Reidy, *Bishop Lancelot Andrewes, Jacobean court preacher: a study in early seventeenth-century religious thought*, Chicago, 1955.

ATTERBURY, FRANCIS

1219 Memoirs and correspondence of Francis Atterbury, D.D., Bishop of Rochester. Ed. by F. Williams. 2 vols. 1869.

Useful though meandering. See also J. Nichols, ed., *The epistolary correspondence . . . of Francis Atterbury* (1662–1732), 5 vols., 1783–98. For a biography of this high church Anglican, in his later years connected with Jacobitism, see H. C. Beeching, *Francis Atterbury*, 1909, bibl.

BANCROFT, RICHARD

1220 [Bancroft, Richard, Archbishop of Canterbury.] Tracts ascribed to Richard Bancroft. Ed. from MSS. in Library of St. John's College, Camb., by A. Peel. Camb. 1953.

BARLOW, THOMAS

1221 The genuine remains of . . . Thomas Barlow, late Lord Bishop of Lincoln. 1693.

BARROW, ISAAC

1222 The theological works of . . . Isaac Barrow. Ed. by John Tillotson. 4 vols.
1683–87. 5th edn. 3 vols. 1741. Later edn. 8 vols. Oxf. 1830. Ed. by
A. Napier. 9 vols. Camb. 1859.

A three-volume edn., with a biography by James Hamilton, was publ. 1840–1.
Barrow was master of Trinity College. See P. H. Osmond, *Isaac Barrow: his life and
times*, 1944.

BARWICK, JOHN

1223 Barwick, P. The life of . . . John Barwick . . . successively dean of Durham
and St. Paul's . . . with . . . an appendix of letters from King Charles I in his
confinement, and King Charles II and . . . Clarendon in their exile, and other
papers . . . from . . . St. John's College [Camb.]. Trans. by H. Bedford. 1724.

Original Latin edn., *Vita Johannis Barwick*, 1721. An abbrev. edn., 1903.

BEVERIDGE, WILLIAM

1224 The works of . . . William Beveridge, Lord Bishop of St. Asaph. With
a memoir of the author by T. H. Horne. 9 vols. 1824. Later edn. 12 vols.
Oxf. 1842–8.

Also publ. 2 vols., 1720.

BLACKBURNE, LAUNCELOT

1225 Sykes, N. '"The Buccaneer Bishop": Launcelot Blackburne, 1658–1743.'
Church Quart. Rev. 130 (1940), 81–100.

Defends Blackburne as a moderate, slightly opportunistic churchman typical of the
period.

BLAKE, MARTIN

1226 Chanter, J. F. The life and times of Martin Blake, B.D. (1593–1673),
vicar of Barnstaple and prebendary of Exeter Cathedral. 1910.

BRAMHALL, JOHN

1227 The works of the most reverend John Bramhall, D.D., sometime Lord
Archbishop of Armagh . . . Ed. by A.W.H. Later edn. 5 vols. Oxf. 1842–5.

Defends Anglican and royalist views against Romanists, sectaries, and Hobbes—with
sermons, letters, and a life of the author. His papers are in H.M.C., R. R. Hastings
MSS., 3 vols., 1928–34. See also J. T. Ball, *The reformed Church of Ireland* (4248),
and no. 4252.

BULL, GEORGE

1228 The works of George Bull, D.D., Lord Bishop of St. David's, collected
and revised by Edward Burton. To which is prefixed the Life of Bishop Bull
by Robert Nelson. 8 vols., Oxf. 1827. Later edn. 6 vols. 1846.

BURNET, GILBERT

1229 Clarke, T. E. S., and Foxcroft, H. C. A life of Gilbert Burnet, Bishop
of Salisbury. Intro. by Sir C. H. Firth. Camb. 1907. Bibl.

Cf. Burnet, *Lives, characters, and a sermon*, ed. by J. Jebb, Dublin, 1803, later edn. 1833.
See also his *History* (341).

BUSHNELL, WALTER

1230 Bushnell, Walter. A narrative of the proceedings of the commissioners appointed by O. Cromwell for ejecting scandalous and ignorant ministers in the case of Walter Bushnell . . . vicar of Box in the county of Wilts. 1660.

Specimen of the attacks on Cromwell's ecclesiastical settlement. See also Sir G. Isham, ed., *The correspondence of Bishop Brian Duppa and Sir Justinian Isham, 1650–1660*, The Northamptonshire Rec. Soc., 1955.

CARTWRIGHT, THOMAS

1231 The diary of Dr. Thomas Cartwright, Bishop of Chester, 1686–87. Ed. by J. Hunter. Camden Soc. 1843.

Important for James II and the revolution.

CASAUBON, ISAAC

1232 Isaac Casaubon 1559–1614. By M. Pattison. 1875. Bibl. 2nd edn. Oxf. 1892.

CHILLINGWORTH, WILLIAM

1233 The works of William Chillingworth. 3 pts. 1727. Ed. by T. Birch. 1742. Later edn. 3 vols. Oxf. 1838.

His *Religion of Protestants*, 1637, illustrates the Laudian interpretation as Chillingworth understood it upon his reconversion from Rome. Cf. *Historical and critical account of the life of William Chillingworth*, by P. Des Maizeaux, 1725. Also A. E. Simpson, 'William Chillingworth', *Hibbert Journal*, 36 (1938), 235–45.

COMBER, THOMAS

1234 The autobiographies and letters of Thomas Comber. Ed. by C. E. Whiting. 2 vols. Surtees Soc. 1941–2.

Comber (1640–1708) was sometime precentor of York and Dean of Durham.

COMPTON, HENRY

1235 Compton, Henry. Episcopalia or letters . . . to the clergy of his diocese. 1686. Ed. by S. W. Cornish. Oxf. 1842.

Cf. E. P. Carpenter, *The Protestant bishop, being the life of Henry Compton, 1632–1713, Bishop of London*, 1956. Many letters to Compton are in Bodleian Libr. Rawl. C 982–5.

COSIN, JOHN

1236 The works of the Right Reverend father in God John Cosin, Lord Bishop of Durham. [Ed. by J. Sansom.] 5 vols. Oxf. 1843–55. Bibl.

Cf. *The correspondence of John Cosin, Lord Bishop of Durham, together with other papers illustrative of his life and times*, edited by G. Ornsby, 2 vols., Surtees Soc., Durham, 1869–72; and P. H. Osmond, *A life of John Cosin, Bishop of Durham*, 1913.

CREWE, NATHANIEL, LORD

1237 Memoirs of Nathaniel, Lord Crewe. Ed. by A. Clark. *Camden Soc. Misc.* ix (1893).

MS. at Bamborough Castle. A flattering biography by an early 18th-century writer. *An examination of the life and character of Nathaniel Crewe* was publ. 1790. A modern biography, based upon extensive research, but not wholly reliable, is C. E. Whiting's *Nathaniel Lord Crewe, Bishop of Durham, 1674–1721, and his diocese*, 1940.

DAVENANT, JOHN

1238 Fuller, M. The life, letters, and writings of John Davenant, D.D. 1572–1641, Lord Bishop of Salisbury. 1897.

Gives considerable quotations from writings, as well as letters.

DODWELL, HENRY

1239 Brokesby, F. The life of Henry Dodwell with an account of his works. 1715.

DONNE, JOHN

1240 The works of John Donne ... with a memoir of his life. Ed. by H. Alford. 6 vols. 1839 (see 2620).

See also E. M. Simpson, *A study of the prose works of John Donne*, 1924, rev. edn., 1948.

DURY, JOHN

1241 Batten, J. M. John Dury, advocate of Christian reunion. Chicago and Lond. 1944.

Well-balanced study but not a definitive biography. Cf. G. Westin's 'Brev från John Durie åren 1636–1638', *Kyrkohistorisk Arsskrift*, 33 (1934), 193–349 (note and correspondence of John Durie with Laud, Hartlib, Roe, etc.); and Westin, *John Durie in Sweden, 1636–1638, documents and letters*, Uppsala, 1936 (issued in parts, 1934–6). See also Brauer (1125), and N. Sykes, *Daniel Ernst Jablonski and the Church of England: a study of an essay towards Protestant union*, 1950.

FERRAR, NICHOLAS

1242 Nicholas Ferrar. Two lives by his brother John and by Doctor Jebb. Ed. by J. E. B. Mayor. Camb. 1855.

Cf. *Nicholas Ferrar, his household and his friends*, Anon., ed. by T. T. Carter, 1892; and *The Ferrar papers*, ed. by B. Blackstone, Camb. and N.Y. 1938. Two works by A. L. Maycock, *Nicholas Ferrar of Little Gidding*, 1938, and *Chronicles of Little Gidding*, 1954, are based on documents in Magdalene College, Camb.

FLEETWOOD, WILLIAM

1243 A compleat collection of the sermons tracts and pieces of all kinds that were written by ... William Fleetwood late Lord Bishop of Ely. 1737. Later edn. Oxf. 1854.

FRAMPTON, ROBERT

1244 The life of Robert Frampton, Bishop of Gloucester. Deprived as a non-juror of 1689. Ed. by T. S. Evans. 1876.

Contemporary, by unknown author.

FULLER, THOMAS

1245 Bailey, J. E. The life of Thomas Fuller, D.D. with notices of his books. his kinsmen, and his friends. 1874.

A full and documented biography and not entirely superseded by later efforts; a modern biography is W. Addison, *Worthy Dr. Fuller*, 1951. For a bibliography see *Camb. Hist. of Eng. Lit.*, vii (1911), 462–3; and S. Gibson, *A bibliography of the works of Thomas*

Fuller, D.D., 1936. On Fuller's *The holy state and the profane state* see no. 2169. See also nos. 1170 and 2442.

GLANVILL, JOSEPH

1246 Glanvill, Joseph. Essays on several important subjects in philosophy and religion. 1676.

For an analysis of Glanvill's intellectual interests and influence see J. I. Cope, *Joseph Glanvill, Anglican apologist*, St. Louis, 1956. See also nos. 2321, 2700, 2909.

GOODMAN, GODFREY

1247 Soden, G. I. Godfrey Goodman, Bishop of Gloucester, 1583–1656. 1953.

Well-documented though partisan account of the bishop who was regarded as a disguised papist in his own time. See Goodman's *Court of James I* (285).

GRANVILLE, DENIS

1248 The remains of Denis Granville, D.D., Dean . . . of Durham, being a further selection from his correspondence, diaries and other papers. Ed. by G. Ornsby. Surtees Soc. Durham. 1865.

The first selection was published in the society's volume of Miscellanies, 1860. See an uncritical *Life* by Revd. R. Granville, Exeter, 1902.

HACKET, JOHN

1249 Hacket, John. Century of sermons. 1675.

With a life by Thomas Plume. Later edn. by M. E. C. Walcott, 1865. Hackett was Bishop of Lichfield and Coventry.

HALES, JOHN

1250 Hales, John. Works . . . now first collected together. Ed. by Sir David Dalyrmple, Lord Hailes. 3 vols. Glasgow. 1765.

Cf. *An account of the life and writings of John Hales*, by P. Des Maizeaux, 1719. Hales, *Golden remains*, was first publ. 1659. See also J. H. Elson, *John Hales of Eton*, 1948.

HALL, JOSEPH

1251 The works of Joseph Hall [Bishop of Norwich]. 1625. Later edn. by J. Pratt. 10 vols. 1808. Ed. by P. Hall. 12 vols. Oxf. 1837–9. Ed. by P. Wynter. 10 vols. Oxf. 1863.

Hall's *Complete poems* were ed. by A. B. Grosart, Manchester, 1879. Cf. *Camb. Hist. of Eng. Lit.*, vol. iv, p. 519. See also T. F. Kinloch, *The life and works of Joseph Hall, 1574–1656*, Lond. and N.Y. 1951. Hall's *The discovery of a new world (Mundus alter et idem)*, *Englished by J. Brown, c. 1609*, was ed. by H. Brown, Camb., Mass. 1937; Hall's *Heaven upon earth and characters of vertues and vices* (pr. 1608) was ed. by R. Kirk, New Brunswick, 1948.

HAMMOND, HENRY

1252 Fell, John. The life of . . . Dr. H. Hammond [Bishop of Oxford]. 1661. Later edn. Oxf. 1856 (with Burnet's life of Sir Matthew Hale).

HERBERT, GEORGE

1253　The works of George Herbert. (See 2627.)

HEYLYN, PETER

1254　Vernon, George. The life of . . . Dr. Peter Heylyn, chaplain to Charles I, and Charles II. 1682.

Vernon's *Life* had been publ. before in the 1681 edn. of Heylyn's *Historical and miscellaneous tracts*. John Barnard replied to the 1682 edn. with *Theologo-historicus, or the true life*, 1683. For works by Heylyn see nos. 289 n., 1171 n., 1266 n. For the diary of Dr. Edward Lake, chaplain to Princesses Mary and Anne, see edition by G. P. Elliott, *Camden Soc. Misc.* i, 1847.

HORNECK, A[NTHONY]

1255　Kidder, Richard. The life of . . . A[nthony] Horneck. 1698.

Repr. in Libr. of Christian biography, 1837. Cf. *Bibliotheca Hornecciana: a catalogue of the library of A. H.*, 1697; and Horneck's *Several sermons*, 2nd edn., 2 vols., 1706. A German by birth, Horneck was a popular preacher.

HUTTON, MATTHEW

1256　The correspondence of Dr. Matthew Hutton, Archbishop of York . . . of Sir Timothy Hutton his son, and Matthew Hutton his grandson. Ed. by J. Raine. Surtees Soc. 1843.

Contains some interesting accounts of expenses at Cambridge University *temp.* James I.

JACKSON, T[HOMAS]

1257　A collection of the works of . . . T[homas] Jackson . . . with the life of the author by E. V[aughan]. Ed. by B. Oley. 3 pts. 1653–7. Later edn. 12 vols. Oxf. 1844.

JOHNSON, SAMUEL

1258　The works of . . . Samuel Johnson. 1710. Later edn. 1713.

See J. Wickham Legg, *E.H.R.* 29 (1914) 723–42, on Johnson's 'degradation' because of publishing anti-popery incitements to sedition, 1686.

JOSSELIN, RALPH

1259　The diary of the Rev. Ralph Josselin, 1616–1683. Ed. by E. Hockliffe. Camden Soc. 1908.

Illustrates the life of the country clergy. For other country clergymen see C. Severn, ed., *Diary of the Rev. John Ward* [Stratford-upon-Avon, 1648–79], 1839, which includes extracts on many subjects from commonplace books.

JUXON, WILLIAM

1260　Marah, W. H. Memoirs of Archbishop Juxon and his times, with a sketch of the archbishop's parish Little Compton. Oxf. 1869.

KEITH, GEORGE

1261　Kirby, E. W. George Keith (1638–1716). N.Y. 1942.

Controversial Scot, 'Christian quaker', and later Anglican clergyman.

KEN, THOMAS

1262 Plumptre, E. H. The life of Thomas Ken, Bishop of Bath and Wells. 2 vols. 1888. Later edn. 2 vols. 1890.

A detailed life, printing eighty-five of Ken's letters, and providing an excellent insight into the Anglo-Catholic point of view. It supersedes all earlier lives, as that by W. Hawkins, 1713, and that by 'A Layman' [i.e. J. L. Anderdon], [1851]. Cf. *The prose works of . . . Thomas Ken,* ed. by W. Benham [1889]. (Earlier editions of works were 1721 and 1838.) See also 'non-Jurors' (1204–6).

KENNET [KENNETT], WHITE

1263 Bennett, G. V. White Kennett, 1660–1728, Bishop of Peterborough. 1957.

First full biography since the *Life* (with letters) by W. Newton, 1730, which was more a political defence of Kennet. Kennet, who was Bishop of Peterborough, was the author of *The compleat history* (262), and *Christian scholar,* 1708. His MSS. are in Br. Mus., Lansdowne 935–1044.

KETTLEWELL, JOHN

1264 [Lee, Francis.] A compleat collection of the works of . . . John Kettlewell . . . to which is prefix'd the life of the author . . . compiled from the collection of G. Hickes and R. Nelson. 2 vols. 1719.

Cf. T. T. Carter's *Life and times of John Kettlewell,* 1895. The *Life* by Lee, which appeared as *Memoirs* in 1718, is useful for the early history of the non-juring movement.

KIDDER, RICHARD

1265 Kidder, Richard. Demonstration of the Messias. 3 pts. 1684–1700. 2nd edn. 3 pts. 1726.

Based on his Boyle lectures, 1693; attempts to 'convert Jews and confute deists'. Kidder, Bishop of Bath and Wells, wrote many sermons and a commentary on the books of Moses. His autobiography was ed. by A. E. Robinson, Somerset Rec. Soc., 1924.

LAUD, WILLIAM

1266 The works of . . . William Laud, . . . Archbishop of Canterbury. Ed. by W. Scott and J. Bliss. 7 vols. in 9. Oxf. 1847–60.

Vol. i, sermons; vols. iii and iv include his devotions and his own account of his trial; vols. vi and vii contain letters of great importance for the reign of Charles I. Other works pertain to his official duties, for which see also H.M.C., *4th Rep.* (House of Lords MSS.), 124–59. Two letters ed. by W. H. Hutton are in *E.H.R.* 45 (1930), 107–9. For notable contemporary comments see William Prynne, *Canterburie's doome . . . 1646,* which is a collection of the documents and of the proceedings on the trial and execution of Laud (for his other writings against Laud see *D.N.B. sub* 'Prynne', and Bruce, no. 747 n.); and Peter Heylyn, *Cyprianus Anglicus, or The history of the life and death [of Laud];* [and] *The ecclesiastical history of England, Scotland and Ireland, from his first rising till his death,* ed. by H. Heylin, 1668. See also W. E. Collins, *Lectures on Archbishop Laud,* with a bibl. of Laudian literature, 1895, a very useful work. See also E. R. Adair, 'Laud and the Church of England', *Church History,* 5 (1936), 121–40. E. C. E. Bourne's *The Anglicanism of William Laud,* 1947, is a vigorous defence of his ideals in church and state. The earlier biographies by W. H. Hutton, 1895, and W. L. Mackintosh, 1907, should be checked by that of Trevor-Roper (467).

LAW, WILLIAM

1267　Law, William. Works. 9 vols. [1753–76]. Priv. repr. edn. by G. Moreton. 1892–3.

See S. Hobhouse editor, *Selected mystical writings of William Law*, 1938 (2nd edn., 1948, bibl.), in one app. of which is an inquiry into the influence on Newton of the ideas of the German mystic, Jacob Boehme. Law, who was a disciple of Boehme, and a nonjuror in 1714, had considerable influence upon 18th-century religious thought. See early lives by R. Tighe, 1813, and C. Walton, 1854; J. H. Overton, *William Law, nonjuror and mystic*, 1881; and S. Hobhouse, *William Law and eighteenth century Quakerism*, 1927. See also brief bibl. in E. Underhill, *Mysticism*, 1911 (12th edn. repr. 1957); and a more extensive one in H. Talon, *William Law*, 1948.

LESLIE, CHARLES

1268　The theological works of . . . Charles Leslie. 2 vols. 1721. Later edn. 7 vols. Oxf. 1832.

LLOYD, WILLIAM

1269　Hart, A. T. William Lloyd, 1627–1717. 1952.

More a compendium of information especially political, on a bishop of the Revolution period.
　　On a 'soldier-bishop', see M. de Haviland, *Dr. Peter Mewes* (1684–1706), Winchester, 1932.

MORE, HENRY

1270　Ward, Richard. The life of . . . Dr. Henry More, later fellow of Christ's College in Cambridge, to which are annex'd divers of his useful and excellent letters. 1710.

Cf. *Collection of several philosophical writings* (2698); and his *Theological works*, 1708. See also no. 2461.

NELSON, ROBERT

1271　Secretan, C. F. Memoirs of the life and times of the pious Robert Nelson. 1860.

Author of *Companion for the festivals and fasts of the Church of England*, 1704 (many later edns.). Nelson was interested in charities. He was also a non-juror.

NICOLSON, WILLIAM

1272　'Diaries.' Ed. by Bishop Ware, *Cumberland and Westmorland Antiq. and Arch. Soc. Trans.*, N.S. 1–6 (1901–6). Pt. vi (1709–10) ed. by R. G. Collingwood, ibid., N.S. 35 (1935). Parts i and ii (1703–4) ed. by T. Gray and E. Birley, ibid., N.S. 46, 50 (1946, 1950).

The early parts (1901–6) give rather full extracts; the later volumes provide virtually the complete texts. The MSS. of Nicolson, Bishop of Carlisle, are described in H.M.C., *2nd Rep.* (1874), p. 125. See also two volumes of *Letters . . . to and from William Nicolson*, 1809. A good biography, though less strong on political aspects, is F. G. James, *North country bishop*, New Haven, 1957, bibl.

PATRICK, SYMON

1273　The auto-biography of Symon Patrick, Bishop of Ely. Oxf. 1839.

Repr. with Patrick's *Works*, ed. by A. Taylor, 9 vols. 1858.

PRESTON, JOHN

1274 Harcourt, E. W., ed. Life of the renowned Doctor Preston writ by his pupil Master Thomas Ball in the year 1628. Oxf. and Lond. 1885.

A Puritan politician. See also I. Morgan, *Prince Charles's Puritan chaplain*, 1957, which should be used with caution.

RAINBOW, EDWARD

1275 [Banks,] [J.] The life . . . of Edw[ard] Rainbow, late Lord Bishop of Carlisle. 1688.

ROUS, JOHN

1276 Diary of John Rous, incumbent of Santon Downham, Suffolk, from 1625 to 1642. Ed. by M. A. E. Green. Camden Soc. 1856.

SACHEVERELL, HENRY

1277 Madan, F., ed. A bibliography of Dr. Henry Sacheverall. [Extracted from the *Bibliographer*, 1883–4, with additions.] Oxf. 1884.

See also *Tryal of . . . Sacheverell before the house of peers*, 1710; and [John Toland,] *High church display'd . . .* 1711.

SANCROFT, WILLIAM

1278 D'Oyly, G. The life of William Sancroft, Archbishop of Canterbury. 2 vols. 1821. Later edn. 1840.

A satisfactory biography. Many of his documents were collected by J. Gutch as *Collectanea Curiosa*, 2 vols., Oxf. 1781. MSS. of Sancroft are in Tanner MSS. at the Bodleian Libr., and in Harl. MSS. (3783–98) at the Br. Mus. See also nos. 971 n., 1281.

SANDERSON, ROBERT

1279 The works of Robert Sanderson. Ed. by W. Jacobson. 6 vols. Oxf. 1854.

The above includes the 1678 life by Izaak Walton. Cf. G. Lewis, *Robert Sanderson, Chaplain to King Charles the First, Regius Professor of Divinity, and Bishop of Lincoln* (English Theologians series), 1924.

SHARP, JOHN

1280 Sharp, T., ed. The life of John Sharp . . . Archbishop of York . . . collected from his diary, letters . . . Ed. by T. Newcome. 2 vols. 1825.

Important for Anne's reign. Sharp's *Works* were publ. in 7 vols., 1754, 5 vols., Oxf. 1829. A. T. Hart's *The life and times of John Sharp, Archbishop of York*, 1949, is a valuable modern biography based upon wide research. This is one of the series of biographies published by the Society for Promoting Christian Knowledge for the Church Historical Society.

SHELDON, GILBERT

1281 Staley, V. The life and times of Gilbert Sheldon, sometime Warden of All Souls College, Oxford, Bishop of London, Archbishop of Canterbury, and Chancellor of the University of Oxford. 1913.

The standard life of the restoration archbishop. See E. A. O. Whiteman, 'Two letter books of Archbishops Sheldon and Sancroft', *Bodleian Library Record*, 4 (1953), 209–15, a description of the MSS.

SOUTH, ROBERT

1282 Memoirs of the life and writings of . . . R. South. 7 vols. Oxf. 1823
Later edn. 2 vols. 1865.

Mainly repr. of *Sermons preached upon several occasions,* 11 vols., 1737–44.

STEWARD, RICHARD

1283 Pocock, Nicholas. Life of Richard Steward. Ed. by T. I. Pocock. 1908.

Life of a royalist divine in exile.

STILLINGFLEET, EDWARD

1284 The life and character of . . . Edward Stillingfleet, Lord Bishop of
Worcester . . . with some account of the works he has published. 1710. Later
edn. 1735.

See his *Works,* 6 vols., 1707–10. See also no. 1299.

TAYLOR, JEREMY

1285 The whole works of . . . Jeremy Taylor . . . with a life of the author.
Ed. by R. Heber. 15 vols. Lond. and Oxf. 1822. Later edn. rev. by C. P.
Eden. 10 vols. 1847–54.

Cf. E. H. May, *A dissertation on the life, theology and times of . . . Jeremy Taylor,* 1892;
and Taylor's *Golden grove: selected passages from the sermons and writings of Jeremy
Taylor,* ed. by L. F. Smith, with a bibl. by R. Gathorne-Hardy, Oxf. 1930. Biographies
are by H. K. Bonney, 1815; R. E. Wilmott, 1847; E. W. Gosse (English Men of Letters),
1904; G. Worley, 1904; and W. J. Brown (in English Theologians series), 1925. Of
recent ones, that by H. R. Williamson, 1952, is popular; that by C. J. Stranks, 1952,
draws upon some newly available MSS., and includes bibliographies in app. Cf.
T. Wood, *English casuistical divinity during the 17th century, with special reference to
Jeremy Taylor,* 1952; P. Elmen, 'Jeremy Taylor and the fall of man', *Modern Lang.
Quart.* 14 (1953), 139–48; and R. Hoopes, 'Voluntarism in Jeremy Taylor and the
platonic tradition', *Hunt. Lib. Quart.* 13 (1950), 341–54.

TENISON, THOMAS

1286 Carpenter, E. Thomas Tenison, Archbishop of Canterbury, his life and
times. 1948. Bibl.

An able scholarly biography drawing upon the MSS. at Lambeth as well as contemporary printed materials. Though less broad in treatment than the title indicates, it
helps correct inaccuracies of such earlier biographies as the anonymous *Memoirs of the
life and times of . . . Thomas Tenison,* c. 1716, and that in Le Neve, *Lives . . . of . . .
bishops* (1217 n.).

THORNDIKE, HERBERT

1287 The theological works of . . . Herbert Thorndike. 6 vols. Oxf. 1844–
56.

His *Epilogue to the tragedy of the Church of England,* 1659, contains the ablest defence
of Anglican church polity at the time of the commonwealth. Vols. v and vi include
other valuable controversial treatises with letters and a life. Cf. T. A. Lacey, *Herbert
Thorndike, 1598–1672* (English Theologians series), 1929; appendix includes list of his
works in print and of Latin MSS.

TILLOTSON, JOHN

1288 The works of Dr. John Tillotson late Archbishop of Canterbury. With the life of the author. 10 vols. 1820.

The above-mentioned life, by T. Birch, had been previously published separately, 1752, 2nd edn., 1753. L. G. Locke, *Tillotson, a study in seventeenth-century literature* (2581), includes a useful bibliography of his writings.

USHER [USSHER], JAMES

1289 Parr, R. The life of . . . James Usher, late Lord Arch-Bishop of Armagh, primate and metropolitan of all Ireland. 1686.

Life—with appendix vindicating the Abp.'s orthodoxy, and 300 letters to and from famous persons at home and abroad. Cf. *The whole works of . . . J. Usher, with a life of the author* . . . ed. by C. R. Elrington and J. M. Todd, 17 vols., Dublin, 1847–64. For the literary history of his *Reduction of episcopacie* see *D.N.B.* See also J. A. Carr's *The life and times of James Ussher, Archbishop of Armagh*, 1895; and no. 4255.

WALTON, BRIAN

1290 Todd, H. J. Memoirs of the life and writings of Brian Walton, Bishop of Chester. 2 vols. 1821.

WILLIAMS, JOHN

1291 Hacket, John. Scrinia reserata: a memorial offered to the great deservings of John Williams, D.D. . . . containing A series of the most remarkable occurrences and transactions of his life . . . 2 pts. 1693.

In two parts, paged separately. See also J. E. B. Mayer, ed., 'Letters of Archbishop Williams and others addressed to him [and] Letters . . . with materials for his life', *Camb. Antiq. Soc.* 2 (1864), 25–66; 3 (1879), 61–106. An early life, in addition to Hacket's, is that of Ambrose Philips, 1700. A recent one is B. D. Roberts, *Mitre and musket: John Williams, Lord Keeper, Archbishop of York, 1582–1650*, 1938. See also N. R. F. Tucker, *Prelate-at-arms, an account of Archbishop John Williams at Conway during the Great Rebellion, 1642–1650*, Llandudno, 1938; and I. Bowen, 'John Williams of Gloddaeth', *Cymmrod. Soc. Trans.* 1927–8 (1929), 1–91.

WILSON, THOMAS

1292 The works of Thomas Wilson . . . with his life. Ed. by C. Cruttwell. 2 vols. Bath. 1781. Later edn. by J. Keble. 7 vols. in 8. Oxf. 1847–63.

Wilson (1663–1755) was bishop of Sodor and Man.

YOUNG, JOHN

1293 The diary of John Young, dean of Winchester, 1616 to the commonwealth. Ed. by F. R. Goodman. 1928.

Diary of the canon of Wells, chaplain to James I and Charles I, and employed by them in important affairs in Scotland.

C. NONCONFORMITY

This section includes the main groups of the 'old dissent', particularly the Independents or Congregationalists, the English Presbyterians, and the Baptists. Some works on 'Puritanism' are included, but others will be found in the section dealing with Anglicanism. The biographical section includes persons representative of all of these groups. See also Chs. XIII–XV *infra* on Wales, Scotland, and Ireland.

1. GENERAL

(a) *Bibliography and Sources*

The literature dealing with these sects is enormous, and new sources are continually being published, especially in the historical societies of the Baptists, Congregationalists, and Presbyterians. The Dr. Williams's Library is the central storehouse for both manuscripts and later works. For bibliographies see Whitley (1341) for the Baptists; Dexter (1316) for Congregationalism; there is no similar work for Presbyterianism. For the period before the civil war the best guide is Champlin Burrage (1308); for 1640–60 probably Masson's *Life of Milton* (2634) is as useful as any one work; Hanbury (1320) is important for both periods. For 1660–88 Baxter (1361), Calamy (1300), and G. L. Turner (1305) are essential, and Bate (1306) is the chief authority for the declaration of indulgence. For 1689–1714 there are valuable materials in Calamy and Heywood (1374), and Gordon (1313 n.) examined minutely the effect of the act of toleration during 1690–2, but the reign of Anne has attracted few nonconformist historians. Of the general historians Neal (1312), and his critics are still useful, and Whitley and Dale are the best studies of the Baptists and Congregationalists respectively within moderate compass; all should be checked by the work of such later scholars as Haller, Mosse, Woodhouse, and Whiting.

In addition to the books enumerated here, works in other sections should often be consulted, for many nonconformist laymen are important in other than ecclesiastical history, as Cromwell or Milton. See Ch. II *supra* and Ch. III esp. § F on Political Theory. For important social, economic, and cultural relationships see the sections devoted to these aspects of the period.

1294   CATALOGUE of the library in Red Cross Street, Cripplegate, founded pursuant to the will of the Reverend Daniel Williams. 2 vols. 1841.

> The library, over 80,000 vols., now at Gordon Square, is a centre for materials on nonconformity. G. F. Nuttall, in his introduction to *Visible Saints* (1329) refers to documents in the Dr. Williams's Library, and to a detailed catalogue by Miss G. Woodward of the library's holdings relating to the history of Dissent before 1800, the compilation of which 'is now complete [1956]'.

The selected sources that follow are arranged in rough chronological order by date of publication, or content:

1295   LEIGHTON, ALEXANDER. An appeal to the parliament, or Sions plea against the prelacie. [Holland? 1628.]

> *S.T.C.*, 15429. This led to Leighton's citation before the Star Chamber. See also no. 747.

1296   PAGITT, EPHRAIM. Heresiography: or A description of the heretickes and sectaries of these latter times. 1645. 6th edn. 1661.

> An unfriendly account of Anabaptists, Brownists, Independents, Familists, Adamites, Antinomians, Arminians, Socinians, Antitrinitarians, Millenaries, Hetheringtonians, Antisabbatarians, Traskites, Jesuits.

Successive editions added to the material and some cuts of heresiarchs were intro-
duced. The 6th edn. is the closing form of the book.

1297   EDWARDS, THOMAS. Gangraena or a catalogue and discovery of
many of the errours, heresies, blasphemies and pernicious practices of the
sectaries of this time, vented and acted in England in these four last years.
3 parts in 1 vol. 1646.

A bitter attack on sectaries by a Puritan, with many curious details of their proceedings.

1298   A COMPLEAT collection of farewel sermons preached by London &
countrie ministers August 17th, 1662. 1663.

1299   STILLINGFLEET, EDWARD. The unreasonableness of separation,
or an impartial account of the history . . . of the present separation from the
communion of the Church of England. 1681.

See also Stillingfleet (1284).

1300   CALAMY, EDMUND. Abridgement of Mr. Baxter's History of his life
and times, with a particular account of the ministers . . . ejected after the
restauration. 1702. Later edns. 2 vols. 1713 and 1727.

In edn. of 1713, the Account forms a separate volume; in edn. of 1727 there is a 'continuation of the Account' which consists of emendations. Samuel Palmer condensed
and rearranged these works in 1775 under the title *The Nonconformists' memorial*
(improved edn., 3 vols., 1802–3); Palmer cannot be implicitly trusted, and reference
should be made to Calamy's originals. An important supplement to the Account, rather
than a revision, is A. G. Matthews, *Calamy revised*, Oxf. 1934. Also by Calamy:
A defence of moderate non-conformity, 3 vols., 1703–5; *An historical account of my own
life*, ed. by J. T. Rutt, 2 vols., 1829; *A caveat against new prophets*, 1708. Cf. J. Walker,
Sufferings of the clergy (1185), and Calamy's reply, *Church and the dissenters compar'd
as to persecution*, 1719.

1301   PEIRCE, JAMES. Vindiciae fratrum dissentientium. 1710.

Trans. as *Vindication of the dissenters in answer to Dr. William Nichols' Defence . . . of
the Church of England* [1718].

1302   UNDERHILL, E. B., ed. The records of a church of Christ, meeting
in Broadmead, Bristol, 1640–1687. The Hanserd Knollys Soc. 1847.

Dr. Underhill's historical introduction deals with the rise of dissent in the Tudor period.
Cf. his *Records of the churches of Christ gathered at Fenstanton, Warboys, and Hexham,
1644–1720* (Hanserd Knollys Soc. Pub., vol. 9), 1854.

1303   [GOULD, G., ed.] Documents relating to the settlement of the Church
of England by the Act of Uniformity of 1662. 1862.

Intro. by P. Bayne.

1304   TURNER, J. H., ed. The Nonconformist register of baptisms, marriages,
and deaths, compiled by the Revs. O. Heywood & T. Dickenson, 1644–1702,
1702–1752, generally known as the Northowram or Coley register. Brighouse.
1881.

See also G. E. Evans, ed., *Vestiges of Protestant dissent, being lists of ministers, sacra-
mental plate, registers . . . pertaining to most of the churches . . . of Unitarian, Liberal
Christian, Free Christian, Presbyterian . . . congregations*, Liverpool, 1897. See also
Parish Registers (2416).

1305 TURNER, G. L., ed. Original records of early Nonconformity. 3 vols. 1911–14.

Vols. i and ii are documents relating to the persecution of Nonconformists during the first half of the reign of Charles II; vol. iii is a commentary. Cf. *The narrative of the persecution of Agnes Beaumont in 1674*, ed. by G. B. Harrison, 1929, a well-known record of the spiritual experience of Nonconformists (first publ. in 1760 with other stories under title: 'An abstract of the gracious dealings of God' . . . ed. by Samuel James).

(b) *Later Works*

1306 BATE, F. Declaration of indulgence, 1672; a study in the rise of organised dissent. 1908. Bibl.

A valuable study.

1307 BOGUE, D. and BENNETT, J. History of dissenters from the revolution (1688–1808). 4 vols. 1808–12. Later edn. 3 vols. 1833–9.

1308 BURRAGE, C. Early English dissenters in the light of recent research (1550–1641). 2 vols. Camb. 1912.

Vol. i is history, vol. ii documents. There is a critical introduction on authorities. A valuable study. Burrage edited *An answer to John Robinson of Leyden, by a Puritan friend* [1609], Camb. (Mass.), 1920. See also by Burrage, *The church covenant idea*, Phila., 1904. Useful articles are: R. K. Merton, 'Puritanism, pietism and science', *Sociological Review*, 28 (1936), 1–30; C. H. George, 'A social interpretation of English Puritanism', *J.M.H.* 25 (1953), 327–42; and two on Puritan thought by J. C. Brauer in *Church History*, 19 (1950), 151–70, and 23 (1954), 99–108. On dissenters of the post-1660 period see Abbott (356 n.).

1309 HETHERINGTON, W. M. History of the Westminster assembly of divines. Edin. and N.Y. 1843. Later edn. by R. Williamson. Edin. 1878.

Essential for the study of the assembly. See also nos. 1333, 1335. Cf. two articles by W. Haller: 'The Word of God in the Westminster Assembly', *Church Hist.* 18 (1949), 199–219; and 'The Word of God in the New Model Army', ibid. 19 (1950), 15–33.

1310 HEXTER, J. H. 'The problem of the Presbyterian Independents', *A.H.R.* 44 (1938), 22–49.

Exposes the fallacy of dividing up Long Parliament members into two rigid groups, Presbyterians and Independents. Cf. G. Yule, *The Independents in the English civil war* (927), which extends Hexter's thesis, but emphasizes the distinction between Independent and Presbyterians in their views on religious toleration. See also Solt (332).

1311 MULLETT, C. F. 'The legal position of English Protestant dissenters, 1689–1767.' *Virginia Law Rev.* 22 (1936), 495–526; 23 (1937), 389–418.

1312 NEAL, D. The history of the Puritans or Protestant Nonconformists (1517–1688). 4 vols. 1732–8. Later edns. by N. Neal. 2 vols. 1754. By J. Toulmin. 5 vols. Bath. 1793–7. Many later edns.

A work that is still of value. The supplementary chapters in the edn. of 1793–7 comprise the history of the English Baptists and Quakers. Vol. i of Neal called forth an answer from Isaac Maddox, *A vindication of the government, doctrine and worship of the Church of England established in the reign of Queen Elizabeth against . . . Neal*, 1733, repr. 1740. At least some of the materials used by Maddox were contributed by

Zachary Grey, who continued the attack on vols. ii–iv of Neal in *An impartial examina-tion* (3 vols., 1736–9); Grey's last two vols. contain valuable documents from the collection of state papers used by Nalson (cf. H.M.C., *Portland Papers*, vol. i). Neal replied in *A review of the principal facts objected to the first volume of the History of the Puritans*, 1734. Joshua Toulmin, *An historical review of the state of the Protestant dis-senters in England from the revolution to the accession of Queen Anne*, Bath, 1814, con-tinues Neal's account to 1702.

1313 SKEATS, H. S. History of the Free Churches of England 1688–1851. 1868. Later edn. 1891.

See also A. Gordon, *Freedom after ejection*, Manchester, 1917, a review (1690–2) of Presbyterian and Congregational Nonconformity in England and Wales, which includes data on some 760 ministers; and B. Nightingale, *The ejected of 1662 in Cumberland and Westmorland*, 2 vols., Manchester, 1911, bibl. and documents.

1314 THUNE, N. The Behmenists and the Philadelphians: a contribution to the study of English mysticism in the seventeenth and eighteenth centuries. Uppsala. 1948.

Study of the small Quaker-like group which existed in England for a few years, and of the influence of Jacob Boehme on Dr. John Pordage and on the founder of the Society, Jane Leade.

1315 WHITING, C. E. Studies in English Puritanism from the restoration to the revolution, 1660–1688. 1931. Bibl.

Twelve learned studies, including sections on the effect of the act of uniformity, the foreign protestants in England, and the minor sects.

2. PURITANS, CONGREGATIONALISTS, AND INDEPENDENTS

(a) *Bibliography and Sources*

1316 DEXTER, H. M. The Congregationalism of the last three hundred years, as seen in its literature. 1880.

The bibliography in the app. has 7,250 titles and is more valuable than the lectures. See also *Congregational History Society Transactions*, 1901+; and *Catalogue* (of the Congregational Library, London), 2 vols., 1895–1910.

1317 SMECTYMNUUS, i.e. S[tephen] M[arshall], E[dmund] C[alamy], T[homas] Y[oung], M[atthew] N[ewcomen], W[illiam] S[purestowe]. An answer to a booke entitled, an humble remonstrance in which, the originall of Liturgy Episcopacy is discussed. 1641.

For the controversy which followed see Masson's *Life of Milton* (2634), ii. 219 seq.

1318 GOODWIN, THOMAS, PHILIP NYE, *et al.* An apologeticall narra-tion. 1643.

A defence of Independency, answered by T. E. and others. Cf. D. Masson's *Life of Milton*, iii. 23 seq.

1319 WALKER, CLEMENT. The compleat history of Independency 1640–60. 1660–1.

Made up of various parts: For 1648, Relations and observations . . ., The history of Independency . . ., and An appendix to the history. For 1649, Anarchia Anglicana:

or the history of Independency, the second part . . . by Theodorus Verax. For 1660, The High Court of Justice . . . Being the third part of the History of Independency written by the same author; and The history of Independency, the fourth and last part . . . by T. M. Esquire. E. M. Morgan (Kirby) cites in her article in *Church Quart. Rev.* 110 (1930), 23–33 the following tracts representing the Erastian view: W. Prynne, *Independency examined, unmask'd and refuted*, 1644; and *Twelve considerable serious questions touching church government*, 1644; D. P. P., *An antidote against the contagious air of Independency*, 1645; Thomas Goodwin, *Calumny arraign'd and cast*, 1645; Prynne, *Diotrophes catechized*, 1645; and John Lightfoote, *A sermon preached before the Honourable House of Commons*, 1645.

1320   HANBURY, B., ed. Historical memorials relating to the Independents and Congregationalists from their rise to the restoration . . . 1660. 3 vols. 1839–44.

Very valuable for literature: consists of lengthy extracts from scarcer early Independent works.

1321   WALKER, W., ed. The creeds and platforms of Congregationalism. N.Y. 1893.

Mainly documents showing the principles of Congregationalists at different times. By same author: *History of the Congregational churches in the United States* (Amer. Church Hist., vol. iii), N.Y. 1894, 6th edn., N.Y. 1907. Cf. *The Cambridge platform of 1648* . . ., ed. by H. W. Foote, Boston, 1949; and *The Savoy declaration of faith and order*, 1658, ed. by A. Peel, 1939.

(b) *Later Works*

1322   CALDER, I. M., ed. Activities of the Puritan faction of the Church of England, 1625–33. 1957.

Introduction and documents surviving from the Feoffees' trial in 1633 illustrating the attempt to purchase impropriated tithes and patronage rights. Cf. her valuable article, 'A seventeenth century attempt to purify the Anglican church', *A.H.R.* 53 (1947–8), 760–75. See also E. W. Kirby, 'The lay feoffees: a study in militant puritanism', *J.M.H.* 14 (1942), 1–25, which is a good discussion of the organization formed in 1625 by English Puritans seeking to provide pulpits for Calvinist clergy.

1323   CRAGG, G. R. Puritanism in the period of the great persecution, 1660–88. Camb. 1957.

Essentially a study of the reactions of the Puritan sects to persecution; less concerned with doctrinal matters. Useful. See also no. 1192, and A. C. Dudley, 'Nonconformity under the Clarendon Code', *A.H.R.* 18 (1913), 65–78.

1324   DALE, R. W. History of English Congregationalism. Ed. by Sir A. W. W. Dale. 1907. Bibl.

Still the best account. Cf. J. A. Houlder, *A short history of the free churches*, 1899; and J. Waddington, *Congregational history*, 5 vols., 1869–80, of which vols. ii and iii relate to the period. On the Congregationalists or Independents in the counties, see W. H. Summers, *History of the Congregational churches in the Berks, South Oxon, and South Bucks Association*, Newbury, 1905; W. Densham and J. Ogle, *Congregational churches of Dorset*, Bournemouth, 1899; J. Brown, *History of Congregationalism . . . in Norfolk and Suffolk*, 1877; T. Coleman, *Memorials of the Independent churches in Northamptonshire*, 1853; A. G. Matthews, *The Congregational churches of Staffordshire*, 1924; and J. Sibree and M. Caston, *Independency in Warwickshire*, Coventry, 1855. For other local materials see § 6, pp. 197–8 (*infra*).

1325 HALLER, W. The rise of Puritanism; or the way to the new Jerusalem as set forth in pulpit and press from Thomas Cartwright to John Lilburne and John Milton. N.Y. 1938. Later edn. N.Y. 1957.

Important study of the effect of the stimulation by such preachers and their associates as Greenham, Dod, Henry Smith, Richard Rogers, Sibbes, and Preston. Also by Haller: *Liberty and reformation in the Puritan revolution*, N.Y. 1955, an excellent study with the thesis that the Puritan revolution triumphed at the cost of the disintegration of Puritanism itself. See also A. Simpson, *Puritanism in Old and New England*, Chicago, 1955; and P. Miller, *The New England Mind* (3341 n.); and no. 960.

1326 HUEHNS, G. Antinomianism in English history, with special reference to the period 1640–1660. 1951. Bibl.

Interesting and scholarly essay upon 17th-century religious radicalism, with references to social as well as political developments.

1327 MATTHEWS, A. G. The Puritans. *In* Christian worship. Ed. by N. Micklem. Oxf. 1936.

See also H. Davies, *The worship of the English Puritans*, 1948, bibl.; and G. S. Wakefield, *Puritan devotion*, 1957, bibl. Other works by Matthews relating to nonconformity are: 'The seventeenth century', in *Congregationalism through the centuries*, 1937; and *Mr. Pepys and nonconformity*, 1954.

1328 MOSSE, G. L. The Holy Pretense: a study in Christianity and reason of state from William Perkins to John Winthrop. Oxf. 1957.

Important study dealing with sincere efforts of Puritans to harmonize religious thinking with the political and the renaissance ideas of the 17th century. See also no. 989.

1329 NUTTALL, G. F. Visible saints: the Congregational way, 1640–1660. Oxf. 1957.

Learned, but somewhat lacking in organization; bibl. footnotes. By same author: *The holy spirit in Puritan faith and experience*, Oxf. 1946; 2nd edn., 1947. See also his *The Welsh saints, 1640–1660*, Cardiff, 1957.

1330 PLUM, H. G. Restoration Puritanism: a study of the growth of English liberty. Chapel Hill. 1943.

Not a major work, but bibliography, pp. 103–23, lists many tracts.

1331 USHER, R. G. 'The deprivation of Puritan ministers in 1605.' *E.H.R.* 24 (1909), 232–46.

Shows that there has been an exaggeration of the number of ministers who were expelled.

3. PRESBYTERIANS

(a) *Sources*

1332 PRESBYTERIAN HISTORICAL SOCIETY. Journal. 1944+.

The Society library is in Regent Square Presbyterian Church.

1333 A DIRECTORY for the publique worship of God, throughout the three kingdoms of England, Scotland and Ireland. Together with an ordinance of parliament for the taking away of the Book of Common-Prayer. 1644–[5]. 2nd edn. Edin. 1645.

Drawn up by the Westminster Assembly; repr. in the *Book of Common Order of the Church of Scotland*, 1868. The other pieces of work have proved even more enduring: *The metrical version of the Psalms*, 1646; *The confession of faith*, 1647; *The two Catechisms*, 1648.

The *Minutes of the Westminster Assembly of divines* were ed. by A. F. Mitchell and J. Struthers, 1874. See also Hetherington, *History of the Westminster Assembly of divines* (1309). A good short account of the assembly, with bibl. by W. A. Shaw, is in *Camb. Mod. Hist.* iv, 1906. See also Carruthers (1335).

1334 C[ORBET], J[OHN]. Interest of England in the matter of religion. 2 pts. 1660.

'Plea by a Presbyterian minister for united Anglo-Presbyterian front' against other sects and popery. Author of other treatises. This one was answered by Roger L'Estrange, *Interest mistaken, or the holy cheat*, 1661. For an early history of Presbyterianism see Peter Heylyn, *Aerius redivivus* (1536–1647), Oxf. 1670.

(b) *Later Works*

1335 CARRUTHERS, S. W. The Westminster Confession of Faith (1646–47). Being an account of the preparation and printing of its seven leading editions. To which is appended a critical text of the Confession, with notes thereon. (Presbyterian Hist. Soc. of England.) Manchester. 1937.

Also by Carruthers: *The everyday work of the Westminster Assembly*, 1943; and *Three centuries of the Shorter Catechism*, Fredericton, N.B. 1957 (includes bibl.). Cf. B. B. Warfield, *The Westminster Assembly and its work*, N.Y. 1931; E. Macrury, *The symbol of division*, Glasgow, 1936, both of which deal with the confession of faith. See also Hetherington (1309).

1336 DRYSDALE, A. H. History of the Presbyterians in England. 1889.

The best general survey. On political activities during the civil war see Hexter (1310); on a Presbyterian minister ejected in 1662 see G. F. Nuttall, ed., *Letters of John Pinney, 1679–1699*, 1939. Cf. G. R. Abernathy, Jr., *The English Presbyterians and the Stuart restoration, 1648–1663*, Phila. 1965.

1337 GRIFFITHS, O. M. Religion and learning. A study in English Presbyterian thought from the Bartholomew ejections (1662) to the foundation of the Unitarian movement. Camb. and N.Y. 1935. Bibl.

1338 HENDERSON, G. D. Presbyterianism. Aberdeen. 1954.

A brief discussion, particularly emphasizing church government, 16th and 17th centuries.

1339 McCRIE, T. Annals of English Presbytery from the earliest period to the present time. 1872.

Cf. J. Meikle, 'The seventeenth century presbytery of Meigle', *Scot. Church Hist. Soc. Records*, 5 (1934), 144–56. See also W. A. Shaw, ed., *Minutes of the Bury Presbyterian classis, 1647–1657*, 2 vols., Chetham Soc. 1896–8, with appendices pertaining to Nottingham, Cornwall, and Cambridge; and A. Gordon, ed., *Cheshire classis: minutes, 1691–1745*, 1919. See also § 6 *infra*.

1340 MURCH, J. History of the Presbyterian and General Baptist churches in the west of England. 1835.

4. BAPTISTS

(a) *Bibliography and Sources*

1341 WHITLEY, W. T., ed. A Baptist bibliography, being a register of the chief materials for Baptist history, whether in manuscript or in print. 2 vols. 1916–22.

Vol. i, 1526–1776; ii, 1777–1837. Gives the titles, etc. of all books by or relating to Baptists in the chronological order of publication, and of MSS. under the years in which their contents begin, with many notes. Extremely valuable. See also E. C. Starr, *A Baptist bibliography, being a register of printed materials by and about Baptists*, 6+ vols., Phila. 1947–59, in progress; titles are arranged in alphabetical order, with cross references to Whitley; vol. vi goes up to *D*.

1342 BAPTIST HISTORICAL SOCIETY. Transactions. Vols. 1–7. 1908–21. Incorporated into *Baptist Quarterly*, 1922+.

Important MS. collections by J. Stennett and B. Stinton are at Dr. Williams's Library and the Angus Library, once at Regent's Park, now at Oxford.

1343 BARBER, EDWARD. A small treatise of baptisme or dipping. [1642?]

Cf. Daniel Featley, *The dippers dipt* [1645] (Wing, F 585).

1344 THE CONFESSION of faith of those churches which are commonly (though falsly) called Anabaptists; presented to the view of all that feare God to examine by the touchstone of the word of truth. 1644. Later edns. 1646 and 1651.

Wing, C 5879. Opponents of the English churches usually supposed that they were akin to the German Anabaptists of the sixteenth century, so quoted largely from continental historians rather than observed what was around them. Both connection and name were repudiated by these Calvinists. Alternative names appeared, 'Baptists' in 1644, 'Antipaedobaptists' in 1646. Cf. *A confession of faith, put forth by the elders and brethren of many congregations of Christians (baptized upon profession of their faith) in London and the country*, 1677, which is a Baptist revision of the Westminster Confession that is still acknowledged by the Strict and Particular Baptists of England and Australia. See also Thomas Grantham, *Christianismus primitivus: or the ancient Christian religion*, 1678, in four parts, incorporating earlier pamphlets, especially the 1660 confession which long remained standard among the General Baptists who originated in 1609.

1345 GOULD, G., ed. Open communion and the Baptists of Norwich. Norwich. 1860.

Text has important legal arguments and judgements. Intro. discusses critically the origin of Baptists in England. Cf. F. Beckwith, 'A Yorkshire manuscript of 1678: William Mitchell's "Difference betwixt Egypt and Canaan"', *Baptist Quart.* 8 (1936), 167–73, 217–22.

1346 WHITLEY, W. T., ed. Minutes of the General Assembly of the General Baptist churches in England, with kindred records; Edited with introduction and notes for the Baptist Historical Society. Vol. i, 1654–1728. Vol. ii, 1731–1811. 1909–10.

1347 McGLOTHLIN, W. J., ed. Baptist confessions of faith. Phila. [1911].

Continental, English, American. Supersedes similar collection ed. by E. B. Underhill, 1854.

(b) *Later Works*

1348 BROWN, L. F. The political activities of the Baptists and fifth monarchy men in England during the interregnum. Washington. 1912. Bibl.

Valuable.

1349 CHRISTIAN, J. T. A history of the Baptists with some account of their principles and practices. Nashville. 1922.

Concerned especially with immersion; vol. ii deals mainly with America. Cf. T. Armitage, *A history of the Baptists*, N.Y. 1887.

1350 CROSBY, T., ed. The history of the English Baptists (to 1714). 4 vols. 1738–40.

Based on materials collected by others; not always clear in his use of terms. Cf. A. Taylor, *The history of the English General Baptists*, 2 vols., 1818, of which the first part deals with the 17th century.

1351 HERIOT, D. B. 'Anabaptism in England during the 17th century.' *Congregational Hist. Soc. Trans.* 12 (1935), 256–71 and 13 (1937), 22–40.

Cf. R. J. Smithson, *The Anabaptists*, 1935.

1352 IVIMEY, J. A history of the English Baptists. 4 vols. 1811–1830.

There are inaccuracies in vols. i and ii, which deal with the period. See also J. M. Cramp, *Baptist history*, 1868, later edns. 1871, 1875, 1905; J. J. Goadby, *Bye-paths in Baptist history*, 1871; and G. A. Lofton, *English Baptist reformation* [1609-1641], Louisville, Ky. 1899.

1353 WHITLEY, W. T. A history of British Baptists. 1923. 2nd edn. 1932.

Probably the best. By the same author, *Baptists of London, 1612–1928*, [1928]. For other regional histories see E. C. Shipley and W. T. Whitley, *Baptists in Yorkshire, Lancashire, Cheshire, and Cumberland*, 1913 (combined separate works publ. in 1912, 1913); an 1846 *History* of the Baptists in the north by D. Douglas; R. Gray *et al.*, eds., *Records of an old [Midland] Association*, [1655], 1905; W. Stokes, *Hist. of the Midland Association of Baptist churches, 1655–1855*, 1855; J. G. Fuller, *A brief history of the Western [Baptist] Association*, Bristol, [1843]; and G. Yuille, *Hist. of the Baptists in Scotland*, Glasgow, 1926. See also Murch (1340) and § 6 *infra*.

1354 UNDERWOOD, A. C. A history of the English Baptists. 1947. 2nd pr. 1956. Bibl.

A concise account, annotated. See also H. C. Vedder, *A short history of the Baptists*, Phila. 1891, later edn. 1907, which was based on much original research.

5. Biographies, Personal Narratives, and Works of Individuals

(a) *Collected Biography*

1355 CLARKE, SAMUEL. A general martyrologie . . . from the creation to our present times. 1651. 3rd edn. 1677.

See also Calamy (1300); and Gordon and Nightingale (1313 n.).

1356 BROOK, B. The lives of the Puritans, containing a biographical account of those divines who distinguished themselves in the cause of religious liberty from the reformation [to 1662]. 3 vols. 1813.

MSS. for a second edn. are in the Congregational Library, Lond.

1357 SHAKESPEARE, J. H. Baptist and Congregational pioneers. 1906.

1570–1646.

1358 TULLOCH, J. English Puritanism and its leaders: Cromwell, Milton, Baxter, Bunyan. Edin. and Lond. 1861.

Cf. Solt (332).

(b) *Individual Biography*

ALLEINE, JOSEPH

1359 Stanford, C. Joseph Alleine: his companions & times; a memorial of 'Black Bartholomew'. 1662. 1861.

ANGIER, JOHN

1360 Oliver Heywood's Life of John Angier of Denton [1605–77], together with Angier's diary. Ed. by E. Axon. Chetham Soc., N.S. 97, 1937.

Includes also the diary of Samuel Angier, a Nonconformist divine.

BAXTER, RICHARD

1361 Orme, W., ed. The practical works of . . . Richard Baxter. 23 vols. 1830.

An earlier folio edn. in 1707 was 4 vols. For list of Baxter's separate works see Wing, B 1176–1455. There is a chronological list of 168 titles in vol. i of Orme. Among the well known are: *Saint's everlasting rest*, 1649; *The reformed pastor*, 1656, abr. edn. by J. T. Wilkinson, 1939, which deals with the Christian ministry; *Christian directory*, 1673, abr. edn. of parts relating to social ethics by J. Tawney, 1925; *The poor man's family book*, 1674, 6th edn., 1697. For Baxter's comments on social conditions see also F. J. Powicke's edn., from an unpubl. MS. dated 1691, of 'The poor husbandman's advocate to rich racking landlords' in *Bull. John Rylands Lib.* 10 (1926), 163–222. Of primary importance is *Reliquiae Baxterianae, or . . . Baxter's narrative of the most memorable passages of his life and times*, ed. by M. Sylvester, 1696; abr. edn. by E. Calamy, 2 vols., 1727; ed. by J. T. Rutt, 2 vols., 1829; abr. edn. by J. M. L. Thomas, under title of the *Autobiography*, 1925. See G. F. Nuttall's pamphlet, *The manuscript of the Reliquiae Baxterianae*, 1954. Several letters of Baxter were edited by F. J. Powicke in *Bull. John Rylands Lib.* 9 (1925), 585–99, and 15 (1931), 138–76, 442–66. The main collection of Baxter's MSS. is in Dr. Williams's Library.

1362 Powicke, F. J. The life of the Reverend Richard Baxter, 1615–1691. 2 vols. 1924–7.

The best account, based on new materials from Dr. Williams's Library; largely supersedes the life in vol. i of Orme. See biographical articles by Powicke in *Bull. John Rylands Lib.* 13 (1929), 63–88, 309–25. See also A. R. Ladell's life, 1925; C. F. Kemp's study of his Kidderminster years, entitled *Pastoral triumph*, N.Y. 1948; H. Martin, *Puritanism and Richard Baxter*, 1954; R. Schlatter, *Richard Baxter and Puritan politics*, New Brunswick, 1957; and J. T. Wilkinson, ed., *Richard Baxter and Margaret Charlton*, being the breviate of [Baxter's] *life of Margaret Baxter, 1681*, 1928.

BROWNE, ROBERT

1363   Burrage, C. The true story of Robert Browne (1550?–1663), Father of Congregationalism, including . . . an extended and improved list of his writings. Oxf. 1906.

Cf. articles by F. I. Cater on Robert Browne in *Congregational Hist. Soc. Trans.*, vols. 2–3 (1905–8). An excellent short life is F. J. Powicke's, *Robert Browne, pioneer of modern Congregationalism*, 1910. See also D. C. Smith, 'Robert Browne, Independent', *Church Hist.* 6 (1937), 289–349, which traces the development of his views on church polity.

BUNYAN, JOHN

1364   The works of that eminent servant in God . . . John Bunyan. 1692. Ed. by G. Offor. 3 vols. Glasgow. 1855.

For other titles and biog. see no. 2592.

BURTON, HENRY

1365   A narration of the life of Mr. Henry Burton . . . written with his own hand. 1643.

CAWTON, THOMAS

1366   The life and death of that holy and reverend man of God Mr. Thomas Cawton. By his son T. Cawton. 1662.

CLARKE, SAMUEL

1367   Whiston, W. Historical memoirs of the life and writings of Dr. Samuel Clarke . . . to which is added . . . I. Dr. Sykes, 'Elogium of Dr. Clarke'. II. Mr. [Thomas] Emlyn's Memoirs of the life and sentiments of Dr. Clarke. 3rd edn. 1748.

CLEGG, JAMES

1368   Kirke, H., ed. Extract from the diary and autobiography of the Rev. James Clegg, Nonconformist minister and doctor of medicine (1679–1755). Buxton. 1899.

His account of his youth is valuable for the history of education.

DELAUNE, THOMAS

1369   A narrative of the tryal and sufferings of Thomas Delaune, for writing and publishing a late book called 'A plea for the Nonconformists' . . . 1684.

GOODWIN, THOMAS

1370   Works. 5 vols. 1681–1704. Later ed. by T. Smith. 11 vols. Edin. 1861–4.

HALL, THOMAS

1371   Powicke, F. J. 'New light on an old English Presbyterian and bookman, . . . Thomas Hall . . . 1610–1665.' *Bull. John Rylands Lib.* 8 (1924), 166–90.

HELWYS, THOMAS

1372   The mistery of iniquity, by Thomas Helwys, 1612. Ed. by W. T. Whitley. (Baptist Hist. Soc.) 1935.

Helwys is credited with forming the first established Baptist congregation in England, 1611. See also no. 1389.

HENRY, PHILIP

1373 [Bates, William.] An account of the life and death of Mr. Philip Henry. 1698. 2nd edn. 1699. 3rd edn., with additions by Matthew Henry. 1712. Ed. by J. B. Williams. 1825.

See Wing, B 1100A. The life, attributed by recent scholarship to Dr. Bates, whose dedication first appears in the 1698 edn., has by some editors been attributed to Henry's son, Matthew. It is based on Henry's own diary and correspondence. The first edn. contains the funeral sermon by Mr. Tallents; to the 1712 edn. is added the funeral sermon for Mrs. Henry preached by Matthew Henry. Cf. *The diaries and letters of Philip Henry of Broad Oak, Flintshire* (1631–96), ed. by M. H. Lee, 1882.

HEYWOOD, OLIVER

1374 The whole works of the Rev. O. Heywood . . . with memoirs of his life. 5 vols. 1827.

Cf. *The Rev. Oliver Heywood, B.A. 1630–1702, his autobiography, diaries* . . . ed. by J. H. Turner, 4 vols., Brighouse, 1881–5; Oliver Heywood's *Life of John Angier of Denton* (1360); and 'Letters of Oliver Heywood and Life of Richard Heywood (1695)', *Congregational Hist. Soc. Trans.* 15 (1945), 18–32. See also J. Hunter's *The rise of the old dissent exemplified in the life of Oliver Heywood*, 1842.

HOWE, JOHN

1375 Calamy, Edmund. Memoirs of the life of the late Revd. Mr. John Howe. 1724.

Cf. *The life and character of John Howe*, by H. Rogers, 1836, new edn. 1863. The *Works* of Howe (publ. in 2 vols., 1724), were ed. by J. Hunt in 8 vols., 1810–22; later edns.

HUSSEY, JOSEPH

1376 Matthews, A. G., ed. Diary of a Cambridge minister. Camb. 1937.

Brief essay with extracts from diary of Joseph Hussey, minister of Emmanuel Congregational Church, Camb. 1691–1719.

INCE, PETER

1377 Jones, T. H. L. The story of the Rev. Peter Ince, M.A., B.D. (of Brasenose College, Oxford), an ejected minister (of Birdbush, Wiltshire). 1936.

JESSEY, HENRY

1378 The life and death of Mr. Henry Jessey, who having finished his testimony, was translated, 4 Sept. 1663 . . . by E. W[histon?]. 1671.

JOLLY, THOMAS

1379 The note book of the Rev. Thomas Jolly, 1671–1693. Extracts from the church book of Altham and Wymondhouses, 1649–1725. Ed. by H. Fishwick. Chetham Soc. 1894.

The spiritual reflections of a Nonconformist.

KIFFIN, WILLIAM

1380 Remarkable passages in the life of William Kiffin: written by himself. Ed. by W. Orme. 1823.

Incorporated in *Life* by J. Ivimey, 1833.

KNOLLYS, HANSERD

1381 Culross, J. Hanserd Knollys, 'a minister and witness of Jesus Christ', 1598–1691. 1895.

MILTON, JOHN

1382 Sewell, A. A study in Milton's Christian doctrine. 1939.

Deals with the posthumously published treatise, *De Doctrina Christiana*, in relation to Milton's intellectual development. Cf. M. Kelley, *This great argument: a study of Milton's De Doctrina Christiana as a gloss upon Paradise Lost*, Princeton, 1941. Cf. Sewell's article, *Mod. Lang. Rev.* 30 (1935), 13–18, and a criticism of his argument by H. J. C. Grierson, ibid. 39 (1944), 97–107. See also nos. 967, 2634.

NEWCOME, HENRY

1383 The diary of the Rev. Henry Newcome from September 30, 1661, to September 29, 1663. Ed. by T. Heywood. Chetham Soc. 1849.

The journal of a Lancashire minister. Cf. *The autobiography [c. 1627–95] of Henry Newcome*, ed. by R. Parkinson, 2 vols., Chetham Soc., vols. 26–7, 1852. The autobiog. is an abstract of a lost diary.

OWEN, JOHN

1384 Works. Ed. by T. Russell. 28 vols. 1826. Ed. by W. H. Goold. 24 vols. 1850–5.

The 1826 edn. contains W. Orme's biography, printed separately in 1820 as *Memoirs of the life* . . . Owen was an influential dissenter.

PETER, HUGH

1385 See no. 487.

PRYNNE, WILLIAM

1386 See nos. 491 and 747 n.

ROBINSON, JOHN

1387 Ashton, R., ed. The works of John Robinson, pastor of the Pilgrim Fathers, with a memoir and annotations. 3 vols. Lond. and Boston (Mass.). 1851.

Among the more important reprints are: *A justification of separation from the Church of England*, Leyden, 1610; *Of religious communion private & publique*, Leyden, 1614; *The peoples plea for the exercise of prophesie*, Leyden, 1618; *A defence of the doctrine propounded by the synode at Dort*, s.l., 1624; *A just and necessarie apologie of certain Christians . . . called Brownists or Barrowists*, Leyden, 1625. Cf. *S.T.C.* 21107–21116. For a life see that by W. H. Burgess, 1920.

ROGERS, JOHN

1388 Rogers, E. Some account of the life and opinions of a Fifth-Monarchy-Man. Chiefly extracted from the writings of John Rogers, preacher. 1867.

SMYTH, JOHN

1389 The works of John Smyth, fellow of Christ's College 1594-8 . . . with notes and biography by W. T. Whitley. 2 vols. Camb. 1915.

Cf. W. H. Burgess, *John Smith the Se-Baptist, Thomas Helwys, and the first Baptist church in England*, 1911. There are interesting comments on this work in Burrage, *Early English dissenters* (1308), vol. i, pp. x–xiii.

STERRY, PETER

1390 Pinto, V. de S. Peter Sterry, Platonist and Puritan, 1613–1672. Camb. 1934. Bibl.

A biographical and critical study, with passages selected from the writings of Cromwell's favourite preacher.

WILLIAMS, ROGER

1391 Winslow, O. E. Master Roger Williams: a biography. N.Y. 1957.

Cf. J. H. Rushbrooke, 'Roger Williams: apostle of soul-freedom', *Baptist Quart.* 8 (1936), 18–31, a speech delivered to the Baptist Society answering arguments of those who claim that Williams was not a Baptist.

6. LOCAL ACCOUNTS

There are various local accounts of groups such as the Baptists in Whitley (1353); Congregationalists in Dale (1324); and Presbyterians in McCrie (1339). See also Skeats (1313). The following titles are arranged by counties, alphabetically. See also Ch. XIII *infra*.

1392 SALT, H. R. Gleanings from forgotten fields, being the story of the Berks Baptist Association 1652–1907. Reading. [1907 n.d.]

Prints the earliest minutes, from MS. in the Gould collection, Regent's Park College.

1393 URWICK, W., ed. Historical sketches of Nonconformity in the county Palatine of Chester. 1864.

He later wrote on Nonconformity in Herts. 1884, and Worcester, 1897.

1394 DAVIDS, T. W. Annals of evangelical Nonconformity in the county of Essex . . . with memorials of the Essex ministers who were ejected . . . in 1660–2. 1863.

See also H. Smith, *The ecclesiastical history of Essex under the Long Parliament and commonwealth*, Colchester, 1932.

1395 BRIGHT, T. The rise of Nonconformity in the Forest of Dean. (Forest of Dean Local History Soc.) Coleford, Gloucestershire. [1954.]

1396 NIGHTINGALE, B. Lancashire Nonconformity, or sketches historical and descriptive of the Congregational and old Presbyterian churches in the county. 6 vols. Manchester. 1890–3.

Has entirely superseded R. Halley's *Lancashire, its Puritanism and Nonconformity*, 2 vols., Manchester, 1869. See W. A. Shaw, ed., *Minutes of the Manchester Presbyterian classis* (1646–60), 3 vols., Chetham Soc. 1890–1, which is 'probably the most perfect of the surviving records of Presbyterianism' for the period it covers; and Shaw's *Materials for an account of the provincial synod of the county of Lancashire, 1646–1660*, Manchester, 1890.

1397 SHAW, W. A., ed. Minutes of the Committee for Plundered Ministers (no. 1109).

See also G. E. Evans, *Record of the Provincial Assembly of Lancashire and Cheshire*, Manchester, 1896.

1398 WILSON, W. The history and antiquities of dissenting churches and meeting houses, in London, Westminster, and Southwark. 4 vols. 1808–14.

The materials used are in Dr. Williams's Library, London, as also the preparation for an enlarged edition. Cf. G. H. Pike, *Ancient meeting-houses or memorial pictures of Nonconformity in Old London*, 1870; C. E. Surman, ed., *Register-booke of the 4th classis in the province of London, 1646–59* (Harleian Soc. 82–3), 1953; and Whitley (1353 n.).

1399 GODFREY, J. T. and J. WARD. The history of Friar Lane Baptist Church, Nottingham, being a contribution towards the history of the Baptists in Nottingham. Nottingham. 1903.

By skilled antiquaries. A fine specimen of a large class of local histories. Cf. H. F. Sanders, 'Early Puritanism and separatism in Nottingham', *Congregational Hist. Soc. Trans.* 12 (1934), 100–11.

1400 NOAKE, J. Worcester sects, or a history of the Roman Catholics and dissenters in Worcester. 1861.

See also W. T. Whitley in *Baptist Quart.*, N.S. 1 (1922–3), 373–83.

1401 MILLER, P. G. E. and JOHNSON, T. H. The Puritans. (Selections from New England Puritan writings.) N.Y. 1938.

A source book on the first century of New England Puritanism. Cf. John Wise, *A vindication of the government of the New-England churches*, Boston, 1717, repr. with intro. by P. Miller, Gainesville, Fla. 1958. For life of Wise, see G. A. Cook, *John Wise: Early American democrat*, N.Y. 1952. See also Ch. XII *infra*.

D. HUGUENOTS AND OTHER REFUGEE GROUPS

I. BIBLIOGRAPHY AND SOURCES

See also Ch. IX *infra*, pp. 342–3, on Foreigners in England. Other examples are J. S. Burn, *History of the French, Walloons, Dutch . . . refugees . . . in England . . . 1846*; and Agnew, *Protestant exiles* (2191 n.).

1402 STRIDE, E. E. 'Bibliography of some [standard] works relating to the Huguenot refugees . . .' *Proc. Huguenot Soc.* 1 (1887), 130–49.

1403 HUGUENOT SOCIETY OF LONDON. Publications. Vol. 1+. 1887+.

See also the Society's *Proceedings*, vol. 1+. 1885+. Among the former there are many church registers; e.g. vol. 2 (1890), A. C. Chamier, ed., *Les actes des colloques des églises françaises et des synodes des églises étrangères refugieés en Angleterre, 1581–1654*; among the latter, see vol. 16 (1938), C. E. Lart, ed., 'Some letters . . . 1585–1685'; and various local studies.

2. LATER WORKS

1404   LEE, G. L. Huguenot settlements in Ireland. 1936. Bibl.

> See also earlier work by T. Gimlette (Dunmore East? 1888), and articles in *Proc. Huguenot Soc.* 6 (1902), 370–432; 8 (1909), 87–139; 10 (1914), 467–84; and 12 (1924), 245–62. On the Huguenots in Scotland see article by A. W. C. Hallen, ibid. 2 (1887–8), 166–81; and A. Fleming, *Huguenot influence in Scotland*, Glasgow, 1953.

1405   SCHICKLER, F. D. G. de (Baron). Les églises du refuge en Angleterre. 3 vols. Paris. 1892.

> Treats of the French-speaking refugee churches. See also his articles in *Proc. Huguenot Soc.* 1 (1887), 95–115; 6 (1902), 268–94. For a general history of the Huguenot refugees see R. Lane Poole, *History of the Huguenots of the dispersion at the recall of the Edict of Nantes*, 1880. Whiting's *Studies in English Puritanism* (1315) contains chapters on foreign protestants in England.

1406   SHAW, W. A. 'English government and the relief of protestant refugees.' *E.H.R.* 9 (1894), 662–83.

> Repr. with additions in *Proc. Huguenot Soc.* 5 (1898), 343–423. See also ibid. 7 (1905), 108–92, and 12 (1924), 263–87, regarding London records relating to the subject; and an article by E. S. de Beer, ibid. 18 (1950), 292–310.

E. QUAKERS

George Fox, the founder of the Quakers, early impressed upon his followers the importance of the use of the pen as well as of the voice in the propagation of their Gospel message. The result was that, according to a modern computation, some four thousand different works were published previous to 1718. Many of them are of permanent importance, not only for the history of Quakerism, but also for the picture they afford of the middle and lower classes. John Whiting produced the earliest ecclesiastical bibliography in 1708, which formed the basis for the elaborate work by Joseph Smith (1407). *The Journal of George Fox* (1427) is the classic of Quakerism and should be studied in the edition prepared by Norman Penney. Next in importance are the *Works* of William Penn. There are valuable short histories by Emmott, Harvy, and Brayshaw, and on the formative period by Lloyd. The work by Braithwaite is difficult to praise too highly.

The Friends' Reference Library, established in 1673, is attached to the head-quarters of the Society of Friends, Friends House, Euston Road, London, N.W. 1, and has the largest collection of Quaker literature in existence. The corresponding collection in America is at Haverford College, Pennsylvania. See also titles in Chs. XIII and XV *infra* on Wales and Ireland.

1. GENERAL WORKS

(a) *Bibliography and Sources*

1407   SMITH, J. A descriptive catalogue of Friends' books or books written by members of the Society of Friends . . . from their first rise to the present time. 2 vols. 1867.

> Vol. i, A–I; vol. ii, J–Z. Cf. Supplement, 1893. These and the next items are important,

Cf. John Whiting's earliest *Catalogue of Friends books*, 1708. See also J. Smith, *Bibliotheca anti-Quakeriana, or a catalogue of books adverse to the Society of Friends . . . together with the answers*, 1873; and C. Furman, *Quaker bibliography for the genealogist; references to biography, genealogy [and] records*, N.Y. 1950[?]. A useful bibliography of MSS. and books is in Lloyd (1417).

1408   JOURNAL of the Friends' Historical Society. 1903+.

Supplements print documents; e.g. no. 26, G. F. Nuttall, *James Nayler, a fresh approach*, 1954; and no. 27, A. W. Braithwaite, *Thomas Rudyard, early Friends' oracle of law*, 1956.

1409   PENNEY, N. 'The first publishers of truth', being early records (now first printed) of the introduction of Quakerism into the counties of England and Wales. 1907.

First pr. in *Jour. Friends' Hist. Soc. Suppl.*, nos. 1–5, 8–11. See also by Penney, *Extracts from state papers relating to Friends, 1654–72*, 1913.

1410   SNELL, B. S., ed. The minute book of the monthly meeting of the Society of Friends for the Upperside of Buckinghamshire, 1669–1690. High Wycombe. 1937. Lond. 1938.

Bucks. Rec. Soc. Pub., vol. 1. On business matters, relief of the persecuted, organization of legal defence, prosecution of perjured informers, dispensing of charity. Cf. *The . . . minute book of the Gainsborough monthly meeting of the Society of Friends 1669–1719*, ed. by H. W. Brace, 3 vols., Hereford, 1948–51. (Lincoln Rec. Soc. Pub., vols. 38, 40, 44.) See Lloyd (1417) for listing of MS. minutes.

(b) *Later Works*

1411   BARCLAY, R. The inner life of the religious societies of the commonwealth. 1876. Later edns. 1877 and 1879.

1412   BRAITHWAITE, W. C. The beginnings of Quakerism. 1912. 2nd edn. rev. by H. J. Cadbury. N.Y. 1955.

Covers 1650–60. Continued in his: *The second period of Quakerism* (1660–1725), 1919. Together these form the best history of Quakerism for the period. Intro. to each vol. by R. M. Jones, who continued the series in *Later periods of Quakerism*, 2 vols., 1921.

1413   EMMOTT, E. B. A short history of Quakerism (to 1725). 1923.

Also by Emmott: *The story of Quakerism*, 1908, repr. frequently. Cf. M. R. Brailsford, *Quaker women, 1650–90*, 1915; A. N. Brayshaw, *The Quakers: their story and message*, 1921, 2nd edn. enl., 1927, 3rd edn., 1938; T. E. Harvey, *The rise of the Quakers*, 1905, 6th imp., 1922; and H. H. Brinton, *Friends for 300 years*, N.Y. 1952.

1414   HIRST, M. E. The Quakers in peace and war. 1923.

Cf. A. Ludgater's articles, 'Sufferings of Essex Quakers' (17th century), *Essex Rev.* 44 (1935), 219–21, and 45 (1936), 165–9; and J. F. Maclear, 'Quakerism and the end of the interregnum', *Church Hist.* 19 (1950), 240–70.

1415   JONES, R. M. Mysticism and democracy in the English commonwealth. Camb. 1932.

See also by Jones *et al.*, *The Quakers in the American colonies*, 1911. Cf. F. B. Tolles, 'The transatlantic Quaker community in the seventeenth century', *Hunt. Lib. Quart.* 14 (1951), 239–58.

1416 KIRBY, E. W. 'The Quakers' efforts to secure civil and religious liberty, 1660–1696.' *J.M.H.* 7 (1935), 401–21.

See also Whiting's chapter on the Quakers in *Studies in English Puritanism* (1315).

1417 LLOYD, A. Quaker social history, 1669–1738. Intro. by H. G. Wood. Toronto, Lond., and N.Y. 1950. Bibl.

Deals with the formative period of Quaker church government and social practice. Based on wide use of MSS.; bibl. of MSS. and books. Cf. two works by L. M. Wright: *The literary life of the early Friends, 1650–1725*, N.Y. 1932; and *Literature and education in early Quakerism*, Univ. of Iowa, 1933. On Quakers in science and industry see Raistrick (2037).

1418 MUSCHAMP, R. 'Historical notes on the Society of Friends or Quakers in Manchester in the seventeenth century.' *Trans. Lanc. and Ches. Antiq. Soc.* 31 (1914), 45–62.

See articles by Muschamp on other Lancashire districts, ibid. 43 (1928), 21–41; 45 (1930), 32–43; and 46 (1931), 78–92. See also G. B. Burnet, *The story of Quakerism in Scotland*, 1952, bibl., and I. Grubb, *Quakers in Ireland*, 1927.

1419 SEWEL, WILLEM. The history of the rise, increase and progress of the Christian people called Quakers . . . with several remarkable occurrences, written originally in Low Dutch by William Sewel and by himself translated into English. 1722. Later edns. 1725.

Originally publ. in Dutch, Amsterdam, 1717: *Histori van de Opkomste, Aanwas, en Voortgang der Christenen bekend by den naam van Quakers*. Valuable. Cf. W. I. Hull, *The rise of Quakerism in Amsterdam, 1655–1665*, Swarthmore, 1938.

2. BIOGRAPHIES, PERSONAL NARRATIVES, AND COLLECTED WORKS

BESSE, JOSEPH

1420 Besse, Joseph. A collection of the sufferings of the people called Quakers [1650–89]. 2 vols. 1753.

Besse also wrote: *Abstract of the sufferings . . .*, 3 vols., 1733–8; *Brief account of many of the prosecutions*, 1736. His various works form an invaluable storehouse of biographical facts. Cf. Henry Tuke, *Biographical notices of members of the Society of Friends*, 2 vols., York, 1813–15, 2nd edn., 2 vols., York, 1826.

BARCLAY, ROBERT

1421 Barclay, Robert. Truth triumphant. 1692. 3 vols. 1717–18.

Collected works. An important work often repr. is *Apology for the true Christian divinity* [Aberdeen?], 1678. For others, see Smith (1407).

BELLERS, JOHN

1422 Fry, A. R., ed. John Bellers, 1654–1725, Quaker, economist and social reformer. His writings reprinted, with a memoir. 1935.

See also H. G. Tibbutt, 'John Crook, 1617–1699: a Bedfordshire Quaker', *Beds. Hist. Rec. Soc. Pub. for 1943*, 25 (1947) 110–28, which includes a bibliography of Crook's writings.

DEWSBURY, WILLIAM

1423   Smith, E. The life of William Dewsbury. 1836.

Cf. *Letters to William Dewsbury and others* (1665–78), ed. by H. J. Cadbury [*Jour. Friends' Hist. Soc.*, Suppl. no. 22], 1949.

ELLWOOD, THOMAS

1424   The history of the life of Thomas Ellwood . . . written by his own hand. Ed. by J. Wyeth. 1714. Ed. by C. G. Crump. 1900. Ed. by S. Graveson. 1906.

Ellwood's works include *Epistle to Friends . . . warning . . .* [against] *George Keith*, 1694, and others relating to the controversy with Keith, who was eventually disowned by the Quakers, and who wrote *Standard of the Quakers examined, or an answer to the Apology of Robert Barclay*, 1702. Others of Ellwood's works are listed in Smith (1407). A short life is B. S. Snell, *Thomas Elwood, the friend of Milton*, repr. 1934.

FELL, MARGARET

1425   A brief collection of remarkable passages and occurrences relating to . . . Margaret Fell, but by her second marriage, Margaret Fox. Together with sundry of her epistles, books and Christian testimonies. 1710.

Cf. I. Ross, *Margaret Fell, mother of Quakerism*, 1949, a biography that reveals much on social history of the lower middle class. See also H. G. Crosfield, *Margaret Fox of Swarthmoor Hall, c.* 1913; M. Webb, *The Fells of Swarthmoor Hall and their friends*, 1865, 2nd edn. Phila. 1884; and no. 2221.

FISHER, SAMUEL

1426   The testimony of truth exalted by the collected labours of . . . Samuel Fisher. s.l. 1679.

Mainly a repr. of *Rusticus ad academicos*, 1660. (Wing, F 1056, 1058.)

FOX, GEORGE

1427   A journal or historical account of the life, travels, sufferings . . . of . . George Fox. Intro. by W. Penn. 1694. Later edns. 2 vols. Camb. 1911. 1 vol. Lond. 1924. Both ed. by N. Penney, rev. 1948. Later rev. by J. L. Nickalls. Camb. 1952.

The first edn. was prepared by T. Ellwood and other Friends. The Cambridge edn. first gives the original manuscript verbatim. For addenda and corrigenda of edn. of 1911 see the *Jour. Friends' Hist. Soc.* 9–21 (1912–24). The *Short journal of George Fox* was ed. by N. Penney, Camb. 1925. Cf. *The Works of George Fox*, 8 vols., Phila. 1831, the most complete collection. Included are the important *Collection of epistles*, 1698, and *Collection of doctrinal books*, 1706. For titles of Fox's works see Wing, F 1739–1944. See also Smith (1407).

1428   Hodgkin, T. George Fox. 1896.

The best short life. Other biographies of Fox are by: J. Marsh, 1847; S. M. Janney, Phila. 1853; W. Tallack, 1868; A. C. Bickley, 1884; H. G. Wood, 1912; R. M. Jones, 1919, 1943; Rachel Knight, 1922. Later studies are A. N. Brayshaw, *The personality of George Fox*, 1933; R. M. Jones, *George Fox, Seeker and Friend*, 1931; and R. H. King, *George Fox and the light within, 1650–1660*, Phila. 1941. In popular style is V. Noble, *The man in leather breeches: the life of George Fox*, N.Y. 1953.

1429   New appreciations of George Fox: a tercentenary collection of studies. 1925. Bibl.

Cf. H. van Etten, *George Fox et les Quakers*, Paris, 1956; and P. Held, *Der Quäker, George Fox: sein Leben, Wirken, Kämpfen, Laiden, Siegen*, Basel, c. 1950, bibl. On cures ascribed to Fox see H. J. Cadbury, *George Fox's Book of miracles*, Camb. 1948; the introduction is valuable.

HAYDOCK, ROGER

1430   A collection of the Christian writings [and] labours . . . of . . . Roger Haydock. 1700.

Cf. T. C. Porteus, 'Roger Haydock of Coppull: A brief biography and ten original letters', *Lancs. and Cheshire Antiq. Soc. Trans.* 52 (1938), 1–66.

HOOTON, ELIZABETH

1431   Manners, E. Elizabeth Hooton, first Quaker woman preacher (1600–72). Intro. by N. Penney. 1914.

Deals with her experiences in New England as well as in England. This forms Supplement 12 of the *Jour. Friends' Hist. Soc.* Cf. L. V. Hodgkin, *A Quaker saint of Cornwall: Loveday Hambly and her guests*, 1927.

HOWGIL, FRANCIS

1432   The dawnings of the gospel-day and its light and glory discovered by . . . Francis Howgil. Ed. by E. Hooks. s.l. 1676.

A reprint of Howgil's tracts, including *The heart of New England hardened through wickedness*, 1659. Cf. *Memoirs of Francis Howgill*, by J. Backhouse, York, 1828. See also Thomas Lurting, *The fighting sailor turn'd peaceable Christian*, 1710, 1813; and lives of James Parnell by H. Callaway, 1846, and C. Fell-Smith, 1906.

NAYLER, JAMES

1433   A true narrative of the examination, tryall and sufferings of James Nayler. 1657.

Cf. *Memoirs of the life, ministry, tryal and sufferings of . . . James Nailer*, 1719. There are lives by J. G. Bevan, 1800; by H. Tuke (1420 n.); by E. Fogelklou (trans. from Swedish by L. Yapp), 1931. Probably the best life is by M. R. Brailsford, 1927.

PENINGTON, ISAAC

1434   Works of the long mournful and sorely distressed Isaac Penington. 2 parts. 1680–81. Later edns. 2 vols. 1761. 4 vols. 1784.

Cf. J. Barclay, ed., *Letters of Isaac Penington*, 1828; J. G. Bexam, ed., *Memoirs of the life of Isaac Penington, to which is added a review of his writings*, 1807, later edn. 1830. See also M. Webb, *The Penns and Peningtons of the seventeenth century in their domestic life, illustrated by original family letters*, 1867, 2nd edn. 1891.

PENN, WILLIAM

1435   A collection of the works of William Penn. To which is prefixed a journal of his life with many original letters. 2 vols. 1726. Later edn. 'Select works.' 5 vols. 1782.

Among the more important works repr. are: *The sandy foundation shaken*, 1668; *The people's ancient and just liberties asserted in the trial of William Penn and William Mead*,

1670; *No cross, no crown; A treatise of oaths; The great ease of liberty of conscience debated*, 1670; *Travels in Holland and Germany*, 1677; *A general description of the province of Pennsylvania*, 1683; *Some fruits of solitude*, 1693; *A brief account of the rise and progress of the people called Quakers*, 1694. Cf. Penn's *My Irish journal, 1669–1670*, ed. by I. Grubb and H. J. Cadbury, 1952. Much material on Penn is contained in Hist. Soc. of Penn., *Memoirs*, etc., 14 vols., Phila. 1826–45. For other titles see Smith (1407), ii and suppl.; Wing; and Peare (1438 n.). Several short texts are repr. in Tolles and Alderfer (1439 n.).

1436 Clarkson, T. Memoirs of the public and private life of William Penn. 2 vols. 1813. Bibl. Later edn. 1849.

The edn. of 1849 has a preface by W. E. Forster, replying to the charges against Penn made by Macaulay (361). This preface was publ. separately as *William Penn and Thomas B. Macaulay*, 1849 (Phila. 1850).

1437 Dixon, W. H. William Penn: an historical biography. 1851. Later edn. 1872.

Concerned with Penn as a statesman, using family and state papers. For documents relating to judicial proceedings against Penn, 1670–1, see *Berks. Arch. Jour.* 37 (1933), 59–75.

1438 Janney, S. M. Life of William Penn, with selections from his correspondence and autobiography. Phila. 1851. 2nd edn. Phila. 1852.

On early biographies see W. I. Hull, *Eight first biographies of William Penn in seven languages and seven lands*, Swarthmore, 1936. See also a 'topical' biography by Hull, 1937. The latest one-volume biography, based on many MS. collections, and including a bibl. of Penn's writings is by C. O. Peare, Phila. and N.Y. 1957. A good popular biography is that of J. W. Graham, 1916. Other useful lives are by J. Stoughton, 1882; M. R. Brailsford, 1930; B. Dobrée, 1932; C. E. Vulliamy, 1933; and W. W. Comfort, Phila. 1914. See also M. Webb, *The Penns and Peningtons* (1434 n.), and A. Pound, *The Penns of Pennsylvania and England*, N.Y. 1932.

1439 Beatty, E. C. O. William Penn as social philosopher. N.Y. and Lond. 1939.

'Detailed survey of his political, economic, and social thought.' Cf. F. B. Tolles, and E. G. Alderfer eds., *The witness of William Penn*, N.Y. 1957, with commentary on selected texts reprinted therein; and J. H. Powell, 'William Penn's writings', *Pennsylvania History*, 11 (1944), 239–59.

ROBERTS, JOHN

1440 Roberts, Daniel. Some memoirs of the life of John Roberts. Exeter. 1746. Later edn. by E. T. Lawrence. 1898. Bibl.

The edn. of 1898 is called *A Quaker of the olden times*, and contains additional genealogical material of the Roberts family.

SANSOM, OLIVER

1441 An account of . . . the life of Oliver Sansom. 1710. Later edn. 1848.

STORY, THOMAS

1442 Journal of the life of Thomas Story. Newcastle-on-Tyne. 1747.

Abridged by J. Kendall, 1786; and rev. by W. Alexander, York, 1832.

WHITEHEAD, GEORGE

1443   The Christian progress of . . . George Whitehead. 4 pts. in 1 vol. 1725.

A very detailed autobiography. Cf. *George Whitehead . . . compiled from his auto-biography*, by W. Beck, 1901.

WHITEHEAD, JOHN

1444   The written Gospel-labours of . . . John Whitehead. Preface by W. Penn. 1704.

Cf. *The life and writings of John Whitehead*, by T. Chalk, 1852.

WHITING, JOHN

1445   Persecution expos'd in some memoirs relating to the sufferings of John Whiting and many others of the people called Quakers . . . in the west of England. 1715. Later edn. 1791.

F. ROMAN CATHOLICISM

The history of the English Catholics in the seventeenth century as a whole remains to be written. The circumstances of the period limited the publication of much except devotional or controversial works. Since the foundation of the Catholic Record Society in 1904 there has become available in print an increasing volume of source material. More lists of members and other biographical materials relating to the various orders, especially that of the Jesuits, have been published also. Of earlier publications, still useful for biography are Dodd (1458), with its continuation by Tierney, and Challoner (1479). Gillow's 'Bibliographical Dictionary' (1460), though incomplete, is valuable. Foley's *Records* (1471) are helpful on the history of the Jesuits and other Catholics in England. Among more recent materials, good examples, besides those published by the Catholic Record Society are family papers such as Crosby Records (1455), and Clark's *Strangers and sojourners at Port Royal* (1465). Shorter histories, making use of newly published materials, are by Matthew (1459), Magee (1483), and Havran (1462 n.). See also Ch. XIII *infra*, nos. 3654–62.

1. BIBLIOGRAPHIES AND SOURCES

Important collections of manuscripts are in the libraries of the London Oratory and The Catholic Cathedral of Westminster (see H.M.C., *5th Rep.*, pt. 1 (1876), 463–76), at the Br. Mus. (transcripts of papal registers 1216–1759 in Add. MSS. 15351–400), and in Stonyhurst College (see H.M.C., *2nd Rep.* (1874), 143–6; *3rd Rep.* (1872), 334–41; *10th Rep.*, pt. 4 (1885), 176–99). For other MS. collections reported by H.M.C. see Upton and Winship, *Guide*, pp. 120–1.

(a) *Bibliographies*

1446   POLLEN, J. H. Sources for the history of Roman Catholics in England, Ireland, and Scotland . . . 1533–1795. (Helps for students of history.) 1921.

See also A. F. Allison and D. M. Rogers, *Catalogue of Catholic books in English printed abroad or secretly in England, 1558–1640*, 2 pts. (*Biographical studies*, III), 1956. See also Gillow (1460); Watkin (1463).

1447 CATHOLIC RECORD SOCIETY. Publications. 1905+.

Includes many Catholic registers and other source materials such as papers on the archpriest controversy, 1621–33, ed. by R. Stanfield (*Misc.* 12 (1921), pp. 132–86); letters of Thomas Fitzherbert, 1608–10, ed. by L. Hicks (vol. 41 for 1941/2 (1948)). For a list of the printed texts in this series see Mullins.

　　Publ. under the auspices of the Society is the new series entitled *Biographical studies*, 1534–1829, ed. by A. F. Allison and D. M. Rogers, vols. 1–4+, Bognor, 1951–8+. Beginning with vol. 4 (1957–8), this series bears the title *Recusant history*. See also *The Catholic Encyclopaedia*, 15 vols., 1907–14.

(b) *General Sources*

Arranged in rough chronological order.

1448 A SUPPLICATION to the kings most excellent maiestie. Anon. s.l. 1604.

A Catholic plea for toleration. For a useful summary of the historical arguments by a Catholic controversialist see [R. Parsons,] *An answere to the . . . reportes . . . by Syr Edward Cooke . . .*, s.l. 1606 (*S.T.C.* 19352).

1449 MR. GEORGE BLACKWEL, (made by Pope Clement 8. Archpriest of England) his answeres upon sundry his examinations . . . 1607.

See also *S.T.C.* 3104 regarding the examination of Blackwell, 1607.

1450 PANZANI, GREGORIO. The memoirs of Gregorio Panzani—giving an account of his agencies in England [1634–1636]. Ed. by J. Berington. Birmingham. 1793.

In the intro. and supplement are accounts of the fortunes of Roman Catholics in England, 1558–1793. Transcript in Br. Mus. Add. MS. 15389. Cf. H.M.C., *3rd Rep.*, pp. 234–6; *The Pope's nuntioes*, 1643; and Berington's *The state and behaviour of English Catholics from the Reformation to 1781*, 2 pts., 1780; 1781. There are transcripts in the P.R.O. of the correspondence of Panzani, Con, and Rossetti.

　　See also Cyprian de Gamaches, *Memoirs of the mission in England of the Capuchin friars of the province of Paris* (1630–69), which is a translation from the French edn. (Paris, 1881) and is printed in vol. ii of *The court and times of Charles I* (287 n.).

1451 PRYNNE, WILLIAM, ed. The popish royall favourite or a full discovery of his majesties extraordinary favours to . . . Papists, priests, Jesuits . . . 1643.

Valuable; publ. by order of Parliament. See also his *New discovery of the prelates tyranny*, 1641. For a parliamentary pamphlet listing Catholic vicars general, 1642, see Wing, V 127–8. See also A.B., *Mutatus polemo*, 1650 (Wing B 21).

1452 CASTLEMAINE, ROGER PALMER, EARL OF. The Catholique apology. 3rd edn. s.l. 1674.

A reasoned defence: contains list of Catholics who died or suffered for the royalist cause during the civil war. Other pamphlets by Castlemaine are listed in Wing (C 1239–51). See also the controversial writings of John Gother, a Catholic divine of the restoration, such as his *Papist misrepresented and represented*, 3 pts., 1665[i.e. 1685]–87 (Wing, G 1324–50), which evoked numerous replies.

1453   JONES, T., ed. A catalogue of the collection of tracts for and against
Popery (published in or about the reign of James II) in the Manchester Library
founded by Humphrey Chetham [including a catalogue compiled by Francis
Peck, 1735]. 2 vols. Chetham Soc. (vols. 48, 64) 1859–65.

1454   BRADY, W. M. Annals of the Catholic hierarchy in England and Scotland, 1585–1876. Rome. 1877. Lond. 1883.

The third vol. (repr.) of *The Episcopal succession in England, Scotland and Ireland* [1400–
1875], 3 vols., Rome, 1876–7, which contains important extracts from continental
archives. Another work of value is John Sergeant's *Abstract of the transactions relating
to the English secular clergy*, 1706, ed. by W. Turnbull under the title of *An account
of the chapter erected by William, titular Bishop of Chalcedon and Ordinary of England
and Scotland*, 1853.

(c) Sources: Diaries and Lists

1455   GIBSON, T. E., ed. Crosby records: (1) A cavalier's note book . . . by
William Blundell . . . captain in the royalist army (1642), 1880; (2) A chapter
of Lancashire recusancy (Blundells of Crosby Hall, 1560–1638), Chetham Soc.
(N.S., vol. 12), 1887; (3) Blundell's diary (Nicholas Blundell, 1702–28). Liverpool. 1895. Later edn. by M. Blundell. Liverpool. 1952.

See also M. Blundell, ed., *Cavalier: letters of Wm. Blundell . . . 1620–98*, 1933; *Personal
records of Thomas Tyldesley* (1712–14), ed. by J. Gillow and A. Hewitson, Preston, 1873;
and 'The notebook of John Southcote' (1623–37), ed. by J. H. Pollen, *Cath. Rec. Soc.
Misc.* I (1905).

1456   POLLEN, J. H., ed. Bedingfield papers. *Cath. Rec. Soc. Misc.* 6 (1909).

Includes diary of Thomas Marwood, 1699–1703, and illustrates life of English Catholics
abroad as well as in England. See also B. Blackstone, ed., *The Ferrar papers*, N.Y. and
Camb. 1938. For other family papers see H.M.C., Coke MSS.; M. F. S. Hervey, *Life
of Thomas Howard, earl of Arundel* (401); and no. 1460 n.

1457   PEACOCK, E., ed. List of Roman Catholics in the county of York
[1604]. 1872.

From a list in the Bodl. Libr. Examples of other lists are J. Huddlestone's 'Obituaries'
(*c.* 1639–63), ed. by J. Gillow in *Cath. Rec. Soc. Misc.* I (1905), 123–32; and J. H.
Matthews, ed., 'Records relating to Catholicism in the South Wales Marches' (ibid.,
Misc. 2 (1906), 289–304), which reprints lists of 1605 and 1688–1717 from P.R.O.
sources. See also pp. 210–11 *infra* on Persecution.

2. General Histories

1458   DODD, C. [i.e. HUGH TOOTELL.] The church of England chiefly
with regard to Catholicks (1500–1688). 3 vols. Brussels. 1737–42. Later edn.
[to 1625] by M. A. Tierney. 5 vols. Lond. 1838–43.

Chief work for Catholic biog. before Gillow (1460). Tierney edn. includes valuable notes
and app. of documents. For MSS. used in preparing this edn. see H.M.C., *3rd Rep.*,
p. 233.
    See also C. Butler, *Historical memoirs respecting English, Irish and Scottish Catholics*,
4 vols., 1819–21, 3rd edn., 4 vols., 1822.

1459   MATHEW, DAVID. Catholicism in England, 1535–1935: portrait of
a minority, its culture and tradition. 1936. 3rd edn. 1955.

Another account is T. Flanagan, *History of the Church in England* (to 1850), 2 vols., 1857. On special topics see W. R. Trimble, 'The embassy chapel question, 1625–1660', *J.M.H.* 18 (1946), 97–107; and A. C. F. Beales, *Education under penalty: English Catholic education* (1547–1689), 1963.

1460 GILLOW, J. A literary and biographical history or bibliographical dictionary of the English Catholics from the breach with Rome in 1534 to the present day. 5 vols. Lond. and N.Y. [1885–1902.]

Valuable though incomplete, especially in vol. 5. Lists writings. A useful volume is B. Hemphill, *The early vicars apostolic of England, 1685–1750*, 1954. *Biographies of English Catholics in the 18th century*, ed. by J. Kirk *et al.*, 1909, contains many 17th-century figures.

Examples of biographical studies on individuals or families are: C. F. R. Palmer, on Philip Thomas Howard, Cardinal of Norfolk, 1867; lives of Mary Ward [1585–1645] by M. C. E. Chambers (ed. by H. J. Coleridge, 2 vols., 1882–5), by M. Salome, 1901, F. A. Gasquet, 1909, and I. F. Coudenhove (tr. by E. Codd, 1939); C. Howard's biog. of Sir John Yorke, 1939, and G. Anstruther's study of the recusant family, *Vaux of Harrowden*, Newport, Mon. 1953.

1461 HARTING, J. H. Catholic London missions from the reformation to the year 1850. 1903.

Much curious and valuable information, especially on chapels, but often inaccurate. See also M. H. A. Stapleton, *History of the post-reformation Catholic missions in Oxfordshire*, 1906.

1462 MEYER, A. O. Clemens VIII und Jakob I von England. Rome. 1904.

Cf. his 'Charles I and Rome', *A.H.R.* 19 (1913), 13–26. A scholarly study, based on MS. sources, is G. Albion, *Charles I and the court of Rome*, 1935. On Henrietta Maria's Franciscan chaplain see E. E. Klaus, *Christopher Davenport*, Lengerich, 1938. See also K. M. Lea's article on Italian hopes to convert James I in *E.H.R.* 47 (1932), 461–77. A recent scholarly monograph is M. J. Havran, *The Catholics in Caroline England*, Stanford (Cal.), 1962, bibl.

1463 WATKIN, E. I. Roman Catholicism in England from the reformation to 1950 (Home University Library). Lond. and N.Y. 1957.

A useful brief history, with select bibliography.

3. SOCIETIES

(a) *Societies, Excluding the Jesuits*

1464 ANSTRUTHER, G. A hundred homeless years: English Dominicans, 1558–1658. 1958.

Has bibliographical footnotes; main emphasis is on the personal. See also vol. 25 (1925) of *Cath. Rec. Soc. Pub.*, 'Dominicana'.

1465 CLARK, R. Strangers and sojourners at Port Royal, being an account of the connections between the British Isles and the Jansenists of France and Holland. Camb. 1932. Bibl.

Valuable. Notes on various English religious establishments in Paris, ed. by G. Daumet, appear in vols. 37, 39 (1910, 1912) of *Mémoires de la Société de l'Histoire de Paris et de l'Ile de France*.

1466 HAUDECŒUR, A. La conservation providentielle du Catholicisme en Angleterre ou histoire du Collège Anglaise, Douai (1563–78), Reims (1578–93), Douai (1593–1793). Reims. 1898.

The only outline of the entire history of the college, 1568–1793; English names often misprinted. Important also are *The Douay College diaries* [1598–1654], ed. by E. H. Burton and T. L. Williams, 2 vols. (*Cath. Rec. Soc. Pub.*, vols. 10–11), 1911–12; F. Febre, *The settling of the English Benedictines at Douai* [1607–1611], 1934; and H. Chadwick, 'The Scots College, Douai, 1580–1613', *E.H.R.* 56 (1941), 571–85.

1467 PETRE, E. Notices of the English colleges and convents established on the continent after the dissolution of religious houses in England. Ed. by F. C. Husenbeth. Norwich. 1849.

A convenient summary. The Catholic Record Society has published many documents pertaining to English Catholics on the continent, of which the following are examples: vol. 29 (1929), Madrid [1611–1767]; *Misc.* 11 (1917), St. Gregory's, Paris [1667–1786]; *Misc.* 3 (1906), St. Omer's College [1667]; vol. 30 (1930), Valladolid [1589–1862].
    See also P. Guilday, *The English Catholic refugees on the continent, 1558–1795*, vol. i (Low Countries), 1914, a scholarly work with a bibliography; J. Kirk, *Historical account of Lisbon College* (with a register compiled by J. Gillow), ed. by W. Croft, Barnet, 1902. On the English in Rome see F. Gasquet (cardinal), *History of the venerable English college*, Rome, 1920; W. Kelly, ed., *The Liber Ruber of the English College, Rome*, vol. i (1943); and B. Jennings, ed., 'Documents from the archives of St. Isidore's College, Rome', in *Analecta Hibernica*, 6 (1934), 203–43. See also p. 210 *infra* on Nuns. For other titles see C. L. Grose (10), 150–1.

1468 THADDEUS, FATHER. The Franciscans in England, 1600–1850. 1898.

Valuable citations from contemporary accounts. List of friars is largely superseded by the official lists published by the Cath. Rec. Soc., vol. 24 (1922).

1469 WELDON, BENNET. Chronological notes, containing the rise, growth, and present state of the English congregation of the Order of St. Benedict. 1881.

A history of the English Benedictines in the 17th century, with lists of monks and obituaries, compiled from MS. memoirs at St. Gregory's Priory, Downside, written *c.* 1709. Cf. *Necrology* (1600–1883) compiled by T. B. Snow, 1883, 2nd edn., by H. N. Birt, 1913; and E. L. Taunton, *The English black monks of St. Benedict*, 2 vols., 1898. For the important Benedictine leader, Father Augustine Baker, see *Memorials*, publ. by the Cath. Rec. Soc., vol. 33 (1933), and a *Life* by P. Salvin and S. Cressy, ed. by Dom Justin McCann, 1932.

1470 ZIMMERMAN, B. Carmel in England: a history of the English mission of the Discalced Carmelites (1615–1819). 1899.

Based on many documents and full for the 17th century. On the Discalced Carmelite nuns in the Netherlands (1617–1819) see A. Hardman, *English Carmelites in penal times*, 1936, and the same author's biog. of Mother Margaret Mostyn, 1625–79, 1937.

(b) *Jesuits*

1471 FOLEY, H., ed. Records of the English province of the Society of Jesus . . . in the sixteenth and seventeenth centuries. 6 vols. 1875–80. Later edn. 7 vols. 1882.

Valuable: largely from the archives of Stonyhurst College, Lancashire. For an early account see H. More, *Historia missionis anglicanae societatis Jesu* [*1580–1635*], in Latin [Saint-Omer], 1660.

1472   NICHOLS, J. G., ed. The discovery of the Jesuits' College at Clerkenwell in March 1627–8. *Camd. Soc. Misc.* ii. 1853.

Cf. *Camden Soc. Misc.* iv for a supplementary note.

1473   OLIVER, G. Collections towards illustrating the biography of Scotch, English and Irish members, S[ocietatis] J[esu]. Exeter. 1838. 2nd edn. 1845.

For other works relating to Catholics in western England see T. N. Brushfield, *The bibliography of the Rev. George Oliver* [s.l., *c.* 1886], repr. from *Devon Trans.* (1885). Examples of more recent biographies are: lives of Father Claude de la Colombière (1641–82) by Sister Mary Philip, 1925, and L. Percy, Paris, 1923; and P. Caraman's *Henry Morse, priest of the plague* (1595–1645), 1957.

1474   TAUNTON, E. L. The history of the Jesuits in England, 1580–1773. 1901.

Not reliable. This work elicited replies such as W. Walsh, *Jesuits in Great Britain: an historical inquiry into their political influence*, 1903.

4. NUNS

1475   HAMILTON, A., ed. The chronicle of the English Augustinian canonesses regular of the Lateran at St. Monica's in Louvain (now at St. Augustine's Priory, Newton Abbot, Devon). 2 vols. Edin. 1904.

Covers period from 1548 to 1644, and includes much genealogical information.

1476   MARY PHILIP, MOTHER. Companions of Mary Ward. 1939.

The foundress of the Institution of the Blessed Virgin Mary, *temp.* James I. See also Gillow (1460).

1477   NEVILLE, ANNE. Abbess Neville's annals of five communities of English Benedictine nuns in Flanders, 1598–1687. Ed. by M. J. Rumsey. *Cath. Rec. Soc. Misc.* 5 (1909).

Other records published by the Catholic Rec. Soc. concern: English Benedictine nuns in Ghent (1627–1811), ed. by A. L. Ward (*Misc.* 11, 1917); English canonesses of the Holy Sepulchre at Liège (1652–1793), ed. by A. J. Kendal and R. Trappes-Lomax (*Misc.* 10, 1915); the 'Blue nuns', Paris (1658–1810), ed. by J. Gillow and R. Trappes-Lomax (vol. 8, 1910); the Poor Clare nuns at Gravelines and other places (1608–1837), ed. by W. M. Hunnybun and J. Gillow (*Misc.* 9, 1914); and English Franciscan nuns (1619–1821), ed. by R. Trappes-Lomax (vol. 24, 1922).

5. PERSECUTION AND MARTYROLOGY

1478   ANSTEY, T. C. A guide to the laws of England affecting Roman Catholics. 1842.

Includes the 17th-century laws, classified and digested. Cf. R. R. Madden, *The history of the penal laws enacted against Roman Catholics*, 1847.

1479 CHALLONER, RICHARD. Memoirs of missionary priests . . . and of
other Catholics . . . that have suffered death in England on religious accounts
[1577–1684]. 2 vols. 1741–2. Later edns. Manchester. 1803. Edin. and Lond.
1878. Ed. by J. H. Pollen. 1 vol. 1924.

> Important. Vol. ii covers the years 1693 to 1684–5. See Pollen's comment on MS.
> sources in intro. to the 1924 edn. For particulars on the various edns. see E. H. Burton,
> *Life and times of Bishop Challoner*, 2 vols., 1909. Cf. M. T. Lomas, *Bishop Challoner*,
> 1936.

1480 DE MARSYS, F. Histoire de la persécution présente des Catholiques en
Angleterre. 3 pts. Paris[?] *c.* 1645.

> Cases on recusancy (1605–1685), ed. by H. Bowler from the London sessions, are printed
> as vol. 34 of *Cath. Rec. Soc. Pub.*, 1934.

1481 DUCKETT, SIR G. F. Penal laws and Test Act. 2 vols. 1882–3.

> Cf. [Henry Care], *Draconica, or an abstract of all the penal laws touching matters of religion*,
> 1687, 3rd edn., 1688. See also the county records transcribed by A. L. Brown, 'King
> James the Second's proposed repeal of the penal laws and test act in 1688; his questions
> to the magistrates of Cumberland, with their answers thereto', *Trans. Cumb. and
> Westmor. Antiq. and Arch. Soc.*, N.S. 38 (1938), 180–94; and similar records in *Hist.
> Coll. Staffordshire* (1939), 158–73; and *Trans. Bristol and Glouc. Arch. Soc.* 61 (1940),
> 287–93.

1482 LAW, T. G., ed. A calendar of the English [Catholic] martyrs of the
sixteenth and seventeenth centuries. 1876.

> For a complete list of contemporary martyrologies see J. H. Pollen in *Cath. Rec. Soc.
> Pub.* 5 (1908), pp. 1–7. Other useful lists are in Foley (1471); and W. Gumbley,
> 'Provincial priors and vicars of the English Dominicans, 1221–1916', *E.H.R.* 38 (1918),
> 243–51.
>   Several lists of 17th-century recusants and martyrs appear in vols. 3–5 (1906–09)
> of the *Cath. Rec. Soc. Misc.* Of individual martyrs examples are: Thomas Holland, S.J.
> (ibid. 8 (1913), 143–9); John Roberts (B. Camm, *A Benedictine martyr*, 1897); John
> Southworth (*Life* by A. B. Purdie, 1930; for Southworth's last speech of 1654, see
> Wing, S 4775).

1483 MAGEE, B. The English recusants: a study of the post-reformation
Catholic survival and the operation of the recusancy laws. 1938.

> By Magee also, 'England's Catholic population in penal times', *Dublin Rev.* 197 (1935),
> 253–68, and 198 (1936), 66–83. Other accounts are: J. M. Stone, *Faithful unto death . . .
> 16th and 17th centuries, from contemporary records*, 1892; and St. G. K. Hyland,
> *A century of persecution*, 1920, which draws upon the Losely MSS. for the period of
> James I and Charles I. See also Jones (3659).

6. Gunpowder Plot

See also *Political History.*

1484 A TRUE AND PERFECT RELATION of the whole proceedings against
the late most barbarous traitors, Garnet, a Jesuite, and his confederats. 1606.

> The official account (*S.T.C.* 11618). See also the controversial tracts evoked by this
> version; namely, *Apologia pro Henrico Garneto ad actionem proditoriam E. Coqui Andreae
> Eudaemon Joannis Cydonii* [i.e. the Jesuit l'Heureux], Cologne, 1610; Robert Abbot's
> answer, *Antilogia adversus apologiam Andreae Eudaemon Joannis*, 1613; and the reply of

Eudaemon-Joannes, *Responsio . . . ad antilogiam*, s.l., 1615. Cf. another account of Garnet's trial in Roger Widdrington, *The tryall and execution of Father H. Garnet* (pr. in Latin in 1616), trans. and publ., 1679 (Wing, W 2087). See also H.M.C., Salisbury MSS. at Hatfield House, vols. 17–18 (1938–40). For an extensive bibliography of the plot see Williamson (1488). Cf. a careful study by P. Caraman, N.Y. 1964.

1485 GERARD, JOHN. The condition of Catholics under James I: Father Gerard's Narrative of the Gunpowder Plot. Ed. by J. Morris. 1871. Later edns. 1872 and 1881.

Life of the Jesuit, Fr. Gerard, consisting mainly of extracts from his autobiography, followed by his 'narrative'. The 1881 edn., practically a new book, is entitled, *The life of Father John Gerard*. These should be checked with the new and complete translation of Gerard's autobiography, ed. by P. Caraman, 1951.

1486 GERARD, J. What was the Gunpowder Plot? The traditional story tested by original evidence. 1897.

An attempt to prove the plot to be chiefly fiction made up by Salisbury. S. R. Gardiner's valuable reply, in which he discusses the nature of historical evidence, *What Gunpowder Plot was*, 1897, produced a rejoinder by Gerard in *The Month*, no. 399. For a review of this discussion see *E.H.R.* 12 (1897), 791–5. See also Gerard's contributions toward a life of Garnet, based on letters in the Stonyhurst Coll., that appeared serially in *The Month*, 1898, and his *Thomas Winter's confession and the Gunpowder Plot*, 1898, in which he treats the confession as a forgery. On connections of European exiles with the plot see an article by A. H. Dodd, *E.H.R.* 53 (1938), 627–50. See also Williamson (1488).

1487 JARDINE, D. A narrative of the Gunpowder Plot. 1857.

Cf. *The identification of the writer of the anonymous letter to Lord Monteagle in 1605*, 1916; and G. B. Morgan's *The great English treason for religion*, 2 vols., Oxf. 1931, which is not entirely reliable.

1488 WILLIAMSON, H. R. The Gunpowder Plot. 1951.

The latest work, with an extensive bibliography, supports Gerard's thesis that the plot was used by the government to push through stronger anti-Catholic legislation.

For monographs on laymen implicated in the plot see T. Longueville, *The life of a conspirator* [Sir Everard Digby], 1895; and D. Carswell, ed., *Trial of Guy Fawkes and others* (Notable British Trials Ser.), Lond. and Edin. 1934.

7. THE POPISH PLOT

1489 COMPLEAT CATALOGUE of all the stitch'd books and single sheets printed since the first discovery of the Popish plot (September, 1678). 1680.

See also Luttrell (344). Among useful MSS. on the subject are H.M.C., Throckmorton (*10th Rep.*, pt. 4), Beaufort (*12th Rep.*, pt. 9), Lindsey (*14th Rep.*, pt. 9), Foljambe (*15th Rep.*, pt. 5), and Fitzherbert (*13th Rep.*, pt. 6). See also bibliographies in Pollock (no. 1497, 1903 edn.), Ronald (365), and Warner (1496).

1490 A COLLECTION of letters and other writings relating to the horrid Popish plott, printed from the originals in the hands of Sir George Treby . . . chairman of the committee of secrecy of the . . . house of commons. 2 pts. 1681.

Important. See also Luttrell (344); and K. Feiling and F. R. D. Needham, 'The journal of Edmond Warcup, 1676–84', *E.H.R.* 40 (1925), 235–60.

1491 [BLOUNT, CH.] Appeal from the country to the city for the preservation of his majesties person . . . and the Protestant religion. 1679. Later edns.

Wing, B 3300. For other Blount titles see Wing, B 3296–3315. Listed in Wing are letters by other writers on the plot, such as G. Burnet (B 5825, 5925) and Robert Ferguson (F 729–66). See also J. Ferguson (363 n.). Other tracts are in the Harleian and Somers collections. See also Warner (1496).

1492 LANGHORN, RICHARD. Mr. Langhorn's memoires, with some meditations and devotions, during his imprisonment . . . and his speech at his execution. 1679.

See also *Tryal of Edward Coleman . . . for conspiring the death of the king*, 1678 (repr. in Cobbett (789), vol. vii). For a *Compendium* of the trials, by Roger Palmer, earl of Castlemaine, see Wing, C 1241. See also bibl. in Warner (1496).

1493 OATES, TITUS. A true narrative of the horrid plot and conspiracy . . . against . . . his sacred majesty, the government, and the Protestant religion. 1679.

Pr. by order of Parliament (Wing, O 59). See the Catholic reply [by John Warner] *A vindication of English Catholicks*, Antwerp, 1680. See also W. C. Abbott, 'Origins of Titus Oates' story', *E.H.R.* 25 (1910), 126–9.

Other contemporary narratives were by Miles Prance (Wing, P 3170, 3174, 3177) and Thomas Dangerfield (Wing, D 192–3). See also Warner (1496).

1494 TRUE AND PERFECT NARRATIVE of the late terrible and bloody murther of Sir Edmondberry Godfrey. 1678.

A. Marks, in *Who killed Sir Edmond Berry Godfrey?* (1905), argues suicide. To the review by J. Pollock (*Law Quart. Rev.* 22 (1906), 431–50) Marks replied in *The Month*, 109 (1907), 36–54. See also J. D. Carr, *Murder of Sir Edmund Godfrey*, 1936.

1495 THE HISTORY OF POPISH—Sham—Plots from the reign of Queen Elizabeth to this present time, particularly of the present Popish plot. 1682.

See also [Henry Care], *History of the damnable popish plot*, 1680, 2nd edn., 1681. For Tory history of the plot see Roger L'Estrange, *A brief history of the times . . .*, 3 pts., 1687–8.

1496 WARNER, JOHN. The history of English persecution of Catholics and the Presbyterian plot. Ed. by T. A. Birrell, with trans. by J. Bligh. 2 vols. 1953–5. Bibl.

Catholic Record Society, vols. 47–8. Texts in Latin and English of the history compiled by a leading protagonist of the English Catholics during the plot, and later chaplain to James II. In the second vol. is a handlist of Warner's extant MSS. and books, including the well-known reply to Oates, *A vindication* (1493 n.).

See also M. V. Hay, *The Jesuits and the Popish plot*, 1934; *The condition of English Catholics under Charles II*, by the Comtesse R. de Courson, ed. by Elizabeth Barker, 1899; and A. M. Crino, *Il Popish plot*, Rome, 1954.

1497 POLLOCK, J. The Popish plot. 1903. Later edn. Camb. 1944.

The bibl. and app. of the 1903 edition are omitted from that of 1944. Deals with the politics of the plot in relation to the religious issues, but does not completely solve the problems. See review by A. Lang in *Valet's tragedy*, 1903, and J. Gerard in *The Popish plot and its newest historian*, 1903. Cf. 'Popish plot', *Church Quart. Rev.* 58 (1904), 137–65.

For a useful monograph on the political implications, with an extensive bibliography, see F. S. Ronalds, *The attempted Whig revolution* (365).

G. UNITARIANISM

As Unitarians stood outside the protection of the law in Great Britain for the period 1603–1714, they were unable to form any lasting organization or to gather congregations for worship. The regular press was closed against them. Except for a brief period under the Commonwealth, publications favouring Unitarian opinions were anonymous and surreptitious and often printed abroad. Materials for the study of Unitarianism in that century are therefore scanty. The story of the Unitarian movement in this period is, accordingly, the story, in the main, of individual thinkers and writers. It must be studied through biography. The *Dictionary of National Biography* gives the lives of most of these Unitarian pioneers, mainly from the hand of the Revd. Alexander Gordon.

The history of many of the Protestant Dissenting congregations which advanced to Unitarianism is set out in special monographs dealing with particular churches. There are valuable bibliographical notes in McLachlan (1506), and in H. McLachlan's *Story of a Nonconformist library*, Manchester, 1923.

1. BIBLIOGRAPHY AND SOURCES

1498 UNITARIAN HISTORICAL SOCIETY. Trans. 1916–18+.

In vol. 1 (1916–18), the editor, W. H. Burgess, listed 'Work in the field of Unitarian history'. See also the *Proceedings* of the American society of the same name, 1925+.

1499 UNITARIAN TRACTS. 5 vols. 1691–1701.

The whole series, publ. by the Unitarian Society, 1791–1802, includes 13 vols. Most of the early literature relating to Unitarians, both writings and biographical material, is contained here. (Biographies include those on John Biddle, Thomas Firmin, and Joshua Toulmin.) See also Th. Emlyn's *Collection of Tracts*, 1719, 2 vols., 1742.

1500 BONET-MAURY, G. Early sources of English Unitarian Christianity. 1884.

Trans. from 1881 Paris edn. by E. P. Hall; includes valuable intro. by J. Martineau and appendix of documents.

1501 BIDDLE [BIDLE], JOHN. A confession of faith touching the Holy Trinity according to the Scriptures. 1648 [1647?] Later edns.

Other writings by Biddle are in *Unitarian Tracts*. See also Wing, B 2877. For lives see *Johannes Bidelli . . . vita* [by John Farrington], 1682; and *A review of the life . . .* by Joshua Toulmin, 1789.

See also the important *Racovian catechisme, wherein you have the substance of the confession of those churches . . . in the kingdom of Poland*, 1652, which is a translation of the Socinian statement from the Polish (c. 1605), and the later edn. by Th. Rees, 1818; and John Crell, *Two books touching one God the Father*, English version (Amsterdam or Lond.), 1665.

1502 [NYE, STEPHEN.] Brief history of the Unitarians, called also Socinians. 1687. Later edn. 1691.

Second edn. in *Unitarian Tracts*. One of the earliest English works using the name 'Unitarians'.

Examples of the leaning toward Unitarianism may be found in works by Locke, Penn, and Milton. For the latter, see his *Last Thoughts on the Trinity, extracted from his* . . . '*Treatise on Christian doctrine*', 1828, and R. K. Allen, *Milton's creative Unitarianism* (Univ. microfilm, no. 5889), Ann Arbor, 1953.

2. LATER WORKS

1503 COLLIGAN, J. H. The Arian movement in England. Manchester. 1913.

An important work. For local history see G. E. Evans, *Vestiges of Protestant dissent* . . . [lists of ministers, registers, etc.] *included in the National Conference of Unitarian, Liberal Christian . . . congregations*, Liverpool, 1897. A useful outline is in W. G. Tarrant, *Unitarianism*, 1912.

1504 GORDON, A. Heads of English Unitarian history, with appended lectures on Baxter and Priestley. 1895.

Other works by this distinguished historian and biographer are: *Addresses biographical and historical*, 1922; *Historical account of Dukinfield chapel*, 1896. Cf. other chapel histories by H. D. Roberts, *Matthew Henry and his chapel*, Liverpool, 1901; by E. Kensett (Horsham), Horsham, 1921; by W. H. Burgess (Dean Row, Cheshire), Hull, 1924.

1505 LINDSEY, T. An historical view of the state of Unitarian doctrine and worship. 1783.

Cf. J. R. Beard, ed., *Unitarianism exhibited in its actual condition . . . in different parts of the world.* 1846.

1506 McLACHLAN, H. The Unitarian movement in the religious life of England. I. Its contribution to thought and learning. 1934.

Histories relating to or by Unitarians are described on pp. 252-68. See also H. J. McLachlan, *Socinianism in seventeenth century England*, Oxf. 1951; E. M. Williams, 'Erastianism in the great rebellion', *Church Quart. Rev.* 110 (1930), 23-33; and no. 1132 n.
    Cf. E. M. Wilbur, *A history of Unitarianism*, 2 vols., Camb. (Mass.), 1945-52 (bibl. footnotes), and Wilbur's translation of Stanislaw Kot's *Socinianism in Poland: the social and political ideas of the Polish antitrinitarians in the 16th and 17th centuries* (first publ. Warsaw, 1932), Boston (U.S.A.), [1957].

1507 WALLACE, R. Antitrinitarian biography (to 1700) . . . to which is prefixed a history of Unitarianism in England during the same period. 3 vols. 1850.

J. Murch deals chiefly with Unitarian churches in his *History of the Presbyterian and General Baptist Churches in the west of England*, 1835.

H. JUDAISM

Since the resettlement of the Jews in England occurred during this century, the sources listed below pertain chiefly to this matter. The chief libraries of works on Jewish history are (1) Jew's College, Tavistock Sq.; and (2) Mocatta Library (the collection of the Jewish Historical Soc. of England), at the Univ. of London. Many valuable articles appear in no. 1510.

1. Bibliography and Sources

1508   ROTH, C. Magna bibliotheca Anglo-Judaica; a bibliographical guide to Jewish history. New edn. rev. and enl. 1937.

Selective and arranged by subject. Roth is a revision of *Bibliotheca Anglo-Judaica*, by J. Jacobs and L. Wolf, 1888. See also J. Bloch, ed., *Journal of Jewish bibliography; a quarterly edited in collaboration with eminent scholars*, N.Y. 1938+.

1509   JEWISH QUARTERLY REVIEW. 1888–1908. New Series. Phila. 1910+.

Index vol. for the first 20 vols., Phila. 1932. A scholarly journal with articles on cultural as well as political and religious matters.

1510   JEWISH HISTORICAL SOCIETY OF ENGLAND. Transactions. 1895+.

Numerous relevant articles are printed here, and also in the Society's *Miscellanies* series, 1925+. In the latter, pt. 2 (1935), is an index to vols. 1–12 of the *Transactions*.

1511   MENASSEH [MANASSEH] BEN ISRAEL. Menassah Ben Israel's mission to Oliver Cromwell. Being a reprint of the pamphlets published by Menasseh Ben Israel to promote the readmission of the Jews to England, 1649–56. Ed. by L. Wolf. 1901.

See also Wing, M 373–81, for titles of Menasseh Ben Israel's pamphlets. For a *Life* see that by C. Roth, Phila. 1935. Examples of other 17th-century pamphlets on the Jews are W. Prynne's *Demurrer*, 1656 (Wing, P 4078); Thomas Violet's *Petition against Jews*, 1661 (see also Wing, V 578–98); and Wing, J 740–3, and S 2066A.

1512   SAMUEL, W. S. 'The first London synagogue of the re-settlement.' *J. H. Soc. E. Trans.* 10 (1921–3), 1–146.

A valuable essay, which includes documents relating to the synagogue established in 1657. See his book of the same title, 1924, and the supplement to both, bearing the title of *Some notes on 17th-century London Jews*, 1937. Documents on the resettlement are printed also in *Bevis Marks records*, ed. L. D. Barnett, 2 vols., Oxf. 1940, and in *Three hundred years: a volume to commemorate the tercentenary of the resettlement of the Jews*, 1957.

2. Later Works

1513   BARON, S. W. A social and religious history of the Jews. 3 vols. N.Y. 1937. Bibl.

Includes extensive bibliography. See also the useful general *History of the Jews in England* by A. M. Hyamson, 1908, 2nd edn. 1928.

1514   HENRIQUES, H. S. Q. The return of the Jews to England. 1905.

By the same author, *The Jews and English law*, 1908. Related to the 18th-century controversy regarding the rights of Jews are D'Blossiers Tovey, *Anglia Judaica: or the history and antiquities of the Jews of England*, Oxf. 1738, and pamphlets by P. C. Webb (*The question whether a Jew . . . was before the . . . late act . . . capable . . . to purchase and hold lands*, 1753), and others. (See list compiled by A. W. Hyamson, *J.H. Soc. E. Trans.* 6 (1908–10), 156–88.)

1515   MARGOLIOUTH, M. History of the Jews in Great Britain. 3 vols. 1851.

Cf. J. Picciotto, *Sketches of Anglo-Jewish history*, 1875.

1516   ROTH, C. A history of the Jews in England. Oxf. 1941.

Excellent brief account by a well-known scholar. Cf. Roth, ed., *Anglo-Jewish letters 1158–1917*, 1938, and M. F. Modder, *The Jew in the literature of England to the end of the nineteenth century*, Phila. 1939.

1517   WOLF, L. The Jewry of the restoration, 1660–1664. 1902.

By the same author see *Cromwell's Jewish intelligencers*, 1891, repr. in *Essays in Jewish history*, ed. by C. Roth, 1934; and articles in *J.H. Soc. E. Trans.* 1 (1895), 55–88; 4 (1903), 177–93.

VI

MILITARY HISTORY

There is no military bibliography covering the period 1603-1714. Useful guides are the catalogue of the War Office Library and its annual supplements (1518 n.), and those for materials in the Public Record Office (1520) and the Br. Mus. (1521). *The Journal of the Society for Army Historical Research* (1533) has published some bibliographical articles. For the period before 1660 the best bibliography still is Cockle (1519), but it should be supplemented by Firth (1519 n.); for the later period, there are useful bibliographies in C. Walton (1535), Atkinson (1567), Parnell (1573), and Taylor (1574). Maseres (1578) should be consulted for tracts relating to the Civil War. On the latter subject see Section D below.

A few foreign works that throw light on English army operations are listed but others should be sought for in the bibliographies mentioned in the section dealing with foreign affairs.

Works on Scottish military history and figures, and some on Ireland are included in this chapter; more of those dealing principally with Ireland are included in the chapter on Ireland.

A. GENERAL

1. BIBLIOGRAPHY

1518 LIST OF WAR OFFICE RECORDS preserved in the Public Record Office. Vol. i, Lists and indexes. 28. 1908.

See also C. T. Atkinson, 'Material for military history in the reports of the Historical Manuscripts Commission', *Jour. Soc. Army Hist. Res.* 21 (1942), 17–34; and F. S. Hudleston, comp., *Catalogue of the War Office library*, 3 pts., 1906–12, with annual suppls. since 1912. See also Pargellis, no. 1258 n.

1519 COCKLE, M. J. D. A bibliography of English military books up to 1642, and of contemporary foreign works. 1900. 2nd edn. [1957.]

Contains books on the art of war, but few historical works. See also Cockle's bibliography of proclamations of military interest, 1511–1641, in *Jour. Soc. Army Hist. Res.* 1 (1922), 165–9, 218–23. See also ibid. 8 (1929), 53–6, a 'Bibliography of the military writing of Sir Charles Firth', supplied by Firth from his full bibliography (318 n.). On regimental histories see Cannon (1633).

2. SOURCES

(a) *Manuscripts*

1520 PUBLIC RECORD OFFICE.

At the Public Record Office are various kinds of military papers, guides to which are found in no. 1518 above, *Lists and Indexes*, 53 (1931), *An alphabetical guide to certain War Office and other military records*. For a partial list of classifications, see Pargellis, pp. 165–7. Examples of 17th-century materials are: *War Office Registers*, some of which date from 1660; Ordnance Office accounts and bill books; and *State Papers, Domestic* 14 and 16, in which appear muster and subsidy rolls from the counties.

1521   BRITISH MUSEUM.

At the British Museum there is an incomplete class catalogue No. 50 (Military) in the Department of Manuscripts. For a list of the general treatises in this catalogue see *Jour. Soc. Army Hist. Res.* 4 (1925), 38–47. Add. MSS. 34217 and 39245 are examples of returns for military levies in the counties.

(b) *Printed Sources*

1522   A COPY OF PAPERS RELATING TO MUSTERS, beacons, subsidies . . . Northampton, A.D. 1586–1623. Ed. by J. Wake. (Northampton Record Soc. Pub. 3.) Kettering. 1926.

Valuable records by a deputy lieutenant. By the same editor is *The Montagu musters book,* . . . *1602–1623* (vol. 7 of the society's publications), Peterborough, 1935.

1523   ACCOUNTS OF THE PARLIAMENTARY GARRISONS of Great Chalfield and Malmesbury, 1645–1646. Ed. by J. H. P. Pafford (*Wilts. Arch. and N.H. Soc., Records Branch*, vol. 2). Devizes. 1940.

First published garrison account book of the civil war.

1524   HARVEY, C. C. 'Military papers of the time of Charles II.' *S.H.R.* 12 (1915), 145–56.

Cf. 'Letters on the administration of James II's army', ed. by G. Davies, *Jour. Soc. Army Hist. Res.* 29 (1951), 69–84.

1525   LESLIE, J. H., ed. 'Old printed army lists.' *Jour. Soc. Army Hist. Res.* 1 (1921–2), 6–9, 56–9, 142–5; 2 (1923), 164–7; 3 (1924), 22–5, 85–8.

Reprint of 1684 list (abridged in Dalton (1529)). See lists of 1661, ibid. 9 (1930), 147–61, 214–42, relating to the earliest British standing army.

1526   TRENCHARD, JOHN. A short history of standing armies in England. 1698.

Repr. with other similar pieces in no. 370 n. This and another pamphlet, *An argument shewing that a standing army is inconsistent with a free government* . . . [by John Trenchard and Walter Moyle], 1697 (reprint in *A collection of state tracts*, 1706), and *The Pamphleteer*, v. 10, 1817, are in controversy with John Somers, *A letter balancing the necessity of keeping a land force . . . with the dangers . . .*, 1697, and Defoe's *Argument shewing that a standing army, with the consent of Parliament, is not inconsistent with a free government*, 1698. See Macaulay (361), ch. xxiii; and E. A. Miller, 'Some arguments used by English pamphleteers, 1697–1700, concerning a standing army', *J.M.H.* 18 (1946), 306–13, in which views from seventeen pamphlets are summarized.

3. LATER WORKS

1527   CLARK, G. N. War and society in the seventeenth century. Camb. 1958.

1528   CLODE, C. M. The military forces of the crown: their administration and government. 2 vols. 1869. Docs.

The standard work on legal enactments and administrative orders relating to the army. By the same author, *Administration of justice under military and martial law*, 1872, docs.

For relationships with Parliament see J. S. Omond, *Parliament and the army, 1642–1904*, Camb. 1933. On recruiting under Queen Anne see article by G. Davies in *Jour. Soc. Army Hist. Res.* 28 (1950), 146–59. See also R. W. Jackson, 'Queen Anne's Irish army establishment in 1704', *The Irish Sword*, I (1950–1), 133–5.

1529 DALTON, C., ed. English army lists and commission registers, 1661–1714. 6 vols. 1892–1904.

These are invaluable guides to the personnel of the army. Cf. the same author's *The Blenheim roll* [1704], 1899; *Irish army lists 1661–1685*, 1907; *The Scots army 1661–1688*, Edin. and Lond. 1909; and documents on the Scottish army in *Maitland Club Misc.* iii, pt. 1 (1843), 71–98.

1530 DAVIES, G. 'The army and the downfall of Richard Cromwell.' *Hunt. Lib. Bull.* 7 (1935), 131–67.

1531 FORTESCUE, J. W. A history of the British army. 13 vols. 1899–1930. Plans. 2nd edn. of vol. i. 1910.

Vol. i to 1713. Deals with formation, administration, and operations of the army. The standard history.

E. W. Sheppard's *Short history of the British army*, 1926, contains a bibl. P. V. Harris, *The British army up to date* [1944], is a useful manual for campaigns and regimental histories.

1532 JOHNSTON, S. H. F. 'The Scots army in the reign of Anne.' *R.H.S. Trans.*, 5th Ser. 3 (1953), 1–21.

Argues the pro-union sentiment of the Scots who served in the English army abroad.

1533 JOURNAL of the Society of [for, after Jan. 1929] Army historical research. Sheffield. 1921+.

1534 LLOYD, E. M. A review of the history of infantry. 1908.

1535 WALTON, C. History of the British standing army, 1660–1700. 1894.

Very complete, though less satisfactory in its account of operations. Appendix of documents; bibl. The third volume of J. S. D. Scott, *The British Army*, 3 vols., 1868–80, deals with the period 1660–89.

B. DISCIPLINE, DRILL, TACTICS, AND EQUIPMENT

There is no comprehensive work on these subjects. There is useful information in Cockle (1519) for the pre-1640 period, and in Walton (1535), Fortescue (1531), and Bland (1547) for the period after 1660. On infantry tactics see Lloyd (1534). For the period 1640–60 see Elton (1542) and Firth (1586).

I. DISCIPLINE, DRILL, TACTICS

1536 MARKHAM, GERVASE. The souldier's accidence; or an introduction to military discipline. 1625.

1537 'ARTICLES OF WAR, 1627.' Ed. by H. Bullock. *Jour. Soc. Army Hist. Res.* 5 (1926), 111–15.

A repr. of articles of 1642, from Thomason Tracts, is ibid. 9 (1930), 117–23; other early articles of war are listed ibid. 4 (1925), 166 ff.

1538 NORTON, ROBERT. The gunner, shewing the whole practice of artillerie, with all the appurtenances thereunto belonging. 1628. Plates.

See also William Eldred, *The gunner's glasse,* 1646, 2nd edn. 1647; and Nathaniel Nye, *The arte of gunnery,* 1647.

1539 BARIFFE, WILLIAM. Military discipline, wherein is discoursed and showne the postures both of musket and pike. 1635. 2nd edn. 1639. 3rd edn. (rev. and enl.). 1643. 6th edn. 1661.

1540 HEXHAM, HENRY. The principles of the art militarie, practised in the warres of the United Netherlands . . . represented by figure. 1637. 2nd edn. in 3 parts. Delft. 1642-3.

1541 WARD, ROBERT. Animadversions of warre, or a militarie magazine of the truest rules and ablest instructions for the managing of warre. 1639. Illus.

Based on wars in the Netherlands and Germany. Important.

1542 ELTON, RICHARD. The compleat body of the art military with a varietie of figures. 1650. 2nd edn. 1659. 3rd edn. 1668.

Mainly concerned with infantry drill: the author served in the parliamentary forces. 3rd edn. has a suppl. by T. Rudd, chief engineer to Charles I.

1543 MONCK, GEORGE (DUKE OF ALBEMARLE). Observations upon military and political affairs. 1671. Ed. by J. Heath. 1761. 1796. Plates.

Probably written about 1644-6.

1544 MILITARY AND MARITIME DISCIPLINE . . . Book I. Military observations or tacticks . . . [by T. Venn]. Book II. An exact method of military architecture . . . [from the works of Andrew Tacquet]. Book III. The compleat gunner . . . 1672.

See also *Abridgment of the military discipline. Printed by his majesty's special command for the use of his majesty's forces,* 1686. This contains 'Rules and articles for the better government of the land forces', a manual of which edns. appeared in Lond. in 1673, and in Edin. in 1675 and 1678. Cf. *The exercise of the foot, with the evolutions . . . By their majesties' command,* 1690.

1545 BOYLE, ROGER (EARL OF ORRERY). Treatise of the art of war. 1677. Diagrams.

Gives some personal experiences in Ireland.

1546 TURNER, JAMES. Pallas armata: military essays of the ancient Grecian, Roman and modern art of war. 1683.

Written in 1670 and 1671.

1547 BLAND, HUMPHREY. A treatise of military discipline. 2nd edn. 1727. 9th edn. 1762.

Bland served under Marlborough, and his book is the best account of British drill and discipline then.
    Cf. Kane (1564).

2. Equipment

(a) *Weapons*

1548 'THE CHARTER OF THE COMPANY OF GUNMAKERS, LON-DON.' (Reprint of the 1637 charter.) *Jour. Soc. Army Hist. Res.* 6 (1927), 79–92.

1549 FFOULKES, C. Arms & Armament: an historical survey of the weapons of the British army. 1945. Illus. Bibl.

By the same author, *The gun-founders of England,* Camb. 1937, which contains a list of English and continental gunfounders, 14th–19th centuries. See also W. Y. Carman, *A history of firearms,* 1955, a useful short account by a staff member of the Imperial War Museum; and J. F. Hayward, *The art of the gunmaker* (vol. i, *1500–1600*), 1962.

1550 FFOULKES, C. and HOPKINSON, E. C. 'Swords of the British Army.' *Jour. Soc. Army Hist. Res.* 13 (1934), 66–70.

By the same authors, *Sword, lance and bayonet,* Camb. 1938, chiefly arms since 1745 and by Ffoulkes, 'Notes on the bayonet', *Jour. Soc. Army Hist. Res.* 18 (1939), 190–8. See a bibl. of works on the bayonet in A. Hutton, *Fixed bayonets,* 1890. On swords see also P. C. Peirce, *A handbook of court and hunting swords, 1660–1820,* 1937.

1551 GROSE, F. Military antiquities respecting a history of the English army from the conquest to the present time. 2 vols. 1786–8. 2nd edn. 1801. 3rd edn. 1812.

Important, though largely pre-17th century. The 2nd edn. includes a treatise on ancient armour and weapons with 61 plates, published separately in 1785.

1552 HALL, A. R. Ballistics in the 17th century. Camb. 1952. Bibl.

See the same author's chapter on 'Military Technology' in vol. iii of Singer (2038).

1553 HOGG, O. F. G. The royal arsenal, its background, origin, and subsequent history. 2 vols. N.Y. 1963.

Valuable lists in appendices. Concentrates especially on Woolwich arsenal, *c.* 1670–1957.

1554 JACKSON, H. J. European hand firearms of the sixteenth, seventeenth and eighteenth centuries, with a treatise on Scottish firearms by C. E. White-law. 1923.

Illus. For pistols see J. N. George, *English pistols and revolvers . . . from the 17th century to the present day,* Onslau, N.C. 1938; I. Glendenning, *Bristol pistols and guns, 1640–1840,* 1951. A manual for identifying hand firearms is H. B. C. Pollard, *A history of firearms,* 1926.

(b) *Uniforms and Medals*

1555 CARMAN, W. Y. British military uniforms from contemporary pictures. 1957.

Chapters 2 and 3 are on the Stuart period.

1556 LUARD, J. A history of the dress of the British soldier. 1852. Illus.

See also C. C. P. Lawson, *A history of the uniforms of the British army . . . to 1760,* 2 vols., 1940–1. Cf. Barnes (1632).

1557   MAYO, J. H. Medals and decorations of the British army and navy. 2 vols. 1897.

With extracts from general orders, royal warrants, etc., relating to their issue. Well illustrated. See also J. S. Farmer, *The regimental records of the British army*, 1901; L. J. Gordon, *British battles and medals: campaign medals, 1588–1949*, Aldershot, 1955; S. N. Milne, *The standards and colours of the army from the restoration*, Leeds, 1893; C. B. Norman, *Battle honours of the British army*, 1911, in which the first two chapters deal with the period.

1558   SUMNER, P. 'Great wardrobe accounts, 1689 to 1702.' *Jour. Soc. Army Hist. Res.* 20 (1941), 139–53.

Other articles by the same author on uniforms of various units are ibid. 13 (1934), 82–106; 14 (1935), 82–101, 177–80; 15 (1936), 151–70.

C. NARRATIVES AND HISTORIES OF MILITARY OPERATIONS

I. GENERAL

The printed narratives of campaigns for the period have limited value because they are not the reports of men of high command. Later historians have had to depend chiefly upon materials of the latter sort as they are available in correspondence. Important works by continental historians which may be consulted are: J. Pelet, *Mémoires militaires relatifs à la succession d'Espagne*, 11 vols. and atlas, Paris, 1835–62; *Feldzüge des Prinzen Eugen von Savoyan*, 20 vols., index vol. and atlas, Vienna, 1876–92; and the older work by J. de Beaurain, *Histoire militaire de Flandre*, 3 vols., Paris, 1755. Useful summaries of the campaigns of William III are to be found in the ninth volume of C. von Clausewitz, *Hinterlassene Werke*, 10 vols., Berlin, 1832–7, 2nd edn. 1862.

See also titles in *Foreign Relations*, and the general histories of the period. The works below are arranged in the chronological order of the operations described, with the exception of the Civil War, for which see nos. 1575–1634. For personal narratives see nos. 1665–1706. See also Ch. XV, *Ireland*.

1559   MONRO, R. Monro his expedition with the . . . Scots regiment (called Mac-Keyes regiment) levied in August 1626 . . . 1637.

Levied for services under Christian IV of Denmark. Cf. J. Beveridge, 'The Scottish expedition in Norway in 1612', *Proc. Soc. Antiq. Scot.*, 6th Ser. 7 (1932–3), 209–23.

1560   BELLER, E. A. 'The military expedition of Sir Charles Morgan to Germany, 1627–9.' *E.H.R.* 43 (1928), 528–39.

Based on state papers and other documents.

1561   SEYMOUR, W. W. On active service. 1939.

Descriptions of various campaigns, 1661–1885, based on accounts of participants, including Kane, Deane, and Christian Welsh. Chaps. 1–2 deal with 1661–1712.

1562   ATKINSON, C. T. 'Charles II's regiments in France, 1672–78.' *Jour. Soc. Army Hist. Res.* 24 (1946), 53–65, 129–36.

See by the same author 'Feversham's account of the battle of Entzheim—1674', ibid. 1 (1921), 33–43.

1563 PARKER, ROBERT. Memoirs of military transactions, 1683–1718, in Ireland and Flanders. Dublin. 1746. 1747.

Much identical with Kane, both having served in the same regiment. Cf. Hist. MSS. Com., *1st Rep.*, p. 129a.
For later accounts of actions in Ireland see H. Mangan, 'Sarsfield's defence of the Shannon, 1690–91', *The Irish Sword*, I (1949–50), 24–32; C. D. Milligan, *The siege of Londonderry*, Belfast, 1951, a scholarly work with bibl.; and D. Murtagh, 'The siege of Athlone', *Jour. Roy. Soc. Antiquaries Ireland*, 83 (1953), 58–81.

1564 KANE, RICHARD. Campaigns of King William and Queen Anne; from 1689 to 1712. Also a new system of military discipline for a battalion of foot in action. 1745. 2nd edn. 1747. Plans.

Important, by a later brigadier-general and governor of Minorca. Similar to Parker. See also *A system of camp discipline . . . To which is added General Kane's campaigns improved by the late Earl of Crawford's and Colonel Dunbar's copies.* Continued to 1757.
See also Frankland–Russell–Astley MSS., Hist. MSS. Com., 1900, with the Cutts and Revett papers 1687–1708, important for the Marlborough wars.

1565 D'AUVERGNE, E. A relation of the most remarkable transactions of the last campaigns . . . in the Spanish Netherlands, 1692–7. 6 pts. 1693–8.

The title varies: 1693–4, *The history of the last campagne in the Spanish Netherlands*; in 1695–7, *The History . . . in Flanders.* The author, a chaplain in the Scots guards, gives valuable detail on the soldier's life, lists of regiments, etc. There is a later introductory *History of the campaign in Flanders . . . 1691*, 1735.
See also W. Sawle, *An imperial relation of all transactions between the army of the confederates and that of the French king . . . in Flanders*, 1691. Useful articles are Sir G. Clark (558); G. Davies, 'The reduction of the army after the peace of Ryswick, 1697', *Jour. Soc. Army Hist. Res.* 28 (1950), 15–28; and S. H. F. Johnston, 'A Scots chaplain in Flanders, 1691–97', ibid. 27 (1949), 3–10.

1566 LANDMANN, KARL VON. Willhelm III von England und Max Emanuel von Bayern in niederländischen Kriege, 1692–7. Munich. 1901.

2. WAR OF THE SPANISH SUCCESSION

1567 ATKINSON, C. T. 'The war of the Spanish Succession.' *Camb. Mod. Hist.* Vol. v. 1908.

Provides a good bibliography. See also bibl. in R. Dunlop's article on Massue de Ruvigny, Henri de, in *D.N.B.*
Numerous important articles by Atkinson, based upon manuscripts, appear in the *Jour. Soc. Army Hist. Res.*, such as 'Gleanings from the Cathcart MSS.', 29 (1951), 20–5, 64–8, 99–102, from MSS. reported on by Hist. MSS. Com., *2nd Rep.*, 1871; 'Notes on the Spanish Succession War', 21 (1942), 83–96, 138–47, based on W.O. IV and other sources in the P.R.O.; 'Queen Anne's war in the West Indies', 24 (1946), 100–9; 183–97. See also an article on Argyll MSS. at Cambridge, by H. W. V. Temperley, *Camb. Hist. Jour.* 1 (1924), 214–17.

1568 BRODRICK, T. A compleat history of the late war in the Netherlands, together with an abstract of the treaty of Utrecht. 2 vols. 1713. Maps. Plans.

See also John Millner, *A compendious journal of all the marches . . . [1701–12], 1733*, a useful daily record.

1569   AN IMPARTIAL INQUIRY INTO THE MANAGEMENT OF THE
WAR IN SPAIN, by the ministry at home . . . Collected from many original
letters and councils of war, never published before. 1712.

'Repr. in 1726 with a new title-page, *The history of the last war in Spain from 1702 to
1710*, is based on [Boyer's] *Annals*, and may have been written by Boyer': *D.N.B. sub*
Massue de Ruvigny, Henri de.

1570   DEANE, J. M. Journal of the campaign in Flanders. Ed. by J. B. Deane.
s.l. 1846.

See also a series of letters by the earl of Orkney describing the battles of Blenheim,
Ramillies, and Malplaquet, ed. by H. H. E. Cra'ster in *E.H.R.* 19 (1904), 307–21.

1571   THE CONDUCT of his grace the Duke of Ormonde in the campaign of
1712. 1715.

One of several pamphlets published this year, of which another is *A vindication*, etc.
MSS. relating to Ormonde in Spain, 1702–4 are in B.M. Add. MSS. 28925, 29591,
38159.

1572   STANHOPE, PHILIP HENRY, LORD MAHON (aft. Earl Stanhope).
History of the war of the succession in Spain. 2 pts. 1832–3. 2nd edn. 1836.
Docs.

1573   PARNELL, A. The war of succession in Spain during the reign of Queen
Anne. 1888. Bibl.

A good account, based on both printed and unprinted sources, but unduly depreciatory
of Peterborough. For the question of the troops available for the peninsula, 1703–7,
see I. F. Burton, 'The supply of infantry', *Bull. Inst. Hist. Res.* 28 (1955), 35–62.

1574   TAYLOR, F. The wars of Marlborough. Ed. by G. W. Taylor. 2 vols.
Oxf. 1921. Maps.

Very good; devoted mainly to 1702–9. Cf. A. H. C. Kearsey, *Marlborough and his
campaigns*, 1929; J. H. P. Belloc, *The tactics and strategy of . . . Marlborough*, Bristol,
1933, which gives a clear account of the main operations; and other titles *sub* Marlborough (1703). For the role of Prince Eugene in mapping strategy see E. Ritter,
Politik und Kriegführing, ihre Beherrschung durch Prinz Eugen, 1704, Berlin, 1934, bibl.

D. THE CIVIL WAR

Both for the general outlines of the Civil War, a knowledge of which is necessary
for the central study of any part of it, and also for the footnotes referring to
authorities, Gardiner (320) and Firth (1586) are indispensable. See also vol. ii
of Wedgwood (300). The same may be said for the notes in *D.N.B.* and in the
biographies of political and military figures. A number of useful studies have
been contributed by Davies (e.g. no. 1585), and the *Journal of the Society for
Army Historical Research* (1533) should be consulted. Owing to the nature of a
civil war, and to the intervention in politics by the New Model Army, military
history is often inseparable from political; both the general sources and later
works for the period, especially those of 1640–60, should be consulted; and those
on the radical political theories listed in *Constitutional History* should be examined

as well. Especially important are pamphlets and newspapers (1578, 3064–74), and it is essential to examine Thomason's collection of tracts at the Br. Mus. (58).

The local historical societies have published many articles and notes on the Civil War as it affected localities, and a number of recent monographs relate to local administrative developments during the period. The examples of local studies listed below can be supplemented by use of the bibliographies in Ch. XI, *Local History*, and Mullins (23 n.).

The titles relating to Wales are in Ch. XIII.

1. GENERAL SOURCES

1575 HOPTON, RALPH. Bellum civile: Hopton's narrative of his campaign in the west [1642–4] and other papers. Ed. by C. E. H. Chadwyck-Healy. Somerset Record Soc. 18 (1902).

Important account by the royalist commander. For a supplement for certain 1643 events, excerpts from Richard Atkyns' *Vindication*, 1669, by P. Young, see *Jour. Soc. Army Hist. Res.* 35 (1957), 3–16, 53–70. See also Symonds (3458).

1576 LUKE, SAMUEL. Journal of Sir Samuel Luke. Ed. by I. G. Phillip. 3 vols. Oxfordshire Record Society. Vols. 29–31. 1950–3.

A Roundhead general's account and letters. From Stowe MSS., Br. Mus., H. G. Tibbutt has edited *The letterbooks, 1644–45 of Sir Samuel Luke*, Bedfordshire Hist. Rec. Soc. 42 (1963). Cf. 'The civil war papers of Sir Will. Boteler, 1642–1655', ed. by G. H. Fowler, *Beds. Hist. Rec. Soc. Pub.* 18 (1936), 1–41; and *Graves memoirs of the civil war*, ed. by F. A. Bates, 1927, which reprints materials relating to the Presbyterian colonial, Richard Graves [Grevis].

1577 MEMORIALS OF THE GREAT CIVIL WAR, 1642–52. Ed. by H. Cary. 2 vols. 1842.

Selected letters from the Tanner MSS. in the Bodleian Library, which contain many others not printed relating to the war 1642–6.

Other important collections of letters relating to the period are *Ormonde Papers . . .* (1641–60), ed. by T. Carte, 2 vols., 1739, from the duke of Ormonde's papers among the Carte MSS. in the Bodleian Library (vol. iii of the ed.'s *Life of James duke of Ormonde*, 3 vols. 1735–6; vols. v and vi of the 1851 edn., 6 vols. Oxf.; *Ruthven Correspondence: Letters and papers of Patrick Ruthven, Earl of Forth and Brentford, and of his family* (1615–62) . . ., ed. by W. D. Macray (Roxburghe Club, 1868), from Rawlinson MSS. A. 148. See also M. Coate, ed., 'An original diary of Colonel Robert Bennett', *Devon and Cornwall N. and Q.* 18 (1935), 251–9; and Nehemiah Wharton, 'Letters of a subaltern officer' ed. by Sir H. Ellis, *Archaeologia*, 35 (1853), 310–34. For notes by John Rushworth on the forming of the New Model Army, ed. by G. Davies, see *E.H.R.* 56 (1941), 103–5. Other documents ed. by Davies are in *J.M.H.* 3 (1931), 64–71.

1578 SELECT TRACTS RELATING TO THE CIVIL WARS IN ENGLAND . . . Ed. by Francis Baron Maseres. 2 vols. 1815.

Contains tracts on political as well as military affairs, such as Th. May, *Breviary of the history of . . . Parliament*, 1650; and no. 457. For light on the campaign of 1644 see *Documents relating to the quarrel between the Earl of Manchester and Oliver Cromwell*, ed. by J. Bruce and D. Masson, Camd. Soc., 1875. Cf. *Camd. Soc. Misc.* viii (1883) and Manchester MSS., H.M.C., *8th Rep.*, pt. ii (180).

1579   SPRIGGE, JOSHUA. Anglia rediviva; . . . being the history of the . . . army under . . . Sir Thomas Fairfax. 1647. 2nd edn. Oxf. 1854.

A history of the new model army by Fairfax's chaplain, who is said to have been helped by Colonel Fiennes. For supplements to the list of officers see *N. and Q.*, 18 Nov. 1893 and 3 March 1894.

Other accounts will be found in *Memorials of the Civil War; correspondence of the Fairfax family* . . ., ed. by R. Bell, 2 vols., 1849 (vols. iii and iv of the Fairfax correspondence, no. 292). See other Fairfax letters in *Jour. Soc. Army Hist. Res.* 5 (1926), 110–25, 160–74.

1580   THE ARMY LISTS OF ROUNDHEADS AND CAVALIERS, containing the names of the officers in the royal and parliamentary armies of 1642. Ed. by E. Peacock. 1863. 2nd edn. (with index). 1874.

Reprints of contemporary pamphlets, with occasional notes. Other lists of royalist officers, by no means complete, are *A list of officers claiming to the sixty thousand pounds . . . granted by his . . . majesty for the relief of his truly loyal and indigent party*, 1663, and *A most true relation of the present state of his majesties army*, 1642.

For a list of parliamentary officers compiled from an account of supplies (text and notes) see G. Davies, 'The army of the Eastern Association', *E.H.R.* 46 (1931), 88–96.

1581   MONCKTON, SIR PHILIP. The Monckton papers. Ed. by E. Peacock. (*Philobiblion Soc. Misc.* 15, no. 5.) *c.* 1884.

Practically memoirs of the first and second civil wars. Appendix contains an account by Col. Edw. Rossiter, 5 July 1648. Indicative of the personal side of the war, of which this is but an example of numerous complaints, is *To the Parliament of England and army: the declaration of Colonel Anthony Weldon*, 1649.

1582   VICARS, J. England's parliamentarie chronicle. 3 vols. 1643–6.

Comprises: *Jehovah Jireh. God in the mount* (1641–Oct. 1642); *God's arke overtopping the world's waves* (July 1643–July 1644); *The Burning-bush not consumed* (Aug. 1644–July 1646). Cf. the same writer's *England's worthies, under whom all the bloudy warres . . . (1642–1647) are related*, 1647, a repr. of which appears in vol. ii of G. Smeeton, *Historical and biographical tracts* (283 n.).

1583   WALKER, SIR EDWARD. Historical discourses upon several occasions . . . with copies of all votes, letters, etc., relating to the treaty at Newport 1648. Ed. by H. Clopton. 1705.

Walker was secretary to Charles I at Newport. On Charles II after Worcester see no. 420 n.

2. GENERAL LATER WORKS

1584   BURNE, A. H. The battlefields of England. Foreword by G. M. Trevelyan. 1950. Maps.

Includes the chief civil war battles, with bibliography for each.

1585   DAVIES, G. 'The parliamentary army under the earl of Essex, 1642–5.' *E.H.R.* 49 (1934), 32–54.

Data on the numerical strength and the components of the army are derived from pay warrants. On relations with the Scots see G. F. T. Jones, 'The payment of arrears to the Army of the Covenant' ibid. 78 (1958), 459–65.

1586 FIRTH, SIR C. H. Cromwell's army: A history of the English soldier during the civil wars, the commonwealth and the protectorate. (Ford Lectures 1900–1.) 1902. 3rd edn. 1921. Illus.

> Invaluable for the army as a whole, 1603–60. For separate regiments, equally valuable is the compilation by Firth, assisted by G. Davies, *The regimental history of Cromwell's army* (1635). Cf. two articles by Firth on the Ironsides, *R.H.S. Trans.* 13 (1899), 17–73, and 15 (1901), 1–45.
>
> W. G. Ross in *Oliver Cromwell and his 'Ironsides' as represented in the so-called 'Squire Papers'*, Chatham, 1889, gives evidence regarding the spuriousness of those papers.

1587 FIRTH, SIR C. H. 'Royalist and Cromwellian armies in Flanders, 1657–1662.' *R.H.S. Trans.*, N.S. 17 (1903), 67–119.

> App. contains new material. See also J. Bourelly, *Cromwell et Mazarin: deux campagnes de Turenne en Flandre . . .*, Paris, 1886.

1588 LINDSAY, J. Civil War in England. 1954.

> Brief narrative of military events in popular style. See also Guttery (1610).
>
> Examples of more limited accounts are: Sir F. Maurice, *The adventures of Edward Wogan*, 1945; and O. Warner, 'The clubmen and the English civil war', *Army Quarterly*, 38 (1939), 287–99.

1589 YOUNG, P. 'King Charles I's army in 1642.' *Jour. Soc. Army Hist. Res.* 17 (1938), 102–9.

> Scholarly article. Others by the same author relating to royalist troops in action appear ibid. 18 (1939), 27–37; 31 (1953), 9–12; 32 (1954), 54–6; 33 (1955), 35–9, 56–60; 35 (1957), 145–51.
>
> Cf. F. J. Varley, 'Oxford army list for 1642–1646', *Oxoniensia*, 2 (1937), 141–51.

3. LOCAL SOURCES AND LATER WORKS

BEDFORDSHIRE

1590 Tibbutt, H. G. Bedfordshire and the first civil war, with a note of John Bunyan's military service. Bedfordshire C.C. (Elstow Moot Hall Leaflets, no. 3). 1956.

BERKSHIRE

1591 Money, W. The first and second battles of Newbury and the siege of Donnington Castle . . . 1643–6. 1881. 2nd edn. 1884.

> Plans; excerpts from documents. See also H. E. Bannard, 'The Berkshire, Buckinghamshire and Oxfordshire committees of 1642–1646', *Berks., Bucks., and Oxon. Arch. Soc.* 31–3 (1927–9), 173–92.

CAMBRIDGESHIRE

1592 Varley, F. J. Cambridge during the civil war, 1642–1646. Camb. 1935.

CHESHIRE

1593 Atkinson, J. A., ed. Tracts relating to the civil war in Cheshire. Manchester. 1909. (Chetham Society, N.S. 65.)

> Repr. of thirty-seven pamphlets.

1594 Malbon, Thomas. Memorials of the civil war in Cheshire and the adjacent counties. Ed. by J. Hall. 1889. (Record Society of Lancashire and Cheshire, vol. 19.)

In the same volume is Edward Burghall's 'Providence Improved', printed from Cole MS., v. 50 (B.M.), which also relates to the civil war. See also Brereton (1670).

1595 Morris, R. H. The siege of Chester, 1643–1646. Ed. by P. H. Lawson. Chester. 1924. Illus. Bibl.

Prints many extracts from authorities.

CORNWALL

1596 Coate, M. Cornwall in the great civil war and the interregnum, 1642–1660. Oxf. 1933.

Excellent.

CUMBERLAND

1597 Tullie, Isaac. A narrative of the siege of Carlisle in 1644 and 1645. Ed. by S. Jefferson. Carlisle. 1840.

See also R. S. Ferguson in *Cumberland and Westmorland Antiq. and Arch. Soc.* 11 (1891), 104–16; and ibid. 7 (1883), 48–63.

DERBYSHIRE

1598 Pole–Gell MSS. H.M.C. *9th Rep.*, pt. ii. 1884.

Papers of Sir John Gell relating to the civil war in Derbyshire. Others are in app. to Stephen Glover's *History . . . of the County of Derby*, ed. by T. Noble, 2 vols., Derby, 1829–33. Excerpts from the records of the Derbyshire committee appear in F. Fisher, 'Civil War papers of the constable of Hope', *Jour. Derbyshire Arch. and N.H. Soc.*, N.S. 23 (1950), 70–7.

DEVONSHIRE

1599 Cotton, R. W. Barnstaple and the northern part of Devonshire during the great civil war (1642–6). 1889.

Good use made of pamphlets.
    Cf. M. Coate, 'Exeter in the civil war and interregnum', *Devon and Cornwall N. and Q.* 18 (1935), 338–52; P. H. Hardacre, 'The end of the civil war in Devon: a royalist letter of 1646', *Trans. Devon. Assoc.* 85 (1953), 95–104.

DORSET

1600 Bayley, A. R. The great civil war in Dorset, 1642–1660. Taunton. 1910. Bibl.

Prints Edward Drake's diary of the siege of Lyme Regis and other documents. Cf. C. H. Mayo, *The minute books of the Dorset standing committee, 1646–50*, Exeter, 1902; G. Bankes, *The story of Corfe Castle* (3161 n.); and H.M.C. (76).

ESSEX

1601 Carter, Matthew. A true relation of the . . . expedition of Kent, Essex, and Colchester, in 1648. 1650. 2nd edn. Colchester. 1789.

Account by a royalist present. Other papers relating to the siege of Colchester are in H.M.C., Round MSS., *apud* Buckinghamshire MSS., 1895; and ibid., Beaufort MSS.,

1891, 281–90; cf. J. H. Round, 'The case of Lucas and Lisle', *R.H.S. Trans.*, N.S. 8 (1894), 157–80. See also H. E. Bannard, 'Essex committees in the civil war', *Essex Rev.* 45 (1936), 101–5.

GLOUCESTERSHIRE

1602 Washbourne, J., ed. Bibliotheca Gloucestrensis: a collection of . . . tracts relating to the city and county of Gloucester during the civil war. Gloucester. 1825.

Published in three parts, 1823–5, then in one vol.; sources, with historical intro.

1603 [Robinson, Richard?] Sieges of Bristol during the civil war. Bristol. 1868.

Cf. article by C. H. Firth and J. H. Leslie, *Jour. Soc. Army Hist. Res.* 4 (1925), 180–203.

HAMPSHIRE

1604 Godwin, G. N. The civil war in Hampshire [1642–5]. 1882. 2nd edn. 1904. Illus.

HEREFORDSHIRE

1605 Webb, J. Memorials of the civil war . . . as it affected Herefordshire and the adjacent counties. Ed. by T. W. Webb. 2 vols. 1879.

Appendix of documents.

HERTFORDSHIRE

1606 Kingston, A. Hertfordshire during the great civil war. 1894.

See also his *East Anglia and the civil war*, 1897, illus.

KENT

1607 Everitt, A. M. The county committee of Kent in the civil war. Leicester. 1957.

Important essay on local organization. For a military operation see H. E. Malden, 'The storm of Maidstone . . . 1648', *E.H.R.* 7 (1892), 533–6.

LANCASHIRE

1608 Broxap, E. The great civil war in Lancashire [1642–51]. Manchester. 1910. Bibl.

Scholarly. See also A. J. Hawkes, 'Wigan's part in the civil war, 1639–1651' (3201 n.). On the composition papers of Lancashire royalists see no. 3197 n.

1609 Ormerod, G., ed. Tracts relating to military proceedings in Lancashire during the civil war. Chetham Soc. 2. 1844.

Cf. E. Robins, *A discourse of the warr in Lancashire*, ed. by W. Beamont, Chetham Soc. 62, 1864.

LEICESTERSHIRE

1610 Guttery, D. R. The great civil war in midland parishes. Birmingham. [1950.]

Concentrates on the effects on the local population of sieges of garrisoned country houses and towns. Scholarly, but undocumented.

1611   Hollings, J. F. Leicestershire during the great civil war. Leicester. 1840. Plan.

> See also E. W. Hensman, *Loughborough during the great civil war*, Loughborough, *c.* 1921, and his 'The east midlands and the second civil war . . . 1648', *R.H.S. Trans.*, 4th Ser. 6 (1923), 126–59; and W. G. Ross, 'The battle of Naseby', *E.H.R.* 3 (1888), 668–79.

LONDON

1612   Clode, C. M. London during the great rebellion. 1892.

> Cf. C. H. Firth, 'London during the civil war', *History*, N.S. 11 (1926), 25–36, which deals with the political role of the city, 1640–60; N. G. Brett-James, 'The fortification of London in 1642/3', *London Top. Rec.* 14 (1928), 1–35; and Pearl (3298).

NORTHAMPTONSHIRE

1613   Page, J. T. 'The great civil war: how it began and ended in Northampton-shire. *Northants Nat. Hist. Soc. . . . Jour.* 28 (1936–8), 87–113, 125–44, 155–75.

> Uses local materials, but without integration.

NORTHUMBERLAND

1614   Terry, C. S. 'The siege of Newcastle-upon-Tyne by the Scots in 1644.' *Archaeologia Aeliana*, 2nd Ser. 21 (1899), 180–258.

> Cf. by the same author 'The visits of Charles I to Newcastle in 1633, 1639, 1641, 1646–7', and 'The Scottish campaign in Northumberland . . . 1644', ibid. 83–145, 146–79.

NOTTINGHAMSHIRE

1615   Wood, A. C. Nottinghamshire in the civil war. Oxf. 1937.

> Based on a variety of sources.

OXFORDSHIRE

1616   Varley, F. J. The siege of Oxford: an account of Oxford during the civil war, 1642–46. 1932. Supplement. 1935.

> A useful collection of facts and a diary of events.

SHROPSHIRE

1617   Farrow, W. G. The great civil war in Shropshire. Shrewsbury. 1926.

> Excellent. See also *Letters and papers of Thomas Mytton* (3455) and J. E. Auden's article on Mytton's case before the county committee in *Shrops. Arch. Soc. Trans.* 48 (1935), 49–60.

SOMERSETSHIRE

1618   See Hopton (1575); also articles by E. Green in *Somerset Arch. and Nat. Hist. Soc.* 14 (1868) and 23–5 (1877–9), and in *Proc. Bath Field Club*, 3, 4, and 6.

STAFFORDSHIRE

1619   Pennington, D. H. and Roots, I. A., eds. The committee at Stafford, 1643–1645. *Staffs. Hist. Coll.*, 4th Ser. 1. Manchester. 1957.

> Valuable. Gives detailed picture of the committee at work. Cf. 'Some letters of the civil war', *Staffs. Hist. Coll.*, 1941, 137–53.

SUSSEX

1620 Thomas-Sanford, C. Sussex in the great civil war and the interregnum, 1642–1660. 1910. Illus.

Uses much source material. Cf. W. H. Blaauw in *Sussex Arch. Coll.* 5 (1852).

WARWICKSHIRE

1621 Walford, E. A. Edgehill: the battle and battlefields. Banbury. 1886. 2nd edn. 1904. 3rd edn. [1923.] Illus. Bibl.

Cf. 'Notes on the battle of Edgehill', by T. Arnold and W. G. Ross, *E.H.R.* 2 (1887), 137–42, 533–43, and an article by G. Davies, ibid. 36 (1921), 30–44, 320. All have bibl. notes.

WILTSHIRE

1622 Pafford, J. H. P., ed. Accounts of the parliamentary garrisons of Great Chalfield and Malmesbury, 1645–46. *Wiltshire Arch. and N.H. Soc. Records*, Ser. 2. Devizes. 1940.

WORCESTERSHIRE

1623 Willis-Bund, J. W. The civil war in Worcestershire (1642–6), and the Scottish invasion of 1651. Birmingham. 1905. Illus.

Cf. by the same ed., *Diary of Henry Townshend*, 2 vols., Worc. Hist. Soc., 1920.

YORKSHIRE

1624 The Hull letters. Documents from the Hull records. 1625–46. Ed. by T. T. Wildridge. Hull. [1886?]

Cf. E. Broxap, 'The sieges of Hull', *E.H.R.* 20 (1905), 457–73.

1625 Drake, Nathan. A journal of the . . . sieges of Pontefract Castle 1644–45. Ed. by W. H. D. Longstaffe. Surtees Soc. Misc. 37. 1861.

Repr. with other narratives in R. Holmes, *The sieges of Pontefract Castle*, Pontefract, 1887.

1626 Firth, Sir C. H. 'The battle of Marston Moor.' *R.H.S. Trans.*, N.S. 12 (1898), 17–79. Bibl.

By the same editor, 'Sir Hugh Cholmley's narrative of the siege of Scarborough' (from Bodl. Libr. Clarendon MSS. 1669), *E.H.R.* 32 (1917), 568–87. Much material on Yorkshire royalists appears in *Yorks. Arch. Soc. Rec. Ser.* 15 (1893), 18 (1895), 20 (1896).

IRELAND AND THE CHANNEL ISLANDS

1627 Hazlett, H. 'The financing of the British armies in Ireland, 1641–49.' *Irish Hist. Studies*, 1 (1938), 21–41.

1628 Saunders, A. C. Jean Chevalier and his times. Jersey. 1937.

Popularly written account, based on Chevalier's diary, regarding events of 1643–51 in Jersey. See no. 96; and 'Journal de Jean Chevalier', ed. by J. A. Messervy, *Société Jersiaise*, [1906]–1914.

SCOTLAND

1629 Akerman, J. Y., ed. Letters from roundhead officers from Scotland to Captain Adam Baynes, 1650–1660. Bannatyne Club. Edin. 1856.

Selected from 10 vols. in Br. Mus. Add. MSS. Other extracts from Baynes correspondence appear in *Proc. Soc. Antiq.* 2 (1849–53) and 3 (1853–6); *Tait's Edinburgh Magazine*, 17–18 (1850–1); and Surtees Soc. Misc. 1 (1860).

1630   Terry, C. S., ed. Papers relating to the Solemn League and Covenant, 1643–7. 2 vols. Scot. Hist. Soc. Publ., 2nd Ser., vols. 16–17. Edin. 1917.

Deals with army administration etc., rather than with operations. Cf. Lord Guthrie, 'The Solemn League and Covenant of the three kingdoms', *S.H.R.* 15 (1918), 292–309.

1631. Douglas, W. S. Cromwell's Scotch campaigns: 1650–51. 1898. Another edn. 1899.

Cf. Sir C. H. Firth, 'The battle of Dunbar', *R.H.S. Trans.*, 2nd Ser. 14 (1900), 19–52. Articles by K. C. Corsar relating to Edinburgh, 1650, are in *S.H.R.* 28 (1949), 43–54, and *Jour. Soc. Army Hist. Res.* 25 (1947), 96–105.

WALES

See Chapter XIII.

E. LISTS AND REGIMENTAL HISTORIES

For bibliographies of regimental histories see the note to Cannon (1633). The histories of some of the earlier regiments that follow are arranged somewhat in order of the establishment of the units.

1632   BARNES, R. M. History of the regiments and uniforms of the British army. 1950. Rev. edn. 1955. Bibl.

Cf. R. M. Barnes, C. K. Allen, and T. B. Beatty, *The uniforms and history of the Scottish regiments of Britain . . . 1625 to the present day* [1956], illus.

1633   CANNON, R., ed. Historical records of the British army, comprising the history of every regiment. 71 vols. 1834–50.

About sixty regimental histories compiled officially, but of varying quality, except that of Packe (1636). A useful list of these and other regimental histories is in the printed catalogue of the Br. Mus. Library (under England, army); in F. S. Hudleston's Catalogue of the War Office Library, part iii, subject index, 1912, with annual supplements; and in the catalogue of the Library of the Royal United Services Institution, 2nd edn., 1908.

Cf. J. H. Lawrence-Archer, *The British army: its regimental records, badges, devices,* 1888; H. M. Chichester and G. Burges-Short, *The records and badges of every regiment and corps in the British army,* 1895, 1900, 1902, illus., which contains useful notes on the services of each regiment and lists of regimental histories.

1634   RAIKES, G. A. History of the Honourable Artillery Company, with maps and illustrations. 2 vols. 1878–9.

Gives particulars of the London trained bands in the civil war. Cf. *The ancient vellum book of the Honourable Artillery Company, being the roll of members, 1611–82,* 1890; and *List of the chiefs, officers . . . of the Honourable Artillery Company,* 1929.

1635   FIRTH, SIR C. H. The regimental history of Cromwell's army. 2 vols. Oxf. 1940.

Arranged with the assistance of Godfrey Davies, this work provides almost an encyclopedic history of the various units. See articles by Firth also in *Jour. Soc. Army Hist. Res.* 6 (1927).

1636 PACKE, E. An historical record of the royal regiment of Horse Guards or Oxford Blues. 1834. 1847. Illus.

Part of the Cannon series above.

1637 ARTHUR, SIR G. C. A. The story of the Household Cavalry. 3 vols. 1909–26. Maps.

Fairly full for 1660–1714.

1638 ATKINSON, C. T. History of the Royal Dragoons, 1661–1934. Glasgow. 1934.

Of special interest are the sections on Tangier. Supersedes C. P. de Ainslie, *Historical record of the First or the Royal Regiment of Dragoons*, 1887.

1639 WHYTE, F. and ATTERRIDGE, A. H. A history of the Queen's Bays, 1685–1929. 1930.

1640 POMEROY, R. L. The regimental history from 1685 to 1922 of the 5th Princess Charlotte of Wales' Dragoon Guards. 2 vols. Edin. and Lond. 1924.

1641 DUNCAN, F. Royal Regiment of Artillery. 2 vols. 1872–73. 3rd edn. 2 vols. 1879.

1642 PORTER, W. and WATSON, C. M. Corps of Royal Engineers. 3 vols. 1889–1915.

1643 AUBREY-FLETCHER, H. L. Foot Guards. 1927.

1644 HAMILTON, SIR F. W. History of the First or Grenadier Guards. 3 vols. 1874. 1877.

1645 DAVIES, G. The early history of the Coldstream Guards. Oxf. 1924. Bibl.

Appendices of documents. Cf. D. Mackinnon, *Origin and services of the Coldstream Guards*, 2 vols., 1833, docs.

1646 DAVIS, J. History of the Second Queen's Royal Regiment. 6 vols. 1887–1906.

Excellent. The first two vols. go to 1715, the first dealing entirely with Tangier.

1647 KNIGHT, H. R. Historical records of the Buffs (East Kent Regiment), 3rd Foot . . . Vol. i (1572–1704). 1905. Cont. by C. B. R. Knight, 3 vols. (1704–1948). 1935–51.

1648 KINGSFORD, C. L. The Royal Warwickshire Regiment (formerly the Sixth Foot). 1921. Maps.

1649 COWPER, L. I., ed. The King's Own . . . 1680–1914. 2 vols. Oxf. 1939. Bibl.

Supersedes the volume in Cannon on the Fourth Foot, or the King's Own Regiment. Uses manuscript sources.

1650 PETRE, F. L. The history of the Norfolk Regiment, 1685–1918. 2 vols. Norwich. 1925. Bibl.

1651 WEBB, E. A. H. History of the 12th (Suffolk) Regiment, 1685–1913. 1914.

By Webb also, *History of the services of the 17th (the Leicestershire) Regiment,* 1911.

1652 EVERETT, SIR H. J. The history of the Somerset Light Infantry . . . 1685–1914. 1934.

1653 FERRAR, M. L. Historical record of the Green Howards . . . 1688–1931. 1931.

1654 ATKINSON, C. T. The South Wales Borderers, 24th Foot, 1689–1937. Camb. 1937.

For another Welsh unit see A. D. L. Cary and S. McCance, *Regimental records of the Royal Welch Fusiliers (late the 23rd foot),* 2 vols., 1921–3.

1655 EVERARD, H. E. E. History of Thos. Farrington's Regiment subsequently designated the 29th (Worcestershire) Foot. Worcester. 1891.

Has some extracts from MSS. records.

Scottish Units

1656 MAXWELL, H. E. Lowland Scots regiments. Glasgow. 1918.

See also F. Adam, *The clans, septs and regiments of the Scottish highlands,* Edin. 1934.

1657 FERGUSON, J. Papers illustrating the history of the Scots Brigade in the service of the United Netherlands (1572–1782) from the archives at the Hague. 3 vols. Scottish Hist. Soc. Edin. 1899–1901.

1658 GROVES, J. P. Royal Scots Greys. 1893.

1659 MAURICE, SIR F. B. The history of the Scots Guards [1642–1914]. 2 vols. 1934.

1660 WEAVER, L. The Royal Scots (the Lothian Regiment) formerly the First of the Royal Regiment of Foot. [1915.] Bibl.

See also J. Mackay, *Mackay's regiment: a narrative of the principal services of the regiment now known as the Royal Scots,* Inverness, 1879, Edin. and Lond. [1885]; and J. C. Leask and H. M. McCance, *Regimental records of the Royal Scots,* Dubl. 1915.

1661 BUCHAN, J. The Royal Scots Fusiliers (1678–1918). Lond. and N.Y. 1925.

Cf. J. P. Groves, *History of the 21st Royal Scots Fusiliers,* Edin. and Lond. 1895.

1662 HOLDEN, R. MacK. The First Highland Regiment. The Argyllshire Highlanders (1689–97). *S.H.R.* 3 (1905), 27–40. Repr. Glasgow. 1905.

See also S. H. F. Johnston, 'The Cameronians at Stenkirk, 1692', *S.H.R.* 27 (1948), 70–6.

Irish Units

1663 GRETTON, G. Le M. The campaigns and history of the Royal Irish Regiment from 1684 to 1902. Edin. and Lond. 1911.

See also C. Litton Falkiner, 'Irish Guards, 1661–1798', *Proc. Roy. Irish Acad.* 24 (1902–4), sec. C. 7–30.

1664 MURRAY, R. H. History of the VIII. King's Royal Irish Hussars, 1693–1927. 2 vols. 1928.

F. BIOGRAPHIES AND PERSONAL MEMOIRS

See also *supra* Ch. II, pp. 51–73 on Political Biography; the chapters on Ireland, Scotland, and Wales; and titles under H.M.C. (Ch. I). Examples are John Lord Belasyse (84), Ormonde (195).

1. 1603–1660

1665 PHILLIPS, C. E. Cromwell's captains. 1938. Bibl.

Essays on Lambert, Hampden, Blake, and Skippon.
See also M. P. Ashley, *Cromwell's generals*, 1954, for an account, intended for the general reader, of the characters of the generals and their relationships.

ALBEMARLE, GEORGE MONCK, DUKE OF

1666 Corbett, J. S. Monk. English Men of Action. 1889.

More recent lively biographies, 1936, are J. D. G. Davies, *Honest George Monck*, and O. M. W. Warner, *Hero of one restoration*. P. Thomas Skinner's *Life of General Monck*, ed. by W. Webster, 1723, 2nd edn. 1724, is a mere compilation.
Still useful is F. P. G. Guizot's *Memoirs of George Monk*, tr. by J. Stuart-Worthy, 1838, from the original French edn., 1837; and A. R. Scoble's translation which contains dispatches of Bordeaux, May 1655–June 1660 and bears the title, *Monck; or The fall of the republic*, 1851.
For the source materials on Monck's career, especially valuable are the papers kept by his secretary William Clarke, the most extensive edn. of which is *Clarke Papers*, ed. by C. H. Firth (4 vols., Camden Society, 1891–1901) from MSS. at Worcester College, Oxf. Other Clarke papers are printed in H.M.C. Leyborne–Popham MSS., 1899. Some were published also in *Puritanism and liberty*, ed. by A. S. Woodhouse, 1938. Valuable for 1655–60 is *The life of General Monck* by Thomas Gumble, Monck's chaplain, 1671.

BELASYSE, JOHN, LORD

1667 A briefe relation of the life . . . of John Lord Belasyse. By Joshua Moore. H.M.C. Ormonde MSS., N.S. ii (1903), pp. 376–99.

Moore was Belasyse's secretary.

BERRY, COLONEL JAMES

1668. A Cromwellian major-general: the career of Colonel James Berry. By J. Berry and S. G. Lee. Oxf. 1938.

Documents. Valuable for army administration and army politics in 1647, and activities in Wales and the Marches, 1655.
For a short note on Major-General James Heane in Dorset by G. S. Fry see *Somerset and Dorset N. and Q.* 23 (1939), 34–9.

BIRCH, COLONEL JOHN

1669 Military memoir of Colonel John Birch, written by his secretary [Roe]. Ed. by J. Webb and T. W. Webb. Camden Soc., N.S. 7. 1873.

Birch was a parliamentary officer.

BRERETON, SIR WILLIAM

1670 'The early life of Sir William Brereton, the parliamentary commander', by R. N. Dore. *Trans. Lanc. and Ches. Antiq. Society*, 63 (1954), 1–26.

Cf. another article on Brereton at Chester and Naseby by Dore, ibid. 67 (1957), 17–44.

CHOLMLEY, SIR HUGH

1671 The memoirs of Sir Hugh Cholmley . . . s.l. 1787. Repr. 1870.

Valuable for social and military history. A recent article on another royalist, Arthur, Lord Capel, by H. Beaumont, is in *Shrops. Arch. and Nat. Hist. Soc. Trans.* 50 (1939), 65–94.

CROMWELL, OLIVER

1672 Cromwell as a soldier. By T. S. Baldock. 1899.

For other biographies of Cromwell see nos. 429–30.

ESSEX, ROBERT DEVEREUX, EARL OF

1673 Lives and letters of the Devereux, earls of Essex, in the reigns of Elizabeth, James I, and Charles I. 1540–1646. By W. B. Devereux. 2 vols. 1853. Illus.

Most of the letters of the last earl, Robert, the parliamentarian, are pr. in *C.S.P. Dom.*, or in the Lords' *Journals*.

FAIRFAX, THOMAS, LORD

1674 Short memorials of the northern actions in which I was engaged [1642–4]; [and] Short memoirs . . . [1645–50]. By Thomas, Lord Fairfax. Ed. by Brian Fairfax. 1699.

Reprinted in various places, such as Maseres (1578), pt. 2; Arber's *English Garner*, viii (62 n.).
The latest scholarly biography by M. A. Gibb, *The lord general; a life of Thomas Fairfax*, 1938, 1940, with bibliography and appendices, does not entirely supersede C. R. Markham's *Life*, 1870. For the *Fairfax correspondence* see nos. 292 and 1579 n.

GRANVILLE [GRENVILLE], SIR RICHARD

1675 The king's general in the west: the life of Sir Richard Granville, 1600–59. By R. Granville. 1908. Illus.

GWYNNE, JOHN

1675 a Military memoirs of the great civil war . . . of J. Gwynne, and an account of the earl of Glencairn's expedition (1653–4). Ed. by Sir W. Scott. Edin. 1822.

Many extracts from *Mercurius Politicus* for 1653–4.

HAMILTON, JAMES AND WILLIAM, DUKES OF

1676 Memoirs of the lives and actions of James and William, dukes of Hamilton. By Gilbert Burnet. 1677. 2nd edn. Oxf. 1852.

See comments on Burnet as an authority on Scottish history by R. Dewar (*S.H.R.* 4 (1907), 384–98), and H. C. Foxcroft (*E.H.R.* 24 (1909), 510–40).

HARRISON, THOMAS

1677 Thomas Harrison, regicide and major-general. By C. H. Simpkinson. 1905. Illus.

Reprints nineteen letters of Harrison. Cf. C. H. Firth's biography of Harrison in *Proc. Amer. Antiq. Soc.* 8 (1893), 390–404.

HUTCHINSON, COLONEL JOHN

1678 Memoirs of the life of Colonel Hutchinson . . . by his widow [Lucy Hutchinson]. Ed. by J. Hutchinson. 1806. Various later edns.

The best of the later edns. is by Sir C. H. Firth, with additional notes, 1906.

LEVEN, ALEXANDER LESLIE, EARL OF

1679 The life and campaigns of Alexander, first earl of Leven. By C. S. Terry. 1899. Bibl.

An important work by an authority on Scottish history.

MELVILL, SIR ANDREW

1680 Memoirs of Sir Andrew Melvill, translated from the French. Ed. by Ameer-Ali Torick. 1918. Illus.

The first French edn. of this autobiography of a soldier of fortune appeared in Amsterdam in 1704. Authenticity somewhat dubious. Cf. J. G. Alger, 'Scottish free lance: Sir Andrew Melville', *Scot. Rev.* 26 (1895), 1–22. For the career of another soldier of fortune on the Continent see *The Relation of Sydnam Poyntz* (1624–36), ed. by A. T. S. Goodrick, 1908 (Camden Soc., 3rd Ser. 14).

MONTROSE, JAMES GRAHAM, MARQUIS OF

1681 Montrose. By J. Buchan. 1928. Latest repr. 1957.

The standard biography, elaborating on the short sketch, 1913, which dealt chiefly with campaigns.

The earliest source, upon which all later biographers have drawn, is *The memoirs of James, marquis of Montrose, 1639–50*, written by his chaplain, George (later Bishop) Wishart, the first part of which (to 1646) was published in Latin in 1647, probably at Amsterdam, and was translated in 1648; a portion of a translation of part two appeared in 1720. For a list of the various edns. see the abridged edn. by J. Sime, 1903. The only complete edn., with notes and appendices, is that ed. by A. S. Murdock and H. M. F. Simpson, 1893.

The chief source for the general biography is Mark Napier's *Memorials of Montrose and his times*, published by the Maitland Club, 2 vols., Edin. 1848–50, which provided the base for Napier's authoritative though partisan *Memoirs of the marquis of Montrose*, 2 vols., Edin. 1856. An earlier work by the same author, *Montrose and the Covenanters*, 2 vols., 1838, contains Montrose's poems. More recent readable biographies are by M. Morris, 1892, and by C. V. Wedgwood, [1952].

NEWCASTLE, DUKE OF

1682 The life of . . . William Cavendish, duke of . . . Newcastle . . . By Margaret Cavendish, duchess of Newcastle. 1667. Edns. by M. A. Lower, 1872, by C. H. Firth, 1886, and a later edn. [n.d.].

The later edns. include also the life of the duchess by herself (see no. 2455 n.). Firth's edn. includes notes and illustrative papers. For references to published letters see Firth's article on Newcastle (*Cavendish*) in *D.N.B.*

OKEY, COLONEL JOHN

1683   Colonel John Okey, 1606–1662. By H. G. Tibbutt. Bedfordshire Hist. Rec. Soc. Publ. 35. Streatley. 1955.

Biography of a parliamentary colonel.

ROSSITER, COLONEL SIR EDWARD

1684   'Colonel Sir Edward Rossiter.' By A. C. Wood. *Linc. Arch. and Arch. Soc.* 41 (for 1932), 219–38.

RUPERT, PRINCE

1685   Memoirs of Prince Rupert and the Cavaliers, . . . from the original MSS. By B. E. G. Warburton. 3 vols. 1849.

Based upon MSS. now in the Br. Mus. (Add. MSS. 18980–2); other important sources on Rupert are letters in the *Pythouse papers*, ed. by W. A. Day, 1879; 'Prince Rupert's journal in England', [1642–46], ed. by Sir C. H. Firth (*E.H.R.* 13 (1898), 729–41), from Clarendon MSS. xxviii, 129.
  For a biography see E. Scott, *Rupert, Prince Palatine*, 1899, 2nd edn., 1900.

SLINGSBY, SIR HENRY

1686   The diary of Sir Henry Slingsby. Ed. by D. Parsons. 1836.

An abridged version, ed. by Sir Walter Scott, was published at Edin. 1806, in *Original memoirs during the civil war*. The MS. is described in H.M.C., *3rd Rep.*, p. 121. An important source (1638–45), by a Yorkshire royalist.

SMITH, SIR JOHN

1687   Britannicae virtutis imago or . . . the life . . . of . . . Major-General Smith. By E. Walsingham. Oxf. 1644.

By the same author are lives of Sir Henry Gage, Oxf. 1645; and Sir John Digby [1605–45], printed in *Camd. Soc. Misc.* xii (1910), 61–149, ed. by G. Bernard.

TURENNE, VISCOUNT DE

1688   The history of Henry de la Tour d'Auvergne, Viscount de Turenne. By A. M. Ramsay. 2 vols. 1735; 1st edn. [Fr.] 2 vols. Paris. 1735.

The second vol. contains the authorities, including Turenne's own *Memoirs* (1643–58) and *Memoirs of the duke of York* (cf. no. 463 n.). A new edn. of Turenne's *Mémoires*, ed. by Paul Marichal, was publ. in two vols. by the Société de l'histoire de France, Paris, 1909–14.

TURNER, SIR JAMES

1689   Memoirs of his own life and times (1632–70). Ed. by T. Thomson. Edin. 1829. Bannatyne Club.

He served under Gustavus Adolphus and in the civil war. See Br. Mus. Add. MS. 12067. Cf. J. D. Mackie, 'Dugald Dalgetty: and Scottish soldiers of fortune', *S.H.R.* 12 (1915), 221–37.

VERE, SIR FRANCIS

1690   Commentaries, being diverse pieces of service wherein he had command. Ed. by W. Dillingham. Camb. 1657. Maps.

Repr. in *Stuart tracts* (62). See biography in C. R. Markham, *The fighting Veres*, 1888, bibl.

WHETHAM, COLONEL NATHANIEL

1691 History of the life of Colonel Nathaniel Whetham. By C. D. Whetham and W. C. D. Whetham. 1907. Bibl.

Relates to the civil war.

WIMBLEDON, EDWARD CECIL, VISCOUNT

1692 Life and times of General Sir Edward Cecil, Viscount Wimbledon (1572–1638). By C. Dalton. 2 vols. 1885.

Valuable biography of a colonel in the Dutch service and a privy councillor.

2. 1660–1714

BERNARDI, MAJOR JOHN

1693 A short history of the life of Major John Bernardi, written by himself. 1729.

In the Dutch service from 1674 and with James II in Ireland.

BERWICK, JAMES FITZJAMES, DUKE OF

1694 Mémoires du Maréchal de Berwick . . . Ed. by l'Abbé L. J. Hooke. 2 vols. Paris. 1778. Engl. trans. 2 vols. 1779. Later French edns. [including Petitot collection].

Constitutes the first authentic edn., following that compiled by l'abbé de Margon, The Hague, 1737, the part of 1715 being Hooke's continuation from Berwick's own writing.
For a good biography of this natural son of James II see C. T. Wilson, *James II and the duke of Berwick*, 1876, and *The duke of Berwick, Marshal of France, 1702–1734*, 1883. Numerous documents are in J. M. C. M. Fitzjames Stuart (Duke de Berwick y de Alba), *El Marischal de Berwick*, Madrid, 1925.

BLACKADER, JOHN, LIEUTENANT-COLONEL

1695 The life and diary of Lieutenant Colonel John Blackader of the Cameronian Regiment. Ed. by A. Crichton. Edin. 1824.

Useful for the Flanders war in Anne's reign; supersedes edn. of 1806 by J. Newton. See also J. Jamieson, 'Lt. Col. John Blackader', *Trans. Stirling Nat. Hist. and Arch. Soc.*, 1925–6, pp. 53–68.
For experiences of private soldiers see *The life and adventures of Matthew Bishop of Deddington in Oxfordshire* [1701–11], 1744, with a useful article on him in *The Retrospective Review*, 2nd Ser. 2 (1828), 42–55; and W. L. Burn, 'A Scots fusilier . . . under Marlborough . . . Sir James Campbell', *Jour. of Soc. for Army Hist. Res.* 15 (1936), 82–97.
A. P. Grubb, *Jean Cavalier*, 1931, is a popular biography of a French protestant who became an officer in the British army and later served as Governor-General of Jersey.

CARLETON, GEORGE

1696 Military memoirs of Captain George Carleton, from the Dutch war, 1672 . . . [to] 1713. 1728. Later edns.

There are several later edns., of which the most recent were ed. by C. H. Hartmann, 1928, and A. M. Lawrence, 1929.
The authorship has been questioned frequently, the authenticity being defended in *D.N.B.* and by Hartmann. The work was attributed chiefly to Swift by A. Parnell

(*E.H.R.* 6 (1891), 97–151); A. W. Secord, in *Studies in the narrative method of Defoe*, Urbana, 1924, concludes that Defoe compiled from contemporary sources a fictitious narrative woven around a genuine person.

DAVIES, MRS. CHRISTIAN

1697   The life and adventures of Mrs. Christian Davies, commonly called Mother Ross. 1740. Repr. 1741. Ed. by J. Fortescue. 1928.

Personal adventures of a woman soldier. Largely fiction, but throws much light on provisioning the army.

DUNDEE, JOHN GRAHAM OF CLAVERHOUSE, VISCOUNT OF

1698   Letters of John Grahame of Claverhouse, Viscount of Dundee . . . 1678–1689. Ed. by G. Smythe. Bannatyne Club. Edin. 1826.

Principal source. See also letters in H.M.C., Buccleuch MSS., *15th Rep.*, pt. 8, 1897, and *Memoirs of the Lord Viscount Dundee . . .*, 1711; 1714; ed. by H. Jenner, 1903; repr. in *Miscellanea Scotica* (3749), vol. iii. Cf. 'Claverhouse's last letter', *S.H.R.* 5 (1908), 505–9, and criticisms by C. S. Terry and J. Anderson, ibid. 6 (1909), 63–70.

M. Napier's *Memorials and letters illustrative of the life and times of John Graham of Claverhouse, Viscount of Dundee*, 3 vols., Edin. 1859–62, based upon manuscript material, but not without bias, is still the standard biography. *Clavers, the despot's champion*, by 'a Southern', 1889, follows it closely.

Later biographies are; C. S. Terry, *John Graham of Claverhouse, Viscount of Dundee, 1648–89*, 1905; M. Barrington (*pseud.*), *Grahame of Claverhouse, Viscount Dundee*, 1911, with maps and bibl.; and *John Graham of Claverhouse*, by A. N. and H. Tayler, 1939. For shorter biographies see those by M. W. Morris (*English Worthies*, 1888) and L. A. Barbé (*Famous Scots*), Edin., [1903].

GORDON, PATRICK

1699   Passages from the diary of General Patrick Gordon of Auchleuchries, 1635–99. Ed. by J Robertson. Aberdeen. 1859. Spalding Club Publ. No. 31.

Gordon was a soldier of fortune in Russian service.

HALKETT, SIR JAMES

1700   A short . . . account [by Sir James Halkett] of . . . the late wars with the Moors. 1922.

Special number of the *Jour. of the Soc. for Army Hist. Res.*, dealing with Tangier, 1680. Pr. from MS. in the Signet Library.

KNIGHT, JOHN, SERJEANT SURGEON

1701   Serjeant surgeon John Knight, surgeon general 1664–1680. By E. M. Calvert and R. T. C. Calvert. 1939.

Knight was surgeon general during the Dutch wars.

MACKAY, HUGH, LIEUTENANT-GENERAL

1702   Memoirs of the war carried on in Scotland and Ireland. Ed. by J. Mackay. Edin. 1833. Bannatyne Club. Docs.

Cf. Br. Mus. Add. MS. 33264. See also J. Mackay's *Life of Lieut.-General Hugh Mackay* [1640?–92], Edin. 1836; 2nd edn., Lond. 1942 (Bannatyne Club).

MARLBOROUGH, JOHN CHURCHILL, DUKE OF

1703 Memoirs of the duke of Marlborough, with his original correspondence. Ed. by W. Coxe. 3 vols. and atlas. 1818–19. 2nd edn. 6 vols. 1820. 3rd edn. by J. Wade. 3 vols. 1847–8.

This work, with Sir G. Murray's edn. of *Letters and dispatches of John Churchill, duke of Marlborough,* 5 vols., 1845, forms one of the most important collections of printed military correspondence for the period (1660–1714). Transcripts of documents at Blenheim made by Coxe are in Br. Mus. Add. MSS. 9128–97. A description, with some extracts, of the Blenheim papers is in H.M.C., *8th Rep.,* pt. 1 (1881), 1–60; see also ibid., *9th Rep.,* pt. 2 (1895), 406–53. Also useful for documents is T. Lediard, *Life of John, duke of Marlborough, illustrated with maps . . . and a great number of original letters* (3 vols., 1736; 2nd edn., 2 vols., 1743), compiled by a close observer, and the chief basis for such early biographies as A. de Vryer, *Histoire van Joan Churchill* (4 vols., Amsterdam, 1738) and *Histoire de Jean Churchill* by M. Madgett and J. F. H. Dutems (3 vols., Paris, 1805–6). *The military history of the late prince Eugene of Savoy and of the late John duke of Marlborough . . . from 1701 to 1706,* by [J. Campbell] (2 vols., 1736–7; 2nd edn., 1 vol., 1742), is based on various authors, but particularly on *Histoire militaire du prince Eugène de Savoy . . ., et duc de Marlborough . . .,* by J. Dumont and J. Russet de Missey (3 vols., The Hague, 1729–47). The latter work was trans. in part by P. Chamerlen, 1736. A defence of the duke by his chaplain in 1704 is Francis Hare, *The conduct of the duke of Marlborough during the present war, with original papers,* 1712; some of Hare's papers are in H.M.C., *14th Rep.,* 1895, Hare MSS. *apud* Buckinghamshire MSS. A poor early biography is J. Banks, *History of John duke of Marlborough,* 1741; 3rd edn., 1755. This and later biographies by A. Alison, 1848, later edns., G. J. Viscount Wolseley, 1894, E. Thomas, 1915, are superseded largely by Sir Winston Churchill's careful but not impartial *Marlborough: his life and times,* 4 vols., 1933–8; rev. edns., Lond. and N.Y. 1934–8, Lond. 1947–8. Extensive bibliographies are included in this work. See comments on Churchill's biography by M. V. Hay, *Winston Churchill and James II of England,* 1934, and Sir J. W. Fortescue, *Quart. Rev.* 262 (1934), 31–43. Brief popular biographies are D. B. Chidsey, *Marlborough,* 1930, N.Y. 1939, Sir J. W. Fortescue, *Marlborough,* 1932, and M. P. Ashley, *Marlborough,* 1939 [Great Lives], 1948. See also no. 473. An important work on military aspects of his career is C. T. Atkinson, *Marlborough and the rise of the British army,* N.Y. 1921 and 1924, maps, illus.; see also Taylor (1574).

PETERBOROUGH, CHARLES MORDAUNT, EARL OF

1704 Account of the earl of Peterborough's conduct in Spain, chiefly since the raising of the siege of Barcelona, 1706 . . . With original papers. By J. Freind. 1707. 3rd edn. 1708.

Freind, who was with Peterborough in Spain as his physician, wrote on his behalf. A reply was *Account of the earl of Galway's conduct in Spain . . .,* 1711, which provoked *Remarks upon the Account* [1711?]. See also *The Comparison or Accounts on both sides fairly stated,* 1711; and *Letters from the earl of Peterborough to General Stanhope in Spain* [1705–7] *from the originals at Chevening,* ed. by [G. D. Warburton], 1834; and no. 1569. Of the biographies, the earliest, with selections from his correspondence, is *A memoir of Charles Mordaunt, earl of Peterborough,* by G. D. Warburton, 2 vols., 1853. F. S. Russell's *The earl of Peterborough and Monmouth,* 2 vols., 1887, embodies new material but is uncritical. W. Stebbing's biography, *Peterborough,* 1890 (English Men of Action Series), is brief but gives an impartial account of Peterborough's conduct in Spain and of the controversies concerning it. C. R. Ballard, *The great earl of Peterborough,* 1929, is popular in style.

ST. PIERRE, COLONEL DE

1705 Military journal of Colonel de St. Pierre (Royal Dragoons) and other manuscripts relating to the war of the Spanish Succession, 1703–13. Ed. by J. E. Renouard James. Chatham. 1882.

Repr. from the *Royal Engineers' Journal*. It deals with operations in Spain and Portugal.

SCHOMBERG, FRIEDRICH VON

1706 Leben Friedrichs von Schomberg oder Schoenburg. By J. F. A. Kazner. 2 vols. Mannheim. 1789.

Contains diary of the German soldier of fortune, and materials on Ireland.

VII

NAVAL HISTORY

The study of naval history, which owes much to the inspiration of Mahan (1722), has produced no conclusive general history for the period. The older work of Clowes (1718) which is now badly out of date, must be used with caution; and Corbett (1719) is limited to the Mediterranean. The publications of the Navy Records Society have added much useful documentary material, both biographical and on naval affairs; and the Pepysian studies by Tanner, Bryant, and others have thrown light upon naval administration in the period of the Restoration, adding to Oppenheim's work on the period before 1660 (1740). The works of Albion (1716), Owen (1818), and Ehrman (1738) are useful monographs, indicating the possibilities of revisions after new research. Valuable material on naval warfare is to be found in Colenbrander (1808), in the Calendars of State Papers, Domestic (256), the House of Lords Papers (162), and others of the H.M.C. series.

Useful bibliographies are those of Callendar (1707) and Manwaring. Many short papers and documents have been printed in *The Mariner's Mirror* (1911+), which is the journal of the Society for Nautical Research.

In addition to the titles in this section, the student should turn to Ch. III, *The Admiralty*, to Ch. VIII, *Trade and Commerce*, and to *Colonial History*, for other titles relating to maritime matters. The sections on *Military History* and *Foreign Relations* contain others that are equally relevant.

A. GENERAL

1. Bibliographies and Guides

1707 CALLENDER, G. A. R. Bibliography of naval history. 2 pts. Historical Association Leaflets 58, 61. 1924, 1925.

Useful, selective guide.

1708 MANWARING, G. E. A bibliography of British naval history. 1930.

The best guide to MS. sources and to periodical literature. Important guides to MS. collections also are: P.R.O. Lists and Indexes, no. 18, *List of Admiralty records*, 1904; P.R.O., *Catalogue of an exhibition of navy records*, 1950; J. R. Tanner *et al.*, eds., *Bibliotheca Pepysiana*, a descriptive catalogue of the library of Samuel Pepys at Magdalene College, Camb. (Navy Records Soc.), 4 vols., 1903–23. For collections reported on by H.M.C. see Cowper MSS. (101), Dartmouth MSS., vols. i–iii (114), Hodgkin (159), Leyborne Popham (203), and Portland MSS., vol. viii (153), especially. Many naval papers also are calendared in *C.S.P. Domestic*. Various collections, especially at the Br. Mus., are listed in *Camb. Mod. Hist.* (7), iv. 906–7, and v. 815–18.

1709 PERRIN, W. G., ed. Admiralty library. Subject catalogue of printed books. Part I. Historical section. 1912.

Still useful as a general bibliography, though it lacks an index. Cf. R. G. Albion,

Maritime and naval history, Mystic, 1955, which is an annotated bibliography, revised from an earlier edition which was privately printed. See also no. 1716.

2. SOURCES (arranged in rough chronological order according to contents)

1710 RALEIGH, SIR WALTER. Judicious and select essayes and observations . . . upon the first invention of shipping; the misery of invasive warre, the navy royall and sea service; with his apologie for his voyage to Guiana. 1650. Later edns.

1711 OPPENHEIM, M., ed. The naval tracts of Sir William Monson. Navy Records Society. 5 vols. 1902–14.

Useful for the period of James I. First printed as a series in Churchill's *Collection of voyages*, vol. iii, 1704; later edn., 1732.

1712 BUTLER [BOTELER], NATHANIEL. Boteler's dialogues. Ed. by W. G. Perrin. Navy Records Soc. 1929.

Written perhaps as early as 1634, and not entirely original. Valuable for contemporary views on the navy. See also in the Navy Records Society's publications, *Extracts from a commissioner's notebook, 1691–94*, ed. by Sir J. K. Laughton, in Misc. 2, 1912.

1713 THOMPSON, SIR E. M., ed. Correspondence of the family of Haddock, 1659–1719. *Camd. Soc. Misc.* viii. 1883.

From Br. Mus. Egerton MSS. 2520–32. Cf. E. H. Meynell, ed., *Letters of the English seamen, 1587–1808*, 1910, an anthology drawing upon publications of the Navy Records Society.

1714 BURCHETT, JOSIAH. Memoirs of transactions at sea during the war with France (1688–97). 1703.

An important memoir by the Secretary to the Admiralty (1695–1742), which is incorporated in his invaluable *Complete history of the most important transactions at sea* (to 1712), 1720. Cf. Luke Lillington, *Reflections on Mr. Burchet's memoirs*, 1704, and *Mr. Burchett's justification*, 1704. On Burchett see G. F. James's article in *Mariner's Mirror*, 23 (1937), 477–95, and his biography of Burchett, 1937.

1715 HODGES, H. W. and HUGHES, E. S., eds. Select naval documents. Camb. 1922. 1936.

Cf. W. C. B. Tunstall, ed., *The anatomy of Neptune from Henry VIII to the present day*, 1936.

3. LATER WORKS

1716 ALBION, R. G. Forests and sea-power: the timber problem of the royal navy, 1652–1862. Camb. (Mass.). 1926. Bibl.

Valuable standard work.

1717 CALLENDER, SIR G. and HINSLEY, F. H. The naval side of British history, 1485–1945. 1952.

Earlier edn. 1924. Among other short histories are C. D. Yonge, *The history of the British navy*, 2 vols., 1863; and D. Hannay, *Short history of the British navy*, 2 vols., 1898–[1909]. See also the history in the Penguin Series by M. Lewis, 1957.

1718 CLOWES, W. L., *et al.* The royal navy: a history. 7 vols. 1897–1903.

The second volume deals with 1603–1714. This is a standard work, contributors to which were C. R. Markham, A. T. Mahan, and H. W. Wilson, but is now badly out of date.

1719 CORBETT, SIR J. S. England in the Mediterranean: a study of the rise and influence of British power within the Straits, 1603–1713. 2 vols. 1904.

Important work. Cf. J. Ehrman, 'William III and the emergence of a Mediterranean naval policy, 1692–4', *Camb. Hist. Jour.* 9 (1949), 269–92. See also no. 1738.

1720 LEDIARD, T. The naval history of England . . . from 1066 to . . . 1734. 2 vols. 1735.

An important early history. Compare S. Colliber, *Columna Rostrata: a critical history of the English sea-affairs*, 1727, 1742; and J. Entick, *A new naval history*, 1757, the latter of which draws upon Lediard but adds several useful documents.

1721 LOW, C. R. History of the Indian navy. 2 vols. 1877.

On the Scottish navy see J. Grant, ed., *The old Scots navy from 1689 to 1710*, Navy Records Soc. 44, 1914.

1722 MAHAN, A. T. The influence of sea power on history, 1660–1783. Boston. 1890. Many edns.

An influential work, dealing especially with naval strategies. Cf. W. D. Puleston, *Mahan*, New Haven, 1939.

1723 PENN, C. D. The navy under the early Stuarts and its influence on English history. Leighton Buzzard and Manchester. 1913. Bibl. Later edn. 1920.

Covers 1603–49. Other useful volumes on special periods are: A. W. Tedder, *The navy of the restoration from the death of Cromwell to the Treaty of Breda*, Camb. 1916, bibl.; E. B. Powley, *The English navy in the revolution of 1688* (1814); and J. R. Tanner, 'Naval preparations of James II in 1688', *E.H.R.* 8 (1893), 272–83.

1724 RITTMEYER, R. Seekriege and Seekriegswesen in ihrer weltgeschicht-lichen Entwicklung. 2 vols. Berlin. 1907–11.

Deals with the 17th and 18th centuries especially. Histories of foreign navies include the standard work by J. C. de Jonge on the Dutch navy (6 vols., Amsterdam, 1833–48); the less reliable M. J. E. Sue's work on the French navy (5 vols., 1835–8); and others cited in Grose (10), p. 64. See also § G, *infra*.

B. ADMINISTRATION AND POLICY

1. SOURCES (chronological order, by content)

See also *Constitutional History*, nos. 754–8.

1725 GARDINER, S. R., ed. Documents illustrating the impeachment of the Duke of Buckingham in 1626. Camd. Soc. 1889.

See also H. Hulme's edition of Sir John Eliot's records of the Devon vice-admiralty (1622–8) in *Camd. Soc. Misc.* xvii, 1940.

1726 TANNER, J. R., ed. Two discourses of the navy, 1638 and 1659, by John Holland; also a discourse of the navy 1660 by Sir Robert Slyngsbie. Navy Records Soc. 1896.

See Slingsby's *Discourse* also in Charnock (1782).

1727 ST. JOHN, OLIVER. The speech . . . of Mr. St. John . . . 1640 . . . concerning ship-money. 1641.

Cf. *An humble remonstrance to his majesty against the tax of ship-money imposed*, s.l. 1641.

1728 BURRELL, ANDREWES. To the right honourable, the High Court of Parliament, the . . . remonstrance of A. Burrell . . . for a reformation of England's navie: England's outguard or England's royal navie surveyed and lamented. 1646(?).

By the author of *A memorable sea fight* . . . [the Downes, 1639], 1649. Burrell's complaint to Parliament evoked *The answer of the commissioners of the navie to a scandalous pamphlet . . . published by Mr. Andrewes Burrell*, 1646.
   See also Giles Greene, *A declaration in vindication of . . . Parliament and the committee of the navy*, 1647; and Burrell's *A cordiall for the calenture: or a declaration advising how England's sea honour may be regained*, 1648 (1649?).

1729 JAMES, DUKE OF YORK (JAMES II). Memoirs of the English affairs: chiefly naval . . . 1660-1673. 1729.

Orders and instructions, as Lord High Admiral. For the year before the restoration see *A letter from the commanders and officers of the fleet: unto General Monck in Scotland*, 1659. On the administration of the duke of York see *The œconomy of his majesty's navy office*, 1717, which includes the rules prepared by Pepys for issue by the duke.

1730 PEPYS, SAMUEL. Memoires relating to the state of the royal navy of England 1679-88. 1690. Later edn. by J. R. Tanner. Oxf. 1906.

Deals with naval administration. See also the *Diary* (2500); *Bibliotheca Pepsyiana* (1708 n.); and Tanner's editions of *Samuel Pepys's naval minutes*, Navy Records Soc., 1926; *Private correspondence and miscellaneous papers of Samuel Pepys, 1679–1703*, 2 vols., 1926, and *Further correspondence, 1662–79*, 1929. E. Chappell edited *Shorthand letters of Samuel Pepys* (1664–5), Camb. 1933, and the important *Tangier papers of Samuel Pepys*, Navy Records Soc., 1935. For evaluations of Pepys see no. 2500 n.

1731 MAYDMAN, HENRY. Naval speculations and maritime politicks: being a modest and brief discourse on the royal navy of England . . . and a projection for a royal marine hospital. Also necessary measures in the war with France. 1691.

See also *The late plot on the fleet detected* . . ., 1689 (Wing, L 555), which relates to the Jacobite invitations for French intervention. It was repr. Edin. 1690.

1732 ST. LO, GEORGE. England's interest, or a discipline for seamen wherein is proposed a sure method for raising qualified seamen. 1694.

One of several similar works by St. Lo. See his *England's Safety* . . ., 1693, in *Somers tracts*, vol. xi. Cf. George Everett, *The pathway to peace and profit . . . for . . . effectual building . . . [the] royal navy*, 1694; Robert Crosfeild, *Justice perverted and innocence and loyalty oppressed*, 1695, on maladministration; and William Hodges, *Great Britain's groans*, 1695, which complains of similar matters. For other titles by Crosfeild and Hodges see Wing.

1733 [TUTCHIN, JOHN.] An historical and political treatise of the navy, 1703.

For works in a similar vein see John Dennis, *An essay on the navy*, 1702; *The present condition of the English navy*, by an anonymous author, 1702; and Wing, S 2190 and R 935A.

1734 REPORT OF THE LORDS committees appointed to take into consideration the reports of the commissioners; so far as relates to the accompts of the Rt. Hon. Edward, Earl of Orford, late treasurer of the navy. 1704.

Cf. *Answers* of the earl, 1704.

1735 JACKSON, G. and DUCKETT, G. F. Naval commissioners . . . 1660–1760. Compiled from the original warrants and returns. [Lewes.] 1889.

See the Admiralty's *List of the lords high admiral and commissioners for executing that office . . . since . . . 1660*, 1892; later edn., 1915. See also no. 755.

1736 MERRIAM, R. D., ed. Queen Anne's navy: documents concerning the administration of the navy of Queen Anne 1702–1714. Navy Records Soc. 1961.

2. LATER WORKS

1737 BRYANT, A. Samuel Pepys. 3 vols. Camb. and N.Y. 1933–8. 2nd pr. 3 vols. 1948–9.

The fullest biography (to 1689) of the diarist (see no. 2500) and secretary for the Admiralty, with vols. ii and iii concerned especially with naval affairs from 1669–89. For other evaluations of Pepys as an administrator see J. Ehrman, 'Pepys' organization and naval mobilization of 1688', *Mariner's Mirror*, 35 (1949), 203–39; and J. R. Tanner, *Samuel Pepys and the royal navy*, Camb. 1920, and 'Samuel Pepys and the Trinity House', *E.H.R.* 44 (1929), 573–87. Tanner has written also 'Pepys and the Popish Plot', ibid. 7 (1892), 281–90, and *Mr. Pepys, an introduction to the diary, together with a sketch of his later life*, 1925. See also no. 1730.

1738 EHRMAN, J. The navy in the war of William III, 1689–1697: its state and direction. Camb. and N.Y. 1953.

Detailed study of conditions in the navy, with operations at sea used as a basis for discussion of administration and policy. An important work from Dutch sources is J. C. M. Warnsinck, *De vloot van den konig-stadhouder, 1689–90*, Amsterdam, 1934.

1739 KEEVIL, J. J. Medicine and the navy, 1200–1900. 2 vols. [1200–1714.] 1957–8. Bibl.

Vol. i goes to 1649, vol. ii to 1714. A useful work with many references to MS. sources. See *The surgeon's mate*, by John Woodall, 1617; and I. G. Powell, 'Early ship surgeons', *Mariner's Mirror*, 9 (1923), 11–15. An early book on diseases of seafaring men by William Cockburn was published in 1696 (Wing, C 4815).

1740 OPPENHEIM, M. A history of the administration of the royal navy and of merchant shipping in relation to the navy from 1509 to 1660. 1896.

Valuable. Cf. A. C. Dewar, 'The naval administration of the interregnum', *Mariner's Mirror*, 12 (1926), 406–30; and W. G. Perrin, 'The lord high admiral and the board of admiralty', ibid. 12 (1926), 117–44; and articles by E. S. de Beer, ibid. 13 (1927), and by O. Murray, ibid. 23–4 (1937–8).

1741   POWELL, I. G. 'The Chatham Chest under the early Stuarts.' *Mariner's Mirror*, 8 (1922), 174–82.

Other articles by Powell relating to naval chaplains, profiteering, and other aspects of naval administration are in vols. 7–10 (1921–4).

1742   RICHMOND, SIR H. The navy as an instrument of policy, 1558–1727. Ed. by E. A. Hughes. Camb. and N.Y. 1953. Bibl.

Excellent. See also his *Statesmen and sea power*, Oxf. 1943, 1947.

1743   TANNER, J. R. 'The administration of the navy from the restoration to the revolution.' *E.H.R.* 12 (1897), 17–66; 13 (1898), 26–54; 14 (1899), 47–70; 14 (1899), 261–89.

Subsequently expanded to form the General Introduction to the Catalogue of Pepysian MSS., vol. i.

C. SEAMANSHIP AND NAVAL WARFARE

1. SEAMANSHIP, SEAMEN, AND NAVIGATION

(a) *Sources* (rough chronological arrangement)

1744   MAINWARING, SIR HENRY. The seamans dictionary. 1644. Later edns.

Written about 1620–3, and imperfect in the early printed edns.; see the modern edn. in vol. ii of G. E. Manwaring, *Life and works of Sir Henry Mainwaring* (Navy Records Soc., 2 vols., 1920–2). See also Nathaniel Boteler's *Dialogues* (1712); and John Smith's *An accidence, or the path-way to experience necessary for all young seamen*, 1626, which bore the title of *A sea grammar* in an enlarged edn. in 1627, and was reprinted often under varying titles, and included in *John Smith's Travels*, Edin. 1910. For a bibliography of English and French nautical dictionaries compiled by L. G. Carr Laughton see *Mariner's Mirror*, 1 (1911), 84–9, 212–15; and 12 (1926), 335–8.

1745   NORWOOD, RICHARD. The seaman's practice. 1637. 5th edn. 1662.

Other works of the early 17th century are: John Tapp, *Seaman's kalendar*, 1601, many later edns.; William Johnson [Janszoon], *The light of navigation*, Amsterdam, 1625; Charles Saltonstall, *The navigator*, 1636, 3rd edn. [1660?]; and Richard Potter, *Pathway to perfect sailing*, 1644.

1746   BARLOW, EDWARD. Barlow's journal of his life at sea in king's ships, East and West Indiamen and other merchantmen (1659–1703). Ed. by B. Lubbock. 2 vols. 1934.

Vivid picture for lower-deck conditions. For ship life as seen by a junior officer under Blake see *The journal of John Weale, 1654–1656*, ed. by J. R. Powell in Naval Misc. 4 (Navy Records Soc. 92), 1952.

1747   STURMY, SAMUEL. The mariner's magazine. 1669. Later edns. 1679. 1684.

A lavishly illustrated tribute to Sturmy is C. E. Kenney, *The quadrant and quill*, 1947. On the use of instruments of navigation see Edmund Gunter in his *Works*, 3rd edn., 1653; 5th edn., 1673. See also P. Perkins, *The seaman's tutor*, 1682.

1748 COLLINS, GREENVILE. Great Britain's coasting pilot: being a survey of the sea coast of England. 1693. Later edns. 1744. 1753. 1792.

First scientific survey of the English coast, but omitting the east coast. On Collins see F. E. Dyer, *Mariner's Mirror*, 14 (1928), 197–219. For charts of other areas see John Seller, *Atlas maritimus*, 1675, and his *English pilot*, 3 vols., 1671–7 (many later edns.), which is largely from Dutch sources.

1749 NEWHOUSE, DANIEL. The whole art of navigation. 2 parts. 1685–1701.

Later edns. of the first part, 1686, 1698. See also Henry Bond, *The boat-swain's art*, 1670, later edn., 1704; Matthew Norwood, *Norwoods system of navigation*, 1685, and other works in Wing, N 1345–6; and Thomas Savery, *Navigation improved, or the art of rowing ships . . .*, 1698.

1750 LIGHTBODY, JAMES. Mariner's jewel. 1695. Later edns. [by 'James Love']. 1705. 1724. 1735.

Probably based on a MS. of Sir John Narbrough; includes a nautical dictionary.

(b) *Later Works*

1751 TAYLOR, E. G. R. The haven-finding art: a history of navigation. 1956. Bibl.

Useful. Chaps. 9 and 10 particularly deal with the period. See also Taylor (3025). Cf. J. B. Hewson, *A history of the practice of navigation*, Glasgow [1951], which has bibliographical footnotes and contains a good deal on the 17th century.

1752 WATERS, D. W. The art of navigation in England in Elizabethan and early Stuart times. New Haven. 1958. Bibl.

Important. The author is concerned with the interrelationship between maritime history and the intellectual and economic developments of the period.

2. NAVAL WARFARE

1753 CORBETT, J. S., ed. Fighting instructions 1530–1816. Navy Records Soc. 1905.

Important. Cf. Jonathan Greenwood, *The sailing and fighting instructions or signals*, [Lond.?], 1714.

1754 BINNING, THOMAS. A light to the art of gunnery. 1676. Later edns.

Cf. Francis Povey, *The sea-gunner's companion*, 1702.

1755 HOSTE, PAUL. L'art des armées navales. Lyon. 1697.

An important treatise on tactics by a Jesuit professor who observed some of the actions. Portions were publ. in English by C. O'Bryen in 1762; a translation by J. D. Boswall, entitled *A treatise on naval tactics*, was pr. in Edin. 1834.

1756 COLOMB, P. H. Naval warfare, its ruling principles and practice historically treated. 1891. Later edns. 1895. 1899.

Concerned especially with strategy.

D. CONSTRUCTION AND SHIPS

1. SOURCES

1757 A TREATISE on rigging written about the year 1625. Ed. by R. C. Anderson. (Society for Nautical Research, Occasional Pub., no. 1.) Southampton. 1921.

From a MS. in Petworth House (see H.M.C., *6th Rep.*, Northumberland MSS.). Also published by the Society (Occasional Pub., no. 3, 1931), *Lengths of masts and yards*, . . . 1640, ed. by G. S. Laird Clowes. Compare Edward Hayward, *The sizes and lengths of rigging for all his majesty's ships and frigates*, 1660. For a general work see Joseph Furtenbach, *Architectura navalis*, 2 vols., Ulm, 1629.

1758 HEYWOOD, THOMAS. A true description of his majesties royal ship built . . . 1637 at Wollwitch in Kent. 1637.

Repr. with additions in 1653 as *The common-wealths great ship*.

1759 BUSHNELL, EDMUND. The compleat ship-wright. 1664. 5th edn. 1688.

Important early work with diagrams.

1760 SUTHERLAND, WILLIAM. The ship-builder's assistant, or marine architecture. 1711.

A larger work by the same author is *Britain's glory, or ship-building unvail'd*, 2 vols. in 1, 1717.

1761 LISTS OF MEN-OF-WAR, 1650–1700. (Society for Nautical Research, Occasional Pub., no. 5.) Camb. 1939.

Part I, 'English Ships', compiled by R. C. Anderson, was separately printed in 1935.

2. LATER WORKS

1762 ABELL, SIR W. S. The shipwright's trade. Camb. 1948.

1763 ANDERSON, R. C. The rigging of ships in the days of the spritsail topmast, 1600–1720. Salem. 1927. Bibl.

By the same author, 'Comparative naval architecture, 1670–1720', *Mariner's Mirror*, 7 (1921), 38–45, 172–81, 308–15. By R. Anderson and R. C. Anderson, *The sailing ship*, 1947.

1764 CHARNOCK, J. History of marine architecture. 3 vols. 1800–2.

Contains much source material, but should be used with caution. Cf. the chapter by G. P. B. Naish on 'Ships and shipbuilding' in vol. iii of Singer (2038). See also *The double bottom, or twin-hulled ship, of Sir William Petty*, ed. by the Marquess of Lansdowne, 1931.

1765 CLOWES, G. S. L. Sailing ships: their history and development. 2nd edn. 2 vols. 1931–2. 4th edn. rev. by E. W. White. 2 vols. 1951–2.

1766 NANCE, R. N. Sailing ship models. 1924. Rev. edn. 1949.

See also H. B. Culver, *Contemporary scale models . . . of the 17th century*, 1926; L. G. C. Laughton, *Old ship figure-heads and sterns*, 1925.

E. MARITIME LAW

1. SOURCES

(Order is roughly chronological with regard to the date of writing, rather than of publication.) See also *Admiralty* (nos. 754, 756).

1767 ADMIRALTY STATUTES: being the public statutes actually in force (1552–1874). Under the authority of the lords commissioners of the admiralty. Ed. by A. V. Dicey. 1875. Later ed. by A. T. Carter. 2 vols. 1905.

Earlier collections of statutes relating to naval matters were publ. in 1742, 1768, and 1810; an official collection was ed. by J. Raithby, 1823.

1768 MARSDEN, R. G., ed. Documents relating to law and custom of the sea (1205–1767). Navy Records Soc. 1915–16.

Valuable collection relating to prize, piracy, etc., chiefly from the public records.

1769 GROTIUS, HUGO. The freedom of the seas, or, the right which belongs to the Dutch to take part in the East Indian trade. Trans. by R. Van D. Magoffin. Ed. by J. B. Scott. N.Y. 1916.

The famous treatise, generally known as *Mare liberum*, was written 1604–5, and first published separately at Leyden in 1609 (see J. Ter Meulen and P. J. J. Diermanse, *Bibliographie . . . de Hugo Grotius* (The Hague, 1950), pp. 210–22). The 1916 edn. is based upon a Latin text of 1635.

The *Mare liberum* was written originally as part of Grotius's *De jure praedae commentarius*, which was not publ. in the author's life-time; the *Mare liberum* evoked replies from Welwod (1770) and Selden (1771).

The larger *De jure praedae . . . commentary of the law of prize and booty*, although the basis for much of the author's best-known treatise, *The law of war and peace* (first publ. 1625), was ed. (in Latin) by H. G. Hamaker, The Hague, 1868; an English trans. from the 1604 text by G. L. Williams was publ. in the 'Classics of International Law', ed. by J. B. Scott for The Carnegie Endowment for International Peace, 2 vols., Oxf. 1950. See H. Klee, *Hugo Grotius and John Selden*, Bern, 1946.

1770 WELWOD, WILLIAM. Abridgment of all sea-lawes. 1613. Later edn. 1636.

Written by Welwod, professor of Civil Law at Aberdeen, as a refutation of Grotius's *Mare liberum*, it inspired an answer by Grotius which was not published until the 19th century (*Bibl. Grotius*, pp. 306–8).

1771 SELDEN, JOHN. Mare clausum seu de Dominio Maris. 1635. Trans. by M. Nedham. 1652.

Written about 1617 or 1618, this is the most famous reply from the British viewpoint to the argument of Grotius which excluded England's claim to the high seas south and east of England.

See also Sir John Borough, *The soveraignty of the British seas, . . . written in the year 1633*, 1651, repr. in 1686 (*D.N.B.*); and ed. by T. C. Wade, Edin. 1920.

1772 ZOUCHE, RICHARD. The jurisdiction of the admiralty of England. 1663.

Zouche was the author also of an early treatise relating to international law, *Juris et juridicii fecialis, sive juris inter gentes* (1014 n.). His work on admiralty jurisdiction was repr. in 1686.

On the admiralty jurisdiction see also Francis Clerke [Clarke], *Praxis curiae admiralitatis Angliae*, 1667, presumably written about 1596, but not publ. until 1666 in Dublin (Wing, C 4440; *D.N.B.*); John Godolphin, *A view of the admiral jurisdiction*, 1661, 2nd edn. 1685; and John Exton, *The maritime dicaeologie, or sea jurisdiction of England*, 1664.

1773 MOLLOY, CHARLES. De jure maritimo et navali: or a treatise of affairs maritime and of commerce. 1676. 4th edn. 1688. 9th edn. 2 vols. 1769.

Was long a standard work.

1774 MEADOWS, PHILIP. Observations concerning the dominion and sovereignty of the seas, being an abstract of the marine affairs of England. 1689.

1775 JUSTICE, ALEX. A general treatise of the dominion and laws of the sea . . . and particularly that excellent body of sea-laws lately published in France . . . with a collection of the marine treaties concluded during the last century. 1705. 3rd enl. edn. [1710?]

2. Later Works

1776 FULTON, T. W. The sovereignty of the sea, an historical account of the claims of England to the dominion of the British seas and of the evolution of the territorial waters. 1911.

Emphasizes 17th-century developments.

1777 HANNAY, D. Naval courts martial (1680–1815). Camb. 1914.

1778 KULSRUD, C. J. Maritime neutrality to 1780: a history of the main principles governing neutrality and belligerency. Boston. 1936.

England and other European states; bibl. footnotes.

1779 ROSCOE, E. S. A history of the English prize court. 1924.

Cf. R. G. Marsden, 'Early prize jurisdiction and prize law in England' (1603–98), *E.H.R.* 25 (1910), 243–63; 26 (1911), 34–56. See also Roscoe (1053).

1780 SENIOR, W. Doctor's Commons and the old court of admiralty. 1922.

By Senior also, *Naval history in the law courts: a selection of maritime cases*, 1927; and article in *Mariner's Mirror*, 13 (1927), 333–47.

F. BIOGRAPHIES AND PERSONAL NARRATIVES

1. Collected Biographies

1781 CAMPBELL, J. The lives of the admirals and other eminent British seamen. 4 vols. 1742–4. Later edn. 8 vols. 1812–17.

Cf. Campbell's *The naval history of Great Britain* . . ., 8 vols., 1818, which is virtually another edn. of the above. Campbell's work, though long a classic, is now practically obsolete. For comments on the various editions, and other naval biographies, see G. F. James, 'Bibliographical aids . . . VI. Collected naval biography', *Bull. Inst. Hist. Research*, 15 (1937–8), 162–75.

1782 CHARNOCK, J. Biographia navalis or impartial memoirs of the lives and characters of officers of the navy . . . from . . . 1660 to the present time. 6 vols. 1794–8.

Cf. C. H. Firth, 'Sailors of the civil war', *Mariner's Mirror*, 12 (1926), 237–59.

2. INDIVIDUAL BIOGRAPHIES AND PERSONAL NARRATIVES

1783 INGRAM, B. S., ed. Three sea journals of Stuart times; the diary of Dawtrey Cooper, captain of the Pelican; the journals of Jeremy Roch, captain of the king's navy; the diary of Francis Rogers, London merchant. 1936.

See also E. H. W. Meyerstein, ed., *Adventures by sea of Edward Coxere*, 1946.

ALLIN, SIR THOMAS

1784 The journals of Sir Thomas Allin, 1660–1678. Ed. by R. C. Anderson. 2 vols. Navy Records Soc. 1939–40.

Valuable. On another officer of the Dutch wars, Sir John Kempthorne, see *Mariner's Mirror*, 12 (1926), 289–317.

BADILEY, RICHARD

1785 Spalding, T. A. A life of Richard Badiley vice admiral of the fleet. 1899.

Chiefly operations in the Mediterranean, 1652–4.

BLAKE, ROBERT

1786 The letters of Robert Blake, together with supplementary documents. Ed. by J. R. Powell. 1937.

Cf. *Lives* by R. Beadon, Lond. and N.Y. 1935; by C. D. Curtis, Taunton, 1934; and Powell's brief sketch, Bridgwater, 1932. Older biographies are those by John Oldmixon, 2nd edn., 1746; W. H. Dixon, 1852, later edn. 1885; and D. Hannay, 1886. See also no. 1807.

DEANE, RICHARD

1787 Deane, J. B. The life of Richard Deane, major-general and general-at-sea in the service of the Commonwealth. 1870.

FAIRFAX, ROBERT

1788 Markham, Sir C. R. Life of Robert Fairfax of Steeton, vice-admiral, alderman and member for York . . . 1666–1725. 1885.

LEAKE, SIR JOHN

1789 Leake, S. M. Life of Sir John Leake rear admiral of Great Britain. Priv. pr. 1750. 2nd edn. by G. A. R. Callender. 2 vols. Navy Records Soc. 1920.

Leake's service at sea covers 1673–1712.

MARTIN, STEPHEN

1790   Life of Captain Stephen Martin 1666–1740. Ed. by Sir C. R. Markham. Navy Records Soc. 1895.

Compiled from Martin's journals. Includes comment on conditions in the navy.

NARBROUGH, SIR JOHN

1791   Dyer, F. E. The life of Admiral Sir John Narbrough (1640–88). 1931.
Useful.

PENN, SIR WILLIAM

1792   Penn, G. Memorials of . . . Sir William Penn, admiral and general of the fleet 1644 to 1670. 2 vols. 1833.

Documents.

PETT, PHINEAS

1793   The autobiography of Phineas Pett. Ed. by W. G. Perrin. Navy Records Soc. 1918.

Covers 1570–1638. Valuable for the history of shipbuilding in England.

RAINBOROWE, THOMAS

1794   Peacock, E. 'Notes on the life of Thomas Rainborowe, officer in the army and navy in the service of the Parliament of England.' *Archaeologia*, 46 (1880), 9–64.

SANDWICH, EDWARD MOUNTAGU, EARL OF

1795   The journal of Edward Montagu, first earl of Sandwich, admiral and general at sea, 1659–1665. Ed. by R. C. Anderson. Navy Records Soc. 1928.

Many documents are included in the *Life* by F. R. Harris, 2 vols., 1912.

TORRINGTON, ARTHUR HERBERT, EARL OF

1796   An impartial account of some remarkable passages in the life of Arthur, earl of Torrington, together with some modest remarks on his tryal, and acquitment. 1691.

Herbert's correspondence, including letters of William III and Burnet, at the time of the Revolution, ed. by Sir E. M. Thompson, is in *E.H.R.* 1 (1886), 522–36.

TORRINGTON, GEORGE BYNG, LORD

1797   Memoirs relating to the Lord Torrington (1678–1705). Ed. by Sir J. K. Laughton. Camden Soc. 1889.

Pr. from Br. Mus. Add. MS. 31958. Cf. *The Byng papers*, ed. by W. C. B. Tunstall, 3 vols., Navy Records Soc., 1930–3, which are important for the War of the Spanish Succession.

G. OPERATIONS AT SEA

1. NAVAL ACTIONS

(a) *General*

See also *Military History*; *Foreign Relations*; *Colonial History*.

1798 ANDERSON, R. C. Naval wars in the Baltic. 1910.

> Authoritative. By the same author, *Naval wars in the Levant, 1559–1853*, Liverpool, 1952.

1799 FISHER, SIR G. Barbary legend: war, trade and piracy in North Africa, 1415–1830. N.Y. 1957.

> Useful; draws upon new materials; attempts without complete success to counteract the traditional views on the 'Barbary pirates'.
> See also: Sir George Carteret, *The Barbary voyage of 1638*, Phila. 1929; G. N. Clark, 'The Barbary corsairs in the 17th century', *Camb. Hist. Jour.* 8 (1944), 22–35; and S. R. H. Rogers, *The Barbary pirates*, 1939.

(b) *1603–1640*

See also Pennington (198).

1800 PENROSE, B., ed. Sea fights in the East Indies, 1602–1639. Camb. (Mass.). 1931.

> Contemporary narratives relating to Anglo-Dutch rivalry.

1801 GLANVILLE, JOHN. The voyage to Cadiz in 1625. Ed. by A. B. Grosart. Camden Soc. 1883.

> Journal of the lord admiral's secretary, printed from Sir John Eliot's MSS. at Port Eliot. Cf. *Two original journals* of Sir R[ichard] Granville of the expedition to Cadiz anno 1625, of the Isle of Rhee . . . anno 1627, 2 pts. in one vol., 1724.

1802 A JOURNALL of all the proceedings of the Duke of Buckingham in the Isle of Ree. 2 pts. 1627.

> See also Edward Herbert, Lord of Cherbury, *Expeditio in ream insulam*, 1656; translation ed. by Edward James Herbert, third earl of Powis, Philobiblon Soc., 1860.

1803 DUNTON, JOHN. The true journall of the Sallee fleet. 1637.

> See Churchill's *Collection of voyages*, vol. iii.

1804 DYER, F. E. 'The ship-money fleet.' *Mariner's Mirror*, 23 (1937), 198–209.

> Narrative of the expedition against the Channel pirates, 1636.

(c) *1642–1676*

1805 HARLOW, V. T., ed. The voyages of Captain William Jackson (1642–5). *Camden Soc. Misc.* xiii. 1924.

> Raids on Spanish shipping in the West Indies.

1806   GARDINER, S. R., ed. Prince Rupert at Lisbon (1649–50). *Camden Soc. Misc.* x. 1902.

> Pr. from Br. Mus. Add. MS. 35251. See also the articles on naval actions of the period of 1648–52 by R. C. Anderson: *E.H.R.* 31 (1916), 406–28; and *Mariner's Mirror,* 9 (1923), 34–46; 14 (1928), 320–8; and 21 (1935), 61–90.

1807   POWELL, J. R. The navy in the English civil war. Hamden (Conn.). 1962.

> Useful documents relating to this period are in J. R. Powell and E. K. Timings, eds., *Documents relating to the civil war 1642–1648,* Navy Records Soc., vol. 105, 1963.
>   Cf. articles on Blake's actions of 1650–1 by Powell, C. D. Curtis, and C. R. Boxer in *Mariner's Mirror,* 18 (1932), 64–80; 20 (1934), 50–66, 448–74; 36 (1950), 212–28. See also C. H. Firth, 'Blake and the battle of Santa Cruz' [1657], *E.H.R.* 20 (1905), 228–50, and Sir Richard Stayner's *Narrative . . . of Santa Cruz,* ed. by Firth in *Naval Record Soc. Misc.* 2, 1912.

1808   COLENBRANDER, H. T. Bescheiden uit vreemde archieven omtrent de groote Nederlandsche Zeeoorlogen, 1652–1676. 2 vols. The Hague. 1919.

> Documents collected chiefly from English and French archives, elucidating the history of the three Anglo-Dutch naval wars. See also the important *Letters and papers relating to the first Dutch war, 1652–1654,* ed. by S. R. Gardiner and C. T. Atkinson, 5 vols., Navy Records Soc., 1898–1912, with an additional volume ed. by Atkinson, 1930; and the documents collected by C. Ballhausen under the title of *Der erste Englisch-Holländische Seekrieg 1652–1654,* The Hague, 1923. On the Dutch admirals, see C. R. Boxer, ed., *The journal of Maarten Harpertszoon Tromp, anno 1639,* Camb. 1930, and his article, 'The Tromps and the Anglo-Dutch Wars, 1652–1674', *History Today* 1953, 836–45.

1809   FIRTH, C. H. 'The capture of Santiago, in Cuba, by Captain Myngs, 1662.' *E.H.R.* 14 (1899), 536–40.

> On activities of Myngs during the protectorate see F. E. Dyer, 'Captain Christopher Myngs in the West Indies', *Mariner's Mirror,* 18 (1932), 168–87.

1810   A TRUE AND PERFECT RELATION of the happy successe & victory obtained against the Turks of Algiers at Bugia, by his majesty's fleet. 1671.

> See also J. S. Bromley, ed., *The Straits voyage or St. David's poem, by John Balthorpe* [1671], Luttrell Soc. Repr., no. 20, Oxf. 1959 (see Wing, B 610).

1811   A TRUE NARRATIVE of the engagement between his majesties fleet and that of Holland (June 1, 1666). 1666.

> Cf. R. C. Anderson, ed., *Naval operations . . . 1666. Navy Records Soc. Misc.* 3, 1927.

1812   ANDERSON, R. C., ed. Journals and narratives of the third Dutch War. Navy Records Soc. 1946.

> Useful for the years 1672–3. Other contemporary accounts of naval engagements and related matters will be found in Wing, E 3696 (1673), J 1244 (1674). Cf. *Relation de ce qui s'est passé entre les armées navales de France et d'Angleterre et celle de Hollande,* 1672–3, Paris, 1674. See also H.M.C., Dartmouth MSS. (114).
>   See also J. S. Corbett, ed., *A note on the drawings . . . illustrating the battle of Sole Bay, . . . , 1672, and the battle of the Texel, 1673* (Navy Records Soc.), 1908; and *The Netherland-historian, containing a true and exact relation of the late warrs . . . 1671 to 1674,* trans. by S. Swart, Amsterdam, 1675.

1813　A LIST of several ships belonging to English merchants taken by French privateers since Dec. 1673, also a brief account touching what application hath been made for redress. Amsterdam. 1677.

(d) *1688–1714*

1814　POWLEY, E. B. The English navy in the revolution of 1688. Camb. 1928. Bibl.

Indicates the navy's decisive role. On the naval policies of 1689–97 see Ehrman (1738).

1815　[STEPHENS, E.] A plain relation of the late action at sea between the English and Dutch and the French fleets. 1690.

Cf. *An account given by Sir John Ashby . . . to the lords commissioners of the engagement at sea . . . June 30th, 1690,* 1691. See also no. 1796.

1816　AN ACCOUNT of the late great victory obtained at sea against the French . . . May 1692. 1692.

Cf. *Admiral Russell's letter to the earl of Nottingham containing an exact . . . relation of the late happy victory . . . 1692* (in *Harl. Misc.*, vol. iv); *A narrative of the victory . . . near La Hogue 1692,* 1744, from the journal of a chaplain, Richard Allyn. Modern commentaries are: G. Toudouze, *La bataille de la Hogue*, Paris, 1899, and six articles by A. de Boislisle, 'M. de Bonrepaus, la marine et le désastre de la Hougue', in *Ann. Bull. Soc. Hist. de Fr.*, 1877.

1817　CARMARTHEN, PEREGRINE OSBORNE, MARQUIS OF. A journal of the Brest expedition. 1694.

An account by a rear-admiral.

1818　OWEN, J. H. War at sea under Queen Anne, 1702–1708. Camb. and N.Y. 1938.

Valuable supplement to the older military accounts. Contemporary narratives are: *An impartial account of all the material transactions of the grand fleet and land forces* [June 29–Nov. 7, 1702], 1793; O. Browning's edn. of Admiral Sir George Rooke's *Journal 1700–1702* (Navy Records Soc.), 1897; and Nathanael Taubman's *Memoirs of the British fleets and squadrons that acted in the Mediterranean 1708 and 1709,* 1710, 1714.

1819　BOURNE, R. M. Queen Anne's navy in the West Indies. New Haven. 1939.

Useful. Cf. W. T. Morgan, 'British West Indies during King William's War', *J.M.H.* 2 (1930), 378–409.

2. PRIVATEERING

See also *Naval Voyages* (below) and *Colonial History.* Titles on piracy are in *Social History*, 'Crime'.

1820　CLARK, G. N. 'English and Dutch privateers under William III.' *Mariner's Mirror*, 7 (1921), 162–7, 209–17.

Deals with attempts to regulate privateering. See also J. Le Pelley's articles on privateers, 1688–1713, ibid. 30 (1944), 22–37, 185–93.

1821 POWELL, J. W. D. Bristol privateers and ships of war. Bristol. 1930.

Cf. W. Branch Johnson, *Wolves of the channel, 1681–1856*, 1931, which is popular in treatment.

H. NAVAL VOYAGES

The voyages listed in this section are principally those made in royal ships, related but indirectly to political or diplomatic developments. For other voyages, see *Economic History, Social History,* and *Colonial History.* For published collections of voyages see nos. 2140 to 2147. The arrangement in the list below is by date of the expedition.

1822 DIGBY, SIR KENELM. Journal of a voyage into the Mediterranean . . . 1628. Ed. by J. Bruce. Camden Soc. 1868.

Virtually a privateering expedition, though commissioned officially.

1823 TEONGE, HENRY. The diary of Henry Teonge, chaplain aboard H.M.S. Assistance, Bristol, & Royal Oak. 1675–9. 1825. Ed. by G. E. Manwaring. 1927.

Excellent account of shipboard life during two Mediterranean voyages.

1824 DAMPIER, WILLIAM. I. A new voyage around the world . . . II. Voyages and descriptions . . . III. A voyage to New Holland [1699]. 3 vols. 1697–1709. Ed. by J. Masefield. 2 vols. 1906.

For the various edns. of the 1697 *New voyage,* the MS. of which is B.M. Sloane MS. 3236, see *D.N.B. sub* Dampier, and N. M. Penzer's preface to a new edn. by Sir A. Gray, 1927. *A voyage to New Holland,* originally publ. in two parts, 1703–9, was ed. by J. A. Williamson, 1939. Reprints of Dampier appear also in most collections of voyages e.g. Callender, Harris, Kerr. Critical comment on Dampier's conduct by a companion of the latter voyage, William Funnell, which appeared as *A voyage round the world . . .,* 1707, was answered by Dampier in his *Vindication,* 1707; the latter provoked John Welbe's *Answer to Captain Dampier's vindication,* [1707?]. On Funnell's charges see also B. M. H. Rogers in *Mariner's Mirror,* 10 (1924), 366–81. The latest scholarly biography is by W. H. Bonner, 1934; others are by W. C. Russell, 1889, and in popular style by C. Wilkinson, 1929.

1825 WAFER, LIONEL. A new voyage and description of the isthmus of America [1680–8]. Ed. by L. E. E. Joyce. (Hakluyt Soc.) Oxf. 1934.

First publ. 1699. Later edns. include Nathaniel Davis, *Expedition to the gold mines,* 1704.

1826 ROGERS, WOODES. A cruising voyage round the world (1708–11). 1712. Later edn. 1718. Ed. by G. E. Manwaring. 1928.

A famous account, often reprinted. An abridged edn. by R. C. Leslie bears the title, *Life aboard a British privateer in the time of Queen Anne.* Rogers's account of the rescue of Alexander Selkirk is said to have inspired Defoe's *Robinson Crusoe.* See also B. H. M. Rogers in *Mariner's Mirror,* 19 (1933), 198–211.

1827 COOKE, EDWARD. A voyage to the South Sea and round the world perform'd in the years 1708, 1709, 1710, and 1711. 2 vols. 1712.

VIII

ECONOMIC HISTORY

Although economic history has been greatly emphasized in recent decades, there is no general survey of the whole field for this period. The most comprehensive surveys are Cunningham (1837) and Lipson (1839). A useful brief survey is Clark (1836). There is, however, a growing number of monographs on a wide variety of subjects, and a growing volume of published source material. For developments of particular significance in the seventeenth century, important works are Clapham (1836 n.), Tawney (1846, 1870 n.), Unwin (1841), and Scott (2128). The *Economic History Review* (1927+), which publishes valuable lists of books and articles, is indispensable.

Many of the sources deal with the subjects of overseas trade, with economic theory, and with governmental policies related thereto (nos. 1832-3 and nos. 2075-6). For industrial change, the student must rely chiefly upon monographs, although more source material is being published. On financial matters, see especially Rogers (1871), Beveridge (1834), Ashton (2062), Dowell (2067), Horsefield (2043), Richards (2057), Shaw (2049 n.), but for public finance see also Ch. III, *Central Administration* (nos. 759-73). On agricultural developments see the separate Section B on *The Land*. Many titles relating to the economic change will be found also in Ch. IX, *Status and Class*, and in *Local History*.

Accounts of voyages which were made chiefly in the interest of economic expansion, under the auspices of private backers, are included in this section (nos. 2140-51); for those made by royal ships see *Naval History*; for those having the character of adventure by individuals, see *Social History* and *Cultural History*.

A. GENERAL WORKS

I. BIBLIOGRAPHY

1828 McCULLOCH, J. R. The literature of political economy. 1845. Repr. 1938.

A valuable bibliography, with extracts and descriptive notes. H. Hall's *Select bibliography for the study . . . of English mediaeval economic history*, 1914, contains many items that are useful also for later periods. Many general titles appear in J. B. Williams's *Guide* (see Pargellis, no. 923). For recent titles see the lists published in *Economic History Review*, 1927+. See also M. A. Arnould, *Vingt années de l'histoire économique et sociale, table analytique . . .*, Paris, 1953.

1829 PALGRAVE, SIR R. H. I., ed. Dictionary of political economy. 3 vols. 1894-9. Ed. by H. Higgs. 3 vols. 1925-6.

The articles and biographies contain short bibliographies. Useful especially for political theory.

1830 SHAW, W. A. Bibliography of the collection of books and tracts on commerce, currency and Poor Law (1557-1763) formed by Joseph Massie (died 1784). 1937.

Historical and bibliographical intro. by Shaw. The collection is from Br. Mus. Lansdowne MS. 1049. A short 'Bibliography . . . modern capitalism', by R. H. Tawney, is in *Econ. Hist. Rev.* 4 (1932–4), 336–56.

2. SOURCES

See Pargellis, pp. 123–5, for suggestions on the types of unpublished source materials on economic history, and where they may be found. See also the bibliographical appendices in Supple (1840). Contemporary works dealing with special subjects are listed in sections on *Land, Trade and Commerce* (e.g. Davenport, Mun, etc.), *Government Regulations*. Useful collections of short documents and excerpts are: A. E. Blank, P. A. Brown, and R. H. Tawney, *English economic history, select documents*, 1914; and R. H. Tawney and E. Power, *Tudor economic documents*, 3 vols., 1924.

1831 HOUGHTON, JOHN. A collection of letters for the improvement of husbandry and trade. 2 vols. 1681–3.

Houghton also started a weekly paper, *A collection for the improvement . . .*, 1691–1703; leading articles from it were repr. by R. Bradley, 4 vols., 1727–8; the stock and share list is repr. in Scott, *Joint stock companies* (2128).

1832 McCULLOCH, J. R., ed. A select collection of scarce and valuable economical tracts. 1859.

Sometimes referred to as 'Overstone's tracts' because the volume was privately pr. by Samuel J. Loyd, Baron Overstone. A valuable collection, including *An apology for the builder . . .*, 1685; and Defoe's *Giving alms no charity . . .*, 1704.
McCulloch published also a *Select collection of scarce and valuable tracts on commerce*, 1859, several items from which are listed (see *Trade and Commerce*, nos. 2078, 2080, 2083). The Economic Hist. Soc. issued a repr. of his *Early English tracts on commerce* [1856], Camb. 1954.

1833 PETTY, SIR WILLIAM. The economic writings of Sir William Petty, together with the observations upon the bills of mortality more probably by Captain John Graunt. Ed. by C. H. Hull. 2 vols. Camb. 1899. Bibl.

Includes *A treatise of taxes*, 1662; *The political anatomy of Ireland . . . to which is added . . . an account of the wealth and expences of England*, 1691; *Political arithmetick . . . concerning the extent and value of lands . . . of Great Britain*, 1690, repr. in Arber (62 n.). On the disputed authorship of the important *Natural and political observations . . . upon the bills of mortality* (1662, 5th edn. 1676), besides Hull's introduction, see W. L. Bevan, 'Sir William Petty: a study in English economic literature', *Publs. Amer. Econ. Assoc.* 9 (1894), 371–472; and Major Greenwood, *Jour. Royal Statistical Soc.* 91 (1928), 79–85. W. F. Willcox, however, in his edn. of 1939 (Baltimore) attributes the original statistical work in the *Natural . . . observations* to Graunt. For *Petty papers* see no. 2907. See also *Population*, § G *infra*. The *Life* by Lord E. G. Fitzmaurice, 1895, includes a list of Petty's works in an appendix. Cf. M. Pasquier, *Sir William Petty, ses idées économiques*, Paris, 1903. See also no. 4289.

3. LATER WORKS: GENERAL

1834 BEVERIDGE, SIR W. H., *et al.* Prices and wages in England from the twelfth to the nineteenth century. Vol. 1. 1939.

The first of a projected four-volume work, containing elaborate price tables for the 'mercantile era'. Until the other volumes are published, the student should still consult the pioneering works by Rogers (1871). See also Gras (1864), Nef (1963), Schumpeter (2064), and Usher (1965).

1835	CHAMBERS, J. D. The vale of Trent 1670–1800. Camb. 1957.

An essay on economic change in one region.

1836	CLARK, G. N. The wealth of England 1496–1760. (Home Univ. Lib.) 1946.

A useful survey with a brief bibliography. Another good short work is J. H. Clapham, *Concise economic history of Britain* (to 1750), Camb. 1930, later edn. 1949.

1837	CUNNINGHAM, W. The growth of English industry and commerce. Camb. 1882. 5th and 6th edns. 3 vols. Camb. 1910–21.

Still useful, though largely superseded by Lipson. A bibliography of Cunningham's works is in his *Progress of capitalism*, Camb. 1916. Sir W. Ashley's series of lectures printed as *The economic organisation of England*, 1914, 3rd edn. enl., 1949 (reissue, 1954), contains relatively little on the seventeenth century, but some useful bibliographical notes are provided. For general medieval background and useful bibliography, see also *Cambridge economic history of Europe*, ed. by J. H. Clapham *et al.*, vols. i–iii of a projected series, Camb. 1941–63.

1838	DOBB, M. H. Studies in the development of capitalism. 1946.

1839	LIPSON, E. The economic history of England. 3 vols. 1915–31. 5th and 6th edns. 3 vols. 1948–56.

Vols. ii and iii, 'The Age of mercantilism', appeared in 1931, after volume i had gone through 5 edns. Probably the best general work for the period. The main ideas are condensed into a single volume in *Growth of English society*, 1949. On economic policies during the Protectorate see M. P. Ashley (2152).

1840	SUPPLE, B. E. Commercial crisis and change in England 1600–1642; a study in the instability of a mercantile economy. Camb. 1959. Bibl.

Valuable analysis of trends in the textile trade and of currency fluctuations especially and their relationship to government policy and economic thought. Cf. J. D. Gould, 'The trade depression of the early 1620's', *Econ. Hist. Rev.*, 2nd Ser. 7 (1954), 81–8; F. J. Fisher, 'The sixteenth and seventeenth centuries: the dark ages in English economic history?', *Economica*, N.S. 24 (1957), 93; E. Hobsbawn, 'The crisis of the 17th century', *Past and Present*, nos. 5, 6 (1954); and H. R. Trevor-Roper, 'The general crisis of the 17th century', ibid., no. 16 (1959).

1841	UNWIN, G. Studies in economic history. Ed. by R. H. Tawney. 1927. Repr. 1958.

Selections from the work of a leader in the field. Important for the seventeenth century are the chapters on the Merchant Adventurers and on the Suffolk cloth industry. See also Fisher (2194).

4. LATER WORKS: ECONOMIC THOUGHT

On some of the practical applications of economic theories, see below under *Banking and Finance, Trade and Commerce,* and *Government Regulation.*

1842	FUZ, J. K. Welfare economics in English Utopias. The Hague. 1952. Bibl.

Deals with welfare ideas in Utopian writings of the period of mercantilism, from Francis Bacon to Bernard Mandeville. Scholarly.

1843 JAMES, M. 'The effect of the religious changes of the sixteenth and seventeenth centuries on economic theory and development.' *In* E. Eyre, ed. *European Civilization*, vol. v (pp. 5–111). 1937.

1844 JOHNSON, E. A. J. Predecessors of Adam Smith: the growth of English economic thought. 1937.

Includes studies of ten typical writers, several from the period; an appendix gives a useful list of the items of economic interest in the *Philosophical Transactions* (1665–1776). A scholarly account, with several chapters on the seventeenth century, is M. Beer, *Early British economics*, 1938. See also Supple (1840); T. S. Ashton, 'The relation of economic history to economic theory', *Economica*, N.S. 13 (1946), 82; and H. F. Kearney, 'The political background to English mercantilism, 1695–1700', *Econ. Hist. Rev.*, N.S. 11 (1959), 484–96.

1845 HECKSCHER, E. F. Mercantilism. 2 vols. 1935. Rev. edn. 2 vols. 1956.

Trans. from German by M. Shapiro, and first publ. in Swedish, 1931. An admirable guide to the study of the practices of the 'age of mercantilism', and in vol. ii, to the theories on the subject. His main points are reviewed in the author's article, 'Mercantilism', in *Econ. Hist. Rev.* 7 (1936), 44–54. Heckscher largely supersedes the classic by G. Schmoller, *The mercantile system and its historical significance* [from *Studien über die wirthschaftliche Politik Friedrichs des Grossen*, 1884], 1896. For a neo-Marxist presentation of mercantilism as an 'ideology' of its age see I. S. Plotnikov, *Merkantilizm*, Leningrad, 1935.

1846 TAWNEY, R. H. Religion and the rise of capitalism. 1926. (Pelican edn.) 1938.

Stimulating but controversial, tending to support Weber (1847), though distinguishing between early and later phases of Puritanism, in arguing the influence of religious changes upon economic activities. Among the numerous critics of the view represented by Tawney is H. W. Robertson, *Aspects of the rise of economic individualism*, Camb. 1933. Cf. C. H. George, 'English Calvinist opinions on usury, 1600–1640', *Jour. Hist. Ideas*, 18 (1957), 455–74; and C. H. and K. George, 'Protestantism and capitalism in pre-revolutionary England', *Church History*, 27 (1958). See also Grose (10), p. 164.

1847 WEBER, M. The Protestant ethic and the spirit of capitalism. 1930.

Trans. from the German *Gesammelte Aufsätze zur Religionssoziologie* (vol. i, 1920), after original printing in article form, 1904–5. A famous essay arguing a strong influence of Calvinism upon the growth of capitalism. This point of view is generally upheld also by E. Troeltsch in various writings, notably his *Social teaching of the Christian churches* (English trans.), 2 vols., 1931.

1848 WILSON, C. '"Mercantilism": some vicissitudes of an idea.' *Econ. Hist. Rev.*, 2nd Ser. 10 (1957), 181–8.

By Wilson also, *Mercantilism* (Historical Assoc. pamphlet no. 37), 1958; and 'The other face of mercantilism', *R.H.S. Trans.*, 5th Ser. 9 (1959), 81–101. Other valuable articles on the theory of mercantilism are: A. V. Judges, 'The idea of a mercantilist state', *R.H.S. Trans.*, 4th Ser. 21 (1939), 41–70; J. Viner, 'English theories of foreign trade before Adam Smith', *Jour. Pol. Econ.* 38 (1930), 249–301, 404–57; and Viner's 'Power versus plenty as objectives of foreign policy in the 17th and 18th centuries', *World Politics*, 1, no. 1 (1948).

B. THE LAND AND ITS USES

Rural development in the seventeenth century was everywhere affected by the commercialization of agriculture. Conditions differed greatly from locality to locality. But land hunger was widespread, and an active land market led to frequent changes in ownership both by purchase and by exchange. Landholders, under the stimulus of higher prices, sought to improve tenures, to make titles more secure, and to increase yields. If the ideas of the 'Improvers' were more evident in their books than in actual farming practices, changes in the latter were not wanting, though here again local differences were marked. In the first edn. of this book, Professor Davies rightly said: 'What literature gives us inadequately is a knowledge of actual farming practices.' It is to help fill this gap that scholars of the past two decades have worked most effectively, often with a new approach and with new techniques. The section on *Local History* (pp. 443–6) points to a veritable revolution in that field. Since the land and its uses are at the heart of local history, much of the work done affects both fields. The Orwins (1865) and G. E. Fussell (1851) were early in the field. Pioneering has been carried forward by W. S. Hoskins, H. P. Finberg, Mrs. Joan Thirsk, and others. The founding of the Agricultural History Society in 1954 has stimulated interest and provided a new outlet for productive research currently under way. Of the projected *Agrarian history of England and Wales*, vol. iv (1500–1640), ed. by J. Thirsk, was publ. Camb. 1967.

1. General

(a) *Bibliography*

Bibliographies of the books on husbandry written in the seventeenth century are included here because many of the works they list do not deal with farming in the narrow sense, but with widely assorted matters concerning the land, its products, and the entire rural economy. The older works from Weston down are still useful, but they have been supplemented, and often corrected by G. E. Fussell (1851), Mrs. Thirsk (1852), and others. In the field of serial publications, the splendid work of E. L. C. Mullins (23 n.) is outstanding. A number of historical journals provide useful lists of books and articles, and often contain excellent bibliographical articles. See especially: *Agricultural History Review*; *Economic History Review*; *Journal of Economic History* (N.Y.). A brief bibliography on farm tools is in vol. iii of Singer (2038).

1849　WESTON, R. Tracts on practical agriculture and gardening with a chronological catalogue of English authors on agriculture. 1769. 2nd edn. 1773.

Contains many errors, but is still useful, giving copies of tracts of which no separate copies now exist.

1850　McDONALD, D. Agricultural writers from . . . 1200 to 1800. Reproductions in facsimile and extracts from their actual writings . . . to which is added an exhaustive bibliography. 1908.

Bibl. is on pp. 199–224. Other useful lists are: C. W. Johnson, 'The early English agricultural writers', *Quarterly Journal of Agriculture*, 12 (Edin. 1841–2); J. Donaldson, *Agricultural biography . . . [with] writings . . . [from 1480]*, 1854; M. F. Moore, *Two select bibliographies of medieval historical study*, 1912, which extends to 1660; M. S. Aslin, *Catalogue of the printed books on agriculture published between 1471 and 1840*, Rothamsted, 1926, which is very good but not exhaustive; V. E. Hitz and I. L. Hawes, *List of publications on agriculture contained in the U.S. Department of Agriculture Library and in part those contained in the Library of Congress*, U.S. Dept. of Agric., Bibl. Contributions, no. 21, Wash. 1930; and E. E. Edwards, *Selected references on the history of English agriculture*, U.S. Dept. of Agric., Bibl. Contributions, no. 24, Wash. 1935. See also App. I in Prothero (1870).

1851   FUSSELL, G. E. Old English farming books from Fitzherbert to Tull, 1523 to 1730. 1947.

A collation of all the editions of the works on farming published in English during the period specified. Mr. Fussell has done by far the best bibliographical work on the subject. His first important work appeared in *The Bookman's Journal*, vols. 12–16 (1925–8). See also his 'Early Farming Journals', *Econ. Hist. Rev.* 3 (1932), 417–22; and 'Agriculture from the restoration to Anne', ibid. 9 (1938–9), 68–74.

1852   THIRSK, J. 'The content and sources of English agrarian history after 1500.' *Agricultural History Review*, 3 (1955), 66–79.

Rich materials on agricultural history are to be found also in publications by national and local historical societies, to which Mullins (23 n.) is the best guide; and in the Historical MSS. Commission *Reports*, for which Upton's *Guide* (p. 13), is useful for many 17th-century subjects.

See also T. J. Bezemer, *Dictionary of terms relating to agriculture, horticulture . . .*, 1934; and the *Catalogues* of the Royal Agricultural Library, Lond., and the Goldsmith's Library, both of which are rich in pamphlet material.

(b) *Sources*

Since England in the seventeenth century remained predominantly rural the sources which provide information on the land and its uses include a wide range of material, sometimes plentiful, often scattered. Diaries are worth examining (see *Social History*, pp. 351–2). Large numbers of deeds, wills, leases, manorial records, and farm accounts exist, both in print and in manuscript, and in both local and national archives. Catalogues of the British Museum, Public Record Office, the Bodleian, and other great libraries point the way to the large collections of manuscripts. Hubert Hall's 'Classified list of agrarian surveys in the P.R.O.', published in *Economica* ii (1922), though primarily medieval, includes much 17th-century material. One type of P.R.O. manuscript as yet scarcely tapped by the student of agricultural and rural history is the great collection of court records that deal with land cases and the affairs of country folk. Records of the Chancery, Star Chamber, and Court of Requests are among those that abound with little-mined ore of the kind, though it is regrettable that as yet the absence of proper indexing and calendaring makes their use a slow process. There is a good typescript index of the Star Chamber records for the reign of James I. *The Calendars of State Papers Domestic* furnish printed abstracts as well as references to the originals in the P.R.O. and are well worth consulting under such entries as corn, enclosures, drainage, and under the headings of individual counties. Local archivists are making progress in getting their MSS. in shape for the scholar's use, and many of them can furnish good handlists, and often typescript calendars. E. L. C. Mullins (23 n.) is the best guide to the printed materials in the serial publications.

Though uneven in quality, many of the contemporary descriptions of counties and regions are exceedingly valuable for their information regarding physical features, varieties of soil, local products, and sometimes their description of farming practices. Some like Blome (3107 n.) and Leigh (3201) deal with the country as a whole. Others are the work of local chorographers, e.g. Aubrey (3254, 3265), Carew (3144), Plot (3232), and Reyce (3249). The best guide to this material is Fussell (2352). See *Local History*.

1853 BAX, RICHARD. 'Account book of Richard Bax, a Surrey yeoman, 1648–1662.' *In* Gleanings after time. Ed. by G. L. Apperson. 1907.

Pages 205–21, repr. from *The Antiquary*.

1854 EYRE, ADAM. 'A dyurnall, or catalogue of all my accions and expenses . . .' *In* Yorkshire diaries. Surtees Society, 65. 1877.

Useful diary of a Yorkshire yeoman. Various records of family accounts, which contain information on estate management and on farming practices are listed under *Social History*. Examples are Fell (2221), Martindale (2458), Shuttleworth (2217), and Verney (2509).

1855 WILLS and inventories.

Besides furnishing many clues to the social and economic status of rural classes and their standard of living, such documents frequently contain information respecting the size and nature of holdings, crops, farm implements, and farm prices. Hundreds of MS. wills are in Somerset House and the diocesan registries, and in the local probate registries of county towns.

Some of the best printed digests of wills are *Lancashire and Cheshire wills*, Chetham Society, 28, 33, 51, 54, Manchester, 1857–61; *North Country wills*, Surtees Society, 2, 26, 38, 104, 110, 112, 121, 142, Durham, 1835–1929. See also *Trans. Lanc. and Cheshire Antiq. Soc.* 46 (1929), and Maddison and others in no. 2420. Examples of printed inventories are F. W. Steer, ed., *Farm and cottage inventories of Mid-Essex, 1635–1749*, Chelmsford, 1950; *Jacobean household inventories, 1606–1620*, Bedfordshire Record Soc. 20 (1928); and G. E. Kirk, ed., 'Wills, inventories and bonds . . . Temple Newsham . . . [Yorks.] 1612–1701', *Thoresby Soc. Misc. for 1933*, 33 (1934). For other titles consult Mullins (23 n.), and no. 2418.

(c) *Later Works*

Almost all of the standard works in economic history contain chapters or sections on agricultural developments in the seventeenth century, e.g. Ashley, Clark, Heaton, Lipson (see § A, pp. 261–3 *supra*). On prices see Beveridge (1834).

1856 ARKHANGEL'SKIY, S. I. Agrarnoe zakonodatel'stva epokh: Velikoy angliyskoy revolutsii 1643–1648. Pt. 1. Moscow. 1935.

'Agrarian legislation of the great English Revolution 1643–1648, Pt. 1.' Part 2, covering period from 1649 to 1660, Moscow and Leningrad, 1940. See also nos. 1946 and 1951.

1857   ASHLEY, SIR W. M. The bread of our forefathers. Oxf. 1928.

An analysis of the grains grown and used in England which adds significantly to social and agricultural history.

1858   BAKER, J. N. L. 'England in the seventeenth century.' *In* An historical geography of England before A.D. 1800. Ed. by H. C. Darby. Camb. 1936.

A good account of weather and climatic conditions as well as grain distribution.

1859   BLOMFIELD, R. The formal garden in England. 1892. 3rd edn. 1901. Repr. of 3rd edn. 1936.

1860   CAMPBELL, M. L. The English yeoman under Elizabeth and the early Stuarts. New Haven. 1942. 1947. Lond. 1960.

Based on a variety of sources; good bibliographical note, which is revised in the 1960 edn.

1861   FORDHAM, M. and T. R. The English agricultural labourer, 1300– 1925. 1925.

See also Fussell (2195); W. A. Hasback, *A history of the English agricultural labourer* (preface by Sydney Webb), 1908; and other works under *Status and Class* in Ch. IX.

1862   FUSSELL, G. E. and ATWATER, V. G. B. 'Agriculture of rural England in the 17th century.' *Economic Geography*, 9 (1933), 387 ff.

G. E. Fussell has been a pioneer in agricultural history. His interest and knowledge extend to every part of the farmer's life and work. See his *Farmer's tools*, 1952; and article in *J.M.H.* 7 (1935), 1–21, 129–40.

1863   GAUT, R. C. A history of Worcestershire agriculture and rural evolution. Worcester. 1939.

Cf. the excellent study by A. Ruston and D. Whitney, *Hooton Pagnell, the agricultural revolution of a Yorkshire village*, N.Y. 1934.

1864   GRAS, N. S. B. The evolution of the English corn market from the twelfth to the eighteenth century. Harvard Economic Studies, 13. Camb. (Mass.). 1915.

Along with Beveridge (1834), Gras furnishes a good corrective to Rogers on corn prices. With E. C. Gras the author also wrote *The economic and social history of an English village—Crawley—Hampshire* (Harvard Economic Studies, 34), 1930, giving a detailed and excellent analysis which uses a village as a 'microcosm of the great world of men and affairs'.

1865   GRAY, H. L. English field systems. Camb. (Mass.). 1915.

A pioneer work, and still useful; contains much important material from 17th-century records. Cf. C. S. and C. S. Orwin, *The open fields*, Oxf. 1938, 1954, 1967; and C. S. Orwin, *The history of English farming*, Edin. 1949.

1866   HABBAKUK, H. J. 'The market for monastic property, 1539–1603.' *Econ. Hist. Rev.*, 2nd Ser. 10 (1958), 362–80.

1867   HOSKINS, W. G. Essays in Leicestershire History. Liverpool. 1950.

Some of these deal with the 16th century, but many of the conditions described carry over into the 17th. See also *The midland peasant*, 1957, with good chapters on both

16th and 17th centuries. Not only Mr. Hoskins's conclusions but his methods of arriving at them make his works of outstanding usefulness.

1868 JOHNSON, A. H. The disappearance of the small landowner. Oxf. 1909.

A classic in its day; somewhat superseded by later researches. Also of some value, though dated, are R. M. Gautier, *History of the English landed interest . . .*, 2 vols., 1892–3, and his *Annals of British peasantry*, 1895.

1869 LENNARD, R. 'English agriculture under Charles II.' *Econ. Hist. Rev.* 4 (1932), 23–45.

Also by Lennard, *Rural Northamptonshire* (3221).

1870 PROTHERO, R. E. [Lord Ernle]. English farming past and present. 1912. 5th edn. 1936.

Something of a classic. Excellent bibliography on farming books. Supersedes his earlier work, *The pioneers and progress of English farming*, 1888. See also his *The land and its people: chapters in rural life and history*, 1925. Cf. M. E. Seebohm, *Evolution of the English farm*, 1927; and R. H. Tawney, *The agrarian problem in the sixteenth century*, 1912.

1871 ROGERS, J. E. T. History of agriculture and prices in England, 1259– 1793. 7 vols. Oxf. 1866–1902.

Vols. v and vi cover period 1583–1702. Both this and the author's *Six centuries of work and wages*, Oxf. 1884, have been largely supplanted by the work of Sir William Beveridge (1834), Gras, and others. Cf. H. L. Lutz, 'Inaccuracies in Rogers' History of Prices', *Quart. Jour. of Econ.* 23 (1908–9), 350 ff. See also A. P. Usher, 'Prices of wheat and commodity price indexes for England 1259–1930', *Harvard Rev. of Econ. Statistics*, 13 (1931), 103 ff.

1872 TROW-SMITH, R. English husbandry. 1951.

See also his *Society and the land*, 1953; and J. Thirsk, *English peasant farming: The agrarian history of Lincolnshire*, 1957.

2. Husbandry, Horticulture, and Gardening

(a) *Sources: General*

Many of the earlier books on farming were wholly or largely translations of the works of continental writers, well sprinkled with quotations from classical authors. But increasingly throughout the 17th century more books came from English pens. They frequently went through many editions, often with additional sections and interpolations. Authors borrowed shamelessly from each other and from their predecessors without acknowledgement and it is difficult to sort out the original from the borrowed. G. E. Fussell (1851) has done the best bibliographical work on the farming books. They are often a mixture of absurd lore and useful suggestions, but are valuable for showing the increasing interest in the improvement of agriculture, and often provide useful observations on local conditions and practices.

Two 16th-century books, frequently republished and widely read in the 17th century are Thomas Tusser, *A hundred good points of husbandry*, 1557 (see Read, no. 2613) and Barnabie Googe's translation of Conrad Heresbach, *Foure bookes of husbandry*, 1577 (Read, no. 2601).

1873 MARKHAM, GERVASE. The English husbandman. 2 parts. 1613, 1615.

Markham wrote voluminously and his books remained popular throughout the century. A general compilation of his writings was published under the title: *A way to get wealth: containing sixe principall vocations or callings in which every good husband or housewife may lawfully imploy themselves*, Part i, 6th edn., 1631. It was revised many times afterward almost always 'enlarged'. Included in it were his *Country contentments*, 1611; *The English huswife*, 1618; and *Farewell to husbandry*, 1620. See nos. 2209, 2255.

1874 PLATTES, GABRIEL. A discovery of infinite treasure . . . in the way of husbandry. 1639.

Repr. under the title of *Practical husbandry improved*, 1656. Plattes, like Markham, was one of the most widely read of the writers on husbandry. Another popular work by him was *The profitable intelligencer, containing many rare secrets and experiments in agriculture*, 1644. Also attributed to Plattes (but thus far no copies have been found) is *A treatise of husbandry*, 1638; *Recreatio agriculturae*, probably 1640; and *Observations and implements in husbandry*, probably 1653. Another book sometimes attributed to Plattes (thought by some to be the work of C. Dymock) is *An essay for the advancement of husbandry . . .*, 1651. See also no. 1886 n.

1875 BLITH, WALTER. The English improver: or, a new survey of husbandry . . . 1649. Later edns. 1649. 1652. 1653.

Some interesting illustrations of farming implements. The 'third Impression much augmented' 1652, which appeared as *The English improver improved: or The survey of husbandry surveyed*, contains 'six newer Peeces of Improvement', among which was the introduction of clover and sainfoin. Often said to be the best treatise on 17th-century agriculture. On Markham and Blith see 'The English improvers', by Sir William Ashley, in *Mélanges d'histoire offerts à Henri Pirenne*, Brussels, 1926. Other early books on improving are Edward Maxey, *A new instruction of ploughing and setting corne*, 1601; and *A direction to the husbandman . . . [on] fertiling [sic] . . .*, 1634 (*S.T.C.*, 6902).

1876 WESTON, SIR RICHARD. A discourse of husbandrie used in Brabant and Flanders: shewing the wonderful improvement of land there; and serving as a pattern for our practice in this commonwealth. Ed. by S. Hartlib. 1650. Later edns.

Especially important for sheep-farming. See also R. Child, *A large letter concerning the defects and remedies of English husbandry*, 1651.

1877 HARTLIB, SAMUEL. Samuel Hartlib his legacie. 1651.

Actually an expansion of Weston (1876), as Hartlib acknowledged, which went through many edns. Repr. by G. Reeve as *Directions left by a gentleman to his sons for the improvement of barren and healthy land*, 1670, 1674. Hartlib's great work was in editing and publishing the works of others, and unlike Markham he did not claim authorship for them, though it is not always clear who their authors were. Among the works sponsored by Hartlib are: *Essay for the advancement of husbandry and learning, or propositions for the erecting a college of husbandry*, 1651 (possibly by Cressy Dymock); *The reformed husbandman*, probably 1651; *Discoverie for division or setting out of land . . . for direction . . . of the adventurers and planters in the fens*, 1653 (possibly also by Dymock); *The compleat husbandman*, 1659. See also nos. 1902 n., 2905, 2934–6. For Dymock see Wing (4).

1878 YARRANTON, ANDREW. The great improvement of lands by clover. 1663.

Cf. G. E. Fussell, 'The first English book on clover and its author', *Ministry of Agriculture Journal*, 41 (1934), 353–8. Other specific types of improvement are dealt with in John S[haw], *Certain plaine . . . demonstrations . . . for the improving . . . of barren land*, 1675; Adolphus [? Adam] Speed, *Adam out of Eden; or an abstract of divers experiments . . .*, 1658 [1659?]; J. Forster, *England's happiness increased . . .* [by planting of potatoes], 1664; *England's improvement . . . and advice . . .* [on hemp and flaxseed], 1691; and Leonard Meager, *A mystery of husbandry: or arable pasture and woodland improved*, 1697.

1879 W[ORLIDGE], J[OHN]. Systema agriculturae: or the mystery of husbandry discovered . . . 1669. Later edns. 1675. 1681. 1687. 1716.

This was the most systematic work on agriculture yet published. In addition to a description of the operations, crops, and implements of the farm, its calendar of monthly directions for husbandmen and the dictionary 'of Rustic terms' are invaluable. The later edns. were 'enlarged' as was the common practice. *The Treatise of husbandry*, 1675, attributed to Worlidge, is probably the second edn. of the *Systema*.

Another popular compilation was J[ohn] B[lagrave], *The epitome of the art of husbandry*, 1669, many later edns.

1880 DONALDSON, J. Husbandry anatomized; or an enquiry into the present manner of tilling and manuring the ground in Scotland. 2 pts. in 2 vols. Edin. 1697–8.

First printed, Edin. 1696. The best contemporary picture of Scottish farming.

1881 M[ORTIMER], JOHN. The whole art of husbandry; or, the way of managing and improving of land. 1707. Later edns. 1708. 1712. 2 vols. 1721. 2 vols. 1761.

The best and most complete work on practical farming which had yet appeared. The second edition has a second part 'containing such additions as are proper for the husbandman and gardiner', and a 'Countryman's kalendar, what he is to do every month in the year'. The 5th edn., 1721, is in 2 vols.; the 6th, 1761, was enl. and rev. by T. Mortimer.

See also Timothy Nourse, *Campania foelix: or a discourse of the benefits and improvements of husbandry*, 1700, which is a section of a book that deals with various aspects of rural community life.

(b) *Special Subjects:*
Accounts, Orchards, Vineyards, Gardens

Quite different from the above 'husbandry books' with their mixture of theory and sometimes impractical hints are descriptions of the way in which farming was actually carried on, either in connection with farm accounts, or in relation to such specialized activities as the development of orchards, vineyards, and gardens. The increasing attention paid to the 'kitchen garden' with its vegetables and medicinal herbs, and to flower gardens, is evident from special chapters in husbandry books as well as from works published separately.

Various titles on 'food' and 'tobacco' are listed in § C, *Industry*.

1882 BEST, HENRY. Henry Best's farming book, or Rural economy in Yorkshire in 1641. Ed. by C. B. Robinson. Surtees Soc. Vol. 33. Durham. 1857.

A detailed account of farming methods and interests among the minor gentry and yeomen of the East Riding.

1883   LODER, ROBERT. Robert Loder's farm accounts, 1610–1620. Camden Soc. 3rd Ser. 53 (1936).

Itemized account of yearly expenditures, profits, and losses of a Berkshire farmer with his shrewd comments on the results, and an excellent critical introduction by G. E. Fussell.

1884   GARDINER, RICHARD. Profitable instructions for the manuring, sowing, and planting of kitchen gardens. 1599. 2nd edn. 1603.

Cf. John Parkinson, *Paradisi in sole, paradisus terrestris,* . . ., 1629, 1656, which deals with various types of gardens and orchards.

1885   LAWSON, WILLIAM. The fruiterer's secrets. 1604.

Repr. in the 1631 edn. of Markham's *Way to get wealth* (1873 n.), with the authorship acknowledged. Also appropriated by Markham for the 1631 edn. were Lawson's *A new orchard and garden*, 1618, and N. F., *The husbandman's faithful orchard*, 1608. Lawson's work was repr. with a preface by E. S. Rohde, 1927.

1886   DESIGNE FOR PLENTY, by universall planting of fruit trees. 1652.

Possibly by Cressy Dymock; repr. in *Samuel Hartlib's legacie* (1877). See also *The countryman's recreation or three books of planting, graffing and gardening*, c. 1640, the author of which was possibly Thomas Barber of Bracemeale, Salop, although the work has frequently been attributed to Gabriel Plattes.

1887   AUSTEN, RALPH. A treatise of fruit trees, showing the manner of planting, grafting, pruning . . . Oxf. 1653. Later edns. 1657. 1665.

In 1658 Austen published *Observations upon some parts of Sir Francis Bacon's history as it concerns fruit-trees*, and the *Observations* were added to the 1665 edn. of the *Treatise*.

1888   SHARROCK, ROBERT. The history of the propagation & improvement of vegetables, . . . Oxf. 1660. 2nd edn. enl. Oxf. 1672.

Reissued 1694, under the title of *An improvement to the art of gardening*. Other works on gardening are by Stephen Blake, 1664 (Wing, B 3139); A. Mollet, *The garden of pleasure* . . ., 1670; and Leonard Meager, *The English gardener*, 1670, many later edns. to 1710. Modern edns. of works from this period are I. Elstor, ed., *The garden book of Sir Thomas Hammer, bart.*, 1933; and *Two manuals of gardening from English manuscript notebooks of the seventeenth century in the library of Rachel McMasters (Miller) Hunt*, 2 vols., Pittsburgh, 1952.

1889   HUGHES, WILLIAM. The compleat vineyard. 1665. Later edns. 1670 and 1683.

The cultivation of the vine on the continental model was a favourite project among literary farmers. The 2nd edn. was enlarged above one half. See also Hughes, *The flower garden*, 1683.

1890   BEALE, J[OHN]. Nurseries, orchards, profitable gardens and vineyards encouraged . . . in several letters . . . directed to Henry Oldenburg, Esq., Secretary of the Royal Society. 1677.

One letter is by Anthony Lawrence, who is sometimes listed as joint author. See also I. B[eale?], *Herefordshire orchards* . . ., 1657, written as letters to S. Hartlib; and the works of J[ohn] W[orlidge], *Vinettum Brittanicum, or a treatise of cider,* 1676; *Systema horti-culturae* [in three books], 1677, and *The most easie method for making . . . cider,* 1687. See also no. 1879.

1891 EVELYN, JOHN. 'Pomona.' Printed as 'An appendix concerning fruit trees in relation to cider', in *Sylva* (1955). 1664. Many later edns.

See also his *Directions for the gardiner at Says-Court* . . . (date uncertain), repr. 1932. Evelyn did a good deal of translating, including *The compleat gardener, with directions concerning melon and orange trees,* from the French of Quintinie (or F. Gentil?), 1693, 'To which is added Kalendarium rusticum . . . and dictionarium rusticum by J. W. gent.' (see no. 1879). *Of gardens,* publ. by Evelyn in 1673, a trans. from the Latin of René Rapin, said to have been made by Evelyn's son.

Other works on fruit trees are Francis Drope, *A short and sure guide in the practice of raising and ordering of fruit trees,* Oxf. 1672; Charles Cotton, *Planter's manual,* 1675, often reprinted; Moses Cook, 1676 (Wing, C 6032); and T. Langford, 1681, 1696 (Wing, L 388–9).

1892 REID, JOHN. The Scots gardner. 2 pts. Edin. 1683. 2nd edn. Edin. 1721.

Repr. with several additional tracts under title *The Scots gardener for the climate of Scotland,* Edin. 1766.

1893 ROHDE, E. S. The story of the garden. 1932.

See also D. B. Green, *Gardener to Queen Anne: Henry Wise (1653–1738) and the formal garden,* 1956, bibl. A brief bibliography on landscape gardening by E. W. Mainwaring is in *Yale University Library Gazette,* 22 (1948), 81–6.

3. ANIMAL HUSBANDRY AND APICULTURE

(a) *Sources*

(1) *Animal Husbandry*

Stock breeding on a wide scale awaited the 18th-century 'Improvers'. But already pioneering was in progress, and some knowledge concerning the care of animals and the treatment of disease, especially among sheep, received attention. Since horsemanship was a skill valued by gentlemen, and racing was already a favourite sport, the care and the training of horses early aroused interest. Widely read, with several edns. in this period, was Leonard Mascall's *Government of cattell* (Read, no. 2604).

1894 MARKHAM, GERVASE. Cavalrice: or the English horseman, contayning all the arte of horsemanship, as much as is necessary for any man to understand, whether he be horse-breeder, horse-ryder, . . . or sadler, etc. 1607.

The most important of Markham's many books on horses. To the seven books of the first and second (1616–17) edns. an eighth book was added in the 1625 edn. Consult also Markham's *Discourse on horsemanship,* 1593, and other similar titles in *S.T.C.* Somewhat more general in nature was his *Cheape and good husbandry for the well-ordering of all beasts and fowles, . . .,* 1614. Helpful hints on the care of poultry and animals were included in many of his husbandry books (1873).

1895 CRAWSHEY, JOHN. The country-man's instructor . . . containing many remedies for the diseases commonly befalling to horses, sheepe, and other cattle. 1635.

> The fifth edn. appeared under the title of *The good husband's jewel* . . ., 1661. Publ. in 1636 were *The English farrier or countryman's treasure* (anonymous), and *The honest and plaine deeling farrier*, by Thomas Grymes. Later works on farriery were by Thomas De la Gray [or DeGray], 1639 (*S.T.C.*, 12205), R. Barrett, 1660 (Wing, B 914), R. Almond, 1673 (Wing, A 2897); and E.R., (?)1680, 1691 (Wing, R 13).

1896 NEWCASTLE, WILLIAM CAVENDISH, 1st DUKE OF. Méthode et invention nouvelle de dresser les chevaux. Antwerp. 1658. Later edn. Lond. 1737.

> Trans. in *A general system of horsemanship*, 2 vols. in 1, 1743. Newcastle wrote a 2nd edn. 1677, with many repr. See also Huth (2253).

1897 LAMBERT, JAMES. The countryman's treasure; showing the nature, causes and cure of all diseases incident to cattel. 1676. 2nd edn. 1683. Later edns.

> See also Michael Harward, *The herds-man's mate* , . ., Dublin, 1673; and *The country-man's companion*, by Philotheos Physiologus (i.e. Thomas Tryon), 1684.

1898 A TREATISE OF OXEN, sheep, hogs, and dogs . . . How to chuse, govern and preserve them in health. 1683.

> Describes the best kind of cattle to buy for various purposes.

1899 BLOME, RICHARD. The gentleman's recreation. In two parts. The first being an encyclopedy of the arts and sciences . . . The second treats of horsemanship, hawking, . . . 1686.

> Interesting passages, especially about different breeds of sheep.

1900 S., A. The husbandman, farmer and grasier's compleate instructor. 1697.

> Attributed uncertainly to Ad. Speed. Deals with buying, selling, breeding, and fattening cattle.

(2) *Apiculture*

The most commonly used supplement to sugar in a 17th-century household was honey; and a few bee hives were among the possessions of almost every farmer. Among the gentry apiculture became something of a fad; hence the popularity of treatises on bees.

1901 BUTLER, CHARLES. The feminine monarchie: or, a treatise concerning bees, and the due ordering of them. Oxf. 1609. Later edn. Oxf. 1634.

> One of the most popular treatises on bee-keeping. The edn. of 1634 adopts phonetic spelling. It was translated into Latin under the title of *Monarchia foeminina, sive apum historia, interprete R. Ricardi*, 1673.

1902 LEVETT, JOHN. The ordering of bees. 1634.

> See Markham's 'The best husbandry of bees' included in his *The making of orchards* (repr. in 1873). Other works on bees are Samuel Hartlib, *Reformed commonwealth of bees . . . with the reformed Virginia silkworm*, 1655, included in the 1655 edn. of *Samuel*

Hartlib his legacie (1877); J. Gedde, *A newe discovery of an excellent method of bee houses and colonies* . . ., 1675, 1676, 1722, reissued and enl., as *The English apiary*, 2 pts., 1721–2; M. Rusden, 1679 (Wing, R 2313), and John Worlidge, 1676 (Wing, W 3594), and his *Complete bee master*, 1698.

(b) *Later Works*

1903 ALLISON, K. J. 'Flock management in the sixteenth and seventeenth centuries.' *Econ. Hist. Rev.*, 2nd Ser. 11 (1958), 98–112.

1904 FUSSELL, G. E. Animal husbandry in eighteenth century England. 1937.

See also his articles: 'Size of English cattle in the 18th century' and 'Animal husbandry in 18th century England' in *Agricul. Hist.* 3 (1929), 160–8; 11 (1937), 96–116, 189–214.

1905 SKEEL, C. A. J. 'Cattle trade between Wales and England.' *R.H.S. Trans.*, 4th Ser. 9 (1926), 135–58.

1906 TROW-SMITH, R. A history of British livestock husbandry to 1700. 1957. Bibl.

Chaps. 5 and 6 deal with the Tudor and Stuart periods.

4. The Manor, Tenure, Enclosures, Drainage

(a) *Bibliography and Sources*

Manorial organization lasted far longer than is sometimes thought, and much longer in some sections than in others. But changes affecting tenure, the exchange and consolidation of holdings, and disputes over lingering manorial obligations are a commonplace throughout the 17th century. They were a part of the struggle by which both landlords and tenants sought to keep or to gain security, and to turn the current shifts in rents and prices to their own advantage. The litigation which often accompanied these efforts called frequently for a restatement of manorial customs (now sometimes being written down for the first time); for more expert surveying; and often for more accurate extents, surveys, and terriers than either landlord or tenant had had before. It is largely the records of these activities, together with leases, deeds of bargain and sale, and the court records that provide the historian with materials for reconstructing this chapter of the past. They abound in manuscript and in print in local collections as well as in the great libraries and national repositories. The most recent and complete bibliography of printed materials is Mullins (23 n.).

(1) *Bibliography*

1907 DAVENPORT, F. G. A classified list of printed original materials for English manorial and agrarian history during the middle ages. Radcliffe College Monographs, no. 6. Boston. 1894.

Contains much material also for the 16th and 17th centuries. Has in general been superseded by later bibliographies, but still has some useful features.

1908 HALL, HUBERT. 'A classified list of agrarian surveys in the P.R.O.'
Economica, 2 (1922), 28–50.

1909 HONE, N. J. The Manor and manorial records. 1906.
Useful bibliography of both printed and manuscript materials.

(2) *Sources*

Many local record offices provide calendars and abstracts of deeds, leases, and
similar materials. Examples are the 'Salt Charters' in the MSS. of the William
Salt Library at Stafford; the 'Exeter deeds and documents' in the Exeter library;
and similar collections in the Essex and Bedford archives. Printed calendars and
abstracts of deeds, leases, bonds, and rentals, of which the following are examples,
are to be had in local publications: *Bradford Hist. and Antiq. Soc. Pub.*, 2nd Ser.,
Pts. 1–3, 1931–6; *Glouc. Notes and Queries*, 6 (1899); *Kent Records*, 7 (1922);
Somerset and Dorset Notes and Queries, 9 (1905); *Sussex Rec. Soc. Pub.*, 29 (1925);
Trans. Cumb. and Westmorland Antiq. Soc., N.S. 14, 38 (1914, 1938). Consult
Mullins (23 n.) for additional material.

(a) Printed Manorial Records

1910 ABSTRACTS of Gloucestershire and Wiltshire post-mortem inquisitions.
The Index Library, 21, 22 (1893, 1897).

These documents are not to be trusted on land values, but they provide a key to land
measurements and to the character of holdings in different localities. The post mortem
inquisitions for all counties are included in the MSS. of the Chancery records in the
P.R.O.

1911 MANORIAL SOCIETY PUBLICATIONS. 14 vols. 1907–26.

The society published several *Monographs* also, 1907–10. Its *Publications* provide
reprints and in some cases facsimile reproductions of contemporary manuals on manorial
principles and practices that were much read though not always followed in practice.
Examples are the anonymous *A manor and court baron*, Repr., no. 3, 1909, which is one
of the best manuals; *A fac-simile reproduction of the order of keeping a court leet and court
baron* (1650 edn.), Repr. no. 8, 1914, another manual; William Barlee, *Concordance of
all written lawes concerning lords of manors, their free tenants, and copieholders*, Repr. no. 6,
1911; and Sir Charles Calthrop, *The relation between the lord of the manor and the copy
holder his tenant* (publ. 1635), Repr. no. 10, 1917. See also *Legal History* (nos. 1090–3).

1912 'ANCIENT CUSTOMS of the manor of Hendon, Middlesex 1685.'
London and Middlesex Archaeol. Soc. Trans., N.S. 7 (1937), 545–92.

Text of presentment. Materials on Hendon surveys are ibid. 234–80, 528–44.

1913 CHARLESWORTH, J., ed. 'Wakefield manor book, 1709.' *Yorks.
Archaeol. Soc. Rec. Ser.* 101. 1939.

Comprehensive account, probably compiled by the deputy steward for the new owner,
the Duke of Leeds. For other Yorkshire records see: T. W. Hall, *A descriptive catalogue
of . . . manorial records relating to lands in . . . the neighborhood of Sheffield*, Sheffield,
1937; Sir. T. Lawson-Tancred, *Records of a Yorkshire manor*, 1937, and his edn. of
Aldborough court rolls publ. in *Yorks. Arch. Jour.* 35 (1941), 201–16.

1914 CUNNINGHAM, W., ed. Common rights at Cottenham and Stretham
in Cambridgeshire. *Camd. Soc. Misc.* xii (1910).
Early 17th century.

1915 COPINGER, W. A. Manors of Suffolk. 7 vols. 1905–12.

Documentary material for a large group of Suffolk manors. Cf. the same author's *County of Suffolk* (3248). For similar works, such as M. Dodds, *History of Northumberland*, see Ch. XI.

1916 FOX, SIR J. C., ed. The Lady Ivie's trial for the great part of Shadwell. Oxf. 1929.

Record of a case in 1684, relating to the title of the dean and chapter of St. Paul's.

1917 GARSIDE, B. The ancient manor courts of Hampton-on-Thames during the 17th century. Pts. 1–2. 1948–9.

Privately printed. Also by Garside and privately printed: *The manor, lordship, and great parks of Hampton Court during the 16th and 17th centuries . . .*, 1951; *People and homes in Hampton on Thames in the 16th and 17th centuries*, 1956; and *The landes and fields of Hampton town during the 17th century*, 1953.

1918 KERRIDGE, E., ed. Surveys of the manors of Philip, first earl of Pembroke and Montgomery, 1631–1632. Devizes. 1953.

Wiltshire Arch. and Hist. Soc., Records Branch, vol. 9. Surveys of some twenty manors, with some useful comment. Cf. two volumes by H. A. Wyndham, Lord Leconfield, on properties of the earls of Northumberland: *Petworth manor in the seventeenth century*, 1954, and *Sutton and Duncton manors*, 1956; see also *Estate accounts of the earls of Northumberland, 1562–1637*, ed. by M. E. James (Surtees Soc. Pub. 163), 1955. Documents relating to several Wiltshire manors are quoted in *The progress notes of Warden Woodward, 1659–75*, ed. by R. L. Rickard (Wiltshire Arch. and Nat. Hist. Soc., Records Branch, 13), 1957.

1919 MARCHAM, W. and MARCHAM, F., eds. Court rolls of the Bishop of London's manor of Hornsey, 1603–1701. 1929.

1920 NORDEN, JOHN. The surveiors dialogue, very profitable for all men to peruse, but especially for gentlemen, farmers, and husbandmen. 1607. Later edns. 1610 and 1618.

The first four books deal with surveys of manors and the relations between lords of manors and tenants; the fifth treats of 'different natures of ground'. An additional vol. in the third edn. includes points to be considered by purchasers.

Other works on surveying are: William Folkingham, *Feudigraphia the synopsis . . . of surveying methodised*, 1610; Aaron Rathborne, *The surveyor*, 1616; O. Wallinby, *Planometria, or the whole art of surveying land*, 1650; and G. Attwell, *The faithful surveyor*, 1662. Often quoted in the period also was John Fitzherbert's 1539 volume on *Surveying*.

1921 ROWE, JOHN. The book of John Rowe, steward of the manors of Lord Bergavenny, 1597–1622. Ed. by W. H. Godfrey. (Sussex Rec. Soc. Pub. 34.) Camb. 1928.

Excellent. Illuminating material on some fifteen Sussex manors at the close of the 16th century is contained in E. Straker's edn. of *The Buckhurst terrier, 1597–1598* (Sussex Rec. Soc. Pub. 39), Lewes, 1933. Accounts of the steward of a north country manor are contained in 'James Jackson's diary, 1650–1683', ed. by F. Grainger, *Westmorland Antiq. and Arch. Soc.*, N.S. 21 (1921), 96–129.

1922 SMITH, JOHN, of Nibley. Lives of the Berkeleys, III. Gloucester.
    1885.

Manors of the hundred of Berkeley in Gloucestershire, described by Smyth, who was
for forty years steward of the hundred.

(b) Enclosures

Enclosures did not create the stir in the 17th century that they did in the 16th
when anti-enclosure legislation was passed, or that they were again to do in the
18th century when the statute books were filled with private parliamentary
enclosure acts. But it has long been known that enclosure continued throughout
the century. Sometimes this occurred in sufficiently large amounts to excite
protest; but oftener it was done by piece-meal methods, and frequently by agreement of both landlord and tenants. Lands long utilized for both arable and
pasture were enclosed, and as well new land was reclaimed from fen, forest, and
waste. There were still some writers who spoke out against the practice, but the
undeniable fact that enclosed land brought greatly increased yields was destined
to win the day in an age which saw the commercialization of agriculture.

1923 TRIGGE, FRANCIS. To the king's most excellent majestie. The
    humble petition of two sisters; the Church and Commonwealth: for the
    restoring of their ancient commons and liberties. 1604.

Trigge's petition against the enclosure of commons belongs to the sheep-breeding,
pasture-farming movement of the reign of Elizabeth.

1924 [CHURTON, R.] An olde thrifte newly revived . . . 1612.

Sometimes attrib. to R. Chambers. See Prothero (1870), 1912 edn., p. 424.

1925 POWELL, ROBERT. Depopulation arraigned, convicted, and con-
    demned by the lawes of God and man. 1636.

Powell complains that the evil of inclosures was never more 'monstrous' than at the
time when he wrote. See on the other side G. Plattes's *Discovery of infinite treasure*
(1874).

1926 HALHEAD, HENRY. Inclosure thrown open; or, depopulation depopu-
    lated, not by spades and mattocks, but by the word of God, the laws of the
    land, and solid arguments. 1650.

The work is prefaced by 'an address to the reader' by J. Sprigge of Banbury. It probably
belongs to a group of pamphlets dealing with the midland counties, where enclosure was
again extremely active.

1927 TAYLOR, SILVANUS. Common good, or, the improvement of com-
    mons, forrests, & chasses by inclosure. (An appendix, shewing the chiefe cause
    of wandring poor in England.) 1652.

'The two great nurseries of idleness and beggery', says Taylor, 'are ale-houses and
commons.' Cf. E.G., *Wast land's improvement, or certain proposals made and tendred to
the consideration of the honourable committee appointed by Parliament, . . .,* 1653, in which
the writer's view is that 'robberies, theft, burglaries, rapes, and murders receive their
nourishment and encouragement' from unenclosed wastes. See also Adam Moore,
Bread for the poor . . ., 1653.

1928 MOORE, JOHN. The crying sin of England, of not caring for the poor, wherein inclosure . . . is arraigned, convicted, and condemned by the word of God. 1653.

This treatise provoked a war of pamphlets. It was answered by 'Pseudomisius' in *Considerations concerning common-fields and inclosures . . . partly to answer some passages in another discourse by Mr. J. Moore under the title of 'The crying sinne . . .'*, 1654. Moore replied with *A scripture-word against Inclosure . . .*, 1656. This second treatise was partly an answer to Joseph Lee (q.v.). Pseudomisius again replied in *A vindication of considerations concerning common-fields and inclosures . . .*, 1656.

1929 LEE, JOSEPH. Εὐταξία τοῦ Ἀγροῦ, or a vindication of a regulated inclosure. Wherein is plainly proved, that inclosure of commons in general, and the inclosure of Catthorpe . . . in particular, are both lawful and laudable. 1656.

In this treatise Lee defends the enclosure of Catthorpe Common. See Wing, L 843A.

1930 CLARK, G. N., ed. 'Enclosure by agreement at Marston, near Oxford.' *E.H.R.* 42 (1927), 87–94.

Note and text of an enclosure record of 1660. Cf. W. H. Hosford, 'An eye-witness's account of a seventeenth-century enclosure', *Econ. Hist. Rev.*, 2nd ser. 4 (1951), 215–20, based on account of the enclosure of the parish of Claythorpe, Lincolnshire.

(c) Drainage

The first great engineering project for the aid of agriculture was the drainage of the fen country, planned and for the most part carried through in the reign of James I. But less spectacular and smaller drainage projects were carried out wherever marsh lands could be recaptured by the industrious and aggressive farmer.

1931 A TRUE REPORT of certaine wonderfull overflowings of waters, now lately in Summerset-shire, Norfolke, and other places in England. 1607.

Anonymous. An enlarged second edn. was entitled, *More strange newes of wonderfull accidents*, n.d. Urging action for reclamation is H.C., *A discourse concerning the drayning of fennes and surrounded grounds in the sixe counteys of Norfolke, Suffolke, Cambridge, with the Isle of Ely, Huntingdon, Northampton, and Lincolne*, 1629. Cf. I.L., *A discourse concerning the great benefit of drayning and embanking*, 1641.

1932 BURRELL, ANDREWES. A briefe relation discovering plainely the true causes why the great levell of fennes . . . have been drowned. 1642.

Burrell, who was employed by the Earl of Bedford on fen drainage, criticizes the engineering works. He refers more particularly to Vermuyden's work in his *Exceptions against Sir C. Virmudens discourse for the drainage of the great fennes . . .*, 1642.

1933 VERMUIDEN [or Vermuyden], SIR CORNELIUS. A discourse touching the drayning of the great fennes lying within the several counties of Lincolne, Northampton, Huntingdon, Norfolke, Suffolke, Cambridge, and the Isle of Ely. 1642.

Vermuyden, who was the engineer employed to drain the fens for the 'Undertakers', in this work defends his methods. See also *The anti-projector or the history of the fen project*, 1646; and *A narrative of all the proceedings in the drainage of the great level of the fens*, by N.N., 1661, repr. in A. Lang's *Social England illustrated* (edn. 1903), pp. 407 ff.

1934 POWELL, SIR NATHANIEL. A remonstrance of some decrees and other proceedings of the Commissioners of Sewers for the upper levels in the counties of Kent and Sussex. 1659.

Thomas Harlachenden 'published' but apparently did not print 'Animadversions' on several material passages in this book: to which Powell replied with *The Animadverter animadverted*, 1663. Both books contain copious extracts from records.

1935 DUGDALE, SIR WILLIAM. History of imbanking and drayning of divers fennes and marshes, both in foreign parts and in this kingdom . . . 1662. Later edn. by C. N. Cole. 1772.

A valuable collection of material. The edn. of 1772 was revised and corrected, and adds three indices. Dugdale's Diary, while making a tour of the district in 1657, remains in Lansdowne MSS. 722. Among the collections of material which he made, the 'Survey of the Fens' (possibly by R. Atkins), drawn up in July, 1605, is preserved in the Harleian MSS. 5011. Cf. W. Dodson, *The designe for the perfect draining of the great level of the fens*, 1665.

1936 MOORE, SIR JONAS. History or narrative of the great level of the fens called Bedford Level: with a large map of the said level, as drained, surveyed, and described. 1685.

As surveyor of the drainage works Moore speaks with authority. See also C. N. Cole ed., *A collection of laws which form the constitution of the Bedford Level Corporation*, 1761, 2nd edn., 1803, which is valuable for texts of documents.

(b) *Later Works*

1937 BERESFORD, M. W. 'Glebe terriers and open field Leicestershire.' *Trans. Leic. Arch. Soc.* 24 (1949), 77–126.

See by the same author, 'Lot Aires', *Econ. Hist. Rev.* 13 (1943), 74–80; and *History on the ground: Six studies in maps, and landscapes*, 1957. The latter is designed primarily perhaps for the general reader. It contains interesting illustrative material for both 16th and 17th centuries and exemplifies the new 'field work' techniques now being applied to the study of the history of the land.

1938 BRADLEY, H. The enclosures of England. N.Y. 1918.

A good case study is D. M. Barratt, 'The enclosure of the manor of Wasperton in 1664', *Univ. of Birmingham Hist. Jour.* 3 (1952), 138–52. A chapter on the century is included in W. H. R. Curtler, *The enclosure and redistribution of our land*, Oxf. 1920.

1939 COATE, M. 'The duchy of Cornwall: its history and administration, 1640–1660.' *R.H.S. Trans.*, 4th Ser. 10 (1927), 135–69.

1940 COOPER, J. P. 'The counting of manors.' *Econ. Hist. Rev.*, 2nd Ser. 8 (1956), 377–89.

1941 DARBY, H. C. 'The draining of the fens. A.D. 1600–1800.' *In* Historical geography of England. Ed. by H. C. Darby. Camb. 1936.

2nd edn. of *The draining of the fens*, Camb. 1956. See also the *Historical account of the great level*, by William Elstobb, engineer for the fourth Duke of Bedford, which was publ. posthumously in 1793.

1942 GAY, E. F. 'The midland revolt and the inquisitions of depopulation of 1607.' *R.H.S. Trans.*, N.S. 18 (1904), 195–244.

Provides basic materials, with tables. Cf. J. D. Gould's note in *E.H.R.* 67 (1952), 392–6. See also D. G. C. Allan, 'The rising in the west, 1628–1631', *Econ. Hist. Rev.*, 2nd Ser. 5 (1952), 76–85, which relates to the enclosing of royal forests; and J. Ghosh, *A history of land tenure in England*, Calcutta, 1924.

1943 GONNER, E. C. K. Common land and inclosure. 1912.

Valuable. Cf. *E.H.R.* 23 (1908), 477–501, for the same author's 'The progress of inclosure during the seventeenth century', with a map showing the enclosed roads in 1675.

1944 HABAKKUK, H. J. 'English landownership, 1680–1740.' *Econ. Hist. Rev.* 10 (1940), 2–17.

Excellent article based upon work done on the landed estates of Northamptonshire and Bedfordshire. See also by the same author, 'The long-term rate of interest and the price of land in the seventeenth century', ibid., 2nd Ser. 5 (1952), 26–45.

1945 HARRIS, L. E. Vermuyden and the fens; a study of Sir Cornelius Vermuyden and the great level. 1953.

Critical assessment of Vermuyden's work based mainly on the minute books of the Bedford Level corporation. Cf. same author's 'Sir Cornelius Vermuyden: an evaluation and an appreciation', *Newcomen Soc. Trans. 1949–51*, 27 (1956), 7–18, which deals critically with criticisms levelled at Vermuyden's work by both contemporary and later writers. Cf. also J. Korthals-Altes, *Sir Cornelius Vermuyden: The life work of an Anglo-Dutchman in land-reclamation and drainage*, 1925. Cf. also S. Wells, *The history of the drainage of the great level of the fens, called Bedford Level; with the constitution and laws of the Bedford Level corporation*, 2 vols., 1830.

1946 HILL, C. 'The agrarian legislation of the interregnum.' *E.H.R.* 55 (1940), 222–50.

Based largely on the research of Professor Arkhangel'skiy of the Univ. of Gorky (no. 1856) with added references from sources not available to him. See also by Hill, 'Professor Lavrovsky's study of a seventeenth-century manor', *Econ. Hist. Rev.* 16 (1946), 125–9, which deals with the crown manor of Barrow on Humber between 1563 and 1803.

1947 HONE, N. J. The manor and manorial records. 1906. 3rd edn. 1925. Illus.

Studies of particular manors are numerous. Examples are to be found in the county historical society publications. See also the *Victoria county histories* (3120).

1948 HOSKINS, W. G. 'The reclamation of the waste in Devon, 1550–1800.' *Econ. Hist. Rev.* 13 (1943), 80–92.

History of enclosures in Devon. See also by the same author: 'The rebuilding of rural England, 1570–1640', *Past and Present*, 4 (1953), 44–56; and *Local history in England*, 1959. See in the latter his useful note on available aerial photographs that are proving so valuable in the study of agricultural and manorial history.

1949 HOLDSWORTH, W. S. A historical introduction to the land law. Oxf. 1927.

Cf. F. Pollock, *The land laws*, 1883. These works should be supplemented by the recent studies of Simpson (1093).

1950 KERRIDGE, E. 'The movement of rent, 1540–1640.' *Econ. Hist. Rev.*, 2nd Ser. 6 (1953), 16–34.

Deals with inflation, sources of income, methods of rent payment.

1951 MADGE, S. J. The Domesday of crown lands: a study of the legislation, survey, and sales of royal estates under the commonwealth. 1938.

Valuable source for agrarian history. Cf. also articles by S. I. Arkhangel'skiy: 'The sale of crown lands in England during the commonwealth and protectorate', *Ist. Marksist*, 60 (1937), 92–114; 'Crown lands in Surrey during the commonwealth and protectorate', *Ist. Zapiski*, 1 (1937), 175–92. See also Coate (1939).

1952 SCRUTTON, T. E. Commons and common fields, or the history and policy of the laws relating to commons and inclosures in England. Camb. 1887.

By the same author, *Land in fetters, or the history and policy of the laws restraining the alienation and settlement of land . . .*, Camb. 1886, several chapters dealing particularly with the 17th century. Cf. E. M. Leonard, 'The inclosure of commonfields in the seventeenth century', *R.H.S. Trans.*, N.S. 19 (1905), 101–46.

1953 THIRSK, J. 'The restoration land settlement.' *J.M.H.* 26 (1954), 315–28.

Pieces together, from the fragmentary evidence of debates in Parliament and from the litigation and later dealings concerning forfeited land, the terms of the settlement which reconciled purchasers of confiscated lands to the restored monarchy. Cf. H. E. Chesney, 'The transference of lands . . . 1640–1660', *R.H.S. Trans.*, 4th Ser. 15 (1932), 181–210.

5. FORESTS

Sources and Later Works

Forests ceased to play the great part in royal and private affairs which they had played in the Middle Ages: but they continued to be of importance as great land-owners sought to protect their hunting preserves from land-hungry enclosers. Likewise concern over the dwindling timber supply led to numerous writings on possible solutions to that problem. There is a short bibliography in the chapter on timber in Albion's *Forests and sea-power* (1716).

1954 DECLARATION from the poor oppressed people of England, directed to all that call themselves or are called lords of manors. 1649.

Br. Mus. 1027, i. 16 (3). Against the cutting down of timber on commons.

1955 EVELYN, JOHN. Sylva: or a discourse of forest-trees and the propagation of timber. 1664. 2nd edn. 1670. 5th edn. 1729. Ed. by A. Hunter. York. 1776.

Long a standard authority; resulted from Charles II's request to the Royal Soc. for study of reforestation. Cf. Moses Cook, *Manner of raising, ordering, and improving forest trees*, 1676, 3rd edn., 1724.

1956 ENGLISH FORESTS and forest trees, historical legendary and descriptive. 1853.

See also J. C. Cox, *The royal forests of England*, 1905, mainly medieval but of some use for later periods; and Sir H. T. Wood, *A history of the Royal Society of Arts*, 1913, rev. by G. K. Menzies, 1935, with a chapter on the society and forestry.

1957 HAMMERSLEY, G. 'The crown woods and their exploitation in the sixteenth and seventeenth centuries.' *Bull. Inst. Hist. Research* 30 (1957), 136–61.

A re-examination of recent studies on the timber crisis between 1540 and 1640. See also C. E. Hart, *The Verderers and speech-court of the Forest of Dean*, Gloucester, 1950.

1958 RICHARDSON, H. G. 'Some remarks on British forest history. II. The sixteenth and seventeenth centuries.' *Trans. Royal Scottish Arboricultural Soc.* Vol. 35.

Has valuable references in footnotes.

1959 TUPLING, G. H. The economic history of Rossendale. Manchester. 1927.

C. INDUSTRY

For industrial developments in general see Cunningham (1837) and Lipson (1839). Of special value for the period is Unwin (1964), in which there is not only a useful appendix of printed works, but also, in App. B, a list of MS. sources for the history of industrial companies of London. Many of the manuscript materials are at the P.R.O., in State Papers Domestic, but others are in Br. Mus., and in the collections reported on by H.M.C. See also Read (11 n.), p. 225. For important recent studies of industrial developments in particular areas, such as Coventry, Exeter, Lincoln, Shrewsbury, and Yorkshire, see Ch. XI, *Local History*. See also § E, *Trade and Commerce*.

I. GENERAL WORKS

1960 COURT, W. H. Rise of the midland industries, 1600–1838. Oxf. 1938. 1953.

Valuable. Cf. R. Jenkins, 'Historical notes . . . Derbyshire industries', *Newcomen Soc. Trans. 1933–34*, 14, pp. 163–77.

1961 HOSKINS, W. G. Industry, trade and people in Exeter, 1688–1800. Manchester. 1935.

Other important studies on 17th-century Exeter are by W. T. MacCaffrey, 1958, and W. B. Stephens, 1958 (2158 n.). Also from the local approach is J. W. F. Hill's *Lincoln*, 1958 (3210 n.).

1962 KRAMER, S. The English craft gilds: studies in their progress and decline. N.Y. 1927. Bibl.

Based on her *English craft gilds and the government*, N.Y. 1905. Cf. J. M. Lambert, *Two thousand years of gild life . . . the gilds and trading companies of Kingston-upon-Hull*, Hull, 1891.

1963 NEF, J. U. 'The progress of technology and the growth of large scale industry in Great Britain, 1540–1640.' *Econ. Hist. Rev.* 5 (1934), 3–24.

Other valuable articles by Nef are: 'Prices and industrial capitalism in France and

England, 1540–1640', ibid. 7 (1937), 155–85; and 'A comparison of industrial growth in France and England from 1540 to 1640', *Jour. Pol. Econ.* 44 (1936), 289–317, 505–33, 643–66. See also no. 2159.

1964 UNWIN, G. Industrial organization in the 16th and 17th centuries. Oxf. 1904. Ed. with intro. and notes by T. S. Ashton. Lond. 1957. Bibl.

Stresses especially changes in the guilds; useful appendices on manuscript and printed sources in the 1957 edn. See also by Unwin, *Gilds and companies of London*, 1908, 3rd edn., 1938; and his 'A seventeenth-century trade union', *Economic Jour.* 10 (1900), 394 ff.

Unwin's conclusions should be compared with those of later scholars. Cf. a useful short article by F. J. Fisher, 'Some experiments in company organization in the early seventeenth century', *Econ. Hist. Rev.* 4 (1933), 177–94. Some references to the century are included in the opening chapter of the *History of trade unionism*, by B. and S. Webb, 1894, 1920.

1965 USHER, A. P. A history of mechanical inventions. 1929. Rev. edn. Camb. (Mass.). 1954.

By Usher also, *Introduction to the industrial history of England*, 1921, one of many brief general accounts. See also G. N. Clark, 'Early capitalism and invention', *Econ. Hist. Rev.* 6 (1936), 143–56. See also 'Technology', nos. 2033–40.

2. COMPANIES

(a) *London Companies (General)*

1966 HERBERT, W. The history of the twelve great livery companies of London. 2 vols. 1837.

A standard work, with many documents, but not always accurate. Also citing much material is W. C. Hazlitt, *The livery companies of London*, 1892, bibl. Slighter histories are by R. J. Cheesewright, [Croydon], 1881; R. J. Blackham, 1937; and W. F. Kahl, Harvard Grad. Sch. Bus. Adm., 1960.

1967 REPORT of the royal commission appointed to inquire into the livery companies of the city of London. 5 vols. 1884.

Parliamentary Papers, 39 (1884). An official report on the companies at the period of the inquiry, containing material on their history and their records.

(b) *London Companies (Particular Trades)*

Because Read (11 n.) provides an extended list arranged alphabetically by trade (pp. 227–31), the following list is intended only as a supplement to Read's. Outstanding among the company histories are H. Welch on the cutlers (Read, no. 2713), A. H. Johnson on the drapers (Read, no. 2715), and C. M. Clode on the merchant taylors (Read, no. 2733). For list of members in 1651 see no. 3289 a. See also companies listed later under particular branches of industry.

1968 REGISTER of apprentices of the worshipful company of clockmakers, 1631 to 1931. [Frome.] 1931.

1969 GIRTIN, T. The golden ram: a narrative history of the clothworkers' company, 1528–1958. 1958. Bibl.

1970 BOYD, P., ed. Roll of the drapers' company of London. Croydon. 1934.

A useful supplement to the standard history by Johnson (Read, no. 2715). A *History of the Company's properties and trusts* was publ. by the company in 2 vols., 1940.

1971 HOWARD, A. L. The worshipful company of glass-sellers of London, from its inception to the present day. 1940.

A few 17th-cent. excerpts.

1972 WALLER, E. C., ed. Extracts from the court books of the weavers' company of London, 1610–1730. Frome. 1931.

Publ. of the Huguenot Soc., vol. 33. Cf. F. Consitt's history of the company (Read no. 2753).

(c) *Companies Outside London*

1973 RUSSELL, W. H., ed. 'The laws of the mercers company of Lichfield [1624].' *R.H.S. Trans.*, N.S. 7 (1893), 109–25.

'Typical of the ordinances . . . made for industrial regulation.' Intro. by W. Cunningham.

1974 MATTHEWS, H. E., ed. Proceedings, minutes, and enrolments of the company of soapmakers, 1562–1642. Ed. by H. E. Matthews. Bristol Rec. Soc. Publ. 10. 1940.

3. Labour, Wages, and Prices

See also the general section, especially Beveridge (1834), and Eden (2530).

1975 'THE RATES OF WAGES of servants, labourers, and artificers, set down and assessed at Okeham [Rutlandshire] . . . 1610.' *Archaeologia*, 11 (1794), 200–4.

Other materials on the same subject, ibid. 204–11. For a Bedfordshire wage assessment, 1684, see *Bedfordshire Hist. Rec. Soc. Publ.* 25 (1947), 129–37. Cf. W. G. Benham, 'Essex wages in Cromwell's time [1651]', *Essex Rev.* 43 (1934), 10–11; the notes of R. K. Kelsall on Herefordshire wages, 1666–1762, *E.H.R.* 57 (1942), 115–19, on Yorkshire, 1669–79, ibid. 52 (1937), 283–9, and Yorkshire, 1679–81, *Yorks. Arch. Jour.* 34 (1939), 310–16; and B. H. Putnam's note on 'Northamptonshire wage assessments, 1560 and 1607', *Econ. Hist. Rev.* 1 (1927), 124–34. See Read (11 n.), pp. 242–3, for list of wage assessments in print. Cf. K. H. Burley, 'A note on a labour dispute in . . . Colchester [1707–15]', *Bull. Inst. Hist. Research*, 29 (1956), 220–30.

1976 CLARK, A. Working life of women in the seventeenth century. 1919. Bibl.

App. has a list of wage assessments. See also F. W. Tickner, *Women in English economic history*, 1923.

1977 COLEMAN, D. C. 'Labour in the English economy of the seventeenth century.' *Econ. Hist. Rev.*, 2nd Ser. 8 (1955–6), 280–95.

Valuable article dealing with employment problems, population statistics, and the 'labouring poor' as viewed by contemporary writers on economic forces. An unpublished thesis by the same author (Lond. 1951) is 'The economy of Kent under the later Stuarts'. On the poor law the standard work is Webb (2535).

1978   DAVIES, M. G. The enforcement of English apprenticeship, 1563–1642. Camb. (Mass.). 1956.

Deals with the problem of enforcing the statutes and with the relationship of economic fluctuations to enforcement policies. See also Kelsall (2157).

1979   GILBOY, E. W. Wages in eighteenth century England. Camb. (Mass.). 1934.

Example of modern methods of studying wages and prices. See also Beveridge (1834) and Rogers (1871).

1980   HILTON, G. W. The truck system, including history of the British truck acts, 1465–1960. Camb. 1960. Bibl.

Study of the history of payment in kind for wages.

1981   KNOOP, D. and JONES, G. P. The London mason in the seventeenth century. Manchester. 1935.

Based on records of the Masons' Company.

1982   PHELPS BROWN, E. and HOPKINS, S. V. 'Wage rates and prices.' *Economica*, 24 (1957), 289–306.

Relates especially to population pressures in the sixteenth century, but useful for background. Cf. E. Phelps Brown and P. E. Hart, 'Wage policy and wage differences', ibid. 22 (1955), 349–54; Y. S. Brenner, 'The inflation of prices in England, 1551–1650', ibid. (1962); and J. D. Gould, on Brenner's article, ibid. 16 (1963), 351–60.

1983   TAWNEY, A. J. and R. H. 'An occupational census of the seventeenth century.' *Econ. Hist. Rev.* 5 (1934), 25–64.

Based on a 1608 muster roll, *Men and armour in Gloucestershire*, publ. 1902. A statistical study is E. J. Buckatzsch, 'Occupations in the parish registers of Sheffield, 1655–1719', ibid., 2nd Ser. 1 (1949), 145–50.

4. SPECIAL BRANCHES OF INDUSTRY

(a) *Textiles*

On particular companies, see also the section above.

(1) *Cotton*

1984   DANIELS, G. W. The early English cotton industry. Intro. by G. Unwin. Manchester. 1920.

Earlier histories of the cotton industry were by R. Guest, Manchester, 1823; and Sir E. Baines, 1835. A useful article relating to the later decades of the century is P. J. Thomas, 'The beginnings of calico printing in England', *E.H.R.* 39 (1924), 206–16.

1985   WADSWORTH, A. P. and MANN, J. de L. The cotton trade and industrial Lancashire, 1600–1780. Manchester. 1931.

Important study, including comparisons with developments in other industries and other countries. Cf. an article by S. Dumbell in *Econ. Jour.* 33 (1932), 362–73.

1986 HORNER, J. The linen trade of Europe. Belfast. 1920.

Cf. A. J. Warden, *The linen trade, ancient and modern*, 1864, 1867. See also an important work by C. Gill, *Rise of the Irish linen industry*, Oxf. 1925.

1987 CHAMBERS, J. D. 'Worshipful company of framework knitters, 1657–1778.' *Economica*, 9 (1929), 296–329.

Cf. *List of members of the worshipful company of framework knitters of England and Wales*, 1932. W. Felkin published a *History of the machine-wrought hosiery and lace manufactures*, 1867. On the Scottish handicraft hosiery industry see an article by I. F. Grant in *S.H.R.* 18 (1921), 277–89.

(3) Wool

See also Friis (2094) on Cokayne's project, and § F, *Government Regulations*.

1988 MAY, JOHN. A declaration of the estate of clothing now used within this realme of England. 1613.

Deals with the growth of, and abuses in, the wool trade.

1989 RAMSAY, G. D., ed. 'The report of the royal commission on the clothing industry, 1640.' *E.H.R.* 57 (1942), 482–93.

From the Portland MSS.; illustrates conflict of interest between London authorities and local clothiers. See also the extracts from the 1656–94 accounts of William Gaby, a middleman, ed. by E. Coward, *Wilts. Arch. and Nat. Hist. Soc. Mag.* 46 (1932–4), 50–7, 336–49.

1990 THE GENTLEMEN WOOL MERCHANTS and serge-makers case. s.l. *c.* 1698.

1991 SMITH, JOHN. Chronicon rusticum-commerciale, or memoirs of wool. 2 vols. 1747. 1757.

Valuable collection includes several papers relating to the 17th-century woollen trade.

1992 BOWDEN, P. J. 'Wool supply and the woolen industry.' *Econ. Hist. Rev.*, 2nd Ser. 9 (1956–7), 44–58.

Shows important relationship between changes in the quality of English wool and the procedures for organizing the industry.

1993 CRUMP, W. B. The yeoman-clothier of the seventeenth century. Bradford. 1932.

Originally published in *The Bradford Antiquary*, N.S. 5 (1932). See also W. B. Crump and G. Ghorbal, *History of the Huddersfield woollen industry*, Huddersfield, 1935. Accounts of other clothiers drawn from contemporary records are E. Moir, 'Benedict Webb, clothier', *Econ. Hist. Rev.*, 2nd Ser. 10 (1957), 256–64; and J. de L. Mann, 'A Wiltshire family of clothiers, George and Hester Wansey, 1683–1714', ibid. 9 (1956), 241–53.
The rise of a London draper, Thomas Cullum, is described by A. Simpson, ibid. 11 (1958), 18–34, and in his *Wealth of the gentry, 1540–1640*, 1961.

1994 HEATON, H. The Yorkshire woollen and worsted industries . . . to the industrial revolution. Oxf. 1920. Bibl.

Important.

1995	LIPSON, E. History of the woollen and worsted industries. 1921.

Valuable work, with bibliographical note. Largely supersedes earlier histories by J. Bischoff, 2 vols., 1842; J. James, 1857; and J. Burnley, 1889. Cf. P. J. Bowden, *The wool trade in Tudor and Stuart England*, N.Y. 1962.

1996	MENDENHALL, T. C. The Shrewsbury drapers and the Welsh wool trade in the XVI and XVII centuries. Oxf. 1953.

By the same author, 'The social status of the more prominent Shrewsbury drapers, 1560–1660', *Trans. Shrop. Arch. Soc.* 54 (1953), 163–70. On the Welsh woollen industry see articles by C. J. Skeel in *Arch. Camb.*, 7th Ser. 2 (1922), 220–57, and 4 (1924), 1–38.

1997	RAMSAY, G. D. The Wiltshire woollen industry in the sixteenth and seventeenth centuries. Oxf. 1943. Repr. 1965.

Scholarly study of a key area. For other studies relating to the west see K. E. Barford, 'The state and the west of England cloth industry . . . Charles I', *Wilts. Arch. and Nat. Hist. Soc. Mag.* 42 (1925); R. Perry, 'The Gloucestershire woollen industry, 1100–1690', *Trans. Bristol and Glouc. Arch. Soc.* 66 (1945), 102; and K. G. Ponting, *A history of the west of England cloth industry*, 1957.

1998	SELLERS, M. 'The textile industries.' *V.C.H. Yorkshire*. Vol. ii. 1912.

Cf. G. Unwin's section on the cloth industry of Suffolk in *V.C.H. Suffolk*, vol. ii, 1907, and his essay on the same subject in his *Studies in economic history* (1841).

(b) *Food and Fish, Tobacco, and Wine*

There is a short bibliography on 'Food' in Singer's *History of technology* (2038), vol. iii, pp. 25–6. Titles on vineyards, orchards, etc., are in the section on *Husbandry* (nos. 1882–91). See also Ch. IX, *Household and Table*.

(1) *Food and Fish*

1999	BENNETT, R. and ELTON, J. History of corn-milling. 4 vols. 1898–1904.

Cf. I. V. Hall, 'John Knight . . . sugar refiner . . . (1654–1679)', *Trans. Bristol and Glouc. Arch. Soc.* 68–9 (1949–50), 110–64. Additional works dealing with cereals and other foods are Ashley (1857), Fisher (2107), Forster (1878 n.), and Gras (1864). See also W. C. Drummond and S. A. Wilbraham (2231).

2000	ELDER, J. R. The royal fishery companies of the seventeenth century. Glasgow. 1912.

Useful. See also the more general *Sea fisheries of Great Britain and Ireland*, by G. L. Alward, Grimsby, 1932. Some contemporary records are printed in 'Sir William Hull's losses in 1641', ed. by A. E. J. Went, *Cork Hist. and Arch. Soc.*, 2nd Ser. 52 (1947), 55–68. A pamphlet, *Royal fishing revived*, 1670, is repr. in Harleian (59), vol. iii.

2001	LOUNSBURY, R. G. The British fishery at Newfoundland, 1634–1763. New Haven. 1934.

A valuable study. For international implications, see H. A. Innis, *The cod fisheries: the history of our international economy*, Oxf. 1940.

2002 RUSSELL, P. Dartmouth: a history of a port and town. 1950.

Useful especially for fishing. Cf. W. B. Stephens, 'The west-country ports and the struggle for the Newfoundland fisheries', *Trans. Devon. Assoc.* 88 (1956), 90–101.

(2) *Tobacco*

2003 T., C. An advice on how to plant tobacco in England. 1615. Repr. Boston. 1930.

2004 BROOKS, J. E. Tobacco, its history illustrated by the books . . . in the library of George Arents, Jr. 5 vols. N.Y. 1937. Illus.

An elaborate publication, covering the period 1507–1698.

2005 MacINNES, C. M. Early English tobacco trade. 1926.

See also W. J. Hardy, 'Tobacco culture in England during the seventeenth century', *Archaeologia,* 51 (1888), 157–66; the articles on the tobacco trade by A. Rive in *William and Mary College Quart. Hist. Mag.*, 2nd Ser. 9 (1929), 1–12, 73–87; and one by N. J. Williams in *Virginia Mag. of Hist. and Biography*, 65 (1957), 403–49. A modern study of the search for a market for colonial tobacco is J. M. Price, *The tobacco venture to Russia*, 1676–1722, Phila. 1961.

(3) *Wine*

2006 [Charleton, Walter.] Two discourses: i. Concerning the different wits of men; ii of the mysterie of vintners. 1669. 3rd edn. 1692.

The second part, which was read to the Royal Society in 1662, was later printed separately, *c.* 1700, as *Vintner's mystery display'd.* See also treatises by John Worlidge on cider, *Vinetum Britannicum* (1890 n.), and by Th. Tryon on brewing, 1690. Several papers concerning the London Vinters' Company were pr. in *Trans. London and Middlesex Arch. Soc.* 3 (1871), 404–91.

2007 SIMON, A. L. The history of the wine trade in England. 3 vols. 1906–9. Illus.

Valuable. Vol. iii deals with the period. See also his *Bibliography* (2233 n.), and titles on vineyards in § B *supra.*

(c) *Metals and Mining*

(1) *General*

There are useful sections on mines and metals in the *Victoria county histories,* for such counties as Cornwall, Derby, Durham, Gloucestershire, Lancaster, Nottingham, Shropshire, Warwick, and York. For some comments on MS. resources, see Read (11 n.), pp. 234–5.

2008 PLATTES, GABRIEL. A discovery of subterraneall treasure. 1639.

Describes assay methods; a pioneer work.

2009 PETTUS, SIR JOHN. Fodinae regales: or the history, laws, and places of the chief mines and mineral works in England, Wales. 1670.

2010 HOUGHTON, THOMAS, ed. The compleat miner; or the collection of the laws, liberties, ancient customs . . . of the several mines and miners in the counties of Derby, Gloucester and Somerset. 3 pts. 1688.

Pt. 1 is a duplicate of *Rara avis in terris, . . .*, 1681. Houghton edited also the *Laws and customs of the mines of the Forest of Dean*, 1689. Cf. *The compleat miner . . .* [Wirksworth and Derbyshire], repr. in *A collection of scarce and valuable treatises upon metals, mines and minerals*, 1740.

2011 JENKINS, R. Links in the history of engineering and technology from Tudor times: the collected papers of Rhys Jenkins. Camb. 1936. Bibl.

Repr. published by the Newcomen Society of papers published in various local and technological journals. Several relate to early metal works, i.e. 'The early tinplate industry', 'The Vauxhall ordnance factory of King Charles I'. See also *Technology*, nos. 2033–40.

(2) *Coal*

2012 GARDINER, RALPH. England's grievance discovered in relation to the coal trade. 1655. Repr. Newcastle. 1786.

Cf. M. A. Richardson's *Reprints of rare tracts*, vol. iii. Also ibid., vol. vii, is a repr. of J.C., *The compleat collier, or the whole art of working coal mines . . . in the northern parts* [1708].

2013 POVEY, CHARLES. A discovery of indirect practices in the coal trade . . . 1700.

Some papers relating to the coal trade, 1671–91, are calendared in H.M.C., *Earl of Lindsey MSS.*, 1942, pp. 155–61.

2014 NEF, J. U. The rise of the British coal industry, 1550–1700. 2 vols. 1932.

The best work on the subject. Useful also are R. L. Galloway, *History of coal mining*, 1882; and P. M. Sweezy, *Monopoly and competition in the English coal trade, 1550–1850*, Camb. (Mass.) 1938. See articles by E. R. Turner in *A.H.R.* 27 (1922), 1–23; and A. Moller, in *R.H.S. Trans.*, 4th Ser. 8 (1925), 79–97.

(3) *Iron*

Useful short bibliographies on the iron industry are in Flinn (2016) and Jenkins (2017). See also the footnotes in Court (1960).

2015 DUDLEY, DUD. Metallum martis: or iron made with pit-coal, sea-cole, etc. 1665. Reprs. [Wolverhampton.] 1851 and 1855.

For a critical comment on Dudley by R. A. Mott, see *Newcomen Soc. Trans.* 15 (1936) 17–37.

2016 FLINN, M. W. 'The growth of the English iron industry, 1660–1760.' *Econ. Hist. Rev.*, 2nd Ser. 11 (1958–9), 144–53.

Presents a revision of the view that the industry was declining in this period; bibl. note. Other valuable articles are B. L. C. Johnson, 'The Foley partnerships: the iron industry at the end of the charcoal era', ibid., 2nd Ser. 4 (1952), 322–37; A. Raistrick and E. Allen, 'The South Yorkshire ironmasters, 1690–1750', ibid. 9 (1939), 168–85; and H. F. Kearney, 'Richard Boyle, ironmaster . . .', *Jour. Roy. Soc. Antiq. Ireland*, 83 (1953), 156–62.

2017 JENKINS, R. 'Iron making in the Forest of Dean.' *Newcomen Soc. Trans.* 6 (1925–6).

Cf. the same author's 'Rise and fall of the Sussex iron industry', ibid. 1 (1920–1). For other articles by Jenkins see the list in his *Collected papers* (2011). See also C. E. Hart, *The free miners of the royal forest of Dean*, Gloucester, 1953.

2018 MacADAM, I. 'Notes on the ancient iron industry of Scotland.' *Proc. Soc. Antiq. Scot.* 21 (1886–7), 89–131.

Cf. R. W. C. Patrick, *Early records relating to mining in Scotland*, Edin. 1878. Articles relating to the industrial history of Neath are pr. in *Neath Antiq. Soc. Trans.*, N.S. 4 (1934), 43–56, 84–5.

2019 NICOLL, J. Some account of the worshipful company of ironmongers. 1851. 2nd edn. 1866.

See also H. G. Nicholls, *Iron-making in the forest of Dean . . .*, 1866; E. Straker, *Wealden iron*, 1931; and M. A. Lower, 'Historical . . . notices on the iron works of . . . Sussex', *Sussex Arch. Coll.* 2 (1849), 169–220.

2020 SCHUBERT, H. R. History of the British iron and steel industry (*c.* 450–1775). 1957.

By the official historian of the Iron and Steel Institute; valuable especially for the technological aspects. See also an article by Schubert in the Institute's *Journal*, 173 (1953); and J. U. Nef's article on iron production, 1540–1650, in *Jour. Pol. Econ.* 44 (1936), 398–403. See also Chambers, *The Vale of Trent* (1835).

(4) Other Metal Industries

2021 HAMILTON, H. The English brass and copper industries to 1800. Intro. by Sir W. Ashley. 1926. Bibl.

See also M. B. Donald, *Elizabethan copper: the history of the company of mines royal 1568–1605*, 1955.

2022 B[adcock], W[illiam]. A touchstone of gold and silver wares; or a manual for goldsmiths. 1677. 2nd edn. 1679.

2023 CHAFFERS, W. Gilda aurifabroram: a history of English goldsmiths and plateworkers. 1883. 1899.

Contains many biographies. Cf. E. Wenham, *Domestic silver of Great Britain and Ireland*, 1931; W. S. Prideaux, *Memorials of the goldsmiths' company*, 1896, 1897; and H. F. Stewart, *History of the worshipful company of gold and silver wyre-drawers*, 1891. A list of *London goldsmiths, 1200–1800*, was compiled by A. Heal, Camb. 1935.

2024 LEADER, R. E. History of the company of cutlers of Hallamshire. 2 vols. Sheffield. 1905–6.

The historian of the London Company is C. Welch (Read, no. 2713). See also G. I. H. Lloyd, *The cutlery trades*, 1913; and E. J. Buckatzsch, 'Occupations of the parish registers of Sheffield, 1655–1719', *Econ. Hist. Rev.*, 2nd Ser. 1 (1949), 145–50. Other titles relating to the silver industry are listed in the bibl. in R. E. Wilson's *Two hundred precious metal years* (1760–1960), 1960.

2025 GOUGH, J. W. Mines of Mendip. Oxf. 1930.

Scholarly account of the lead mines from early times. By Gough also, *Mendip mining laws*, Somerset Rec. Soc. Publ. 45 (1931); and *The superlative prodigall, a life of Thomas Bushell*, Bristol, 1932, which is the biography of a courtier and mine developer in Somerset and Wales. Cf. R. S. France, ed., *The Thieveley lead mines, 1629–1635*, Lancashire and Cheshire Rec. Soc., Preston, 1951. Useful articles on lead mining are by F. N. Fisher, *Derbyshire Arch. and Nat. Hist. Soc.*, N.S. 25 (1952), 74–118; and

A. Raistrick, *Newcomen Soc. Trans.* 14 (1935), 119–62. The diary of a Scottish supplier of lead ore, Sir James Hope [1649], is in the *Scottish Rec. Soc. Publ.*, 3rd Ser. 50 (1958), 129–97.

2026 LEWIS, G. R. The stannaries: a study of the English tin miner. Boston. 1908. Bibl.

An important work. Thomas Pearce ed. *The laws and customs of the stannaries in . . . Cornwall and Devon*, 1725. See also A. K. H. Jenkin, *The Cornish miner*, 1927.

(d) *Glass*

A short bibliography on glass manufacture appears in Singer, *Technology* (2038), vol. iii, pp. 242–4.

2027 NERI, ANTONIO. Art of glass. 1662.

Trans. from the Italian edn., Florence, 1592. Repr. 1826.

2028 POWELL, E. J. Glass-making in England. Camb. 1923.

2029 THORPE, W. A. A history of English and Irish glass. 2 vols. 1929. Bibl. 2nd edn. 1949.

Thorpe also wrote *English glass*, 1935. Cf. M. S. D. Westropp, *Irish glass*, 1920; J. C. Harrington, *Glassmaking at Jamestown*, Richmond (U.S.A.), 1952. A brief *History of the Vauxhall and Radcliff glass houses, 1670–1800*, by W. H. Bowles, was privately pr. in 1926. See also no. 2738.

(e) *Paper*

For printing see *Cultural History*.

2030 COLEMAN, D. C. The British paper industry, 1495–1860. N.Y. 1958.

Scholarly; shows development especially in the latter half of the 17th century. Cf. a series of articles on early paper-making by R. Jenkins, repr. in his *Collected papers* (2011).

2031 SHORTER, A. H. Paper mills and paper makers in England, 1495–1800. Paper Publications Society. 1957.

Valuable. Stresses geographical factors that influenced locations of the industry.

(f) *Clockmaking*

2032 HILL, R. N. Early British clocks from ca. 1600 to ca. 1800. (The Connoisseur.) 1949.

For a contemporary treatise see W[illiam] D[erham], *Artificial clock-makers: a treatise of watch and clock work*, 1696, later edns., 1700, 1734. See also nos. 1039–41 in Grose (10).

5. TECHNOLOGY AND ENGINEERING

(a) *Sources*

2033 WORCESTER, EDWARD SOMERSET, second MARQUIS OF. A century of the names [and?] scantlings of such inventions as at present I can call to mind to have tried and perfected. 1663.

Commonly referred to as *Century of inventions*. See H. Dircks, *The life, times, and* scientific labours of the second marquis of Worcester, 1865; and W. H. Thorpe, 'The marquis of Worcester and Vauxhall', *Newcomen Soc. Trans.* 13 (1932–3), 75–88.

2034 MOXON, JOSEPH. Mechanick exercises, or the doctrine of handy-works. 1677. Repr. in 2 vols. 1683. Later edns. 1693. 1700.

A repr. of the first edn., with a preface by T. L. Devinne, was publ. in 1896, 2 vols., N.Y. For works by Moxon on other subjects see Wing, M 2998–3027a.

2035 H[ALE], T[HOMAS]. An account of several new inventions. 1691.

Includes 'New Invention of mill'd lead . . . for ships.'

(b) *Later Works*

2036 MERTON, R. K. 'Science and the economy of seventeenth-century England.' *Science and Society*, 3 (1939), 3–27.

Deals with technological developments relating to the scientific achievements of the period. See also Merton (2920), Clark (1965 n.), Nef (1963), Jenkins (2011), and S. B. Hamilton, 'Captain John Perry, 1670–1732', *Newcomen Soc. Trans.* 27 (1956), 241–53. On patents see no. 2160.

2037 RAISTRICK, A. Quakers in science and industry . . . during the 17th and 18th centuries. 1950.

Valuable.

2038 SINGER, C. *et al.*, eds. A history of technology. Vol. iii. From the renaissance to the industrial revolution. 1957. Bibl.

The five-volume series, Oxf. 1954–8, deals with general European as well as British developments. The series is valuable, though there are omissions and there is insufficient 'synthesis'. The bibliography for vol. iii contains a list of periodicals bearing on the history of technology. A single-volume history, following the pattern of Singer, is T. K. Derry and T. I. Williams, *Short history of technology*, N.Y. 1961.

2039 WAILES, R. Windmills in England, a study of their origin [and] development. 1948.

By the same author, *The English windmill*, 1954.

2040 WILLIAMSON, F. 'George Sorocold of Derby: a pioneer of water supply.' *Journ. Derbyshire Arch. and Nat. Hist. Soc.*, N.S. 10 (1936), 43–93.

Cf. F. Williamson and W. B. Crump, 'Sorocold's water works at Leeds, 1694', *Thoresby Soc. Publ.* 37 (1940), 166–82; and W. D. Bushell, *Hobson's conduit: the new river at Cambridge*, Camb. 1938.

D. FINANCE

Especially valuable in the following section for coinage are Feaveryear (2048), Oman (2049 n.), and Shaw (2049 n.); on banking, Richards (2057); on government borrowing, Ashton (2062). Horsefield is representative of the trends of recent scholarship. See also Supple (1840). On prices see Beveridge (1834). The titles relating to disbursements and to the Exchequer and the Treasury have been included in Ch. III, *Central Administration*. See also *Economic Thought* (nos.

1846–7); and, below, *Trade and Commerce*. There are valuable bibliographies especially rich in reference to MS. materials in Horsefield and Richards. For the principal official records see nos. 759–63.

1. GENERAL

2041   FENTON, ROGER. A treatise of usury. 1612.

Still influential in the seventeenth century is the *Discourse on usury* published by Thomas Wilson in 1572 (repr. with a valuable introduction by R. H. Tawney, 1925; see Read, no. 2955). An examination of Fenton's treatise is Sir Robert Filmer's *Quaestio quodlibetica, or . . . whether it may be lawfull to take use for money*, 1653. For interpretations of the question in the history of economic thought see Tawney (1846).

2042   CULPEPPER, SIR THOMAS. Tract against usurie. 1621.

Written against the importation of money for the purposes of usury.

2043   HORSEFIELD, J. K. British monetary experiments, 1650–1710. 1960. Bibl.

Valuable study of financial background at the mid century, and of coinage policies and the developments in banking. Bibliography lists many contemporary treatises. By the same author, 'Inflation and deflation in 1694–1696', *Economica*, N.S. 23 (1956), 229–43.

2. COINAGE AND MONEY

(a) *Sources*

2044   McCULLOCH, J. R., ed. A select collection of scarce and valuable tracts on money. 1856.

Repr. includes Rice Vaughan's *Discourse of coin and coinage* (publ. 1675 but written c. 1630–5); *A speech . . . by Sir Robert Cotton . . . touching the alteration of coin . . . 1626*, 1651; a tract by Sir William Petty, 1695; and Loundes (2047).

2045   SHAW, W. A., ed. Select tracts and documents illustrative of English monetary history, 1626–1730. 1896. Repr. 1935.

Includes, besides some of those in McCulloch, H. Robinson's *England's safety*, 1641; selections from state papers, 1649–51; and Newton's mint reports 1701–25 (see H.M.C., *8th Rep.*, 1881, pp. 63–92, and *6th Rep.*, 1887, pp. 330–40).

2046   VIOLET, THOMAS. An appeal to Caesar, wherein gold and silver is proved to be the kings majesties royal commodity. 2 vols. 1660.

Objects to shipments of gold and silver as merchandise. See his *Humble declaration . . . touching the transportation of gold and silver*, 1643, repr. at Hull, 1812. See also Sir Dudley North, *Discourses upon trade, principally . . . the interest, coynage, clipping, increase of money*, 1691, later edn. by J. H. Hollander, Baltimore, 1907. See Shaw (2045).

2047   L[OWNDES], W[ILLIAM]. A report containing an essay for the amendment of the silver coins. 1695.

Repr. in McCulloch. Lowndes, who was secretary to the Treasury, wrote also *A further essay*, 1695. John Locke, who had published his first treatise on coinage in 1692 (*Consideration of the consequences of . . . raising the value of money*, repr. in McCulloch), replied to Lowndes with *Further considerations . . .*, 1695. See C. R. Fay, 'Locke versus Lowndes', *Camb. Hist. Jour.* 4 (1933), 143–55; and his 'Newton and the gold standard', ibid. 5 (1935), 109–17.

(b) *Later Works*

2048 FEAVEARYEAR, A. E. The pound sterling: a history of English money. Oxf. 1931. Rev. edn. Oxf. 1963.

Useful, with several chapters on the period. An early account, '*Chronicum preciosum*', was publ. by William Fleetwood, bishop of Ely, in 1707 (repr. in his collected works, 1737). Selections from documents relating to coinage were edited by I. M. Shrigley, *The price of gold* . . . (1694–1931), 1935; and by M. Butchart, *Money* . . . (1640–1935), 1935.

2049 RUDING, R. Annals of the coinage of Britain and its dependencies. 3 vols. 1817–19. 3rd edn. 3 vols. 1840. Illus.

Still useful. See also C. W. C. Oman, *Coinage of England*, Oxf. 1931.
   On currency see W. A. Shaw, *The history of currency, 1252–1894*, 1895; B. E. Supple, 'Currency and commerce in the early seventeenth century', *Econ. Hist. Rev.* 10 (1957), 239–55; and Craig (766).

3. BANKING

(a) *Bibliography and Sources*

2050 STEPHENS, T. A. A contribution to the bibliography of the Bank of England. 1897.

A brief list of MS. sources is in C. L. Grose (10), p. 94. See also Richards (2057) for list of numerous MSS.

2051 VAN DILLEN, J. G., ed. History of the principal banks accompanied by extensive bibliographies of the history of banking in eleven European countries. The Hague. 1934.

Valuable. Includes R. D. Richards, 'First fifty years of the Bank of England'.

2052 BRIEF ACCOUNT of the intended Bank of England. 1694.

Excellent argument on the expected benefits. Attributed to William Paterson by Wing; by others, to Michael Godfrey, author of *Short account of the bank of England*, 1695. On earlier projects relating to land banks, see Hugh Chamberlen, *Proposal to make England rich and happy*, 1690. Cf. Defoe's *Essay on projects*, 1697, which contains a suggestion for a national bank as well as savings banks and other matters.

2053 MURRAY, ROBERT. A proposal for the more easie advancing to the crown any fixed sum of money to carry on the war against France; and payment of the debts contracted thereby. 1696.

(b) *Later Works*

2054 CLAPHAM, J. H. The Bank of England. 2 vols. Camb. 1944.

Valuable, largely superseding Rogers (2058) and earlier histories. Vol. i covers the period 1694–1797.

2055 HOLDEN, J. M. The history of negotiable instruments in English law. 1955. Bibl.

Cf. the same author's article on bills of exchange in *Law Quart. Rev.* 67 (1951), 230–48; and R. de Roover, *L'évolution de la lettre de change*, Paris, 1953.

2056 PRICE, F. G. HILTON. A handbook of London bankers with some account of their predecessors, the early goldsmiths. 1876. Later edn. 1890–1.

By the same author, *Temple Bar, or some account of 'ye Marygold', No. 1 Fleet Street*, 1875, which is a sketch of the banking house of Messrs. Child & Co. On other early bankers and banking see J. B. Martin, '*The Grasshopper' in Lombard Street*, 1892 (includes repr. of *The mystery of the new fashioned goldsmiths* . . ., 1676); Lady A. Archer Houblon, *The Houblon family*, 2 vols., 1907; and D. K. Clark's chapter in *Essays in honor of William Cortez Abbott*, Camb. (Mass.) 1941, and her essay on Edward Backwell in *Econ. Hist. Rev.* 9 (1938), 45–55.

2057 RICHARDS, R. D. The early history of banking in England (to 1833). 1929. Bibl.

Excellent. In this and other writings, Richards shows the close interaction of Exchequer practice and the development of banking; see his *Early English banking schemes*, 1928; his article on Edward Backwell in *Econ. Hist.* 1 (1925), 335–55; and 'The lottery in the history of English government finance', *Econ. Jour.* 3 (1934), 57–76. His article, 'The Stop of the Exchequer', in *Econ. Hist.* 2 (1933), 45–62, should be compared with A. Browning's article on the same subject in *History*, 14 (1930), 333–7. See also A. V. Judges, 'The origins of English banking', ibid. 16 (1931), 138–45; and C. L. Grose, 'The Dunkirk money', *J.M.H.* 5 (1933), 1–18.

2058 ROGERS, J. E. T. The first nine years of the Bank of England. Oxf. 1887.

Still useful, though largely superseded by Clapham. See also W. M. Acres, *The Bank of England from within, 1694–1700*, 2 vols., 1931; and A. C. Carter, 'The Huguenot contribution to the early years of the funded debt', *Proc. Huguenot Soc. London*, 19 (1955), 21–41.

2059 THOMAS, S. E. The rise and growth of joint stock banking. Vol. i. Britain to 1860. 1934.

Begins with 1694. See also Scott (2128), Davis (2137), and the South Sea Company (2138).

2060 WRIGHT, C. and FAYLE, C. E. A history of Lloyd's from the founding of Lloyd's coffee house to the present day. 1928.

Also on Lloyds are: R. S. Sayers, *Lloyd's bank in the history of English banking*, N.Y. and Oxf. 1957; M. M. Beeman, *Lloyd's*, 1938; and N. Lane, 'The origin of Lloyd's', *History Today*, Dec. 1957, 848–53. See also *Insurance* (2101).

4. PUBLIC FINANCE

(a) *Government Borrowing*

References to MS. sources are in Richards (2057), Horsefield (2043), and in Ch. III, *Central Administration*. Various fiscal records of the period after 1664, relating to the mint, the clerk of the patents, etc., are calendared in H.M.C., *Earl of Lindsey*, 1942 (pp. 69–115, 162–83). See also *Banking*, above.

2061 OXFORD, ROBERT HARLEY, EARL OF. An essay upon publick credit. 1710.

Sometimes attributed to Defoe. Repr. in J. R. McCulloch, ed., *A select collection of* . . . *tracts* . . . *on the national debt*, 1857.

2062 ASHTON, ROBERT. The crown and the money market. 1603–1640. Oxf. 1960. Bibl.

An excellent study of deficit finance, especially with reference to the customs farm and to the corporation of London. See the author's articles on the early Stuart period, *Econ. Hist. Rev.*, N.S. 8 (1955–6), 310–22, and 10 (1957), 15–29. See also Dietz (767).

2063 HARGREAVES, E. L. The national debt. 1930.

Contains a bibliography of contemporary works. The early chapters relate to the seventeenth century.

2064 SCHUMPETER, E. B. 'English prices and public finance.' *Rev. of Econ. Statistics* (1938), 28–37.

Cf. J. M. Price, 'Notes on some London price currents', *Econ. Hist. Rev.*, N.S. 7 (1954), 240–50, and no. 1982.

(b) *Taxation*

(1) *General*

2065 A REVENUE LETTER-BOOK. Being correspondence . . . [2 Jan. 1689/90 to 15 Dec. 1692], of their Majesties' agents for bringing in of taxes. (Publ. Board of Inland Revenue.) 1933.

Only 75 copies were printed.

2066 EXETER IN THE SEVENTEENTH CENTURY: tax and rate assessments 1602–1699. Ed. by W. G. Hoskins. Exeter. (Devon and Corn. Rec. Soc.) 1957.

2067 DOWELL, S. A history of taxation and taxes in England from the earliest times to the present day. 4 vols. 1884. 2nd edn. 4 vols. 1888.

Standard work, though much out of date. See also Hughes (770), and Hughes's article, 'The English stamp duties, 1664–1764', *E.H.R.* 56 (1941), 234–64.

2068 KENNEDY, W. English taxation, 1640–1799; an essay on policy and opinion. 1913.

Studies effects of taxation especially. Earlier works are Sir John Sinclair, *The history of the public revenue of the British empire*, 3 pts., 1785–9, later edn., 3 vols., 1803–4; and J. Stevens, *The royal treasury of England, or an historical account of all taxes*, 1725, later edn., 1733.

(2) *Customs and Other Special Taxes*

2069 HALL, H. History of the custom-revenue in England from the earliest times to . . . 1827. 2 vols. 1885.

Still the standard general account. On MSS. see p. 108. Important materials on the customs farm early in the 17th century are included in Tawney (477), pp. 282–310, 315–54. Cf. H. Atton and H. H. Holland, *The king's customs*, 1908. William Edgar ed. in 1714 *Vectigalium systema: or a complete view of . . . the revenue . . . called customs.*

2070 HOON, E. E. [Mrs. Cawley.] Organization of the English customs system, 1696–1786. N.Y. 1938. 2nd edn. Newton Abbot. 1968.

Important. For a summary of an unpublished thesis, by C. C. Crews on the last period of the customs farm, see *Bull. Inst. Hist. Research*, 14 (1936), 118–21.

2071 MARSHALL, L. M. 'The levying of the hearth tax, 1662–1688.' *E.H.R.* 51 (1936), 628–46.

Also valuable, with an intro. by P. Styles, is M. Walker, ed., *Warwick County Records: Hearth tax returns, I. Warwick,* 1957. See also Marshall (2163).

2072 GORDON, M. D. 'The collection of ship money in the reign of Charles I.' *R.H.S. Trans.,* 3rd Ser. 4 (1910), 141–62.

Based on A.O. Declared Accounts, assessments in Council Register, and instructions to sheriffs. For evidence from local records see 'The ship money papers of Henry Chester and Sir Will. Boteler, 1637–1639', ed. by F. G. and M. Emmison, *Beds. Hist. Rec. Soc. Publ.* 18 (1936), 43–88; papers for Walsall, in *Hist. Coll. Staffs.,* 1932, pp. 103–20; and see *C.S.P. Dom.* See also *Naval History.*

E. TRADE AND COMMERCE

1. GENERAL

Numerous tracts, in addition to those listed below, are printed in McCulloch (1832); some appear in *Economic Thought,* nos. 1842–8. Especially significant for the earlier period see Malynes, Missledon, and Mun; for the later, Child, Coke, Davenant, and Charles King. See also no. 2097. A short collection on voyages is in Cox, *Guide to . . . travel* (2351), vol. iii, 325–8. For trade in special commodities, see *Industry* above. See also *Colonial History.*

(a) *Bibliography and Sources*

2073 CLARK, G. N. Guide to English commercial statistics, 1696–1782. (R.H.S. Guides and Handbooks No. 1.) 1938.

Useful. Contains a catalogue of materials by B. Franks. A useful list of contemporary sources for the first half of the century is in Supple (1840).

2074 WILLIAMS, N. J., ed. Tradesmen in early-Stuart Wiltshire. Publ. by Wilts. Arch. and Nat. Hist. Soc. Records Branch, 15 (1960).

Lists from Exchequer records, 1607, 1620, 1637.

2075 MISSELDEN, EDWARD. Free trade, or the means to make trade flourish. 1622.

Analyses the trade decline of the period. Misselden wrote also *The circle of commerce, or the balance of trade,* 1623. He expresses the view of the Merchant Adventurers.

2076 MALYNES, GERALD DE. The center of the circle. 1623.

Answer to Misselden's *Circle.* Malynes, a member of 'The Staple' and a prolific writer, publ. in 1602 a *Treatise on the canker of England's commonwealth,* and in 1622, *The maintenance of free trade,* replying to Misselden's pamphlet of the year. A follower of Malynes's ideas, largely, is Sir Ralph Maddison, *Great Britain's remembrancer,* written 1640, publ. 1655. For an analysis of Malynes's views see J. D. Gould, 'The trade crisis of the early 1620s and English economic thought', *Jour. of Econ. Hist.* 15 (1955), 121–33.

2077 MUN, THOMAS. England's treasure by foreign trade. 1664.

A classic, parts of which were written *c.* 1623, and others possibly 1635–40, though published posthumously. Repr. in McCulloch; latest edn. by B. Blackwell, for the Economic History Soc., 1933.

For comments on the date see J. D. Gould in *Jour. Econ. Hist.* 15 (1955), 160–1; and B. E. Supple, 'Thomas Mun and the commercial crisis, 1623', *Bull. Inst. Hist. Research*, 27 (1954), 91–4. See also R. de Roover, 'Thomas Mun in Italy', ibid. 30 (1957), 80–5, and the analysis of Mun's place in developing economic theory in Supple (1840). Mun's *Discourse of trade*, 1621, was repr. in McCulloch, *Early English tracts* (1832 n.) and in 1952.

2078 OBSERVATIONS TOUCHING TRADE and commmerce with the Hollander, and other nations. 1653.

Attributed at the time of publication to Sir Walter Raleigh, and repr. in his *Remains*, 1661, *Miscellaneous Works*, 2 vols., 1751, and McCulloch, *Select . . . tracts on commerce* (1832 n.). Raleigh's authorship has been doubted, however (*D.N.B.*), and the pamphlet has been attributed also to John Keymor [Keymer] (Wing, K 391; *Br. Mus. Cat. Pr. Books*). In it appears a comparison of English and Dutch trade, and suggestions for advancing the former.

2079 SMITH, WILLIAM. An essay for recovery of trade, viz. i for regulating the manufacture of wool. ii against the corruptions practised upon tin and lead. iii for the advancement of fishing and plantations. 1661.

On the wool trade see also W.S., *The golden fleece*, 1656, and the arguments of the clothier, William Carter, on the advantages of native woollen manufactures, *England's interest by trade asserted . . .*, 1663(?), 1671, 1689; and *England's interest asserted in improvement of its native commodities . . .*, 1669. On trade and fishing see John Smith, *The trade and fishing of Britain displayed*, 1661.

2080 FORTREY, SAMUEL. England's interest and improvement consisting in the increase of the store and trade of this kingdom. Camb. 1663. Later edns. Lond. 1713. 1744.

Repr. McCulloch; also ed. by J. H. Hollander, Baltimore, 1907.

2081 CHILD, JOSIAH. New discourse of trade, wherein are recommended several weighty points, relating to companies of merchants. 1693. Later edns. 1740. 1775.

The first draft of this book was the 1668 publication, *Brief observations concerning trade . . .*; several chapters were added in *Discourse about trade*, 1690. See also no. 3402 n. On Child's writings see W. Letwin, *Sir Josiah Child*, Boston (Mass.), 1959, which includes a repr. of the *Brief observations*, 1668, and a bibl. of Child's writings.

2082 COKE, ROGER. Discourse of trade. 1670.

Discusses the decline of England's trade at the period. Coke wrote, among other works, *A treatise wherein is demonstrated that the church and state of England are in equal danger with the trade of it*, 1671. Others who wrote on ways to improve England's trade at this period were Robert Murray, *A proposal for the advancement of trade*, 1676 (see Wing); and Andrew Yarranton, *England's improvement by sea and land*, 2 vols., 1677–81.

2083 [PETYT, WILLIAM.] Britannia languens; or a discourse of trade. 1680. 1689.

Strongly critical of the East India Company. Repr. in McCulloch, *Select . . . tracts . . . commerce* (1832 n.).

2084 KING, GREGORY. Of the naval trade of England A° 1688. Ed. by G. E. Barnett. Baltimore. 1936.

Ed. with King's well-known tract of 1656, *Natural and political observations* (2171), this statistical report on trade had remained in MS. form (Bodleian Libr., Rawl. MSS. D. 919). The manuscript was seen, however, and utilized by Davenant (q.v.) for his *Essay* relating to the balance of trade.

2085 B[ARBON], N[ICHOLAS]. Discourse of trade. 1690. Repr. edn. by J. H. Hollander. Baltimore. 1905.

Of this period also are the several essays by the Bristol merchant, John Cary, *Irish and Scotch trade*, Bristol, 1695; *East India trade*, Bristol, 1695; and others (see C. L. Grose, p. 80); and Sir Francis Brewster, *Essays on trade and navigation*, 1695.

2086 DAVENANT, CHARLES. Political and commercial works . . . relating to the trade and revenue of England. Ed. by Sir C. Whitworth. 5 vols. 1771.

Includes his *Essay on the East India trade*, 1696; *Essay upon the probable methods of making a people gainers in the ballance of trade*, 1699; *Discourse upon grants and resumptions* [Irish], 1700; and *Reflections upon . . . the trade to Africa*, 1709. A list of the writings of Davenant, a commissioner of excise, has been compiled by D. Waddell and printed in *The Library*, 5th Ser. 11 (1956), 206–12. Several letters, ed. by G. Davies and M. Scofield, are in *Hunt. Lib. Quart.* 4 (1941), 309–42. A biographical sketch by Waddell is in *Econ. Hist. Rev.*, N.S. 11 (1959–60), 279–88. See Waddell's article, 'An English economist's view of the union, 1705', *S.H.R.* 35 (1956), 144–9.

2087 POVEY, CHARLES. Unhappiness of England as to its trade by sea and land truly stated. 1701.

See also an anonymous pamphlet of this year, *Proposals and reasons for constituting a council of trade*.

2088 WOOD, WILLIAM. A survey of trade in four parts. 1718.

The first parts deal with advantages and characteristics, the third relates to colonies and plantations, and the fourth, to current disadvantages affecting trade.

2089 KING, CHARLES, ed. The British merchant, or commerce preserv'd. 3 vols. 1721.

Actually collected from a periodical, 1713–14, to which numerous merchants contributed. Attacked the views of Defoe that were contributed during this period to *Mercator*. An influential pamphlet.

2090 DEFOE, DANIEL. Plan of the English commerce, being a complete prospect of the trade of this nation. 1728. Later edn. 1730. Repr. Oxf. 1928.

Cf. Defoe's *General history of trade*, 1713.

(b) *Later Works*

Important chapters appear in Cunningham (1837), Lipson (1839), and Unwin (1841). On fairs and markets, see the general works listed in Gross (11). See also Read (1959 edn.), nos. 2987, 2994, and 3015.

2091 ANDERSON, A. An historical and chronological deduction of the origin of commerce. 2 vols. 1764. Later edn. by W. Coombe. 4 vols. 1787–9.

Much important material in the form of annals. Cf. D. Macpherson's *Annals of commerce, manufacturers, fisheries and navigation*, 4 vols., 1805, which is a continuation of Anderson to 1800.

2092 CHALMERS, G. An estimate of the comparative strength of Britain during the present and four preceding reigns and of the losses of her trade from every war since the revolution. 1782. Later edns. 1794. 1804.

The edns. of 1802 and later include Gregory King's *Natural and political observations* (2171).

2093 DAVIS, R. The rise of the English shipping industry in the seventeenth and eighteenth centuries. 1962.

Important, dealing with causes of expansion, organization of trade, etc. Related articles by Davis are 'English foreign trade, 1660–1700', *Econ. Hist. Rev.*, N.S. 7 (1954), 150–66, and 'Merchant shipping in the economy of the late seventeenth century', ibid., N.S. 9 (1956–7), 59–71. J. H. Andrews has compiled a study on foreign trade for the year 1701 in *Mariner's Mirror*, 41 (1955), 232–5; and from certain Kentish ports in *Arch. Cant.* 66 (1953), 37–44; 69 (1955), 125–31. For Anglesey ports see D. Thomas, *Anglesey shipbuilding down to 1840*, 1933; for those of Cardiganshire see no. 3578.

2094 FRIIS, A. Alderman Cockayne's project and the cloth trade: the commercial policy of England in its main aspects, 1603–1625. Copenhagen and Lond. 1927.

Important for wool trade and for more general commercial developments. For the effects of the evolving corn market on trade, see Gras (1864).

2095 HEWINS, W. A. S. English trade and finance chiefly in the seventeenth century. 1892.

Still useful as a survey, but needing to be supplemented by works of recent scholarship. See also Supple (1840) and M. P. Ashley (2152).

2096 JONES, R. J. C. British merchant service; being a history of the British mercantile marine . . . 1898.

Government policies illustrated by selected documents are described in H. C. Hunter, *How England got its merchant marine, 1066–1776*, N.Y. and Lond. 1935. General accounts are H. Moyse-Bartlett, *History of the merchant navy*, 1937; and F. H. Shaw, *Flag of the seven seas*, 1953.

2097 PAPILLON, A. F. W. Memoirs of Thomas Papillon of London, merchant (1623–1702). Reading. 1887.

Useful for trade and politics in London, *temp.* Charles II. Includes letters and excerpts from accounts. See also no. 3402, and I. Scouloudi, 'Thomas Papillon . . .', *Proc. Huguenot Soc. London*, 18 (1947), 49–72. Biographies of several 17th-century figures are included in H. R. Fox Bourne, *English merchants*, 2 vols., 1866; 1886. See also M. Priestley, 'London merchants and opposition politics in Charles II's reign', *Bull. Inst. Hist. Research*, 29 (1956), 205–19; Tawney's important study of the merchant, Lionel Cranfield, *Business and Politics under James I* (477); and the Cranfield papers (H.M.C.) in no. 108.

2098 SUTHERLAND, L. S. 'The law merchant in England in the 17th and 18th centuries.' *R.H.S. Trans.*, 4th Ser. 17 (1934), 149–76.

Deals with the growth of the special body of mercantile law from the point of view of the requirements of merchants. See also *Legal History*.

2099 WESTERFIELD, R. B. Middlemen in English business, particularly between 1660 and 1760. Trans. Connecticut Academy of Arts and Sciences, 19. New Haven. 1915. Bibl.

The accounts of a Hereford mercer, John Noble, for 1691 to 1694, ed. by F. C. Morgan, *Trans. of the Woolhope Club*, 1944 and 1945, were repr. Hereford, 1947. For the accounts of a mercer of Worcester, 1643, see *Worcs. Arch. Soc. Trans.*, N.S. 14 (1937), 45–60.

2100   WILLIAMS, N. J. Contraband cargoes: seven centuries of smuggling. 1959. Hamden (Conn.). 1961.

Footnotes are included in the 1961 edn. See also Atton and Holland (2069 n.); and R. G. Albion's article on 'Smuggling' in *Encyclop. of the Social Sciences*. A popular account is *Smugglers*, by H. M. Shore, Baron Teignmouth, and C. G. Harper, 2 vols., 1923. An essay on American smuggling, 1660–1760, is included in W. J. Ashley, *Surveys: historical and economic*, 1900.

2. INSURANCE

2101   MARTIN, F. The history of Lloyds and of marine insurance. 1876. Bibl.

For later histories of Lloyds see no. 2060.

2102   RELTON, F. B., ed. An account of the fire insurance companies . . . in Great Britain and Ireland during the 17th and 18th centuries, including the Sun Fire Office: also of Charles Povey, the projector of that office. 1893.

Includes documents and bibl. of Povey's writings.

3. DOMESTIC COMMERCE

For ships, navigation, and seamen see also *Naval History*. Titles in *Local History* should also be checked.

(a) *Sources*

2103   BROOKS, F. W., ed. The first order book of the Hull Trinity House, 1632–1665. Yorks. Arch. Soc. Rec. Ser. for 1941. [1942.]

Records of the gild of seamen. See also *Calendars* [of other Trinity House docs.], ibid. Misc. 5 (1951), pp. 1–45 and 47–67.

2104   McGRATH, P., ed. Merchants and merchandise in 17th-century Bristol. Bristol Rec. Soc. Publ. 19. Bristol. 1955.

Selection of documents and excerpts to illustrate mercantile activities, as well as to indicate the types of sources in existence.

2105   WILLAN, T. S., ed. The navigation of the Great Ouse between St. Ives and Bedford in the seventeenth century. Bedfordshire Hist. Rec. Soc. Publ. 24. Streatley. 1946.

For other titles on river navigation see Cox's *Guide* (2351), vol. iii, pp. 325–8, and no. 2109.

(b) *Later Works*

2106   CHAPLIN, W. R., comp. The corporation of Trinity House of Deptford Strond from . . . 1660. 1952.

Cf. A. S. Harvey, *The 'Trinity House' of Kingston upon Hull*, Hull [1950].

2107 FISHER, F. J. 'The development of the London food market 1540–1640.' *Econ. Hist. Rev.* 5 (1935), 46–64.

Valuable. See also his article on London as a centre of consumption in *R.H.S. Trans.* 4th Ser. 30 (1948), 37–50. On shipment of farm produce in other parts of the country see an able article by G. E. Fussell, *Agric. Hist.* 20 (1946), 77–86.

2108 OWEN, SIR D. J. The origin and development of the ports of the United Kingdom. 1939.

Cf. E. Harris, *Swansea, its port and trade* . . ., Cardiff, 1934, and articles by W. B. Stephens on 'Exeter's commercial policies, 1625–88', *Trans. Devon. Assoc.* 86 (1954), 137–60, and by B. Hall on Newcastle and the north-east coast, *Bull. Inst. Hist. Research*, 12 (1934), 56–60.

2109 WILLAN, T. S. The English coasting trade, 1600–1750. Manchester. 1938. Bibl.

By the same author, *River navigation in England 1600–1750*, Milford and Lond. 1936; *Navigation of the river Weaver in the 18th century*, publ. by Chetham Soc., 1951; and his articles on the Severn valley, 1600–1710, *Econ. Hist. Rev.* 8 (1937), 68–79, and East Anglia, 1600–1750, in *Norfolk Archaeology*, 26 (1938), 296–309. See also I. G. Philip, 'River navigation at Oxford during the civil war and commonwealth', *Oxoniensia*, 2 (1937), 152–65.

4. FOREIGN AND COLONIAL

See also *Colonial History* and *Foreign Relations*. For trade in certain commodities see also *Industry* above; see also *Trading Companies* (nos. 2127–39).

The titles in this section are arranged after the general ones, roughly as they relate to particular countries or areas. A brief bibliography is in Ramsay. A bibliography containing many titles relating to Dutch commerce and trading companies is W. Ph. Coolhaas, ed., *A critical survey of studies on Dutch colonial history*, The Hague, 1960, originally publ. in French in *Rev. d'histoire des colonies*, 44 (1957), 311–448.

(a) General

2110 CLARK, G. N. 'War trade and trade war, 1701–1713.' *Econ. Hist. Rev.* 1 (1928), 262–80.

2111 FISHER, F. J. 'London's export trade in the early seventeenth century.' *Econ. Hist. Rev.*, 2nd Ser. 3 (1950), 151–61.

2112 RAMSAY, G. D. English overseas trade during the centuries of emergence. 1957. Bibl.

The best general account of the developments in foreign trade during three centuries, the late 15th to the later 18th; stresses non-English sources; a valuable modern supplement to vol. ii of Lipson (1839). See also Innes (3326).

2113 SCHUMPETER, E. B. English overseas trade statistics, 1697–1808. 1960.

Intro. by T. S. Ashton. See also J. M. Price, 'Multilateralism and bilateralism . . . *c.* 1700', *Econ. Hist. Rev.*, 2nd Ser. 14 (1962), 240–74; and J. Sperling, 'The international payments mechanism . . .', ibid. 446–68.

(b) *Particular Countries and Areas*

2114 MOODY, T. W. The Londonderry plantation. 1939.

Cf. T. Phillips, *Londonderry and the London companies, 1609–1629*, 1928.

2115 COKE, ROGER. Reasons of the increase of the Dutch trade wherein is demonstrated from what causes the Dutch . . . manage trade better than the English. 1671.

Second part of his *Treatise* (2082 n.).

2116 BARBOUR, V. 'Dutch and English merchant shipping in the seventeenth century.' *Econ. Hist. Rev.* 2 (1930), 261–90.

Concerned more with ships than with policies. See also her *Capitalism in Amsterdam in the seventeenth century*, Baltimore, 1951; repr. Ann Arbor, 1963.

2117 CLARK, G. N. and EYSINGA, W. J. M. 'The colonial conferences between England and the Netherlands in 1613 and 1615.' 2 vols. *Bibliotheca Visseriana Dissertationum Jus Internationale Illustrantum*, 15, 17 (1940–51). Leyden. 1952.

See also no. 683 and D. H. Smit's edn. of notes by the secretary to the Dutch trade delegation, 1628–30, 'A. Boot's journal . . .', *Hist. Genootschap Utrecht Bijd. en Mededeel*, 67 (1936), 62–109.

2118 WILSON, C. Profit and power: a study of England and the Dutch Wars. 1957. Bibl.

Attempts to show that the wars developed from England's internal economic problems as well as from economic rivalry. See also Colenbrander (676), Elias (686), and Japikse (690).

2119 PRIESTLEY, M. 'Anglo-French trade and the "unfavourable balance" controversy, 1660–1685.' *Econ. Hist. Rev.*, 2nd Ser. 4 (1951), 37–52.

Suggests caution in accepting contemporary assertion that the balance was highly unfavourable. Cf. D. G. E. Hall, 'Anglo-French trade relations under Charles II', *History*, 7 (1922), 17–30. On a scheme for smuggling in French goods, see article by W. H. Manchée, *Proc. Huguenot Soc. of London*, 5 (1935–6), 406–27. See also Clark, *The Dutch alliance* (683), and A. L. Horniker, 'Anglo-French rivalry in the Levant from 1583 to 1612', *J.M.H.* 18 (1946), 289–305.

2120 CHAPMAN, A. B. W. 'The commercial relations of England and Portugal, 1487–1807.' *R.H.S. Trans.*, 3rd Ser. 1 (1907), 157–79.

Published separately also, with bibl. and list of MS. sources, as part ii in a volume bearing the same title, with V. M. Shillington as author of part i, on the medieval period. For the text of correspondence relating to the British factory at Lisbon, 1696–7, ed. by A. R. Walford, see *Hist. Assoc. Lisbon Branch Ann. Repts.* 2 (1938), 99–149.

2121 McLACHLAN, J., ed. 'Documents illustrating Anglo-Spanish trade between the commercial treaty of 1667 and the Asiento contract of 1713.' *Camb. Hist. Jour.* 4 (1932–4), 299–311.

Notes and extracts. See her *Trade and peace with old Spain* (665). See also C. Nettels, 'England and the Spanish American trade, 1680–1715', *J.M.H.* 3 (1931), 1–32; and H. Koenigsberger, 'English merchants in Naples and Sicily in the seventeenth century', *E.H.R.* 62 (1947), 304–26, which is based largely upon state papers and other P.R.O. materials.

2122 BRINKMANN, C. 'England and the Hanse under Charles II.' *E.H.R.* 23 (1908), 683–708.

See also P. Simpson, 'Die Handelsniederlassung der englischen Kaufleute in Elbing', *Hansische Geschichtsblatter* 22 (1916), 87–143.
See also titles on the Eastland Company.

2123 UNGER, W. S. 'Trade through the Sound in the seventeenth and eighteenth centuries.' *Econ. Hist. Rev.*, 2nd Ser. 12 (1959), 206–21.

A review article, making use of *Tabeller øver Skipsfort og Varetransport gennen Øresund* (1497–1783), ed. by N. E. Bang and K. Korst, 7 vols., Copenhagen and Leipzig, 1906–53. On the reliability of the latter, see Ramsay (2112), p. 256.

2124 NIKIFOROV, L. A. *Russko-Angliyskiye otnosheniya pri Petre I.* [Moscow.] 1950.

See also S. J. Arkangel'skiy, 'Anglo-gollandskaya tergovlya s Moskvoy v 17 veke' ['Anglo-Dutch trade with Moscow in the 17th century'], *Ist Sbornik*, pt. 5 (1936), 5–38; S. Konovalov (652); and Lubimenko (653).

2125 FOSTER, SIR W. E. England's quest of eastern trade. 1933.

Good short introduction. Cf. J. Broderick, 'Japanese and English in the 17th century', *The Month*, 178 (1942), 113–25.
For India and the East Indies see also *Colonial History* (3376–418).

2126 PARES, R. Merchants and planters. Supp. 4 to *Econ. Hist. Rev.* 1960.

See also F. Cundall, *The Darien venture*, N.Y. 1927; and C. R. Boxer, 'English shipping in the Brazil trade, 1640–65', *Mariner's Mirror*, 37 (1951) 197–230; and *Colonial History*, nos. 3352, 3353.

5. TRADING COMPANIES

For Darien see *Scotland*; for the East India Company see Ch. XII, *India*. After the general titles, the titles below are in alphabetical order by the company names.

(a) *General*

2127 CARR, C. T., ed. Select charters of trading companies, A.D. 1530–1707. Selden Soc. 1913.

Valuable, with important introduction.

2128 SCOTT, W. R. The constitution and finance of English, Scottish, and Irish joint-stock companies to 1720. 3 vols. Camb. 1910–12. Bibl.

Valuable; still the fullest account, but should be supplemented by more recent monographs. *Early chartered companies, 1296–1858*, by G. Cawston and A. H. Keane, 1896, includes some documents. See also K. G. Davies, 'Joint-stock investment in the later seventeenth century', *Econ. Hist. Rev.*, 2nd Ser. 4 (1952), 283–301.

2129 SKEEL, C. A. J. 'The Canary Company [1665–67].' *E.H.R.* 31 (1916), 529–44.

(b) *Eastland Company*

2130 SELLERS, M., ed. The acts and ordinances of the Eastland Company. Royal Hist. Soc. 1906.

See also *Reasons humbly offered by the . . . Eastland Merchants against giving a general liberty . . . to export the English woollen manufacture*, 1689. A valuable modern study, with documents, is R. W. K. Hinton, *The Eastland trade and the common weal in the seventeenth century*, Camb. 1959.

(c) *Hudson's Bay Company*

2131 RICH, E. E., ed. Hudson's Bay Company minutes [1671–84]. 3 vols. 1942–6.

Hudson's Bay Company Record Series, publ. by the Champlain Record Soc. (1938+), vols. v, viii, ix. Also ed. by Rich in the Society's Record Series, vols. xi and xx (1948–57), are the *Copy-booke of letters outward* (1680–96). See also *Charters, statutes, orders in council . . . relating to the Hudson's Bay Company*, publ. by the company, Lond. 1949. Other MS. records are in the archives of the company (see C. L. Grose, p. 87). The best history is that by E. E. Rich, vol. i (1670–1763), publ. by the Hudson's Bay Record Society, 1958, bibl.; earlier histories are by G. Bryce, 1900; B. Willson, 2 vols., 1900; Sir W. Schooling, 1920; and D. MacKay, 1937.

(d) *Levant Company*

2132 WOOD, A. C. A history of the Levant Company. 1935. Bibl.

Covers the entire history, to 1825, but does not entirely supersede M. Epstein's *Early history of the Levant Company* [to 1640], *c.* 1908. On the company papers (1606–1833) at the P.R.O. see *Lists and Indexes*, No. 19 (1904), pp. 109–11. See also Dr. John Covel's diaries (ed. by J. T. Bent, Hakluyt Soc. 87, 1893); G. F. Abbott, *Under the Turk in Constantinople, a record of Sir John Finch's embassy 1672–81*, 1920; A. C. Wood, 'The English embassy at Constantinople, 1660–1762', *E.H.R.* 40 (1925), 533–61; and G. Ambrose, 'English traders at Aleppo, 1658–1756', *Econ. Hist. Rev.* 3 (1931), 246–67.

(e) *Merchant Adventurers*

2133 WHEELER, JOHN. A treatise of commerce, wherein are shewed the commodities arising by a wel ordered . . . trade such as that of the Merchantes Adventurers is proved to bee. Middleburgh. 1601. Later edn. Lond. 1601. Ed. by G. B. Hotchkiss. N.Y. 1931.

A short history, written by the secretary of the company, partly in defence against the Hanseatic merchants and others. Also by Wheeler, *The lawes, customs and ordinances of the . . . Merchantes Adventurers*, 1608, repr. ed. by W. E. Lingelbach (Univ. of Pennsylvania Translations and Reprints . . ., 2nd Ser. 2), [Phila.] 1902.

For an answer to Wheeler's *Treatise* see Thomas Milles, *The customers replie . . .*, 1604. Other pamphlets dealing with the relationship of this early chartered company to the freedom of trade are *A discourse consisting of motives for enlargement . . . of trade . . .*, 1645; *Reasons offered by the Merchant Adventurers . . . at Hull for the preservation of their societies . . .*, 1661; see also *Cat. of Thomason Tracts*, i. 417, 500.

2134 LINGELBACH, W. E. 'The internal organisation of the Merchant Adventurers of England.' *R.H.S. Trans.*, N.S. 16 (1902), 19–67.

Cf. G. Unwin's chapter on 'The Merchant Adventurers' Company in the reign of Elizabeth' in no. 1841; and C. te Lintum, *De Merchant Adventurers in de Nederlanden*, The Hague, 1905.

2135 McGRATH, P., ed. Records relating to the Society of Merchant Venturers of the city of Bristol in the seventeenth century. (Bristol Rec. Soc. Publ. 17) Bristol. 1951 [1952].

Selections, the first of two volumes. The petitions of the Merchant Venturers, 1698–

1803, ed. by W. A. Minchinton, are in Bristol Rec. Soc. Publ. 23 (1963). See articles by McGrath in *Mariner's Mirror*, 36 (1950), 69–80; and *Trans. Bristol and Glouc. Arch. Soc.* 72 (1954), 105–28. The standard account is J. Latimer, *The history of the society of Merchant Venturers of the city of Bristol*, Bristol, 1903.

For records of the Newcastle Merchant Adventurers, ed. by J. R. Boyle and F. W. Denby, see Surtees Soc., vols. 93 and 101, Durham, 1895–9 (excerpts); for those of York, 1356–1917, ed. by M. Sellers, see ibid., vol. 129 (1918).

(f) *Royal African Company*

2136 Certain considerations relating to the Royal African Company of England. 1680.

From Br. Mus. 712. f. 19 (1). A volume of tracts relating to the African trade is Br. Mus. 8223. 1. 4. For descriptions of the records of the company see K. G. Davies (2137) and H. Jenkinson, 'Records of the English African companies', *R.H.S. Trans.*, 3rd Ser. 6 (1912), 185–220. See also Davenant (2086 n.).

2137 DAVIES, K. G. The Royal African Company. 1957.

Authoritative work, relating the company's activities to the economic developments of the years 1672–1713. See also W. R. Scott, 'The constitution and finance of the Royal African Company', *A.H.R.* 8 (1902–3), 241–59; G. F. Zook, 'The Company of Royal Adventurers trading into Africa [1662–72]', *Jour. of Negro Hist.* 4 (1919), 134–231 (separately pr., Lancaster, Pa. 1919); and J. W. Blake, 'The farm of the Guinea Company in 1631', in *Essays in British and Irish history*, ed. by H. A. Cronne *et al.*, 1949. On the slave trade see Donnan (3419 n.). On disputes with Jewish merchants of the Netherlands see an article by W. S. Samuel in *Jewish Hist. Soc. of Engl. Trans.* 14 (1935), 39–79. On the Scottish company see G. P. Insh (3929), and his edn. of its *Papers* (1696–1707), Edin. 1924.

(g) *South Sea Company*

2138 CARSWELL, J. The South Sea bubble. 1960.

Based upon company records and other MSS. Early chapters relate to the late Stuart period, and biographical sketches of directors are contained in the appendix. For a list of contemporary pamphlets, see *Camb. Mod. Hist.* vi. 872–4. H. M. Hyde's biog. of John Law (3928), contains much new material. See Law's *Money and trade considered*, Edin. 1705; and P. Harsin's edition of Law's *Œuvres complètes*, 3 vols., Paris, 1934. Useful articles on the company are by R. D. Richards in *Econ. Hist.* 1 (1933), 348–74, and E. Donnan in *Jour. of Econ. and Bus. Hist.* 2 (1930), 419–50. See also no. 3929.

(h) *Virginia Company*

2139 KINGSBURY, S. M., ed. The records of the Virginia Company of London. 4 vols. Wash. 1906–35.

Vols. i–ii contain the court books (1619–24), and vols. iii and iv contain documents. In the first vol. is a list of the company records. Other works relating to this company can be found in the bibliographies in *Colonial History*, Ch. XII.

6. VOYAGES

The following section contains the largest number of titles from the separate section on *Voyages and Travels* in the original edition of this bibliography. For travels mainly to the European continent, and of a private rather than a commercial nature, see Ch. IX, *Travel*; for voyages in ships of the royal navy, such as those of Dampier or Rogers, see Ch. VII, *Naval Voyages*. Others relating to the West Indies and to the East are in *Colonial History*.

In the present section are (*a*) Collections of voyages, the chronological arrangement of which will give some indication of the interest of the age in exploration; and (*b*) later works of a general nature. The most famous of the collections is Purchas (2140), with Churchill's (2143) possibly next in importance. An analysis of the contents of the chief collections is in Appendix I to the *Catalogue* of the Royal Geographical Society; the 17th-century collections are briefly described in chapters 2 and 3 of E. Lynam, ed., *Richard Hakluyt and his successors, a volume issued to commemorate the centenary of the Hakluyt Society* (the Society's second Ser., no. 93), 1946.

No complete list of particular voyages is provided here. The Hakluyt Society, which continues to publish fresh material, includes most of the accounts of significance for the period. The list of its titles is in Mullins (23 n.), pp. 148–76. Important 17th-century voyages to particular areas, as printed in the Hakluyt Society volumes, in addition to the Purchas collection are: Africa, the Levant and the Red Sea, Ser. 1, vol. 87, Ser. 2, vols. 6, 17, 100; the East Indies and the Orient, Ser. 2, vols. 66, 74, 75, 82, 85, 88; the western hemisphere, particularly in search of the north-west passage, Ser. 1, vols. 5, 18, 27, 59, 63, 88, 89, and Ser. 2, vol. 60. For those relating to colonial America see the bibliographies in *Colonial History*. For listings by period and by area E. G. Cox's *Guide to . . . Travel* (2351) is of some value. Outside of the Hakluyt series, most of the well-known narratives have been reprinted in such collections as Churchill or Pinkerton; a few are in the *Harleian Miscellany* (59). For individual names the student is referred to *D.N.B.*, the *S.T.C.* (3), and Wing (4).

(a) *Collections of Voyages*

2140 PURCHAS, SAMUEL, ed. Hakluytus posthumus or Purchas his pilgrimes . . . 4 vols. 1625. Later edn. 20 vols. (Hakluyt Soc. Extra Ser. 14–33.) Glasgow. 1905–7.

> Usually added as a fifth volume is *Purchas his pilgrimage* (1613, 4th edn., 1626). A bibliographical note is included in the 1905 edn. C. Wild ed. excerpts under the title of *Purchas his pilgrimes in Japan*, 1939.
> For Hakluyt see Read, nos. 3136–7.

2141 RAY, JOHN, ed. A collection of curious travels and voyages . . . 2 vols. 1693. Later edns.

> Period, 16th and 17th centuries. The 1738 edn. is combined with the account of Ray's own travels.

2142 HACKE, WILLIAM, comp. A collection of original voyages, containing: I. Capt. Cowley's voyage round the globe. II. Capt. Sharpe's journey over the isthmus of Darien . . . III. Capt. Wood's voyage through the straits of Magellan. IV. Mr. Robert's adventures among the Corsairs of the Levant. 1699.

> Repr. in 1729 in *Collection* . . . (4 vols.), which includes a number of Dampier's voyages (see no. 1824). See also Exquemeling, *Bucaneers of America* (3347). Originals of Cowley Sharp, and Wood are Br. Mus. Sloane MSS. 46, 54, 3833.

2143 CHURCHILL, AWNSHAM and JOHN, eds. A collection of voyages and travels ... 4 vols. 1704. Maps. Later edns. 6 vols. 1732. Maps. 8 vols. 1744–7. Maps.

Contains a prefatory essay on the history of navigation. The 1744–7 edn. includes as vols. vii and viii the so-called Harleian collection, *A collection of voyages and travels ... compiled from the library of the late earl of Oxford*, 2 vols., 1745. Churchill includes important 16th- and 17th-century European as well as English travels; brief description in Lynam. Cf. John Locke, *The whole history of navigation* [1704], and Locke's *Works*, vol. x (10th edn.), 1801.

2144 HARRIS, JOHN, ed. Navigantium atque itinerantium bibliotheca; or a compleat collection of voyages and travels. 2 vols. 1705. Maps. Later edn. by John Campbell. 2 vols. 1744–8. Maps.

Harris's collection, ranging chiefly from the 15th to the 18th century, contains selections from some 400 writers, including parts from Hakluyt and Purchas. The so-called second edn., by Dr. John Campbell, is virtually a new collection, in terms of rearrangement of the narratives, and induction of some new material (see Lynam). A minor collection of this period, including several accounts from Spanish and Portuguese sources, was publ. as a *New collection of voyages ...*, by John Stevens, 2 vols., 1708–10, later edn., 1711.

2145 ASTLEY, THOMAS, publ. A new general collection of voyages and travels. 4 vols. 1745–7. Maps.

Editorship frequently attributed to John Green. Includes 15th- to 18th-century narratives, foreign as well as English, with many notes. Based largely on Astley is J. H. Moore's *New and complete collections of voyages and travels ...*, 2 vols. [1785?] A minor collection, containing little new material, is the compilation by the bookseller, John Newbury, *The world displayed, or a curious collection of voyages and travels selected from the writers of all nations ...*, 20 vols., 1759–61, maps. See also collections by J. Knox, 7 vols., 1767; and W. F. Mavor, 20 vols., 1796–1802, enl. edn., 28 vols., 1810.

2146 CALLANDER, J., ed. Terra australis cognita: or voyages to the Terra Australis ... 3 vols. Edin. 1766–8. Maps.

Covers 16th to 18th centuries. Based largely upon C. de Brosses, *Histoire des navigations aux terres australes*, 2 vols., Paris, 1756. Cf. R. H. Major, ed., *Early voyages [to 1727] to Terra Australis* (Hakluyt Soc., vol. 25), 1859.

2147 PINKERTON, J., ed. A general collection of the best and most interesting voyages and travels ... 17 vols. 1808–14. Maps. Bibl.

Vols. ii and iii relate to the British Isles; vol. xvii contains a 'Catalogue of books' for each country. Another useful later collection is R. Kerr, *General history and collection of voyages and travels*, 18 vols., Edin. 1811–24.

(b) *Later Works*

2148 BARROW, J. A chronological history of voyages into the Arctic regions ... 1818.

Cf. N. M. Crouse, *In quest of the western ocean*, N.Y. 1928, bibl., and his *Search for the northwest passage*, N.Y. 1934; and L. J. Burpee, *The search for the western sea ...*, 1907, rev. edn., 2 vols., 1936. Also on the north-west passage are R. B. Bodilly, *The voyage of Captain Thomas James ... 1631*, 1928; and M. Christy, 'Captain William Hawkeridge ...', *Mariner's Mirror*, 13 (1927), 51–78.

2149 BURNEY, J. A chronological history of north-eastern voyages of discovery. 1819. Maps.

Also by Burney, *A chronological history of the discoveries in the South Sea or Pacific Ocean*, 5 vols., 1803–17. D. Henry compiled *An historical account of all the voyages round the world performed by English navigators*, 4 vols., 1773–4, vols. 5–6, 1775–84.

2150 HEAWOOD, E. A history of geographical discovery in the seventeenth and eighteenth centuries. Camb. 1912.

Cambridge Geographical Series.

2151 MURRAY, H. Historical account of discoveries and travels in Asia from the earliest ages to the present time. 3 vols. Edin. 1820. Bibl.

Murray ed. John Leyden's *Historical account of discoveries . . . in Africa*, 2 vols., Edin. 1817; and wrote *Historical account of discoveries . . . in North America . . .*, 2 vols., 1829, both with bibl. With others he publ. also *Narrative of discovery . . . in Africa . . .*, Edin. 1830, and *Narrative of discovery . . . in the Polar Seas*, Edin. 1830.

F. GOVERNMENT REGULATION

For the theory of government regulation see the general section in this chapter, particularly the titles on *Mercantilism*; see also *Public Finance* and *Trade and Commerce*. For ordinances see *Constitutional History*. The titles in the section below are representative of particular areas of regulation; those relating to the poor are in Ch. IX, *Social Problems*.

2152 ASHLEY, M. P. Financial and commercial policy under the Cromwellian protectorate. 1934. 2nd edn. 1962.

Valuable study of relationships between government and economic developments, with separate chapters on taxes, public finance, commercial classes, trade, depression. Cf. G. D. Ramsay, 'Industrial laissez-faire and the policy of Cromwell', *Econ. Hist. Rev.* 16 (1946), 93–110.

2153 BARNES, D. G. History of the English corn laws . . . 1660–1846. 1930. Bibl.

First two chapters on the period. C. R. Fay, *The corn laws and social England*, Camb. 1932, also is concerned chiefly with the later centuries.

2154 BERESFORD, M. W. 'The common informer, the penal statutes and economic regulation.' *Econ. Hist. Rev.* 10 (1957), 221–37.

Also by Beresford, 'The beginning of retail tobacco licenses, 1632–41', *Yorks. Bull. Econ. Soc. Research*, 7 (1955), 128–43.

2155 CHERRY, G. L. 'The development of the English free-trade movement in Parliament, 1689–1702.' *J.M.H.* 25 (1953), 103–19.

Written to correct the over-emphasis on the influence of pamphleteers in the interest of freer trade. But see also H. F. Kearney, 'The political background of English mercantilism, 1695–1700', *Econ. Hist. Rev.*, 2nd Ser. 11 (1958–9), 484–96.

2156 HARPER, L. A. The English navigation laws: a seventeenth-century experiment in social engineering. N.Y. 1939. Bibl.

Chief emphasis is on the later decades; appendices include useful tables. For other interpretations of the relationships between legislation and economic crises in the earlier periods see Hinton (2130 n.) and Supple (1840). On the 1631 act see G. N. Clark's interpretive article in *History*, N.S. 7 (1922–3), 282–6. Bieber (779) deals with some of the problems of enforcement.

2157 KELSALL, R. K. Wage regulation under the statute of artificers. 1938.

Useful for administrative aspects, especially in eastern and north-eastern England. See Kelsall's articles on the subject (1975 n.); and M. G. Davies (1978). On earlier problems of enforcement see B. Putnam, *The enforcement of the statute of labourers*, N.Y. 1908.

2158 LOHMANN, F. Die staatliche Regelung der englischen Wollindustrie. Leipsic. 1900.

Should be checked by the work of later scholars. Several chapters in Heaton (1994) relate to government regulation. See also R. M. Lees, 'Constitutional importance of the commissioners for wool, 1689: an administrative experiment . . .', *Economica*, 40 (1933), 147–68, 264–74.

2159 NEF, J. U. Industry and government in France and England, 1540–1640. Phila. 1940. N.Y. 1957.

Nef's thesis is that in England greater freedom in industrial enterprise accompanied progress in constitutional government. See D. O. Wagner, 'Coke and the rise of economic liberalism', *Econ. Hist. Rev.* 6 (1935–6), 30–44.

2160 PRICE, W. H. The English patents of monopoly. Boston (Mass.). 1906.

A useful monograph, with sections relating to the period. See also E. W. Hulme, *Early history of the English patent system*, 1909, and D. S. Davies, 'The early history of the patent specification', *Law Quart. Rev.* 50 (1934), 86–189, 260–74. Cf. Clark (1965 n.) and Churchill (1021).

G. POPULATION

No conclusive study of population throughout the century has been made. In Ch. IX, *Biography*, are references to the types of materials from which statistical studies can be drawn. The fourth volume of *Victoria County History of Wiltshire*, 1959, includes studies for several medieval years and tables for the period since 1800. Other titles in *Local History* are of use.

Although depopulation was a matter of concern in the Stuart period, official reports of the problems relate chiefly to enclosures and the decline of cultivated acreage (see Gay, no. 1942). On the statistical attempts by John Graunt in 1662 and Sir William Petty, using bills of mortality, see Petty (1833). See also Bell (3292). Edmund Halley's papers on 'The degrees of mortality of mankind', based upon statistics from Breslau, in Silesia, and publ. by the Royal Society in 1693, were repr. in 1942 (C. H. Evans, ed., Baltimore). On the reliability of the most well-known contemporary figures for England in the last decade of the century by King (2171), see D. V. Glass, 'Gregory King's estimates of population, 1695', in *Population Studies*, III; and Jones (2162).

The titles listed below illustrate additional types of population studies that are now available.

2161 THE INHABITANTS of London in 1638. (The Society of Genealogists.) 1931.

Ed. by T. C. Dale from MS. 272 in the Lambeth Palace Library. See also Dale (3294).

2162 JONES, P. E. and JUDGES, A. V. 'London population in the late 17th
century.' *Econ. Hist. Rev.* 6 (1935), 45–63.

Estimates based upon various contemporary records are compared with those by King.
Cf. N. G. Brett-James, 'The London bills of mortality in the seventeenth century',
Lond. and Middlesex Arch. Soc. Trans., N.S. 6 (1930), 284–309. An article by I. Scouloudi
on alien immigration into London is in *Proc. Huguenot Soc. of London,* 16 (1937–8),
27–49.

2163 MARSHALL, L. M. Rural population of Bedfordshire, 1671–1921,
based on the hearth tax returns of 1671 and the census returns of 1801 and
1921. (Bedfordshire Hist. Rec. Soc. 16.) 1924.

Valuable, illustrating the statistical use of the hearth tax returns. (Cf. 2071.) See also
C. A. F. Meekings, *Surrey hearth tax, 1664* (Surrey Rec. Soc. Publ. 17), 1942; and
M. M. B. Weinstock, *Hearth tax returns, Oxfordshire, 1665* (Oxfordshire Rec. Soc.
Publ.), 1940. For estimates on Exeter's population in the century, see *Devon and
Cornwall N. and Q.* 20 (1939), 210–14.

Other local studies, based on church records and on assessments of the period are:
for Nottinghamshire towns, by A. C. Wood, *Trans. Thoroton Soc.* 40 (1936), 109–13,
and 41 (1937), 18–26; for a Warwickshire village, 1698, by P. Styles, *Univ. of Birmingham Hist. Jour.* 3 (1951), 33–51; and W. G. D. Fletcher, *Religious census of Shropshire
in 1676* [1891?].

IX

SOCIAL HISTORY

Aspects of social history of the seventeenth century are revealed by almost every-
thing that was written in the period, and only a selected number of these aspects
are dealt with in this chapter. Many sources in other parts of the volume are
useful for studying social history. An attempt has been made in this section to
suggest types of sources, rather than to provide complete lists. Letters, diaries,
household accounts, records of family events such as marriages and births, reveal
much about the daily habits of the upper and middle classes, and in rarer
instances for those of lower degree. Allusions in literature, and the comments
of travellers, are helpful, though somewhat less reliable. From official records
such as those of quarter sessions much can be learned. For the well-to-do and
those who attached themselves to the royal court, guides on conduct have more
meaning than for the rest. Manners and tastes, however, were being influenced
by the widening horizons of the age, an important aspect of the period.

The culture of the Tudor age extended well into the century, and for the early
years the bibliographies in *Shakespeare's England* (2181) still are helpful. There
is no general social history for the middle or late years, although there have been
studies focusing on special periods, such as Bryant (2176) for the Restoration
period. Macaulay's sketch of the state of England in 1685 (361) is still valuable,
as is the first volume of Lecky for conditions at the close. The outlines for a
comprehensive study are suggested by Trevelyan (2185) but the details still need
to be filled in. For this purpose there is an increasing quantity of source material
available—literary, personal, and official—and these relate to the countryside as
well as to the better-known region of London. Jordan (2539) provides an example
of conclusions to be drawn from new materials.

Several subjects of a social nature have been treated more particularly in other
sections. Matters of wealth, occupations, and population are in *Economic History*;
education, music, art, literature, and the press are in *Cultural History*. On legal
matters there is much of value in Holdsworth (1024) and other titles in *Legal
History*; and for the affairs of individuals as well as of communities, much is to
be found in the sections on *Local Government* in Ch. III, and in *Local History*.
Biographical material occurs in many chapters. In the *Reports* of the Historical
Manuscripts Commission there are numerous materials rich in social history.
Examples are Gawdy (142), Le Fleming (138), Montagu of Beaulieu (184),
Rutland (211), and Verulam (149).

A. GENERAL

Although there are no general bibliographies, the bibliographies in Notestein
(2183) and in several chapters of no. 9 n. are useful.

1. SOURCES

See also sermons (nos. 1110–12).

2164 EBURNE, RICHARD. A plaine path-way to plantations. 1624. Later edn. by L. B. Wright. Ithaca. [1962.]

2165 CARY, WALTER. The present state of England. 1627.

2166 COTTON, SIR ROBERT. Danger wherein the kingdom now standeth. 1628.

2167 EARLE, JOHN. Microcosmography: or a peece of the world discovered in essays and characters. 1628. Many later edns. Ed. by P. Bliss. 1811. Ed. by S. T. Irwin. Bristol. 1897. 1903.

> One of the most well known of the 'books of character'. See also Sir Thomas Overbury, *The Overburian characters*, 1614, 1615, ed. by W. G. Paylor (Percy Reprints, vol. 13), Oxf. 1936. Because of the bibliographies in the 1811 and 1897 edns. of Earle many similar character books are omitted, but see Halliwell-Phillipps (2168); G. Murphy, *A bibliography of English character-books 1608–1700*, 1925; and C. N. Greenough, *A bibliography of the Theophrastian character in English*, Camb. (Mass.) 1947.

2168 HALLIWELL-PHILLIPPS, J. O., ed. Books of characters, illustrating the habits and manners of Englishmen from the reign of James I to the restoration. 1857.

> Repr. *The wandering Jew telling fortunes to Englishmen*, 1649; *The man in the moone telling strange fortunes*, 1609; J. Stephens's *Essayes and characters, ironicall and instructive*, 1615; D. Lupton's *London and the country carbonadoed and quartered into several characters*, 1632.

2169 FULLER, THOMAS. The holy state and the profane state. Camb. 1642. Later edn. by M. Walten. 2 vols. N.Y. 1938 (Columbia Univ. studies in English and comparative literature no. 136).

> See W. E. Houghton, *The formation of Thomas Fuller's holy and profane states*, Camb. (Mass.) 1938; and no. 2145.

2170 OSBORNE, FRANCIS. The works of Francis Osborne. 7th edn. 1673. 8th edn. 1682. 1689. 1701. 11th edn. 2 vols. 1722.

> The edn. of 1673, though called the 7th (? of *Advice to a son*), is probably the 1st collected edn. of Osborne's works; that of 1722, the last and best, contains his letters to Col. William Draper, 1653–7. His *Advice to a son*, first publ. in two parts, 1656–8, was ed. by E. A. Parry, 1896; ed. by L. B. Wright (Folger Documents, no. 2), Ithaca, 1962.

2171 KING, GREGORY. Natural and political observations and conclusions upon the state and conditions of England. 1696. Ed. by G. E. Barnett. Baltimore. 1936.

> Good contemporary description of population and wealth. See nos. 1833, 2162. The two volumes ed. by G. B. Harrison, *A Jacobean journal, being a record of those things most talked of during the years 1603–1606*, 1941, and *Second Jacobean journal* (1607–1610), 1958, are compilations in chronological order of items from contemporary materials, but are of limited value for the scholar.

2172 SHAFTESBURY, ANTHONY ASHLEY COOPER, EARL OF. Sensus communis; an essay on the freedom of wit and honour. In a letter to a friend. 1709.

2173 HAZLITT, W. C., ed. Fugitive tracts written in verse which illustrate the condition of religious and political feeling in England . . . Second series, 1600–1700. 2 vols. 1875.

This is an example of various collections of materials relating to social history. Others worth examining are: C. Hindley, ed., *The old book collector's miscellany* (3 vols., 1871–3), which contains minor literary pieces mainly illustrating social history; and *Social England illustrated: a collection of xviith century tracts*, with intro. by A. Lang, Westminster, 1903, which is repr. from *An English garner* (62 n.). Volumes iv and v of R. B. Morgan's *Readings in English social history*, Camb. 1921–2, pertain to the period. See also J. Ashton (2174). Collections of letters are mentioned in § F, *Biography*, below.

2. Later Works

2174 ASHTON, J. Social life in the reign of Queen Anne, taken from original sources. 2 vols. 1882. 1904. Illus.

Valuable. See also for this period W. H. Irving's excellent *John Gay's London*, Camb. (Mass.) 1928; L. Melville (*pseud.*), *In the days of Queen Anne*, 1929; and J. R. Sutherland, *Background for Queen Anne*, 1939. Much biographical material is contained in the two latter works.

2175 BASTIDE, C. The Anglo-French entente in the seventeenth century. 1914.

Virtually a translation of the Paris edition of 1912. Cf. L. Charlanne, *L'influence française en Angleterre au xviie siècle*, Paris, 1906.

2176 BRYANT, ARTHUR. The England of Charles II. 1934.

Strong emphasis on social history, from the sources. See also Beloff (356). On the social ideas of religious groups see Schlatter (1148) and Lloyd (1417).

2177 COATE, MARY. Social life in Stuart England. 1924. Bibl.

See also the famous third chapter of Macaulay (361), and the comment by Sir C. Firth in *History*, 17 (1932), 201–19. *Court and society from Elizabeth to Anne*, by William D. Montagu, duke of Manchester, 2 vols., 1864, is loosely assembled from Montagu family papers and applies to society in general as well as to the court. Still of some use is W. C. Sydney, *Social life in England* (1660–1690), 1892. In T. Burke, *The English townsman as he was and as he is*, 1946, parts of ch. 2 deal with the period.

2178 DEXTER, H. M. The England and Holland of the Pilgrims. Ed. by M. Dexter. Lond., N.Y., and Boston. 1906.

A valuable study.

2179 FOLGER BOOKLETS on Tudor and Stuart civilization. Ithaca, N.Y. 1958+.

A useful series published by the Folger Shakespeare Library consisting of brief essays on a variety of subjects, with illustrations from the sources. Included are: 1. D. Mason, *Music in Elizabethan England*; 11. V. A. La Mar, *Travel and roads . . .*; 12. J. R. Hale, *The art of war . . .*; 13. A. J. Schmidt, *The yeoman . . .*; 15. B. Penrose, *Tudor and early Stuart voyaging*; 17. E. C. Eyler, *English gardens and garden books*.

2180 GILLESPIE, J. E. Influence of oversea expansion on England to 1700. N.Y. 1920. (Columbia University Studies.) Bibl.

2181   LEE, S., ed. Shakespeare's England, being an account of the life and manners of his age. 2 vols. Oxf. 1916.

Valuable bibl. notes for each chapter.

2182   MATHEW, D. The Jacobean age. 1938.

Interesting study of the background of the period. For later years see the brief introductory surveys for the periods of Charles II and Anne in Ogg (364) and Trevelyan (385).

2183   NOTESTEIN, W. The English people on the eve of colonization, 1603–30. N.Y. and Lond. 1954. (New American Nation Series.) Bibl. Repr. N.Y. 1962.

Well-documented commentary on classes and institutions that incorporates much from recent scholarship. For background see also L. B. Wright, *Middle-class culture in Elizabethan England*, 1935, bibl.

2184   TRAILL, H. D., ed. Social England: a record of the progress of the people in religion, laws, learning, arts, industry, commerce, science, literature and manners. 6 vols. 1893–7. Illustrated edn. Lond. and N.Y. 1901–4.

Vol. iv is devoted to 1603–1714. Comprehensive; a co-operative work, of which some parts are unsatisfactory and some are out of date. More specialized aspects are treated in W. T. O'Dea, *The social history of lighting*, 1958, bibl., and G. Roberts, *The social history . . . of the southern counties*, 1856.

2185   TREVELYAN, G. M. English social history. 1942. 1944. 2nd edn. [1946]. Illustrated edn. in 4 vols. 1949–52.

A rich panorama. Of the illustrated edn., vol. ii and part of vol. iii deal with the century. *Studies in social history: a tribute to Trevelyan*, ed. by J. H. Plumb, 1955, contains essays by Rowse, Notestein, Hoskins, Wedgwood, Habakkuk, and Plumb. Also useful are *Life and work of the people of England*, by D. Hartley, and M. M. Elliot (1925; N.Y. 1929, illus.); and the briefer *Picture source book for social history: seventeenth century*, by M. Harrison and A. A. M. Wells, 1953.

2186   TROTTER, E. Seventeenth century life in a country parish. Camb. 1919. Bibl.

Drawn mainly from North Riding quarter sessions records. See also F. H. West, *Rude forefathers: the story of an English village 1660–66*, 1949, which is based on account books of Upton-by-Southwell.

B. STATUS AND CLASS

1. SOURCES

Contemporary materials include those relating to families, their pedigrees and titles, heraldry, treatises on particular classes, and various literary materials ranging from plays to sermons. Examples of such types are listed below, and others may be found under *Biography* (§ F, below), *Literature* (2578 to 2689), and *Economic History* (1854, 1855, 1860). See also *House of Lords* (811, 849).

(a) *Pedigrees and Heraldry*

2187 HOLME, RANDLE. The Academy of armory, or a storehouse of armory and blazon. Chester. 1688. Illus.

Repr. 1905 with an additional vol. ed. by I. H. Jeayes from Holme's work in Harl. MSS. 2033–5. Cf. J. Guillim, *A display of heraldry*, 1610, 6th edn. 1724; and T. Moule, *Bibliotheca heraldica Magnae Britanniae*, 1822, which lists many works on heraldry.

2188 ST. GEORGE, SIR HENRY. Wiltshire visitation pedigrees 1623. Ed. by G. D. Squibb. (Harleian Soc. Pub. 105–106.) 1954.

This is one of the official reports to the College of Heralds on the pedigrees and arms of county families. An invaluable source for social and local history as well as for genealogy. See no. 2417.

By the same ed., *Reports of heraldic cases in the Court of Chivalry, 1623–1732* (Harleian Soc. Pub. 107), 1956. Reports on men subject to knighthood compositions and other levies, *temp.* Charles I, are in Sir Richard Norton's letter-book (Br. Mus. Add. MS. 21922), and in other collections, e.g. Add. MS. 38139, S.P. 16, xlvi, 2, and clxxxix, 46; *Sussex Arch.* 16 (1864), 45–51. Several have been printed by local historical societies (see Mullins, 23 n.).

(b) *Literary Sources*

2189 TAYLOR, JOHN. 'A Brood of Cormorants', in *Works* (2367 n.).

Examples of other literary sources revealing class structure are ballads such as those in *A Kentish garland*, ed. by J. H. L. Devaynes, 2 vols., Hertford, 1881–2; plays, e.g. *George a Green, the pinner of Wakefield* [1599], ed. by F. W. Clarke, Malone Society Reprints, 1911; and Nathaniel Newbury's sermon, *The yeoman's prerogative*, 1652 (Wing, N 847).

2190 HERBERT, GEORGE. A priest to the temple, or the country parson. 1652. 2nd edn. 1671. 3rd. 1675. 4th. 1701.

Also in *Works* (2627).

(c) *Other Sources*

2191 SHAW, W. A. Letters of denization and acts of naturalization for aliens in England and Ireland, 1603–1700. Lymington. 1911.

Intro. explains the history of the law and documentary sources. Cf. J. S. Burn, *History of French, Walloon, Dutch and other foreign protestant refugees settled in England . . .*, 1846; W. D. Cooper's *Lists of foreign protestants and aliens resident in England 1618–1688*, Camden Soc., 1862; D. C. A. Agnew, *Protestant exiles from France in the reign of Louis XIV*, s.l. 1866; and E. E. Stride, *A bibliography of works relating to the Huguenot refugees*, Lymington, 1886. See also nos. 1402–6.

2192 POWELL, THOMAS. Tom of all trades: the plaine pathway to preferment . . . in all professions, trades, arts and mysteries. 1631.

Second edn., 1635, under the title of *The art of thriving*.

2. LATER WORKS

2193 FINCH, M. E. The wealth of five Northamptonshire families. 1540–1640. Northamptonshire Rec. Soc. Publ. 19 (1954–5). Oxf. 1958.

Important well-documented study. Cf. P. Laslett, 'The gentry of Kent in 1640', *Camb.*

Hist. Jour. 9 (1948), 148–64; J. E. Mousley, 'The fortunes of some gentry families of Elizabethan Sussex', *Econ. Hist. Rev.*, 2nd ser. 11 (1958–9), 467–83. A. Simpson uses family records for *The wealth of the gentry, 1540–1660: East Anglian studies*, Chicago, 1961; and a single family case is presented in A. F. Upton, *Sir Arthur Ingram, c. 1625–1640: a study of the origins of an English landed family*, Oxf. 1961. See also Gay's articles on the Temple family (2506); also nos. 2217, 2222.

2194   FISHER, F. L., ed. Essays in the economic and social history of Tudor and Stuart England, in honour of R. H. Tawney. Camb. 1961.

Includes an essay by L. Stone on the finances of the earl of Salisbury, and others of use for the Stuart period. See also E. L. Klotz and G. Davies, 'The wealth of the royalist peers and baronets . . .', *E.H.R.* 58 (1943), 217–19; J. P. Cooper, 'The fortune of Thomas Wentworth, earl of Strafford', *Econ. Hist. Rev.*, 2nd ser. 11 (1958–9), 227–48; and K. S. Van Eerde, 'The creation of the baronetage in England', *Hunt. Lib. Quart.* 22 (1958–9), 313–22.

2195   FUSSELL, G. E. and K. R. The English countryman: his life and work. A.D. 1500–1900. 1955.

Also by G. E. Fussell, *The English rural labourer: his house, furniture, clothing, and food from Tudor to Victorian times*, 1949, bibl. Both of these works present a good picture of a neglected class. See also W. G. Hoskins, *The midland peasant*, N.Y. 1957. For yeomen and other rural classes see Campbell (1860) and nos. 1873, 1882.

2196   MATHEW, D. The social structure in Caroline England. Oxf. 1948.

Valuable but not infallible. Useful articles on related subjects are: C. R. Mayes, 'The sale of peerages in early Stuart England', *J.M.H.* 29 (1957), 21–37; T. C. Mendenhall, 'The social status of the more prominent Shrewsbury drapers, 1560–1660', *Shrops. Arch. and N.H. Soc. Trans.* 54 (1953), 163–70; and D. Ross, 'Class privilege in seventeenth-century England', *History*, 28 (1943–4), 148–55, the latter of which comments particularly on the governmental role of the squirearchy. A picture of three influential classes is given in E. Dakers (Jane Lane, *pseud.*), *Puritan, rake and squire*, 1950.

2197   STONE, L. The crisis of the aristocracy 1558–1641. Oxf. 1965.

Important study of economic and social change.

2198   TAWNEY, R. H. 'The rise of the gentry, 1558–1640', *Econ. Hist. Rev.* 11 (1941), 1–38.

An important article setting forth economic factors as a cause for the shift of political power from the aristocracy. A controversial answer to Tawney's thesis is H. R. Trevor-Roper, *The gentry, 1540–1640* (Camb. 1953, *Econ. Hist. Rev.*, Suppl. no. 1). Articles relating to the ensuing debate are: by Tawney, 'The rise of the gentry: a postscript', *Econ. Hist. Rev.* 7 (1954), 91–7; and 'Harrington's interpretation of his age', *Proc. of the Brit. Acad.*, 1941; by L. Stone, 'The anatomy of the Elizabethan aristocracy', *Econ. Hist. Rev.* 18 (1948), 1–53, and 'The Elizabethan aristocracy, a re-statement', ibid., 2nd Ser. 4 (1952), 302–21; by Trevor-Roper, 'The Elizabethan aristocracy, an anatomy anatomized', ibid. 3 (1951), 279–98, two essays in his *Historical essays*, 1957, and his 'Oliver Cromwell and his parliaments' in no. 927 n. See also no. 2197. Tending to support Trevor-Roper is J. P. Cooper, 'The counting of manors', *Econ. Hist. Rev.*, 2nd Ser. 8 (1956), 377–89, and critical of his view is C. Hill (325 n.). Independent critical comments on the points at issue are: J. H. Hexter, 'Storm over the gentry', *Encounter*, May 1958, repr. in his *Reappraisals in history*, Evanston, 1961 (N.Y. 1963); and P. Zagorin, 'The social interpretation of the English revolution', *Journal of Econ. Hist.* 19 (1959), 376–401.

C. SOCIAL AND DOMESTIC LIFE

1. General: Manners and Customs

(a) *Bibliographies and Sources (alphabetically arranged)*

See also periodicals of the later years, *The Tatler* (3089) and *Spectator* (3090) especially. See also *Social Reform*, nos. 2512–19.

2199 NOYES, G. E. Bibliography of courtesy and conduct books in seventeenth-century England. New Haven. 1937.

Cf. J. E. Mason, *Gentlefolk in the making: studies in the history of English courtesy literature and related topics from 1531 to 1744*, Phila. 1935.

2200 ALLESTREE, RICHARD. The whole duty of man. 1658. 1659–60. 1660. 1661. Later edns.

Cf. no. 1159 n. Also attributed to Allestree, though sometimes to Lady Dorothy Pakington, Archbishop Sterne, and others, is *The gentleman's calling* (1660, two edns.; 1662, 1664, 1667, etc.). See also *The academy of complements, wherein ladyes, gentlewomen scholars and strangers may accommodate their courtly practice with most curious ceremonies* (1640, 1645, 1650, 1658 and later edns.), and other similar works listed in Br. Mus. Pr. Cat. *sub* Academy. The 1685 edn. has title: *The academy of complements or a new way of wooing*. See also *The new academy of complements . . . with an exact collection of the newest and choicest songs a la mode*, 1713, comp. by L[ord] B[uckhurst], Sir C[h.] S[edley], Sir W[m.] D['Avenant], and others.

2201 ASHTON, J., ed. Humor, wit and satire of the seventeenth century. 1883.

Mainly a repr. of ballads.

2202 BLOUNT, THOMAS. The academy of eloquence formula's . . . to speak and to write fluently. 1654. 2nd edn. 1656. 5th edn. 1683.

2203 BRATHWAITE, RICHARD. The English gentleman, containing sundry excellent rules . . . tending to direction of every gentleman. 1630. 1633. 1641.

Also by Brathwaite, *The English gentlewoman . . . expressing what habilliments doe best attire her, . . .* 1631, 1641. Cf. Nicholas Breton, *The court and country, or a briefe discourse between the courtier and the countryman*, 1618; Jean Gailhard, *The compleat gentleman*, 2 vols., 1678; Henry Peacham, *The compleat gentleman . . .*, 1622 (ed. by G. S. Gordon, Oxf. 1906); and *The truth of our times*, 1638. For a volume written about 1729 see Defoe's *The compleat English gentleman*, ed. by K. D. Bülbring, 1890. See also Walker (2944).

2204 GILDON, CHARLES. The postman robb'd of his mail: or, the packet broke open. 1719.

Cf. C. G[ildon], *The post-boy robb'd of his mail: letters of love and gallantry*, 1692, 2nd edn., 1706. See also no. 2431.

2205 HAWKINS, FRANCIS, trans. Youth's behaviour, or decency in conversation amongst men . . . newly turned into English. *Ca.* 1641. 10th edn. 1672.

From French original. [Robert Codrington], *Youth's behaviour or decency in conversation amongst women* was added as a second part in 1664 edn. Cf. Richard Head, *Proteus redevivus: or the art of wheedling or insinuation obtain'd by general conversation*, 1675; also, *The rules of civility, or certain ways of deportment observed in France amongst all persons of quality . . .*, 1671, later edns. 1678, 1685; and S. C., *The art of complaisance . . .*, 1673, 2nd edn., 1677.

2206   MADDEN, SIR F., ed. A relation of some abuses which are committed against the Commonwealth . . . composed especiallye for the benefit of this countrie of Durhame, December the xxvith, 1629. *Camd. Soc. Misc.* iii. 1855.

Includes 'vanities . . . drinking, smoking, and apparel'.

2207   MALCOM, J. P., comp. Miscellaneous anecdotes illustrative of the manners and customs of Europe during the reigns of Charles II, James II, William III and Q. Anne. 1811.

This volume, and the same compiler's *Anecdotes of the manners and customs of London* (2 vols., 1811; 3-vol. edn. the same year), are mainly quotations from ephemeral literature.

2208   MARKHAM, FRANCIS. The booke of honour. 1625.

2209   MARKHAM, GERVASE. The English housewife. 1618. 1631. 1637. 5th edn. 1649. Later edns.

Also appeared as Book II of 1615 and 1623 edns. of *Countrey Contentments* (1876, 2255). See also [Daniel Rogers], *Matrimoniall honour: or the mutuall crowne and comfort of godly, loyall and chaste marriage*, 1642.

2210   NORTHUMBERLAND, HENRY PERCY, EARL OF. Advice to his son by Henry Percy, ninth earl of Northumberland. Ed. by G. B. Harrison [1930]. Ed. by L. B. Wright. Ithaca. 1962.

Excellent example of this type of source. See also John Heydon's *Advice to a daughter in opposition to the advice to a sonne*, 1658, 2nd edn., 1659; 'Richard [Vaughan] earl of Carbery's "Advice to his son"' (*c.* 1651), ed. by V. B. Heltzel, *Hunt. Lib. Bull.* 11 (1937), 59–105; William Higford, *Institutions, or advice to his grandson*, 1658, 1660, [1818]; and 'Sir Peter Leicester's precepts to his son', ed. by E. M. Halcrow, *Trans. Lanc. and Ches. Antiq. Soc.* 62 (1953), 68–72.

2211   PRYNNE, WILLIAM. Healthes sicknesse, or a compendious discourse proving the drinking of healthes to be sinfull. 1628.

Also by Prynne, *The unloveliness of love-locks*, 1628. Cf. Thomas Hall, *Comarum ἀκοσμεία, The loathsomenesse of long haire . . .*, 1654.

(b) *Later Works*

2212   BRAND, J. Observations on popular antiquities. Newcastle-upon-Tyne. 1777. Ed. by H. Ellis, 2 vols. 1813. Ed. by W. C. Hazlitt, 3 vols. 1870. 2 vols. 1905.

See also M. von Boehn, *Modes and manners*, trans. from the German by J. Joshua, 4 vols., 1932–5, which includes English as well as European materials, the third and fourth vols. dealing with the 17th and 18th centuries.

2213 HOLE, C. The English housewife in the seventeenth century. 1953. Bibl.

Excellent for many aspects of home life; well documented. See her earlier *English home-life, 1500–1800,* 1947. Also helpful is R. M. Bradley, *The English housewife in the 17th and 18th centuries,* 1912. See also nos. 2304–14.

2214 POWELL, C. L. English domestic relations, 1487–1653. N.Y. 1917.

Monograph from legal and literary point of view, with bibl. Cf. Elizabeth Godfrey [pseud.; Jessie Bedford], *Home life under the Stuarts, 1603–1649,* 1903, 1925; and L. L. Schücking, *Die Familie im Puritanismus,* Leipzig, 1929. See also W. and M. Haller, 'The puritan art of love', *Hunt. Lib. Quart.* 5 (1942), 235–72, based upon sermons.

2. HOUSEHOLD AND TABLE

Material relating to this subject appears in *Economic History* (1853–4); in many of the biographical collections (e.g. 2488, 2509) and in the sections immediately preceding this one. In addition to contemporary comments, estate accounts and inventories are mines of material, of which relatively few have been available in print until recent years. The examples of this type that are cited below are arranged in rough chronological order according to content.

Most of the titles relating to *Houses* appear under *Architecture* (2762–5). For *Gardens* see nos. 1884, 1888, 1893.

(a) *Sources*

2215 PLAT[T], SIR HUGH. Delightes for ladies. 1608.

First publ. 1602. Repr. facs. with intro. and bibl. by G. E. and K. R. Fussell. 1948.

2216 GOUGE, WILLIAM. Of domesticall duties. 2nd edn. 1626. 3rd edn. 1634.

See also F. B., *The office of the good housewife,* 1672; [C. R.], *The housekeeper's guide in the prudent managing of their affairs,* 1706.

2217 HARLAND, J., ed. The house and farm accounts of the Shuttleworths of Gawthorpe Hall, in the county of Lancaster . . . (1582–1621). 4 vols. Manchester. 1856–8.

Chetham Soc. vols. 35, 41, 43, 46. Vol. 31 of the same series (1853–4) contains the Derby household books ed. by F. R. Raines under title of *The Stanley papers.* Cf. E. L. Lodge, ed., *Account book of a Kentish estate, 1616–1704,* 1927, papers of the Toke family; and Lambert estate papers, 1590–1614, in *The Stockwell papers,* ed. by J. Rutherford (Southamp. Rec. Soc.), 1933.

2218 ORNSBY, G., ed. Selections from the household books of the Lord William Howard of Naworth Castle, 1612–40. Surtees Soc. Durham. 1878.

See also no. 2225.

2219 STEER, F., ed. Farm and cottage inventories of Mid-Essex, 1634–1749. 1950.

Gives texts of 250 inventories, with useful introduction. Numerous examples of this type of source appear in publications of the local historical societies, e.g. *Beds. His. Rec. Soc. Pub.* 20 (1938), 1–43; *Yorks. Arch. Jour.* 34 (1939), 170–203. See also Loder (1883).

2220 WALKER, J. W., ed. 'Hackness manuscripts and accounts', *Yorks. Arch. Soc. Rec. Ser.* 95 (1938).

Accounts from 1658 to 1724; also extracts from the diary of Lady Margaret Hoby. See also accounts of the Dentons in *Arch. and Arch. Soc. for Bucks.* 11 (1921–6), 135–44, 186–98, 244–55.

2221 FELL, SARAH. The household account book of Sarah Fell, of Swarthmoore Hall. Ed. by N. Penney. Camb. 1920.

The entries date from 1673 to 1678.

2222 MYDDLETON, W. M., ed. Chirk Castle Accounts, 1605–66. Privately pr. 1908. Id. 1666–1753. Manchester. 1931.

Reveals much on household management. Cf. 'Extracts from the journal and account book of Timothy Burrell, 1683–1714', ed. by R. W. Blencowe, *Sussex Arch. Coll.* 3 (1850), 117–72; 'A 17th-century account book [William Freke, 1619–30]', ed. by G. W. Prothero, *E.H.R.* 7 (1892), 88–102; and 'The account-book of James Wilding 1682–8', ed. by E. Gordon Duff, *Oxf. Hist. Soc. Coll.*, 1st Ser., 1885, 249–68.

(b) *Later Works*

2223 PERCIVAL, Mac I. Old English furniture and its surroundings from restoration to regency. 1920. Illus.

Also on furnishings see G. M. Ellwood, *English furniture and decoration 1680–1800*, 1909, later edns. 1923, 1933, illus.; C. H. Hayward (2737 n.); P. Macquoid and R. Edwards, *Dictionary of English furniture* (2736 n.); R. W. Symonds, *Furniture making in seventeenth . . . century England*, 1955, and his 'Charles II, couches, chairs and stools', *Connoisseur*, 93 (1934), 15–34, 86–95. For some curiosa regarding home life see J. G. Squiers, *Secret hiding-places*, 1933. See also nos. 2732–43.

2224 QUENNEL, M. and C. H. B. A history of everyday things in England. Part 2, 1500–1799. 1918. 3rd edn. 1937. Illus.

Excellent collection. Cf. R. Bayne-Powell, *Housekeeping in the eighteenth century*, 1956, and W. G. Hoskins, 'The rebuilding of rural England, 1570–1640', *Past and Present*, no. 4 (1953).

2225 THOMSON, G. S. Life in a noble household, 1641–1700. Lond. and N.Y. 1937.

From household accounts of the first duke of Bedford. See also no. 2505. Compare G. R. Batho, 'Henry, ninth earl of Northumberland and Syon House, Middlesex, 1594–1632', *Trans. Anc. Mon. Soc.*, N.S. 4 (1956), 95–109; the 1678 accounts of the earl of Ailesbury in *Beds. Hist. Rec. Soc. Pub.* 32 (1951), 108–42; H. J. Habakkuk, 'Daniel Finch, 2nd earl of Nottingham: his house and estate', in *Studies in social history, a tribute to G. M. Trevelyan*, ed. by J. H. Plumb, 1955; and E. Mercer, 'The houses of the gentry', *Past and Present*, no. 5 (1954).

(c) *Special Subjects*

(1) *Cookery*

(a) Bibliographies and Sources

2226 OXFORD, A. W. English cookery books to the year 1850. Oxf. 1913.

See also G. Vicaire, *Bibliographie gastronomique*, Paris, 1890, English edn. 1954; and Hazlitt (2232). Other titles are in *Economic History*, nos. 1857, 1999, and 2038.

2227   ASTRY, DIANA. 'Diana Astry's recipe book *c.* 1700', ed. by B. Stitt, *Beds. Hist. Rec. Soc. Pub.* 37 (1956), 83–167.

Other ladies' recipe books: Mrs. Susanna Avery, *A plain plantain: country wines, dishes & herbal cures from a 17th-century household MS. receipt book,* ed. by R. G. Alexander, 1922, with a bibl. on herbals; *The receipt book of Mrs. Ann Blencowe, 1694,* with intro. by G. Saintsbury, 1925.

2228   DIGBY, SIR KENELM. Closet of . . . Sir Kenelme Digby opened, whereby is discovered . . . excellent directions for cookery. 1669. 3rd edn. 1677. Ed. by A. MacDonell. 1910.

Other examples are Robert May, *The accomplisht cook . . .,* 1660, numerous later edns.; William King, *Art of cookery,* 1708; William Rabisha, *The whole body of cookery dissected,* 1661; and M. P[arsons], *The ladies cabinet opened: wherein is found hidden severall experiments in preserving and conserving, physicke and surgery, cookery and huswifery,* 1639.

2229   TRYON, TH. Wisdom's dictates, or aphorisms and rules, physical, moral and divine for preserving the health of the body and peace of the mind to which is added . . . 75 noble dishes. 1691. 1696.

Also concerned with health is Thomas Moffett, *Healths improvement,* 1655.

2230   WOLLEY [WOOLLEY], HANNAH. Queen-like closet or rich cabinet, stored with all manner of rare receipts for preserving, candying and cookery. 1670. Later edn. with suppl. 1672–4.

She also wrote *Ladies directory,* 1661; *Cook's guide,* 1664; *Ladies delight,* 1672; and *Gentlewoman's companion, or a guide to the female sex,* 1675, 1682.

(*b*) Later Works

2231   DRUMMOND, J. C. and WILBRAHAM, A. The Englishman's food: a history of five centuries of English diet. 1939. Rev. edn. 1957. 1958.

Four chapters in Part ii deal with the period; scholarly, bibl. footnotes. See also J. R. Ainsworth-Davis, *Cooking through the centuries,* 1931, bibl.

2232   HAZLITT, W. C. Old cookery books and ancient cuisine. 1886. 1902.

Prints some extracts; short bibl. Cf. H. Simpson, 'Four centuries of English cookery', *Roy. Inst. Gr. Brit. Proc.* 29, pt. 4 (1937), 548–72; and J. Ferguson, 'Bibliographical notes on histories of inventions and books of secrets 1650–1700', *Trans. Glasgow Arch. Soc.,* N.S. 6 (1916), 1–78; 7 (1924), 1–77.

(2) *Drink*
(*a*) Bibliography and Sources

2233   SIMON, A. Bibliotheca Bacchica, bibliographie raissonnée des ouvrages imprimés avant 1800 . . . Lond. and Paris. 1927.

Cf. his earlier *Bibliotheca vinaria: a bibliography of books and pamphlets dealing with viticulture, wine-making, distillation, the management, sale, taxation, use and abuse of wine and spirits,* 1913; and no. 2007.

2234   GALLOBELGICUS, [pseud.] Wine, beere and ale, together by the eares. Tr. Mercurius Britannicus. 1629. Title: Wine, beere, ale and tobacco, contending for superiority. 1630.

See also by the poet, John Taylor, *Ale ale-vated into the ale-titude,* 1651, 1653. Taylor's *Drinke and welcome,* 1637, is repr. in *Ashbee reprints,* 1871.

2235 SCRIVENER, MATTHEW. A treatise against drunkenness. 1685.

Cf. Richard Carr, *Epistolae medicinales*, 1691 (Engl. trans., 1714), in which are letters on over-indulgences; Bishop Peter Browne, *A discourse of drinking healths*, Dublin and Lond. 1716; and Daniel Duncan, *Wholesome advice against the abuse of hot liquors*, 1706.

(b) Later Works

2236 BICKERDYKE, J. [C. H. Cook.] The curiosities of ale and beer. 1886. 1889.

See also Simon (2007).

2237 WEBB, S. and B. The history of liquor licensing in England, principally from 1700 to 1830. 1903.

(3) Coffee, Tea, and Chocolate

2238 THE WOMENS PETITION against coffee. 1674.

Cf. *The mens answer to the womens petition against coffee*, 1674. Both are repr. in *Old English coffee houses* (2240 n.). See Charles II's *Proclamation for the suppression of coffee houses*, 1675, which was countermanded in eleven days; and *The character of a coffee house*, 1673 (Wing, C 1968).

2239 [CHAMBERLAYNE, JOHN.] The manner of making coffee, tea, and chocolate . . . newly done out of French and Spanish. 1685.

Sometimes attributed to the same author, *The natural history of coffee, thee, chocolate, tobacco*, 1682. See also Robert Morton, *Lines appended to the nature, quality and most excellent vertues of coffee*, [1670?]; John Ovington, *Essay on the nature and qualities of tea*, 1699, 1705; and Henry Stabbe, *The Indian nectar or a discourse concerning chocolate*, 1662.

2240 AYTON, E. The penny universities; a history of the coffee houses. 1956.

Includes valuable source material but without documentation. See also the brief *Old English coffee houses*, 1954, which includes reprints of several tracts; and S. H. Twining, *The house of Twining 1706–1956*, 1956, superseding his 1931 history of the firm of coffee and tea merchants. Cf. E. F. Robinson, *The early history of coffee houses in England*, 1893; and W. R. Dawson, 'The London coffee-houses and the beginning of Lloyd's', *Brit. Arch. Assoc. Jour.* 40 (1934), 104–27, 133–4.

2241 UKERS, W. H. All about coffee. N.Y. 1922. 2nd edn. N.Y. 1935. Bibl.

By the same author, *All about tea*, 2 vols., N.Y. 1935, bibl.

(4) Tobacco

For the tobacco trade see no. 2005.

2242 BRAGGE, W. Bibliotheca nicotiana: a first catalogue of books about tobacco. [Birmingham.] 1874. 2nd edn. 1880.

See also Brooks (2004).

2243 JAMES I, KING. A counterblaste to tobacco. 1604.

2244 [DEACON, JOHN.] Tobacco tortured, or the filthy fume of tobacco refined. 1616.

Examples of other contemporary pamphlets are: C. T., *An advice* (2003); Tobias Venner, *A briefe . . . treatise concerning the taking of the fume tobacco*, 1621; Raphael Thorius, *Hymnus tabaci*, 1626, 1628 (trans. by Peter Hausted, 1651); and Aegidius Everaerdts, [Giles Everard], *Panacea or the universal medicine . . . tobacco*, 1659.

2245 FAIRHOLT, F. W. Tobacco: its history and associations. 1859. Later edn. 1876.

Cf. G. L. Apperson, *The social history of smoking*, [1914]; W. J. Hardy, 'Tobacco culture in England during the seventeenth century', *Archaeologia*, 51 (1888), 157–66; and A. Rive, 'The consumption of tobacco since 1600', *Econ. Hist.* 1 (1926–9), 57–75.

(5) *Servants*

2246 [WOLLEY, HANNAH.] The compleat servant maid, or the young maiden's tutor. 1677. 3rd edn. 1683. 4th edn. 1685. Later edns.

Attributed by Wing to Hannah Wolley. See also Thomas Fosset, *The servant's dutie, or the calling and condition of servants . . .*, 1613.

2247 DEFOE, DANIEL. The great law of subordination consider'd or the insolence and insufferable behaviour of servants in England duly enquir'd into. 1724.

Reissued the same year with title: *The behaviour of servants in England inquired into.*

2248 STUART, D. M. The English Abigail. 1946.

Based on sources. Briefer but useful is D. Marshall's sketch, *The English domestic servant in history*, 1949.

3. AMUSEMENTS

(a) *General*

2249 BROWN, THOMAS. Amusements, serious and comical, calculated for the meridian of London. 1700. Ed. by A. L. Hayward. 1927.

See also J. Beeverell, *Délices de la grande Bretagne et d'Irlande*, 1707 (extracts publ. as *The pleasures of London*, 1940); and R. Bell, 'Social amusements under the restoration', *Fortnightly Rev.* 2 (1865), 193–205, 299–309, 460–75.

2250 LENNARD, R. V., ed. Englishmen at rest and play, 1558–1714. Oxf. 1931.

Includes sources; treats of Sunday observance, watering places, country inns, and a variety of other matters. See also I. Brooke, *Pleasures of the past*, [1955]; and H. Morley, *Memoirs of Bartholomew fair*, 1859.

(b) *Sports*

(1) *Bibliographies and Sources*

2251 WESTWOOD, T. and SATCHELL, T., eds. Bibliotheca piscatoria: a catalogue of books on angling, the fisheries, and fish-culture. 1883.

Valuable; a suppl. was publ. in 1901 as a *List of books . . . to supplement the Bibliotheca piscatoria*. Cf. B. Dean *et al.*, eds., *A bibliography of fishes*, 3 vols., N.Y. 1916–23.

2252 HARTING, J. E. Bibliotheca accipitraria: a catalogue of books . . . relating to falconry. 1891.

Well arranged; includes foreign as well as English books.

2253 HUTH, F. H. Works on horses and equitation: a bibliographical record of hippology. 1887.

2254 THIMM, C. A. A complete bibliography of fencing and duelling. 1896.

Enlarged from his work of 1891, and afterwards included in his *Fencing and duelling as practised by all European nations from the middle ages to the present day*, Hampton Hill, 1897.

2255 MARKHAM, GERVASE. Country contentments, in two bookes: the first containing the whole art of riding . . . the second intitled the English huswife. 1615. 5th edn. 1633.

Country contentments had appeared alone in 1611. Extracts from the second part were ed. by Constance, Countess De La Warr [*c.* 1908].

2256 THE KINGES MAJESTIES DECLARATION to his subjects concerning lawfull sports to be used. 1618. Later edn. 1633.

The proclamation commonly called *The book of sports*, to which the Puritans objected. Repr. in *Somers tracts* (61); cf. J. Tait, 'The declaration of sports for Lancashire [1617], *E.H.R.* 32 (1917), 561–8; and L. A. Govett, *The king's book of sports . . . with a reprint of the declarations and a description of the sports then popular*, 1890.

2257 STOKES, WILLIAM. The vaulting master, or the art of vaulting reduced to a method. 1641. 2nd edn. Oxf. 1652.

2258 WALTON, IZAAK. The compleat angler, or the contemplative man's recreation. 1653. 5th edn. 1676. 100th edn. by R. B. Marston. 2 vols. 1888. Illus. Bibl.

The edn. of 1676 is the first in which Charles Cotton's *The Compleat angler* . . . Part ii, 1676, and Robert Venables's *The experienc'd angler*, 1662, are joined to Walton's treatise with the common title, *The universal angler*. The 100th edn. has a complete bibliographical note.
    Cf. T. Westwood, *The chronicle of the 'Compleat angler' of Izaak Walton and Charles Cotton, being a bibliographical record*, 1864. See also a repr. of Venables, with Gervase Markham's *The pleasures of princes*, preface by H. G. Hutchinson, 1927.

2259 COX, NICHOLAS. The gentleman's recreation: in four parts, viz. hunting, hawking, fowling, fishing. 1674. 4th edn. 1697. 6th edn. 1721. Illus.

Added to the 1697 edn. was 'A perfect abstract of all the forest laws', based on Manwood's book, 1696. See also Simon Latham, *Falconry and the falcon's lure and cure*, 1615 (later edn. 1633); Edmund Bert, *An approved treatise of hawkes and hawking*, 1619 (later edn. by J. E. Harting, 1891); Francis Barker, *Several ways of hunting, hawking and fishing*, [1671]; and Richard Blome, *The gentleman's recreation*, 1686.

2260 PARKYNS, SIR THOMAS. Προγυμνάσματα. The inn-play; or, Cornish-hugg-wrestler. 1713. 2nd edn. corr. and enl. 1714. 3rd edn. 1714. Last edn. [? 1800].

(2) Later Works

2261 CASTLE, E. Schools and masters of fence from the middle ages to the eighteenth century. 1885. Later edns. 1892. 1910. Bibl.

2262 HACKWOOD, F. W. Old English sports. 1907.

Cf. J. Strutt, *Glig-Gamena Angel-Deod, or the sports and pastimes of the people of England*, 1801 (later edn. by W. Hone, 1875; and by J. C. Cox, 1903). A good modern work with bibl. is C. Hole, *English sports and pastimes*, 1949. Cf. M. Kloeren, *Sport und Rekord, Kultursoziologische Untersuchungen zum England des sechzenten bis achtzehnten Jahrhunderts*, Leipzig, 1935, bibl.

2263 KIRBY, C. and E. 'The Stuart game prerogative.' *E.H.R.* 46 (1931), 239–54.

Implications of the revisions of the game code.

2264 HORE, J. P. The history of Newmarket and the annals of the turf . . . to the end of the seventeenth century. 3 vols. 1886.

Detailed; contains many extracts from state papers, memoirs, etc. Popular, but based on good contemporary and secondary authorities, is *Bridleways through history*, by V. Bathhurst, Lady Apsley, 1936, rev. edn., 1948.

(c) Games and Gambling

(1) Sources

2265 ANNALIA DUBRENSIA. [Poems] upon the yeerely celebration of Mr. Robert Dovers' Olimpick games upon Cotswold-Hill [ed. by Matthew Welbancke?]. 1636. Later edn. by A. B. Grosart. Manchester. 1877.

2266 COTTON, CHARLES. The compleat gamester, or instructions how to play at billiards, trucks, bowls and chess . . . cards . . . dice. 1674. 5th edn. 1725.

Both this work and Theophilus Lucas, *Memoirs of the lives . . . of the most famous gamesters . . . in the reigns of Charles II* [to Anne], 1714, are repr. in C. H. Hartmann, ed., *Games and gamesters of the restoration*, 1929.

(2) Later Works

2267 ASHTON, J. A history of English lotteries. 1893. Illus.

See also his *History of gambling in England*, 1898. C. H. L. Ewen, in *Lotteries and sweepstakes*, 1932 (bibl.), describes the activities more as business than as amusement.

2268 GOMME, A. B., LADY. The traditional games of England, Scotland, and Ireland. 2 vols. 1894–8.

Also J. Marshall, *The annals of tennis*, 1878. Cf. F. P. Magown, Jr., 'Scottish popular football, 1424–1815', *A.H.R.* 37 (1931), 1–13; and his *History of football . . . to 1871*, Bochum-Langendreer, 1938.

2269 HARGRAVE, C. P. A history of playing cards and a bibliography of cards and gaming. Boston and N.Y. 1930.

See also *Playing cards of various ages and countries* (selected from the collection of Lady Charlotte Schreiber, vol. i, English and Scottish, Dutch and Flemish), 1892.

A catalogue of this collection, now in the Br. Mus., was made by F. M. O'Donoghue, 1901. Cf. W. H. Willshire's catalogue, *Playing and other cards* [in the Br. Mus.], 1876–7.

(d) *Dancing*

2270 BEAUMONT, C. W. A bibliography of dancing. 1929.

Br. Mus. books; alphabetical arrangement. See also P. D. Magriel, *A bibliography of dancing*, N.Y. 1936, with a supplement, 1941, which uses subject arrangement. See also John Playford, *The English dancing-master* (2781).

2271 WEAVER, JOHN. An essay towards an history of dancing. 1712.

Cf. his *Orchesography, or the art of dancing by characters and demonstrative figures* (trans. from the French of Feuillet), 1706, 1710.

2272 VUILLIER, G. A history of dancing. Lond. and N.Y. 1898.

Trans. from French edn., Paris, 1898. Ch. 14, by J. Grego, deals with the dance in England; ch. 15, with Irish and Scottish dancing. Cf. R. St. Johnston, *A history of dancing*, 1906; C. J. Sharp and H. C. Macilwaine, *The Morris book*, 1907, 1911; and A. M. Cowper Coles, *Old English country dance steps*, 1909.

(e) *Theatre*

For titles pertaining to drama as a literary form see Ch. X, *Literature*. See also *Music*.

(1) *Bibliography and Sources*

The sources are arranged in chronological order by date of publication.

2273 BAKER, B. M. Theatre and allied arts; a guide to books dealing with the history, criticism, and technic of the drama and theatre . . . N.Y. 1952.

See her *Dramatic bibliography*, N.Y. 1933.

2274 LOWE, R. W. A bibliographical account of English theatrical literature. From the earliest times to the present day. 1888.

Includes many contemporary pamphlets. See also M. S. Steele, *Plays and masques at the court during the reigns of Elizabeth, James and Charles*, New Haven, 1926, an annotated list in chronological order.

2275 HERBERT, SIR HENRY. The dramatic records of Sir Henry Herbert, master of the revels, 1623–1673. Ed. by J. Q. Adams. New Haven. 1917.

Cf. C. C. Stopes, *The seventeenth-century accounts of the masters of the revels*, 1922; and accounts cited by F. P. Wilson in *Bodleian Lib. Rec.* 5 (1955), 217–21. See also P. Simpson and C. F. Bell, *Designs of Inigo Jones for masques and plays at court* (2704).

2276 PRYNNE, WILLIAM. Histrio-mastix. The players scourge or actors tragedie, divided into two parts. 1633.

The celebrated work by the controversial Puritan. For bibliographies of his writings see Kirby (491 n.), Wood (2427, 3rd edn., P. Bliss, vol. iii, 844 ff.), and *Documents relating to the proceedings against Prynne* (747 n.).

One reply to Prynne is Sir Richard Baker's *Theatrum redivivum*, 1662. A document on Sir William Davenant and the revival of the drama during the protectorate, ed. by C. H. Firth, is in *E.H.R.* 18 (1903), 319–21.

2277 COLLIER, JEREMY. A short view of the immorality and profaneness of the English stage. 1698. 5th edn. 1730.

For a bibl. of the controversy on the immorality of the English stage see *Camb. Hist. Eng. Lit.* viii, 432–4; also J. Ballein, *Jeremy Collier's Angriff auf die englische Bühne*, Marburg, 1910; J. W. Krutch, *Comedy and conscience after the restoration*, N.Y. 1924, 1949; and Sister Rose Anthony, *The Jeremy Collier stage controversy, 1698–1726*, Milwaukee, 1937. One example of replies to Collier is John Dennis, *The usefulness of the stage to the happiness of mankind, to government and to religion*, 1698.

2278 [WRIGHT, JAMES.] Historia histrionica: an historical account of the English stage. 1699.

In part a reply to Collier *supra*, this work includes useful historical material (repr. in Robert Dodsley's *Select collection* (2666), ed. Hazlitt, xv, and in Lowe's edn. of *Cibber's Apology* (2291), and elsewhere).

Another valuable contemporary history is [John Downes], *Roscius Anglicanus, or an historical review of the stage* [1641–1706], 1708, many edns.; ed. by M. Summers [1927?], with extensive notes. For another arrangement of illustrative works see W. C. Hazlitt, ed., *The English drama and stage under The Tudor and Stuart princes, 1543–1664*, 1869.

(2) Later Works

2279 AVERY, E. L. *et al.*, eds. The London stage 1660–1800. Parts 1–5. Carbondale (Ill.). 1960+.

A major work undertaking to provide, season by season, not only the record of the plays performed but of the actors, and other related matters. Valuable introductions. First publ. are two vols. of Part 2 (1700–17, 1718–29), and additional vols. for 1729–76. The work will largely supersede J. Genest, *Some account of the English stage* (1660–1830), 10 vols., Bath, 1832.

2280 BENTLEY, G. E. The Jacobean and Caroline stage. 6 vols. Oxf. 1941–. (5th vol. 1956.) Bibl.

Useful earlier works are Th. Betterton, *History of the English stage from the restoration to the present time* (1741; rev. edn., Boston, 1814), the authorship of which has also been attributed to William Oldys and to Edmund Curll; and D. E. Baker, *The companion to the play-house*, 2 vols., 1764 (later edns. entitled *Biographica dramatica . . .*; ed. by I. Reed, 1782 and 1801; ed. by S. James, 3 vols., 1812). See also A. W. Green, *The inns of court and early English drama*, New Haven, 1931; R. R. Reed, *Bedlam on the Jacobean stage*, Camb. (Mass.), 1952; G. F. Sensabaugh, 'Love ethics in platonic court drama, 1625–1642', *Hunt. Lib. Quart.* I (1937), 277–304; and A. Thaler, *Shakespere to Sheridan*, Camb. (Mass.), 1922.

2281 CHAMBERS, E. K. The Elizabethan stage. 4 vols. Oxf. 1923. Bibl.

Cf. F. G. Fleay, *A chronicle history of the London stage, 1559–1642*, 1890, repr. N.Y. 1909; and F. E. Schelling, *Elizabethan drama 1558–1642*, 2 vols., 1908, bibl.; later edn., 2 vols., N.Y. 1959. See also P. Reyher, *Les masques anglais: étude sur les ballets et la vie de cour en Angleterre 1512–1640*, Paris, 1909, bibl.

2282 CLARK, W. S. The early Irish stage (to 1720). Oxf. 1955. Bibl.

For Scotland see R. Lawson, *Story of the Scots stage*, Paisley, 1917, bibl.

2283 GRAY, C. H. Theatrical criticism in London to 1795. N.Y. 1931.

Useful, but not definitive. Cf. D. F. Smith, *The critics in the audience of the London theatres from Buckingham to Sheridan* [1671–1779], Albuquerque, 1953.

2284 HOTSON, J. L. Commonwealth and restoration stage. Camb. (Mass.). 1928.

Important. Has contemporary material in appendix. Cf. A. M. Summers, *Restoration theatre*, 1934; S. Rosenfeld, 'The restoration stage in newspapers and journals, 1660–1700', *Mod. Lang. Rev.* 30 (1935), 445–59; and G. W. Whiting, 'Condition of the London theatres, 1679–83', *Mod. Phil.* 25 (1928), 195–206.

2285 KNIGHTS, L. C. Drama and society in the age of Jonson. 1937. N.Y. 1951.

2286 NICOLL, A. A history of restoration drama, 1660–1700. Camb. 1923. Rev. edn. 1952. Bibl.

Valuable. Continued in his: *A history of early eighteenth-century drama, 1700–1750*, Camb. 1925, 2nd edn., 1929, bibl. See also his *English theatre: a short history*, 1936; and no. 2661.
    Cf. K. Lynch, *Social mode of restoration comedy*, N.Y. 1926; E. Boswell [Murrie], *The restoration court stage (1660–1702)*, Camb. (Mass.), 1932; and S. M. Rosenfeld, *Strolling players and drama in the provinces, 1660–1765*, Camb. 1939.

2287 MYERS, A. M. Representation and misrepresentation of the Puritan in Elizabethan drama. 1931.

Cf. E. K. Maxfield, 'The Quakers in English stage plays before 1800', *P.M.L.A.* 45 (1930), 256–73; H. Silvette, 'The doctor on the stage . . . seventeenth-century English drama', *Annals of Med. Hist.*, N.S. 8 (1936), 520–40; 9 (1937), 62–87, 174–88, 264–79, 371–94, 482–507; and J. H. Smith, *The gay couple in restoration comedy*, Camb. (Mass.), 1948.

2288 ROLLINS, H. E. A contribution to the history of the English commonwealth drama. 1921. Repr. from *Studies in Phil.* 3 (1921).

Based on materials from the Thomason collection. L. B. Wright deals with another special aspect in 'The reading of plays during the Puritan revolution', *Hunt. Lib. Quart.* 6 (1934), 73–108.

(3) *Actors and Actresses*

2289 NUNGEZER, E. A dictionary of actors and of other persons associated with the public representation of plays in England before 1642. New Haven. 1929.

Bibl. Valuable reference work. Does not include playwrights. Cf. H. B. Baker, *English actors from Shakespeare to Macready*, 2 vols., N.Y. 1879.

2290 HEYWOOD, THOMAS. An apology for actors. 1612.

Repr. in *Somers tracts* (61), edn. 1809–15, vol. iii, 574–600, and ed. by J. D. Collier, 1841. Cf. I. G. [John Green?], *A refutation of the 'Apology for Actors'*, 1615 (repr., with Heywood's *Apology*, in *Scholar's facsimiles and reprints*, N.Y. 1941). See also *The actors' remonstrance or complaint for the silencing of their profession . . .*, 1645, repr. in 1868 (in Ashbee), and 1873.

2291 CIBBER, COLLEY. An apology for the life of Mr. Colley Cibber, comedian. 1740. Later edn. by R. W. Lowe. 2 vols. 1889.

The edn. of 1889 repr. *A brief supplement to Colley Cibber, Esq.; his lives of the late famous actors and actresses, by A. Aston* [London? 1748]. See also *The dramatic works* (no. 2673); and R. H. Barker, *Mr. Cibber of Drury Lane*, N.Y. 1939, bibl.

2292 WILSON, J. H. All the king's ladies: actresses of the restoration. Chicago. 1958. Bibl.

List of actresses, 1660–89, with biog. notes. See also R. Gilder, *Enter the actress*, 1931; and H. W. Lanier, *The first English actresses*, N.Y. 1931.

(f) *Clubs and Societies*

2293 HARRINGTON, SIR JOHN. The Rota or a model of a free state. 1660.

By same author, *The censure of the Rota upon Mr. Milton's book*, 1660. Rota was a political club.

2294 DEFOE, DANIEL. The secret history of the October club. 1711.

Cf. [Ward, Edw.] *Secret history of the Calves-Head club*, 1703, 2nd edn., 1703, later edns.; and his anon. *Secret history of clubs*, 1709; also James Puckle, *The club*, 1713.

2295 ALLEN, R. J. Clubs of Augustan London. Camb. (Mass.). 1933.

Definitive, with bibl. footnotes.
    See also [James Caulfield], *Memoirs of the celebrated persons composing the Kit-Cat Club*, 1821, illus.; and John Timbs, *Club life of London; with anecdotes of the clubs, coffee houses and taverns of the metropolis during the 17th, 18th and 19th centuries*, 2 vols., 1866, new edns., 1872, 1908.

2296 KNOOP, DOUGLAS and JONES, G. P. A short history of freemasonry to 1730. Manchester. 1940.

Scholarly.

(g) *Spas and Watering Places*

For a short bibliography see Cox (2351), vol. iii, pp. 306–11.

2297 JORDEN, EDW. Discourse of naturall bathes and minerall waters. 1631. 2nd edn. 1632. 3rd edn. 1669.

Also Lodwick Rowzee, *The Queenes welles . . . a treatise of the nature and vertues of Tunbridge water*, 1632, 1670, 1671; Edward Ward, *A step to the bath with a character of the place*, 1700; and *The queen's famous progress* [to Bath], 1702.

2298 ADDISON, W. English Spas. 1951.

Uses contemporary sources but footnotes are somewhat incomplete. On Bath see P. R. James, *The baths of Bath in the sixteenth and early seventeenth centuries*, Bristol, 1938; A. Barbeau's excellent *Life and letters at Bath in the 18th century*, 1904, trans. from Paris ed., *Une ville d'eaux Anglaise*, 1904; and F. Shum, *A catalogue of Bath books*, Bath, 1913.

4. DRESS

2299 FAIRHOLT, F. W., ed. Satirical songs and poems on costume from the 13th to the 19th century. Percy Soc. 1849.

Cf. [Thos. Jeanson], *Artificiall embellishments, or art's best directions how to preserve beauty or procure it*, Oxf. 1665.

2300 CUNNINGTON, C. W. and P. Handbook of English costume in the 17th century. 1955. Bibl. Illus.

An excellent guide. By the same authors, *The history of underclothes*, 1951. Cf. I. Brooke, *English costume in the seventeenth century*, 1934, 1950, and her *Dress and undress: The restoration and eighteenth century*, 1958. Fine illustrations are in N. Bradfield, *Historical costumes of England*, 1938, 1958, bibl.; and *Picture book of English costume* (Victoria and Albert Museum), 1937.

    Other useful older works are: J. Strutt, *A complete view of the dress and habits of the people of England*, 2 vols., 1796–9, 2nd edn., 1842; J. R. Planché, *History of British costume*, 1834, 3rd edn., 1874, and his *Cyclopedia of costume*, 2 vols., 1876–9; F. W. Fairholt, *Costumes in England*, 1846 (2 vol. edn. by H. A. Dillon, 1885); and G. Hill, *History of English dress*, 2 vols., 1893. See also nos. 2212 n. and 2706.

2301 KELLY, F. M. and SCHWABE, R. Historic costume, 1490–1790. 1925. 1929. Bibl. Illus.

Includes continental as well as English fashions. By the same authors, *Short history of costume and armour, chiefly in England*, 2 vols., 1931. Popular in style but useful is D. C. Calthrop, *English costume*, 4 vols., 1906 (reissued in one vol. 1907, repr. 1926), illus.

2302 McCLINTOCK, H. F. Old Irish and highland dress. Dundalk. 1943. Illus.

2303 EVANS, J. English jewellery from the fifth century to 1800. 1921. Illus.

Cf. her *History of jewelry, 1100–1870*, [1953], which includes English jewellery; H. Clifford Smith, *Jewellery* (The Connoisseur's library), 1908; and J. F. Hayward, *English watches*, 1956.

5. WOMEN AND THEIR PLACE

(a) *Sources*

See also nos. 2213, 2215–16, 2943.

2304 RICH, BARNABY. The excellency of good women. 1613.

See also his *Faultes, faults and nothing else but faultes*, 1606, and *Roome for a gentleman, or the second part of Faultes*, 1609. Numerous examples of works of this sort are listed in the bibliography of Camden (2309).
    Examples of marriage sermons are one of 1607, *The merchant royall*, with intro. by S. Pargellis (Herrin, Illinois, 1945), and T. Gataker, *A good wife God's gift; and A wife indeed, two marriage sermons*, 1623.

2305 [ALLESTREE, RICHARD?] The ladies calling. 2 pts. Oxf. 1673. 8th edn. 1705.

Included in his *Works*, 1684, later edns. (see no. 2200). Regarding the authorship see *D.N.B.*, *sub* Pakington, Dorothy.

2306 WONDERS OF THE FEMALE WORLD . . . to which is added a pleasant discourse of female pre-eminences, or the dignity and excellence of that sex above the male. 1683.

Cf. [François Poulain de la Barre], *The woman as good as the man, or The equality of both sexes*, trans. by A. L., 1677 (from French edn., Paris, 1673).

2307 [ASTELL, MARY?] An essay in defence of the female sex. 1696. 3rd edn. 1697.

Doubts about her authorship of this work have been expressed in F. M. Smith's *Mary Astell*, N.Y. 1916, but see H. MacDonald's Dryden bibliography (2624 n.), no. 287.

Mary Astell is the author of other important works, especially *Serious proposal to the ladies for the advancement of their true and greatest interest* (1694, 4th edn. enl., 1697), in which she proposed ways to pursue intellectual interests. See also *The whole duty of a woman, written by a lady*, 1701.

2308 H., N. The ladies dictionary; being a general entertainment for the fair sex. 1694.

Cf. *The ladies library*, publ. by Sir Richard Steele (3 vols., 1714; later edns. to 1772), compiled from 17th-century authors, and attributed to Mrs. Mary Wray.

(b) *Later Works*

2309 CAMDEN, C. The Elizabethan woman [1540–1640]. 1952. Bibl.

Ambitious in scope; scholarly but based too exclusively upon literary sources. See also Clark, *Working life of women* (1976). W. Notestein's essay on 'The English woman 1580 to 1650' in Plumb (2185 n.) is excellent. Popular in style is G. Hill, *Women in English life from medieval to modern times*, 2 vols., 1896. Good sections on the Stuart period are in M. Phillips and W. S. Tomkinson, *English women in life and letters*, Oxf. 1926.

2310 FUSSELL, G. E. and K. R. The English country woman: a farmhouse social history, 1500–1900. 1953. Illus.

Includes good treatment of the Stuart period, with wide use of contemporary sources. See also R. G. Griffiths, 'Joyce Jeffreys of Ham Castle: a 17th-century business gentlewoman', *Worc. Arch. Soc. Trans.*, N.S. 10 (1934), 1–32, 11 (1935), 1–13, and 12 (1936), 1–17.

2311 GAGEN, J. E. The new woman: her emergence in the English drama (1600–1730). N.Y. 1954.

Useful, based on detailed studies of particular works to illustrate social history.

2312 GRAHAM, R. 'Civic position of women at common law before 1800', in her English ecclesiastical studies (1929), pp. 360–77.

A few 17th-century illustrations, chiefly on parish offices.

Cf. I. O'Mattey, *Women in subjection: a study of the lives of English women before 1832*, 1933.

2313 REYNOLDS, M. The learned lady in England, 1650–1760. Boston. 1920. Bibl.

See also A. Wallace, *Before the bluestocking*, 1929, which deals with the women of the 17th and 18th centuries who represent changing social and intellectual interests. See also E. M. Williams, 'Women preachers in the civil war', *J.M.H.* 1 (1929), 561–9.

2314 SIX BRILLIANT ENGLISH WOMEN. [1930.]

Six vols. in Representative women series [1927–8], bound together. Includes V. M. Sackville-West, 'Aphra Behn'; B. Dobrée, 'Sarah Churchill', etc.

Other examples of biographical collections relating to women are: G. Ballard, *Memoirs of several ladies of Great Britain*, 1752, 1775; L. S. Costello, *Memoirs of eminent*

English women, 4 vols., 1844, which includes much contemporary material; M. E. Tabor, *Four Margarets*, 1929, which includes Margaret Fell and Margaret Godolphin.

6. Superstitions and Beliefs

(a) *General*

See also Thorndike (2833) in *Science*, and other works on the thought of the period.

2315 PITT, MOSES. Account of Anne Jeffries . . . who was fed for six months by a small sort of airy people called fairies, and of the cures she performed with salves . . . she received from them. 1696.

Repr. in J. Morgan, *Phoenix Britannicus*, 1732, and C. S. Gilbert, *Cornwall* (3145).

2316 KIRK, ROBERT. Secret commonwealth: or a treatise displaying the chiefe curiosities as they are in use among diverse of the people of Scotland to this day. Edin. 1815. Ed. by A. Lang. 1893.

The author, a 17th-century clergyman and scholar, was interested in Gaelic folk-lore. The 1815 edn. is called a repr. of a 1691 tract, but Lang and other scholars doubt publication before 1815. Cf. D. B. Smith, 'Mr. Robert Kirk's notebook', *S.H.R.* 18 (1921), 237–48; and M. M. Rossi, 'Text-criticism of Robert Kirk's "Secret commonwealth"', trans. by M. I. Johnston, *Edin. Bibl. Soc. Trans.* 3 (1957), 253–68.

2317 DALYELL, J. G. Darker superstitions of Scotland. Edin. 1834. Glasgow. 1835.

Includes evil eye, amulets, divination, etc., as well as witchcraft. For other titles see Grose (10), pp. 122–3; see also Lea (2320 n.).

(b) *Witchcraft*

(1) *Bibliography and Sources*

2318 BURR, G. L. 'The literature of witchcraft.' *Papers of the Amer. Hist. Assoc.* 4 (1890), 235–66.

See also J. Winsor, 'The literature of witchcraft in New England', *Proc. Amer. Antiq. Soc.*, N.S. 10 (1896), 351–73.

2319 BLACK, G. F. A calendar of cases of witchcraft in Scotland, 1510–1727. N.Y. 1938.

Repr. from *N.Y. Pub. Lib. Bull.* 41, 42 (1937–8). Cf. the same author's *Some unpublished Scottish witchcraft trials*, N.Y. 1941.

2320 POTTS, THOMAS. The wonderfull discoveries of witches in the countie of Lancaster . . . 1612. 1613.

This is the fullest of all English witch accounts, and has been repr. in *Somers tracts*, iii (1810); Chetham Society 6 (1845), ed. with notes by J. Crossley; and ed. by G. B. Harrison, 1929.

See also Matthew Hopkins, *The discovery of witches*, 1647 (repr. with notes by A. M. Summers, 1928). For the titles of many other sources of this type see the appendices in Notestein (2327). See also the sections on England and Scotland in vol. iii of H. C.

Lea, *Materials towards a history of witchcraft*, ed. by A. C. Howland, 3 vols., Phila. and Lond. 1939.

2321 GLANVILL, JOSEPH. Sadducismus triumphatus, or a full and plain evidence concerning witches and apparitions, in two parts, the first treating of their possibility, the second of their real existence. 1681. Various later edns. to 1726.

A popular book by the famous philosopher and member of the Royal Society, which incorporates his earlier publication, *Some philosophical considerations touching witches and witchcraft*, 1666, which in its 4th edn., 1668, was entitled *A blow at modern sadducism*. For other comments on Glanvill see nos. 2700, 2909.

Milder works in general support of Glanvill's point of view are Richard Bovet's *Pandaemonium* (1684, repr. with notes by M. Summers, Aldington, 1951); and John Beaumont, *Historical, physicological and theological treatise of spirits . . .*, 1705. For a discussion of the literary controversy here represented see Notestein.

2322 WEBSTER, JOHN. Displaying of supposed witchcraft. 1677.

The chief attack on Glanvill's point of view. For a biographical article on the rationalist author by W. S. Weeks see *Trans. Lanc. and Ches. Antiq. Soc.* 39 (1923), 55–107.

2323 HUTCHINSON, FRANCIS. An historical essay concerning witchcraft. 1718. Enl. edn. 1720.

Based upon systematic study of the evidence, this essay marks the close of the literary controversy and the triumphs of the sceptical point of view.

(2) *Later Works*

2324 CAMPBELL, J. Witchcraft and second sight, in the highlands and islands of Scotland. Glasgow. 1902.

By the same author, *Superstitions of the highlands*, Glasgow, 1900.

2325 EWEN, C. L., ed. Witch hunting and witch trials: the indictments for witchcraft from records of 1373 assizes held for the home circuit, 1559–1736. 1929.

Evidences from four eastern shires, amassed in scholarly fashion. See also by Ewen, *Witchcraft and demonianism . . . derived from . . . the courts of England and Wales* (1538–1717), 1933, his privately printed essay, *Witchcraft in the Star Chamber*, 1938, and a Berkshire case reported in *Berks. Arch. Jour.* 40–1 (1936–7), 207–13.

Less scholarly in treatment is P. W. Sergeant, *Witches and warlocks*, 1936, which deals with the celebrated Lancashire and Essex trials among others.

2326 KITTREDGE, G. L. Witchcraft in old and new England. Camb. (Mass.). 1929. N.Y. 1958.

Based on wide use of the sources, especially of the Tudor–Stuart period. Somewhat controversial in interpretations.

2327 NOTESTEIN, W. A history of witchcraft in England from 1558 to 1718. Amer. Hist. Assoc. Washington. 1911. Bibl.

Still the most authoritative factual account of the trials and the literature relating to witchcraft in 17th-century England.

Scholarly but more popular in style is C. Hole's *Mirror of witchcraft*, 1957, which defines various phenomena by excerpts from numerous sources.

2328   SUMMERS, M. The history of witchcraft and demonology. 1926. 2nd
edn. 1956. Bibl.

Undependable and over-credulous, but containing useful information. See also by
Summers, *Geography of witchcraft*, 1927, and *A popular history of witchcraft*, 1937.

7. TASTE

See also *Fine Arts, Literature,* and other sections in Ch. X; for gardens see
Economic History, nos. 1888–93.

2329   ALLEN, B. S. Tides in English taste 1619–1800. A background for the
study of literature. (See no. 2555.)

Vol. i covers the Stuart period, with comment on tastes in fashion, the fine arts, china,
gardens, among others.
    Cf. T. Ashcroft, *English art and English society* (1660 to the present), 1936, which is
less thorough and not well documented. On changing taste in furniture see J. Gloag,
Time, taste and furniture, 1925. See also nos. 2732–43.

2330   CARRITT, E. F. A calendar of British taste from 1600 to 1800 [1948?].

Pts. i and ii cover the period, with a chronological arrangement of contemporary comment on manners, taste, music, poetry. Good for illustrating changes in taste.

2331   OGDEN, H. V. S. and M. S. English taste in landscape in the seventeenth
century. Lond. and Ann Arbor. 1955. Illus.

Concerned with taste, not just a history of painting, and based on extensive research.
Contains chapter on treatises on landscapes, elaborate notes and illustrations.

D. THE COURT

See also *Political History,* nos. 285, 287; *Theatre, Music,* and the biographical
sections, nos. 388–526 and 2431–2511.

1. SOURCES

(in roughly chronological order according to contents)

2332   NICHOLS, J., ed. The progresses, processions and magnificent festivi-
ties of King James the First, his royal consort, family and court; collected from
original manuscripts, scarce pamphlets . . . comprising forty masques and
entertainments; ten civic pageants; numerous original letters; and annotated
lists of the peers, barons and knights who received those honours during the
reign of King James. 4 vols. 1828. Illus.

2333   ARMSTRONG, A[RCHIE]. A banquet of jeastes. Pt. I. 1630. 4th edn.
1634. Pt. II. 1633. Later edns.

See *S.T.C.* Best edn. is by T. H. Jamieson, Edin. 1872.

2334   W[AKER], N[ATHANIEL]. The refin'd courtier, or a correction of
several indecencies crept into civil conversation. 1663. 1679.

2335 GRAMMONT, ANTHONY HAMILTON, COUNT DE. Memoirs of the life of Count de Grammont, containing in particular the amorous intrigues of the court of England [1662–4]. Translated by A. Boyer, 1714. Many later edns. Ed. by G. Goodwin. 2 vols. 1903. Ed. by C. H. Hartmann. 1930.

Important portrayal of the court which originally appeared in French in 1713; not factually accurate. Scholarly studies by W. Kissenberth (Rostock, 1907) and Ruth Clark, *Anthony Hamilton . . .,* 1921. See also chronology of the *Memoirs* in App. A of Cunningham (2347).

2336 AULNOY, MARIE CATHERINE, COMTESSE D'. Memoirs of the court of England [1675]. 1707. 1708. Trans. by Mrs. W. A. Arthur and ed. by G. D. Gilbert. 1913. 1927.

First edn., 2 vols., Paris, 1695. Gilbert's edn. includes app. on Lucy Walter.
Cf. *Memoires of the dutchess Mazarine,* 1676 (1st edn. in French, Cologne, 1675); and Hartmann (2348).

2337 CAMPANA DE CAVELLI, EMILIA, MARQUISE. Les derniers Stuarts et le château de Saint-Germain en Laye: documents inédits et authentiques. 2 vols. Paris. 1871.

Contains documents from many foreign archives to illustrate the lives of James II and Mary of Modena, 1673–89 (see *Edin. Rev.* (1882), 291–321). See also *The Stuart papers relating chiefly to Queen Mary of Modena and the exiled court of King James II,* ed. by F. Madan, 2 vols., Roxburghe Club, 1889 (pr. from Bodl. Libr. MSS. Add. C. 106–7). Other MSS. are B.M. Add. MSS. 34638, 28224–26 (Carlyll family papers).

2338 SPANHEIM, E. VON. 'Account of the English court in 1704.' Ed. by R. Doehner. *E.H.R.* 2 (1887), 757–73.

French text is in app. to *Relation de la cour de France en 1690,* ed. by E. Bourgeois, Paris, 1900.

2. GENERAL LATER WORKS

2339 OAKES-JONES, H. 'The king: his ancient royal bodyguards.' *Jour. Soc. Army Hist. Res.* 16 (1937), 63–86.

Includes excerpts from various contemporary accounts of the coronations of Charles II and James II. Cf. Kearsley (722).

2340 PETHERICK, MAURICE. Restoration rogues. 1951.

Contains various accounts of court intrigues, in addition to chapters on well-known figures from the lower classes.
A biography of one such adventurer which has historical value is W. C. Abbott, *Colonel Thomas Blood, crown-stealer,* 1911, repr. in his *Conflicts with oblivion* (2437).

2341 PICKEL, M. B. Charles I as patron of poetry and drama. 1936. Bibl.

Though the emphasis is on literature, the author depicts the court before the civil war as a literary and artistic centre in the Renaissance tradition. A doctoral thesis. Cf. E. S. de Beer's article on the efforts of Charles II to establish English rather than French fashions, *Journ. Warburg Courtauld Inst.* 2 (1938), 105–15.

2342 WELSFORD, E. The fool: his social and literary history. 1935. Bibl.

Includes scattered material on court fools of the period. Cf. R. H. Hill, *Tales of the esters,* Edin. and Lond. 1934.

3. BIOGRAPHIES

For the biographies of kings, queens, ministers, and state officials see *supra* Ch. II, § F, nos. 388–526. See also the general biographical titles in § G of this chapter. The biographies of the court ladies in most cases are not satisfactory.

2343 CHANCELLOR, E. B. The lives of the rakes. 6 vols. 1924–5.

Collective biography in popular style, based on Grammont and other familiar sources, vols. i and ii dealing with the restoration period. Cf. [T. Longueville], *Rochester and other literary rakes . . .*, 1902, 1903; R. S. Forsythe, *A noble rake: the life of Charles, fourth Lord Mohun*, Camb. (Mass.), 1929.

A collective biography of the chief court ladies, *temp.* Charles II, is F. D. P. Senior, *The king's ladies*, 1936.

2344 WILSON, J. H. The court wits of the restoration. Princeton. 1948.

Informative collective biography, concerned especially with literary trends.

CLEVELAND, BARBARA VILLIERS [PALMER], DUCHESS OF

2345 A memoir of Barbara, duchess of Cleveland. By G. S. Steinman. Oxf. 1871. *Addenda*. Oxf. 1874 and 1878.

By the same author, an account of her rival, Jane Myddleton, *Some particulars contributed towards a memoir of Mrs. Myddleton*, [Oxf.] 1864, addenda, [Oxf.] 1880. See also P. W. Sergeant, *My lady Castlemaine*, 1912; and the latest popular biography, drawing upon the State Papers as well as on the standard printed sources, M. Gilmour's *The great lady: a biography of Barbara Villiers, mistress of Charles II*, 1944, bibl. G. S. Steinman, in *Althorp memoirs*, Oxf. 1869, gives biographical sketches of several other court ladies.

GODOLPHIN, MARGARET

2346 The life of Mrs. Godolphin. By John Evelyn. Ed. by Bishop S. Wilberforce. 1847. Later edns. 1888. 1904. 1938.

The 1938 edn., by H. Sampson, is the best. It presents a character sketch of a maid of honour untainted by the restoration vices. Cf. W. G. Hiscock, *John Evelyn and Mrs. Godolphin*, 1951.

GWYN, NELL

2347 The story of Nell Gwyn and the sayings of Charles II. By P. Cunningham. 1852. Later edn. by H. B. Wheatley. 1892. Ed. by G. Goodwin. Edin. 1908. Ed. with intro. by J. Drinkwater [Navarre Soc.]. 1927.

Appeared first in *Gentleman's Magazine*, 1851, and has been basic to most of the biographies, even though it is not without inaccuracies. Popular biographies drawing upon contemporary materials were published by L. Mellville, 1923, and A. I. Dasent, 1924. J. H. Wilson, *Nell Gwyn, royal mistress*, N.Y. 1952, is based upon scholarly research and includes Nell's letters in app.

HENRIETTA, DUCHESS OF ORLEANS

2348 Charles II and Madame. By C. H. Hartmann. 1934.

Includes even more correspondence than was included in J. M. Cartwright's [Mrs. H. Ady's] *Madame: A life of Henrietta, daughter of Charles I and duchess of Orleans*, 1894, 4th edn., 1903. Some of the letters were ed. by Ch. Baillon (comte de) in *Henriette-Anne d'Angleterre*, Paris, 1886. See also the less reliable *Histoire de Mme. Henriette d'Angleterre*, by Marie M. (de la Vergne), Comtesse de la Fayette, Amsterdam, 1720; various later edns., repr. Paris, 1925; trans. as *Secret history of Henrietta* . . . by J. M. Shelmerdine, N.Y. 1929.

Other popular biographies of court ladies by C. H. Hartmann are *La Belle Stuart* . . . *Frances Teresa* . . . *duchess of Richmond and Lennox*, 1924; and *The vagabond duchess* . . . *Hortense* . . . *duchesse Mazarin*, 1926.

PORTSMOUTH, LOUISE DE KÉROUALLE, DUCHESSE DE

2349   Louise de Kéroualle, duchesse de Portsmouth, 1649–1734. Ed. by H. Forneron. Paris. 1886. 1891. Engl. trans. 1887.

Based upon French archives, but slight and inaccurate, especially in the translation. A better brief account, based on newly discovered MSS., is J. M. P. J. Lemoine and André Lichtenberger, 'Louise de Kéroualle, duchesse de Portsmouth', *Rev. des Deux Mondes*, 5th Ser. 14 (1903), 114–46.

There are several popular biographies, largely based upon such unreliable contemporary accounts as the *Secret history of the duchess of Portsmouth*, 1690. The most recent is that by John Lindsey (pseud.), *Charles II and Madame Carwell*, Melrose, 1937.

STUART, LADY ARABELLA [ARBELLA]

2350   Arbella Stuart, royal lady of Hardwick and cousin of King James. By P. M. Handover. 1957. Bibl.

Reinterprets, in the light of recent research on the period, the earlier biographies. Still valuable for use of original sources are E. Cooper, *Life and letters of Lady Arabella Stuart*, 2 vols., 1866, biographies by E. T. Bradley, 2 vols., 1889, and M. Lefuse, 1913, and that by B. C. Hardy, 1913, which is based upon additional MS. correspondence.

E. TRAVEL

1. GENERAL

The titles in this section relate to travel in its social aspects, the economic aspects being treated elsewhere. For voyages primarily commercial in nature, either exploratory or in connection with specific enterprises, see *Trade and Commerce* (nos. 2140–51); for those relating to foreign affairs or carried out by ships of the Crown see *Naval History* (nos. 1822–7). Contemporary descriptions with a large amount of social interest are listed in this section. For roads in general and observations chiefly topographical in nature see *Local History*, nos. 3098, 3100, 3107–15. For river travel see *Trade and Commerce*, no. 2108 n. The titles of sources below are arranged roughly in accordance with the date of travel or writing, rather than date of publication.

(a) *Bibliography and Sources*

2351   COX, E. G. A reference guide to the literature of travel. 3 vols. Seattle. 1935–49.

The first volume relates to the old world, the second to the new world, and the third to England, with Scotland. A useful reference work, with titles arranged chronologically within topics.

2352 FUSSELL, G. E. The exploration of England: a select bibliography of travel and topography, 1570–1815. 1935.

An excellent selected list arranged chronologically according to date of writing, with a list of other bibliographies at the end. Portions on the 17th and 18th centuries appeared earlier in *The Library*, 4th Ser. 10 (1928), 84–103, and 13 (1933), 292–311. See also Fordham (3100).

2353 CHAMBERLAYNE, EDWARD. Angliae notitia; or, the present state of England. 1669.

A sort of Whitaker's Almanack; very useful. Went through 22 edns., 1669–1707, being continued by J. Chamberlayne from 1704 onward. The title changed after 1708 to *Magnae Britanniae notitia*, the final (38th) edn. being in 1755. Ref. to *N. and Q.*, 6th Ser. 12; 7th Ser. 1 and 2.

There was a rival publication by Guy Miège, *The new state of England*, 1691, the title of which after 1707 became *The present state of Great Britain*.

2354 HOWELL, JAMES. Instructions for forrein travel. 1642. Later edn. 1650.

The 1650 edn. contains app. on travel to Turkey and the Levant. See repr. ed. by E. Arber (English Reprints), 1869.

Cf. Edward Leigh, *Three diatribes or discourses. First of travel, or a guide for travellers into foreign parts*, 1671, which was publ. in 1680 under title of *The gentleman's guide* (repr. in *Harleian Miscellany*, vol. x, 1813 suppl.). See also Th. Harbin, *The traveler's companion, containing variety of useful yet pleasant matters relating to commerce*, 1702.

2355 RAY, JOHN. Itineraries.

Pr. in *Selected remains of . . . John Ray . . . with his life*, by W. Derham, 1760; also in E. Lankester, ed., *Memorials of John Ray*, 1746. For other works of this type, see *Topography* (nos. 3107–15).

(b) *Later Works*

2356 PARKES, J. Travel in England in the seventeenth century. 1925. Illus. Bibl.

A good survey. See also V. A. La Mar, *Travel and roads in England*, Wash. 1960. Popular in style is T. Burke, *Travel in England*, 1942, 1946, 1949. For foreign travel see nos. 2385–2407.

On the Post Office see nos. 775–6.

2. LAND TRAVEL

(a) *Roads*

See also Ogilby (3109) and other titles listed under *Topography*.

(1) *Bibliography and Sources*

2357 BALLEN, D. Bibliography of roadmaking and roads in the United Kingdom. 1914.

Enlargement of a 1906 bibl. compiled by S. and B. Webb.

2358 PROCTOR, T. A profitable worke to this whole kingdom concerning the mending of all highways. 1610.

Cf. text of the earliest (1622) turnpike bill, with note by F. G. Emmison, which points out that the turnpike era began before the famous act of 1663, *Bull. Inst. Hist. Research*, 12 (1934), 108–12.

(2) *Later Works*

2359 SCOTT-GILES, C. W., comp. The road goes on: a literary and historical account of the highways, byways and bridges of England. 1946. Bibl.

Excerpts from printed literary materials, part relating to the period, and repr. of some 17th-cent. maps. Designed for the general reader.

2360 THOMPSON, G. S. 'Roads in England and Wales in 1603.' *E.H.R.* 33 (1918), 234–43.

Lists of roads and distances to London from various localities. See also La Mar (2356 n).

2361 WEBB, B. and S. The story of the king's highway. 1913. Bibl. notes. Vol. v of no. 930.

The best and most comprehensive. Early chapters are valuable for information on road use and maintenance prior to the 18th century.

In popular style, but based on the sources is T. W. Wilkinson, *From track to by-pass*, 1934. S. Gilbert, in *From trackway to turnpike*, Oxf. 1928, limits his account to East Devon. Intended for the general reader are G. G. Jackson, *From track to highway: a book of British roads*, 1935; and J. Oliver, *The ancient roads of England*, 1936.

(b) *Inns, Carriages, and Coaches*

(1) *Sources*

2362 PEACHAM, HENRY. Coach and sedan, pleasantly disputing. 1636. Repr. 1925.

2363 TAYLOR, JOHN. The carrier's cosmographie, or a brief relation of the inns, ordinaries, . . . etc. 1637.

See article based on Taylor's observations in *Sussex Arch. Coll.* 79 (1938), 61–73. A 1685 inn inventory is printed in *Arch. Cant.* 46 (1934), 97–101.

(2) *Later Works*

2364 RICHARDSON, A. E. and EBERLEIN, H. D. The English inn, past and present; a review of its history and social life. 1925. Illus.

Richardson, drawing on the same materials, but with less emphasis on development, published *The old inns of England*, 1934.

See also C. G. Harper, *The old inns of old England*, 2 vols., 1906; and T. Burke, *The English Inn*, Lond. and N.Y. 1930, 1931. H. E. Popham, *The taverns in the town*, 1937, is limited to old inns of London.

2365 STRAUSS, R. Carriages and coaches: their history and their evolution. 1912.

Most of the books on coaches relate to the turnpike travel of the next century.

3. TRAVELLERS

The narratives and records of their observations left by travellers of this century is so voluminous that only a selection of the most noteworthy ones can be presented here. For other titles see Cox or Fussell. See also the sections on *Literature* and *Biography* for figures such as Evelyn, Thornby, George Fox. Defoe (3110) and several others are in Ch. XI, *Topography*. See also *Scotland*. The titles listed below are arranged by dates of travel.

(a) *English Travellers in England*

(1) *Sources*

2366 MORYSON, FYNES. An itinerary written by Fynes Moryson, gent. . . . first in the Latin tongue, and then translated . . . into English. 1617.

Ten years of travel in European countries and in parts of the British Isles. His account of the British travel is in the first of three parts. Much of the Scottish part is repr. in P. H. Brown's *Early Travellers* (Edin. 1891), pp. 80–90. Other parts are repr. in C. Hughes, *Shakespeare's Europe*, 1903.

2367 TAYLOR, JOHN. The pennyles pilgrimage. 1618.

This account of the Water Poet's trip by foot from London to Edinburgh is the first of various travels reported in an amusing style. This, with various water trips, such as *A very merry wherry voyage*, 1622, and *A new discovery by sea*, 1623, appears in his collected *Works*, 1630.
  See other titles in Cox (2351).

2368 A RELATION OF A SHORT SURVEY of twenty-six counties observed in a seven weeks' journey . . . [1634] by a captain, a lieutenant and an ancient [from Norwich]. Ed. by L. G. W. Legg. 1904.

From Lansdowne MS. 213 in Br. Mus. An earlier printing is in *Reprints of rare tracts*, Newcastle, 1849, and portions have been printed in various places. See Legg's edn. of a second tour of 1635 by the lieutenant is in *Camd. Soc. Misc.*, xvi (1936), 1–97.

2369 BRERETON, SIR WILLIAM. Notes on a journey through Durham and Northumberland [1635]. Reprints of rare tracts. Newcastle. 1844.

See also Brereton's 'Travels in England, Scotland and Ireland', which is bound with his 'Travels in Holland', etc., in Chetham Soc. Publ. 1 (1844), ed. by E. Hawkins.
  See also the later travels of Ralph Thoresby in northern England and Scotland, accounts of which occur in his *Diary* and his *Letters*, both ed. by J. Hunter, 4 vols., 1830–2, and in Brown (3940). Compare also Macky (2371). Extracts from Thomas Baskerville's accounts of his travels in numerous counties are printed in H.M.C., *Manuscripts of the Duke of Portland*, vol. ii (1893), 263–314.

2370 FIENNES, CELIA. The journeys of Celia Fiennes. Ed. by C. Morris. 1947. 1949.

More complete and accurate than the 1888 edn. by E. W. Griffiths under the title of *Through England on a side-saddle*.
  This diary by the daughter of Nathaniel Fiennes is possibly the most well-known travel diary; it is full of observations, 1685–1703. For the most famous *tour*, see Defoe (3110).

2371 [MACKY, JOHN.] A journey through England in familiar letters from a gentleman here to his friend abroad. 2 vols. 1714–22.

A third vol. on Scotland appeared in 1723, 2nd edn. 1729. The author, a Whig intelligencer (see his *Memoirs*, no. 372 n.), explained in vol. ii that its appearance had been delayed for political reasons, and was now published to refute Misson (2380).

(b) *Foreign and Colonial Travellers in England*

(1) *Sources*

In addition to the selected titles in this section see others mentioned in Ascoli (2382), Cox (2351), Rye (2383), and Smith (2384). Most of the general travel narratives which include accounts of other countries in addition to England are omitted, since they will be found in Cox. See also Shaw (2191).

2372 WALDON, F. F. 'Queen Anne and "The four kings of Canada", a bibliography of contemporary sources.' *Canadian Hist. Rev.* 16 (1935), 266–75.

Relates to visiting Indian chiefs, 1710.

2373 SULLY, MAXIMILIEN, DE BÉTHUNE, DUC DE. Memoirs of the Duc de Sully . . . Trans. by C. Lennox. Rev. edn. 4 vols. 1856.

From the French edn. (Amsterdam, 1638), of which the best edn. is that in vols. xvi–xvii of J. F. Michaud and J. J. F. Poujoulat, *Nouvelle collection des mémoires . . .*, 1854. Includes account of the duke's embassy to England in 1603.

Less valuable, except for the court, are the observations of Le Sieur J. Puget de La Serre on the entry of the Queen Mother of France into England in 1638 (a French edn. 1638, English versions 1639 and 1756), repr. in *Antiquarian Repertory*, 4 (1775), 520 ff.

2374 SORBIÈRE, SAMUEL DE. A voyage to England [1663], containing many things relating to the state of learning, religion, and other curiosities. 1709.

Trans. from the 1st edn. (Paris, 1664), entitled *Relation d'un voyage en Angleterre . . .* The author, who had translated Hobbes, aroused considerable discussion by his criticism of English religion and government. Cf. Bishop Thomas Sprat's *Observations on M. de Sorbière's voyage*, 1665; J. J. Jusserand, *A French ambassador*, 1892, pp. 62–4; and the critical study by A. Morize in *Rev. d'hist. de la France littéraire*, 14 (1907), 231–75.

Somewhat more exact observations, though more limited in scope, are those by Samuel Chappuzeau, *L'Europe vivante, ou relation nouvelle, historique & politique de tous ses estats* [1666], Geneva, 1666, 1667. See also Balthasar de Monconys, 'Voyage en Angleterre' [1663] in his *Journal des voyages*, 3 pts., Lyon, 1665–6, many edns.

2375 'RELAZIONI ITALO-INGLESI NEL SEICENTO.' In P. Rebora, *Civiltà italiana e civiltà inglese.* Florence. 1936.

Pages 147–80. Includes narratives by Italian observers of the fire of London, the 1688 revolution, and a 'voyage' in England, 1667–8.

2376 JOUVIN [JOREVIN] DE ROCHEFORT, ALBERT. 'Description of England and Ireland [1666?].' *Antiquarian repertory*, iv (1809 edn.), 549–622.

From his *Le Voyageur d'Europe* (7 pts., Paris, 1672–6). Includes Scotland also. Various parts have been reprinted. By another French traveller, [François Larchier,] *Les Voyages d'un homme de qualité en Angleterre*, Lyon, 1681.

2377 MAGALOTTI, COUNT LORENZO. Travels of Cosmo the third, grand duke of Tuscany, through England . . . [1669]. Trans. from Italian. 1821. Views.

The narrator, a learned Italian, travelled as the duke's secretary. Valuable.

2378 LETI, GREGORIO. Del teatro britannico o vero historia . . . della Grand Bretagna. 1683. 5 vols. Amsterdam. 1684.

By a Milanese who was in England, 1680–1. The book offended English Catholics and was later suppressed.

2379 MURALT, BÉAT L. DE. Letters describing the character and customs of the English and French nations [1694–5]. 2 vols. 1726.

Trans. from French edn. (Cologne and Zurich, 1725). Modern edns.: Bern, 1897; Lond. and Paris, 1933.
Interesting observations by an astute traveller from Bern. Brought forth various replies because more favourable to England than to France.

2380 MISSON DE VALBOURG, HENRI. Memoirs and observations in his travels over England with some account of Scotland and Ireland [1697]. 1719.

Trans. by J. Ozell from the French *Mèmoires et observations* . . ., The Hague, 1698. Valuable comments by a French protestant refugee. Authorship is sometimes attributed (*D.N.B.*) to his brother, F. Maximilien Misson. See attempted refutation by Macky (2371).

2381 UFFENBACH, ZACHARIAS CONRAD VON. Merkwürdige reisen durch Niedersachsen, Holland, und Engelland [1710]. 3 vols. Ulm. 1753.

Parts of vols. ii and iii contain useful observations on England. Translations of several portions have been published as: *Cambridge under Queen Anne*, ed. by J. E. B. Mayor, Camb. 1911; *Oxford in 1710*, ed. by W. H. Quarrel and W. J. C. Quarrel, Oxf. 1928; and *London in 1710*, ed. by W. H. Quarrel and M. Mare, 1934. Cf. Georges L. Le Sage, *Remarques sur . . . l'Angleterre, faites par un voyageur . . . dans les années 1710 et 1711*, Amsterdam, 1715; and his similar work with dates 1713–14, Amsterdam, 1715.

(2) *Later Works*

2382 ASCOLI, G. Grande Bretagne devant l'opinion française au XVIIe siècle. 2 vols. in 1. Paris. 1930.

Exhaustive study with excellent bibl. Valuable for travel and intellectual contacts. Much more specialized is E. Philips, 'French interest in Quakers', *P.M.L.A.* 45 (1930), 238–55.

2383 RYE, W. B. England as seen by foreigners in the days of Elizabeth and James the First. 1865.

Recent books covering several centuries are H. Ballam and R. Lewis, eds., *The visitor's book: England and the English as others have seen them* (1500–1950), 1950; W. D. Robson-Scott, *German travellers in England, 1400–1800*, Oxf. 1953; and F. M. Wilson, *Strange island: Britain through foreign eyes, 1395–1940*, 1955.

2384 SMITH, E. Foreign visitors in England, and what they have thought of us: being some notes on their books and their opinions during the last three centuries. 1889. Bibl.

Cf. A. G. H. Bachrach, 'Some Dutch contacts with the Bodleian library in the seventeenth century', *Bodl. Lib. Rec.* 4 (1952), 149–60.

(c) *English Travellers Abroad*

The travels relating chiefly to diplomatic missions are listed in the section on Foreign Relations (pp. 73–99). See also *Naval History* (nos. 1822–7) and voyages listed in *Economic History* (nos. 2140–51). The most complete bibl. is vol. i of Cox (2351), which deals with the eastern hemisphere. The selected titles below are arranged roughly by date of the travels. For the period after 1700 see Pargellis (nos. 1786 and 1787). For travel in Russia, see vol. ii of F. V. Adelung, *Kritisch-literärische Übersicht der Reisenden in Russland bis 1700*, Amsterdam, 1960.

(1) *Sources*

2385 SHERLEY, SIR ANTHONY, SIR ROBERT, and SIR THOMAS. The three brothers, or the travels and adventures of Sir Anthony, Sir Robert, and Sir Thomas Sherley in Persia, Russia, Turkey, Spain, etc. 1825.

Based on early tracts. See Purchas, pt. ii (2140); E. P. Shirley, *The Sherley brothers, an historical memoir* . . . (Roxburghe Club, Chiswick, 1848), based largely on MSS. in P.R.O.; *Gentleman's Mag.* 22 (1844), 473–83, 594–8.

Sir Thomas Sherley's *Discours of the Turkes* [1606–07] was ed. by E. D. Ross in *Camd. Soc. Misc.* xvi (1936). By the same editor, *Sir Anthony Sherley and his Persian adventures*, 1933, based upon early narratives. For other titles see Cox, i. pp. 95, 247.

2386 MUNDY, PETER. The travels of Peter Mundy in Europe and Asia, 1608–1667. Ed. by R. C. Temple. 5 vols. in 6. Camb. 1907–36. Maps. Bibl.

Hakluyt Soc., Ser. II, vols. 17, 35, 45, 46, 55, 78; from Bodl. Lib. Rawl. MS. A. 315, and Br. Mus. Harl MS. 2286. Valuable. European sections, as private traveller, in 1st and 4th parts; elsewhere commercial.

2387 CORYATE, THOMAS. Coryats crudities, hastily gobled up in five moneths travells in France, Savoy, Italy, Rhetia . . ., Switzerland, some parts of high Germany, and the Netherlands. 1611. Later edns. 3 vols. 1776. 2 vols. Glasgow. 1905.

Coryat's letters from India are included in 1776 edn. 'The first, and for long . . . the only handbook for continental travel.' See Kerr, vol. ix (2147 n.), Purchas, pts. 1 and 2.

2388 OVERBURY, SIR THOMAS. Sir Thomas Overbury, his observations in his travailes upon the state of the XVII Provinces . . . [1609]. 1626. Later edn. 1651.

Repr. in *Harl. Misc.*, vol. vii.

2389 MORYSON, FYNES. An itinerary . . . containing his ten yeeres travell through the twelve dominions of Germany, Bohmerland, Sweitzerland, Netherland, Denmarke, Poland, Italy, Turkey, France, England, Scotland and Ireland . . . 1617. Repr. 4 vols. Glasgow. 1907–8.

'Invaluable to the social historian.' The MS. of an unfinished part of this work is in the library of Corpus Christi College, Oxford; parts were ed. by C. Hughes under the title of *Shakespeare's Europe*, 1903.

2390 HERBERT, [SIR] THOMAS. A relation of some yeares travaile . . . [1626–] into Afrique and the greater Asia. 1634. Later edns. 1638. 1665. 1677.

The third and fourth edns. were much enlarged by the author. Herbert's account of the first English embassy, that of Sir Dodmore Cotton, is important. An abridged version was ed. by Sir W. Foster, *Travels in Persia, 1627–1629*, 1928. See also *The journal of Robert Stodart*, ed. by E. Ross, 1935, for a report by another member of Cotton's company in 1627.

2391 WADSWORTH, JAMES. The English Spanish pilgrime, or a new discovery of Spanish popery and Jesuiticall stratagems. 1629. 2nd edn. 1630.

The 1630 edn. includes 'Further observations . . . concerning Spaine'. Reprints 1674 and 1684 under the title, *Memoirs and travels of . . . Wadsworth*. The author, an ex-Jesuit, visited Spain, 1609–18, and 1622, and was afterwards employed as an informer against Romanism (*D.N.B.*). Compare the anti-Catholic bias in a report of other Mediterranean area travels in W. Lithgow, *Rare adventures and painefull peregrinations*, ed. by B. J. Lawrence, 1928.

2392 BRERETON, SIR WILLIAM. Travels in Holland, the United Provinces, England, Scotland, and Ireland, 1634–1635. Ed. by E. Haskins. Chetham. Soc. 1 (1844).

2393 EVELYN, JOHN. The state of France as it stood in the ixth yeer of the present monarch Louis XIIII . . . 1652.

For other commentaries on France and on Italy before 1660 see *Francis Mortoft, his book* [1658–9], ed. by M. Letts (Hakluyt Soc., Ser. II, 57 (1925)); and John Raymond's *Itinerary contayning a voyage through Italy* [1646–7], 1648.

2394 HEYLYN, PETER. A full relation of two journeys: the one into the mainland of France, the other into some of the adjacent islands. 1656. Later edns. with varying titles. 1657. 1673. 1679.

His satirical journal, *France painted to life*, was published without his consent, 1656, 2nd edn., 1657.

2395 RAY, JOHN. Observations . . . made in a journey through the Low Countries, Germany, Italy and France, with a catalogue of plants not native of England . . . [1663]. 1673. 2 vols. 1738.

With this narration by the famous naturalist in the 1673 edn. is Francis Willughby's *Voyage through a great part of Spain*. Reprints of Ray and Willughby are in Harris, ii (2144).

2396 WHELER, GEORGE. A journey into Greece . . . [1675–6] in company of Dr. Spon of Lyons. 1682. Maps.

French trans., 2 vols., Amsterdam, 1689. Dr. Jacob Spon's account was publ. in Lyons in 3 vols., 1678. See also John Burbury, *Relation of a journey of . . . Lord Henry Howard from London to Vienna and thence to Constantinople . . .* [1665,] 1671.

2397 PITTS, JOSEPH. True and faithful account of the religion and manners of the Mohammetans, in which is a particular relation of their pilgrimage to Mecca [1678–94]. Exeter. 1704. 3rd edn. 1731.

Said to be the first Englishman to reach Mecca.

2398 BURNET, GILBERT. Some letters containing an account of . . . Switzerland, Italy, Germany, etc. [1685–6]. Rotterdam. 1686.

A Lond. edn., 1688, adds 'Three letters concerning . . . Italy [1687]' (separately publ. the same year). See Burnet's *Tracts* (2 vols., 1689), and Harris, ii (2144).

Cf. Richard Lassels, *The voyage of Italy*, ed. by S. Wilson, Paris, 1670, 1698. See Harris, ii.

2399 KER [CARR], WILLIAM. Remarks on the government of several parts of Germany, Denmark, Sweden . . . [and] the United Provinces. Amsterdam. 1688.

Written by an English consul at Amsterdam. Printed in *The memoirs of John Ker* . . . [1727]. See also Molesworth (980).

2400 BROMLEY, WILLIAM. Remarks in the grand tour of France and Italy. 1692.

An edn. of 1705 was unauthorized. See the same author's *Several years travels through Portugal, Spain, Italy, Germany* . . . 1702; see also Joseph Addison, *Remarks on several parts of Italy* (1701–3), 1705, 1718; and John Dryden, Jr., *A voyage to Sicily and Malta* (1700–1), 1776.

2401 MAUNDRELL, HENRY. A journey from Aleppo to Jerusalem at Easter, A.D. 1697. Oxf. 1703. Later edn. 1714.

The 1714 edn. includes an account of his travels to Mesopotamia in 1699. See Harris, vol. ii (2144); Pinkerton, vol. x (2147); Moore, vol. ii (2145 n.); *World displayed*, vol. xi (2145 n.).

2402 LISTER, [DR.] MARTIN. A journey to Paris in the year 1698. 1699. Later edn. Paris. 1875.

The author was interested in hygienic as well as artistic aspects of Paris life. See Pinkerton, vol. iv (2147). Edn. of 1873 published with annotations by Société des Bibliophiles Français. Satirized by M. Sorbière [pseud. for Wm. King], *A journey to London, in the year 1698* . . . [1698].

2403 NORTHLEIGH, JOHN. Topographical descriptions with historico-political and medico-physical observations made in two several voyages through most parts of Europe. 1702.

See Harris, vol. ii (2144). Cf. Ellis Veryard [M.D.], *An account of divers choice remarks, as well geographical, as historical, political, mathematical, physical, and moral; taken in a journey through the Low Countries, France, . . . as also a voyage to the Levant*, 1701.

2404 SLOANE, HANS. A voyage to the islands of Madera, Barbados, Nieves, S. Christophers and Jamaica, with the natural history . . . of the last of those islands. 2 vols. 1707–25. Maps.

Excellent for its natural history as well as for the travel account by the well-known member of the Royal Society.

(2) Later Works

2405 HOWARD, C. M. English travelers of the Renaissance. N.Y. 1913. Lond. 1914. Bibl.

Deals with 16th to early 18th century. See also B. Penrose, *Urbane travelers, 1591–1635* (Phila. and Lond. 1942), which includes biographical sketches of Fynes Moryson, Coryate, Herbert, and others. Also, C. E. Maxwell, *English traveller in France 1698–1815*, 1932. M. H. Braaksma, in *Travel and literature* (Groningen, 1938), evaluates several English narratives of the period as works of literature. See also the articles by M. Letts, 'Seventeenth-century travel in Europe', *Notes and Queries*, 11th Ser. 12 (1915), 42–4 and passim; 12th Ser. 1 (1916), 61–4 and passim. See also Frantz (2559).

2406   STOYE, J. W. English travellers abroad, 1640–1667: their influence in English society and politics. 1952.

See also G. Bonno, 'Les relations intellectuelles de Locke avec la France', *Univ. of Cal. Publ. in Mod. Philology*, 38 (1955), 37–264, which deals with travels of Locke on the continent and effects of French culture on him.

2407   WALKER, J. 'The English exiles in Holland during the reigns of Charles II and James II.' *R.H.S. Trans.*, 4th Ser. 30 (1948), 111–25.

Well-documented account of political and religious exiles.

F. BIOGRAPHY

I. BIBLIOGRAPHIES AND GUIDES

This section includes the lives and writings or the family papers of persons whose careers were too varied to be listed in other sections. Biographical lists in other parts of the volume should be examined by the student. Space does not permit the citing of genealogies, but these may be traced through Marshall (2409) and similar works. For heraldry see nos. 2187–8. Some examples of the variety of source materials available to the social historian, as well as the genealogist, are listed. Most of the following biographical works have been selected because they either contain documentary matter or reveal much on the customs and spirit of the age. Most family histories have been excluded (see Thomson, no. 2418). For bibliographies of biography see Stauffer (2583). See also H.M.C. (nos. 72–255) and *D.N.B.* (54).

2408   HAYDN, J. *Beatson's political index modernised: the book of dignities.* 1851. 1890.

For Beatson, see no. 52. See also the various publications of the Public Record Office; F. M. Powicke, ed., *Handbook of British chronology* (56); and H. B. George, *Genealogical tables illustrative of modern history*, ed. by J. H. R. Weaver, 1930.

2409   MARSHALL, G. W. The genealogist's guide to printed pedigrees. 1879. 4th edn. Guildford. 1905.

Valuable reference to wide variety of printed materials. See also W. P. W. Phillimore, *How to write the history of a family: a guide*, 1887, 1888; supplement, 1896, 1900. Useful periodicals are *Miscellanea Genealogica et Heraldica*, 31 vols., 1868–1938; *The Genealogist*, 45 vols., 1877–1922; and *The Ancestor*, 12 numbers, 1902–5.

2410   HARRISON, H. G. Select bibliography of English genealogy, with brief lists for Wales, Scotland and Ireland. 1937.

A useful manual. Cf. G. Gatfield, *Guide to printed books relating to English and foreign heraldry and genealogy*, 1892.

2411   RICHES, P. M. An analytical bibliography of universal collected biography, comprising books published in the English tongue in Great Britain and Ireland, America and the British dominions. 1934.

A guide to lives in many collective volumes. For diaries see E. F. MacPike, *English,*

Scottish and Irish diaries, journals, commonplace books . . . 1550–1900, 1941, and nos. 2434–6. For 17th-century biographies see Stauffer (2583).

2412 THOMSON, T. R. A catalogue of English family histories. 1928. 2nd edn. 1935.

Among those useful for the period are E. C. Legh, Lady Newton, ed., *The house of Lyme*, 1917; C. Dalton, *History of the Wrays of Glentworth*, 2 vols., 1880–1; and *Parentalia, or memoirs of the . . . Wrens* (2760 n.).

2. GENERAL FAMILY HISTORY

(a) *Sources*

2413 INQUISITIONS POST MORTEM. Stewart-Brown, R., ed. Cheshire inquisitions post mortem. Stuart period, 1603–1660. 3 vols. (Record Soc. Lancs. and Cheshire.) 1934–5.

An example, of which others may be found in the publications of local historical societies. Records of the family relationships and properties at the death of a supposed tenant in chief of the king. The MSS. at the P.R.O., Chancery and Exchequer, run to 5 Charles I; printed calendars in *Lists and Indexes*, Nos. 23, 26, 31, and 33 (1907–9). See also no. 3105.

2414 LOCAL LISTS. Jewson, C. B., ed. Transcript of three registers of passengers from Great Yarmouth to Holland and New England, 1637–1639. (Norfolk Record Soc. 25.) Norfolk. 1954.

Other examples of lists of names are: C. S. A. Dobson, ed., *Oxfordshire protestation returns, 1641–2* (Oxfordshire Rec. Soc. 36), 1955; J. W. Clay, 'The gentry of Yorkshire at the time of the civil war', *Yorks. Arch. Jour.* 23 (1914–15), 349–94; 'Norwich subscriptions to the voluntary gift of 1662', *Norfolk Rec. Soc. Pub.* 1 (1931), 69–86. The hearth-tax returns, of which a number have been printed by the local record societies, also are useful (e.g. Oxfordshire for 1665, Oxfordshire Rec. Soc. 21 (1940)). See no. 2163 and Mullins (23 n.). See also Dale (3294).

2415 MARRIAGE LICENCES. Glencross, R. M., ed. A calendar of the marriage licence allegations in the registry of the Bishop of London (1597–1648; 1660–1700). 2 vols. 1937–40.

Published by the British Record Society Index Library (vols. 62, 66), which has published many similar volumes for other regions. The Harleian Society also has published many registers (cf. its 'London Marriage Licences'); and 17th-century marriage records have been printed by such record societies as those of Gloucestershire, Lancashire, Sussex, and Yorkshire (see Mullins, 23 n.).

2416 PARISH REGISTERS. Marshall, G. W. Parish registers: a list of those printed or of which MS. copies exist in printed collections, together with references to extracts therefrom, printed and manuscript. 1881. Repr. with suppls. 1900–8 (Parish Register Soc. 30, 50, 61).

Annexed also to 3rd edn. of Marshall's *Genealogist's guide* (2409). Other guides to these important records of baptisms, marriages, and burials are by G. F. Matthews, 1908, A. M. Burke, 1908, suppl., 1909, and J. C. Cox, 1910, as well as earlier ones. Various types of parish records are described in Thompson (3304). Important printed registers, in addition to those published by numerous local societies, and the Harleian Society,

Register Section (vols. 1–85, 1877–1955, listed in Mullins, pp. 190–7), are Phillimore's parish register series, 1896+, and that of the Parish Register Society, 1896+. Parish registers are included at times in the publications of county historical societies (see *Local History*).

2417 VISITATIONS OF HERALDS. Harleian Society Publications. 1869+.

The heraldic visitations of the 17th century are particularly important, not only for family pedigrees, but for what they indicate about the movement of families into the ranks of the gentry, as indicated by the reports for such years as 1623, 1634, 1664, 1681. A few visitation records have been published also by county societies. See no. 2188, and references to separate counties in *Local History*.

2418 WILLS AND ADMINISTRATIONS. Index of wills proved in the prerogative court of Canterbury. (British Record Society Index Library.) 11 vols. 1893–1958.

Vols. iii–xi cover the years 1558–1693. Two other series on 'P.C.C.' in the Index Library are *Index to the act books of the archbishops of Canterbury* [1663–1859], 1929–38; and *Index to administrations* [Canterbury, 1649–60], 2 vols. in 4, 1944–53; and other volumes in the Index Library provide indexes to courts in various other places. Of even greater interest are collections of abstracts, of which the following are examples: J. and G. F. Matthews, eds., *Abstracts of probate acts in the prerogative court of Canterbury* [1620–55], 7 vols., 1911–14; J. H. Morrison's abstracts from the single *Register Scroope* [1630], 1934; A. Maddison, *Lincolnshire wills*, 2 vols., Lincoln, 1888–91; F. A. Crisp, ed., *Abstracts of Somerset wills* (3240 n.); and other volumes in the publications of the Chetham Society, Surtees Society, and Thoresby Society. See also no. 1855. For obituaries see Musgrave (2419 n.).

(b) *Later Works*

2419 BURKE, J. A genealogical and heraldic history of the commoners of Great Britain and Ireland. 4 vols. 1833–8.

Continued as a periodical published at irregular intervals, under the title of *A genealogical and heraldic dictionary of the landed gentry of Great Britain and Ireland*. Of less value for the 17th century is *Musgrave's Obituary*, ed. by G. J. Armytage, 6 vols. (Harleian Society, 44–9), 1899–1901.

2420 HUNTER, J. Familiae minorum gentium. Ed. by J. W. Clay. 4 vols. (Harleian Soc., vols. 37–40.) 1894–6.

Chiefly relates to the northern shires. Good examples for others are: J. Comber, *Sussex genealogies* (3259 n.); W. Rye, *Norfolk families* (3216 n.); and A. R. Maddison, *Lincolnshire pedigrees* (3209 n.).

2421 LE NEVE, J. Monumenta anglicana; being inscriptions on the monuments of several eminent persons deceased (1600–1718). 5 vols. 1717–19.

An earlier work by J. Weever, *Ancient funerall monuments . . .*, was printed in 1631. See also by Le Neve, *Memoirs British and foreign of the lives . . . of the most illustrious persons who dy'd in . . . 1711*, 1712. A similar collection for 1712 was publ. by him in 1714.

2422 SHAW, W. A. The knights of England: a complete record . . . of all the orders of chivalry in England, Scotland, Ireland, and of knights bachelors. 2 vols. 1906.

Cf. W. C. Metcalfe, *A book of knights banneret, Knights of the Bath, and knights bachelor*

(1426–1660), 1885; and G. W. Marshall, *Le Neve's pedigrees of knights* (1660–1714). Harleian Soc., 1873.

3. PEERS AND BARONETS

See also §B, *Status and Class*, pp. 31517.

2423 BURKE, SIR J. B., *et al.* A genealogical and heraldic history of the peerage and baronetage. 1826+.

Title for early volumes was *A genealogical and heraldic dictionary*; publication became annual after 1847. See also by the same, *A Genealogical history of the dormant, abeyant, forfeited and extinct peerages of the British Empire*, first publ. 1831, later edns. 1840, 1846, 1866, 1883; and their *Genealogical and heraldic history of the extinct and dormant baronetcies . . .*, 1841, later edns., 1844, 1866.

2424 C[OKAYNE], G. E. Complete peerage of England, Scotland, Ireland, Great Britain and the United Kingdom. 8 vols. 1887–98. New edn. rev. and enl. by V. Gibbs, H. A. Doubleday, and others. 14 vols. 1910–59.

Cokayne is the most complete peerage, the new edn. being more accurate. Other useful peerages are Sir William Dugdale, 3 vols., 1675–6; A. Collins, 1709 and many edns. (best edn., enl., by Sir S. E. Brydges, 9 vols., 1812); and J. E. Doyle, *Official baronage of England* [1066–1885], 3 vols., 1886. The best for Ireland is J. Lodge, rev. edn., 7 vols., Dublin, 1789.

2425 C[OKAYNE], G. E. Complete baronetage [1611–1800]. 6 vols. Exeter. 1900–9.

Invaluable, but contains some errors. For some additional lines of descent see T. Wotton, *The English baronetage*, 4 vols. in 5, 1741 (later edn. by E. Kimber and R. Johnson, 8 vols., 1771); and W. Betham, *Baronetage of England*, 5 vols., Ipswich and Lond. 1801–5.

4. UNIVERSITY AND SCHOOL LISTS

In the books below many biographical details, in addition to those supplied by the university or school records, have been added by the editors. See also the important Inns of Court registers in *Legal History*, and titles on many schools in the section on *Education* in Ch. X.

2426 FOSTER, J., ed. Alumni Oxonienses, being the matriculation register of the university 1500–1714. 4 vols. Oxf. 1891–2.

There is a later series of 4 vols. for 1715–1886, 1887–8. Cf. *The historical register of the University of Oxford . . . an alphabetical record of University honours . . .* [to 1900], Oxf. 1900; and A. Clark, ed., *Register of the University of Oxford*, vol. ii, 1571–1622, 2 vols. in 5, Oxf. Hist. Soc., 1885–9. Most of the colleges have separate printed registers.

2427 WOOD, ANTHONY à. Athenae Oxonienses, an exact history of all the writers and bishops who have had their education in the University of Oxford. To which are added the Fasti or annals of the said university. 2 vols. 1691. 2nd edn. 1721. Later edn. by P. Bliss. 4 vols. 1813–20.

Valuable biographical sketches, with lists of works; should be supplemented by reference to Foster. Wood's MSS. are in the Bodleian Libr. See A. Clark's edn. of *The life and times of Anthony Wood, antiquary, of Oxford, 1632–95, described by himself*, 5 vols., Oxf. Hist. Soc., Oxf. 1891–1900.

2428 VENN, J. and VENN, J. A., comps. Alumni Cantabrigienses. Part I [to 1751]. 4 vols. Camb. 1922–7.

By the same authors, *The book of matriculation and degrees* [1544–1659], Camb. 1913. See also J. R. Tanner, *The historical register of the University of Cambridge* (to 1910), Camb. 1917. The work of the Venns virtually supersedes the earlier *Athenae Cantabrigienses* (1500–1611), by C. H. Cooper and T. Cooper, 3 vols., Camb. 1858–1913.

2429 HARWOOD, T. Alumni Etonenses, or a catalogue of the provosts and fellows of Eton College and King's College, Cambridge, 1443–1797. Birmingham. 1797.

See also R. A. Austen-Leigh, ed., *The Eton College register, 1698–1752*, Eton, 1927.

2430 BARKER, G. F. R., and STENNING, A. H., eds. The record of old Westminsters. 2 vols. 1928.

5. BIOGRAPHIES AND PERSONAL PAPERS

(a) *Collective Biographical Materials*

(1) *Collections of Letters (Miscellaneous)*

See also Collins (259) and Ellis (260). For correspondence relating to particular families see P. Finch, ed., *History of Burley-on-the-Hill, Rutland*, 2 vols., 1901; E. C. Legh, Lady Newton, eds., *Lyme Letters, 1660–1760*, 1925 (Legh of Lyme); and *Trevelyan papers*, ed. by J. P. Collier, Sir W. C. Trevelyan, and Sir C. E. Trevelyan, 2 vols., Camden Soc., 1872–3.

2431 BRYANT, A., ed. Postman's horn. An anthology of the letters of latter seventeenth-century England. 1936.

The interest varies, as in any artificial selection, but the collection has value. Cf. *Call back yesterday*, a collection compiled by Lady Charnwood, 1937. See also no. 2204.

2432 SCOTT, SIR W. Private letters of the seventeenth century. Ed. by D. Grant. 1947.

The well-known *Ho-Elianiae or Familiar letters*, by James Howell, 3 vols., 1645–50 (ed. by J. Jacobs, 2 vols., 1892; 4 vols., Boston and N.Y. 1907), contains a few authentic letters, but represents otherwise the literary effort of the author while he was in prison. See intro. by Jacobs, and *D.N.B.* They have more value for literary or social history than for biography.

2433 [WALKER, JOHN.] Letters written by eminent persons in the 17th and 18th centuries, to which are added Hearne's journeys to Reading and to Whaddon Hall . . . and lives of eminent men by John Aubrey. 2 vols. 1813.

Taken from Hearne, Smith, and Ballard collections at the Bodleian. A somewhat similar collection is R. Warner, *Original letters from Richard Baxter, Matthew Prior, Lord Bolingbroke, Alexander Pope, etc.*, 2 pts., 1817–18.

(2) *Collected Diaries*

2434 MATTHEWS, WILLIAM. British diaries: an annotated bibliography of British diaries written between 1442 and 1942. Berkeley. 1950.

See also M. Bottrall, *Everyman a phoenix: studies in seventeenth-century autobiography*, [1958]. Earlier lists are in *Camb. Hist. Engl. Lit.* See also Riches (2411).

2435　D'OYLEY, E., ed. More English diaries. 1938.

Includes extracts from diaries of Dr. John Dee, Capt. Thos. James, Sir Henry Slingsby, Sir John Reresby, Dr. Claver Morris. See also A. A. W. H. Ponsonby, *English diaries* [1923]; *More English diaries* [16th–19th centuries], 1927; and *Scottish and Irish diaries* [1927]. J. Aitken edited *English diaries of the XVI, XVII and XVIII centuries*, 1941 (Pelican Books).

2436　HODGSON, J. C., ed. North country diaries. 2 vols. Surtees Soc. Durham. 1910–15.

A number of short diaries, of which John Ashton's (vol. i) gives some details about the Bishops' War, 1639. The *Journal of Sir Wm. Brereton* [1635] is reprinted in vol. ii. Relating to the north also, ed. by C. Jackson *et al.*, is *Yorkshire diaries and autobiographies in the seventeenth and eighteenth century*, 2 vols., Surtees Soc., Durham, 1877–86; vol. i contains diaries, etc. of Adam Eyre, John Shaw, James Fretwell, John Hobson, and Heneage Dering; vol. ii, those of Jonathan Priestley, Sir Walter Calverley.

(3) *Collected Biographies*

On biographies written before 1700, see Stauffer (2583).

2437　ABBOTT, W. C. Conflicts with oblivion. Camb. (Mass.). 1924. 2nd edn. Camb. (Mass.) 1935.

Includes Pepys, Cromwell, Col. Thom. Blood.

2438　ADAMS, P. W. A history of the Adams family of North Stafford. 1914.

This is cited because it relates to a yeoman family. For others of this class see D. S. Boutflower on the Boutflower family, Newcastle, 1930; and Sir G. Sitwell on the *Hurts of Haldworth*, Oxf. 1930.

2439　AUBREY, JOHN. Brief lives, chiefly of contemporaries, set down by John Aubrey, between the years 1669 and 1696. 2 vols. 1813. Later edns. By A. Clark, 2 vols. Oxf. 1898. By A. Powell. 1949. By O. L. Dick. Ann Arbor. 1957.

One of the outstanding collections. Cf. *E.H.R.* 11 (1896), 328–35, for a note by Mr. Clark on Aubrey's biographical collections. The edn. of 1813 is entitled: *Letters written by eminent persons . . . and lives of eminent men.* The letters are pr. from Ballard and other MSS. in the Bodleian. Cf. *The scandal and credulities of John Aubrey*, ed. by J. Collier, 1931; and A. Powell's *John Aubrey and his friends*, 1948.

2440　CLARKE, S. The lives of sundry eminent persons in this later age. In two parts. I. of divines. II. of nobility and gentry of both sexes . . . to which is added his own life. 1683.

Characters, rather than biographies, of pious men and women. For several character sketches see also D. N. Smith, *Characters from the histories and memoirs of the seventeenth century*, Oxf. 1918. Other early collections are: Clement Barksdale, *Memorials of worthy persons*, 3 vols., 1661–70; and *Bibliographica Brittanica*, 6 vols., 1747–66 (5-vol. edn. 1778–93).

2441　DOBRÉE, B., ed. From Anne to Victoria: essays by various hands. 1937.

Repr. N.Y. 1967. Includes A. S. Turberville's 'John Churchill, Duke of Marlborough'; W. Connely's 'Addison and Steele'; J. Hayward's 'Jonathan Swift'; B. C. Brown's 'Sarah, Duchess of Marlborough'; G. D. H. Cole's 'Daniel Defoe', etc. Cf. Dobrée's *Essays in biography, 1680–1726*, Milford, 1925, which includes studies of Sir George Etherege, Sir John Vanbrugh, and Addison.

See also A. W. Fox, *Men and marvels in the 17th century*, N.Y. 1937; and H. R. Williamson, *Four Stuart portraits*, 1949, comprising Launcelot Andrewes, Sir John Eliot, Sir Balthazar Gerbier, and Col. Thomas Rainsborough.

2442 FULLER, THOMAS. The history of the worthies of England. 1662. Later edns. By J. Nichols. 2 vols. 1811. By P. A. Nuttall. 3 vols. 1840. By J. Freeman. (1st edn. abr.) [1952.]

A classic collection. For biographies of Fuller, and bibliographies, see no. 1245.

2443 JOHNSON, CHARLES. A general history of the lives and adventures of the most famous highwaymen, murderers, street-robbers, etc. . . . and of the most notorious pyrates. 1734. Later edns. 1742 and 1839.

Repr. in 1926 edn. of A. Smith's *History of . . . highwaymen* (2546). Cf. *A bibliography of the works of Captain Charles Johnson*, by P. Gosse, 1927.

2444 NOTESTEIN, W. Four worthies: John Chamberlain, Anne Clifford, John Taylor, Oliver Heywood. 1956. New Haven. 1957.

By same author: *English folk: A book of characters*, 1938. Both are readable volumes based on diaries and letters. The latter includes sketches of Thos. Tyldesley, Alice Thornton, Leonard Wheatcroft, Adam Eyre, and others.

2445 PITTS, T., pseud. The western martyrology or bloody assizes containing the lives, trials and dying speeches of all those eminent Protestants that suffered in the west of England . . . with the life and death of George L[ord] Jeffreys. The fifth edn. (by Pitts). 1705.

This is the usual title and permanent form. The 1st edn. has not been found; it has sometimes been attributed to John Tutchin and John Dunton, and probably was entitled *A collection of the dying speeches*, etc. (see Term Catalogue, ii. 258). The 3rd edn. is *A new martyrology . . . life and death of George Lord Jeffrey*, 1689; 4th edn. 1693 (ed. by 'Th. Pitts'). It is included in *Notable British trials*, [1929] (1062 n.).

2446 PRINCE, J. Danmonii orientales illustres: or the worthies of Devon. Exeter. 1701. Later edn. 1810.

2447 SANFORD, J. L. and TOWNSEND, M. The great governing families of England. 2 vols. Edin. 1865.

A standard work.

2448 WALTON, IZAAK. The lives of Dr. John Donne, Sir Henry Wotton, Mr. Richard Hooker, Mr. George Herbert . . . [The life of Dr. Sanderson . . .] 2 vols. 1670. 1678. Later edns. By T. Zouch. 2 vols. York. 1817. By A. Dobson. 2 vols. 1898. Later edns. 1927. 1951.

This is the first collected edn. of these four lives; and the first edn. of the life of Sanderson. A. S. Collins' ed. *The lives of Herbert and Wotton*, 1934. Cf. J. E. Bult, *A bibliography of Izaak Walton's 'Lives'*, Oxf. 1930; and D. Novarr, *The making of Walton's 'Lives'*, 1959.

(b) *Lives and Papers of Individuals or Families*

ASSHETON, NICHOLAS

2449 The journal of Nicholas Assheton of Downham in the County of Lancaster (1617–18). Ed. by F. R. Raines. Chetham Soc. 1848.

The diary of a sporting gentleman.

ASTON FAMILY

2450 Clifford, A., ed. Tixall letters; or the correspondence of the Aston family ... during the seventeenth century. 2 vols. 1815.

See the same author's *Tixall poetry*, [1813].

BARNES, AMBROSE

2451 Memoirs of the life of Mr. Ambrose Barnes, late merchant and sometime alderman of Newcastle upon Tyne. Ed. by W. H. D. Longstaffe. Surtees Soc. 1867.

Dedication by M. R. dated 1716.

BRISTOL, JOHN HARVEY [HERVEY], FIRST EARL OF

2452 The diary of John Harvey, first earl of Bristol, with extracts from his book of expenses 1688 to 1742. Wells. 1894.

His letter-books and Sir T. Harvey's letters were publ., 3 vols., Wells, 1894.

BROCKBANK, REVD. THOMAS

2453 The diary and letter book of the Rev. Thomas Brockbank, 1671–1709. Ed. by R. Trappes-Lomax. (Chetham Soc. Pub., N.S. 89.) 1930.

Correspondence with relatives and friends, of limited historical value. For another clergyman, see E. M. Walker, ed., 'Letters of the Rev. George Plaxton, M.A., rector of Berwick-in-Elmet' (1706–1709/10), *Thoresby Soc. Publ.* 37 (1936), 30–104.

BURY, MRS. ELIZABETH

2454 Bury, S. Account of the life and death of Mrs. Elizabeth Bury chiefly collected out of her own diary (1644–1720). Bristol. 1720.

CAVENDISH FAMILY

2455 Bickley, F. The Cavendish family. 1911. N.Y. and Boston. 1914.

Cf. White Kennet, *A sermon preached at the funeral of ... William duke of Devonshire ... with some memoirs of the family of Cavendish*, 1708. On the duke of Newcastle see no. 1682. On Margaret (Lucas), duchess of Newcastle, see lives by R. W. Goulding, 1925, and D. Grant, Toronto, 1957; also H. T. E. Perry, *The first duchess of Newcastle and her husband as figures in literary history*, Boston, 1918.

CHESTERFIELD, PHILIP STANHOPE, SECOND EARL OF

2456 Letters of Philip, second earl of Chesterfield ... with some of their replies. 1829.

Interesting private letters, mainly 1656–89. Cf. *Philip Stanhope, second earl of Chesterfield. His correspondence with various ladies among whom is notably Barbara Villiers, later Lady Castlemaine and Duchess of Cleveland, and letters exchanged with Sir Charles Sedley, John Dryden, Charles Cotton, Mr. Bates*, 1930.

The 1930 edn., which omits most letters of political significance, gives the texts from the letter-book in the Br. Mus.

CHETHAM, HUMPHREY

2457 Raines, F. R., and Sutton, C. W. Life of Humphrey Chetham, founder of the Chetham Hospital and Library, Manchester. 2 vols. Chetham Soc. 1903. Bibl.

CLIFFORD, LADY ANNE

2458   The diary of the Lady Anne Clifford (1590–1676). Ed. by V. Sackville-West. 1923.

Diary extends from 1603 to 1619. Cf. G. C. Williamson, *Lady Anne Clifford, Countess of Dorset, Pembroke, and Montgomery, 1590–1676*, Kendal, 1922; and Notestein, *Four Worthies* (2444).

COKE, ROGER

2459   Coke, Roger. Detection of the court and state of England during the last four reigns. 2 vols. 1694. Later edn. 3 vols. 1719.

Has some family memoirs and remarks on trade; otherwise unreliable gossip. Edn. of 1719 has a continuation to 1714.

COLSTON, EDWARD

2460   Garrard, T. Edward Colston, the philanthropist, his life and times. Bristol. 1852.

CONWAY, VISCOUNTESS and MORE, HENRY

2461   Conway Letters: the correspondence of Anne, Viscountess Conway, Henry More, and their friends 1642–84. Ed. by M. H. Nicolson. New Haven. 1930.

CORNWALLIS, JANE [MEAUTYS], LADY

2462   The private correspondence of Jane, Lady Cornwallis, 1613–1644. From the originals in the possession of the family. [Ed. by Lord Braybrooke.] 1842.

Contains some interesting anecdotes and occasional notices of public affairs. Lady Cornwallis was afterwards the wife of Nathaniel Bacon. Concerning her brother see A. C. Bunten, *Sir Thomas Meautys, secretary to Lord Bacon, and his friends*, 1918.

COURTHOP, SIR GEORGE

2463   The memoirs of Sir George Courthop [1616–85]. Ed. by Mrs. S. C. Lomas. *Camden Soc. Misc.* xi. 1907.

Ed. from an 18th-century transcript in G. J. Courthope's possession.

CREWE, JOHN

2464   Lawson, P. H., ed. 'The commonplace book of John Crewe of Utkinton, co. Chester, circa 1640–1650.' *Jour. Chester and North Wales Arch. Arch. Hist. Soc.*, N.S. 26 (1925), 133–53.

Another brief record is 'The diary of Sir Thomas Dawes, 1644', ed. by V. B. Redstone, *Surrey Arch. Colls.* 37 (1926), 1–36. See also a diary of John Cruwys, 1682–8, in *Devon and Corn. N. and Q.* 18 (1935), 259–64.

DE LA PRYME, ABRAHAM

2465   The diary of Abraham de la Pryme, the Yorkshire antiquary. Ed. by C. Jackson. (Surtees Soc. 54.) 1870.

D'EWES, SIR SIMONDS

2466 The autobiography [to 1636] and correspondence [to 1649] of Sir Simonds D'Ewes during the reigns of James I and Charles I. Ed. by J. O. Halliwell. 2 vols. 1845.

The autobiography of a Puritan antiquary. Valuable. Contains also 'The Secret history of the reign of King James' (Harl. MS.), and 'An account of the journey of the Prince's servants into Spain, A.D. 1623', by Sir Richard Wynne.

EVELYN, JOHN

2467 Memoirs illustrative of the life and writings of John Evelyn, comprising his Diary from the year 1641 to 1705–6, and a selection from his familiar letters (1642–1704). Ed. by W. Bray. 2 vols. 1818. Later edn. by H. B. Wheatley. 4 vols. 1879. Ed. by A. Dobson. 3 vols. 1906. Ed. by E. S. de Beer. 6 vols. Oxf. and Lond. 1955.

Most edns. of the diary contain correspondence of Charles I and Charles II with Sir E. Nicholas (1641–55), letters between Hyde and Sir R. Browne (1646–59), and other correspondence of Browne (1640–51).

The 1955 edn. of the diary is the most complete. The observations of a cultured gentleman, Evelyn's comments provide a rich source on many aspects of his period. See also his *Memoires for my grandson*, transcribed and ed. by G. Keynes, 1926, and W. Upcott's edn. of *The miscellaneous writings of John Evelyn*, 1825. G. L. Keynes compiled a bibl. of Evelyn's writings (Camb. 1937). See also no. 2346.

2468 Smith, H. M. The early life and education of John Evelyn. Oxf. 1920.

Other works on Evelyn include: G. Boas's 'John Evelyn, "Virtuoso": in the light of recent research', *Essays by divers hands* (Trans. Royal Soc. Literature), 3rd Ser. 28 (1956), 106–22; F. E. Bowman's 'Studies in the life of John Evelyn (1620–1706)', *Harvard Summaries of Theses* (1935), 308–11; and C. Marburg, *Mr. Pepys and Mr. Evelyn*, Phila. and Lond. 1935. See also Lord Ponsonby, *John Evelyn, fellow of the Royal Society*, 1932. On the Evelyn family and its various branches see H. Evelyn, *History of the Evelyn family*, 1915; see also W. G. Hiscock, *John Evelyn and his family circle*, 1955.

FINCH, SIR JOHN and BAINES, SIR THOMAS

2469 Malloch, A. Finch and Baines. A seventeenth-century friendship. Camb. 1917.

Sir John Finch [1626–82] and Sir Thomas Baines [1622?–80], who were interested in science and in cultural advances of their times. Finch was a brother of Anne, Viscountess Conway (see no. 2461).

FREKE, MRS. ELIZABETH

2470 Mrs. Elizabeth Freke her diary, 1671–1714. Cork. 1913.

FURSE, ROBERT

2471 'Diary and family book of Robert Furse, yeoman, 1593.' Ed. by H. Carpenter. *Trans. Devon. Assoc.* 26 (1894).

An uncommon type of source from this social class. On matters relating to land see also 'The book of John Rowe' (1921). See also Adam Eyre (1854) and E. Brockbank, *Richard Hubberthorne of Yeland, yeoman-soldier-quaker, 1628–62*, 1929.

GAWDY, PHILIP

2472 Letters of Philip Gawdy 1579–1616. Ed. by I. H. Jeayes. Roxburghe Club. 1906.

Pr. from Br. Mus. Add. MSS. 27395–9 and Egerton MSS. 2713–22. Cf. H.M.C., Gawdy MSS. (142).

GREENE, JOHN

2473 The diary of John Greene (1635–57). Ed. by E. M. Symonds. *E.H.R.* 43 (1928), 385–94, 598–604; 44 (1929), 106–17.

On his terms at Lincoln's Inn, on family happenings, the plagues, civil war.

GUISE FAMILY and THOS. RAYMOND

2474 Autobiography of Thomas Raymond [and] Memoirs of the family of Guise of Elmore, Gloucestershire. Ed. by G. Davies. Camden Soc. 1917.

Guise memoirs pr. from transcript in the Bodl. Libr., Raymond from Bodl. Lib. Rawl. MS. D. 1150.

HALKETT, ANNE, LADY

2475 The autobiography of Anne, Lady Halkett. Ed. by J. G. Nichols. Camden Soc. 1875.

Important for the duke of York's escape and for royalist activities in Scotland, 1649–54. There is an interesting article on Lady Halkett in *Blackwood's Mag.*, Nov. 1924.

HANMER, SIR THOMAS

2476 The correspondence of Sir Thomas Hanmer . . . with a memoir of his life. Ed. by Sir H. Bunbury. 1838.

Useful for 1710–14 events, as well as for social history.

HARLEY, LADY BRILLIANA

2477 Letters of the Lady Brilliana Harley, wife of Sir Robert Harley. Ed. by T. T. Lewis. Camden Soc. 1854.

Covers 1625–43. Most interesting letters of a Presbyterian, mainly written to her son at Oxford. Other letters and narratives of the sieges of Brampton Castle, 1643–4, are in Bath MSS. (80).
See a short sketch in Notestein, *English folk* (2444 n.).

HERBERT FAMILY

2478 The life of Edward Lord Herbert of Cherbury written by himself (to 1624). Ed. by H. Walpole. Strawberry Hill Press. 1764. Later edn. by Sir W. Scott. 1824. Ed. by Sir S. Lee. 1886. 1907.

See also R. Warner, ed., *Epistolary curiosities . . . letters . . . illustrative of the Herbert family*, 2 vols., Bath, 1818.

HOBY, LADY MARGARET

2479 Diary of Lady Margaret Hoby, 1599–1605. Ed. by D. M. Meads. Boston. 1930.

HOLLES FAMILY

2480 Holles, Gervase. Memorials of the Holles family. Ed. by A. C. Wood. Camden Soc. 1937.

Cf. 'A fragment of the autobiography of Gervase Holles', transcr. with notes by Wood, *Lincoln Arch. and Arch. Soc.* 41 (1934), 50–60, a hitherto unpublished fragment of the autobiography, written by Holles during his exile in Holland after the civil war. Cf. also Wood, 'The Holles Family', *R.H.S. Trans.*, 4th Ser. 19 (1936), 145–64.

ISHAM FAMILY

2481 'The diaries (home and foreign) of Sir Justinian Isham, 1704–1736', ed. by H. I. Longden. *R.H.S. Trans.*, 3rd Ser. 1 (1907), 181–203.

See also *The correspondence of Bishop Brian Duppa and Sir Justinian Isham, 1650–1660*, ed. by Sir G. Isham (Northampton Rec. Soc.), Lamport, 1955. Duppa was Bishop of Salisbury at the time.

KNATCHBULL FAMILY

2482 Vellacott, P. C. 'The diary of a country gentleman in 1688.' *Camb. Hist. Journ.* 2 (1926), 48–62.

Sir John Knatchbull and the revolution in Kent. See also Sir T. Matthew, *The life of Lady Lucy Knatchbull*, ed. from a 1642 MS. by D. Knowles, 1932.

KNYVETT, THOMAS

2483 The Knyvett letters, 1620–1644. Ed. by B. Schofield. (Norfolk Rec. Soc.) Norfolk and Lond. 1949.

Letters of a Norfolk royalist, Thomas Knyvett of Ashwellthorpe, to his wife; mainly concerned with personal affairs, but of more than local significance.

LANSDOWNE, GEORGE GRANVILLE, LORD

2484 Handasyde, E. Granville the polite; the life of George Granville, Lord Lansdowne, 1666–1735. 1933.

Includes some particulars on Jacobitism, 1711–12. On another Jacobite family see H. Tayler, *Lady Nithsdale and her family*, 1939.

LAPTHORNE, RICHARD

2485 Portledge papers, being extracts from the letters of Richard Lapthorne ... London, to Richard Coffin . . . Devon [1687–97]. Ed. by R. J. Kerr and I. C. Duncan. 1928.

LISTER, JOSEPH

2486 Autobiography of Joseph Lister of Bradford in Yorkshire to which is added a contemporary account of the defence of Bradford and capture of Leeds by the parliamentarians in 1642. Ed. by T. Wright. 1842.

LOWE, ROGER

2487 The diary of Roger Lowe of Ashton-in-Makerfield, Lancashire, 1663–74. Ed. by W. L. Sachse. New Haven and Lond. 1938.

Diary of a shopkeeper. Cf. R. C. Latham, 'Roger Lowe, shopkeeper and nonconformist', *History*, 26 (1941), 19–35.

MARTINDALE, ADAM

2488 Life of Adam Martindale. Ed. by R. Parkinson. Chetham Soc. Publs. 1845.

A nonconformist country minister, whose life is representative of his social class.

MAYNWARING [MAINWARING], ARTHUR

2489 The life and posthumous works of Arthur Maynwaring. Ed. by J. Old-mixon. 1715.

MILDMAY, SIR HUMPHREY

2490 Ralph, P. L. Sir Humphrey Mildmay, royalist gentleman: glimpses of the English scene, 1633–1652. New Brunswick. 1947.

Life of the country gentleman based on his diary and account books.

MONMOUTH, ROBERT CAREY, EARL OF

2491 Memoirs of the life of Robert Carey [to 1626] . . . written by himself. Ed. by John, Earl of Cork and Orrery. 1759. Later edn. by Sir W. Scott. Edin. 1808. Ed. by G. H. Powell. 1905.

MORDAUNT FAMILY

2492 Halstead, R. (pseud. for Henry Mordaunt, 2nd earl of Peterborough). Succinct genealogies of the noble and ancient houses of . . . Mordaunt of Turvey. 1685.

Of extreme rarity; useful for Peterborough's own life and times.
Cf. *Private diarie of Elizabeth, Viscountess Mordaunt* (1656–78), Duncairn, 1856. For Peterborough see no. 1704.

MORRIS, CLAVER

2493 The diary of a west country physician, 1684–1726. Ed. by E. Hobhouse. 1934.

NEWDIGATE, SIR RICHARD

2494 Newdigate-Newdegate, Lady. Cavalier and Puritan in the days of the Stuarts compiled from the private papers and diary of Sir Richard Newdigate . . . with extracts from MS. news-letters (1675–89). 1901.

NEWTON, SAMUEL

2495 Diary of Samuel Newton, alderman of Cambridge (1662–1717). Ed. by J. E. Foster. (Camb. Antiq. Soc.) Camb. 1890.

Also useful for Cambridge in the period is the *Autobiography of Matthew Robinson*, ed. by J. E. B. Mayor, Camb. 1856; Robinson was a fellow of St. John's College, Cambridge, and vicar of Burneston, Yorks.

OGLANDER, SIR JOHN

2496 A royalist's notebook. The commonplace book of Sir John Oglander, Kt. of Nunwell (1585–1655). Ed. by F. Bamford. 1936.

See also W. H. Long's edn., 1888, entitled *The Oglander memoirs*, which contain a good deal of local history for the Isle of Wight. Letters and memoirs are used in C. F. Aspinwall-Oglander, *Nunwell symphony*, 1945.

OSBORNE, DOROTHY

2497 Letters from Dorothy Osborne to Sir William Temple 1652–54. Ed. by E. A. Perry. 1888. Later edn. 1914. Ed. by G. C. Moore Smith. Oxf. 1928.

The 1928 edn. contains corrected chronology and is the definitive edn. Cf. Julia G. Longe's *Martha, Lady Giffard, her life and correspondence (1664–1722): a sequel to the Letters of Dorothy Osborne*, 1911. See also no. 512.

OXINDEN, HENRY and PEYTON, SIR THOMAS

2498 The Oxinden letters, 1607–1642; being the correspondence of Henry Oxinden of Barham and his circle. Ed. by D. Gardiner. 1933.

Excellent picture of the squirearchy on the eve of the civil war.
    Cf. the same editor's *The Oxinden and Peyton letters, 1642–1670*, 1937, which extend the picture of country life into more troubled times, and contain the letters of Sir Thomas Peyton of Knowlton.

PASTON, LADY KATHERINE

2499 The correspondence of Lady Katherine Paston, 1603–1627. Ed. by R. Hughey. (Norfolk Rec. Soc. 14.) 1941.

Reveals personal and business affairs of a well-known Norfolk family.

PEPYS, SAMUEL

2500 Diary of Samuel Pepys, 1660–1669. Ed. by H. B. Wheatley. 10 vols. 1893–9.

This famous diary by a civil servant and observer of London life, existing in MS. form at Oxford, has had three major editors: Richard, Lord Braybrooke (using transcriptions of John Smith and including some correspondence), 2 vols., 1825; M. Bright, using his own transcription, 6 vols., 1875–9; and Wheatley, based on Bright but more complete. A fourth edn. has been proposed. For the 'Second diary' relating to Tangier see *Naval History*, no. 1730 n. For letters see J. Smith, ed., *The life, journals and correspondence . . .*, 2 vols., 1841, additional ones in R. Howarth, ed., *Letters and the second diary*, 1932; and H. T. Heath, ed., *The letters of Samuel Pepys and his family circle*, 1955. For official papers on naval matters see no. 1730. For a description of the Pepys MSS., see Grose (10), p. 306.
    Of the biographies the most scholarly is Bryant (1737); those in more popular style include E. Moorhouse, 1922, P. Lubbock, 1923, and P. Hunt, Pittsburgh, 1958. Pepys and his varied activities have been the subject of numerous monographs and articles, such as *Occasional papers read by members of the Samuel Pepys Club*, 2 vols., 1917–25; M. Astin, *Mrs. Pepys: her book*, 1929; Marburg, *Mr. Pepys and Mr. Evelyn* (2468 n.); and U. T. Holmes, *Samuel Pepys in Paris*, Chapel Hill, [1954]. See also E. Chappell, *Eight generations of the Pepys family, 1599–1800*, 1936.

PRIDEAUX, HUMPHREY

2501 Letters of Humphrey Prideaux sometime dean of Norwich to John Ellis sometime under-secretary of state. 1674–1722. Ed. by E. M. Thompson. Camden Soc. 1875.

Pr. from Br. Mus. Add. MSS. 28929. Gives much amusing gossip, especially about Oxford 1674–85. The life of Prideaux, attributed to T. Birch, 1748, is useful. For other letters of Prideaux, see Pine Coffin MSS. (100).

RAWDON, MARMADUKE

2502   Anon. The life of Marmaduke Rawdon of York. Ed. by R. Davies. Camden Soc. 1863.

Of importance for trade with the Canary Islands. Cf. 'Memoirs of Sir Marmaduke Rawdon, Kt. 1582–1646', ed. by H. F. Killick, *Yorks. Arch. Jour.* 25 (1919), 315–30.

RERESBY, SIR JOHN

2503   Memoirs of Sir John Reresby: the complete text and a selection of his letters. Ed. by A. Browning. Glasgow. 1936.

Earlier and less complete edns. were 1734; by J. J. Cartwright, 1875; and by A. Watt, 1904. Reresby (1634–89), Yorkshire squire and M.P., a moderate Tory and friend of Halifax, provides valuable comments, especially on local affairs; they are fullest after 1678. The MS. is in the Br. Mus.

RUGG, THOMAS

2504   The diurnal of Thomas Rugg, 1659–1661. Ed. by W. L. Sachse. Camden Soc. (3rd Ser. 91.) 1961.

Observations of political as well as social interest.

RUSSELL FAMILY

2505   Berry, M. Some account of the life of Rachael Wriothesley, Lady Russell . . . followed by a series of letters from Lady Russell to Lord Russell [1672–82] . . . [and] eleven letters from Dorothy Sidney Countess of Sunderland to George Saville Marquis of Hallifax in the year 1680. 1819.

Originals in the possession of Duke of Devonshire. Of the many edns. of Lady Russell's letters the most complete, with new letters, is Lord John Russell's, 2 vols., Camden Soc., 1853.

Important recent studies based upon their household and business papers are by G. S. Thomson: *Life in a noble household* (2225); *The Russells in Bloomsbury, 1669–1771*, 1940; and *Family background, Four studies of the Russells* (15th–18th centuries), 1949.

TEMPLE FAMILY OF STOWE

2506   Gay, E. F. 'The Temples of Stowe and their debts. Sir Thomas Temple and Sir Peter Temple, 1603–1653.' *Hunt. Lib. Quart.* 2 (1939), 399–438.

Biographical sketches of family members and account of their litigations. Cf. by same author: 'The rise of an English country family: Peter and John Temple to 1603', ibid. 1 (1938), 367–90; and 'Sir Richard Temple: the debt settlement and estate litigation, 1653–1675', ibid. 6 (1943), 255–91.

The three articles present a valuable record of the family's financial affairs.

THORNTON, MRS. ALICE

2507   The autobiography of Mrs. Alice Thornton of East Newton, co. York. Surtees Soc. 1875.

Covers 1629–69; revealing for the life of a gentlewoman. Cf. Notestein (2444 n.).

THROCKMORTON, SIR FRANCIS

2508   Barnard, E. A. B. A seventeenth-century country gentleman (Sir Francis Throckmorton, 1640–80). Camb. 1944. 1949.

A consecutive narrative of a young man's activities 'based on a ledger which records his day-to-day expenditures from the age of eleven' until after his marriage.

VERNEY FAMILY

2509   Memoirs of the Verney family from the letters . . . at Claydon House.
Vols. i and ii by Frances Parthenope, Lady Verney, vols. iii and iv by Margaret
Maria, Lady Verney. 4 vols. 1892–9. 3rd edn. 2 vols. 1925.

> A valuable history of a county family during the 17th century. See also no. 229. Some
> of the papers were printed in vols. 31 and 56 of the first Camden Ser., ed. by J. Bruce.
> See also Lady M. M. Verney's edn. of *Verney letters of the 18th century*, 2 vols., 1930.

WARWICK, MARY RICH, COUNTESS OF

2510   Autobiography of Mary [Rich] Countess of Warwick. Ed. by T. C. Croker.
1848.

> Illustrates social life and religion. Lives by C. F. Smith, 1901; and M. E. Palgrave, 1901.

WYNN FAMILY

2511   Calendar of Wyn (of Gwydir) papers, 1515–1690. In the National Library
of Wales and elsewhere. 1926 [1927].

> A family of great influence in Wales and at court. For Sir Richard Wynn's travel to
> Spain see no. 2466 n.

G. SOCIAL REFORM AND PROBLEMS

For religious societies concerned with such matters see *Ecclesiastical History*
(1207–10); for problems relating primarily to education or to health, see Ch. X,
Education, and *Science*. See also *Political Theory* in Ch. III.

1. GENERAL SOCIAL REFORM

(a) *Sources*

No bibliography exists in print, but Bahlman (2515) refers to a typed bibliography dealing with societies for the reformation of manners compiled by D. M.
Davies in 1938 and deposited in the library of University College, London.

2512   [CHAMBERLAYNE, EDWARD.] England wants: or several proposals
probably beneficial for England humbly offered to the consideration of all good
patriots in both houses of Parliament. 1667.

> Repr. in *Somers tracts*, vol. ix.

2513   [PRESTON, RICHARD GRAHAM, VISCOUNT.] Angliae speculum
morale; the moral state of England with several aspects it beareth to virtue
and vice. 1670.

2514   STEPHENS, EDWARD. The beginning and progress of a needful and
hopeful reformation. 1691.

> See also Woodward (1207); *A help to a national reformation*, 1700; and William Bisset's
> sermon, *Plain English*, 1704, which points out defects in societies for moral reform.

(b) *Later Works*

2515 BAHLMAN, D. W. The moral revolution of 1688. New Haven. 1957.

Bibl. footnotes. Scholarly essay relating the development of the movement for social reform to the new order in church and state *temp.* William III and Anne. See also nos. 1207–10.

2516 BERENS, L. H. The digger movement in the days of the commonwealth as revealed in the writings of Gerrard Winstanley, the digger. 1906.

See also no. 966.

2517 CLARK, G. N. Science and social welfare in the age of Newton. Oxf. 1937. Repr. with cor. Oxf. 1949.

Lectures, some of which are repr. from *Econ. Jour.* and *Econ. Hist. Rev.*, which are concerned chiefly with scientific developments but deal also with social controls and with the beginning of a scientific approach to social problems. Clark replies to B. Hessen, *The social and economic roots of Newton's Principia*, Sydney, 1946 (repr. of an article in *Science at the cross-roads*, 1931).

2518 JAMES, M. Social problems and policy during the Puritan revolution, 1640–1660. 1930.

A valuable monograph drawing upon pamphlets, literature especially.
  Cf. W. Schenk, *The concern for social justice* (994) and Troeltsch (1847 n.). For the post-1660 period see Schlatter (1148). See also Wilson (1848 n.).

2519 MUELLER, W. R. The anatomy of Robert Burton's England. Berkeley and Los Angeles. 1952.

Has bibl. footnotes. The author's aim is to treat Burton as an analyser of society.

2. THE POOR AND POOR LAW

A description of the statutes and pamphlet literature will be found in Eden (2530); and numerous pamphlets are listed in Webb (2535) and Marshall (2533).
  See also records of the Quarter Sessions; *Calendar of State Papers, Domestic*; and *Acts of the Privy Council*.

(a) *Sources*

2520 ORDERS AND DIRECTIONS . . . for the better administration of justice . . . and how . . . the lawes and statutes tending to the reliefe of the poore . . . are executed . . . 1630 [1631?].

The official 'Book of Orders'. See also [Samuel Carter], *Legal provisions for the poor, or a treatise of the common and statute laws concerning the poor* . . ., 1710. For a review of the principal statutes see Eden (2530).

2521 DOWNAME, JOHN. The plea of the poor, or a treatise of beneficence poore . . . and almsdeeds. 1616.

2522 S., M. Greevous grones for the poore done by a well-willer who wisheth that the poore of England might be so provided for as none should neede to go a begging. 1621.

This work, which is quoted in Eden, has been ascribed to Thomas Dekker and Michael Sparke.

2523 STANLEYE'S REMEDY: or a way how to reform wandring beggers, theeves, high-way robbers and pick-pockets. 1646.

Purports to be from the pen of a repentant highwayman. From this period also came: *Unum necessarium or the poore man's case* . . . by John Cooke (solicitor general), 1648; Peter Chamberlen, *The poore man's advocate*, 1649, with proposals for employment of the poor and an inquiry into public expenditure; and I. D. (John Keymor), *Clear and evident way of enriching the nations of England and Ireland and for setting very great numbers of poore on work*, 1650, which urges employment in the fishing industry.

2524 H[AINES], R[ICHARD.] Prevention of poverty: or a discourse of the causes of the decay of trade, fall of lands, and want of money. 1674.

Proposes cultivation of flax and hemp. Haines's *Proposals for building in every county a working-almshouse or hospital as the best expedient to perfect the trade and manufactory of linen cloth*, 1677, is repr. in *Harleian Misc.* (59), vol. iv.

2525 FIRMIN, THOMAS. Some proposals for the imploying of the poor and for the prevention of idleness. 1678. Later edn. 1681.

Included in *Collection of pamphlets concerning the poor*, 1787. In the latter also are Richard Dunning, *Bread for the poor* . . ., Exeter, 1698; and Defoe (2528). See also Matthew Hale, *A discourse touching provision for the poor*, 1683, 1695, 1927.

2526 NORTH, ROGER. A discourse of the poor, shewing the pernicious tendency of the laws now in force for their maintenance and settlement. 1753.

Written between 1660 and 1688. See also John Bellers, *Essays about the poor, manufacturers, trade, plantations* . . ., 1699, and other similar pamphlets (Wing, B 1829, 1832).

2527 CARY, JOHN. An account of the proceedings of the corporation of Bristol, in execution of the act of Parliament for the better employing and maintaining the poor of that city. 1700.

For other works on this corporation see E. E. Butcher in Bristol Rec. Soc., 1932; and Webb, *Local government:* statutory authorities, p. 114 n. Examples of reports on other localities are: [John Fransham], *Exact account of the charge for supporting the poor of* . . . *Norwich*, 1720; E. L. Guilford, 'Extracts from . . . Nottingham', *Trans. Thoroton Soc.* 30 (1926), 108–36, and 31 (1927), 85–104; A. Fessler, 'The official attitude toward the sick poor . . . Lancashire', *Trans. Lancs. Ches. Hist. Soc.* 102 (1951), 85–113; and S. A. Cutlack, 'The Gnosall records, 1679–1837', *Coll. Hist. Staff.* for 1936, 1–141. See also no. 2531.

2528 DEFOE, DANIEL. Giving alms no charity, and employing the poor a grievance to the nation. 1704.

(b) *Later Works*

2529 BURN, R. The history of the poor laws. 1764.

The author was a J.P. in Westmorland.

2530 EDEN, SIR F. M. The state of the poor, or a history of the labouring classes in England . . . with respect to diet, fuel, and habitation. 3 vols. 1797. Abr. edn. by A. G. L. Rogers. 1928.

Valuable for documents and for extracts from pamphlets, etc. Index of 1928 edn. serves as a brief bibl.

2531   HAMPSON, E. M. Treatment of poverty in Cambridgeshire, 1597–1834.

An important monograph, based on extensive study of parish records.

2532   LEONARD, E. M. The early history of English poor relief. Camb. 1900.

Important older work. Cf. her article, 'The relief of the poor by the state regulation of wages', *E.H.R.* 13 (1898), 91–3. See also Godfrey (2538 n.).

2533   MARSHALL, D. English poor in the 18th century: a study in social and administrative history. 1926. Bibl.

Author used MSS. of Cambridgeshire and Lancashire. Cf. her 'Old poor law, 1662–1795', *Econ. Hist. Rev.* 8 (1937–8), 38–47.

2534   NICHOLLS, SIR G. A history of the English poor law. 2 vols. 1854. Later edn. by H. G. Willink and Timakay. 3 vols. 1898–9.

Valuable. Nicholls wrote also on the poor laws of Scotland and Ireland. See also Gray (2537a); and C. J. Ribton-Turner, *History of vagrants and beggars*, 1887.

2535   WEBB, B. and WEBB, S. The old poor law (Part I of English poor law history, 3 vols., in *English Local Government*). 1927.

Invaluable; cites official records as well as pamphlet literature. See also Savidge (1203 n.).

3. Hospitals and Charities

2536   BERNARD, RICHARD. The ready way to good works, or a treatise of charitie. 1634.

2537   H[ARTLIB], S[AMUEL.] London's charity enlarged, or stilling the orphan's cry by the liberality of Parliament. 1650.

2537a   GRAY, B. K. A history of English philanthropy from the dissolution of the monasteries to the taking of the first census. 1905.

Has bibl. footnotes. Cf. H. Levy, 'The economic history of sickness and medical benefit before the Puritan revolution', *Econ. Hist. Rev.* 13 (1943), 42–57. See also Portus (1209).

2538   HOBSON, J. M. Some early and later houses of pity. 1926.

Arranged by counties and useful for reference, but Stuart period is not always differentiated. See also *The endowed charities of the city of London, reprinted . . . from . . . reports of the commissioners for inquiry concerning charities,* 1829, which has a detailed table of contents and index. On the *Reports* of the commissioners [for England and Wales], 1818–37, see Pargellis, p. 269. W. H. Godfrey, *The English Almshouse,* [1955], is largely architectural in focus, but contains information on numerous almshouses founded in the 17th century.

2539   JORDAN, W. K. Philanthropy in England, 1480–1660: a study of the changing pattern of English social aspirations. N.Y. 1959.

See also his related volumes, *The charities of London,* N.Y. 1960; and *The forming of the charitable institutions of the west of England,* Phila. 1960; and *Charities of rural England,* N.Y. 1961. Jordan's studies, based upon extensive use of wills of donors, is a notable contribution to the history of social change. A fourth volume on other counties is projected. See further his studies of Kentish institutions in *Arch. Cant.* 65 (1961), and Lancashire in Chetham Soc., 3rd Ser. 9 (1962).

2540 MOORE, SIR N. The history of St. Bartholomew's hospital. 2 vols. 1918.

There is a short history by Sir D'A. Power, 1923, who wrote also *Dr. William Harvey and St. Bartholomew's Hospital*, 1924. Histories of St. Thomas's have been written by F. G. Parsons, 3 vols., 1932–6, and by C. Graves, 1947. On the Royal Hospital at Chelsea, opened in 1694, see [Th. Faulkner], *Historical . . . account*, 1805. See also R. Kirk, *Mr. Pepys upon the state of Christ-Hospital*, 1935.

2541 MULLETT, C. F. 'Sir William Petty on the plague.' *Isis*, 28 (1938), 19–25.

Reports on Petty's proposals concerning this London problem. See also pamphlets of 1696–1708 regarding a proposed dispensary described by B. Boyce in *Rev. English Studies*, 14 (1938), 453–8.

4. CRIME, POLICE, AND PRISONS

(a) *Sources*

(Arranged in chronological order by date of publication)

2542 MYNSHUL, GEFFRAY. Essayes and characters of a prison and prisoners. 1618. Later edn. Edin. 1821.

Cf. William Fennor, *The compters common wealth, or a voiage made to an infernall iland* . . . 1617; John Clavell, *A recantation of an ill-led life, or a discovery of the highway law*, 1634; and W. Bagwell, *The merchant distressed* (observations while a prisoner for debt in 1637), verse, 1644. See also A. V. Judges, ed., *The Elizabethan underworld: a collection of Tudor and early Stuart tracts and ballads*, 1930.

2543 HARRIS, ALEXANDER. The oeconomy of the Fleete, or an apologiti-call answere of Alexander Harris (late warden) unto xix articles sett forth against him by the prisoners. Ed. by A. Jessup. Camd. Soc. 1879.

Cf. William Leach, *Proposalls for an act for speedy setting at large all prisoners*, 1649, and his *Proposals for an act for the more speedy satisfaction of creditors*, 1650. See also G[eorge] F[idge], *The English gusman*, 1652.

2544 HEAD, RICHARD. The English rogue described in the life of Meriton Latroon, a witty extravagant, being a compleat history of the most eminent cheats of both sexes. 1665. Parts 2–4 [by Francis Kirkman]. 1668–1671. Repr. 1928.

2545 PITT, MOSES. The cry of the oppressed, being a true account of the unparallel'd sufferings of multitudes of poor imprisoned debtors in most of the gaols in England. 1691.

A plea for prison reform.

2546 SMITH, ALEXANDER. The history of the lives of the most noted highwaymen, footpads, shop-lifts and cheats of both sexes, in and about London and other places. 1711. 2nd edn. 2 vols. 1714. 5th edn. 3 vols. 1719–20. Ed. by A. L. Hayward. 1926.

Reprinted in various collections, including *The complete Newgate calendar*, ed. by J. LeRayner and G. T. Crook, 5 vols., 1926. See also Johnson (2443).

(b) *Later Works*

2547   GOSSE, P. History of piracy. 1932. 2nd edn. 1954.

By the same author, *The pirate's Who's who, giving particulars of the lives . . . of the pirates and buccaneers*, 1924; and *My private pirate library*, 1926, with a bibl.
   On the Atlantic buccaneers see A. H. C. Prichard, *The Buccaneers*, 1929, and S. R. H Rogers, *The Atlantic Buccaneers*, 1939. For the notorious Captain William Kidd, see accounts of his trial in *Collection of State tracts* (370), and Notable British Trials series (1062 n.); and recent lives by C. P. Milligan, Phila. 1932, and H. T. Wilkins, 1937.

2548   IVES, G. A history of penal methods, criminals, witches, lunatics. 1914.

Cf. H. W. Bleackley, *The hangmen of England*, 1929.

2549   LEE, W. L. M. History of police in England. 1901.

Cf. A. Solmes, *The English policeman, 871–1935*, 1936.

2550   PIKE, L. O. A history of crime in England. 2 vols. 1873–6.

A standard work. Cf. R. Fuller, *The beggar's brotherhood*, 1936, which deals largely with the 16th and 17th centuries. On figures connected with the court, see Petherick (2340).

2551   WEBB, S. and WEBB, B. English prisons under local government. 1922.

See no. 930. See also E. G. O'Donoghue, *Bridewell hospital, palace, prison, schools*, 2 vols., 1923–9; and W. E. Hooper, *The history of Newgate and the Old Bailey . . .*, 1935. On the Fleet, see J. Ashton, *The Fleet: its river, prison, and marriages*, 1888.

X

CULTURAL HISTORY

Cultural history as represented in this chapter relates mainly to intellectual developments rather than to social, but special aspects of intellectual interest have been included elsewhere in Ch. III, § F on Political Theory, Ch. VIII, pp. 262–3 on Economic Theory, and Ch. V, pp. 160–4 on Religious Thought. Because the literary studies for the period are so extensive and so specialized, it has been deemed unnecessary to go beyond citing the major works related to such studies, and the most important titles relating to the major literary figures. In the selection of contemporary authors as well as of later works, the purpose has been to indicate broad developments in ideas and tastes rather than to deal in an exhaustive way with particular ideas or authors. A special group of titles (nos. 2918–22) indicates something of the impact of science at this point. There is no satisfactory survey for the history of thought in general.

A. GENERAL WORKS

1. BIBLIOGRAPHIES

The bibliographies in the section on *Literature* include numerous works of value for the background of the period. On the works published in the century, *S.T.C.* (3) and Wing (4) are the chief guides. Clues to what was being read may be found in library catalogues (see nos. 17–20), and Jayne (2553). Of value for general cultural as well as more specialized studies are the magazines, *Isis* (2814) with its bibliographies; and *Journal of the History of Ideas*, vol. 1+, N.Y., 1940+.

2552 CORDASCO, F. A register of 18th-century bibliographies and references. Chicago. 1950.

Lists for the years 1926–48 publications of a bibliographical nature relating to English literature, bookselling, and other subjects. Though slight and somewhat uncritical, the work has some value for the 17th century.

2553 JAYNE, S., ed. Library catalogues of the English Renaissance. Berkeley, Cal. 1956.

Describes many MS. catalogues of the years 1500–1640, as an approach to the reading interests of the period. See also the publications of individual English libraries; e.g. those of the Bristol Reference Library, which include catalogues of *Early Printed English Books, 1496–1640*, *Foreign Books 1473–1700*, and *English Books 1641–1700*, Bristol, 1954–8. See also lists of books in two private libraries of the century, in *The Library*, 4th Ser. 2 (1922), 1–12; 13 (1933), 89–98.

2554 STUDIES IN PHILOLOGY. Vol. 1+. Chapel Hill. 1906+.

Publishes a valuable annual bibliography on the Renaissance, which includes items on England of general as well as literary interest. Cf. no. 2572.

2. LATER WORKS

2555 ALLEN, B. S. Tides in English taste, 1619–1800. A background for the study of literature. 2 vols. Camb. (Mass.). 1937. Later edn. 2 vols. 1958.

Cf. V. de S. Pinto, *The English renaissance, 1510–1688, with a chapter on literature and music . . .*, 1938, bibl. (vol. ii of *Intro. to English literature*, ed. by B. Dobrée; rev. edn. 1951). L. Stephen, *History of English thought in the eighteenth century*, 2 vols., 1876 (later edns.), begins with the restoration period.

2556 BAUMER, F. L. 'The conception of Christendom in Renaissance England.' *Jour. Hist. Ideas*, 6 (1945), 131–56.

Also by Baumer, 'England, the Turk, and the common corps of Christendom', *A.H.R.* 50 (1944), 26–48; and 'The Church of England and the common corps of Christendom'. *J.M.H.* 16 (1944), 1–21.

2557 BETHEL, S. L. The cultural revolution of the seventeenth century. Lond. and N.Y. 1951.

Is concerned chiefly with theological doctrines and poetry; has bibl. footnotes. See also C. Hill, *Intellectual origins of the English revolution* (325 n.); and Willey (2569).

2558 EMERY, C. 'John Wilkins' universal language.' *Isis*, 38 (1947–8), 174–85.

Includes extracts from his *Essay toward a real character and a philosophical language*, 1668. On the subject of dialect and language in the period see also H. Hulme, 'Derbyshire dialect', *Derbyshire Arch. and Nat. Hist. Soc.*, N.S. 14 (1940), 88–103; J. I. Cope, 'Seventeenth-century Quaker style', *P.M.L.A.* 71 (1956), 725–54; and R. F. Jones, 'Science and language in England of the mid-seventeenth century', *Jour. Eng. and German Philol.* 31 (1932), 315–31, and no. 2919. See also J. Laird, 'George Dalgarno', *Aberdeen Univ. Rev.* 23 (1935), 15–31.

2559 FRANZ, R. W. The English traveller and the movement of ideas, 1660–1732. 2 vols. Lincoln, Neb. 1934.

For European influences see also L. Charlanne, *L'Influence française en Angleterre au xviie siècle*, Paris, 1906; G. van Alphen (681); and D. Stimson, 'Hartlib, Haak and Oldenburg: intelligencers' (2905 n.). For non-European influences see S. C. Chew, *The crescent and the rose: Islam and England during the renaissance*, N.Y. 1937; W. W. Appleton, *A cycle of Cathay: the Chinese vogue in England during the seventeenth and eighteenth centuries*, N.Y. 1951; and R. P. Bond, *Queen Anne's American kings*, Oxf. 1952.

2560 HARRIS, V. All coherence gone. Chicago. 1949. Bibl.

Examines the controversy over the idea of decay. Cf. Tuveson (3010).

2561 HOUGHTON, W. E. 'The history of trades: its relation to seventeenth-century thought.' *Jour. Hist. Ideas*, 2 (1941), 33–60.

2562 LOVEJOY, A. O. The great chain of being: a study of the history of an idea. Camb. (Mass.). 1936. 1953.

Lectures delivered at Harvard in 1933. Included with Lovejoy's *Essays in the history of ideas* (Balt. 1948), relating chiefly to later centuries, is a bibl. of Lovejoy's writings.

2563 MAYO, T. F. Epicurus in England, 1650–1725. Dallas, Texas. 1934. Bibl.

Examines the impact of Epicurean philosophy on literature and religious thought especially.

2564 NICOLSON, M. H. The breaking of the circle; studies in the effect of the 'new science' upon seventeenth-century poetry. Evanston. 1950.

By the same author, *Science and imagination*, Ithaca, 1956. See also nos. 2919, 2921.

2565 SENCOURT, R. [R. E. G. GEORGE.] Outflying philosophy: a literary study of the religious elements in the poems and letters of John Donne and in the works of Sir Thomas Brown and of Henry Vaughan . . . [1923].

Cf. L. J. Mills, *One soul in bodies twain*, Bloomington, 1938, a scholarly study of the friendship theme.

2566 SMITH, P. A history of modern culture. N.Y. 2 vols. 1930–[1939]. Bibl.

Useful. Vol. i covers 1543–1687; vol. ii, 1687–1776.
Cf. P. Hazard, *La crise de la conscience européenne (1680–1715)*, 3 vols., Paris, 1935; and essays on ideas by R. Metz and others in *Seventeenth-century studies presented to Sir Herbert Grierson*, Oxf. and N.Y. 1958.

2567 SOLT, L. F. 'Anti-intellectualism in the Puritan revolution.' *Church Hist.* 25 (1956), 306–16.

Examines the hostility of the Levellers and others toward traditional ideas.

2568 WILEY, M. L. The subtle knot: creative scepticism in the seventeenth century. Camb. (Mass.). 1952.

2569 WILLEY, B. The seventeenth-century background. 1934. Later edn. N.Y. 1950.

Stimulating studies on the thought of the period. By Willey also, *The religion of nature*, 1957. See also Bredvold, *Intellectual milieu of . . . Dryden* (2625 n.); and Westfall (2922).

2570 WILLIAMSON, G. 'Mutability, decay and seventeenth-century melancholy.' *Jour. Engl. Lit. Hist.* 2 (1935), 121–50.

Also by Williamson, 'Richard Whitlocke, learning's apologist', *Philological Quart.* 15 (1936), 254–72. See also L. Babb, *The Elizabethan malady . . . melancolia* [1580–1640], East Lansing, 1951, bibl.

B. LITERATURE

Rich though the seventeenth century is in literary history, the student should be reminded that the early decades are virtually an extension of the 'Elizabethan Age', and the later decades provide the beginning of the 'Augustan Age'. Any distinctively literary characteristics for the period that lies between tend to be obscured by the conflicts growing out of the political and religious currents of the times. The works which are listed in this section have been chosen as guides to the abundant bibliographical material, to the main branches of the literature of the century, and to the best editions and bibliographies for representative

writers. Because the relationship between history and literature is so close, these
materials will serve to illustrate not only the literary ideas and tastes of the period
but also the influence of the times upon the fabric of its literature. Both con-
tribute to an understanding of the century.

Useful chapters dealing with these relationships will be found in Clark (267),
M. Ashley (265), and no. 2579. See also MacClure (1110) and Mitchell (1112).

I. GENERAL

(a) *Bibliography and Reference*

2571 [ANNUAL] BIBLIOGRAPHY of English language and literature. Compiled by members of the Modern Humanities Research Association. Ed. by
A. C. Paues *et al.* Camb. 1921+.

Cf. S. A. Allibone, *Critical dictionary of English literature* . . ., 3 vols. 1859–71. 2 suppl.
vols. by J. F. Kirk, Phila. 1891; and *The year's work in English studies*, publ. by The
English Assoc. 1919+. See *Cambridge bibliography of English literature* (6), and the
bibls. in *Camb. Hist. Engl. Lit.* (2579).

2572 ENGLISH LITERATURE, 1660–1800: a current bibliography. Compiled by R. S. Crane, C. B. Woods, G. S. Alleman, *et al. Philological Quarterly.*

An annual publication, Iowa City, 1926+. The bibls. from 1926 to 1960 have
been separately publ. as *English literature, 1660–1800, a bibliography of modern
studies*, Princeton, 1950–62.
Cf. J. W. Hebel, *English seventeenth-century literature: a brief working bibliography*,
N.Y. 1929; A. Esdaile, *The sources of English literature: a guide for students*, Camb.
1928; and G. W. Cole, *A survey of the bibliography of English literature 1473–1640*,
Chicago, 1930.

2573 FREEMAN, R. English emblem-books. 1948.

A bibl. to 1700.

2574 PRICE, M. B. and PRICE, L. M. The publication of English literature
in Germany in the eighteenth century. Berkeley. 1934.

See also E. J. Simmons, *English literature and culture in Russia (1553–1840)*, Camb.
(Mass.), 1935; and J. F. Bense, *Anglo-Dutch relations* . . ., The Hague, 1925.

2575 ENGLISH LITERARY HISTORY. Baltimore. [1934+.]

A useful periodical.
Other outstanding serial publications which should be consulted for literary history
are: *English Journal* (Chicago, 1912+); *Essays and Studies* . . . *English Association*
(1910+); *Journal of English and German Philology* (Urbana, 1897+); *Modern Language
Journal* (N.Y. 1916+); *Modern Language Notes* (Balt. 1886+); *Modern Language
Quarterly* (Seattle, 1940+); *Modern Language Review* (Camb. 1905+ superseding *Mod.
Lang. Quart.*, Lond. 1897–1904); *Modern Philology* (Chicago, 1903+); *Oxford Biblio-
graphical Society Proceedings and Papers* (Oxf. 1922+); *Publications of the Modern
Language Assoc. of America* (1884/5+); *Review of English Studies* (1925+); *Studies in
Philology* (Chapel Hill, 1906+); and *Seventeenth-Century News Letter* (Sampson, N.Y.
1942+).
See also *Huntington Library Quarterly* (1937+, formerly *Hunt. Lib. Bull.*, 1931–7);
Notes and Queries (43); *Philological Quarterly* (2572); and *London Times Literary Supple-
ment* (1902+).

(b) *Anthologies*

2576 COFFIN, R. P. T. and WITHERSPOON, A. M. Seventeenth-century prose and poetry. N.Y. 1946. 1961.

2577 WHITE, H., WALLERSTEIN, R. C., and QUINTANA, R. Seventeenth-century verse and prose. 2 vols. N.Y. 1951, 1952.

Vol. i, 1600–60; vol. ii, 1660–1700. Includes brief general bibls. as well as bibls. for individual writers.

(c) *Later Works*

2578 BUSH, D. English literature in the earlier seventeenth century, 1600–1660. Oxf. 1945. Bibl.

In *Oxford history of English literature*, ed. by F. P. Wilson and B. Dobrée. An excellent guide. Cf. C. V. Wedgwood, *Seventeenth-century English literature* (Home University Library), 1950, bibl.

2579 CAMBRIDGE HISTORY OF ENGLISH LITERATURE. Ed. by Sir A. W. Ward and A. R. Waller. 15 vols. Camb. 1907–32. Bibl. Later edn. 15 vols. Camb. 1949–53. Repr. 15 vols. Camb. 1963.

Bibliographies omitted from later edns. Less inclusive, but well organized, is B. Ford, ed., *A guide to English literature*, vols. i–iv, 1957, new edn., 1961–2 (Penguin Books), of which vols. iii–iv relate to the period.

2580 GRIERSON, H. J. C. Cross currents in English literature of the seventeenth century. 1929.

Still useful. Examples of the treatment of special subjects are: B. Boyce, *The Theophrastan character in England to 1642*, Camb. (Mass.), 1947; and his *Polemic character, 1640–1661*, Lincoln, 1955; and A. Beljame, *English men of letters and the English public ... 1600–1774*, trans. 1948 from the 1881 Paris edn. See also H. Brown, 'The classical tradition in English literature: a bibliography', *Harvard Studies and Notes in Philol. and Lit.* 18 (1935), 7–46.

2581 LOCKE, L. G. Tillotson; a study in seventeenth-century literature. Copenhagen. 1954. Bibl.

On pulpit oratory in its literary aspects see also Mitchell (1112). On Tillotson see no. 1288. See also Richardson, *English preachers and preaching* (1112 n.).

2582 SLOANE, W. Children's books in England and America in the seventeenth century. N.Y. 1955.

An annotated checklist is appended. Cf. E. M. Field, *The child and his book*, 1891, later edn., 1895.

2583 STAUFFER, D. A. English biography before 1700. Camb. (Mass.). 1930. Bibl.

By same author, *The art of biography in the eighteenth century*, Princeton and Lond. 1941, bibl. supplement, 1941. See also D. N. Smith, ed., *Characters from the histories and memoirs of the seventeenth century with an essay on the character*, Oxf. 1918; and V. de S. Pinto, ed., *English biography in the 17th century*, 1951.

2584 WELLEK, R. and WARREN, A. Theory of literature. N.Y. 1949.

2585 WHITE, H. C. English devotional literature, prose, 1600–1640. Madison. 1951.

See also L. M. Wright, *The literary life of the early Friends, 1650–1725,* N.Y. 1932.

2. PROSE

(a) *Anthologies*

2586 SHAABER, M. A. Seventeenth-century English prose. N.Y. 1957.

See also in Pelican Books, K. Muir, ed., *Elizabethan and Jacobean prose, 1550–1620,* 1956; P. Ure, ed., *Seventeenth-century prose,* 1956; and J. W. Hebel *et al.,* eds., *Prose of the English renaissance,* N.Y. 1952.

2587 SPINGARN, J. E., ed. Seventeenth-century critical essays. 3 vols. Oxf. 1908–9. Bibl. Reissued. 3 vols. Bloomington, Ind. 1957.

Extracts and repr. of essays, prefaces, etc. Cf. J. Haslewood, *Ancient critical essays upon English poets and poesy,* 2 vols., 1811–15; and N. Drake, *Essays . . . illustrative of the Tatler, Spectator, and Guardian,* 3 vols., 1805.

(b) *Non-Fictional Prose*
(1) *General Works*

2588 HAZLITT, W. The collected works of William Hazlitt. Ed. by A. R. Waller and A. Glover. 12 vols. 1902–4. Ed. by P. P. Howe. 21 vols. 1930–4.

Includes *Lectures on the comic writers.*

2589 KRAPP, G. P. Rise of English literary prose. 1915.

A basic work. For Scottish prose, see J. H. Millar, *Scottish prose of the 17th and 18th centuries,* Glasgow, 1912.

(2) *Individual Writers*

See Sir Francis Bacon (403, 2695). John Dryden is listed under 'Poets' (2624–5) as is Milton (2633–4). For the diarists see John Evelyn (2467), Samuel Pepys (2500), and nos. 2434–6. For 'Characters' and biography see Earle (2167), and Ch. IX *supra.* Writers in the fields of political theory, religion, science, and scholarship may be traced through the index. Travel narratives are mainly in Ch. IX.

ADDISON, JOSEPH. 1672–1719

2590 The work of Joseph Addison. Ed. by R. Hurd. 6 vols. 1811. 6 vols. 1854–6. 1893 (Bohn Standard Lib.).

The *Letters* were ed. by W. Graham, Oxf. 1941. Lives are by L. Aikin, 1843; W. J. Courthope, N.Y. 1884, later edn. 1911; and P. Smithers, Oxf. 1954. For bibl. see *C.B.E.L.* ii. 601–7, v. 460–1.

BROWNE, SIR THOMAS. 1605–1642

2591 Works. Ed. by G. Keynes, 6 vols., 1928–31.

Includes *Religio Medici,* 1642, *Pseudodoxia epidemica,* 1646, and *Hydriotaphia,* 1658, as well as others, and letters; vols. v and vi were repr. with corrections, 1946. Still of some value is the earlier edn. by S. Wilkins, 4 vols., 1835–6, 1852. Biographies include those of Samuel Johnson, 1756, and Sir E. Gosse, 1905; a good critical study is by F. L. Huntley, Ann Arbor, 1962. For bibl. see G. Keynes, Camb. 1924; and *C.B.E.L.* i. 834.

BUNYAN, JOHN. 1628–1688

2592 The works of that eminent servant of Christ . . . John Bunyan. Ed. by C. Doe. 1672.

The first complete *Works* were ed. by G. Offor, 3 vols., Glasgow, 1855. Of his most famous work, *The pilgrim's progress*, 1678, the first critical edn. was by Offor, 1847; the definitive text is in the edn. by J. B. Wharey, Oxf. 1928. The standard biography is H. Talon, *John Bunyan: the man and his works*, 1951 (trans. by B. Wall from Paris edn., 1948). An earlier life by J. Brown, 1885, was rev. by F. M. Harrison, 1928. A bibl. was compiled by F. M. Harrison (Bibliog. Soc.), 1932. See also *C.B.E.L.* ii. 490–5, v. 447–8.

BURTON, ROBERT. 1577–1640

2593 The anatomy of melancholy, what it is, with all the kindes, causes, symptomes, prognosticks, and several cures of it. Oxf. 1621. Later edn. by A. H. Bullen and A. R. Shilleto, 3 vols. 1893 and 1923. By H. Jackson. 3 vols. 1932.

Cf. 'Robert Burton and the "Anatomy of Melancholy"', Papers by Sir W. Osler, E. Bensly, and others', ed. by F. Madan, *Oxf. Bibliog. Soc. Proc. and Papers*, 1 (1925) 163–246. For bibl. see *C.B.E.L.* i. 829–30, v. 340.

DEFOE, DANIEL. 1660–1731

2594 Novels and selected writings. (Shakespeare Head edn.) 14 vols. Oxf. 1927–8.

The best modern edn. See also *Romances and narratives*, ed. by G. A. Aitken, 16 vols., 1895–6. Defoe's *Letters* (see vols. iv–v of Portland MSS., no. 153), were ed. by G. H. Healey, Oxf. 1955. Of the biographies, the best is by J. R. Sutherland, 1937, 1954, but also good is J. R. Moore, Chicago, 1958. For bibl. see *C.B.E.L.* ii. 495–514, v. 448–50, and those in the biographies. See also Defoe's *Review* (3084); his *Tour* (3110); and political writings (376, 982).

DENNIS, JOHN. 1657–1734

2595 The critical works of John Dennis. Ed. by E. N. Hooker. 2 vols. Baltimore. 1939–43.

His *Miscellanies in verse and prose* were publ. in 1693; his *Select works*, 2 vols., 1718; *Original letters, familiar, moral, and critical*, 2 vols., 1721. See H. G. Paul, *John Dennis, his life and criticism*, N.Y. 1911, bibl.; and a bibl. including plays and works in *C.B.E.L.* ii. 571–2.

SELDEN, JOHN. 1584–1654

2596 Table-talk, being the discourses of John Selden, Esq., or his sense of various matters . . . relating especially to religion and state. Ed. by R. Milward. 1689. Later edns. By S. H. Reynolds. Oxf. 1892. By Sir F. Pollock. 1927.

The 1927 edn. includes an account of Selden and his work by Sir E. Fry. For bibl. see *C.B.E.L.* i. 721, 874. See also no. 1075.

STEELE, RICHARD. 1672–1729

2597 Tracts and pamphlets by Richard Steele. Ed. with notes and commentary by R. Blanchard. Baltimore. 1944.

Cf. *Correspondence*, ed. by Blanchard, 1941. The standard life, with a bibl., is by

G. A. Aitken, 2 vols., 1889; others are by H. A. Dobson, 1886; W. Connely, 1934. See also J. C. Loftis, *Steele at Drury Lane*, 1952. Bibls., besides 'Aitken, are R. Blanchard, 'The Christian hero, a bibliography', *Library*, 10 (1929); and *C.B.E.L.* ii. 608–12, v. 461–2.

SWIFT, JONATHAN. 1667–1745

2598   Prose works of Jonathan Swift. Ed. by T. Scott. 12 vols. 1897–1908.

The definitive edn. in progress is *Prose Works*, ed. by H. Davis, 14 vols., Oxf. 1939+. The *Poems* were well ed. by Sir H. Williams, 3 vols., Oxf. 1937, rev. 1958, and in 2 vols., ed. by J. Harrell, Lond. 1958. *Correspondence* was ed. by F. E. Ball, 6 vols., 1910–14, and in special sets by D. Nichol Smith, Oxf. 1935, and H. Davis, Oxf. 1935. The standard lives are by John Forster, 1875; by H. Craik, 2 vols., 1894; and by Sir L. Stephen, 1882; see also J. M. Murry, N.Y. 1955. Of the numerous works of criticism, useful outside of the field of literature, are L. A. Landa, *Swift and the church of Ireland*, Oxf. 1954; and R. Quintana, *The mind and art of Jonathan Swift*, 1936, 1953; and no. 4254. For bibl. see H. Terrink, The Hague, 1937; and *C.B.E.L.* ii. 581–96 and v. 456–60.

TEMPLE, SIR WILLIAM. 1628–1699

2599   The works of Sir William Temple, Bart. (512).

The *Essays on ancient and modern learning* were ed. by J. E. Spingarn, Oxf. 1909; J. A. Nicklin ed. the *Essays* also, 1911. Cf. *Early essays and romances*, ed. by G. C. Moore Smith, Oxf. 1931. Biographies by C. Marburg [Kirk], New Haven, 1932, and H. E. Woodbridge, N.Y. 1940, include bibls.; see also *C.B.E.L.* ii. 569–70.

(c) *Fiction*

(1) *General Works*

2600   ESDAILE, A. A list of English tales and prose romances printed before 1740. 2 pts. in 1 vol. 1912.

See also C. C. Mish, *English prose fiction 1600–1640*. *English prose fiction 1641–1660*, Charlottesville, 1952+, publ. as supplements to Esdaile; a third part carries the supplements to 1700 (in progress).

2601   BAKER, G. A. The history of the English novel. 10 vols. 1929–39.

Vols. ii and iii relate to the period; vol. iii was repr. 1942. See also C. E. Morgan, *The rise of the novel of manners* (1600–1740), N.Y. 1911, with good bibl.; and I. P. Watt, *The rise of the novel, studies in Defoe, Richardson and Fielding*, 1957. E. Bernbaum, in *The Mary Carleton narratives, 1663–1673* (Camb., Mass. 1914), examines the group of accounts as fictional biography, anticipatory of later novels.

2602   GOVE, P. B. The imaginary voyage in prose fiction. N.Y. 1941.

Includes an annotated check list of 215 imaginary voyages, 1700–1800.

2603   MACCARTHY, B. G. Women writers: their contribution to the English novel, 1621–1744. Oxf. 1944.

With a second vol. on later writers (1744–1818), and with a bibl., the work was repr. under the title of *The female pen*, 2 vols., Cork and N.Y. 1946–7.

(2) *Individual Writers of Fiction*

See above, Bunyan (2592), Defoe (2594), and Swift (2598).

BEHN, APHRA [AMIS?]. 1640–1689

2604 The works of Aphra Behn. Ed. by M. Summers. 6 vols. 1915. N.Y. 1967.

> The novels were separately ed. also by E. A. Baker, 1913. There are lives by V. Sackville-West, 1927; G. Woodcock, 1948; and E. Hahn, 1951. Comments on this somewhat controversial writer of plays and tales are in Baker (2601), MacCarthy (2603), and other literary histories. Her reputation as a novelist rests chiefly on *Oroonoko*, 1688. For bibl. see *C.B.E.L.* ii. 417–18, v. 439.

3. POETRY

The bibliographies in the general section of this chapter should be consulted. There are selected bibliographies also in most of the works of criticism which follow.

(a) *Anthologies*

See also the general anthologies (2576–7).

2605 BALD, R. C. Seventeenth-century English poetry. N.Y. 1959.

> See also J. W. Hebel and H. H. Hudson, ed., *The poetry of the English renaissance, 1509–1660*, N.Y. 1929, 1932, which has good notes; and R. G. Howarth, *Minor poets of the seventeenth century*, N.Y. 1931.

(b) *General*

2606 BUSH, D. Mythology and the renaissance tradition in English poetry Minneapolis. 1932. Repr. N.Y. 1957.

> On other general characteristics see T. R. Glover, *Poets and Puritans*, 1915, 1923. See also E. E. Stoll, *Poets and playwrights: Shakespeare, Jonson, Spencer, Milton*, Minneapolis, 1930.

2607 SHARP, R. L. From Donne to Dryden: the revolt against metaphysical poetry. Chapel Hill. 1940. Repr. 1955.

> Deals with changes in form as well as in content. As examples of one type of change see V. de S. Pinto's commentary on the poet-rakes in *Restoration carnival*, 1954.

2608 SPENCER, T. and VAN DOREN, M. Studies in metaphysical poetry. N.Y. 1939. Bibl.

> Cf. R. Tuve, *Elizabethan and metaphysical imagery; renaissance poetic and twentieth-century critics*, Chicago, 1947; and I. Husain, *The mystical element in the metaphysical poets of the seventeenth century*, Edin. 1948.

2609 WALLERSTEIN, R. C. Studies in seventeenth-century poetic. Madison (Wis.). 1950.

> On other special aspects see also M. Praz, *Studies in seventeenth-century imagery*, 2 vols., 1939–47; and J. Miles, *The primary language of poetry in the 1640's*, Berkeley, 1948.

2610   WHITE, H. C. The metaphysical poets: a study in religious experience. N.Y. 1936.

See also L. L. Martz, *The poetry of meditation*, New Haven, 1954, 2nd edn., 1962, bibl. Martz edited also *The meditative poem, an anthology of seventeenth-century verse*, N.Y. 1963.

2611   WILLIAMSON, G. The Donne tradition: a study in English poetry from Donne to the death of Cowley. Camb. (Mass.). 1930. N.Y. 1958. Bibl.

(c) *Individual Poets*

BUCKINGHAM, JOHN SHEFFIELD, DUKE OF. 1648–1721

2612   The works of . . . John Sheffield, late Duke of Buckingham. Ed. by J. Henley. 1721. Later edn. by A. Pope. 2 vols. 1723. 2 vols. 1729 and 1753.

See the article in the *D.N.B.* on the various edns. of his works and the censorship of them by the government. Cf. no. 412.

BUTLER, SAMUEL. 1612–1680

2613   Collected works. Ed. by A. R. Waller and R. Lamar. 3 vols. Camb. 1905–28.

The poetical works, ed. by R. B. Johnson, 2 vols., 1893, bibl. *Hudibras*, of which the first part was publ. anonymously in 1663, was publ. in 3 parts in 1678. The most recent bibl. notes are in the Waller–Lamar edn. A good modern criticism is E. A. Richards, *Hudibras in the burlesque tradition*, N.Y. 1937.

CAMPION, THOMAS. d. 1620

2614   Works. Ed. by P. S. Vivian. Oxf. 1909. Ed. by W. R. Davis. N.Y. 1967.

First collected edn. by A. H. Bullen, 1889. His *First book of airs* (c. 1613) was republ. in 1925. For criticism see T. MacDonagh, *Thomas Campion and the art of English poetry*, Dublin, 1913; and M. M. Kastendieck, *England's musical poet, Thomas Campion*, N.Y. 1938.

CAREW, THOMAS. 1594?–1640

2615   The poems of Thomas Carew. Ed. by Rhodes Dunlap. Oxf. 1949. 1957.

Includes his court masque, *Coelum Britannicum*. For interpretation see Williamson (2611), Grierson (2580), and E. I. Selig, *The flourishing wreath*, New Haven, 1958.

CHAPMAN, GEORGE. 1559?–1634

2616   The works of George Chapman. Ed. by R. H. Shepherd. 3 vols. 1873. Later edns. 3 vols. 1874–5 and 1889.

In edn. of 1874, vol. i is Plays; ii, Poems; iii, Iliad and Odyssey. Modern edn. of *Poems*, by P. B. Bartlett, N.Y. and Lond. 1941. A standard modern edn. of *Plays and poems*, by T. M. Perrott, 2 vols., 1901–14, was not completed. For biography and interpretation see A. C. Swinburne, 1875; H. Ellis, 1934; N. von Pogrell, Hamburg, 1939; and J. Jacquot, Paris, 1951. Modern critical studies of his dramatic works are by J. W. Weiler, N.Y. 1949, and E. Rees, Camb. (Mass.), 1954. For bibl. see S. A. Tannenbaum, N.Y. 1938, suppl., N.Y. 1946.

COWLEY, ABRAHAM. 1618-1667

2617 English writings of Abraham Cowley. Ed. by A. R. Waller. 2 vols. Camb. 1905-6.

Earlier edns., 1668; and by A. B. Grosart, 2 vols., Edin. 1876-81. For biog. and criticism see T. Sprat's life in the 1668 edn.; J. Loiseau, Paris, 1931; A. H. Nethercote, 1931; Williamson (2611); and *C.B.E.L.* i. 458.

CRASHAW, RICHARD. 1612 or 1613-1649

2618 The poems . . . of Richard Crashaw. Ed. by L. C. Martin. Oxf. 1927. 2nd edn. Oxf. 1957.

The most authoritative text, with an account of all MSS. Earlier edns. were ed. by W. B. Turnbull, 1858, A. B. Grosart, 2 vols., 1872-3, and A. R. Waller, 1904. For biog. and criticism see A. Warren, *Richard Crashaw*, Baton Rouge, 1939, repr. Ann Arbor, 1957; R. C. Wallerstein, *Richard Crashaw: a study of style and poetical development*, 1935, 1959. Shorter comments are by White (2610) and Williamson (2611). Bibl. is in *C.B.E.L.* i. 456-7.

DAVENANT, SIR WILLIAM. 1606-1668

2619 The works of Sir William D'Avenant, Kt. Consisting of those which were formerly printed and those which he designed for the press, now published out of the author's originall copies. 1673.

Selected poems were ed. by D. Bush, Camb. (Mass.) 1943; his *Discourse upon Gondibert*, 1650, with Hobbes's *Answer*, 1650, were republished in vol. ii of Spingarn, *Critical essays* (2587). See C. M. Dowlin, *Sir William Davenant's Gondibert . . .*, Phila. 1934. The *Dramatic works* were ed. by J. Maidment and W. H. Logan, 5 vols., Edin. 1872-4. For lives see A. Harbage, Phila. 1935 (bibl.), E. Marchant, Oxf. 1936, and A. H. Nethercot, Chicago, 1938; for bibl., see *C.B.E.L.* i. 453-5, v. 221.

DONNE, JOHN. 1573-1631

2620 Works . . . with a memoir of his life. Ed. by H. Alford. 6 vols. 1839.

Includes sermons, the Devotions, some poems, and letters. The *Complete poetry and selected prose* were ed. by J. Hayward, 1929, rev. edn. 1930; by R. S. Hillyer, N.Y. 1946; and by C. M. Coffin, N.Y. 1952. The standard edn. of *The Poems* is by H. J. C. Grierson, 2 vols., Oxf. 1912, 1 vol., Oxf. 1929. Important recent studies are H. Gardner, *John Donne: the divine poems*, Oxf. 1952; and T. Redpath, ed., *The songs and sonnets*, 1956. For bibl. see G. L. Keynes, Camb. 1914, 3rd edn., 1958; and *C.B.E.L.* i. 441-4, v. 216-19. On Donne's sermons and essays see no. 1240.

2621 Gosse, E. W. The life and letters of John Donne. 2 vols. 1899.

For the basic life by Izaak Walton see no. 2448. Other biographies are by H. I'A. Fausset, 1924, and E. Hardy, 1942. See also R. C. Bald, *Donne and the Drurys*, Camb. 1959. Useful critical studies are by Williamson (2611); T. S. Eliot, 'The metaphysical poets', in *Homage to John Dryden*, 1924; T. Spencer et al., *A garland for John Donne*, Camb. (Mass.) 1931; and I. Husain, *The dogmatic and mystical theology of John Donne*, 1938.

DRAYTON, MICHAEL. 1563-1631

2622 The works of Michael Drayton . . . now first collected. 1748. Later edn. 4 vols. 1753. Ed. by R. Hooper. 3 vols. 1876. Ed. by J. W. Hebel. 5 vols. Oxf. 1931-41.

The *Poems* were ed. by J. P. Collier, Roxburghe Club, 1856; and the *Minor poems* by

C. Brett, 1907. Bibliographies are O. Elton, *Michael Drayton, a critical study with a bibliography*, 1905; *Camb. Hist. Eng. Lit.* iv (1909); and a bibl. by S. A. Tannenbaum, N.Y. 1941.

DRUMMOND OF HAWTHORNDEN, WILLIAM. 1585–1649

2623 The works of William Drummond of Hawthornden. [Ed. by J. Sage and T. Ruddeman.] Edin. 1711. Later edn. The Poetical Works. Ed. by L. E. Kastner. 2 vols. Manchester. 1913.

The poems were first pr. in Edin. in 1616 (possibly private pr. in 1614?). For biography see D. Masson, *Drummond of Hawthornden*, 1873; A. Joly, *William Drummond de Hawthornden*, Lille, 1934; and F. R. Fogle, *A critical study of Drummond*, 1952. For bibl. see *C.B.E.L.* i. 444–5, v. 219.

DRYDEN, JOHN. 1631–1700

2624 Works of John Dryden. Ed. by Sir W. Scott. 18 vols. Edin. 1808 and 1821. Rev. edn. by G. Saintsbury. 1882–93.

In progress, under the editorship of E. N. Hooker and H. T. Swedenberg (21 vols.? Berkeley, Cal. 1956+) is a complete new edn. of the poems and plays. The *Poems* have been ed. by W. D. Christie, 1870, 1904; by J. Sargeaunt, 1910, 1935; by G. R. Noyes, rev. edn., Boston, 1950; and by J. Kingsley in 4 vols., Oxf. 1958. The *Songs* were ed. by C. L. Day, Camb. (Mass.), 1932. Dryden's *Letters* were ed. by C. E. Ward, Durham, N.C., 1942. For his prose works see the edn. by E. Malone, 3 vols. in 4, 1800, and W. P. Ker's edn. of *The essays*, 2 vols., Oxf. 1900, 1926. For plays, see M. Summers, ed., *The dramatic works of John Dryden*, 6 vols., 1931–2. *A Bibliography* . . . by H. Macdonald, Oxf. 1939, should be supplemented with additions by J. M. Osborn in *Modern Philology*, 39 (1941), 69–98, 197–212, 313–19; see also *C.B.E.L.* ii. 262–75, v. 404–7.

2625 Johnson, Samuel. Life of John Dryden. (The lives of the poets, I.) 1781. Later edns. Oxf. 1905. 1937.

An excellent, well-documented modern *Life* is by C. E. Ward, Chapel Hill, 1961. See also J. M. Osborn, *John Dryden, some biographical facts and problems*, N.Y. 1940. For critical studies see M. Van Doren, *The poetry of John Dryden*, N.Y. 1928, later edn., Camb. 1931; T. S. Eliot, *John Dryden*, 1932; and S. H. Monk, ed., *John Dryden, a list of critical studies* [1895–1948], Minneapolis, 1950. Of major importance is L. I. Bredvold, *The intellectual milieu of John Dryden*, Ann Arbor, 1934, 1936.

GAY, JOHN. 1685–1732

2626 The poetical works of John Gay, including 'Polly', 'The beggar's opera', and selections from the other dramatic works. Ed. by G. C. Faber. 1926. Bibl.

Gay's *Works* were ed. in 4 vols., Dublin, 1770, and in a later edn., with Dr. Johnson's preface, in 6 vols., London, 1795; the poetical works were ed. by J. Underhill, 2 vols., 1893 and 1905. Gay's *Present state of wit*, 1711, was ed. by D. F. Bond, Ann Arbor (Augustan Reprint Soc.), 1947. On Gay see P. F. Gaye, 1938; and W. H. Irving, Durham, N.C. 1940. For bibl. see *C.B.E.L.* ii. 292–4, v. 410–11.

HERBERT, GEORGE. 1593–1633

2627 The works of George Herbert. Ed. by F. E. Hutchinson. Oxf. 1941.

The standard edn. Selected poems were ed. by D. Brown, 1960. Izaak Walton's life is in no. 2448; a recent one is by M. Bottrall, 1954. Other modern studies, in addition to works on the metaphysical poets, are R. Tuve, *A reading of George Herbert*, 1951, and

M. Chute, *Two gentle men, George Herbert and Robert Herrick*, 1959. G. H. Palmer compiled a useful but incomplete Herbert bibl., Camb. (Mass.) 1911. See also *C.B.E.L.* i. 451–3, v. 220–1.

HERRICK, ROBERT. 1591–1674

2628 Poetical works. Ed. by L. C. Martin. Oxf. 1956.

The standard edn. *Hesperides, or the works both human and divine of Robert Herrick*, was publ. in 1648. Other edns. of the works are by W. C. Hazlitt, 1869, by A. B. Grosart, 1876, by A. W. Pollard, 1891, and by F. W. Moorman, 1915.

Lives of Herrick are by F. W. Moorman, 1910, 1924; and F. Delattre, Paris, 1912. See also N. Roeckerath, *Der Nachruhm Herricks und Waller*, Leipzig, 1931, and M. Chute, *Two gentle men, George Herbert and Robert Herrick*, 1959. For bibl. see *C.B.E.L.* i. 449–50, v. 220; and a *Concise bibliography* by S. A. and D. R. Tannenbaum N.Y. 1949.

JONSON, BEN. 1573–1637

2629 Works. Ed. by C. H. Herford and P. and E. M. Simpson. 11 vols. Oxf. 1925–52.

An older edn. of complete works, ed. by W. Gifford, 9 vols., 1816, was repr. by F. Cunningham, 3 vols., 1871, 9 vols., 1875. Letters are included in vol. i of the 1925–52 edn. *Notes* of his conversations with William Drummond of Hawthornden were published in 1842 (Shakespeare Soc.) and ed. by P. Sidney, 1906. Early lives appear in Fuller's *Worthies* and Aubrey's *Lives*; later biographies are by M. Castelain, Paris, 1907, G. Smith (English men of letters), 1919, and in the latest edn. of the *Works*. For critical studies see White *et al.* (2577). On Jonson the dramatist see M. Kerr, Phila. 1912, and R. G. Noyes, Camb. (Mass.), 1935.

For bibl. see S. A. Tannenbaum, N.Y. 1938, suppl., N.Y. 1947; and *C.B.E.L.* i. 613–19, v. 296–300.

LOVELACE, RICHARD. 1618–1658

2630 The poems of Richard Lovelace. Ed. by C. H. Wilkinson. 2 vols. Oxf. 1925. 1 vol. 1930.

See C. H. Hartmann, *The Cavalier spirit and its influence in the life and work of Richard Lovelace, 1618–58*, Lond. and N.Y. 1925. Bibl. is in *C.B.E.L.* i. 460.

MANDEVILLE, BERNARD. 1670?–1733

2631 The fable of the bees. Ed. by F. B. Kaye. 2 vols. Oxf. 1924. Bibl.

The fullest bibl. of Mandeville's writings is the essay by F. B. Kaye, repr. from the *Journal of English and Germanic Philology*, 20 (1921); suppl. in *Notes and Queries*, 146 (1924), 317–21. See also *C.B.E.L.* ii. 599–601, v. 460.

MARVELL, ANDREW. 1621–1678

2632 The poems and letters of Andrew Marvell. Ed. by H. M. Margoliouth. 2 vols. Oxf. 1927. Rev. edn. 2 vols. Oxf. 1952.

The definitive edn. H. Macdonald ed. *The poems*, 1953. See also D. Davison, *Andrew Marvell: selected poetry and prose* (with an intro. on his times and his poetry), 1952. Early lives are by Aubrey and Anthony Wood (*Athenae Oxonienses*). Modern ones are by A. Birrell (English men of letters), 1905; P. Legouis, Paris, 1928; and M. C. Bradbrook and M. G. Lloyd Thomas, Camb. 1940. The best bibls. are in the Margoliouth edn., and in Legouis. Cf. *C.B.E.L.* i. 460–1, v. 222–3. See also nos. 868, 974.

MILTON, JOHN. 1608–1674

2633 The works of John Milton. Ed. by F. A. Patterson *et al.* 18 vols. N.Y. 1931–8. Index. 2 vols. N.Y. 1940.

Older *Works*, ed. by J. Mitford, 8 vols., 1851. Of *Complete prose works*, being ed. by D. M. Wolfe *et al.* in a projected 8 volumes, vols. i–iv have appeared, New Haven, 1953–66. For poetical works, see the edn. by H. J. Todd, 6 vols., 1801, with numerous later edns.; that by H. F. Fletcher, with facsimile reproductions, 4 vols., Urbana, 1943–8; and M. Y. Hughes, ed., *Complete poems and major prose*, N.Y. 1957.
  Milton bibls., including many works of criticism, are in *Camb. Hist. Eng. Lit.* vii, 1911, and *C.B.E.L.* i. 463–73, v. 225–37. These should be supplemented by D. H. Stevens, *Reference guide* [1800–1930], Chicago, 1930, addenda by H. F. Fletcher, Urbana, 1931.

2634 Masson, D. The life of John Milton. 7 vols. 1859–94. Repr. 7 vols. N.Y. 1946.

The classic biography. H. Darbishire ed. *The early lives of Milton*, 1932 (reprints of six early biographies). An excellent modern one is by J. H. Hanford, N.Y. and Lond. 1949. Valuable also is H. F. Fletcher, *The intellectual development of John Milton*, of which vols. i–ii (Urbana, 1956–61) cover the years to 1632. See also J. M. French, ed., *Life records*, 5 vols., New Brunswick, N.J. 1949–58; and a life of Milton's wife, Marie Powell, by R. von R. Graves, 1943. See also no. 478. Other titles relating to Milton's views on political and religious issues may be located through the index.

MORE, HENRY. 1586–1661

2635 More, H. Philosophicall poems . . . Camb. 1647. Later edn. by A. B. Grosart. Blackburn. 1878.

For an article on, and bibl. of, Platonists and latitudinarians see *Camb. Hist. Engl. Lit.* viii, 1912. Cf. *The philosophical writings of Henry More*, ed. by F. I. Mackinnon, 1925. See also nos. 1270, 2461, 2698.

OLDHAM, JOHN. 1653–1683

2636 The works of Mr. John Oldham, together with his remains. 4 pts. 1686. Later edn. by E. Thompson. 3 vols. 1770.

His *Satyrs upon the Jesuits: written in the year 1679 upon occasion of the plot, together with the Satyr against vertue* . . . was publ. in 1681. See limited bibl. by H. F. Brooks, *Oxford Bibl. Soc. Proc. and Papers*, 5 (1936), 1–38.

POPE, ALEXANDER. 1688–1744

2637 The works of Alexander Pope. Ed. by W. Elwin and W. J. Courthope. 10 vols. 1871–89.

Also *Correspondence*, ed. by G. Sherburn, vols. i–ii, iv–v, Oxf. 1956+. For lives see vol. v of *Works*, 1889; G. Sherburn, *The early career of Alexander Pope*, Oxf. 1934; and those of L. Stephen, 1880, and B. Dobrée, 1951. For critical studies see J. E. Tobin, *Pope: a list of critical studies*, N.Y. 1945. For bibl. see G. A. Aitken, *Notes on the bibliography of Pope*, 1914; R. H. Griffiths, *Alexander Pope: a bibliography*, 2 pts., Austin, Texas, 1922–7; and *C.B.E.L.* ii. 294–305, v. 411–13.

PRIOR, MATTHEW. 1664–1721

2638 The literary works. Ed. by E. B. Wright and M. K. Spears. 2 vols. Oxf. 1959. Bibl.

Prior's *Poems*, first publ. in an unauthorized collection, 1707, with a second collection

1716, were publ. in a single vol., 1718. Various later edns., including that by R. B. Johnson, 2 vols., 1892. For lives see no. 490.

QUARLES, FRANCIS. 1592–1644

2639   The complete works in prose and verse . . . [Ed. by A. B. Grosart.] 3 vols. Edin. 1880.

J. Horden compiled *Francis Quarles, 1592–1644; a bibliography of his works to the year 1800* (Oxford Bibl. Soc. Pub., N.S. 2), 1953.

RALEIGH, SIR WALTER. *c.* 1552–1618

2640   Poems. Ed. by A. M. C. Latham. Boston and N.Y. 1929.

See also no. 494.

ROCHESTER, JOHN WILMOT, SECOND EARL OF. 1647–1680

2641   Collected works. Ed. by J. Hayward. 1926.

Poems were ed. by J. Thorpe, Princeton, 1950, and by V. de S. Pinto, Camb. 1953. For bibl. see Prinz (495 n.). See also *The Rochester–Savile Letters*, ed. by J. H. Wilson (338 n.). For lives see V. de S. Pinto, 1935, C. W. S. Williams, 1935, and no. 2343.

SEDLEY, SIR CHARLES. 1639–1701

2642   Poetical and dramatical works. Ed. by V. de S. Pinto. 2 vols. 1928.

For biography, see V. de S. Pinto, 1927. An earlier critical biography is by K. M. Lissner, Halle, 1905. Sedley, along with Rochester (2641), and Charles Sackville, earl of Dorset, was one of the restoration wits.

SHIRLEY, JAMES. 1596–1666

2643   Dramatic works and poems. Ed. by A. Dyce. 6 vols. 1833.

The *Poems* were ed. by R. L. Armstrong, N.Y. 1941. Cf. A. H. Nason, *James Shirley dramatist*, N.Y. 1915, bibl. For bibl. see *C.B.E.L.* i. 638–40, v. 306; and a *Concise bibliography* by S. A. and D. R. Tannenbaum, N.Y. 1946.

SUCKLING, SIR JOHN. 1609–1642

2644   The works of Sir John Suckling in prose and verse. Ed. by A. H. Thompson. N.Y. 1910.

The first collection, *Fragmenta aurea*, was publ. in 1646. Other edns. were in 1676, etc.; and that by W. C. Hazlitt, 2 vols., 1874. His plays are discussed in A. Harbage, *Cavalier drama*, 1936.

TRAHERNE, THOMAS. 1637?–1674

2644a Centuries, poems, and thanksgivings. Ed. by H. M. Margoliouth. Oxf. 1958.

The standard edn., superseding others by B. Dobell, 1903 and 1908; and G. I. Wade, 1932. See lives by H. Q. Iredale, Oxf. 1935; and by G. I. Wade, with selective bibl. by R. A. Parker, Princeton, 1944.

VAUGHAN, HENRY. 1622–1695

2645   Works. Ed. by L. C. Martin. 2 vols. Oxf. 1914. Rev. edn. Oxf. 1957.

The standard edn. The *Poems* [1646] were ed. by E. K. Chambers, 2 vols. 1896, 1905; and the *Complete Works* by A. B. Grosart, 4 vols., Blackburn, 1871. For biography see

F. E. Hutchinson, Oxf. 1947. Bibl. in *C.B.E.L.* i. 461–2, v. 223–4; and E. L. Marilla, *A comprehensive bibliography*, Tuscaloosa, 1948.

WALLER, EDMUND. 1606–1687

2646 Poems. Ed. by G. Thorn-Drury. 1893. 2 vols. 1905.

The standard edn. with biographical intro. Original publication, 1645; later edns., 1664 etc. For bibl. see *Camb. Hist. Eng. Lit.* vii, 1911; and *C.B.E.L.* i. 455–6.

WITHER, GEORGE. 1588–1667

2647 [Works] repr. by Spenser Society. 20 vols. Manchester. 1870–83.

Poems, ed. by J. M. Gutch, 3 vols., Bristol, 1820. The standard modern edn. of his early verse, *Juvenilia*, is by F. Sidgwick, 1902. J. M. French ed. Wither's *The history of the pestilence* [1625], Camb. (Mass.) 1932. Early lives are in Aubrey (2439) and *Ath. Oxon.* (2427). For bibl. see *C.B.E.L.* i. 446–9.

WOTTON, SIR HENRY. 1568–1639

2648 Reliquiae Wottonianae, or a collection of lives, letters, poems, with characters of sundry personages, . . . by . . . Henry Wotton. 1651.

For Wotton's correspondence see no. 574. Lives are by I. Walton (2448), and by A. W. Ward, Westminster, 1898.

(d) *Ballads and Songs*

(1) *Bibliography*

The major collections of 'popular' ballads and songs are listed in *C.B.E.L.* i. 272–3, 403–8; a bibliography of 'broadside' ballads is given on pp. 720–1. Among the latter the most useful are *Bibliotheca Lindesiana, catalogue of a collection of English ballads*, 1890; Lemon (57 n.); Fortescue's catalogue of the Thomason collection (58); and J. O. Halliwell [Phillipps], *Catalogue of a unique collection of ancient broadside ballads*, 1856 (a sales catalogue of a collection now known as the Euing Ballads, Univ. of Glasgow Library). H. E. Rollins compiled an *Analytical index to the ballad entries 1557–1709 in the register of the Stationers Company*, Chapel Hill, 1924.

(2) *Collections of Ballads*

2649 A COLLECTION of old ballads. [Ed. by A. Philips?] 3 vols. 1723–5. Repr. 1872.

Other early collections are in the Harleian Miscellany (59), and T. Percy, *Reliques of ancient English poetry*, 3 vols., 1765, many later edns.

2650 CHAPPEL, W., ed. A collection of national English airs. 2 vols. 1840.

Reissued as *Popular music of the olden time*, 2 vols., 1855–9; ed. by H. E. Wooldridge, 2 vols., 1893.

2651 CHILD, F. J., ed. English and Scottish popular ballads. 5 vols. in 10 pts. Boston (Mass.). 1883–98.

Actually the second edn. of a work originally published 1857–8; contains excellent bibl. and guides to the sources. The latest edn. is 5 vols. in 3, N.Y. 1956. See B. H. Bronson,

The traditional tunes of the Child ballads; with their texts (2770). Cf. E. K. Wells, *The ballad tree, a study of British and American ballads* . . ., N.Y. 1950.

2652　DURFEY, T. Wit and mirth . . . merry ballads and songs. 6 vols. 1719–20. Repr. 6 vols. in 3. N.Y. 1959.

Cf. C. L. Day, *The songs of Thomas Durfey*, Camb. (Mass.), 1933.
For other collections of ballads illustrative of manners see J. W. Draper, ed., *A century of broadside elegies*, 1928; J. W. Ebsworth, ed., *Westminster drolleries*, Boston, Lincs. 1875, and *Merry drollery complete*, and *Choice drollery*, Boston, Lincs. 1875 and 1876.

2653　FIRTH, C. H., ed. Naval songs and ballads. Navy Rec. Soc. 1908.

Cf. *Early naval ballads of England*, ed. by J. O. Halliwell, Percy Soc., 1841.

2654　MAIDMENT, J., ed. Ballads and other fugitive poetical pieces chiefly Scottish . . . Edin. 1834.

See also articles by C. H. Firth on Scottish ballads relating to the history of the century in *S.H.R.* 3 (1906), 257–73, and 6 (1909), 113–28.

2655　NOYES, R. G. and LAMSON, R. Broadside ballad versions of the songs in restoration drama. Camb. (Mass.). 1937.

Cf. F. S. Boas, ed., *Songs and lyrics from the English masques and light operas*, 1949; and W. Thorpe, ed., *Songs from the restoration theatre*, Princeton, 1934.

2656　ROLLINS, H. E., ed. Old English ballads, 1553–1625. Camb. 1920.

Illustrates the struggle between Catholics and Protestants. He also ed. *A Pepysian garland* (1595–1639), Camb. 1922; *Cavalier and Puritan* (1640–1660), N.Y. 1923; *The Pepys ballads*, 8 vols., Camb. (Mass.) 1929–32; and another collection relating to superstitions, *The pack of Autolycus*, Camb. (Mass.) 1927.

2657　ROXBURGHE BALLADS. Ed. by W. Chappell and J. W. Ebsworth. 9 vols. Hertford. 1871–99.

A very useful collection. Two smaller selections from this collection were publ. by J. P. Collier, 1847, and, in two vols., by C. Hindley, 1873–4.

2658　SHIRBURN BALLADS, 1585–1616. Ed. by A. Clark. Oxf. 1907.

From MS. of the Earl of Macclesfield. See H. E. Rollins, 'Notes on the Shirburn ballads', *Journal of Amer. Folk Lore*, 1917.

2659　WILKINS, W. W., ed. Political ballads of the seventeenth and eighteenth centuries [1641–　　]. 2 vols. 1860.

Cf. C. H. Firth, 'Ballad history of the reigns of James I and Charles I', *R.H.S. Trans.*, 3rd Ser. 5 and 6 (1911–12). Other collections relating chiefly to political matters are: F. W. Fairholt, ed., *Poems and songs relating to George Villiers, Duke of Buckingham and his assassination*, Percy Soc., 1850; *The Rump; or an exact collection . . . relating to the late times* (1639–1661), 2 vols. in 1, 1662, repr., 2 vols., 1874, index and notes by H. F. Brooks, *Oxford Bibl. Soc. Proc. and Papers*, 5 (1939), 281–304; T. Wright, ed., *Political ballads published . . . during the commonwealth*, Percy Soc., 1841 (from the Thomason collection); F. B. Fawcett, ed., *Broadside ballads of the restoration period* [Osterly Park Ballads], 1930; *Poems on affairs of state*, 4 pts., 1689, 5th edn., 1703–7, index in *N. and Q.*, 5th Ser. 6 (18 Nov.–30 Dec. 1876); *Whig and Tory, or wit on both sides . . . upon all remarkable occurrences from the change of ministry to this time*, 1712, reissued 1715 as *A Tory pill to purge Whig melancholy; Political merriment*, 3 pts., 1714–15; and *A pill to purge state melancholy*, 3rd edn., 1716. See also J. W. Ebsworth, ed., *The Bagford ballads: illustrating the last years of the Stuarts*, 2 vols., Hertford, 1878.

4. DRAMA

For works dealing with drama as an amusement and its relation to social history, and with the development of the theatre, see *Social History* (2273–92). The titles below relate to dramatic literature and its writers.

(a) *Bibliography*

2660 GREG, W. W. A bibliography of the English printed drama to the restoration. Bibliographical Society. 4 vols. 1939–59.

A major reference work, listing plays in print before the beginning of 1660; useful appendices in vol. iii; vol. iv includes introduction and index. Also by Greg, and pr. by the Bibliographical Society, are: *A hand-list of English plays written before 1643 and printed before 1700*, 1900; and *A list of masques . . . written before 1643 and printed before 1700*, 1902. Greg's 4-vol. work supersedes others for the period before 1643. See also Harbage, *Annals* (2671 n.).

2661 WOODWARD, G. L. and McMANAWAY, J. G., comp. A check list of English plays, 1641–1700. Chicago. 1945. Suppl. by F. T. Bowers. Charlottesville. 1949.

Alphabetical listing by author if known, otherwise by title. See also M. Summers, *A bibliography of restoration drama*, [1934]; and the *Short-title catalogue* [of plays, 1660–1900], in vol. vi of A. Nicoll, *History of English drama 1660–1900*, Camb. 1959 (see also no. 2286). For other lists and collections of plays see *C.B.E.L.* i. 487–92, ii. 392–3, v. 241, 432.

(b) *Sources*

(1) *Contemporary Criticism*

2662 LANGBAINE, GERARD. The lives and characters of the English dramatick poets. Also an exact account of all the plays . . . printed in the English tongue [to 1698]. Ed. by Ch. Gildon. 1699.

Said to be begun by Langbaine, and 'improved and continued' by Gildon. First publ., without Gildon's revision, 1691. This work is the basis for numerous later lists.

2663 RYMER, THOMAS. A short view of tragedy. 1693.

Cf. Rymer's *The tragedies of the last age considered and examined*, 1678, later edn. 1692.

(2) *Collections of Plays*

2664 EVANS, H. A. English masques. 1897. Later edn. 1925.

Includes texts of 10 Jonson masques, Daniel, Campion, Shirley, and Davenant, with brief introductions.

2665 DILKE, C. W., ed. Old English plays being a selection from the early dramatic writers. 6 vols. 1814–16.

Contents listed in Lowndes, p. 1883.

2666 DODSLEY, R. A select collection of old plays. 12 vols. 1744. 2nd edn. by I. Reed. 12 vols. 1780. 3rd edn. by J. P. Collier. 12 vols. 1825–7. 4th edn. by W. C. Hazlitt. 15 vols. 1874–6.

Cf. R. Straus, *Robert Dodsley, poet, publisher and playwright*, Lond. and N.Y. 1910, with bibl.

2667 THE MERMAID SERIES: the best plays of old dramatists. Various editors. 1887–1909.

Contain generally select plays but sometimes the complete plays of the following: Beaumont and Fletcher, Chapman, Congreve, Dekker, Dryden, Farquhar, Ford, Greene, Heywood, Jonson, Marlowe, Massinger, Middleton, Otway, Shadwell, Shirley, Steele, Vanbrugh, Webster, and Wycherley. Later reprints of selected volumes, e.g. Dryden, Farquhar, 1949, 1950.

Other collections are: J. H. L. Hunt, *The dramatic works of Wycherley, Congreve, Vanbrugh, and Farquhar . . .*, 1849, 1851; J. Maidment and W. H. Logan, eds., *Dramatists of the restoration*, 14 vols., Edin. 1872–9; and C. F. T. Brooke and N. B. Paradise, eds., *English drama, 1580–1642*, Boston and N.Y. 1933.

(c) *Later Works*

2668 BOWERS, F. T. Elizabethan revenge tragedy: 1587–1642. Princeton. 1940.

Cf. H. H. Adams, *English domestic or homiletic tragedy, 1575–1642*, N.Y. 1943; and C. Leech, *Shakespeare's tragedies and other studies in seventeenth-century drama*, 1950. See also Schelling (2281 n.).

2669 DOBRÉE, B. Restoration comedy, 1660–1720. Oxf. 1924.

By Dobrée also, *Restoration tragedy*, Oxf. 1929. Cf. T. H. Fujimura, *The restoration comedy of wit*, Princeton, 1952; and G. H. Nettleton, *English drama of the restoration and eighteenth century*, N.Y. 1914. See also Krutch, *Comedy and conscience after the restoration* (2277 n.); and Nicoll, *History of the restoration drama* (2286).

2670 ELLIS-FERMOR, U. M. The Jacobean drama, an interpretation. 1936. Later edns. 1947. 1953. 4th edn. 1958.

Biographical notes. See also F. G. Fleay, *A biographical chronicle of the English drama, 1559–1642*, 2 vols., 1891, and no. 2281 n. An older standard work is Sir A. W. Ward, *History of English dramatic literature down to Queen Anne*, 2 vols., 1875, later edn., 3 vols., 1899.

2671 HARBAGE, A. Cavalier drama: an historical and critical supplement to the study of the Elizabethan and restoration stage. 1936.

Concentrates especially on the period of 1625–69. See Bentley (2280); Rollins (2288); Reyher, *Les masques anglais* (2281 n.); and E. Welsford, *The court masque*, Camb. 1927. By Harbage also, *Annals of English drama, 975–1700*, 1940, 1964; and *Thomas Killigrew, cavalier dramatist*, 1930, 1935.

(d) *Individual Dramatists*

Several writers of plays are listed elsewhere, e.g. John Dennis in the section on Prose (2595); and in the section on Poetry, Chapman (2616), Dryden (2624), Gay (2626), and Jonson (2629). The index should be used for names.

BEAUMONT, FRANCIS (1585?–1616) and FLETCHER, JOHN (1579–1625)

2672   The comedies and tragedies written by Francis Beaumont and John
Fletcher, gentlemen. Ed. by J. Shirley. 1647.

Later edns. of collected plays are by A. Dyce, 11 vols., 1843–6; by A. Glover and
A. R. Waller, 10 vols., Camb. 1905–12; also by J. St. L. Strachey, 2 vols., 1904 (Mermaid ser.). Critical studies are by A. C. Sprague, Camb. (Mass.) 1926; J. H. Wilson,
Columbus, 1928; D. M. MacKeithan, Austin, 1938; W. W. Appleton, 1956. Bibls.
are by A. C. Potter, Camb. (Mass.) 1890; by S. A. Tannenbaum, N.Y. 1948, suppl.,
N.Y. 1948; and those in *Camb. Hist. Eng. Lit.* vi (1910), and *C.B.E.L.* i. 632–6, v.
304.

CIBBER, COLLEY. 1671–1757

2673   Dramatic works of Colley Cibber. 5 vols. 1736. Later edn., with life by
D. E. Baker. 5 vols. 1777.

For life see no. 2291. Modern biographies are by F. D. Senior, 1928; and R. H. Barker,
N.Y. 1939. See also De W. C. Croissant, *Studies in the work of Colley Cibber*, Lawrence,
Kans. 1912, bibl. For bibl. see *C.B.E.L.* ii. 430–1.

CONGREVE, WILLIAM. 1670–1729

2674   The works of Mr. William Congreve. 3 vols. 1710. Many later edns.
Ed. by M. Summers. 4 vols. 1923. Ed. by F. W. Bateson. 1930.

The *Comedies* were ed. by G. S. Street, 2 vols., 1895; and by B. Dobrée, 2 pts., 1925–8.
Lives are by E. Gosse, 1888, rev. edn., 1924; D. C. Taylor, 1931. For bibl. see J. C.
Hodges, N.Y. 1941; a list of plays by Z. Haraszti in *P.M.L.A., More Books*, 9 (1934),
81–95; and *C.B.E.L.* ii. 414–16, v. 438–9.

DEKKER, THOMAS. 1570?–1641 [1632?]

2675   The dramatic works of Thomas Dekker. [Ed. by R. H. Shepherd.] 4 vols.
1873.

His non-dramatic works were ed. by A. B. Grosart, 5 vols. 1884–6 (Huth Library). For
bibl. see *Camb. Hist. Eng. Lit.* iv, 1910; S. A. and D. R. Tannenbaum, N.Y. 1939,
suppl., N.Y. 1945; and *C.B.E.L.* i. 619–22, v. 300–1.

ETHEREGE, SIR GEORGE. 1635?–1691

2676   The works of Sir George Etherege, containing his plays and poems. 1704.
Later edn. by A. W. Verity. 1888.

Two volumes of a projected 3-vol. edn. by H. F. B. Brett-Smith, Oxf. 1927+, have
appeared. Etherege's *Letterbook* was ed. by S. Rosenfeld, 1928. For biography see
V. Meindl, *Sir George Etheredge . . .* , Vienna, 1901. Recent critical studies are by
F. S. [McCamic] Tinker, Cedar Rapids, 1931, and D. Underwood, New Haven, 1957.
For bibl. see *C.B.E.L.* ii. 410, v. 439.

FARQUHAR, GEORGE. 1678–1707

2677   The dramatic works of George Farquhar. Ed. by A. C. Ewald. 2 vols.
1892.

The original collection of plays under the same title was publ. in 2 vols. in 1736.
C. Stonehill ed. *The complete works*, 2 vols., 1930. Cf. D. Schmid's biography, Vienna,
1904; and *C.B.E.L.* ii. 416, v. 439.

FORD, JOHN. 1586–1639

2678 The dramatic works of John Ford. Ed. by H. Weber. 2 vols. Edin. 1811. Later edn. by W. Gifford. 2 vols. 1827. Rev. by A. Dyce. 3 vols. 1869. 1895.

For life see M. J. Sargeaunt, Oxf. 1935; for recent critical studies, see G. F. Sensabaugh, Stanford and Lond. 1944; H. J. Oliver, Melbourne, 1955; and C. Leech, 1957. Bibls. are S. A. Tannenbaum, N.Y. 1941; and *C.B.E.L.* ii. 637–8, v. 305–6.

HEYWOOD, THOMAS. d. 1650?

2679 The dramatic works of Thomas Heywood. Ed. by R. H. Shepherd. 6 vols. 1874.

The standard authority is A. M. Clark, *Thomas Heywood, playwright and miscellanist*, Oxf. 1931. For bibl. see that by Clark, published by the Oxf. Bibl. Soc., *Proc. and Papers*, 1 (1925); and *C.B.E.L.* i. 622–4.

LEE, NATHANIEL. 1653?–1692

2680 The works of ... Nathaniel Lee. 2 vols. 1713. Later edn. 3 vols. 1733–4.

Works, ed. with introduction by T. B. Stroup and A. L. Cooke, 2 vols., New Brunswick, N.J. 1954–5.

MARSTON, JOHN. 1575?–1634

2681 The works of John Marston. 1633. Ed. by J. O. Halliwell. 3 vols. 1856. Ed. by A. H. Bullen. 3 vols. 1887.

The standard modern edn. of the plays is by H. H. Wood, 3 vols. Edin. 1934–9. For bibl. see *C.B.E.L.* i. 627–8, and S. A. Tannenbaum, *Concise bibliography*, N.Y. 1940.

MASSINGER, PHILIP. 1583–1640

2682 The dramatic works. Ed. by T. Coxeter. 4 vols. 1759. Reissued 1761. Later edns.: By J. M. Mason. 4 vols. 1779. By W. Gifford. 4 vols. 1805. By F. Cunningham. 1 vol. 1871.

Cf. S. R. Gardiner, 'The political element in Massinger', *Contemporary Review*, August, 1876; and critical studies by M. Chelli, Lyon, 1924, and Paris, 1926; and by B. T. Spencer in *Seventeenth-century studies*, ed. by R. Shafer, Princeton, 1933. For bibl. see S. A. Tannenbaum's *Massinger*, N.Y. 1938; and *C.B.E.L.* i. 630–2, v. 302.

OTWAY, THOMAS. 1652–1685

2683 The works of Mr. Thomas Otway ... consisting of his plays, poems, and love-letters. 2 vols. 1712. Later edns.: By T. Thornton. 3 vols. 1813. By M. Summers. 3 vols. 1926. By J. C. Ghosh. 2 vols. Oxf. 1932.

For critical study see R. G. Ham, *Otway and Lee*, New Haven, 1931. Bibl. in *C.E.B.L.* ii. 413–14, v. 438.

SHADWELL, THOMAS. 1642?–1692

2684 Complete works ... Ed. by M. Summers. 5 vols. 1927.

Earlier *Dramatic works*, 4 vols., 1720. For his life see A. S. Borgman, *Thomas Shadwell: his life and comedies*, N.Y. 1928. Bibl. is in *C.B.E.L.* ii. 411–12, v. 437–8.

SHAKESPEARE, WILLIAM. 1564-1616

2685   Mr. William Shakespeare's comedies, histories, and tragedies. Published according to the true originall copies. 1623.

Of the numerous later edns. of the *Works*, important ones are by H. H. Furness and H. H. Furness, Jr., *New variorum edition*, 20 vols., Phila. 1871-1919, which is the fullest; and 'The Arden Shakespeare', ed. by W. J. Craig *et al.*, 37 vols., 1899-1924, which has excellent annotations (new edn. in progress, 1951+).

For criticism, see *A companion to Shakespeare studies*, ed. by H. Granville-Barker and G. B. Harrison, Camb. 1934, as well as Lee, *Shakespeare's England* (2181). An important biographical account is by E. K. Chambers (2 vols., Oxf. 1930, abridged, 1933).

Standard bibliographical studies are by W. Jaggard, Stratford-on-Avon, 1911; H. C. Bartlett, *Mr. William Shakespeare. Original and early editions . . .*, New Haven, 1922; Chambers (*supra*); and W. Esbisch and L. L. Schücking, *A Shakespeare bibliography*, Oxf. 1931. Annual bibls. are publ. in *Shakespeare Survey* (Camb. 1946+), and *Shakespeare Quarterly* (N.Y. 1950+). See also Read (1959 edn.), nos. 3643-6, and *C.B.E.L.* i. 539-608, v. 257-91.

TOURNEUR, CYRIL. 1575?-1626

2686   Works. Ed. by A. Nicoll. 1930.

Earlier edn. by J. C. Collins, 2 vols., 1878. For bibl. see *C.B.E.L.* i. 628-9, v. 302-3, and S. A. Tannenbaum, N.Y. 1946.

VANBRUGH, SIR JOHN. 1664-1726

2687   Complete works . . . Plays. Ed. by B. Dobrée. Letters. Ed. by G. Webb. 4 vols. 1927-8.

Earlier edn. of *Plays*, 2 vols., 1719, 1730, 1734, 1735; later edn. by W. C. Ward, 2 vols., 1893. Cf. M. Dametz, *John Vanbrughs Leben und Werke*, Vienna, 1898; and *C.B.E.L.* ii. 414. See also no. 2759.

WEBSTER, JOHN. 1580?-1625?

2688   Complete works. Ed. by F. L. Lucas. 4 vols. 1927. Bibl.

Earlier *Works*, ed. by A. Dyce, 4 vols., 1830. Cf. F. E. Pierse, *John Webster, the period of his work*, 1905, and *The collaboration of Webster and Dekker*, New Haven, 1909; and a modern life by C. Leech, 1951. For bibl. see *C.B.E.L.* i. 629-30, v. 303.

WYCHERLEY, WILLIAM. 1640?-1716

2689   The works of the ingenious Mr. William Wycherley. 1713. Later edns. By W. C. Ward. 1888. By M. Summers (Complete Works). 4 vols. 1924.

These are edns. of the plays. Various edns. of poems have been publ. from 1704 onwards. For lives see C. Perromat, Paris, 1921; and W. Connely, 1930. Bibl. in *C.B.E.L.* ii. 410-11, v. 437.

C. PHILOSOPHY

Because many of the men interested in philosophical problems in the period are known also for their literary efforts, or their contributions to political theory, religious or scientific thought, the works of some of them have been listed in other sections of this volume. Some biographies are listed in Ch. II, pp. 49-73 *supra* on Biography. Authors can be located by the index. Among them are such figures as John Selden, Robert Greville, Lord Brooke, Sir Thomas Browne, Sir Kenelm Digby, James Harrington, Jeremy Taylor, Robert Boyle, Samuel Parker, and Sir Isaac Newton.

There is no complete bibliography on the philosophy of the century. Though uncritical and not up to date, that in Sorley (2694) is still useful. The *Journal of Philosophy* (N.Y. 1904+) should also be consulted.

1. GENERAL WORKS

2690   CARRÉ, M. H. Phases of thought in England. Oxf. 1949.

Includes several useful chapters relating to the century. See also Burtt, *Metaphysical foundations of modern physical science* (2820), Koyré (1830), and Newton (2842, 2853, 2861).

2691   CASSIRER, E. The Platonic renaissance in England. Trans. by J. P. Pettegrove. Edin. 1953.

First publ. in Berlin, 1932, and probably the best brief account. For fuller treatment, see J. Tulloch, *Rational theology* . . . (1141). Other less inclusive works are: F. J. Powicke, *The Cambridge Platonists*, 1926; and W. C. de Pauley, *The candle of the Lord, studies in the Cambridge Platonists*, 1937.

2692   COLIE, R. L. Light and enlightenment: a study of the Cambridge Platonists and the Dutch Arminians. Camb. 1957.

Also on religious concepts are W. Schenk, 'The religion of the spirit in seventeenth-century England', *Church Quart. Rev.* 140 (1945), 12–28; and G. R. Cragg, *From Puritanism to the age of reason* (1192).

2693   LAMPRECHT, S. P. The role of Descartes in seventeenth-century England. Studies in the History of Ideas III. N.Y. 1935.

Argues that Descartes deeply influenced every English thinker of consequence between 1640 and 1700. Cf. J. K. Ryan's article on one of the less well-known writers, 'Anthony Legrand (1629–1699): Franciscan and Cartesian', *New Scholasticism*, 9 (1935), 226–50.

2694   SORLEY, W. R. A history of English philosophy. Camb. 1920. Repr. 1937. Bibl.

Useful, especially for its bibliography.

2. PHILOSOPHERS

The list is arranged in rough chronological order, rather than alphabetically. The names of other important figures may be found *supra* in Ch. V, Ch. III § F on Political Theory, and §§ B and F of this chapter.

BACON, FRANCIS

2695   The advancement of learning. 1605.

This work, with his *Novum Organum*, 1620, represents the most influential of Bacon's philosophical writings. Both were incorporated in the collection which he entitled *Instauratio magna*, other parts of which were publ. between 1620 and 1653 (see bibl. in Sorley, pp. 324–7). See Spedding (403), vols. i–v; a single-volume edn. of *The Philosophical Works* was ed. by J. M. Robertson, 1905. Useful commentaries are F. H.

Anderson, *The philosophy of Francis Bacon*, Chicago, 1948; and, also by Anderson, *Francis Bacon: his career and his thought*, Los Angeles, 1962. See also nos. 403, 2904.

HERBERT OF CHERBURY, EDWARD, LORD

2696   De veritate. Trans. with an intro. by M. H. Carré. Bristol. 1937.

First publ. in 1624. See also *Lord Herbert of Cherbury's 'De religione laici'*, ed. and trans. by H. R. Hutcheson, New Haven and Lond. 1944.

HOBBES, THOMAS

2697   Works. Ed. by Sir W. Molesworth (968 n.).

Philosophical writings include *De cive*, publ. as *Elementorum philosophiae, sectio tertia*, Paris, 1647, with the English version publ. in 1651 as *Philosophicall rudiments concerning government and society; De corpore*, part one of the *Elementorum philosophiae*, 1655, English trans., 1656; and *De homine*, part two of the *Elementorum philosophiae*, 1658. These three parts, as well as various essays on mathematics and science, were repr. under the title of *Opera philosophica*, 3 parts, Amsterdam, 1668. On Hobbes as a philosopher see works by G. Lyon, *La philosophie de Hobbes*, 1893, and J. Laird, *Hobbes* (Leaders of Philosophy), 1934. S. I. Mintz, *The hunting of Leviathan*, Camb. 1962, deals with some contemporary reactions to Hobbes.
See also biographies listed in no. 968.

MORE, HENRY

2698   Collection of several philosophical writings. 2nd edn. 1662. Ed. by F. I. MacKinnon. N.Y. 1925.

A famous Cambridge Platonist. For other titles on More see nos. 1270, 2461, 2635. See also M. Nicolson, 'George Keith and the Cambridge Platonists', *Philosophical Rev.* 39 (1930), 36–55.

CUDWORTH, RALPH

2699   True intellectual system of the universe. 1678. 2nd edn. 2 vols. 1743. 3 vols. 1845.

Attack by an influential Cambridge Platonist on the materialism of Hobbes, but in a vein that aroused much theological controversy. See also J. A. Gregory, 'Cudworth and Descartes', *Philosophy*, 17 (1933), 454–69. A scholarly exposition of his philosophy is J. A. Passmore, *Ralph Cudworth, an interpretation*, Camb. 1951.

GLANVILL, JOSEPH

2700   Popkin, R. H. 'Joseph Glanvill: a precursor of Hume', *Jour. Hist. Ideas*, 14 (1953), 292–303.

Cf. articles on Glanvill by C. F. Mullett, *Hunt. Lib. Quart.* 1 (1938), 447–56; and D. Krook, ibid. 18 (1955), 261–78. See also nos. 2321, 2909.

LOCKE, JOHN

2701   Works. See *Political Theory*, no. 978.

Chief among his philosophical works is his *Essay concerning human understanding*, 1690, many later edns.; R. I. Aaron and J. Gibb ed. an early draft of the essay, with excerpts from Locke's journals, Oxf. 1936. Cf. J. Gibson, *Locke's theory of knowledge and its historical relations*, Camb. 1917, 1960. Modern biographies are by R. I. Aaron, N.Y. and Oxf. 1937, 1955; and M. Cranston, N.Y. 1957. See also *Education*, no. 2946. For his ideas on toleration see no. 1121.

BURTHOGGE, RICHARD

2702 Philosophical writings of Richard Burthogge (1638–1698). Ed. by M. W. Landes. Chicago and Lond. 1921.

Includes sketch of his life and a short bibl. His *Organum vetus et novum, or a discourse of reason and truth*, was publ. in 1678; *An essay upon reason . . .*, 1694.

BERKELEY, GEORGE

2703 Treatise concerning the principles of human knowledge. Dublin. 1710. Many later edns.

The best edn. of the *Works*, the greater portion of which belong to the eighteenth century, is that by A. C. Fraser, 4 vols., Oxf. 1871, 4 vols., Oxf. 1901. B. Rand ed. *Correspondence of George Berkeley . . . Sir John Percival*, Camb. 1914. See also a *Bibliography*, by T. E. Jessop, 1934, and J. Wild, *George Berkeley, a study of his life and philosophy*, Camb. (Mass.) 1936. For other titles see Pargellis, nos. 2531–2.

D. FINE ARTS

I. FINE ARTS EXCLUDING ARCHITECTURE

(a) *General*

(1) *Bibliography and Sources*

The best guide to modern work in the whole area is the *Annual bibliography of the history of British art* (1934+). Camb. 1936+. Older references appear in sections of *C.B.E.L.* (6), vols. i and ii. For painting see Ogden (2708).

The major periodicals, each published with elaborate illustrations, are: *Burlington Magazine*, 1903+; the annual volumes of the *Walpole Society*, Oxf. 1912+; and *Country Life*, 1897+, which is useful chiefly for architecture. *The Connoisseur*, 1901+, deals with a wide range of subjects in the arts and in crafts. For an index to more than a hundred art periodicals see *The Art Index* (1929+), N.Y. 1933+.

See also Ch. IX *supra*, especially p. 335 on Taste and pp. 327–30 on Theatre.

2704 JONES, INIGO. Designs by Inigo Jones for masques and plays at court. A descriptive catalogue of drawings for scenery and costumes . . ., with introduction and notes by P. Simpson and C. F. Bell. Walpole Society 12. 1924.

2705 VERTUE, GEORGE. Notebooks relating to the history of art in England. 6 vols. Walpole Society. 1930–47.

A major source for the period, and the chief basis for Horace Walpole's *Anecdotes of painting . . . and incidental notes on other arts*, 4 vols., 1762–71; later edns. by J. Dallaway, 5 vols., 1826; by R. Wornum, 3 vols., 1849; a 5th vol., New Haven, 1937. Frequent comments on the arts appear in the writings of John Evelyn (2467) and Samuel Pepys (2500).

(2) *Later Works*

2706   EDWARDS, R. and RAMSEY, L. G. G., eds. The Connoisseur period
guides to the houses, decorations, furnishings and chattels of the classic
periods. Vol. ii. The Stuart period. 1957. Illus.

Brief bibls. with each chapter.

2707   OXFORD HISTORY OF ENGLISH ART. Vol. vii. English art, 1553–
1625. Ed. by E. Mercer. Oxf. 1962. Vol. viii. English art, 1625–1714. Ed.
by M. D. Whinney and O. Millar. Oxf. 1957.

An important work, in progress, providing the best survey for the period, with bibls.

(b) *Painting, Drawing, Engraving*

(1) *Bibliography*

2708   OGDEN, H. V. S. and M. S. A bibliography of seventeenth-
century writings on the pictorial arts in English. In *Art Bulletin*, 29 (1947),
196–201.

Gives a complete list of printed and MS. sources. Cf. Luigi Salerno, 'Seventeenth-
century English literature on painting', in *Journal of the Warburg and Courtauld Institutes*, 14 (1951), 234–58. See also Whinney and Millar (2707).

(2) *Later Works*

(a) Catalogues (other than sales or exhibitions)

Public collections. The latest edns. of the catalogues of the National Gallery,
Lond.; National Portrait Gallery, Lond.; the Tate Gallery, Lond.; National
Maritime Museum, Greenwich; Scottish National Portrait Gallery, Edin.

2709   GOODISON, J. W. Catalogue of Cambridge portraits: I. The University Collection. Camb. 1955.

2710   MILLAR, O. British pictures in the Royal Collection. Vols. i and ii.
The Tudor, Stuart, and early Georgian pictures. 1963–4.

2711   POOLE, R. L. Catalogue of portraits in the possession of the university,
colleges, city and county of Oxford. 3 vols. Oxf. 1912–25.

Private collections

2712   BAKER, C. H. C. Catalogue of the Petworth Collection. 1920.

2713   GOULDING, R. W. and ADAMS, C. K. Catalogue of pictures belonging to His Grace the Duke of Portland. Camb. 1936.

2714   SCHARF, G. Catalogue of the collection of pictures at Woburn Abbey.
1889.

(b) Collecting

2715   LUGT, F. Répertoire des catalogues de ventes publiques. I. *c.* 1600–
1825. The Hague. 1938.

2716 HERVEY, M. F. S. The life, correspondence, and collections of Thomas Howard, Earl of Arundel. Camb. 1921.

See also Ogden (2331).

(c) Drawings

2717 BINYON, L. Catalogue of drawings by British artists and artists of foreign origin working in Great Britain, in the British Museum. 4 vols. 1898–1907.

Cf. J. Woodward, *Tudor and Stuart drawings*, 1951.

(d) Engravings

2718 CHARRINGTON, J. Catalogue of the engraved portraits in the library of Samuel Pepys, F.R.S., now belonging to Magdalene College. Camb. 1936.

2719 HIND, A. M. Engraving in England in the sixteenth and seventeenth centuries. II. The reign of James I. Camb. 1955.

Later volumes in preparation.

2720 O'DONOGHUE, F. and HAKE, H. M. Catalogue of engraved British portraits in the British Museum. 6 vols. Oxf. 1908–25.

2721 SMITH, J. C. British mezzotinto portraits. 5 vols. and album. 1878–83.

(e) Exhibitions

2722 GRAVES, A. A century of loan exhibitions (1813–1912). 5 vols. 1913–15.

With indices of owners and portraits.

2723 CATALOGUES of the: National Portrait Exhibitions, South Kensington, 1866–8 (3 vols.); Royal House of Stuart, New Gallery, Lond., 1889; British Art, Royal Academy, Lond., 1934; British Portraits, Royal Academy, 1956–7.

(f) Miniatures

2724 LONG, B. S. British miniaturists. 1929.

In dictionary form with list of earlier literature. Cf. Torben Holck Colding, *Aspects of miniature painting*, Copenhagen, 1953 (with full bibl.).

(g) Painting

2725 BAKER, C. H. C. Lely and the Stuart portrait painter. 2 vols. 1912.

Summarized and revised in C. H. C. Baker and W. G. Constable, *English painting of the sixteenth and seventeenth centuries*, Florence and N.Y. 1930, with full bibl., and C. H. C. Baker and M. R. James, *British painting*, Boston and N.Y. 1933.

2726 CAW, J. L. Scottish painting past and present, 1620–1908. Edin. 1908.

2727 ENGLEFIELD, W. A. D. The history of the Painter-Stainers Company of London. 1923.

2728 SAINSBURY, W. N. Original unpublished papers illustrative of the life of Sir Peter Paul Rubens. 1859.

2729 WATERHOUSE, E. K. Painting in Britain 1530–1790. Lond. and Baltimore. 1953. Bibl.

(c) *Sculpture*

There is no general survey for the period, nor a specialized bibliography. In the *Oxford history* (2707) are listed the few contemporary sources that include comments on this branch of art. See also *Architecture*.

2730 ESDAILE, K. A. English monumental sculpture since the renaissance. 1927.

Excellent. Also by her are *Monuments in English churches*, 1937; *English church monuments 1510–1840*, 1946; and 'John Bushnell' in *Walpole Society*, 15 (1927), 21–45, and 21 (1933), 105–7. See also M. Whinney, *Sculpture in Britain, 1530–1830*, 1964.

2731 GUNNIS, R. Dictionary of British sculpture, 1660–1830. 1953.

Contains much information, though because of its dates it does not completely supersede E. B. Chancellor, *Lives of the British sculptors*, 1911. A slighter *Dictionary*, covering the 13th to the 20th centuries, is by M. H. Grant, 1953. H. Faber has done a biography of *Caius Gabriel Cibber*, Oxf. 1926.

(d) *Decorative Arts*

See also Ch. VIII, *Industry*; and Ch. IX, *Taste*.

(1) *General*

2732 JOURDAIN, M. English decoration and furniture of the early renaissance (1550–1650). 1924.

Also by Jourdain, but under the pseud. of Francis Lenygon, *Decoration and furniture of English mansions in the seventeenth and eighteenth centuries*, 1909, with a list of books printed on the subject before 1800; and *Decoration in England from 1660 to 1770*, 1914, rev. edn. (1640–1760), 1927.
  The author publ. under her own name also *English interiors in smaller houses, 1660–1830* [1923]; and *English interior decoration, 1500–1830* [1950].

2733 MULLINER, H. H. The decorative arts in England 1660–1780. 1924.

Cf. A. Vallance, *Art in England during the Elizabethan and Stuart periods*, 1908.

2734 STRATTON, A. The English interior. 1920.

Architectural and decorative features.

(2) *Furniture*

2735 JOURDAIN, M. Furniture in England from 1660 to 1760. 1914.

Publ. under pseud. of F. Lenygon (see 2732). Cf. no. 2223.

2736 MACQUOID, P. History of English furniture. 4 vols. 1904–8. Illus.

Vols. iii and iv relate to the period; supersedes the *History* by F. Litchfield, 1892. See also by Macquoid and R. Edwards, *The dictionary of English furniture*, 3 vols., 1924–7 (rev. edn. by Edwards, 3 vols., 1954). A *History of English furniture* was publ. by the Victoria and Albert Museum, 1955.

2737 SYMONDS, R. W. English furniture from Charles II to George II. 1929. Illus.

By Symonds also, *Furniture making in seventeenth- and eighteenth-century England*, 1955. Cf. C. H. Hayward, *English period furniture* (1500–1800), 1936, later edn., Phila. [1949?].

(3) *Glass and Pottery*

2738 HARTSHORNE, A. Old English glasses. 1897.

Useful chapters on the period, though the fullest modern work is by Thorpe (2029). Useful also are J. Bles, *Rare English glasses of the 17th and 18th centuries*, 1924 (illus.); and D. R. Guttery, *From broad glass to cut crystal*, 1956. See also *Glass making*.

2739 JEWITT, Ll. The ceramic art of Great Britain from prehistoric times ... 2 vols. 1878. Later edn. 1 vol. *ca.* 1883. Illus.

See the handbooks by A. H. Church, *English porcelain*, 1885 (2nd edn., 1904); and *English earthenware*, 1904, 1911. See also no. 2706; and R. L. Hobson's *Catalogue of the collection of English porcelain in the British Museum*, 1903.

(4) *Silver and Pewter*

2740 OMAN, C. C. English domestic silver. 1934. 4th edn. 1959.

Also by Oman, *The English silver in the Kremlin, 1557–1663*, 1961. See also J. F. Hayward, *Huguenot silver in England, 1688–1727*, 1959, bibl.

2741 COTTERELL, H. H. Pewter down the ages. 1932.

Ch. 4 is on the 17th century. Cf. the same author's illustrated articles, 'Great pewter collections', in *Apollo*, 19 (1934), 95, 192–9, and 20 (1934), 19–24. See also H. J. L. J. Massé, *Pewter plate*, 1904; and C. Welch, *History of the Pewterers*, 2 vols., 1902.

(5) *Textiles*

2742 KENDRICK, A. F. English decorative fabrics of the sixteenth to eighteenth centuries. Benfleet. 1934. Illus.

Cf. articles on needlework of the period by J. L. Nevinson in *Apollo*, 24 (1936), 279–83 and *Embroidery*, 4 (1936), 77–80. See also C. G. E. Hunt, *Tudor and Stuart fabrics*, Leigh-on-Sea, 1961. On carpets see C. E. C. Tattersall, *A history of British carpets*, Benfleet, 1934, illus. See also no. 2706.

2743 THOMSON, W. G. Tapestry weaving in England. Lond. and N.Y. 1914.

Previously publ. in 6 pts. in *Art Journal*, 1911. See also his *History of tapestry*, 1906, rev. edn., 1930.

2. ARCHITECTURE

(a) *Reference Works and Sources*

There is no complete bibliography for the period, but useful select lists are in Summerson (2755) and Whinney and Millar (2707). *A short bibliography of architecture*, by A. J. Stratton, was publ. by The Historical Association, 1923. Valuable surveys of buildings are by the Royal Commission on Historical Monuments (2748) and, for London, the *Survey of London* (3300); *Country Life* (see p. 392) is valuable for homes outside of London. See also *Scotland* (3975, 3978).

2744 WOTTON, SIR HENRY. The elements of architecture. 1624.

Also in *Reliquiae Wottonianae* ed. by I. Walton, 1651, 1672, 1685, and repr. in *Somers tracts*, iii.
For comments by English architects, see section (c) below.

2745 PALLADIO, ANDREA. Architecture . . . in four books . . . to which are added several notes and observations by Inigo Jones. Tr. by N. Du Bois. 15 pts. 1715.

There were many edns. of this influential work, first publ. in Venice in 1570; an edn. of pt. 1 appeared in England in 1663, and went through several other edns. before 1708. See also John Evelyn's *Whole body of ancient and modern architecture, with L. B. Albert's treatise on statues* . . ., 1680, which is his translation of Roland Freart's *Parallel*, 1650, and was licensed for publication as early as 1663. For Evelyn's own 'Account of architects . . .', see his *Miscellaneous writings* (2467 n.).

2746 KIP, JOHANNES. Britannia illustrated, or views of the Queen's palaces, as also . . . seats of the nobility and gentry . . . 1707. 1720.

Fine engravings by Kip, from drawings of Leonard Knyff.

2747 CAMPBELL, COLIN. Vitruvius Britannicus, or the British architect. 3 vols. 1715–25. Illus.

Vols. i–ii, publ. in 1715, and iii, 1725, are invaluable for their illustrations of the important buildings of the later part of the 17th century. The series was continued to seven volumes by others, 1767–1808.
    For university architecture see David Loggan, *Oxonia illustrata*, Oxf. 1675; and his *Cantabrigia illustrata*, Camb. 1690.

2748 ROYAL COMMISSION ON HISTORICAL MONUMENTS [to 1714]. Reports and inventories. 1910+.

Illustrated catalogues for England, Scotland, and Wales, by counties, with 8 vols. on London. In progress. Useful illustrations are also in *V.C.H.* (3120). For London see also the London County Council's *Survey of London* (3300).

2749 WREN SOCIETY. Ed. by A. T. Bolton and H. D. Hendry. 20 vols. 1924–43. Illus.

Valuable set, relating not only to Wren's works but to developments in architecture generally, 1660–1715.

(b) *Later Works*

2750 BLOMFIELD, R. A history of renaissance architecture in England 1500–1800. 2 vols. 1897. Illus.

An abridged edn., *Short history*, was publ. in 1900. Less valuable, but with useful illustrations, is *Later renaissance architecture in England*, by J. Belcher and N. Macartney, eds., 2 vols., 1901. See also G. H. Birch, *London churches of the 17th and 18th centuries*, 1896.

2751 CROSSLEY, F. H. Timber building in England from early times to the end of the seventeenth century. 1951. Illus.

Deals chiefly with earlier periods, but has valuable illustrations. Cf. W. Taylor, *Old halls in Cheshire*, Manchester, 1884.

2752   GOTCH, J. A. Architecture of the renaissance in England (1560–1635). 2 vols. 1894.

Illustrations are in the text. By Gotch also, *Early renaissance architecture in England* (1500–1625), 1901, 2nd edn., 1914. Still of some value is A. W. Hakewill, *Architecture of the seventeenth century*, pts. 1–3 [1856].

2753   INNOCENT, C. F. The development of English building constructions. Camb. 1916.

Valuable also is Knoop and Jones (1981). Other titles relating to building construction are: W. G. Bell, *A short history of the tylers and bricklayers . . . of London*, 1938; and N. Lloyd, *History of English brickwork*, 1934. See also J. Lang, *Rebuilding St. Paul's after the great fire of London*, 1956.

2754   PEVSNER, N. The buildings of England. 1951+.

A survey which provides a guide book to the chief buildings of interest, county by county. In progress (Penguin Books).

2755   SUMMERSON, J. Architecture in Britain, 1530–1830. 1953.

The best general survey; has bibl. references for each chapter. See also A. Stratton, *Introductory handbook to the styles of English architecture*, 2 vols., 1928–9, which was rev. and enl. for the 5th edn., 2 vols. in one, 1946; and R. J. Willis and J. W. Clark, *The architectural history of the university of Cambridge and of the colleges of Cambridge and Eton*, 4 vols., Camb. 1886.

(c) *Architects*

2756   COLVIN, H. M. Biographical dictionary of English architects, 1660–1840. 1954.

Valuable, with lists of works and references; largely supersedes the *Dictionary of architecture*, ed. by W. Papworth for the Architectural Publication Society, 1848–92.

JONES, INIGO

2757   Gotch, J. A. Inigo Jones. 1928.

This is the best biography, superseding that by P. Cunningham, 1848; some useful illustrations are in the brief volume by S. C. Ramsey, 1924. See also W. J. Loftie, *Inigo Jones and Wren*, 1893; W. Kent, *The designs of Inigo Jones*, 1727, repr. 1835; and no. 2704.

PRATT, SIR ROGER

2758   Gunther, R. T., ed. The architecture of Sir Roger Pratt . . . from his notebooks. 1928.

Pratt was Charles II's commissioner for the rebuilding of London after the fire. For other less well-known figures of the century, see J. A. Gotch, *A complete account of the buildings erected by Sir Thomas Tresham* [d. 1605], Northampton, 1883; M. J. Batten, 'The architecture of Dr. Robert Hooke, F.R.S.', *Walpole Soc.* 25 (1937), 83–113. See also Hooke's *Diary* (2908 n.); and J. Lees-Milne, *The age of Inigo Jones*, 1953.

VANBRUGH, SIR JOHN

2759 Whistler, L. Sir John Vanbrugh: architect and dramatist, 1664–1726. 1938.

By the same author, *The imagination of Sir John Vanbrugh and his fellow artists*, 1954. Another brief life is by C. A. Barman, 1924. See Vanbrugh's *Letters*, ed. by G. F. Webb, vol. iv of the *Works* (2687).

WREN, SIR CHRISTOPHER

2760 Summerson, J. Sir Christopher Wren. 1953.

One of the better modern biographies, although not definitive. The best sources for Wren's life are S. Wren, ed., *Parentalia, or memoirs of the family of the Wrens*, 1750, compiled by Wren's son and grandson, portions of which were republ. in 1903 as *Life and works of Sir Christopher Wren*, ed. by E. J. Enthoven; and the *Wren Society* volumes. The early *Memoirs . . . of Sir Christopher Wren*, by J. Elmes (1823, rev. edn., 1952), is now largely obsolete. Other modern biogs. are by G. F. Webb, 1937, and G. Bolton, 1956. For others see Colvin.

2761 Royal Institute of British Architects. Sir Christopher Wren: bicentenary memorial volume. 1923.

Articles by various authors. The R.I.B.A. also published in 1952: *Wren, authenticated and attributed works: alphabetical list. . . .* Recent scholarly works of criticism are V. Fürst, *The architecture of Sir Christopher Wren*, 1956, illus.; and E. F. Sekler, *Wren and his place in European architecture*, [1956]. A useful select bibl. is in Sekler.

(d) *Houses*

2762 AMBLER, L. Old halls and manor houses of Yorkshire. 1913. Illus.

See also Crossley (2751) and *Country Life*, p. 392.

2763 DAVIE, W. G. and DAWBER, E. G. Old cottages and farmhouses in Kent and Sussex. 1900.

The authors published similar volumes for the Cotswold district, 1905, and Surrey, 1908. Cf. J. A. Gotch, *Old Halls . . . Northants*, 1936; H. and F. C. Batsford, *The English cottage*, 1938, 3rd edn., 1950; M. S. Briggs, *The English farmhouse*, 1953; M. W. Barley, 'Farmhouses and cottages', *Econ. Hist. Rev.*, 2nd Ser. 7 (1955), 291–306; and D. Morand, *The minor architecture of Suffolk*, 1929, one volume in a series, *Minor domestic architecture of England*.

2764 GOTCH, J. A. The growth of the English house (1100–1800). 1909. 2nd edn. 1928.

Cf. his *The English home from Charles I to George IV . . .*, 1918. See also H. Field and M. Bunney, *English domestic architecture of the xvii and xviii centuries*, 1905, rev. edn., 1928; A. E. Richardson and H. D. Eberlein, *The smaller English house (1660–1830)*, 1925; N. Lloyd, *History of the English house . . .*, 1931, rev. edn., 1949, with good illustrations; and S. O. Addy, *Evolution of the English house*, 1898, rev. edn. by J. N. Summerson, 1933.

2765 TIPPING, H. A. English homes. Period III (1558–1649). 2 vols. 1922–7. Period IV (1649–1736). 2 vols. 1920–8.

The home of the Hollands, 1605–1820, by G. S. Fox-Strangways, earl of Ilchester, 1937, deals with Holland House in London. Other famous homes are described in the volumes of *Country Life*.

E. MUSIC

In order to give greatest bibliographical help to general historians, for whom this selection is prepared, predominance is given to more recent publications.

1. REFERENCE WORKS

2766 BLUME, F., ed. Die Musik in Geschichte und Gegenwart. Allgemeine Enzyklopädie der Musik. Kassel and Basel. 1949+ (9 vols. to 1961; A–Onslow).

Highly regarded; ed. secures British and American authorities to write on British musical subjects. Bibliographies.

2767 GROVE, G. Grove's dictionary of music and musicians. 4 vols. 1878–89. 5th edn. by E. Blom. 9 vols. 1954. Supplementary vol. 1961.

Standard work. Reviewers generally disappointed with 5th edn. See, e.g. P. H. Lang, *Musical Quarterly*, 41 (1955), 215–22.

Other valuable general reference works include: W. Apel, *Harvard dictionary of music*, Camb. (Mass.) 1944 (excludes biography); T. Baker, *Baker's biographical dictionary of musicians*, N.Y. 1900, 5th edn. by N. Slonimsky, N.Y. 1958; N. Dufourcq, ed., *Larousse de la musique. Dictionnaire encyclopédique*, 2 vols., Paris, 1957–8; K. Riemann, *Riemann musik lexikon*, Leipzig, 1882, 12th edn. by W. Gurlitt, vol. 1, *Personenteil A–K*, Mainz, 1959, vol. 2, *Personenteil L–Z*, Mainz, 1961; P. Scholes, *The Oxford companion to music*, 1938, 9th edn., 1955.

2768 PULVER, J. A. A biographical dictionary of old English music. 1927.

Needs revision but still useful, as is also Pulver's *A Dictionary of old English music and musical instruments*, 1923.

2. SOURCES

(a) *Music*

Much of the music and several treatises written in the 17th century remain in manuscript, or have until recently, while what was printed in the 17th century frequently remains in rare or unique copies, sometimes reproduced in later times. For general description of types of available materials, and catalogues, see 'Libraries and Collections' in Grove (2767). Finding early edns. is aided by E. B. Schnapper, ed., *The British union-catalogue of early music printed before the year 1801: A record of the holdings of over one hundred libraries throughout the British Isles*, 2 vols., 1957. Among the notable collections, in England: British Museum, Bodleian, Royal College of Music, Royal Academy of Music, Fitzwilliam Library, St. Michael's College, Tenbury; and in the United States: Library of Congress, New York Public, Folger Shakespeare, and H. E. Huntington. More detailed information about particular works appears in the reference works listed above, especially Blume (2766) and Grove (2767), and in biographies and other studies listed below. A few of the more famous works published in the 17th century, and more recent edns. and collections, are listed in this section.

It should be remembered that well-done phonograph records are a valuable form of the publishing of music; in some cases phonograph records have been produced from manuscripts never published. Scholarly reviews of records appear in such journals as *Musical Quarterly* (2806).

2769 BARNARD, JOHN, ed. The first booke of selected church musick, consisting of services and anthems, such as are now used in the cathedrall, and collegiat churches of this kingdome . . . 1641.

No complete set, of all ten books for the different voices, is known; on attempts to remedy this, and on the importance of the work see, e.g. Fellowes, *English cathedral music* (2795), Walker (2809), and Scholes, *Oxford companion* (2767 n.).

2770 BRONSON, B. H. The traditional tunes of the Child ballads with their texts, according to the extant records of Great Britain and America. Vols. i–ii. Princeton. 1959–62.

A 'monumental work' to be completed in four volumes; see review for evaluation and references: C. M. Simpson, *Journal of the American Musicological Society*, 12 (1959), 88–90. Bronson's work, with Dean-Smith's (2792) will serve as an excellent guide into the subject of folk music.

2771 BYRD, WILLIAM. Works. Ed. E. H. Fellowes. 20 vols. 1937–50.

See also the important, corrective, article by J. Kerman, 'Byrd's Motets: Chronology and Canon', *Journal of the American Musicological Society*, 14 (1961), 359–82. Byrd, with John Bull and Orlando Gibbons, wrote the music in *Parthenia or the maydenhead of the first musicke that ever was printed for the virginalls*, c. 1612; several other edns. in the 17th century; facsimile edn. by O. Deutsch, 1942; other edns. by K. Stone, N.Y. 1951, and T. Dart, c. 1960. A related volume, *Parthenia In-violata, or mayden-musicke for the virginalls and bass-viol . . .*, 1625(?) has been printed (N.Y. 1961) in facsimile from the apparently unique copy in the New York Public Library, with prefatory matter by T. Dart, R. J. Wolfe, and S. Beck.

2772 COPERARIO, GIOVANNI. Rules how to compose. A facsimile edition of a manuscript from the library of the Earl of Bridgewater (*circa* 1610) now in the Huntington Library . . . with an introduction by M. F. Bukofzer. Los Angeles. 1952.

2773 FELLOWES, E. H., ed. The English madrigal school. 36 vols. 1913–24.

See also E. H. Fellowes, *The English madrigal composers*, 1921, 2nd edn., 1948.

2774 FELLOWES, E. H., ed. The English school of lutenist song writers. 2nd Ser. 32 vols. 1920–32.

2775 FROST, M. English and Scottish psalm and hymn tunes c. 1543–1677. 1953.

Valuable. Includes bibl.

2776 MACE, THOMAS. Musick's monument; or a remembrancer of the best practical musick, both divine, and civil . . . 1676. Facsimile: vol. i (Parts I and II, and Part III through chapter 9). Paris. 1958.

Valuable in many ways, but long out of date, when published, as a guide to the lute; see D. Gill, 'The Lute and Musick's Monument', *Galpin Society Journal*, 3 (1950), 9–11, and E. D. MacKerness, 'Thomas Mace and the Fact of Reasonableness', *Monthly Musical Record*, 85 (1955), 211–13, 235–9. For information on instruction on the lute c. 1670 see T. Dart, 'Miss Mary Burwell's Instruction Book for the Lute', *Galpin Society*

Journal, 11 (1958), 3–62; commentary and text. See also G. Hayes, 'Music in the Boteler Muniments', *Galpin Society Journal*, 8 (1954), 43–6.

2777 MORLEY, THOMAS, ed. The first booke of consort lessons, made by divers exquisite authors for six instruments to play together, the treble lute, the pandora, the citttern, the base-violl, the flute and treble-violl. 1599. 2nd edn. 1611. Ed. S. Beck. N.Y. 1959.

Beck's reconstructed edn. reviewed by J. A. Westrup, *Music and Letters*, 42 (1961), 81–3.

2778 MORLEY, THOMAS. A plaine and easie introduction to practical musicke . . . 1597. 2nd edn. 1608. Facsimile edn. 1937. Modernized edn., by A. Harman. 1952.

On deficiencies in the 1952 edn. see review by R. Stevenson, *Journal of the American Musicological Society*, 6 (1953), 74–7.

2779 MUSICA BRITANNICA. A national collection of music. 1951+.

Various eds. Volumes are devoted to (ix) *Jacobean Consort Music*, (xv) *Music of Scotland 1500–1700*, and works by (ii) Locke and C. Gibbons, (v) Tomkins, (vi) Dowland, (vii) Blow, and (xiv) Bull.

2780 PLAYFORD, JOHN. A breefe introduction to the skill of musick. 1654.

Many edns., numbered and unnumbered, with varying titles and content; 2nd edn., 1655; Purcell rev. the edn. designated the 12th, 1694. Much has been written and remains to be written on this important work; see, e.g. I. Spink, 'Playford's "Directions for Singing after the Italian Manner"', *Monthly Musical Record*, 89 (1959), 130–5. On Playford see Humphries and Smith (2802) and references there. Many more instruction books were published than can be listed here. A bibl. of treatises on violin instruction publ. in England 1658–1731 is given by D. D. Boyden in 'A Postscript to "Geminiani and the First Violin Tutor"', *Acta Musicologica*, 32 (1960), 40–7.

2781 PLAYFORD, JOHN. The English dancing master: or, plaine and easie rules for the dancing of country dances, with the tune to each dance. 1651 [1650].

Many later edns. Facsimile, with introduction, bibl., and notes, by M. Dean-Smith, 1957.

2782 PURCELL, HENRY. Works. 1878+. 31 vols. by 1962.

Some of Purcell's works were publ. in his own time; see Westrup (2810). The character of the editing in the collected edn. varies greatly between that of the volumes publ. in the later decades of Victoria and the middle of the 20th century; see T. Dart, 'Purcell's Chamber Music', *Proceedings of the Royal Musical Association*, 85 (1959), 81–93. Several of the early volumes are being revised, and vol. ix, *Dioclesian*, ed. M. Laurie, appeared in 1961.

2783 SABOL, A. J., ed. Songs and dances for the Stuart masque. An edition of sixty-three items of music for the English court masque from 1604 to 1641. Providence, R.I. 1959.

See also: J. P. Cutts, ed., *La musique de scène de la troupe de Shakespeare. The King's Men sous le règne de Jacques Ier*, Paris, 1959, with *Addenda et Corrigenda* (6 pp.), 1961; for critical reservations see review by F. W. Sternfeld, *Music and Letters*, 41 (1960), 300–03.

2784 SIMPSON, CHRISTOPHER. The division-violist. 1659. Revised edn. 1667. Ed. N. Dolmetsch. 1955.

> Simpson also wrote a more general work, *The principles of practical musick*, 1665; 2nd edn., rev. and enl., *A Compendium . . .*, 1667; and many more edns. The publisher of *The division-violist*, Playford, had earlier published *Musicks recreation on the lyra viol*, 1652.

(b) *General*

Beyond what has been listed in the preceding section, materials for the history of music may be found in nearly every type of sources. Collections often having relevance to some aspect of the subject include those of the Public Record Office (a very wide variety of classifications), municipal records, and family archives. The *Calendar of State Papers, Domestic*, the *Calendar of Treasury Books*, the publications of the Historical Manuscripts Commission and of local history societies, and the like, are often useful, but sometimes deficient because of their editors' lack of interest in music. Fellowes (2795), Scholes (2807), Woodfill (2811), and the biographies, especially Westrup (2810), indicate the character and location of many of the sources. Titles of a few of the more important published non-musical sources follow.

2785 LAFONTAINE, H. C. DE, ed. The King's musick. A transcript of records relating to music and musicians (1460–1700). 1909.

> Very useful, but incomplete and not always accurate, from Lord Chamberlains' records preserved in the Public Record Office. See also 'Lists of the King's Musicians from the Audit Office Declared Accounts', *Musical Antiquary*, I–III (1909–12); contains much more than names of musicians.

2786 NORTH, ROGER. Roger North on music. Transcribed and ed. by J. Wilson. 1959.

> Valuable from the restoration into the 18th century; see review by J. A. Westrup, *Music and Letters*, 41 (1960) 176–7.

2787 RIMBAULT, E. F., ed. The old cheque-book, or book of remembrance of the Chapel Royal. Camden Society, 2nd Ser., vol. 3. 1872.

> Unsystematic notations concerning appointments, deaths, arrangements for special occasions, etc. New edn. needed. Microfilm in Public Record Office, 1955. Recent studies of the Chapel Royal in the 17th century include: chapter 7 in Woodfill (2811); W. K. Ford, 'The Chapel Royal at the restoration', *Monthly Musical Record*, 90 (1960), 99–106; J. A. Westrup, 'The Chapel Royal under James II', *Monthly Musical Record*, 70 (1940), 219–22.

3. MODERN STUDIES

Especially in the last quarter century much of the best work has appeared in journals. Of these, the ones most frequently contributing to knowledge of music in Britain in the 17th century are listed below; examples of the types of articles that they publish are given throughout the whole section on music.

2788 BUKOFZER, M. F. Music in the baroque era. N.Y. 1947.

> Too often scholars have tended to forget that British music has been a part of, rather

than independent of, the musical history of Western Europe. Reading of Bukofzer will help correct this. See also P. H. Lang, *Music in western civilization*, N.Y. 1941. The relevant volumes of the *New Oxford history of music*, ed. J. A. Westrup *et al.*, 1954+, may appear soon, and should be useful.

2789 BURNEY, C. A general history of music from the earliest ages to the present period. 4 vols. 1776–89. New edn. with notes by F. Mercer. 2 vols. 1935.

The 18th-century printings should be used when possible. Contains source materials for the Stuart period.

2790 DAY, C. L. and MURRIE, E. B. English song-booke 1651–1702: a bibliography with a first-line index of songs. 1940.

See also Day and Murrie, 'English song-books, 1651–1702, and their publishers', *The Library*, 4th Ser. 16 (1936), 355–401.

2791 DEAN, W. Handel's dramatic oratorios and masques. 1959.

Published too late for inclusion in Pargellis and Medley, to whose period Handel chiefly belongs, this outstanding work gives a concise recent guide to the enormous bibl. of Handel.

2792 DEAN-SMITH, M. A guide to English folk song collections 1822–1952 with an index to their contents, historical annotations and an introduction. Liverpool. 1954.

Reviewed: B. H. Bronson, *Journal of the American Musicological Society*, 8 (1955), 57–8. See also E. A. White, compiler, and M. Dean-Smith, ed., *An index of songs contributed to the Journal of the Folk Song Society, 1899–1931, and its Continuation The Journal of the English Folk Dance and Song Society, to 1950*, 1951. See Bronson (2770).

2793 DENT, E. J. Foundations of English opera: a study of musical drama in England during the seventeenth century. Camb. 1928.

2794 EVANS, W. M. Henry Lawes, musician and friend of poets. 1941.

See also E. F. Hart, 'Introduction to Henry Lawes', *Music and Letters*, 32 (1951), 217–25, 328–44.

2795 FELLOWES, E. H. English cathedral music from Edward VI to Edward VII. 1941. 2nd edn. 1945.

Introductory; see also: C. H. Phillips, *The singing church. An outline history of the music sung by choir and people*, 1945; and two articles by J. A. Westrup, both in *Monthly Musical Record*: 'Church music at the restoration', 71 (1941), 131–5, and 'Parish church music in the seventeenth century', 72 (1942), 227–31.

2796 FELLOWES, E. H. Orlando Gibbons. Oxf. 1925. 2nd edn. 1951.

2797 FELLOWES, E. H. William Byrd. 1936. 2nd edn. 1948.

2798 GALPIN, F. W. Old English instruments of music; their history and character. 1910. 3rd edn. revised 1932. (A new revised edn. announced.)

One of Galpin's important achievements, on which the society named in his memory now builds (see next item).

2799 GALPIN SOCIETY JOURNAL. 1948+.

'Occasional'; annual to date. Valuable articles on many aspects of the history, and connected with the history, of musical instruments. For examples of the type of article published, in addition to those cited throughout this section, see: E. Halfpenny, 'The English 2- and 3-Keyed Hautboy', 2 (1949), 10–26, and E. Halfpenny, 'Biographical notices of the early English woodwind-making school', 12 (1959), 44–52.

2800 HAWKINS, SIR JOHN. A general history of the science and practise of music. 5 vols. 1766. 3rd edn. 2 vols. 1875.

Contains some source material for Stuart period.

2801 HOLLANDER, J. The untuning of the sky: ideas of music in English poetry 1500–1700. Princeton. 1961.

Concerned 'not so much with musical practices as with beliefs about music's power, its place in the world-view of the times'. For another important study of music and literature see B. Pattison, *Music and poetry of the English renaissance*, 1948.

2802 HUMPHRIES, C. and SMITH, W. C. Music publishing in the British Isles from the earliest times to the middle of the nineteenth century: a dictionary of engravers, printers, publishers and music sellers, with a historical introduction. 1954.

Bibl. Invaluable. Supersedes F. Kidson, *British music publishers, printers, and engravers*, 1900.

2803 LEFKOWITZ, M. William Lawes. 1960.

2804 MANIFOLD, J. S. The music in English drama from Shakespeare to Purcell. 1956.

See also F. W. Sternfeld, 'The use of song in Shakespeare's tragedies', *Proceedings of the Royal Musical Association*, 86 (1960), 45–59.

2805 MUSIC AND LETTERS. 1920+. Quarterly.

Excellent articles and reviews. Another English quarterly, *Music Review*, Camb. 1940+, occasionally has relevant material, as does the more popular monthly, *Musical Times*, 1844+. The *Proceedings of the (Royal) Musical Association*, 1874+, annual, contain many important papers; see, e.g. I. Spink, 'English cavalier songs, 1620–1660', 86 (1960), 61–78. The *Monthly Musical Record*, 1871–1960, bimonthly since 1956, and concluded with the issue of November–December 1960, contains many valuable articles, a number of which are cited in this section.

2806 MUSICAL QUARTERLY. N.Y. 1915+.

Reviews as well as articles occasionally offer substantial contributions; 'Quarterly Book List' gives titles from many countries. The *Journal of the American Musicological Society*, Boston, Mass. 1948+ (three numbers a year, now Richmond, Va.), includes extensive reviews. See also *Musica Disciplina*, 1946+; quarterly, Camb. (Mass.), March 1946–June 1947; irregularly since, in Rome.

2807 SCHOLES, P. A. The puritans and music in England and New England 1934.

Scholes, *Music and puritanism*, Vevey, 1934, contains some material not in the above.

2808 STEVENS, D. Thomas Tomkins 1572–1656. 1957.

See also L. A. Gill, 'The Anthems of Thomas Tomkins . . .', *Musica Disciplina*, 11 (1957), 153–86.

2809 WALKER, E. A history of music in England. Oxf. 1907. 3rd edn., rev. and enl. by J. A. Westrup. Oxf. 1952.

The reviser of the third edn., Westrup, has written many articles about music in Stuart England, of which several are listed elsewhere in this section; among others are: 'Domestic music under the Stuarts', *Proceedings of the Musical Association*, 68 (1942), 19–53; 'Foreign musicians in Stuart England', *Musical Quarterly*, 27 (1941), 70–89; and 'Amateurs in seventeenth-century England', *Monthly Musical Record*, 69 (1939), 257–63.

2810 WESTRUP, J. A. Purcell. 1937. 4th edn. 1960.

Outstanding among many biographies. Much was published in 1959 to celebrate the tercentenary of Purcell's birth; e.g. the June 1959 issue of *Musical Times* (vol. 100); J. A. Westrup, 'Purcell and Handel', *Music and Letters*, 40 (1959), 103–8; and I. Holst, ed., *Henry Purcell 1659–1695: essays on his music*, 1959. See also R. E. Moore, *Henry Purcell and the restoration theatre*, Camb. (Mass.) and Lond. 1961; review by P. Brett, *Music and Letters*, 43 (1962), 162–4.

2811 WOODFILL, W. L. Musicians in English society from Elizabeth to Charles I (Princeton Studies in History, vol. 9). Princeton. 1953.

An exploration of a large part of the field in the decades about 1600, from historians', rather than musicians', points of view; indicates wide variety of sources, and prints original contemporary material.

F. SCIENCE

The section indicates the works that will guide the student toward the best knowledge of English science in the 17th century as it is now understood. The list of general works begins with surveys of the history of science and narrows down to works concerned primarily with the seventeenth century. Books dealing with the individual sciences are followed by a section on scientists who cannot be listed conveniently under any of the prior headings. Secondary works are given the most attention. The student who wishes to go beyond the major sources listed should let the secondary works guide him. A final section on the social relations of science deals with the Royal Society and with the broader implications of science.

1. GENERAL

(a) *Bibliographies*

2812 SARTON, G. A guide to the history of science. Waltham (Mass.). 1952.

A basic guide by the master of contemporary historians of science.

2813 GUERLAC, E. Science in Western civilization. N.Y. 1952.

The syllabus of a course at Cornell University with extensive bibls.

2814   ISIS. International review devoted to the history of science and civilization. Camb. (Mass.). 1913+.

This most important of the journals devoted to the history of science publishes a continuing series of exhaustive critical bibls. on the history of science.

(b) *General Works*

2815   OSIRIS. Studies on the history and philosophy of science and on the
history of learning and culture. Bruges. 1946+.

See also *Isis* (2814).

2816   ANNALS OF SCIENCE. A quarterly review of the history of science
since the renaissance. Lond. 1936+.

2817   ARCHIVES INTERNATIONALES d'histoire des sciences. Nouvelle
série d'Archeion. Paris. 1947+.

Previous titles, *Archivio di storia della scienza*, Rome, 1919–27; and *Archeion*, 1927–43.

2818   REVUE D'HISTOIRE DES SCIENCES ET LEUR APPLICA-
TIONS: organe de la section d'histoire des sciences. Paris. 1947+.

2819   BOAS, M. 'The establishment of the mechanical philosophy.' *Osisis*, 10
(1952), 412–541.

An important treatment of the new conception of nature.

2820   BURTT, E. A. The metaphysical foundations of modern physical science.
Rev. edn. [1949].

A classic discussion of 17th-century scientific thought. Publ. in 1925 as *The metaphysic
of Sir Isaac Newton*.

2821   BUTTERFIELD, H. The origins of modern science. 2nd edn.   N.Y.
1957.

Another excellent survey of the period, perhaps less difficult than Hall. Bibl.

2822   COLLINGWOOD, R. G. The idea of nature. Oxf. 1945.

2823   DAMPIER, W. C. A history of science and its relations with philosophy
and religion. 4th edn. Camb. 1948; N.Y. 1949.

One of the best single-volume histories of science.

2824   DIJKSTERHUIS, E. J. Die Mechanisierung des Weltbildes. Tr.
from Dutch by H. Habicht. Berlin. 1956.

An important treatment of the change in physical thought.

2825   GLANSDORFF, M. Essai sur l'avènement de la raison expérimentale.
Brussels. 1948.

2826   GUNTHER, R. W. T. Early science in Oxford. (Oxf. Hist. Soc.) 14
vols. Oxf. 1921–45. Illus.

Vols. 1 and 2 are vols. 77 and 78 of Oxford Hist. Soc. Pubs. By same author: *Early* science in Cambridge, Oxf. 1937; 'Oxford colleges and their men of science through the centuries', in *The book of Oxford* (British Medical Assoc. 1936). Gunther's works are masses of undigested factual information, together with important reprints of classics.

2827 HALL, A. R. The scientific revolution. 1954.

Excellent study of the 16th and 17th centuries. Bibl.

2828 JOHNSON, F. R. A study of the English scientific writings from 1500 to 1645. Baltimore. 1937. Bibl.

Huntington Library pubn.

2829 KOYRÉ, A. Études galiléennes. Paris. 1939.

Though not about England, fundamental to understanding science in the 17th century, including English science. Cf. his 'Galileo and the scientific revolution of the seventeenth century', *Philosophical Review*, 52 (1943), 333–48.

2830 KOYRÉ, A. From the closed world to the infinite universe. Baltimore. 1956.

An interpretation of changing scientific thought in the 17th century.

2831 PLEDGE, H. T. Science since 1500: a short history of mathematics, physics, chemistry, biology. 1939.

A good short account of the modern period.

2832 PRIOR, M. E. 'Bacon's man of science.' *Jour. Hist. Ideas*, 15 (1954), 348–70.

Study of the ideal image which Bacon created of the new scientist.

2833 THORNDIKE, L. A history of magic and experimental science. Vols. vii and viii, The seventeenth century. N.Y. 1958.

Two new volumes in Thorndike's massive survey in 8 vols., which began in 1923. See also his 'Newness and craving for novelty in seventeenth century science and medicine', *Jour. Hist. Ideas*, 12 (1951), 584–96, a treatise on words used in scientific and pseudo-scientific titles.

2834 WIGHTMAN, W. P. D. The growth of scientific ideas. Edin. and Lond. 1950. New Haven. 1951.

An excellent interpretative account.

2835 WOLF, A. A history of science, technology, and philosophy in the 16th and 17th centuries. 1935. New edn. 1950.

A mine of factual information but low on interpretation.

2. MATHEMATICS

(a) Sources

2836 NAPIER, JOHN, of Merchistoun. Mirifici logarithmorum canonis descriptio, ejusque usus, in utraque trigonometria; ut etiam in omni logistica mathematica; amplissimi facillimi et expeditissimi explicatio. Edin. 1614. Diagr.

Cf. Napier's *Rabdologiae, seu numerationis per virgulas*, Edin. 1617.

2837 BRIGGS, HENRY. Arithmetica logarithmica sive logarithmorum chiliades triginta, pro numeris . . . ad 20,000 et a 90,000 ad 100,000 . . . 1624. Later edn. by A. Vlacq. Gouda. 1628.

Vlacq added the logarithms from 20,000 to 90,000 omitted by Briggs, as well as tables of trigonometrical functions. Substantially all modern tables of logarithms are based on this work.

2838 OUGHTRED, WILLIAM. Clavis mathematicae denuo limata, sive potius fabricata. 1631. 4th edn. 4 pts. Oxf. 1667.

The title is taken from edn. of 1667. Original title was *Arithmeticae in numeris et speciebus institutio*. A textbook of arithmetic and algebra. Cf. F. Cajori, *W. Oughtred*, Chicago and Lond. 1916; also his 'Oughtred's ideas and influence on the teaching of mathematics', *Monist*, 25 (1915), 495–530, and his 'The works of William Oughtred', ibid. 441–66.

2839 WALLIS, JOHN. Opera mathematica. 3 vols. Oxf. 1693–9.

A precursor of the calculus. Cf. J. F. Scott, *The mathematical work of John Wallis*, 1938.

2840 BARROW, ISAAC. The mathematical works of Isaac Barrow. Ed. W. Whewell. Camb. 1860.

Another precursor of the calculus; Newton's teacher. Cf. J. M. Child, *The geometrical lectures of Isaac Barrow, translated, with notes and proofs, and a discussion on the advance made therein on the work of his predecessors in the infinitesimal calculus*, Chicago and Lond. 1916, which claims that Barrow discovered the calculus. For a reply cf. F. Cajori, 'Who was the first inventor of the calculus?', *American Mathematical Monthly*, 26 (1919), 15–20.

2841 GREGORY, JAMES. Tercentenary memorial volume, containing his correspondence with John Collins and his hitherto unpublished mathematical manuscripts . . . Ed. by H. W. Turnbull. 1939.

2842 NEWTON, ISAAC. Opera quae exstant omnia. 5 vols. Ed. S. Horsley. 1779–85. Mathematical works in vol. i.

See also under astronomy and physics. Cf. H. W. Turnbull, *The mathematical discoveries of Newton*, Lond. and Glasgow, 1945. For the controversy over invention of the calculus cf. *Commercium epistolicum de re mathematica inter celeberrimos praesentis seculi mathematicos*, 1713, and especially edn. of 1856 by Lefort and Biot; Cantor (2847); K. I. Gerhardt, 'Leibniz in London', trans. with notes by J. M. Child, *Monist*, 27 (1917), 524–59; J. M. Child, 'Barrow, Newton, and Leibniz, in their relation to the discovery of the calculus', *Science Progress*, no. 98 (1930), 295–307; J. E. Hofmann, 'Studien zur Vorgeschichte des Prioritätestreites zwischen Leibniz und Newton und die Entdeckung der höheren Analysis', *Abhandlung der Preussische Akademie der Wissenschaften. Mathematisch-naturwissenschaftliche klasse*, Berlin, 1943; Brewster (2864 n.); More (2864 n.).

(b) *Later Works*

2843 SCRIPTA MATHEMATICA. A quarterly journal devoted to the philosophy, history and expository treatment of mathematics. N.Y. 1932+.

2844 BOYER, C. B. The concepts of the calculus. N.Y. 1949.

Now the standard work on the historical development of the calculus.

2845 BRUNSCHVICQ, L. Les étapes de la philosophie mathématique. 3rd edn. Paris. 1929.

Many valuable insights on Newton.

2846 CAJORI, F. A history of the conceptions of limits and fluxions in Great Britain from Newton to Woodhouse. Chicago and Lond. 1919.

2847 CANTOR, M. Vorlesungen über Geschichte der Mathematik. 4 vols. Leipzig. 1880–1908. Diag.

The standard modern history of mathematics. The Stuart period is contained in vols. ii and iii. Cf. F. Cajori, *A history of mathematics*, 2nd edn., N.Y. 1919; D. E. Smith, *History of mathematics*, 2 vols., Boston and N.Y. 1923–5; D. J. Struik, *A concise history of mathematics*, 2 vols., N.Y. 1948, 2nd edn. rev., 1 vol., N.Y. n.d.; W. W. Rouse Ball, *A short account of the history of mathematics*, 1888, 3rd edn., 1901, and *A history of the study of mathematics at Cambridge*, Camb. 1889. Also E. T. Bell, *The development of mathematics*, N.Y. 1940.

2848 LORIA, G. Guida allo studio della storia delle matematiche. 2nd edn., revised and augmented. Milan. 1946.

By one of the modern masters of the discipline. Cf. his *Storia delle matematiche*, 3 vols., Turin, 1929–33; revised edn. in 1 vol., Milan, 1950. See also G. Sarton, *The study of the history of mathematics*, Camb. (Mass.) 1936.

2849 TAYLOR, E. G. R. The mathematical practitioners of Tudor and Stuart England. Camb. 1954.

Excellent work with biographical sketches and annotated source bibls.

3. ASTRONOMY

(a) *Sources*

2850 HORROX, JEREMIAH. Opera posthuma. Ed. John Wallis. 1673.

2851 HALLEY, EDMOND. Catalogus stellarum australium. 1679.

Other works: 'Astronomiae cometicae synopsis', *Phil. Trans. Roy. Soc.* 23 (1704–5), 1882–99 (Eng. trans., 1705), which predicts the return of 'Halley's' comet; 'Journal of a voyage made for the discovery of the rule of variation of compass . . . 1699 and 1700' in Alex. Dalrymple, *Collection of voyages*, 1775; *Astronomical tables, with precepts both in English and Latin for computing the places of the sun, moon, planets, and comets*, 1752 (1st edn. in Latin, 1745). Cf. *Correspondence and papers of Edmond Halley, preceded by an unpublished memoir of his life by one of his contemporaries and the 'Eloge' by D'Ortous de Mairan*, ed. E. F. MacPike, Oxf. 1932. See also MacPike's *Hévélius, Flamsteed and Halley: three contemporary astronomers and their mutual relations*, 1937. For bibl. see *Bull. of Bibl.*, 4 (1905), 52–7.

2852 FLAMSTEED, JOHN. Historia coelestis Britannica. 3 vols. 1725.

3rd vol. contains his famous 'British catalogue' of stars. An earlier form of *Historia*, publication of which began in 1706 under auspices of the Royal Society, was publ. in 2 parts in 1712. Cf. F. Bailey, *An account of the Rev. John Flamstead, the first astronomer-royal*, 1835, which includes his autobiography and correspondence.

2853 NEWTON, ISAAC. A treatise of the system of the world. 1728.

Also in Latin, *De mundi systemate*, 1728. This is Book iii of the *Principia* (2861).

Cf. P. E. B. Jourdain, 'Newton's hypothesis of ether and of gravitation', *The Monist*, 25 (1915), 79–106, 233–54, 418–40; and A. Koyré, 'La gravitation universelle de Kepler à Newton', *Archives internationales d'histoire des sciences*, 4 (1959), 638–53.

(b) *Later Works*

2854   ABETTI, G.   The history of astronomy. Tr. from Italian by B. B. Abetti. N.Y. 1952.

Cf. A. Berry, *A short history of astronomy*, N.Y. 1899.

2855   JOHNSON, F. R.   Astronomical thought in renaissance England. Baltimore. 1937.

An excellent work that will introduce the student to the new astronomy.

2856   KING, H. D.   The history of the telescope. Camb. (Mass.). 1955.

2857   McCOLLEY, G.   'The seventeenth-century doctrine of a plurality of worlds.' *Annals of Science*, 1 (1936), 385–430.

2858   STIMSON, D.   The gradual acceptance of the Copernican theory. N.Y. 1917.

2859   ZINNER, E.   Die Geschichte der Sternkunde. Berlin. 1931.

4. PHYSICS AND MECHANICS

(a) *Sources*

2860   BOYLE, ROBERT.   The spring and weight of the air. 1660.

The experiments leading to Boyle's law were publ. in the 2nd edn., 1662. For Boyle's exposition of the mechanical philosophy see *Origin of forms and qualities*, 1666, *Mechanical origine or production of divers particular qualities*, 1675, *A free enquiry into the vulgarly received notion of nature*, 1686. See *Works*, ed. Birch (2872).

2861   NEWTON, ISAAC.   Philosophiae naturalis principia mathematica. 1687. Diagrams. Later edns. By R. Cote. Camb. 1713. By H. Pemberton. 1726.

The 2nd and 3rd edns. appeared during Newton's lifetime and were revised by him. Eng. trans. by A. Motte, 1729; edn. F. Cajori, Berkeley, 1946. The *Principia* was the most important book on physical science of the age and one of the greatest of all time.
    Cf. W. W. Rouse Ball, *An essay on Newton's Principia*, Lond. and N.Y. 1893; P. E. B. Jourdain, 'The principles of mechanics with Newton', *The Monist*, 24 (1914), 187–224, 515–64; A. R. Hall, 'Newton on the calculation of central forces', *Annals of Science*, 13 (1957), 62–71; F. Cajori, 'Newton's twenty years' delay in announcing the law of gravitation', *Sir Isaac Newton 1727–1927; a bicentenary evaluation of his work; a series of papers prepared under the History of Science Society* . . . (Baltimore, 1928), 127–88; A. Koyré, 'The significance of the Newtonian synthesis', *Jour. of Genl. Education*, 4 (1950), 256–68, and his 'An unpublished letter of Robert Hooke to Isaac Newton', *Isis*, 43 (1952), 312–27, very important.

2862   NEWTON, ISAAC.   Opticks: or a treatise of the reflexions, refractions, inflexions and colours of light. 1704. 2nd edn. 1717. 3rd edn. 1721. Latin edn. Samuel Clarke trans. 1706.

See edn. based on 4th Lond. edn. with a foreword by A. Einstein, an introduction by Sir E. Whittaker, a pref. by I. B. Cohen, and an analytical table of contents prepared by D. H. D. Roller, N.Y. 1952. Cf. *Optical lectures*, 1728, a trans. of part of *Lectiones opticae*, fully publ. in 1729. See also M. Roberts and E. H. Thomas, *Newton and the origin of colours*, 1934; A. R. Hall, 'Sir Isaac Newton's note-book, 1661–65', *Camb. Hist. Jour.* 9 (1948), 239–50, and his 'Further optical experiments of Isaac Newton', *Annals of Science*, 11 (1955), 27–43; L. Rosenfeld, 'La théorie des couleurs de Newton et ses adversaires', *Isis*, 9 (1927), 44–65, and his 'Le premier conflit entre la théorie ondulatoire et la théorie corpusculaire de la lumière', *Isis*, 11 (1928), 111–22.

2863 NEWTON, ISAAC. Opera quae exstant omnia. Ed. by S. Horsley. 5 vols. 1779–85. Diagr.

Also *Newton's philosophy of nature; a selection from his writings*, ed. by H. S. Thayer, N.Y. 1953. *Papers and letters on natural philosophy, and related documents*, ed. by I. B. Cohen and R. E. Schofield, Camb. (Mass.) 1958, includes Fontenelle's *Éloge* and excellent introductory articles. *The Leibniz–Clarke correspondence, together with extracts from Newton's Principia and Optics*, ed. by H. G. Alexander, N.Y. 1956. See also A. R. Hall and M. B. Hall, eds., *Unpublished scientific papers of Isaac Newton . . .*, N.Y. 1962.

Cf. E. Cassirer, 'Newton and Leibniz', *Philosophical Review*, 52 (1943), 366–91; F. Rosenberger, *Isaac Newton und seine physikalischen Principien*, Leipzig, 1895; L. Bloch, *La philosophie de Newton*, Paris, 1908; A. J. Snow, *Matter and gravity in Newton's physical philosophy*, 1926, and his 'The role of mathematics and hypothesis in Newton's physics', *Scientia*, 42 (1927), 1–10. I. B. Cohen, *Franklin and Newton* (Phila. 1956) is a very important discussion of Newton's philosophy. Also, E. W. Strong, 'Newton's "Mathematical way"', *Jour. Hist. Ideas*, 12 (1951), 90–110; and his 'Newton and God', ibid. 13 (1952), 147–67; H. R. Burke, 'Sir Isaac Newton's formal conception of scientific method', *New Scholasticism*, 10 (1936), 93–115; A. Koyré, 'Expérience et hypothèse chez Newton', *Bulletin de la Société Française de Philosophie* (1956); A. C. Crombie, 'Newton's conception of scientific method', *Bull. Inst. Phys.* 8 (1957), 350–62. For bibl. see G. J. Gray, *A bibliography of the works of Sir Isaac Newton*, Camb. 1888; 2nd edn. enl., Camb. 1907; and H. Zeitlinger, 'A Newton bibliography', *Isaac Newton 1642–1727, a memorial volume*, ed. by W. J. Greenstreet, 1927; *A descriptive catalogue of the Grace K. Babson collection of the works of Sir Isaac Newton and the material relating to him*, N.Y. 1950.

2864 NEWTON, ISAAC. The correspondence of Isaac Newton. Ed. by H. W. Turnbull and J. F. Scott. Vols. i–iii. Camb. 1959–61.

The Royal Society's definitive edn. projected in 6 vols. Until complete see S. P. and S. J. Rigaud, eds., *Correspondence of scientific men of the seventeenth century . . . printed from the originals in the collection of . . . the Earl of Macclesfield*, 2 vols., Oxf. 1841–62, which has correspondence of other men beside Newton. Also *Correspondence of Sir Isaac Newton and Professor Cotes, including letters of other eminent men . . . other unpublished letters and papers by Newton*, ed. by J. Edleston, 1850. J. Pelseneer, 'Lettres inédites de Newton', *Osiris* 7 (1939), 523–55; 'Une lettre inédite de Newton à Pepys (23 décembre, 1693)', ibid. 1 (1936), 497–9; 'Une lettre inédite de Newton', *Isis*, 12 (1929), 237–54. See also W. G. Hiscock, ed., *David Gregory, Isaac Newton and their circle, extracts from David Gregory's memoranda, 1677–1708*, Oxf. 1937.

The basic biography, not really superseded by more recent works, is D. Brewster, *Memoirs of the life, writings, and discoveries of Sir Isaac Newton*, 2 vols., 1855. See also A. De Morgan, *Essays on the life and work of Newton*, ed. P. E. B. Jourdain, Chicago, 1914; and biographies by L. T. More, 1934, J. W. N. Sullivan, 1938, and E. N. da C. Andrade, 1950. Cf. William Stukeley, *Memoirs of Sir Isaac Newton's life, being some account of his family and chiefly of the junior part of his life*, ed. by A. H. White, 1936. Also *The Royal Society: Newton tercentenary celebrations 15–19 July 1946*, Camb. 1947.

(b) *Later Works*

2865   CAJORI, F. A short history of physics. Rev. edn. N.Y. 1929.

Compact but reliable. On ballistics see Hall (1552). See also M. von Laue, *Geschichte der Physik*, 2nd edn., Bonn, 1947.

2866   DUGAS, R. Histoire de la mécanique. Neuchâtel. 1950.

An outstanding recent history of mechanics. Also his *La mécanique au xviie siècle*, Neuchâtel, 1954.

2867   KOYRÉ, A. Documentary history of the problem of fall from Kepler to Newton. Phila. 1955.

2868   MACH, E. The science of mechanics; a critical and historical account of its development. Trans. by P. E. B. Jourdain. Chicago and Lond. 1915.

Perhaps the most important work on the history of mechanics. See also his *The principles of physical optics*, trans. by J. S. Anderson and F. A. Young, 1926.

2869   MILLINGTON, E. C. 'Theories of cohesion in the seventeenth century.' *Annals of Science*, 5 (1945), 253–69.

2870   RONCHI, V. Storia della luce. Bologna. 1939. Fr. trans. Paris. 1956.

The outstanding history of optics.

5. CHEMISTRY

(a) *Bibliography and Sources*

2871   FERGUSON, J. Bibliotheca chemica, a catalogue of the alchemical books in the collection of the late James Young of Kelly and Durris. 2 vols. Glasgow. 1906.

One of the best tools of the historian of chemistry.

2872   BOYLE, ROBERT. The works of the Honourable Robert Boyle. Ed. by Thomas Birch. 5 vols. 1744.

Especially *The sceptical chymist: or chymico-physical doubts and paradoxes, touching the experiments whereby vulgar spagyrists are wont to endeavor to evince their salt, sulphur, and mercury, to be the true principles of things* . . ., Oxf. 1661. 'Marks a turning-point in the history of chemistry'—Sir Edward Thorpe.

   Cf. M. Boas, *Robert Boyle and seventeenth-century chemistry*, N.Y. 1958, bibl.; a new evaluation both of Boyle's works and of seventeenth-century chemistry, it replaces the standard biography by L. T. More, N.Y. 1944. See also T. S. Kuhn, 'Robert Boyle and structural chemistry in the seventeenth century', *Isis*, 43 (1952), 12–36; and T. L. Davis 'Boyle's conception of element . . .', ibid. 16 (1931), 82–91; R. S. Westfall, 'Unpublished Boyle papers relating to the scientific method', *Annals of Science*, 12 (1956), 63–73, 103–17; M. S. Fisher, *Robert Boyle, devout naturalist; a study in science and religion in the seventeenth century*, Phila. 1945; and R. E. Maddison, 'A summary of former accounts of the life and work of Robert Boyle', *Annals of Science*, 13 (1957), 90–108. For bibl. see J. F. Fulton, *A bibliography of the Honourable Robert Boyle*, Oxf. 1932.

(b) *Later Works*

2873 CHYMIA: annual studies of the history of chemistry. Phila. 1948+.

2874 COLEBY, L. J. M. 'John Francis Vigani, first professor of chemistry in in the University of Cambridge.' *Annals of Science*, 8 (1952), 46–60.

Cf. G. H. Turnbull, 'Peter Stahl, the first public teacher of chemistry at Oxford', ibid. 9 (1953), 265–70; and P. George, 'The scientific movement and the development of chemistry in England', ibid. 8 (1952), 302–22.

2875 FARBER, E. The evolution of chemistry. N.Y. 1952.

2876 McKIE, D. 'Some notes on Newton's chemical philosophy written upon the occasion of the tercentenary of his birth.' *Philosophical Magazine and Journal of Science*, 33 (1942), 847–70.

Cf. T. S. Kuhn, 'Newton's 31st query and the degradation of gold', *Isis*, 42 (1951), 296–8; T. S. Kuhn and M. Boas, 'Newton and the theory of chemical solution', ibid. 43 (1952), 123–5. M. Boas and A. R. Hall, 'Newton's chemical experiments', *Archives internationales d'histoire des sciences*, 11 (1958), 113–52.

2877 METZGER, H. La doctrine chimique en France. Paris. 1923.

Fundamental work on 17th-century chemistry. Cf. her *Newton, Stahl, Boerhaave . . .*, Paris, 1930, and two articles in *Archeion*, 11 (1929), 13–25, 190–7.

2878 PATTERSON, T. S. 'John Mayow in contemporary setting.' *Isis*, 15 (1931), 47–96, 504–46.

Cf. H. Guerlac, 'John Mayow and the aerial nitre', *Actes du Congrès International d'Histoire des Sciences* (Jerusalem, 1953), 332–49, and J. R. Partington, 'The life and works of John Mayow (1641–1679)', *Isis*, 47 (1956), 217–30, 405–17, which take issue with and correct Patterson's interpretation. Also D. McKie, 'Fire and the Flamma Vitalis: Boyle, Hooke and Mayow', *Science, Medicine and History*, Oxf. 1953, pp. 469–88.

6. BIOLOGICAL SCIENCES

(a) *Sources*

2879 HOOKE, ROBERT. Micrographia, or some physiological descriptions of minute bodies made by magnifying glasses. 1665.

Reproduced as vol. xiii of Gunther, *Early Science in Oxford* (2826). One of the first publications of microscopic observations. See also Gunther (2886) and no. 2908.

2880 GREW, NEHEMIAH. The anatomy of plants. 1682.

Grew used the microscope to study the structure of plants.

2881 RAY, JOHN. Historia plantarum generalia. 3 vols. 1686–1704.

Sachs says this 'treats of the whole of theoretical botany in the style of a modern textbook'. See also his *Synopsis methodica stirpium Britannicarum*, 1690 and 1724; *Synopsis methodica animalium*, 1693; *Methodus insectorum*, 1705; *Historia insectorum*, 1710; all of them were landmarks in the history of biology.

Cf. the excellent biography by C. E. Raven, Camb. 1942. Also I. P. Stevenson, 'John Ray and his contributions to plant and animal classification', *Jour. of the Hist. of Med. and Allied Sciences*, 2 (1947), 250–61. A bibl. was compiled by G. Keynes, 1951.

2882 WILLUGHBY, FRANCIS. Ornithologiae libri tres. 1676.

See also his *De historia piscium libri quinque*, 2 vols., 1685–6. Both of these works were as much the work of Ray as of Willughby and constitute further dimensions of his achievement.

(b) *Later Works*

2883 ARBOR, A. R. Herbals, their origin and evolution, a chapter in the history of botany, 1470–1670. Camb. 1912. Bibl.

2884 CLAY, R. S. and COURT, T. H. The history of the microscope. 1932.

2885 NORDENSKIOLD, E. A history of biology. Trans. by L. B. Eyre. N.Y. 1928.

The standard work. Cf. C. Singer, *A history of biology*, rev. edn., N.Y. 1950.

2886 RAVEN, C. E. English naturalists from Neckam to Ray. Camb. 1947.

Dealing chiefly with developments before 1660 is R. W. T. Gunther, *Early British botanists*, Oxf. 1922.

2887 SACHS, J. VON. History of botany, 1530–1860. Trans. by H. E. F. Garnsey. Oxf. 1890 and 1906.

A basic work.

7. MEDICINE

(a) *Bibliography and Sources*

2888 GARRISON, F. H. and MORTON, L. T. A medical bibliography; a checklist of texts illustrating the history of medical sciences. 1943.

Cf. F. H. Garrison, (1) 'Medical and scientific periodicals of the 17th and 18th centuries'; (2) 'Medicine in the *Tatler, Spectator*, and *Guardian*', *Bull. Inst. Hist. Medicine*, 2 (1934), 285–343, 477–503. See also *A catalogue of the printed books in the Wellcome Historical Medical Library*, vol. 1, Books printed before 1641, 1962.

2889 MERRETT, CHRISTOPHER. Catalogus librorum . . . in Musaeo Harveano. 1660.

The earliest catalogue of the library of the Royal College of Physicians. See also Royal College of Physicians of London, *Catalogue of the library*, 1912. Cf. W. B. Taylor, *Catalogue of the library of the Society of Apothecaries*, ed. by J. E. Harting, 1913.

2890 ROYAL COLLEGE OF PHYSICIANS. Pharmacopoea Londinensis in qua medicamenta antiqua et nova usitatissima, sedulo collecta, accuratissime examinata . . . discribuntur. Opera medicorum collegii Londinensis. 1618.

There are many edns. and trans. Cf. N. Culpeper, *A physicall directory, or a translation of the London dispensatory . . . with many hundred additions*, 1649. See W. R. Munk, *The roll of the Royal College of Physicians of London, comprising biographical sketches of all the eminent physicians*, 2 vols., 1861, later edn., 3 vols., 1878. Also *The statutes of the Colledge of Physicians in London*, 1693. Cf. C. C. Gillispie, 'Physick and philosophy; a study of the influence of the College of Physicians of London upon the foundation of the Royal Society', *J.M.H.* 19 (1947), 210–25.

2891 HARVEY, WILLIAM. Guilielmi Harveii opera omnia; a Collegio Medicorum Londinensi edita. 1766. Later edn. by R. Willis. 1847.

Edn. of 1847 is a trans. from the Latin. See especially *De motu cordis*, 1628, and *Exercitationes de generatione animalium*, 1651. Cf. G. L. Keynes, ed., *The anatomical exercises of Dr. William Harvey*, 1928, and his *Bibliography of the writings of William Harvey*, Camb. 1928, rev. edn. 1953; and *Memorials of Harvey, including a letter and autographs in facsimile*, ed. by J. H. Aveling, 1875. For biography see D'A. Power, *William Harvey*, 1897; a brief one by A. Malloch, N.Y. 1929; and an important scholarly one by L. Chauvois, N.Y. 1957, bibl. See also H. P. Bayon, 'William Harvey, physician and biologist; his precursors, opponents and successors', *Annals of Science*, 3 (1938), 59–118, 435–56; 4 (1939), 65–106; 5 (1939), 329–89; and his 'William Harvey (1578–1657): his application of biological experiment, clinical observations, and comparative anatomy to the problems of generation', *Jour. of the Hist. of Med. and Allied Sciences*, 2 (1947), 51–96; and also D. Fleming, 'William Harvey and the pulmonary circulation', *Isis*, 46 (1955), 319–27.

2892 WILLIS, THOMAS. Opera omnia. Amsterdam. 1682.

Trans. as *Dr. Willis's practice of physick*, 1684.

2893 CULPEPER, NICHOLAS. The English physician enlarged with 269 medicines made of English herbs. 1652. 1653.

Cf. G. A. Gordon, ed., *Culpeper's works . . .*, 3 vols., 1802.

2894 LOWER, RICHARD. Tractatus de corde. 1669.

Reproduced in Gunther, *Early Science in Oxford*, vol. ix. Harvey's most important successor in the 17th century. Cf. F. Gotch, *Two Oxford physiologists*, Oxf. 1908, studies of Lower and Mayow; and E. H. and P. M. Hoff, 'The life and times of Richard Lower, physiologist and physician (1631–1691)', *Bull. Inst. Hist. Medicine*, 4 (1936), 517–35. For bibl. see J. F. Fulton, 'A bibliography of two Oxford physiologists, Richard Lower (1631–1691) and John Mayow (1643–1679)', *Oxford Bibliographical Society Proceedings and Papers*, 4 (1935), 1–62.

2895 TYSON, EDWARD. Ourang-outgang, sive homo sylvestris, or the anatomy of a pygmy. 1699.

Really deals with the chimpanzee; one of a series of monographs relating to single species by a pioneer in comparative anatomy. Cf. M. F. Ashley-Montagu, *Edward Tyson, M.D., F.R.S., 1650–1708, and the rise of human and comparative anatomy in England; a study in the history of science*, Phila. 1943.

2896 SYDENHAM, THOMAS. Opera omnia. Ed. by W. A. Greenhill. 1846. Later edn. in Eng. trans. by R. G. Latham. 2 vols. 1848–50.

A pioneer in clinical medical study. Cf. J. D. Comrie, *Selected works of Thomas Sydenham with short biography and explanatory notes*, 1922; J. F. Payne's biography, 1900; and R. M. Yost, Jr., 'Sydenham's philosophy of science', *Osiris*, 9 (1950), 84–105.

2897 BOYLE, ROBERT. Medicinal experiments: or, a collection of choice remedies, for the most part simple, and easily prepared. 1692.

Three vols. were publ. 1692–4.

(b) *Later Works*

2898 BULLETIN of the history of medicine. Baltimore. 1939+.

Preceded by *Bulletin of the Institute of the History of Medicine*, 1933–8. Other journals are *Annals of Medical History*, N.Y. 1917–42; and *Medical History*, Lond. 1957+.

2899 FOSTER, M. Lectures in the history of physiology during the sixteenth, seventeenth, and eighteenth centuries. Camb. 1924.

Should be used with care.

2900 GARRISON, F. H. Introduction to the history of medicine. 4th edn. N.Y. 1929.

2901 SHRYOCK, R. H. The development of modern medicine. Phila. 1936. Rev. edn. N.Y. 1947.

One of the best surveys. A more synthetic treatment is A. Castiglioni, *A history of medicine*, trans. by E. B. Krumbhaar, N.Y. 1941.

2902 SINGER, C. The evolution of anatomy. 1925.

A valuable survey. Cf. F. J. Cole, *A history of comparative anatomy*, 1944.

8. Individual Scientists

Men not fully covered under any of the prior headings. See also nos. 1901, 1955.

2903 WARD, J. The lives of the professors of Gresham College. 1740.

Contains much useful information.

2904 BACON, FRANCIS. Novum organum. 1620.

Cf. *The advancement of learning* (2695); *New Atlantis*, 1627; and *Works* (Spedding, no. 403). See B. Farrington, *Francis Bacon, philosopher of industrial science*, N.Y. 1950; S. B. L. Penrose, *The reputation and influence of Francis Bacon in the seventeenth century*, N.Y. 1934. R. F. Jones, *Ancients and moderns* (St. Louis, 1936) has a great deal about his influence. For a biography see M. Sturt, 1932. Also see R. W. Gibson, *Francis Bacon, a bibliography of his works and of Baconiana to the year 1750*, Oxf. 1950; supplement, Pasadena, 1959.

2905 HARTLIB, SAMUEL. A discourse of husbandrie used in Brabant and Flanders. 3rd edn. 1654.

Hartlib was a great promoter of scientific and practical knowledge. See nos. 1877, 2934, 2961. Also see G. H. Turnbull, 'Samuel Hartlib's influence on the early history of the Royal Society', *Notes and Records of the Royal Society*, 19 (1953), 101–30; and D. Stimson, 'Hartlib, Haak and Oldenburg, intelligencers', *Isis*, 31 (1939–40), 309–26.

2906 WILKINS, JOHN. Mathematical and philosophical works. 2 vols. 1802.

First publ. in 4 pts., 1707–8. One of the early enthusiasts behind the Royal Society. Cf. D. Stimson, 'Dr. Wilkins and the Royal Society', *J.M.H.* 3 (1931), 539–63; and G. McColley, The Ross–Wilkins controversy', *Annals of Science*, 3 (1938), 153–89.

2907 PETTY, WILLIAM. The Petty papers. Some unpublished writings of Sir William Petty. Ed. by Marquis of Lansdowne. 2 vols. 1927.

Another amateur of great ability and wide interests. See also *The Petty–Southwell correspondence, 1676–1687*, ed. Marquis of Lansdowne, 1928; and E. Strauss, *Sir William Petty: portrait of a genius*, Lond. and Glencoe (Ill.), 1954.

2908 HOOKE, ROBERT. Lectures de potentia restitutive, or of spring, explaining the power of springing bodies . . . [1678].

Contains the well-known Hooke's law. A universal genius, Hooke dabbled in and contributed to nearly every field of research. See also no. 2879.

   Cf. *Life and work of Robert Hooke*, vols. vi, vii, viii, x, and xiii of Gunther, *Early Science in Oxford* (2826). See also M. 'Espinasse, *Robert Hooke*, Berkeley, 1956; E. N. da C. Andrade, 'Robert Hooke', *Proc. Royal Soc.* A, 201, 439–73; L. D. Patterson, 'Hooke's gravitation theory and its influence on Newton', *Isis*, 40 (1949), 327–41, 41 (1950), 32–45, and her 'Pendulums of Wren and Hooke', *Osiris*, 10 (1952), 277–321. A. Koyré replies to the first in 'A note on Robert Hooke', *Isis*, 41 (1950), 195. D. J. Lysaght, 'Hooke's theory of combustions', *Ambix*, 1 (1927), 93–108. *The Diary of Robert Hooke, 1672–1680*, was ed. by H. W. Robinson and W. Adams, 1935.

2909 GLANVILL, JOSEPH. Essays on several important subjects in philosophy and religion. 1676.

   Cf. *Plus ultra: or, the progress and advancement of knowledge since the days of Aristotle*, 1668. Glanvill was an important publicist and defender of the scientific cause. See F. Greenslet, *Joseph Glanvill, a study in English thought and letters of the seventeenth century*, N.Y. 1900, bibl.; M. E. Prior, 'Joseph Glanvill, witchcraft, and seventeenth-century science', *Modern Philology*, 30 (1932), 167–93; J. I. Cope, *Joseph Glanvill, Anglican apologist*, St. Louis, 1956. See also nos. 2321, 2700.

9. THE SOCIAL RELATIONS OF SCIENCE

(a) *The Royal Society*

2910 THE RECORD of the Royal Society. 4th edn. 1940.

Contains chronological lists of officers, fellows, prizes, etc. See also *Notes and records of the Royal Society*, n.d.

2911 PHILOSOPHICAL TRANSACTIONS of the Royal Society. 1665+.

Vols. i–xxix cover 1665–1716. Cf. a general index by P. H. Maty, 1787; an abridgement to 1700, ed. by John Lowthorp, 1705; and another 1700–20, by H. Jones. For other abridgements, etc., see Lowndes, pp. 2143–7.

2912 SPRAT, THOMAS. The history of the Royal Society of London for the improving of natural knowledge. 1667. Later edn. with critical apparatus by J. I. Cope and H. W. Jones. St. Louis. 1958.

An early defence of the Royal Society.

2913 BIRCH, T. The history of the Royal Society of London. 4 vols. 1756–7.

A transcription of the minutes to 1887. Cf. C. R. Weld, *A history of the Royal Society, with memoirs of the presidents*, 2 vols., 1848; based on Birch through the early period.

2914 JOHNSON, F. R. 'Gresham college: precursor of the Royal Society.' *Jour. Hist. Ideas*, 1 (1940), 413–38.

2915 ORNSTEIN, M. The role of scientific societies in the seventeenth century. 3rd edn. by A. E. Cohn. Chicago and Camb. 1938.

Incomparable as a reference book for the history of scientific academies and a valuable addition to the history of science.

2916   STIMSON, D. Scientists and amateurs: a history of the Royal Society.
N.Y. 1948.

A readable informative history. Cf. her 'The critical years of the Royal Society, 1672–
1703', *Journal of the Hist. of Med. and Allied Sciences*, 2 (1947), 283–98, and 'Amateurs
of science in 17th-century England', *Isis*, 31 (1939–40), 32–47. See also the valuable
study by H. Lyons, *The Royal Society, 1660–1940, a history of its administration under
its charters*, Camb. 1944.

2917   SYFRET, R. H. 'The origins of the Royal Society.' *Notes and Records
of the Royal Society*, 5 (1948), 75–137.

Argues that the famous 'invisible college' was not identical with the group from which
the Royal Society grew. For the other side see D. Stimson, 'Comenius and the "invisible
college"' (2933 n.).

(b) *The Impact of Science*

See also B. Willey (2569), S. L. Bethel (2557), G. N. Clark (2517), G. R. Cragg
(1192), and W. E. H. Lecky (1132).

2918   HOUGHTON, W. E., Jr. 'The English virtuoso in the seventeenth century.' *Jour. Hist. Ideas*, 3 (1942), 51–73.

A study of the motivations behind the amateurs in science.

2919   JONES, R. F. 'Science and criticism in the neo-classical age of English
literature' (pp. 41–74). 'Science and English prose style in the third quarter of
the seventeenth century' (pp. 75–110). 'Science and language in England of
the mid-seventeenth century.' *The seventeenth century. Studies in the history
of English thought and literature from Bacon to Pope*. By R. F. Jones and others
writing in his honor. Stanford. 1951.

2920   MERTON, R. K. 'Science, technology and society in seventeenth century England.' *Osiris*, 4 (1938), 360–632.

Pioneering sociological study of the values which helped promote the growth of the
scientific movement and shifts in the foci of scientific interest. See also no. 2036.
Cf. his 'Puritanism, piety and science', *Sociol. Rev.* 28 (1936), 1–30, 'Some economic
factors in seventeenth-century English science', *Scientia*, 62 (1937), 142–52, and 'Science
and the economy of seventeenth-century England', *Science and Society*, 3 (1939), 3–27.

2921   NICOLSON, M. 'The "new astronomy" and English literary imagination.' *Studies in Philology*, 32 (1935), 428–62.

Cf. her 'The telescope and imagination', *Modern Philology*, 32 (1935), 233–60; 'A world
in the moon, a study of the changing attitude toward the moon in the seventeenth and
eighteenth centuries', *Smith College studies in modern language*, 17 (1936), and 'The
microscope and English imagination', ibid. 16 (1935). See also no. 2564.

2922   WESTFALL, R. S. Science and religion in seventeenth-century England. New Haven. 1958.

G. EDUCATION

A general history of education for the period has not been written, and certain
types of schools, such as writing schools and dames' schools, have still to be
studied. There is a growing number of books on individual local schools, and

on the universities and their separate colleges. Rich collections of source materials at the universities await use for the study of particular aspects of seventeenth-century interest and practice.

1. GENERAL

(a) *Bibliography*

2923 ADAMSON, J. W. Guide to the history of education (Helps for students of history). 1920.

> See also his chapter and bibl. in vol. ix of *Camb. Hist. Eng. Lit.* (2579). Some bibliographical notes on early education in Great Britain, by W. C. Hazlitt, were pr. in vols. 35 and 36 of *The Antiquary* (1899).

2924 HEAL, A. The English writing-masters and their copy-books 1570–1800; a biographical dictionary and bibliography. Camb. 1931.

2925 RAVEN-HART, H. E., and JOHNSTON, M. 'Bibliography of the registers (printed) of the universities, inns of court, colleges, and schools of Great Britain and Ireland.' *Bull. Inst. Hist. Research*, 9 (1932), 19–30, 65–83, 154–70.

2926 WATSON, F. 'The curriculum and text books of English schools in the first half of the seventeenth century.' *Trans. of the Bibliog. Soc.* 6, pt. ii (1903), pp. 159–267.

> A full bibl. See also Watson's *English Grammar Schools* (2969); and A. W. Tuer, *History of the horn-book*, 2 vols., 1896, 1897.

(b) *Sources*

On the 'education of gentlemen', see also Peacham and Brathwaite, in *Social History* (no. 2203). Articles on education appear also in the literary periodicals toward the end of the period, such as *Spectator* (3090), nos. 157, 168, 307; *Tatler* (3089), nos. 63, 173, 197; *Guardian* (3091), nos. 72, 94.

2927 LEACH, A. F., ed. Educational charters and documents 598–1909. Camb. 1911.

> Leach compiled also *Documents illustrating early education in Worcester, 685–1700*, Worc. Hist. Soc., 1913; and *Early Yorkshire Schools*, Yorks. Arch. Soc. Rec. Ser. 27 (1899) and 33 (1903). The introductions are valuable, as are Leach's chapters on schools in various volumes of the *Victoria County History* (3120).

2928 SHADWELL, L. L. Enactments in Parliament, specially concerning the universities of Oxford and Cambridge, the colleges and halls therein, and the colleges of Winchester, Eton and Westminster. Oxf. Hist. Soc. 4 vols. Oxf. 1912.

> Vol. i, 37 Edward III–13 Anne.

2929 BACON, FRANCIS, Viscount St. Albans. The two bookes of Francis Bacon of the advancement . . . of learning . . . 1606.

> The first English edn. of the work. See also the *Works* (403).

2930 BRINSLEY, JOHN. Ludus literarius: or, the grammar schoole. 1612. 1627. Later edn. by E. T. Campagnac. Liverpool. 1917.

Excellent contemporary comment. See also Brinsley's *Consolation for our grammar schooles*, 1622, repr. and ed. by T. C. Pollock, N.Y. 1943.

2931 MINSHEU, JOHN. Ἡγεμὼν εἰς τὰς Γμῶσσας id est Ductor in Linguas: the guide into tongues. 1617.

See also Hezekiah Woodward, *A light to grammar*, 1641.

2932 MORRICE, THOMAS. An apologie for schoolemasters, tending to the advancement of learning and the vertuous education of children. 1619.

Cf. Edmund Coote, *The Englishe schoolemaister*, first publ. 1596, with edns. in 1627, 1630, and later.

2933 COMENIUS, JOHN AMOS. The great didactic. Trans. and ed. by M. W. Kearinge. 1910.

This major work of the Moravian educator, though written about 1628–32, was publ. in Latin in Amsterdam, 1657. His *Janua linguarum reserata*, written in 1628, and publ. in England in 1632 (many later edns. on the Continent) was widely discussed by those interested in educational reform, such as Hartlib (q.v.). Also important was Comenius's *Informatory of the mother school*, publ. in Germany in 1633, and in Amsterdam in 1657, and recently ed. by E. M. Eller as *The school of infancy*, Chapel Hill, N.C. 1956. Documents relating to his 1641 visit to England have been ed. by R. F. Young, *Comenius in England*, 1932. In commemoration of that visit is the collection of essays and addresses, *The teacher of nations . . .*, ed. by N. J. T. M. Needham, Camb. 1942. See also M. Spinka's biography, *John Amos Comenius*, Chicago, 1943, with a good bibl.; D. Stimson, 'Comenius and the invisible college', *Isis*, 23 (1935), 373–88; M. Spinka, 'Comenian pansophic principles', *Church History*, 22 (1953), 155–65; and Turnbull (2934 n.).

2934 HARTLIB, SAMUEL. A description of the famous kingdom of Macaria. 1641.

Hartlib publ. his trans. of two works by Comenius under the title *A reformation of schools designed in two excellent treatises*, 1642–8. Other works by Hartlib are: *Considerations tending to the happy accomplishment of England's reformation in church and state*, 1647; *London's charity inlarged* (2537); and *The true and readie way to learn the Latine tongue*, 1654. See other writings in G. H. Turnbull, ed., *Hartlib, Dury, and Comenius*, Liverpool, 1947. Important treatises influenced by Hartlib are nos. 2935–7. See also no. 2905.

2935 MILTON, JOHN. Of education. To Master Samuel Hartlib. 1644. 1673. Ed. by O. Browning. Camb. 1883. 1895.

There are numerous other edns. of this famous 'Tractate on Education', such as that by O. M. Ainsworth, New Haven, 1928. See also Fletcher (2634 n.).

2936 PETTY, SIR WILLIAM. The advice of W.P. to Mr. S. Hartlib for the advancement of some particular parts of learning. 1647. 1648.

Repr. in *Harl. Misc.* (59), vol. vi. Sets forth Petty's idea of universal schools, in line with Hartlib's views.

2937 DURIE [or DURY], J[OHN]. The reformed school. [1649?]

Cf. Dury's *The reformed librarie-keeper, with a supplement to the reformed school* [1650]. See a modern edn. of both *The reformed school* and the supplement by H. M. Knox,

Liverpool, 1958. Dury, like Milton and Petty, shows the influence of Hartlib. See also John Hall's *Humble Petition to the Parliament of England concerning the advancement of learning*, 1649.

2938 DELL, WILLIAM. 'The right reformation of learning, schools and universities.' In *Select works of William Dell*. 1773.

The pamphlet, printed *c.* 1650, criticized both the influence of classical writers and the exclusiveness of the universities.

2939 WEBSTER, JOHN. Academiarum examen, or the examination of academies wherein is discussed . . . academick and scholastick learning. 1654.

Advocates university reform. For replies to some points by Bishop Seth Ward, see Ward's *Vindiciae academiarum*, 1654. See also Abraham Cowley, *Propositions for the advancement of experimental philosophy*, 1661 (repr. in his *Essays*, 1886), proposing a 'philosophical college'.

2940 HOOLE, CHARLES. A new discovery of the old art of teaching schoole, in four small treatises. 1660. Later edn. by E. T. Campagnac. Liverpool. 1913. Bibl. index.

2941 N[EDHAM], M[ARCHAMONT]. A discourse concerning schools and schoolmasters. 1663.

2942 BURNET, GILBERT. Thoughts on education. 1761.

Written about 1668. See J. Clarke, *Bishop Gilbert Burnet as educationist . . .*, Aberdeen, 1914.

2943 MAKIN, MRS. BATHSUA. An essay to revive the antient education of gentlewomen in religion, manners, arts and tongues. 1673.

See also George Savile, Marquis of Halifax, *The lady's new years gift, or advice to a daughter*, 1688, repr. with annotation and bibl. in H. C. Foxcroft's *Life of Halifax* (452), ii. 379–424.

2944 WALKER, OBADIAH. Of education, especially of young gentlemen. Oxf. 1673. 6th edn. 1699.

Cf. Stephen Peyton, *Guardian's instruction, or The gentleman's romance . . .*, 1688, repr. 1897; and Peyton's *New instructions to the guardian*, 1694. For others, see G. C. Brauer, *The education of a gentleman: theories of gentlemanly education in England, 1660–1775*, N.Y. 1959.

2945 WASE, CHRISTOPHER. Considerations concerning the free schools as settled in England. Oxf. 1678.

Information about grammar schools.

2946 LOCKE, JOHN. Some thoughts concerning education. 1693. Later edn. by R. H. Quick. Camb. 1898.

Repr., together with *Of the conduct of the understanding*, in *The educational writings of John Locke*, ed. by J. W. Adamson, 1912, 1922. An edn. from Locke's first draft (Br. Mus., Add. MS. 38771) was publ. by F. G. Kenyon, *John Locke, Directions concerning education . . .*, Oxf. 1933.

2947 WOTTON, WILLIAM. Reflections upon ancient and modern learning. 1694. 2nd edn. 1697. 3rd edn. 1705.

> The 2nd and 3rd edns. are prefixed to Richard Bentley's *Dissertation upon the epistles of Phalaris*; the 3rd edn. includes also Wotton's *Defence* in answer to objections by Sir W. Temple and others.
>
> Wotton's own early education is described in *Essay on the education of children in the first rudiments of learning*, written in 1672 by his father, Henry Wotton, and publ. in 1753. Cf. Th. Tryon, *New method of educating children*, 1695.

2948 AINSWORTH, ROBERT. The most natural and easie way of institution, containing proposals for making a domestic education less chargeable to parents, and more easie and beneficial to children. 1698. 1699. 1736.

> See also [Th. Baker], *Reflections upon learning . . .*, 1699, 1700, and later edns.; and F[rancis] B[rokesby], *Of education with respect to grammar schools and the universities*, 1701.

2949 WESLEY, SAMUEL. A letter from a country divine to his friend in London concerning the education of dissenters in their private academies . . . 1702. 3rd edn. 1706.

> Written in 1693. Samuel Palmer replied with *A defence of the dissenters education*, 1703; Wesley answered in *Defence of a letter*, 1704; Henry Sacheverell entered the controversy with *Nature and mischief of prejudice and partiality stated*, Oxf. 1704; and Palmer's *Vindication*, 1705, was in reply to both Sacheverell and Wesley; Wesley answered with *A reply to Mr. Palmer's 'Vindication'*, 1707.

2950 MAIDWELL, LEWIS. Essay upon the necessity and excellency of education, with an account of erecting the royal mathematical schole. 1705. Repr. with intro. by J. M. Patrick. Los Angeles. 1955.

2951 AN ACCOUNT OF CHARITY-SCHOOLS in Great Britain and Ireland: with the benefactions thereto. 1704. 13th edn. with additions. 1714.

> Titles of edns. vary; the first edn. is appended to Richard Willis, *Sermon . . ., June 8, 1704*; the 1705 title was *An account of the methods whereby the charity-schools have been erected and managed.*
>
> Also on the charity schools see James Talbott, *Christian school master . . .*, 1707, 1711, 1811, and William Dawes, *Excellence of the charity of charity-schools*, 1713.

(c) *Later Works*

2952 ADAMSON, J. W. Pioneers in modern education, 1600–1700. Camb. 1905. Bibl.

> Scholarly. See also his *Short history of education*, Camb. 1905; and his chapter in *Camb. Hist. Engl. Lit.*, vol. ix, chap. 15. Cf. M. L. Clarke, *Classical education in Britain, 1500–1900*, Camb. 1959; and L. Stone, 'The educational revolution in England, 1560–1649', *Past and Present*, no. 28 (July 1964), 41–80.

2953 BEALES, A. C. F. 'Popish schools under James I.' *Month*, N.S. 7 (1952), 199–209.

> Scholarly article. A similar study by Beales on the period of Charles I is ibid., N.S. 10 (1953), 12–27.

2954   DE MONTMORENCY, J. E. G.   State intervention in English education (to 1833). Camb. 1902.

> Useful. See also his *Progress of education in England*, 1904. More general in treatment, with stress on the 18th century, is A. E. Dobbs, *Education and social movements, 1700–1850*, 1919.

2955   DOWLING, P. J.   Hedge schools of Ireland. 1935. Bibl.

> Sketches popular education in Ireland to 1831. For other titles see C. L. Grose (10), p. 114, and *Irish History*.

2956   EDWARDS, E.   Lives of the founders of the British Museum; with notices of its chief augmentors and other benefactors 1570–1870. 1870.

2957   GARDINER, D.   English girlhood at school: a study of women's education through twelve centuries. 1929.

> Useful. Cf. M. Reynolds, *The learned lady in England, 1650–1760*, Boston, 1920, bibl.

2958   LAMBLEY, K.   The teaching and cultivation of the French language in England during Tudor and Stuart times. Manchester. 1920.

> Excellent.

2959   McLACHLAN, H.   English education under the test acts, being a history of the nonconformist academies, 1622–1820. Manchester. 1931. Bibl.

> Valuable material on new schools which opened after the closing of the universities to dissenters. Cf. J. W. A. Smith, *The birth of modern education: the contribution of the dissenting academies, 1660–1800*, 1954; and W. T. Whitley, 'Private schools, 1660–1689', *Congreg. Hist. Soc. Trans.* 12 (1934), 172–85.

2960   MORGAN, A.   Rise and progress of Scottish education. Lond. and Edin. 1927.

> See also earlier histories by Grant (3973); J. Strong, Oxf. 1909; and Kerr (3977).

2961   TURNBULL, G. H.   Samuel Hartlib: a sketch of his life and his relations to J. A. Comenius. 1920.

> Cf. H. Dircks, *A biographical memoir of Samuel Hartlib . . . with bibliographical notice of works published by him*, 1865; and no. 2934.

2962   VINCENT, W. A. L.   The state and school education 1640–1660 in England and Wales. 1950. Bibl.

> Based on printed sources, but very useful. App. A. lists the grammar schools in existence in England and Wales between 1600 and 1660. Cf. F. Watson, 'The state and education during the commonwealth', *E.H.R.* 15 (1900), 58–72.

2963   WATSON, F.   The beginnings of the teaching of modern subjects in England. 1909.

> Valuable, especially for bibliographical notes. Cf. F. A. Yeldham, *The teaching of arithmetic through four hundred years (1535–1935)*, 1936; and D. K. Wilson, *The history of mathematical teaching in Scotland to the end of the eighteenth century*, 1935.

2. Schools and Schoolmasters

No attempt is made here to list all titles on schools. Useful lists of registers in print are in Raven-Hart (2925); lists of schools, with their histories, are in Mullinger (2967) and Vincent (2962). A few recent titles not in those lists have been included with the list of more general titles below. For schools in particular counties see *Victoria County History*, sections on 'schools' (3120).

2964   ACKERMANN, R. The history of the colleges of Winchester, Eton, and Westminster, with the Charter-house, the schools of St. Paul's, Merchant Taylors', Harrow, and Rugby, and the free-school of Christ's Hospital. 1816.

Standard separate histories are Sir H. C. Maxwell Lyte on Eton, 1875, 4th edn., 1911 (not superseded by G. Hollis's *Eton*, 1960); H. B. Wilson on Merchant Taylors', 2 vols., 1812–14, which should be checked by the 1929 (Oxf.) *Merchant Taylors' School*; J. Sargeaunt's *Annals of Westminster School*, 1898, which should be compared with L. E. Tanner's history, 1934; and E. H. Pearce, *Annals of Christ's Hospital*, 1901, as well as the later account by E. Blunden, 1923.

2965   CARLISLE, N. A concise description of the endowed grammar schools in England and Wales, ornamented with engravings. 2 vols. 1818.

Arranged alphabetically by shires.

2966   HAZLITT, W. C. Schools, school-books, and schoolmasters. 1888.

Much miscellaneous information. See the same author's 'Farther contributions . . .', *The Antiquary*, N.S., no. 109 (1899–1900). See also G. F. R. Barker's *Memoir of Richard Busby (1606–95)*, 1895, for an account of a headmaster at Westminster School.

2967   MULLINGER, J. B. 'English grammar schools.' *Camb. Hist. Eng. Lit.* vii (1911), chap. xiv.

The bibl. includes a list of the chief public schools (to 1650) and of histories of them. Recent histories include C. R. Forder on Paston Grammar School (Norfolk), 1934, and J. B. Oldham on Shrewsbury School, Oxf. 1952.

2968   PARKER, I. Dissenting academies in England. Camb. 1914. Bibl.

Has a list of academies in appendix.

2969   WATSON, F. The English grammar schools to 1660, their curriculum and practice. Camb. 1908.

By Watson also, *Old Grammar Schools*, Camb. 1916; and articles in *Gentleman's Mag.* 291 (1901), 229–44; 293 (1902), 286–97, 553–69; 295 (1903), 428–43; and *Trans. Bibl. Soc.* 6 (1903), 159–267.

3. Universities and Colleges

(a) *General*

For matriculates, with biographical notes, see Foster, *Alumni Oxonienses* (2426), and Venn, *Alumni Cantabrigienses* (2428); for registers, see Raven-Hart (2925).

2970   COSTELLO, W. T. The scholastic curriculum at early seventeenth-century Cambridge. Camb. (Mass.). 1958. Bibl.

Based on much MS. material; valuable for intellectual interests of the time.

2971 CURTIS, M. H. Oxford and Cambridge in transition, 1558–1642. Oxf. 1959.

Excellent, with special emphasis upon the impact of religious and social change. Cf. P. Allen, 'Scientific studies in 17th-century English universities', *Jour. Hist. Ideas*, 10 (1949), 219–53.

2972 WORDSWORTH, C. Social life at the English universities in the eighteenth century. Camb. 1874. Abr. edn. 1928.

Cf. his valuable *Scholae academicae: some account of the studies at the English universities in the eighteenth century*, Camb. 1877. Both works contain seventeenth-century material. Chiefly Cambridge examples are included in J. Venn, *Early collegiate life*, Camb. 1913. Cf. *College life in the time of James I as illustrated by an unpublished diary of Sir Symonds D'Ewes* [ed. by J. H. Marsden], 1851.

(b) *Oxford University*

2973 MADAN, F. Oxford books: a bibliography of printed works relating to the university and city of Oxford or printed or published there. Oxf. 3 vols. 1895–1931.

Cf. his *Rough list of manuscript materials relating to the history of Oxford contained in the printed catalogues of the Bodleian and college libraries*, Oxf. 1887.

2974 STATUTES OF THE COLLEGES of Oxford with royal patents of foundation; injunction of visitors . . . 3 vols. Oxf. and Lond. 1853. Suppl. 1855.

See also *Statutes of the University of Oxford codified . . . 1636 under the authority of Archbishop Laud*, ed. by J. Griffiths and C. L. Shadwell, Oxf. 1888. Laud's account of his chancellorship is in vol. v of his *Works* (1266), having been printed first in vol. i of H. Wharton's edn. of *Laud's remains*, 1700. See also Shadwell (2928).

2975 THE REGISTER of the visitors of the University of Oxford 1647–1658 . . . with some account of the state of the university during the commonwealth. Ed. by M. Burrows. Camd. Soc. N.S. 29. 1881.

See also *The Restoration visitation . . .*, ed. by F. J. Varley, *Camden Misc.* xviii, 3rd Ser. 79 (1948).

2976 WOOD, ANTHONY À. The history and antiquities of the University of Oxford. Ed. by J. Gutch. 2 vols. in 3. Oxf. 1792–6.

First publ. in Latin as *Historia et antiquitates . . .*, 2 vols., Oxf. 1674. See also A. Clark, ed., *The life and times of Anthony Wood, 1632–1695, described by himself*, 5 vols., Oxf. 1891–1900, abr. ed. by L. Powys, 1932. Less valuable than Wood's history is John Ayliffe, *Antient and present state of the University of Oxford*, 2 vols., 1714, 1723.

2977 MALLETT, SIR C. E. A history of the University of Oxford. 3 vols. 1924–7.

The best history; vol. ii relates to the period. See also R. Ackermann, *History of the University of Oxford*, 2 vols., 1814. On science at Oxford, see Gunther (2826).

2978 CLARK, A., ed. The colleges of Oxford: their history and traditions. 1891. 2nd edn. 1892.

A series of *University of Oxford college histories* was publ. by Robinson, 19 vols., 1898–

1903; and various separate histories have been published by the Oxf. Hist. Soc.: G. C. Brodrick, *Merton*, 1885; T. Fowler, *Corpus Christi*, 1893; D. Macleane, *Pembroke*, 1897; *Brasenose College quarter centenary monographs*, 3 vols., 1909–10; W. C. Costin, *St. John's*, 1958. See also J. R. Magrath, *Queen's College*, 2 vols., Oxf. 1921. Relating to the founding of Wadham College are *Letters of Dorothy Wadham, 1609–18*, ed. by R. B. Gardiner, 1904.

2979 RELIQUIAE BODLEIANAE or some genuine remains of Sir Thomas Bodley containing his life, the first draught of the statutes of the publick library at Oxford (in English) and a collection of letters. 1703.

See also *The Bodleian Library in the seventeenth century*, Oxf. 1951, an exhibition guide with useful notes; and articles in the *Bodleian Quart. Record*, 8 (1935), 6–15, 55–65; and *Bodleian Library Record*, 5 (1955), 130–46.

2980 YOUNG, R. F. A Bohemian philosopher at Oxford in the seventeenth century. 1925.

On the career of George Ritschel. See the author's article on Ritschel and other scholars in *E.H.R.* 38 (1923), 72–84. Cf. F. S. Boas, ed., *The diary of Thomas Crosfield*, 1935.

2981 MAGRATH, J. R., ed. The Flemings in Oxford, being documents selected from the Rydal papers in illustration of the lives and ways of Oxford men, 1650–1700. Oxf. Hist. Soc. 3 vols. Oxf. 1904–24.

See also Fleming MSS. (138).

2982 WOODWARD, MICHAEL. 'The annual progress of New College, by Michael Woodward, warden, 1659–1675.' *Records of Buckinghamshire*, 13 (1935), pp. 77–137.

Ed. by G. Eland; useful for economic information also.

2983 WARTON, T. Life and literary remains of Ralph Bathurst, Dean of Wells and President of Trinity College in Oxford. 1761.

2984 BLOXAM, J. R., ed. Magdalen College and King James II, 1686–1688. A series of documents. Oxf. Hist. Soc. Oxf. 1886. Bibl. of MSS.

Useful. Cf. H. G. Rawlinson, ed., 'Three letters of Dr. Richard Traffles', *Oxoniensia*, 79 (1942), 93–101; and E. D. Tappe, 'The Greek college at Oxford, 1699–1705', ibid. 19 (1954), 92–111.

2985 HEARNE, THOMAS. Remarks and collections. Ed. by C. E. Doble, D. W. Ronnie, and H. E. Salter. 11 vols. Oxf. Hist. Soc. Oxf. 1885–1921.

Notes on a wide range of subjects, 1705–35, and used by Hearne for his historical works. A selection was publ. by P. Bliss, *Reliquiae Hearnianae*, 2 vols., Oxf. 1857, and 3 vols., Lond. 1869.

(c) *Cambridge University*

2986 BOWES, R. Catalogue of books . . . relating to the university, town and county of Cambridge from 1521 to 1893. Camb. 1894.

Cf. A. T. Bartholomew, *Catalogue of the books . . . relating to the university . . . bequeathed . . . by J. W. Clark*, Camb. 1912; and G. R. Barnes, *List of books printed in Cambridge at the University Press, 1521–1800*, Camb. 1935.

2987   DOCUMENTS relating to the University and colleges of Cambridge. 3 vols. 1852.

Another collection useful for the period is *Cambridge University transactions during the puritan controversies of the 16th and 17th centuries*, ed. by J. Heywood and T. Wright, 2 vols., 1854.

2988   CLARK, J. W., ed. Endowments of the University of Cambridge. Camb. 1904.

Valuable. See also H. F. Howard, *An account of the finances of the college of St. John the Evangelist in the University of Cambridge, 1511–1926*, Camb. 1935.

2989   COOPER, C. H. Annals of Cambridge. 5 vols. Camb. 1842–53. Enl. edn. of vol. 5. Camb. 1908.

Vols. iii and iv cover 1603–1714. See also his *Memorials of Cambridge*, 2 vols., Camb. 1858–60. Thomas Fuller's *History of the University of Cambridge*, originally a part of his *Church history* (1170), was publ. in 1655, and in a later edn. by J. Nichols, in 1840.

2990   MULLINGER, J. B. The University of Cambridge. 3 vols. Camb. 1873–1911.

Valuable. Also by Mullinger, *Cambridge characteristics in the seventeenth century . . .* 1867. An earlier account is R. Ackermann, *History of Cambridge . . .*, 2 vols., 1815.

2991   UNIVERSITY OF CAMBRIDGE college histories. 16 vols. 1898–1906.

For other college histories see T. Baker (ed. by J. E. B. Mayor), *St. John*, 2 vols., Camb. 1869; J. Venn, *Biographical history of Gonville and Caius College*, 4 vols., Camb. 1897–1912; T. A. Walker, *Peterhouse*, Camb. 1906, new edn. 1935; W. H. S. Jones, *St. Catherine's College*, Camb. 1936. For registers, see Raven-Hart (2925).

2992   WORTHINGTON, JOHN. Diary and correspondence. Ed. by J. Crossley and R. C. Christie. Chetham Soc. 3 vols. 1847–86.

Dr. John Worthington was Master of Jesus College, and Vice-chancellor. The documents, mainly from Harl. MS. 7045, and covering 1632–7, include letters from S. Hartlib and others from Baker MSS., Camb. Univ. Libr., and Br. Mus., Add. MS. 32498. Cf. R. C. Christie, ed., *Bibliography of the works written and edited by Dr. J. Worthington*, Chetham Soc., N.S. 13 (1888). On another distinguished Cambridge scholar, Isaac Barrow, see nos. 1222, 2840. See also T. A. Walker, ed., *Memoirs of Joseph Beaumont, Master of Peterhouse 1663–1699 . . .*, Camb. 1934.

2993   MAYOR, J. E. B. Cambridge under Queen Anne, illustrated by memoir of Ambrose Bonwicke and diaries of Francis Burnham and Zacharias Conrad von Uffenbach. Camb. 1911.

The Bonwicke memoir, with the title *Life of Ambrose Bonwicke by his father*, was separately pr. in Camb. 1870.

2994   MONK, J. H. The life of Richard Bentley, Master of Trinity College [Cambridge]. 1830. Later edn. 2 vols. 1833.

The *Correspondence* of Bentley, the classical scholar, was ed. by C. Wordsworth, 2 vols., 1842; A. T. Bartholomew ed. *Richard Bentley, D.D., a bibliography of his works and all the literature called forth by his acts or writings*, Camb. 1908. A short life by Sir R. C. Jebb is in *English Men of Letters Series*, 1882.

(d) *Other Universities*

For Ireland, see *Irish History*. See also *Scottish History*.

2995 MORGAN, A. and HANNAY, R. K., eds. Charters, statutes . . . University of Edinburgh. 1937.

See articles relating to the period in *Univ. Edinburgh Jour.* 7 (1935), 213–19; and 9 (1938), 153–9; and see Grant (3972).

2996 COUTTS, J. History of the University of Glasgow. Glasgow. 1909.

See also H. M. B. Reid, *Divinity professors in the University of Glasgow*, Glasgow, 1923; and J. D. Mackie, *The University of Glasgow, 1451–1951*, Glasgow, 1954.

2997 HANNAY, R. K., ed. 'Visitation of St. Andrews University in 1690.' *S.H.R.* 13 (1916), 1–15.

See also W. C. Dickinson (3967 n.) and *The College of St. Salvador: commemoration of the 500th anniversary of the foundation, 1950 . . .*, Edin. 1952. See also Cant (3968).

H. SCHOLARSHIP

In the seventeenth century there was a continuation of the interest in scholarly work which had gained impetus in the Tudor period. The religious and political controversies of the age directed attention to church history, constitutional and legal history, and political theory, subjects which are dealt with in other chapters of this volume (Chs. III, IV, V). In addition, scholarship relating to language, both classical and English, produced some notable works. In historical studies, possibly spurred by the founding of the Society of Antiquaries in Elizabeth's reign, possibly also by social changes which attracted attention to local history, a new school of historical scholarship developed. In addition to such classics in royal biography as Lord Herbert of Cherbury's *Henry VIII*, Robert Cotton's *Henry III*, and Bacon's *Henry VII*, written essentially as manuals for statesmen, the period produced important publications from official manuscripts and some of the earliest of county regional histories. See also Camden's *Annals* (262 n.) and similar titles in Ch. II; and local histories in Ch. XI. There are useful chapters as well as bibliographies in vols. vii and ix of *Camb. Hist. Eng. Lit.* (2579).

I. BIBLIOGRAPHY AND REFERENCE

2998 KENNEDY, A. G. A bibliography of writings on the English language from the beginning of printing to the end of 1922. Camb. (Mass.) and New Haven. 1927.

Important also are the bibls. in Duff (3006) and Evans (3006 n.).

2999 SPARGO, J. W. 'Some reference books of the sixteenth and seventeenth centuries: a finding list.' *The Papers of the Bibliographical Society of America*, 31 (1937), 133–75.

Also publ. Lond. 1937. Annotated bibl. of some 123 works, not limited to English.

2. HISTORIOGRAPHY, OLD ENGLISH AND CLASSICAL STUDIES

(a) *Sources* (see also individual writers below)

3000 ROWLANDS, RICHARD [alias VERSTEGGEN, RICHARD.] Restitution of decayed intelligence in antiquities concerning the English nation. Antwerp. 1605. 1628. 1634. 1653. Lond. 1673.

Early period of English history; the chief work of Rowlands. For others, see *D.N.B.*

3001 BRAITHWAIT, RICHARD. A survey of history, or a nursery for gentry. 1638.

Extols history as a general study. On another contemporary commentator on history, see J. J. Murray, 'John Hales on history', *Hunt. Lib. Quart.* 19 (1956), 231–43.

3002 THE OPINIONS OF SEVERAL LEARNED ANTIQUARIES, viz. Dodridge, Agor, Tate, Camden, Holland, Cotton, Selden. Touching the antiquity . . . of the High Court of Parliament. 1658. 1685.

On the origin of this publication, and its influence, see E. Evans in *History*, 23 (1938), 206–21.

3003 BENTLEY, RICHARD, ed. Q. Horatius Flaccus, ex recensione et cum nutis atque emendationibus Richardi Bentleii. 2 vols. Camb. 1711. Various later edns. 2 vols. Berlin. 1869.

On Bentley's contributions to classical scholarship see no. 3006.

(b) *Later Works*

3004 ADAMS, E. N. Old English scholarship in England from 1566–1800. New Haven. 1917.

Useful. Deals with the growth of old English studies and the scholars who forwarded them.

3005 DOUGLAS, D. C. English scholars, 1660–1730. 1939. 2nd edn. rev. 1951.

Valuable critical study of the work of such historical scholars as Dugdale, Gale, Hickes, Wanley, Brady, Wharton, Madox, Rymer, and others.
  See the author's article on medievalists in *R.H.S. Trans.*, 4th Ser. 21 (1939), 21–39. On some of the problems of early antiquarians see the article by J. Butt, *Eng. Assoc. Essays & Studies for 1938*, 24 (1939), 64–79.

3006 DUFF, J. D. and ALDIS, H. G. 'Scholars and antiquaries. I. Bentley and classical scholarship. II. Antiquaries.' *Camb. Hist. Eng. Lit.* 9 (1912), ch. xiii.

The bibls. are especially valuable, listing the names of many less well-known scholars. Cf. vol. ii of Sir J. E. Sandys, *History of classical scholarship*, 3 vols., Camb. 1906–8, and H. R. Steeves, *Learned societies and English literary scholarship*, N.Y. 1913, bibl. Valuable bibl. and early chapters are in J. Evans, *History of the Society of Antiquaries*, Oxf. 1956.

3007 FOX, L., ed. English historical scholarship in the sixteenth and seventeenth centuries. (The Dugdale Society.) 1956.

Collection of valuable papers prepared for the tercentenary of the publication of Dugdale's *Warwickshire*. Included are R. B. Wernham, 'The public records in the sixteenth and seventeenth centuries'; M. Maclagan, 'Genealogy and heraldry in the sixteenth and seventeenth centuries'; P. Styles, 'Politics and historical research in the early seventeenth century'; a valuable chapter by H. A. Cronne on Sir Henry Spelman and Dugdale; and others. Cf. T. D. Kendrick, *British antiquity*, which deals with 'antiquarianism' from Geoffrey of Monmouth to the newer scholarship of the early seventeenth century.

3008   FUSSNER, F. S. The historical revolution: English historical writing and thought, 1580–1640. 1962.

Bibl. footnotes. See also Pocock (991) and Pocock's article in *Camb. Hist. Jour.* 10 (1951), 186–204; and Merchant (3603).

3009   STARNES, D. T. and NOYES, G. E. The English dictionary from Cawdrey to Johnson, 1604–1755. Chapel Hill. 1946.

On the makers, sources, and compilations of dictionaries in the period.

3010   TUVESON, E. L. Millenium and Utopia. Berkeley. 1949.

Examines the influence of religious views of the apocalypse upon the idea of progress. On the idea of decay, see Harris, *All coherence gone* (2560).

(c) *Individual Scholars*

See also Aubrey (2439), Coke (1079), Kennett (262), Selden (1075), Sibbald (3965), Wood (2976), and others.

ARCHER, SIMON

3011   Styles, P. Sir Simon Archer. Oxf. 1946. Dugdale Soc. Occasional Papers, no. 6.

ASHMOLE, ELIAS

3012   Memoirs of the life of that learned antiquary Elias Ashmole drawn up by himself by way of diary with an appendix of original letters. Ed. by C. Burman. 1717.

Repr. in *The lives of those eminent antiquaries Elias Ashmole and William Lilly*, 1774. Cf. *The diary and will of Elias Ashmole*, Oxf. 1927. The MS. together with other autobiographical matter is in Bodl. Libr., Ashmole MS. 1136. Cf. A. L. Humphreys, *Elias Ashmole* (repr. from the *Berks., Bucks., and Oxon. Arch. Jour.*), Reading, 1925; and D. Wright's *Elias Ashmole: founder of the Ashmolean Museum*, 1924. Ashmole's *The institution, laws and ceremonies of the most noble Order of the Garter* appeared in 1672 with engravings by Hollar.

AYLIFFE, JOHN

3013   Gibson, S. A neglected Oxford historian (John Ayliffe, 1676–1732). *In* Oxford essays presented to H. E. Salter. Oxf. 1934.

On a 17th-century historian of Cambridgeshire see W. M. Palmer, *John Layer (1586– 1640) of Shepreth*, Camb. 1935 (Camb. Antiq. Soc. Publ., no. 53).

BAXTER, WILLIAM

3014   J. E. Auden, trans. 'The life of William Baxter. Written by himself for the sake of his children.' *Shrops. Arch. and Nat. Hist. Soc. Trans.* 42 (1923–4), 127–40.

Addenda and corrigenda, ibid. 43 (1925–6), 142.

CHETHAM, HUMPHREY

3015 Raines, F. R. and Sutton, C. W. Life of Humphrey Chetham: founder of the Chetham Hospital and library, Manchester. 2 vols. Manchester. 1903.

Chetham Soc., N.S., vols. 49–50. Vol. ii mainly an appendix of documents. See also article by J. Rogan on Thomas Machell, antiquary, *Trans. Cumb. and West. Arch. Soc.*, N.S. 55 (1956), 132–53.

DODSWORTH, ROGER

3016 Denholm-Young, N. and Craster, H. H. E. 'Roger Dodsworth and his circle.' *Yorks. Arch. Jour.* 32 (1934), 5–32.

Includes bibl. description of Dodsworth's MS. works. See the same author's article of the same title in *Bodleian Quart. Rec.* 7 (1934), 409–19. For the relationship of Dodsworth to Dugdale and especially the former's work on the *Monasticon*, see Douglas (3005).

DUGDALE, SIR WILLIAM

3017 The life, diary [1643–86] and correspondence [1635–86] of Sir William Dugdale. Ed. by W. Hamper. 1827.

For a more complete bibl. of Dugdale's works, with notes on his life and his MS. sources, see *Sir William Dugdale, 1605–1686*, by F. Maddison, D. Styles, and A. Wood, Warwick, 1953. An important evaluation of his work is in Douglas (3005). Dugdale's *History of St. Paul's Cathedral*, publ. in 1658, was republ. in 1716, and, ed. by H. Ellis, in 1818. See also his *Warwickshire* (3261); and his important work on fen drainage (1935).

POCOCK, EDWARD

3018 Twells, L. The life of Dr. Edward Pocock, the celebrated orientalist.

In vol. i of 2 vols. entitled *The lives of Dr. Edward Pocock . . .* [1816]. For bibl. of the two scholars of the name, see no. 3006.

SPELMAN, SIR HENRY

3019 Gibson, E. 'Life of Sir Henry Spelman Kt.' *in* Gibson's edn. of *The English works of Sir Henry Spelman*. 2 pts. 1723. Later edn. 1727.

Bishop Gibson had publ. the posthumous works, *Reliquiae* (1013), in 1698. On Spelman as an historian see F. M. Powicke's lecture in *Proc. Brit. Acad.* 16 (1930), 345–77; and Fox (3007). See also *Legal History*, nos. 1097, 1098.

THORESBY, RALPH

3020 The diary of Ralph Thoresby (1677–1724) [and] letters of eminent men addressed to Ralph Thoresby. Ed. by J. Hunter. 4 vols. 1830–2.

Cf. D. H. Atkinson, *Ralph Thoresby the topographer; his town and times*, 2 vols., Leeds, 1885–7.

3. MAPS AND GEOGRAPHY

See also *Topography* (3107–15), especially such works as Camden (3107) and Gough (3111). On MS. collections, see Pargellis, pp. 370–1.

(a) Lists of Maps

3021 FORDHAM, SIR H. G. Studies in carto-bibliography. 1914.

Cf. Chubb (53), and Chubb's lists of maps for several counties, i.e. Wiltshire, Gloucestershire, Somerset, Norfolk. Other collections for different counties are Fordham, *Hertfordshire maps: a descriptive catalogue . . . 1579–1900*, Hertford, 1907, his list for Cambridgeshire, 1908, and his *Road-books* (3100); H. Whitaker, ed., *A descriptive list of the printed maps of Yorkshire . . . 1577–1900*, Wakefield, 1933, and his list for Lancashire, Manchester, 1938; and F. G. Emmison, ed., *Catalogue for maps in the Essex record office, 1566–1855*, Chelmsford, 1947. See also Taylor (3025).

3022 INGLIS, H. R. G., MATHIESON, J., and WATSON, C. B. B. The early maps of Scotland, with an account of the Ordnance Survey. Edin. 1934. 2nd edn. Edin. 1936.

See also *The maps of Edinburgh, 1544–1929*, by W. Cowan and C. B. B. Watson, Edin. 1932.

(b) Geography and Map-making

3023 BAKER, J. N. L. 'Academic geography in the seventeenth and eighteenth centuries.' *Scot. Geog. Mag.* 51 (1935), 129–44.

See also Darby (3117).

3024 GOBLET, Y. M. La transformation de la géographie politique de l'Irelande au XVIIᵉ siècle dans les cartes et essaies anthropo-géographiques de Sir William Petty. 2 vols. Paris. 1930.

3025 TAYLOR, E. G. R. Late Tudor and early Stuart geography. 1934. Bibl. Repr. N.Y. 1968.

A sequel to her *Tudor geography, 1485–1583*, and useful especially for the bibl. By Taylor also, 'The geographical ideas of Robert Hooke', *Geog. Jour.* 89 (1937), 525–38; 'Robert Hooke and the cartographical projects of the late seventeenth century . . .', ibid. 90 (1937), 529–40. Cf. R. H. Hill, 'The king's map-maker (John Ogilby)', *Blackwoods*, 236 (1934), 632–48; and no. 3109.

3026 WAGNER, H. R. The cartography of the northwest coast of America to the year 1800. 2 vols. Berkeley. 1937.

Scholarly. An annotated list of maps is in vol. ii. See also F. Mood, 'The English geographers and the Anglo-American frontier in the seventeenth century', *Univ. of Calif. Pub. in Geography*, 6 (1944), 363–96; and W. P. Canning, *The southeast in early maps*, 2nd edn., Chapel Hill, 1964(?).

I. PRINTING AND PUBLISHING

1. GENERAL

(a) Catalogues and Guides

See also Ch. I, *Bibliography*, especially nos. 3, 4, 13.

3027 STUDIES IN BIBLIOGRAPHY: Papers of the Bibliographical Society of the University of Virginia. Vol. 1 (1948–9)+. Charlottesville.

Contains many valuable articles on printers, booksellers, and publishing, as well as a checklist of bibliographies.

3028 THE LIBRARY, Transactions of the Bibliographical Society. Vol. 1 (1889)+.

A quarterly review, London. G. W. Cole compiled *An index to bibliographical papers* [of the Bibliographical Society and the Library Association] . . . *London, 1877–1932,* Chicago, 1933. Articles useful for the period include E. F. Bosanquet, 'English seventeenth-century almanacks', 4th Ser. 10 (1930), 361–97; S. L. C. Clapp, 'Subscription publishers prior to Jacob Tonson', 4th Ser. 13 (1932), 158–83; A. F. Johnson, 'The king's printers, 1660–1742', 5th Ser. 3 (1949), 33–8.

3029 ALDIS, HARRY G. List of books printed in Scotland before 1700 . . . with brief notes on the printers and stationers. Edin. 1904.

See also R. H. Carnie and R. P. Doig, 'Scottish printers and booksellers 1668–1755: a supplement', *Studies in Bibliography,* 12 (1958), 131–59; and W. J. Couper's edn. of parts of the MS. by George Chalmers, 'Historical account of printing in Scotland (1507–1707)', *Rec. Glasgow Bibl. Soc.* 7 (1923), 62–89.

3030 BERRY, W. T. and JOHNSON, A. F. Catalogue of specimens of printing types by English and Scottish printers and founders, 1665–1830. 1935.

See also A. F. Johnson, *A catalogue of engraved and etched English title-pages* . . . (to 1691), 1934.

3031 CATALOGUE OF A COLLECTION of works on publishing and bookselling in the British library of political and economic science. 1936.

Cf. *Catalogue of an exhibition of books illustrative* . . . *of printing and bookselling in England, 1477–1800,* 1912. See also 'English provincial presses III', by W. H. Allnutt, *Bibliographica,* 2 (1896), 276–308; and no. 2790 n.

3032 DIX, E. R. McC. Catalogue of early Dublin printed books, 1601–1700 2 vols. 1898–1905.

See also by Dix, 'Earliest Dublin printers and the Company of Stationers of London', *Trans. Bibl. Soc.* 7 (1904), 75–85; and J. Anderson, *Catalogue of early Belfast-printed books, 1694 to 1830,* Belfast, [1886], enl. edn. Belfast, 1890.

(b) *Sources*

3033 JACKSON, W. A., ed. Records of the court of the Stationers' Company, 1602–1640. 1957.

See Arber's transcript (3 n.). Also by Jackson, 'Variant entry fees of the Stationers' Company', *Papers Bibl. Soc. America,* 51 (1957), 103–10; C. Blagden, 'Charter Trouble', *Book Collector,* 6 (1957), 369–77. See also S. Hodgson *The Worshipful Company of Stationers and Newspaper Makers,* 1953; and C. Blagden's *The Stationers' Company* . . ., Camb. (Mass.) 1960.

3034 MOXON, JOSEPH. Mechanik exercises on the whole art of printing. 1683. Ed. by H. Davis and H. Carter. Oxf. and N.Y. 1958.

The original edn. is vol. ii of no. 2034. Moxon was a well-known type-maker who wrote books on various subjects.

3035 HODGSON, N. and BLAGDEN, C. The notebook of Thomas Bennet and Henry Clements (1686–1719) with some aspects of booktrade practice. Oxf. 1956.

Oxf. Bibl. Soc. Pub., N.S. 6. An excellent picture of the London book trade.

(c) *Later Works*

3036 ALBRIGHT, E. M. Dramatic publication in England 1580–1640. A study of conditions affecting content and form of drama. 1927. Bibl.

Includes material on censorship, copyright, printing-houses, as well as other matter relating particularly to the drama. Cf. W. W. Greg (2660).

3037 DAHL, F. 'Amsterdam—cradle of English newspapers', *The Library*, 5th Ser. 4 (1949), 166–78.

Cf. A. F. Johnson, 'The exiled English church at Amsterdam and its press', ibid., 5th Ser. 5 (1951), 219–42.

3038 GREG, W. W. Some aspects and problems of London publishing between 1550 and 1650. Oxf. 1956.

The Lyell lectures; bibl. footnotes. Cf. F. R. Johnson, 'Notes on English retail book-prices, 1550–1640', *The Library*, 5th Ser. 5 (1950), 83–112.

3039 JOHNSON, J. and GIBSON, S. Print and privilege at Oxford to the year 1700. Oxf. and Lond. 1946.

Contains an app. of documents; useful. Cf. F. Madan, 'The Oxford press, 1650–75 . . .' *The Library*, 4th Ser. 6 (1925), 113–47; also by Madan, *A brief account of the University Press at Oxford . . .*, Oxf. 1908, and no. 2973.

3040 JONES, J. I. History of printing and printers in Wales to 1810 . . . also . . . in Monmouthshire to 1923. Cardiff. 1925.

Cf. L. C. Lloyd, 'The book trade in Shropshire . . . to *c.* 1800', *Shrops. Arch. Soc. Trans.* 48 (1936), 65–142, 145–98; and Lloyd's 'Paper-making in Shropshire', ibid. 49 (1938), 121–87.

3041 PLOMER, H. R. Short history of English printing, 1476–1898. 1900. Rev. edn. 1920.

See also Rostenberg (3049).

3042 REED, T. B. History of the old English letter foundries. 1887. Rev. edn. by A. F. Johnson. 1952.

A standard work.

3043 SIMPSON, P. Proof-reading in the sixteenth, seventeenth and eighteenth centuries. 1935.

Useful.

3044 UPDIKE, D. B. Printing types; their history, forms and use; a study in survivals. 2 vols. 1922. 2nd edn. 2 vols. Lond. and Camb. (Mass.). 1937. 3rd edn. Edin. 1962.

Valuable both on history and on typography. See also A. F. Johnson, *Type designs; their history and development*, 1934, 2nd edn. 1959, bibl.

3045 WILES, R. McK. Serial publication in England before 1750. Camb. 1956. Bibl.

An appendix includes a list of books published as fascicules before 1750. On literary magazines see W. J. Graham, *The beginnings of English literary periodicals . . . 1665–1715*, 1926.

2. Printers, Publishers, and Booksellers

3046 CURWEN, H. History of booksellers. 1873.

See also H. R. Plomer's *Dictionary of the booksellers and printers* (13 n.); F. A. Mumby, *Publishing and bookselling, a history*, 1930, bibl.; J. Lawler, *Book auctions in England in the seventeenth century*, 1898; and A. W. Pollard, 'English book sales, 1676–1680, 1681–1686', *Bibliographica*, 1 (1895), 373–84; 2 (1896), 112–26.

3047 GIBSON, S. A bibliography of Francis Kirkman. Oxf. 1949.

Details of the books printed by Kirkman, an important publisher of the restoration period. Cf. C. E. Kenney, 'William Leybourne, 1626–1716', *The Library*, 5th Ser. 5 (1950), 159–71.

See also by various authors articles on Nathaniel Ponder, ibid., 4th Ser. 15 (1934), 257–94; Thomas Chard, a stationer, ibid., 2nd Ser. 4 (1923–4), 219–37, and 4th Ser. 21 (1940), 26–43; William Fitzer, ibid., 4th Ser. 24 (1943–4), 142–64; and Humphrey Moseley, *Oxf. Bibl. Soc. Proc. and Papers*, 2 (1929), 61–142.

3048 PLANT, M. The English book trade: an economic history of the making and sale of books. 1939.

3049 ROSTENBERG, L. Literary, political, scientific, religious and legal publishing, printing and bookselling in England, 1551–1700. 2 vols. N.Y. 1965.

Important. By the same author, 'William Dugard: pedagogue and printer of the commonwealth', *Papers Bibl. Soc. Amer.* 52 (1958), 179–204. On a Quaker publisher of the same period see H. E. Terry, 'Giles Calvert's publishing career', *Friends' Hist. Soc. Jour.* 35 (1939), 45–9.

3050 'WILLS of Thomas Bassadyne and other printers in Edinburgh, 1577–1687.' *Bannatyne Club Misc.* 2 (1836), 185–296.

Cf. J. M. Henderson, 'James Fraser, 1645–1731', *Aberdeen Univ. Rev.* 25 (1938), 138–46.

3. Freedom of the Press

(a) *Sources*

3051 MILTON, JOHN. Areopagitica: a speech for the liberty of unlicens'd printing. 1644.

The most celebrated argument for freedom of the press in the century. Many edns. See *Works* (2633).

3052 L'ESTRANGE, ROGER. Considerations and proposals in order to the regulation of the press. 1663.

L'Estrange attacks freedom of expression. See other titles by L'Estrange in Wing and in *Camb. Hist. Eng. Lit.*, vol. ix. See also G. Kitchin, *Sir Roger L'Estrange, a contribution to the history of the press in the seventeenth century*, 1913, bibl.; and nos. 3076, 3078.

3053 BLOUNT, CHARLES (under pseud. Philopatris.) Just vindication of learning: or a humble address to the high court of parliament in behalf of the liberty of the press. 1679.

Blount used large parts of *Areopagitica* in his *Reasons humbly offered for the liberty of unlicens'd printing*, 1693. His *Just vindication* is included in the 1695 edn. of his *Miscellaneous works*.

3054 BOHUN, EDMUND. The diary and autobiography of Edmund Bohun
. . . with an introductory memoir. Ed. by S. Wilton Rix. Beccles. 1853.

Bohun was licenser of the press 1692–3.

(b) *Later Works*

3055 CLYDE, W. M. The struggle for the freedom of the press from Caxton
to Cromwell. 1934.

See also by Clyde, 'Parliament and the press, 1643–7', *The Library*, 4th Ser. 13 (1933),
399–424, and 14 (1933), 39–58; F. S. Siebert, 'Regulation of the press in the seventeenth century', *Journalism Quart.* 13 (1936), 381–93, and 'The regulation of newsbooks,
1620–1640', ibid. 16 (1939), 151–60; and J. Walker, 'The censorship of the press . . .
Charles II', *History*, 35 (1950), 219–38. Cf. C. R. Gillett, *Burned books: neglected chapters
in British history and literature*, N.Y. 1932.

3056 FREEMAN, E. 'A proposal for an English academy in 1660.' *Modern
Lang. Rev.* 19 (1924), 291–300.

Concerns a proposal, attributed to Robert Hooke, for improving and licensing of books.

3057 HANSON, L. W. Government and the press, 1695–1763. 1936. Bibl.

Useful. On government monopoly of the news after 1660, see P. Fraser (752).

J. NEWSPAPERS

The circulation of news became increasingly important through the century. In
addition to the newsletters distributed by professional writers such as John
Chamberlain (287), Henry Muddiman, and others (see Fraser, no. 752), there
were early corantos that provided news from abroad and, by the 1640s, series of
pamphlets reporting on domestic issues, especially developments in Parliament.
Often strongly partisan in tone, some of the journals became virtually official
organs of the government. Periodicals of a more literary nature began to appear
near the close of the century. Because there are numerous lists of large collections, and several good bibliographical studies of the development of the press,
no attempt is made here to provide more than a representative list of the newspapers of the period. Useful chapters and bibls. are in *Camb. Hist. Eng. Lit.*,
vols. vii and ix.

I. CATALOGUES AND LISTS

3058 CRANE, R. S. and KAYE, F. B. A census of British newspapers and
periodicals, 1620–1800. Chapel Hill. 1927.

Valuable, indicating those available in American libraries and those not. Alphabetical
arrangement, with an index by years, and with a geographical index also. See also useful
lists of journals before 1647 in the appendices of Frank (3094); and *Bibliotheca Lindesiana, collations and notes*, no. 5: *catalogue of English newspapers, 1641–1666*, Aberdeen,
1901.

3059 [MUDDIMAN, J. G.] Tercentenary handlist of English and Welsh
newspapers, magazines and reviews. 1920. 1933.

Arranged by years, covering 1620–1920. Additions and corrections are in *N. and Q.*, 12th Ser. 8 (1921) and 10 (1922), and vol. 167 (1934), 113–16, 187–8.

Lists for special periods are D. C. Collins, *Handlist of news pamphlets, 1590–1610*, Walthamstow, 1943; and G. A. Cranfield, *Handlist of English provincial newspapers and periodicals, 1700–1760*, Camb. 1952.

3060 DAHL, F. A bibliography of English corantos and periodical newsbooks 1620–1642. 1952. Bibl.

Published for the Bibliographical Society. Also by Dahl, *Dutch corantos 1618–1650*, The Hague, 1946. Cf. W. P. Van Stockum, Jr., ed., *The first newspapers of England printed in Holland 1620–21*, The Hague, 1914; and L. W. Hanson, 'English newsbooks, 1620–1641', *The Library*, 4th Ser. 18 (1938), 355–84.

3061 MILFORD, R. T. and SUTHERLAND, D. M. A catalogue of English newspapers and periodicals in the Bodleian Library, 1622–1800. Oxf. 1936.

Also publ. in *Oxf. Bibl. Soc. Proc. and Papers*, 4 (1935), 167–344; largely supersedes the annotated catalogue publ. in 1865. For newspapers 1641–63 in the Thomason Collection, Br. Mus. (58), see vol. ii, pp. 371–460.

For collections in other libraries see *An exhibition from the London Press Club's collection of English newspapers of the seventeenth and eighteenth centuries; a catalogue* [St. Bride Foundation Institute], 1931; *The Britwell handlist or short title catalogue of the principal volumes . . . in the library of Britwell Court, Buckinghamshire*, 2 vols., 1933; A. J. Gabler, 'Checklist of English newspapers and periodicals before 1801', *Huntington Lib. Bull.* 2 (1931), 1–67; H. M. Bruner, comp., *Catalogue of English pamphlets in the Sutro Library*, Part II, San Francisco, 1941; and P. Stewart, *British newspapers and periodicals, 1632–1800 . . . at the University of Texas*, Austin, 1950.

3062 WEED, K. K. and BOND, R. P. Studies of British newspapers and periodicals from their beginnings to 1800: a bibliography. Chapel Hill. 1946.

Section iv includes an alphabetical list of individual newspapers and periodicals, as well as of editors, publishers, etc. Most of the significant works on the subject that were published before 1941 are listed by the authors. See also Bond, ed., *Studies in the early English periodical* (1700–1760), Chapel Hill, 1957; and Wiles (3045).

3063 COUPER, W. J. Edinburgh periodical press . . . vol. i., Introduction and bibliography, 1642–1711; vol. ii, Bibliography, 1711–1800. 2 vols. Stirling. 1908. Facsimiles.

Annotated and chronologically arranged.

2. NEWSPAPERS AND JOURNALS

3064 THE HEADS of several proceedings in this present Parliament . . . Nov. 22–29, 1641.

Publ. by John Thomas, the first of numerous publications of similar title, that appeared, sometimes intermittently, during the months before 1643. For lists of early journals of this period, published under similar titles such as *Diurnall occurrences in Parliament, A perfect diurnall . . .*, and their publishers, see Coates (862 n., pp. 404–6), and Frank (3094). By the close of 1642, Samuel Pecke's *Perfect diurnall* (3065) had become fairly reliable.

3065 A PERFECT DIURNALL of some passages in Parliament . . . 26 June 1643, 8 Oct. 1649. Ed. by Samuel Pecke.

A stabilized journal that developed from earlier series published under the joint editorship of Pecke and Francis Coles. Neutral in politics, and the earliest example of well-informed editing. See Frank (3094) and P. Radin, ed., *An annotated bibliography of F. Cole's* [sic] *'A Perfect Diurnall'*, San Francisco, 1939.

3066 MERCURIUS AULICUS ... 8 Jan. 1643–7 Sept. 1645. Ed. by John Berkenhead.

Royalist and satirical. Preceded by a first issue (1 Jan. 1643) at Oxford under title of *Oxford Diurnall*. See F. J. Varley's account, *Mercurius Aulicus*, Oxf. 1948.

3067 THE KINGDOMES WEEKLY INTELLIGENCER ... 3 Jan. 1643–9 Oct. 1649. Ed. by Richard Collings.

Presbyterian. After closing in 1649, the paper reappeared in July 1650, and ran, after some early irregularity, for six years as *The Weekly Intelligencer*.

Also ed. by Collings and Presbyterian in tone, though more critical of the king, was *Mercurius Civicus* ... 11 May 1643–10 Dec. 1646, an illustrated paper.

3068 THE MODERATE INTELLIGENCER ... 6 March 1645–May 1649. Ed. by John Dillingham.

Presbyterian royalist. Actually a substitute for Dillingham's earlier journal *The Parliament Scout*, first issued 20–7 June 1643 (*The Parliament Scout's Discovery* 9–15 June 1643), and discontinued in Feb. 1645. A new series of the *Moderate Intelligencer* ran briefly 1652–3. See also no. 3072.

3069 MERCURIUS BRITANICUS ... 29 Aug. 1643–18 May 1646. Ed. by Thomas Audley (to No. 51) and Marchamont Nedham.

Parliamentary and satirical. For Nedham's changes in politics in his editorial career see *Mercurius Pragmaticus* (3071) and *Mercurius Politicus* (3074), and his pamphlet, *The case of the Commonwealth* ... (969 n.). In criticism of the contemporary press, especially of *Mercurius Britanicus* are John Cleveland's *Character of a London diurnal*, 1644, and *A character of a diurnal-maker*, 1654.

3070 PERFECT OCCURRENCES ... 1–8 August 1645–12 Oct. 1649. Ed. by Henry Walker [Luke Harruney, anagram].

Continuation of a publication appearing in Jan. 1644 as *Occurrences of Certain Special ... Passages*, later in the year, as *Perfect Occurrences of Parliament*, with Walker as partial editor. By 1645 Walker's paper came to resemble Pecke's *Perfect Diurnal*, which was published on a different day of the week, but the *Occurrences* was more anti-royalist. (See Frank, pp. 108, 327.)

3071 MERCURIUS PRAGMATICUS ... 21 Sept. 1647–28 May 1650. (Variations in title.) Ed. by Samuel Sheppard, John Cleveland, and Marchamont Nedham.

Royalist. Various authors used the same title in 1649 and 1650.

3072 THE MODERATE ... 29 June 1648–25 Sept. 1649. Ed. by Gilbert Mabbot.

Chief organ of the Levellers, opposing Presbyterian periodicals of similar titles. Mabbot as censor, having refused licence to Dillingworth's *Moderate Intelligencer* (June 1648), issued his own paper first (no. 171) as a continuation of that paper, changing the title after three weeks.

3073   A BRIEFE RELATION . . . 2 Oct. 1649–22 Oct. 1650. Ed. by Walter Frost.

Edited by the Secretary of the Council of State, this was one of the official or semi-official organs of the commonwealth, supplanting more critical journals that suffered under the new licensing acts. Also printing official news were: *Severall (or 'Perfect') Proceedings* . . . 9 Oct. 1649–27 Sept. 1655, ed. by Henry Walker (after early issues by Henry Scobell, clerk to Parliament); and *A Perfect Diurnall of . . . the Armies* . . . 17 Dec. 1649–24 Sept. 1655, ed. by Samuel Pecke (originally by John Rushworth).

3074   MERCURIUS POLITICUS . . . 13 June 1650–12 April 1660. Ed. by Marchamont Nedham and John Canne [1659].

Official, Nedham having been induced to change sides (see 3069). The most complete newspaper of the interregnum. Virtually the same paper, but printed on a different day of the week, was *The Publicke Intelligencer* . . . 8 Oct. 1655–9 April 1660 [4 June 1660], with the same editors and printers.

3075   THE PARLIAMENTARY INTELLIGENCER . . . 26 Dec. 1659–31 Aug. 1663. Ed. by Henry Muddiman.

Renamed *Kingdoms Intelligencer* in 1661. A Thursday issue, begun in 1660, was *Mercurius Publicus*, ed. by Muddiman and Giles Dury. Muddiman virtually succeeded to Nedham's monopoly of the news (3074).

3076   THE INTELLIGENCER . . . 31 Aug. 1663–29 Jan. 1666. Ed. by Sir Roger L'Estrange.

See *The Newes* (3 Sept. 1663–25 Jan. 1666) as the Thursday edn.

3077   THE LONDON GAZETTE. 16 Nov. 1665 to date. Ed. by Henry Muddiman, Charles Perrot, *et al.*

First issued as the *Oxford Gazette*, with the title changed on 5 Feb. 1666, this journal has outlasted all of its early contemporaries. It was virtually the only English newspaper from 1665 to 1679.

3078   THE OBSERVATOR . . . 13 April 1681–9 March 1687. Ed. by Sir Roger L'Estrange.

Satirical opponent of Oates and Shaftesbury, licensed by the Secretaries of State. Other journals relating chiefly to the Oates excitement are the pro-Oates journals, *Domestic Intelligence* . . . 9 July 1679–15 April 1681, ed. by Benjamin Harris, and *The True Protestant Mercury*, 28 Dec. 1680–25 Oct. 1682, ed. by Thomas Vile; and the opposing *Heraclitus Ridens* . . . 1 Feb. 1681–22 Aug. 1682 (repr. 1713), ed. by Thomas Flatman, and *The Loyal Protestant* . . . 9 March 1681–20 March 1683, ed. by Nathaniel Thompson. See also no. 3083.

3079   THE MERCHANTS REMEMBRANCER. 23 May 1681 to *c.* 1700. Ed. by James Whiston.

Of great value for trade and prices. Existing sets very incomplete.

3080   PRESENT STATE OF EUROPE, or the monthly account of occurrences . . . 1692–1696.

Title varies; trans. of the periodical edited by J. Dumont and H. Basnage, *Lettres Historiques* . . . 90 vols., The Hague, 1692–1736.

3081 THE POST-MAN . . . 11 Aug. 1694–1723.

Begun as *Account of Publick Transactions in Christendom*, and continuing from Oct. 1695 as the *Post-Man* and *Post-Boy*. The latter was publ. until 1735. Both were Tory and Jacobite journals, by various eds.

3082 THE DAILY COURANT. 11 March 1702–1735. By various eds.

Non-partisan(?); first English daily.

3083 THE OBSERVATOR. 1 April 1702–1712. Ed. by John Tutchin.

Important Whiggish journal, to be distinguished from the earlier paper of the same title (3078). Other Whig papers were the *Flying Post* (1695–1731), by various eds.; and the *London Post* (1699–1705), ed. by Benjamin Harris and others. A Tory reply to Tutchin's paper was Charles Leslie's *Rehearsal* (1704–09).

3084 A WEEKLY REVIEW of the affairs of France. [19 Feb. 1704–July 1712.] Ed. by Daniel Defoe.

Appearing under various title changes, Defoe's Whiggish *Review* was outstanding as a journal of opinion. See a facsimile repr., with intro. by A. W. Secord, 9 vols. in 22, N.Y. 1938.

3085 THE DUBLIN GAZETTE. 1706 to date.

Official. See article by D. Hipswell in *N. and Q.*, 8th Ser. 11 (1897), 495.

3086 THE EDINBURGH GAZETTE. 25 March 1707 to date.

Official. On previous unofficial issues in 1699 and 1706, as well as 1680, see *Publs. Edin. Bibl. Soc.* 12 (1925), 84–88. A variant title, 1708–1713, was *The Scots Postman*. Other Scottish papers were the *Edinburgh Courant*, Feb. 1705(?)–22 March 1710; and *Scots Courant*, 1710(?)–20(?).

3087 THE EXAMINER. 3 Aug. 1710–26 July 1714. By various eds.

Principal Tory journal, with writing by Swift, Bolingbroke, etc. Cf. *The prose works of . . . Swift* (2598).

3088 THE MEDLEY. 5 Oct. 1710–7 Aug. 1712. By various eds. Ed. by Arthur Maynwaring and John Oldmixon.

Whig. In 1712 the *Medley* reprinted the five issues of Joseph Addison's *The [Whig] Examiner* (1710), his reply to no. 3087. See also Oldmixon, *Memoirs of the press . . . 1710–1740*, 1742.

3089 THE TATLER. 12 April 1709–Jan. 1711. Ed. by Richard Steele. Later edn. by G. A. Aitken. 4 vols. 1898–9.

Consult G. A. Aitken's *Life of Steele*, 2 vols. 1889, which contains a full bibl. A precursor of the *Tatler* as a literary magazine was *Athenian Mercury*, 1691–7.

3090 THE SPECTATOR. 1 March 1711–6 Dec. 1712. Contin. 18 June–20 Dec. 1614. Ed. by Joseph Addison, Richard Steele, and others. Later edns. by G. A. Aitken. 8 vols. 1898. By D. F. Bond. 5 vols. Oxf. 1965.

Cf. E. Partridge, *An original issue of 'The Spectator' . . .* [with an account of its founding], San Francisco, 1939. John Gay wrote a comment on *The Tatler*, *The Spectator*, and similar publications in *The present state of wit in a letter to a friend*, 1711.

3091 THE GUARDIAN. 12 March 1713–1 Oct. 1713. Ed. by Richard Steele and others.

Whig. See also Steele's Whiggish journal, *The Englishman*, 6 Oct. 1713–Feb. 1714. R. Blanchard included a second series, 1715, in his edition of *The Englishman . . .,* N.Y. 1955.

3092 MERCATOR; or commerce retrieved. 1 May 1713–20 July 1714.

Attributed to Daniel Defoe, supporting trade to France.

3. LATER WORKS

For titles relating to censorship see *Freedom of the press* (3051–7).

3093 BOURNE, H. R. F. English newspapers: chapters in the history of journalism. 2 vols. 1887.

Still useful for a general account, though chapters on the 17th century should be supplemented by later works, such as Frank. A briefer general account is H. Herd, *The march of journalism: the story of the British press from 1622 to the present day,* [1952]. On Scottish journalism see W. J. Couper (3063); and his article in *Scottish N. and Q.,* 3rd Ser. 12, pp. 190–3.

3094 FRANK, J. The beginnings of the English newspaper. Camb. (Mass.). 1961. Bibl.

Valuable. Concentrates on the years 1641–60; useful lists are in appendices. On the ancestry of the press see M. A. Shaaber, *Some forerunners of the newspaper in England, 1476–1622,* 1929.

3095 MORISON, S. The English newspaper: some account of the physical development of journals printed in London between 1622 and the present day. Camb. 1932.

Important.

3096 STEVENS, D. H. Party politics and English journalism. Menasha, Wis. 1916. Bibl.

Relates to the years 1702–1742. Cf. articles pertaining to the period: G. B. Needham, 'Mary de la Rivière Manley, Tory defender', *Hunt. Lib. Quart.* 12 (1949), 253–88; M. E. Ransome (912 n.); J. R. Sutherland, 'The circulation of newspapers . . . 1700–30', *Library,* 4th Ser. 15 (1934), 110–24. Excerpts and commentary are included in W. B. Ewald, *The newsmen of Queen Anne,* Oxf. 1956.

3097 WILLIAMS, J. B. [i.e. J. G. Muddiman.] A history of English journalism to the foundation of the *Gazette* [1666]. 1908. Bibl.

Useful, though tinged with bias toward Royalism. See also the same author's chapter in *Camb. Hist. Eng. Lit.* vii (1911), and his 'Newsbooks and letters of news of the restoration', *E.H.R.* 23 (1908), 252–76. Williams published under his own name (J. G. Muddiman) his study of the *Gazette's* editor, Henry Muddiman, using the title of *The king's journalist, 1659–1689,* 1923. See also Fraser (752).

XI

LOCAL HISTORY

To the wide and varied field of local history there is no complete guide. For books published before 1918 Humphreys (3104) is still a good general guide, and Gross (3102) remains valuable for municipalities. For later works, the Historical Association's handlist (3103) is helpful. The older general histories, usually of separate counties, must now be supplemented with newly published documentary materials and with monographs on particular localities or subjects. The volumes dealing with earlier periods in this bibliographical series should be consulted for additional titles. Parish registers and records of quarter sessions are dealt with mainly in other sections of this volume (2416 and 936), with the introductions to the latter being of special value for the light they shed on local government. The *Victoria County History* (3120), still in progress, is invaluable.

To assist students in the expanding field of local history, two recent series of publications are useful. The Standing Conference for Local History (of the National Council of Social Science, London), has published in a 'Local History Series' the following pamphlets: No. 1. *A plan for the study of local history*, 1949; No. 2. *The compilation of county bibliographies*, 1948; No. 3. *A selection of books on English local history*, 1949; No. 4. *A directory of authorities and organizations for the assistance of local historians*, 1950. The *Guide to the reports on collections of manuscripts . . . Part I, Topographical*, published by the Historical Manuscripts Commission (p. 12) indicates the location of records at the time of its publication, 1914. The Commission's National Register of Archives publishes reports on accessions to local archives and activities there in its *Bulletin*, Lond. 1948+; and the *List of accessions to repositories*, Stationery Office, 1958+. See also Mullins (23 n.) and no. 3103. For suggestions on the use of local archives, see Hoskins (3118).

On the materials in university and other local libraries, see *supra* pp. 4–5. See also Ch. V, and § E of this chapter on Diocese and Parish. On maps see Ch. X, pp. 432–3, and no. 53. In Ch. VI are local histories of the civil war.

A. GENERAL: BIBLIOGRAPHIES AND GUIDES

3098 ANDERSON, J. P. The book of British topography: a classified catalogue of the topographical works in . . . the British Museum relating to Great Britain and Ireland. 1881.

Cf. W. Upcott, *A bibliographical account of the principal works relating to English topography*, 3 vols., 1818.

3099 BRITISH RECORDS ASSOCIATION. List of record repositories in Great Britain. 1956.

A new edn. was being prepared by 1961 (see M. Bond, 'The Archivist and his records', in *History Today*, 11 (1961), 501–5. See also F. G. Emmison and I. Gray, *County records*

(Historical Assoc., Special Ser. S. 3, 1948); and L. J. Redstone and F. W. Steer, *Local records: their nature and care* (Soc. of Local Archivists, 1953). See also P. Hardacre, 'County record offices in England and Wales: a list of guides and references', *Amer. Archivist*, 25 (1962), 477–83. W. V. Daniel and F. J. Nield, *Manual of British topography: a catalogue of county and local histories, pamphlets, etc.*, 1909, is a bookseller's catalogue that includes many useful items.

3100 FORDHAM, H. G. The road-books and itineraries of Great Britain, 1570–1850. A catalogue, with an introduction and a bibliography. Camb. 1924.

By the same author, *Notes on British and Irish itineraries*, Hertford, 1912; and a separate volume on *Roadbooks . . . of Ireland*, Dublin, 1923. See also Fussell (2352), and vol. iii of Cox (2351).

3101 GOMME, G. L., ed. Index of archaeological papers, 1665–1890 [with annual supplements to 1908]. 1907.

Arranged under authors; valuable, though not exhaustive. Succeeding Gomme, from 1929, were the *Bull. Inst. Hist. Research, Supplements*, 1930+ (23), and Milne (14). See also Mullins (23 n.).

3102 GROSS, C. A bibliography of British municipal history. *Harvard Hist. Studies*, No. 5. N.Y. 1897.

Standard work; the best on towns to 1897. For London see also C. W. F. Goss, *The London directories, 1677–1855, a bibliography*, 1932.

3103 HISTORICAL ASSOCIATION [OF LONDON]. English local history handlist: a short bibliography and list of sources for the study of local history and antiquities. Special Ser. S. 2. 1947. 2nd edn. 1952.

A useful checklist. See also A. H. Thompson, *A short bibliography of local history* (Hist. Assoc. Leaflet, No. 72), 1928. Still useful is 'A list of works relating to British genealogy and local history, *N.Y. Publ. Lib. Bull.* 14 (1910).

3104 HUMPHREYS, A. L. A handbook to county bibliography: being a bibliography of bibliographies relating to the counties and towns of Great Britain and Ireland. 1917.

The chief guide to materials published earlier. See also F. J. C. Hearnshaw, *Municipal records*, 1918.

3105 INDEX OF INQUISITIONS preserved in the Public Record Office. Vol. iii, James I; iv, Charles I and later. Lists and indexes. Nos. 31, 33. 1909.

Cf. no. 2413. For other useful materials at the P.R.O., see 'Calendar and inventory of parliamentary surveys preserved among the records of the augmentation office', *Rep. of the Deputy Keeper*, vii. 124; viii. 52, 1846–7.

3106 THIRD REPORT OF THE ROYAL COMMISSION on public records appointed to inquire into and report on the state of the public records and local records of a public nature of England and Wales . . . Vol. 3 (3 pts.). H.C. 1919 (Cmd. 367, Cmd. 368, Cmd. 369), xxviii. 1, 53, 189.

The first and second Reports (1912, 1914) also should be consulted. See also *Report of the committee appointed to enquire as to the existing arrangements for the collection and custody of local records* (Parl. Papers 1902, vol. xlix), 1902.

B. GENERAL: TOPOGRAPHY AND LOCAL HISTORY

1. DESCRIPTIVE WORKS (arranged in roughly chronological order)

3107 CAMDEN, WILLIAM. Britannia, siue florentissimorum regnorum Angliae, Scotiae, Hiberniae chorographica descriptio. 1586. 6th edn. 1606. English tr. 1610. Enl. by Richard Gough. 3 vols. 1789.

The best-known of various similar works in this and the next century. Cf. Richard Blome, *Britannia*, 1673. Michael Drayton's 'Poly-Olbion', 1612–22, appears in vol. iv of his *Works*, Oxf. 1933. For early maps see John Speed, *Theatre of the empire of Great Britaine*, 1611, and nos. 3021–6.

3108 NORDEN, JOHN. England. An intended guyde for English travailers, showing in generall, how far one citie & many shire-townes in England, are distance from other. 1625.

Norden wrote also descriptions of various counties under the title of *Speculum Britanniae*, parts of which have been publ. variously: Cornwall, 1728; Essex (Camden Soc., 1840); Hertfordshire, 1598; Middlesex, 1593; Northampton . . . in 1610, 1720. See Read, p. 355.

3109 OGILBY, JOHN. Britannia. Or an illustration of the kingdom of England and the dominion of Wales by a geographical and historical description of the principal roads. 1675. 2nd edn. 1698. Maps.

Important. This was followed in 1699 by his popular *Traveller's Guide*, of which there were many later edns. Cf. Sir H. G. Fordham's bibl. article on Ogilby and later itineraries in *The Library*, 4th Ser. 6 (1925), 157–78. Other travel descriptions are by Samuel Dunstar, 1699, and James Brome, 1700, 1707. John Adams compiled *Index villaris, or an alphabetical table of all the cities, market-towns, parishes, villages and private seats in England and Wales*, 1680, 1690.

3110 DEFOE, DANIEL. A tour through the whole island of Great Britain. 3 vols. 1724–7. Ed. by G. D. H. Cole. 2 vols. 1927.

Compiled from observations made during frequent travels *temp.* Queen Anne. Cf. Defoe's letters in H.M.C., Portland MSS. iv. For other travel works see nos. 2366–84.

3111 GOUGH, R. British topography, or an historical account of what has been done for illustrating the topographical antiquities of Great Britain and Ireland. 2 vols. 1780.

Originally publ. in 1768 as *Anecdotes of British topography*. Gough's collection of books and MSS. is in the Bodleian Library (Western MSS.); see *Catalogue*, Oxf. 1814.

3112 NICHOLS, JOHN, *et al.* Bibliotheca topographica Britannica. 10 vols. 1780–1800.

Last two vols., 1791–1800, bear the title, *Miscellaneous antiquities*. See also *Collectania topographica et genealogica*, ed. by J. Gough Nichols *et al.*, 8 vols., 1834–43, and followed by 3 vols., entitled *The topographer and genealogist*, 1846–58.

3113 GOMME, G. L., ed. Gentleman's magazine library: being a classified collection of the chief contents of the Gentleman's Magazine, 1731–1868. 29 vols. in 30. 1883–1905.

Vol. xii is the first of the topographical volumes. Valuable.

3114 LEWIS, S. A topographical dictionary of England . . ., with atlas. 4 vols. 1831. 3rd edn. 5 vols. 1835. 5th edn. 4 vols. 1842.

A valuable work, though not without error.

3115 LYSONS, D. and S. Magna Britannia; being a concise topographical account of the several counties of Great Britain. 6 vols. [1806]–22.

Alphabetically arranged, but not completed beyond Devon. Cf. E. W. Brayley, J. Britton, *et al.*, *The beauties of England and Wales . . .*, 18 vols., 1801–15.

2. LATER WORKS

3116 COX, J. C. The royal forests of England. 1905.

Useful.

3117 DARBY, H. C., ed. An historical geography of England before 1800. Camb. 1936. Repr. 1963.

Includes good sections on 17th-century England and London. Cf. F. Walker, 'Geographical factors in the civil war in East Anglia', *Geography*, 24 (1939), 171–81. On maps, see T. Chubb (53).

3118 HOSKINS, W. G. Local history in England. N.Y. 1959.

Valuable as an introduction to the resources and procedures for the study of English local history; includes much bibl. data. Cf. E. F. Jacob, 'Local history: the present position and possibilities', *History*, N.S. 34 (1949), 193–203; and D. M. Meads, 'Searching local records', *Rev. Engl. Studies*, 4 (1928), 173–90, 201–22.

3119 MEREWETHER, H. A. and STEPHENS, A. J. The history of the boroughs and municipal corporations of the United Kingdom. 3 vols. 1835.

Includes valuable material, but interpretations are not always correct.

3120 VICTORIA HISTORY of the counties of England. Ed. by W. Page, H. A. Doubleday, and others. Westminster. 1900+.

A standard work, monumental in scope and still in progress. The series is complete for ten or more counties (see below). There are several recent popular series, such as two under the editorship of B. V. Fitzgerald, *The county books*, 60 vols., 1947–56; and *The regional books*, 1952+ (in progress).

C. SEPARATE COUNTIES, CITIES, AND TOWNS

1. BEDFORDSHIRE

(a) *Bibliography*

3121 TURNER, R. Guide to the Bedfordshire record office. Bedford. 1957.

(b) *Local Societies and Journals*

3122 THE BEDFORDSHIRE HISTORICAL RECORD SOCIETY. Publications. Aspley Guise. 1913+.

Valuable. Among the volumes useful for the seventeenth century are vols. 16, 18, 20, 24, 26, 27, 31.

3123 THE BEDFORDSHIRE MAGAZINE. A quarterly miscellany and review of Bedfordshire life and history. Luton. 1947+.

Also a miscellany is *Bedfordshire Notes and Queries*, 3 vols., Bedford, 1886–93.

(c) *County and Town Histories and Records*

The *V.C.H. Bedfordshire* (3120) is complete in 3 vols. and index, 1904–14. See also F. A. Blaydes, ed., *Genealogia Bedfordiensis* (1538–1700), 1890; and Harleian Soc. (2417), vol. 19 (1884).

3124 FISHER, T. Collections historical, genealogical, and topographical for Bedfordshire. 1812–36.

3125 PARRY, J. B. Select illustrations, historical and topographical, of Bedfordshire. 1827.

Deals with Bedford, Ampthill, Houghton, Luton, and Chicksand.

Bedford. T. A. Blyth, *The history of Bedford and visitors' guide*, [1873]. Cf. *Schedule of the records of the corporation of Bedford*, Bedford, 1883; and G. Parsloe, ed., *The minute book of the Bedford corporation, 1647–1664* (Bedfordshire Hist. Rec. Soc. Publ. 26), Streatley, 1949. See also Parsloe (956).

Luton. W. Austin, *The history of Luton*, 2 vols., 1928. Cf. H. Cobbe, *Luton church, historical and descriptive*, 1899.

2. BERKSHIRE

(a) *Bibliography*

3126 HILL, F. Guide to the Berkshire record office. Reading. 1952.

(b) *Local Societies and Journals*

3127 BERKSHIRE ARCHAEOLOGICAL AND ARCHITECTURAL SOCIETY. Quarterly journal. 3 vols. Reading [1889–95].

Continued by the *Berks., Bucks., and Oxon. Archaeological Journal*, 1895–1930; then as the *Berkshire Archaeological Journal*, 1930+.

3128 NEWBURY DISTRICT FIELD CLUB. Transactions. Newbury. 1871+.

See also *Berkshire Notes and Queries*, vol. 1, pts. 1–4, 1890–1.

(c) *County and Town Histories and Records*

V.C.H. Berkshire is complete in 4 vols. and index, 1906–27. See H.M.C. (240) for records of Berkshire corporations, Abingdon, and Reading. County pedigrees are in Harl. Soc. (2417), vols. 56–7 (1907–8), and in a volume by W. Berry 1837.

3129 ASHMOLE, ELIAS. The history and antiquities of Berkshire, with a description of Windsor. 3 vols. 1719. Later edn. 1 vol. Reading. 1736.

Cf. W. N. Clarke, *Parochial topography of the hundred of Wanting*, Oxf. 1924; and Cooper King, *History of Berkshire*, 1887.

Newbury. History and antiquities of Newbury and environs, including 28 parishes in . . . Berks., Speenhamland, 1839; and W. Money, *History of the borough of Newbury*, Oxf. 1887.
Reading. J. M. Guilding, ed., *Reading records: diary of a corporation*, 4 vols., 1892–6. Cf. C. Coates, *History and antiquities of Reading*, Reading, 1802, suppl., 1810.
Wallingford. J. K. Hedges, *The history of Wallingford*, 2 vols., 1881; abr., 1893.
Windsor. R. R. Tighe and J. E. Davis, *Annals of Windsor . . .*, 2 vols., 1858, based on documents.

3. BUCKINGHAMSHIRE

(a) *Bibliography*

3130 [GOUGH, HENRY.] Bibliotheca Buckinghamensis. *Archit. and Arch. Soc. for the Co. of Bucks.* Aylesbury. 1890.

Also, *A calendar of deeds and other records in . . . the museum, Aylesbury*, Buckinghamshire Arch. Soc., Records Branch, Publ. 5, 1944.

(b) *Local Societies and Journals*

3131 ARCHITECTURAL AND ARCHAEOLOGICAL SOCIETY FOR THE COUNTY OF BUCKINGHAM. Records of Buckinghamshire. Aylesbury. 1858+.

Records Branch (Buckinghamshire Archaeological Society, later styled Buckingham Record Society), Publications, 1937+.

(c) *County and Town Histories and Records*

The *V.C.H. Buckinghamshire* is complete in 4 vols. and index, 1905–28. See no. 936 for quarter sessions. For pedigrees see Harl. Soc. (2417), vol. 58.

3132 LIPSCOMB, G. The history and antiquities of the county of Buckingham. 4 vols. 1831–47.

Useful, though old and not always accurate. Of somewhat less value are J. J. Sheahan *History and topography of Buckingham*, 1862; and R. Gibbs, *Buckinghamshire, a record of local occurrences* (1400–1800), 4 vols., Aylesbury, 1878–82. Some papers relating to county administration are in G. Eland, ed., *Papers from an iron chest at Doddershall, Bucks*, Aylesbury, 1937.

3133 GIBBS, R. Buckinghamshire, a history of Aylesbury and its boroughs and hundreds. Aylesbury. 1885.

Buckingham. B. Willis, *The history and antiquities of the town, hundred, and deanery of Buckingham*, 1755.
Newport Pagnell. O. Ratcliffe, *History and antiquities of Newport Pagnell*, Olney, 1900, and F. W. Bull, *History of Newport Pagnell*, Kettering, 1900.
Wendover. L. H. West, *History of Wendover*, Aylesbury, 1909.
Wycombe. R. W. Greaves, *The first ledger book of High Wycombe* (1475–1734), Buckingham Rec. Soc. Publ. 9 (1947), 1956.

4. CAMBRIDGESHIRE

(a) *Bibliography*

3134 BOWES, R. A catalogue of books printed at or relating to the university, town and county of Cambridge from 1521 to 1893. Camb. 1894.

Cf. A. T. Bartholomew, *Catalogue . . . of the books and papers bequeathed to the university by J. W. Clark*, Camb. 1912.

(b) *Local Societies and Journals*

3135　CAMBRIDGE ANTIQUARIAN SOCIETY. Antiquarian communications. Vols. 1–6. Camb. 1859–88. Continued as Proceedings, vol. 7+ (new Ser., 1+), 1893+. Also Publications. Octavo series, 1851+. Quarto series, 1840–9, 1908–51.

See also *East Anglian* (3246), and *Fenland Notes and Queries* (3188), and Cambridge Society, *Monographs*, Camb. 1951+.

3136　CAMBRIDGE AND HUNTINGDONSHIRE ARCHAEOLOGICAL SOCIETY. Transactions. Ely. 1904+.

(c) *County and Town Histories and Records*

V.C.H. Cambridgeshire and the Isle of Ely, vols. i–iv, and an index volume have appeared, 1938–60. For pedigrees see Harl. Soc. (2417), vol. 41.

3137　BLOMEFIELD, F. Collectanea Cantabrigiensia, or collections relating to Cambridge University, town and county. Norwich. 1750.

3138　CARTER, E. The history of the county of Cambridge. Camb. 1753.

Very general in its treatment is E. Conybeare, *A history of Cambridgeshire* (Popular County Histories), 1897. See also W. M. Palmer, *Cambridge subsidy rolls, 1250–1695*, Norwich, 1912.

Cambridge. C. H. Cooper, *Annals of Cambridge*, 5 vols., Camb. 1842–1908. Vol. v was ed. by J. W. Cooper. Useful, especially vols. iii–iv. Of less value is A. Gray, *The town of Cambridge*, Camb. 1925. See also T. D. Atkinson and J. W. Clark, *Cambridge described . . .*, 1897; and *The Charters of . . . Cambridge* (to 1685), ed. by F. W. Maitland and M. Bateson, Camb. 1901. Two volumes, with maps of the city, were publ. by the Royal Commission on Historical Monuments, 1959.

Wisbech. W. Watson, *Historical account of . . . Wisbech and . . . towns and villages, drainage of the fens, etc.*, Wisbech, 1827.

5. CHESHIRE

(a) *Bibliography*

3139　COOKE, J. H. Bibliotheca Cestriensis, or a biographical account of books, maps, plates . . . relating to, printed or published in, or written by authors resident in Cheshire. Warrington. 1904.

Cf. *A list of books relating to Cheshire history*, 1853–5.

(b) *Local Societies and Journals*

3140　ARCHITECTURAL, ARCHAEOLOGICAL, AND HISTORICAL SOCIETY for the county, city and neighbourhood of Chester. Journal. Chester. 1849–85, 1887+.

Name of society varies; since 1915 it has been Chester and North Wales (Architectural) Archaeological and Historic Society.

See also nos. 3197–9; *The Cheshire Sheaf*, Chester, 1880+; *The Palatine Note-book*, 4 vols., Manchester, 1881–4; and *Chester Notes and Queries*, Stockport, 1886–1912 (continuing the *Advertiser Notes and Queries*, 5 vols., Stockport, 1881–5).

(c) *County and Town Histories and Records*

For heraldic visitations see Harl. Soc. (2417), vols. 59, 93; for quarter sessions see no. 936.

3141 ORMEROD, G. History of the county palatine and city of Chester 3 vols. 1819. Revised by T. Helsby. 3 vols. 1875–82.

The standard history of Chester. Also useful is J. P. Earwaker, *East Cheshire . . . or a history of the hundred of Macclesfield*, 2 vols., 1877–80. William Webb's *Description of Cheshire, in 1621* is included in D. King, *The vale royal*, 1656.

Chester. J. Hemingway, *History of the city of Chester*, 2 vols., Chester, 1831. A shorter history is by G. L. Fenwick, Chester, 1896. See also A. Hopkins, *Selected rolls of Chester city courts*, Manchester, 1951; and M. J. Groombridge, ed., *Calendar of Chester city council minutes, 1630–42* (Lancs. and Chesh. Rec. Soc. Publ. 106), 1956. See also Atkinson (1594) and Morris (1596).

6. CORNWALL

(a) *Bibliography*

3142 BOASE, G. C. and COURTNEY, W. P. Bibliotheca Cornubiensis: a catalogue of works relating to the county of Cornwall. 3 vols. 1874–82.

(b) *Local Societies and Journals*

See also nos. 3155–6.

3143 ROYAL INSTITUTION OF CORNWALL. Journal and Reports. Truro. 1864+.

See also *The Cornish Magazine*, by H. T. Quiller-Couch, 2 vols., Truro, 1898–9.

(c) *County and Town Histories and Records*

V.C.H. Cornwall is still incomplete. The first vol. and parts of vol. ii have appeared, 1906–56.

3144 CAREW, RICHARD. The survey of Cornwall. 1602. Ed. by Tonkin. 1811. See also Norden, *Speculum Britanniae . . . Cornwall* (3108).

3145 GILBERT, C. S. An historical and topographical survey of Cornwall. 2 vols. Plymouth. 1817–20.

Cf. G. C. Boase, *Collectanea Cornubiensia*, Truro, 1890. Biographical material on M.P.s is printed in *Western Antiquary* (3156 n.); and in W. H. Tregellas, *Cornish worthies*, 2 vols., 1884. See also J. L. Vivian, *The visitations of Cornwall*, Exeter, 1887.

3146 POLWHELE, R. History of Cornwall, civil, military, etc. 7 vols. Falmouth and Lond. 1803–16.

The best of the older histories of Cornwall. For Cornwall in the civil war period see Coate (1596).

Trig Minor. J. MacLean, *The parochial and family history of the deanery of Trig Minor,* 3 vols., Bodmin, 1863–79, is based on original sources. His *History of the parish of St. Tudy* was pr. in Exeter, 1879.

7. CUMBERLAND

(a) *Bibliography*

There is no important bibliography. The counties of Westmorland and Cumberland are both dealt with in some works. (See nos. 3262–3.)

(b) *Local Societies and Journals*

3147 CUMBERLAND AND WESTMORLAND ANTIQUARIAN AND ARCHAEOLOGICAL SOCIETY. Transactions. Kendal. 1866–1900. 1901+. Publications. Kendal. 1877+.

The latter series includes numerous important 17th-century records, especially those of the Fleming family.

(c) *County and Town Histories and Records*

The first two vols. of *V.C.H. Cumberland* were published 1901–5.

3148 FERGUSON, R. S. History of Cumberland. 1893.

For family pedigrees of the 1615 visitation, see Harl. Soc. (2417), vol. 7, 1872. On members of Parliament see no. 917.

3149 HUTCHINSON, W. The history of the county of Cumberland and some places adjacent. 2 vols. Carlisle. 1794.

The standard history is no. 3263. Incomplete is S. Jefferson, *History and antiquities of Cumberland*, 2 vols., Carlisle, 1840–2. See also Fleming (3262 n.).

Carlisle. R. S. Ferguson and W. Nanson, eds., *Some municipal records of the city of Carlisle*, Lond. and Carlisle, 1887. In the records publications of no. 3147. Cf. W. H. Chippindall, *History of the township of Ireby*, Chetham Soc., N.S. 95 (1935).

8. DERBYSHIRE

(a) *Bibliography*

3150 ORMEROD, J. A select catalogue of books about the county. Derby. 1930.

See also Cox (3152 n.).

(b) *Local Societies and Journals*

3151 DERBYSHIRE ARCHAEOLOGICAL AND NATURAL HISTORY SOCIETY. Journal. 1879+.

Of less value is *Nottinghamshire and Derbyshire Notes and Queries*, 6 vols., Derby, 1892–8.

(c) *County and Town Histories and Records*

For the *V.C.H. Derbyshire* vols. i, ii have appeared, 1905–7.

3152 COX, J. C. Three centuries of Derbyshire annals as illustrated by the records of the quarter sessions. 2 vols. 1890.

Cf. *Calendar of the records of the county of Derby*, 1899. These two works supply a valuable guide to the various kinds of county records. See also I. H. Jeayes, *A descriptive catalogue of Derbyshire charters*, 1906.

3153 GLOVER, S. History of the county of Derby. Ed. by T. Noble. 2 vols. Derby. 1829. 2 vols. Derby. 1831–2.

Derby. W. Hutton, *History of Derby*, 1791, later edn. 2 vols., 1817.

9. DEVONSHIRE

(a) *Bibliography*

3154 DAVIDSON, J. Bibliotheca Devoniensis: a catalogue of the printed books relating to the county of Devonshire. Exeter. 1852. Supplement. 1861.

On the city of Exeter, see W. Harte, *A bibliography of Exeter*, Historical Assoc., Leaflet No. 9 [1908].

(b) *Local Societies and Journals*

3155 DEVON AND CORNWALL RECORD SOCIETY. Publications. Exeter. 1906+.

3156 DEVONSHIRE ASSOCIATION for the Advancement of Science, Literature and Art. Transactions. Plymouth. 1863+.

Valuable. See also *Devon Notes and Queries*, Exeter, 1901–9, continued as *Devon and Cornwall Notes and Queries*, 1909+; *Notes and Gleanings* [for Devon and Cornwall], 5 vols., Exeter, 1888–92; and *The Western Antiquary, or Notebook for Devon, Cornwall and Somerset*, 12 vols., and supplement, Plymouth, 1882–95.

(c) *County and Town Histories and Records*

Vol. i of *V.C.H. Devon* has appeared, 1906. Much Devonshire material is contained in works in military history and in naval history. On quarter sessions see Hamilton (938 n.). For pedigrees, 1620, see Harl. Soc. (2417), vol. 6 (1872).

3157 HOSKINS, W. G. and FINBERG, H. P. R. Devonshire studies. 1952.

Chiefly relating to the land. See also Prince (2446).

3158 POLWHELE, R. A history of Devonshire. 3 vols. Exeter. 1797.

Cf. Sir William Pole, *Collections towards a description of the county of Devon*, 1791; and Tristram Risdon, *The chorographical description . . . of Devon . . . and Exeter*, 2 vols., 1714, rev. edn. 1811; originally publ. in 1630.

Barnstaple. J. B. Gribble, *Memorials of Barnstaple*, Barnstaple, 1830. Also useful are J. R. Chanter and T. Wainwright, *Barnstaple records*, 2 vols., Barnstaple, 1900, which contains excerpts from the local records; Chanter's *Sketches of the literary history of Barnstaple*, Barnstaple, 1866; and Cotton (1599).

Exeter. G. Oliver, *The history of the city of Exeter*, Exeter, 1821, 1861. Valuable modern works are: Hoskins (1961); W. B. Stephens, *Seventeenth-century Exeter, 1625–1688*, Exeter, 1958; and W. T. MacCaffrey, *Exeter, 1540–1640*, Camb. (Mass.) 1958. Numerous articles on Exeter and its officials have been printed in no. 3156 and n. See also H.M.C. (240).

Honiton. A. Farquharson, *The history of Honiton*, Exeter, 1868.

Okehampton. W. B. Bridges *et al.*, *Account of the barony and town of Okehampton*, rev. edn. by W. H. K. Wright, Tiverton, 1889.

Plymouth. R. N. Worth, *History of Plymouth*, 1872, 1890. Worth also ed. *Calendar of Plymouth municipal records*, Plymouth, 1893. See also Plymouth Institution [and Devon and Cornwall Natural History Society], *Transactions*, vols. 1–[16], 1830–1915/16.

Tiverton. W. Harding, *A history of Tiverton*, 2 vols., Lond. and Tiverton, 1845–7.

Totnes. W. Cotton, *A graphic and historical sketch of the antiquities of Totnes*, 1850.

10. DORSETSHIRE

(a) *Bibliography*

3159 MAYO, C. H. Bibliotheca Dorsetiensis: being a carefully compiled account of printed books and pamphlets relating to . . . the county of Dorset. 1885.

Cf. E. A. Fry and G. S. Fry, *Dorset records . . .*, Dorchester, 1878; and *Report of the County Records Committee for the county of Dorset*, Dorchester, 1878. See also R. Douch, *A handbook of local history, Dorset*, [Bristol] 1952.

(b) *Local Societies and Journals*

3160 DORSET NATURAL HISTORY and Antiquarian Field Club. Proceedings. Sherborne. 1877–1950.

In 1928 name changed to *Dorset Natural History and Archaeological Society*. See also no. 3238 n.

(c) *County and Town Histories and Records*

Vol. ii of *V.C.H. Dorset* has appeared, 1908. Dorset pedigrees are in Harl. Soc. (2417), vol. 20 (1885).

3161 HUTCHINS, J. History and antiquities of the county of Dorset. 2 vols. 1774. 3rd edn. by W. Shipp and F. W. Hodson. 4 vols. Westminster. 1861–70.

Standard county history. For Dorset during the civil war see Bayley (1600). See also H.M.C. (76).

Corfe Castle. G. Bankes, *The story of Corfe Castle*, 1853.

Dorchester. C. H. Mayo, ed., *The municipal records of the borough of Dorchester*, Exeter, 1908. Mayo also described, with extracts, *The municipal records of . . . Shaftesbury*, Shaftesbury, 1889.

Poole. J. Sydenham, *The history of the town and county of Poole*, Poole, 1839.

Weymouth. H. J. Moule, *A descriptive catalogue of the charters, minute books . . . of Weymouth and Melcombe Regis, 1252–1800*, Weymouth, 1883. See also *H.M.C.* (240).

11. DURHAM

(a) *Bibliography*

There is no general bibliography for the county.

3162 HANDLIST OF HALMOTE COURT BOOKS, palatinate of Durham and bishopric estates. Durham. 1956.

See also *Handlist of rentals of wards and townships among the Halmote Court records of the palatinate of Durham and bishopric estates*, Durham, 1956.

(b) *Local Societies and Journals*

3163 DURHAM AND NORTHUMBERLAND ARCHITECTURAL AND ARCHAEOLOGICAL SOCIETY. Transactions. Sunderland. 1863+.

3164 SURTEES SOCIETY. Publications. [1835+].

Valuable for material relating to the history of north England, chiefly Durham, Northumberland, and Yorkshire. For the 17th century, for example, vol. 34 contains records from the court of High Commission; vol. 111, records on royalist compositions; vol. 135, protestation returns of 1641. For others, see Mullins (23 n.).

(c) *County and Town Histories and Records*

Vols. i–iii of *V.C.H. Durham* have appeared, 1905–28.

3165 HUTCHINSON, W. The history and antiquities of the county palatine of Durham. 3 vols. Newcastle. 1785–94. Later edn. 3 vols. Durham. 1823.

3166 SURTEES, R. The history and antiquities of the county palatine of Durham. 4 vols. 1816–40. New edn. in progress. Sunderland. 1908+.

Durham. C. E. Whiting, ed., *Durham civic memorials: the order book of the corporation of Durham* (1602–66), Surtees Soc. Pub. 160 (1952).
Newcastle. R. Welford, *History of Newcastle and Gateshead*, 3 vols., 1884–7.

12. ESSEX

(a) *Bibliography*

3167 VICTORIA COUNTY HISTORY. Essex. Vol. vi. Bibliography. 1959.

This is an excellent bibl., organized by subject, person, and place. See also A. Cunningham, *Catalogue of books, maps and manuscripts relating to . . . the county of Essex*, Braintree, 1902; G. A. Ward, *Essex local history: a short guide to books and manuscripts*, Chelmsford, 1950; and Read (11 n.), pp. 368–9.

3168 EMMISON, F. G. Guide to the Essex Record Office. Essex Record Office. Publ. no. 1, 2. 2 pts. in 1 vol. Chelmsford. 1947–8.

See also H.M.C., *Tenth Rep.*, app. 4 (239). The Essex Record Office issues a series of *Publications* from the records, 1946+.

(b) *Local Societies and Journals*

3169 ESSEX ARCHAEOLOGICAL SOCIETY. Transactions. Colchester. 1858+.

Also valuable is *Essex Review*, Chelmsford, 1892+; see papers on economic and military matters of the 17th century in vols. 17, 18; on Little Baddow in vol. 43.

(c) *County and Town Histories and Records*

Vols. i–iv and vi of *V.C.H. Essex* have been published. 1903–63. For pedigrees 1612 and 1634, see Harl Soc. (2417), vols. 13, 14 (1878–9).

3170 EDWARDS, A. C. English history from Essex sources, 1550–1750. (Essex Record Office Publ. 17.) Chelmsford. 1952.

Cf. *County maps of Essex,* 1576–1852, Essex Record Office Publ. 25 (1955).

3171 MORANT, P. History and antiquities of the county of Essex. 2 vols. 1768. Repr. 2 vols. Chelmsford. 1816.

The best of the older histories of the county. Relying heavily on Morant is T. Wright, *History and topography of . . . Essex,* 2 vols., 1836.

3172 SMITH, H. The ecclesiastical history of Essex under the Long Parliament and commonwealth. Colchester. 1932.

Colchester. T. Cromwell, *History . . . of the ancient town . . . of Colchester,* 2 vols., 1825. See also P. Morant's *History . . . of Colchester,* bound with his *History of Essex.* Three works by J. H. Round are *The history . . . of Colchester Castle,* Colchester, 1882; 'Colchester during the commonwealth', *E.H.R.* 15 (1900), 641–64; and 'Cromwell and the electorate', *Nineteenth Century,* 46 (1899), 947–56.

13. GLOUCESTERSHIRE

(a) *Bibliography*

3173 AUSTIN, R. Catalogue of the Gloucestershire collection, books, pamphlets, and documents in the Gloucester Public Library relating to the county of Gloucester. Gloucester. 1928.

Also by Austin, *Catalogue of the Gloucestershire books collected by Sir Francis Hyett of Painswick,* Gloucester, [1949]. See also I. E. Gray and A. T. Gaydon, *Gloucestershire quarter sessions archives,* Gloucester, 1958; and F. A. Hyett and W. Bazeley, *The bibliographer's manual of Gloucester literature,* 3 vols., Gloucester, 1895–7, suppl. by F. A. Hyett and R. Austin, 2 vols., Gloucester, 1915–16.

(b) *Local Societies and Journals*

3174 BRISTOL AND GLOUCESTERSHIRE ARCHAEOLOGICAL SOCIETY. Transactions. [Bristol.] 1876+.

See also *Gloucestershire Notes and Queries* [1878]–1905, 1913–14; and *Bristol Record Society,* Bristol, 1930+.

(c) *County and Town Histories and Records*

V.C.H. Gloucestershire, vol. ii, was publ. 1907. For pedigrees of 1623 see Harl. Soc. (2417), vol. 21 (1885).

3175 BIGLAND, R. Historical collections relative to the county of Gloucester. 2 vols. 1786–92.

Cf. R. Atkyns, *The ancient and present state of Gloucestershire,* 1712, repr. 1768; and S. Rudder, *A new history of Gloucestershire,* Cirencester, 1779. Of uneven quality are the essays in H. P. Finberg, ed., *Gloucester studies,* Leicester, 1957. See also Willcox, *Gloucestershire* (931).

3176 SMYTH, JOHN. The Berkeley manuscripts. Ed. by Sir John Maclean. 3 vols. Gloucester. 1883–5.

Publ. by the Bristol and Glouc. Arch. Soc., these volumes include Smyth's *Lives of the Berkeleys*, and his description of the hundred of Berkeley. See also H.M.C. (216).

Bristol. J. Latimer, *The annals of Bristol in the 17th century*, Bristol, 1900. Cf. W. Barrett, *History and antiquities of the city of Bristol*, Bristol, 1789; and S. Seyer, *Memoirs historical and topographical of Bristol and its neighbourhood*, 2 vols., Bristol, 1821–3. Published by the Bristol Record Society are *Bristol Charters, 1509–1899*, ed. by R. C. Latham, 1947; and several volumes of Deposition Books (1643–54), ed. by H. E. Nott and E. Ralph, 1935–48. On the Merchant Venturers see no. 2135.

Gloucester. W. H. Stevenson, *Calendar of records of the corporation of Gloucester*, Gloucester, 1893. Cf. The calendar of the letter books, 1619–60, in H.M.C. (240); and T. D. Fosbroke, *Original history of . . . Gloucester*, 1819.

14. HAMPSHIRE
(a) *Bibliography*

3177 GILBERT, H. M. and GODWIN, G. N. Bibliotheca Hantoniensis: a list of books relating to Hampshire. Southampton. 1891.

(b) *Local Societies and Journals*

3178 HAMPSHIRE FIELD CLUB AND ARCHAEOLOGICAL SOCIETY. Papers and proceedings. Southampton. 1890+.

Called Hampshire Field Club until 1899. Also the *Hampshire Notes and Queries*, 9 vols., Winchester, 1883–98; and *Hampshire Record Society Publications*, 12 vols., 1889–99. The Winchester Cathedral Records were publ. in conjunction with the latter.

3179 SOUTHAMPTON RECORD SOCIETY. Publications. Southampton. 1905+.

Valuable for town history.

(c) *County and Town Histories and Records*

V.C.H. Hampshire is complete in 5 vols. and index, 1900–14. For pedigrees see Harl. Soc. (2417), vol. 64; and Berry (3180 n.). For the Isle of Wight see no. 3279.

3180 WOODWARD, B. B., WILKS, T. C., and LOCKHART, C. S. M. A general history of Hampshire. 3 vols. 1861–9.

The best of the older histories of the county, including the Isle of Wight. Of some use also is R. Warner, *Collections for the history of Hampshire*, 6 vols., 1795. For county pedigrees, there is a collection by W. Berry, County genealogies series, 1833; for civil war history, see Godwin (1604).

Crawley. N. S. B. Gras and E. C. Gras, *The economic and social history of an English village—Crawley, Hampshire* (1864 n.).

Portsmouth. W. H. Saunders, *Annals of Portsmouth, 1595–1865*, 1880. Cf. R. East, *Extracts from records . . . of the borough of Portsmouth*, 1891. The *Oglander Memoirs* (2496) should be consulted also.

Southampton. J. S. Davies, *History of Southampton*, Southampton, 1883. The corporation records are described in *H.M.C.* (240), and several series are in process of publication by the Southampton Record Society: Assembly books, 1602–16, 4 vols., ed. by J. W. Horrocks, 1917–25; Court leet records, 1603–24, ed. by F. J. C. Hearnshaw and D. M. Hearnshaw, 1908; Book of examinations and depositions, 1622–44, 4 vols., ed. by R. C. Anderson, 1929–36. For other types, see Read (11 n.), p. 373.

Winchester. G. W. Kitchin, *Winchester*, 1890. Also good is J. Milner, *History and survey of the antiquities of Winchester*, 2 vols. [1798?]; 3rd edn., 2 vols., 1839. See also *The diary of John Young* (1293), by a dean of the cathedral.

15. HEREFORDSHIRE

(a) *Bibliography*

3181 ALLEN, J. Bibliotheca Herefordiensis; or a descriptive catalogue of the books, pamphlets, maps, prints . . . relating to the county of Hereford. Hereford. 1821.

See also, by County Libraries, *Herefordshire books: select list of books in the local collection*, 1955.

(b) *Local Societies and Journals*

3182 CANTILUPE SOCIETY. [Publications.] Hereford. 1906+.

The Cantilupe Society, jointly with the Canterbury and York Society, is concerned with publishing episcopal registers.

(c) *County and Town Histories and Records*

One volume of *V.C.H. Hereford* has been published, 1908. For the county and city records, see H.M.C., *Thirteenth Report* (240). For parliamentary history see Williams (917); for military history see Webb (1605).

3183 DUNCUMB, J., COOKE, W. H., *et al.* Collections toward the history and antiquities of the county of Hereford. 6 vols. Hereford. 1804–1912 (in progress).

The best county history to date.

Hereford. J. Price, *An historical account of the city of Hereford*, 1796. There is a *Catalogue of and index to MSS. papers . . . of the city of Hereford*, Hereford, 1894.
Leominster. G. F. Townshend, *The town and borough of Leominster*, 1863.

16. HERTFORDSHIRE

(a) *Bibliography*

None of importance.

(b) *Local Societies and Journals*

3184 EAST HERTFORDSHIRE ARCHAEOLOGICAL SOCIETY. Transactions. Hertford. 1901+.

Also *St. Albans Architectural and Archaeological Society Transactions*, St. Albans, 1885+, called since 1895 *St. Albans and Hertfordshire Architectural and Archaeological Society*. See also no. 3283 n.

(c) *County and Town Histories and Records*

V.C.H. Hertford is complete in 4 vols. and index, 1902–14. For the quarter sessions records see no. 936. Hertfordshire pedigrees are in Harl. Soc. (2417), vol. 22. See no. 1606 for military history.

3185 CHAUNCY, H. Historical antiquities of Hertfordshire. 1700. Later edn. 2 vols. 1826.

Based upon much manuscript material.

3186 CLUTTERBUCK, R. History and antiquities of the county of Hertford. 3 vols. 1815–27.

Also useful is J. E. Cussans, *History of Hertfordshire*, 3 vols., 1870–81.

Hertford. L. Turner, *History of the ancient town and borough of Hertford*, Hertford, 1830.
Hitchin. R. L. Hine, *The history of Hitchin*, 2 vols., 1927–9.
St. Albans. A. E. Gibbs, *The corporation records of St. Albans*, St. Albans, 1890, containing excerpts.

17. HUNTINGDONSHIRE

(a) *Bibliography*

3187 NORRIS, H. E. Catalogue of the Huntingdonshire books collected by Herbert E. Norris. Cirencester. 1895.

Cf. County Library, *Catalogue of the local history collection* [at] *Gazeley House, Huntingdon*, Huntingdon, 1950.

(b) *Local Societies and Journals*

3188 FENLAND NOTES AND QUERIES. A quarterly antiquarian journal for the Fenland in the counties of Huntingdon, Cambridge, Lincoln, Northampton, Norfolk, and Suffolk. Peterborough. 1889–1909.

See also no. 3136.

(c) *County and Town Histories and Records*

V.C.H. Huntingdon is complete in 3 vols. and index, 1926–32.

3189 TURNER, G. J., ed. A calendar of the feet of fines relating to the county of Huntingdon (1194–1603). Camb. Antiq. Soc. 37. Camb. 1913.

The Huntingdonshire visitation of 1613, ed. by Sir H. Ellis, is in Camden Soc., 1849. For Protestation returns, see vol. 5 (1936) of no. 3136.

18. KENT

(a) *Bibliography*

3190 CHURCHILL, I. J., ed. A handbook to Kent records. Kent Arch. Soc., Records Branch, 2 (1914).

See also J. R. Smith, *Bibliotheca Cantiana, a catalogue of a . . . collection of books and manuscripts relative to the county of Kent . . . offered for sale*, 1837, later edn. 1851. The edn. of 1851 includes Sussex and Surrey as well.

(b) *Local Societies and Journals*

3191 KENT ARCHAEOLOGICAL SOCIETY. Archaeologia Cantiana.
1858+. Kent Records. 1912+.

Outstanding among the county publications. Of slight value is *Kentish Note Book*,
2 vols., Gravesend, 1891–4.

(c) *County and Town Histories and Records*

Vols. i–iii of *V.C.H. Kent* have appeared, 1908–32. The records of some Kentish
towns are described in H.M.C. (240). For pedigrees see Harl. Soc. (2417), vols.
42 and 54. For military history see Everitt (1607).

3192 HASTED, E. A history and topographical survey of the county of Kent.
4 vols. Canterbury. 1778–99. 12 vols. 1797–1801. New edn. of pt. 1 by
H. H. Drake. 1886.

The best older history. Edn. of 1797–1801 contains Hasted's 'History of Canterbury'.
The brief modern *History of Kent* by F. W. Jessup, 1958, is somewhat uneven.

3193 [PHILIPOT, JOHN and PHILIPOT, THOMAS.] Villare Cantianum
or Kent surveyed and illustrated. 1659. 1664. 2nd edn. rev. 1776.

Parts written by John Philipot, but published by his son Thomas, under the latter's
name. See also William Lambarde, *A perambulation of Kent*, 1576, 1596, 1656, etc.;
and Richard Kilburne, *A topographie or survey of the county of Kent*, 1695.

3194 TEICHMAN-DERVILLE, M. The level and the liberty of Romney
Marsh in the county of Kent. An inquiry into the origins . . . of the two
reputed corporations . . . with some account of their ancient courts and early
forms of land drainage administration. Ashford. 1936.

Canterbury. William Somner, *Antiquities of Canterbury*, Canterbury, 1640, 1703.
Chislehurst. E. A. Webb, G. W. Miller, and J. Beckwith, *History of Chislehurst*, 1899.
Dover. J. Lyon, *History of the town and port of Dover and Dover castle, with some account
   of the Cinque Ports*, 2 vols., Dover, 1813–14. Cf. S. P. H. Statham, *The history of the
   castle, town and port of Dover*, 1899; J. B. Jones, *Annals of Dover*, Dover, 1916, and
   his *Records of Dover*, Dover, 1920.
Knole. J. Bridgman, *An historical and topographical sketch of Knole*, 1817, 1821. See
   also V. Sackville-West, *Knole and the Sackvilles*, 1922, repr. 1923.
Sandwich. W. Boys, *Collections for an history of Sandwich in Kent. With notices of the
   other Cinque Ports and members, and of Richborough*, Canterbury, 1792; based on local
   records.

19. LANCASHIRE

(a) *Bibliography*

3195 FISHWICK, H. The Lancashire library; a bibliographical account of
books on topography . . . and miscellaneous literature relating to the county
palatine. 1875.

Cf. A. J. Hawkes, *Lancashire printed books. A bibliography . . . down to . . . 1800*, Wigan,
1925. The Manchester Public Libraries published *Reference Library subject catalogue*,
Manchester, 1957, with a special section on parish registers (see Read, p. 378). See also

A. Sutton, *Bibliotheca Lancastriensis: a catalogue of books on* . . . *Lancashire, with an appendix of Cheshire books,* Manchester, 1894, 2nd edn. 1898.

3196 FRANCE, R. S. Guide to the Lancashire Record Office. Lancashire Record Publications, no. 2. Preston. 1948.

(b) *Local Societies and Journals*
See also Cheshire (3140).

3197 CHETHAM SOCIETY. Remains historical and literary . . . of Lancaster and Chester. [Manchester.] 1844+.

An important series. Examples are civil war tracts, 1844; Norris papers (Liverpool), 1846; the Moore rental, 1847; Farington papers, 1856; quarter sessions, 1917; and W. K. Jordan, *Social institutions, 1480–1660,* 1962.

3198 HISTORIC SOCIETY OF LANCASHIRE AND CHESHIRE. Proceedings. Liverpool. 1849+.

Called *Transactions* after 1855. See also *Lancashire and Cheshire Antiquarian Society Transactions,* Manchester, 1884+; and *Lancashire and Cheshire Historical and Genealogical Notes,* 3 vols., Leigh, 1879–83.

3199 RECORD SOCIETY FOR . . . LANCASHIRE AND CHESHIRE. Publications. 1879+.

Has published many papers relating to property and estates, including 3 vols. on inquisitions post mortem, Cheshire, 1934–8; some Lancashire quarter sessions (1616–23), 1901; 2 vols. on 'plundered ministers', 1893–6; and 6 vols. on royalist composition papers, 1891–1942.

(c) *County and Town Histories and Records*

V.C.H. Lancashire is complete in 8 vols. 1906–14. On the Lancashire lieutenancy, see no. 932; on parliamentary history, see no. 917. Lancashire visitations are in Chetham Soc., vols. 82, 84, 85, 87 (1871–3). See also Shuttleworth (2217).

3200 BAINES, E. A history of the county palatine and duchy of Lancashire. 2 vols. Manchester and Lond. 1824. Best edn. by J. Croston. 5 vols. Manchester. 1888–93.

See also M. Gregson, *Portfolio of fragments relative to the history and antiquities of the county palatine and duchy of Lancaster,* Liverpool, 1817, 2nd edn., 1824; and Kenyon MSS., H.M.C. (209).

3201 LEIGH, CHARLES. The natural history of Lancashire, Cheshire and the Peak in Derbyshire. Oxf. 1700.

Clitheroe. W. S. Weeks, 'Clitheroe in the seventeenth century', *Lanc. and Ches. Antiq. Soc. Trans.,* vols. 41 (1924), 44–78; 42 (1925), 81–119; 43 (1926), 72–124; and Read (11 n.), no. 4499.
Lancaster. R. Simpson, *History and antiquities of the town of Lancaster,* 1852. See also 'Rolls of the freemen of the borough of Lancaster, 1688–1840' [A–L], *Rec. Soc. for Lanc. and Ches.,* 87 (1935).
Liverpool. J. A. Picton, *Memorials of Liverpool,* 2 vols., 1873, 1875, rev. edn. 2 vols., 1907. See also *Sir E. Moore, Liverpool in King Charles the Second's time* (1667–8), ed. by W. F. Irvinge, 1899.

Rossendale. G. H. Tupling, *The economic history of Rossendale*, Manchester, 1927.
Salford. J. G. de T. Mandley, ed., *The portmote or court leet records of . . . Salford* (1597–1669), 2 vols., Chetham Soc. (vols. 46, 48), 1902.
Whalley. T. D. Whitaker, *A history of the original parish of Whalley, and the honor of Clitheroe*, 4th edn. by J. G. Nichols and P. A. Lyons, 2 vols., 1872–6.
Wigan. A. J. Hawkes, *Wigan's part in the civil war and in the events which immediately preceded it*, Wigan, 1932. Cf. G. H. Tupling, 'The causes of the civil war in Lancashire', *Lanc. and Ches. Antiq. Soc. Trans.* 65 (1955), 1–32. For Wigan history, see D. Sinclair, *History of Wigan*, 2 vols., Wigan, 1882–[3].

20. LEICESTERSHIRE

(a) *Bibliography*

None of importance.

(b) *Local Societies and Journals*

3202 LEICESTERSHIRE ARCHAEOLOGICAL SOCIETY. Transactions. Leicester. 1855+.

From 1855 to 1917 called *Leicestershire Architectural and Archaeological Soc.* In 1955 changed to *Leicestershire Archaeological and Historical Soc.*

3203 LEICESTER LITERARY AND PHILOSOPHICAL SOCIETY. Transactions. Leicester. 1835; 1879–80; 1884–5; 1886+.

See also *Leicestershire and Rutland Notes and Queries*, 3 vols., Leicester, 1891 [1889]–95.

(c) *County and Town Histories and Records*

Vols. i–v of *V.C.H. Leicester* have appeared, 1907–64.

3204 NICHOLS, J. History and antiquities of the county of Leicester. 4 vols. in 8 pts. 1795–1815.

For economic matters, see W. G. Hoskins, *Essays in Leicestershire history*, Liverpool, 1950; and the same author's *Midland peasant*, 1957, and *Provincial England*, N.Y. 1963.

3205 THROSBY, J. Memoirs of the town and county of Leicester. 6 vols. Leicester. 1777.

Cf. Throsby, *History and antiquities of the ancient town of Leicester*, 1791.

Langton. J. H. Hill, *The history of the parish of Langton*, Leicester, 1867.
Leicester. H. Stocks and W. H. Stevenson, ed., *Records of the borough of Leicester . . .* [vol. iv] 1603–88, Camb. 1923. Cf. H. Hartropp, *Register of the freemen of Leicester . . .*, Leicester, 1927; and his *Roll of the mayors of . . . Leicester*, Leicester, [1936]. J. C. Jeaffreson published *An index to the ancient manuscripts . . . of Leicester*, Westminster, [1878]. The best town history is J. Thompson, *History of Leicester . . . to the end of the seventeenth century*, 1849.

21. LINCOLNSHIRE

(a) *Bibliography*

3206 CORNS, A. R., ed. Bibliotheca Lincolniensis. A catalogue of the books, pamphlets, etc. relating to the city and county of Lincoln . . . in . . . the city of Lincoln Public Library. Lincoln. 1904.

See also Lincolnshire Archives Committee, *Archivists' reports*, nos. (1)–7. July 1948–March 1956, (1950)–1956.

(b) *Local Societies and Journals*

3207 LINCOLNSHIRE ARCHITECTURAL AND ARCHAEOLOGY SOCIETY. Papers. Lincoln. 1850–1937. New ser. 1938+.

Changed in 1935 to *Lincolnshire Associated Architectural Societies.*
See also *Lincolnshire Magazine* (Lindsey Local History Society), Lincoln, 1932–9,which was superseded, 1947+, by *Lincolnshire Historian* (Lincolnshire Local History Society). Also useful is *Lincolnshire Notes and Queries*, Horncastle, 1888–1936.

3208 LINCOLN RECORDS SOCIETY. Publications. Lincoln. 1911+.

Vol. 1 of the series is R. E. G. Cole, ed., *Lincolnshire church notes made by Gervase Holles, 1634–1642.* A parish register series is in progress. See also quarter sessions (936).

(c) *County and Town Histories and Records*

Vol. ii of *V.C.H. Lincoln* has been published, 1906.

3209 ALLEN, T. History of the county of Lincoln. 2 vols. 1834.

See Read (11 n.), nos. 4549–50 on county and church records. For family history, see A. Gibbons, *Notes on the visitation of Lincolnshire, 1634*, Lincoln, 1898; and A. R. Maddison, *Lincolnshire pedigrees*, 4 vols., Harl. Soc., 1902–6.

3210 BREARS, C. Lincolnshire in the 17th and 18th centuries. 1940.

Compiled from numerous local records. Cf. F. V. Brooks, 'The vicissitudes of a Lincoln-shire manor during the civil war and the commonwealth', *E.H.R.* 58 (1943), 344–56; and J. Thirsk, *English peasant farming*, 1957. On fen drainage, see nos. 1931–45.

Boston. R. W. K. Hinton, ed., *The port books of Boston, 1601–40*, Linc. Rec. Soc. Publ. 50 (for 1954–5), 1956. The best history of Boston is by P. Thompson, 1856.
Grantham. E. Turnor, *Collections for the history . . . of Grantham*, 1806.
Lincoln. J. W. F. Hill, *Tudor and Stuart Lincoln*, 1956.

22. NORFOLK

(a) *Bibliography*

3211 QUINTON, J. Bibliotheca Norfolciensis: a catalogue of . . . works relating to Norfolk in the library of J. J. Colman . . . Norwich. 1896.

3212 RYE, W. An index to Norfolk topography. Index Soc. Publ. 10. 1881. Suppl. 1896. App. (later books). 1916.

By Rye also, *An index rerum to Norfolk antiquities*, Norwich, 1899; and *Norfolk handlists*, Norwich, 1924.

(b) *Local Societies and Journals*

3213 NORFOLK AND NORWICH ARCHAEOLOGICAL SOCIETY. Norfolk Archaeology. Norwich. 1847+.

Cf. *Norfolk Antiquarian Miscellany*, 3 vols., Norwich, 1877–87, 2nd Ser., pts. 1–3, Norwich, 1906–8.

3214 NORFOLK RECORD SOCIETY. [Publications.] Fakenham and Lond. 1931+.

Valuable series. Examples for the period are vol. 14 (1941), Paston correspondence, 1607–27; vols. 22 (1951), and 27 (1956), miscellanies.

(c) *County and Town Histories and Records*

Vols. i and ii of *V.C.H. Norfolk* appeared, 1901–6. See also Gawdy papers (H.M.C., no. 142); and P. Millican's articles on the Gawdys in *Norf. Arch.* 26 (1938) and 27 (1941). For quarter sessions see no. 936.

3215 BLOMEFIELD, F. and PARKIN, C. Topographical history of . . . Norfolk. 5 vols. Fersfield. 1739–75. 11 vols. Lond. 1805–10. Index by J. N. Chadwick. King's Lynn. 1862.

The best complete history of the county. A *Supplement*, ed. by C. R. Ingleby, was publ. in 1929.
    Other general histories are *History and antiquities of the county of Norfolk*, 10 vols., Norwich, 1781 (an anon. rearrangement of Blomefield); and R. H. Mason, *History of Norfolk*, 1884. [John Norden,] *The chorography of Norfolk*, was ed. by Mrs. I. Hood, Norwich, 1938.

3216 RYE, W. A history of Norfolk. 1885.

See also *Norfolk records: A collection of record references derived from indexes in the Public Record Office, London*, ed. by W. Rye and W. D. Selby (*Norf. and Norwich Arch. Soc.*), 2 vols., 1886–92; Rye, *Norfolk families*, 2 vols., Norwich, 1913; the Norfolk visitations in Harl. Soc. (2417), vols. 32, 85, 86; Rye, ed., *State papers relating to musters, beacons* . . . (1626 to civil war), Norwich, 1907; and H. Le Strange, *Norfolk official lists*, Norwich, 1890.

3217 SAUNDERS, H. W., ed. The official papers of Sir Nathaniel Bacon of Stiffkey, Norfolk, as justice of the peace 1580–1620. Camd. Soc. 1915.

King's Lynn. B. Mackerell, *The history and antiquities of . . . King's Lynn . . .*, 1738; see also W. Richards, *History of Lynn*, 2 vols., Lynn, 1812; H. J. Hillen, *History of the borough of King's Lynn*, 2 vols., Norwich, 1907; and *A calendar of the freemen of Lynn, 1292–1836*, Norwich, 1913.
Launditch. G. A. Carthew, ed., *The hundred of Launditch and deanery of Brisley*, 3 pts., Norwich, 1877–9, useful as an addition to Blomefield.
Norwich. B. Mackerell, *History of the city of Norwich*, 2 vols. 1737; W. Hudson and J. C. Tingey, ed., *The records of the city of Norwich*, 2 vols., Norwich and Lond. 1906–10, with emphasis on the medieval period; W. L. Sachse, ed., *Minutes of the Norwich court of mayoralty, 1630–1631* (Norf. Rec. Soc. 15), 1942. See also P. Millican, *The register of the freemen of Norwich, 1548–1713*, Norwich, 1934; and B. Cozens-Hardy and E. A. Kent, *The mayors of Norwich, 1403–1835*, Norwich, 1938. W. Rye, ed., *The Norwich rate book* (1633–4), 1903.
Yarmouth. Henry Manship, *History of Great Yarmouth*, ed. by C. R. Palmer, 2 vols., Great Yarmouth, 1854–6. Manship's history, written by the Elizabethan town clerk, is contained in vol. i; Palmer continued the history, utilizing town records, and also H. Swinden's *History and antiquities of . . . Great Yarmouth*, Norwich, 1772. See also C. J. Palmer, *The perlustration of Great Yarmouth*, 3 vols., Great Yarmouth, 1872–5; and *Calendar of the freemen of Great Yarmouth* (Norf. and Norwich Arch. Soc.), Norwich, 1910.

23. NORTHAMPTONSHIRE
(a) *Bibliography*

3218 TAYLOR, J. Bibliotheca Northantonensis. Northampton. [1869?] 2nd edn. 1884.

A bibl. account of what has been written or printed relating to Northamptonshire (25,000 references). Original printing limited to six copies.

(b) *Local Societies and Journals*

3219 NORTHAMPTONSHIRE RECORD SOCIETY. Publications. Hereford. 1924+. Northamptonshire past and present. Northampton. 1948+.

The publications include quarter sessions records (1630–58), ed. by J. Wake, in vol. 1; papers relating to musters, etc. (1586–1623), ed. by J. Wake, vol. 3 (1926). See Mullins (23 n.). Cf. *Northamptonshire Notes and Queries*, Northampton, 1884–96, new series, 1906–31.

(c) *County and Town Histories and Records*

Vols. i–iv of *V.C.H. Northamptonshire* have been published, 1902–37, with a valuable supplementary volume by O. Barron, *Northamptonshire families*, 1906.

3220 BAKER, G. History and antiquities of the county of Northampton. 2 vols. 1822–41.

Incomplete, but useful. See also J. Bridges, *History and antiquities of Northamptonshire, compiled from the manuscript collections of Sir Peter Whalley*, 2 vols., 1791. For additional family history see W. C. Metcalfe, ed., *The visitations of Northamptonshire*, 1887; Harl. Soc. (2417), vol. 87; and H.M.C., *Buccleuch MSS.* 3 (1926).

3221 LENNARD, R. Rural Northamptonshire under the commonwealth. Oxf. 1916.

See also Norden, *Speculi Britanniae . . . Northamptonshire 1610* (3108); and Finch (2193). Many useful 17th-cent. items, especially on witches, are in J. Taylor, ed., *Tracts . . . relating to Northamptonshire*, 2 vols., Northampton, 1870–81. On the clergy, with indexes and biographical sketches, see H. I. Longden, *Northampton and Rutland clergy from 1500*, 16 vols., Northampton, 1939–52.

Northampton. C. A. Markham and J. C. Cox, eds., *Records of the borough of Northampton*, 2 vols., 1898.
Peterborough. See Mellows (954). For Peterborough records of various types see Northamp. Rec. Soc. 9 (1939) and 18 (1956).

24. NORTHUMBERLAND
(a) *Bibliography*

None of importance.

(b) *Local Societies and Journals*

Cf. no. 3163.

3222 SOCIETY OF ANTIQUARIES OF NEWCASTLE-ON-TYNE. Archaeologia Aeliana. Newcastle. 1822+.

Valuable series. For M.P.s, 1559–1831, see 4th Ser. 23 (1945); on county and town officials, see vols. 17, 18, 20, 22. For Newcastle see no. 3224.

(c) *County and Town Histories and Records*

3223 A HISTORY OF NORTHUMBERLAND . . . issued under the direction of the Northumberland county history committee. 15 vols. Newcastle. 1893–1940 (in progress).

An excellent modern work by various authors.

3224 HODGSON, J. and HINDE, J. H. A history of Northumberland. 7 vols. Newcastle. 1820–58.

See also R. Welford, *Men of mark 'twixt Tyne and Tweed*, 3 vols., 1895.

Newcastle-upon-Tyne. R. Welford, *History of Newcastle and Gateshead*, vol. iii, 16th and 17th centuries, 1887. An older history by John Brand was publ. in 2 vols., 1789. See also the publications of the Newcastle upon Tyne Records Committee, 1920+, including: *Newcastle council minute book, 1639–1656*, extracts ed. by M. H. Dodds, 1920; *Register of freemen*, ed. by Dodds, 1923.

25. NOTTINGHAMSHIRE

(a) *Bibliography*

None of importance.

(b) *Local Societies and Journals*

3225 THOROTON SOCIETY. Transactions. Nottingham. 1898+. Record series. Nottingham. 1903+.

See also *Nottinghamshire and Derbyshire Notes and Queries* (3151 n.).

(c) *County and Town Histories and Records*

Vols. i, ii of *V.C.H. Nottingham* have been published, 1906–10. For county records see no. 936; for pedigrees see Harl. Soc. (2417), vol. 4 (1871), and Thoroton Soc. Rec. Ser. 13 (1949).

3226 THOROTON, ROBERT. The antiquities of Nottinghamshire. 1677. 3 vols., with additions by J. Throsby. 1790. 1797.

The classic older history. There are briefer ones by C. Brown, 1891, and A. C. Wood, Nottingham, 1947.

Newark-on-Trent. C. Brown, *A history of Newark-on-Trent*, 2 vols., 1904–7. Cf. article by C. G. Parsloe in *R.H.S. Trans.*, 4th Ser. 22 (1940), 171–98.

Nottingham. Records of the borough of Nottingham, ed. by W. H. Stevenson *et al.*, 9 vols., Lond. and Nottingham, 1882–1956, with vols. iv–vi relating to 1547–1760. For town history, see C. Deering, *Nottingham vetus et nova* . . ., Nottingham, 1751; and J. Blackner, *History of Nottingham*, Nottingham, 1815.

26. OXFORDSHIRE

(a) *Bibliography*

3227 CORDEAUX, E. H. and MERRY, D. H., eds. A bibliography of printed works relating to Oxfordshire (excluding the university and the city of Oxford). Oxf. 1955.

Cf. F. Madan, *Oxford books: a bibliography of printed works relating to Oxford*, 2 vols., Oxf. 1895–1912.

(b) *Local Societies and Journals*

3228 NORTH OXFORDSHIRE ARCHAEOLOGICAL AND NATURAL HISTORY SOCIETY. Banbury. [1856]+.

Called since 1888 *Oxfordshire Archaeological Society*. See also *Oxford Architectural and Historical Society*, Oxf. 1835–1900.

3229 OXFORD HISTORICAL SOCIETY. Publications. Oxf. 1885+.

Valuable.

3230 OXFORD RECORD SOCIETY. Oxford Record Series. Oxf. 1919+.

Publications include many records of estates and parishes.

(c) *County and Town Histories and Records*

Vols. i–iii, v–viii of *V.C.H. Oxford* have appeared, 1907–64. For parliamentary history see W. R. Williams (917); for the University, see *Cultural History*; for pedigrees see Harl. Soc. (2417), vol. 5.

3231 FALKNER, J. M. A history of Oxfordshire. 1899.

Cf. J. M. Davenport, *Oxfordshire lords lieutenant, high sheriffs, . . .*, Oxf. 1868, rev. edn. by T. M. Davenport, Oxf. 1888; and White Kennett, *Parochial antiquities . . . in the counties of Oxford and Bucks.*, Oxf. 1685, enl. edn. 2 vols., Oxf. 1818.

3232 PLOT, ROBERT. The natural history of Oxfordshire. Oxf. 1677. Later edn. by J. Burman. 1705.

Oxford. Anthony à Wood, *The ancient and present state of the city of Oxford*, with additions by John Peshall, 1773. Also Wood, *Survey of the city of Oxford*, ed. by A. Clark, Oxf. Hist. Soc., 3 vols., 1889–99; *Oxford council acts, 1583–1701*, ed. by H. E. Salter and M. G. Hobson, 3 vols., Oxf. Hist. Soc. 87, 95, N.S. 2 (1928–39); and J. E. T. Rogers, ed., *Oxford city documents financial and judicial, 1268–1665*, ibid. 18 (1891).

Wotton. C. Ponsonby, *Wotton: the history of an Oxfordshire parish*, Oxf. 1947.

27. RUTLANDSHIRE

(a) *Bibliography*

None of importance.

(b) *Local Societies and Journals*

See Leicestershire, no. 3203 n.

(c) *County and Town Histories and Records*

V.C.H. Rutland is complete in 2 vols. and index, 1908–36. For family pedigrees see Harl. Soc. (2417), vols. 3, 73.

3233 BLORE, T. History and antiquities of the county of Rutland. Vol. i. Stamford. 1811.

Only vol. i printed. See also James Wright, *History and antiquities of the county of Rutland*, 1684.

28. SHROPSHIRE

(a) *Bibliography*

None of importance.

(b) *Local Societies and Journals*

3234 SHROPSHIRE ARCHAEOLOGICAL AND NATURAL HISTORY SOCIETY. Transactions. Shrewsbury. 1878+.

Many source materials have been printed; valuable notes on members of Parliament. See also *Shropshire Notes and Queries*, 3 vols., Shrewsbury, 1886–7; later series, 8 vols., Shrewsbury, 1892–9.

(c) *County and Town Histories and Records*

Vol. i of *V.C.H. Shropshire* has appeared, 1908. The County Record Office has published *A guide to Shropshire records*, Shrewsbury, 1952. On family pedigrees see Harl. Soc. (2417), vols. 28, 29. For quarter sessions see no. 936.

3235 EYTON, R. W. Antiquities of Shropshire. 12 vols. 1854–60.

Less valuable is T. F. Dukes, ed., *Antiquities of Shropshire, from an old manuscript of Edward Lloyd . . .*, Shrewsbury, 1846.

3236 HURLBURT, C. History and description of the county of Salop. 2 vols. Shrewsbury. 1837.

J. B. Blakeway published *Sheriffs of Shropshire*, Shrewsbury, 1831.

Shrewsbury. H. Owen and J. B. Blakeway, *A history of Shrewsbury*, 2 vols., 1825. Cf. M. Peele, 'Shrewsbury Burgesses, 16th–17th centuries', *Trans. Shrop. Arch. Soc.* 48 (1937), 213–32; H. Beaumont, 'Shrewsbury and ship money', ibid. 49 (1937), 27–41; and H. Johnstone, 'Two governors of Shrewsbury during the great civil war and the interregnum', *E.H.R.* 26 (1911), 267–77.

29. SOMERSETSHIRE

(a) *Bibliography*

3237 GREEN, E. Bibliotheca Somersetensis: a catalogue of books, . . . connected with the county of Somerset. 3 vols. Taunton. 1902.

Cf. A. L. Humphreys, *Somersetshire parishes: a handbook of historical reference to all places in the county*, 2 vols., 1906.

(b) *Local Societies and Journals*

3238 SOMERSET ARCHAEOLOGICAL AND NATURAL HISTORY SOCIETY. Proceedings. Taunton and Shrewsbury. 1849+.

Vol. 83 (1939) contains biographical sketches of county M.P.s, 1258–1832. Cf. *Notes and Queries for Somerset and Dorset*, Sherborne, 1890+; and *Western Antiquary* (3156 n.).

3239 SOMERSET RECORD SOCIETY. Publications. 1887+.

Includes quarter sessions records (1607–77) in 4 vols. (1907–19); Hopton's civil war narrative, vol. 18 (1902).

(c) *County and Town Histories and Records*

Vols. i–ii of *V.C.H. Somerset* have appeared, 1906–11. For quarter sessions see no. 936; for pedigrees see Harl. Soc. (2417), vol. 11.

3240 COLLINSON, J. History and antiquities of the county of Somerset. 3 vols. Bath. 1791.

Cf. W. Phelps, *History . . . of Somersetshire*, 2 vols., 1836–9. For family history see F. A. Crisp, ed., *Abstracts of Somerset wills from the collection of Rev. Frederick Brown*, 6 vols., priv. pr., s.l., 1887–90.

3241 GERARD, THOMAS. A particular description of Somerset [1633]. Ed. by E. H. Bates. Somerset Rec. Soc. vol. 15 (1900).

See also C. E. H. Chadwick Healey, *The history of the part of West Somerset comprising the parishes of Luccombe . . .*, 1901. On county politics see Barnes (928), and his article in *R.H.S. Trans.*, 5th Ser. 9 (1959), 103–32.
Bath. R. Warner, *The history of Bath*, Bath, 1801.
Dunster. H. C. Maxwell Lyte, *A history of Dunster*, 2 vols., 1909.
Taunton. J. Toulmin, *History of the town of Taunton*, Taunton, 1791; ed. by J. Savage, Taunton, 1822. See also R. G. H. Whitty, *The court of Taunton in the sixteenth and seventeenth centuries*, Taunton, 1934.

30. STAFFORDSHIRE

(a) *Bibliography*

3242 SIMMS, R. Bibliotheca Staffordiensis; or a bibliographical account of books relating to the county of Stafford. Lichfield. 1894.

(b) *Local Societies and Journals*

3243 WILLIAM SALT ARCHAEOLOGICAL SOCIETY: Collections for a history of Staffordshire. Birmingham. 1881+.

In 1935 became *Staffordshire Record Society*.
Valuable series, including 2 vols. on parliamentary history, 1917–20; heraldic visitations, 1614 and 1663–4 (1884–5), and many materials on estates and family history.

(c) *County and Town Histories and Records*

Vols. i, iv, v, and viii of *V.C.H. Stafford* have appeared, 1908–63. For pedigrees see Harl. Soc. (2417), vol. 63; for quarter sessions, see no. 936.

3244 PLOT, ROBERT. The natural history of Staffordshire. Oxf. 1686.

Cf. Sampson Erdeswicke, *A survey of Staffordshire* [before 1603?], ed. by R. Rawlinson, 1717, and by T. Harwood, 1820 and 1844.

3245 SHAW, S. History and antiquities of Staffordshire. 2 vols. 1798–1801.

'The best history of the county.' See also A. Peel, 'A Puritan survey of the church in Staffordshire in 1604', *E.H.R.* 26 (1911), 338–52.
Litchfield. T. Harwood, *The history and antiquities of . . . Litchfield . . .*, Gloucester 1806; see also H. Thorpe's study in *Staff. Rec. Soc.* 1950–1 (1954), 139–211.

Newcastle-under-Lyme. T. Pape, *Newcastle-under-Lyme in Tudor and early Stuart Times*, Manchester, 1938; and no. 955.
Tamworth. C. J. Palmer, *History of the town and castle of Tamworth*, Tamworth, 1845.

31. SUFFOLK

(a) *Bibliography*

None of importance, but see Copinger (3248).

(b) *Local Societies and Journals*

3246 THE EAST ANGLIAN, or Notes and Queries Connected with . . . Suffolk, Cambridge, Essex, and Norfolk. Lowestoft. 1864–1910.

See also *Suffolk Green Books*, Wells and Woodbridge, 1894–1929.

3247 SUFFOLK INSTITUTE of Archaeological and Natural History. Proceedings. Bury St. Edmunds. 1853+.

The 1st vol. is called *Proceedings of the Bury and West Suffolk Archaeological Institute.* A useful series, including a vol. on ship-money returns of 1639–40, 1904.

(c) *County and Town Histories and Records*

Vols. i and ii of *V.C.H. Suffolk* have appeared, 1907–11.

3248 COPINGER, W. A., ed. County of Suffolk. Its history as disclosed by existing records . . . 5 vols. 1904–6.

Cf. Copinger's *The manors of Suffolk* . . ., 7 vols., 1905–11.

3249 REYCE, ROBERT. Suffolk in the xviith century: being the breviary of Suffolk by R[obert] Reyce. Ed. by Lord Francis Harvey. 1902.

See also R. Loder, ed., *The journal of William Dowsing of Stratford, parliamentary visitor . . . for demolishing the superstitious pictures . . . within . . . Suffolk* (1643–4), Woodbridge, 1786; later edn. by C. H. Evelyn White, Ipswich, 1885.

3250 SUCKLING, A. The history and antiquities of . . . Suffolk. 2 vols. 1846–8.

The best older history, but incomplete. See also J. J. Raven, *History of Suffolk*, 1895. For family history, see J. J. Howard, *The visitation of Suffolk* [1561], 2 vols., 1866–71; W. C. Metcalfe, *The visitations of Suffolk*, Exeter, 1882; and J. J. Muskett, *Suffolk manorial families*, 3 vols., Exeter, 1900–14.

Orford. R. A. Roberts, 'The borough business of a Suffolk town (Orford), 1559–1660', *R.H.S. Trans.*, 4th Ser. 14 (1931), 95–120.
Ipswich. W. H. Richardson, ed., *The annals of Ipswich . . . by Nath[ll] Bacon . . .* [1654], Ipswich, 1884. Cf. J. Wodderspoon, *Memorials of Ipswich*, Ipswich, 1850.

32. SURREY

(a) *Bibliography*

3251 JENKINSON, C. H. *et al.* Guide to the archives . . . relating to Surrey. 6 vols. *Surrey Rec. Soc.* 23, 24, 26, 28, 29, 31–2 (1925–31).

Deals with Surrey records in P.R.O.; also local parish, manor, and borough records; vol. 32 provides a guide to quarter sessions records.

See also Smith (3190 n.); and M. Stephenson, *A catalogue of books in the library of the Surrey Archaeological Society*, Surrey Arch. Soc. Trans. 10 (1891); also, *A catalogue of works relating to Surrey in the Minet Library*, Camberwell, 1901, suppl. 1923.

(b) *Local Societies and Journals*

3252 SURREY ARCHAEOLOGICAL SOCIETY. Collections. 1858+.

3253 SURREY RECORD SOCIETY. Publications. 1913+.

(c) *County and Town Histories and Records*

V.C.H. Surrey is complete in 4 vols. and index, 1902–14. For quarter sessions see no. 936; for pedigrees see Harl. Soc. (2417), vols. 43, 60, and Berry (3255 n.). On members of Parliament, see Smith (917).

3254 AUBREY, JOHN. The natural history and antiquities of the county of Surrey. 5 vols. 1718–19.

Valuable, based upon Aubrey's tour *c.* 1672–3; notes of inscriptions in parish churches, etc.

3255 MANNING, O. and BRAY, W. History and antiquities of the county of Surrey. 3 vols. 1804–14.

The standard older history. See also E. W. Brayley, *A topographical history of Surrey*, 5 vols., 1850; later edn. by E. Walford, 4 vols., 1878–81. For families see W. Berry, *County genealogies: pedigrees of Surrey families*, 1837.

Bletchingley. A. U. M. Lambert, *Blechingly: a parish history*, 2 vols., 1921. By Lambert also, *Godstone, a parish history*, 1929.

Guildford. The history of Guildford, the county town of Surrey . . ., Guildford, 1777; 1801.

33. Sussex

(a) *Bibliography*

3256 BUTLER, G. S. Topographica Sussexiana; an attempt towards forming a list of the various publications relating to the county of Sussex. *Sussex Arch. Soc. Coll.* 15–18 (1863–6); continued to 1882 by F. E. Sawyer, ibid. 32–3 (1882–3).

See also Smith (3190 n.).

(b) *Local Societies and Journals*

3257 SUSSEX ARCHAEOLOGICAL SOCIETY. Collections. 1848+.

Valuable. See also the society's quarterly journal, *Sussex Notes and Queries*, 1927+.

3258 SUSSEX RECORD SOCIETY. Publications. Lewes. 1902+.

Has published much material on estates, parish and archdeaconry registers, etc. Vol. 5 (1905–6) is 'West Sussex protestation returns, 1641–2'.

(c) *County and Town Histories and Records*

Vols. i–iv, vii, and ix of *V.C.H. Sussex* have appeared, 1905–53. For pedigrees see no. 3259 n.; for military history see Thomas-Sanford (1620); for quarter sessions see no. 936.

3259 HORSFIELD, T. W. History, antiquities and topography of the county of Sussex. 2 vols. Lewes. 1835.

> Cf. J. Dallaway, *History of the western division of the county of Sussex*, 2 vols. (in 3 pts.), 1815–30; 2nd edn. of pt. 3 by E. Cartwright, 1832; and M. A. Lower, *A compendious history of Sussex*, 2 vols., Lewes, 1870. For family history see W. Berry, *County genealogies . . . Sussex*, 1830; J. Comber, *Sussex genealogies*, 3 vols., Camb. 1931–3; and Harl. Soc., vols. 53 and 89 (1905, 1937).
>
> *Chichester.* A. Hay, *History of Chichester*, Chichester, 1804.
>
> *Lewes.* L. F. Salzman, 'The town book of Lewes, 1542–1701', *Sussex Rec. Soc. Publ.* 48 (1947); see also T. W. Horsfield, *The history and antiquities of Lewes*, 2 vols., Lewes, 1824–7.
>
> *Pagham.* L. Fleming, *History of Pagham in Sussex*, 3 vols., Sussex, 1949–50.
>
> *Rye.* W. Holloway, *History and antiquities of the ancient town and port of Rye, with incidental notices of the Cinque Ports*, 1847. See also L. A. Vidler, *A new history of Rye*, 1934.
>
> *Winchelsea.* W. D. Cooper, *History of Winchelsea*, 1850.

34. WARWICKSHIRE

(a) *Bibliography*

None of importance.

(b) *Local Societies and Journals*

3260 DUGDALE SOCIETY. Publications. Oxf. 1921+.

> Mainly local history and records. See also *Warwickshire antiquarian magazine*, 8 pts., Warwick, 1859–77. For others, of less value for the period, see Read (11 n.), p. 402.

(c) *County and Town Histories and Records*

V.C.H. Warwick has been published in 6 vols. with index, 1904–51. Vol. vii, *City of Birmingham* was published 1964; an eighth volume is projected. For pedigrees see Harl. Soc. (2417), vols. 12, 62 (1877–1911); for quarter sessions see no. 936.

3261 DUGDALE, WILLIAM. The antiquities of Warwickshire. Maps. 1656. Later edn. by W. Thomas. 2 vols. 1730.

> The 1730 edn. continued Dugdale's work into the 18th century. See also F. L. Colvile, *Worthies of Warwickshire*, 1870.
>
> *Coventry.* M. D. Harris, *Life in an old English town: a history of Coventry*, 1898. An older history is by B. Poole, 1870. On town records see J. C. Jeaffreson, *A calendar of the books, charters . . . of the city of Coventry*, Coventry, 1896; and M. D. Harris, 'Unpublished documents . . . Coventry', *R.H.S. Trans.*, 4th Ser. 3 (1920), 103–24; and her edn. of *Coventry leet books*, 4 vols., Coventry, 1907–13. On a town guild, see Dugdale Soc., vols. 13, 19 (1935, 1944).
>
> *Warwick.* T. Kemp, ed., *The Black book of Warwick*, Warwick, 1898. Mainly Elizabethan material, some 17th century.

35. WESTMORLAND

(a) *Bibliography*

None of importance.

(b) *Local Societies and Journals*

See Cumberland, no. 3147.

(c) *County and Town Histories and Records*

3262 FLEMING, SIR DANIEL. Description of the county of Westmorland [1671]. Ed. by Sir G. F. Duckett. 1882.

> Cf. Fleming's *Description of the county of Cumberland* [1671] ed. by R. S. Ferguson, Kendal, 1889. Both publ. for Cumb. and Westm. Arch. Soc. from MS. in Bodleian Library.

3263 NICOLSON, J. and BURN, R. History and antiquities of the counties of Westmorland and Cumberland. 2 vols. 1777.

> Index vol. publ. by Cumb. and Westm. Arch. Soc., 1934. Cf. R. S. Ferguson, *History of Westmorland*, 2 vols., 1894.

> *Appleby.* J. F. Curwen, ed., *The later records relating to North Westmorland or the barony of Appleby*, Kendal, 1932. See by Curwen also, *Records relating to the barony of Kendale*, 3 vols., Kendal, 1923–6 (Cumb. and Westm. Arch. Soc., vols. 4–6).

36. WILTSHIRE

(a) *Bibliography*

None of importance.

(b) *Local Societies and Journals*

3264 WILTSHIRE ARCHAEOLOGICAL AND NATURAL HISTORY SOCIETY. Magazine. Devizes. 1854+.

> See also *Wilts. Record Society*, Publications, 1896–1903, and 1939+. A Records Series began, 1937+.

(c) *County and Town Histories and Records*

Vols. i (pt. 1), and ii–vii of *V.C.H. Wiltshire* have appeared, 1953–7. For pedigrees see Harl. Soc. (2417), vols. 105, 106; and Marshall (3266 n.).

3265 AUBREY, JOHN. Collections for the natural and topographical history of Wiltshire. Ed. by Thomas Phillips. 2 vols. 1821–38. With extensions by John Britton. 1847. Further extended by J. E. Jackson. Devizes. 1862.

3266 HOARE, R. C., *et al.* Modern history of Wiltshire. 6 vols. 1822–45.

> See G. W. Marshall, *The visitation of Wiltshire, 1623*, 1882. On town records see M. Rathbone, 'List of Wiltshire borough records . . .', *Wilts. Arch. and Nat. Hist. Soc.*, Rec. Branch, 5 (1951).
> *Bewdley.* P. Styles, 'The corporation of Bewdley under the later Stuarts' (956 n.).

Calne. A. W. Mabbs, 'Guild steward's book of the borough of Calne, 1561–1688', *Wilts. Arch. and Nat. Hist. Soc.*, Rec. Branch, 7 for 1951 (1953). Cf. A. E. W. Marsh, *History of the borough and town of Calne*, Calne, 1903.

Chippenham. F. H. Goldney, *Records of Chippenham* [excerpts], Chippenham, 1889.

Devizes. E. B. H. Cunnington, *Some annals of the borough of Devizes*, 2 vols., Devizes, 1925–6; also his *Rival mayors in Devizes in the reign of Queen Anne*, Devizes, 1934; and J. Waylen and R. D. Gillman, *Annals of Devizes*, 1908.

Marlborough. J. Waylen, *A history . . . of Marlborough*, 1854.

Salisbury. H. Hall, ed., *The commonwealth charter of the city of Salisbury*, [*12*] *September 1656*, in *Camd. Soc. Misc.* xi, 1907, which incidentally 'furnishes the missing clue to the origin of the important commonwealth committee on municipal charters'. Cf. B. L. K. Henderson, 'The commonwealth charters', in *R.H.S. Trans.*, 3rd Ser. 6 (1912), 129–62. For a history of Salisbury see R. Benson and H. Hatcher, *Old and New Sarum or Salisbury*, 1843.

37. WORCESTERSHIRE

(a) *Bibliography*

3267   BURTON, J. R. and PEARSON, F. S., eds. Bibliography of Worcestershire. Part I. Acts of Parliament relating to the county. Part II. Being a classified catalogue of books, and other printed matter. 2 vols. *Worc. Hist. Soc.* 1898–1903.

See also C. L. Nichols, *Bibliography of Worcestershire*, Worcester, 1899.

(b) *Local Societies and Journals*

3268   WORCESTERSHIRE ARCHAEOLOGICAL SOCIETY. Transactions. Worcester. 1923+.

3269   WORCESTERSHIRE HISTORICAL SOCIETY. Publications. Worcester. 1893–1916. 1926+.

(c) *County and Town Histories and Records*

V.C.H. Worcester has been completed in 4 vols. and index, 1901–24. For quarter sessions records see no. 936. For parliamentary history see Williams (917).

3270   HABINGTON, THOMAS. A survey of Worcestershire. Ed. by J. Amphlett. 2 vols. *Worc. Hist. Soc.* 2, 3 (1895–9).

Survey of parishes, 1560–1647.

3271   [NASH, T. R.] Collections for the history of Worcestershire. 2 vols. 1781–2, 2nd edn. and suppl. 1799. Index publ. by *Worc. Hist. Soc.* 5 (1894–5).

On agricultural history see R. C. Gaut, *History of Worcestershire agriculture . . .*, Worcester, 1939; on families, see W. C. Metcalfe, ed., *Visitation of the county of Worcester, 1682–1683*, Exeter, 1883, and Harl. Soc. (2417), vol. 90.

Worcester. M. Hollings, *The red book of Worcester*, Worc. Hist. Soc. 1 vol. in 4 [1934–50].

38. YORKSHIRE

(a) *Bibliography*

3272   BOYNE, W. The Yorkshire library: a bibliographical account of books on topography relating to the county of York. 1869.

See also Clay (3274 n.). W. T. Freemantle compiled *A bibliography of Sheffield and vicinity to . . . 1700*, Sheffield, 1911; and G. E. Kirk compiled *Yorkshire Archaeological Society: Catalogue* [of books, etc. in the Society's library], Wakefield, 1935–6. See also E. Hailstone, *Catalogue of a collection of historical and topographical works, and civil war tracts relating to the county of York*, Bradford, 1858.

(b) *Local Societies and Journals*

See also no. 3164.

3273 BRADFORD HISTORICAL AND ANTIQUARIAN SOCIETY. The Antiquary. Bradford. 1881+.

Publishes also a Local Record Series, e.g. 'West Yorkshire deeds', vol. 2 (1931–6). Other useful series, primarily local in focus, are *Halifax Antiquarian Society, Papers*, Halifax, 1901+; *East Riding Antiquarian Society, Transactions*, Hull, 1893+; *North Riding Record Society, Publications*, 13 vols., 1884–97; and *Thoresby Society, Publications*, Leeds, 1889+.

3274 YORKSHIRE ARCHAEOLOGICAL AND TOPOGRAPHICAL ASSOCIATION. Yorkshire Archaeological and Topographical Journal. 1870+. Record Series. 1885+. A series of extra vols. 1892+. Extra series. 1935+.

The record series includes many parish records, indexes to wills in the York registry, etc. Royalist composition papers are in 3 vols. (1893–6); for quarter sessions of the West Riding see no. 936.

See C. T. Clay, *Catalogue of the publications of the Record Series*, vol. 113 (1948). Cf. *Yorkshire Notes and Queries*, Bingley, 1885–90; continued as *Yorkshire County Magazine*, 1891–4.

(c) *County and Town Histories and Records*

Vols. i–iii and index of *V.C.H. Yorkshire* have appeared, 1907–25; 2 vols. and index complete *V.C.H. North Riding*, 1914–23; *City of York*, 1961. On quarter sessions records of north and west ridings see no. 936; for pedigrees see no. 3275 n.

3275 CARTWRIGHT, J. J. Chapters in the history of Yorkshire being a collection of original letters, papers and public documents. Wakefield. 1872.

More 'complete' county histories are by T. Allen, 3 vols., 1828–31; and T. Baines, 2 vols., 1871–7. See also J. Hunter, *South Yorkshire*, 2 vols., 1828–31. On parliamentary history see Gooder (917). For family history see diaries in no. 2436 and n.; and pedigrees in Harl. Soc., vols. 37–40, Surtees Soc., vol. 36 (1859), and J. Foster, *Pedigrees of . . . Yorkshire*, 3 vols., 1874.

3276 WHITAKER, T. D. The history and antiquities of the deanery of Craven. 3rd edn. by A. W. Morant. 1878.

Also by Whitaker, *A history of Richmondshire . . .*, 2 vols., 1823.

Beverley. J. Dennett, 'Beverley borough records, 1575–1821', *Yorks. Arch. Soc., Rec. Ser.* 84 (1933).

Hooton Pagnell. A. Ruston and D. Whitney, *Hooton Pagnell, the agricultural evolution of a Yorkshire village*, 1934.

Hull. Thomas Gent, *Annales regioduni Hullini, or the entertaining history of . . . Kingston-upon-Hull*, 1735; repr. Hull, 1869; T. T. Wildridge, *Old and new Hull*, Hull, 1884; B. N. Reckitt, *Charles the first and Hull*, 1952. For town records, see *The Hull letters*

(1624). For records of economic interest from Hull's Trinity House see Brooks (2103). Cf. J. M. Lambert, *Two thousand years of gild life*, Hull, 1891.

Leeds. J. G. Clark, ed., 'The court books of the Leeds corporation, 1662–1705', *Thoresby Soc. Publ.* 34 for 1933 (1936). Cf. *A select bibliography of items relating to the official history of Leeds*, [Leeds,] 1952. *A municipal history of Leeds* was publ. by J. Wardell, 1846.

Pontefract. R. Holmes, ed., *The booke of entries of the Pontefract corporation, 1653–1726,* Pontefract, 1882.

Ripon. Ripon millenary record, 2 vols., 1886–91.

Wakefield. S. H. Waters, *Wakefield in the seventeenth century* (1550–1710), Wakefield, 1933.

York. F. Drake, *Eboracum; or the history and antiquities of the city of York,* 1736. 'Valuable.' Cf. 'From an old York chronicle [1578–1709]', *Yorks. Arch. Soc. Proc.* 1 (1935), 36–41; A. Raine, 'Proceedings of the commonwealth committee for York and Ainsty', *Yorks. Arch. Soc., Rec. Ser.* 118 (1953), 1–30; and M. Sellers, 'York in the sixteenth and seventeenth centuries', *E.H.R.* 12 (1897), 437–47.

39. ISLANDS
Channel Islands

3277   GUERNSEY and JERSEY.

Guernsey. Société Guernesiaise, Reports and transactions, Guernsey, 1882+. Name of Society varies: founded in 1882 as *The Guernsey Society of Natural Science; Guernsey Society of Natural Science and Local Research* (1889–1921). Cf. sections on the islands of Jersey, Guernsey, and the Isle of Wight included in R. Warner's *Collections . . . Hampshire* (3180 n.).

Jersey. Société Jersiaise pour l'étude de l'histoire, Bulletins, St. Helier, 1875–1939. A 1685 survey of the island is in vol. 12 (1935), 413–46. See also A. C. Sanders, *Jersey in the 17th century,* Jersey, 1931, and no. 1628.

Isle of Man

3278   CUBBON, W., ed. A bibliographical account of works relating to the Isle of Man . . . 2 vols. 1933–9.

For a history, see R. H. Kinvig, *History of the Isle of Man,* 1944. Several 18th-century titles are in Pargellis, p. 396. See also *Manx Society, Publications,* Douglas, 1859–95.

Isle of Wight

3279   [WORSLEY, SIR RICHARD.] The history of the Isle of Wight. 1781.

The island is dealt with in various works on Hampshire (3178–80); see also *The Oglander memoirs* (2496); and Sir F. Black, *Parliamentary history of the Isle of Wight,* Newport, 1929.

D. LONDON AND MIDDLESEX

As London was the stage on which much of English history was acted in the Stuart period, many general sources and later works are often of far greater importance for its history than works specifically devoted to that subject.

For bibliographies of the latter see nos. 3098–3106, as well as those below. Others may be found in library or sale catalogues; in addition to that on the Guildhall Library, there are those of the libraries of the London County Council, the Bishopsgate Institute, the University of London (Goldsmiths' Library at the University Offices, London section of the library at University College), which all have large general collections, while the libraries of the City of Westminster and most of the metropolitan Boroughs, and the Minet Library at Camberwell (covering all London south of the Thames, see no. 3251 n.) have good local ones.

Sotheby's catalogue of the library of Edward Tyrrell, sold in April 1864, is the most valuable in that class: it gives the titles of many tracts, a most important type of source for London in this period; for them see, for 1640–60, the Br. Mus. Cat. of Thomason Tracts; before and after those dates the footnotes to Sharpe (3299) and the *V.C.H.* (3120), Bell's bibliographies (3291–2), and the above library catalogues, with that of the London Institution [1835]. For literary sources, see the bibliographies in *Camb. Hist. Eng. Lit.* (2579). A useful list of statutes and charters is prefixed to Pulling's *Laws, customs . . of London*, 1842. For maps and views see Grace (3280).

In other sections are numerous works containing matter important for the London region. For London livery companies see Unwin, *Gilds and companies* (1964 n.); nos. 1966–72; and Jones (3281). On population see nos. 1833, 2161–2; on social life and problems see *Social History*. For the county, see no. 936 for Middlesex quarter sessions and notes on county records; for families of Middlesex, see Harl. Soc., vols. 15, 17, and 65 (1880–1941). The *V.C.H. Middlesex*, vol. ii, appeared in 1911 and vol. iii in 1962; and vol. i of *V.C.H. London* in 1909.

1. Bibliographies and Guides

3280   CRACE, J. G., ed. A catalogue of maps, plans and views of London . . . collected . . . by F. Crace. 1878.

The best bibl. on maps; another is included in A. M. Hinds, *Wenceslaus Hollar and his views of London*, 1922. Useful collections of maps and prints are at the Guildhall, the London Museum, Sir John Soane's Museum, and Bishopgate Institute. N. G. Brett-James published *Three maps of 17th-century London*, 1928.

3281   JONES, P. E. and SMITH, R. Guide to the records in the Corporation of London Record Office and the Guildhall Library muniment room. 1951.

For more detail see *Analytical index to the series of records known as the Remembrancia* (9 vols., 1579–1664), ed. by W. H. and H. C. Overall, 1878, the index being virtually a calendar of these valuable records; and *Catalogue of the Guildhall Library*, 1889. See also A. H. Thomas, *Mayor's court rolls*, [1924].

On parochial records see E. Freshfield, *A discourse on some unpublished records of the city of London*, 1887. See also nos. 2416 and 3309.

3282   SMITH, J. E. A catalogue of Westminster records deposited at the town hall. 1900.

Many excerpts. See also Manchee (3297). For registers of St. Margaret's, see A. M. Burke, ed., *Memorials of St. Margaret's* (1539–1660), 1914.

2. Local Societies and Journals

3283   HOME COUNTIES MAGAZINE: devoted to the topography of London, Middx., Essex, Herts, Bucks, Berks, Surrey, and Kent. 1899–1912.

Continuation of *Middlesex and Hertfordshire Notes and Queries*, 4 vols., 1895-8. See also *Middlesex County Records Society*, 1886-92.

3284 LONDON AND MIDDLESEX ARCHAEOLOGICAL SOCIETY. Transactions. 1860+.

Publications include: *Facsimile reproductions of Ogilby and Morgan's Map of the city, 1677*, ed. by C. Welch; and, in N.S. 4, a study of the parliamentary surveys of crown lands, 1649-59, in London and Middlesex.

3285 LONDON TOPOGRAPHICAL SOCIETY. Publications. 1911+.

Includes much 17th-century material, with valuable notes, maps, etc., in its [annual] *London Topographical Record*, 1899+.

3. HISTORIES AND RECORDS

(a) *Sources*

3286 STOW, JOHN. The survey of London . . . Begunne first by . . . John Stow [1598] . . . finished by A. M[unday], H. D[yson] and others. 1633. Later edn. by John Strype. 2 vols. 1720. Ed. by C. L. Kingsford. 2 vols. Oxf. 1908.

Other 17th-century descriptions are: Jean Puget de La Serre, *Histoire de l'entrée de la reine mère* . . . (2373 n.); J. Howell, *Londinopolis*, 1657; William Gough, *Londinum triumphans* [1682]; and T. DeLaune, *The present state of London*, 1681, rev. edn. 1690. On Stow's survey see A. Bonner, in *Trans. London and Middx. Arch. Soc.*, N.S. 8 (1938), 70-4.

3287 [BIRCH, W. DE GRAY], ed. Historical charters and constitutional documents of the city of London. 1884. Bibl. 1887.

For the royal charter, see *The royal charter of confirmation granted by King Charles II to the city of London,* . . . ed. by S. G. Gent, 1680; later edns. 1738, 1745. The second edn., by J.E., has sometimes been catalogued as a new book. See also *The pleadings, arguments and other proceedings in the court of King's Bench upon the Quo Warranto touching the charter of the city of London*, 1690, 1696. Among the pamphlets relating to these proceedings are *The modest enquiry* [1683]; Thomas Hunt, *A defence of the charter* . . ., [1683]; and *A display of tyranny*, 2 pts., 1689-90. For others see Gross (3102).

3288 BRYDALL, JOHN. Camera regis, or a short view of London. Containing the antiquity . . . officers, courts, customs, franchises . . . 1676. 1678.

Useful for constitutional history of the city. See the earlier *Reports of speciall cases touching . . . London*, by Sir Henry Calthrop, 1655, later edn. 1670; and *Lex Londinensis* [1680]. See also Thomas (3281 n.). The best description for the close of the century is William Bohun, ed., *Privilegia Londini: or the laws, customs, and priviledges of the city of London*, 1702, 3rd edn., 1723.

3289 COLSONI, F. Le guide de Londres pour les étrangers (1693). Ed. by E. S. de Beer. Camb. 1951.

Publ. by London Topograph. Soc. Cf. 'London in 1689-90, by the Rev. R. Kirk', in *Trans. London and Middx. Arch. Soc.* 6 (1930-2), 322-42, 487-97, 652 ff.; and 7 (1934-6), 133-57, 305-15; and Z. C. von Uffenbach, *London in 1710* (3281 n.).

3289a WHITEBROOK, J. C., ed. London citizens in 1651. 1910.

Transcribed from Harl. MS. 4478, list of members of 22 companies; with a repr. of a tract giving names of the grand jury of the London quarter sessions, Oct. 1681.

(b) *Later Works*

3290 BEAVEN, A. B. The aldermen of the city of London. 2 vols. 1908–13.

Cf. G. E. Cokayne, *Some account of the lord mayors and sheriffs of . . . London* [1601–25], 1897; and J. J. Baddeley, *The aldermen of Cripplegate ward*, 1900.

3291 BELL, W. G. The great fire of London in 1666. 1920. Bibl. Rev. edn. 1951.

Valuable. Largely derived from MSS. and other sources previously unexplored. Appendices comprising documents, a repr. of the official account in *The London Gazette*, No. 85, Sept. 1666, and lists of the churches and halls destroyed and those preserved. Gives much information both about the state of London before the fire and about the rebuilding. For a few additional references and conclusions see E. Jeffries Davis, in *History*, N.S. 8 (1923), 40–3; and Bell's article, ibid. N.S. 12 (1927), 117–29. For poems on the fire and rebuilding, see R. A. Aubin, *London in flames, London in glory*, New Brunswick, 1943. See also J. Lang, *Rebuilding St. Paul's* (2753 n.); T. F. Reddaway, *The rebuilding of London after the great fire*, 1940, later edn., 1951; A. H. Thomas, 'The rebuilding of London after the great fire', *History*, N.S. 25 (1940), 97–112; and G. Whitteridge, 'The fire of London and St. Bartholomew's hospital', *Lond. Topographical Rec.* 20 (1952), 47–78. John Evelyn's plan for rebuilding after the fire, *London revived*, was ed. by E. S. de Beer, Oxf. 1938. Cf. P. Mills and J. Oliver, *Survey of building sites . . . after the great fire*, 2 vols., London Topograph. Soc. Publ., 1946–56.

3292 BELL, W. G. The great plague in London in 1665. 1924. Bibl.

Based entirely upon contemporary sources, it supersedes all accounts published since Defoe's *Journal of the plague year*, 1722, which the author shows to be essentially a work of fiction, though it incorporates material from the Lord Mayor's orders and the bills of mortality. Cf. *History*, N.S. 10 (1925), 65–7. See also *London in plague and fire, 1655–1666; selected source materials*, Boston, 1957, ed. by R. Bartel; Nathaniel Hodges, *Loimologia, or an Historical account of the plague in London in 1665*, 1720; and W. Kelly, 'Visitations of the plague at Leicester', *R.H.S. Trans.* 6 (1877), 395–447.

3293 BRETT-JAMES, N. G. The growth of Stuart London. Lond. and Middx. Arch. Soc. 1935.

By same author: *Maps* (3280 n.); 'Some extents and surveys of Hendon', part 5, *Trans. Lond. and Middx. Arch. Soc.*, N.S. 7 (1937), 528–44; 'A 17th-century "L.C.C."', ibid., N.S. 5 (1928), 380–412; and 'A speculative London builder of the seventeenth century, Dr. Nicholas Barbon', ibid., N.S. 6 (1929), 110–45. Cf. W. Besant, *London in the time of the Stuarts*, 1903. On London's economic growth see F. J. Fisher (2107). On churches see J. Clayton, *The works of Sir Christopher Wren . . . churches . . . London and Westminster* (Wren Soc. Publ. 9), 1932.

3294 DALE, T. C., ed. The inhabitants of London in 1638 (2161).

Lists householders (and rentals) in 93 out of 107 parishes. See also by Dale, *Members of the city companies in 1641* (Soc. of Genealogists), 1934; *Returns made by parishes . . . of persons assessed for payment of the poll tax of 1641* (Soc. of Genealogists), 6 pts. 1934–9, and *The inhabitants of Westminster in the reign of Charles I* (ibid.), 1935. Cf. *A collection of the names of merchants . . . of London*, 1677 (repr. edn. by J. C. Hotten under title of *The little London directory of 1677*, 1863). Also useful for biography are

R. R. Sharpe, ed., *Calendar of wills proved and enrolled in the court of Husting*, 2 vols., 1889–90; other London wills listed in Brit. Rec. Soc., P.C.C., vols. 5, 6; and G. M. Glencross, ed., *Calendar of marriage license allegations . . . London*, vol. 1, 1597–1648 (Brit. Rec. Soc. Index Lib. 62), 1937.

On the important population studies by John Graunt and Sir William Petty, 1662–76, based on the yearly bills of mortality (original bills in Guildhall Library and Br. Mus.), see Petty (1833). For discussions of the bills see Maitland (3296), and Bell (3292).

3295 DASENT, A. I. The history of St. James's Square and the foundation of the west end of London. Lond. and N.Y. 1895.

The author used the rate-books of the parish, and family MSS. of owners of property there. Appendices print documents. Other useful studies of areas are C. L. Kingsford, *The early history of Picadilly, Leicester Square, Soho . . .*, Camb. 1926; and C. T. Gatty, *Mary Davies and the manor of Ebury*, 2 vols., 1921. On the centre of the city, see S. Perks, *History of the mansion house*, Camb. 1922, and his *Essays on old London*, Camb. 1927. For others see Pargellis (11 n.), no. 3253.

3296 MAITLAND, WILLIAM, *et al.* The history of London . . . including the several parishes. 1739. Later enl. edn. 2 vols. 1756.

Vol. i is chiefly narrative and vol. ii is descriptive; both include useful documents. Examples of London parish histories, most of them with excerpts from the records: J. and H. S. Storer, and T. Cromwell, *History . . . of the parish of Clerkenwell*, 1828; another by W. J. Pinks, Clerkenwell, 1865; G. W. Hill and W. H. Frere, *Memorials of Stepney* (1579–1662), Guildford, 1890–1; E. Freshfield, ed., *Parish of St. Bartholomew Exchange: vestry minutes* (1567–1676), *account books* (1596–1698), 2 vols., 1890–5; also by Freshfield, *Parish of St. Christopher le Stocks: the register book* (1558–1780), *vestry minutes . . .* [and] *accounts*, 6 vols., 1882–95, and *The vestry book of . . . St. Margaret Lothbury*, 1571–1677, 1887, as well as his article on St. Stephen Coleman Street in *Archaeologia*, 50 (1887), 17–57; T. Mason, *Catalogue of books and documents . . . parish of St. Martin-in-the-Fields*, 1895, and its parish records partially ed. by J. V. Kitto, 1901, and by J. McMaster, 1916; F. H. W. Sheppard, *Local government in St. Marylebone, 1688–1835*, Fairlawn, N.J., 1958; and W. S. Simpson, *Chapters in the history of old St. Paul's*, 3 vols., 1881–94, and documents on St. Paul's ed. by Simpson in Camden Soc., N.S. 26 (1880).

3297 MANCHÉE, W. H. The Westminster city fathers (the Burgess Court of Westminster), 1585–1901. 1924.

Includes extracts from minutes, 1610–15 (later vols. of the period are lost). Compare with ch. iv on Westminster in Webb, *Local government* (930), vol. ii.

3298 PEARL, V. London on the outbreak of the puritan revolution: city government and national politics, 1625–1643. 1961.

Valuable. For later in the period see C. M. Clode, *London during the great rebellion* (1612); and Clode's *Memorials of the . . . Merchant Taylors*, 1875; also Sharpe (q.v.).

3299 SHARPE, R. R. London and the kingdom. 3 vols. 1894–5.

Important, based mainly on Guildhall archives, with documents 1603–83 in vol. iii, app.

3300 SURVEY OF LONDON, issued by the . . . London County Council. [In progress.] 32+ vols. 1900–64+.

Valuable series; deals mainly with buildings and antiquities, arranged by parishes. A useful topographical dictionary is H. B. Wheatley [and P. Cunningham], *London past and present*, 3 vols., 1891, based on Cunningham's *Handbook of London*, 2 vols., 1849; rev. 1850.

E. DIOCESE AND PARISH

Sections on local ecclesiastical history are included in *The Victoria History of the Counties* (3120). Several types of church records, including parish registers and others useful for genealogical purposes, are described in nos. 2415–16, 2418, and 3304. Local materials relating to non-Anglican religious groups in this bibliography are in the sections relating to those groups in *Ecclesiastical History*; and some materials on parishes have been cited in the previous portions of the present chapter. Mullins (23 n.) should be referred to for publications by local societies. See also the reports of the Historical Manuscripts Commission (241–4); and Webb, *English local government* (930).

I. GENERAL

3301 DIOCESAN HISTORIES. S.P.C.K. 21 vols. 1880–1902.

Brief histories, by various authors. For a fuller listing see Gross (11), no. 820*b*. See also G. Hill, *English dioceses: a history of their limits*, 1900.

3302 EPISCOPALIAN VISITATION returns for Cambridgeshire, 1638, 1662. Ed. by W. M. Palmer. Camb. 1930.

An important type of diocesan record in the period. See also a preliminary article by Palmer in *Camb. and Hunt. Arch. Soc. Trans.* 4 (1929), 313–411; and W. P. Kennedy's 'List of visitations' (1107). Other examples are: *Visitation articles, archdeaconry of Berkshire*, Oxf. 1635; Buckingham, 1662 (*Bucks. Rec. Soc.* 7 (1943), publ. 1947); Carlisle, 1612 (*Cumb. and Westm. Ant. and Arch. Soc. Trans.*, N.S. 49 (1950), 148–55), and 1703–4 (ibid. 1877); Durham, 1662–71 (*Arch. Aeliana*, 4th Ser. 34 (1956), 92–109); Essex, 1685 (*Essex Arch. Soc. Trans.*, N.S. 21 (1934)); Notts. 1603 (*Thoroton Soc. Trans.* 46 (1942), 3–14); and Salisbury, 1607 (*Wilts. Arch. and Nat. Hist. Mag.* 50 (1943), 170–87).

3303 PHILIPS, E. 'A list of printed churchwardens' accounts.' *E.H.R.* 15 (1900), 335–41.

See a good survey with extracts representing numerous parishes in J. C. Cox, *Churchwardens' accounts*, 1913. Based chiefly on such accounts, is B. Garside, *Parish affairs in Hampton town during the seventeenth century*, Hampton, 1954. Examples of good published accounts are I. L. Gregory, ed., *The Hartland church accounts, 1597–1706*, 1950; C. Drews, ed., *Lambeth churchwardens' accounts, 1504–1645, and vestry book, 1610* (Surrey Rec. Soc. Publ. 20), 1950; H. Johnstone, ed., *Churchwardens' presentments* (Chichester and Lewes), 2 vols. (Sussex Rec. Soc. 49–50), 1948–50; H. Peet, ed., *Liverpool vestry books, 1681–1834*, 2 vols., Liverpool, 1912–15; H. R. Plomer, ed., *Churchwardens' accounts of St. Nicholas, Strood*, Pt. 2, 1603–62 (Kent Records 5, for 1915, 1927). See also S. A. Peyton, ed., *Churchwardens' presentments in Oxfordshire . . .* (Oxfordshire Rec. Soc. 10), 1928.

3304 THOMPSON, A. H. Parish history and records. 1919. Rev. edn. 1926.

In 'Helps for students of history' series. On several London parishes see Freshfield (3281 n.) and Maitland (3296). On parish registers see also no. 2416; and C. L. Grose (10), no. 1428. A good work on parish finance is S. Ware, *The Elizabethan parish*, Baltimore, 1908.

2. PARTICULAR DIOCESES AND PARISHES

3305 DART, J. The history and antiquity of the cathedral church of Canterbury. 1726.

Several docs. relating to Canterbury in the 17th cent. are pr. in *Arch. Cant.* 42 (1930), 93–139, and 49 (1938), 195–222.

3306 BROWNBILL, J., ed. List of clergymen in the diocese of Chester, 1691. Chetham Soc., N.S. 3. Manchester. 1915.

Cf. J. R. Beresford, ed., 'Churchwardens' accounts of Holy Trinity, Chester, 1532 to 1633', *Chester, North Wales A.A. Hist. Soc. Jour.*, N.S. 38 (1951), 95–172; and J. V. H. Burne, 'History of Chester cathedral in the reigns of James I and Charles I', ibid. 39 (1952), 59–91.

3307 GIBBONS, A., ed. The Ely episcopal records: a calendar and concise view of the episcopal records preserved in the muniment room of the palace at Ely. 1891.

A *History . . . of the . . . cathedral church of Ely*, by J. Bentham, was publ. Camb. 1771, 2nd edn., Norwich, 1812.

3308 FOSTER, C. W., ed. The state of the church in the reigns of Elizabeth and James I as illustrated by documents relating to the diocese of Lincoln. Lincoln Rec. Soc. 23+. Horncastle. 1926+.

Vol. i, 1571–1607; vol. ii, 1608–25. Cf. K. Major, *A handlist of the records of the bishops of Lincoln and of the archdeacons of Lincoln and Stow*, 1953; and J. H. Srawley, *Michael Honywood, dean of Lincoln, 1660–81*, Lincoln minster pamphlets, no. 5 [1951].

3309 CALENDAR OF THE ALLEGATIONS in the registry of the Bishop of London, 1597–1700. 1934.

Brit. Rec. Soc. Publ. See also J. Dodd, 'Troubles in a city parish under the protectorate [i.e. St. Botolph without Aldgate]', *E.H.R.* 10 (1895), 41–54. See also Richard New-court, *Repertorium ecclesiasticum parochiale Londinense*, 2 vols., 1708–10; and G. L. Hennessy, *Novum repertorium ecclesiasticum parochiale Londinense*, 1898. Various London parishes have been included in the Register Series of the Harleian Society.

3310 WILLIAMS, J. F. and COZENS-HARDY, B., eds. Extracts from the two earliest minute books of the dean and chapter of Norwich Cathedral, 1566–1649. Norfolk. 1953.

Norfolk Rec. Soc. 24. Cf. E. H. Carter, *Norfolk incumbents for the period 1660–1720 . . .*, Norwich, 1936; and his *Norwich subscription books* (1637–1800), 1937. For Peterborough see Mellows (954) and Longden (3221 n.).

3311 BARRATT, D. M., ed. Ecclesiastical terriers of Warwickshire parishes. Vol. i [A–Li]. Oxf. 1955.

Dugdale Soc. Publ. 22. Series of terriers, Elizabeth to Anne. Several articles on Staffordshire parish surveys are in *Hist. Coll. Staffordshire*, 1938, pp. 203–63, and 1944, pp. 1–86; see also *Worc. Hist. Soc. Publ.* 34 (1924).

3312 DART, J. Westmonasterium: the history and antiquities of the abbey church of St. Peter's, Westminster. 2 vols. *c.* 1742. Plates.

Cf. H. F. Westlake, *Westminster Abbey*, 2 vols., 1923; and *The marriage, baptismal and burial registers . . . of St. Peter, Westminster*, Harl. Soc., 1876; and *Allegations for marriage licenses* (1558–1669), ibid. 1886.

3313 STEPHENS, W. R. W. and MADGE, F. T., eds. Documents relating to the history of the cathedral church of Winchester in the seventeenth century. Hampshire Record Soc. 1897.

Cf. A. W. Goodman and W. H. Hutton, *The statutes governing the cathedral church of Winchester given by King Charles I*, Oxf. 1925; and F. R. Goodman, *Reverend landlords and their tenants*, Winchester, 1930.

3314 LAWTON, G. Collectio rerum ecclesiasticarum de diocesi eboracensi; or collections relative to . . . the diocese of York [and] . . . the diocese of Ripon. 2 vols. 1840. New edn. 1 vol. 1842.

E. W. Crossley compiled indexes to documents in the consistory court of York, 1427–1658, and in the court of the dean of York, 1604–1722 (Yorks. Arch. Soc. Rec. Ser. 73), Leeds, 1928. For Ripon minster fabric accounts, 1661–76, see the society's vol. 118 (1953), pp. 85–150. Many notes on ecclesiastical affairs are in *Yorks. Arch. Jour.*; see also Yorkshire Parish Register Society's series of published registers, 1899+.

XII

COLONIAL HISTORY

Other sections containing titles relating to colonial history are *Constitutional History* (nos. 742–4, 777–82), *Economic History* (especially commercial companies and voyages), and *Naval History*. The general sections on social life and cultural development likewise include titles of value for the corresponding aspects of colonial history.

Only selected bibliographies and guides, with a few representative titles of later works, are included for the mainland North American colonies.

A. GENERAL AND MISCELLANEOUS

1. BIBLIOGRAPHIES, GUIDES, AND SOURCES

Most of the bibliographies listed under *American Colonies* contain titles relating to the whole subject of colonization, such as that by A. P. C. Griffin (3334). Probably the best series of bibliographies is in the *Cambridge history of the British empire* (3322). See also the select bibliographies in M. Jensen, ed., *American colonial documents*. [1607]–1776 (vol. ix of *English Historical Documents*), 1955. The chapter on *Economic History*, especially *Trade and Commerce*, includes numerous titles related to the beginnings of empire. The major trading companies are listed there.

3315 LEWIN, P. E. Subject catalogue of the library of the Royal Empire Society, formerly Royal Colonial Institute. 4 vols. 1930–7.

Important; topographically arranged.

3316 HIGHAM, C. S. S. The colonial entry-books: a brief guide to the colonial records in the Public Record Office before 1696. (Helps for students of history series.) 1921.

Probably the most convenient guide. See also the 1911 *List of Colonial Office records* [in the P.R.O.]; and *Catalogue of the printed books in the library of the Colonial Office* (1896; suppl., 1907).

3317 ACTS OF THE PRIVY COUNCIL, colonial series (1613–1783). Ed. by W. L. Grant and J. Munro. 6 vols. Stationery Office. 1908–12.

This series, with the next two entries, provide valuable official source material, and useful introductions. See also *Journals of the Commissioners for Trade and Plantations* (777).

3318 CALENDARS OF STATE PAPERS, colonial series. (1) America and West Indies [1574–1714], ed. by W. N. Sainsbury *et al.*, *c.* 38 vols., 1860+; (2) East Indies, China, and Japan [1513–1634], ed. by W. N. Sainsbury, 5 vols., 1862–92.

3319   LABAREE, L. W., ed. Royal instructions to British colonial governors, 1670–1776. 2 vols. N.Y. and Lond. 1935.

See also 'List of commissions and instructions . . . 1609–1784', *Amer. Hist. Assoc. Rep.*, 1911, i. 393–528; and *A.H.R.*, 3 (1898), 170–6.

3320   STOCK, L. F., ed. Proceedings and debates of the British parliaments respecting North America. 5 vols. (to 1754+). Wash. 1924–41+.

Vol. i, 1542–1688; ii, 1689–1742.

2. LATER WORKS

3321   ANDERSON, J. S. M. The history of the Church of England in the colonies and foreign dependencies of the British empire. 3 vols. 1845–56. Later edn. 1856.

Cf. L. B. Wright, *Religion and empire, 1558–1625*, 1943.

3322   CAMBRIDGE HISTORY OF THE BRITISH EMPIRE. Ed. by J. H. Rose, A. P. Newton, *et al.* 8 vols. in 9. Camb. 1926–59.

For the vols. on India see no. 3390.

3323   CRUMP, H. J. Colonial admiralty jurisdiction in the seventeenth century. 1931.

Excellent treatise on the development of admiralty jurisdiction in the American colonies and the West Indies. See also Doty (756).

3324   EGERTON, H. E. A short history of British colonial policy. 1897. 5th edn. 1918. 9th edn. 1932. Bibl.

A standard work. On special aspects see also G. H. Gutteridge, *The colonial policy of William III and the West Indies*, Camb. 1922; C. R. Fay, *Imperial economy and its place in the formation of economic doctrine, 1600–1932*, 1934; K. E. Knorr, *British colonial theories, 1570–1850*, Toronto, 1944; and E. E. Rich, 'The first earl of Shaftesbury's colonial policy', *R.H.S. Trans.*, 5th Ser. 7 (1957), 47–70.

3325   GIBB, A. D. Scottish empire. Macklehose. 1937.

On the role played by Scotsmen in the history of the empire. Cf. G. P. Insh, 'Some notes on the literature of Scots colonisation', *Glasgow Bibl. Soc. Rec.* 8 (1928), 57–63.

3326   INNES, A. D. The maritime and colonial expansion of England under the Stuarts. 1932.

For one aspect of colonial trade see A. M. Wilson, 'The logwood trade in the seventeenth and eighteenth centuries', in *Essays in the history of modern Europe*, ed. by D. C. MacKay, N.Y. 1936.

3327   LUCAS, C. P., ed. Historical geography of the British colonies. 7 vols. in 11. Oxf. 1888–1920. Many edns.

Vol. ii, by Lucas, West Indies, 1890, later edn. by C. Atchely, 1905; vol. iii, by Lucas, West Africa, 1894, 1900; vol. v, pt. 4, Newfoundland, by J. D. Rogers, 1911.

3328   NEWTON, A. P. The colonizing activities of the English puritans. Intro. by C. M. Andrews. New Haven. 1914.

By Newton also: *The British empire to 1783*, 1935.

3329 WILLIAMSON, J. A. A short history of British expansion. 1922.
2 vols. 1930. Later edns. 1945–53. Bibl.

> Vol. i, *The old colonial empire,* is a standard authority. See also Beer (3336); G. B. Hertz,
> *The old colonial system,* Manchester, 1905; and J. T. Adams, *Building the British empire,*
> 1938. M. Wright, *The development of the legislative council, 1606–1945,* 1946, is vol. i
> of *Studies in colonial legislatures.*

B. AMERICAN COLONIES (MAINLAND)

I. BIBLIOGRAPHIES AND GUIDES

The existence of a number of detailed bibliographies to some extent atones for
the relatively few entries which limitations of space permit. With regard to the
sources an attempt has been made to show the kind of available material. In
choosing the later works two principles have been adopted: to cover the wide
field as adequately as possible, and to give fair representation to the different
schools of American historians. A comprehensive list of bibliographies is Beers
(3333 n.). The most complete, up to 1954, is *The Harvard Guide to American
History* (3334); A. P. C. Griffin (3332) is invaluable for the publications of
historical societies, and Grace Griffin for the annual output of historical literature.
For Canada see publications of the Hudson's Bay Record Society (2131).

Books dealing with the relations of the colonies and the home government
will be found in the section devoted to central administration in *Constitutional
History*. An excellent collection of sources, with good bibliographical sections
is Jensen (see p. 483).

3330 ANDREWS, C. M. Guide to the materials for American History to 1783,
in the Public Record Office of Great Britain. 2 vols. Wash. 1912–14.

> Cf. by Andrews and F. G. Davenport: *Guide to the manuscript materials for the history
> of the United States to 1783 in the British Museum, in minor London archives, and in the
> libraries of Oxford and Cambridge,* Wash. 1908. See also 'Guide to the items relating to
> American history in the reports of the English Historical Manuscripts Commission', ed.
> by J. F. Jameson, *American Hist. Assoc. Rep. for 1898* (1899), pp. 611–708; and G. G.
> Griffin's *Guide to manuscripts relating to American history in British depositories, repro-
> duced for the Division of Manuscripts of the Library of Congress,* Library of Congress,
> 1946. More recent listings of MSS. and locations are in B. R. Crick and M. Alman,
> *A guide to manuscripts relating to America in Great Britain and Ireland,* 1961.

3331 HANDBOOK OF MANUSCRIPTS in the Library of Congress. Wash.
1918.

> For supplements (1932, 1939), and for guides to MSS. in other libraries and in local
> archives, see Pargellis, pp. 452–3. See also Hale (20).

3332 GRIFFIN, A. P. C., ed. Bibliography of American historical societies
(the United States and the Dominion of Canada, to 1905). *A.H.A. Rep. for
1905,* vol. ii. 2nd edn. Wash. 1907.

> First edn. 1895, pp. 675–1236. Invaluable.

3333 GRIFFIN, G. G., ed. Writings on American history, 1906–8. A bibliography of books and articles on United States and Canadian history during the
year. Wash. and N.Y. 1908.

A vol. for 1902 was ed. by E. C. Richardson and A. E. Morse, Princeton, 1904; for 1903 by A. C. McLaughlin, W. A. Slade, and E. D. Lewis, Wash. 1905. After 1906 an annual publication of great value. From 1918 on, publ. as vol. 2 of *Annual rep.* of A.H.A. as an annual bibl. on American and Canadian history. See also H. P. Beers, *Bibliographies of American history: a guide to materials for research* (2nd edn., N.Y. 1942).

3334 HANDLIN, O. *et al.*, eds. The Harvard guide to American history. Camb. (Mass.). 1954.

The most complete guide, with a full index. There are various specialized bibls. but little annotation. Useful bibls. are included in the vols of the New American Nation series that relate to the period (3335 n.).

2. LATER WORKS

Because the history of the colonies on the mainland of North America has been treated so intensively by American historians, with numerous bibliographies and guides available, the titles selected for inclusion here are those of representative works only. The sources have been omitted almost entirely, and all of the specialized bibliographies. For other titles, especially the best for particular regions or colonies, see Pargellis, pp. 458–79. Invaluable both for articles and bibliography is *The American Historical Review* (25). See also *Canadian Historical Review* (28).

3335 ANDREWS, C. M. The colonial period of American history. 4 vols. New Haven. 1934–8. Bibl.

Indispensable for the development of colonial policy by the author of numerous works on British colonial policy and its consequences. The work of earlier authorities is the somewhat dated but still useful American Nation series ed. by A. B. Hart *et al.*, 28 vols., N.Y. and Lond. 1904–18; it should be supplemented by the volumes in the New American Nation series, ed. by H. S. Commager and R. Morris, N.Y. 1954+ (in progress).

3336 BEER, G. L. The origins of the British Colonial system, 1578–1660. N.Y. 1908. 1922.

Continued in *The old colonial system*, 2 vols., N.Y. 1912, repr. 1933 and 1958, which influenced all historical writing on economic policies, superseding earlier studies.

3337 LABAREE, L. W. *Royal government in America.* New Haven. 1930.

Largely supersedes E. B. Greene, *The provincial governor in the English colonies of North America*, N.Y. 1898. For other titles see *Central Administration, Board of Trade* in Ch. III *supra*. For a short survey of the colonial constitution see A. B. Keith, *The first British empire*, 1930.

3338 OSGOOD, H. L. The American colonies in the seventeenth century. 3 vols. N.Y. 1904–7.

Still the standard work for institutional and religious history. Continued in his *The American colonies in the eighteenth century*, 4 vols., N.Y. 1924. For ecclesiastical policy see A. L. Cross, *The Anglican episcopate and the American colonies*, N.Y. 1902, bibl.; and for the church in the colonies, see W. S. Perry, ed., *Historical collections relating to the American colonial church*, 5 vols. in 4, Hartford, 1870–8.

The first vol. of E. Channing's *History of the United States*, 6 vols., N.Y. 1905–36, which deals with the period to 1660, is now out of date, although Channing's work supersedes that of the earlier historians such as Bancroft, 10 vols., 1834–74. Still of some use for its bibl. references to MS. materials is J. Winsor's *The narrative and critical history of America*, 8 vols., N.Y. 1884–9.

3339 PROWSE, D. W. The history of Newfoundland from the English, colonial, and foreign records. 1895. Bibl. Later edn. 1896.

The principal authority. Cf. R. G. Lounsbury, *The British fishery at Newfoundland, 1634–1763*, New Haven, 1934.

3340 SCHLESINGER, A. M. and FOX, D. R., eds. A history of American life. 12 vols. N.Y. 1927–44.

Emphasizing economic and social history, vol. ii by T. J. Wertenbaker is *The first Americans, 1607–1690*, 1927, and vol. iii by J. T. Adams is *Provincial society, 1690–1763*, 1927. See E. B. Greene, *Provincial America*, vol. vi, 1905. Useful single volumes on colonial manufactures are those by V. S. Clark, Wash. 1916; and R. M. Tryon, Chicago, 1917.

3341 TYLER, M. C. History of American literature, 1607–1765. 2 vols. N.Y. 1878. 1897. Vol. i reissued Ithaca, 1949.

An excellent early work, still useful for its bibliographies. For later interpretations see P. Miller, *The New England mind*, 2 vols., N.Y. 1939–53; and E. A. J. Johnson, *American economic thought in the seventeenth century*, 1932.

C. WEST INDIES

1. BIBLIOGRAPHIES AND GUIDES

3342 CUNDALL, F. (1) Bibliographia Jamaicensis. Kingston, Jamaica. 1902. With supplement 1908. (2) Bibliography of the West Indies (excluding Jamaica). Kingston. 1909. With supplements 1915 and 1919.

Very useful, though uncritical and not claiming to be exhaustive; hand-list arranged in chronological order of publication under geographical headings. A useful commentary on West Indian historiography, though excluding works on biography and the slave trade, is E. V. Goveia, *A study on the historiography of the British West Indies to the end of the nineteenth century*, Mexico, 1956.

3343 PARES, R. 'Public records in British West India Islands.' *Bull. Inst. Hist. Research*, 7 (1930), 149–57.

Best guide to local records; for those in Great Britain see Higham (3316). See also J. de Dampierre, *Essai sur les sources de l'histoire des Antilles françaises 1492–1664*, Paris, 1904 (vol. 6 of Mémoires et documents publiés par la Société de l'École des Chartes); and *List of works in the New York Public Library relating to the West Indies* (in vol. 16 of *Bull. of N.Y. Publ. Lib.*), N.Y. 1912. For a special collection of sources see E. M. Oldham, 'The Hunt collection on the West Indies', *Boston Publ. Libr. Quart.* 11 (1959), 21–32.

2. GENERAL ACCOUNTS

3344 GAGE, THOMAS. The English American, his travail by sea and land: or A new survey of the West Indies. 1648. Later edns. 1699. By A. P. Newton. 1928.

Personal description of travels in Mexico; a very popular book, which is believed to have influenced Cromwell's West Indian policy.

See also, for geographical information and some of historical value, John Ogilvy, *America, being the latest . . . description of the New World*, 1671 (repr. 1851, Kingston, Jamaica, under title of *A description and history of Jamaica*).

3345 DU TERTRE, J. B. Histoire générale des Antilles habitées par les François. 4 vols. Paris. 1667–71. Maps. Plates.

Invaluable for early relations of French and English in West Indies up to 1668. Many documents quoted at length. Du Tertre made several voyages to the West Indies. His first work was publ. in 1654 under the title: *Histoire générale des isles de S. Christophe, de la Guadaloupe*. For critical discussion see de Dampierre (1824).

3346 HARLOW, V. T., ed. Colonising expeditions to the West Indies and Guiana 1623–1667. Hakluyt Soc., 2nd Ser. 56. 1925.

See also Jean Baptiste Labat, *Nouveau voyage aux isles de l'Amérique . . .*, 6 vols., Paris, 1722, which is based on the author's observations for eleven years beginning in 1694. See also Hans Sloane (2404).

3347 EXQUEMLIN, ALEXANDRE O. [or JOHN ESQUEMELING]. Bucaniers of America. 1684. Various later edns. 1699. Enl. 1911. 1951. Maps.

Informative on local affairs in the West Indian colonies as well as on piracy. Translated from the original Dutch (Amsterdam, 1678), it has been the source of numerous later compilations. For critical discussion see de Dampierre (1824) and Haring (3351).

3348 THOMAS, DALBY. An historical account of the rise and growth of the West India collonies, and of the great advantages they are to England, in respect to trade. 1690.

A typical mercantilist argument. Repr. in *Harl. Misc.* ix. 403–45. For the point of view of a Barbadian see the pamphlet, *The groans of the plantations*, by [Edward Littleton], 1689.

3349 CARIBBEANA, being miscellaneous papers relating to the history, genealogy, topography, and antiquities of the British West Indies. Ed. by V. L. Oliver. 6 vols. 1909–19. Maps. Plans. Ports.

A quarterly magazine containing a valuable if miscellaneous collection of transcripts of original MSS., both public and private, parish registers, genealogical trees, etc. Much material for 17th century.

For documents on Irish migration in this century see article by A. Gwynn in *Analecta Hibernica*, 4 (1932), 140–86.

3350 EDWARDS, B. The history, civil and commercial, of the British colonies in the West Indies. 2 vols. 1793. 3rd edn. 3 vols. 1801. 5 vols. 1819.

The 'standard' history, but more valuable for later periods than for the 17th century. Still useful, though dull, is T. Southey, *Chronological history of the West Indies*, 3 vols., 1827. The best popular account is Lucas (3327).

3351 HARING, C. H. The buccaneers in the West Indies in the seventeenth century. 1910. Bibl.

An important study, with a critical bibl. Cf. V. Barbour, 'Privateers and pirates in the West Indies', *A.H.R.* 16 (1911), 529–66.

3352 NEWTON, A. P. European nations in the West Indies, 1493–1688 [Pioneer histories]. 1933.

For special periods see A. P. Watt, *Une Histoire des colonies anglaises aux Antilles* (*1649–60*), Paris, 1925; Henri R. du Motey, *Guillaume d'Orange et les origines des Antilles Françaises*, Paris, 1908, which is based partly on MS. sources and partly on Du Tertre; articles on the West Indies in international politics by A. P. Newton in *History*, 19 (1935), 302–10, W. G. Bassett (abstr. of a thesis) in *Bull. Inst. Hist. Research*, 13 (1935), 48–50, and W. T. Morgan in *J.M.H.* 2 (1930), 378–409. On the naval aspects see Bourne (1819).

3353 THORNTON, A. P. West India policy under the restoration. Oxf. 1956.

An important modern study, dealing with international as well as domestic problems. By Thornton also, an article on the early slave trade, 1660–85, in *William and Mary Quart.*, 3rd Ser. 10 (1955), 399–409. See also Pares (2126).

3354 WILLIAMSON, J. A. The Caribbee Islands under the proprietary patents. 1926.

Important for new light from MS. sources. See also no. 3375, by the same author. Useful material on the 17th and 18th centuries is in L. M. Penson, *The colonial agents of the British West Indies*, 1924, bibl. and docs. Cf. H. H. Wrong, *Government of the West Indies*, Oxf. 1923, bibl.

3. BAHAMAS

3355 MALCOLM, H., ed. Historical documents relating to the Bahama Islands. Nassau. 1910.

See also Malcolm's *List of documents relating to the Bahama Islands in the British Museum and the Record Office, London*, Nassau, 1910.

3356 HASSAM, J. T. The Bahama Islands: notes on an early attempt at colonization. Camb., Mass. 1899.

Deals with the history of the islands in the 17th century, and quotes original docs. In *Mass. Hist. Soc. Proc.*, 2nd Ser., vol. 13. One early record is *Company of adventurers for . . . the plantation of the islands of Eleutheria, formerly called Bahama: articles and orders*, 1647.

4. BARBADOS

3357 FOSTER, NICHOLAS. A briefe relation of the late horrid rebellion acted in the island Barbadas. 1650. Later edn. 1879.

An example of the stream of pamphlets called forth by the Cavalier–Roundhead struggle in the Barbados. See Cundall, *Bibl.* (3342), p. 1. Other contemporary materials have been printed in *Barbados Mus. and Hist. Soc. Jour.*, vol. 1+, 1934+.

3358 LIGON, RICHARD. A true and exact history of the island of Barbados. 1657.

Rather a description of the island and life there than a history; written by Ligon, after three years on the island, while he was in debtor's prison in London. Regarding the value of *Some memoirs of the first settlement of the island of Barbadoes* [by William Duke?], 1741 (repr. 1939), see Williamson (3354).

3359 THE LAWS OF BARBADOES. Comp. by W. Rawlin. 1699.

A collection of the Acts made by the clerk to the Assembly. There are several later collections of the Acts of Assembly, but with only the laws currently in force printed *in extenso*. Cf. R. Pares, a series of articles on Barbados history from records of the prize courts in *Barbados Mus. and Hist. Soc. Jour.* 6 (1938–9), 10–20, 59–66.

3360 SCHOMBURGK, R. H. The history of Barbados, comprising a geographical and statistical description of the island; and a sketch of the historical events since the settlement. 1848. Maps. Plates.

A book of great learning and authority, though recent research has added much to our knowledge of the early history of Barbados; see V. T. Harlow's *A history of the Barbadoes 1625–85*, Oxf. 1926; N. D. Davis, *The Cavaliers and the Roundheads of Barbados, 1650–1652*, Georgetown, Br. Guiana, 1887; and articles by the latter preserved in the Royal Colonial Institute, Lond. See also W. S. Samuel, *A review of the Jewish colonists in Barbadoes* [1680], 1936 (publ. also in *Jewish Hist. Soc. Trans.* 13 (1936), 1–111).

5. BERMUDA

3361 ACTS OF ASSEMBLY made and enacted in the Bermuda or Summer Islands from 1690 to 1714. 1719.

Also, Reginald Gray, ed., *Acts of . . . Bermuda, 1690–1883*, 2 vols., 1884.

3362 LEFROY, J. H. Memorials of the discovery and early settlement of the Bermudas or Somers Islands, 1515–1685. 2 vols. 1877–9.

An exhaustive treatment of the subject, with a repr. of early descriptions and official docs. See also his edn. of Nathaniel Butler's history from Br. Mus. MS. Sloan 750 in Hakluyt Soc. Pub., no. 65 (1882); and *The journal of Richard Norwood, surveyor of Bermuda* (1639–40), ed. by W. F. Craven and W. B. Hayward, N.Y. 1945.

3363 WILKINSON, H. C. The adventurers of Bermuda: a history of the island from its discovery until the dissolution of the Somers Island Company in 1682. Oxf. 1933. 2nd edn. N.Y. 1958.

Reliable account of the Somers Island Company to the annulment of its charter. For important articles by W. F. Craven on Bermuda history see *William and Mary College Quart. Hist. Mag.*, 2nd Ser., vols. 17–18 (1937–8).

6. JAMAICA

3364 BLOME, RICHARD, ed. A description of the island of Jamaica with the other isles and territories in America . . . Taken from the notes of Sir Thomas Linch . . . governor of Jamaica and other experienced persons. 1672. Later edn. 1678. Maps.

See also Wing, B 3215. For other 17th-century accounts of Jamaica see Cundall, *Bibl. Jamaica*, pp. 14–16.

3365 LAWS OF JAMAICA: passed by the Assembly and confirmed by his Majesty in Council, April 17th, 1684. To which is added the State of Jamaica, as it now is under the government of Sir Thomas Lynch. 1684. Map.

In 1698 a second volume was published: *The continuation of the Laws of Jamaica . . .*

confirmed . . . December 26th 1695. See also: *Acts of the Assembly passed in the island of Jamaica from 1681 to 1737 inclusive,* 1738; and *Journals of the Assembly of Jamaica, 1663–1826,* 15 vols., Jamaica, 1811–29.

3366 VENABLES, GENERAL ROBERT. The narrative of General Venables . . . Ed. by C. H. Firth. Camden Soc. 1900.

Has an app. of documents relating to the conquest of Jamaica. See also other narratives on the English attacks on Jamaica and St. Domingo, ed. by I. A. Wright (*Camden Soc. Misc.* xiii, xiv, 1923–26); and *Some account of General Robert Venables* [with a diary of his widow], Chetham Soc. Misc. 4 (1872).

See also F. Cundall and J. L. Pietersz, eds., *Jamaica under the Spaniards, abstracted from the archives of Seville,* Kingston, Jamaica, 1919.

3367 CRUIKSHANK, E. A. The life of Sir Henry Morgan, with an account of the English settlement on the island of Jamaica, 1655–1688. Toronto and Lond. 1935.

Of general as well as biographical interest. Other lives of Morgan, pirate and lieutenant-governor of Jamaica, are by M. P. Allen, N.Y. 1931, and R. Forbes, 1948. Cf. no. 3681.

3368 [LONG, E.] The history of Jamaica. 3 vols. 1774.

Though prejudiced, still of value. See the scholarly *History of Jamaica* by W. J. Gardner, 1873. An important article is F. Strong, 'The causes of Cromwell's West Indian expedition', *A.H.R.* 4 (1899), 228–45, which portrays the expedition as part of a far-seeing deliberate policy.

3369 WHITSON, A. M. The constitutional development of Jamaica, 1660–1729. Manchester. 1929.

Clear narrative supported by docs. Of value on the constitutional side also are F. Cundall, *The governors of Jamaica in the seventeenth century,* 1936, and *The governors . . . in the first half of the eighteenth century,* 1937.

7. Leeward Islands

3370 DAVIES, JOHN, trans. The history of the Caribby-Islands . . . with a Caribbian vocabulary, rendered into English by John Davies of Kidwelly. 1666.

Chiefly deals with natural history, but has some details about the early relations of French and English in St. Christopher. A translation from the 2nd edn. of [César de Rochefort], *Histoire naturelle et morale des îles Antilles de l'Amérique . . .,* Rotterdam, 1665. See de Dampierre (1824). See also *Les particularitez de la défaite des Anglois . . . dans l'Isle de S. Cristophe, en l'Amérique, par les François,* Paris, 1666, which was the first of several printed pamphlets in Paris with news of the Anglo-Dutch war (see Cundall's *Bibl. of West Indies,* p. 14); and J. Langford, *A briefe account of the sufferings of the servants of the Lord called Quakers* [in Antigua, 1660–1695], 1706. See also the sections on Antigua and Nevis in Besse's *Sufferings of the Quakers* (1420).

3371 ACTS OF ASSEMBLY passed in the Charibbee Leeward Islands, from 1690 to 1730. 1734.

Consists of two parts: Acts of the General (federal) Assembly, 1690–1705, and Acts of Antigua, 1668–1730. Only those acts which were in force at the time of publication are printed *in extenso.* Similar collections were printed for each of the other Leeward Islands.

3372 HIGHAM, C. S. S. The development of the Leeward Islands under the restoration, 1660–1688. Camb. 1921. Maps. Bibl.

Compare C. S. S. Higham's 'The early days of the church in the West Indies', *Church Quart. Rev.* 92 (1921), 106–30; 'The accounts of a colonial governor's agent in the seventeenth century', *A.H.R.* 28 (1923), 263–70; 'Some Treasurer's accounts of Monserrat, 1672–1681', *E.H.R.* 38 (1923), 87–90; and 'The general assembly of the Leeward Islands', ibid. 41 (1926), 190–209, 366–88. See also V. T. Harlow, *Christopher Codrington, 1668–1710*, Oxf. 1928. Based on the MS. letter-book of a settler and agent at St. Kitts is J. C. Jeaffreson, ed., *A young squire . . . from the papers [1676–86] of Christopher Jeaffreson . . .*, 2 vols., 1878.

3373 OLIVER, V. L. The history of the island of Antigua. 3 vols. 1894–9.

There is a short hist. intro., consisting almost entirely of transcripts of docs.; the book itself is chiefly genealogical in emphasis.

8. Surinam and Guiana

3374 SANFORD, ROBERT. Surinam justice . . . being a publication of that perfect relation of the . . . disturbances in the colony . . . set forth by Wm. Byam . . . couched in the answer thereto by Robert Sanford. 1662.

Reprints an extremely rare pamphlet by Governor Byam, *A narrative of the late troubles in Surinam*. For further pamphlets on Surinam, with criticism, see Williamson (3375), p. 150. Cf. Cundall's *Bibl. of West Indies*, p. 72. A description by George Warren, 1667, is repr. in *Harl. Coll.* (59). Useful for the loss of Surinam is Jean Clodoré, *Relation de ce qui s'est passé dans les Isles et Terre-Ferme de l'Amérique*, 2 vols., Paris, 1671.

3375 WILLIAMSON, J. A. English colonies in Guiana and on the Amazon, 1604–1668. Oxf. 1923. Map.

Critical discussion of authorities. For further discussion of contemporary authorities see G. Edmundson, 'The Dutch in Western Guiana', *E.H.R.* 16 (1901), 640–75; and his 'The Dutch on the Amazon', ibid. 18 (1903), 642–63. See also Harlow (3346).

D. EAST INDIES, INDIA, AND THE EAST

The following bibliography is limited to the English in India, and the activities of the East India Company during the seventeenth century, though a few books are included which throw light on the condition of India during that period. The Dutch collections of documents have been omitted, but reference may be made through Moreland (3376 n.). A valuable guide to the sources for the period is Khan (3376). There is a growing number of documents available in print, both from the India Office in England (see nos. 3377, 3381–2), and from repositories in India (see *Proceedings of . . . the Indian Historical Records Commission*, no. 3378; and the various journals of the Royal Asiatic Society and its affiliates, no. 3380), as well as an increasing volume of studies by Indian historians.

A selection of titles on voyages to India and the East is included in this section. Reference should be made also to Stock, *Joint Stock Companies* (2128) and other works dealing with trade to this region in Ch. VIII, *Trade and Commerce*.

I. General Accounts

(a) *Bibliographies and Guides*

3376 KHAN, SHAFAAT AHMAD. Sources for the history of British India in the seventeenth century. Bombay. 1926.

Valuable bibl. of documents in all the chief repositories; less complete for the Indian Record Offices. See also vol. iv of Lewin (3315).

For Dutch sources see W. H. Moreland, 'Dutch sources for Indian history, 1590–1650', *Jour. of Indian History*, no. 5 (1923), 222–32; and *Jour. of Asiatic Society of Gr. Britain*, i, o.s. 345, 353. A useful guide on dates, native dynasties, and terms is C. H. Philips, ed., *Handbook of Oriental history*, 1951.

For general purposes see also the bibls. in the *Camb. hist. of India* (3390), and the section on 'East Indies' in the Br. Mus. Catalogue. There are also good bibls. in the 3rd edn. of *The Oxford history of India*, by V. A. Smith, ed. and rev. by P. Spear *et al.*, N.Y. 1958.

3377 FOSTER, W. A guide to the India Office records, 1660–1858. 1919.

Valuable introduction on the record system, superseding G. C. M. Birdwood, *Report on . . . records of the India Office*, 1878. See also *A catalogue of the library of the Hon. East-India Company*, 2 vols., 1845–51, which notes many pamphlets; F. C. Danvers, ed., *List of marine records of the late East India Company; preserved in the Record Department of the India Office*, 1895; and *Press list of India Office records from the earliest date to 1630*, s.l., 1891.

3378 PROCEEDINGS of the [first] meeting of the Indian Historical Records Commission . . . In progress, annual volume. Calcutta. 1919+.

See also 'Bibliography of Indian history and Oriental research for 1938', publ. as a suppl. to the *Jour. of the Bombay Hist. Soc.* 5 (1939).

3379 DOWSON, J., ed. The history of India as told by its own historians: The Muhammadan period. 8 vols. 1867–77.

Ed. from the papers of Sir H. M. Elliot, it gives some guide to native historians of India; the first vol. only of a projected *Bibliographical index to the historians on Mohammedan India* was publ. in 1849.

(b) *Sources*

3380 ROYAL ASIATIC SOCIETY. JOURNAL. Vol. 1+. 1834+.

Began as *Transactions*, 3 vols., 1823–33. Separate *Journals* published by several branches have printed documents and bibliographical articles; e.g. Bombay, vol. 1 (1841)+; Ceylon, vol. 1 (1845)+; North China branch, vol. 1 (1858)+; Straits branch, vols. 1–86 (1878–1922), which was superseded by the Malayan branch, vol. 1 (1923)+.

A *Catalogue of printed books published before 1932 in the Library of the Royal Asiatic Society* was pr. in 1940.

Official Records

3381 THE ENGLISH FACTORIES IN INDIA . . . A calendar of documents in the India Office, British Museum, and Public Record Office. 17 vols.+ Oxf. 1906–55+.

Vols. 1–13 (1906–27), dealing with the years 1618–69, were ed. by W. Foster. Four volumes of a new series, ed. by Sir C. Fawcett and continued by Sir P. Cadell, and dealing with the years 1670–84, have been publ., Oxf. and Lond. 1936–55. See also nos. 3399–401.

3382 SAINSBURY, E. B., ed. A calendar of the court minutes . . . of the East India Company (1635–1679). Oxf. 1907–38.

Includes also abstracts of docs. in East India series at P.R.O. and references to Indian affairs in S.P. Dom. Continues in part the Cal. S.P., Colonial series, East Indies.

Voyages

Numerous accounts of voyages have been printed, many by the Hakluyt Society. (See Mullins, pp. 148–76, and *India* in the index.) Others have appeared in the *Journal of Indian History*. For some primarily of a commercial nature, see *Economic History*, pp. 306–9. See also Cox and Wing.

The following titles are representative only, and are arranged in rough chronological order according to the period of the voyage.

3383 A TRUE AND LARGE DISCOURSE of the voyage of the whole fleete of ships set forth the 20 of April 1601 . . . wherein is set doune the order and manner of their trafficke. 1603.

See also B. Corney, ed., *The voyage of Sir Henry Middleton to Bantam* (Hakluyt Soc. 19 (1855)), which is a repr. of *The last East-Indian voyage*, 1606. It deals with the second voyage of the East India Company, the only East Indian voyage of the 17th century of which a separate narrative was published. See Purchas (2140), pt. 1.

3384 FOSTER, W., ed. Early travels in India, 1583–1619. 1921. Bibl.

Reprints travels of Fitch, Mildenhall, Hawkins, Finch, Wittington, Coryat, Terry, with intro.

Other well-known early voyages are those of Sir James Lancaster to the East Indies, 17th century (Hakluyt Soc., Ser. 1, vol. 66 (1877)); John Jourdain in Arabia, India, and Malaya, 1608–17 (ibid., Ser. 2, vol. 16 (1905)).

3385 FOSTER, W., ed. The embassy of Sir Thomas Roe to the court of the Great Mogul, 1615–19. 2 vols. [Hakluyt Soc., Ser. 2, vols. 1–2.] Rev. edn. Oxf. 1926.

From Roe's journal and correspondence, esp. Br. Mus. Add. MSS. 6115, 19277. The intro. to the 1899 edn. contains a bibl. of the voyage. Cf. *A voyage to India* by Edward Terry, 1655, the author of which was chaplain to Roe.

3386 A TRUE RELATION of the unjust cruel and barbarous proceedings against the English at Amboyna. 1624.

Contains also the Dutch *True declaration* . . ., and E.I.C. reply. For various edns. and related pamphlets, see B.M. *Catalogue of printed books*, *sub* Amboyna; for criticism, see Hunter, *Hist. Br. India* (3392), vol. i, ch. 10.

Concerning Amboyna see also *A remonstrance . . . of the directors of the Netherlands East India Company . . .* [with the English E.I.C. reply], 1632; and Abraham Van Golt, *Belga-Britannus; . . . the affair of Amboyna set in a true light . . . in answer to a pamphlet called Dutch alliances*, 2 pts., 1712.

3387 FRYER, JOHN. A new account of East-India and Persia (1672–1681). 1698. Later edn. by W. Crooke. 3 vols. Hakluyt Soc., Ser. 2, vols. 19, 20, 39. 1909–15.

For travels of an agent of the French E.I. Co. about the same time see *Travels of the Abbé Carré in India and the Near East, 1672–74*, tr. by Lady Fawcett and ed. by Sir C. Fawcett, 3 vols., Hakluyt Soc., 1947–8.

3388 OVINGTON, JOHN. A voyage to Suratt, 1689. 1696. Repr. 1929.

For Ovington's essay on tea, 1699, see Wing, O 700. Other later titles of interest are Charles Lockyer, *An account of trade in India . . . with descriptions of Fort St. George*, 1711; and Daniel Beeckman, *A voyage to and from the island of Borneo* [1714], 1718.

See also Alexander Hamilton, *A new account of the East Indies* [*1688–1723*], 2 vols., Edin., 1727; repr. 2 vols., 1930; and *The Norris embassy to Aurangzib* [*1699–1702*], by Harihar Das, ed. by S. C. Sarker, Calcutta, 1959.

(c) *Later Works*

3389 BALLARD, G. A. 'The effect of the Anglo-Dutch wars of the seventeenth century on Indian Ocean developments.' *Mariner's Mirror*, 12 (1926), 264–88.

Cf. other articles on related subjects, ibid., pp. 69–94, 169–95; and J. C. De, 'The Anglo-Dutch duel in eastern waters, 1652–54', *Journal of Indian Hist.* 19 (1940), 79–90.

3390 CAMBRIDGE HISTORY OF INDIA. Ed. by E. J. Rapson, W. Haig, and H. H. Dodwell. 5 vols. Camb. 1922–37. Supplementary vol. Camb. 1953.

Vol. v, 'British India, 1497–1858', 1929, is also vol. iv of *Camb. hist. of the British empire* (3322). This is the standard single volume account. A different *Cambridge shorter history of India*, also ed. by Dodwell *et al.*, Camb. 1934, is excellent. See also the volume on India (in 2 parts) by P. E. Roberts (vol. vii) in Lucas, *Historical geography* (3327); later 1 vol. edn. under title of *History of British India*, 1923, 2nd edn. 1938, 3rd edn., completed by T. G. P. Spear, 1952.

3391 DUFF, J. G. A history of the Mahrattas. 3 vols. 1826. Later edn. rev. by S. M. Edwardes. 2 vols. 1921.

Classical history of the Mahrathas, based on materials in part no longer extant. Cf. R. Orme, *Historical fragments of the Mogul empire, the Morrattoes, the English . . .* [from 1659], 1782, later edn., 1805; H. G. Rawlinson, *Shivági The Maráthá*, Oxf. 1915, which is a life based on Indian chronicles and records, with bibl. intro.; C. A. Kincaid and Rao Bahadur D. B. Parasnis, *History of the Maratha people*, 3 vols., Bombay, 1918–25, an important modern work; and J. Sarkar, *House of Shivaji*, 2nd edn. rev., Calcutta, 1948. For early rules, chronological tables, etc., see Philips, *Handbook* (3376 n.).

3392 HUNTER, W. W. *A history of British India*. 2 vols. 1899–1900.

The standard history for the 17th century, based on original material; the second vol., with bibl. intro., was completed by P. E. Roberts. See also Hunter, *The Indian empire*, 1893, and his edn. of the *Imperial gazeteer of India*, 9 vols., 1881, various later edns. The ambitious 19th-century *History of British India* by James Mill (3 vols., 1817; 5th edn. by H. H. Wilson, 10 vols., 1858) has been corrected on many points by later scholars. A useful later history is by G. Dunbar, 1936. See also E. J. Thompson and G. T. Garratt, *Rise and fulfilment of British rule in India*, 1934.

3393 KEITH, A. B. A constitutional history of India, 1600–1935. 1936.

The original Benares edn., 1933, covered the years 1600–1919. Cf. C. G. H. Fawcett, *The first century of British justice in India* (1672 to the late 18th century), Oxf. and Lond. 1934; K. V. Punnaiah, *The constitutional history of India from the advent of the East India Company to the present time*, Allahabad, 1938.

3394 MAJUMDAR, R. C., RAYCHAUDHURI, H. C., and DATTA, K. An advanced history of India. 1946. Bibl.

Valuable modern work with extensive bibls.; treatment of the English settlements in 17th century is brief.

3395 SMITH, V. A. Akbar, the Great Mogul, 1542–1605. Oxf. 1917. Bibl.

An important monograph with a critical bibl., dealing with records written in Persian and Turkish, as well as European accounts.

2. ECONOMIC AND SOCIAL HISTORY

3396 KHAN, SHAFAAT AHMAD. The East India trade in the seventeenth century, in its political and economic aspects. Oxf. 1923.

Deals only with trade between India and England. Cites many contemporary pamphlets. Cf. D. Macpherson, *The history of European commerce with India*, 1812; C. J. Hamilton, *Trade relations between England and India, 1600–1896*, Calcutta, 1919; and Bal Krishna, *Commercial relations between India and England, (1601–1757)*, 1924.

3397 MORELAND, W. H. India at the death of Akbar: an economic study. 1920. Bibl.

By the same author, *From Akbar to Aurangzeb*, 1923, bibl. The two volumes are valuable studies of economic conditions prior to and shortly after the arrival of the Europeans. Cf. H. G. Rawlinson, *British beginnings in western India, 1579–1657* [Surat], Oxf. 1920, docs.

3398 OATEN, E. F. European travellers in India during the fifteenth, sixteenth, and seventeenth centuries: the evidence afforded by them with respect to Indian social institutions, and the nature and influence of Indian governments. 1909. Bibl.

See Oaten's article on Anglo-Indian literature in *Camb. Hist. Eng. Lit.*, vol. xiv pp. 366–79.

3. EAST INDIA COMPANY

In addition to the titles in the general section, *English factories* (3381) and Sainsbury (3382), the following relate particularly to the company.

(a) *Sources*

3399 GRIGGS, W. and BIRDWOOD, G. Relics of the honourable East India Company. 1909.

Facsimile reproductions of early documents, including plan of Bombay harbour in 1626. Cf. H. Stevens, ed., *The dawn of British trade to the East Indies* [court minutes, 1599–1603], 1886.

3400 SHAW, J., ed. Charters relating to the East India Company, 1660–1761. Madras. 1887.

Repr., with preface and additions from an earlier collection [Madras? 1774] made from documents lost after that publication. For early letters see G. Birdwood and W. Foster, eds., *The register of letters . . . of the governor and company of merchants . . . trading into* the East Indies, *1600–1619*, 1893; and F. C. Danvers and W. Foster, eds., *Letters received by the East India Company* (1602–17), 6 vols., 1896–1902.

3401 TEMPLE, R. C., ed. The diaries of Streynsham Master, 1675–1680. 2 vols. 1911.

India Records Series; journeys of inspection. See also *Annals of the honourable East-India Company* [1600–1707/8], by J. Bruce (the company's historiographer), 3 vols., 1810; and R. C. Temple, L. M. Anstrey, and B. P. Scattergood, *The Scattergoods and the East India Company* [1681–1723], Bombay, 1935. On Bruce see W. Foster in *S.H.R.* 9 (1912), 366–75. On Thomas Pitt see biography by C. N. Dalton, Camb. 1915, and documents in Hakluyt Soc., Ser. 1, vol. 78, 1889.

3402 [PAPILLON, THOMAS.] East India trade a most profitable trade to this kingdom. 1677. 1681. 1696.

Generally attributed to Papillon, and representing the mercantilist answer to attacks such as *Two letters concerning the East India Company*, 1676. For authorship and dates see Wing, P 307, T 2087. See also no. 2097.

Other important tracts revealing the differing viewpoints include: Josiah Child [under the pseud. Philopatris], *A treatise wherein is demonstrated: I. That the East India trade is the most national of all foreign trades* . . . 1681, 1689 (repr. in *Somers Tracts*, viii, different titles for two 1689 edns.); and a reply, *A discourse concerning the East Indian trade* (*Somers Tracts*, x); Child's *New discourse* (2081); *Companies in joynt-stock unnecessary and inconvenient*, 1691; *A regulated company more material than a joint-stock in the East India trade*, 1700; *The allegations of the Turky Company* [against the E.I.C.], 1681; and *The Answer of the East India Company* [to the allegations], 1681.

3403 AN ACCOUNT of some transactions in . . . the House of Commons and before the Privy Council . . . relating to the East India Company. 1693.

Somers Tracts, x. 618. See also *A collection of debates* . . . [1694–5] *upon the inquiry into the late briberies* . . ., 1695; *The examinations* . . . *of Sir Thomas Cooke*, 1695. See also *the argument of the lord chief justice* . . . *concerning the great case of monopolies between the East India Company* . . . *and Thomas Sandys*, 1698, and Cobbett, *State trials* (1060), x. 372–554.

3404 DAVENANT, CHARLES. An essay on the East-India trade. 1696.

Repr. in vol. i of his *Works* (2086); provoked replies such as *An answer to a late tract entituled* . . ., 1697; *England and East India inconsistent* . . ., 1697; and Thomas Smith [a weaver], *Reasons humbly offered for the pasing* [sic] *a bill for the hindering the home consumption of the East India silks*, 1697; N.C., a weaver of London, *The great necessity and advantage of preserving our own manufactures*, 1697; and [Gardner, —], *Some reflections on a pamphlet entituled, England and East India inconsistent in their manufactures*, 1696. See also Wing, S 175. Other pamphlets of the period are listed in Thomas (3407), pp. ix–x.

3405 [MARTIN, HENRY?] Considerations upon the East India trade. 1701. Later edns. 1720 and 1856.

Included in McCulloch (1832). On authorship see Thomas (3407), app. B.

(b) *Later Works*

3406 FOSTER, W. The East India House, its history and associations. 1924.

Includes some reprints. Also by Foster, 'Charles I and the East India Company', *E.H.R.* 19 (1904), 456–63. Cf. H. A. Young, *The East India Company's arsenals and manufactories*, 1937; and B. Willson, *Ledger and sword, or the Honourable Company of Merchants of England trading to the East Indies*, 2 vols., 1903. R. Walcott deals with political pressures by the rival companies, 1700–1, in *E.H.R.* 71 (1956), 223–39.

3407 THOMAS, PARAKUNNEL J. Mercantilism and the East India trade: an early phase of the protection v. free trade controversy. 1926. Bibl.

Bibl. lists many tracts, as well as collections of MSS. The conclusions should be compared with those of others.

4. Particular Regions

3408 HEDGES, WILLIAM. Diary . . . during his agency in Bengal (1681–7). Ed. by R. F. Barlow and H. Yule. 3 vols. 1887–9.

Hakluyt Soc., Ser. 1, vols. 74, 75, 78. See also Thomas Bowrey, *A geographical account . . . Bay of Bengal* (1669–79), ed. by R. C. Temple, ibid., Ser. 2, vol. 12, 1905. A *Bibliography of Bengal Records, 1632–1858*, being a list of English records in print, has been publ. (2nd edn., Calcutta, 1925).

3409 WILSON, C. R., ed. The early annals of the English in Bengal. 3 vols. Lond. and Calcutta. 1895–1917.

First vol. has extracts from original records, 1704–10. Also ed. by Wilson, *Old Fort William in Bengal, a selection of official documents* (Indian Rec. Ser.), 2 vols., 1906. For observations made by a company factor in Bengal see S. A. Khan, ed., *John Marshall in India* [1668–72], 1927.

3410 ANDERSON, P. The English in Western India, being the early history of the factory at Surat, of Bombay, and the subordinate factories on the western coast. 1854.

See also S. A. Khan, *Anglo-Portuguese negotiations relating to Bombay, 1660–1677*, 1922 (repr. from *Jour. of Indian Hist.* 1, 1922), which is largely source-material; A. R. Ingram, *The gateway to India: the story of Methwold and Bombay*, 1938; B. M. Malabari, *Bombay in the making, 1661–1726*, 1910, bibl.; and R. and O. Strachey, *Keigwin's rebellion (1683–4)*, Oxf. 1916.

3411 FORREST, G. W., ed. Selections from the letters, despatches, and other state papers, preserved in the Bombay Secretariat. 4 vols. Bombay. 1885–99.

Vol. i of the 'Home Series' contains 17th-century material. Forrest's *Alphabetical catalogue of the contents of the Bombay Secretarial records (1630–1780)*, Bombay, 1887, contains little on the century. See also A. F. Kindersley, *Handbook of the Bombay government records*, Bombay, 1921; and S. T. Sheppard, ed., *Bombay in the days of Queen Anne*, 1933, Hakluyt Soc., Ser. 2, vol. 72, account by John Burnell.

3412 LOVE, H. D., ed. Vestiges of old Madras, 1640–1800. (Indian Rec. Ser.) 4 vols. 1913.

Vol. i has 17th-century matter; vol. iv is index. See also J. T. Wheeler, ed., *Madras in the olden time . . . compiled from original records*, 3 vols., Madras, 1861–2, the first vol. covering 1639–1702; W. Foster, *The founding of Fort St. George*, 1902; and A. T. Pringle, ed., *Selections from the consultations of the agent governor and council of Fort St. George*, 5 vols., Madras, 1893–5.

3413 RECORDS OF FORT ST. GEORGE. Madras. 1908+.

Systematic publication of Madras records *in extenso*, including for the 17th-century consultations, dispatches, letters, and sundry books. See Lewin (3315), vol. iv, for list. There is also a Dutch series, *Press lists of ancient documents*, 47 vols., 1891–1910.

See H. H. Dodwell's *Report* on the records, Madras, 1916, and the earlier *Handbook to the Madras records*, by J. T. Wheeler, Madras, 1861.

3414 KNOX, ROBERT. An historical relation of the island Ceylon; together with an account of the . . . captivity [of] the author. 1681. Later ed. by J. Ryan. Glasgow. 1911.

A classic; first account of Ceylon in English.

3415 HALL, D. G. E. Early English intercourse with Burma (1587–1743). 1928.

Scholarly. Cf. J. Anderson, *English intercourse with Siam in the seventeenth century*, 1890.

3416 MORSE, H. B. The chronicles of the East India Company trading to China, 1635–1834. 4 vols. Oxf. 1926. Suppl. 1929.

See also P. Auber, *China, an outline of the . . . British and foreign embassies to, and intercourse with, that empire*, 1834.

3417 RIESS, L. 'History of the English factory at Hirado [1613–22], with an introductory chapter on the origin of English enterprise in the Far East.' *Trans. of the Asiatic Soc. of Japan*, 26 (1898), 1–114.

An appendix, pp. 163–218, contains original docs. See also T. Rundall, ed., *Memorials of the empire of Japan in the sixteenth and seventeenth centuries* (Hakluyt Soc., Ser. 1, vol. 8), 1850; E. M. Satow, ed., *The voyage of Captain John Saris to Japan 1613* (ibid., Ser. 2, vol. 5), 1900; E. M. Thompson's edn. of *Diary of Richard Cocks, Cape merchant in the English factory in Japan, 1615–22*, 2 vols. (ibid., Ser. 1, vols. 66–7), 1883.

3418 JACKSON, E. L. St. Helena: The historic island from its discovery to the present date. 1903.

Contains a section on St. Helena records. See also H. R. Janisch, *Extracts from the St. Helena records* (ed. by B. Grant), St. Helena, 1885; and the anonymous *Relation of the retaking of . . . St. Helena, and three Dutch East India ships*, 1673, repr. in Arber's *English Garner* (62 n.), vol. ii, p. 431.

E. AFRICA

For the Royal African Company see *Economic History*, nos. 2136–7.

3419 KEITH, A. B. West Africa. Oxf. 1933.

Accounts of settlements, as well as of the slave trade. For the latter subject see the important *Documents illustrative of the history of the slave trade to America*, ed. by E. Donnan, 3 vols., Wash. 1930–2. A journal of an early exploration into Senegambia, 1689–90, was ed. by T. G. Stone, *E.H.R.* 39 (1924), 89–95.

3420 ROUTH, E. M. G. Tangier, England's lost Atlantic outpost, 1661–1684. 1912. Bibl.

The best account of the English occupation. See also W. B. T. Abbey, *Tangier under British rule, 1661–1684*, Jersey, 1940; H. A. Kaufman, ed., *Tangier at high tide: the journal of John Luke 1670–1673*, Geneva and Paris, 1958, bibl.; and E. G. Troyte-Bullock, 'Col. Bullen Reymes' diary', *Somerset and Dorset N. and Q.* 22 (1938), 207–12, 215–30. See also *Naval History*, 1730 n.

3421 FOSTER, W. 'An English settlement in Madagascar in 1645–46.' *E.H.R.* 27 (1912), 239–50.

Cf. S. E. Howe, 'Un rêve anglais: Madagascar colonie britannique' [1639], *Rev. Hist. des Colonies*, 27 (1934), 1–32.

XIII

WALES

There is as yet no standard history of Stuart Wales. Williams (3488) devotes about 40 pp. to the period; Dodd (3478) deals with six selected topics; Morrice (3604) is purely biographical and literary, and largely superseded on the former side by the Welsh biographical dictionary (3429), which is indispensable, and on the latter by Parry (3605). The historical atlases (3536) provide an essential background. Otherwise the history of the period is to be sought in monographs and articles in learned journals. For materials relating to Wales in the Historical Manuscripts Commission see nos. 102, 156, 255.

A. BIBLIOGRAPHIES, CALENDARS, CATALOGUES, AND DICTIONARIES

3422 BIBLIOGRAPHICA CELTICA: register of publications relating to Wales and the Celtic peoples and languages. Series I (1909–28), 9 vols., 1910–34. Series 2 (1929–38), 2 vols., 1939, 1952. Series 3 (1953–7), 1954–8 (in progress). Aberystwyth, National Library of Wales.

3423 BLACKWELL, H. 'Bibliography of local and county histories.' *Old Welsh Chips*, ed. E. Poole, Brecknock, 1888, 138–45; 171–81, 198–216, 224–30.

3424 BREESE, E. Kalendars of Gwynedd. 1873.

Lists of lord lieutenants, sheriffs, constables of castles, etc., for the three shires of Gwynedd. Not always reliable, but incorporates valuable notes by W. W. E. Wynne of Peniarth, the antiquary (1801–80), based on MSS. in the Peniarth collection, now in Nat. Lib. of Wales.

3425 CAMBRIAN BIBLIOGRAPHY, containing an account of the books printed in the Welsh language or relating to Wales, from 1546 to 1800. By W. Rowlands. Ed. by D. Silvan Evans. Llanidloes. 1869.

Written in Welsh. Useful. A continuation by C. Ashton, also in Welsh, gives a list of books printed 1801–10. (Published by National Eisteddfod Association, Oswestry, 1908.) See also emendations and supplementary information on some of the 16th- and 17th-century titles in J. H. Davies, 'Early Welsh bibliography', *Cymmrod. Soc. Trans.*, 1897–8, 10–22.

3426 CARDIFF FREE LIBRARIES. Catalogue of printed books in the Welsh department. By J. Ballinger and J. I. Jones. 1898.

3427 DAVIES, J. H. 'Bibliography of Quaker literature relating to Wales.' *Welsh Bibliog. Soc. Journ.* I (1912–15), 203–25.

With biographical annotation. Additional titles for Merioneth in B. Owen, 'Llyfryd diaeth crynwyr Meirionydd', ibid. 7 (1950–3), 1–17.

3428 DAVIES, W. Ll. 'Short-title list of Welsh books, 1546–1700.' *Welsh Bibliog. Soc. Journ.* 2 (1916–23), 176–88, 210–28, 254–69; 4 (1932–6), 59–73.

Also by Davies, 'Short-title list of eighteenth-century Welsh books', part 1, 1701–10, ibid. 4 (1932–6), 123–32; and 'Welsh books entered in the stationers' company register', part 1, 1554–1660, ibid. 2, 167–74.

3429 DICTIONARY OF WELSH BIOGRAPHY. Ed. by J. E. Lloyd and R. T. Jenkins. Cymmrod. Soc. 1959.

First publ. in Welsh, 1952. Full bibl. with each article.

3430 HARRIES, E. R. Bibliography of the county of Flint. Pt. 1. Flint County Library. 1953.

3431 JENKINS, R. T. and REES, W. A bibliography of the history of Wales. Cardiff. 1931. 2nd edn. 1962.

The second edn. was publ. by the Univ. of Wales, Board of Celtic Studies.

3432 LIBRARY ASSOCIATION, Wales and Monmouthshire branch. Subject index to Welsh periodicals. Vol. 1 (1931), ed. A. ap Gwynn. Vols. 2–4 (1932–7), ed. A. ap Gwynn and I. Lewis. Cardiff. 1931–8.

3433 NATIONAL LIBRARY OF WALES.

(*a*) Calendars of deeds and documents. Vol. 1. The Coleman deeds. Ed. F. Green. Aberystwyth. 1921. Vol. 2. The Crosswood deeds. Ed. F. Green. Aberystwyth. 1927. Vol. 3. The Hawarden deeds. Ed. F. Green. Aberystwyth. 1931.

(*b*) Calendar of Wynn (of Gwydir) papers, 1515–1690. Aberystwyth. 1926.

An indispensable source for 17th-century social and political history, especially of the three shires of Gwynedd.

(*c*) Catalogue of MSS. Vol. 1. Additional MSS. in the collections of Sir John Williams. Aberystwyth. 1921.

Mainly pre-17th century.

(*d*) Catalogue of tracts of the civil war and commonwealth period relating to Wales and the border counties. Aberystwyth. 1911.

Many titles have been added since the catalogue was completed.

(*e*) Clenennau letters and papers in the Brogyntyn collection. Part 1. Ed. by T. J. Pierce. Aberystwyth. 1947.

(*f*) Handlist of manuscripts in the National Library of Wales. 2 vols. and index. Aberystwyth. 1943–51. In progress.

Descriptive accounts of accessions are published from time to time in *N.L.W. Journ.* (3474).

(*g*) 'The popish plot.' *N.L.W. Journ.* 6 (1949–50).

List of 72 tracts of the period 1678–86 in N.L.W., by J. H. Evans. Only five of these concern Wales, but others are listed in Matthews (3511), iv. 155–9, and in *Welsh Bibliog. Soc. Journ.* 4 (1932–6), 243–52.

(*h*) 'The Plas Yolyn collection of Morgan Llwyd's papers.' Ed. by E. D. Jones. *Merioneth Hist. Soc. Journ.* 3 (1959), 286–95.

Cf. T. E. Ellis and J. H. Davies, eds., *Gweithiau Morgan Llwyd* [The works of M. Ll.], 2 vols., Bangor, 1899–1908.

3434   OWEN, B. 'Llyfryddiaeth morwyr Cymru.' *Welsh Bibliog. Soc. Journ.* 3 (1928–31), 99–104, 180–5.

A bibl. of Welsh seamen.

3435   OWEN, E., ed. A catalogue of the manuscripts relating to Wales in the British Museum. 4 pts. 1900. 1903. 1908. 1922.

Cymmrodorion Record Series, 4.

3436   REES, W. 'Bibliography of . . . the municipal history of Wales and the border.' *Bull. Bd. of Celtic Studies*, 2 (1923–5), 321–82; 3 (1926–7), 72.

3437   SHANKLAND, T. 'List of MS. records of the trustees for the maintenance of ministers, now at Lambeth Palace Library, relating to Wales, 1649–60.' *Bull. Bd. of Celtic Studies*, 1 (1921), 55–63.

3438   UNIVERSITY OF WALES, Board of Celtic Studies. History and Law Series.

  1. A catalogue of Star Chamber proceedings relating to Wales. Ed. by I. ab O. Edwards. Cardiff. 1929.
  Unreliable, but indispensable.

  8. A review of the records of the Conway and Menai ferries. By H. R. Davies. Cardiff. 1942.

  10. Correspondence and minutes of the S.P.C.K. relating to Wales, 1699–1740. Ed. by M. Clement. Cardiff. 1952.

  12. A survey of the duchy of Lancaster lordships in Wales, 1609–13. Ed. by W. Rees. Cardiff. 1953.

  14. Calendar of Salusbury correspondence, 1553–*c*. 1700. Ed. by W. J. Smith. Cardiff. 1954.

  15. Exchequer proceedings concerning Wales *in tempore* James I. Ed. by T. I. J. Jones. Cardiff. 1955.
  See also nos. 3471 and 3476.

3439   WILLIAMS, O. Bibliography of the county [Denbighshire]. Part 2: historical and topographical sources. Wrexham. 1937. 2nd edn. Ruthin. 1951.

3440   WILLIAMS, P. The council in the marches of Wales under Elizabeth I. Cardiff. 1958.

Has a useful bibl., superseding that in C. A. J. Skeel (3497).

B. POLITICAL AND GENERAL HISTORY

1. SOURCES

From the time of the final incorporation of Wales into England (1536–42), the basic sources for English and Welsh political history are the same. A survey of public records relating to Wales is printed in *Y Cymmrodor*, 10 (1890), 157–206.

For a note on those later removed to the National Library of Wales see W. Ll. Davies, *The National Library of Wales*, Aberystwyth, 1937, 83. The sources listed below are in general those throwing light on Welsh reactions to British public events.

(a) General

3441 'BULKELEY MANUSCRIPTS.' (i) Civil war period. *Arch. Camb.* 1846, 326–33, 385–9. (ii) 1681–1706. Ibid. 1851, 229–37.

Originals in University College Library, Bangor (Baron Hill MSS.).

3442 'OLD HERBERT PAPERS at Powis Castle and in the British Museum.' Ed. by M. C. Jones. *Montgom. Coll.* 20 (1887).

On the Middletons of Chirk Castle see no. 2222.

3443 'PRYCE (NEWTOWN HALL) CORRESPONDENCE.' Ed. by E. Powell. Ibid. 31 (1900), 65–114; 32 (1901), 65–96.

Uncompleted, but covers period 1555–1698.

(b) Pre-Civil War

3444 ROBERTS, PETER. Y Cwtta Cyfarwydd. Ed. by D. R. Thomas. 1883.

A chronicle for the years 1607–46, kept by a St. Asaph public notary. Appended is the register note-book of T. Rowlands, Vicar-choral, for the years 1595–1607 and 1646–53.

3445 'ROBERT PARRY'S DIARY.' *Arch. Camb.* 1915, 109–39.

A Denbighshire lawyer's jottings on public and private events, 1559–1613.

3446 'THE DIARY OF WALTER POWELL of Llantilio Crosenny' (Mon.). Ed. by J. Bradney-Bristol. 1907.

Covers period 1603–54.

3447 'TWO WELSH CATHOLIC ÉMIGRÉS discuss the accession of James I.' Ed. by A. H. Dodd. *Bull. of Bd. of Celtic Studies*, 8 (1935–7), 344–58.

See also 'A Spy's report, 1604', ibid. 9 (1937–9), 154–67, 247.

3448 VAUGHAN, W. The spirit of detraction. 1611.

His views on contemporary Welsh politics at pp. 321 sqq. Cf. nos. 3583 and 3680.

(c) Civil War and Interregnum

Many titles in no. 3433 (*d*) are relevant.

3449 'AN ACCOUNT OF THE CIVIL WAR IN NORTH WALES.' Ed. by R. Williams. *Arch. Camb.* 1846, 33–42.

Transcribed from contemporary notebook (now lost) of William Maurice of Llansilin.

3450 'CORRESPONDENCE DURING THE GREAT REBELLION.' Ed by W. W. E. W[ynne]. Ibid. 1875, 201–10, 307–24.

3451 EOS CEIRIOG, sef casgliad o bêr caniadau Huw Morus. Ed. by W. Davies. Gwrecsam (Wrexham). 1823.

The verses of the leading Welsh cavalier poet. Other cavalier rhymes collected in: Hen gerddi gwleidyddol, ed. J. H. Davies (Cymdeithas Llên Cymru, Cardiff, 1901); 'Caniadu'r gwrthryfel mawr', *Cymru*, Caernarfon, 21 (1901), 213–19. Cf. *Seren Gomer*, Tonypandy, N.S. 4 (1902), 169–72; 'Dau gywydd' (1653), *Ang. Antiq. Soc. Trans.* 1938, 50–6.

3452 HISTORIA BELLOMARISEI, or the history of the town and burrough of Beaumaris. By John Williams, c. 1669. *Arch. Camb.* suppl., 1917, app. ii.

Contains valuable contemporary account of the civil war in Anglesey.

3453 'INEDITED LETTERS . . .' *Hist. Soc. Lancs. and Cheshire Trans.*, N.S. 1 (1861), 200–99.

Extensive transcripts from letter-book of John Jones, the Welsh regicide, 1651–60. Originals now in N.L.W. (Plas Yolyn MSS.). See J. Lloyd, 'Colonel John Jones, Maesygarnedd', *Merioneth Hist. Soc. Journ.* 2 (1954), 95–104.

3454 [LEWIS, JOHN, of Glasgrug.] Contemplations upon these times, or The Parliament explained to Wales. Written by . . . a cordiall well-wisher of his countries happinesse. 1646. Cardiff. 1907. Issued by 'Cymdeithas Llen Cymru' (Society of Welsh Literature).

An appeal to Wales on behalf of Parliament.

3455 'MYTTON MANUSCRIPTS, letters and papers of Thomas Mytton of Halston' (1642–55). Ed. by S. Leighton. *Montgom. Coll.* 7 (1874), 353–76; 8 (1875), 293–311.

Valuable for civil war campaigns in North Wales, especially Montgomeryshire; on the latter see also ibid. 22 (1888), 179–210; 23 (1889), 71–80.

3456 'NEWS-LETTERS OF THE CIVIL WAR PERIOD relating to Shropshire and Wales.' Transcr. by E. Rowley-Morris. *Bye-gones relating to Wales and the Border Counties*, Oswestry, 1888, 126–8, 141, 163–4, 170–1, 184–6, 236–8; 1889–90, 203–6, 516–20; 1893–4, 499–501.

See also transcripts of news-letters from South Wales, 1650, by R. P. Stearns, in *Essex Inst. Hist. Coll.* (Mass.), 1935–6, 62–73 (reprints in B.M.), and by J. H. Matthews in *Cardiff Records* (3511), vol. iv, 149–55.

3457 'ORIGINAL LETTERS.' *Arch. Camb.* 1853, 62–9.

On civil war campaigns in West Wales.

3458 SYMONDS, R. Diary of the marches of the royal army (1644–5). Ed. by C. E. Long. Camden Soc. 1859.

Covers Charles I's march through Wales, with valuable topographical notes.

3459 PHILLIPS, J. R. Memoirs of the civil war in Wales and the marches. 2 vols. 1874.

Vol. ii consists of documents. See also no. 3481.

3460 'RUPERT'S LETTERS TO ANGLESEY and other civil war correspondence.' Ed. by N. Tucker, *Anglesey Antiquarian Soc. Trans.*, 1958, 16–32.

From Baron Hill MSS.

3461 'A TRUE CHARACTER OF THE DEPORTMENT . . . of the principal gentry within the counties of Carmarthen, Cardigan and Pembroke.' *c.* 1661. *Cambrian Register*, 1 (1795 (1796)), 164–7.

An attack on the conduct of the West Wales gentry during the civil wars and interregnum, repr. (ed. E. J. Jones) *Nat. Lib. of Wales Journ.* 11 (1959), 142–6.

3462 A WORD FOR GOD. Or a testimony on truths behalf. 1655.

Anti-Cromwellian Welsh puritan manifesto. Analysis of signatures in A. H. Dodd, 'A Welsh remonstrance, 1655', *Bull. Bd. of Celtic Studies*, 17 (1956–8), 219–92.

3463 'UNPUBLISHED CORRESPONDENCE between Archbishop Williams and the Marquis of Ormond' (1643–6). *Arch. Camb.* 1869, 305–43.

See also no. 1291.

3464 YONGE, W. England's shame . . . 1663.

On Yonge see *Welsh Bibliog. Soc. Journ.* 3 (1925–31), 89–91.

(d) *The Restoration and After*

3465 BARDDONIAETH EDWARD MORRIS. Ed. by H. Hughes. Liverpool. 1902.

Verses of a popular poet, some of them political in character. A shorter selection ed. by O. M. Edwards, Llanuwchllyn, 1904.

3466 DINELEY, THOMAS. The account of the official progress of . . . the first duke of Beaufort through Wales, 1684. Ed. by R. W. Banks. 1883.

Facsimile with Dineley's original sketches. Earlier transcript (ed. by C. Baker), 1864.

3467 GLORIA CAMBRIAE: or the speech of a bold Briton. 1702. Somers Tracts. 1814, 11.

Speech by Robert Price of Giler against the alienation of Welsh lordships to Bentinck.

3468 LLOYD, W. (dean of Bangor). A sermon at the funeral of Sir Edmund Berry Godfrey, Oct., 1678. A sermon preached before the king at White-hall, Nov., 1678. 1679.

3469 WYNNE, W. The history of Wales. 1697.

Powel's *Historie of Cambria*, 1584, brought up to date, with comments on contemporary developments. On the author see R. T. Jenkins in *Bull. Bd. of Celtic Studies*, 6 (1931–3). 153–9.
    See also Percy Enderbie, *Cambria triumphans, shewing the origin and antiquity of that . . . nation . . . to King Charles . . .*, 1661, later edn. 1810, which is 'an over-enthusiastic but ill-informed attempt to cover the same ground'.

2. Historical and Archaeological Journals

For journals dealing with county history and ecclesiastical history see sections D and F respectively. Articles from periodicals have been listed only when they embody important documentary material or when they deal with important events not recorded in publications of a more general character.

3470 ARCHAEOLOGIA CAMBRENSIS. 1846+. The journal of the Cambrian Archaeological Association. Index to first four series 1846–64, 1892. Index to fifth ser., 1884–1900, 1902.

3471 BULLETIN OF THE BOARD OF CELTIC STUDIES of the University of Wales. Cardiff. 1923+.

3472 HONOURABLE SOCIETY OF CYMMRODORION. *Y Cymmrodor.* 1877+. Transactions. 1892+.

An index to both publications to 1912 published as supplement to *Transactions*, 1911–12.

3473 LIVERPOOL WELSH NATIONAL SOCIETY. *Transactions.* Liverpool. 1885–1912.

3474 NATIONAL LIBRARY OF WALES. *Journal.* Aberystwyth. 1939+.

3475 WELSH BIBLIOGRAPHICAL SOCIETY. *Journal.* Carmarthen. 1910+.

3476 WELSH HISTORY REVIEW. Cylchgrawn Hanes Cymru. Univ. of Wales, Bd. of Celtic Studies, Hist. and Law Committee. Cardiff. 1960+.

3. Monographs and Articles

3477 BIRCH, T. An inquiry into the share which King Charles I had in the transactions of the Earl of Glamorgan (1645–6). 1747. Later edn. 1756.

Based partly on Rinuccini memoirs. Cf. S. R. Gardiner, 'Charles I and the Earl of Glamorgan', *E.H.R.* 2 (1887). See also J. H. Round, *Studies in peerage and family history*, 1901, ch. 9.

3478 DODD, A. H. Studies in Stuart Wales. Cardiff. 1952.

By the same author, 'The pattern of politics in Stuart Wales', *Cymmrodor. Soc. Trans.* 1948 (1949), 8–91; 'Wales and the Scottish succession', ibid. 1937 (1938), 201–25; 'Wales in the second bishops' war', *Bull. Bd. of Celtic Studies*, 13 (1946–8), 92–5; 'Colonel Thomas Trafford', ibid. 14 (1950–2), 300–2; 'The tragedy of Colonel John Bodvel', *Caerns. Hist. Soc. Trans.* 6 (1945), 1–22; and '"Tuning" the Welsh bench, 1680', *Nat. Lib. of Wales Journ.* 6 (1949–50), 249–59.

3479 DODD, A. H. 'Wales's parliamentary apprenticeship', *Cymmrodor. Soc. Trans.* 1942 (1944), 8–72.

Also by Dodd, 'Wales in the parliaments of Charles I', ibid. 1945 (1946), 16–49; 1946–7 (1948), 59–96; and 'Welsh opposition lawyers in the Short Parliament', *Bull. Bd. of Celtic Studies*, 13 (1946–8), 106–7.

3480 MATHEW, D. 'Wales and England in the early seventeenth century.' *Cymmrodor. Soc. Trans.* 1955 (1956), 36–49.

3481　PHILLIPS, J. R. Memoirs of the civil war in Wales and the marches, 1642–1649. 2 vols. 1874.

2nd edn. in 1 vol., 1878, omitting documents. The only comprehensive narrative of the civil war in Wales, but confused and prejudiced.
For partial revisions see 3482, 3486, 3541. See also Morris (1596).

3482　REES, J. F. Studies in Welsh history. Cardiff. n.d.

Nos. 5, 6, and 7 are on the civil war.

3483　RICHARDS, T. 'Declarasiwn 1687: tipyn o hanes a barn Cymru amdano.' *Cymdeithas hanes y bedyddwyr, Trafodion*, 1924, 27–37.

Welsh reactions to the declaration of indulgence. Also by Richards, *Piwritaniaeth a pholitics, 1689–1719*, Gwrecsam (Wrexham), 1927, which deals with religion and politics in post-revolution Wales.

3484　TERRY, W. H. Judge Jenkins. 1929.

See also T. Richards, 'The indiscretion of Anthony Wood', *Y Cymmrodor*, 26 (1926), 55–63. Many pamphlets on and by Jenkins in no. 3433d. Cf. nos. 953 n. and 1082.

3485　TIBBOTT, G. 'Welshmen with Prince Charles in Spain 1623', *Nat. Lib. of Wales Journ.* 1 (1939–40), 91–4.

3486　TUCKER, N. North Wales in the civil war. Denbigh. 1958.

See also his articles on civil war colonels: *Caerns. Hist. Soc. Trans.* 13 (1952), 1–8 (Carter), 19 (1958), 38–41 (Wynne), *Denbs. Hist. Soc. Trans.* 4 (1955), 27–37 (Robinson), 5 (1956), 7–34 (Salesbury), *Flints. Hist. Soc. Publications*, 1957, 42–53 (Mostyn).

3487　VAUGHAN, H. M. 'Oliver Cromwell in South Wales, 1648–9.' *Cymmrodor Soc. Trans.* 1936 (1937), 41–60.

3488　WILLIAMS, D. History of modern Wales. 1950.

Chapters 7–10 are on Stuart Wales. See also Wynne (545).

C. LEGAL AND ADMINISTRATIVE HISTORY

For writings on local administration see § D, such as 3511, 3565.

3489　BOWEN, I., ed. The statutes of Wales. 1908.

A very useful collection of the statutes relating to Wales, 1215–1902.

3490　DODDRIDGE [or DODERIDGE], SIR JOHN. The history of the ancient and moderne estate of the principality of Wales, dutchy of Cornwall, and earldom of Chester. 1630. 1714.

Written by Doddridge (1555–1628) in the early part of the reign of James I to urge the revival of the principality.

3491　LEWIS, E. A., ed. 'Three legal tracts concerning the courts leet in Wales.' *Bull. Bd. of Celtic Studies*, 9 (1937–9), 345–56.

3492   LEWIS, T. H. 'The justice of the peace in Wales.' *Cymmrodor. Soc. Trans.* 1943–4 (1945), 120–32.

An examination of the distinctive features of the office in Wales, 16th to 18th centuries.

3493   LLOYD, R. L. 'Welsh masters of the bench of the Inner Temple from early times until the end of the 18th century.' Ibid. 1938 (1939), 155–245.

3494   MATHEW, D. 'The Welsh influence among the legal advisers of James II.' Ibid. 1938 (1939), 119–23.

3495   OWEN, GEORGE. 'A dialogue of the government of Wales' and 'Treatise of Lordshipps Marcher'. In Description of Pembrokeshire, 3, 1–119, 127–286.

Written in 1603; publ. by Cymmrodorion Society in 3 pts., 1892–1906.

3496   OWEN, H. The administration of English law in Wales and the marches. 1900. Bibl.

A valuable sketch.

3497   SKEEL, C. A. J. The council in the marches of Wales. 1904.

See also her 'The St. Asaph cathedral library MS. of the instructions to the earl of Bridgewater, 1633', *Arch. Camb.* 1917, 177–92; Hancock, T. W., ed., 'The court of the marches: Montgomeryshire cases, 1617', *Montgom. Coll.* 19 (1886), 251–6. See also no. 3440.

3498   VAUGHAN, R. Practica Walliae. 1672.

3499   VAUGHAN, W. The Golden-grove. 1600. 2nd edn. 1608.

A Welsh writer's views on the government of the country. Cf. no. 3583.

3500   WILLIAMS, W. R. The history of the great sessions in Wales, 1542–1830, together with the lives of the Welsh judges. Brecknock. 1899.

The same author's *Parliamentary history* (917) should be used with great caution.

3501   WILLIAMS, W. Ll. An account of the kings court of great sessions in Wales. 1916.

A paper read before the Cymmrodorion Society in 1911.

D. COUNTY AND FAMILY HISTORY AND TOPOGRAPHY

The numerous parish, municipal, and family histories which have appeared in the publications of county or local historical societies or as separate publications, are not included here unless their significance is more than local. The Welsh biographical dictionary (3429) contains many valuable 'family' articles. Many of the Welsh county record offices have issued reports on the MS. material in their custody; e.g. M. Bevan-Evans, *Guide to the Flintshire Record Office*, Mold, 1955; M. Elsas, 'Local archives of Great Britain: the Glamorgan Record Office', *Archives*, 3 (1950), 7–16; W. O. Williams, *Guide to the Caernarvonshire Record*

Office, Caernarvon, 1952, and *An introduction to the county records*, Caernarvon, 1950; see also reports of county archivists and record committees: Carmarthen, 1953; Merioneth, 1954 sq.; Monmouth, 1905, 1939 sq. For fuller information on local history see no. 3431; the following are also relevant to this section: nos. 255, 3423, 3430, 3436, 3438, and 3441–3.

I. SOURCES

3502 'APPORTIONMENT OF TAXES, Denbighshire, 1675.' Ed. by R. Williams. *Arch. Camb.* 1881, 329–30.

Similar documents for Carmarthenshire transcr. by A. W. Matthews in *Carmarth. Antiq. Soc. Trans.* 8–10 (1914–15); see also 'Memorandum on the payment of subsidies in Wales temp. James I' in J. H. Matthews (3511), iv. 143–5.

3503 BENNETT, J. H. E. and LAWSON, P. H. 'An index of the wills proved in the peculiar court of Hawarden, . . . 1554–1800.' *Flints. Hist. Soc. Journ.* 4 (1906), 41–100.

3504 'CAERNARVONSHIRE AND THE RESTORATION: four letters.' Ed. by A. H. Dodd, *Caerns. Hist. Soc. Trans.* 11 (1950), 36–9.

3505 CLARK, G. T. Cartae et alia munimenta quae ad dominium de Glamorgan pertinent. 4 vols. Dowlais (vol. i), Cardiff (vols. ii–iv), 1885–93. 6 vols. Cardiff. 1910.

See also his 'Manorial particulars of the county of Glamorgan', *Arch. Camb.* 1877, 349–69; 1878, 1–21, 114–34; and T. Richards, ed., 'Glamorgan loyalists of 1696', *Bull. Bd. of Celtic Studies*, 3 (1926), 137–49.

3506 DWNN, LEWYS. Heraldic visitations of Wales, and part of the marches. Ed. by Sir S. R. Meyrick. 2 vols. Llandovery. 1846.

The fullest printed collection of Welsh pedigrees, made by Dwnn as deputy herald-at-arms between 1586 and 1613.
   Other useful collections of pedigrees in: *Llyfr Baglan*, by John Williams, *c.* 1600–7, ed. by J. A. Bradney, 1910; Bradney (3538); J. Buckley, *Genealogies of the Carmarthenshire sheriffs, 1539–1759*, 2 vols., Carmarthen, 1910–13; J. E. Lloyd (3551); J. Y. W. Lloyd, *The history of Powys Fadog*, 6 vols., 1881–7, and his article on Denbighshire sheriffs (3552); W. V. Lloyd (3553). See also G. T. Clark, *Limbus patrum Morganniae . . .*, 1886; J. E. Griffith, *Pedigrees of Anglesey and Caernarvonshire families*, Horncastle, 1914. Cf. F. Jones, 'An approach to Welsh genealogy', *Cymmrod. Soc. Trans.* 1948 (1949), 303–455.

3507 FRANCIS, G. G. Charters of Swansea . . ., 1215–1837. 1867.

3508 'HISTORY OF THE BULKELEY FAMILY.' Ed. by E. G. Jones and B. D. ROBERTS. *Anglesey Antiq. Soc. Trans.* 1948, 1–99.

Original MS. in Nat. Lib. of Wales.

3509 LEET PROCEEDINGS of the borough of Newtown, 1665–83. Transcr. and ed. by E. A. Lewis and J. C. Davies. *Montgom. Coll.* 47 (1941–2), 183–204; 48 (1943–4), 11–29.

See also 'Leet proceedings of the manor courts in North Radnorshire, 1688', ed. by E. A. Lewis. *Radnorshire Soc. Trans.* 4 (1943), 18–23; 5 (1944), 4–15.

3510 LETTERS . . . RELATING to the family of George, Lord Jeffreys . . . Ed. by W. H. W. Powell. *Home Counties Mag.* 12 (1910), 3–17, 81–91.

Corresp. between the judge and his family and friends in North Wales. Cf. no. 1038.

3511 MATTHEWS, J. H., ed. Cardiff records, being materials for the history of the county borough from the earliest times. 6 vols. Cardiff. 1898–1911. Maps.

See also S. Leighton, ed., *The records of the corporation of Oswestry*, [1884?], repr. from *Trans. of Shropshire Arch. Soc.*, 1879–84 (the town, though in Shropshire, has strong connections with Wales). Other collections of municipal records surveyed in: *Anglesey Antiq. Soc. Trans.* 1932, 75–90; 1933, 59–60 (Beaumaris, 1691–3, ed. by H. Owen); *Arch. Camb.* 1921, 425–43 (Ruthin, ed. by J. Fisher); *Nat. Lib. of Wales Journ.* 7 (1951–2), 33–45, 120–37 (Newtown, Pemb., ed. by B. G. Charles); ibid. 9 (1955–6), 157–79 (Haverfordwest, ed. B. G. Charles).

3512 'MERIONETHSHIRE ELECTION AGREEMENT, 1671.' Ed. by G. E. Evans. *Arch. Camb.* 1919, 220–1.

Cf. 'Montgomery election petition, 1685', *Montgom. Coll.* 21 (1887), 267–72.

3513 OWEN, GEORGE. The description of Pembrokeshire (1603). Ed. by H. Owen. Cymmrodorion record series, no. 1. 4 parts, paged as 2 vols. 1892.

Parts 1 and 2 deal with Pembrokeshire, the latter (which is incomplete) to be supplemented by B. G. Charles, 'The second book of George Owen's Description of Pembrokeshire', *Nat. Lib. of Wales Journ.* 5 (1947–8), 265–85. Parts 3 and 4 include other works by Owen.

3514 PARKINS, W. T. 'The lords of Mold.' *Cheshire Sheaf*, 2 (1880–2).

Repr. (ed. by H. Taylor) *Flintshire Hist. Soc. Publications*, 6 (1916–17), 37–62. The principal documents for the 17th century are printed in full, 42–61.

3515 'PEMBROKESHIRE HEARTHS IN 1670.' *W. Wales Hist. Rec.* 9 (1920–3), 217–40; 10 (1924), 177–216; 11 (1926), 113–38 (index 139–40).

From lay subsidy rolls.

3516 REES, W. Charters of the borough of Newport in Gwynllwg. Newport. 1950.

Cf. nos. 3507, 3511, 3565.

3517 REGISTRA ANTIQUA DE LLANTILIO CROSSENNY ET PENRHOS IN COMITATU MONUMETHENSI, 1577–1644. Ed. by J. A. Bradney. 1916.

A copy of the original parish registers made by Walter Powell, the author of the diary, 1603–54. Other ancient Monmouthshire transcr. and ed. by Bradney as separate publications are those of Caerwent and Llanfair Discoed, 1920; Grosmont, 1921; Llanbadog, 1919; Llanddewi Rhydderch, 1919; Llanfihangel Ystern Llewern, 1920. Other registers of the 17th century and earlier published separately are those of Conway (ed. A. Hadley, 1900), Kegidog (ed. E. A. Crisp, 1890), Llansannan (ed. R. Ellis, 1904), Llantrithyd (ed. H. S. Hughes, 1888); complete transcripts also appear in the following journals: *Arch. Camb.* 1888 (Erbistock); *Anglesey Antiq. Soc. Trans.* 1924 (Trefdraeth); *Montgom. Coll.* 30-2 (1897–1902), (Mallwyd), 32-3 (1902–4), (Trefeglwys), 34-5 (1905–10), (Llanllugan), 39 (1915–20), (Kerry); *Northern Flintshire*, 1 (1913), (Meliden, etc.); *Parish Register Soc.* 52 (1904), (Glasbury); *Welsh Gazette*, 1903–5 (Lampeter). Others print excerpts and descriptions. See also *Llandaff records* (5 vols., Cardiff and Lond. 1905–14), vol. i. For nonconformist registers see nos. 3569, 3673.

3518 SURVEY OF THE LORDSHIP OF BROMFIELD AND YALE, 1620. By J. Norden.

Printed in part in *Arch. Camb.* suppl. 1877 (original documents) and in J. Y. W. Lloyd (3506 n.), vols. ii and iii.

Other manorial surveys of 17th century in *Arch. Camb.* 1900, 1–23, 110–28 (Radnorshire, ed. J. Lloyd); *Nat. Lib. of Wales Journ.* 6 (1949–50), 385–90 (Uwchmynydd, ed. E. Evans); *Wales*, 3 (1896), 69–73 (Denbigh, ed. E. Owen).

Cf. J. O. Halliwell, ed., *An ancient survey of Penmaenmawr*, 1859, later edn. 1906; and no. 3438 (12), duchy of Lancaster.

2. County Historical Journals

Only the publications of the main county historical societies are included here. Many smaller field clubs and local antiquarian societies publish their own proceedings, and columns of historical 'notes and queries' in the local press are sometimes reprinted as an annual volume: for a full list the new edition of the *Bibliography* of Welsh history (3431) should be consulted. There is also much material for Welsh history in the historical journals of the English border shires.

3519 ANGLESEY ANTIQUARIAN SOCIETY AND FIELD CLUB. *Transactions.* Llangefni. 1913+. Index from 1911 to 1938 in 1938 vol.

3520 BRECKNOCK SOCIETY. *Transactions . . . and Records.* Cardiff. 1928–9. Revived as *Brycheiniog*. Cardiff. 1955+.

3521 CAERNARVONSHIRE HISTORICAL SOCIETY. *Transactions.* Caernarvon. 1939+.

3522 CARDIGANSHIRE ANTIQUARIAN SOCIETY. *Transactions [and Archaeological Record].* Aberystwyth. 1909–39. Revived as *Ceredigion*. Llandyssul. 1950+.

3523 CARMARTHENSHIRE ANTIQUARIAN SOCIETY AND FIELD CLUB. *Transactions.* Carmarthen. 1905–39. Revived as *The Carmarthen Antiquary*. Llandyssul. 1941+.

3524 DENBIGHSHIRE HISTORICAL SOCIETY. *Transactions.* Conway. 1952–6. Denbigh. 1957+.

3525 FLINTSHIRE HISTORICAL SOCIETY. *Publications.* Prestatyn. 1911–13. 1922–5. *Journal.* Prestatyn. 1913–20. *Publications.* Caernarvon. 1951+.

3526 MERIONETH HISTORICAL AND LOCAL RECORD SOCIETY. *Journal.* Bala. 1950+.

3527   MORGANNWG. Transactions of the Glamorgan Local History Society. Cardiff. 1957+.

3528   THE PEMBROKE HISTORIAN. Journal of the Pembrokeshire Local History Society. Haverfordwest. 1959+.

3529   POWYS-LAND CLUB. COLLECTIONS, HISTORICAL AND ARCHAEOLOGICAL, RELATING TO MONTGOMERYSHIRE. Lond. 1868–1945. No imprint. 1948–   . Since 1946 (49) called *Montgomeryshire Collections*. Index, vols. 1–28, 1895. Vols. 29–40 (1896–1928) include supplements (paged 1–648) entitled *Montgomeryshire Records*, containing much valuable source-material.

3530   RADNORSHIRE SOCIETY. *Transactions*. Llandrindod Wells. 1931+.

3531   SOUTH WALES AND MONMOUTH RECORD SOCIETY. *Publications*. Newport, Mon. 1932+.

3532   HISTORICAL SOCIETY OF WEST WALES. *West Wales Historical Records*. Carmarthen. 1910–29.

3. Topographical Works

See also nos. 3458, 3466.

3533   BOWEN, E. G. Wales, a study in geography and history. Cardiff. 1941.

3534   LEWIS, S. A topographical dictionary of Wales. 2 vols. 1833. 4th edn. 1849.

> To be corrected from *Rhestr o enwau lleoedd* (Gazetteer of Welsh place-names) ed. E. Davies, Cardiff, 1957. See also lists of Welsh parishes, hundreds, manors, and lordships in *Report of Royal Commission on land in Wales and Monmouthshire*, 1896, appendices G and M (C–8242), 361–76, 437–75.

3535   LHUYD, EDWARD. Parochialia, being a summary of answers to 'parochial queries in order to a geographical dictionary of Wales'. *c.* 1696–9. Ed. by R. H. Morris. 3 pts. *Arch. Camb.* suppl. 1909–11.

> See also F. V. Emery, 'A new reply to Lhuyd's *Parochial Queries*', *Nat. Lib. of Wales Journ.* 10 (1957), 395–402, and 'A map of Edward Lhuyd's "parochial queries" . . . 1696', *Cymmrod. Soc. Trans.* 1958 (1958), 41–53. Cf. also Owen (3513), 'A description of Wales' (Pt. 4, vol. 2, 287–716) (incomplete). On Lhuyd cf. Gunther (3599).

3536   REES, W. An historical atlas of Wales. Cardiff. 1951.

> See also M. Davies, *Wales in maps*, Cardiff, 1951; J. I. Jones, *Atlas hanesyddol o Gymru* Caerdydd (Cardiff), 1952.

4. Monographs and Articles

3537   BELL, H. I. Two Denbighshire MSS. *Bull. of Bd. of Celtic Studies*, 5 (1929–31), 45–54.

> Description (with excerpts) of court book of Chirkland manors and order book of Denbighshire quarter sessions, 1675–81.

3538 BRADNEY, J. A. A history of Monmouthshire. 4 vols. 1904–32.

The county is surveyed parish by parish and family by family, but the work was never completed. It may be supplemented by: W. Coxe, *Historical tour in Monmouthshire*, 2 vols., 1801, and by D. Williams, *History of Monmouthshire*, 1794. Cf. A. Clark, *Raglan Castle and the civil war in Monmouthshire*, Chepstow, 1953.

3539 DAVID, W. 'The antiquities of St. Fagans, with specific reference to the battle of 1648.' *Cardiff Naturalists' Soc. Trans.* 9, 1877.

A decisive battle of the 2nd civil war in Wales.

3540 DAWSON, J. W. Commerce and customs: a history of the ports of Newport and Caerleon. Newport. 1932.

3541 DODD, A. H. 'Anglesey in the Civil War.' *Ang. Antiq. Soc. Trans.* 1952, 1–33.

Also by Dodd, 'Caernarvonshire in the civil war', *Caerns. Hist. Soc. Trans.* 13 (1953), 1–34; 'The civil war in east Denbighshire', *Denbs. Hist. Soc. Trans.* 1954, 41–89; 'Flintshire politics in the seventeenth century', *Flints. Hist. Soc. Publ.* 14 (1953–4), 22–46; and 'Welsh and English in east Denbighshire: a historical retrospect', *Cymmrodor. Soc. Trans.* 1940, 34–65. See also no. 904 n.

3542 DODD, A. H., ed. A history of Wrexham. Wrexham. 1957.

3543 FENTON, R. A historical tour through Pembrokeshire. 1811. Repr. Brecon. 1903.

See also E. Laws, *The history of Little England beyond Wales* [*i.e.* South Pembrokeshire], 1888. Also, A. L. Leach, *The history of the civil war (1642–1649) in Pembrokeshire*, 1937.

3544 HANBURY, F. P. J. Coldbrook Park. The Hanbury and Herbert families. Privately printed. Newport. 1925.

3545 JONES, B. P. From Elizabeth I to Victoria: the government of Newport (Mon.), 1550–1850. Newport. 1957.

3546 JONES, E. D. 'Gleanings from the Radnorshire file of the Great Sessions papers, 1691–9.' *Radnorshire Soc. Trans.* 13 (1943), 7–34.

3547 JONES, E. G. 'Some notes on the principal county families of Anglesey in the sixteenth and early seventeenth centuries.' *Anglesey Antiq. Soc. Trans.* 1940, 46–61.

By the same author, 'County politics and electioneering 1558–1625', *Caerns. Hist. Soc. Trans.* 1 (1939), 39–46.

3548 JONES, ENID S. (Lady Clement Jones). Trevors of Trevalyn and their descendants.

Privately printed. 1955.

3549 JONES, T. A history of the county of Brecknock. 2 vols. Brecknock. 1805–9. Plates. Repr. 1 vol. Brecon. 1898.

3550   LEWIS, E. A. 'Schedule of the quarter sessions records of the county of Montgomery at the National Library of Wales (1614–1737).' *Montgom. Coll.* 46 (1940), 156–82; 47 (1941–2), 26–63.

With extensive excerpts.

3551   LLOYD, J. E., ed. A history of Carmarthenshire. 2 vols. Cardiff. 1935. 1939.

Vol. ii covers period from 1536.

3552   LLOYD, J. Y. W. 'The sheriffs of Denbighshire (1541–1700).' *Arch. Camb.* 1869, 1–29, 97–117, 202; 1870, 170–92.

3553   LLOYD, W. V. The sheriffs of Montgomeryshire, 1540–1639. Repr. from *Montgom. Coll.* 2–6 (1869–73), and continued to 1658, ibid. 27 (1893), 147–214.

Cf. 'E.A.', 'Genealogical notes on the sheriffs of Carmarthenshire', *Carmarthenshire Antiq. Soc. Trans.* 3 (1906–7), 29, 33–6, 76, 79–80, 84–7; 4 (1908–9), 3–4, 7, 13–14.

3554   MAHLER, M. A history of Chirk Castle and Chirkland. 1912.

On Chirk Castle in civil wars see pp. 163–97. Cf. G. M. Griffith, 'Chirk Castle election activities, 1600–1750', *Nat. Lib. of Wales Journ.* 10 (1957–8), 18–50.

3555   MEYRICK, SIR S. R. The history and antiquities of the county of Cardigan. 1810. Illus. Repr. Brecon. 1907.

3556   MOSTYN, LORD, and GLENN, T. A. History of the family of Mostyn of Mostyn. 1925.

3557   NICHOLAS, T. Annals and antiquities of the counties and county families of Wales. 2 vols. 1872.

3558   OWEN, E. 'The decline of the Tudors of Penmynydd.' *Ang. Antiq. Soc. Trans.* 1934, 48–60; 1935, 80–9.

3559   OWEN, H. Old Pembroke families. 1908.

See also J. R. Phillips, *Memories of the ancient family of Owen of Orielton, county Pembroke,* 1886.

3560   PIERCE, T. J. 'The old borough of Nefyn, 1555–1882.' *Caerns. Hist. Soc. Trans.* 18 (1957), 36–53.

3561   RICHARDS, T. 'Richard Edwards of Nanhoron: a restoration study.' *Caerns. Hist. Soc. Trans.* 8 (1947), 27–34.

3562   ROBERTS, G. 'The parliamentary history of Beaumaris, 1555–1832.' *Anglesey Antiq. Soc. Trans.* 1933, 97–109.

On Beaumaris see also nos. 3452 and 3511 n.

3563   STEEGMAN, J. Portraits from Welsh houses. Vol. 1, Houses in North Wales. Nat. Museum of Wales. Cardiff. 1957.

3564 WHITFIELD, W. E. B. 'The Glynnes of Hawarden.' *Flints. Hist. Soc.
Journ.* 4 (1916), 41–110.

See also G. Roberts, 'The Glynnes and Wynns of Glynllifon', *Caerns. Hist. Soc. Trans.*
9 (1948), 25–40; cf. no. 3569, 49–114.

3565 WILLIAMS, J., ed. Records of Denbigh and its lordship. Vol. 1 [all
publ.]. Wrexham. 1860.

Cf. his *Ancient and modern Denbigh*, Denbigh, 1856. Both have valuable excerpts from
municipal archives, but need to be treated with caution.

3566 WILLIAMS, J. G. 'Sir John Vaughan of Trawscoed.' *Nat. Lib. of
Wales Journ.* 8 (1953–4), 33–48, 121–46, 225–43.

On the local and family background of this eminent judge see pp. 225–43, and cf.
J. M. Howells, 'The Crosswood estate, 1547–1947', *Ceredigion*, 3 (1956), 70–88.

3567 WILLIAMS, J. The history of Radnorshire. Repr. from *Arch. Camb.*
Tenby. 1859. Later edn. Brecknock. 1905.

3568 WILLIAMS, R. History and antiquities of the town of Aberconway.
Denbigh. 1835.

On Conway Castle in civil wars and after see pp. 52–69.

3569 WILLIAMS, W. S. Arfon y dyddiau gynt. Repr. from *Cymru*. Caernarfon. 1914–15.

Essays on Caernarvon Castle in the civil war, and kindred subjects.

E. SOCIAL, ECONOMIC, AND CULTURAL HISTORY

1. SOURCES
See also no. 3438 (8).

3570 BUSHELL, T. A just and true remonstrance of his majesties mines-
royall in the principality of Wales. 1641.

Cf. G. E. Evans, 'King Charles and the Cardiganshire mines', *Old Wales* (ed. W. R.
Williams), Tal y bont, Brecon, 1 (1905–6), 333–7, 370–5 (letters of Charles I, 1638–43).
See also no. 3591.

3571 'THE CARREGLWYD BUILDING ACCOUNT, 1636.' Ed. by
D. Knoop and G. P. Jones. *Anglesey Antiq. Soc. Trans.* 1934, 27–43.

3572 'CORRESPONDENCE OF DR. JOHN DAVIES OF MALLWYD
and Sir Simonds D'Ewes.' Transcr. by E. Owen and trans. from Latin by
G. Hartwell-Jones. *Y Cymmrodor*, 17 (1904), 164–85.

On Davies, cf. no. 3600.

3573 'THE CORRESPONDENCE OF JOHN LEWIS, GLASGRUG,
with Richard Baxter and with Dr. John Ellis, Dolgelley.' Ed. by G. F. Nuttall.
Merioneth Hist. Soc. Journ. 2 (1953–6), 95–104.

On the proposed college for Wales cf. R. Baxter, *Certainty of the world of spirits*, 1691,
128–9; J. Lewis (3624), 30–1; H. Peter, *A good work for magistrates*, 1651.

3574 'THE DIARY OF BULKELEY OF DRONWY, ANGLESEY, 1630–6.' Ed. (with intro. and index) by H. Owen. *Anglesey Antiq. Soc. Trans.* 1937, 26–172.

See also 'Anglesey', ed. by T. Wright, *Arch. Camb.* 1882, 45–75 (transcr. of 17th-century MS. attacking social habits and institutions).
    Cf. nos. 3444–5.

3575 ELLIS, M. 'Cyflwyniad Rowland Vaughan, Caergai, i'w gyfieithiad o *Eikon Basilike.*' *Nat. Lib. of Wales Journ.* 1 (1939–40), 141–4.

Dedication of Welsh translation by a literary champion of crown and church.

3576 JONES, E. D. 'The Brogyntyn Welsh MSS.' *Nat. Lib. of Wales Journ.* 5 (1947–8), 233–64; 6 (1949–50), 1–42, 149–61, 223–48, 309–28; 7 (1951–2), 1–11, 85–101, 165–98, 277–315; 8 (1953–4), 1–32.

A repertory of Welsh poetry and scholarship of the 17th century; copious extracts illustrative of social life are printed in the original and translated.

3577 JONES, M. G., ed. 'Two accounts of the Welsh trust, 1675 and 1678.' *Bull. Bd. of Celtic Studies,* 9 (1937–9), 71–80.

An important Welsh educational trust; see also Wynne (3469), 288, and *Cymmrodor. Soc. Trans.* 1904–5 (1906), 82–3.

3578 'THE PORT OF CARDIFF and its member ports, 1606–10.' Ed. (with tabular analysis) by W. Rees. *S. Wales and Mon. Rec. Soc.* 3 (1954), 69–91.

Cf. also 'The port books of Cardigan in Elizabethan and early Stuart times', ed. (with tabular analysis, 1603–99) by E. A. Lewis, *Cardiganshire Antiq. Soc. Trans.* 7 (1930), 21–49; 9 (1933), 36–62; M. I. Williams, 'A contribution to the commercial history of Glamorgan, 1666–1735', *Nat. Lib. of Wales Journ.* 9 (1955–6), 188–215, 334–53 (tabular shipping lists for the period).

3579 'THE REGISTERS OF THE CORVISORS OF RUTHIN, 1570–1671.' Ed. by E. D. Jones. *Nat. Lib. of Wales Journ.* 7 (1951–2), 239–45.

3580 SUMMERS, H. H. C. 'The poor, 1685–1734.' *Montgom. Coll.* 38 (1918), 147–52.

Transcripts of indentures of apprenticeship, Oswestry.

3581 TAYLOR, J. A short relation of a long journey . . . encompassing the principalities of Wales. 1653. Spenser Soc. repr. 1876.

Cf. C. Cotton, *A voyage to Ireland in burlesque,* 1670.

3582 'TWO MACHYNLLETH TOLL BOOKS', 1632. Transcr. and ed. by E. Evans. *Nat. Lib. of Wales Journ.* 6 (1949–50), 78–103.

An important source for the trade in sheep and cattle through north and central Wales.

3583 VAUGHAN, WILLIAM. The golden fleece. 1626.

Pt. 2, ch. 6 contains criticisms of social and economic life in 17th-century Wales. Cf. nos. 3448, 3680.

3584 WALLER, W. An essay on the values of the mines, late of Sir Carbery Price. 1698.

An important source of lead mining in Cardiganshire; see also D. Jenkins, 'The Pryse family of Gogerddan (3)', *Nat. Lib. of Wales Journ.* 8 (1953–4), 353–68. Cf. nos. 3570, 3591.

2. LATER WORKS

(a) *General*

There is a sketch of Welsh 17th-century society in Dodd no. 3478, 1–48.

3585 OWEN, L. 'The population of Wales in the sixteenth and seventeenth centuries.' *Cymmrod. Soc. Trans.* 1959, 99–113.

Cf. D. Williams, 'A note on the population of Wales, 1536–1801', *Bull. Bd. of Celtic Studies*, 8 (1937), 359–63.

3586 PEATE, I. C. The Welsh house: a study of folk culture. *Y Cymmrodor*, 48 (1940). 3rd edn. Liverpool. 1946.

Valuable information on Welsh houses of the period is preserved and often illustrated in the inventories of the Royal Commission on Ancient Monuments in Wales and Monmouthshire (Montgomery, 1911; Flint, 1912; Radnor, 1913; Denbigh, 1914; Carmarthen, 1917; Merioneth, 1921; Pembroke, 1925; Anglesey, 1937; Caernarvon east, 1956). See also C. Fox and Lord Raglan, *Monmouthshire houses*, Cardiff, 1951–4, pts. 2 and 3; W. J. Hemp and C. Gresham, 'Park, Danfrother, and the unit system', *Arch. Camb.* 1942–3, 96–112 (with plans).

(b) *Agriculture, Industry, and Commerce*

No general economic history of Wales has been written in English, and only a very brief one in Welsh: B. B. Thomas, *Braslum o hanes economaidd Cymru*, Caerdydd (Cardiff), 1941. See also nos. 3513, 3518.

3587 DAVIES, D. J. An economic history of south Wales prior to 1800. Cardiff. 1935.

3588 EMERY, F. V. 'West Glamorgan farming, *c.* 1580–1620.' *Nat. Lib. of Wales Journ.* 10 (1957–8), 17–32.

Cf. B. E. Howells, 'Pembrokeshire farming, *c.* 1580–1620', ibid. 9 (1955–6), 239–50, 313–33, 413–39. On cattle trade see no. 1905.

3589 EVANS D. J. 'A note on Dr. John Ellis and the drapers of Shrewsbury.' *Mer. Hist. Soc. Journ.* 2 (1953–6), 69–71.

See also Mendenhall (1996); on records of the Shrewsbury shearmen see *Nat. Lib. of Wales Journ.* 8 (1954), 110.

3590 FRANCIS, G. G. The smelting of copper in the Swansea district. 1881.

Documents for 17th century, 58–96.

3591 GOUGH, J. W. The superlative prodigall. A life of Thomas Bushell. Bristol. 1932.

Cf. no. 3570. Also by Gough, *The mines of Mendip*, Oxf. 1930.

3592 JONES, T. I. J. 'A study of rents and fines in south Wales in the 16th and early 17th centuries.' *Harlech Studies*, ed. by B. B. Thomas. Cardiff. 1938.

3593 SKEEL, C. A. J. 'Social and economic conditions in Wales and the border in the early seventeenth century, as illustrated by Harl. MS. 4220.' *Cymmrod. Soc. Trans.* 1916–17 (1918), 119–44.

3594 WILKINS, C. History of the iron steel [etc.] trades of Wales. Merthyr Tydfil. 1903.

See also by Wilkins, *The South Wales coal industry and its allied industries* . . . Cardiff, 1888. Early chapters of both deal with the 17th century. Cf. no. 3544 (on a family of Quaker ironmasters).

3595 WILLIAMS, W. O. 'The Anglesey gentry as business men in Tudor and Stuart times.' *Anglesey Antiq. Soc. Trans.* 1948, 100–14.

(c) *Culture and Education*

3596 BRADNEY, J. [A.] A history of the free grammar school . . . of Llantilio-Crossenny . . . Monmouth, founded . . . 1654. 1924.

Other 17th-century foundations described in: C. Campbell, 'Some records of the free grammar school of Deythur, . . . Montgomery, 1690–1900', *Y Cymmrodor*, 43 (1932), 37–52; W. S. Davies, 'Bishop Gore's school' (Swansea, 1682), *Swansea Grammar School Mag.*, special no., 1932, 1–32; E. M. Jones, 'The free grammar school of Beaumaris' (1603), *Ang. Antiq. Soc. Trans.* 1922, 36–46; W. B. Jones, 'Hawarden grammar school' (1606), *Flints. Hist. Soc. Journ.* 1916–17, 6–84; G. Parry, 'Hanes ysgol Botwnnog' (1616), *Cymmrod. Soc. Trans.* 1957, 1–17 (cf. no. 3649); A. H. Williams, 'The origins of the old endowed grammar schools of Denbighshire', *Denbs. Hist. Soc. Trans.* 2 (1953), 17–69: Wrexham (1603), 44–7, Ruabon (1632), 47–52 (cf. *N.L.W. Journ.* 9 (1955–6), 264), Llanrwst (*c.* 1605–12), 57–63. See also no. 3609 (Monmouth, 1615), and J. Morgan, *David Hughes, founder of Beaumaris free school*, Caernarvon, 1883.

3597 CLEMENT, M. The S.P.C.K. and Wales, 1690–1740. Cardiff. 1954.

Cf. no. 3438 (10). See also T. Shankland, 'Sir John Phillipps and the charity-school movement in Wales, 1699–1737', *Cymmrod. Soc. Trans.* 1904–5 (1906), 74–216.

3598 GRIFFITHS, G. M. 'Educational activity in the diocese of St. Asaph, 1500–1650.' *Hist. Soc. Church in Wales Journ.* 3 (1953), 64–77.

3599 GUNTHER, R. T. Life and letters of Edward Lhuyd. Oxf. 1945.

Cf. no. 3535. See also A. H. Dodd, 'The early days of Edward Lhuyd', *Nat. Lib. of Wales Journ.* 6 (1949–50), 305.

3600 JAMES, J. W. 'Dr. John Davies of Mallwyd, 1578–1644.' *Hist. Soc. Church in Wales Journ.* 1 (1947), 40–52.

The leading Welsh philologist of his day; see also *Nat. Lib. of Wales Journ.* 7 (1951–2), 2–10, and cf. no. 3572.

3601 JONES, E. D. 'Robert Vaughan of Hengwrt.' *Merioneth Hist. Soc. Journ.* 1 (1949–51), 21–30.

See also T. A. Glenn, 'Robert Vaughan of Hengwrt and Robert Vaughan the engraver', *Arch. Camb.* 1934, 291–301.

3602 JONES, J. H. 'John Owen, Cambro-Britannus.' *Cymmrod. Soc. Trans.* 1940 (1941), 130–43.

Also by Jones, 'John Owen, the epigrammatist', *Greece and Rome*, 10 (1941), 65–73; and 'John Owen, Plas du', *Y Llenor*, Cardiff, 17 (1938), 215–20.

3603 MERCHANT, W. M. 'Lord Herbert of Cherbury and seventeenth-century historical writing.' *Cymmrod. Soc. Trans.* 1956 (1957), 47–63.

3604 MORRICE, J. C. Wales in the seventeenth century. Its literature and men of letters and action. Bangor. 1918.

3605 PARRY, T. Hanes llenyddiaeth Gymraeg hyd 1900. Cardiff. 1944.

English trans. by H. I. Bell: *A history of Welsh literature*, Oxf. 1955.

3606 RICHARDS, T. The Puritan visitation of Jesus College, Oxford, and the principalship of Dr. Michael Roberts (1648–57). 1924.

From the *Cymmrod. Soc. Trans. 1922–3*. See also E. G. Hardy, *Jesus College*, 1899; Sir L. Jenkins, *The life of Francis Mansell*, 1854.

3607 ROBERTS, H. P. 'Nonconformist academies in Wales.' *Cymmrod. Soc. Trans.* 1928–9 (1930), 1–98.

See also G. D. Owen, 'James Owen a'i academi', *Y Cofiadur*, 1952, 3–36; and notes in *Welsh Bibliog. Soc. Journ.* 3 (1925–31), 89–95. Cf. no. 3630.

3608 SHANKLAND, T. 'A list of the free-schools of Wales, 1650–1660.' *Seren Gomer*, Tonypandy, N.S. 22 (1901), 326–8.

Cf. W. A. L. Vincent, *The state and school education, 1640–60*, 1950; T. Richards, *Religious developments in Wales, 1654–62*, 1923, pp. 54–68.

3609 WARLOW, W. M. A history of the charities of William Jones at Monmouth and Newland. Bristol. 1899.

F. ECCLESIASTICAL HISTORY

In addition to the titles given below, much material on individual churches and local religious developments is printed in the journals listed in B2, D2, and F2, or separately published. Full particulars in no. 3431.

I. SOURCES

The records of the Church in Wales have been deposited in the National Library of Wales; a survey of them by J. C. Davies is printed in *Nat. Lib. of Wales Journ.* 4, 1945–6. Religious works in Welsh are listed in Parry (3605). Foley (1471) contains much material on Welsh recusants of the period in vols. iv and v, and Besse (1420) contains records of the early Welsh Quakers. See also nos. 3437, 3457, and 3463.

3610 AN ACT FOR THE PROPAGATION of the gospel in Wales, 1649; together with the proceedings of the commissioners for North Wales. Privately printed for 'Cymdeithas Llen Cymru' (The Welsh Literature Society). Cardiff. 1908.

The proceedings are printed from Bodley MS. Rawlinson C. 261, the official minute-book.

3611   CHARLES, T. and OLIVER, D., eds. The works of the late Rev. Walter Cradock, with a short account of his life. Chester. 1800.

Cf. J. M. Jones, 'Walter Cradoc a'i cyfoeswyr', *Y Cofiadur*, Wrexham, 15 (1938), 3–48.

3612   [DAVIES, RICHARD.] An account of the convincement, exercises, services, and travels of . . . Richard Davies with some relation of ancient friends and the spreading of truth in North-Wales. 1710. 7th edn. 1844.

An interesting autobiography. Cf. *John Ap John and early records of Friends in Wales*, by W. G. Norris, ed. by N. Penney, 1907.

3613   DIARIES AND LETTERS OF PHILIP HENRY. Ed. by M. H. Lee. 2 vols. 1882.

3614   'DOCUMENTS RELATING TO TITHE . . . belonging to the dean and chapter of St. Asaph' (1647–9). Ed. by E. R. Morris. *Arch. Camb.* 1887, 29–47.

3615   EDWARDS, C. 'An afflicted man's testimony . . .' 1691. *Cymru Fydd*, Dolgellau, 2 (1889), 337–51.

On Edwards see G. J. Williams, introduction to Edwards's *Hanes y ffydd ddifuant*, Cardiff, 1936; S. Lewis in *Efrydiau Catholig*, 4 (1949), 45–52.

3616   [ERBURY, W.] The testimony of William Erbury, left upon record for the saints of suceeding [*sic*] ages . . . Whereunto is added The honest heretick, giving his tryal at Westminster . . . 1658.

See also by Erbury, *The sword doubled* [*etc.*], 1652; *The north star* [*etc.*], 1653.

3617   FORTY-SIXTH ANNUAL REPORT OF THE DEPUTY KEEPER OF PUBLIC RECORDS. 1886. App. 1.

Ecclesiastical appointments in Wales, *temp.* Charles II, from patent rolls. Repr. *Arch. Camb.* 1886, 139–44, 228–40, 308–15.

3618   GORDON, A. 'An anonymous MS.' *Welsh Bibliog. Soc. Journ.* 3 (1925–31), 81–7.

Sermon notes of a Flintshire parson, 1657–1702.

3619   GRIFFYTH, ALEXANDER. Strena Vavasoriensis. A New-years-gift for the Welch itinerants. 1654.

An attack on the Propagation Act (3610) and on Vavasour Powell, 'metropolitan of the itinerants' (see 3631, 3666). Cf. his *Mercurius Cambro-Britannicus: or, News from Wales*, 1652; *A true and perfect relation of the whole transaction concerning the petition of the six counties of South-Wales*, 1654.

3620   GWEITHIAU MORGAN LLWYD [The works of M. Ll.]. Ed. by T. E. Ellis (vol. i) and J. H. Davies (vol. ii). 2 vols. Bangor. 1899–1908.

A complete edn. of the Welsh and English works of the Puritan mystic of Wrexham (1619–59). The full (Welsh) introduction to vol. ii is an important study of the history of the period.

3621 H[UGHES], J[OHN]. Allwyd neu agoriad paradwys i'r Cymry. Liège 1670. Ed. by J. Fisher. Cardiff. 1929.

R.C. tract. See also G. Bowen, 'Llyfr y resolusion neu directori Christianogol,' *Nat. Lib. of Wales Journ.* 11 (1959–60), 147–9 (another work by Hughes); and for other Welsh R.C. tracts and translations, ibid. 3 (1943–4), 69–75; *Efrydiau Catholig*, 2 (1947), 11–35, 4 (1949), 28–44; *Welsh Bibliog. Soc. Journ.* 7 (1950–3), 201–2.

3622 JENKINS, DAVID. A scourge for the Directorie . . . 1647.

Attack on the Westminster Assembly. On Jenkins see no. 3484.

3623 JONES, T. Y gwir er gwaethed yw . . . 1684.

Anti-popish tract (cf. no. 3422 (g)). See also L. Owen, *The Jesuites looking-glass*, 1629; E. Price, *Eye salve for England*, 1667; Anon., *The pope's down-fall at Abergavenny*, 1679.

3624 LEWIS, JOHN. *ΕΥΑΓΓΕΛΙΟΓΡΑΦΑ* [Evangeliographa], or some seasonable and modest thoughts in order to . . . promoting . . . the gospel, especially in Wales. 1656.

Dedicated to Cromwell. Cf. no. 3454.

3625 LLANDAFF RECORDS. See no. 3517 n.

See also: 'Bishop Francis Goodman's instructions to the diocese of Llandaff', ed. by G. Gruffydd, *Hist. Soc. Church in Wales Journ.* 4 (1954), 14–22; 'William Beaw, D.D., bishop of Llandaff', ed. by C. Waldron, *Red Dragon* (Cardiff), 9 (1886), 67–72 (letter to Abp. Tenison on state of diocese, 1699); A. Williams, ed., 'A Welsh parish in the interregnum', *E.H.R.* 9 (1894), 339–43 (contemp. account by incumbent of Merthyr Tydfil, a parish of Llandaff). Cf. no. 3645.

3626 'LLANCEVELACH NONCONFORMISTS. Annals and registers of Tirdunkin chapel, 1666 et seq.' Ed. by G. E. Evans. *Carmarthenshire Antiq. Soc. Trans.* 15 (1921), 50–4; 16 (1922), 11.

Unfinished, but complete to *c.* 1708. Cf. 'Records of Independent church at Pant-têg, Abergwili', *c.* 1690–1714, ed. by E. D. Jones, *Cofiadur*, 23 (1953), 24–31. See also no. 3673.

3627 McCANN, J. and CONNOLLY, H., eds. Memorials of Father Augustine Baker. *Cath. Rec. Soc. Publications*, 33 (1933).

Includes his autobiography.

3628 'THE MERIONETH MINISTERS' PETITION TO OLIVER CROMWELL.' Ed. by E. D. Jones. *Merioneth Hist. Soc. Journ.* 2 (1953–6), 156–7.

3629 MYLES, JOHN. An antidote against the infection of the times. 1656. Ed. by T. Shankland. *Cymdeithas Hanes y Bedyddwyr, Trafodion.* 1904.

An attack on the Quakers. On Myles see also nos. 3673, 3674.

3630 OWEN, JAMES. Moderation still a virtue. 1704.

A defence of the dissenting academies; cf. no. 3607. See also G. Owen, *Some account of . . . Mr. James Owen*, 1809.

3631 POWELL, VAVASOR. The bird in the cage, with an epistle to the Welsh churches, and a brief narrative. 1661. Later edn. 1662.

The 'Narrative' is a defence of the proceedings of the commission of 1650 for the propagation of the Gospel in Wales. *The life and death of Vavasor Powell*, s.l., 1671, contains Powell's autobiography; the editor is thought to have been Edward Bagshaw the younger. Cf. Alexander Griffith, *Strena Vavasoriensis* (3619), a hostile account; and David Davies, *Vavasor Powell, the Baptist evangelist of Wales in the seventeenth century*, 1896. Cf. no. 3666.

3632 'THE PERSONALITY OF A WELSH CLERIC.' Ed. by F. Jones. *Hist. Soc. Church in Wales Journ.* 1 (1947), 154–62.

3633 PRICHARD, R. Cannwyll y Cymry. Ed. by S. Hughes. 1672. Many later edns.

Popular and influential religious verse in Welsh, written before 1644. See also J. Ballinger, 'Vicar Prichard', *Y Cymmrodor*, 13 (1900), 51–75; D. G. Jones, *Y Ficer Prichard a Canwyll y Cymru*, Caernarfon, 1946.

3634 PRYCE, A. I. The diocese of Bangor during three centuries. Cardiff. 1929.

Tabular list of presentations to livings, with valuable introduction. See also: 'A breviat of all the presentments against the clergie of the diocese of Bangor . . . 1623', *Arch. Camb.* 1863, 283–5; H. Humphreys (bp.), 'Ymofion i'w hateb gan brocatorion, wardenied a swyddogion eraill . . . 1690', in A. O. Evans, *A few episcopal visitation queries*, Bangor, 1937; J. Pring, *Papers, documents, law proceedings, etc. respecting the maintenance of the choir of the cathedral at Bangor, as provided for by an act of Parliament passed in 1685*, Bangor, 1819.

3635 THE RECORDS OF A CHURCH OF CHRIST MEETING AT BROADMEAD, BRISTOL. Ed. by E. B. Underhill. Hanserd Knollys Soc. 1847. Another edn. by N. Haycroft. 1865.

An indispensable source for the origins of Welsh separatism.

3636 WYNNE, R. A short narrative of the proceedings against the bishop of St. Asaph [Eddard Jones]. 1702.

2. JOURNALS OF WELSH ECCLESIASTICAL HISTORY

3637 Y COFIADUR. Cylchgrawn Cymdeithas Hanes Annibynwyr Cymru. (Journal of Welsh Congregational Historical Society.) Wrexham. 1923–8. Llandyssul. 1946+.

3638 CYMDEITHAS HANES Y BEDYDDWYR CYMRU, *Trafodion* (Proceedings of the Welsh Baptist Historical Society). Various imprints. 1906+.

3639 EFRYDIAU CATHOLIG (Catholic Studies). Aberystwyth. 1946–9.

3640 HISTORICAL SOCIETY OF THE CHURCH IN WALES. *Journal*. Cardiff. 1949+.

3. Monographs and Articles

(a) *General*

3641 BALLINGER, J. The Bible in Wales. 1906.

Traces the history of the Welsh versions of the Bible to 1900, with a complete bibl. See also T. Llewelyn, *Historical account of the British or Welsh versions and editions of the Bible*, 1768, which includes the dedications of Salesbury (1567), Morgan (1588), and Parry (1620).

3642 RICHARDS, T. The religious census of 1676. *Cymmrodor. Soc. Trans.* suppl. 1925–6.

(b) *The (Anglican) Church in Wales*

3643 BARNARD, E. A. S. 'Bishop Lewes Bayly and his son Thomas.' *Cymmrod. Soc. Trans.* 1928–9 (1930), 99–132.

See also ibid. 1945, 32–3, and H. Grey-Edwards in *Carmarth. Antiq. Soc. Trans.* 27 (1937), 70–4.

3644 BEVAN, W. L. St. David's. Diocesan Histories, S.P.C.K. 1889.

The companion volumes for the other Welsh dioceses are now superseded. On St. David's see also: W. M. Williams and I. Jones, 'An inventory of records at the palace of Abergwili', *Bull. Bd. of Celtic Studies*, 9 (1939), 7–9, 358–66; W. T. Morgan, 'The consistory courts in the diocese of St. David's 1660–1858', *Hist. Soc. Church in Wales Journ.* 7 (1957), 1–24; T. Richards, 'The troubles of Dr. William Lucy', *Y Cymmrodor*, 38 (1927), 142–83.

3645 BIRCH, W. DE G. Memorials of the see and cathedral of Llandaff. Neath. 1912.

3646 DODD, A. H. 'The Church in Wales in the age of the reformation' (15th–17th centuries). Welsh Church Congress handbook. Cardiff. 1953. Pp. 18–41.

Cf. H. O. Wakeman, 'The Laudian movement in Wales', *Cymru Fydd*, Dolgellau, 3 (1890), 275–85.

3647 HART, A. T. William Lloyd, 1627–1717. Bishop, politician, author and prophet. 1952.

3648 JAMES, J. W. A church history of Wales. Ilfracombe. 1945.

See also J. E. Hirsch-Davies, *A popular history of the Church in Wales*, 1911; D. A. Jones, *The Church in Wales*, Carmarthen, 1938.

3649 MORGAN, J. Coffadwriaeth . . . Henry Rowland, escob Bangor (1598–1616). Bangor. 1910.

Bishop and educationist.

3650 RICHARDS, T. 'Two studies in the history of Bangor diocese.' *Arch. Camb.* 1925, 32–74.

See also no. 3634. Also by Richards, 'The Whitford leases. A battle of wits', *Cymmrod. Soc. Trans.* 1925 (1926), 1–75. Cf. W. H. Howse, 'Contest for a Radnorshire rectory in the seventeenth century', *Hist. Soc. Church in Wales Journ.* 7 (1957), 69–79.

3651 THOMAS, D. R. The history of the diocese of St. Asaph. 1874. 3 vols. Oswestry. 1908–13.

See also no. 3614.

3652 WILLIS, B. Survey(s) of the cathedral-church(es) of St. David's, 1717; Llandaff, 1715; St. Asaph, 1720 (2nd edn., ed. E. Edwards, 2 vols., Wrexham, 1801); Bangor, 1721.

Each survey includes brief accounts of the successive bishops and cathedral dignitaries.

3653 WRIGHT, E. G. 'Humphrey Humphreys' (Bishop of Bangor). *Anglesey Antiq. Soc. Trans.* 1949, 66–76, and *Hist. Soc. Church in Wales Journ.* 2 (1950), 72–86.

See also his 'Dean John Jones, 1650–1727', *Anglesey Antiq. Soc. Trans.* 1952, 34–43.

(c) *Catholic Recusants*

See also nos. 1446–97, 3447, and 3483.

3654 ATTWATER, D. The Catholic church in modern Wales. 1935.

3655 BOWEN, G. 'Gwilym Pue, bardd Mair, a theulu'r Penrhyn.' *Efrydiau Cath.* 2 (1947), 11–35.

A study of a 17th-century recusant bard and his background. See also, on John Roberts, no. 1482 n.

3656 CANNING, J. H. 'The Titus Oates plot in South Wales and the Marches.' *St. Peter's Mag.*, Cardiff, 1923, 3–7, 38–47, 74, 94–101, 127–35, 159–68, 189–97, 219–26, 249–55, 278–82, 308–14, 342–7; 1924, 2–6, 38–42, 70–7, 99–105.

Fully documented and illustrated; invaluable. Other short (sometimes incomplete) articles on 17th-century recusancy in South Wales by J. M. Cronin, ibid. 1924, 1926–7, 1929, and by R. Hodges, 1925–6.

3657 CLEARY, J. M. 'The Catholic resistance in Wales.' *Blackfriars*, 37 (1957), 111–25.

See also by Cleary, *The Catholic recusancy of the Barlows of Slebech in Pembrokeshire*, Newman Ass., Cardiff Circle, 1956.

3658 ELLIS, T. P. The Catholic martyrs of Wales. 1933.

Cf. F. E. Ll. Jones, *Blessed Philip Powell: a Catholic martyr of Breconshire*, Brecon, 1946.

3659 JONES, E. G. Cymru a'r hen ffydd. Caerdydd (Cardiff). 1951.

Lectures on the regional distribution of recusancy; more detailed local studies in: *S. Wales and Mon. Rec. Soc. Publications*, 3 (1954), 49–67, 4 (1957), 59–110 (Glamorgan and Monmouth, Eliz. and Jas. I, ed. by F. H. Pugh, with map); *Cath. Rec. Soc. Publications*, 2 (1906), 289–303 (S. Wales marches, 17th and 18th centuries, ed. by J. H. Matthews); *Cymmrod. Soc. Trans.* 1945 (1946), 114–33 (Denbigh, Flint, and Montgomery, 1581–1625, ed. by E. G. Jones); *Montgom. Coll.* 55 (1957), 10–33 (Montgomery, ed. by T. B. Trappes-Lomax). List of priests in: *S. Wales and Mon. Rec. Soc.* 1 (1932), 193–9 (Monmouth, 1678, ed. by W. Rees); *Cath. Rec. Soc. Publications*, 9 (1911), 106–7 (N. Wales, 1692, ed. by R. Stanfield).

3660 JONES, E. G. 'Hugh Owen of Gwenynog.' *Anglesey Antiq. Soc. Trans.* 1938, 42–9.

An eminent Anglesey convert and translator of à Kempis; see also S. Lewis in *Efrydiau Cath.* 4 (1949), 28–32, G. Bowen in *Welsh Bibliog. Soc. Journ.* 7 (1950–3), 201–2.

3661 LLOYD, D. T. 'Rome and Wales.' *Dock Leaves*, Pembroke Dock, winter, 1952, 7–15.

A report on Welsh recusant material in the Vatican archives.

3662 THOMAS, D. 'St. Winifred's well and chapel, Holywell.' *Hist. Soc. Church in Wales Journ.* 8 (1958), 15–31.

A notable place of pilgrimage.

(d) *Puritans and Protestant Dissenters*

See nos. 3427, 3478, 3483, 3561, 3607.

3663 BEBB, W. A. 'John ap John, apostol y crynwyr.' *Cymru*, Gwrecsam, 61 (1921), 70–1, 87–9, 116–18, 156–8; 62 (1922), 79–81, 119–20, 142–3, 187–8.

The apostle of Quakerism in Wales; cf. no. 3612 n.

3664 DODD, A. H. 'New England influences in early Welsh Puritanism.' *Bull. Bd. of Celtic Studies*, 16 (1954), 30–7.

See also by Dodd 'The background of the Welsh Quaker migration to Pennsylvania', *Merioneth Hist. Soc. Journ.* 3 (1957–60), 111–27.

3665 JAMES, J. S. Hanes y bedyddwyr yng Ghymru. 4 vols. Caerfyrddin (Carmarthen). 1893–8.

The standard history of the Welsh Baptists. Cf. also J. Davies, *History of the Welsh Baptists*, Pittsburgh, 1835; J. Thomas, *History of the Baptist Association in Wales* (1650–1790), 1795. Reassessment of origins in T. Richards, 'Y dechreuadau: golwg newydd', *Cymdeithas Hanes y Bedwyddwyr, Trafodion*, 1948–9, 5–30. Regional studies in: E. G. Bowen, 'Bedyddwyr Cymru tua 1714', ibid. 1957, 5–14 (with map), W. T. Whitley, 'Radnorshire Baptists 1646–1776', *Radnorshire Hist. Soc. Trans.* 5 (1935), 28–39 (with map). See also Nuttall, *The Welsh saints* (1329 n.).

3666 JONES, R. T. 'Vavasor Powell and the protectorate.' *Congregational Hist. Soc. Trans.* 17 (1953), 41–50.

See also his 'Vavasor Powell a'r bedyddwyr', *Cymdeithas a Hanes y Bedyddwyr Cymru, Trafodion*, 1948–9, 38–43. Cf. no. 3631.

3667 KENRICK, W. B. Chronicles of a nonconformist family; the Kenricks of Wynn Hall [Denbighshire], Exeter and Birmingham. Birmingham. 1932.

3668 LLOYD, S. The Lloyds of Birmingham. 1907.

Chaps. 1–3 on Montgomeryshire background of this family of Quaker bankers; see also R. J. Lowe, *Farm and its inhabitants, with an account of the Lloyds of Dolobran*, privately printed, 1883.

3669 REES, T. History of Protestant nonconformity in Wales from its rise in 1633 to the present time. Later edn. 1883.

3670 REES, T. M. A history of the Quakers in Wales. Carmarthen. 1925.

See also: R. Jones, *Crynwyr bore Cymru*, *Abermaw* (Barmouth), 1931; E. S. Whiting, E. R. Morris, and J. Hughes, *The background of Quakerism in Wales and the border* (with map), Malvern, 1952; F. J. Gibbins, 'Historical survey of the yearly meetings for Wales', *The Friend*, N.S. 10, 1870. Regional studies in: *Caerns. Hist. Soc. Trans.* 2 (1940), by B. Owen; *Carmarth. Antiq. Soc. Trans.* 4 (1908–9), 14–16, 18–21, 27–8, 35–9, 46–9, 55–6, 61–5, 72–3 (by G. E. Evans); *Radnorshire Soc. Trans.* 11 (1941), 31–6 (by H. D. Phillips); *W. Wales Hist. Rec.* 9 (1923), 1–32 (Pembrokeshire, by D. Salmon); *Y Geninen*, Caernarvon, 7 (1889), 251–5, 8 (1890), 62–5, 130–2, 198–9 (Merioneth, by E. Griffith); *Friends Hist. Soc. Journ.* 14 (1917), 56–7 (Monmouthshire meeting, 1680).

3671 RICHARDS, T. History of the Puritan movement in Wales from 1639 to 1653. 1920.

See also his regional reassessments of Puritanism in no. 3551, ii. 133–84; *Flints. Hist. Soc. Publications*, 13 (1952–3), 53–71; *Merioneth Hist. Soc. Journ.* 2 (1953–6), 105–19; *Anglesey Antiq. Soc. Trans.* 1954, 34–58. Cf. also P. Davies, 'Episodes in the history of Brecknockshire dissent', *Brycheiniog*, 3 (1957), 11–36.
  Also by Richards, *Religious developments in Wales 1654–62*, 1923; *Wales under the penal code, 1662–87*, 1925; *Wales under the indulgence, 1672–5*, 1928.

3672 RICHARDS, T. Cymru a'r uchel gomisiwn, 1633–40. Lerpwl (Liverpool). 1928.

Welsh cases before the high commission court. By Richards also, 'Eglwys Llanfaches', *Cymmrodor. Soc. Trans.* 1941, 150–84, which deals with the pioneer separatist church of Wales (cf. T. M. Rees in *Congregational Hist. Soc. Trans.* 13 (1938), 87–97); and 'Henry Maurice, piwritan ac annibynwr', *Y Cofiadur*, 1928, 15–67, concerning a post-restoration Puritan leader.

3673 SHANKLAND, T. John Myles. *Cymdeithas Hanes y Bedyddwyr Cymru, Trafodion*, 1910–11, 8–16.

The founder of the Baptist community in Wales; see also D. R. Phillips, 'Cefndir hanes eglwys Ilston', ibid. 1928, 1–107 (list of members of this pioneer Baptist church, 1649–70, 100–7). On Myles cf. no. 3674.
  By Shankland also, 'Stephen Hughes a'i cyfnod', *Y Berniad*, Lerpwl (Liverpool), 2 (1912), 175–85, dealing with the Puritan author, editor, and translator.

G. EMIGRATION AND COLONIZATION

See also no. 3604.

3674 BICKNELL, T. W. 'John Myles. Religious toleration in Massachusetts.' *Mag. of New England Hist.* Boston (Mass.). 1892.

Cf. nos. 3629, 3673.

3675 BROWNING, C. H. The Welsh settlement of Pennsylvania. Phila. 1912.

See also T. A. Glenn, *Welsh founders of Pennsylvania*, Oxf. 1913, and *Merion in the Welsh tract*, Morriston, Pa. 1896; H. M. Jenkins, *Historical collections relating to Gwynedd*, Phila. 1884.

See also N. R. Burr, 'The Welsh episcopalians of colonial Pennsylvania and Delaware', *Hist. Mag. of Protestant Episcopal Church*, New Brunswick, N.J. 8 (1939); J. Clement, 'Griffith Hughes, S.P.G. missionary to Pennsylvania . . .', ibid. 17 (1948); and F. J. Dallett, 'Griffith Hughes dissected', *Barbados Museum and Hist. Soc.* 23 (1955).

3676   DODD, A. H. The character of early Welsh emigration to the United States. Cardiff. 1953. 2nd edn. 1957. With map.

Pp. 1–16, 33–5 are on this period; see also B. Owen, 'Yr ymfudo o sir Gaernarfon i'r Unol Daleithiau', *Caerns. Hist. Soc. Trans.* 13 (1952), 42–4.

3677   LEVICK, J. John ap Thomas and his friends. Phila. 1886.

3678   PALMER, A. N., ed. 'The adventures of a Denbighshire gentleman in the seventeenth century in the east Indies.' *Arch. Camb.* 1902, 277–86.

Descriptive letter from Madras, 1658, to Denbighshire relatives, by a servant of the East India Co.

3679   ROBERTS, H. 'Brief journal of . . . travels from Pennsylvania to England and Wales.' (1697–8.) *Pennsylvania Mag. of Hist. and Biog.* 1894.

Repr. with modernized spelling in *Wales*, Wrexham, ed. O. M. Edwards, 3 (1896), 335–6, 370–3.

3680   VAUGHAN, WILLIAM. Cambrensium Caroleia. 1625.

A plea for the author's colony of Cambriol, on which see E. R. Williams, *Some studies in Elizabethan Wales* (Newtown, n.d.), ch. 14. Other relevant works by Vaughan are: *Directions for health . . .* 1600, 7th edn. 1633; *The Newlanders cure*, 1630. Cf. nos. 3448, 3583.

3681   WILLIAMS, W. Ll. Sir Henry Morgan. *Cymmrod. Soc. Trans.* 1903–4, 1–42.

Buccaneer and deputy governor of Jamaica; see corrections in *Dict. Welsh Biog.*, p. 645. Cf. no. 3367.

XIV

SCOTLAND

A. REFERENCE

See also *Scottish Historical Review* (50).

3682 ALDIS, H. G. A list of books printed in Scotland before 1700, including those printed furth of the realm for Scottish booksellers. *Edin. Bibliog. Soc.*, no. 6 (1904).

Cf. 'A century of books printed in Glasgow, 1638–1686', *Glasgow Bibliog. Soc. Records*, 5 (1920), 31–95.

3683 BLACK, G. F. List of works relating to Scotland [in New York Public Library]. N.Y. 1916.

3684 CRAIGIE, W. A., ed. A dictionary of the older Scottish tongue. Oxf. 1933+ (in progress).

3685 GOULDESBROUGH, PETER, KUP, A. P., and LEWIS, IDWAL. Handlist of Scottish and Welsh record publications. Brit. Rec. Assoc. Pub. 1954.

Excludes official publications.

3686 GRANT, W., ed. The Scottish national dictionary, designed partly on regional lines and partly on historical principles, and containing all the Scottish words known to be in use or to have been in use since *c.* 1700. Aberdeen. 1931+ (in progress).

3687 HINDLE, C. J. A bibliography of the printed pamphlets of Lady Eleanor Douglas, the 17th-century prophetess. Edin. 1934.

Reprinted from *Edin. Bibliog. Soc. Papers*, 15 (Oct. 1934), 35–54.

3688 LIVINGSTONE, MATTHEW. A guide to the public records of Scotland deposited in H.M. General Register House, Edinburgh. Edin. 1905.

See also 'Accessions of public records to the register house since 1905', *S.H.R.* 26 (1947), 26–46; J. M. Thomson, *The public records of Scotland*, Glasgow, 1922; H. M. Paton, *The Scottish records, their history and value*, Edin. 1933.

3689 MEIKLE, H. W., BEATTIE, W., and WOOD, H. H. Scotland: a select bibliography. Camb. 1950.

The most comprehensive of the short bibliographies; but J. D. Mackie, *Scottish history*, Camb. 1956, gives valuable comments on the books listed.

3690 MITCHELL, A., and CASH, C. G. Contribution to the bibliography of Scottish topography. 2 vols. Scot. Hist. Soc., 2nd ser., xiv–xv (1917).

Vol. i, Topographical; ii, Topical—Industries, Maps, Travellers, etc. Valuable. Continued (on different plan) in P. Hancock, *A bibliography of books on Scotland, 1916–50*,

Edin. 1960. See also H. R. G. Inglis, J. Mathieson, and C. B. B. Watson, *The early maps of Scotland*, Edin., 2nd edn., 1936.

3691 NATIONAL LIBRARY OF SCOTLAND. Catalogue of MSS. acquired since 1925. Vol. i. Edin. 1938.

3692 SCOTLAND: GENERAL REGISTER HOUSE. Index to register of deeds, 1661–85. 25 vols. Edin. 1929–59 (in progress).

Deeds recorded in 'Books of council and session', valuable for biographical and other research. The parallel 'Registers of sasines', recording transactions in heritable property, are indexed for certain counties.

3693 SOURCES AND LITERATURE OF SCOTS LAW. Stair Soc. i. (1936).

Sections contributed by experts. Indispensable for every branch of Scottish history.

3694 STUART, MARGARET, and PAUL, J. B. Scottish family history. Edin. 1929.

The essential guide to writings on Scottish families. J. P. S. Ferguson, *Scottish family histories held in Scottish libraries*, Edin. 1960, includes more recent books.

3695 TERRY, C. S. A catalogue of the publications of Scottish historical and kindred clubs and societies, and of the volumes relative to Scottish history issued by H.M. Stationery Office, 1780–1908, with a subject-index. Glasgow. 1909.

The same author's *Index to the papers relating to Scotland described or calendared in the Historical MSS. Commission's Reports*, Glasgow, 1908, is no substitute for the indexes to the individual reports. Both Terry's works were continued to 1927 in C. Matheson, *A catalogue of the publications of Scottish . . . societies . . . the reports of the royal commission on historical MSS.*, Aberdeen, 1928.

3695a TERRY, C. S. The rising of 1745, with a bibliography of Jacobite history, 1689–1788. Scottish history from contemporary writers. 1900. 1903.

The later edn. has a revised and enlarged bibl.

B. GENERAL HISTORY

In this period, when ecclesiastical and civil affairs were inextricably intertwined, the division between political and ecclesiastical history is purely formal. There are no bibliographies dealing with the 'political' history of Scotland in the 17th century. There are valuable materials relating to Scottish history in the *Reports of the Historical Manuscripts Commission* (see nos. 248–54 and p. 26). A useful collection of documents and extracts is W. C. Dickinson and G. Donaldson, eds., *A source book of Scottish history*, vol. iii (1567–1707), Edin. 1954.

1. SOURCES

3696 AN ACCOUNT of the proceedings of the estates in Scotland, 1689–90. 2 vols. Edin. 1954–5. Ed. by E. W. M. Balfour-Melville. Scot. Hist. Soc. Pub., 3rd Ser., vols. xlvi–xlvii.

3697 ACCOUNTS OF THE MASTER OF WORKS for building and repairing royal palaces and castles. Vol. i, 1529–1615. Ed. H. M. Paton. Edin. 1957.

3698 THE ACTS OF THE PARLIAMENTS OF SCOTLAND. Ed. by T. Thomson and C. Innes. 12 vols. Edin. 1814–75.

Vols. iv–xii cover 1593–1707. The reissue of vols. v and vi is much fuller. Vol. xii has an index to the whole.

3699 ANALECTA SCOTICA. Ed. by J. Maidment. 2 vols. Edin. 1834–7.

Miscellaneous items, unarranged, but largely 17th century. Cf. *Historical fragments relative to Scottish affairs from 1635–1664*, ed. [J. Maidment], 3 parts, Edin. 1832–3.

3700 ANNALS AND CORRESPONDENCE of the Viscount and the first and second Earls of Stair. By J. M. Graham. 2 vols. Edin. and Lond. 1875.

Part of vol. i has valuable original documents. For biography see A. J. G. Mackay, *Memoir of Sir James Dalrymple, first Viscount Stair*, Edin. 1873. See also no. 3828.

3701 THE ARGYLE PAPERS (1640–1723). Ed. by J. Maidment. Edin. 1834.

Cf. *Letters to the Argyll family (1520–1685)*, ed. A. Macdonald, Maitland Club., Edin. 1839; and no. 3730 n.

3702 THE ARNISTON MEMOIRS . . . 1571–1838. Edited from the family papers. Ed. by G. W. T. Omond. Edin. 1887.

A few 17th-cent. documents, but mainly later.

3703 A BOOK OF SCOTTISH PASQUILS, 1568–1715. Ed. by [J.] [Maidment]. Edin. 1868.

Mainly 17th century.

3704 CHRONOLOGICAL NOTES of Scottish affairs from 1680 till 1701, being chiefly taken from the diary of Lord Fountainhall. By Sir John Lauder, Lord Fountainhall. Ed. by Sir W. Scott. Edin. 1822.

From a small vol. in Advocates' Library, Edin., compiled by Robert Mylne, who suppressed some passages and inserted others with 'perverse assiduity'. See Scott's Introduction; also Fountainhall's *Historical notices*, Bann. Club, vol. i, pp. x, xi.
Cf. *Historical observes of memorable occurents in church and state* [1680–1686], Bann. Club, Edin. 1840, ed. by A. Urquhart and D. Laing, and *Historical notices of Scottish affairs selected from the manuscripts of Sir J. Lauder of Fountainhall* [1661–1688], Bann. Club, 2 vols., Edin. 1848, ed. by David Laing; and *Journals of Sir John Lauder, Lord Fountainhall, with his observations on public affairs and other memoranda, 1665–1676*, ed. by D. Crawford, Scot. Hist. Soc., 1 vol., Edin. 1900. These works form a valuable criticism of the government by a Presbyterian.

3705 CORRESPONDENCE OF GEORGE BAILLIE of Jerviswood, 1702–1708. Ed. by Gilbert Elliot, second Earl of Minto. Bann. Club. Edin. 1842.

3706 CORRESPONDENCE OF COLONEL N. HOOKE, agent from the court of France to the Scottish Jacobites in the years 1703–1707. Ed. by W. D. Macray. 2 vols. Roxburghe Club. 1870–1.

Ed. from transcripts in the Bodleian Library. See also *Secret history of Colonel's Hooke's negociations in Scotland in 1707, being the original letters and papers*, by N. Hooke, Edin. 1760.

3707 CORRESPONDENCE OF SIR ROBERT KERR, first Earl of Ancram, and his son William, third Earl of Lothian [1616–1667]. Ed. by D. Laing. Uniform with Bann. Club publications. 2 vols. Edin. 1875.

Kerr was a Covenanter and filled high offices of state while his party was in the ascendant. From the original letters preserved at Newbattle Abbey.

3708 CORRESPONDENCE OF THE SCOTS COMMISSIONERS in London, 1644–6. Ed. by H. W. Meikle. Roxburghe Club. 1917.

Letters from the representatives of Scotland in the Committee of both kingdoms.

3709 THE CROMWELLIAN UNION: papers relating to the negotiations for an incorporating union between England and Scotland, 1651–1652, with an appendix of papers relating to the negotiations in 1670. Ed. by C. S. Terry. Scot. Hist. Soc. Edin. 1902.

Similar collections for 1651–9 on Scotland and the commonwealth and Scotland and the protectorate. Ed. C. H. Firth. Scot. Hist. Soc., vols. 18, 31, Edin. 1895, 1899.

3710 IN DEFENCE OF THE REGALIA, 1651–2. Being selections from the family papers of the Ogilvies of Barras. Ed. by D. G. Barron. 1910.

3711 DIARY OF ALEXANDER BRODIE, 1652–80, and of his son James Brodie, 1680–85. Ed. D. Laing. Spalding Club. Aberdeen. 1863.

3712 DIARY OF ANDREW HAY OF CRAIGNETHAN, 1659–60. Ed. A. G. Reid. Scot. Hist. Soc. Edin. 1901.

3713 DIARY OF ALEXANDER JAFFRAY. Ed. J. Barclay. 1833. Aberdeen. 1856.

A Scottish commissioner to Charles II in 1649–50; afterwards a Quaker.

3714 DIARY OF SIR ARCHIBALD JOHNSTON of Wariston, 1632–9, 1650–4, 1655–60. Ed. G. M. Paul, D. H. Fleming, and J. D. Ogilvie. 3 vols. Scot. Hist. Soc. Pub. lxi, 2nd Ser. 18, 3rd Ser. 34. Edin. 1911, 1919, 1940.

A portion for 1639 is in *Scot. Hist. Soc. Pub.* xxvi, Edin. 1896.

3715 DIARY OF THE CORRESPONDENCE OF SIR THOMAS HOPE, 1633–45. Ed. T. Thomson. Bann. Club. Edin. 1843.

Lord Advocate under Charles I. Letters by him are in *Miscellany* of Scot. Hist. Soc. i. Cf. *S.H.R.* 3 (1905–6).

3716 DIARY OF MR. JOHN LAMONT of Newton, 1649–71. Ed. G. R. Kinloch. Maitland Club. Edin. 1830.

Of special value to genealogists.

3717 DIARY OF PUBLIC TRANSACTIONS AND OTHER OCCURRENCES, chiefly in Scotland, from January 1650 to June 1667, by J. Nicoll. Ed. D. Laing. Bann. Club. Edin. 1836.

3718 DIARY OF THE PROCEEDINGS IN THE PARLIAMENT AND PRIVY COUNCIL of Scotland, May 21, 1700–March 7, 1707, by Sir D. Hume of Crossrigg, one of the senators of the College of Justice. Bann. Club. Edin. 1828.

See: *Domestic details of Sir David Hume of Crossrig . . . 1697 . . . 1707*, Edin. 1843, ed. by W. B. D. D. T[urnbull].

3719 THE DIPLOMATIC CORRESPONDENCE OF JEAN DE MON-TEREUL and the brothers De Bellièvre, French ambassadors in England and Scotland, 1645–48. Ed. by J. G. Fotheringham. 2 vols. Scot. Hist. Soc. Edin. 1898–9.

Of great value for the period it covers. From the original ciphered dispatches in the French Foreign Office.

3720 THE GRAMEID: an heroic poem descriptive of the campaign of Viscount Dundee in 1689, and other pieces. By J. Philip. Ed. by A. D. Murdoch. Scot. Hist. Soc. Edin. 1888.

Translation from the Latin.

3721 THE HAMILTON PAPERS; being selections from original letters in the possession of His Grace the Duke of Hamilton and Brandon relating to the years 1638–1650. Ed. by S. R. Gardiner. Camd. Soc. 1880.

Cf. *Camd. Soc. Misc.* ix for other letters.

3722 HIGHLAND PAPERS. Ed. J. R. N. Macphail. 4 vols. Scot. Hist. Soc. Edin. 1914–34.

Includes some papers of general political interest, especially in the late seventeenth century. Cf. *Loyall dissuasive and other papers concerning the affairs of Clan Chattan, 1691–1705*, by Sir A. Macpherson, ed. A. D. Murdoch, Scot. Hist. Soc., Edin. 1902; *Papers illustrative of the political condition of the Highlands of Scotland, 1689–96*, ed. J. Gordon, Maitland Club, Glasgow, 1845; *Raid on Glenkindie in 1698*, in Third Spalding Club Miscellany 2 (1940), 89–114.

3723 THE HISTORICAL WORKS OF SIR JAMES BALFOUR . . . Lord Lyon King at arms to Charles the First, and Charles the Second . . . from the original manuscripts . . . in the Advocates' Library. Ed. by J. Haig. 4 vols. Edin. 1825.

The last three vols. (1604–52) are valuable as the work of one who in his later years was in close contact with the administration. Royalist in sympathies, but critical. Up to 1640 called by the author 'Annales', and after 'Memories and passages of State', the volumes form a chronological whole.

3724 HISTORY OF SCOTS AFFAIRS FROM 1637 to 1641. By James Gordon, parson of Rothiemay. Ed. by J. Robertson and G. Grub. 3 vols. Spalding Club. Aberdeen. 1841.

Written from a royalist point of view.

3725 THE HISTORY OF THE TROUBLES OF GREAT BRITAIN, containing a particular account of the most remarkable passages in Scotland,

from the year 1633 to 1650. With an exact relation of the wars carried on . . .
by . . . Montrose . . . To which is added The true causes . . . which contributed
to the restoration of King Charles II . . . by D. Riordan of Muscry. Translated
into English by Capt. J. Ogilvie. By Robert Menteth. 1735.

The 1st edn. is entitled *Histoire des troubles . . . par Messire Robert Mentet de Salmonet*,
Paris, 1661. It also contains Riordan's *Relation des veritables causes . . .* Royalist in
sympathies.

3726 THE HISTORY OF THE TROUBLES AND MEMORABLE
TRANSACTIONS IN SCOTLAND from the year 1624 to 1645 . . . From
the original MS. of John Spalding, then commissary clerk of Aberdeen. 2 vols.
Aberdeen. 1792. Later edns. 2 vols. Bann. Club. Edin. 1828–9. Ed. by
[J. Skene]. 2 vols. Spalding Club. Aberdeen. 1850–1. Ed. by J. Stuart.

The 1st edn. is unscholarly and incomplete. Spalding had strong royalist leanings. The
edn. 1850–1, called *Memorialls of the troubles in Scotland and England*, has the best text.

3727 THE HISTORY OF THE UNION OF GREAT BRITAIN. By
Daniel Defoe. Edin. 1709. Later edn. Lond. 1786.

Of the first importance. Defoe was commissioned by the English Government to reside
in Edinburgh while the Treaty of Union was being discussed in the Scottish Parliament.
Edn. of 1786 has 'An essay containing a few strictures on the Union', by J. L. de Lolme.

3728 JOURNAL OF THE HON. JOHN ERSKINE of Carnock, 1683–7.
Ed. W. Macleod. Scot. Hist. Soc. Edin. 1893.

Important for Argyll's insurrection in 1685.

3729 A LARGE DECLARATION concerning the late tumults in Scotland,
from their first originalls: together with a particular deduction of the seditious
practices of the prime leaders of the Covenanters: collected out of their owne
foule acts and writings . . . By the King. By [W. Balcanquhall]. 1639.

The official defence of the policy of Charles I by a Laudian.

3730 THE LAUDERDALE PAPERS. Vol. i, 1639–1667; vol. ii, 1667–1673;
vol. iii, 1673–1679. Ed. by O. Airy. 3 vols. Camd. Soc. 1884–5.

Important as containing the correspondence of those responsible for the administration.
Selected from Brit. Mus. Add. MSS. 23119–34, 35125. Cf. Mr. Airy's letters addressed
to the Earl of Lauderdale [1660–9] in *Camd. Soc. Misc.* viii, 1883, and his articles on
Lauderdale in *E.H.R.*, July 1886, *Quarterly Rev.*, July 1884, and on Archbishop Sharp
in the *Scottish Rev.*, July 1884. A collection of letters from Lauderdale to John, 2nd
earl of Tweeddale, and others, is in *Scot. Hist. Soc. Misc.*, vi, 111–240 (Edin.
1939). See also *Letters from Lady Margaret Kennedy to John, duke of Lauderdale*, Bann.
Club, Edin. 1828; *Letters from Archibald, earl of Argyll, to John, duke of Lauderdale,
1663–70*, ed. G. Sinclair and C. K. Sharpe, Bann. Club, Edin. 1829; 'Letters from
John, earl of Lauderdale and others, to Sir John Gilmour', in *Scot. Hist. Soc. Misc.*
v, 109–94 (Edin. 1933).

3731 LETTERS FROM JAMES, EARL OF PERTH, . . . to his sister the
countess of Erroll and other members of his family. Ed. W. Jordan. Camd.
Soc. 1845.

Covers Dec. 1688–Apr. 1696.

3732 LETTERS AND STATE PAPERS during the reign of King James the Sixth (1578-1625). Ed. by J. Maidment. Abbotsford Club. Edin. 1838.

Chiefly from MSS. collected by Sir J. Balfour.

3733 THE LETTERS AND JOURNALS of Robert Baillie, Principal of the University of Glasgow, 1637–1662. 2 vols. Edin. 1775. Later edn. 3 vols. Bann. Club. Edin. 1841–2. Ed. by D. Laing.

First edn. has only a selection; that of Laing is complete. Supplies a vivid presentation of leading events and persons, English as well as Scottish, from a Presbyterian point of view. App. to vol. i has original papers 1633–9; ii, 1639–46; and iii, 1647–61.

3734 LETTERS AND PAPERS illustrating the relations between Charles the Second and Scotland in 1650. Ed. by S. R. Gardiner. Scot. Hist. Soc. Edin. 1894.

Consists of extracts from the *Brief Relation*, the official organ of the Council of State, and from the State Papers in the Public Record Office, London, and from MSS. in the Bodleian.

3735 A COLLECTION of letters addressed by prelates and individuals of high rank in Scotland and by two bishops of Sodor and Man to Sancroft, Archbishop of Canterbury, in the reigns of Charles II and James VII, ed. from the originals in the [Tanner MSS.] Bodleian Library, Oxford. Ed. by W. N. Clarke. Edin. 1848.

3736 LETTERS, ILLUSTRATIVE OF PUBLIC AFFAIRS in Scotland, addressed by contemporary statesmen to George, Earl of Aberdeen, Lord High Chancellor of Scotland. 1681–4. Ed. by J. Dunn. Spalding Club. Aberdeen. 1851.

MSS. at Haddo House in possession of the Earl of Aberdeen.

3737 LEVEN AND MELVILLE PAPERS: letters and state papers chiefly addressed to George, Earl of Melville, Secretary of State for Scotland, 1689–1691. Ed. by W. L. Melville. Bann. Club. Edin. 1843.

The most important work for the period it covers.

3738 THE LOCKHART PAPERS: containing memoirs and commentaries upon the affairs of Scotland from 1702 to 1715, by George Lockhart, Esq., of Carnwath. Ed. [A. Aufrere]. 2 vols. 1817.

Valuable for Jacobitism.

3739 MEMOIR touching the revolution in Scotland (1688–90), presented to King James II at St. Germains (1690). By Colin Lindsay, earl of Balcarres. Ed. by A. W. Crawford, Lord Lindsay. Bann. Club. Edin. 1841.

3740 THE MEMOIR of James and William, dukes of Hamilton. By G. Burnet. Oxf. 1852.

Cf. *The Memoirs of . . . Montrose* (1681 n.).

3741 MEMOIRS OF HIS OWN TIME (1632–70). By Sir James Turner. Bann. Club. Edin. 1829.

3742 MEMOIRS OF THE LIFE of Sir John Clerk of Penicuik, baronet, baron of the exchequer, extracted by himself from his own journals, 1676–1755. Ed. J. M. Gray. Scot. Hist. Soc. Edin. 1892. Roxburghe Club. 1895.

Clerk was one of the commissioners for the union.

3743 MEMOIRS OF HENRY GUTHRY, late bishop of Dunkel, in Scotland: wherein the conspiracies and rebellion against King Charles I, to the time of the murther of that monarch, are . . . related. 1702. Glasgow. 1747, 1748. Ed. by G. Crawfurd.

3744 MEMOIRS OF THE AFFAIRS of Scotland from the restoration of King Charles II. By Sir George Mackenzie of Rosehaugh. Ed. T. Thomson. Edin. 1821.

Mackenzie was Lord Advocate.

3745 MEMOIRS OF NORTH BRITAIN. By John Oldmixon. 1715.

Useful for Glencoe and the Darien Company.

3746 MEMOIRS OF MR. WILLIAM VEITCH and George Brysson, written by themselves, with other narratives illustrative of the history of Scotland from the restoration to the revolution. Ed. by T. McCrie. Edin. and Lond. 1825.

Valuable for the accounts of the risings against the government. Interesting as reflecting the spirit of the times is *Memorialls; or The memorable things that fell out within this island of Brittain from 1638 to 1684; by the Rev. Mr. Robert Law*, ed. by C. K. Sharpe, Edin. 1818.

3747 MEMORIALS AND LETTERS relating to the history of Britain in the reign of James the First. By Sir David Dalrymple, Lord Hailes. Glasgow. 1762. Later edn. Glasgow. 1766.

Mainly from Wodrow MSS. The 2nd edn. was 'corrected and enlarged'. From the Balfour MSS. in the Advocates' Library, Edin.

3748 MINUTE-BOOK kept by the war committee of the covenanters in the stewartry of Kirkcudbright in 1640 and 1641. Kirkcudbright. 1855.

3749 MISCELLANEA SCOTICA. A collection of tracts, relating to the history, antiquities, topography and literature of Scotland. 4 vols. Glasgow. 1818–20.

Vol. i contains 'Authentic narrative of the massacre of Glencoe, contained in a Report of the Commission given by his Majesty for inquiring into the slaughter of the men of Glencoe'. Cf. *Miscellany of the Abbotsford Club*, Edin. 1837; *Miscellany of the Bannatyne Club*, ed. by D. Laing, 3 vols., Edin. 1827, 1836, 1855; and *Spottiswoode Miscellany*, ii, ed. by J. Maidment, Spots. Soc., Edin. 1845. See also *Miscellany of the Maitland Club*, ed. by J. Dennistoun, A. Macdonald, and Joseph Robertson, 4 vols., Edin. 1833–47, in vol. ii of which part i has documents relative to schools, and part ii contains papers relative to Montrose.

3750 MISCELLANY of the Scottish History Society, I, II, III, 1893, 1904, 1919.

I has: civil war papers, 1643–50; letters to Archbishop Sharp from the Duke and

Duchess of Lauderdale and Lord Hatton; diary of John Turnbull, 1657–1704; Master-man papers, 1660–1719. II has: Correspondence of George Graeme, Bishop of Dun-blane and of Orkney, 1602–38; narratives of Hamilton's expedition in 1648; papers of Robert and Gilbert Burnet and Archbishop Robert Leighton. III has: Dundee court martial records, 1651; Bishop of Galloway's correspondence, 1679–85; diary of Sir James Hope, 1646–54; contributions to the distressed church of France, 1622; Forbes baron court book, 1659–78.

3751 MORE CULLODEN PAPERS. Ed. D. Warrand. Vol. i (to 1704), ii (1704–25). Inverness. 1923–5.

Culloden Papers (Lond. 1815) contain very few items before 1715.

3752 THE POLITICAL WORKS of Andrew Fletcher, Esq. 1732. Glasgow. 1749.

Fletcher was a prominent opponent of the union of 1707. See 'A bibliography of Andrew Fletcher of Saltoun, 1653–1716', by R. A. S. Macfie, Edin. Bibl. Soc. Pub. iv (1901). Cf. no. 3793.

3753 THE REGISTER OF THE PRIVY COUNCIL of Scotland. Ed. by J. H. Burton, D. Masson, P. H. Brown, and H. Paton. Edin. H.M. Stationery Office. 1877–1933 [in progress].

Vol. i begins with the year 1545. Vols. vi (first series)–vol. xiv (third series) deal with the period to 1681. The most valuable source of information regarding the administration in the successive reigns.

3754 REGISTRUM MAGNI SIGILLI regum Scotorum. The register of the great seal of Scotland [from 1306]. Ed. by T. Thomson, Sir J. B. Paul, J. Maitland Thomson, J. Horne Stevenson, and W. K. Dickson. Edin. 1814–1914.

Vol. vi (1593–1608)–vol. xi (1660–8).

3755 REPORT ON THE EVENTS and circumstances which produced the union of the kingdoms of England and Scotland; on the effects of this great national event, on the reciprocal interests of both kingdoms . . . [with appendix]. By [J.] [Bruce]. 2 vols. [1799.]

Appendix contains original documents dealing with projected unions before 1707. A limited number only were pr. for official use. Cf. Seafield (3757).

3756 ROYAL LETTERS and other historical documents . . . from the family papers of Dundas of Dundas. Ed. by W. Macleod. 1 vol. Edin. 1897.

3757 SEAFIELD CORRESPONDENCE [1685–1708]. Ed. by J. Grant. Scot. Hist. Soc. Edin. 1912.

Valuable. Cf. *S.H.R.* 10, p. 47. *Letters relating to Scotland in the reign of Queen Anne* [1702–8], ed. by P. H. Brown, Scot. Hist. Soc., Edin. 1915, include much Seafield correspondence; valuable for the Union.

3758 A SELECTION FROM THE PAPERS of the Earls of Marchmont in the possession of the Right Honble. Sir George Henry Rose, illustrative of events from 1685–1750. Ed. by G. H. Rose. 3 vols. 1831.

Sir Patrick Hume, 1st Earl of Marchmont (1641–1724), was Lord Chancellor of Scotland (1696–1702), and Lord High Commissioner in 1698 and 1702.

3759 SHORT ABRIDGEMENT of Britane's distemper 1639–49. By Patrick Gordon. Ed. by J. Dunn. Spalding Club. Aberdeen. 1844.

3760 SIEGE OF THE CASTLE of Edinburgh 1689. Ed. by R. Bell. Bann. Club. Edin. 1828.

Cf. C. S. Terry's 'Siege of Edinburgh Castle in 1689', *S.H.R.* 2 (1904–5). The Le Fleming MSS., Hist. MSS. Comm., 1890 (138) has many news-letters from Edinburgh 1689–90.

3761 THE STAGGERING STATE of the Scots statesmen . . . from 1550 to 1650. By Sir John Scott of Scotstarvet. Ed. by [W. Goodall]. Edin. 1754. Later edn. by C. Rogers. Edin. 1872.

Cf. *Scotstarvet's trew relation*, ed. G. Neilson, *S.H.R.* 11, 12, 13, 14 (1913/14–1916/17).

3762 STATE PAPERS and miscellaneous correspondence of Thomas [Hamilton], earl of Melros. Ed. by J. Maidment. 2 vols. Abbotsford Club. Edin. 1837.

Mainly from Balfour MSS. in Advocates' Library, Edinburgh, consisting of letters of Privy Council to James VI and others, and chiefly relative to the period 1603–25.

3763 STATE PAPERS AND LETTERS addressed to William Carstares, confidential secretary to K. William during the whole of his reign . . . relating to public affairs in Great Britain, but more particularly in Scotland, during the reigns of K. William and Q. Anne. Ed. by J. McCormick. Edin. 1774.

3764 THE EARL OF STIRLING'S REGISTER of royal letters relative to the affairs of Scotland and Nova Scotia from 1615 to 1635. Ed. by C. Rogers. 2 vols. Edin. 1885.

William Alexander, earl of Stirling, was Secretary of State for Scotland from 1626 till his death in 1640. MSS. in General Register House and Advocates' Library, Edin.

3765 THE STUART PAPERS at Windsor. Being selections from unprinted royal archives. Ed. by A. N. and H. Tayler. 1939.

Cf. H.M.C. (221).

3766 THE TREATY of union of Scotland and England, 1707. Ed. by G. S. Pryde. Edin. 1950.

On an earlier proposal for union see the treatise written about 1604 by Sir Thomas Craig, *De unione regnorum Britanniae tractatus*, ed. (with translation) from MS. in Advocates' Library, by C. S. Terry, Scot. Hist. Soc., Edin. 1909.

2. LATER WORKS

3767 BROWN, P. H. History of Scotland to the present time. 3 vols. Camb. 1899–1905. Later edn. 3 vols. Camb. 1911.

Out of date in its approach and emphasis, but not yet superseded. Fuller but less coherent than Brown is J. H. Burton, *History of Scotland*, 9 vols., Lond. and Edin. 1853, 1867–70; later eds., 1873 and 1876.

3768 BROWN, P. H. The legislative union of England and Scotland. Oxf. 1914.

Appendix of documents in P.R.O. and B.M. Cf. P. H. Brown's and W. L. Mathieson's articles in *S.H.R.* 4 (1906–7); C. W. T. Omond, *The early history of the Scottish union question*, 2nd edn., 1906; J. Mackinnon, *The union of England and Scotland*, 1896; and *The union of 1707, a survey of events*, by various authors, intro. by P. H. Brown, 1907.

3769 BUCHAN, J., BARON TWEEDSMUIR. The massacre of Glencoe. 1933.

Cf. J. Paget (361 n.).

3770 CORSAR, K. C. 'The surrender of Edinburgh castle, December 1650.' *S.H.R.* 28 (1949), 43–54.

3771 COWAN, S. The lord chancellors of Scotland . . . to the treaty of union. 2 vols. 1911.

3772 CUNNINGHAM, A. The loyal clans. Camb. 1932.

An important study of highland history in relation to government policy.

3773 DAKERS, E. (K.). The reign of King Covenant. 1956.
Critical of the covenanters.

3774 DICEY, A. V., and RAIT, R. S. Thoughts on the union between England and Scotland. 1920.

The classical commentary. Cf. 'The constitutional necessity for the union of 1707', by W. S. McKechnie, *S.H.R.* 5 (1907–8), 52–66; and Nobbs (383).

3775 ELDER, J. R. The Highland host of 1678. Glasgow. 1914.

3776 FLEMING, D. H. Critical reviews relating chiefly to Scotland. 1912.

The miscellaneous writings of a scholar noted equally for his strong Presbyterian prejudices and his strict accuracy in facts.

3777 GIBB, A. D. Scotland resurgent. Stirling. 1950.

'Nationalist' criticism of the union of 1707.

3778 LANG, A. A history of Scotland from the Roman occupation. 4 vols. Edin. and Lond. 1900–7.

The 2nd edn. of vols. i and ii (1900, 1903) contains the author's corrections. Cf. J. D. Mackie, *Andrew Lang and the house of Stuart, being the author's Andrew Lang Lecture delivered . . . 21 Nov. 1934*, 1935.

3779 MACKENZIE, A. M. The Scotland of Queen Mary and the religious wars, 1513–1638. Edin. 1936. The passing of the Stewarts, 1638–1748. Glasgow. 1937.

Nationalist and anti-Presbyterian. The author's *Scottish pageant*, 1513–1625 and 1625–1707 (2 vols., Edin. 1948–9) gives extracts from sources, with spirited commentary.

3780 MATHIESON, W. L. Politics and religion. A study in Scottish history from the reformation to the revolution (1550–1695). 2 vols. Glasgow. 1902.

Scotland and the union. A history of Scotland from 1695 to 1747. Glasgow. 1905.

The best account of the period. On Jacobitism see G. H. Jones (386), and Petrie (387).

3781 OMOND, G. W. T. The lord advocates of Scotland from the close of the fifteenth century to the passing of the reform bill. 2 vols. Edin. 1883.

3782 SALOMON, F. Frankreichs Beziehungen zu dem Schottischen Aufstand, 1637–40. Berlin. 1890.

3783 TEMPLE, R. C. New light on the mysterious tragedy of the 'Worcester', 1704–5. 1930.

3784 TERRY, C. S., ed. 'Free quarters in Linlithgow, 1642–7.' *S.H.R.* 14 (1916–17), 75–80.

3785 TERRY, C. S. The Pentland rising and Rullion Green. Glasgow. 1905.

Drummond's official dispatch is printed *S.H.R.* 3 (1905–6), 449–52; Terry discusses it, ibid. 4 (1906–7), 114–16.

3786 WEDGWOOD, C. V. 'Anglo-Scottish relations, 1603–40.' *R.H.S. Trans.* 4th Ser. 32 (1950), 31–48; also 'The covenanters in the first civil war.' *S.H.R.* 39 (1960), 1–15.

See also nos. 1629–31. An inadequate attempt at a new approach is D. Mathew, *Scotland under Charles I*, 1955.

3. BIOGRAPHY

ARGYLL, ARCHIBALD, FIRST MARQUESS OF

3787 Willcock, J. The great marquess. Life and times of Archibald, 8th earl and 1st (and only) marquess of Argyll (1607–1661). Edin. and Lond. 1903.

ARGYLL, ARCHIBALD, NINTH EARL OF

3788 Willcock, J. A Scots earl of covenanting times: being life and times of Archibald, 9th earl of Argyll (1629–1685). Edin. 1907.

ARGYLL, JOHN, DUKE OF

3789 Campbell, R. The life of the most illustrious prince, John, duke of Argyle and Greenwich. 1745.

BALCARRES, ANNA, COUNTESS OF

3790 Lindsay, A. W., earl of Crawford and of Balcarres. Memoir of Lady Anna Mackenzie, countess of Balcarres, and afterwards of Argyll (1621–1706). Edin. 1868.

CAMERON OF LOCHEIL, SIR EWEN

3791 Memoirs of Sir Ewen Cameron of Locheil [1629–1696]. By John Drummond. Ed. by J. Macknight. Abbotsford and Maitland Clubs. Edin. 1842.

Said to be written in 1733.

CARSTARES, WILLIAM

3792 William Carstares: a character and career of the revolutionary epoch
(1649–1715). By R. H. Story. 1874.

Contains family papers. Carstares's letters to Harley, 1702–7, are in Portland MSS.
viii, Hist. MSS. Comm. (153).

FLETCHER, ANDREW

3793 Mackenzie, W. C. Andrew Fletcher of Saltoun. His life and time. Edin.
1935.
Cf. no. 3752.

GRIERSON, SIR ROBERT (d. 1733)

3794 The laird of Lag. By A. Fergusson. Edin. 1886.

HAY, JOHN

3795 Inglis, J. A. Sir John Hay, 'the incendiary', 1578–1654, clerk register of
Scotland, provost of Edinburgh. Glasgow. 1937.

LAUDERDALE, JOHN, SECOND EARL OF

3796 Mackenzie, W. C. The life and times of John Maitland, duke of Lauderdale (1616–82). Lond. and N.Y. 1923.

LINDSAY, JOHN, FIRST EARL OF

3797 John, first earl of Lindsay. By J. Lindsay. Edin. 1935.

MACKENZIE OF ROSEHAUGH, SIR GEORGE

3798 Sir George Mackenzie, King's Advocate, of Rosehaugh. His life and
times. By A. Lang. 1909.

MORAY, SIR ROBERT

3799 The life of Sir Robert Moray: soldier, statesman and man of science
(1608–73). By A. Robertson. 1922.

RAMSAY, JAMES

3800 'The frowning cavalier.' *Blackwood's Magazine*, 238 (Oct. 1935), 548–62.
Scottish officer under Gustavus Adolphus.

URQUHART, SIR THOMAS

3801 Sir Thomas Urquhart of Cromartie. By J. Willcock. 1899.

Not a purely literary treatment; dated but still useful.

C. CONSTITUTIONAL HISTORY

I. BIBLIOGRAPHY AND SOURCES

See *Sources and literature of Scots law* (3693).

3802 COURT BOOK of the barony of Urie. 1604–1747. Ed. by D. G. Barron.
Scot. Hist. Soc. Edin. 1892.

3803 COURT BOOK of Shetland, 1602–4. Ed. G. Donaldson. Scot. Rec. Soc. Edin. 1954.

3804 MISCELLANY OF THE SCOTTISH BURGH Record Society. Ed. by Sir J. D. Marwick. Edin. 1881.

For records of particular burghs, see *Local History*.

3805 MELROSE REGALITY RECORDS, 1547–1706. Ed. C. S. Romanes. Scot. Hist. Soc., 2nd Ser. 6, 8, 13. 3 vols. Edin. 1914–17.

3806 RECORDS OF THE BARON COURT of Stitchill, 1655–1807. Ed. by C. B. Gunn. Scot. Hist. Soc. Edin. 1905.

3807 RECORDS OF THE CONVENTION of the royal burghs of Scotland, 1597–1711 [vols. ii–iv]. Ed. by Sir J. D. Marwick. 3 vols. Edin. 1870–80.

Valuable for the light the records throw on the institutions of the burghs with which they respectively deal. There is a separate index to all the five volumes (1295–1738), Edin. 1890.

3808 RECORDS OF THE COUNTY of Banff, 1660–1760. Ed. by A. and H. Tayler. New Spalding Club. Aberdeen. 1922.

3809 RECORDS OF THE SHERIFF COURT of Aberdeenshire. Ed. by D. Littlejohn. 3 vols. New Spalding Club. Aberdeen. 1904–7.

Vols. ii and iii give the records 1598–1660, with lists of officials to 1907.

3810 REPORT UPON THE SETTLEMENT of the revenues of excise and customs in Scotland A.D. 1656. By Robert Tucker. Ed. by J. A. Murray. Bann. Club. Edin. 1825.

3811 REVENUE OF THE SCOTTISH CROWN, 1681. By Sir William Purves. Ed. by D. M. Rose. Edin. 1897.

An account of the rents due to the crown, with a comparison between the rental in 1681 and that of 1603. Drawn up by the King's solicitor.

2. LATER WORKS

3812 FOSTER, J. Members of Parliament, Scotland, 1357–1882. 1882. 2nd edn. revised and corrected. 1882.

A new work, containing biographies of all members of the Scottish Parliaments, is in preparation.

3813 LOVAT-FRASER, J. A. 'Constitutional position of the Scottish monarch prior to the union.' *Law Quar. Rev.* 17 (1901), 252–62.

3814 PAGAN, T. The convention of royal burghs. Glasgow. 1926.

3815 RAIT, R. S. The Parliaments of Scotland. Glasgow. 1924.

Indispensable. Cf. C. S. Terry, *The Scottish Parliament, its constitution and procedure, 1603–1707*, Glasgow, 1905; J. D. Mackie and G. S. Pryde, *The estate of the burgesses in the Scots Parliament and its relation to the convention of royal burghs*, St. Andrews, 1923;

'The judicial proceedings of the Parliaments of Scotland, 1660–1688', by W. B. Gray, in *Juridical Review*, 36 (1924), 135–51; 'The Scottish Parliament, 1690–1702: a study of Scottish parliamentary government', by K. Stewart, ibid. 39 (1927), 10–37, 169–90, 291–312, 408–33; and E. B. Thomson, *The Parliaments of Scotland, 1690–1702*, Lond. and N.Y. 1929.

3816 THOMSON, THOMAS. Memorial on old extent. Ed. by J. D. Mackie. Stair Soc. Edin. 1946.

Deals with the electoral law of Scottish shires.

D. LEGAL HISTORY

1. REFERENCE

3817 MAXWELL, L. F. A bibliography of Scottish law from earliest times to November 1936. Together with a list of Roman law books in the English language. Being vol. v of Sweet and Maxwell's legal bibliography. 1937. 2nd edn. 1957.

See no. 1002. See also *Sources and literature of Scots law* (3693).

2. SOURCES

3818 ANCIENT CRIMINAL TRIALS in Scotland (1488–1624). Ed. by R. Pitcairn. 3 vols. Bann. Club. Edin. 1833.

Compiled from the original records and MSS. with historical illustrations, etc. Continued in *Selected justiciary cases, 1624–50*, ed. S. A. Gillon (Stair Soc., vol. 16, Edin. 1953), and *Records of the proceedings of the Justiciary Court, Edinburgh, 1661–1678*, ed. W. G. Scott-Moncrieff (Scot. Hist. Soc., vols. 48, 49, Edin. 1905).

3819 HOPE'S 'MAJOR PRACTICKS', 1608–33. Ed. by J. A. Clyde. 2 vols. Stair Soc. publ. Edin. 1937–8.

3820 THE INSTITUTIONS of the law of Scotland. By George Mackenzie. Edin. 1684. 8th edn. 1758.

3821 INSTITUTIONS of the law of Scotland. By James Dalrymple, Lord Stair. Edin. 1681; 1693.

3822 JUSTICIARY RECORDS of Argyll and the Isles, 1664–1705. Ed. by J. Cameron. Stair Soc. publ. Edin. 1949.

3823 THE OLD MINUTE BOOK of the faculty of procurators in Glasgow, 1668–1758. Ed. by J. S. Muirhead. Glasgow. 1948.

3824 ROLMENT OF COURTIS. By H. Bisset. Ed. P. J. Hamilton-Grierson. 3 vols. Scot. Text Soc., N.S. 10, 13, 18 (1920–6).

Compilation of the forms of civil action in early 17th century.

3825 THE ACTS OF SEDERUNT of the lords of council and session from 15 Jan. 1553 to 11 July 1790. By A. Tait. Edin. 1790.

The acts of sederunt are concerned principally with the rules of the court of session.

The court's proceedings, known as the Acts and Decreets, are unprinted except for selected items reproduced in J. Balfour, *Practicks* (Edin. 1754), and W. M. Morison, *Dictionary of decisions*, 38 vols., 1801–4.

3826 DE VERBORUM SIGNIFICATIONE. By J. Skene. Edin. 1597. 1681.

A law dictionary, still useful.

3. LATER WORKS

3827 BRUNTON, G., and HAIG, D. Historical account of the senators of the college of justice from its institution in 1532. Edin. 1832.

3828 CAMPBELL, A. H. The structure of Stair's Institutions, being the twenty-first lecture on the David Murray foundation in the University of Glasgow. Glasgow Univ. publ. no. 98. Glasgow. 1954.

Cf. J. Thomson, 'The first Viscount Stair', *Juridical Review*, 36 (1924), 33–59; and J. L. Duncan, 'The life and times of Viscount Stair', ibid. 46 (1934), 103–20.

3829 ENCYCLOPAEDIA of the laws of Scotland. By John Chisholm. 14 vols. Edin. 1896–1904. Ed. by J. L. Wark. 16 vols. and index, with 3 suppl. vols. Edin. 1926–52.

Generally known as *Green's Encyclopaedia*.

3830 ERSKINE, JOHN. An institute of the law of Scotland. Edin. 1773.

3831 AN INTRODUCTION to Scottish legal history. By various authors. Stair Soc. publ. Edin. 1958.

The best general guide to the history of the law and the law courts.

3832 MACKAY, A. J. G. The practice of the court of session. 2 vols. Edin. 1877–9.

Vol. i, history, constitution and jurisdiction of the court, and procedure in ordinary actions.

3833 McMILLAN, A. R. G. The evolution of the Scottish judiciary. Edin. 1941.

Cf. 'The judicial system of the commonwealth of Scotland', in *Juridical Review*, 49 (Sept. 1937), 232–55.

E. ECCLESIASTICAL HISTORY

1. BIBLIOGRAPHY AND SOURCES

3834 OGILVIE, J. D. 'A bibliography of the Glasgow Assembly, 1638.' *Glasgow Bibliog. Soc. Records*, 7 (1923), 1–12.

Cf. the same author's bibls. of the Bishops' Wars, 1639–40, ibid. 12 (1936), 21–40, and the Resolutioner–Protester controversy, 1650–9, *Edinburgh Bibliog. Soc. Publs.* 14 (1928), 57–85; and his 'The national petition, October 18, 1637', ibid. 12 (1925), 105–31.

3835 ACTS AND PROCEEDINGS of the general assemblies of the kirk of Scotland from the year 1560[-1618]. Ed. by T. Thomson. 3 vols. Bann. Club, 81; Maitland Club, 49. Edin. 1839-45.

Commonly referred to as *The booke of the universall kirk of Scotland*. Not official records, for original MSS. were burned in 1834, but a partial reconstruction from later transcripts, including a selection ed. by Alex. Peterkin and publ. in 1839. Later records are printed as follows: *Records of the Kirk of Scotland, containing the acts and proceedings of the several assemblies from the year 1638 downwards, as authenticated by the clerks of assembly, with notes and historical illustrations* [to 1654], by A. Peterkin, Edin. 1838; *Acts of the general assembly of the Church of Scotland, 1638-1842*, ed. by T. Pitcairn and others, Church Law Society, Edin. 1843; *Records of the commissions of the general assemblies of the Church of Scotland* (1646-52), ed. by A. F. Mitchell and J. Christie, 3 vols., Scot. Hist. Soc., Edin. 1892-1909. It should be noted that the general assembly did not meet between 1618 and 1638 and between 1653 and 1690.

3836 'An "Advertistment" about the service book, 1637.' By J. M. Henderson. *S.H.R.* 23 (1925-6), 199-204.

Illustrates the preparation for opposition to Charles I.

3837 ANALECTA, or materials for a history of remarkable providences; mostly relating to Scotch ministers and Christians. By R. Wodrow. 4 vols. Maitland Club. Edin. 1842-3.

3838 THE BLAIRS PAPERS, 1603-1660. Ed. by M. V. Hay. Lond. and Edin. 1929.

From Roman Catholic archives. See also W. F. Leith, ed., *Memoirs of Scottish Catholics during the XVIIth and XVIIIth centuries, selected from hitherto inedited MSS.*, 2 vols., 1909.

3839 BREIFFE NARRATION of the services done to three noble ladyes (1631-49). By Gilbert Blackhall. Ed. by J. Stuart. Spalding Club. Aberdeen. 1844.

Roman Catholic priest's activities. Cf. 'Priest errant', *Cornhill Mag.* 159 (Mar. 1939), 322-53.

3840 CERTAINE RECORDS touching the estate of the Kirk in the years 1605 and 1606. By John Forbes. Ed. by D. Laing. Wodrow Soc. Edin. 1846.
Valuable.

3841 ECCLESIASTICAL RECORDS OF ABERDEEN. Selections from the records of the kirk session, presbytery and synod of Aberdeen (1562-1681). Ed. by J. Stuart. Spalding Club. Aberdeen. 1846.

Similar selections: Presbytery of St. Andrews and Cupar, 1641-98, ed. G. R. Linloch, Abbotsford Club, Edin. 1837; Synod of Fife, 1611-87, ed. C. Baxter, Abbotsford Club, Edin. 1837; Synod of Dunblane, 1662-88, ed. J. Wilson, Edin. and Lond. 1887; Presbytery of Lanark, 1623-1709, ed. J. Robertson, Abbotsford Club, Edin. 1839; Presbyteries of Inverness and Dingwall, 1643-88, ed. W. Mackay, Scot. Hist. Soc., Edin. 1896; Presbytery of Strathbogie, 1631-54, ed. J. Stuart, Spalding Club, Aberdeen, 1843; Exercise of Alford, 1662-88, ed. T. Bell, New Spalding Club, Aberdeen, 1897; Synod of Argyll, 1639-61, ed. D. C. MacTavish, Scot. Hist. Soc., Edin. 1943-4. See *Sources and literature of Scots law* (3693), 156-62, for lists of MS. and printed records of church courts.

3842   HIND LET LOOSE, or an historical representation of the testimonies
of the Church of Scotland. By Alexander Shields. s.l. 1687. Later edns.
Edin. 1744. Glasgow. 1770 and 1797.

Represents the position of the extreme Covenanters. The first edn. pr. in Holland
without the author's name. Cf. *Faithful contendings displayed, being an historical relation
of the state and actings of the suffering remnant of the Church of Scotland, who subsisted
in select Societies . . . 1681 to 1690*, by M. Shields, ed. by J. Howie, Glasgow, 1780.

3843   THE HISTORIE OF THE KIRK of Scotland, 1558–1637, by John
Row, minister at Carnock; with additions and illustrations by his sons . . .
Ed. by B. Botfield. Maitland Club. [Edin.] 1842. Later edn. by D. Laing.
Wodrow Soc. Edin. 1842.

The Wodrow Soc. edn. has the better text. Presbyterian viewpoint.

3844   THE HISTORY OF THE CHURCH of Scotland, beginning the year
of our Lord 203, and continued to the end of the reign of James VI. By John
Spottiswoode. 1655. Later edn. by M. Russell and M. Napier. 3 vols.
Spottiswoode Soc. and Bann. Club. Edin. 1847–51.

Of the first importance for the period, containing original documents; royalist and
episcopal in sympathies, but moderate in tone. For proof that grave liberties have been
taken with some documents see *Proc. Soc. Antiq. of Scotland*, 60 (1925–6), 317, 344–7.

3845   THE HISTORY OF THE SUFFERINGS of the Church of Scotland
from the restauration to the revolution . . . From the public records, original
papers, and manuscripts of that time, and other well attested narratives. By
R. Wodrow. 2 vols. Edin. 1721–2. Later edn. by R. Burns. 4 vols. Glasgow.
1828–30.

Consists largely of transcripts from the Register of the Privy Council of Scotland (see
no. 3753) relative to ecclesiastical affairs. The author was a zealous Presbyterian.

3846   JAMES GORDON'S DIARY, 1692–1710. Ed. by G. D. Henderson
and H. H. Porter. *3rd Spalding Club Publ.* Aberdeen. 1949.

Episcopalian after the revolution.

3847   'LETTERS TO JOHN MACKENZIE of Delvine from Alexander
Monro, 1690–1698.' Ed. by W. K. Dickson. *Scot. Hist. Soc. Misc.* v, 195–290.

The writer had been deprived by the Presbyterians of his office of Principal of Edinburgh
University. Cf. R. K. Hannay, 'The visitation of the college of Edinburgh in 1690', in
Book of the Old Edinburgh Club (p. 560), viii, 79–100.

3848   LIFE OF MR. ROBERT BLAIR, minister of St. Andrews, containing
his autobiography, 1593–1636, with supplement . . . to 1680 by Mr. W[illiam]
Row. Ed. by T. McCrie. Wodrow Soc. Edin. 1848.

3849   THE MAKING of the Scottish Prayer Book of 1637. By G. Donaldson.
Edin. 1954.

Prints the text of the book and the drafts on which it was based.

3850 MEMOIRS OF THE REV. JOHN BLACKADDER, composed chiefly from memoirs of his life and ministry written by himself. Ed. by A. Crichton. Edin. 1823.

Illustrates the fate of a minister *temp.* Charles II. Cf. H. Macpherson, 'John Blackadder', *Scot. Church Hist. Soc. Records*, 4 (1932), 162–75.

3851 NAPHTALI or the wrestlings of the Church of Scotland . . . from the reformation . . . until 1667. By Sir James Stewart and James Stirling. S.l. 1667. Several reprs., the last Perth, and Kirkcudbright. 1945.

Andrew Honeyman, Bishop of Orkney, wrote a reply in two parts: *A survey of the insolent and infamous libel entituled Naphtali*, s.l., 1668, and *Survey of Naphtali*, Edin. 1669.

3852 NARRATIVE of Mr. James Nimmo, 1654–1709. Scot. Hist. Soc. Edin. 1889.

Reflections of a Covenanter.

3853 ORIGINAL LETTERS relating to the ecclesiastical affairs of Scotland, chiefly written by, or addressed to, His Majesty King James the Sixth, 1603– 1625. Ed. by D. Laing. 2 vols. Bann. Club. Edin. 1851.

3854 RECORDS OF THE DIOCESE of Argyll and the Isles, 1560–1860. By J. B. Craven. Kirkwall. 1907.

3855 REGISTER OF THE CONSULTATIONS of the ministers of Edinburgh and some other brethren of the ministry, 1652–1660. Ed. by W. Stephen. 2 vols. Scot. Hist. Soc., 3rd Ser. 1, 16. (1921, 1930.)

Illustrates the divisions between Resolutioners and Protesters.

3856 A RELATION of proceedings concerning the affairs of the Kirk of Scotland, from August 1637 to July 1638. By John Leslie, Earl of Rothes. Ed. by J. Nairne and D. Laing. Bann. Club. Edin. 1830.

Defends the proceedings of the Covenanters against Charles I. MS. in Advocates' Library, Edin.

3857 REPORTS ON THE STATE of certain parishes in Scotland in 1627. Maitland Club. Edin. 1835.

3858 SCOTTISH LITURGIES of the reign of James VI. Ed. by G. W. Sprott. Edin. 1871. Later edn. Edin. and Lond. 1901.

The first edn. has a fuller introduction. The second contains the ordinal of 1620.

3859 THE SECRET AND TRUE HISTORY of the Church of Scotland from the restoration to the year 1678, by the Rev. Mr. James Kirkton, to which is added an account of the murder of Archbishop Sharp, by James Russell, an actor therein. Ed. by C. K. Sharpe. Edin. 1817.

A vivid narrative written from the covenanting point of view, with notes from the opposite point.

3860 THE TRUE HISTORY of the Church of Scotland from the beginning of the reformation, unto the end of the reign of King James VI ... By David Calderwood. [Rotterdam.] 1678. Later edn. by T. Thomson. 8 vols. Wodrow Soc. Edin. 1842–9.

The first edn. was a condensed history printed from a manuscript prepared by the author for the press. The Wodrow Society edn. is from the MS. in the Br. Mus. Presbyterian: of the first importance for the contemporary documents it contains.

2. LATER WORKS

3861 BELL, W. F. 'South Perthshire and the covenanting struggle.' *Scot. Church Hist. Soc. Records*, 1 (1926), 57–74.

Cf. S. A. Burrell, 'The covenant idea as a revolutionary symbol, 1596–1637', *Church History*, 27 (1958), 338–50.

3862 BELLESHEIM, A. History of the Catholic church in Scotland. Ed. by D. O. H. Blair. 4 vols. Edin. 1887–90.

Vols. iii–iv, 1560–1878. The translator has taken occasional liberties with the text. Cf. P. F. Anson, *The Catholic church in modern Scotland, 1560–1937*, 1937; and 'Scottish Catholicism during [the] seventeenth century', in *Bonaventura*, 1 (1937), 106–15.

3863 BURNET, G. B. The story of Quakerism in Scotland, 1650–1850; with an epilogue ... 1850–1950, by W. H. Marwick. 1952.

Cf. J. Torrance, 'The early Quakers in northeast Scotland', in *Banff F.C. Trans. for 1936*, 67–87, and 'The Quaker movement in Scotland' in *Scot. church Hist. Soc. Records*, 3 (1929), 31–42. See also D. Butler, *George Fox in Scotland*, Edin. 1913.

3864 BURNET, G. B. The Holy Communion in the reformed church of Scotland, 1560–1960. Edin. and Lond. 1960.

Deals with the 'externals' of the service. A well-documented study.

3865 CAMPBELL, W. M. The triumph of Presbyterianism. Edin. 1958.

3866 CARRUTHERS, S. W. 'The Solemn League and Covenant (1643): its text and its translators.' *Scot. Church Hist. Soc. Records* 6 (1938), 32–51.

Cf. D. H. Fleming, *Some subscribed copies of the Solemn League and Covenant*, Edin. Bibl. Soc., Edin. 1918; 'The subscribing of the National Covenant in 1638', in *History of the old Greyfriars Church*, by W. M. Bryce, Edin. 1912.

3867 CHRISTIE, G. 'Scripture exposition in Scotland in the seventeenth century.' *Scot. Church Hist. Soc. Records*, 1 (1926), 97–111.

3868 CONNELL, J. A treatise on the law of Scotland respecting tithes and the stipends of the parochial clergy, with an appendix containing illustrative documents not before published. 3 vols. Edin. 1815. Later edn. 2 vols. Edin. 1830.

The 2nd edn. is 'considerably enlarged'.

3869 COOPER, J. 'Notes on a proclamation by King Charles I.' *Scot. Ecclesiological Soc. Trans.* 7 (1922–3), 48–56.

Dismissing the Glasgow Assembly, 1638.

3870   CORMACK, A. A. Teinds and agriculture. Oxf. 1930.

3871   CRAVEN, J. B. History of the church in Orkney, vol. ii (1558–1662), iii (1662–1688). Kirkwall. 1893, 1897.

3872   CUNNINGHAM, J. The church history of Scotland . . . to the present century. 2 vols. Edin. 1859. 2nd edn. 1882.

A convenient summary. Still useful, though older, is G. Grub, *An ecclesiastical history of Scotland . . . to the present time*, 4 vols., Edin. 1861. Grub was a Scottish Episcopalian.

3873   DEFOE, DANIEL. Memoirs of the Church of Scotland . . . [from the reformation to the union] with an appendix of some transactions since the union. 1717. Perth. 1844. Edin. 1848.

3874   DONALDSON, M. E. M. Scotland's suppressed history. 1935.

A somewhat intemperate rejoinder to the Presbyterian interpretation of the period.

3875   FLEMING, A. Huguenot influence in Scotland. Glasgow. 1954.

Cf. D. E. Easson, 'French protestants in Edinburgh', *Proc. Huguenot Soc. London*, 18 (1950), 325–44.

3876   FOSTER, W. R. Bishop and presbytery; the church of Scotland, 1661–1688. 1958.

A study of ecclesiastical administration. Cf. J. Hunter, *The diocese and presbytery of Dunkeld, 1660–1689*, 2 vols., Lond. and N.Y. 1917, a documented study.

3877   FULTON, A. The 1633 and 1635 editions of the old Scottish 'Psalm Book'. Manchester. 1934.

Also publ. *Presbyterian Hist. Soc. Journ.* 5 (1935), 173–94.

3878   GOLDIE, F. A short history of the Episcopal Church in Scotland, from the restoration to the present time. 1952.

Cf. T. Hannan, 'The Scottish consecrations in London in 1610', *The Church Quarterly Review*, vol. 71, pp. 387–413; and D. J. S. Simpson, 'The consecrations of bishops for Scotland in 1610', *Hibbert Journ.* 37 (1939), 448–56.

3879   HENDERSON, G. D. Religious life in seventeenth-century Scotland. Camb. 1937.

Several of the chapters are reprinted from periodicals. Cf. the same author's 'The Aberdeen doctors', *Aberdeen Univ. Rev.* 26 (1938), 10–19; and D. Anderson, *The Bible in seventeenth-century Scottish life and literature*, 1936. See also J. D. Ogilvie, 'The Aberdeen doctors . . .' and 'The cross petition', *Edin. Bibliog. Soc. Papers*, 11 (1921), 73–86, and 15 (1934), 55–76.

3880   HEWISON, J. K. The Covenanters. A history of the Church in Scotland from the reformation to the revolution. 2 vols. Glasgow. 1908. Later edn. 2 vols. Glasgow. 1913.

The writer had strong covenanting sympathies. Some errors have been corrected in the 1913 edn.

3881 HUTCHISON, M. The reformed Presbyterian church in Scotland, 1680–1876. Paisley. 1893.

Cf. 'The literature of the Scottish reformed Presbyterian church' and 'A reformed Presbyterian bibliography', in *Scot. Church Hist. Soc. Records*, 5 (1935), 227–37, and 6 (1938), 299–304.

3882 THE INNES REVIEW. Glasgow. 1950+.

Contains articles and documents on post-reformation Roman Catholicism.

3883 INNES, A. T. The law of creeds in Scotland. Edin. 1867. Later edn. 1902.

3884 KEITH, R. A large new catalogue of the bishops of the several sees . . . of Scotland down to the year 1688. Edin. 1755. Later edn. by M. Russell. Edin. 1824.

3885 MACGREGOR, G. 'Ecclesiastical usages in early seventeenth-century Scotland.' *Church Quart. Rev.* 150 (1950), 155–72.

3886 MACINNES, J. The evangelical movement in the Highlands of Scotland, 1688–1800. Aberdeen. 1951.

Of much wider interest than the title suggests. Cf. J. Macleod, 'A northern nonconformist: Rev. Roderick Mackenzie of Avoch', *Scott. Church Hist. Soc. Records*, 6 (1938), 252–64.

3887 MACLEAN, D. 'The presbytery of Ross and Sutherland, 1693–1700.' *Scot. Church Hist. Soc. Records*, 5 (1935), 251–61.

Also by Maclean, 'Roman Catholicism in the reign of Charles II', ibid. 3 (1929), 43–54; and *The counter-reformation in Scotland, 1560–1930*, 1931.

3888 MACMILLAN, W. The worship of the Scottish reformed church, 1550–1638. 1931.

A thorough study. Cf. W. D. Maxwell, *History of worship in the Church of Scotland*, 1955; P. Millar, *Four centuries of Scottish psalmody*, Oxf. 1949.

3889 MAXWELL, T. 'Presbyterian and episcopalian in 1688.' *Scot. Church. Hist. Soc. Records*, 13, 25–37.

Discusses respective strengths of the two parties.

3890 MECHIE, S. The office of Lord High Commissioner. Edin. 1957.

3891 MEIKLE, J. 'The seventeenth-century presbytery of Meigle.' *Scot. Church Hist. Soc. Records*, 5 (1934), 144–56.

3892 NAPIER, M. The case for the crown in re the Wigtown martyrs. Edin. 1863.

Controversy over the alleged execution of two women by drowning in 1685 continued in A. Stewart, *History vindicated in the case of the Wigtown martyrs*, Edin. 1867, 2nd edn., 1869; *History rescued, in answer to 'History vindicated'*, by M. Napier, Edin. 1870; and *The new examen* (361 n.).

3893   SCOTT, H. Fasti ecclesiae Scoticanae. The succession of ministers in the parish churches of Scotland from the reformation, 1560, to the present time. 6 vols. Bann. Club. 1866–71.

New and enlarged edn., 7 vols. Edin. 1915–28; vol. viii, Edin. 1950, contains additions and corrections.

3894   SCOTT, J. 'Baptists in Scotland during the commonwealth.' *Scot. Church Hist. Soc. Records*, 3 (1929), 174–85.

3895   THOMSON, J. H. The martyr graves of Scotland. 2 vols. Edin. 1875, 1877. 2nd edn. by M. Hutchinson. 1 vol. Edin. and Lond. 1903.

The edn. of 1903 is much enlarged, and contains a list, previously unprinted, of the Dunnottar prisoners.

3896   WALKER, P. Six saints of the Covenant, Peden, Semple, Welwood, Cameron, Cargill, Smith. Ed. by D. H. Fleming. 2 vols. 1901.

Lives originally publ. 1724–32. Repr. in 1827 as *Biographia Presbyteriana*. See also R. Wodrow, *Select biographies*, ed. by W. K. Tweedie, 2 vols., Wodrow Soc., Edin. 1845–7. A similar volume is *Selections from Wodrow's biographical collections: divines of the north-east of Scotland*, New Spalding Club, Aberdeen, 1890.

3897   WILLCOCK, J. 'Sharp and the restoration policy in Scotland.' *R.H.S. Trans.*, N.S. 20 (1906), 149–69.

3. BIOGRAPHY

CLARK, JAMES

3898   Couper, W. J. 'The writings and controversies of James Clark, minister at Glasgow, 1702–1724.' *Glasgow Bibl. Soc. Records*, 11 (1933), 73–95.

DURHAM, JAMES

3899   Christie, G. 'A bibliography of James Durham: 1622–1658.' *Edin. Bibliog. Soc. Publs.* 11 (1918), 35–46.

Also by Christie, 'James Durham as courtier and preacher', *Scot. Church Hist. Soc. Records*, 4 (1932), 66–80.

FORBES, PATRICK

3900   Snow, W. G. S. The time, life, and thought of Patrick Forbes. 1951.

GORDON, JOHN

3901   Taylor, T. F. A profest papist: Bishop John Gordon. 1958.

Bishop of Galloway 1689–1726.

HENDERSON, ALEXANDER

3902   Aiton, J. The life and times of Alexander Henderson, giving a history of the Church of Scotland and of the covenanters during the reign of Charles I. Edin. 1836.

Cf. R. L. Orr, *Alexander Henderson: churchman and statesman*, 1919; *Lives of Alexander Henderson and James Guthrie, with specimens of their writings*, by T. McCrie, Edin. 1846.

LEIGHTON, ROBERT

3903. Butler, D. The life and letters of Robert Leighton, restoration bishop of Dunblane and archbishop of Glasgow. 1903

Cf. W. West, ed., *The whole works as yet recovered of Robert Leighton*, 6 vols., 1869–75. Also E. A. Knox, *Robert Leighton, archbishop of Glasgow*, 1930.

LIVINGSTON, JOHN

3904 Philip, R. G. 'The life and preaching of John Livingston, 1603–1672.' *Scot. Church Hist. Soc. Records*, 4 (1932), 150–61.

OGILVIE, JOHN

3905 Brown, W. E. John Ogilvie. 1925.

Jesuit executed for treason in 1615. Cf. T. Collins, *Martyr in Scotland*, 1955.

RENWICK, JAMES

3906 Shields, A. The life and death of . . . James Renwick. Edin. 1724.

Reprinted in vol. ii of *Biographia Presbyteriana* in 1827 and 1837. Sixty-one of Renwick's letters are in *A collection of letters*, Edin. 1764.

RUTHERFORD, SAMUEL

3907 Gilmour, R. Samuel Rutherford. A study . . . in the history of the Scottish covenant. Edin. and Lond. 1904.

Another life by T. Murray, Edin. 1828. Cf. Rutherford's *Lex rex: the law and the prince*, 1644.

SHARP, JAMES

3908 Stephen, T. Life and times of Archbishop Sharp. 1839.

SHIELDS, ALEXANDER

3909 Macpherson, H. The Cameronian philosopher, Alexander Shields. 1932.

WISHART, GEORGE

3910 Quig, G. 'Montrose's chaplain: Rev. George Wishart, D.D.' *Scot. Church Hist. Soc. Records*, 5 (1935), 40–9.

WODROW, ROBERT

3911 Sharp, L. W., ed. Early letters of Robert Wodrow, 1698–1709. Edin. 1937.

Cf. W. J. Couper, 'Robert Wodrow (1679–1734)', *Scot. Church Hist. Soc. Records*, 3 (1929), 112–34; 'Robert Wodrow and his critics', ibid. 5 (1935), 238–50.

F. ECONOMIC HISTORY

I. BIBLIOGRAPHY

3912 SCOTT, W. R. Scottish economic literature to 1800. Glasgow. 1911.

Cf. also T. Keith, *Bibliography of Scottish economic history*, Pub. Hist. Assoc. of Scotland, v (1914); W. H. Marwick, 'A bibliography of Scottish economic history', *Econ. Hist. Rev.* 3 (1931), 117–37, and 'A bibliography of works on Scottish economic history published during the last twenty years', ibid. 2nd Ser. 4 (1952), 376–82.

2. Sources

3913   THE ACCOUNT BOOK of Sir John Foulis of Ravelston, 1671–1707. Ed. by A. W. C. Hallen. Scot. Hist. Soc. Edin. 1894.

3914   CHAMBERLAIN'S ACCOUNT, 1650, Dunnottar. Transcribed by D. Christie. Third Spalding Club Miscellany, 2 (1940), 185–212. Aberdeen.

3915   COMPT BUIK of David Wedderburne, merchant of Dundee, 1587–1630, together with the shipping lists of Dundee, 1580–1618. Ed. by A. H. Millar. Scot. Hist. Soc. Edin. 1898.

Cf. C. Innes, ed., *Ledger of Andrew Halyburton . . . Together with the book of customs and valuations of merchandises in Scotland, 1612*, Edin. 1867 (ledger for 1492–1503).

3916   THE DARIEN PAPERS : being a selection of original letters and official documents relating to the establishment of a colony at Darien by the Company of Scotland trading to Africa and the Indies, 1695–1700. Ed. by J. H. Burton. Bann. Club. Edin. 1849.

Cf. Sir Paul Rycaut, *The original papers and letters relating to the Scots Company, trading to Africa and the Indies: from the memorial given in against their taking subscriptions at Hamburgh, by Sir Paul Ricaut, His Majesty's resident there . . .*, s.l. [Edin.], 1700; Francis Borland, *The history of Darien. Giving a short description of that country, an account of the attempts of the Scotch nation to settle a colony in that place . . . with some practical reflections upon the whole* [written c. 1700], Glasgow, 1779; *Papers relating to the ships and voyages of the company of Scotland trading to Africa and the Indies, 1696–1707*, Scot. Hist. Soc., 1924; and J. Scott, ed., *A bibliography of printed documents and books relating to the Scottish Company, commonly called the Darien Company*, Edin. Bibliog. Soc. Publ. vi, pt. i, Edin. 1904.

3917   DIARY and general expenditure book of William Cunningham of Craigends (1673–80). Ed. by J. Dodds. Scot. Hist. Soc. Edin. 1887.

3918   THE HOUSEHOLD BOOK of Lady Grisell Baillie, 1692–1733. Ed. by R. Scott-Moncrieff. Scot. Hist. Soc. Edin. 1911.

3919   RECORDS OF A SCOTTISH cloth manufactory at New Mills, Haddingtonshire, 1681–1703. Ed. by W. R. Scott. Scot. Hist. Soc. Edin. 1905.

3920   THE RECORDS OF THE TRADES HOUSE of Glasgow, 1605–1678. Ed. by H. Lumsden. Glasgow. 1910.

Cf. G. Crawford, *A sketch of the rise and progress of the Trades' House of Glasgow, its constitution, funds, and bye-laws*, Glasgow, 1858; and *Inventory of charters, deeds, old minute books and other records belonging to the Trades House of Glasgow* [Glasgow, 1909].

3921   ROYAL LETTERS, charters and tracts relating to the colonization of New Scotland, 1621–38. Ed. by D. Laing. Bann. Club. Edin. 1867.

3922   THE WRITINGS OF WILLIAM PATERSON, founder of the Bank of England, with biographical notices of the author . . . Ed. by S. Bannister. 2 vols. 1858. 3 vols. 1859.

Cf. S. Bannister, *William Paterson, the merchant statesman and founder of the Bank of England; his life and trials*, Edin. 1858, 2nd edn., 1859. Also, J. S. Barbour, *A history of William Paterson and the Darien Company, with illustrations and appendices*, Edin. and Lond. 1907.

3. LATER WORKS

3923 BAIN, E. Merchant and craft guilds: a history of the Aberdeen incorporated trades. Aberdeen. 1887.

3924 CONACHER, H. M. 'Land tenure in Scotland in the seventeenth century.' *Juridical Rev.* 50 (1938), 18–50.

Cf. J. H. Romanes, 'The land system of the Scottish burgh', ibid. 47 (1935), 103–19.

3925 DAVIDSON, J. and GRAY, A. Scottish staple at Veere: a study of the economic history of Scotland. 1909.

Cf. M. P. Rooseboom, *The Scottish staples in the Netherlands*, The Hague, 1910.

3926 FRANKLIN, T. B. The history of Scottish farming. Edin. 1952.

Quite inadequate on this period. J. A. Symon, *Scottish farming*, Edin. and Lond. 1959, is almost equally inadequate.

3927 GRANT, I. F. The economic history of Scotland. Vol. ii of Economic history of Britain, ed. by J. F. Rees. 1934.

A good brief review is J. Mackinnon, *The social and industrial history of Scotland from the earliest times to the union*, 2 vols., 1920–1.

3928 HYDE, H. M. John Law: the history of an honest adventurer. 1948.

3929 INSH, G. P. The company of Scotland trading to Africa and the Indies. Lond. and N.Y. 1932.

The standard work on the venture. Cf. the same author's *Scottish colonial schemes, 1626–1686*, Glasgow, 1922; and *The Darien scheme*, 1947. Also F. R. Hart, *The disaster of Darien*, 1929, which prints many documents from Spanish sources; F. Cundall, *The Darien venture*, N.Y. 1926; and T. C. Pears, 'The design of Darien', *Journ. of the Dept. of History of the Presbyterian Church in the U.S.A.* 17 (1936), 9–108.

3930 KEITH, T. Commercial relations of England and Scotland, 1603–1707. Camb. 1910.

Cf. articles by this author in *S.H.R.* 5 (1907–8), 273–84; 6 (1908–9), 32–48; 10 (1912–13), 250–71.

3931 KERR, A. W. History of banking in Scotland. 1884. 3rd edn. 1918. 4th edn., rev. and enl. 1926.

Cf. C. A. Malcolm, *The bank of Scotland, 1695–1945*, Edin. 1949.

3932 LUMSDEN, H. and AITKEN, P. H. History of the hammermen of Glasgow. Paisley. 1912. 1915.

Cf. H. Lumsden, *History of the skinners, furriers and glovers of Glasgow*, Glasgow, 1937.

3933 LYTHE, S. G. E. The economy of Scotland, 1550–1625. Edin. and Lond. 1960.

3934 MARWICK, J. D. Edinburgh guilds and crafts (1616–1872). Scot. Burgh. Rec. Soc. Edin. 1909.

For articles on particular guilds and crafts in Edinburgh see *Book of the Old Edinburgh Club*, p. 560.

3935 SCOTT, W. R. 'The fiscal policy of Scotland before the union.' *S.H.R.* 1 (1903–4), 407–15. 'Scottish industrial undertakings before the union.' Ibid. 2 (1904–5), 53–60, 287–97, 406–11; and 3 (1905–6), 71–6.

3936 SÉE, H. and CORMACK, A. A. 'Commercial relations between France and Scotland in 1707.' *S.H.R.* 23 (1925–6), 275–9.

G. SOCIAL HISTORY

1. SOURCES

See also Ch. IX, *supra*, which includes many titles useful for Scotland.

3937 THE BOOK OF RECORD: a diary written by Patrick, first Earl of Strathmore, and other documents relating to Glamis Castle, 1684–9. Ed. by A. H. Millar. Scot. Hist. Soc. Edin. 1890.

From MSS. at Glamis.

3938 'THE DIARY of Sir William Drummond of Hawthornden, 1657–1659.' Ed. by H. W. Meikle. *Scot. Hist. Soc. Misc.* vii (1941).

3939 DOMESTIC ANNALS of Scotland from the reformation to the revolution (vols. i and ii) [and] Domestic annals . . . to the rebellion of 1745 (vol. iii). By R. Chambers. 3 vols. Edin. 1859–61. 3rd edn. 3 vols. Edin. and Lond. 1874.

Consists of quotations from contemporaries.

3940 EARLY TRAVELLERS in Scotland (to 1689). Ed. by P. H. Brown. Edin. 1891.

Contains the impressions of travellers from England and the continent. The *Tours* of Thomas Kirk, 1677, and Ralph Thoresby, 1681, were ed. by P. H. Brown in 1892 and Lowther's Journal, 1629, in 1894. Cf. Sir A. Mitchell's 'List of travels and tours in Scotland (1296–1900)', repr. from the *Proceedings of the Society of Antiquaries of Scotland*, vol. 35, Edin. 1902, and continued in vol. 39.

3941 THE JOURNAL of Thomas Cuningham of Campvere, 1640–54. Ed. by E. J. Courthope. Edin. 1928.

3942 JOURNEY to Edenborough in Scotland. By Joseph Taylor. Ed. by W. Cowan. Edin. 1903.

The journey took place in 1705.

3943 PAPERS RELATING to the Scots in Poland, 1576–1793. Ed. by A. F. Steuart. Scot. Hist. Soc. Edin. 1915.

Cf. J. H. Burton, *The Scot abroad*, Edin. and Lond., new edn., 1881. Cf also *The Scots in Germany*, Edin. 1902; *The Scots in . . . Prussia*, Edin. 1903; *The Scots in Sweden*,

Edin. 1907, all by Th. A. Fischer; and Sir John Lauder's 'Journals in France, 1665–1667', in *Journals of Sir John Lauder*, ed. by D. Crawford (Scot. Hist. Soc.), Edin. 1900; Fr. edn. by J. Plattard, *Un étudiant écossais* . . ., Paris, 1935.

3944 SCOTLAND before 1700, from contemporary documents. Ed. by P. H. Brown. Edin. 1893.

Cf. C. Rogers, *Social life in Scotland from early to recent times*, 3 vols., Grampian Club, Edin. 1884–6.

3945 SCOTTISH DIARIES and memoirs, 1550–1746. Ed. by J. G. Fyfe. Stirling. 1928. Toronto. 1935.

3946 SELECTIONS from the family papers preserved at Caldwell (1496–1853). Ed. by [? William Mure]. 3 vols. Maitland Club. Glasgow. 1854.

3947 A SHORT ACCOUNT of Scotland. By T. Morer. 1702.

2. LATER WORKS

3948 ADAM, F. The clans, septs and regiments of the Scottish Highlands. With a foreword by T. Innes of Learney. Edin. 1934. 3rd edn. 1935.

Cf. R. Bain, *The clans and tartans of Scotland*, 1938.

3949 BICKLEY, F. The Leiths of Harthill. The story of some turbulent lairds and a royalist martyr. 1937.

3950 CORMACK, A. Poor relief in Scotland. Aberdeen. 1923.

3951 DUNBAR, E. D. Social life in former days, chiefly in the province of Moray. 2 vols. Edin. 1865–6.

Cf. D. Anderson, 'Aspects of social life in Scotland in the seventeenth century', *Gaelic Soc. Glasgow Trans.* 4 (1934), 47–67.

3952 FINLAYSON, C. P. 'Illustrations of games by a seventeenth-century Edinburgh student.' *S.H.R.* 37 (1958).

3953 JOHNSTON, T. The history of the working classes in Scotland. Glasgow. 1922. 3rd edn. 1935.

3954 McKENZIE, J. 'School and university drama in Scotland.' *S.H.R.* 34 (1955), 103–21.

3955 MACKINTOSH, J. The history of civilisation in Scotland. 4 vols. Aberdeen and Lond. 1878–88. Later edn. 4 vols. Paisley and Lond. 1892–6.

An unscholarly work, but of use for its collection of facts. The 2nd edn. was revised but is far from immaculate.

3956 MAXWELL, S. and HUTCHISON, R. Scottish costume, 1550–1850. 1958.

3957 MICHEL, F. Les Ecossais en France; les français en Ecosse. 2 vols. 1862.

3958 MOORE, M. F. 'The education of a Scottish nobleman's sons in the seventeenth century.' *S.H.R.* 31 (1952), 1–15, 101–15.

3959 REID, R. C. 'John Maxwell of Castlemilk.' *Dumfries and Galloway Nat. Hist. and Antiq. Soc. Trans.*, 3rd Ser. 19 (1936), 187–204.

3960 TAYLER, H. The seven sons of the provost. Lond. and Edin. 1949.

Compiled from original letters. Mainly post-1714.

3961 WARRACK, J. Domestic life in Scotland, 1488–1688. 1920.

H. CULTURAL HISTORY

1. Sources

3962 CATALOGUE OF THE GRADUATES . . . of the University of Edinburgh, 1587–1858. Ed. by D. Laing. Bann. Club. Edin. 1858.

See also no. 2995.

3963 FASTI ACADEMIAE mariscallanae Aberdonensis: selections from the records, 1593–1830. Ed. by P. J. Anderson. 3 vols. New Spalding Club. Aberdeen. 1889–98.

Vol. iii is an index by J. F. K. Johnstone. Cf. P. J. Anderson, ed., *Officers and graduates of University and King's College*, Aberdeen, 1893; and *Roll of alumni in Arts University and King's College 1596–1860*, Aberdeen, 1900; also C. Innes, ed., *Fasti Aberdonenses: selections from the records of the University and King's College of Aberdeen, 1494–1854,* 1854.

3964 JAMES GREGORY tercentenary memorial volume. Containing his correspondence with John Collins and his hitherto unpublished mathematical MSS., together with addresses and essays communicated to the Royal Society of Edinburgh, July 4, 1938. Ed. by H. W. Turnbull. Edin. 1939.

3965 THE MEMOIRS of Sir Robert Sibbald (1641–1722). Ed. by F. P. Hett. 1932.

3966 MUNIMENTA almae universitatis Glasguensis: records of the University of Glasgow from its foundation till 1727. Ed. by C. Innes. 3 vols. Maitland Club. Glasgow. 1854.

3967 GEORGE STRACHAN: memorials of a wandering Scottish scholar of the seventeenth century. Ed. by G. L. Dellavida. *Third Spalding Club Publ.* 1956.

Cf. W. C. Dickinson, ed., *Two students at St. Andrews, 1711–1716*, Edin. 1952.

2. Later Works

3968 CANT, R. G. The University of St. Andrews. Edin. 1946.

Brief. See also J. M. Anderson, *The University of St. Andrews*, Cupar, 1878.

3969 CAW, J. L. Scottish portraits, with an historical and critical introduction and notes. 2 vols. Edin. 1903.

Cf. *Scottish painting past and present, 1620–1908*, Edin. 1908.

3970 FARMER, H. G. A history of music in Scotland. 1947.

3971 FINLAY, I. Scottish crafts. 1948.

Cf. *Art in Scotland*, Oxf. 1948; *Scottish gold and silver work*, 1956.

3972 GRANT, A. The University of Edinburgh during its first three hundred years. 2 vols. Edin. 1884.

3973 GRANT, J. History of the burgh and parish schools of Scotland. 1876.

Deals only with burgh schools. See also D. Mackinnon, 'Education in Argyll and the Isles, 1638–1709', *Scot. Church Hist. Soc. Records*, 6 (1936), 46–54.

3974 GRANT, J. 'Archibald Hislop, stationer, Edinburgh, 1668–1678.' *Edin. Bibliog. Soc. Publs.* 12 (1924), 35–51.

3975 HAY, G. The architecture of Scottish post-reformation churches, 1560–1843. Oxf. 1957.

3976 HILL, O. Scottish castles of the 16th and 17th centuries. 1953.

3977 KERR, J. Scottish education. School and university. From early times to 1908. Camb. 1910. Later edn. 1913.

See also Morgan (2960).

3978 MacGIBBON, D., and ROSS, T. The castellated and domestic architecture of Scotland from the twelfth to the eighteenth century. 5 vols. Edin. 1887–92. The ecclesiastical architecture of Scotland from the earliest Christian times to the seventeenth century. 3 vols. Edin. 1896–7.

3979 MACKENZIE, D. A. Scottish folk-lore and folk life. Studies in race, culture and tradition. 1935.

3980 MAXWELL, J. S. Shrines and homes of Scotland. Glasgow. 1937.

3981 MEIKLE, H. W. Some aspects of later seventeenth-century Scotland. Being the fourteenth lecture on the David Murray foundation in the University of Glasgow. Glasgow. 1947.

3982 MITCHELL, W. S. History of Scottish bookbinding. Edin. 1955.

3983 PANNIER, J., ed. 'Français du sud-ouest étudiants à Glasgow en 1622.' *Soc. Hist. Protestantisme Français Bull.* 85 (avril–juin 1936), 166–70.

3984 RAIT, R. S. The universities of Aberdeen. Aberdeen. 1895.

3985 READ, J. 'Scottish alchemy in the seventeenth century.' *Chymia*, 1 (1948), 139–51.

3986 SMALL, J. W. Scottish woodwork of the sixteenth and seventeenth centuries. Edin. 1878.

3987 STEWART, I. H. The Scottish coinage. 1955.

Cf. E. Burns, *The coinage of Scotland from David I to Queen Anne*, 3 vols., Edin. 1887;
R. W. Cochran-Patrick, *Records of the coinage of Scotland*, 2 vols., Edin. 1876.

I. LOCAL HISTORY

1. REFERENCE

3988 ORDNANCE GAZETTEER of Scotland: A survey of Scottish topography, statistical, biographical and historical. Ed. by F. H. Groome. 6 vols.
Edin. 1882–5. Later edns. 6 vols. Lond. 1894[95]. 3 vols. Lond. 1903.

The notice of each important town is furnished with a bibl. A very useful work.

2. SOURCES

For lists of local records see *Sources and literature of Scots law* (3693). Local
court records appear with the sources for constitutional history, *supra*. Only the
outstanding among the other printed records are listed below. There is a fuller
list in Conyers Read (11 n.), 2nd edn., 424–7, most of the items in which relate
to the seventeenth century.

3989 RECORDS OF OLD ABERDEEN, 1157–1903. Ed. by A. M. Munro.
2 vols. New Spalding Club. Aberdeen. 1899, 1903.

Extracts from records of council, convener court, hammermen, etc. Also from the
borough records, ed. by J. Stuart, are *Extracts from the council register of the burgh of
Aberdeen*, vol. ii, 1570–1625, Spalding Club, Aberdeen, 1848; and 2 vols. under the same
title, covering 1625–1747, publ. by Scottish Burgh Rec. Soc., Edin. 1871–2. See also
L. B. Taylor, ed., *Aberdeen council letters*, vol. i (1552–1633), Oxf. and Lond. 1940;
vol. ii (1634–44), Oxf. 1950; vol. iii (1645–59), Lond. 1952; vol. iv (1660–9),
Lond. 1954; vol. v (1670–5), Lond. 1957. The 'Register of burgesses of guild and
trade of the burgh of Aberdeen, 1399–1631', was publ. in *New Spalding Club Misc.* i,
Aberdeen, 1890.

3990 AYR BURGH ACCOUNTS 1534–1624. Transcribed and ed. by G. S.
Pryde. Scottish Hist. Soc. Publ., vol. 28. Edin. 1937.

3991 THE VALUATION of the county of Aberdeen for the year 1667. Ed.
by A. and H. Tayler. Third Spalding Club Publ. Aberdeen. 1933.

3992 RECORDS OF THE COUNTY OF BANFF, 1660–1760. Compiled
by the late J. Grant and ed. with an introd. by A. and H. Tayler. New
Spalding Club Publ. Aberdeen. 1922.

3993 REGISTER OF THE BURGESSES of the burgh of the Canongate
from 27th June, 1622 to 25th September, 1733. Ed. by H. Armet. Scottish
Record Soc. Publ. Edin. 1951.

3994 EXTRACTS FROM THE BURGH RECORDS of Dunfermline in the
16th and 17th centuries. Ed. by A. Shearer. Dunfermline. 1951.

3995 EXTRACTS FROM THE RECORDS of the burgh of Edinburgh, 1589–1689. Ed. by M. Wood. 7 vols. Lond. and Edin. 1927–54.

See also in Scot. Hist. Rec. Soc. Publ. the following: M. Wood, ed., *Edinburgh poll tax returns for 1694*, Edin. 1951; F. J. Grant and C. B. B. Watson, eds., *Register of apprentices of the city of Edinburgh, 1583–1666, 1666–1700*, 2 vols., Edin. 1906, 1929; and C. B. B. Watson, ed., *Roll of Edinburgh burgesses and guild brethren, 1406–1700*, Edin. 1929.

3996 EXTRACTS FROM THE RECORDS of the burgh of Glasgow, 1573–1717. Ed. by J. D. Marwick and R. Renwick. 4 vols. Scot. Burgh Rec. Soc. Glasgow. 1876–1908.

See also J. R. Anderson, ed., *The burgesses and guild brethren of Glasgow, 1372–1750*, Scot. Rec. Soc. Publ., Edin. 1925.

3997 RECORDS OF INVERNESS. Vol. ii. Ed. by W. Mackay and G. S. Laing. Aberdeen. 1924.

3998 EXTRACTS FROM THE RECORDS of the . . . burgh of Lanark, with charters . . . 1150–1722. Ed. by R. Renwick. Glasgow. 1893.

3999 CHARTERS AND DOCUMENTS relating to the burgh of Peebles, with extracts from the records of the burgh, 1165–1710. Ed. by W. Chambers. Scot. Burgh Rec. Soc. Edin. 1872.

Cf. R. Renwick, ed., *The burgh of Peebles: gleanings from its records, 1604–52*, 2nd edn., Peebles, 1912; and *Extracts from the records of the burgh of Peebles, 1652–1714*, Scot. Burgh Rec. Soc., Glasgow, 1910.

4000 ROTHESAY TOWN COUNCIL RECORDS, 1653–1766. 2 vols. 1935.

Transcribed by M. B. Johnston at the instance of John, fourth Marquis of Bute.

4001 EXTRACTS FROM THE RECORDS of the . . . burgh of Stirling, 1519–1752. Ed. by R. Renwick. 2 vols. Glasgow. 1887–9.

Cf. *The Stirling guildry book, 1592–1846*, ed. by W. B. Cook and D. B. Morris, Stirling, 1916.

4002 A DESCRIPTION of the Western Islands of Scotland *circa* 1695. By Martin Martin. Including A voyage to St. Kilda, by the same author, and A description of the Western Islands of Scotland, by Sir Donald Monro. Stirling. 1934. 4th edn. by D. J. Macleod.

3. LATER WORKS

For the history of Edinburgh, use should be made of the *Book of the Old Edinburgh Club* (1908+). There is an index to vols. i–xx. For parish histories, see Mitchell and Cash (3690).

4003 BARRY, G. History of the Orkney islands. Edin. 1805. 2nd edn. Lond. 1908.

4004 BARTY, A. B. The history of Dunblane. Stirling. 1944.

4005 BROWNE, J. A history of the Highlands and of the Highland clans. 4 vols. Glasgow. 1838. Later edns. 4 vols. Lond. 1849. 4 vols. Edin. and Lond. s.a.

Contains a catalogue of Gaelic and Irish MSS. in the libraries of Great Britain and Ireland.

4006 BUCHAN, J. W. and PATON, H. A history of Peeblesshire. 3 vols. Glasgow. 1925–7.

4007 DONALDSON, G. Shetland life under Earl Patrick. Edin. 1958.

4008 EYRE-TODD, G. History of Glasgow. Vol. ii–iii. Glasgow. 1931–4.

4009 GILLESPIE, J. H. Dundonald: a contribution to parochial history. 2 vols. Glasgow. 1939.

4010 GILLIES, W. A. In famed Breadalbane. Perth. 1938.

4011 GRAHAM, J. Condition of the Border at the union. Glasgow. 1902. 2nd edn. Glasgow. 1907.

The 'union' is that of 1603. Based on Lord Muncaster's MSS. in *Hist. MSS. Comm. Report X*, pt. iv.

4012 GREGORY, D. The history of the Western highlands and Isles of Scotland, 1493–1625. Edin. 1836. Later edn. Lond. 1881.

The 2nd edn. is a reprint. The work draws largely on the Privy Council register, the register of the Privy Seal, and the Denmylne MS. in the Advocates' Library, Edin.

4013 IRVING, J. History of Dumbartonshire. Dumbarton. Rev. edn. 1917–24.

4014 LIDDELL, R. H. R. 'Saint Madoes and its clergymen: notes on a Perthshire parish, 1640–88.' *S.H.R.* 25 (1927–8), 255–69.

4015 MACKERLIE, P. H. History of the lands and their owners in Galloway. 5 vols. Edin. 1870–8. 2 vols. Paisley. 1906.

4016 McKERRAL, A. Kintyre in the seventeenth century. Lond. and Edin. 1948.

4017 MAXWELL, A. The history of old Dundee. Dundee. 1884.

4018 METCALFE, W. M. History of the county of Renfrew. Paisley. 1905.

4019 PATERSON, J. History of the counties of Ayr and Wigtown. 5 vols. Edin. 1863–6.

Cf. A. I. Dunlop, ed., *The royal burgh of Ayr* . . . (Ayrshire Arch. and Nat. Hist. Soc.), Edin. 1953.

4020 SHAW, LACHLAN. The history of the province of Moray. 3 vols. Glasgow. 1882.

4021 WARDEN, A. J. Angus or Forfarshire. 5 vols. Dundee. 1880.

J. GENEALOGY

I. Sources

Among MS. sources, the records of testaments are especially valuable. There are indexes published by the Scottish Record Society. Throughout the period an increasing number of parish registers become available: cf. *Detailed list of the old parochial registers of Scotland*, Edin. 1872. The testaments are with the national records in the [old] Register House, the parish registers in the custody of the Registrar General in the New Register House. See also Stuart and Paul (3694).

4022 INQUISITIONUM AD CAPELLAM DOMINI REGIS RETOR-
NATARUM . . . ABBREVIATIO. Ed. by Thos. Thomson. 3 vols. Edin.
1811–16.

Records of *retours*, the findings of juries concerning the inheritance of land held of the crown and generally the 'service of heirs'.

2. Later Works

4023 THE SCOTS PEERAGE, founded on Wood's edition of Sir Robert
Douglas's *Peerage of Scotland*, containing a historical and genealogical account
of the nobility of that kingdom. With armorial illustrations. Ed. by Sir J. B.
Paul. 9 vols. Edin. 1904–14.

Has full references to the sources, and an ample index.

4024 GENEALOGICAL COLLECTIONS . . . made by Walter Macfarlane.
2 vols. Scot. Hist. Soc. Glasgow. 1900.

4025 FRASER, J. Chronicles of the Frasers . . . the true genealogy of the
Frasers, 916–1674. Ed. by W. Mackay. Scot. Hist. Soc. Edin. 1905.

Useful for the middle of the 17th century.

4026 FRASER, WILLIAM.

His memorials of various Scottish noble families contain much useful material, including
numerous transcripts of documents. All of them were published in Edinburgh between
1859 and 1897, as follows: *Montgomeries, earls of Eglinton*, 2 vols., 1895; *Maxwells of
Pollok*, 2 vols., 1863; *The chiefs of Colquhoun*, 2 vols., 1869; *The Lennox*, 2 vols., 1874;
The earls of Cromartie, 2 vols., 1876; *The red book of Menteith*, 2 vols., 1880; *The Douglas
book*, 4 vols., 1885; *Family of Wemyss*, 3 vols., 1888; *Memorials . . . earls of Haddington*,
2 vols., 1889; *The Melvilles, earls of Melville, and the Leslies, earls of Leven*, 3 vols., 1890;
The earls etc. of Annandale, 2 vols., 1894; *Lords Elphinstone, Balmerino, Coupar*, 2 vols.,
1897.

4027 LINDSAY, LORD. Lives of the Lindsays, or a memoir of the house
of Crawford and Balcarres. 4 vols. Wigan. 1840. 3 vols. Lond. 1849. 1858.

4028 MACDONALD, A. and MACDONALD, A. The clan Donald. 3 vols.
Inverness. 1896–1904.

4029 MACKECHNIE, HECTOR. The Lamont clan. Edin. 1938.

4030 MACKINTOSH, A. M. Historical memoirs of the house and clan of Mackintosh and of the clan Chattan. 2 vols. 1880.

4031 PATON, H. The Clan Campbell: abstracts of entries relating to Campbells in the sheriff court books of Argyll, Perth, particular register of Sasines, books of council and session, register of deeds, parish registers, and miscellaneous. 8 vols. Edin. 1913–22.

Vols. i and iii, sheriff court of Argyll; ii, sheriff court of Perth; iv, miscellaneous; v, particular register of Sasines; vi, books of council and session, and register of deeds; vii, parish registers; viii, books of council and session, and acts and decreets.

4032 SETON, B. G. The house of Seton: a study of lost causes. 2 vols. Edin. 1941.

4033 SOMERVILLE, J. Memorie of the Somervilles; being a history of the baronial house of Somerville. Ed. by Sir W. Scott. 2 vols. Edin. 1815.

Preface and notes by Scott. MS. in the possession of the family. The 'Introduction' is dated 1679.

4034 TAYLER, H. History of the family of Urquhart. 1946.

Ill-arranged, but contains some useful 17th-century material.

4035 THE WEDDERBURN BOOK. 2 vols. s.l. 1898.

XV

IRELAND

The seventeenth century saw the destruction of medieval Norman Gaelic civilization. Out of the chaos there emerges an upper-class British protestant colonial society and a Catholic Anglo-Irish middle class and proletariat. Between these two in the north-east there is found by the end of the century a Scottish Presbyterian tenantry confronted by a substantial Catholic Gaelic proletariat whose traditions go back to an independent pre-Norman society of a thousand years earlier. The clash of reformation and counter-reformation only accentuates this difference. The politics of this struggle dominates every aspect of life. While the British win the military conflicts, eject their opponents from administrative office and reduce them to the level of inferior citizens, they cannot eradicate them. The flight to Catholic Europe secures unassailable centres to strengthen the resistance. In the armies of France, of Spain, and of Austria, are found the military-minded sons of the expropriated Irish aristocracy. In the colleges of the counter-reformation are educated the spiritual missioners who return to confirm the faith of their persecuted relatives in Ireland. It is these exiles who assist in preserving so many aspects of an older tradition modernized in the new European traditions of post-reformation Western Europe. In the following sections an attempt is made to conform to the general plan of this bibliography but the special circumstances described above necessitate some variations in presentation.

A. REFERENCE

1. BIBLIOGRAPHY

This section corresponds to several sections in Ch. I. It includes bibliography of bibliography (§ A 1 a), catalogues and bibliographies (§ A 1 b), library resources (§ A 1 c), and pamphlet collections (§ A 1 d). It is assumed here that reference will first be made by readers to works in Ch. I.

(a) *Bibliography of Bibliography*

4036   EAGER, A. R. A guide to Irish bibliographical material being a bibliography of bibliographies. 1964.

> Of earlier works, particularly notable is K. Povey, 'The sources for a bibliography of Irish history, 1500–1700', in *Irish Hist. Studies*, 1 (1939), 393–403. As early as 1903 J. King had attempted a classification, *Subject index of Irish bibliography*, 1903. D. J. Clarke and P. J. Madden (Read, no. 5680) should be consulted for printing; R. M. Elmes (Read, no. 5686) catalogues topographical prints. The whole subject is transformed with the publication for the National Library of Ireland of R. J. Hayes, *Manuscript sources for the history of Irish civilisation*, grouped under persons (and institutions), subjects, places, date, 11 vols., Boston (Mass.), [1966].

(b) *Catalogues and Bibliographies of British History*

After the *Bibliographies* of British history by C. Gross *et al.* (11), the catalogues of Pollard and Redgrave (3) and Wing (4) present the most substantial body of known contemporary literature. The eighteenth-century works of Nicolson and Harris (Gross, no. 50) and of Tanner (ibid., no. 52) are still the best starting-point in investigation. More selective are W. S. Mason, *Bibliotheca Hibernicana* (Pargellis, no. 3441); E. R. McC. Dix and C. W. Dugan, eds., *Books printed in Dublin in the 17th century*, Dublin, 1898–1902; R. Dunlop in *Camb. Mod. Hist.*, iv, 913–18; v, 829–37; vi, 913–24; R. H. Murray, *Ireland, 1603–1714*, 1920; and J. F. Kenney (p. 567, *infra*).

4037   'Writings on Irish History', 1937+. In *Irish Hist. Stud.* 1+ (1938+).

> Published annually, beginning with 1936, a fairly complete list on materials for Irish history, of which the successive contributors have been J. Carty, R. D. Edwards, T. W. Moody, K. Povey, R. B. McDowell, P. Henchy, T. P. O'Neill, F. X. Martin, L. Bieler, A. MacCabe, J. Barry, E. Semple, D. Kennedy, H. Hornsby, M. Henchy. From this list is selected annually the material on Irish history for the annual *International bibliography of historical sciences* (1 n.).
> Lists restricted by subject are R. I. Best on Irish Gaelic philology and literature (Read no. 5676); R. de Hae and B. Ni Dhonnchadha on modern Irish Gaelic (Eager, no. 2375), Dublin published books 1700–91 (Eager, no. 67), J. Alden's Irish supplement to Wing (4), and C. L. Grose (10).

4038   WALSH, M. O'N. 'Check list of Irish books printed abroad 1470–1700.' In *The Irish Book*, ii (1), pp. i–viii, 1–36 (Dublin, 1963).

> Valuable.

4039   SIMMS, J. G. 'Report on the compilation of a bibliography of source material for the history of Ireland 1685–1702.' In *Analecta Hibernica*, no. 22, pp. 1–10 (Dublin, 1960).

(c) *Library Resources*

Of library resources the general catalogues are now largely outdated by the unpublished card catalogues of the various institutions. The National Library of Ireland has the greatest and most accessible collection for Irish history.

Among the works listed in Ch. I, § B 1, see especially *B.M. Cat.* (17), *ASLIB*, *American lib. resources*, Ash, and Crick and Alman. Hamer's *Guide* (19 n.) lists the main repositories with Irish material in the United States; Hale (20) links to libraries in the United States and Canada the Irish as well as the British documentation in photocopies.

Published catalogues still notable are the 1905 list of the New York Public Library, the 1916 and 1918 Catalogues of the Cambridge University Library, Bradshaw, and Dublin Municipal Public Libraries, Gilbert Collections (Pargellis, nos. 3443, 3445, 3447; for 'Charleville Hall' (ibid., p. 12) read 'Pearse St.'). Other published catalogues, noted by Eager, nos. 50–126, are: Belfast Linen Hall, 1917, and Public (F. J. Bigger, 1930, and J. S. Crone); Camb. (Mass.), Public, 1920; Chicago, Public, 1942; Cork University, 1914; Lowell (Mass.), city, 1910; Wigan, Public, 1896. The unpublished catalogues of the following are valuable: Belfast (Queen's Univ.); California, San Marino (Huntington); Dublin (Irish Folklore Commission); Dublin, Killiney (Franciscan); Dublin (Marsh's); Dublin (Nat. Lib. Ire.); Dublin (Trinity College); Dublin (Univ. Coll.); Illinois, Chicago (Newberry); London (Soc. of Genealogists); Londonderry (Magee Univ.); Massachusetts, Cambridge (Harvard U. Widener Lib.); Pennsylvania, Philadelphia (Free); Rhode Island, Providence (Public, C. J. Fox collection); Washington, D.C. (Folger-Shakespeare); Washington, D.C. (Lib. of Congress).

(d) *Pamphlet Collections*

To the cautionary implications for the Pargellis (pp. 11–12) three-fold classification, may be extended the conclusion of L. M. Cullen that the historian has too frequently seen problems 'with the prejudices and myopia of contemporaries' (*Irish Hist. Stud.* 14 (1964), 145).

Special subjects include: Roman Catholicism (in Maynooth College Library (see *infra*, no. 4046, *An Leabharlann*, 14 (1956), 51–7); and in Franciscan Library, Killiney, see *Archiv. Hib.* 18 (1955), 150–6); Protestant episcopalianism (Cashel Diocesan Library; Dublin, Archbishop Marsh's Library; see Eager, nos. 429, 98); Presbyterianism (Londonderry, Magee Univ. College Library).

Individual collections include: Bradshaw in Cambridge University Library (Pargellis, no. 3445); E. R. McC. Dix in Dublin, Nat. Lib. Ire. (both invaluable on printers); C. H. Earbery in the A. Crofton Collection in Trinity College, Dublin Library (mainly economics, see Friends of the Library of T.C.D., *Annual Bulletin*, 1956); J. T. Gilbert in Dublin Public (mainly political, Pargellis, no. 3447); C. Halliday in Dublin Royal Irish Academy (Pargellis, p. 423); P. Power in Dublin, University College (Catholic Irish abroad).

General collections are also in Dublin, Nat. Lib. Ire. (Pargellis, p. 422); Dublin, Trinity College; and, among others in Illinois, Chicago, Newberry; California, San Marino, Huntington, and in Washington, D.C., Folger. Not all material is in *S.T.C.* (3) or in Wing (4) or in supplements such as Alden (4 n.). Walsh (4038) is impressive on printing abroad. After 1700 in addition to Arber, *The term catalogues* (4 n.), Bent (Pargellis, no. 3), and the Catalogues printed in Ireland from 1700 (*supra*, p. 565) there is Nat. Lib. Ire. MS. 216, Irish books 1575–1744.

2. PERIODICALS AND SOCIETY PUBLICATIONS

Apart from R. R. Madden, *History of Irish periodical literature* (Pargellis, no. 3452) no one since 1867 attempted to survey this subject until Kenney (*infra*, p. 567) in 1929 in his opening chapter, 'History in Ireland', traced the breakdown of the Gaelic literary organization in the seventeenth century and noted sporadic developments from the Stuart restoration to the national movements of the early 20th century.

(a) *Bibliographies and Guides*

Not until the beginning in 1786 of the *Transactions of the Royal Irish Academy* (Read, no. 5669) is there any continuity in the history of publication societies.

Apart from lists and indexes of the publications of individual organizations, and the catalogues of some libraries, there are no adequate bibliographies and guides. D. MacCartney, 'The writing of history in Ireland, 1800–30', in *I.H. Stud.* 10 (1957), 347–62, marks a beginning. Cf. K. T. Hoppen, ibid. 14 (1964), 99–118.

(b) *Serial Publications*

Of the serials listed in Read, 2nd edn., pp. 478–9, no specifically historical periodical appeared until *Irish Historical Studies* (39) in 1938. As in contemporary Britain, 'antiquities' dominated cultural interests until the mid nineteenth century. Revolutionary national movements tended to weaken cultural societies. British organizations (Pargellis, Ch. I, § E, 3) absorbed more Irish workers until the mid twentieth century. Local periodicals catered for general Irish history. More recently have emerged Catholic diocesan publications. The serials listed below are supplementary to those in Ch. I, pp. 6–7, *supra*, and in Read and in Pargellis (Ch. XIII, § C).

4040   HISTORICAL STUDIES: papers read before the [biennial] Irish Conference of historians. London. 1958+.

4041   DUBLIN HISTORICAL RECORD: proceedings of the Old Dublin Society. Dublin. 1938+.

4042   COLLECTANEA HIBERNICA: sources for Irish history. Dublin. 1958+.

Mainly ecclesiastical.

4043   STUDIA HIBERNICA: Dublin. 1961+.

Gaelic and historical.

4044   ZEITSCHRIFT FÜR CELTISCHE PHILOLOGIE. Halle. 1897+.

4045   THE IRISH BOOK. Dublin. 1959+.

Succeeding *The Irish Book Lover* (Dublin, 1909–57), both including papers of the Bibliographical Society of Ireland; Dublin. Vol. 1+ (1918+).

4046   AN LEABHARLANN: Journal of the Library Association of Ireland. Dublin. 1930+.

3. GENERAL WORKS OF REFERENCE

General guides include J. F. Kenney, *The sources for the early history of Ireland*, vol. i, ecclesiastical, N.Y. 1929; R. H. Murray, *Ireland, 1603–1714* (Helps for students of history), 1920; and C. Maxwell, *A short bibliography of Irish history* (Historical Assoc., leaflet no. 23), 1921.

Guides on particular subjects include one on economics, 1700–83, by H. R. Wagner (Pargellis, no. 3451); one by E. O'Reilly for Gaelic literature (Pargellis, no. 3443).

4047 PATENTEE OFFICERS IN IRELAND 1173–1826 including high
sheriffs 1661–84 and 1761–1816. By J. L. J. Hughes. Dublin. Irish Manuscripts Commission. 1960.

Alphabetical list compiled from the *Liber Munerum Publicorum Hiberniae* (Pargellis,
no. 3477).

4048 BIBLIOGRAPHIE DE LA RÉFORME, 1450–1648. Ouvrages parus
de 1940 à 1955. 2me fasc. (incl.) Irlande, ed. by A. Gwynn, pp. 51–61. Leiden.
1960.

4049 BREATNACH, R. A. 'The end of a tradition: a survey of eighteenth
century Irish literature.' In *Studia Hibernica*, 1 (1961), 128–50.

4050 FALLEY, M. D. Irish and Scotch-Irish ancestral research: a guide to
the genealogical records, methods and sources in Ireland. Vol. i (repositories
and records). Vol. ii (bibliography and family index). Evanston, Illinois.
1961.

For local and family history see also W. MacArthur, 'Bibliography of histories of Irish
counties and towns' (Pargellis, no. 3444), and J. B. Burke, *Landed gentry* . . . , 4th edn.
by L. G. Pine, 1958.

4051 'A HANDLIST OF IRISH DIOCESAN HISTORIES.' In *Irish
Catholic Historical Committee Proceedings*. 1957.

For the Irish abroad see, in addition to M. O'N. Walsh (4038), C. McNeill (4330), and
other titles in § K of this chapter.

4052 CARTY, J., ed. Ireland: a documentary record, 1607–1782. Dublin.
1949.

Other documentary collections are: J. Lodge, ed., *Desiderata Curiosa Hibernica*, 2 vols.,
Dublin, 1772, which includes state papers and some tracts (cf. *E.H.R.* 22 (1907), 104–30,
527–52); A. Thom, ed., *Collection of tracts and treatises illustrative . . . of Ireland*, 2 vols.,
Dublin, 1860–1; H. Morley in 1890 (Read, no. 5805); C. Maxwell in 1923 (ibid.,
no. 5752); and E. Curtis and R. B. McDowell in 1943 (ibid., no. 5840).

4053 MAC MANUS, F., ed. After the flight, being eyewitness sketches from
Irish history from 1607 to 1916. Dublin. 1938. 1940.

Cf. M. J. MacManus, ed., *Irish cavalcade, 1530–1850*, Dublin, 1939, 1943.

4054 HAYES-McCOY, G. A., ed. Ulster and other Irish maps, *c.* 1600.
Dublin. Ir. MSS. Comm. 1964.

By R. Bartlett (Barthelet), Francis Candell. See also the atlases described by T. Chubb
(53). For place-names see Y. M. Goblet, *A topographical index of the parishes and town-
lands of Ireland in Sir W. Petty's MSS. Barony Maps and 'Hiberniae Delineatio'*, Dublin,
Ir. MSS. Comm., 1932.

4055 WILLIS, J. Lives of illustrious and distinguished Irishmen. 6 vols.
Dublin. 1840–7.

See also *D.N.B.*, and other collections on Irish biography by R. Ryan, 1821; E. O.
Blackburne [Casey], 1877; A. J. Webb, *Compendium of Irish biography*, Dublin, 1878;
and J. S. Crone, *Concise dictionary of Irish biography*, Dublin, 1928, 1937. See also

Eager, no. 34, on the forthcoming work of the Nat. Lib. Ire., *National bibliography and Dictionary of Irish biography*.

4056   O CLEIRIGH, M. Focloir no sanasan nua. Louvain. 1643.

A rudimentary philological work on Gaelic Irish, which was trans. in *Rev. Celt.*, 1880. Cf. *Arch. Celt. Lex.* i (111), 348. Cf. no. 4316. See also F. O'Molloy, *Grammatica Latino-Hibernica*, Rome, 1677. There are no other dictionaries apart from those listed in Ch. § I, D.

4057   LHUYD, EDWARD. Archaeologia Britannica, i (1707).

Cf. E. G. Quin in Friends of the Library of T.C.D. *Ann. Bull.* (1951), pp. 7–10; also B. Ó Cuív in *Éigse*, 11 (1964), 74–6.

4058   WALSH, PETER. A prospect of the state of Ireland. 1682.

The author's historical methods were influenced by the chronological studies of R. Bellarmine and J. Ussher, as were those of Geoffrey Keating in his early 18th-century history of Ireland, *Forus feasa ar Eirinn* (Read, no. 5805 a). Cf. R. O'Flaherty, *Ogygia* (ibid., no. 6157).

4. MANUSCRIPTS

The §§ F (MSS.) and G (Historical Manuscripts Commission) of Ch. I *supra*, correspond to this one, the publications of the Irish Manuscripts Commission being the main additions to § G.

(a) *Manuscripts: General*

In addition to *Archives* (63) and other works listed in Ch. I, § F 1 *supra*, such as the National Register of Archives *Bulletin* and *Accessions*, important materials are listed in Crick and Alman (p. 10, *supra*), Hamer (19 n.) and Hale (20). Reference has already been made to recent works like Nat. Lib. Ire., *Manuscript sources of Irish civilization* (4036 n.), A. R. Eager (4036), M. D. Falley (4050), but earlier publications worthy of study include E. Bernard in 1697 (Gross (11), no. 498), W. Nicolson in 1724 (ibid., no. 50), and T. Tanner in 1748 (ibid., no. 52).

(b) *Government Official Archives*
See § F 2 of Ch. I.

For the period before 1922, the main Irish governmental archives were preserved in England. In addition to repositories in London (4065–6) see also the Stuart MSS. (221). For the 17th century subsidiary material was preserved in Ireland. Owing to the existence of Irish records in the Vatican and elsewhere in Europe, the references below are arranged in alphabetical order chiefly by towns and institutions. For Edinburgh, see *Scotland*, no. 3688. For the principal European archives, see Thomas and Case, *Guide to diplomatic archives* (529), and Ch. II *supra*, § G on Foreign Relations. Cf. Nat. Lib. Ire., *Manuscript sources* (4036 n.).

Local official archives in Ireland having relevant material include:

Dublin Municipal (cf. Read, nos. 5708, 6115, 6121; guilds, nos. 5956, 6089–90, 6094, 6101); and see Gilbert (*infra*, 4077 n.).
Galway Municipal, University College Library, Galway.
Waterford Municipal, see Pender (4144).

4059 BELFAST. Public Record Office of Northern Ireland.

For guides see D. A. Chart in *I.H. Stud.*, 1 (1938), 42–57, and K. Darwin in *Archives*, 6 (1963), 108–16. See *Report of the deputy keeper of the records of Northern Ireland*, 1924+, Belfast, 1925+. Cf. H.M.C., *Record repositories in Great Britain* (*recte* in the United Kingdom), p. 39 (1964).

4060 DUBLIN. National Library of Ireland and National Archives.

See *Report of the council of trustees*, 1932+. The Report for 1932–3 (1933) provides a *Handlist of MSS. in the library*; that for 1949–50 (1951) lists MSS. in the Bibliothèque National that relate to Ireland; those for 1950–1 and 1951–2 list filmed copies of MSS. relating to Ireland (see Read, nos. 5694–5).

For the D. Comyn collection, see Eager, no. 70.

Also attached to the Nat. library is the Genealogical Office, formerly the Ulster King-of-Arms' Office. Cf. article by T. U. Sadleir, *Genealogists' Mag.* 6 (1934), 434–8; and Falley (4050).

4061 DUBLIN. Ordnance Survey records.

The list by J. G. Hanlon in *Jour. R.S.A.I.* (1856–67), iv–ix, is differentiated between MSS. transferred to the Royal Irish Academy and those remaining in the Ordnance Survey by R. D. Edwards in *Analecta Hibernica*, no. 23.

4062 DUBLIN. Public Record Office of Ireland.

A *Short guide* by M. Griffith is in *I.H. Stud.* 8 (1952), 45–58. Much of the material described in the guides by H. Wood, Dublin, 1919, and R. H. Murray, Lond. 1919, was destroyed by fire in 1922. Cf. H. Wood in *R.H.S. Trans.*, 4th Ser. 13 (1930), 17–49. The *Reports of the deputy keeper of the public records, Ireland*, Dublin, 1869+, contain valuable apps.

The Griffith guide and the deputy keeper's reports 55–9 (1928–62) describe the material surviving the 1922 losses.

4063 IRELAND. J. T. Gilbert, ed. Facsimiles of national MSS. of Ireland. 4 vols. Dublin. 1874–84.

Important. Useful also is Gilbert's *Account* of the facsimiles, Lond. 1884, which gives descriptions and calendars of representative documents in the collection.

For repositories of public records in Ireland see also Belfast (4059), Dublin (4060–2), and Maynooth (4084).

4064 IRELAND. Public records reports. For the Irish Record Commission 1810–30 see M. C. Griffith in *I.H. Stud.* 7 (1950), 17–38.

Cf. Read, no. 5722, and Pargellis, no. 3437. While largely superseded since the establishment of the Public Record Office of Ireland in 1867 (see no. 4062), data on some repositories is not elsewhere available. Most of the I.R. Comm.'s records ultimately passed to the P.R.O. Ireland (surviving the destruction of 1922), but some reached the Royal Irish Academy and Trinity College, Dublin, as well as Maynooth College.

4065 LONDON. House of Lords Record Office.

A report on appeals in Irish Courts, 1710–30, by L. McRedmond appears in *Analecta Hibernica*, no. 23. Earlier and other material from the British parliament's archives are described in H.M.C., House of Lords MSS. (162). See also Bond (783).

4066 LONDON. Public Record Office.

See nos. 65–6. Besides Port books, Privy Council registers, State Papers Domestic (for the *Calendars* see no. 256), there are the important State Papers Ireland. For these there is the *Calendar of state papers* . . . *Ireland, 1603–1670*, ed. by C. W. Russell, J. P. Prendergast, and R. P. Mahaffy, 13 vols., 1870–1910. The Irish state papers after 1670 are included in the English calendars (no. 256). There are also State Papers Ireland Supplementary (including DE RENZY), and there is Irish material in virtually every collection, notably in the foreign dispatches from Flanders, France, Spain, Venice. Among papers received on deposit or by gifts see Thomas Carew of Crowcombe, Manchester (N. Rich), Shaftesbury. Changes in dynasties, 1603, 1649, 1660, 1689, led to lacunae in collections. Editors of calendars were not always perceptive of the manner in which former custodians and departments artificially built up their records.

4067   MADRID. (*a*) Archivo Historico Nacional.

See J. Ranson in Ir. Cath. Comm., *Proc.*, 1955, pp. 22–4. Cf. J. Silke in *Studia Hibernica*, 3 (1963), 179–90; and M. Walsh (4176).

(*b*) Ministry of External Affairs. Fonds Santa Sede.

See B. Curtin in *Archivium Hibernicum*, 26 (1963), 40–9.

4068   PARIS. (*a*) Archives des Affaires Étrangères; (*b*) Archives National; (*c*) Dépôt de la Guerre.

For Paris also see no. 4086. Cf. 4060 n.; also, T. J. Walsh in Ir. Cath. Comm. *Proc.*, 1955.

4069   PORTUGAL. For the records in government archives, see V. de Santarem, ed., *Quadro elementar des relacões polit. e diplomat. de Portugal* (1842+).

4070   ROME. (*a*) Sacra Congregationis de Propaganda Fide.

See B. Jennings in *Archivium Hibernicum*, 22 (1959), 28–139.

(*b*) Vatican: Arcivio Segreto.

See K. Fink, *Das Vaticanische archive*, Rome, 1951. Cf. E. Mac Fhinn in *Analecta Hibernica*, 16 (1946).

4071   SIMANCAS. ARCHIVO GENERAL.

See J. Silke (noted in 4067), also C. Mooney in Ir. Cath. Hist. Comm. *Proc.*, 1955, pp. 18–21. Cf. Nat. Lib. Ire., *Rep. Council of Trustees*, 1952.

(c) *Other Libraries and Repositories*

The National Library of Ireland and the Public Record Offices Dublin and Belfast undertake some of the functions performed in Great Britain by the National Register of Archives and the British Records Association. Apart from official archives, institutions known to possess relevant materials are here listed under the towns in which they are located. See also Edinburgh (3691); Galway (p. 569, *supra*).

Collections in the United States are: Chicago Public Library, the J. D'Alton Collection; Harvard University's Widener Library; Huntington Library at San Marino, Cal., Hastings MSS. (155), and Ellesmere Collection listed in *Anal. Hibern.* 8 (1938), 431–42, and portions of the Stowe MSS. (see a *Catalogue* by C. O'Connor, 1818, and see Br. Mus., and Dublin, Royal Irish Academy, 4077, *infra*).

4072 ARMAGH: (*a*) County Museum; (*b*) Church of Ireland diocesan registry office; (*c*) Public Library (see *Catalogue* of MSS. by J. Dean, Armagh, 1928).

4073 BELFAST: (*a*) The Linen Hall Library; (*b*) Presbyterian Historical Society Library; (*c*) Public Libraries (Catalogue of F. J. Bigger collection, 1930).

4074 BRUSSELS. Bibliothèque Royale.

Another collection in Belgium is at Louvain; see Killiney (4080).

4075 CARRICKMACROSS, Lough Fea Library.

Although the library's collection has been dispersed, a useful *Catalogue* by E. P. Shirley was publ. in 1872 (Read, no. 5725).

4076 COPENHAGEN. Kongelige Bibliotek.

4077 DUBLIN. Franciscan Collections, described in Killiney (4080) and Pargellis, no. 3439.

Marsh's Library. *Catalogue*, by J. R. Scott and N. J. D. White, Dublin, 1913.
Public Libraries. J. T. Gilbert Collection (Pargellis, no. 3447).
Representative Church (of Ireland) Body. *Catalogue* of MSS. by J. B. Leslie, Dublin, 1938.
Royal Irish Academy. *Catalogue* by T. F. O'Rahilly, Dublin, 1926+; catalogue of non-Gaelic MSS. in preparation; Stowe MSS. See Pargellis, p. 423.
Society of Friends.
Trinity College. *Catalogues* by T. K. Abbott, Dublin, 1900, and by Abbott and E. J. Gwynn, Dublin, 1921. See also R. H. Murray, *Short guide* . . . (Helps for Students of History, no. 32), Lond. 1920; Pargellis, no. 3439; and Eager, no. 164.

4078 FERMOY. St. Colman's College.

4079 KILKENNY. St. Kieran's College.

4080 KILLINEY. Franciscan Library. Guide in *Arch. Hib.* 18 (1955). Cf. no. 4133.

4081 LONDON. British Museum. *Catalogue of Irish MSS.*, by S. H. O'Grady, R. Flower, and M. Dillon, 3 vols., 1909–53; see also R. Flower in *Anal. Hibern.* 2 (1931), 310–29, on Irish annals.

Heralds College of Arms. See Pargellis, nos. 83, 450.
Lambeth Palace. Carew MSS., *Calendar* by J. S. Brewer and W. Bullen, 6 vols., 1867–73, vol. 6 relating to 1603–24. Cf. *E.H.R.* 42 (1927), 261–7. On the Carte MSS. see no. 4085. See also Pargellis, no. 81.

4082 LONDONDERRY. Magee University Library.

4083 MANCHESTER. John Rylands Library. See Eager, no. 355.

4084 MAYNOOTH. Royal College of St. Patrick Library.

Catalogue of Irish MSS., Pt. 1, by P. Walsh, Maynooth, 1943. See also Eager, nos. 207, 390.

4085   OXFORD. Bodleian Library. See C. McNeill on Irish materials in the
Rawlinson Collection, *Analecta Hibernica*, 1 (1930), 1–178 and 2 (1931), 1–291;
also ibid. 4 (1932), 1–98; and *Report . . . upon the Carte and Carew Papers in the
Bodleian and Lambeth libraries*, by T. D. Hardy and J. S. Brewer, 1864; and
the *30th Report* and *32nd Report* of the deputy keeper of public records of
England. See also Pargellis, no. 81, and *supra*, no. 71.

4086   PARIS. Bibliothèque Nationale. See no. 4060, *supra*.

Bibliothèque Ste Geneviève.

Also in France, see the Bibliothèque Municipale at Troyes.

4087   SHEFFIELD. City Libraries. Guide, 1956.

4088   THURLES. Holy Cross Monastery.

4089   VATICAN CITY. Bibliotheca Apostolica Vaticana.

Cf. L. MacFarlane in *Archives*, 4 (1959). Transcripts from the Vatican archives have
been reprinted in the *Archivium Hibernicum*, publ. by the Catholic Record Society of
Ireland, Dublin, 1912+. See also articles by P. J. Corish, in *Irish Theol. Quart.* 21
(1954), 375–81; and by C. Giblin, *Archiv. Hibern.* 18 (1955), 67–144; also no. 4060,
supra; and Eager, no. 353.

4090   WINDSOR. Windsor Castle Library.

(d) *British and Irish Historical Manuscripts Commissions*

A three-fold sub-division has been adopted: (1) collections of general impor-
tance; (2) municipal collections and other organizations; (3) collections of sub-
sidiary interest. In addition to the Hist. MSS. Comm. reports listed in Ch. I,
§ G, *supra*, some supplementary materials are given here. For the Irish MSS.
Comm. reference may be made to the 1966 catalogue published by the Dublin
Stationery Office.

(1) *Collections of General Importance*

In addition to the list below, see Historical MSS. Commission *Reports* (Ch. I)
nos. 101 (Coke, Cowper); 117 (Buckhurst, Cranfield, De la Warr, Sackville);
162 (House of Lords); 190 (Nalson, Portland); 195 (Ormonde); 200 (Egmont,
Perceval); 212 (Cecil, Salisbury); 221 (Stuart); 225 (Downshire, Trumbull);
253 (Laing).
   See also National Library of Ireland (4060); Dublin Genealogical Office
(4060 n.); and Dublin Registry of Deeds (4132); the Huntington Library (p. 571,
supra); Rawlinson MSS. (4085); Simms (4039).

4091   ACTA SANCTORUM HIBERNIAE. By J. Colgan. 1645. Facsimile
reproduction. Intro. by B. Jennings. I.M.C. Dublin. 1948.

4092   ANALECTA HIBERNICA. Including the reports of the Irish Manuscripts Commission. 1+. Dublin. 1930+.

4093   ANNALS OF LOUGH CÉ. By W. M. Hennessy. Rolls Ser. 2 vols.
1871. Trans. by W. M. Hennessy. 2 vols. Dublin. 1940.

Chiefly earlier than 1603, but valuable. See Read, no. 5782.

4094 'CENSUS OF IRELAND (*c.* 1659).' Ed. by S. Pender. I.M.C. Dublin. 1939.

4095 CHICHESTER LETTER-BOOK, 1612–14. Ed. by R. D. Edwards. In *Analecta Hibernica*, 8 (1938).

4096 THE CHRONICLE OF IRELAND, 1584–1608. By Sir James Perrott. Ed. by H. Wood. I.M.C. Dublin. 1933.

Favourable to the government of Mountjoy's successor, Chichester.

4097 THE CIVIL SURVEY, 1654–6. Ed. by R. C. Simington.

Vols. i, ii (1931, 1934), Co. Tipperary; vol. iii (1937), Cos. Donegal, Derry, and Tyrone; vol. iv (1938), Co. Limerick; vol. v (1940), Co. Meath; vol. vi (1942), Cos. Waterford, Cork (Muskerry), Kilkenny city, city valuations *c.* 1663–4; vol. vii (1945), Co. Dublin; vol. viii (1952), Co. Kildare; vol. ix (1953), Co. Wexford; vol. x (1961), Miscellanea. I.M.C.
Cf. *Analecta Hibernica*, 16 (1946) on missing volumes. See also no. 4118.

4098 CLARKE, G. Report on the war correspondence, 1690–1. By N. B. White. In *Analecta Hibernica*, 10 (1941).

4099 COMMONWEALTH STATE ACCOUNTS, 1650–6. Ed. by E. Mac-Lysaght. Ibid. 15 (1944).

4100 COURTS OF CLAIMS, 1661–9, Office of general registrar. By R. C. Simington. Ibid. 16 (1946), 377–85.

4101 THE DANISH FORCE IN IRELAND, 1690–1. Ed. by K. Danaher, J. G. Simms, and [J. Jordan]. I.M C. Dublin. 1962.

4102 D'AVAUX. Négociacions de M. le Comte (J. A. de M.) d'Avaux en Irlande, 1689–90. [Vol. i, facsimile reproduction of London printing 1844, ed. A. C. H. Gordon.] Introduction by J. Hogan. 1934. Supplementary vol. [ii]. By J. Hogan and L. Tate. I.M.C. Dublin. 1958.

Important for relations with James II and France.

4103 DOWN SURVEY MAPS. By R. Rochford (1787). Reports by C. McNeill, R. C. Simington. In *Analecta Hibernica*, 8 (1938).

See also *Down survey superimposition on townland maps* (by R. Johnson and R. C. Simington), Co. Tipperary, 1955, Cos. Carlow, Roscommon, 1956, Cos. Louth, Wexford, 1958, Co. Dublin, 1959, Co. Galway, 1962, Co. Clare, 1963. Nat. Lib. Ire. See also Goblet (4054 n.).

4104 ENGLISH PARLIAMENT. Orders for Ireland, 1642–5. Ed. by J. Hogan. Ibid. 4 (1934).

4105 FINGAL MSS. A light to the blind, 1685–1714. H.M.C. Ser. 14.

Now in Nat. Lib. Ire.

4106 FRANCO-IRISH WAR CORRESPONDENCE, 1688–91. Ed. by L. Tate. In *Analecta Hibernica*, 21 (1959).

Includes Tyrconnell correspondence.

4107   IRISH REBELLION. Letters and papers, 1642–6. Ed. by J. Hogan.
I.M.C. Dublin. 1935.

Allegedly collected for A. Annesley, first Earl of Anglesey.

4108   JACOBITES. Irish outlaws. 1690–8. Ed. by J. G. Simms. In *Analecta Hibernica*, 22 (1960).

4109   LEABHAR MUIMHNEACH. Ed. by T. Ó. Donnchadha. I.M.C. Dublin. 1940.

Munster genealogies to the early 18th century.

4110   LOFTUS, DUDLEY. Annals. 1180–1625. Report by N. B. White in *Analecta Hibernica*, 10 (1941).

4111   O'MELLAN, TURLOCH. Diary of O'Neill forces, 1641–7. Ed. by T. Ó. Donnchadha. Ibid. 3 (1931).

4112   OUTLAWS, 1641–7. Ed. by R. C. Simington and J. MacLellan. Ibid. 23 (1966).

4113   REPRESENTATIVE CHURCH BODY. Report by G. Fitzgerald. Ibid. 23 (1966).

Cf. no. 4077 n.

4114   RINUCCINI, G. B. Commentarius Rinuccinianus . . . by R. B. O'Ferrall and R. D. O'Connell. Ed. by S. J. Kavanagh. Vols. i–vi. I.M.C. Dublin. 1932–49.

See also nos. 210, 4179–80.

4115   ROCHESTER. Correspondence in 1702 of Lord Lieutenant, the earl of. Report to H.M.C. on King's Inns, Dublin MS. In Nat. Lib. Ire.

4116   STAPLETON, T. Catechismus seu Doctrina Christiana Latino-Hibernica. Brussels. 1639. Facsimile reproduction. Ed. by J. F. O'Doherty. I.M.C. Dublin. 1945.

4117   STRAFFORD INQUISITION. CO. MAYO. Ed. by W. O'Sullivan. I.M.C. Dublin. 1958.

4118   SURVEY AND DISTRIBUTION, Books of. Ed. by R. C. Simington and B. MacGiolla Choille. 4 vols. Dublin. 1949–65.

Vol. i, Co. Roscommon; vol. ii, Co. Mayo; vol. iii, Co. Galway; vol. iv, Co. Clare.

4119   THE TANNER LETTERS. Documents of Irish affairs in the sixteenth and seventeenth centuries extracted from the Thomas Tanner Collection in the Bodleian Library, Oxf. By C. McNeill. I.M.C. Dublin. 1943.

4120   TYRCONNELL. Letterbook of Richard Talbot, Lord Tyrconnell, 1689–90. Ed. by L. Tate. In *Analecta Hibernica*, 4 (1932), 99–133.

Cf. ibid. 1 (1930), 38–44; 4 (1932), 134–8; 21 (1959), 203–29.

4121 ULSTER PLANTATION. Survey of 1608. Ed. by J. Hogan. Orders, 1608–12. Ed. T. W. Moody. In *Analecta Hibernica*, 3 (1931); 8 (1938).

4122 VALUATIONS OF TOWNS, *c.* 1663–4. Ed. by R. C. Simington. Kells, Co. Meath, ibid. 22 (1960). Cork and Waterford in *The Civil Survey*, 6 (see no. 4097).

4123 VATICAN ARCHIVES. Irish material. Report by E. MacFhinn in *Analecta Hibernica*, 16 (1946).

4124 WADDING. Papers of Luke Wadding, 1614–38. Ed. by B. Jennings. I.M.C. Dublin. 1953.

Cf. Read, no. 6067.

4125 WEST INDIES. Irish settlers. Ed. by A. Gwynn. In *Analecta Hibernica*, 4 (1932).

4126 WILD GEESE IN SPANISH FLANDERS, 1582–1700. Document relating chiefly to Irish regiments from the Archives Générales du Royaume, Brussels, and other sources. Ed. by B. Jennings. I.M.C. Dublin. 1964.

4127 ZOILOMASTIX. By P. O'Sullivan Beare. Selection ed. by T. J. O'Donnell. I.M.C. Dublin. 1960.

(2) *Municipal Corporations and Other Organizations*

See also *supra*, no. 246, for Cork, Dublin, Galway, Kilkenny, Limerick.

4128 ATHY. Report on borough records to H.M.C. unpublished.

Transferred to I.M.C.; now in Nat. Lib. Ire.

4129 COLERAINE. Corporation petition to the viceroy, 1677[–8]. In *Analecta Hibernica*, 12 (1943).

4130 DE PRAESULIBUS HIBERNIAE. By John Lynch. Ed. by J. F. O'Doherty. 2 vols. I.M.C. Dublin. 1944.

4131 DERRY. Derry diocese temporalities [1639]. By John Bramhall. In the O'Kane papers. *Analecta Hibernica*, 12 (1943).

Marginalia on Derry diocese, by G. Downham, ibid. 12 (1943).

4132 DUBLIN. King's Hospital. Ibid. 15 (1944).

Nat. Lib. Ire. Genealogical Office. Will abstracts, ed. by P. B. Eustace (Mrs. Phair), ibid. 17 (1949); see also no. 4060 n.
Registry of Deeds. Abstracts of wills, i (1708–45), by P. B. Eustace, I.M.C., Dublin, 1956; and Eustace's *Guide*, in *Analecta Hibernica*, 23 (1966).
Trinity College. See no. 238 (H.M.C., Ser. 3, 7).

4133 FRANCISCAN ORDER. Reports. In *Analecta Hibernica*, 2 (1931), 87–91, and 3 (1931), 219–24. See also nos. 244 (H.M.C., Ser. 65), 4080.

4134 GALWAY. Report on ecclesiastical wardenship. By E. MacLysaght. In *Analecta Hibernica*, 14 (1944).

On Galway corporation see no. 246 (H.M.C., Ser. 14).

4135   IRISHTOWN, KILKENNY. Corporation, 1550–1628.

Incomplete report to H.M.C. Now in Nat. Lib. Ire.

4136   IRISH COLLEGES ABROAD. See H.M.C., no. 244, and *Topographical Index to 1914* (H.M.C.).

On Jesuits in Ireland see also no. 244.

4137   KILMAINHAM. Royal Hospital. Report by J. Ainsworth. In *Analecta Hibernica*, 23 (1966).

4138   KINSALE CORPORATION. Report, ibid. 15 (1944).

4139   LONDON CITY RECORD OFFICE. Schedule of lands in Ulster, 1613. Ed. by T. W. Moody. Ibid. 8 (1938).

4140   MONTGOMERY, G. Survey of the bishoprics of Derry, Raphoe and Clogher. Ibid. 2 (1943).

4141   OSSORY. Diocese in 1679. By Bishop T. Otway. In unpublished report to H.M.C. now in Nat. Lib. Ire.

4142   QUAKER RECORDS, DUBLIN. Abstracts of Wills. By P. B. Eustace and O. C. Goodbody. I.M.C. Dublin. 1957.

4143   VALUATION OF IRISH TOWNS. *c.* 1663–4. Cork and Waterford in *The Civil Survey*, 6 (1942). Kells, Co. Meath, in *Analecta Hibernica*, 22 (1960).

4144   WATERFORD. Corporation Council Books. 1662–1700. Ed. by S. Pender. I.M.C. Dublin. 1964.

See no. 246 (H.M.C., Ser. 14); and the unpublished report transferred to I.M.C. For valuation, see no. 4143.

(3) *Collections of Subsidiary Interest*

Many of the collections reported to H.M.C. are mentioned above in no. 247. Of special interest are nos. 72, 73, 75, 80, 87, 89, 90, 97, 101, 106, 118, 155, 159, 196, 203, 210, 245.

4145   THE ADAMS RENTAL, 1697. Co. Westmeath. By P. Walsh. In *Analecta Hibernica*, 10 (1941).

4146   ANNESLEY Collection, Castlewellan, Co. Down. Report, ibid. 16 (1946).

See also H.M.C., no. 73.

4147   BOWEN, Bowenscourt, Kildorrery, Co. Cork. MSS. Ibid. 15 (1944).

4148   BROWN, Clonboy, O'Brien's Bridge, Co. Clare. (Pearce, Quaker family in Limerick.) Ibid.

4149 CAREW, SHAPLAND. Ed. by A. K. Longfield (Mrs. H. G. Leask). I.M.C. Dublin. 1946.

4150 COLCLOUGH. Tintern Abbey, Saltmills, Co. Wexford. *Analecta Hibernica*, 20 (1958).

4151 CONNER, Dunnonanway. Co. Cork. Ibid. 15 (1944).

4152 DILLON. Clonbrook, Co. Galway. Ibid. 20 (1958).

4153 DONERAILE (St. Leger). Ibid. 15 (1944), 20 (1958).

4154 DOWDALL DEEAS. Pippard and Blundell MSS. (Lancashire R.O., Preston). Ed. by C. McNeill and A. J. Otway Ruthven. I.M.C. Dublin. 1960.

4155 DUNALLY, Kilboy, Co. Tipperary. Ed. by T. U. Sadlier. In *Analecta Hibernica*, 12 (1943).

Families of Harrison, Prittie, Sadlier.

4156 DUNSANDLE (Daly, Viscount). Formerly O'Madden Country. Ibid. 15 (1944).

4156a FERMANAGH GENEALOGIES. Ed. by E. MacNeill and C. Ó Cadhla. Ibid. 3 (1931).

4157 GENEALOGICAL COLLECTIONS. Guide by S. Pender. Ibid. 7 (1935).

See also *Genealogical tracts*, by Dubhaltach MacFirbhisigh, ed. by T. Ó Raifeartaigh, I.M.C., Dublin, 1932; *Gormanston*, Preston genealogies supp. to H.M.C., *4th Report* (unpublished), now in Nat. Lib. Ire.; 'Linea Antiqua', Irish genealogies *c.* 1710, by Roger O'Ferrall, in *Analecta Hibernica*, 10 (1941); see also no. 4166.

4158 HERBERT. Cahirnane, Killarney. Eyre, Hedges, White families. *Analecta Hibernica*, 15 (1944).

See *Herbert correspondence*, Chirbury, Powis, Dolguog [and Castleisland, Co. Kerry], ed. by W. C. Smith, I.M.C., Cardiff and Dublin, 1963.

4159 INCHQUIN (O'Brien) MSS. Ed. by J. Ainsworth. I.M.C. Dublin. 1961.

Cf. *Analecta Hibernica*, 15 (1944). Cf. no. 4177.

4160 IRISH MONASTIC AND EPISCOPAL DEEDS, A.D. 1200–1600. Ed. N. B. White. I.M.C. Dublin. 1936.

From original docs. at Kilkenny Castle, now in Nat. Lib. Ire. App. includes some 17th-century materials on monastic property after the dissolution.

4161 KENMARE (BROWNE) MSS. Ed. by E. MacLysaght. I.M.C. Dublin. 1942.

Now in the possession of Mrs. B. Grosvenor, Kenmare House, Killarney.

4162 KILDARE (FITZGERALD) CORRESPONDENCE, 1620–32. Transferred by H.M.C. with 3 unpubl. vols. of Duke of Leinster MSS. to I.M.C.,
and now in Nat. Lib. Ire.

4163 LANE, SIR G. *Analecta Hibernica*, 15 (1944).

4164 LONGFIELD. Mallow, Co. Cork. Ibid.

4165 MAC CARTHAIGH RIABHACH, BOOK OF, or the book of Lismore.
Facsimile edn. by R. A. S. Macalister. I.M.C. Dublin. 1950.

Used by M. Ó Cléirigh, 1629.

4166 MACLYSAGHT, Raheen, Tuamgraney, Co. Clare. Families of Arthur,
Brown, Reddan. *Analecta Hibernica*, 15 (1944).

See also O'Donnell genealogies, ed. by P. Walsh, ibid. 8 (1938).

4167 MANSFIELD, Newbridge, Co. Kildare and Waterford. Also Lattin of
Kildare. Ibid. 20 (1958).

See also Nugent, Farrenconnell, Mount Nugent, Co. Cavan; and Westmeath, ibid.

4168 Ó CLÉIRIGH. Book of genealogies. Ed. by S. Pender. Ibid. 18
(1951).

4169 O'GRADY. Killballyowen, Kilmallack, Co. Limerick. Ibid. 15
(1944).

Also, O'Shee, Power. Gardenmorris, Kilmacthomas, Co. Waterford; and Sheestown,
Co. Kilkenny; Cloran, Co. Tipperary, ibid. 20 (1958).

4170 [O'NEILL] Leabhar Cloinne Aodha Buidhe. Ed. by T. Ó Donnchadha.
I.M.C. Dublin. 1931.

Historical rights of O'Neill of Ulster.

4171 ORRERY (Roger Boyle, Earl of). Calendar, 1660–90. Ed. by E. Mac-
Lysaght. I.M.C. Dublin. 1941.

Cf. no. 4213.

4172 PII ANTISTITIS ICON. Life of F. Kirwan (Kirouan), bishop of
Killala, 1645–61, by John Lynch, St. Malo, 1669. Facsimile edn. by R. I. Best.
I.M.C. Dublin. 1951.

Supersedes 1884 edn. by C. P. Meehan.

4173 ROCHE OF FERMOY. *Analecta Hibernica*, 15 (1944).

See also Segrave of Cabra, Dublin, ibid. 15 (1944); and Shirley, ibid. 20 (1958). For
Shirley, cf. Ser. 4, Ettington MSS., H.M.C.

4174 SARSFIELD, COL. Dominick, Viscount Kilmallock, 1688–91.

Unpubl. H.M.C. report in Nat. Lib. Ire.

4175   SMYTH. Dumcree, Co. Westmeath. *Analecta Hibernica*, 20 (1958).

See also Ussher, Co. Waterford, ibid. 15 (1944); and Vigors, Burgage, Leighlinbridge, Co. Carlow, ibid. 20 (1958).

4176   SPANISH KNIGHTS OF IRISH ORIGIN. i, 1607–1786 (1960); ii, 1617–1889 (1965). Ed. by M. Walsh. I.M.C. Dublin.

4177   WYNDHAM (PETWORTH). *Analecta Hibernica*, 23 (1966).

Now in Nat. Lib. Ire. Cf. no. 4159.

B. POLITICAL HISTORY

Many of the sources for English political history of the Stuart period are useful also for the history of Ireland. Already referred to are materials in the reports of the Historical Manuscripts Commission (see no. 247) and numerous public records, such as the State Papers (4066) and the various foreign series (see § A of this chapter, pp. 569–73). For the earliest years of the Stuart period, certain mainly Tudor materials are useful, such as Perrott (4096) and Barnaby Rich (Read, nos. 5817 and 5819). Already listed in § A *supra* are the many important sources, such as Carty (4052) and Gilbert (4063). Especially for the years before 1660 are the Strafford inquisition (4117); Kildare correspondence (4162); the collection of letters in nos. 4107 and 4119; commonwealth accounts (4099); O'Mellan (4111); Outlaws, 1641–7 (4112); and Rinuccini (4114); and for the later decades, Orrery (4171); *Négociacions . . . d'Avaux* (4102); Jacobites (4108); and Rochester (4115). The Ormonde papers (195, 4212) are invaluable.

Among the general histories of Ireland, Bagwell (4191) is the best modern history; Dunlop's chapters as well as his bibliographies (4196) are important and good brief accounts are by Beckett (4192) and Curtis (4194). Coonan (4195) throws light on the complicated problems of the mid century, as do Murray (4202) and Simms (4204) on the period for 1689 and William III.

1. SOURCES

The arrangement is roughly in chronological order according to contents. Materials relating chiefly to the plantations are in § G *infra* on Economic History.

4178   COX, SIR RICHARD. Hibernia Anglicana, or the history of Ireland, from the conquest thereof by the English to this present time. 2 vols. 1689.

App. has docs. valuable for period of Charles I. Cox, who wrote to persuade William III to conquer Ireland, was later lord chancellor of Ireland (see no. 4241 n.). Cf. the *Annála Rioghachta Eireann: annals of the kingdom of Ireland by the four masters . . . to 1616*, ed. by John O'Donovan (4317).

4179   BELLINGS, SIR RICHARD. History of the Irish confederation and war in Ireland (1641–9). With original documents, correspondence of this confederation, and of the administration of English government in Ireland. Ed. by Sir J. T. Gilbert. 7 vols. Dublin. 1882–91.

Many docs. from the Carte Coll. in the Bodleian. For an earlier edn. of the second and third books of Bellings's account see *Desiderata Curiosa Hibernica* (4052 n.). Written from the viewpoint of the Anglo-Irish constitutional party.

4180 A CONTEMPORARY history of affairs in Ireland (1641–52): containing the . . . narrative, entitled an 'Aphorismical discovery of treasonable faction'. Ed. by Sir J. T. Gilbert. 3 vols. Dubl. Irish Arch. Soc. 1879.

From MS. F. 3. 28 in Trinity Coll., Dublin, by an author who styled himself secretary to Owen Roe O'Neill. Although considered unreliable by Carte, this account has value as representing the native or 'old Irish' view of events.

On the mission of the papal nuncio, Rinuccini, see nos. 210, 4107, and 4114. See also M. J. Hynes, *Mission of Rinuccini*, Dublin, 1932; and Wadding (4124). Also, Fr. Luke Wadding commemorative volume, ed. Franciscan fathers, Killiney, Dublin, 1957.

4181 TEMPLE, SIR JOHN. The Irish rebellion: or a history of the beginnings and first progress of the general rebellion . . . 1641. Together with the barbarous cruelties and bloody massacres which ensued thereupon. 2 pts. 1646. Later edns. 1674. 1679. 1724.

Temple, after the restoration, was embarrassed by the 1674 edn., and disclaimed responsibility. The 1678 edn., produced posthumously, in the popish plot atmosphere, enlarges the original text. Strongly anti-Catholic, it is described in *D.N.B.* as rather a partisan pamphlet than a historical treatise. Cf. Jones (4245).

4182 CLARENDON, EDWARD HYDE, EARL OF. The history of the rebellion and civil wars in Ireland. 1719. Later edn. Dublin. 1720.

Incorporated in Bandinel's edn. of Clarendon's *History of the rebellion* (305), 1849. See also *Clarendon state papers* (257); and Birch (4193). Cf. MSS. 23–4, 190 in no. 4077 (Dublin Public Lib., Gilbert). A biased account, redolent of the popish plot, is Edmund Borlase, *History of the execrable Irish rebellion* (1641–62), 1680, later edn., Dublin, 1743.

4183 CLANRICARDE, ULICK DE BURGH, MARQUIS OF. The memoirs of Ulick, marquis of Clanricarde . . . lord lieutenant of Ireland and commander in chief of the forces of King Charles . . . during the rebellion. 1757.

Letters covering Oct. 1641–Aug. 1643; later letters on the treaty with the duke of Lorraine, 1651–Aug. 1652. The latter section was separately printed in 1722 as *Memoirs of . . . Clanricarde . . . relating to the treaty between the duke of Lorraine and the Irish commissioners*. B.M. Add. MS. 42063 has 1643–7 letters. Cf. § F *infra*, on Military History, for other titles relating to the rebellion.

4184 DUNLOP, R. Ireland under the commonwealth. Being a selection of documents relating to the government of Ireland from 1651 to 1659. With historical introduction and notes. 2 vols. Manchester. 1913.

4185 L[EYBURN], G[EORGE]. Memoirs . . . being a journal of his agency for Prince Charles in Ireland in the year 1647. 1722.

4186 [LYNCH, JOHN.] Cambrensis eversus, seu potius historica fides in rebus Hibernicis Giraldo Cambrensi abrogata . . . qui etiam aliquot res memorabiles Hibernicas veteris et novae memoriae passim e re nata huic operi inseruit. [St. Malo?] 1662. Later edn. with trans. and notes by M. Kelly. 3 vols. Dublin (Celtic Soc.). 1848–52.

Lynch, 'an eminent man of letters', expresses the views of the Anglo-Irish Catholic constitutional party. He 'defends the Cessation of 1643, the peaces of 1646 and 1648, condemns the nuncio'. *D.N.B.* Cf. P. J. Corish in *I. H. Stud.* 8 (1952–3), 171–2, 217–36. See also no. 4318.

4187 FRENCH, NICHOLAS [Bishop of Ferns]. The historical works of, ...
now first collected, with an introduction containing notices historical and
descriptive of the Irish colleges of Louvain. Ed. by S. H. Bindon. 2 vols.
Dublin. 1846.

Includes (1) *Narrative of . . . Clarendon's settlement and sale of Ireland* (publ. Louvain,
1668, repr. Lond. 1704); (2) *The bleeding Iphigenia* (Louvain, 1675); (3) *The unkinde
desertor of loyall men and true friends* (Louvain, 1676). The desertor is Ormonde. Cf.
P. J. Corish, 'Bishop Nicholas French and the second Ormonde peace, 1648-9', *I.H.
Stud.* 6 (1948), 83–100.

4188 SAMSON, THOMAS. A narrative of the late popish plot in Ireland.
1680.

Includes also a report on Catholics killed in 1641–52. Cf. [John Bury,] *A true narrative
of the late designs of the papists*, 1679; *The information of John Macnamara . . . touching
the popish plot in Ireland*, 1680; and the narrative by David Fitzgerald (Wing, F 1072)
and James Carroll (Wing, C 644). See also Moran (4274), and C. L. Grose (10),
no. 2450 n.

4189 AN ACCOUNT OF THE TRANSACTIONS of the late King James
in Ireland, wherein is contain'd the Act of Attainder passed at Dublin, in
May 1689. 1690.

See also the important *Négociacions . . . d'Avaux* (4102).

4190 [STORY, GEORGE WALTER.] A true and impartial history of the
most material occurrences in the kingdom of Ireland during the last two years.
1691. Later edn. 1693.

Account by 'an eye witness', continued to March 1692 in the second edn. See also
Walter Harris, *History of the life and reign of William . . . king of England, in which the
affairs of Ireland are more particularly handled . . .*, 2nd edn., Dublin, 1749, with an app.
of documents.

2. LATER WORKS

4191 BAGWELL, R. Ireland under the Stuarts. 3 vols. 1906–16. Repr. 1962.

Covers the period 1603–90, with main emphasis on political events. Still the 'standard'
history, but should be supplemented by new scholarly work coming from Ireland. Comparisons with Froude (Pargellis, no. 3468) and Lecky (4200) are still useful, and, for the
international viewpoint, with Ranke (275).

4192 BECKETT, J. C. A short history of Ireland. 1952. Rev. edn. 1958. Bibl.

Also by Beckett, *Protestant dissent in Ireland, 1687–1780* (4256). His work suggests
useful new approaches.

4193 BIRCH, T. An inquiry into the share which King Charles I had in the
transactions of the earl of Glamorgan . . . in the years 1645 and 1646. 1747.
Later edn. 1756.

Birch used the copy of the Rinuccini memoirs (4114) in the possession of the earl of
Leicester; he issued *An appendix to an inquiry . . . 1755.* J. Boswell replied in *The case
of the royal martyr considered with candour*, 1758. Cf. S. R. Gardiner, 'Charles I and the
earl of Glamorgan', *E.H.R.* 2 (1887), 687–708.

4194   CURTIS, E. A history of Ireland. 1936. 6th edn. 1950.

Probably the best general account.

4195   COONAN, T. L. The Irish Catholic confederacy and the Puritan revolution. N.Y. 1954. Bibl.

Detailed account of events *c.* 1635–53, and based on wide use of sources. Valuable, including comment on political theory as well as on the narrative; sympathetic with the Irish. Cf. R. L. Schuyler, 'Ireland and the English Parliament . . .', *Pol. Sci. Quart.* 41 (1926), 489–519. But see Beckett in *Hist. Stud.* 2 (1959). On the controversy regarding evidences of the massacres in 1641–2, see M. Hickson, *Ireland in the seventeenth century,* 1884, and articles by R. Dunlop in *E.H.R.* 1 (1886), 740–3 and 2 (1887), 338–40, 527–33. Cf. T. Fitzpatrick, *The bloody bridge . . . 1641,* Dublin, 1903; for unpublished studies of the alleged massacres, see the Fitzpatrick MSS., University College, Dublin, Library. See also Meehan (4231).

4196   DUNLOP, R. Ireland to the settlement of Ulster. Camb. Mod. Hist. iii, ch. xviii. 1905.

Cont. 1611–59, ibid. iv, ch. xviii, 1906; 1660–1700, ibid. v, ch. x [3], 1908; ibid. vi, ch. xiv, 1909. All are by Dunlop and have excellent bibls. See also his introduction to *Ireland under the commonwealth* (4184), and his short history, *Ireland from the earliest times . . .,* 1922.

4197   FALKINER, C. L. Illustrations of Irish history and topography, mainly of the seventeenth century. 1904.

Cf. Falkiner, *Essays relating to Ireland . . .,* 1909.

4198   HAMILTON, ERNEST W., LORD. The Irish rebellion of 1641, with a history of the events which led up to and succeeded it. 1920.

Cf. F. Warner, *The history of the rebellion and civil war in Ireland* [1641–60], 1767, 1768.

4199   KEARNEY, H. F. Strafford in Ireland, 1633–41. N.Y. 1960.

Good on administrative history. Cf. W. H. A. O'Grady, *Strafford and Ireland,* 2 vols. Dublin, 1923. See also Strafford's *Letters and despatches* (506), and nos. 4087, 4117.

4200   LECKY, W. E. H. History of Ireland in the eighteenth century. Vol. i. 1877. 5 vols. 1892. Repr. 1908–12.

First vol. deals with the later Stuarts; includes social as well as political history. Somewhat dated but still useful.

4201   MURPHY, D. Cromwell in Ireland. A history of Cromwell's Irish campaign. 1883.

App. of documents. Valuable.

4202   MURRAY, R. H. Revolutionary Ireland and its settlement, with an introduction by Rev. J. P. Mahaffy. 1911. Maps. Bibl.

Valuable for period of James II and William III, especially on European relations, but sometimes inaccurate.

4203   PRENDERGAST, J. P. The Cromwellian settlement of Ireland. Dublin. 1865. Later edns. Dublin. 1875 and 1922.

Somewhat disappointing. Also by Prendergast, *Ireland from the restoration to the revolution, 1660 to 1690*, 1887. On the land settlements compare with Simms (q.v.). On the lieutenancy of the earl of Essex see no. 4207.

4204 SIMMS, J. G. The Williamite confiscation in Ireland. 1956.

Important evaluation of evidence regarding Catholic land losses.

3. Correspondence, Journals, and Biographies

See also Chichester (4095); Radcliffe (493); Rochester (4115); Strafford (506). An Irish equivalent of the Welsh biographical dictionary is overdue. Still needing biographers are Chichester and Sir John Davies.

CLARENDON, HENRY HYDE, EARL OF

4205 The state letters of . . . Clarendon, lord lieutenant of Ireland during the reign of James the Second and . . . diary, 1687–90. Ed. by J. Douglas. 2 vols. Oxf. 1763. Repr. Dublin. 1765. Later edn. by S. W. Singer. 2 vols. Lond. 1828.

The 1828 edn., under title of *The correspondence of . . . Clarendon*, includes letters of his brother Lawrence, earl of Rochester, and various family matters.

CORK, RICHARD BOYLE, EARL OF

4206 Lismore papers. Ed. by A. B. Grosart. 10 vols. 1886–8.

Formerly preserved in Lismore Castle, now in the National Library of Ireland. The first series (5 vols.) contains the earl's diary, 1611–43. The second series contains correspondence to and from him. A modern biography is needed, although of some use is D. Townshend, *The life and letters of the great earl of Cork*, 1904. For Grosart's editorial methods see T. Ranger in *I.H.Stud.* 10 (1957).

ESSEX, ARTHUR CAPEL, EARL OF

4207 Letters written by . . . Essex, lord lieutenant of Ireland in . . . 1675. 1770. Later edn. Dublin. 1773.

Life prefixed; based upon B.M. Stowe MSS. 200–17. Cf. *Essex papers* (1672–7), ed. by O. Airy and C. E. Pike, 2 vols., Camden Soc., 1890, 1913. There are Essex papers in B.M. Add. MS. 36786, as well as Stowe, and in the Bodl. Libr. Western MSS. 11839, 30231–5; see Grose (10), no. 2401. See also C. E. Pike, 'Intrigue to deprive . . . Essex of the lord lieutenancy of Ireland', *R.H.S. Trans.*, 3rd Ser. 5 (1911), 89–103.

GRANARD, EARLS OF

4208 Memoirs of the earls of Granard. By John Forbes. Ed. by George A. H. Forbes, earl of Granard. 1868.

App. of docs. for Irish history. Cf. H.M.C., *2nd report*, 210–17.

LUCAN, PATRICK SARSFIELD, EARL OF

4209 Life of Patrick Sarsfield, earl of Lucan, with a short narrative of the principal events of the Jacobite war in Ireland. By J. Todhunter. 1895.

In Duffy's New Irish Library, vol. vii. Cf. modern biog. by A. Curtayne (Noted Irish Lives Ser.), 1934, bibl. For Col. Dominick Sarsfield, see no. 4174.

O'NEILL, HUGH [EARL OF TYRONE]

4210 Fate and fortunes of Hugh O'Neill, earl of Tyrone, and Rory O'Donel, earl of Tyrconnel; their flight from Ireland and death in exile. By C. P. Meehan. Dublin (Lond.). 1868. 1870. Rev. edn. 1886.

App. has docs. from Carew MSS. and from those of the Irish college at Salamanca, now in Maynooth College. See also P. Walsh, *Will and family of H. O'Neill*, Dublin, 1930. A popular biography, based on good materials, is S. O'Faslaín, *The great O'Neill . . .*, 1943; counteracts the 'hagiographical aura' of earlier lives. Cf. no. 4170.

O'NEILL, OWEN ROE

4211 Owen Roe O'Neill. By J. F. Taylor. 1896.

To be used with some caution. Cf. E. O'Neill, *Owen Roe O'Neill* (Noted Irish Lives Ser.), Dublin and Lond. 1937.

ORMONDE, JAMES BUTLER, DUKE OF

4212 The life of James duke of Ormond; containing an account of . . . Ireland under his government; with an appendix and a collection of letters. By Thomas Carte. 3 vols. 1735-6. 2nd edn. (best). 6 vols. Oxf. 1851.

The title is that of the second edn. An 'indispensable work' for the period 1610-88, by the great collector whose MSS. (now at the Bodl. Libr.) are so rich a resource for Irish history (see no. 4085). For the official papers transcribed for the P.R.O. and P.R.O.I. see *Reps. dep. keeper publ. rec.* 32, app. 1 (1871). See also no. 195. Ormonde might be described as 'the Clarendon of Ireland' in the period after 1660.

Useful also, but not definitive, is the *Life* by Winifred G., Lady Burghclere, 2 vols., 1912.

ORRERY, ROGER BOYLE, FIRST EARL OF

4213 A collection of the state letters of . . . Roger Boyle, the first earl of Orrery, lord president of Munster in Ireland . . . Ed. by T. Morrice. 1742. Later edn. 2 vols. Dublin. 1743.

Contains also Orrery corresp. (1660-8) with Ormonde, and a favourable biog. by his chaplain, Morrice. See also the important *Calendar*, ed. by E. MacLysaght (4171).

RAWDON, SIR GEORGE

4214 Sir George Rawdon, a sketch of his life and times. By M. Beckett. Belfast. 1935.

A favourable view. Rawdon was active in Irish politics, from *temp.* James I until after the restoration.

C. CONSTITUTIONAL HISTORY

The question of rulership, involving traditions of Gaelic-Irish independence, and of constitutional liberties among the English, was the great question in successive crises during the century. Behind the question of the ruler there were also the religious conflicts and the struggle for political power and land ownership; after 1649 the latter was particularly prominent. Official papers included in nos. 4215 and 4220-1 are valuable for this subject, as are the later works of MacNeill (4216), Ball (4240), Bagwell (4191), and Kearney (4199).

The Confederation of Kilkenny, as well as the Commonwealth Parliaments and that of James II should be included in the parliamentary history. On the first the work of Meehan, though incomplete, has not yet been replaced. Much more analysis is needed on the editions both of statutes and of journals of the Parliaments; Moody's study for that of James I (4224) is valuable; the accounts on that of 1689 (4226) are incomplete.

On local government, except for Bolton, almost nothing has been done.

Reference should be made to various works in Ch. III *supra*, such as *Bibliotheca Lindesiana*, vol. ii (716) for royal proclamations; *Acts of the Privy Council* (735); on Parliaments, Porritt, vol. ii (890), Oldfield (898), vol. vi, and the state papers. For governments of towns see § J *infra* on Local History.

1. GENERAL

4215 LASCELLES, R. Liber munerum publicorum Hiberniae ab an. 1152 usque ad 1827, or, the establishments of Ireland. 2 vols. 1824–30. 2nd edn. 1852.

Index, *Reports of the deputy keeper of public records in Ireland*, 9, Dublin, 1877. Imperfect, but the chief source for Irish official appointments; includes excerpts from journals and sessional papers. Cf. Hughes, *Patentee officers* (4047). For chief governors see *Handbook of British chronology*, 2nd edn. (Royal Hist. Soc.).

4216 MacNEILL, J. G. S. Constitutional and parliamentary history of Ireland till the Union. 1917.

Based on secondary materials. Cf. Molyneux (4233).

2. EXECUTIVE

See also Chichester (4095), Kearny (4199), Bonnell (4250), and the papers of various lords lieutenant in § B 3 *supra* above.

4217 HOGAN, J. 'The Irish law of kingship.' *Proc. R.I.A.* 40, Sect. C (1932), 186–254.

Davies, 'The case of tanistry' in no. 4236 *infra* is considered historically in W. F. T. Butler, *Gleanings from Irish history*, 1925.

4218 HUGHES, J. L. J. 'The chief secretaries in Ireland, 1566–1921.' *I.H. Stud.* 8 (1952), 59–72.

Cf. *Handbook* (4215).

4219 WOOD, H. 'The offices of secretary of state and keeper of the signet or privy seal.' *Proc. R.I.A.* 38, Sect. C (1928), 51–68.

For some printed records of the Irish Council, see no. 4107.

3. JUDICIARY

4220 COURT OF CASTLE CHAMBER. Records, in possession of the earl of Egmont. 2 vols. in 3. H.M.C. 1905–9.

H.M.C. *Reports 7* and *17*, in which the entry books are calendared. Vol. i is 1573–1620; vol. ii contains entries of the 17th–18th centuries. Cf. H. Wood, 'The court of Castle chamber, or star chamber of Ireland', *Proc. R.I.A.* 32, Sect. C, no. 10 (1914), 152–70. See also V. W. Treadwell, 'The Irish court of wards under James I', *I. H. Stud.* 12 (1960).

4221 HIS MAJESTIES DIRECTIONS for the ordering and setling of the courts, and course of justice, within his kingdom of Ireland. Dublin. 1622.

To be edited for Ir. MSS. Comm. by G. J. Hand and V. W. Treadwell. On appeals in Irish courts, 1710–30, see no. 4065. See also Ball (4240), O'Flanagan (4241), and other titles in *Legal History*, § D.

4. LEGISLATURE

For relations with the English Parliament, see no. 4104, as well as the titles in Ch. III *supra*, § D on Parliament.

(a) *Parliament in Ireland*

4222 THE STATUTES AT LARGE passed in the Parliament held in Ireland (1310–1800). 20 vols. Dublin. 1786–1801.

An earlier collection, compiled by Sir Richard Bolton, from 3 Edward II to 11 James I, was publ. in Dublin, 1621. See also *A collection of all the statutes now in use in the kingdom of Ireland* . . ., Dublin, 1678, which contains the Acts of Settlement and Explanation. For the Acts of the Parliament of 1689, not included in the 1786–1801 publication, consult Davis, *The Patriot Parliament* (4226 n.).

4223 BALL, J. T. Historical review of the legislative systems operative in Ireland from the invasion of Henry II to the union, 1172–1800. 1888. Later edn. Dublin. 1889.

Cf. R. D. Edwards and T. W. Moody, 'The history of Poynings' Law 1495–1615', *I.H. Stud.* 2 (1941), 415–24.

4224 MOODY, T. W. 'The Irish Parliament under Elizabeth and James I: a general survey.' *Proc. R.I.A.* 45 (1939), 41–81.

Apps. listing parliamentary boroughs 1560–1613, and the Catholic and Protestant members returned in 1613. Cf. Treadwell (4227 n.).

4225 MOUNTMORRES, H. R. MORRES, LORD. The history of the principal transactions of the Irish Parliament (1634–66). 2 vols. 1792.

Includes Sir Robert Southwell's life of the 1st duke of Ormonde and some papers on finance and trade.

4226 A TRUE ACCOUNT of the whole proceedings of the Parliament in Ireland beginning March 25, 1689. 1689.

Cf. *The journal of the proceedings of the Parliament*, 1689; *A journal of the proceedings of the pretended Parliament* (*Somers Tracts*, iv, ed. 1750); *An exact list of the lords spiritual and temporal who sate in the pretended Parliament*, 1689. A 'polemical' account is T. O. Davis, *The Patriot Parliament of 1689*, ed. by Sir C. G. Davis (The New Irish Library), 1893 (first pr. in the *Dublin Magazine* in 1843). Cf. T. D. Ingram, *Two chapters of Irish history*, 1888, which presents 'a clever piece of special pleading'. See also C. Preston, 'The Irish Parliament of 1689', *Irish Eccl. Rec.* 70 (1948), 715–30; and D. Savory, 'The all-Irish "Patriot Parliament" of 1689', *Proc. Huguenot Soc. London*, 19 (1953), 56–64.

(b) *House of Lords*

4227 JOURNALS OF THE HOUSE OF LORDS of the kingdom of Ireland from . . . 1634 to . . . 1800. 8 vols. Dublin. 1779–1800.

A journal from 17 March 1640 to 5 March 1641 with variations from the above is in H.M.C., *Various 8* (Clements MSS.), pp. 200–14. See also V. Treadwell, 'The House of Lords in the Irish Parliament of 1613–1615', *E.H.R.* 80 (1965), 92–107, which prints, from B.M. Add. MS. 4792, an index to the last Lords' journal of 1613–15.

(c) *House of Commons*

4228 THE JOURNALS OF THE HOUSE OF COMMONS of the kingdom of Ireland . . . 1613 . . . 1800. App. and Index. 20 vols. Dublin. 1796–1800.

See J. P. Prendergast, on Sir Audley Mervyn, Speaker, 1661–6, in *R.H.S. Trans.* 3 (1874), 421–54. *An account of the sessions of Parliament in Ireland, 1692*, was pr. in 1693.

4229 BURTCHAELL, G. D. Genealogical memoirs of the members of Parliament for the county and city of Kilkenny. Dublin. 1888.

Cf. S. R. Lowry-Corry, earl of Belmore, *Parliamentary memoirs of Fermanagh and Tyrone* (1613–1885), Dublin, 1887. Several lists of M.P.s are mentioned in Grose (10), no. 2420.

(d) *Confederation of Kilkenny*

4230 DARCY, PATRICK. Model of civil government [1642]. In Bellings (4179), ii, pp. 73–89.

Darcy's draft of the constitution for the revised government of Ireland is contained also in *Commentarius Rinuccinianus* (4114), i. 320–6. See Coonan (4195), ch. x, and Meehan, *infra*.

4231 MEEHAN, C. P. The confederation of Kilkenny. Dublin. 1846. Later enl. edn. Dublin. 1882.

See also Bellings (4179) and no. 4180; for an evaluation of the principal contemporary sources on the Irish Catholic confederacy see Coonan (4195). The Barbarini MSS., Nat. Lib. Ire., contain materials on diplomatic representatives to the confederation from the Holy See. See also J. F. O'Doherty, 'The confederation of Kilkenny', in *Blessed Oliver Plunket, Historical Studies*, Dublin (For the League of Prayer for the Canonization of Blessed Oliver Plunket), 1937.

5. POLITICAL THEORY

4232 DAVIES, SIR JOHN. A discovery of the true causes why Ireland was never . . . brought under obedience of the crowne of England, untill the beginning of his majesties happie raigne. [Lond.] 1612.

Various later edns., of which good ones are by G. Chalmers, *Historical tracts, . . .*, 1786; and by A. B. Grosart, *Works of Sir John Davies*, 3 vols., 1869–76.

4233 MOLYNEUX, WILLIAM. The case of Ireland's being bound by Act of Parliament in England stated. Dublin. 1697 or 1698. Later edn. Dublin. 1725.

Edn. of 1725: 'To which is added the case of tenures upon the commission of defective titles (Trin. 13 Caroli Regis), argued by all the judges of Ireland. With their resolutions and the reasons' (no. 4237, *infra*). The original autograph is in Trinity College, Dublin, no. 890 in Abbott's *Catalogue*. The author 'accepts the superior position of the English Parliament but argues that the alternatives are a legislative union or a greater freedom for Ireland'.

For replies to Molyneux see [John Cary], *Answer*, 1698, and [William Atwood], *History*, 1698. On Molyneux's arguments see Clark, *Later Stuarts* (267), 320–1.

D. LEGAL HISTORY

1. REFERENCES AND SOURCES

For bibliography see vol. iv of Maxwell and Maxwell (1002). Manuscript materials on Irish common-law cases exist in the archives of the House of Lords, Westminster, and there are printed abstracts of many such cases in the King's Inns, Dublin, and in the National Library of Ireland. Records of many ecclesiastical appeals exist in the papal archives at Rome, particularly of the Holy Office and the Congregatio de Propaganda Fide; some abstracts have been printed in *Archivium Hibernicum* and *Collectanea Hibernica*. For Brehon law there are the resources of Gaelic Irish linguistic materials in the Br. Mus. (Cat. Irish MSS.), Trinity College, Dublin (Cat. Irish MSS.), the Royal Irish Academy (Irish MSS.), and the National Library of Ireland.

4234 A REPERTORY of the inrolments of the patent roles of Chancery, in Ireland; commencing with the reign of King James I. Ed. by J. C. Erck. Dublin. 1846.

Only the first part of this work was published. Cf. J. Ainsworth, 'Some abstracts of chancery suits relating to Ireland', *Jour. R.S.A.I.* 69 (1939), 39–44.

4235 CALENDAR of the patent and close rolls of Chancery in Ireland of the reign of Charles the First. First to eighth year inclusive. Ed. by J. Morrin. Dublin. 1863.

Sharply criticized in 'On the history, position, and treatment of the public records of Ireland', by an Irish Archivist, i.e. Sir J. T. Gilbert (2nd edn., Lond. 1864).

4236 DAVIES, SIR JOHN. Le primer report des cases et matters en ley resolues et adiudges en les courts de roy en Ireland. Dublin. 1615. Later edns. Lond. 1628 and 1674. Dublin. 1762 [a trans.]. Edin. 1907 (The English Reports, vol. 80).

See also Grosart edn. of *Works* (4232 n.).

4237 BARRY, JAMES. The case of tenures upon commission of defective titles, argued by all the judges of Ireland, with their resolution, and the reasons of their resolution. Dublin. 1637.

Cf. no. 4233 n. above.

2. HISTORIES AND TREATISES

4238 MacNEILL, E. 'Ireland and Wales in the history of jurisprudence.' *Studies*, 16 (1927), 254–8, 605–15.

Also see his article in *Jour. R.S.A.I.* 57 (1927), 154–5. On the exchequer in Ireland see G. E. Howard's treatises, 1759–60, 1776, in Grose (10), no. 2422.

4239 BADE, E. S. 'A princely judgment. The earl of Ormond's case.' *Minnesota Law Rev.* 23 (1939), 925–40.

Analyses judicial processes involved.

3. Courts and Justices

4240 BALL, F. E. The judges of Ireland, 1221–1921. 2 vols. 1926.

Includes biog. sketches and gives an account of legal developments. There are notes by Ball on the judiciary, 1660–85, in *Jour. Cork Hist. Arch. Soc.*, 2nd Ser., vols. 7–9 (1901–3).

4241 O'FLANAGAN, J. R. The lives of the lord chancellors and keepers of the great seal of Ireland. 2 vols. 1870.

Cf. C. J. Smyth, *Chronicle of the law officers of Ireland containing lists of the lord chancellors and keepers of the great seal, masters of the rolls . . . from the earliest period*, Dublin, 1839. On individuals see R. Caulfield, *Autobiography of Richard Cox . . . lord chancellor of Ireland*, 1860 (see Cox's *Hibernia Anglicana*, no. 4178); and F. W. X. Fincham, 'Letters concerning Sir Maurice Eustace' (1660–5), *E.H.R.* 35 (1920), 251–9. Lists of lawyers prepared by T. U. Sadleir are in the possession of the Ir. MSS. Comm.

4242 BOLTON, SIR RICHARD. A justice of peace for Ireland, consisting of two bookes: whereunto are added many presidents of indictments of treasons, felonies . . . Dublin. 1638. 1683.

E. RELIGIOUS HISTORY

Many of the collections referred to in § A of this chapter relate to matters of religion. Besides the important Vatican Archives (4089), and those in other places on the continent (e.g. 4067, 4068, 4070, 4071), the repositories in Ireland have much evidence to offer on the various religious groups, whether the official Church of Ireland, the Roman Catholics, or some branch of Protestant dissent. Useful titles will be found also in Ch. V *supra*. See also Gwynn's bibliography (4048).

Parochial records are described in *Reports of the deputy keeper of the public records, Ireland* (4062), vols. 13–28 (1881–96), *passim*, and a *Handlist of Irish diocesan histories* (4051). See also § J *infra* on Local History. For land distributions see § G *infra* on Economic History.

I. General

4243 EDWARDS, R. D. Church and state in Tudor Ireland. A history of penal laws against Irish Catholics, 1534–1603. Dublin. 1935. Bibl.

'Standard' for the 16th century, and provides background for study of the Stuart period. Also important for background is *Irish monastic and episcopal deeds* (4160).

4244 KILLEN, W. D. The ecclesiastical history of Ireland from the earliest period to the present times. 2 vols. Belfast. 1875.

Cf. M. J. Brenan, *An ecclesiastical history of Ireland . . .*, 2 vols., Dublin, 1840; rev. edn. Dublin, 1864.

2. CHURCH OF IRELAND

(a) *Sources*

See no. 4077, especially J. B. Leslie's catalogue of the MSS. relating to the Representative Church Body. On pamphlets see p. 566. The bibl. in no. 4249 is valuable.

4245 JONES, HENRY. A remonstrance of divers remarkable passages concerning the church and kingdom of Ireland, to the honourable House of Commons in England. 1642.

> Based on the personal experiences of Jones and on extracts out of the depositions now preserved in Trinity College Dublin Library (repr. in Somers Tracts, vol. v, pp. 573–624). Also by Jones, who was bishop of Neath, *A remonstrance* [*relation?*] *of the beginning and proceedings of the rebellion of county Cavan*, 1642. (See Wing, J 943, 944.) Repr. in Somers Tracts, vol. v, and in no. 4180. Coonan (4195) considers Jones 'an unreliable witness', owing to his deep interest in the forfeitures and transplantations.

4246 [KING, WILLIAM.] Archbishop of Dublin. The state of the protestants of Ireland under the late King James's government: in which their carriage towards him is justified, and the . . . necessity . . . of submitting to their present majesties is demonstrated. 1691. 4th edn., with additions. 1692.

> Cf. Charles Leslie's *An answer to a book entituled the state* . . ., 1692. See also no. 4253.

4247 COTTON, HENRY. Fasti ecclesiae Hibernicae: the succession of the prelates and members of the ecclesiastical bodies in Ireland. 6 vols. Dublin. 1845–78.

> Vol. vi is a suppl. by C. P. Cotton. Contains brief biographies and matters relating to appointments. See also J. D'Alton, *Memoirs of the archbishops of Dublin*, Dublin, 1838. Succession lists also in R.C.B. library (nos. 4077 n., 4113).

(b) *Later Works*

4248 BALL, J. T. The reformed Church of Ireland (1537–1889). 1886. Rev. edn. 1890.

> Useful, especially on ecclesiastical legislation. Cf. J. C. Beckett, 'The government and the Church of Ireland under William III and Anne', *I. H. Stud.* 2 (1941), 280–302.

4249 PHILLIPS, W. A., ed. History of the Church of Ireland. 3 vols. 1933–4.

> A collaborative history. Still useful, with more details, is R. Mant, *History of the Church of Ireland* (from the reformation to 1801), 2 vols., 1840, 2nd edn., 1841. The first vol. goes to 1689; both vols. include documents, and represent the Anglican view. See also T. Olden, *The Church of Ireland*, 1902.

(c) *Biographies*

See also Cotton (4247).

BONNELL, JAMES

4250 The exemplary life . . . of James Bonnell, . . . late accomptant-general of Ireland. By William Hamilton. Dublin. 1703. Later edns. 1707 (Lond.). 1718.

Sermon at Bonnell's funeral, 1699. See also C. L. Falkiner, ed., 'Some letters of Toby and James Bonnell (1660–90)', *E.H.R.* 19 (1904), 122–8, 299–306; and J. A. Carr, 'James Bonnell', *Churchman*, N.S. 14 (1900), 11–26. Bonnell was a figure in administrative history, *temp.* William III.

BEDELL, WILLIAM

4251 Memoir of the life and episcopate of William Bedell, lord bishop of Kilmore. Printed . . . from . . . MS. in the Harleian Collection. By A. Clogy or Clogie. Ed. by W. W. Wilkins. 1862. Later edn. by E. S. Shuckburgh. Camb. 1902.

Edn. of 1902, entitled *Two biographies of William Bedell . . .*, includes as the second *The true relation of the life and death of William Bedell*, by W. Bedell, Jr. (ed. by T. W. Jones for Camden Soc., 1872; original in Bodl. Lib. Tanner MS. cclxxvii). 'This is the most trustworthy source.' Gilbert Burnet's *Life*, based on information supplied by Clogie, was publ. in 1685, 3rd edn., Dublin, 1758.

BRAMHALL, JOHN

4252 Life of Archbishop Bramhall, prefixed to his Works. By John Vesey, archbishop of Tuam. Dublin. 1676. Later edns. Dublin. 1677. Ed. by G. Ingram. Bury St. Edmonds. 1841.

The 1841 edn. is repr. from the Dublin edn. of 1677, with notes. The *Works*, to which Vesey's biog. was a prefix, were pr. in 4 vols., Dublin, 1676 (see no. 1227). See also E. Berwick, ed., *The Rawdon papers, consisting of letters . . . to and from J. Bramhall, Primate of Ireland*, 1819. There are biographies by W. B. Wright, 1899, and W. J. S. Simpson, 1927, as well as in no. 1227.

KING, WILLIAM

4253 A great archbishop of Dublin [William King], 1650–1729; his autobiography . . . and a selection from his correspondence. Ed. by C. S. King. 1906.

The King MSS., H.M.C., *Reports* 2 (231 seq.) and 3 (416 seq.) (see no. 247), are now at Trin. Coll. Lib., Dublin. A Latin autobiog. was pr. in *E.H.R.* 13 (1898), 309–23; a diary kept during his imprisonment 1689, ed. by H. J. Lawlor, was repr. from the *Jour. R.S.A.I.*, Dublin, 1903. Cf. J. C. Beckett, 'William King's administration of the diocese of Derry, 1691–1703', *I.H. Stud.* 4 (1944), 164–80; and J. M. Hone, in *Dublin Mag.* 9 (1934), 51–6. For MSS. collected by King see no. 4095 *supra*.

SWIFT, JONATHAN

4254 Jonathan Swift, dean and pastor. By R. W. Jackson. 1939.

See also Landa, *Swift and the Church of Ireland* (2598 n.); and Lecky, *Leaders*, 1871 edn. (Pargellis (II), no. 3545).

USHER [USSHER], JAMES

4255 Life . . . By C. R. Elrington. Dublin. 1847. 1848.

See no. 1289. A corrected copy of the life and of vols. xv and xvi of the correspondence, with an index by Bishop Reeves, is in Trin. Coll. Lib., Dublin (see Abbott's Cat., nos. 1072–5).

3. NONCONFORMITY

(a) *General*

4256   BECKETT, J. C. Protestant dissent in Ireland, 1687–1780. 1948.

Studies in Irish Hist., vol. 2. Cf. A. S. de Blacam, 'The other hidden Ireland', *Studies*, 23 (1934), 439–54.

4257   SEYMOUR, St. J. D. The Puritans in Ireland, 1647–1661. Oxf. 1921.

On the organization of the Puritan Church; list of ministers in app.

(b) *Presbyterianism*

See also no. 4073; and Hill (4292). There are pamphlets at Londonderry (see no. 4082, and p. 566 *supra*).

4258   KILLEN, W. D., ed. A true narrative of the rise and progress of the Presbyterian church in Ireland (1623–70). [By Patrick Adair.] Also the History of the church in Ireland since the Scots were naturalized. By the Rev. A. Stewart. Belfast. 1866.

On errors in this edn. see *Northern Whig*, Oct. and Nov., 1867. Other contemporary material is in: [James Kirkpatrick], *Historical essay on the loyalty of the Presbyterians in Great Britain and Ireland . . . to 1713* [Belfast], 1713; and Th. Witherow, *Historical and literary memorials of Presbyterianism in Ireland, 1623–1731*, 1879.

4259   REID, J. S. History of the Presbyterian Church in Ireland, comprising the civil history of the province of Ulster from the accession of James the first. 3 vols. Belfast. 1834. Later edn. by W. D. Killen. Belfast. 1867.

Cf. W. T. Latimer, *A history of the Irish Presbyterians*, Belfast [1893], later edn. 1902; and O. A. Marti, 'Passive resistance of the Scotch-Irish Presbyterians during the period of revolution, 1660–1672', *Jour. of Religion*, 8 (1928), 581–602. See also C. E. Pike, 'The origin of the regium donum', *R.H.S. Trans.*, 3rd Ser. 3 (1909), 205–69; and Eager, no. 679.

(c) *Quakers*

See also Dublin, Society of Friends (4077).

4260   RUTTY, J. and WIGHT, T. A history of the rise and progress of the people called Quakers in Ireland (1653–1751). Dublin. 1751. Later edn. Lond. 1800.

See also *A journal of the life, travels, suffering . . . of . . . William Edmundson*, Dublin, 1715 (many repr.), an autobiography useful for political and social as well as religious history; and Eustace and Goodbody, *Quaker Records, Dublin, abstract of wills* (4142).

(d) *Huguenots*

4261   LEE, G. L. The Huguenot settlements in Ireland. 1936.

Also useful is A. Carré, *L'influence des Huguenots français en Irlande aux xviie et xviiie siècles*, Paris, 1937. In H. J. Lawlor, *Fasti of St. Patrick's, Dublin* (Dundalk, 1930) is an app. by T. P. le Fanu on the Huguenots who met there.

4. ROMAN CATHOLICISM

For sources relating to Roman Catholicism in England and also in Ireland, see Pollen (1446) and the Catholic Record Society (1447), as well as those mentioned in the introductory paragraphs of this section on p. 590. For pamphlets see p. 566. References to dioceses will be found in § J *infra* on Local History.

(a) *Sources (General)*

See also Rinuccini (nos. 210 and 4114); also nos. 4123, 4179, 4180, and French (4187).

4262   ROTHE, DAVID. Analecta sacra nova et mira de rebus Catholicorum in Hibernia . . . gestis. Pt. i. Cologne. 1616. Pts. i and ii. Cologne. 1617. Pt. iii, entitled *De processu martyriali*. Cologne. 1619. Ed. by P. F. Moran. Dublin. 1884.

Rothe, the learned Roman Catholic bishop of Ossory, attacks the Irish ecclesiastical policy of Elizabeth and James I. Cf. M. V. Ronan, 'A contemporary English transcript of the *Analecta Sacra* of David Rothe, bishop of Ossory (1618–1650)', *R.I.A. Proc.* 42, Sect. C (1935), 193–8.

4263   WALSH, PETER. The history and vindication of the loyal formulary or Irish remonstrance . . . received by his majesty . . . 1661. Against all the calumnies and censures . . . With a true account of the delusory Irish remonstrances . . . 1666. 1674.

Walsh, a Franciscan, but an Ormondist in the conflict of the civil war period, was denounced by the supporters of the papal nuncio. His position was also maintained by Raymond Caron, *Loyalty asserted, and the late remonstrance . . . of the Irish clergy and layty confirmed . . .*, 1662.

4264   MORAN, P. F., ed. Spicilegium Ossoriense: being a collection of original letters and papers illustrative of the history of the Irish church from the reformation to the year 1800. 3 vols. Dublin. 1874–84.

Important collection on affairs of the Irish Catholics. There are numerous miscellaneous docs. also in D. MacCarthy, ed., *Collections of Irish church history from the MSS. of the late Laurence F. Renehan*, 2 vols., Dublin, 1861–74. On officials, are Brady, *The episcopal succession* (1454), and Cotton (4247). See also biographies, *infra*. A good collection on a great Catholic family is no. 4161.

4265   HAGAN, J., ed. 'Miscellanea Vaticano-Hibernica.' In *Archiv. Hibern.*, 1914–22.

Papers from Vatican archives pr. *in extenso*, with brief calendars in English. See nos. 4089, 4123.

4266   O'REILLY, M. W. P. Memorials of those who suffered for the Catholic faith in Ireland in the sixteenth, seventeenth and eighteenth centuries. 1868.

Collected and edited from original sources. See also C. L. Grose (10), no. 2449 n.; and *Summarium beatificationis martyrii D. O'Harley, C. O'Devany et sociorum*, Rome, 1914.

(b) *Later Works* (*General*)

4267 BELLESHEIM, A. Geschichte der Katholischen Kirche in Irland.
3 vols. Mainz. 1890–1. Bibl.

Vol. ii relates to the years 1509–1690. A portion of this work was trans. by W. McLough-
lin as *The papal nuncio Archbishop Rinuccini* . . ., Dublin, 1908. Cf. P. F. Moran, *History
of the Catholic archbishops of Dublin* [to 1641], Dublin, 1864; and M. O'Conor, *The
history of the Irish Catholics from* . . . *1691 to the revolution*, Dublin, 1813.

4268 EDWARDS, R. D. 'Irish Catholics and the Puritan revolution.' In
Father Luke Wadding commemorative volume. Dublin. 1957.

Cf. J. MacCaffrey, 'The position of the Irish Catholics during the reign of James I',
Irish Theol. Quart. 10 (1915).

4269 PARNELL, H. B. A history of the penal laws against the Irish Catholics,
from . . . 1689 to the union. 1808. 4th edn. 1825.

See also R. D. Edwards, 'The history of the penal laws against the Catholics in Ireland
(1534–1691)', *Bull. Inst. Hist. Research,* 11 (1934), 185–9; W. P. Burke, *The Irish priests
in penal times (1660–1760),* Waterford, 1914; and C. Meehan, ed., *The Geraldines, earls
of Desmond and the persecution of the Irish Catholics* (trans. from the Latin of Daniel
Daly), Dublin, 1847; M. V. Ronan, *The Irish martyrs of the penal laws,* 1935; and J. G.
Simms, 'Land owned by Catholics in Ireland in 1688', *I. H. Stud.* 7 (1951), 180–90.
Cf. no. 4243.

(c) *Orders*

4270 BURKE (*seu* DE BURGO), THOMAS. Hibernia dominicana. Cologne
[Kilkenny]. 1762. Suppl. 1772.

See Read, no. 6008. A history of the Dominican order in Ireland. On the Jesuits, see
E. Hogan, ed., *Ibernia Ignatiana, seu Ibernorum societatis Jesu patrum monumenta collecta*
. . . (*1540–1607*), Dublin, 1880. Cf. H.M.C., *Rep. 10,* app. v. Regarding the Carmelite
friars, see J. P. Rushe, *Carmel in Ireland,* 2nd edn., 1903. Cf. *Archivium Hibernicum,*
25 (1962).

4271 MEEHAN, C. P. The rise and fall of the Irish Franciscan monasteries,
and memoirs of the Irish hierarchy in the seventeenth century. Dublin (Lond.).
1869. 5th edn. Dublin [1877].

To be used with some caution. On the Franciscans MSS. at Dublin and Killiney see
nos. 4077, 4080, 4133, as well as H.M.C., no. 244. See also a report on a visitation
c. 1615, ed. by B. Jennings, *Analecta Hibernica,* 6 (1934), 12–131; W. D. O'Connell,
'Franciscan reorganization in Munster during the early seventeenth century', *Jour. Cork
Hist. and Arch. Soc.,* 2nd Ser. 44 (1939), 37–45; the papers of Father Luke Wadding,
author of *Annales minorum* (Read, no. 6067), an important figure at the papal court
(4124); and B. Millett, *The Irish Franciscans, 1651–65,* Rome, 1964.

(d) *Biography*

4272 D'ALTON, J. Illustrations, historical and genealogical, of King James's
Irish army list, 1689. Dublin. 1855. Best edn. 2 vols. Dublin. 1861.

Valuable for Irish support for James II and for the history of the principal Roman
Catholic families in Ireland.

4273   MARTIN, F. X. Friar Francis Lavalan Nugent (1569–1635). 1962.

See also various memoirs in Brady (1454), Butler (1458 n.); Lynch's biography of
Bishop Kirwan in no. 4172; P. Power, *Bishop of penal times: being reports and letters of
John Brenan, bishop of Waterford (1671–1693), and bishop of Cashel (1677–1693)*,
Dublin, 1932, Cork, 1933 (also in *Irish Eccles. Rec.*, 1932). There are biographical
sketches by J. Corboy on Fathers David Galway (d. 1634), *Irish Monthly*, 62 (1944),
58–67; James Archer (d. 1625), Henry Fitzsimon (d. 1643), and Christopher Holywood
(d. 1626) in *Studies*, 32 (1943), 260–6, and 33 (1944), 99–107, 543–9.

4274   MORAN, P. F. Memoirs of the Most Rev. Oliver Plunket, Archbishop
of Armagh . . . Dublin. 1861. 1895.

From original documents. See also articles by R. D. Edwards, P. Walsh, *et al.*, in
Blessed Oliver Plunkett, Historical Studies, Dublin, 1937; A. Curtayne, *The trial of Oliver
Plunkett*, 1953; and the various narratives of the Popish Plot (4188).

(e) *Irish Colleges Abroad*
See also § K *infra*.

4275   BOYLE, P. The Irish college in Paris, 1578–1901. Dublin. 1901.

Contains accounts of other Irish colleges in France, as well. Cf. J. O'Boyle, *Irish colleges
on the continent*, Dublin, 1935; and J. Corboy, 'The Irish College at Salamanca', *Irish
Eccles. Rec.*, 5th Ser. 63 (1944), 247–53. See also no. 4338, French (4187), and Read
(nos. 6110, 6111).

F. MILITARY AND NAVAL HISTORY

A number of the sources relating to the wars of the century have been referred
to in § A of this chapter, and in the general political history, § B. In the general
chapter on Military History, Ch. VI, a number of titles should be consulted, such
as nos. 1518, 1519, 1529 n., 1545, 1563, and 1627; and in that on Naval History,
Ch. VII, see Tanner (1723 n.), and nos. 1731, 1738, and 1814. For the period
of 1689–90, the Clark MSS. are valuable (Trinity College, Dublin, see no. 4077),
as are the letters of James II to Hamilton (MSS. at Royal Irish Acad., Dublin,
no. 4077). See also *The Irish Sword, the Journal of the Military History Society
of Ireland* (Dublin, 1949+), especially D. C. Lineham, 'Index to the MSS. of
military interest in Nat. Lib. Ire.', ibid. 2 (1954–6), 33–9. See also Nat. Lib.
Ire. MS. 660, Captain T. Phillips, 'Military survey of Ireland, 1685'; D. Bryan,
'Irish wars', in *University Review*, 1 (no. 10, Dublin, 1956); G. A. Hayes-McCoy,
'O'Mellan's account of the battle of Benburb, 1646', in *Féilsgríbhinn Torna*, Cork,
1947; D. Murtagh, 'The Irish Jacobite army, 1688–92' (Univ. Coll. Galway MS.).

On naval history, see A. T. Lawlor, *Irish maritime survey*, Dublin, 1945;
J. R. Powell, 'The parliamentary squadron at the siege of Duncannon in 1645',
Irish Sword, 2 (1945); D. Bryan, 'The Irish admiralty, 1642–3', *An Cosantóir*,
7 (1947).

4276   BERNARD, NICHOLAS, Dean of Ardagh. The whole proceedings of
the siege of Drogheda in Ireland . . . with a relation of such passages as have
fallen out there. 1642. Later edn. Dublin. 1736.

Edn. of 1736 has appended G. Walker's account of the siege of Londonderry (q.v.).
Bernard's is 'a vivid narrative with details of importance'.

4277 CUFFE, MAURICE. The siege of Ballyally Castle in the county of Clare. Ed. by T. C. Croker. Camden Soc. 1841.

The volume, which includes also O'Kelly's *Macariae exicidium* (4281), bears the title of *Narratives illustrative of the contests in Ireland in 1641 and 1690.* See also other important accounts in Bellings (4179), Temple (4181), Clarendon (4182), Clanricarde (4183), Murphy (4201), and Ormonde (4212).

4278 CASTLEHAVEN, JAMES LORD AUDLEY, EARL OF. Memoirs, . . . his engagement and carriage in the wars of Ireland (1642–1651). 1680. Later edns. 1681, 1684 (with app.). Ed. by C. O'Connor. Waterford. 1753.

Attacked by Arthur Annesley, earl of Anglesey, in *A letter from a person of honour in the country*, 1681 (Wing, A 3170). See also *The history of the warr in Ireland . . . by a British officer of the regiment of Sir John Clotworthy*, ed. by E. H[ogan], Dublin, 1873.

4279 DAVIES, ROWLAND, Dean of Ross. Journal of the Very Rev. Rowland Davies . . . Ed. by R. Caulfield. Camden Soc. 1857.

Covers the period of 8 March 1689 to 29 Sept. 1690. The part on the battle of the Boyne was pr. in *Ulster Jour. Arch.* 4 (1856), 85–96. See also the important D'Avaux (4102); and the army lists in D'Alton (4272).

4280 WALKER, GEORGE. True account of the siege of Londonderry. 1689.

Publ. in German at Hamburg, and in Dutch at Antwerp the same year. In reply John Mackenzie wrote *Narrative of the siege . . . to rectify the mistakes . . . of Mr. Walker's account*, 1690 (ed. by W. D. Killen, Belfast, 1861); which was answered (though dated 1689) by *A vindication of the true account.* Mackenzie's *Narrative* was attacked anonymously in *Mr. John Mackenzie's Narrative . . . a false lible*, 1690; and Mackenzie replied with *Dr. Walker's invisible champion foiled*, 1690. Parts of all of the above are pr. in J. Hempton, *Siege and history of Londonderry*, Londonderry, 1861. Walker's *True account*, the *Vindication*, and various letters and other contemporary materials, were ed. by P. Dwyer under the title of *The siege of Londonderry in 1689, as set forth in the literary remains of Colonel the Rev. George Walker*, 1893. On Walker, governor of Londonderry, and killed at the Boyne in 1690, see W. S. Kerr, *Walker of Derry*, Londonderry, 1938.

On Londonderry see also T. Witherow, ed., *Two diaries of Derry* (by Richard, a naval officer, and Capt. Thomas Ash) [Lond.?], 1888; Witherow's *Derry and Enniskillen in . . . 1689*, Belfast, 1873, 3rd edn., Belfast, 1885; and W. R. Young, *Fighters of Derry*, 1932.

4281 O'KELLY, CHARLES. Macariae excidium, or the destruction of Cyprus, being a secret history of the war of the revolution in Ireland. Ed. by T. C. Croker. Camden Soc. 1841. Later edn. by C. O'Callaghan. [Irish Arch. Soc.] Dublin. 1850.

The 1841 edn. was publ. with Cuffe (4277); the 1850 edn. is the best. Another edn. was publ., Dublin, 1894, under title of *The Jacobite war in Ireland*, with editors listed as E. Hogan and E. Plunket (Count). See also the Jacobite narrative from the Fingal MSS. (4105); the Franco-Irish war corresp. (4106); I. Dumont de Bostaquet, *Mémoires inédits*, ed. by C. Read and F. Waddington, Paris, 1864; and Lucan (4209).

4282 STEVENS, JOHN. Journal . . . containing a brief account of the war in Ireland, 1689–91. Ed. by R. H. Murray. Oxf. 1912. Bibl.

Pr. from B.M. Add. MS. 36296. See also Capt. W. M'Carmick, *A true account of the actions of the Inniskilling men*, 1691 (ed. by W. T. Latimer, [Belfast?], 1896); George Story (4190); and William King (4246). Cf. C. L. Grose (10), nos. 3267–8. Another anonymous *History*, 1690, is in Wing (H 2190).

4283 MACARTNEY-FILGATE, E. The war of William III in Ireland, being a narrative of the campaigns of Duke Schomberg, of the king, and of General de Ginckel. (Military Soc. Ireland.) Dublin. 1905.

D. C. Boulger, *The battle of the Boyne*, 1911, is based on research in Paris, but is uncritical. Useful also are the Tyrconnell letter-book (4120), and P. W. Sergeant, *Little Jennings and fighting Dick Talbot, a life of the duke and duchess of Tyrconnel*, 2 vols., 1913.

G. ECONOMIC HISTORY

For bibliography see P. L. Prenderville, in *Econ. Hist. Rev.* 3 (1931–2), 402–16; and L. W. Hanson, *Contemporary printed sources for British and Irish economic history, 1701–1750*, Camb. 1963. On natural resources see Ch. XI *supra*, § B on Topography. Consult also Ch. VIII *supra*.

I. GENERAL

4284 O'BRIEN, G. A. T. The economic history of Ireland in the 17th century. Dublin and Lond. 1919.

Cf. O'Brien's volume on the 18th century (Pargellis, no. 3522); and D. A. Chart, *An economic history of Ireland*, Dublin, 1920.

2. PLANTATIONS AND CONFISCATIONS

(a) *Sources*

Important modern publications by the Commissioners of Irish MSS. include records of forfeitures following the 1641 rebellion, the *Civil survey* (4097), and *The book of survey and distribution* (4118). See also nos. 4103, 4121, 4122.

4285 O'BRIEN, G. A. T., ed. Advertisements for Ireland, being a description of the state of Ireland in the reign of James I. Dublin. 1923.

Valuable, possibly written by Sir Henry Bourchier, later earl of Bath. Cf. Barnaby Rich, *A short survey . . .*, 1609, and *A new description*, 1610, ed. by E. Hogan, 1878.

4286 LOWRY, T. K., ed. The Hamilton manuscripts: containing some account of the settlements . . . in the county of Down . . . in the reigns of James I and Charles I; with memoir . . . By Sir James Hamilton, Viscount Claneboye. Belfast. [1867.]

Cf. D. A. Chart, 'The break-up of the estate of Con O'Neill, Castlereagh, county Down, temp. James I.', *R.I.A. Proc.* 48 (1942), 119–51; and no. 4170. *The Montgomery manuscripts*, comp. by William Montgomery (d. 1707) and ed. by J. McKnight, Belfast, 1830 (enl. edn. by G. Hill, Belfast, 1869), provide 'a vivid sketch of Scottish settlements in Co. Down' and of later developments in Ulster.

4287 PETTY, SIR WILLIAM. The history of the survey of Ireland, commonly called the Down Survey . . . A.D. 1655–6. Ed. by T. A. Larcom. [Irish Arch. Soc.] Dublin. 1851.

Ed. from MSS. in Trin. Coll. Lib., and others. See also (4097); and letters of Petty and others, publ. by M.H., 1660, under title of *Reflections upon persons and things in Ireland...*

4288 GOOKIN, VINCENT. The great case of transplantation in Ireland discussed. 1655 [1654?].

On the authorship of the tract and Petty's supposed share in it see Lord E. Fitzmaurice's *Life of Petty*, p. 32 n., and S. R. Gardiner's article, 'The transplantation to Connaught', *E.H.R.* 14 (1899), 700–34. Arguing for total transplantation is Richard Lawrence, *The interest of England in the Irish transplantation stated . . .*, 1655; to which Gookin replied with a *Vindication* of his views, 1655. On one post-Cromwellian estate see *The Adams rental* (4145).

4289 PETTY, SIR WILLIAM. The political anatomy of Ireland, with the establishment for that kingdom when the late duke of Ormond was lord lieutenant . . . To which is added Verbum sapienti; or an account of the wealth and expenses of England . . . [1672]. 1691. Later edn. 2 pts. 1719.

Repr. in Hull's edn. of Petty's *Works* (see 1833), vol. i. Petty attempted to present quantitative facts relating to the issues. See also French (4187). Hugh Reily, in *Ireland's case briefly stated* (2 pts., s.l., 1695) presents the argument in favour of the Roman Catholics. The title varies in later edns., as *The impartial history of Ireland . . .*, Lond. 1754; and *The genuin history of Ireland . . . from 1676 . . .*, Dublin [1799]. See also *The report of the commissioners appointed by parliament to enquire into the Irish forfeitures . . . 15th of Dec. 1699*, 1700 (repr. in vol. ii of *A collection of State tracts*, 1705–7).

(b) *Later Works*

4290 BONN, M. J. Die englische Kolonisation in Irland. 2 vols. Stuttgart and Berlin. 1906.

Useful. Cf. *E.H.R.* 21 (1906), 772–8.

4291 BUTLER, W. F. T. Confiscation in Irish history. Dublin. 1917.

Cf. *Case of the forfeitures fairly stated*, 2nd edn., 1700. On the years 1690–1703, see J. G. Simms, *The Williamite confiscation* (4204), and his article on Catholic landholders (4269 n.).

4292 HILL, G. An historical account of the plantation in Ulster at the commencement of the 17th century, 1608–20. Belfast. 1877.

Also valuable are C. Maxwell, 'The colonization of Ulster', in *History* 1 (1916); and T. W. Moody, *The Londonderry plantation . . .*, Belfast, 1939. The latter is concerned with both the expropriated and the planters, as well as with political matters. See also F. Boyle, 'Studies in Ulster history', *Irish Eccles. Rec.*, 5th Ser. 43 (1933), 155–81, and 44 (1934), 347–58; S. R. L. Corry, earl of Belmore, *The history of two Ulster manors . . .*, Dublin, 1881; S. Ó Ceallaigh, *Gleanings from Ulster history*, Cork and Oxf. 1951; T. W. Moody's articles in *Bull. Inst. Hist. Research*, 12 (1934), 178–83; *Analecta Hibernica*, 8 (1938), 179–311; *I. H. Stud.* 1 (1938–9), 59–63, 251–72.

3. TRADE AND FINANCE

4293 LAWRENCE, RICHARD. The interest of Ireland in its trade and wealth stated. 2 pts. in 1 vol. Dublin. 1682.

Cf. William Temple, *Essay upon the advancement of trade in Ireland*, Dublin, 1673 (repr. in his *Miscellanea*, 1680); and John Collins, *Plea for bringing in of Irish cattel, and keeping out fish caught by foreigners*, 1680.

4294 MURRAY, A. E. The history of the commercial and financial relations between England and Ireland from the period of the restoration. 1903.

Includes political considerations relating to these matters. See also M. Dillon, *The history and development of banking in Ireland* . . ., 1889; T. J. Kiernan, *History of the financial administration of Ireland to 1817*, 1930; J. O'Donovan, *The economic history of live stock in Ireland*, Dublin, 1940; and two articles on Drogheda trade in 1683 by J. T. Dolan, *County Louth Arch. Jour.* 3 (1912–15), 83–103, 250–8.

4. INDUSTRY

4295 CROMMELIN, SAMUEL-LOUIS. An essay towards improving the hempen and flaxen manufactures in the kingdom of Ireland. Dublin. 1705.

See also W. R. Scott, 'The king's and queen's corporation for the linen manufacture in Ireland [1690]', *R.S.A.I. Proc.* 31 (1901); C. Gill, *The rise of the Irish linen industry*, Oxf. 1925; and W. Carter, *Linen: the story of an Irish industry*, 3rd edn., Belfast, 1954.

4296 WEBB, J. J. Guilds of Dublin. 1929.

Cf. H. F. Berry, ed., 'Records of the Dublin gild of merchants [1438–1671]', *Jour. R.S.A.I.* 30, Dublin, 1900; and E. M. Fahy, 'The Cork goldsmith's company, 1657', *Jour. Cork Hist. and Arch. Soc.* 58 (1953), 33–8. See also materials on Dublin gilds in Read, nos. 6090, 6094, 6101.

4297 CUNNINGHAM, W. 'The repression of the woollen manufacture in Ireland.' *E.H.R.* 1 (1886), 277–94.

See also C. H. Oldham, *The woolen industry of Ireland*, Dublin, 1909; and A. K. Longfield, 'History of tapestry-making in Ireland in the 17th and 18th centuries', *Jour. R.S.A.I.* 68 (1938), 91–105.

5. POPULATION

4298 O'HART, J. Irish and Anglo-Irish landed gentry when Cromwell came to Ireland; or a supplement to Irish pedigrees. Dublin. 1884. Later edn. 1892.

Based on docs. in the P.R.O., Dublin, viz. *Books of survey and distribution* (see no. 4118).

4299 WILLOUGHBY, CHARLES. 'Observations on the bills of mortality and the increase of the people in Dublin.' [1690.] Ed. by W. R. W. Wilde. *Proc. Roy. Irish Acad.* 6 (1858), 399–415.

See also Pender's edn. of a census *c.* 1659, based upon poll money ordinances, 1660–1, no. 4094.

H. SOCIAL HISTORY

No titles relating to genealogical materials are listed below. Reference should be made to Falley (4050), Wills (4055), and the numerous collections referred to in *Anal. Hib.* (e.g. nos. 4155, 4157, 4158). The general chapter on Social History (England), Ch. IX *supra*, is useful also for Ireland. For the theatre see § I of this Chapter, *infra*.

1. Topography and Travel

Among English and foreign travellers who have left some account of their Irish visits are Moryson (2366; and Read, no. 5810); Brereton (2392), Jouvin (2376), and Misson de Valbourg (2380). See also Cox (2351); E. McCracken, 'The woodlands of Ireland', *I. H. Stud.* 11 (1959); D. B. Quinn, *The Elizabethans and the Irish*, N.Y., Ithaca, 1966.

4300 FORDHAM, SIR H. G. The road-books and itineraries of Ireland 1647–1850; a catalogue. Dublin. 1923.

For maps *c.* 1600, see Hayes-McCoy (4054); see also Y. M. Goblet's index of parishes etc. (4054 n.).

4301 WOODHOUSE, J. A guide for strangers in the kingdome of Ireland; wherein the high-wayes and roads . . . is truly set down. 1647. Later edn. 1683. Map.

See also C. L. Falkiner (Read, no. 5850).

4302 BOATE, GERARD. Ireland's naturall history: being a true . . . description of its situation, greatness, shape, and nature; of its hills, woods . . . metalls . . . 1652. Later edns. Dublin. 1726. Dublin. 1860.

French version: *Histoire naturelle d'Irlande*, Paris, 1666.

4303 EACHARD, LAURENCE. An exact description of Ireland, chorographically surveying all its provinces and counties. 1691. Maps.

See also Thomas Dineley, *Observation in a voyage through the kingdom of Ireland . . . in 1681*. Ed. by J. Graves, Dublin, 1870.

2. Social and Domestic

4304 LODGE, J. The peerage of Ireland; or a genealogical history of the present nobility of that kingdom . . . 4 vols. Dublin. 1754. Later edn. by M. Archdall. 7 vols. Dublin. 1789.

Irish peers are included also in *G.E.C.* (2424). C. R. Mayes, in 'The early Stuarts and the Irish peerage', *E.H.R.* 73 (1958), 227–51, points out that the enlargement of the Irish peerage was regarded as a means of curbing the power of Irish nationalist and Catholic leadership.

4305 BLAKE, M. J., ed. Blake family records, 1600–1700. A chronological catalogue with notes. 1905.

Other collections of value for social as well as political history are the Kenmare MSS. (4161), Orrery papers (4171). See also *infra*, no. 4329.

4306 FITZGERALD, B. The Anglo-Irish: three representative types: Cork, Ormonde, Swift, 1602–1745. 1952.

See also F. E. Ball, 'Some notes on the household of the dukes of Ormonde', *Proc. Roy. Irish Acad.* 38 (1928); D. F. Gleeson, *The last lords of Ormond, a history of the 'countrie of the three O'Kennedys'*, 1938; and O'Hart, *Irish and Anglo-Irish landed gentry* (4298).

4307 MacLYSAGHT, E. Irish life in the seventeenth century: after Cromwell. Dublin. 1939. Rev. edn. Oxf. 1950.

On costume see H. F. McClintock, *Old Irish and Highland dress* (2302). See also J. P. Gannon, *A review of Irish history in relation to the social development of Ireland*, 1900.

I. CULTURAL HISTORY

In the reference section (A) above are several titles that relate especially to Ireland's cultural development. See Best, on Gaelic philosophy and literature (4037 n.), and Dix and Dugan, *Books printed in Dublin in the 17th century* (p. 565 *supra*). On maps see Hayes-McCoy (4054). On philosophy see M. Corcran, *Rythmus Pan-Sophicus sive metrica totius philosophiae Synopsis Divi Th. Aquinatis menti coaptata*, Morlaix, 1690; and J. Stearne, *Animi medela seu de beatitudine et miseria*, Dublin, 1658. On science see B. Connor, *Dissertationes medico-physicae de montis Vesuvii incendio*, Oxf. 1695; J. Stearn, Θανατολογία *(Thanatologia) seu de morte*, Dublin, 1659; Sir W. Petty, *Discourse concerning duplicate proportion, with a new hypothesis of elastique motions*, 1674; K. T. Hoppen, 'The Dublin Philosophical Society and the new learning in Ireland', *I.H. Stud.* 1964; and Y. M. Goblet, *La Transformation de la géographie politique de l'Irlande au XVIIe siècle*, 2 vols., Paris, 1930. See also Ch. X *supra*, especially the section on science, and the quarterly review, *Studies* (Dublin, 1912+).

1. LITERATURE

4308 HULL, E. A textbook of Irish literature. 2 vols. Dublin. 1906–8.

See Breatnach's article (4049) which views the 17th–18th centuries as seeing 'the end of a tradition'. See also D. Hyde, *A literary history of Ireland*, 1899; and C. G. Duffy, *The ballad poetry of Ireland*, 3rd edn., Dublin, 1845. See also J. C. MacErlean, *The poems of David O'Bruadair*, 3 vols., 1910–17 (Irish Texts Soc.); O. J. Bergin, ed., 'Páirlement Chloinne Tomáis' in *Gadelica*, I (1912–13); C. Ó Cadla, ed., 'Páirliament na mBan' in *An Lochrann*, Dublin, 1909; Colm Ó Lochlainn, *Irish street ballads*, 1939.

4309 O'REILLY, E. A chronological account of nearly four hundred Irish writers . . . to the year 1750. Iberno-Celtic Soc. Trans. I. Dublin. 1820.

Cf. M. O'N. Walsh (4038) on Irish books printed abroad before 1700. See also 'Seventeenth-century writers' in W. Harris, ed., *The whole works of Sir J. Ware* (Read, no. 5916). Various writings by Swift can be checked by the index to this bibliography.

4310 STOCKWELL, LA TOURETTE. Dublin theatres and theatre customs (1637–1820). Kingsport (Tenn.). 1938. Bibl.

Good. See also W. S. Clark, *The early Irish stage* (2282); and James Shirley, *St. Patrick for Ireland*, 1640.

4311 WALSH, P. Irish men of learning. By Colm Ó Lochlainn. Dublin. 1947.

Cf. A. S. Green, *The making of Ireland and its undoing, 1200–1600*, Lond. 1908, 1909, which deals with education and scholarship, among other subjects, but in an 'uncritical' manner. See also *John Dunton, The Dublin scuffle*, 1699.

2. FINE ARTS AND MUSIC

See Eager (4036), nos. 2036–8, and elsewhere.

4312 JOPE, E. M. 'Scottish influence in the north of Ireland: castles with Scottish features, 1580–1640.' *Ulster Jour. of Arch.*, 3rd Ser. 14 (1952), 31–47.

See also M. J. Craig, *Dublin* (4322 n.); A. K. Longfield, 'Tapestry making' (4297); and H. G. Leask, *Irish castles*, Dundalk, 1941.

4313 FLOOD, W. H. G. A history of Irish music. Dublin. 1905. 3rd edn. Dublin. 1913.

Some of the titles listed under *Music* in Ch. X deal with the British Isles, rather than England alone; see Schnapper (p. 400), and Humphries and Smith (2802). See also D. O'Sullivan, [*Turlough*] *Carol'an, an Irish harper*, 2 vols., 1958; and D. O'Sullivan, *Irish folk music and song*, Dublin (Irish Life and Culture), 1952.

3. EDUCATION

See also § K *infra*, on *The Irish Abroad*.

4314 BURTCHAELL, G. B. and SADLEIR, T. U., eds. Alumni Dublinenses. A register of the students, graduates, professors, and provosts of Trinity College in the University of Dublin (1593–1846). 1924. New edn. with suppl. (1593–1860). Dublin. 1935.

Important also are W. Urwick, *The early history of Trinity College Dublin, 1591–1600, as told in contemporary records*, 1892; and J. P. Mahaffy, *An epoch in Irish history: Trinity College Dublin, its foundations and early fortunes, 1591–1660*, 1903. See also J. W. Stubbs, *The history of the University of Dublin from its foundation to the end of the 18th century*, Dublin, 1889; W. S. Ferguson, *Church control over the grammar schools in Ireland, c. 1540–1714*, Bulletin Ir. Committee on Hist. Sciences, 1946; R. B. McDowell and D. A. Webb, 'Courses in Trinity College, Dublin', *Hermathena*, Dublin, 1947; M. V. Ronan, *Erasmus Smith endowment*, Dublin, 1947.

4315 CORCORAN, T. Studies in the history of classical teaching, Irish and continental 1500–1700. Dublin. 1911.

Includes '*William Bathe, S.J., of Dublin (1564–1614) and his method of language teaching*'. Also by Corcoran, 'Early Irish educators: I. Thomas White of Clonmel (1556–1622)', *Studies*, 29 (1940), 545–69, 30 (1941), 59–74; and *State policy in Irish education . . . 1536–1816, exemplified in documents . . .*, Dublin, 1916.

4. SCHOLARSHIP AND HISTORIOGRAPHY

See also *supra* p. 602.

4316 JENNINGS, B. Michael O'Cleirigh, chief of four masters, and his associates. Dublin and Cork. 1936.

For O'Cleirigh as a student of language as well as of Irish history see no. 4056. See also D. Ryan, *The sword of light, from the four masters to Douglas Hyde, 1636–1938*, 1939, dealing with the history of the Irish language. See also John Colgan's *Acta Sanctorum Hiberniae* (4091); and J. F. Kenney, 'History in Ireland' in *Sources* (Read, no. 5699).

4317 O'DONOVAN, J., ed. Annála rioghachta Eireann. Annals of the kingdom of Ireland by the Four Masters . . . to 1616. 7 vols. Dublin. 1851.

One of the principal works of O'Cleirigh and his collaborators (see *D.N.B.*). On his studies of genealogies, see no. 4168. On one of his sources, see no. 4615. See also G. Keating (Read, 5805a). Other historians include Dudley Loftus (4110); Philip O'Sullivan Beare (4127, and Read, nos. 5898–9); Usher (see *Hermathena*, 1956); Luke Wadding (4124) and *Fr. L. Wadding commemorative volume*, 1957. See also *Archivium Hibernicum, or Irish historical records* (Cath. Rec. Soc. of Ireland), Dublin, 1912+.

4318 LYNCH, JOHN [GRATIANUS LUCIUS]. Alithinologia [St. Malo]. 1664. Alithinologia supplementum [St. Malo]. 1667.

Works against R. B. O'Ferrall (*supra*, 4114). See also Lynch (4186). Cf. P. J. Corish in *I. H. Stud.*, 1953. Also by Lynch, the biography of Bishop Kirwan, *Pii Antistitis Icon* (4172), and *De Praesulibus Hiberniae* (4130). See also especially Sir James Ware (1594–1666), *The annals of the affairs of Ireland* . . . [to Elizabeth, and cont.], repr. with other works of Ware in *The antiquities and history of Ireland*, Lond. 1704; later edns. by W. Harris, Dublin, 1739, 1746, 1764 (see Read, nos. 5913–16); and the later work of Peter Walsh (4058); O'Flaherty (4052 n. and Read, no. 6157); and Edward Lhuyd (4057). On Walsh and Keating (*supra*, 4058 n.) also see Cox (4178) and Clanricarde (4183 n., intro. to 1722 edn.).

5. PRINTING AND NEWSPAPERS

On printing, see the work of E. R. McC. Dix and J. Anderson on printers in Dublin and Belfast in no. 3032, as well as Dix and Dugan's *Books* (p. 565 *supra*). See also Eager (4036), nos. 1757–2001.

4319 MADDEN, R. R. The history of Irish periodical literature, from the end of the seventeenth to the middle of the nineteenth century. 2 vols. 1867.

Of slight value before 1714. Cf. E. R. McC. Dix, *Tables relating to some Dublin newspapers of the eighteenth century* . . ., Dublin, 1910. See also nos. 3058 and 3062. J. W. Phillips compiled 'A trial list of Irish paper makers, 1690–1800', *Library*, Mar. 1958. There are lists also in *Ir. Independent*, Jan. 18–20, 1905 (Eager, no. 267), and *Ir. Book Lover*, 4 (1912–13), 97–8 (Eager, no. 269). See also R. L. Munter, *A hand-list of Irish newspapers, 1685–1750* (Camb. Bibl. Soc., 1960); and his *The history of the Irish newspaper, 1685–1760*, Camb. 1967. The catalogue of the H. Bradshaw Irish collection in Cambridge systematically lists local printing under towns (cf. *supra*, § A, p. 565).

J. LOCAL HISTORY

Reference should be made to the extensive list of titles on Irish local and family history in Read (1959 edn., pp. 512–18). Descriptions of various local records are in § A, pp. 569–73 *supra*; and in H.M.C., no. 246. See also *Report of the commissioners appointed to inquire into the municipal corporations of Ireland*, F, Parl. Papers, 1835, vols. 27–8; 1836, vol. 24. Important recent publications are the *Civil Survey* (4097) and *Down Survey maps* (4103). See also Y. M. Goblet, *Les noms de lieux Irlandais dans l'œuvre géographique de Sir W. Petty*, Paris, 1930.

I. BIBLIOGRAPHIES

4320 O'NEILL, T. P. Sources of Irish local history. Dublin. 1958.

See also the bibl. of histories of Irish counties and towns, by W. MacArthur, which appeared in a series of articles in *Notes and Queries*, 6 Feb. 1915–30 Dec. 1916 (Ser. 11, vols. 11–12; Ser. 12, vols. 1–2). See also Eager (4036). A select bibl. on Dublin, compiled by J. J. Bouch, was publ. in *Lord Mayor's Handbook, Dublin municipal annual* (1942), 79–89; one on Connaught, by J. Coleman, is in *Jour. Galway Arch. and Hist. Soc.* 5 (1908), 28–34, 239; and one on Ulster by E. R. McC. Dix and John S. Crone, in *Ulster Jour. Arch.*, 2nd Ser., vols. 6–13 (1900–7). See also D. F. Gleeson, 'Sources for local history in the period 1200 to 1700', *Jour. Cork Hist. Soc.*, 1941; Hayes, *MS. Sources* (4046 n.); Dublin, Ordnance survey (4061); C. T. McCready, *Dublin*, Dublin, 1892; W. Kavanagh, *Bibliography of County Galway*, Galway, 1965; and Falkiner (Read, 2nd edn., no. 6133), Gale (Read, 1st edn., no. 4098), and MacLeod (Read 2nd edn., no. 6154).

2. CIVIL DIVISIONS

The arrangement below is according to provinces, with counties and towns in alphabetical order within those regions.

CONNAUGHT

4321 O'Flaherty, Roderick. Chorographical description of west or H-Iar Connaught. 1684. Ed. by J. Hardiman. Dublin. 1846.

On Galway, see nos. 246, 4118, 4134, and 4152; also J. Hardiman's *History*, Dublin, 1820, repr. 1926; M. D. O'Sullivan, *Old Galway*, Camb. 1942; and T. M. O'Flynn, *Leitrim*, Dublin, 1937. For Sligo, there are histories by W. G. Wood-Martin, Dublin, 1889, and T. O'Rorke, Dublin, [1890].

LEINSTER

4322 Calendar of ancient records of Dublin in possession of the municipal corporation. Ed. by J. T. Gilbert. 17 vols. Dublin. 1889–1916.

Vols. iii–vii deal with the period. On Dublin records, see nos. 246, 4060–2, and 4077; a county history is by F. E. Ball, Dublin, 1902–6; city histories are by W. Harris, Dublin, 1766, J. T. Gilbert, 3 vols., Dublin, 1854–5, and M. J. Craig, from 1660 to 1860, Lond. 1952. H. F. Berry edited 'Minute book of the corporation of Dublin, 1567–1611', *Proc. R.I.A.* 30, Sect. C, Dublin, 1912.

For Louth, there are 17th-century materials in *Proc. R.I.A.* 33, Sect. C (1916–17), 499–504; and *Jour. County Louth Arch. Soc.* 1 (1904–7), 61–73, and 2 (1908–11), 24–6. For Wexford, county and town, see P. H. Hore's history, 5 vols., 1900–11. See also O'Hanlon (Read, no. 6159); Sir H. Piers, *Westmeath*, 1682, ed. by C. Vallancey in *Collectanea de rebus Hibernicis*, Dublin, 1770.

MUNSTER

4323 The council book of the corporation . . . of Cork [1609–43, 1690–1800]. Ed. by R. Caulfield. Guildford. 1876.

Extracts. Also ed. by Caulfield, Co. Cork corporations books as follows: Cork city, 1876; Youghal, 1878; Kinsale, 1879. Descriptive is C. Smith, *Ancient and present state of the county and city of Cork*, 2 vols., Dublin, 1750, later edn., with additions, Cork, 1893–4; valuable is W. O'Sullivan, *Economic history of Cork*, Lond. 1937; and materials on forfeited lands in *Cork Hist. and Arch. Soc. Jour.*, 2nd Ser. 37–41 (1932–6). Cf. no. 4143. For Clare, see J. Frost's *History*, Dublin, 1893. Other county histories by C. Smith are: Kerry, 1756; Waterford, 1746 (2nd edn., 1774, see Read, no. 6174). For Limerick there is M. Lenihan's history, Dublin, 1866 (notes in Br. Mus. Add. MSS. 31878–88), 2nd edn., 1884. *Waterford during the civil war*, by T. Fitzpatrick, Waterford, 1912, is valuable. R. H. Ryland's history of the city and county was publ. in 1824; see also nos. 246, 4144, an article by S. Pender in *Cork Hist. and Arch. Soc. Jour.*, 2nd Ser. 44

(1939), 75–88; and a list of mayors, 1365–1649, in *Jour. R.S.A.I.* 65 (1935), 313–19. D. F. Gleeson, *The last lords of Ormond*, 1938, is important. See also Butler (Read no. 6120).

ULSTER

4324 Benn, G. History of the town of Belfast. 2 vols. in 1. Belfast. 1877–80.

See also R. M. Young, ed., *Historical notices of old Belfast . . .*, Belfast, 1896; and histories of Ulster by R. Colles, 4 vols., 1919–20, and Cyril Falls, 1936. On the Ulster plantation see nos. 4054, 4059, 4121, and 4292. See also R. M. Young, ed., *Belfast town book*, 1892; Carrickfergus (Read, no. 6155); W. Harris and C. Smith, *Co. Down*, 1744 (2nd edn., Dublin, 1757); T. Colby, *Ordnance Survey, Co. Londonderry*, Dublin, 1837; E. P. Shirley, *Monaghan* (Read, no. 6171).

3. ECCLESIASTICAL CENTRES

See *Handlist of diocesan histories* (4051) and nos. 4140–1; also *Archivium Hibernicum* (4089 n.); Ware-Harris (4318 n.); J. Lynch, *De praesulibus Hiberniae* (4130); John O'Heyn (Read, no. 5988); J. M. Hartry, *Triumphalia . . .* (written *c.* 1640, Read, no. 5973). The bishops are listed in *Handbook of British chronology*, 2nd edn., 1961.

4325 ARMAGH PROVINCE

See *Seanchas Ardmhacha* (Read, no. 5671); *Clogher Record*, Monaghan, 1953+; R. Hayes, ed., *Register of Derry Cathedral . . . 1642–1703*, Dublin, 1910; and L. P. Murray, *History of the parish of Creggan* (17th–18th centuries), Dundalk, 1940.

4326 CASHEL PROVINCE

W. M. Brady, *Clerical and parochial records of Cork, Cloyne, and Ross . . .*, 3 vols., Dublin, 1863–4. Cf. A. Webster, *Diocese of Cork*, Dublin, 1920; and W. Holland, *History of West Cork and the diocese of Ross*, Skibbereen, 2nd edn., 1950. Also, D. F. Gleeson and A. Gwynn, *A history of the diocese of Killaloe*, Dublin, 1962.

4327 DUBLIN PROVINCE

See *Reportorium Novum* (Read, no. 5667). Also, W. M. Mason, *History and antiquities of the . . . cathedral church of St. Patrick, near Dublin, 1190–1819*, Dublin, 1819; J. Mills, ed., *The registers of [the parish of] St. John, Dublin, 1616–19*, Parish Register Soc. of Dublin, 1906; and W. Carrigan, *History of the diocese of Ossory*, 4 vols., Dublin, 1905.

4328 TUAM PROVINCE

On the wardenship of Galway see no. 4134. See also J. Fahey, *The history of the diocese of Kilmacduagh*, Dublin, 1893; and P. K. Egan, *The parish of Ballinasloe*, Dublin, 1960.

4. FAMILY HISTORY

The first modern Irish demographic revolution, 1534–1706, substituted generally a new colonial landed class for the families listed in C. Read (ch. 13, sect. G) and in Roger O'Ferrall, 'Linea Antiqua' (4157 n.). Those who took service abroad are partly recorded in Jennings (4126) and Walsh (4176). Those deprived under Cromwell and under William III are usually in the Outlawry lists (4112 and 4108 respectively), and the details are in the Dublin P.R.O.I. (4062), those in print being noted above (4118); cf. O'Hart (4298). The 'census' of 1659 (4094) sums up the position in 27 counties by barony and parish. The new owners are usually listed in the crown rental for 1706 (Q.R.O. MSS. in 4062), the most successful of them being in Aaron Crossly, *Peerage of Ireland*, Dublin, 1725, and in Lodge (4304), as well as among the parliamentary commoners listed for Queen Anne and George I (913). Other families are in the Dublin Registry of Deeds and Genealogical Office Archives (cf. M. D. Falley, *supra*, no. 4050, vol. i, pp. 51, 137), whose will abstracts are listed for the Irish MSS. Comm. (4132). The archives of those families who survived the second modern Irish demographic revolution, 1849–1923, not listed for the United Kingdom Hist. MSS. Comm. and National Register of Archives (Ch. I, *supra*), are noted for the Belfast P.R.O.N.I. (4059), the Dublin P.R.O.I. and Nat. Lib. Ire. in Hayes, *MS. Sources* (4036); those listed for the Irish MSS. Comm. appear alphabetically above in § A, sub-section 4 d, or are in the unpublished boxes of family papers in the archives of the Dublin Irish Land Commission. Outside of Ulster, the change was mainly of landowners only. Members of many Irish families remained as tenants in the same localities and are listed with the newer families by Mac Lysaght (4329). For the Irish who followed James II to Europe after his defeat by William III see J. D'Alton (4272), C. E. Lart, *The pedigrees and papers of James Terry, Athlone herald, 1690–1725*, Exeter, 1938.

4329 MacLYSAGHT, E. Irish families, their names, arms, and origins. Dublin. 1957.

> Supplementary volumes: Galway, 1960; Dublin, 1964. J. Ainsworth, 'Abstracts of Irish wills in the prerogative court of Canterbury', *Jour. R.S.A.I.* 78 (1948), 24–37. On the Dublin Genealogical Office see nos. 4060 n. and 4132. See also references to wills in Falley (4050), vol. ii, part 3, ch. 15.

K. THE IRISH ABROAD

Still unwritten is the record of those who left Ireland for countries of Catholic Europe, to join centres of learning and religious activity there, or to enlist in the armies of Catholic monarchs of the continent or in the cause of the Jacobites. A few studies have been done regarding those others who migrated across the Atlantic. For other source materials relating to expatriates in European countries, most of them waiting to be searched, see § A of this chapter. See also Eager, nos. 3781–3803.

I. WRITINGS

4330 McNEILL, C. Publications of Irish interest . . . by Irish authors on the continent . . . prior to the eighteenth century. Bibliog. Soc. Ire. 4 (1930), 3–42.

> Cf. Walsh's checklist of Irish books printed abroad (1470–1700), no. 4038. See also Colgan (4091), French (4187), Lynch (4172, 4186, 4318), Ó Cleirigh (4056, 4316), O'Sullivan Beare (4127; Read, nos. 5898–9), Wadding (4124). See also nos. 4077, 4116.

2. ACTIVITIES

(a) *In Europe*

4331 BIGGER, F. J. 'Irish in Rome in the 17th century.' *Ulster Jour. Arch.*
5 (1899), 115–38.

See also p. 610.

4332 MACSWINEY, V. E. P. Articles on Irish in the service of Spain and
Naples. *Proc. R.I. Acad.* 37, Sect. C. (1924–7), 158–74; and *Jour. R.S.A.I.*,
6th Ser. 17 (1927), 7–20.

See also no. 4176 and pp. 609–10 *infra*; also W. O. Cavenagh on Irish in imperial service,
Jour. R.S.A.I., 6th Ser. 16 (1926), 95–105, and 17 (1927), 117–26.

4333 O'CALLAGHAN, J. C. History of Irish brigades in the service of France
from the revolution . . . [1688] to the revolution in France [1789]. Glasgow.
1870.

Cf. C. N. Watts, 'The Irish troops in the service of France, 1691–1791', *Roy. United
Serv. Inst. Jour.* 62 (1917). See also R. Hayes, *Old Irish links with France*, 1940, and
Biographical dictionary of Irish in France, 1949.

4334 O'CONOR, M. Military history of the Irish nation [1550–1750], comprising a memoir of the Irish brigade in the service of France, with official
papers relative to the brigade. Dublin. 1845.

Cf. nos. 4210–11 on Hugh O'Neill, Rory O'Donnell, and Owen Roe O'Neill. See also
'Lord Iveagh and other Irish officers at Collège des Grassins, Paris, 1684–1710', *Ir.
Eccles. Rec.*, 1901.

4335 REDMOND, J. R. 'Military and political memoirs of the Redmond
family during the Jacobite era in the services of France, Portugal, the Empire
and Spain.' In *Jour. Cork Hist. Arch. Soc.*, 2nd Ser., vols. 27–30 (1921–5).

See also nos. 4108, 4126, and 4176; and Sir C. Oman, 'The Irish troops in the service
of Spain, 1709–1818', *Roy. United Serv. Inst. Jour.* 63+ (1918+). See also J. Henning,
'Irish soldiers in the 30 years war', *Jour. R.S.A.I.*, 1952.

(b) *In America*

See also Gwynn, no. 4125.

4336 GLASGOW, M. Scotch-Irish in northern Ireland and in the American
colonies. N.Y. 1936.

Cf. W. F. Dunaway, *The Scotch-Irish in colonial Pennsylvania*, Phila. 1944. See also
articles by M. J. Murphy relating to Ulster settlers in America in *Ulster Jour. Arch.*,
2nd Ser. 2 (1896), 17–32; and notes in *Jour. R.S.A.I.*, 5th Ser. 12 (1903), 385–92; 6th
Ser. 2 (1913), 21–6; vol. 95 (1965), 39–50, where E. Evans points out that the term
'Scotch-Irish' is unusual before 1850.

4337 MYERS, A. C. Immigration of Irish Quakers into Pennsylvania, 1682–
1750, with their early history in Ireland. Swarthmore, Pennsylvania. 1902.

See also J. J. Williams, *Whence the 'Black Irish' of Jamaica*, N.Y. 1932; A. Gwynn,
'Irish on the Amazon', in *Proc. R.I. Acad.*, 1932–4; C. Wittke, *The Irish in America*,
Baton Rouge, Louisiana, 1956.

3. INSTITUTIONS

(a) *Spain and Portugal*

4338 O'DOHERTY, D. J. 'Students of the Irish college, Salamanca.' *Arch. Hib.* 2 (1913), 1–36; 3 (1914), 87–112; 4 (1915), 1–58, 96–130.

List of students, with places of birth, etc. The archives are now in Maynooth College, Ireland. See also no. 244 and, in § A, nos. 4077, 4136; and see P. J. Corish in *Arch. Hib.*, 1965. For Irish colleges at Alcalá, Madrid, Santiago da Compostella see Kenney (p. 567 *supra*), 1. 29. For Seville see J. J. Silke in *Arch. Hib.*, 1961. For Salamanca language-teaching see W. Bathe, *Janua Linguarum*, 1611, in Corcoran (4315).

4339 LISBON, IRISH COLLEGES. For secular, Dominican, and Franciscan foundations see Kenney, 1. 29.

(b) *Flanders, Spanish and later Austrian Netherlands*

On the Irish in the Low Countries, now Belgium, see J. P. Spelman in *I.E. Record*, 1885–6; J. Brady in *Arch. Hib.*, 1949; and B. Jennings, ibid. 1952.

4340 CORCORAN, T. Facultates Lovanienses, 1426–1797 praecipue qua nomen Hibernicum spectant. Dublin. 1939.

Cf. B. Jennings, 'Irish in Louvain University', in S. O'Brien, ed., *Measgra M. Uí Chleirigh*, Dublin, 1944.

4341 MOONEY, C. 'St. Anthony's Irish Franciscan college.' *Ir. Book Lover*, 1940; *I.E. Record*, 1942.

See Kenney, 1. 29; B. Jennings, *M. Ó Cleirigh* (4316); C. Giblin, ed., *Liber Lovaniensis, 1629–1717*, Dublin, 1956; T. O'Donnell, ed., *Fr. J. Colgan essays*, Dublin, 1959. For the Irish secular college, Louvain, see Kenney, 1. 29; also B. Jennings and F. Jones in *Arch. Hib.* 16. (1952) For the Irish Dominican college see Kenney.

4342 JENNINGS, B. 'Irish college, Douai.' *Arch. Hib.* 1943.

Cf. J. Brady in *Measgra M. Uí Chleirigh*, Dublin, 1944, and in *Arch. Hib.*, 1947. Cf. Kenney.

4343 JENNINGS, B. 'Irish college, Antwerp, 1694–1700.' *Arch. Hib.* 16 (1952).

Cf. *Principium ac progressu collegii pastoralis Hibernorum* (Antwerp, 1680), quoted in Kenney, 1. 29; J. Brady, 'Douai, Antwerp', *Arch. Hib.*, 1947; B. Jennings, 'Irish in Malines', *I.E. Record*, 1951; *Arch. Hib.* 23 (1960); J. Brady, 'Tournai Irish College', *Arch. Hib.* 14 (1949). Cf. Kenney, 1. 29. For Irish Benedictine nuns at Ypres, see Kenney. See also B. Jennings, 'St. Triden', *Arch. Hib.*, 1962–3.

(c) *France*

See T. J. Walsh in *Cork Hist. Jour.*, 1953, and *Irish Cath. Hist. Comm. Proc.*, 1955. See also C. Mooney, *Irish Franciscan relations . . . 1224–1850*, Dublin, 1951.

4344 WALL, T. 'Irish in Paris University.' *I.E. Record*. 1944.

Cf. P. Boyle in *Arch. Hib.* 5 (1916); T. Corcoran, *In universitati Parisiensi, 1578–1793*, Dublin, 1943. Cf. Kenney, 1. 29. See also Boyle (4275).

4345 PARIS, IRISH COLLEGE. See Kenney, 1. 29.

4346 WALSH, T. J. 'Irish college, Bordeaux.' *Cork Hist. Jour.* 1947.

Cf. Kenney, 1. 29. And see, for Irish Franciscans, Boulay, Kenney, 1. 29, and *Arch. Hib.*, 1944; B. Jennings, ed., 'Irish college, Lille', *Arch. Hib.* 16 (1952) (cf. Kenney, 1. 29); P. Hurley, 'A bishop of Cork and the Irish at Nantes', in *Dublin Rev.*, 1892, quoted by Kenney, 1. 29; F. Finegan, 'The Irish college of Poitiers, 1674–1762', in *I.E. Record*, 1965. For the Irish secular college at Rouen, see Kenney, 1. 29; for that at Toulouse see Kenney. Cf. T. J. Walsh, in *Cork Hist. Jour.*, 1954.

(d) *Rome, Prague, Poland*

4347 CORISH, P. J. 'The beginnings of the Irish college, Rome.' In The Franciscan Fathers Killiney, *Father Luke Wadding commemorative volume.* Dublin. 1957.

Cf. J. Hanly in *I.E. Record*, 1964; *Arch. Hib.*, 1964; Kenney, 1. 29.

4348 CLEARY, A. Father Luke Wadding and St. Isidore's. Rome. 1925.

Also, C. Giblin, B. Egan, and C. MacGrath, 'Rome graduates', *I.E. Record*, 1942. Cf. Kenney, 1. 29.

4349 KEARNS, C. 'Archives of the Irish Dominican college, San Clemente, Rome.' *Arch. Hib.* 1955.

Cf. Kenney, 1. 29; C. Giblin, ed., 'A guide to Irish material in Vatican Lib. MSS. Barberini Latini', *Arch. Hib.* 18; B. Millett, 'Archives of Propaganda Fide', in *Ir. Cath. Hist. Comm. Proc.*, 1956, and in *Collectanea Hibernica*, 1964–5. Also, B. Egan, 'Notes on propaganda printing press and F. Aolloy', ibid. 2 (1959); F. Molloy, *Lucerna fidelium*, ed. P. Ó Suilleabhain, Dublin, 1967; B. Jennings, 'Rome theses' in *Collectanea Hibernica* 2 (1959).

4350 WALL, T. 'Bards and Bruodins.' In Fr. Luke Wadding. 1957.

Cf. B. Jennings, 'Irish Franciscans at Prague', in *Arch. Hib.* 9 (1942); *Studies*, 1939; B. Jennings, 'Willun', *Arch. Hib.*, 1951 (Kenney, 1. 29); B. Jennings, 'Poland', *Arch. Hib.*, 1957.

INDEX

Subject headings appear in italics, as do titles of major modern serial publications. Page references are indicated by p. or pp.; all other figures refer to numbered items. Names of editors, unless they have contributed importantly, have usually been omitted.

Aaron, R. I.: Locke, 2701.
Abadie, Jacques: hist. of the late conspiracy, 372.
Abbey, Charles J.: Eng. church, 1187.
Abbey, W. B. T.: Tangier, 3420.
Abbot, George: bibl., 1214.
Abbot, Robert: antilogia, 1484.
Abbott, Edwin: Bacon, 403.
Abbott, George F.: Finch's embassy to Constantinople, 698.
Abbott, Richard: narrative, 1070.
Abbott, Th. Kingsmill: cat. Trin. Coll. MSS., 4077.
Abbott, Wilbur Cortez: Col. Thos. Blood, 2340; conflicts, 2437; conspiracy and dissent, 356; Gibraltar, 667; long parl. of Chas. II, 827; Titus Oates' story, 1493; pol. parties, 919; ed. Cromwell bibl., writings, 429; essays in honour of, 925.
Abell, Sir Westcott S.: shipwright's trade, 1762.
Aberdeen, burgh of, recs., 3989; co. of, recs., 3809, 3991; presb. and synod of, recs., 3841.
Aberdeen University, recs., 3963; hist., 3984.
Abernathy, G. R., Jr.: Eng. Presb., 1336.
Abetti, G.: hist. of astron., 2854.
Abstracts of Gloucester and Wiltshire post-mortem inquisitions, 1910.
Academy of complements, The, 2200.
Account of charity schools, 2951.
Account of proceedings of the house of peers, 846.
Account of some transactions . . . E. India Co., etc., 3403.
Account of the transactions of the late King James in Ir., 4189.
Account of victory at sea, 1816.
Accounts of the net public income, 760.
Ackermann, Rudolph: hist. Camb., 2990; hist. of the colleges, 2964; hist. Oxf., 2977.
Acres, W. Marston: bank of Eng., 2058.
Act for the propagation of the gospel in Wales, 3610.
Actes et mémoires . . . Nimègue, 546.

Acton, Lord (John Emerich Edward Dalberg): secret hist. of Chas. II, 421; hist. essays, 421.
Actors and actresses, 2289–92.
Actors' remonstrance, the, 2290.
Acts of assembly . . . Bermuda, 3361.
Acts of assembly . . . Leeward Is., 3371.
Acts of the privy council, 735.
Adair, Edward Robert: extraterritoriality of ambassadors, 557; sources for hist. of the council, 733; arts., 557, 619, 733, 830, 1266.
Adair, Patrick: Presb. ch. in Ir., 4258.
Adam, Frank: clans, septs, and regts., 1656, 3948.
Adams, C. K.: cat. Portland coll., 2713.
Adams, Eleanor Nathalie: Old Eng. scholarship, 3004.
Adams, H. H.: domestic tragedy, 2668.
Adams, James Truslow: building the Br. empire, 3329; provincial society, 3340.
Adams, John: index villaris, 3109.
Adams, Jonas: court leet, 952.
Adams, Joseph Q.: ed. Herbert's recs., 2275.
Adams, P. W.: Adams family, 2438.
Adams, Walter: ed. Hooke, 2908.
Adamson, John W.: guide to education, 2923; hist. of educ., etc., 2952; ed. Locke's educ. writings, 2946.
Addison, Joseph: remarks on Italy, 2400; works and letters, 2590; ed. The Spectator, 3090, Whig Examiner, 3088; lives of, 2441, 2590.
Addison, W.: Fuller, 1245; Eng. spas, 2298.
Addleshaw, G. W. O.: high church tradition, 1188.
Addy, S. O.: Eng. house, 2764.
Adelung, Friedrich von: bibl. on travel in Russia, p. 344.
Admiralty, 754–8; court of, 1053; laws concerning, 786; library, 1709; recs. and lists, 1708, 1735.
Admiralty statutes, 1767.
Ady, Mrs. Henry: *see* Cartwright, Julia M.
Aerssen, François van: embassy to Eng., 674.
Africa, 3419–21; trade to, 2136–7.

E., J.: Lords' proceedings, 844.

E., T.: letter from a parliament man, 872.

Eachard, John: grounds of contempt of the clergy, 1174.

Eager, Alan Robert: Irish bibl., 4036.

Earle, Erasmus: papers, 125.

Earle, John: microcosmography, 2167.

Earwaker, J. P.: East Cheshire, 3141.

Easson, D. E.: French protestants, 3875.

East, Robert: Portsmouth recs., 3180.

East Anglian, 3246.

East Hertfordshire Archaeological Society, trans., 3184.

East India Company, 3381, 3382, 3399–3407; cal. court minutes, 3382.

East Indies, 3376–3418.

East Riding Antiquarian Soc., trans., 3273.

Eaton, John: liber valorum, 1179.

Eberlein, Harold Donaldson: Eng. inn, 2364; smaller Eng. house, 2764.

Ebsworth, Joseph Woodfall: Westminster drolleries, 2652; ed. Bagford ballads, 2659; Roxburghe ballads, 2657.

Eburne, Rich.: plaine path-way, 2164.

Ecclesiastical appointments in Wales, 3617.

Ecclesiastical centres, Ireland, 4325–8.

Ecclesiastical history, 1104–1517; Ireland, 4243–75; Scotland, 3834–3911; Wales, 3610–73.

Ecclesiastical law, 1096–1101.

Echard (Eachard), Laurence: descr. of Ir., 4303; hist. of Eng., 263; hist. of the revolution, 263.

Economic history, 1828–2163; Ireland, 4284–99; Scotland, 3912–36; Wales, 3570–1, 3578, 3582, 3584, 3585, 3587–95.

Economic History Review, 31.

Economic Journal, 32.

Economica, 33.

Eden, Ch. Page: ed. Taylor, 1285.

Eden, Sir Frederick Morton, Bart.: state of the poor, 2530.

Edgar, Wm.: vectigalium systema, 2069.

Edgcumbe family: letters, 126.

Edie, C. A.: succession and monarchy, 983.

Edinburgh, borough of, 3995; maps, 3022.

Edinburgh Courant, 3086.

Edinburgh Gazette, 3086.

Edinburgh Review, 34.

Edinburgh University, 2995, 3962, 3972.

Edinger, Geo. A.: Prince Rupert, 498.

Edleston, Joseph: ed. Newton corresp., 2864.

Edmondes, Sir Th.: letterbook, 127; papers, 543.

Edmundson, Geo.: Anglo-Dutch rivalry, 685; Dutch in Guiana, 3375.

Edmundson, Wm.: autobiog., 4260.

Education, 2923–97; in Ireland, 4314–15; in Scotland, 3962, 3966, 3968, 3972, 3973, 3977; in Wales, 3596–3608.

Edwardes, Stephen M.: ed. Duff, 3391.

Edwards, A. D.: Essex sources, 3170.

Edwards, Bryan: Br. colonies in W. Ind., 3350.

Edwards, C.: testimony, 3615.

Edwards, E. E.: bibl. on Eng. agr., 1850.

Edwards, Edward: founders of the Br. Mus., 2956; ed. Raleigh, 494.

Edwards, I. ab O.: Star Chamber proc. Wales, 3438.

Edwards, Rich.: life, 3561.

Edwards, R. Dudley: church and state in Tudor, Ire., 4243; Ir. Cath. and the Puritan revol., 4268; penal laws, 4269; Poynings' law, 4223; Plunket, 4274; ed. Chichester letter-book, 4095.

Edwards, Ralph: dict. of furniture, 2223, 2736; ed. Connoisseur period guides, 2706.

Edwards, Thomas: gangraena, 1297.

Efrydiau Catholig, 3639.

Egan, B.: Ir. abroad, 4348, 4349.

Egan, P. K.: parish of Ballinasloe, 4328.

Egerton, Hugh Edward: Br. col. policy, 3324; Br. foreign policy, 573.

Egerton, Th., Lord Ellesmere: legal papers, 128; observations on Coke's reports, 1008; auth. (?) certaine observations, 1049; privileges and prerogatives, 1049.

Egerton papers, the, 284.

Eglinton family: letters, 129.

Egmont MSS., 4220.

Ehrenpreis, Irvin: ed. Swift's enquiry, 377.

Ehrman, J.: naval policy of Wm. III, 559, 1738; Pepys' organization, 1737; Wm. III's Mediterranean policy, 1719.

Eikon basilike, authorship of, 418.

Ekelbad, Johan: letters, 633.

Eland, G.: ed. Buckinghamshire docs., 3132; ed. Woodward, 2982.

Elder, John R.: highland host, 3775; royal fishery company, 2000.

Eldred, Wm.: gunner's glasse, 1538.

Elias, J. E.: voorspel van den eersten Engelschen oorlog, 686; tweede Engelschen oorlog, 686.

Eliot, Sir John: lives, 440, 2441; writings, 440; family papers, 130; recs. of Devon vice-admiralty, 1725.

Eliot, T. S.: on Donne, 2621; Dryden, 2625.

Green, Mary Anne Everett: princesses of England, 393; ed. com. for advance of money, 761; com. for compounding, 761; letters of Henrietta Maria, 454; Rous's diary, 1276.

Greene, Evarts Boutell: provincial Amer., 3340; provincial governor, 3337.

Greene, Giles: declaration in vindication of Parliament, 1728.

Greene, John: diary, 2473.

Greenhill, Wm. A.: ed. Sydenham's works, 2896.

Greenough, C. N.: bibl. of Theophrastian character, 2167.

Greenslet, F.: Joseph Glanvill, 2909.

Greenstreet, W. J.: ed. Newton memorial vol., 2863.

Greenwood, Jonathan: sailing and fighting instructions, 1753.

Greenwood, Major: Petty, 1833.

Greenwood, Wm.: county courts, etc., 953.

Greg, Walter Wm.: bibl. of printed drama, and hand-list of plays, 2660; Lond. publishing, 3038; recs. from pr. council registers, 735.

Gregg, Pauline: John Lilburne, 468.

Grego, Joseph: dancing, 2272.

Gregory, David: memoranda of, 2864.

Gregory, Donald: western highlands, 4012.

Gregory, I. L.: ed. Hartland ch. accts., 3303.

Gregory, Jas.: corresp. and MSS., 2841, 3964.

Gregory, J. A.: Cudworth and Descartes, 2699.

Gregson, Matthew: co. of Lancaster, 3200.

Grenville, Geo. Nugent Temple, Lord Nugent: Hampden, 453.

Gretton, Geo. le M.: Royal Irish Regiment, 1663.

Gretton, Mary Sturge: Oxfordshire J.P.s, 943.

Greville, Robert, Lord Brooke: life, 409.

Grew, Marion E.: Portland, 489.

Grew, Nehemiah: anatomy of plants, 2880.

Grey, Anchitel: parl. debates, 869.

Grey, Ford, earl of Tankerville: life, 510; confession, 350; secret history, 350.

Grey, Zachary: defence of historians, 274; impartial examination of Neal, 1312.

Grey-Edwards, Henry: Bishop Bayley, 3643.

Gribble, J. B.: memorials of Barnstaple, 3158.

Grierson, Herbert Jones Clifford: cross currents in Eng. lit., 2580; Milton's views on liberty, 967; ed. Donne's poems, 2620.

Grierson, Sir Robert: life of, 3794.

Griffin, Appleton Prentiss Clark: ed. bibl. Amer. hist. societies, 3332.

Griffin, Grace Gardner: MSS. relating to Amer. hist., 3330; ed. writings on Amer. hist., 3333.

Griffith, Alexander: strena Vavasoriensis, etc., 3619.

Griffith, D. M.: const. law, 710.

Griffith, G. M.: Chirk Castle election, 3554; art., 3598.

Griffith, J. E.: pedigrees, 3506.

Griffith, John: papers *temp.* Jas. I., 148.

Griffith, M.: guide to P.R.O. Ir., 4062; Ir. rec. com., 4064.

Griffiths, John: ed. stat. of Oxf., 2974.

Griffiths, Olive M.: religion and learning, 1337.

Griffiths, R. G.: Joyce Jeffreys, 2310.

Griffiths, Reginald Harvey: bibl. of Pope, 2637.

Griggs, Wm.: relics of East India Co., 3399.

Grimblot, Paul: ed. Wm. III and Louis XIV, 584.

Grimston, Sir Harbottle: personal and family papers, 149.

Groen van Prinsterer, Guillaume: ed. archives l'Orange-Nassau, 673.

Groombridge, M. J.: ed. Chester council min., 3141.

Groome, Frances Hindes: ordinance gazetteer of Scot., 3988.

Grosart, Alexander Balloch: ed. annalia Dubrensia, 2265; Cowley, 2617; Crashaw, 2618; Davies, 4232; Dekker, 2675; Eliot, 440; Glanville, 1801; Herrick, 2628; Lismore papers, 4206; Marvell, 868; More, 2635; Quarles, 2639; Vaughan 2645.

Grose, Clyde Leclare: Anglo-Dutch alliance, 689; Anglo-Portuguese marriage, 416, 662; bibl. of Br. hist., 10; bibl. of Jacobitism, 386; Ch. II, 421; Dunkirk money, 2057; Eng. and Dunkirk, 590; Louis XIV and Ch. II, 591; religion in Restoration Eng., 1187.

Grose, Francis: military antiquities, 1551.

Gross, A.: der streit um das widerstandsrecht, 319.

Gross, Ch.: bibl. of Brit. hist., 11; bibl. Br. municipal hist., 3102.

Gross, Lothar: ed. reportorium der diplomatischen vertrevter, 540.

Grosvenor, Sir Rich.: parl. diary, 861.

Index

PRINTED IN GREAT BRITAIN
AT THE UNIVERSITY PRESS, OXFORD
BY VIVIAN RIDLER
PRINTER TO THE UNIVERSITY